Third Edition
SOCIOLOGY

John J. Macionis
Kenyon College

Prentice Hall, Englewood Cliffs, New Jersey 07632

Library of Congress Cataloging-in-Publication Data

MACIONIS, JOHN J.
  Sociology/John J. Macionis.—3rd ed.
    p. cm.
  Includes bibliographical references and index.
  ISBN 0-13-820358-X
  1. Sociology. I. Title.
HM51.M166 1991
301—dc20   90–45058
                    CIP

Acquisitions editor: *Nancy Roberts*
Editorial/production supervision: *Marianne Peters*
Interior and cover design: *Meryl Poweski*
Prepress buyer: *Debra Kesar*
Manufacturing buyer: *Mary Ann Gloriande*
Photo researcher: *Chris Pullo*
Photo editor: *Lorinda Morris-Nantz*
Cover art: Jean Baraud, *Outside of the Theatre du Vaudeville, Paris,*
1849–1936, French. Private Collection. Photo from Three Lions.

 © 1991, 1989, 1987 by Prentice-Hall, Inc.
A Division of Simon & Schuster
Englewood Cliffs, New Jersey 07632

Printed in the United States of America
10 9 8 7 6 5 4 3 2

ISBN 0-13-820358-X

PRENTICE-HALL INTERNATIONAL (UK) LIMITED, *London*
PRENTICE-HALL OF AUSTRALIA PTY. LIMITED, *Sydney*
PRENTICE-HALL CANADA INC., *Toronto*
PRENTICE-HALL HISPANOAMERICANA, S.A., *Mexico*
PRENTICE-HALL OF INDIA PRIVATE LIMITED, *New Delhi*
PRENTICE-HALL OF JAPAN, INC., *Tokyo*
SIMON & SCHUSTER ASIA PTE. LTD., *Singapore*
EDITORA PRENTICE-HALL DO BRASIL, LTDA., *Rio de Janeiro*

Contents

Brief Contents

Contents   ix

BOXES

CRITICAL THINKING

CROSS-CULTURAL COMPARISON

SOCIOLOGY OF EVERYDAY LIFE

SOCIETY IN HISTORY

PROFILE

Preface

Since the first edition appeared in 1987, *Sociology* has invited students from all backgrounds, in colleges and universities across North America and around the world, to discover a fresh and exciting way to look at their world and themselves. This is a tall order for a single book: one of the greatest challenges of developing this text has been to systematically address the diversity of students—black, white, Hispanic, Asian, and Native American; male and female; "traditional" younger students as well as "non-traditional" older learners—that enroll in the introductory course. My interest in meeting this challenge grew out of my twenty-year teaching career in a wide range of academic settings, including large universities, small colleges, community colleges, and even a prison and a police academy. But the most important reason to strive for inclusiveness is that it is *good sociology*, since a text that is inviting to *all* categories of students provides a better learning experience for *each* as it portrays the rich variety of American society.

Human society cannot be reduced to simplistic summaries or easy formulas. This text, therefore, realistically explores the social patterns of our world in their complexity. Topics are presented from various points of view, and each theoretical approach is systematically linked to ongoing research. Virtually every page of this book contains imaginative, class-tested examples and illustrations to help all types of students readily share in the vital insights of sociology.

The third edition of *Sociology* is the result of two years of intensive effort. During that time, I have worked harder on refining this text than on anything in my life. The task was guided by hundreds of comments about the book from instructors and students alike, pointing out what has worked well and making suggestions for improvements. Prentice Hall has also made an unprecedented commitment to craft a book of the highest possible quality, without gimmicks and without compromise. We invite your careful consideration of what I hope you will agree is our best work yet.

THE ORGANIZATION OF THIS TEXT

Part I introduces the foundations of sociology. Beginning students first come to know sociology as a perspective, an invigorating point of view that illuminates the surrounding world in a new way. The *sociological perspective* is presented in Chapter 1, so that readers will understand and appreciate the way of thinking that informs the remainder of the text. Chapter 2 explains *sociological investigation*, or the "doing of sociology." This chapter explains how the logic of science is applied to understanding human society and brings to life important research strategies with extended examples of actual sociological work. As readers learn what sociologists *do*, they are transformed from passive bystanders to active, critically thinking participants in the debates found in subsequent chapters.

These beginning discussions also reveal sociology's concern with values as well as facts. As instructors are well aware, most sociologists have been moralists as much as scientists. In every chapter, this text explores the fascinating controversies that are at the center of the discipline.

Part II presents the foundations of social life. Chapter 3 introduces the central concept of *culture*, emphasizing the many ways of life that make up our world. Cultural diversity is a theme carried forward into the rest of the text. Chapter 4 links culture to the concept of *society* and presents four enduring models for understanding the structure and dynamics of human societies. Assigned in sequence, this unique chapter provides students with the background necessary to comprehend more fully the ideas of important thinkers that appear in subsequent chapters. Alternatively, instructors may integrate one or more of the chapter's four parts at various points in the course. Chapter 5 focuses on *socialization*, explaining how we gain our humanity from social experience. Chapter 6 provides a close-up look at the patterns of *social interaction* that make up our everyday lives.

Chapter 7 offers full-chapter coverage of *groups and organizations*, additional important elements of social structure. Chapter 8 completes the unit by investigating how the operation of society promotes both *deviance and conformity*.

Part III provides a detailed analysis of various kinds of social inequality. Because of its importance to human life, three chapters are devoted to *social stratification*. Chapter 9 presents major concepts and theoretical analyses of social inequality. This chapter richly illustrates how stratification has changed historically and highlights cross-cultural variations today. Chapter 10 surveys dimensions of inequality in American society, assessing how American perceptions of inequality square with the facts. Chapter 11 extends the analysis of social stratification to the world as a whole, placing American society in global context and revealing the extent of differences in wealth and power between rich and poor societies. *Race and ethnicity*, important dimensions of social inequality both in North America and around the world, are discussed in Chapter 12. The focus of Chapter 13 is *sex and gender*. Here we explain the biological foundation of sex and sexuality and how societies transform the distinction of sex into systems of gender stratification. Chapter 14, *Aging and the Elderly*, investigates topics of increasing concern to most industrial societies including the United States.

Part IV includes a full chapter on each social institution. Chapter 15, *Family*, presents the rich diversity of family life both in the United States and in the world as a whole. Chapter 16, *Education*, traces the emergence of widespread formal schooling in industrial societies. Here again, American educational patterns are made more meaningful through contrasts with those of many other societies. Chapter 17 discusses *religion*, revealing how the timeless human search for ultimate purpose and meaning has affected social life in countless ways. Chapter 18, *Politics and Government*, now presents a significant discussion of the military, war, and peace. Chapter 19 focuses on *the economy and work*, highlighting what industrialization, postindustrialization, and the emergence of a global economy mean for the lives of Americans. Chapter 20, *Health and Medicine*, argues that health is as much a social issue as it is a matter of biological processes. As with each institution, this chapter explains the historical emergence of medicine as we know it today, analyzes current practices from different points of view, and compares American systems to those found in other societies.

Part V examines important dimensions of social change. Chapter 21 focuses on the historical and contemporary impact of *population growth and urbanization* in the United States and throughout the world. Chapter 22 explains how people seek (and resist) social change through various forms of *collective behavior and social movements*. Chapter 23 concludes the text with an analysis of *social change and modernity*, explaining how and why societies change, and critically analyzing the benefits and liabilities of contemporary social patterns. This chapter also answers a question central to sociology from its inception: what is distinctive about modern societies?

ESTABLISHED FEATURES OF *SOCIOLOGY*

Although texts introducing sociology have much in common, they are not all the same. The extraordinary success of *Sociology* results from a distinctive combination of features.

Writing style. Perhaps most important, this text offers a writing style that has been widely praised by students and faculty alike as elegant and engaging. *Sociology* is an inviting text that encourages students to read—even beyond their assignments.

Rich and varied examples. American sociologist George Herbert Mead once described the ideal teacher as a person able to transform simple information into real knowledge. Mead's insight applies as much to books as to teachers; on virtually every page of *Sociology*, therefore, rich and illuminating illustrations show students the power of applying sociology to their everyday lives.

Revealing human variety. *Sociology* celebrates human diversity. This means recognizing the rich social weave that is American society. Beyond the United States, the text takes every opportunity to reveal the cultural variety of the entire globe.

Focus on women and men. *Sociology* does more than devote a full chapter to the important concepts of sex and gender. Rather than limiting the discussion of gender to one part of the book, this text "mainstreams" gender into *every* chapter, showing how the topic at hand differently affects the lives of men and women. In addition, a special effort has been made to incorporate recent sociological research concerned with gender throughout the text.

Theoretically clear and balanced. *Sociology* makes theory easy. The discipline's major theoretical approaches are introduced in Chapter 1 and are systematically reapplied in subsequent chapters. In addition to the social-conflict, structural-functional, and symbolic-interaction paradigms, other theoretical models are used in many chapters, including social exchange analysis, ethnomethodology, cultural ecology, and sociobiology.

Chapter 4 offers unique, easy-to-understand introductions to important social theorists *before* their work is discussed in later chapters. Gerhard and Jean Lenski describe the history of human societies, and Max Weber, Karl Marx, and Emile Durkheim provide their distinctive insights in four sections that may be assigned together or read separately at different points in the course.

Recent sociological research. Ongoing research continuously renews the discipline of sociology. This text blends classic sociological statements with the latest research, as reported in the leading publications in the field. On average, two-thirds of the citations in each chapter represent material published since 1980.

Engaging chapter introductions. One of the most popular features of earlier editions has been the engaging vignettes that begin each chapter. These openings spark the interest of the reader and introduce important themes. For this edition, seventeen of the vignettes are new.

Learning aids. To increase student comprehension, **key concepts** are identified by boldfaced type and are followed by a precise definition. An alphabetical listing of key concepts with definitions appears at the end of each chapter and again in the **Glossary** at the end of the book. Each chapter also contains a numbered **Summary** to help students to review material and assess their understanding. Chapters conclude with lists of **Suggested Readings** describing books of lasting importance and highlighting recent publications on the topic at hand.

Illustrations. The photography and artwork in *Sociology* have been carefully developed by the author and a resource team at Prentice Hall as elements of the learning package. The text's illustration program includes photographs and paintings by diverse artists that present ideas with particular power and effectiveness. They expand the visual experiences of students by highlighting differing ways of life within American society and around the world.

Boxes. Although boxes are common to most introductory texts, *Sociology* provides a wealth of uncommonly good boxes. Like the illustration program, the boxes have been prepared by the author as an integral part of the text in order to highlight central themes. *Critical Thinking* boxes teach students to ask sociological questions about their world and to evaluate important, controversial issues. *Cross-Cultural Comparison* boxes provoke students to think about their own way of life by examining the fascinating cultural diversity found around the world. *Sociology of Everyday Life* boxes show that, far from being detached from daily routines, many of sociology's most important insights involve familiar, everyday experiences. *Society in History* boxes link the present to the past, reminding us that modern social patterns are often quite unlike those taken for granted by earlier generations. Finally, *Profile* boxes introduce many of the men and women who have shaped the discipline of sociology.

CHANGES IN THE THIRD EDITION

After years of intense work, I was deeply gratified by the warm reception given the first edition of *Sociology*. By all accounts this was the most successful new sociology text of the 1980s and is now used at over 500 colleges and universities across North America and around the world. The second edition of the book afforded the opportunity to make a number of improvements, including the introduction of the Annotated Instructor's Edition. Based on the generous comments of students and faculty alike, this third edition has been extensively revised to reflect several themes that will almost certainly have great importance in the 1990s.

Emphasis on critical thinking. Today's sociology courses are no longer designed merely to convey facts; instructors now seek to stimulate students to be active learners. Critical thinking skills involve the ability to challenge common assumptions, formulate questions, identify and weigh appropriate evidence, and reach reasoned conclusions.

By encouraging critical thinking skills, this text empowers students to discover as well as to learn, to seek out contradictions as well as consistent arguments, and to make connections among the various dimensions of social life. These goals have guided the line-by-line revision of *Sociology* and are reflected in features such as the *Critical Thinking* boxes that appear in most chapters.

Highlighting the social diversity of American society. American college students have never been as diverse as they are in the 1990s. This has brought change to disciplines—especially sociology. The third edition of *Sociology* recognizes this diversity by incorporating variables of sex, race, ethnicity, and social class in each chapter. Surprisingly, perhaps, many sociology texts speak only of "generic" Americans, which is, at best, a short-hand fiction. *Sociology* is richer for continuously showing how topics have different significance to various categories of readers and for encouraging students to intellectually reach beyond their own lives. Moreover, photography, artwork, and graphics have been carefully prepared to present the diversity of American society.

Placing American society in global perspective. Sociology has long revealed how individual lives are shaped by placement in their own society. As we approach the new century, sociology is extending its reach by showing how American society is itself affected by our country's placement in the world as a whole. The world is learning about America faster than we are learning about the world. Currently there are seven times as many foreign students studying in the U.S. as there are Americans studying abroad. Including extensive cross-cultural material in an introductory sociology course is a sensible and significant way to help prepare our students for living in a world that is becoming increasingly interdependent.

During the fall of 1988, I visited twelve nations around the world as an instructor for Semester-at-Sea, a ship-based college program administered by the University of Pittsburgh. This wonderful experience, in which faculty and students join together using the world as a classroom, expanded my thinking in more ways than could ever be expressed here. I have tried to incorporate some of the excitement and rewards of global education into this third edition of *Sociology*. This is especially true with respect to the "Pacific Rim," including Japan, North and South Korea, Taiwan (Republic of China), Hong Kong, and the People's Republic of China. Similarly, the dramatic changes that have rippled across Eastern Europe and the reorganization of Soviet society are thoroughly integrated in many of the chapters of this new edition. This global emphasis does not lessen the text's focus on American society; it simply enriches the analysis.

A new chapter on global stratification. One obvious way in which the third edition of *Sociology* introduces students to the larger world is the addition of Chapter 11, "Global Inequality." This discussion supplements the two stratification chapters found in earlier editions by explaining American society's position in a world of unequal wealth and power. "Global Inequality" offers various explanations of how global inequality developed, what it means for Americans, and considers what developments are likely during the coming century.

New topics. This edition of *Sociology* also offers many new or expanded discussions, including how gender affects sociological research (Chapter 2), the controversy over making English the official language of the United States (Chapter 3), why American crime rates are so high by world standards (Chapter 8), how wealthy black Americans differ from their white counterparts (Chapter 10), how advertising often perpetuates racial stereotypes (Chapter 12), the "mommy-track" controversy surrounding women in corporate America (Chapter 13), the debate over limiting health care for the very old (Chapter 14), the development of urban magnet schools (Chapter 16), the American military and the evolving arms race (Chapter 18), the reasons for *perestroika* in the Soviet Union (Chapter 19), the social causes of eating disorders (Chapter 20), the expansion of Third World cities to unprecedented size (Chapter 21), why social movements are becoming national and international in scope (Chapter 22), and the dilemma faced by some traditional societies that are able to achieve a higher standard of living only by sacrificing their cultural past (Chapter 23).

The latest statistical data. You can count on finding the most current statistical data—in many cases for 1989 and 1990—in the third edition of *Sociology*. In addition, this revision incorporates the latest research findings; on the average, two-thirds of each chapter's citations are of material published since 1980.

SUPPLEMENTS

This text is the heart of a complete learning package that includes a wide range of proven instructional aids as well as many new ones. As the author of the text, I have supervised all of the supplements, ensuring their quality and compatibility with the text. The supplements for *Sociology*, Third Edition, have been completely revised to improve each one and provide more substantial material. In addition, the list of supplements has been greatly expanded in this edition to respond to the needs of students and instructors. Seasoned instructors, who have avoided supplements in the past because they lacked depth, are invited to examine those that accompany this edition of our text.

The Annotated Instructor's Edition. The AIE is a complete student text that has been annotated on every page by the author with additional material. Annotations are *not* pedagogical gimmicks intended for inexperienced teachers. They include summaries of research findings, statistics that allow comparisons between American society and other nations of the world, insightful quotations, and high-quality survey data from the National Opinion Research Center's (NORC) General Social Survey.

Data File. This is an "instructor's manual" that will be of interest even to long-time instructors. The *Data File* provides far more than chapter outlines and discussion questions; it contains statistical data about American society and other nations of the world, brief summaries of important developments and significant research, and "briefs" on topics that expand every chapter of the text. The *Data File* has been prepared by Stephen W. Beach (Avila College) and John J. Macionis.

Social Survey. *Social Survey* is a software program that allows instructors and students alike to investigate American society with the best source of survey data available, the NORC General Social Survey. John J. Macionis and Jere Bruner (Oberlin College) have prepared over 100 data sets that correspond to the chapters of *Sociology*, Third Edition; Jere Bruner has written an easy-to-understand manual to accompany the software. *Social Survey* allows analysis of survey responses by sex, race, income level, education, age, and a host of other variables. *Social Survey* is executed on the CHIPendale 1 microcomputer program developed by James A. Davis (Harvard University) and is available to operate on the IBM and Apple families of personal computers.

Seeing Ourselves: Classic, Contemporary, and Cross-Cultural Readings in Sociology. This widely-adopted collection of sixty-five readings is edited by John J. Macionis and Nijole V. Benokraitis (University of Baltimore). Clusters of articles are organized to correspond to the chapter sequence of *Sociology*. *Seeing Ourselves* combines classic sociological statements (by Durkheim, Marx, Mead, Weber, and others), contemporary research findings, and cross-cultural inquiry to provide excep-

tional flexibility for instructors who wish to supplement reading assignments in the text with primary sources.

Test Item File. Prepared by Edward Kick, University of Utah, and available in both printed and computerized forms, this completely new file contains 2,300 questions for *Sociology*, Third Edition. Tests are made up of multiple-choice, true/false, and essay questions. The answers are page-referenced to the text. *Prentice-Hall DataManager* is a test generator and classroom management system designed to provide maximum flexibility in producing and grading tests and quizzes. MicroTest III, MacIntosh Version, is available for MacIntosh users.

Prentice Hall Color Transparencies: Sociology Series I and II. The 93 transparencies in these two series are taken from illustrations and charts in the text and other sources. The transparencies are accompanied by the *Instructor's Guide to Prentice Hall Color Transparencies: Sociology Series I and II*, a guide giving background information and suggestions for using the transparencies.

Film/Video Guide: Prentice Hall Introductory Sociology. Prepared by Peter Remender, University of Wisconsin of Oshkosh, the guide describes films and videos appropriate for classroom viewing for each text chapter (more than 160 films and videos are included). Summaries, discussion questions, and rental sources are provided for each film and video. Half of the entries are new to this edition of the text.

Prentice Hall's Video Library. We offer a wide selection of videos in sociology for classroom viewing. Videos are available in ½″ VHS, ½″ BETA, and ¾″ tape. A complete listing is available from your Prentice Hall representative. *Video Lecture Series*: John J. Macionis, David Popenoe, and Erich Goode, three notable authors in the field of sociology, address key topics in the introductory course in this thought-provoking video.

Study Guide. Prepared by Henry Borne for this edition, each chapter in this new study guide offers a topical outline, a chapter summary, learning objectives, and chapter review questions with an answer key. *Study Guide for Non-Native Speakers*: Designed for students whose first language is not English, this new guide includes the same material as the regular study guide but adds information on vocabulary, idioms, and culture.

Critical Thinking Audiocassette Tape. This 60-minute cassette shows students how to develop their critical thinking and study skills, with an emphasis on how to ask the right questions and how to analyze what is read.

ABC News/Prentice Hall Video Library for Sociology. Video is the most dynamic supplement you can use to enhance a class. But the quality of the video material and how well it relates to your course still makes all the difference. Prentice Hall and ABC News are now working together to bring you the best and most comprehensive video ancillaries available in the college market.

Through its wide variety of award-winning programs—*Nightline, Business World, On Business, This Week with David Brinkley, World News Tonight,* and *The Health Show*—ABC offers a resource for feature and documentary-style videos related to the chapters in *Sociology.* The programs have extremely high production quality, present substantial content, and are hosted by well-versed, well-known anchors.

Prentice Hall and its authors and editors provide the benefit of having selected videos on topics that will work well with this course and text and include notes on how to use them in the classroom. An excellent video guide in the *Data File* carefully and completely integrates the videos into your lecture. The guide has a synopsis of each video showing its relation to the chapter and discussion questions to help students focus on how concepts and theories apply to real-life situations.

A Contemporary View. *The New York Times* and Prentice Hall are sponsoring *A Contemporary View,* a program designed to enhance student access to current information of relevance in the classroom. Through this program, the core subject matter provided in the text is supplemented by a collection of current articles from one of the world's most distinguished newspapers, *The New York Times.* These articles demonstrate the vital, ongoing connection between what is learned in the classroom and what is happening in the world around us. To enjoy the wealth of information of *The New York Times* daily, a reduced subscription rate is available. For information, call toll-free 1-800-631-1222.

Prentice Hall and *The New York Times* are proud to co-sponsor *A Contemporary View.* We hope it will make the reading of both textbooks and newspapers a more dynamic, involving process.

A Year That Changed the World. *The New York Times* and Prentice Hall are also sponsoring *A Year That Changed the World,* a collection of articles from *The New York Times* covering the dramatic changes in China,

the Soviet Union, Eastern Europe, and South Africa from May 1989 to July 1990. The implications of these changes are covered in specific chapters in *Sociology,* but it was also thought helpful to gather together in one place the headline articles that chronicled the events of this amazing year.

ACKNOWLEDGMENTS

The conventional practice of designating a single author obscures the efforts of dozens of women and men that have resulted in *Sociology,* Third Edition. Nancy Roberts, sociology editor at Prentice Hall and valued friend, has provided enthusiasm, support, and sound advice throughout the revision process. Susanna Lesan has played a major part in the development of *Sociology* since its first edition. Here, again, her exceptional editorial eye has smoothed many of the rough edges and added some needed straight lines. She is one of the best editors in college publishing, and I am grateful to have worked with her and learned from her. Sharon Chambliss, supplements editor, has taken charge of the greatly expanded list of supplements for this edition, a challenge that she has met with humor and intelligence. Many members of the Prentice Hall sales staff, and especially Robert Thoresen, have made suggestions that have improved this book. I am grateful to John Jones, national sales manager, and all the members of the sales team for their enthusiastic efforts on behalf of this text.

The production of *Sociology* was supervised by Marianne Peters. She expended extraordinary time and energy, kept track of countless details, and tolerated no compromises along the way. Books of this quality are simply not possible without the talent and dedication of people such as Marianne. Meryl Poweski is responsible for the interior and cover design of the book and created each of the pages with exceptional skill. Development editors Marilyn Miller, Julie Nord, Tracy Ronvik, and Martha Wiseman have all contributed to making the text easy to read and understand. Copyediting of the manuscript was provided by Diana Drew, Ilene McGrath, and Amy Macionis. Chris Pullo served as photo researcher and Joelle Burrows provided assistance with the fine art, both under the supervision of Lorinda Morris-Nantz, head of the Prentice Hall Photo Archives. Special thanks is due to Paul Liebhart, an extraordinary photographer and friend, who has captured much of the world on film as few others have done. This edition has made extensive use of Paul Liebhart's images. I am grateful to Paul, and also to my traveling companions Mike and Ruth Verbois, all of the Brooks Photographic Institute of Santa Barbara.

The marketing program for this book is the work of Roland Hernandez; I thank him for his exceptional interest in the new edition. I also wish to extend my sincere gratitude to Bill Webber, Susan Willig, Charlyce Jones Owen, Will Ethridge, and Ed Stanford for all that they have done to make this text what it is today.

All of the editions of *Sociology* have benefited from the critical evaluation of many of my colleagues. The following have reviewed some or all of the manuscript:

Igolima Amachree, Western Illinois University
Richard Barash, Rancho Santiago College
Stephen Beach, Avila College
Nijole Benokraitis, University of Baltimore
Paul R. Benson, Tulane University
Philip Berg, University of Wisconsin-LaCrosse
Dallas A. Blanchard, University of West Florida
Rudee Devon Boan, Gardner-Webb College
Charles Bolton, Portland State University
Brent Bruton, Iowa State University
Jean H. Cardinalli, Monroe Community College
Gregg Carter, Bryant College
Frank Clemente, Pennsylvania State University
Peter Conrad, Brandeis University
Sheila Cordray, Oregon State University
Harold Cox, Indiana State University
Harrold Curl, Mount Vernon Nazarene College
Dennis K. Dedrick, Georgetown College
Joseph DeMartini, Washington State University
John Farley, Southern Illinois University
Joe R. Feagin, University of Texas
Juanita M. Firestone, University of Texas at Austin
Alvin J. Fischer, Camden County College
Kevin Fitzpatrick, University of Alabama-Birmingham
Don C. Gibbons, Portland State University
Norval D. Glenn, University of Texas
Ann Goetting, Western Kentucky University
Phillip Gonzales, University of New Mexico
Edith E. Graber, Lindenwood College
H. James Graham, Mott Community College
Marshall J. Graney, University of Tennessee
Linda M. Grant, Southern Illinois University
L. Sue Greer, University of Pittsburgh
Patricia A. Gwartney-Gibbs, University of Oregon
Maureen Hallinan, University of Notre Dame
Charles L. Harper, Creighton University
Jessie D. Harper, St. Cloud State University

Barbara Heisler, Cleveland State University
Cedric Herring, Texas A&M University
Gary Hodge, Collin County Community College
Paul Hsu, Austin Peavy State University
Kathy Hughes, Henderson Community College
Janet C. Hunt, University of Maryland
Faye Johnson, Middle Tennessee State University
Norris R. Johnson, University of Cincinnati
Ronald L. Johnstone, Central Michigan University
Edward L. Kain, Southwestern University
Alice A. Kemp, University of New Orleans
Ross A. Klein, Skidmore College
Marlene Lehtinen, University of Utah
Hugh F. Lena, Providence College
Linda Lindsey, Maryville College
Larry Lyon, Baylor University
William Marsiglio, University of Florida
Wilfred G. Marston, University of Michigan
Greg Matoesian, Fontbonne College
John D. McCarthy, Catholic University
Allan McCutcheon, University of Delaware
Alan McEvoy, Wittenberg University
Meredith B. McGuire, Trinity University
Virginia McKeefery-Reynolds, Northern Illinois University
Roger McVannan, Broome Community College
Dwayne Monette, Northern Michigan University
Wilbert E. Moore, University of Denver
Peter Morrill, Bronx Community College
Charles W. Mueller, University of Iowa
David M. Neal, University of North Texas
Sharon Nero, University of Wisconsin-Stout
Alvaro L. Nieves, Wheaton College
Anthony M. Orum, University of Texas
Albert L. Reese, Bainbridge College
Franklyn Robbins, Community College of Rhode Island
Dorothy M. Roe, Milwaukee Area Technical College
Howard Sacks, Kenyon College
Beth Anne Shelton, SUNY Buffalo
Anson Shupe, University of Texas
Jan Smith, Ohio Wesleyan University
Karen Cole Smith, Sante Fe Community College
Kevin B. Smith, Lamar University
Eve Spangler, Boston College
Michael Stein, University of Missouri
George F. Stine, Millersville University
Teresa A. Sullivan, University of Texas
M. L. Taylor, University of Texas-Arlington
Verta Taylor, The Ohio State University

Vickie H. Taylor, Danville Community College
Kendrick S. Thompson, Northern Michigan University
Robert Thornburrow, Paris Junior College
Susan Tiano, University of New Mexico
Andrew Treno, Clarke College
Theodore C. Wagenaar, Miami University
Pamela Barnhouse Walters, Indiana University
Philo C. Wasburn, Purdue University
David L. Westby, Pennsylvania State University
Craig C. White, Fairmont State College
John Wilson, Duke University
Richard Withers, Alderson Broaddus College
Anthony L. Wolf, Bucks County Community College
Wayne S. Wooden, California State Polytechnic
  University-Pomona

Although mentioned above, particular credit is due to Anne Goetting (Western Kentucky University) and Dennis K. Dedrick (Georgetown College, KY) for extensive comments offered during the course of this revision.

I also wish to thank the following colleagues for sharing their wisdom in ways that have improved this book: Doug Adams (The Ohio State University), Kip Armstrong (Bloomsburg State College), Rose Arnault (Fort Hays State University), Philip Berg (University of Wisconsin, La Crosse), Bill Brindle (Monroe Community College), Karen Campbell (Vanderbilt University), Gerry Cox (Fort Hays State University), Harrold Curl (Mount Vernon Nazarene College), James A. Davis (Harvard University), Helen Rose Fuchs Ebaugh (University of Houston), Heather Fitz Gibbon (The College of Wooster), Kevin Fitzpatrick (University of Alabama-Birmingham), Andrew Foster (Kenyon College), Charles Frazier (University of Florida), Karen Lynch Frederick (Saint Anselm College), Steven Goldberg (City College, City University of New York), Jeffrey Hahn (Mount Union College), Peter Hruschka (Ohio Northern University), Glenna Huls (Camden County College), Harry Humphries (Pittsburg State University), Cynthia Imanaka (Seattle Central Community College), Patricia Johnson (Houston Community College), Ed Kain (Southwestern University), Irwin Kantor (Middlesex County College), Thomas Korllos (Kent State University), Michael Levine (Kenyon College), Don Luidens (Hope College), Larry Lyon (Baylor University), Li-Chen Ma (Lamar University), Alan Mazur (Syracuse University), Meredith McGuire (Trinity University), Jack Melhorn (Emporia State University), Toby Parcel (The Ohio State University), Daniel Quinn (The Ohio State University), Nevel Razak (Fort Hays State College), Virginia Reynolds (Indiana University of Pennsylvania), Laurel Richardson (The Ohio State University), Howard Schneiderman (Lafayette College), Ray Scupin (Linderwood College), Harry Sherer (Irvine Valley College), Glen Sims (Glendale Community College), Len Tompos (Lorain County Community College), Daryl Tukufu (Memphis State University), Christopher Vanderpool (Michigan State University), Marilyn Wilmeth (Iowa University), Stuart Wright (Lamar University), and Frank Zulke (Harold Washington College).

I also wish to thank members of my department at Kenyon College—Rita Kipp, George McCarthy, Sharon Minor King, Howard Sacks, Ric Sheffield, J. Kenneth Smail, David Suggs, Edward Schortman, and Patricia Urban—who provide a daily environment of intellectual stimulation. Sharon Duchesne, a valued member of our department family for over a decade, provided skillful editorial and secretarial help.

Carol Singer, Government Documents Librarian at Kenyon College, has served as a consultant and research assistant in the preparation of this revision. She is responsible for the appearance of only the most recent data in the third edition, as in earlier editions.

This book is dedicated to all teachers of sociology who are devoting their lives to helping others understand their place in American society and in the larger world.

John J. Macionis

1

The Sociological Perspective

On a spring evening in New York's Central Park in 1989, a twenty-eight-year-old woman was jogging after a day of work in the city's financial district. Passing a grove of sycamore trees, she was no longer alone. The quiet setting suddenly exploded into a chase as she was pursued by a gang of six young boys. Flushed with terror and anger, the woman stumbled into a gully where she fought off her attackers while being battered with a pipe and stabbed with a knife. Overpowered and seriously wounded, she was then repeatedly raped. Left for dead, she lay helpless and broken until found three hours later. Having lost most of her blood, she reached a local hospital in a coma. Months of intensive medical care and a courageous desire to live now promise a physical recovery.

Many Americans reacted to this incident with disbelief. Partly, this was because of the brutality of the attack, and partly because the boys were only fourteen to sixteen years of age. But most curiously, the offenders offered no sensible explanation for their crime beyond the excitement of what they termed a night of "wilding." Perhaps more than anything else, this terrible event provoked people everywhere to confront again the basic question: *What makes people do the things they do?*

There are, of course, many ways to look at human events. The *perspective*—or point of view—that is used identifies certain facts as most important and suggests how these facts can be woven together into meaning. The police officers investigating the "wilding" case used one perspective. They focused on piecing together what happened and on identifying and apprehending the individuals involved. This point of view is concerned primarily with describing an event and establishing a course of action to be undertaken in accordance with the law.

A psychiatrist offers another perspective that might be applied to the behavior of the boys. From a psychiatrist's point of view, the important issue is the state of mind that could lead an individual to an act of such

1

One way to grasp the power that society has in shaping the lives of individuals is to imagine how your life would be different had you been born in the place of one of these children.

wanton violence. In this case, the psychiatric perspective would identify a different set of facts and prescribe a response based on appropriate medical principles.

A sociologist brings still another perspective to understanding human behavior, one that is probably less familiar to Americans than the two already mentioned. In this case, a sociologist attempting to make sense of the incident might note that the offenders were males, that they were teenagers, and that they were of an economically disadvantaged minority. Notice that the facts highlighted by the sociological perspective are different in a crucial way from those noted by law enforcement officials or psychologists. The police are concerned with the facts specific to this one situation. Knowing that an offender is male is useful only insofar as it leads to identifying *which* male was involved. Likewise, psychiatrists seek out the personal traumas that may have contributed to an explosive outburst by a specific individual. Both police and psychiatrists share the assumption that, in important respects at least, every crime and every person are unique. In contrast, a sociologist looks beyond any *particular* event or person to seek an understanding of how and why some *category* of people behaves differently from another.

These brief comparisons introduce the important idea that, to a large degree, the reality that we perceive is a result of the perspective that we employ. This chapter introduces the sociological perspective, which helps to explain how social forces affect all human events.

DEFINING THE SOCIOLOGICAL PERSPECTIVE

A distinctive perspective is central to the discipline of **sociology**, which is defined as *the scientific study of human social activity*. As an academic discipline, sociology is continually learning more about how human beings as social creatures think and act. This knowledge is drawn largely from scientific research, which is the subject of Chapter 2 ("Sociological Investigation"). As explained later in this chapter, sociologists also use various theoretical approaches to guide their work. But all sociologists use one basic point of view in their quest to understand the social world.

Seeing the General in the Particular

Peter Berger (1963) describes the sociological perspective as *seeing the general in the particular*. This means that sociologists see general social patterns in the behavior of particular individuals. We recognize that each individual is in some ways unique, but we also see that general social forces shape us into various *kinds* of people. In the case just described, the sociological perspective leads us to wonder if violent crime may be more common among males, the young, and the disadvantaged, for example, than among females, older people, and the more privileged. Sociological research has confirmed that this is indeed the case.

To change the example slightly, what are the odds of becoming the *victim* of a violent crime resulting in death? A look at Figure 1–1 provides several sociological insights. All categories of people are vulnerable to deadly violence, of course, but not to an equal degree. Notice, first, a general pattern involving race: *blacks* are more likely to become victims of homicide than are *whites*. The overall rate of victimization for blacks (32.4 cases for every 100,000 people in this category for the year 1986) is almost six times higher than the rate for whites (5.7 per 100,000). But notice that for both races, *males* are more likely to become victims than are *females*, evidence that our sex also affects our lives. Among whites, males (8.6) are almost three times more likely than females (3.0) to fall victim to homicide. For blacks, males (55.0) have a rate over four times higher than that for females (12.1). As Chapter 8 ("Deviance") explains, the toll of violent crime is especially heavy among black males who are disadvantaged within American society.

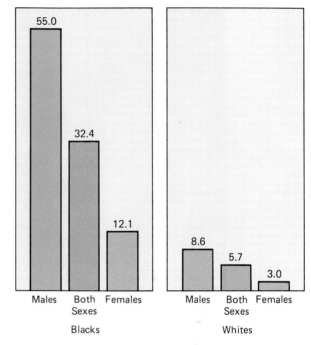

Figure 1–1   Rate of Death by Homicide, by Race and Sex, for Americans

Rates indicate the number of deaths by homicide for every 100,000 people in each category for 1986.

(*U.S. Bureau of the Census*)

Clearly, then, the particular life experiences we have are shaped by the general categories of society into which we fall.

Seeing the Strange in the Familiar

The sociological perspective can also be described as *seeing the strange in the familiar*. This does not mean that sociologists focus on the bizarre elements of society. Rather, sociological observation involves detaching oneself from familiar ways of thinking in order to gain new insights that at first may seem strange. Using the sociological perspective leads us to observe that, in the words of Peter Berger (1963:23), "things are not what they seem."

Most people in American society take the social world so much for granted that they rarely "see" how society affects us at all. Using the sociological perspective,

Black students who attend expensive colleges in the United States are often a numerical minority. For this reason, they typically have a heightened sociological perspective, that is, they are keenly aware of social patterns that the white majority takes for granted.

therefore, requires a bit of practice. The effort, however, results in a new level of understanding that is far richer than simple "common sense."

Some students enter a first course in sociology with a vague idea that sociology is, in one way or another, the complicated study of the obvious. The following examples should convince you that what the sociological perspective reveals is often quite different from what most people would claim to be the "obvious" facts of social life.

Why Did You Come to This Particular College?

Without using a sociological perspective, students are likely to respond to this question with diverse, personal answers:

I wanted to stay close to home.
This college has the best women's basketball team.
A journalism degree from this university ensures a good job.
My girlfriend goes to school here.
I wasn't accepted at the school I really wanted to attend.

Such responses are certainly real to the people expressing them, but do they tell the complete story?

The sociological perspective provides additional insights that may not be readily apparent.

To approach the issue sociologically, we must first step back from personal reasons that tell us only about *particular* situations and seek more *general* explanations. We must ask what students as a *category* of people have in common. A look around a college classroom provides one answer. Although people of all ages attend college, most students are relatively young—generally between eighteen and twenty-four years of age. A pattern in American society links college attendance to this period of life. Something more is involved, however, because fewer than half of college-age Americans are actually enrolled in college. In fact, only about 37 percent of eighteen to twenty-four-year-olds were enrolled in 1989.

What else do college students have in common? We might look next at family income. Traditionally, students who attend college come from families with annual incomes that are several thousands of dollars a year above the American average. Not surprisingly, then, those racial and ethnic categories of Americans with higher incomes are most represented on campuses. While about 38 percent of whites in this age range are in college, only about 26 percent of blacks and 23 percent of Hispanics are enrolled (U.S. Bureau of the Census, 1988a).

Of course, just as there are differences among students, so there are differences among America's colleges and universities. These, too, can be categorized, in terms of cost, for instance. Some colleges are much more

SOCIOLOGY OF EVERYDAY LIFE

What's in a Name? Social Forces and Personal Choice

On July 4, 1918, twins were born to Abe and Becky Friedman in Sioux City, Iowa. The first to be born was named Esther Pauline Friedman; her sister was named Pauline Esther Friedman. Today, these women are known to almost every American, but by new names adopted later: Ann Landers and Abigail ("Dear Abby") Van Buren.

These two women are not the only Americans to have changed their names to further their careers—it is a practice especially common among celebrities. At first glance, this may seem to be simply a matter of particular preferences. However, examining the list below from a sociological perspective uncovers a general pattern. Historically, women and men of various national backgrounds have tended to adopt not just any name, but *English-sounding* names. Why? Because American society has long accorded high social prestige to those of Anglo-Saxon background. How many of these well-known people can you identify from their original names?

1. Michael James Vijencio Gubitosi
2. Cherilyn Sarkisian
3. Cheryl Stoppelmoor
4. Robert Allen Zimmerman
5. Margarita Carmen Cansino
6. John Bongiovi
7. Frederick Austerlitz
8. George Kyriakou Panayiotou
9. Ana Mae Bullock
10. Issur Danielovitch Demsky
11. Mladen Sekulovich
12. Gerald Silberman
13. Bernadette Lazzarra
14. Karen Ziegler
15. Ramon Estevez
16. Henry John Deutschendorf, Jr.
17. Allan Stewart Konigsberg
18. Judy Cohen
19. Eugene Maurice Orowitz
20. William Claude Dukenfield

1. Robert Blake; 2. Cher; 3. Cheryl Ladd; 4. Bob Dylan; 5. Rita Hayworth; 6. Jon Bon Jovi; 7. Fred Astaire; 8. George Michael; 9. Tina Turner; 10. Kirk Douglas; 11. Karl Malden; 12. Gene Wilder; 13. Bernadette Peters; 14. Karen Black; 15. Martin Sheen; 16. John Denver; 17. Woody Allen; 18. Juice Newton; 19. Michael Landon; 20. W. C. Fields

expensive than others, and going away to school costs more than attending college while living at home.

More than three-fourths of the almost 13 million college students in the United States attend schools that receive substantial government funding (U.S. Center for Education Statistics, 1988a). These schools include locally funded community colleges, which generally offer two-year programs, as well as four-year state colleges. In both cases, 1990 annual tuition for students living at home averaged over $1,500; for those paying room and board the total was above $5,000. Private four-year colleges and universities, however, were even more expensive: tuition, room, and board costs averaged about $13,000, with the most expensive schools exceeding $20,000 per year. Because most of the costs of a college education in the United States are paid by students and their families, students from families of more modest means are likely to select local two-year colleges or four-year state schools. In addition, many of the growing number of older students with job and family responsibilities also favor these schools, taking advantage not only of lower costs but of part-time and evening programs. Private four-year colleges and universities are typically chosen by younger, more affluent students who are able to study full time.

More choice in purchasing a formal education clearly depends on more income. It may initially seem strange to explain personal choice in terms of social forces. In doing this, the sociological perspective does not detract from anyone's autonomy. Rather, it *adds* to our individual power by helping to explain how society links our lives to those of countless others. The box further illustrates how social forces affect a seemingly personal matter: the choice of names.

Why Do People Get Divorced?

The question of why people divorce can be more fully and accurately answered if we consider not only particular reasons but general social trends. Particular people divorce because they fall out of love or their relationships

The "Wilding" Controversy: Are Sociologists Bleeding Hearts?

In the weeks following the "wilding" incident in New York's Central Park, the American press presented divergent views about how much personal responsibility should be assigned to the boys who committed the crime.

On one side of the controversy, a number of sociologists, social workers, and various other professionals pointed out that a wide range of social factors—including gender, youth, race, and social background—had to be considered in assessing responsibility. Not everyone was convinced, however. Indeed, several nationally known commentators took the opportunity to belittle sociology by arguing that the discipline's concern for social forces served only to obscure the basic issue: these were *bad* kids because they had committed a morally *repulsive* act, and they should be *punished*. Never mind, they added, what the "bleeding hearts" say.

George F. Will, a Pulitzer prize–winning journalist, no doubt spoke for many when he denounced "psycho-socio babble" that made society, rather than the boys, responsible for the attack. Sociologists, Will contended, confused the issue by their "dispersal of responsibility into a fog of 'socio-economic factors.' " From Will's point of view, the problem was simpler: there are good people and evil people.

Will, of course, has a point. Especially when a particular event causes pain and anguish, people want to know who is to be blamed and punished. In this case, six young boys

were arrested and charged with the crimes. Thus, the perceived evil was addressed, and people's passionate sense of anger and injustice served. But is this the whole picture?

Sociologists would have to say no, and they also have a point. To begin, we must state clearly that sociological analysis is *not* a plea to turn loose people who commit violent crimes. But we must be prepared to face the truth that no human behavior is the product solely of what philosophers (and George Will) call simple "free will" or "choice." On the contrary, all human behavior involves choices, but within a constellation of influential social forces (not to mention whatever biological and psychological forces may also be at work). "Simple" is one thing that human beings are not.

Gender is one such social force. Would anyone imagine girls to be as likely as boys to commit this kind of crime? The fact is that American males engage in nine times as many violent crimes as females do, as Chapter 8 ("Deviance") explains. And what about age? Are middle-aged men as likely as teenagers to "choose" to commit this crime? Hardly, as evidenced by the fact that Americans between the ages of fifteen and twenty-four represent only one-sixth of the population but account for almost half of all violent crimes. Likewise, we know that categories of Americans who are poor—including blacks and other disadvantaged minorities—are involved in more violence, both as victims and offenders,

than are more affluent people. Finally, we might well consider the fact that crimes such as the Central Park attack are remarkably *American*. More assaults and murders occur in New York and other American cities in a typical week than occur in most large, European cities in almost a year. And in American society, sexuality is all too often linked to rape and other brutal violence.

In short, no society can exist without demanding that people take at least some personal responsibility for their actions. Americans typically respond to morally outrageous behavior by wanting to attach blame to specific people. To blame "society" is to blame everyone and no one. But in this cultural climate of individualism, sociology provides a needed dose of realism. Embedded in society from the moment of our birth, we learn to think, feel, and act as products of a larger social world. To think sociologically is not, therefore, to become a "bleeding heart." It is to understand ourselves and the world around us more fully and accurately. If our desire is to control crime effectively, we must not only punish individuals but address the situations that encourage people to make evil choices.

SOURCE: Inspired by George F. Will's column "No Psycho-Socio Babble Lessens the Fact That Evil Was the Crux of Central Park Rape," *The Philadelphia Inquirer*, May 1, 1989; Edwin M. Yoder, Jr., "Offering Sociology as Theology," *The Philadelphia Inquirer*, May 5, 1989; and J. Anthony Lukas, "Wilding—As American as Tom Sawyer," *The New York Times*, May 28, 1989, Sec. 4, p. 15.

are ruined by financial problems, career stress, alcoholism, or infidelity. The fact that more general forces are also at work is suggested by a tenfold increase in the divorce rate over the last hundred years.

One important change in American society during this period has been the growing proportion of women in the labor force. In 1900, only about one in five women worked outside of the home. By the end of the 1980s, about three in five did so (U.S. Bureau of Labor Statistics, 1989a). This fact, along with the women's movement, greater educational opportunity, technological advances in birth control, and greater affluence for most Americans, provides women today with a far wider range of choices and opportunities. Similarly, divorce no longer carries the sinful stigma it had a century ago. As a result, both women and men feel less bound to remain in unsatisfying marriages. The sociological perspective again helps to show how general changes within society as a whole often set the stage for the choices made by particular women and men.

Seeing the Individual in Context

Especially in individualistic North American society, people learn to view their lives in very personal terms. We emphasize personal choice in our lives by making claims such as "I went to college because I wanted to be a nurse" or "My parents decided to get a divorce because they fought all the time." Our everyday awareness carries a heavy load of personal responsibility, so that we pat ourselves on the back when we enjoy success and kick ourselves when things go wrong. Proud of our individuality, even in painful times, we resist the idea that we act in socially patterned ways. Indeed, when life goes awry we are often intent on attaching personal blame to someone.

For this reason, a tragic event such as the Central Park attack described at the beginning of this chapter often provokes controversy about how much responsibility should be attached to the offenders. The box looks critically at the spirited debate that appeared in the American press following this crime.

Suicide: The Most Individual Act

There is perhaps no more compelling demonstration of how social forces affect human behavior than the study of suicide. What, after all, could be more personal than the act of taking one's own life? Perhaps this is why Emile Durkheim, a pioneer of sociology writing a century ago, chose this as a topic of study. He was able to show that social forces are at work even in the apparent isolation of a self-destructive act.

Durkheim, who lived in France, examined records of suicide in various regions of Central Europe.[1] These records clearly showed that some categories of people were much more likely than others to choose to commit suicide. Specifically, Durkheim found, males, Protestants, wealthy people, and the unmarried all had significantly higher suicide rates than did females, Catholics and Jews, the poor, and married people. Durkheim explained these differences in terms of the degree of *social integration* typical of these various categories. That is, low suicide rates were found to characterize those types of people who commonly have stronger social bonds with others. On the other hand, high suicide rates were found for those categories of people who are more typically individualistic and autonomous.

Within male-dominated societies of Europe, males certainly have more autonomy than females do. Whatever advantages this freedom may afford, reasoned Durkheim, it also means that males kill themselves with greater frequency. Likewise, Catholic and Jewish practices foster stronger social ties and greater conformity than do individualistic Protestant doctrines. The result is that Protestants have a higher suicide rate than Catholics or Jews. The wealthy clearly have much more freedom than do the poor, but with the predictable result in terms of suicide rates. Finally, single people have fewer social bonds than married people do, which, consistent with Durkheim's theory, explains their greater likelihood of suicide.

A century later, statistical evidence continues to support Durkheim's analysis (Pescosolido & Georgianna, 1989). Figure 1–2 on page 8 shows suicide rates for four categories of Americans. With 13.9 recorded instances of suicide for every 100,000 people in this category in 1986, whites have a rate twice as high as that of blacks (6.5). Also, for each racial category, suicide is more common to males than to females. White males (22.3) are almost four times more likely than white females to take their own lives. Among blacks, males (11.1) are about five times more likely than females to do so. Following Durkheim's argument, we conclude that the

---

[1] This discussion is a much abbreviated account of Durkheim's (1966; orig. 1897) considerably more complex analysis of suicide.

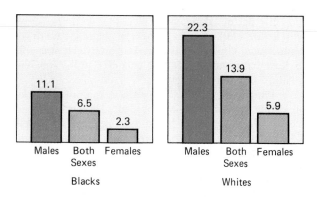

Figure 1–2 Rate of Death by Suicide, by Race and Sex, for Americans

Rates indicate the number of deaths by suicide for every 100,000 people in each category for 1986.

(*U.S. Bureau of the Census*)

higher suicide rate among whites, males, and especially white males is due to their greater affluence and autonomy in American society. In contrast, poorer people and those with limited social choices are more socially rooted and have correspondingly lower rates of self-destruction.

In this way, we see how even the most personal actions of individuals are guided by the impersonal operation of society. Social forces are complex, of course, as a comparison of Figure 1–1 and Figure 1–2 shows. We can see that social forces linked to race produce very different patterns with regard to death from homicide and suicide. Blacks and other disadvantaged categories of Americans suffer disproportionately from homicide; whites, as a privileged category, suffer from suicide. On the other hand, gender operates consistently: males are more prone to both homicide and suicide than are females. The precise patterns may change, but in all such cases we are able to see how society is at work in our lives.

The first part of this chapter has argued that human beings fashion their own lives only within a powerful and complex social environment. It is easy to understand this if we imagine how different our lives would be had we been born in ancient China, medieval England, or contemporary Bangladesh. Using the sociological perspective, each chapter of this book will help to explain how our lives within American society in the late twentieth century are distinctively *modern* and *American*.

THE SOCIOLOGICAL PERSPECTIVE IN EVERYDAY LIFE

As we have explained, most Americans tend to overlook the power of social forces. Yet there are some kinds of situations that do prompt us to view the world sociologically even before we take a first course in sociology.

Sociology and a World of Diversity

A Japanese student who has just arrived on an American college campus is likely to notice social patterns that Americans take for granted. The strangeness of the surroundings helps a foreigner see that people's behavior is not only a result of individual choice but also reflects patterns of the larger society. In the same way, of course, encountering the social diversity of our world heightens an American's awareness of social forces. Moreover, confronting other societies often prepares us to look at American society with new eyes when we return home. A similar broadening of perspective occurs when we confront unfamiliar social environments within our own society—visiting strange neighborhoods, for example, or meeting people whose beliefs and patterns of behavior are quite different from our own.

Sociology and Marginality: Race, Gender, and Age

Sociologists often use the term **social marginality** to refer to *the state of being excluded from social activity as an "outsider."* All people experience social marginality from time to time; for some categories of Americans, however, being an outsider is commonplace. The more intense their social marginality, the more likely they are to make use of the sociological perspective.

No person who is black, for example, could live very long in the United States without being aware of how much race affects personal experiences. But because whites constitute the dominant majority of American society, whites think about race only occasionally. When they do, they may consider race an issue that applies only to blacks rather than to themselves as well. This social blindness probably accounts for the accusation of some whites that nonwhites exaggerate the importance

Because elderly Americans are often viewed as social outsiders, they tend to be more sociological in their outlook than younger people. In Japan, however, the elderly play a central part in social life; as a result, they probably adopt a sociological perspective less readily.

of race. But within a primarily white society, nonwhites are forced to be more aware of race than are whites.

In a similar way, women of all races are more likely to see the world sociologically than are men. For the past two decades, women who have personally experienced some of the limitations that American society imposes on females have been getting together to compare notes. The result has been a growing awareness that any particular woman's experience of social inequality is not unique but reflects general social forces. Some men, because of their dominant social position, have failed to see patterns of sexual inequality. Like the whites noted above, they have sometimes accused women of exaggerating the problem. In the 1970s, American women described their growing recognition of sexual inequality as "consciousness raising." In this case, "raising one's consciousness" involves gaining a sociological perspective.

The elderly often perceive social patterns more acutely than do young people. Whereas this may be partly due to wisdom gained over a lifetime, another important factor is that the elderly often experience considerable social marginality. As Chapter 14 ("Aging and the Elderly") explains, Americans tend to define growing old as the loss of the capacity to engage in many important human activities, including physical recreation, work, and even sex. Since most elderly people are indeed physically and mentally capable of all these things, they understand more clearly than the young the degree to which society defines what individuals are and how they should think and act.

In short, people who are placed on the outside of social life—due to their race, sex, age, or a host of other factors—are likely to be aware of social patterns that others take for granted. They have stepped back from society (perhaps more accurately, society has stepped back from them) and therefore have a more sociological view of the world.

Sociology and Social Crisis

American sociologist C. Wright Mills (1959) suggested that times of social disruption foster widespread sociological thinking. In this century, the 1930s stand out as a decade of heightened sociological awareness. Following the stock market crash of 1929, the Great Depression resulted in unemployment for about one-fourth of the labor force. Under such circumstances, most unemployed workers could not help but see general social forces at work in their particular lives. Rather than claiming, "Something is wrong with me; I can't find a job," they were likely to say, "The economy has collapsed; there are no jobs to be found!"

People very quickly develop a sociological perspective when the established patterns of society begin to shake and crumble. The decade of the 1960s was another period when the sociological awareness of Americans was enhanced. The civil rights, women's liberation, antiwar, and hippie movements all challenged accepted social patterns in a highly visible way. This social climate called attention to the ways in which personal experiences

American society encourages us to view individuals as responsible for their successes and failures. This explains our tendency to view advantaged people as especially capable and disadvantaged people as personally undeserving.

were being shaped by forces beyond the people themselves—the political, economic, military, and technological elements of "the system." Although the merits of these movements may be debated, there is no doubt that, by pointing to social forces that affect the lives of all Americans, they each contain an element of the sociological perspective.

Worth noting, too, is that the converse is often true: sociological thinking sometimes fosters social disruption. In other words, gaining a sociological understanding of how "the system" works may well provoke attempts to change it in some way. For example, as American women and men have confronted the power of gender, many have actively tried to reduce the traditional separation of men's and women's lives.

As these everyday examples suggest, an introduction to sociology is an invitation to learn a new way of looking at familiar patterns of social life. At this point, we might well consider whether this invitation is worth

accepting. In other words, what are the benefits of learning to use the sociological perspective?

The Benefits of the Sociological Perspective

The knowledge that has been amassed within sociology is immense and can be readily applied to our lives in countless ways. There are, however, four general ways in which the sociological perspective can enrich our lives.

The first benefit of using the sociological perspective is learning that our world contains a remarkable variety of human social patterns. North Americans represent only about 5 percent of the world's population, and, as the remaining chapters of this book explain, the rest of humanity lives in ways that often differ dramatically from our own. As members of any society, people define their ways of life as proper and often "natural." But looking over the course of human history, and examining the world today, we find countless competing versions of correct behavior. *The sociological perspective helps us to recognize human diversity and to begin to understand the challenges of living within a diverse world.*

The second benefit comes from realizing that, within particular societies, people come to accept as "true" certain ideas that may or may not be factual. *The sociological perspective challenges our familiar understandings of ourselves and of others, so that we can critically reconsider what has been assumed to be "true."*

As we have already seen, a good example of a widespread but misleading "truth" is that Americans are "autonomous individuals," independent of others and personally responsible for their lives. By thinking this way, we are sometimes too quick to praise particularly successful people as being personally superior to those who have not fared as well. On the other side of the coin, people who do not measure up may be unfairly condemned as personally deficient. A sociological approach encourages us to ask whether these beliefs are actually true and, to the extent that they are not, why they are so widely held.

As we consider American society in global context, we might also wonder if the American conception of "success," with its emphasis on materialism rather than, for instance, spiritual well-being, is the best way by which to judge others, as well as to evaluate our own lives.

The third benefit provided by the sociological perspective involves understanding that, for better or worse, American society operates in a particular and deliberate way. No one is able to live with complete disregard for society's "rules of the game." In the game of life, we may decide how to play our cards, but it is society that deals us the hand. The more effective player is generally one who better understands how the game works. Here again, sociology is valuable. *The sociological perspective allows us to recognize both the opportunities and the constraints that affect our lives.* Knowledge of this kind

is power. Through it, we come to understand what we are likely and unlikely to accomplish for ourselves, and we are able to see how the goals we adopt can be realized more effectively.

Of course, the more we understand about the operation of society, the more we can take an active part in shaping social life. On the other hand, with little awareness of how society operates, we are likely passively

PROFILE

C. Wright Mills (1916–1962)

Charles Wright Mills managed to cause a stir with most everything he did. Even arriving for a class at New York's Columbia University—astride his motorcycle and clad in a sweatshirt and boots—he was likely to turn some heads. During the conservative 1950s, Mills not only dressed a bit out of the mainstream; he produced a number of books that critically questioned most of what Americans took for granted. In the process, he won both followers and adversaries.

Mills's most enduring contribution was his insistence that people actually use what he described as the "sociological imagination" in their daily lives. For him, sociology was

not to be a dry enterprise detached from life but a vital process by which people became engaged in their social world. His hopeful vision was for a sociologically aware society forging a more gentle and just way of life.

The following excerpt provides the first step in Mills's vision.[2] Here he suggests that we must learn to understand our individual lives in terms of the social forces that have shaped them.

> When a society becomes industrialized, a peasant becomes a worker; a feudal lord is liquidated or becomes a businessman. When classes rise or fall, a man is employed or unemployed; when the rate of investment goes up or down, a man takes new heart or goes broke. When wars happen, an insurance salesman becomes a rocket launcher; a store clerk, a radar man; a wife lives alone; a child grows up without a father. Neither the life of an individual nor the history of a society can be understood without understanding both.

[2] In this excerpt, Mills uses male pronouns which appear as he wrote them. Of course, his point applies to all people. It is interesting, and even ironic, that an outspoken critic of society such as Mills reflected the conventional practices of his time in his writing as far as gender was concerned.

Yet men do not usually define the troubles they endure in terms of historical change. . . . The well-being they enjoy, they do not usually impute to the big ups and downs of the society in which they live. Seldom aware of the intricate connection between the patterns of their own lives and the course of world history, ordinary men do not usually know what this connection means for the kind of men they are becoming and for the kinds of history-making in which they might take part. They do not possess the quality of mind essential to grasp the interplay of men and society, of biography and history, of self and world. . . .

What they need . . . is a quality of mind that will help them to [see] . . . what is going on in the world and . . . what may be happening within themselves. It is this quality . . . that . . . may be called the sociological imagination.

. . . The first fruit of this imagination—and the first lesson of the social science that embodies it—is the idea that the individual can understand his own experience and gauge his own fate only by locating himself within his [society].

SOURCE: C. Wright Mills, *The Sociological Imagination* (New York: Oxford University Press, 1959), pp. 3–5; also "Legend of the Left," *Newsweek*, Vol. 63 (May 11, 1964):91–92.

to accept the status quo. *The sociological perspective, therefore, empowers us as active members of our world.* For some, this may mean embracing society as it is; others, however, may attempt nothing less than trying to change the entire world in some way. The discipline of sociology advocates no one particular political orientation. Indeed, sociologists are widely spread across the political spectrum. But evaluating any aspect of social life—whatever one's eventual goal—depends on the ability to identify social forces and to assess their consequences.

Some thirty years ago, C. Wright Mills (1959) pointed out the importance of what he termed the "sociological imagination" in helping people to confront actively the forces of society. This important sociologist is highlighted in the profile box on the previous page. Others will be featured in boxes throughout this book.

THE ORIGINS OF SOCIOLOGY

Like individual "choices," major historical events rarely "just happen." They are typically products of powerful social forces. So it was with sociology itself. Having described the discipline's distinctive perspective and its benefits, we can now consider how and why this point of view emerged in the first place.

Although people have thought about society since the beginning of human history, sociology is one of the youngest academic disciplines—far younger than history, physics, or economics, for example. It was only in 1838 that the French social thinker Auguste Comte, introduced in the box, coined the term *sociology* to describe a new way of looking at the world.

Science and the Development of Sociology

The nature of society was an issue of major importance in the writings of brilliant thinkers of the ancient world, including the Greek philosophers Plato (427–347 B.C.E.) and Aristotle (384–322 B.C.E.).[3] Similarly, the Roman emperor Marcus Aurelius (121–180), the medieval theo-

---

[3] Throughout this text, the abbreviation B.C.E. designates "before the common era." This terminology is used in place of the traditional B.C. ("before Christ") in recognition of the religious plurality of American society. Similarly, in place of the traditional A.D. (anno Domini, or "in the year of our Lord"), the abbreviation C.E. ("common era") is employed.

logian St. Thomas Aquinas (c. 1225–1274), the great English playwright William Shakespeare (1564–1616), and a host of others reflected on human society in their writings. Yet, as Emile Durkheim noted toward the end of the last century, none of these social thinkers approached society with a sociological point of view.

> Looking back in history . . . we find that no philosophers ever viewed matters [with a sociological perspective] until quite recently. . . . It seemed to them sufficient to ascertain what the human will should strive for and what it should avoid in established societies. . . . Their aim was not to offer us as valid a description of nature as possible, but to present us with the idea of a perfect society, a model to be imitated. (1972:57; orig. 1918)

In other words, prior to the birth of sociology, philosophers and theologians were primarily concerned with imagining the "ideal" society, as it ought to be. None attempted an analysis of "real" society, as it actually was. This is what marked the birth of sociology: pioneers of the discipline such as Auguste Comte and Emile Durkheim reversed these priorities. Although they were certainly concerned with how human society could be improved, their major goal was to understand how society actually operates.

The key to achieving this goal, according to Comte, lay in the development of a scientific approach to studying society. Comte divided historical efforts to understand society into three distinct stages (1975; orig. 1851–1854). At least from the medieval period in Europe, people's view of the world around them was heavily shaped by religion. Society was widely held to be an expression of God's will—at least insofar as human beings, under the guidance of the church, were capable of fulfilling a divine plan. Comte considered this to exemplify the *theological stage* in humanity's understanding of society.

With the Renaissance, this theological approach to society gave way to what Comte termed the *metaphysical stage*. During this period, people were less likely to see society as the work of supernatural forces and placed more emphasis on the forces of nature. For instance, the English philosopher Thomas Hobbes (1588–1679) suggested that society reflected not God as much as a rather selfish human nature.

What Comte heralded as the final, *scientific stage* in the long quest to understand society actually had its roots in the work of natural scientists such as the Polish astronomer Copernicus (1473–1543), the Italian astronomer and physicist Galileo (1564–1642), and the English

Auguste Comte (1798–1857)

What sort of person would try to invent *sociology?* Certainly someone living in times of momentous change. Comte grew up in the shadow of the French Revolution, which brought sweeping changes to his country. And if that wasn't sufficient, there was another revolution going on: factories and other kinds of industrial technology were reshaping much of European society. Just as people enduring a storm cannot help but think of the weather, so those living during Comte's lifetime had become very conscious of the state of society.

Drawn from a small town to the intense activity of Paris, Comte became deeply involved in the exciting events of his time. Perhaps most of all, however, he sought a way to understand the human drama that was all around him. His hope was that, with knowledge of how society operates, people would be able to build a better future for themselves. Thus, he was interested in both how society is held together (which he called *social statics*) and in how society changes (*social dynamics*). From the Greek and Latin words meaning "the study of society," Comte came to describe his work as *sociology*.

---

physicist and mathematician Isaac Newton (1642–1727). Comte's contribution came in applying this new scientific approach to the study of society itself.

This approach is often called **positivism,** which may be defined as *a path to understanding the world based on science.* As a positivist, Comte believed that society would be found to conform to invariable laws, much as the physical world operates according to gravity and other laws of nature.

When sociology became established as an academic discipline in the United States at the beginning of this century, early sociologists such as Lester Ward (1841–1913) were strongly influenced by Comte's ideas. Even today, most sociologists continue to view science as a crucial element of sociology. But during the century since Comte's death, sociologists have learned that science cannot be applied to the social world in the same way that it is applied to the physical world. As we shall explain in Chapter 2 ("Sociological Investigation"), the causes of human behavior are often far more complex than the causes of events in the natural world. In other words, human beings are more than physical objects. We are creatures with considerable imagination and spontaneity, so that our behavior can never be fully explained by any rigid "laws of society."

Social Change and the Development of Sociology

We have already suggested that the birth of sociology was provoked by revolutionary changes in society itself. European societies were experiencing striking transformations during the seventeenth and eighteenth centuries. As the social ground trembled under their feet, people were understandably less likely to take society for granted.

The sociological perspective was sparked by three basic and interrelated changes. First, rapid technological innovation in eighteenth-century Europe soon led to the spread of factories and an industrial economy. Second, these factories drew millions of people from the countryside, causing an explosive growth of cities. Third, people in these expanding industrial cities soon began to entertain new ideas about the world, leading to important political developments. We shall briefly describe each of these three changes in turn.

The Rise of the Industrial Economy

During the Middle Ages, most people in Europe tilled fields near their homes or engaged in small-scale *manu-*

The Industrial Revolution drew people in Europe and North America away from small towns to rapidly growing industrial cities. The discipline of sociology developed in precisely the areas of the world in which traditional social patterns were disrupted in this way.

facturing (a word derived from Latin words meaning "to make by hand"). Thus, most people worked where they lived, and homes were often centers of commercial endeavors such as baking, making furniture, and sewing garments.

Early in the eighteenth century, as new sources of energy, including steam power, were harnessed to large machines, factories began to appear. Instead of laboring at home, on land their families had worked for generations in tightly knit communities, workers became part of a largely anonymous industrial labor force, working away from home, often for strangers who owned and controlled the factories. In this way, factories and the expanding industrial economy shook medieval society to its foundations. The inevitable result of the rising industrial economy was the rapid breakdown of long-established ways of life within countless small communities. Further, factories drawing people from the country-side also produced cities.

The Growth of Cities

The factories that sprouted across England and other areas of Western Europe became magnets attracting peo-ple in need of work. This "pull" was made all the more powerful by an additional "push" from the countryside. As the English textile industry expanded, farmland was transformed into grazing land to raise sheep—the source of wool. In the process known as the "enclosure move-ment," countless people pushed from the countryside flooded into the cities in search of employment in facto-ries.

Not surprisingly, these now-industrial cities soon became bigger than ever before. Settlements during the Middle Ages had been mere towns: small, self-contained worlds, often within defensive walls. As late as 1700, the dawning of the industrial era, London was the largest city in Europe, with only 500,000 people. Two centuries later, London's population had increased thirteen times over to 6.5 million (Chandler & Fox, 1974).

Urban growth of this kind took place across the European continent, dramatically changing people's lives in the process. Not only were cities full of strangers, but the tremendous influx of people simply overwhelmed the city's capacity to absorb them. Widespread social problems—including pollution, crime, and inadequate housing—were the order of the day. These were the kinds of social crises that stimulated the development of the sociological perspective.

Political Changes

During the Middle Ages, as Comte noted, most people thought of society as an act of divine will. The feudal nobility, for instance, claimed to rule by "divine right," as if the entire social order were simply God's plan for humanity. Such a view of society is clearly evident in lines from the old Anglican hymn "All Things Bright and Beautiful":

> The rich man in his castle,
> The poor man at his gate,
> He made them high and lowly
> And ordered their estate.

As we look back now, a transformed economy and the rapid growth of cities seems to have made changes in political thought inevitable. By the sixteenth century, the political conservatism that had characterized the medieval era was succumbing to a spirited attack on every kind of tradition, especially the notion that society was an expression of divine will. In the writings of Thomas Hobbes, John Locke (1632–1704), and Adam Smith (1723–1790), we find less concern with the moral obligations of people to society and more support for the idea that society is the product of self-interest. Indeed, the key phrases in the new political climate surrounded the individual: *individual liberty* and *individual rights*. Echoing the thoughts of John Locke, the American Declaration of Independence, which celebrated the separation of the American colonies from England, is a clear statement of these new political ideas. Here we read that all people have "certain unalienable rights," including "life, liberty, and the pursuit of happiness." The political revolution in France that began soon afterward in 1789 was, of course, an even more dramatic effort to break with political and social traditions.

As he surveyed his own society after the French Revolution, the French social and political thinker Alexis de Tocqueville was only slightly exaggerating when he exclaimed that the changes we have described amounted to "nothing short of the regeneration of the whole human race" (1955:13; orig. 1856). In this context, it is easy to see why Auguste Comte and other pioneers soon developed the new discipline of sociology. Sociology flowered in precisely those societies that had experienced the most pronounced social changes. France, Germany, and England underwent a truly revolutionary social transformation, and in all three sociology had emerged by the end of the nineteenth century. On the other hand, in societies touched less by these momentous events—including Portugal, Spain, Italy, and Eastern Europe—there was little development of the sociological perspective.

Individual sociologists reacted differently to the new social order, just as they respond differently to society today. Some found the emerging modern world to be deeply disturbing. One response, exemplified by Auguste Comte, was conservative. He feared that people would

This drawing suggests the apprehension as well as the excitement of early scientists breaking away from conventional understandings of the universe. Pioneering sociologists set out to explore the operation of human society, generating new and often controversial ideas.

be overpowered by change and uprooted from long-established local communities; he sought a rebirth of traditional family, community, and morality.

Different criticism of these massive changes was offered by the German social critic Karl Marx (1818–1883), whose ideas are introduced in Chapter 4 ("Society"). Marx worried little about the loss of traditional social patterns, which he detested. But neither could he condone the concentration of the great wealth produced by industrial technology in the hands of a small elite, while the masses commonly faced only hunger and misery.

Clearly, the beliefs of Comte and Marx were strikingly different. Yet they shared the conviction that society cannot be understood simply in terms of individual choice. Rather, the sociological perspective that animates the work of each reveals that the essential issues involve not particular people but general social patterns that influence us all even today.

The major issues within the discipline of sociology—topics featured in subsequent chapters of this book—include precisely these general social patterns. Culture, social class, race, ethnicity, gender, the family, and religion—all show us the ways in which individuals are guided, united, and divided within the larger arena of society.

SOCIOLOGICAL THEORY

The discipline of sociology involves more than a distinctive point of view. Linking specific observations in a meaningful way involves another element of the discipline: theory. In the simplest terms, a **theory** is *an explanation of the relationship between two or more specific facts.* To illustrate the use of theory in sociology, recall Emile Durkheim's study of suicide. Durkheim attempted to explain the fact that some categories of people (males, Protestants, the wealthy, and the unmarried) have higher suicide rates than others (females, Catholics, Jews, the poor, and the married). He did this by linking one fact—suicide rates—to another fact—the degree of social integration characteristic of these various categories of people. Through systematic comparisons, Durkheim refined his theory of suicide, showing that people with low social integration are more prone to take their own lives.

To illustrate further, how might we explain the sociological observation that more men than women enroll in college science courses? One possible theory is that the sciences are more attractive to males than to females; perhaps males simply have a greater innate interest in science. A second theoretical approach suggests that the educational system has some formal or informal policy that limits the enrollment of women in science courses. Still another possibility is that American society encourages males to develop an interest in science while simultaneously discouraging this interest in females.

As this example shows, there is usually more than one theoretical explanation for any particular social pattern. Therefore, merely linking facts together does not ensure that a theory is correct. In order to evaluate a theory, sociologists make use of various methods of scientific research, which the next chapter describes in detail. Sociologists use research methods to gather more and more information so that they are able to confirm some theories while rejecting or modifying others. Early in this century, for example, the rapid growth of cities provoked theories linking urban living to pronounced impersonality and even mental illness. As we shall explain in Chapter 20 ("Health and Medicine"), however, research has subsequently shown that living in a large city does not necessarily result in being socially isolated, nor does it diminish mental health. Theory, then, is never static; it is continually being refined through sociological research, just as it is in other types of science.

In attempting to develop theories about human society, sociologists face a wide range of choices. What issues should they choose to study? How should facts be linked together to form theories? Questions such as these are not answered in a haphazard fashion. Rather, theory building is guided by a general framework called a theoretical paradigm (Kuhn, 1970). As applied to sociology, a **theoretical paradigm** is defined as *a set of fundamental assumptions about society that guides sociological thinking and research.*

We suggested earlier that two of sociology's founders—Auguste Comte and Karl Marx—made sense of the emerging modern society in rather different ways. Such differences continue to exist among sociologists today. Some are more concerned with how society manages to maintain itself over time; others focus on how societies change. Similarly, some direct attention to what joins people together, while others investigate how society divides people according to sex, race, or social class. Moreover, some sociologists seek to understand the operation of society as it exists, while others see their work as encouraging what they consider to be desirable social change.

In short, sociologists often disagree about what the most interesting questions are, and even when they address the same questions, they may still disagree about the answers. Nonetheless, sociological theory is far from chaotic, because sociologists do agree that three major theoretical paradigms allow for effective analysis of virtually all dimensions of society.

The Structural-Functional Paradigm

The **structural-functional paradigm** is *a theoretical framework based on the assumption that society is a complex system whose parts work together to promote stability.* Stability is perhaps the key feature of this model of society. As its name suggests, the structural-functional paradigm has two components. First, society is composed of various kinds of **social structure,** defined as *a relatively stable pattern of social behavior.* Social structure ranges from broad patterns including the family and religious systems to forms of greeting and other patterns that characterize face-to-face social contact. Second, all structures are related in terms of their **social functions,** which refer to *consequences for the operation of society as a whole.* Thus all the elements of society—from religious belief to a simple handshake—have important functions that help society to persist, at least in its present form.

The structural-functional paradigm owes much to the ideas of Auguste Comte, who was concerned about how his own society could remain unified while undergoing massive change. Another who advanced this theoretical approach was the English sociologist Herbert Spencer

PROFILE

Herbert Spencer (1820–1903)

Herbert Spencer's most memorable idea was his assertion that the future would be characterized by "the survival of the fittest." Many people link this immortal phrase to the model of species evolution developed by the natural scientist Charles Darwin (1809–1882). The idea was actually Spencer's, however, and he was referring to society, not the human species. But Spencer's remark shows how deeply early sociological thought was influenced by comparisons between the social and natural worlds.

Spencer's view of society, which came to be known as *social Darwinism,* was that success would come to the most intelligent, ambitious, and productive people, who were likely to survive at the expense of the less able. This was good, Spencer claimed, because this process would steadily improve society as it evolved.

The key to successful societal evolution, he argued, was simply not to meddle with society, especially its free-market economy. For this, Spencer was widely applauded by many early industrialists who endorsed the idea of big business free of any government regulation or social conscience. Indeed, John D. Rockefeller, who gobbled up companies to gain control of much of the American oil industry early in this century, often repeated Spencer's words to young children in Sunday school, maintaining that the growth of giant businesses is merely the "survival of the fittest."

But there were others who objected to the idea that society was simply a jungle in which people could use whatever advantage they could muster in complete selfishness. Many found in the new industrial America a pressing need for social welfare programs that would assist the poor. From Spencer's point of view, of course, welfare damaged society by favoring its least worthy members.

Gradually, Spencer's doctrine of social Darwinism has been discredited among social scientists, although it remains influential in American society. In part, this is a matter of fact: we now know that personal ability is only a partial explanation of success, and favoring the rich and powerful is not necessarily in the interest of society as a whole. In addition, as a matter of values, Spencer's ideas have been widely dismissed as a remarkably heartless view of society with little room for any human compassion.

(1820–1903), introduced in the box. A student of both the human body and society, Spencer asserted that the two have much in common. The structural parts of the human body include the skeleton, muscles, and various internal organs. All of these body parts are interdependent, and each one has a function that contributes to the survival of the human organism. Likewise, reasoned Spencer, the elements of human society are interdependent and work to keep society operating. This approach, then, leads sociologists to identify the various parts of society, asking what part each plays in the operation of the whole.

Several decades after the death of Comte, Emile Durkheim continued the development of the structural-functional paradigm in France. Like Spencer, his English counterpart, Durkheim investigated ways in which modern societies maintain their social integration. Because of the importance of his ideas to later chapters, Durkheim's analysis of social structures and their functions will be detailed in Chapter 4 ("Society").

As sociology developed within the United States, the approach of Herbert Spencer and Emile Durkheim was carried forward by Talcott Parsons (1902–1979). As the major proponent of the structural-functional paradigm in American sociology, Parsons attempted to identify the major functions any and all societies had to perform in order to survive, and how they accomplished them.

A contemporary American sociologist whose work is largely guided by the structural-functional paradigm is Robert K. Merton. Merton (1968) has shown that any part of society can have many functions, some more obvious than others. The **manifest functions** of any element of social structure are *consequences that are recognized and intended by people within the society.* On the other hand, **latent functions** are *consequences that are largely unrecognized and unintended.* The rapid proliferation of automobiles during this century illustrates this distinction. One of their manifest functions is transporting people and goods from one place to another. Another is serving as what we commonly call a *status symbol.* This means that a domestic economy car will get you where you're going just as an expensive foreign model will, but each makes a different statement about one's taste and bank account. Autos also have important latent functions. Because they allow people to travel about in relative isolation, autos reinforce the American emphasis on personal autonomy. This is one reason that private automobiles have long been favored by most Americans over public transit systems.

Merton has a further point: it is unlikely that *all* the effects of a single element of social structure will be useful. Merton identified these effects as **social dysfunctions,** or *undesirable effects on the operation of society.* One of the dysfunctions of the American reliance on private automobiles is that, with more than 180 million of them, air quality has become poor, especially in large cities. No doubt, too, the easy travel made possible by cars has contributed to a decline in the strength of traditional families and local neighborhoods, changes lamented by many Americans.

Critical evaluation. Despite its strong influence on the discipline of sociology, recent decades have revealed limitations of the structural-functional paradigm. In the process of focusing attention on ways in which society is unified, critics point out, structural-functionalism tends to pay less attention to powerful divisions based on social class, race, ethnicity, and sex, and especially ignores how such divisions often generate tension and conflict. In addition, the structural-functional emphasis on social stability tends to push aside concern for the important processes of conflict and social change. Overall, then, the general character of this paradigm is conservative. As a critical response, another theoretical orientation in sociology has developed: the social-conflict paradigm.

The Social-Conflict Paradigm

The **social-conflict paradigm** is *a theoretical framework based on the assumption that society is a complex system characterized by inequality and conflict that generate social change.* This approach complements the structural-functional paradigm by highlighting not social integration but social differences, especially inequality. Guided by this paradigm, sociologists investigate how factors such as social class, race, ethnicity, sex, and age are linked to unequal distribution of valuable resources, including money, power, education, and social prestige. Therefore, rather than identifying how social patterns can be functional for society as a whole, this approach investigates how they are useful to some people and harmful to others.

In this way, the social-conflict paradigm leads sociologists to view society as an arena in which conflict emerges from the incompatible interests of various categories of people. Not surprisingly, dominant categories— the rich in relation to the poor, whites in relation to nonwhites, and males in relation to females—typically try to protect their privileges by supporting the status quo. Those with fewer privileges commonly counter these efforts by attempting to bring about a more equitable distribution of social resources.

To illustrate, Chapter 16 ("Education") explains how American secondary schools prepare some students for college and emphasize vocational training for others. The structural-functional paradigm would suggest that society as a whole might benefit from such "tracking" if, for instance, different types of education are provided to students with varying academic abilities. The social-conflict paradigm provides a contrasting insight: this practice confers privileges on some that it denies to others, thereby perpetuating social inequality and promoting conflict between favored and disadvantaged categories of people.

Research has shown that American students are placed in college-preparatory tracks not so much for their

Karl Marx maintained that ideas about the world should be linked to action intended to improve the human condition.

intelligence as for the privileged background of their families. Virtually ensured of becoming part of the minority of Americans with a college education, most are likely to enter occupations that will provide both prestige and a high income. In the process, of course, the privileges of one generation are passed to another. In contrast, schools commonly fill vocational tracks with students from less privileged backgrounds, sometimes with little regard for their actual abilities. They receive no preparation for college, and thus, like their parents before them, they are likely to enter occupations that provide little prestige and low income. Furthermore, research shows that the alleged foundation of this practice—the academic ability of those involved—is difficult to determine apart from social background (Bowles & Gintis, 1976; Oakes, 1982, 1985). The overall result is that the concept of "ability" is often used to justify a practice that really amounts to perpetuating privilege.

Other important examples of social conflict in American society are strikes and other kinds of labor unrest, the civil rights movement, and the more recent movement seeking social equality for women. Overall, then, rather than viewing society as relatively stable, the social-conflict paradigm shows how social structure fosters continual conflict involving forces of change and resistance to change.

Finally, many sociologists who make use of the social-conflict paradigm attempt not only to understand society as it is but also to reduce social inequality. This was the goal of Karl Marx, the social thinker who has had a singularly important influence upon the development of the social-conflict paradigm in sociology. Marx had little patience with those who sought to use science only to understand how society works. In a well-known declaration (inscribed on his monument in London's Highgate Cemetery), Marx maintained: "The philosophers have only interpreted the world, in various ways; the point, however, is to change it."

Critical evaluation. The social-conflict paradigm has developed rapidly in recent decades to become a major part of sociology. As the paradigm itself would lead us to expect, more traditional sociological thinkers have voiced criticisms. One general concern is that this approach highlights power struggles as the dominant way in which society is held together but gives little attention to social unity involving functional interdependence and shared values. In addition, the social conflict approach is often criticized for explicitly advocating change, thereby giving up at least some claim to scientific objectivity. In response, advocates of this approach respond that *all* social analysis has political consequences, albeit different ones.

An additional criticism, which applies equally to both the structural-functional and social-conflict paradigms, is that they approach society in terms of broad generalities. A third theoretical paradigm views society more in terms of face-to-face social interaction.

The Symbolic-Interaction Paradigm

Both the structural-functional and social-conflict paradigms share a **macro-level orientation**, meaning *a concern with large-scale patterns that characterize society as a whole.* They approach society as you might investigate a city from the windows of a helicopter—noting, for example, that highways facilitate traffic flow from one place to another, or that there are striking contrasts between the neighborhoods of the rich and the poor. The symbolic-interaction paradigm, however, differs, providing a **micro-level orientation**, meaning *a concern with small-scale patterns of social interaction in specific settings.* Exploring urban life in this way means being at street level, observing, for example, face-to-face interaction in public parks or how people respond to a homeless person they pass on the street. The **symbolic-interaction paradigm**, then, is *a theoretical framework based on the assumption that society involves interaction by which individuals actively construct reality in everyday life.*

How are the lives of millions of distinct individuals woven together into the drama of society? One answer, discussed in detail in Chapter 3 ("Culture"), is that people interact in terms of shared symbols and meanings. Only in rare situations do we respond to each other in direct, physical terms, as when someone ducks to avoid a punch. Mostly, we respond to others according to the meanings we attach to them. For example, if we define a homeless man on a city street as "just a bum looking for a handout," we may ignore him. On the contrary, if defined as a "fellow human being in need," he becomes part of a situation that actively engages us. Similarly, a police officer walking nearby may generate a sense of security in some pedestrians and a feeling of nervous anxiety in others. Sociologists guided by the symbolic-interaction approach view society as a complex mosaic of subjective perceptions and responses.

The development of the symbolic-interaction para-

digm was greatly influenced by Max Weber (1864–1920), a German sociologist who emphasized the importance of understanding society as it is subjectively perceived by individuals. Weber's approach to understanding society is considered at length in Chapter 4 ("Society").

From this foundation, others have developed a number of related approaches to understanding society. Chapter 5 ("Socialization") discusses the ideas of American sociologist George Herbert Mead (1863–1931), who explored how the human personality gradually emerges as a result of social experience. Chapter 6 ("Social Interaction in Everyday Life") presents the work of American sociologist Erving Goffman (1922–1982). Goffman's approach to understanding society is described as *dramaturgical analysis* because it emphasizes how human beings resemble actors on a stage as we deliberately foster certain impressions in the minds of others. Other contemporary sociologists, including George Homans and Peter Blau, have developed an approach called *social-exchange analysis.* This shows how social interaction is often guided by what each one stands to gain and lose from others. In Chapter 15 ("Family") this approach is applied to the process of courtship, in which individuals typically seek mates who offer them at least as much—in terms of physical attractiveness, intelligence, and social background—as they offer in return.

Critical evaluation. The symbolic paradigm helps to overcome a limitation typical of all macro-level approaches to understanding society. Society is indeed composed of broad social patterns, such as "the family" and "social inequality." The existence of social structure, however, does not negate society's foundation in people actively engaging one another in social interaction. Put another way, as a micro-approach, this paradigm attempts to convey more of how we as individuals actually *experience* society. At the same time, all social experience is affected by social structure, just as what you choose to do in the future will be guided (although not determined) by your past life.

The structural-functional paradigm, the social-conflict paradigm, and the symbolic-interaction paradigm are three major frameworks that guide the efforts of sociologists to develop an understanding of society. Their important characteristics are summarized in Table 1–1. As we have noted, certain kinds of questions suggest the use of a particular theoretical paradigm. In many cases, however, the greatest benefits come from linking the sociological perspective to all three, as we shall now illustrate with an analysis of sports in American society.

Table 1–1 THE THREE MAJOR THEORETICAL PARADIGMS: A SUMMARY

Theoretical Paradigm	Orientation	Image of Society	Illustrative Questions
Structural-functional	Macro-level	A system of interrelated parts that is relatively stable based on widespread consensus as to what is morally desirable; each part has functional consequences for the operation of society as a whole	How is society integrated? What are the major parts of society? How are these parts interrelated? What are the consequences of each for the operation of society?
Social-conflict	Macro-level	A system characterized by social inequality; any part of society benefits some categories of people more than others; conflict-based social inequality promotes social change	How is society divided? What are major patterns of social inequality? How do some categories of people attempt to protect their privileges? How do other categories of people challenge the status quo?
Symbolic-interaction	Micro-level	An ongoing process of social interaction in specific settings based on symbolic communications; individual perceptions of reality are variable and changing	How is society experienced? How do human beings interact to create, sustain, and change social patterns? How do individuals attempt to shape the reality perceived by others? How does individual behavior change from one situation to another?

Sports: An Illustration of the Three Theoretical Paradigms

Sports seem indispensable to social life in North America. Almost every American has engaged in some type of sport, from gym classes throughout the school years to continued participation in sports by many adults well into old age. In the United States, the sale of sporting goods is a multibillion-dollar industry, and more and more Americans observe and discuss sporting events each year. Television brings sports to American living rooms, not only as part of newscasts, but as regular programming averaging more than three hours a day (Coakley, 1990).

What new insights can the sociological perspective provide about this important and familiar element of American society? Each of the three major theoretical paradigms in sociology provides part of the answer.

The Functions of Sports

A structural-functional approach directs attention to various functions of sports for society as a whole. The manifest functions of sports include providing both recreation, and a relatively harmless way to "let off steam," and contributing to the physical fitness of the population. Sports have important latent functions as well, from fostering social relationships to generating tens of thousands of jobs. Perhaps the most important latent function of sports is encouraging specific attitudes and patterns of behavior that are central to American society.

For example, the personal effort and discipline essential to success in sports are necessary in achieving success in other areas as well. Being a team player and playing by the rules are other important social skills developed through participating or watching sporting events. Probably most significantly, sports generate the sense of personal competition that individualistic Americans value so much in celebrating a "winner" (Spates, 1976a; Coakley, 1990). When he said, "Winning is not everything, but making the effort to win is," Vince Lombardi was speaking not only as a football coach; he was also speaking as a typical American.

Sports also have dysfunctional consequences, of course. For example, colleges and universities intent on having winning teams may recruit students for their athletic ability rather than for their academic aptitude.

The painting *Pastime* by Gerald Garston suggests that baseball—the Great American Pastime—is more than mere diversion and entertainment. In addition, it provides valuable lessons about how we as Americans are expected to think and behave.

This can adversely affect the academic standards of the school and may also leave the athletes themselves little time to learn anything but their sport. Len Bias, a University of Maryland basketball star who died tragically from cocaine use in 1986, earned no academic credits during his last semester—a situation far from rare among athletes who must practice from four to five hours a day (Bingham, 1987). The tragedy of Len Bias is all the greater because he was part of the 1 percent of male college players who earn a professional sports contract. For too many others, the long-term benefits of attending college are meager. As sociologist Harry Edwards points out about his own university, "I've known athletes . . . who are functional illiterates who have been here for four years. If this is going on at [the University of California at] Berkeley, which is supposed to have such integrity,

imagine what's going on at the jock-factory schools" (cited in Bowen, 1985:64).

In sum, the structural-functional paradigm suggests that sports contribute in many ways to the operation of American society. Perhaps the most important of these is teaching and celebrating the ideas of competition and personal success central to our way of life.

Sports and Social Conflict

A social-conflict analysis of sports would begin by pointing out that sports are closely related to patterns of American social inequality. Some sports, such as tennis, swimming, golf, and skiing, are expensive, so participation is largely limited to the well-to-do. On the other hand, the sports with mass appeal, including football, baseball, and basketball, are accessible to average people of modest means. In other words, the games people play are likely to reflect broader patterns of economic inequality.

Within the United States, sports are also overwhelmingly oriented toward males. Sexual discrimination has traditionally limited the opportunities of females in most sports, even when they have the talent, interest, and economic means to do so. When the first modern Olympic Games were held in 1896, for example, women were excluded from all competition (Mangan & Park, 1987). Until quite recently, girls were also barred from Little League teams in most parts of the country. This exclusion has been defended by ungrounded sexual stereotypes that claim that girls either lack the ability to engage in sports or risk losing their femininity if they do so. Joan Benoit, a gold medalist marathon runner in the 1984 Olympic Games, conceded that becoming a serious athlete seemed somehow "wrong" for an American woman: "When I first started running I was so embarrassed I'd walk when cars passed me. I'd pretend I was looking at the flowers" (cited in Coakley, 1986:115).

Thus, we observe a social pattern within American society by which males are encouraged to be athletes and females are expected to be attentive observers and cheerleaders. In 1989, 57 percent of male high-school seniors claimed to be active in sports, compared to 31 percent of senior females (U.S. Congress, 1989). But the fitness movement and political efforts by women resulting in government legislation are reducing this inequity, already evident in the sizable increase of high-school women in sports programs from about 300,000 in 1970 to 1.8 million by 1984 (Coakley, 1986:116). In addition, more women now play professionally than ever before, and enjoy growing spectator interest. Still,

Sociologist Harry Edwards has helped professional baseball officials recognize and respond to social barriers that have historically excluded nonwhites from management positions.

women continue to take a backseat to men in professional sports—particularly in those that provide the most earnings and social prestige.

It is true that nonwhites in American society have enjoyed a greater opportunity to earn high incomes in professional sports than in many other occupations. This is a relatively recent development, however. In professional baseball, the first of the major American sports to admit nonwhite players, only in 1947 was the "color line" broken by Jackie Robinson. By 1985, however, blacks accounted for one in five professional baseball players, just over half of all football players, and three-fourths of all basketball players (Coakley, 1986:145).

According to Harry Edwards (1973), the increasing proportion of black males in professional sports is largely due to the fact that individual athletic performances can be measured precisely. For this reason, white prejudice cannot easily diminish the achievement of nonwhite athletes. In addition, faced with continuing discrimination in many areas of life, many blacks look to careers in athletics as a chance to escape disadvantage.

Nonetheless, racial discrimination continues to shape professional sports in the United States. For example, while nonwhite players are now common, as the 1990s begin almost all managers, head coaches, and owners of sports teams are still white. In 1987, Al Campanis, a vice-president of the Los Angeles Dodgers baseball team, stated on national television that while blacks are good athletes, they may lack the "necessities" to become team managers and executives. The furor that followed this racist remark revealed to Americans that forty years after Jackie Robinson's great achievement nonwhites continue to be excluded from professional sports beyond the playing fields (Jones, 1987). One response was that Peter Ueberroth, the baseball commissioner, hired Harry Edwards as a special consultant to help black and Hispanic former players find new jobs in baseball management (Litsky, 1987).

Furthermore, nonwhite players are unlikely to play in the starring positions in professional sports. For example, about 70 percent of black players in the major leagues play in the outfield (Staples, 1987). Figure 1–3 on page 24 shows the proportion of white and black players in the various positions within professional football and basketball and of Hispanic players, as well, for baseball. Clearly, in all three sports, the central positions have the highest proportion of white players.

On a broader level, the social-conflict paradigm raises the question of what category of people benefits most from the operation of professional sports teams. Although millions of Americans watch professional sports, the vast profits these teams produce are controlled by the small number of people—predominantly white males—who own the teams as income-generating property. Though the people living in a city may speak of a professional team as "ours," the reality is that the team is controlled by an owner who would not hesitate to move it to another city in search of higher profits.

In the last decade or so, professional athletes have managed to gain a larger share of what their teams earn. By 1989, for example, the average salary of major-league baseball players had risen to about $490,000—seventeen times higher than the average in 1970, and far higher than salaries of even the baseball greats of the past. Nonetheless, baseball and other professional sports provide high income to only a tiny proportion of nonwhite Americans. Furthermore, in all professional sports, the lion's share of both power and profits continues to be held by the few owners.

In sum, the social-conflict paradigm analyzes professional sports in terms of patterns of social inequality. As noted earlier, sports may reflect the importance of competition and achievement to all Americans, but they are also bound up with extensive inequalities based on sex, race, and economic power.

Sports as Interaction

Any sports event is also a complex pattern of social interaction. In part, the participants' behavior is guided by

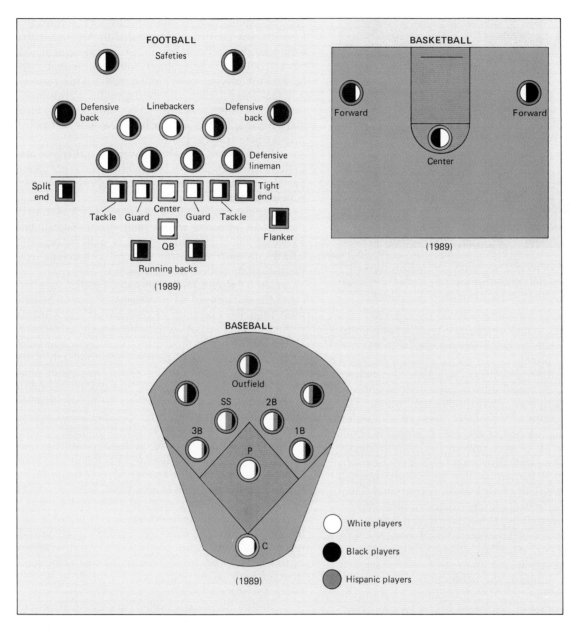

Figure 1–3 Race and Professional Sports: Patterns of Discrimination
These diagrams show the proportion of white and black players for each position in professional
football and basketball, and the proportion of white, black, and Hispanic players for each
position in professional baseball. In each case, the central positions—outlined in blue—
have the highest proportion of white players.

(*Coakley, 1990; Baseball data compiled by* USA Today, *August 10, 1989:11c*) their assigned positions and by the rules of the game. Like all human behavior, however, sports are also partly spontaneous. For this reason, each game is a unique event that unfolds in ways that cannot be predicted. According to the symbolic-interaction paradigm, sports are less a "system" than an ongoing process.

The symbolic-interaction paradigm also draws attention to the fact that each player is likely to understand the game at least somewhat differently. This is especially true with regard to competition—a key element in American sports. For people who have very competitive personalities, the heightened pressure that accompanies a sports event increases motivation to perform well. Some may even play the game simply for the thrill of outperforming opponents. For others, love of the game may be greater than the need to be a winner; these people may actually perform less well under pressure. Still others use sports to build personal friendships and may fear that competition will alienate players from one another (Coakley, 1986).

Although observers tend to think of a team as a single entity, team members are distinct human beings who are likely to "shape their own realities" as they perceive one another in terms of particular prejudices and jealousies, as well as respect. Furthermore, the behavior of any single player is likely to change over time. A rookie, for example, can be expected to feel quite self-conscious during the first few games in the big leagues. In time, however, a more comfortable sense of really being a member of the team may emerge. This process of coming to feel at home in professional sports was slow and agonizing for Jackie Robinson, who initially was only too aware that many white players, and millions of white baseball fans, resented his presence in major-league baseball (Tygiel, 1983). In time, however, his outstanding performance as a player and his confident and cooperative manner off the field won him the respect of the entire nation.

Furthermore, in spite of varied motives and perceptions, each player is expected to display team spirit and other elements of good sportsmanship. The dramaturgical approach of Erving Goffman (1959) suggests that American athletes typically embrace the ideals of honesty, hard work, and, above all, the will to win. In reality, of course, many fall quite short of these ideals. For instance, frequent news accounts since the mid-1980s have documented the involvement of both amateur and professional athletes with illegal drugs, which has prompted controversial calls for mandatory drug testing. The ideal image of the athlete was also shaken in 1989 by the expulsion from baseball of Cincinnati Reds manager Pete Rose. A model athlete who had earned the nickname "Charlie Hustle," Rose was found to have engaged for years in illegal wagering on baseball games, including those of his own team.

We now recognize that sports is a complex activity that has many levels of meaning. It is a social ritual that affirms American values (as the structural-functional paradigm suggests), a form of social inequality that advantages some categories of Americans in relation to others (as the social-conflict paradigm helps to show), and an endeavor that illustrates how individual men and women engage each other in the ongoing human drama of reality construction (as the symbolic-interaction paradigm indicates). The same holds for countless other dimensions of social life; these three theoretical paradigms will be systematically used to explore significant elements of American society throughout the text.

Overall, the differences in these paradigms do not imply that one is more correct than another. Applied to various social issues, the different theoretical paradigms generate fascinating debates and controversies, many of which are found in later chapters. It is the goal of the remainder of this book to convey the broadest range of understanding that the sociological perspective offers.

SUMMARY

1. The sociological perspective provides the means to recognize that the lives of individuals are shaped by the forces of society. This point of view may be described as "seeing the general in the particular."
2. Because Americans tend to see events as the product of individual will, the impact of social forces on individual lives goes largely unrecognized. Therefore, revealing how social forces shape everyday life can also be described as "seeing the strange in the familiar."
3. Emile Durkheim was able to show how social forces affect even the most personal of our actions. He did this by demonstrating that suicide is more com-

mon among some categories of people than among others.

4. The sociological perspective sometimes arises naturally, as when we enter an unfamiliar setting. Similarly, socially marginal people are likely to perceive the effects of society more than do others. During periods of social crisis, everyone is more likely to view the world sociologically.

5. There are four general benefits to using the sociological perspective. First, it challenges our familiar understandings of the world; second, it makes us aware of the diversity of human social behavior; third, it reveals constraints and opportunities that affect our lives; and fourth, it encourages more active participation in society.

6. Auguste Comte gave sociology its name in 1838. Whereas previous social thought focused on what society ought to be, sociology was based on the use of scientific methods to understand society as it is.

7. Sociology emerged as a reaction to the rapid transformation of European society during the eighteenth and nineteenth centuries. The rise of an industrial economy, the explosive growth of cities, and the emergence of new political ideas combined to direct attention to the operation of society.

8. Sociological insights are linked together in meaningful ways by sociological theory. Theory building is guided by one or more theoretical paradigms.

9. The structural-functional paradigm is a framework for exploring how social structures function to promote the stable operation of society. This approach tends to minimize the conflict linked to social inequality and to view social change as the exception rather than the rule.

10. The social-conflict paradigm suggests that the conflict generated by social inequality promotes ongoing social change. On the other hand, this approach tends to minimize the extent of social integration and social stability.

11. In contrast to these two macro-level approaches, the symbolic-interaction paradigm is a micro-level framework for studying patterns of social interaction within specific situations. At this level of analysis, society is seen as subjective, highly variable, and at least somewhat unpredictable.

12. The three major theoretical paradigms provide different, but complementary, analyses of sports. The structural-functional paradigm emphasizes that sports encourage typically American patterns of behavior. The social-conflict paradigm links sports to patterns of social inequality. The symbolic-interaction paradigm focuses on the subjective, largely spontaneous interplay of individual human beings in sports, as in all social life.

13. Because each paradigm highlights different dimensions of any social issue, the richest understanding is derived from applying all three.

KEY CONCEPTS

latent functions the unrecognized and unintended consequences of any social pattern

macro-level orientation a concern with large-scale patterns that characterize society as a whole

manifest functions the recognized and intended consequences of any social pattern

micro-level orientation a concern with small-scale patterns of social interaction within specific settings

positivism Comte's system for understanding the world based on science

social-conflict paradigm a theoretical framework based on the assumption that society is a complex system characterized by inequality and conflict that generate social change

social dysfunction the undesirable consequences of any social pattern for the operation of society

social function the consequences of any social pattern for the operation of society

social marginality the state of being excluded from social activity as an "outsider"

social structure a relatively stable pattern of social behavior

sociology the scientific study of human social activity

structural-functional paradigm a theoretical framework

based on the assumption that society is a complex system whose parts work together to promote stability

symbolic-interaction paradigm a theoretical framework based on the assumption that society involves interaction by which individuals actively construct reality in everyday life

theoretical paradigm a set of fundamental assumptions that guides thinking and research

theory an explanation of the relationship between two or more specific facts

SUGGESTED READINGS

These two paperbacks are readable classics that describe the sociological perspective and the benefits of learning to think sociologically.

C. Wright Mills. *The Sociological Imagination.* New York: Oxford University Press, 1959.

Peter Berger. *An Invitation to Sociology.* Garden City, NY: Anchor Books, 1963.

This paperback provides supplementary readings that follow the chapter flow of this book. For each topic, classic essays from sociological literature are accompanied by works emphasizing contemporary and cross-cultural issues.

John J. Macionis and Nijole V. Benokraitis, eds. *Seeing Ourselves: Classic, Contemporary, and Cross-Cultural Readings in Sociology.* Englewood Cliffs, NJ: Prentice Hall, 1989.

This collection of essays examines the potential contribution of sociology to various areas of social life and points to factors that have limited the discipline's significance in the past.

Edgar F. Borgatta and Karen S. Cook. *The Future of Sociology.* Newbury Park, CA: Sage Publications, 1988.

This recent sociological analysis of suicide in modern Japan supports Durkheim's contention that social forces are at work even in the most personal of actions.

Mamoru Iga. *The Thorn in the Chrysanthemum: Suicide and Economic Success in Modern Japan.* Berkeley: University of California Press, 1986.

George C. Homans, a senior American sociologist, reflects on his discipline, on American society, and on the ways his own life was shaped by membership in one of Boston's most privileged families.

George Caspar Homans. *Coming to My Senses: The Autobiography of a Sociologist.* New Brunswick, NJ: Transaction Books, 1984.

The following two books describe the history of sociology. The first is a general intellectual history of the discipline focusing on sociology's European roots. The second details the development of American sociology at the University of Chicago in the years after World War I.

Randall Collins and Michael Makowsky. *The Discovery of Society.* New York: Random House, 1984.

Martin Bulmer. *The Chicago School of Sociology: Institutionalization, Diversity, and the Rise of Sociological Research.* Chicago: University of Chicago Press, 1984.

Although better known as a civil rights activist, W. E. B. DuBois also made a contribution to early American sociology.

Dan S. Green and Edwin D. Driver, eds. *W. E. B. DuBois on Sociology and the Black Community.* Chicago: University of Chicago Press, 1978.

A comprehensive sociological analysis of sports is found in this paperback.

Jay J. Coakley. *Sport in Society: Issues and Controversies.* 4th ed. St. Louis: Times Mirror/Mosby College Publishing, 1990.

This useful paperback book for the beginning student includes a discussion of theoretical paradigms in sociology as well as information about how to gather data for writing papers.

Pauline Bart and Linda Frankel. *The Student Sociologist's Handbook.* 4th ed. New York: Random House, 1986.

Information about career possibilities in sociology is available free from the American Sociological Association, 1722 N Street NW, Washington, D.C. 20036. Ask for:

Careers in Sociology. Washington, D.C.: American Sociological Association.

Bettina J. Huber. *Career Possibilities for Sociology Graduates.* Washington, D.C.: American Sociological Association.

第三次全国人口普查
簸桥公社顺江大队第一普查组
流动登记站

2

Sociological Investigation

The Buffalo Creek winds for some seventeen miles through the hills of West Virginia, past more than a dozen small settlements that were home to five thousand people in the winter of 1972. Logan County had long made its living mining coal, and the hard lives of many of the miners had finally begun to improve. Wages were up, and some were making needed improvements to their homes, which had been cheaply built by the coal company decades earlier. But all this was to change at eight o'clock on the morning of February 26th.

A long-time company practice had been to dispose of "slag"—a mixture of clay, mine dust, low-quality coal, and other debris produced by the mining operations—into the headwaters of the Buffalo Creek. Hundreds of thousands of tons each year had built up into a massive, makeshift dam. Behind this they pumped the black water used in the coal processing to form a lake twenty acres in size and as much as forty feet deep.

In retrospect, it was a disaster waiting to happen. After several days of rain, the entire mass suddenly broke loose, forming a monstrous wave of mud that snaked down the creek bed, utterly demolishing everything in its path. In two hours, every building along Buffalo Creek was gone. Since there had been no warnings, some pronounced the fact that only 125 people died to be a miracle. But few of the survivors felt lucky; most were left stunned, and all were homeless.

In the months that followed, millions of dollars of relief poured into the area, and survivors were resettled in temporary shelters. As the physical injuries healed, some hoped the tragedy would recede into a bitter memory. Sociologist Kai Erikson, investigating the event as part of a legal action on behalf of hundreds of residents, was troubled. A year had passed, but he found the people still experiencing trauma, now of a different kind. Torn loose from their homes, rehoused without regard for traditional neighbors, most of the people of Buffalo Creek felt lost. Many had trouble working or sleeping; some even wondered why they should stay alive. Although difficult for some of the people to put into words, they

had, essentially, lost the social fabric vital to human life.

Erikson's account of the disaster and its aftermath, in the award-winning *Everything in Its Path* (1976), beautifully illustrates how the sociological perspective can reveal patterns (and often problems) that other points of view overlook. His efforts were instrumental in helping the people of Buffalo Creek rebuild their sense of community. Most important for our purposes, his work demonstrates the *doing* of sociology—the process of *sociological investigation*.

Many people think of scientific research only in terms of laboratory experiments involving precise equipment and careful measurements. But as Erikson's experience suggests, sociological investigation can, and often does, occur anywhere that social life is found. As this chapter explains, sociologists sometimes do make use of laboratories, but the rich variety of human life provides the special challenge of adapting scientific techniques to countless different settings and tasks.

This chapter introduces the most common ways in which sociological research is carried out. Included, too, are the problems that typically test the skills and imagination of even the most seasoned men and women in this field of study. We shall begin with the basics.

THE BASICS OF SOCIOLOGICAL INVESTIGATION

Two simple requirements underlie the process of sociological investigation. Chapter 1 ("The Sociological Perspective") has suggested the first: *Look at the world using the sociological perspective.* As we do so, the surroundings suddenly become strange, full of curious patterns of behavior that call out for further study.

Notice how Kai Erikson did exactly this when he entered the Buffalo Creek area in the months after the flood. Most of the physical injuries had healed. Moreover, many of the buildings were being reconstructed. But using his sociological imagination, Erikson could perceive that the *social* structures of the community were still in ruins.

This brings us to the second requirement for a sociological investigator: *Be curious and ask questions.* What social patterns characterize a particular setting? Why are they important? Who supports them? Who opposes them? How do the people involved understand their own lives?

These two requirements—seeing the world sociologically and asking questions—are fundamental to sociological investigation. They are only the beginning, however. As they draw us into the social world, they stimulate our curiosity. But then there is the often more difficult matter of finding answers. To understand the kind of answers sociology offers, we must consider how we come to recognize any piece of information as being "true."

Ways of Knowing: Science and "Truth"

Saying we "know" something can mean any number of things. Most Americans, for instance, claim to believe in the existence of God. Probably most have never had direct contact with God, but they are believers all the same. This kind of knowing is often called "faith." A second kind of knowing is based on the pronouncement of a recognized expert. When we want to know how to spell a word correctly, for example, we turn to a dictionary because we presume that the book's editors are spelling experts. In still other cases, people who are not "experts" sometimes define what is "true" through simple agreement. This basis for knowing can be called "consensus." Americans "know" that sexual intercourse among young children is wrong, for instance, because virtually everyone agrees that this is the case. Of course, people in other times and places may agree on a different "truth." The Trobriand Islanders of New Guinea, for instance, shrug off sexual intercourse among young children as a harmless act.

There are, in short, many paths to "truth." As a final example, imagine that you are a Peace Corps volunteer helping people in a small, traditional society grow more food. Early in your visit, you observe local farmers placing a dead fish directly on top of the ground where they have planted a seed. Curious about this practice, you are told that their tradition is to make a gift to the god of the harvest. A local elder adds, in a tone of warning, that one year when there were no fish to use as gifts, the corn harvest suffered.

According to this system of knowledge, which reflects the three ways of knowing just described, using fish as gifts to the harvest god makes sense. But, with scientific training in agriculture, you would probably see a different "truth" in this situation: the decomposing fish fertilize the ground, producing a better crop.

Knowledge of the chemical benefits of fertilizer represents science, a fourth way of knowing. **Science** can be defined as *a logical system that bases knowledge on direct, systematic observation.* Instead of being based

The Emergence of Clowns by Roxanne illustrates the story of creation according to the Santa Clara Pueblo. Life began, they believe, when four clowns emerged onto the earth's surface, each facing in a different direction. All of the various peoples that make up American society have beliefs of this kind, although they are sometimes dismissed as mere "myth." Such accounts do address basic truths, however: the human search for our origins and ultimate purpose in the universe. These are truths that science cannot address.

on faith, the supposed wisdom of "experts," or simply general agreement, scientific knowledge is based on **empirical evidence**—that is, *evidence that we are able to verify with our senses.*

Our Peace Corps example does not mean, of course, that members of technologically advanced societies routinely reject all ways of knowing except science. A medical researcher seeking an effective treatment for cancer, for example, may still practice her religion as a matter of faith, seek the advice of experts in making financial decisions, and derive many opinions on politics from those around her. Yet none of this is fundamentally important to her work as a scientist. Science, then, is in some respects at odds with the "common sense" that guides our everyday lives.

Common Sense versus Scientific Evidence

Here are six statements that many North Americans consider "true" on the basis of common sense, yet each is at least partly contradicted by scientific evidence.

1. **Poor people are far more likely to break the law than are rich people.** Chapter 8 ("Deviance") explains that people of all social backgrounds break the law. However, the actions of those with less social privilege are more likely to come to the attention of law enforcement officials and to show up in official crime statistics.

2. **The United States and Canada are middle-class societies in which most people are more or less equal.** Those expressing this opinion are probably unaware that the richest 5 percent of North Americans control half of the continent's total wealth. Chapter 10 ("Social Class in America") provides details.

3. **Most poor people ignore opportunities to work.** While this may be true of some poor people, Chapter 10 ("Social Class in America") explains that about half of the American poor are actually children and elderly people.

4. **Differences in the social behavior of males and females is "human nature."** Much of what we call "human nature" is produced by the society in which we are raised, as Chapter 3 ("Culture") explains. Further, as Chapter 13 ("Sex and Gender") shows, some societies' definitions of "masculine" and "feminine" vary from those we take for granted.

5. **People change as they grow old, losing many former interests in favor of concerns about their health.** Chapter 14 ("Aging and the Elderly") reports that the scientific study of aging reveals little

personality change as we grow older. Although problems of personal health do increase in old age, the majority of the elderly suffer from no serious health problems.

6. **Most people marry because they are in love.** Surprising as it may be to Americans, research has shown that in most societies marriage has little to do with love. In addition, as Chapter 15 ("Family") reveals, even Americans typically decide that they "love" someone who is a socially suitable marriage partner.

These examples suggest that much of what we accept as true is at least partially *false*. Moreover, we are brought up to believe traditional truths, bombarded by "expert advice," and pressured to accept the opinions of friends. We must learn to evaluate critically what we see, read, and hear in order to separate what is true from what is not.

As a scientific discipline, sociology can help us to do exactly that. Like all ways of knowing, science has limitations, as we shall see. A scientific sociology, however, can lead us to evaluate many kinds of information more accurately.

THE ELEMENTS OF SCIENCE

Sociologists view society scientifically in much the same way that natural scientists see the physical world. The work of social scientists lies in identifying the parts of society and how they are interrelated. This suggests that a sociologist might ask questions such as the following:

What segments of the population are most likely to vote in national elections?
Are abused children at risk to become child abusers themselves?
Are city dwellers less neighborly than people living in rural areas?

Notice how each of these questions links parts of the social world together. The goal of sociological investigation is to provide specific answers to such questions by gathering empirical evidence.

The following sections of this chapter introduce a number of important elements of scientific investigation. First, we shall consider the important ideas of *concept*, *variable*, and *measurement*.

Concepts, Variables, and Measurement

Sociology uses concepts to identify elements that make up a society. A **concept** is *an abstract idea that represents an aspect of the world, inevitably in a somewhat ideal and simplified form.* "Society" is itself a concept, of course. Sociologists also make use of concepts to describe parts of societies, including "religion" and "the economy." Concepts can also be applied to individuals, as when we speak of their "sex," "race," or "social class."

A **variable** is simply *a concept that has a value that changes from case to case.* The familiar variable "price" varies from item to item in a supermarket. Similarly, the concept "social class" varies as people are described as "upper class," "middle class," "working class," or "lower class."

Closely related to the use of variables is **measurement**, meaning *the process of determining the value of a variable in a specific case.* Some variables are easily measured, as when we determine our weight by stepping on a scale. Measuring sociological variables, however, is often more difficult than making physical measurements.

For example, how would you measure something as complex as "social class"? We can do this crudely by looking at how a person dresses, by hearing patterns of speech, or by noting a home address. More precisely, we might investigate a person's income, occupation, and education. But a variable can sometimes be measured in more than one way. A particular man may have a very high income, leading us to define him as "upper class." Yet he may earn his high income selling automobiles, an occupation that seems more "middle class." Finally, he might have only an eighth-grade education, suggesting that he be considered "lower class." To resolve this particular dilemma, sociologists sensibly (although somewhat arbitrarily) combine these into a single composite measurement of social class that is described in Chapters 9 ("Social Stratification") and 10 ("Social Class in America").

A related problem arises when sociologists wish to describe all Americans with regard to some variable such as income. Because it is impractical to provide a measurement of the income of *every* person, sociologists make use of one or more statistical measures often called *descriptive statistics.* The box explains how this is done.

This example shows that how a variable is defined affects what its value is. Therefore, researchers must specify definitions carefully. **Operationalizing a variable** means *specifying exactly what is to be measured in assigning a value to a variable.* In measuring social class, for

Three Useful (and Simple) Statistical Measures

We often describe people, things, or numbers in terms of averages: the average age of Americans, the average price of a gallon of gasoline, or the average winning from state lotteries. In sociological research, three different statistical measures are used to describe what is average or typical.

Assume that we wish to describe the salaries paid to seven members of the local city council:

$14,250	$64,000
$21,750	$23,000
$23,000	$14,000
$18,500	

The simplest of the three statistical measures is the **mode**, defined as *the value that occurs most often in a series of numbers*. In this example, the mode is $23,000, since that value occurs twice, while the others occur only once. If each value were to occur only once, there would be no mode; if two values each occurred twice, there would be two modes. The mode is easy to identify yet is rarely used in sociological research because it provides information about only some, rather than all, of the values.

A more common statistical measure is the **mean**, which is *the arithmetic average of a series of numbers*, calculated by adding all the values together and dividing by the number of cases. The sum of the seven incomes here is $178,500 which, divided by 7, results in a mean income of $25,500. Notice, however, that the mean income is actually higher than the income of six of the seven members of the council. This is because the mean has the drawback of being strongly influenced by any extremely high or low value (in this case, the $64,000 income). The mean therefore reflects every case but gives a distorted picture of any distribution of values that has any extreme scores.

The **median** is *the value that occurs midway in a series of numbers or, simply, the middle case*. Here the median income for the seven people is $21,750, since three incomes are higher and three are lower. (With an even number of cases, the median would be halfway between the two middle cases.) Here, therefore, the median gives a better picture of the income of the group as a whole. Whenever there appear to be extreme cases, as with research involving income in American society, the median is likely to be used by sociologists to describe what is average.

---

example, researchers must decide exactly *what* will be measured. If variables such as income, occupational prestige, and education are involved, researchers must determine *how* they will be measured and how these variables will be combined into a composite measure of "social class." When reporting results of their research, then, sociologists should explain how all variables used in a study are operationalized, so that other people, and especially other researchers, will understand exactly how conclusions were reached.

Reliability and Validity of Measurement

Beyond carefully operationalizing variables, useful measurement involves two other considerations. **Reliability** is *the quality of consistency in measurement*. If, for example, repeated measurements of a person's social class produced differing values, the measurements would not be reliable. An unreliable technique for measurement is of little use in sociology, just as a scale giving inconsistent readings of weight would be useless in physics.

But consistency is no guarantee of validity in measurement. **Validity** means *the quality of measurement gained by actually measuring what one intends to measure*. Say you want to measure how religious people are, and you decide to do so by asking how often they attend religious services. Notice that while you are really interested in *religiosity*, what you are actually measuring is *attendance at services*, which may not be the same. This is because people may engage in religious rituals for any number of reasons. Moreover, many devout believers avoid organized religion altogether. Thus, even when yielding consistent results (and thus having reliability), any measurement can still miss the real target (and therefore lack validity). Because the process of measurement is so crucial to sociological investigation, researchers must always treat these as important issues.

Relationships among Variables

The real payoff in sociological investigation comes from determining the relationships among variables. The sci-

Men who drink a lot of coffee are more likely to die from a heart attack than are tea drinkers. Does this mean that coffee causes heart disease? No—the link between those two variables is spurious. Both coffee drinking and heart disease are caused by a third variable, high levels of occupational *stress*.

entific ideal is relating variables in terms of **cause and effect,** which means that *change in one variable is caused by change in another.* A familiar cause-and-effect relationship occurs when you put a tray of water into the freezer. The lower temperature causes a change in the state of the water, which turns to ice. *The variable that has caused the change* (in this case, the lower temperature of the freezer) is called the **independent variable.** *The variable that is changed* (the state of the water) is called the **dependent variable.** The value of the second variable, in other words, is dependent on the value of the first. Although information about cause is highly useful, it is worth remembering that few dimensions of social life are likely to have a single cause.

Sometimes people incorrectly think that a cause-and-effect relationship exists just because two variables seem to be related. But even though change in one variable is accompanied by change in another, there may be no causal link between them. For example, the fact that more cars are stolen when the temperature goes up does not mean that heat turns human beings into thieves. Rather, drivers are more likely to leave car windows open in warm weather.

As a more complex example, consider the fact that official rates of juvenile delinquency are higher among young people who live in crowded housing. We

might operationalize the variable "juvenile delinquency" to mean a person under the age of eighteen having a police record, and operationalize the variable "crowded housing" to mean living with less than a set amount of square feet of living space per person. We might be tempted to conclude that crowding causes tensions that promote delinquency. Viewed this way, crowded housing is the independent variable, and delinquency is the dependent variable. But does the fact that the two vary together indicate a causal connection?

Not necessarily. *When two (or more) variables are related in some way,* they are said to demonstrate **correlation.** We know there is some relationship between these two variables because they change together, as shown in Part (a) of Figure 2–1 on page 35. While this *may* mean that crowding causes delinquency, there are other possibilities as well. Think for a minute about what kind of people both live in crowded housing and do mischief more likely to be officially defined as delinquent. In simple terms, the answer is people with less power and choice, the poor. Thus, the fact that crowded housing and juvenile delinquency tend to be found together may mean that *both* are caused by the third factor, poverty (Fischer, 1984). The relationships among these three variables are shown in Part (b) of Figure 2–1. In other words, the initial correlation between crowding and de-

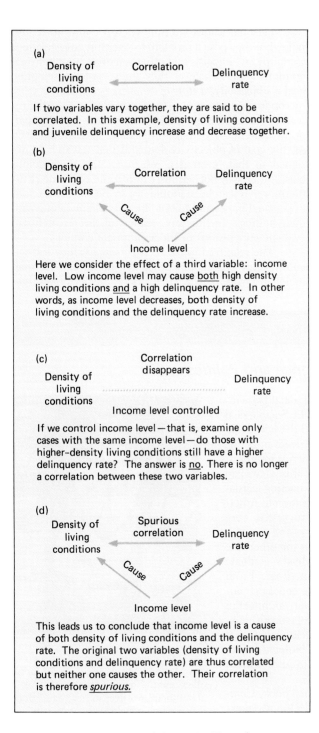

(a)

Density of living conditions   Correlation   Delinquency rate

If two variables vary together, they are said to be correlated. In this example, density of living conditions and juvenile delinquency increase and decrease together.

(b)

Density of living conditions   Correlation   Delinquency rate

Cause   Cause

Income level

Here we consider the effect of a third variable: income level. Low income level may cause both high density living conditions and a high delinquency rate. In other words, as income level decreases, both density of living conditions and the delinquency rate increase.

(c)

Correlation disappears

Density of living conditions   Delinquency rate

Income level controlled

If we control income level—that is, examine only cases with the same income level—do those with higher-density living conditions still have a higher delinquency rate? The answer is no. There is no longer a correlation between these two variables.

(d)

Density of living conditions   Spurious correlation   Delinquency rate

Cause   Cause

Income level

This leads us to conclude that income level is a cause of both density of living conditions and the delinquency rate. The original two variables (density of living conditions and delinquency rate) are thus correlated but neither one causes the other. Their correlation is therefore _spurious._

Figure 2–1   Correlation and Cause: An Example

linquency is "explained away" by the fact that change in each is independently caused by a third variable, income. The term **spurious correlation** means _a false or indirect link: a relationship between two (or more) variables not based on direct cause and effect._

Identifying a correlation as spurious is often a tricky task, but one that can be solved through the use of scientific **control**, in this case meaning _the ability to neutralize the effect of one variable so that the relationships among other variables can be more precisely determined._ In order to examine the relationship between housing density and delinquency while _controlling_ the effect of income, we would measure the first two variables only among persons of a single income level. If the relationship between crowding and delinquency still exists, we have evidence supporting the conclusion that crowded homes do in fact cause delinquency. If the relationship disappears, as shown in Part (c) of the figure, we can rule out a cause-and-effect relationship between the two. Research has, in fact, shown that most, although perhaps not all, of the relationship between crowding and delinquency disappears if the effects of income are controlled. So we have now sorted out the relationship among the three variables, as illustrated in Part (d) of the figure. Crowded housing and juvenile delinquency have a spurious correlation, and the evidence suggests that both are caused by a lower level of income.

In summary, correlation means only that two variables vary together. Cause and effect implies correlation and something more: that change in one of the variables actually causes change in the other. To conclude that a relationship of cause and effect exists between two variables, three factors must be demonstrated: (1) the two variables are correlated; (2) the independent (or causal) variable precedes the dependent variable in time; and (3) no evidence exists that a third variable is responsible for a spurious correlation between the two.

Identifying cause-and-effect relationships is valuable because it makes possible the scientific goal of _prediction,_ using some facts to predict others. The natural sciences have an easier time with prediction, since laboratory conditions allow extensive control of a number of variables. The sociologist faces a considerably more difficult task. In a world of countless social forces, to which each of us may react in a unique way, relationships of simple cause and effect are rare. Sometimes sociologists must be satisfied with demonstrating only correlation. When relationships of cause and effect can be shown, they are usually complex, involving many variables.

The Ideal of Objectivity

Assume that ten people who work for a magazine in Ames, Iowa, are putting together a story about that city's best restaurant. With their employer paying all the expenses, they set out for a week of fine dining. When they get together to compare notes, will one restaurant be everyone's clear favorite? Perhaps, but that hardly seems likely.

In terms of the logic of science, each of the ten would probably operationalize the concept "best restaurant" somewhat differently. For one, it might be a place that serves good home cooking at reasonable prices; for another, the choice might turn on a rooftop view of the city; for yet another, attentive service might be the deciding factor. Like so many other things in our lives, the best restaurant may well be mostly a matter of individual taste.

Personal values are fine when it comes to restaurants, but they pose a problem to scientific investigation. Certainly, sociologists and other scientists have personal opinions about whatever they study, but the scientific goal is **objectivity,** *a state of complete personal neutrality in conducting research.* This is an ideal rather than a reality, however, since complete neutrality on the part of a researcher is virtually impossible to achieve. Even so, the goal of objectivity demands that research be designed so that, even if a researcher has unconscious biases, they will not seriously distort the outcome. Furthermore, researchers should try to become conscious of personal biases and to state them explicitly along with their findings. In this way, readers of the research can evaluate conclusions in the appropriate context.

The relationship between personal values and scientific study greatly concerned the influential German sociologist Max Weber. He expected the personal values

CRITICAL THINKING

The Samoa Controversy: The Interplay of Science and Politics

Margaret Mead (1901–1978) is probably the most important of all American anthropologists. (Like sociology, anthropology studies human behavior, but with a focus on preindustrial rather than modern societies.) Several years after her death, however, her work became the center of controversy, raising questions about the interplay of science and politics.

Mead began her career by studying how children grew up in Samoa, an island in the South Pacific. Her research showed that, far from being a simple biological process, growing up varies significantly from one culture to another. These results became an important part of a raging debate as to whether biology or environment has a greater influence on human behavior.

The dominant position early in this century was that biology was more influential. The political conse-quences of this type of social Darwinism (see Chapter 1, "The Sociological Perspective") included the belief that people with more privileges might be in some basic way superior to others. Scientists supporting this view had even played a part in enacting legislation restricting immigration to America of peoples they suggested were "inferior."

A leading figure on the other side of the debate was Mead's graduate school mentor, Franz Boas. From him, Mead gained the belief that environment is the primary architect of human behavior. Not surprisingly, both Boas and Mead feared that what they viewed as false biological doctrine was being used to justify unfair social policies.

Margaret Mead's first book, *Coming of Age in Samoa* (1928), was powerful ammunition for the environmental side of what Chapter 5

One of the pioneers of social research was Margaret Mead, whose work among other cultures helped Americans think about their own lives in new ways. But can research conclusions—especially about controversial topics—be separated from the personal values of the researcher?

of the sociologist to play a part in at least the selection of topics to be studied. What other than personal values would lead one person to study world hunger, another to investigate population migration in Canada, and yet another to examine religious cults?

Yet, Weber argued, while research may be *value-relevant*, it must be carried out dispassionately if we are to uncover the truth *as it is* rather than as we think *it should be*. This, for Weber, is the essential difference between the world of science and the world of politics. Weber charged researchers, whatever the political implications of their work, to strive to be *value-free*. This means they should have an open-minded readiness to accept the results of their investigations, no matter what those results might be.

Most sociologists accept Weber's argument, but few are confident that we can ever be entirely aware of our own biases. Our social identities affect the way we think, how we see the world, and what we find to be morally good or socially dangerous. Moreover, sociologists are not "average" people; most are male, white, urban, and highly educated. In addition, although the opinions of sociologists cover the full political spectrum, sociologists generally are more liberal than the population as a whole, and even more liberal than members of many other academic disciplines (Wilson, 1979). Thus, as researchers, all sociologists must guard against personal bias distorting their work. As a consumer of research, you should be aware that personal values can and do affect sociological research, just as your own values affect your interpretation of this work.

One way to limit distortion caused by personal values is through the **replication** of research, meaning that *other researchers repeat the same study*. The same results obtained by subsequent study increase confidence that the original research was conducted objectively. In-

("Socialization") presents as the "nature-nurture debate." After reporting that growing up in Samoa revealed little of the turbulence typical of adolescence in the United States, Mead concluded that environment far outweighs biology in shaping humanity. She subsequently made similar claims regarding the significance of sex: environment, not biology, produces what we call "masculine" and "feminine." If true, then no category of people is inherently better than another or, for that matter, is inherently *anything*.

Mead's research helped discredit biological views of human behavior by the middle of this century. Yet shortly after her death, Derek Freeman, a researcher who had also conducted research in Samoa, reported different findings and further claimed that Mead selectively represented Samoan society according to her personal politics. According to Freeman, Samoan society reveals that growing up is not the stress-free process that Mead described. This provides support for the position that society is a competitive arena in which biological forces do play a part.

Scholars are still divided as to the truth. To some, Mead was a young (twenty-four years of age when she arrived in Samoa in 1925) and unseasoned researcher prompted by her teacher to produce evidence supporting an environmental doctrine of human behavior. Her conclusions are too "neat," critics claim, suggesting that she saw only what she was looking for in her research. To those critics, her work had more to do with personal politics than with scientific facts.

To others, Freeman is the villain in the controversy. Without denying that research has progressed in more than a half-century since Mead's work was begun, many believe her conclusions are mostly sound. It is Freeman, Mead's defenders charge, who appears rigidly committed to a view that human behavior is largely determined by biology and who has sought fame and fortune by attacking the work of a great scientist.

There is, probably, some truth on both sides of this recent controversy. On one point, however, there can be agreement: human beings are passionate and often political creatures who are unlikely to achieve the scientific goal of complete objectivity in research.

SOURCE: Based on Margaret Mead, *Coming of Age in Samoa* (New York: Dell, 1961 [orig. 1928]); Derek Freeman, *Margaret Mead and Samoa: The Making and Unmaking of an Anthropological Myth* (Cambridge: Harvard University Press, 1983); Annette B. Weiner, "Ethnographic Determinism: Samoa and the Margaret Mead Controversy," *American Anthropologist*, Vol. 85, No. 4 (December 1983): 909–919; and Lowell Holmes, "A Tale of Two Studies," *American Anthropologist*, Vol. 85, No. 4 (December 1983):929–935.

deed, the need for replication in scientific investigation is probably the reason that the search for knowledge is called *re*search in the first place. The box on pages 36–37 describes a recent controversy arising from replication of well-known research.

Some Limitations of Scientific Sociology

Science was first applied to the study of the natural world. The logic of science can also be applied to the social world, but only if we recognize several important limitations.

1. **Sociologists can rarely make precise determinations of cause and effect. Thus human behavior cannot be predicted with the precision of the natural sciences.** Astronomers are able to predict the behavior of the heavenly bodies with remarkable precision; they know years in advance, for example, when Halley's comet will next be visible from the earth. Human bodies, however, are more than physical matter; they contain creative minds, so that no two individuals are likely to react in the same way to the same social surroundings. Therefore, sociologists speak of "probabilities" that categories of people will act in some manner, while rarely speaking of certainties, especially about the behavior of an individual.

2. **We all react to the world around us, so the mere presence of researchers may affect the behavior that is being studied.** An astronomer gazing at a comet has no effect whatever on it, but people often react to being observed. Some may become anxious or defensive; others may try to "help" the researcher by providing the answers or actions they think are expected of them.

3. **Social patterns are constantly changing; what is true in one time or place may not be true in another.** Atoms and molecules do not consciously shape their environment; but human beings do, in remarkably variable ways. The study of social life, therefore, must acknowledge diversity and change.

4. **Because sociologists are part of the social world they study, objectivity in social research is especially difficult.** Chemists, for example, are not often personally affected by what goes on in test tubes. But sociologists study the society in which they live. Therefore, sociologists usually have even greater difficulty in controlling—or even in recognizing—personal values that may distort their work.

The Importance of Subjective Interpretation

The logic of science cannot eliminate all elements of subjectivity from research. But in the minds of some

A basic lesson of social research is that being observed affects human behavior. Researchers can never be sure precisely how this will occur: some people become shy as the subject of attention, while others become highly animated. In neither case does the researcher witness natural behavior.

This celebrated photograph by Harold E. Edgerton of a golf swing suggests an important concern in sociological research: Analyzing patterns of human behavior—even in minute detail—is of little value without also understanding what motivates the action.

sociologists, eliminating subjectivity would be undesirable even if it were possible. This is so for two reasons.

First, science is basically a series of procedures to guide research, rather like a recipe used in cooking. Just as something more than recipes is required to make a great chef, so scientific procedures will never, by themselves, produce a great sociologist. In both cases, an additional requirement is an inspired personal imagination. Robert Nisbet (1970) has pointed out that the greatest human insights have come not from science itself but from the lively thinking of creative human beings. The genius of physicist Albert Einstein and of sociologist Max Weber resulted not only from their skillful use of the scientific method but also from their curiosity and imagination.

Second, science is insufficient for comprehending the vast and complex range of human motivations and feelings, including greed, love, pride, and despair. Science helps us to gather facts about human behavior, but it can never fully embrace the process by which human beings build a world of subjective meanings (Berger & Kellner, 1981). Moreover, no scientist's data speak for themselves; sociologists are always faced with the ultimate task of *interpretation*: creating meaningful expla-

nations of the facts that confront them. In this sense, sociology is an art as well as a science.

Politics, Ethics, and Gender in Research

Some sociologists reject Max Weber's goal of value-free research in favor of making their work explicitly political. Alvin Gouldner (1970a, 1970b), who claims that political neutrality is a "storybook picture" of research, argues that all aspects of social life—from national decision making to everyday relationships between women and men—inevitably have political implications. In other words, *social* must also mean *political*, since any particular social arrangement is likely to benefit some people more than others. As part of a political world, Gouldner claims, research is inevitably shaped by political values and has political consequences.

If sociologists have no choice about their work being political, Gouldner continues, they do have a choice about *which* values are worth supporting. Moreover, they have an obligation to support these political objectives. Although this viewpoint is not limited to sociologists of any one political orientation, it is especially

CRITICAL THINKING

Gender and Sociological Investigation

A society's attitudes and behavior in relation to people's sex—that is, being male or female—have enormous significance for everyday life. This is the issue of gender, which is detailed in Chapter 13 ("Sex and Gender") and raised in every other chapter as well. Here, our concern is the implications of gender for sociological investigation. Margrit Eichler (1988) points out four dangers to sound research that involve gender.

1. **Androcentricity.** Androcentricity (*andro* is the Greek word for "male"; *centricity* means "being centered on") refers to approaching any issue from a male perspective. This problem arises, for instance, when a researcher treats a topic as if only males are important and the female half of humanity simply does not matter. Research about the labor force, for instance, has long fo-

cused on the paid work of males while overlooking the housework traditionally common to the lives of women. Would anyone disagree that research that claims to inform us about human behavior but does not apply to men is of limited value? This is no less true in the case of women.

Eichler points out that the parallel problem of *gynocentricity*—seeing the world from a female perspective—is equally dangerous to sociological investigation. However, this is less frequent than androcentricity in male-dominated American society.

2. **Overgeneralizing.** Information drawn only from members of one sex supports conclusions only about that sex. Historically, however, sociologists have used data from males as the basis for claims about all humans. An example

of overgeneralizing is gathering information about communities or organizations from public officials or other prominent persons, who are likely to be men, and using this as the basis for conclusions about the settings in general.

Here, again, the problem can also occur in reverse. For example, in an investigation of childrearing practices, collecting data only from females would support conclusions about "motherhood" but not about the more general issue of "parenthood."

3. **Gender insensitivity.** This problem occurs when research fails to consider the variable of sex at all. As will be seen throughout this book, social forces often affect males and females differently. To illustrate, failing to consider the importance of sex

strong among those influenced by the ideas of Karl Marx. As noted in Chapter 1 ("The Sociological Perspective") Marx asserted that while it is important to understand the world, the crucial task is to change it (1972:109; orig. 1845).

The values that can influence research also include those involving gender—the ways in which societies define males and females. Sociologists are becoming increasingly aware that gender-related issues pose serious hazards to sociological investigation, as the box explains.

Sociologists must also be mindful of how their research affects those directly involved. The American Sociological Association—the major professional association of sociologists in North America—has established formal guidelines for the conduct of research (1984). As already noted, technical competence and awareness of bias are of paramount importance in conducting all research. Sociologists must also strive to protect the rights,

privacy, and safety of anyone involved in a research project. Sociologists are obligated to terminate any research, however useful its possible results, if they note potential danger to participants. In cases of even minimal danger, sociologists must ensure in advance that all participants understand and accept the risks. All subjects in research are entitled to full anonymity, even if sociologists come under legal pressure to release confidential information. Moreover, sociologists must accurately present the purpose of their work to subjects, especially if it involves working for a particular political organization or a business. Such affiliations must also be disclosed in the publication of the research. Since any private or public agency may seek to constrain the research process, a sociologist must ensure that acceptance of funding will not require violating any of the ethical guidelines mentioned here.

After completing research, sociologists should re-

in a study of growing old in America would lead to omitting important information, such as the fact that a majority of elderly males live with spouses, while elderly females, who usually outlive their husbands, typically live alone.

4. **Double standards.** Researchers must be careful to evaluate attitudes or behaviors of both sexes consistently. Double standards are often evident in language, as when a researcher investigating families describes a couple as "man and wife." This problem involves more than words because a researcher may define a man as the "head of household" and treat him accordingly, while assuming that a woman (whose life may be much the same) is his wife and simply engaged in family "support work." Such double standards will invariably

undermine an objective analysis of the issue at hand.

5. **Interference.** Beyond the four problems outlined by Eichler that affect researchers, the attitudes of *subjects* concerning gender also shape the research process. The problem of "interference" occurs as subjects react to the sex of the researcher rather than to the research itself. For instance, while conducting research in Sicily, Maureen Giovannini (1989) reported that many males guided by local traditions responded to her as a *woman* rather than in the sex-neutral sense of being a *researcher*. In this setting, gender issues effectively prevented many activities (such as private conversations with males) that were deemed inappropriate for single females. In addition, Giovannini was also denied access to places

considered by locals to be "off-limits" to members of her sex.

None of the issues raised here implies that researchers cannot deliberately focus their work on one sex or the other. Indeed, the pervasive attention to males at the expense of females common in the past has led many of today's researchers to make special efforts to investigate the lives of women. But researchers—and others who read their work—must think critically about how gender can, and often does, shape the process of sociological investigation.

SOURCE: Based on Margrit Eichler, *Nonsexist Research Methods: A Practical Guide*, Boston: Allan & Unwin, 1988; also Maureen Giovannini, "Female Anthropologist and Male Informant: Gender Conflict in a Sicilian Town," in John J. Macionis and Nijole V. Benokraitis, eds., *Seeing Ourselves: Classic, Contemporary, and Cross-Cultural Readings in Sociology*, Englewood Cliffs, NJ: Prentice Hall, 1989:30–35.

port their findings in full, with a precise description of how the study was conducted. Sociologists should also clearly indicate their organizational affiliations and sources of funding, attempt to provide all possible interpretations of their data, and point out the limitations of their conclusions (American Sociological Association, 1984).

THE METHODS OF SOCIOLOGICAL RESEARCH

A **research method** is *a systematic strategy for carrying out research*. Four of the most commonly used methods of sociological investigation are introduced here. None is better or worse than any other; but in the same way that a carpenter selects a particular tool for a particular

task, distinctive strengths and weaknesses make each method suitable for certain kinds of research.

Experiments

The logic of science is clearly expressed in the **experiment**—*a research method that investigates cause-and-effect relationships under highly controlled conditions*. Experimental research tends to be *explanatory*, meaning that it is concerned not just with *what* happens but with *why*. Experiments are typically devised to test a specific **hypothesis**—*an unverified statement of a relationship between any facts or variables*. In everyday language, a hypothesis is simply a hunch or educated guess about what the research will show. Of course, a hypothesis must be tested. An ideal experiment involves three steps leading to accepting or rejecting a hypothesis using

Natural disasters, such as the earthquake that devastated Armenia in the Soviet Union in 1989, provide opportunities for field research that could never be created in a laboratory. Such studies show that disasters destroy not only buildings but the fabric of social life, causing human suffering that continues long after physical structures have been repaired.

empirical evidence. First, the dependent variable is measured; second, the dependent variable is exposed to the effects of the independent variable; and third, the dependent variable is measured again to see what, if any, change has taken place.

Successful experiments depend on careful control of all factors that might affect what is being measured. This is easiest in a laboratory, an artificial setting specially constructed for this purpose. But experiments in an everyday location—"in the field," as sociologists say—have the advantage of allowing researchers to observe subjects

in their natural setting. In addition, field experiments can investigate phenomena that could never be artificially created in a laboratory. Kai Erikson's field research in Buffalo Creek, described at the beginning of this chapter, illustrates a field experiment. Erikson set out to assess—and later confirmed—the hypothesis that damage to the Buffalo Creek community went a great deal beyond the destruction of property. Of course, the inability to control the field environment means that hypotheses are typically more general than they might be in a laboratory setting. Moreover, most field experiments are difficult to replicate because similar conditions (such as the Buffalo Creek flood) may never occur again.

In the laboratory or in the field, subjects may change their behavior if they are aware of being part of a research project, as one classic experiment discovered. In the late 1930s, the Western Electric Company studied factors affecting workers' productivity at its Hawthorne factory near Chicago (Roethlisberger & Dickson, 1939). One experiment tested the hypothesis that increasing the available lighting would raise productivity. First, worker productivity (the dependent variable) was measured; then lighting (the independent variable) was changed; finally, worker productivity was measured again. Productivity increased, and the hypothesis was confirmed. But when lighting was subsequently reduced, productivity *again* increased, contradicting the initial hypothesis. In time, the researchers realized that the workers were working harder simply because they knew that they were being studied. Since then, the term Hawthorne effect has been used to refer to *any distortion in research caused by subjects' awareness that they are the focus of study.*

A Laboratory Experiment: The Stanford County Prison

The social dynamics of prisons is an important topic of study, although social scientists are typically unable to carry out this kind of research "in the field." Philip Zimbardo nonetheless sought to investigate the issue of prison violence by creating a prison environment in an artificial "laboratory" (Zimbardo, 1972; Haney, Banks, & Zimbardo, 1973).

Zimbardo was skeptical of the common-sense idea that prison violence is caused by prisoners who are in jail precisely because of antisocial or violent behavior. Moreover, he doubted that prison guards are simply the kind of people who enjoy pushing other people around. On the contrary, Zimbardo suspected that, placed within the prison setting, even the healthiest and most emotionally stable people would be prone to violent behavior. This led to the following hypothesis: *The character of prison itself, and not the personalities of prisoners and guards, is the cause of prison violence.* Thus, the prison itself was treated as the independent variable capable of causing change in the dependent variable, violent behavior.

To test this hypothesis, Zimbardo's research team first placed an ad in a local newspaper in Palo Alto, California, offering young men $15 a day to help with a two-week research project. Each of the seventy who responded was given a series of physical and psychological tests. The researchers selected the twenty-four deemed the healthiest, both physically and mentally. Then the men were randomly assigned to two groups; half were designated "prisoners" and half became "guards." The guards and prisoners were to spend the next two weeks in the "Stanford County Prison," an approximation of a prison specially constructed in the basement of the psychology building on the Stanford University campus.

The "prisoners" were surprised when the Palo Alto police "arrested" them at their homes soon afterward. After being searched and handcuffed, they were taken to the local police station to be fingerprinted. Then they were transported to the "prison" on the Stanford campus. There each met other "prisoners," as well as the "guards," who had been instructed to keep the prison secure at all times. Zimbardo and his associates sat back with a video camera to see what would happen next.

The experiment soon became more than anyone had bargained for. The researchers could see both the "guards" and the "prisoners" beginning to act in stereotypical fashion, quickly losing their sense of basic human decency. The guards began to insult and abuse the prisoners, forcing them to engage in humiliating tasks such as cleaning out toilets with their bare hands. The prisoners reacted to the setting with bitterness and hostility. Within the first four days, five prisoners had to be removed from the study "because of extreme emotional depression, crying, rage, and acute anxiety" (1973:81). Before the end of the first week, the situation had deteriorated so badly that the researchers cancelled the experiment. Zimbardo explains (1972:4): "The ugliest, most base, pathological side of human nature surfaced. We were horrified because we saw some boys (guards) treat others as if they were despicable animals, taking pleasure in cruelty, while other boys (prisoners) became servile, dehumanized robots who thought only of escape, of their own individual survival and of their mounting hatred for the guards."

Philip Zimbardo's research helps explain events such as the takeover of the federal detention center in Oakdale, Louisiana in 1987. According to Zimbardo, frequent violence is a product of the dehumanization inherent in prison life.

What unfolded in the "Stanford County Prison" supported Zimbardo's hypothesis that prison violence is caused by the social character of prisons themselves, rather than by the personalities of guards and prisoners. Zimbardo's findings further raise obvious questions about the way we as a society operate prisons, and they point to the need for basic prison reform. In addition, the experiment also shows how research itself can threaten the physical and mental well-being of subjects. Such dangers are not always predictable (Zimbardo apparently did not expect his research to unfold in quite the way it did), nor as immediately apparent as they were in this case. Therefore, researchers must consider carefully the potential harm to subjects at all stages of their research and end any study, as Zimbardo responsibly did, if subjects appear to be psychologically or physically threatened.

Survey Research

A **survey** is *a research method in which subjects respond to a series of items or questions* in a questionnaire or an interview. Perhaps the most widely used of all research methods, surveys are particularly suited to studying what cannot be observed directly, such as political attitudes, religious beliefs, or the private lives of couples. Like experiments, surveys can be used to investigate the relationship among variables. They are also useful for *descriptive* research, in which subject responses help a sociologist to describe a social setting, such as an urban neighborhood or a gambling casino.

Population and Sample

In survey research, a **population** is defined as *the people about whom a researcher seeks knowledge*. We might wish, for example, to learn how much schooling is typical of adults living in a particular city. In this case, all the adults in the city are the survey population. Sometimes every adult in the country can be the survey population,

as in the familiar polls that are taken during political campaigns. Contacting each of such a vast number of people is a virtual impossibility, of course. Researchers get around this problem by using a **sample,** meaning *a part of a population, selected to be representative of the entirety, from whom data are obtained*. The precise proportion of a population within the sample varies. The box describes the beginnings of polling organizations, which are now able to represent the entire population of the United States with a carefully selected sample of about fifteen hundred people.

The logic of sampling is actually something we use all the time. If you were to wander around a party, noticing five or six people bored to the point of distraction, you might conclude that the party is a flop. Such a conclusion actually involves making an inference about *all* of the people (the "population") after observing only *some* of the people (the "sample"). But how can we know if those in a sample actually represent the entire population?

The most common assurance is a technique called *random sampling*, in which every element in the popula-

---

SOCIOLOGY OF EVERYDAY LIFE

National Political Surveys

Over 91 million Americans voted in the presidential election of 1988. The close race ended with little suspense, however, because before the first vote had been cast, surveys had predicted that George Bush would handily defeat Michael Dukakis.

Such surveys, commonly called *polls*, are now routine in American politics. But how can information drawn from about fifteen hundred people predict what tens of millions of people will do, at least within a few percentage points? The key to accurate prediction is selecting a sample that represents the population as a whole, which today's pollsters are generally able to do.

National polls had a rocky beginning. In 1936, a survey by the *Literary*

Digest predicted that Republican Alfred E. Landon would defeat Democrat Franklin Delano Roosevelt by a considerable margin. They could hardly have been more wrong, and Landon lost to Roosevelt in a historic landslide. The reason for such an embarrassing error was simply that the magazine's sample was not representative of the voting population. The *Digest* mailed survey ballots to some 10 million people (far more than would be included in a poll today), drawing names obtained from telephone listings and automobile registrations. Such sources introduced a major bias, since, especially then, people who owned a telephone and a car were more affluent and therefore more likely to be Republicans.

The incorrect prediction made by the *Literary Digest* did nothing for the popularity of that magazine, which soon went out of business. But another poll had accurately predicted the decisive Roosevelt victory. That survey was conducted by a novice pollster named George Gallup (1902–1984), who went on to become the best-known national survey researcher in the United States. Today, polls by the Gallup organization and others routinely provide information about elections and a host of other political issues.

SOURCE: Information on Gallup and the *Literary Digest* poll adapted from Earl Babbie, *The Practice of Social Research*, 3rd ed. (Belmont, CA: Wadsworth, 1983), pp. 141–143.

---

tion has an equal chance of being selected for the sample. In this case, the laws of probability make a representative sample likely and, just as important, give us some idea of exactly *how* likely. Random samples are generally produced by computers. Novice researchers, however, sometimes make the mistake of assuming that "randomly" walking up to people on the street will produce a random sample. This, unfortunately, is unlikely for two reasons. First, wherever one might be in a city, some kinds of people would be more likely than others to be there. Second, few people find everyone equally approachable, which again introduces a bias.

Although good sampling is far from simple, it offers a considerable savings in time and expense. We are spared the tedious task of contacting everyone in a population, while obtaining essentially the same results.

Questionnaires and Interviews

Selecting the subjects is only the first step in carrying out a survey. Also required is a specific plan for asking questions and recording answers. Surveys employ two general techniques: questionnaires and interviews.

A **questionnaire** is *a series of questions or items to which subjects are asked to respond.* In most cases, the researcher provides possible responses to each item so that the subject need select only one (similar to multiple-choice examination questions). Analyzing results obtained in this way is easy because the responses have been limited by the researcher. A questionnaire presenting set responses to the subject has a *closed-ended format.*

In some cases, however, a researcher may want subjects to respond in an entirely free way. In an *open-ended format,* subjects are able to express their responses however they wish, offering the researcher more subtle shades of opinion. Of course, one later has to make sense out of what can be a bewildering array of answers.

How to present questions to subjects is another part of the research strategy. Most often, a questionnaire is mailed to respondents, who are asked to complete the form and then to return it. This technique is called a *self-administered survey.* Since no researcher is present when subjects respond to such a questionnaire, the format must be both inviting and clear if it is to be usefully completed. Finally, a self-administered questionnaire should always be pretested with a small group of people before sending it to all the subjects. This small investment of time and money may avoid the costly problem of finding out—too late—that instructions or questions were unclear to respondents.

Using the mail has the advantage of bringing a large number of people over a wide geographical area into a study at relatively little expense. At the same time, questionnaires received by mail are often ignored, so that fewer than half are typically completed and returned. And even a 50 percent return rate may require follow-up mailings to coax reluctant subjects. Worth remembering, too, is that many subjects are not capable of completing a questionnaire on their own. Included in this category are young children, many hospital patients, and perhaps as many as one-third of adults who simply have too much difficulty with reading and writing (Kozol, 1985a).

An **interview** is *a series of questions or items administered personally by a researcher to respondents.* The most useful interviews have an open-ended format, allowing the researcher to ask follow-up questions, both to probe a bit more deeply and to clarify the subject's responses. In doing so, however, the researcher must avoid influencing the subject, which can be as easy as raising an eyebrow as a person begins to answer. The advantage of an interview is that a subject is more likely to complete a questionnaire if contacted personally by the researcher. One disadvantage is that tracking people down and personally interviewing them is costly and time-consuming, especially if all subjects do not live in the same area.

However questions are asked, wording can have a surprisingly significant effect on the answers given (Fowler, Jr., & Mangione, 1989). Words or phrases with an emotional impact are especially likely to influence the subject's response. For example, a person might endorse the statement "I approve of having my child taught by people representing all political opinions" and yet reject the same statement with the words "including radicals" added to the end. Similarly, "welfare mothers" is an emotionally loaded reference to "women who receive public assistance." In other cases, the wording of questions suggests what other people think, thereby subtly guiding the respondent. People would be more likely to respond positively to the question "Do you *agree* that the police force is doing a good job?" than they would to the question "Do you *think* that the police force is doing a good job?" simply because the phrase "do you agree" suggests that most other people endorse the statement. In short, researchers must strive to use language that suggests no "correct" response.

Researchers should also avoid items that are actually two questions in one, such as, "Do you think that the government should spend less money for military defense and more for domestic social programs?" The problem here, of course, is that a subject could very well agree with only part of the question, so that saying either yes or no would distort the actual opinion the researcher is seeking.

Surveys at Work: A Study of American Couples

Couples are a basic social unit in most societies of the world. In 1975, two American sociologists, Philip Blumstein and Pepper Schwartz, began a large and complex investigation of couples in the United States: how they make decisions, what importance sex has in their lives, and how factors such as jobs and money shape their relationships. This research culminated in the publication of *American Couples* (1983), a book that provides many rich insights into close human relationships in our society.

Blumstein and Schwartz operationalized the concept *couple* to mean two individuals who (1) live together and (2) have had a sexual relationship for at least some period of time. Aware that most previous research had considered only married couples, they enlarged their focus to include cohabiting heterosexual couples as well as male and female homosexual couples.

Blumstein and Schwartz faced a mammoth task in gathering data on a topic involving tens of millions of Americans—especially since some of the information involved normally private matters such as sexual relationships. Their study is an excellent example of how questionnaires and interviews can generate information on a complex issue.

Building a sample. There is, of course, no complete listing of American couples from which to easily draw a random sample. Blumstein and Schwartz were also aware that many homosexual men and women are quite secretive about their relationships, fearing negative public reaction to their sexual orientation. Thus, these researchers employed several strategies to make their sample as representative as possible.

First, Blumstein and Schwartz acquired as many subjects as they could, knowing that a larger number would increase the chances that their sample would represent the entire population of couples. They were fortunate that word of their research was carried in national news reports, and they also appeared on several national television shows. They were soon swamped with offers to participate from couples across the country. Questionnaires were sent to volunteers by return mail.

Second, Blumstein and Schwartz tried to ensure that all types of couples were included in the study.

Even a large sample is not representative if some categories of people are more likely to volunteer their participation than others. Judging that homosexual couples were less likely to volunteer, Blumstein and Schwartz made use of contacts within the homosexual communities of Seattle (their own city) and San Francisco (where many homosexuals tend to be more open about their sexual orientation). The researchers also asked participants to suggest others who might be willing to join the research. This procedure, often called *snowball sampling*, can quickly increase the number of subjects.

Third, to further broaden the range of participants, Blumstein and Schwartz appeared before a variety of civic associations including the PTA and the Rotary Club, indicating their need for subjects and leaving questionnaires to be completed by those who wished to do so.

Fourth and finally, the researchers even alerted the general public to the study by walking through neighborhoods and by leaving flyers in supermarkets and movie theaters. In the end, the researchers distributed almost twenty-two thousand questionnaires.

While Blumstein and Schwartz's sample was certainly large and diverse, they still had no guarantee that it was representative of the entire population of American couples. Mindful of this possible shortcoming, they included in their report the following evaluation:

> [The sample] does not represent all of the couples in the United States, and it would be misleading if our findings were applied to all groups within the country. For instance, a large number of our couples come from the New York, San Francisco, and Seattle areas. More important, our couples are primarily white and disproportionately well educated. We have more high salaries and prestigious occupations among our couples than would be found in the general population. Thus, we need to be tentative about applying our findings to working-class or poor people, or people with only a grade-school education (1983:548).

Notice that the limitations of any sample can be reduced to the extent that the researchers carefully assess their work and include this information in their formal results.

The use of questionnaires. Since they sought a large number of participants, Blumstein and Schwartz sensibly chose a questionnaire to collect information. The questionnaire, containing some thirty-eight pages of specific questions, had to be carefully prepared and clearly worded. A closed-ended format lessened the work of compiling the responses.

From the almost twenty-two thousand questionnaires Blumstein and Schwartz distributed, more than twelve thousand came back—a return rate of about 55 percent, which is excellent in light of the length of the questionnaire. Follow-up mailings might have increased the return rate, but ethical concerns led the researchers to protect the privacy of volunteers by destroying all names and addresses after questionnaires were initially mailed.

The use of interviews. Blumstein and Schwartz also conducted interviews to gain a deeper understanding of the lives of couples in their study. For example, information on the history of each couple's relationship could not easily be explored using a questionnaire. The time needed to locate subjects and to conduct the interviews required Blumstein and Schwartz to employ a research staff in this phase of their work. In all, 320 couples were interviewed for periods of time ranging from two and one-half to four hours.

Because the researchers wished to interview subjects personally rather than by telephone, couples were interviewed only in limited areas surrounding Seattle, San Francisco, and New York City. So that the couples selected for interviews would be as representative as possible, Blumstein and Schwartz categorized them according to education, duration of the relationship, and sexual orientation and then randomly selected samples from each category.

Researchers traveled to the home of the couple to ensure that participants would be as comfortable as possible and also to spare them unnecessary inconvenience. Two interviewers were employed, so that partners could be interviewed separately as well as together, yielding more candid responses to many questions. Couples with small homes presented the researchers with a challenge, since privacy was mandatory. Blumstein and Schwartz explain, "Some couples had only one suitable room, and so several interviews were conducted without heat, or with a flashlight, in backyards and even bathrooms. We came to call these our bathtub interviews" (1983:20).

The interviews contributed depth and detail to the research that questionnaires alone could never have provided. But face-to-face questions about personal topics required special care on the part of researchers. On the one hand, they wanted to avoid influencing the responses of the participants, while on the other, they did want to encourage openness by being nonjudgmental about what each participant revealed. In the end, the research team concluded that they had been largely successful: they had learned things many subjects had never revealed

Researchers must be aware that, among many of the world's people, personal issues such as sexuality are not normally discussed. Some of the questions asked by Blumstein and Schwartz might well have offended many Japanese. If this research were to be done in Japan, researchers might learn facts that subjects had never shared, even with their spouses.

to anyone else, even to partners. Of course, this makes the ethical issue of protecting privacy all the more important.

Findings. Among the more interesting conclusions of this study was that, even within a loving relationship, money means power. The researchers found that the partner with the higher income generally steered the relationship, a blow to the common-sense view that love encourages relational equality. In this regard, however, homosexual women were an exception. Perhaps because American women do not usually judge their personal worth by their income, Blumstein and Schwartz reasoned, lesbian couples tended to be the most egalitarian of couples.

Another finding was that couples varied greatly in terms of sex outside of the relationship, which Blumstein and Schwartz describe with the neutral term "nonmonogamy." As Table 2–1 on page 48 shows, in all types of partnerships the likelihood of nonmonogamy increases over time. But married couples tend to have more fidelity than heterosexual couples simply living together. Further differences emerge among homosexual couples, none of whom can legally marry. Lesbians have

Table 2–1 SEXUAL ACTIVITY AMONG AMERICAN COUPLES, BY TYPE OF RELATIONSHIP, DURATION OF RELATIONSHIP, AND SEX OF RESPONDENT

	Married Couples					Cohabiting Heterosexual Couples					Homosexual Couples				
	Reported Sexual Activity outside Relationship						Reported Sexual Activity outside Relationship					Reported Sexual Activity outside Relationship			
Years Together	Females		Males			Years Together	Females		Males		Years Together	Females		Males	
	Yes	No	Yes	No			Yes	No	Yes	No		Yes	No	Yes	No
Under 2	13%	87%	15%	85%		Under 2	20%	80%	21%	79%	Under 2	15%	85%	66%	34%
2–10	22	78	23	77		2–10	42	58	47	53	2–10	38	62	89	11
Over 10	22	78	30	70		Over 10*	no data		no data		Over 10	43	57	94	6

* Too few cohabiting couples had been together for more than ten years.

SOURCE: Adapted from Philip Blumstein and Pepper Schwartz, *American Couples* (New York: William Morrow, 1983), p. 276. © 1983 by Philip Blumstein and Pepper W. Schwartz. Adapted by permission of William Morrow & Co.

CRITICAL THINKING

Table Reading: An Important Skill

A table provides a great deal of information in a small amount of space, so learning to read tables can increase your reading and information-gathering efficiency. When you spot a table, look first at the title to see what information it contains. In Table 2–1, for example, the title is presented at the top, indicating that the table reports the sexual activity of American couples. In many cases, the title of a table will also indicate all the variables that are used in organizing the data. Here, sexual patterns are described in terms of three additional variables: (1) the type of relationship involved (married couples, cohabiting heterosexual couples, and homosexual couples); (2) the duration of the relationship (under 2 years, 2 to 10 years, over 10 years); and (3) the sex of the respondent (males and females).

These three variables form the three major parts of the table, and six categories of people are found within each part. For each category, the proportion of people who reported sexual activity outside of the relationship is presented, along with the pro-portion that reported no such activity. For each category, two percentages are provided, which add to 100 percent.

Looking at the first part of the table, we can see that 13 percent of females married for less than two years reported having sexual activity outside of their relationship, while 87 percent reported no such activity. For women married between two and ten years, 22 percent reported being nonmo-nogamous, while 78 percent reported no instance of nonmonogamy. The same percentages hold for women married for more than ten years. Comparable information is provided for the other categories of people as well.

This table provides numerous interesting insights. First, for all types of relationships, the longer the couple has been together, the more likely is nonmonogamy. Second, regardless of the type of relationship, males are more likely than females to be non-monogamous. Third, the likelihood of nonmonogamy varies among the different types of couples. Overall, married couples are the most likely to remain monogamous; cohabiting heterosexual couples are somewhat more likely to be nonmonogamous. Notice, finally, that the pattern among homosexuals differs sharply by sex. Gay males are the most likely of all couples to be nonmonogamous; the proportion of nonmonogamous lesbians is higher than that of married females and slightly lower than that of cohabiting heterosexual females.

Finally, when reading tables or any research results, a critical reader should be alert for any clues to the overall quality of the work. Important items include the identity and back-ground of the researchers themselves (are they sociologists? newspaper reporters?), as well as bibliographic information (where was the research published—by an established journal? by a group with some vested interest in the topic?). The research presented here is sound on both counts. Of course, this is not always the case, so that critical thinking skills involve assessing the research itself as well as its results.

only slightly less sexual involvement outside their relationships than do cohabiting heterosexuals. Gay men, on the other hand, were found to have far more (although, as noted in Chapter 20, "Health and Medicine," this pattern changed during the 1980s).

Participant Observation

Participant observation is *a method in which researchers systematically observe people while joining in their routine activities.* This method is useful for studying social life within virtually any setting, ranging from night clubs to religious seminaries. Participant observation is also widely used by cultural anthropologists to study other societies. Cultural anthropology is closely related to sociology, except that whereas sociologists typically focus their attention on their own society, cultural anthropologists apply the method of participant observation—which they call *fieldwork*—to small, technologically simple societies. Cultural anthropologists describe an unfamiliar culture in an *ethnography*; a sociologist may study a particular category of people or a particular setting as a *case study*.

Sociologists are likely to choose participant observation when they have only a vague understanding of the social patterns they wish to investigate. Thus, studies of this kind are often descriptive and sometimes even *exploratory*. They usually begin with few, if any, specific hypotheses to test, since researchers are often not sure what the important questions will turn out to be. Compared to experiments and survey research, then, participant observation has fewer hard-and-fast rules. Indeed, the research plan must be flexible enough to adapt to unexpected circumstances. Initially, then, a researcher is likely to be concerned with gaining entry into what may be an unfamiliar social setting. In time, observations give rise to many specific questions, and answers are organized into a detailed description of a way of life.

As its name suggests, participant observation has two sides. On the one hand, gaining an "insider's" look depends on becoming a participant in the setting—"hanging out" with others, attempting to act, think, and even feel the way they do. In contrast to other research methods, participant observation requires a researcher to become immersed in a social setting, not for a week or two, but usually for a period of years. On the other hand, for the duration of the study, the researcher must also maintain the role of "observer," standing back from the action and applying the sociological perspective to social patterns that others take for granted.

Participant-observation research is well suited for exploring an unfamiliar setting. Doing so, however, usually requires extensive preparation, as anthropologists who routinely study other cultures know well. Before entering this urban community in Bombay, India, a researcher would need new language skills and at least a basic understanding of a complex and distinctive culture. To minimize these difficulties, researchers usually study communities with which they have at least some previous experience.

Obviously, not all observational research need involve participation in the social setting under study. When it does, however, the twin roles of "insider" participant and "outsider" observer must be a matter of careful compromise. Such tensions are commonly featured in the daily record of how the research proceeds, called *field notes*. As the basis of the final research report, these notes allow others to understand not only a researcher's conclusions but something of the research experience itself.

Sociologists working alone in this kind of study must use extraordinary care in their work, since the results depend on the interpretations of a single scientist. Moreover, participant observation is typically an example of **qualitative research,** meaning *research based heavily on subjective impressions.* In contrast, most surveys are examples of **quantitative research,** which *emphasizes the analysis of numerical data.* Because personal impressions play such a central role in participant observation, this method may be criticized as lacking scientific rigor. Yet its personal approach is also a strength; while a highly visible team of sociologists attempting to administer formal surveys may disrupt many social settings, a sensitive participant-observer can often gain considerable insight into people's natural behavior.

A Case Study: Street Corner Society

A classic illustration of participant observation was carried out in the late 1930s by William Foote Whyte. As a graduate student at Harvard University, Whyte was fascinated by the lively street life of a nearby, rather run-down section of Boston. He embarked on a four-year study of this neighborhood, which he called "Cornerville" to protect the privacy of its inhabitants.

Cornerville was the home of first- and second-generation Italian immigrants. Many were poor and lived quite differently from the more affluent Bostonians with whom Whyte was familiar. Indeed, to many, Cornerville was a place to be avoided: a poor, chaotic slum that was the home of racketeers. Unwilling to accept this prevailing view of Cornerville, Whyte set out to discover for himself exactly what kind of life went on inside this community. His celebrated book, *Street Corner Society* (1981; orig. 1943), reports that Cornerville was actually a highly organized community, with its own code of values, complex social patterns, and distinctive social conflicts.

Whyte's research demonstrates some of the advantages of the participant-observation method as well as some of its pitfalls. Whyte could have taken his clipboard and questionnaire to one of Cornerville's community centers and asked local residents to tell him about their lives. Or he could have asked members of the community to come to his office at Harvard for interviews. In either case, the information he gathered would certainly have been misleading, since as we have already seen, the awareness of being observed often alters the behavior of subjects. Many Cornerville residents would probably have refused to talk to him at all under those circumstances. Whyte realized that he had to downplay the role of observer if people were to be comfortable in his presence. He therefore tried to become part of Cornerville's everyday social patterns.

One night early in his study, Whyte joined a group of people in Cornerville who frequented a gambling establishment. After listening to a man tell a long tale about how gambling was organized, Whyte commented naively, "I suppose the cops were all paid off?" The man's reaction taught Whyte something about the tension between being a participant and being an observer:

> The gambler's jaw dropped. He glared at me. Then he denied vehemently that any policeman had been paid off and immediately switched the conversation to another subject. For the rest of that evening I felt very uncomfortable. The next day [a local acquaintance] explained the lesson of the previous evening. "Go easy on that 'who,' 'what,' 'why,' 'when,' 'where' stuff, Bill. You ask those questions and people will clam up on you. If people accept you, you can just hang around, and you'll learn the answers in the long run without even having to ask the questions." (1981:303)

Gaining insider status—becoming a participant—was thus the crucial first step in Whyte's research. But how could an upper-middle-class Anglo-Saxon graduate student from Harvard become part of the life of a poor Italian immigrant community like Cornerville?

The problem of "breaking in" is common to research of this kind. Trying to gain entry into a strange social environment can be difficult, embarrassing, and often even dangerous, as Whyte soon found out. Accepting some questionable advice from a young instructor at Harvard, Whyte decided to drop in to a local bar, offer to buy a woman a drink, and encourage her to talk about Cornerville. Entering a night spot that evening, he could find no women alone. Presently, however, he noticed one man talking with two women, providing what he thought was a good opportunity:

> I approached the group and opened with something like this:
> "Pardon me. Would you mind if I joined you?" There was a moment of silence while the man stared at me. Then he offered to throw me down the stairs. I assured him that this would not be necessary, and demonstrated as much by walking right out of there without any assistance. (1981:289)

This experience taught Whyte another important lesson: the researcher must be sensitive to the danger of imposing in any way upon the subject. Attempting to force an entry as Whyte did is not only awkward for the researcher but represents an unfair intrusion into the lives of other people.

Fortunately, Whyte's research soon took a turn for the better when he met a young man named "Doc" in the local community agency. Whyte explained his difficulty to Doc, who took Whyte under his wing as a friend to be introduced to others in the area. This was the real start of Whyte's research because, with Doc's help, he soon became a regular among the people of Cornerville.

Whyte's friendship with Doc illustrates the importance that a *key informant* can play in field research. Key informants introduce a researcher to a community, and they can also suggest how and where to find specific information. The use of a key informant has its dangers, however. Because any key informant is familiar with only part of a community, any assistance is likely to be selective. Moreover, a researcher identified with an unpopular key informant may actually encounter resistance from some others. Thus, while a key informant may be invaluable at the outset, the participant-observer must immediately seek a broader range of contacts.

Over several years of research, Whyte gradually settled in as a comfortable resident of Cornerville. He soon learned that it was not the disorganized slum some believed it to be. Many immigrant members of the community participated in a wide range of civic associations in the hope of becoming "established" Americans. Moreover, a number of their children were in college with an eye toward future success. To be sure, there were social divisions in Cornerville, and even a few criminals, as there are in virtually every community. Yet Whyte was able to see that this distinctive section of Boston was composed mostly of people who, though poor, were working hard to build a future for themselves.

In sum, participant observation is a method embracing tensions and contrasts. Its lack of rigid planning allows the flexibility needed in an unfamiliar setting, but this very aspect challenges any researcher's discipline and ingenuity. Sympathetic understanding of a setting requires involvement, while the rigorous work of the scientific observer demands detachment. Especially if a researcher works alone, this method can often be used with minimal funding; but the length of time involved makes this the most personally costly type of research. Perhaps for all these reasons, participant-observation research is far rarer than other methods described in this chapter. Yet the depth of understanding gained through research of this kind has greatly enriched our knowledge of many types of human communities.

Secondary Analysis

Each of the methods of conducting sociological investigation described so far involves researchers personally collecting their own data. Doing so is not always possible, however, and it is often not necessary. In many cases, sociologists engage in **secondary analysis,** which is *a research method involving analysis of data originally collected by others.*

The data most widely used in this way are statistics gathered by government agencies of many countries. The Bureau of the Census is continuously gathering information about the people of the United States, much of which is of interest to sociologists. Similar information is available from Statistics Canada, a branch of the Canadian government. Data about other societies in the world are found in various publications of the United Nations and The World Bank. A wide range of such information is as near as the college library.

Most census data are obtained by questionnaires sent and returned through the mail. In some urban areas, however, this strategy produces too few responses, so trained researchers are likely to follow up by conducting personal interviews.

Secondary analysis may also involve a researcher using data originally collected by others. The obvious advantage of using available data—whether government statistics or the results of other research studies—is the savings in time and money that would otherwise be needed to gather the information from scratch. Using data collected by others means that sociologists with low budgets can undertake research that might otherwise be impossible. Moreover, the quality of data available from government agencies is generally better than what even well-funded researchers could hope to obtain on their own.

Still, secondary analysis has characteristic problems. For one thing, although Census Bureau data are generally quite precise, many original researchers provide no basis to evaluate the accuracy of their data. Was information gathered in a systematic way that encouraged unbiased responses? Was all information accurately recorded? Using data collected by others is thus sometimes a bit like buying a used car. Although bargains are common, the potential for error and distortion means that "what you see may not be what you get."

Emile Durkheim's nineteenth-century study of suicide, described in Chapter 1 ("The Sociological Perspective"), is one of the best-known sociological investigations making use of existing records. But Durkheim's research also illustrates some of the dangers of this approach. He used official records of suicide among various segments of European society. Whether a death was actually a suicide is often uncertain, however. Many accidents may be incorrectly classified as suicides; perhaps more commonly, actual suicides may be recorded as accidents or deaths due to other causes.

Sociologists today who utilize official crime statistics are always on guard against distortions. Researchers have learned, for example, that many crimes are not reported to police. And to complicate matters, the likelihood of reporting varies according to the type of crime. Homicides, for example, typically do come to the attention of police, but, as Chapter 8 ("Deviance") explains, most rapes remain unreported.

A second problem is that available data may have been collected for purposes different from those of a subsequent researcher. Questions may have been phrased and presented to respondents in a way not exactly suited to the current researcher's goals, or subjects may not be the ideal sample. Obviously, we are dealing with a trade-off here. Any shortcomings in the data must be balanced against the ease by which they are obtained by the researcher.

Historical Research: A Tale of Two Cities

Since we are all trapped in the present, secondary analysis is especially useful in historical research. An example of historical sociology involving new analysis of existing data is the study *Puritan Boston and Quaker Philadelphia*, carried out by E. Digby Baltzell (1979). While visiting the campus of Bowdoin College in Maine, Baltzell was startled to learn that a larger number of notable Americans had graduated from that small school than from his own, much bigger University of Pennsylvania. This sparked Baltzell's sociological imagination, leading him to investigate historical patterns of achievement in New England in relation to those in Pennsylvania.

Baltzell set out to test his hunch that New England had produced far more than its share of national leaders in diverse fields such as politics, law, and the arts, while his native Pennsylvania had produced few such people. Realizing that he would have to rely on information compiled by others, Baltzell turned to the *Dictionary of American Biography*, twenty volumes of historical, biographical information on over thirteen thousand men and women. Baltzell knew that by using this source he was limiting himself to considering only those people the editors of the *Dictionary* had deemed worthy of inclusion. Accepting some inevitable bias, however, he proceeded, confident that there was no better source of the information he needed.

Baltzell's next step was to assess each person's achievement. Here, again, he cleverly relied on existing judgments, basing his rankings on the stated policy of the *Dictionary* to make the length of each biography proportional to the person's importance. All such ratings are open to argument, of course, but Baltzell could hardly have done better entirely on his own.

By the time Baltzell had identified the seventy-five Americans with the longest biographies, a striking pattern had emerged. Massachusetts had the most, claiming twenty-one of the seventy-five top achievers; overall, the New England states had thirty-one such entries. In contrast, Pennsylvania had only two; and the entire Middle Atlantic region, only twelve. Closing in on the explanation, Baltzell soon realized that almost all the great achievers from Massachusetts were actually from the city of Boston. In stark contrast, there was little such achievement in the history of his own city of Philadelphia.

What might explain the disparity? Baltzell drew inspiration from the German sociologist Max Weber (1958; orig. 1904–1905), whose own research showing how attitudes toward achievement are influenced by religion is detailed in Chapter 4 ("Society"). Baltzell turned his attention to the two very different religious environments that have historically dominated Boston and Philadelphia. Here he found the key to this historical puzzle: based on religious conviction in both cases, the Puritan founders of Boston sought public achievement just as fervently as their Quaker counterparts in Philadelphia avoided it.

Both cities were founded by religious refugees fleeing persecution in England. But the ways the groups viewed the world were quite at odds. Convinced of humanity's innate sinfulness, Boston's Puritans built a rigid society on family, church, and school to regulate people's behavior. Hard work glorified God, and public prominence was the most reassuring sign that one had received God's blessing. Thus, Puritanism fostered a hierarchical and disciplined life in which achievement was vigorously sought and highly respected.

In contrast to the Puritans, Philadelphia's Quakers built a way of life on the notion that human beings are inherently good. They saw little need for strong social institutions to "save" individuals from sinfulness. Moreover, believing all people to be equal, the Quakers celebrated personal modesty and discouraged anyone from standing apart from others.

Baltzell therefore imagined Boston and Philadelphia as two social "test tubes": Puritanism was introduced into one, Quakerism into the other. From our vantage point centuries later, we can see what "chemical reactions" occurred in each case. Without claiming that either religion is in any absolute terms "better" than the other, Baltzell convincingly argues that the two belief systems set into motion different orientations toward individual achievement that shaped the history of each region.

As in all research, of course, Baltzell's historical data do not prove his conclusions in any absolute sense. The best we can say is that Baltzell's theory is consistent with the data, and as always, we must look to additional research to provide further support for or cast doubt on these conclusions. Especially when dealing with events far removed from the present, researchers must make considerable use of their skills of interpretation. This reminds us that, in the end, sociological investigation is a complex weave of scientific skills, personal values, and a lively and practiced imagination.

Four major methods of sociological investigation have now been introduced and are summarized in Table 2–2. A final consideration is how the specific facts obtained through sociological investigation are related to theory.

Table 2–2 FOUR RESEARCH METHODS: A SUMMARY

Method	Application	Advantages	Limitations
Experiment	For explanatory research that specifies relationships among variables; generates quantitative data	Provides greatest ability to specify cause-and-effect relationships; replication of research is relatively easy	Laboratory settings have artificial quality; unless research environment is carefully controlled, result may be biased
Survey	For gathering information about issues that cannot be directly observed, such as attitudes and values; useful for descriptive and explanatory research; generates quantitative or qualitative data	Sampling allows surveys of large populations using questionnaires; interviews provide in-depth responses	Questionnaires must be carefully prepared and may produce low return rate; interviews are expensive and time-consuming
Participant Observation	For exploratory and descriptive study of people in a "natural" setting; generates qualitative data	Allows study of "natural" behavior; usually inexpensive	Time-consuming; replication of research is difficult; researcher must balance roles of participant and observer
Secondary analysis	For exploratory, descriptive, or explanatory research whenever suitable data are available	Saves time and expense of data collection; makes historical research possible	Researcher has no control over possible bias in data; data may not be suitable for current research needs

The Interplay of Theory and Method

The methods of sociological investigation we have described guide the discovery of facts about our social world. Facts, however, are not the final goal of research; as suggested in Chapter 1 ("The Sociological Perspective"), what we are really after is the development of theory—combining facts into meaning.

In sociological investigation, the discovery of facts and theory are related in two ways. **Deductive logical thought** *begins with general ideas about the world that produce specific hypotheses suitable for scientific testing.* From a general understanding of some issue the researcher *deduces* a specific hypothesis and selects a method by which to test it. Of course, the data collected may or may not support the hypothesis. Data supporting the hypothesis suggest that the general theory is on the right track. Data refuting the hypothesis suggest that the theory must be revised or perhaps rejected entirely. The deductive logical model, then, proceeds from the general (theory) to the specific (facts used for evaluation).

Philip Zimbardo's Stanford County Prison experiment illustrates the operation of this model. Zimbardo began with the general idea that prisons themselves affect human behavior. He then designed a specific hypothesis: extremely healthy young men placed in a prison setting would display some violent behavior. Zimbardo confirmed this hypothesis when violence erupted soon after the experiment began. Had his experiment produced amicable behavior between "prisoners" and "guards," his original theory would clearly have required reformulation.

A second type of logical thought works in the other direction. **Inductive logical thought** *begins with specific observations that a researcher attempts to link together into general theory.* In other words, a researcher confronted with specific facts uses inductive reasoning to organize them into a more general theory about human behavior.

E. Digby Baltzell's research provides an illustration of the inductive logical model. He began with the observation that one New England college had produced a surprising number of high achievers. He then collected additional facts from two regions of the United States and gradually organized them into a distinctive pattern. Finally, he interpreted this pattern as evidence of the general importance of religious values to historical achievement.

In most cases, researchers make use of *both* types of logical thought, as represented in Figure 2–2. Researchers often begin with general ideas that lead (deduc-

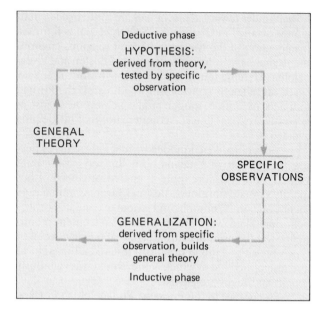

Figure 2–2 Deductive and Inductive Logical Thought

tively) to hypotheses, which in turn are evaluated on the basis of specific observations. These observations then lead (inductively) to the modification of the original ideas into a somewhat different theory.

PUTTING IT ALL TOGETHER: THE STEPS IN SOCIOLOGICAL INVESTIGATION

The following ten steps are guidelines for carrying out any research project in sociology.

1. **Define the topic you wish to investigate.** The ideas for social research can come to you anywhere and at any time if you remain curious and observe the world around you from the sociological perspective. As Max Weber suggested, the issue chosen for study is likely to have some personal significance to you.

2. **Find out what has already been written about the topic.** You are probably not the first person to have an interest in the particular issue. Spend enough time in the library to learn what theories and methods of sociological investigation have been applied to your topic. Theory guides the kinds of

questions you ask, and research methods provide strategies for finding answers. In looking over the research that has already been done on the topic, be especially mindful of problems that may have come up before.

3. **Assess the requirements for carrying out research on the topic.** What resources are necessary to support your research? How much time will you need? Can you do the work yourself? If not, how much help will you need? What expenses will you have along the way? What sources of funding might be available to support your research? It is important that you be able to provide answers to all these questions before you actually begin to design the research project.

4. **Specify the questions you are going to ask.** Are you seeking to explore an unfamiliar social setting? To describe some category of people? Or to investigate the link between several variables? If your study is exploratory, identify general questions that will guide your work. If it is descriptive, specify the population and the characteristics of interest. If your study is explanatory, state the hypothesis to be tested and carefully operationalize each variable.

5. **Consider the ethical issues involved in the research.** Not every study will raise major ethical issues, but you should be sensitive to this matter at the outset of your research. Will you promise anonymity to the subjects? If so, how will you ensure that anonymity will be maintained? Can your research cause harm to anyone? How might you design the study to minimize the chances for such harm?

6. **Decide which research method you will use.** Consider all major research strategies—as well as innovative combinations of approaches—before deciding how to proceed. Keep in mind that the appropriate method is largely related to the kind of questions you are asking as well as to the resources available to support your research.

7. **Put the method to work to gather data.** The collection of data is carried out according to the research method you have chosen. Be sure to record all information accurately and in a way that will make sense to you later (it may be some time before you actually write up the results of your work). Remain keenly aware that various sources of bias can weaken the research.

8. **Interpret the findings.** Organize your data in terms

This painting by René Magritte can be interpreted to mean that insight is the ultimate goal of sociological investigation. This is achieved only by combining research skills with human imagination.

of the initial questions and decide what answers the data suggest. If your study involved a specific hypothesis, the data should provide you with a basis to confirm, reject, or modify the hypothesis. Keep in mind that there may be several ways to interpret the results of your study, consistent with different theoretical paradigms, and you should consider them all. Also be on guard against the ever-present danger that your personal values or your expectations at the outset will affect how you make sense out of the data you have collected.

9. **State your conclusions based on your findings.** Prepare a final report indicating what you have learned from the research. Consider the contributions of your work both to sociological theory and to improving sociological methods of research. What is the value of your research to other people in general? Finally, evaluate your own work. What problems arose during the research process? What questions are left unanswered? Note any ways in which your own biases may have affected your conclusions.

10. **Publish your research!**

SUMMARY

1. Sociology is more than a perspective; sociological investigation uses the logic of science to learn actively about the social world.

2. Science is an important foundation of all sociological research and, more broadly, helps us to critically evaluate information we encounter every day.

3. Two basic requirements for sociological investigation are (1) using the sociological perspective to view the surrounding world and (2) being curious and asking questions about society.

4. Science is a particular way of knowing based on empirical evidence. As such, science often contradicts our common sense.

5. Measurement is the process of determining the value of a variable in any specific case. Sound measurement has both reliability and validity.

6. Science seeks to specify the relationship among variables. Ideally, researchers seek relationships of cause and effect, in which an independent variable can be used to predict change in a dependent variable. Often, however, research involves only correlation.

7. The scientific ideal is objectivity. Although the issues studied typically reflect personal interests, value-free research depends on suspending personal values and biases as much as possible. Issues involving gender often generate bias.

8. The logic of science was developed primarily through study of the natural world. Applying science to the study of human behavior involves various considerations and limitations.

9. Curiosity and imagination, vital to research, spring from the human mind and not from science. Since human reality is a matter of meanings, the process of interpretation is inherent in all sociological investigation.

10. Many sociologists argue that research inevitably involves political values, and some maintain that therefore sociological research should encourage desirable social change.

11. Ethical guidelines are necessary because sociological research can affect subjects for good or ill.

12. Experiments attempt to specify the relationship between two (or more) variables and are best carried out under controlled conditions.

13. Surveys solicit subject responses to items or questions. Two major tools are questionnaires and interviews.

14. Participant observation involves direct observation of a social setting for an extended period of time. The researcher is both a participant in the setting and a careful observer of it.

15. Secondary analysis, or making use of available data, is often preferable to collecting one's own data; it also allows study of historical issues.

16. Theory and research are closely interrelated. Deductive thought moves from general ideas to evaluating specific hypotheses. Inductive thought organizes specific observations into general ideas. Most sociological investigation is characterized by both types of logical thought.

KEY CONCEPTS

cause and effect a relationship between two variables in which change in one (the independent variable) causes change in another (the dependent variable)

concept an abstract idea that represents some aspect of the world, inevitably in a somewhat ideal and simplified form

control the ability to neutralize the effect of one variable so that the relationships among other variables can be more precisely determined

correlation a relationship between two (or more) variables

deductive logical thought a logical process in which general theory yields specific hypotheses suitable for scientific testing

dependent variable a variable that is changed by another (independent) variable

empirical evidence evidence we are able to verify with our senses

experiment a research method that investigates cause-and-effect relationships under highly controlled conditions

Hawthorne effect any distortion in research caused by subjects' awareness that they are being studied

hypothesis an unverified statement of a relationship between any facts or variables

independent variable a variable that causes change in another (dependent) variable

inductive logical thought a logical process in which specific research observations are organized into general theory

interview a series of items or questions administered personally by a researcher to respondents

mean the arithmetic average of a series of numbers

measurement the process of determining the value of a variable in a specific case

median the value that occurs midway in a series of numbers or, simply, the middle case

mode the value that occurs most often in a series of numbers

objectivity the state of complete personal neutrality in conducting research

operationalizing a variable specifying exactly what is to be measured in assigning a value to a variable

participant observation a method in which researchers systematically observe people while joining in their routine activities

population the people about whom a researcher seeks knowledge

qualitative research research based heavily on subjective impressions

quantitative research research that emphasizes the analysis of numerical data

questionnaire a series of questions or items to which subjects are asked to respond

reliability the quality of consistency in measurement

replication the process by which a study is repeated by other researchers

research method a systematic strategy for carrying out research

sample part of a population, selected to be representative of the entirety, from whom data are obtained

science a logical system that bases knowledge on direct, systematic observation

secondary analysis a research method involving analysis of data originally collected by others

spurious correlation a relationship between two (or more) variables not based on direct cause and effect

survey a research method in which subjects respond to a series of items or questions in a questionnaire or interview

validity the quality of measurement gained by actually measuring what one intends to measure

variable a concept with a value that changes from case to case

SUGGESTED READINGS

The following books introduce the process of sociological investigation in terms that are easy for beginning students to understand.

Earl Babbie. *The Practice of Social Research*. 5th ed. Belmont, CA: Wadsworth, 1989.

Morton M. Hunt. *Profiles of Social Research: The Scientific Study of Human Interactions*. New York: Russell Sage Foundation/Basic Books, 1986.

Floyd J. Fowler, Jr., and Thomas W. Mangione. *Standardized Survey Interviewing: Minimizing Interviewer-Related Error*. Newbury Park, CA: Sage, 1989.

This recent book focuses on one central research strategy.

Danny L. Jorgensen. *Participant Observation: A Methodology for Human Studies*. Newbury Park, CA: Sage, 1989.

These books explore the neglected issue of how gender and sexism can affect the research process.

Tony Larry Whitehead and Mary Ellen Conaway, eds. *Self, Sex, and Gender in Cross-Cultural Fieldwork*. Urbana, IL: University of Illinois Press, 1986.

Margrit Eichler. *Nonsexist Research Methods: A Practical Guide*. Winchester, MA: Unwin Hyman, 1988.

How the political environment can shape science is evident in this study of the Soviet Union, in which sociological research is controlled by the Central Committee of the Communist party.

Vladimir Shlapentokh. *The Politics of Sociology in the Soviet Union*. London/Boulder, CO: Westview Press, 1987.

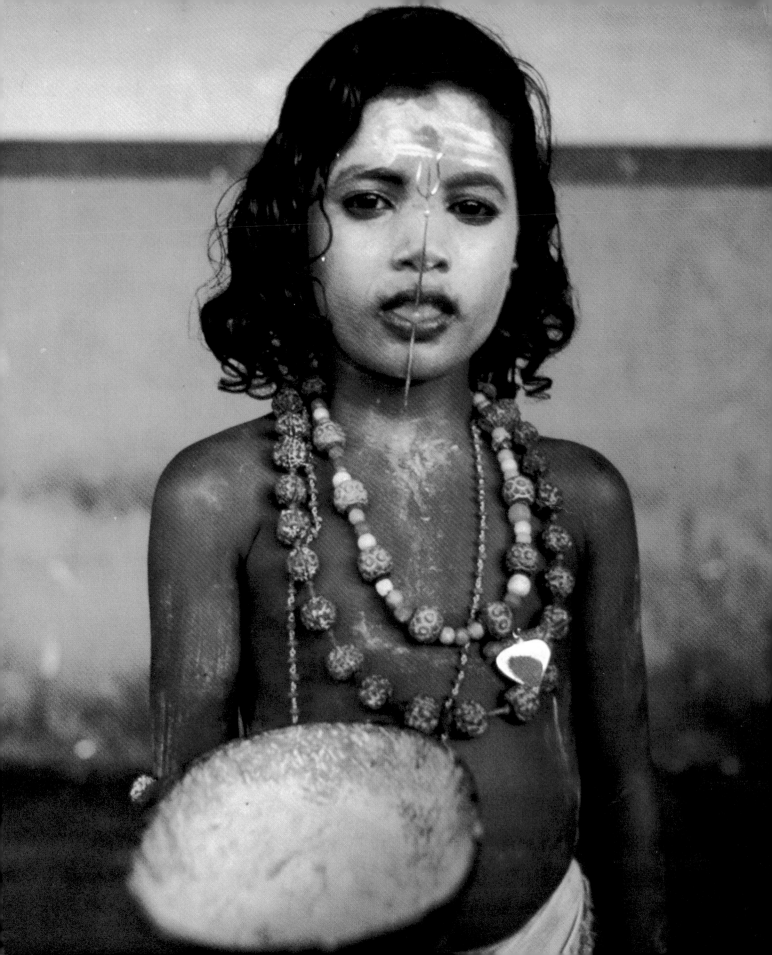

3

Culture

A small aluminum motorboat chugged steadily along the muddy Orinoco River, deep in the vast tropical rain forest of southern Venezuela. American anthropologist Napoleon Chagnon was nearing the end of a three-day journey to the home territory of the Yąnomamö, one of the few technologically simple societies remaining on earth.

Some twelve thousand Yąnomamö live in scattered villages along the border between Venezuela and Brazil. Their way of life contrasts sharply with our own. The Yąnomamö are spirit worshippers who have no form of writing. Until recent contact with outsiders, they used hand-crafted weapons such as the bow and arrow to hunt for food. Thus Chagnon would be as strange to them as they to him.

By two o'clock in the afternoon, Chagnon had almost reached his destination. The hot sun made the humid air almost unbearable. The anthropologist's clothes were soaked with perspiration; his face and hands were swollen from the bites of innumerable gnats that swarmed around him. But he hardly noticed, so preoccupied was he with the fact that in just a few moments he was to come face to face with people unlike any he had ever known.

Chagnon's heart pounded as the boat slid onto the riverbank near a Yąnomamö village. Sounds of activity came from nearby. Chagnon and his guide climbed from the boat and walked toward the village, stooping as they pushed their way through the dense undergrowth. Chagnon describes what happened next:

> I looked up and gasped when I saw a dozen burly, naked, sweaty, hideous men staring at us down the shafts of their drawn arrows! Immense wads of green tobacco were stuck between their lower teeth and lips making them look even more hideous, and strands of dark green slime dripped or

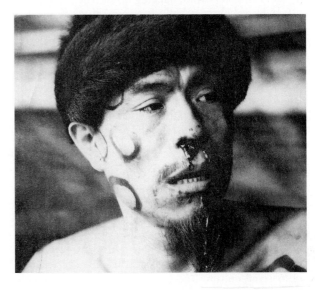

hung from their nostrils—strands so long that they clung to their [chests] or drizzled down their chins.

My next discovery was that there were a dozen or so vicious, underfed dogs snapping at my legs, circling me as if I were to be their next meal. I just stood there holding my notebook, helpless and pathetic. Then the stench of the decaying vegetation and filth hit me and I almost got sick. I was horrified. What kind of welcome was this for the person who came here to live with you and learn your way of life, to become friends with you? (1983:10)

Fortunately for Chagnon, the Yąnomamö villagers recognized his guide and withdrew their weapons. Reassured that he would at least survive the afternoon, Chagnon was still shaken by his inability to make any sense of the people surrounding him. And this was to be his home for a year and a half! He wondered why he had forsaken physics to study human culture in the first place.

All 5 billion people living on our planet are members of but one biological species: *Homo sapiens*. Even so, any of us can be overwhelmed by how different we are from one another, differences not of biology but of culture. Upon his arrival at the Yąnomamö village, Chagnon experienced a severe case of culture shock: *the personal disorientation that may accompany exposure to an unfamiliar way of life*. Like most of us, Chagnon had been raised to keep his clothes on, even in hot weather, and to use a handkerchief when his nose was running—especially in front of others. The Yąnomamö clearly had other ideas about how to live. The nudity that embarrassed Chagnon was customary to the Yąnomamö. The green slime hanging from their nostrils was caused by inhaling a hallucinogenic drug, a practice common among friends. The "stench" from which Chagnon recoiled in disgust no doubt smelled like "Home Sweet Home" to the inhabitants of that Yąnomamö village.

Human beings the world over have very different ideas about what is pleasant and unpleasant, polite and rude, true and false, right and wrong. This capacity for startling difference is a wonder of our species: the expression of human culture.

WHAT IS CULTURE?

Culture may be defined as *the beliefs, values, behavior, and material objects shared by a particular people*. As this definition suggests, sociologists distinguish between nonmaterial culture: *the intangible creations of human*

society (ideas ranging from altruism to zen), and material culture: *the tangible products of human society* (objects ranging from armaments to zippers). The terms *culture* and *society* are obviously similar, but their precise meanings are different. Culture is a way of life or social heritage that certain people have in common. Society, the topic of the next chapter, is the interaction among people within a geographical or political boundary, which is guided by culture. Although the two concepts have different meanings, neither society nor culture can exist without the other.

Culture is expressed in everyday life in what we wear to work, when and what we eat, and how we enjoy spending our free time. In addition, our culture leads us to sleep in houses of wood and brick, while people of other cultures live in igloos of ice or tepees made of animal skins. Culture provides the framework within which life becomes meaningful, based on standards of success, beauty, and goodness, and reverence for a divine power, the forces of nature, or long-dead ancestors. Culture also shapes our personalities—what we commonly (yet inaccurately) describe as "human nature." The Yąnomamö are fierce and warlike, and they strive to develop these "natural" qualities in their children. The Tasaday of the Philippines, in contrast, have been described as so peace-loving that their language has no word for violence. Both the American and the Japanese cultures stress achievement and hard work; but Americans value competition and individualism, while the Japanese emphasize cooperation and self-denying obedience to authority. In short, our culture affects virtually every dimension of our lives, from the power of enormous corporations to the most subtle facial expression.

Sociologically speaking the concept of culture is broader than that used in common speech. In everyday conversation, "culture" usually refers to art forms associated with elites, such as classical forms of literature, music, dance, and painting. Here, however, the term refers to *everything* that is part of a people's way of life—Motown as well as Mozart, fish sticks as well as fine cuisine, ping pong as well as polo.

No cultural element is "natural" in human beings, although most people around the world view their particular way of life as just that. What is naturally human is the capacity to create culture, which we learn to do as members of a society. And although culture is largely transmitted from generation to generation, every element of culture is a human product that is subject to change.

Every other species of living creatures—from ants to antelopes—behaves in uniform ways. Indeed, to a world traveler, the enormous diversity of humanity stands

People around the world have created highly diverse ways of life. This is evident in outward differences of appearance: compare the women shown here from Iran, Kenya, Greece, and Egypt and the men from Taiwan, Peru, India, and Indonesia. Less obvious, but of even greater importance, are the internal differences, since culture also shapes our self-concept and innermost personal feelings.

out in contrast to, say, cats, which are everywhere strikingly alike. The way of life of most living things is largely a matter of biological forces we call *instincts*, strategies for survival that change only over very long periods of time. A few animals—most notably chimpanzees and other related primates—have some basic elements of culture, such as the use of tools, and to teach simple skills to their offspring. But our creative ability to shape the world far exceeds that of any other form of life, so that *only humans rely on culture rather than instinct to ensure the survival of their kind* (Harris, 1987).

To understand how this came to be, we must briefly review the history of our species on the earth.

Culture and Human Intelligence

In a universe scientists estimate to be 15 billion years old, our planet is a relatively young 4.5 billion years of age, and the human species is a wide-eyed infant of only 250,000. We can trace our ancestry to the first forms of life that emerged a billion years after the earth was formed. Our history took a crucial turn when the mammals we call primates developed some 65 million years ago.

Early primates gradually evolved into highly intelligent life forms, with the largest brains relative to body weight of all living creatures. The human line diverged from that of our closest primate relatives, the great apes, about 12 million years ago. Our common lineage remains apparent, however, in characteristics that the human species shares with chimpanzees, gorillas, and orangutans of today: great sociability, leading to affectionate and long-lasting bonds for childrearing and mutual protection; the ability to walk upright (normal in humans, but less commonly used by other primates); and hands that grasp and manipulate objects with great precision.

Studying fossil records, scientists have concluded that the first creatures with clearly human characteristics existed about 2 million years ago. The mental capacity of these distant ancestors was sufficient to develop certain fundamentals of culture, including the use of fire, tools, weapons, and simple shelters. Such "stone age" achievements may seem modest, but they mark a major event in human history. At this point, our ancestors had embarked on an evolutionary course in which culture—made possible as the human brain enlarged—became the primary strategy for survival.

It is worth emphasizing that all humans, including those "ancient" ancestors, are newcomers to the earth, at least in an evolutionary time frame. To make this clear, Carl Sagan (1977) suggests that we imagine the entire 15-billion-year history of our universe as a single calendar year. The life-giving atmosphere of our planet did not develop until the fall of that year, and the earliest humanlike beings did not appear until December 31, the last day of the year, at about 10:30 at night! Yet not until 250,000 years ago—or minutes before the end of Sagan's "year"—did our own species finally emerge. These *Homo sapiens* (derived from Latin meaning "thinking person") continued to evolve until, just 40,000 years ago, creatures who looked very much like ourselves lived on the earth. With brains as large as our own, these "modern" *Homo sapiens* developed culture at a rapid pace, as the wide range of tools and cave art from this period suggests. Still, what we call civilization, based on permanent settlements and specialized occupations, began in the Middle East only about 12,000 years ago (Hamblin, 1973; Wenke, 1980). In terms of Sagan's "year," this flowering of human culture occurred during the final *seconds* before midnight on New Year's Eve. And what of our modern, industrial way of life? At only 300 years of age, it is just a millisecond in Sagan's "year."

Human culture, therefore, is linked to the biological evolution of human beings. It is a strategy for survival that began as our ancestors gradually moved from the trees to the ground, where walking upright and hunting in organized groups held obvious advantages. Second, the human ability to create a complex and variable way of life—as opposed to merely responding to biological forces—developed extremely slowly over millions of years as the size of the human brain increased. The essence of this transformation was that the biological forces we commonly call *instincts* were gradually replaced by a more efficient survival strategy: *human beings gained the mental power to actively fashion the natural environment for themselves.* At this point, human nature was no longer instinct but culture, setting us apart from other forms of life (Barash, 1981). Ever since, humans have made and remade their worlds in countless ways, which explains today's fascinating (and, as Napoleon Chagnon's experiences show, sometimes disturbing) diversity in human ways of life.

THE COMPONENTS OF CULTURE

Although cultures vary greatly, they all have five components in common: symbols, language, values, norms, and material culture. We shall begin with the one that underlies the rest: symbols.

Symbols

Human beings live within a world not just of objects and action, but of *meaning*. The human world, in short, is *symbolic*. A symbol is *anything that carries a particular meaning recognized by members of a culture*. A whistle, a wall of graffiti, a flashing red light, and a fist raised in the air can all serve as symbols. The human capacity to create and manipulate symbols is evident in the various ways a simple wink of the eye can convey interest, understanding, or insult.

As the basis of culture, symbols are the foundation of everyday reality. We become so familiar with the symbols of our own culture that we usually take them for granted. Often, however, we gain a sense of the importance of our symbolic world when a symbol is used in an unconventional way. Imagine, for example, a priest appearing before a church congregation dressed like a Hell's Angel.

Another way to understand the power of symbols is to enter a society with an unfamiliar culture. The essence of culture shock is an inability to properly attach meaning to what is around us. Like Napoleon Chagnon confronting the Yąnomamö, we feel lost, unsure of how to act, and sometimes frightened—a consequence of being outside the symbolic web of culture that unites individuals in meaningful social life.

The variability of symbols means that an action or object with important symbolic meaning within one culture may have a very different meaning, or no meaning at all, in another. To people in North America, a baseball bat symbolizes sport and relaxation, but the Yąnomamö would probably see it as a well-carved club that arouses thoughts of hunting or war. A dog is a beloved household pet to millions of Americans but a regular meal to millions of Chinese. Likewise, the cows that are sacred to millions of Hindus in India are routinely consumed as "quarter-pounders" by hungry Americans. Thus symbols that bind together people of one society can also separate people who live within the various societies of the world.

In practice, behavior that seems trivial to us may spark offense among people of other societies. An American sitting with one leg draped casually across the other, for instance, will insult an Iranian who holds the Islamic belief that the bottom of one's foot is unclean. Look to the box on page 64 for further illustrations of this problem.

To some degree, of course, symbolic meanings also vary even within a single society. The fur coat, prized as a symbol of success by one person, may represent the inhumane treatment of animals to another. Similarly, opening a door for a woman may signify a common courtesy in the minds of some men yet symbolize male condescension and dominance to many women.

Cultural symbols often change over time. Blue jeans were first sturdy and inexpensive clothing worn by people engaged in physical labor. In the 1960s, this fact made jeans popular among students—many of whom wore them to mask their affluence. Just a decade later, however, "designer jeans" became much the opposite: fashionable "status symbols" of big clothing budgets.

In sum, symbols are the means by which human beings make sense of their lives. In a world of cultural diversity, the use of symbols may cause embarrassment and even conflict, but without symbols our existence would be meaningless indeed.

Language

Helen Keller (1880–1968) was blind and deaf from infancy. Thus cut off from the symbolic world around her, she was literally apart from society. Only when her teacher, Anne Mansfield Sullivan, succeeded in introducing language did Helen Keller's world begin to open to the full range of human possibility. Helen Keller, who later became a renowned educator herself, recalls the moment she acquired language:

> We walked down the path to the well-house, attracted by the smell of honeysuckle with which it was covered. Someone was drawing water, and my teacher placed my hand under the spout. As the cool stream gushed over one hand, she spelled into the other the word *water*, first slowly, then rapidly. I stood still, my whole attention fixed upon the motions of her fingers. Suddenly I felt a misty consciousness as of something forgotten—a thrill of returning thought; and somehow the mystery of language was revealed to me. I knew then that "w-a-t-e-r" meant the wonderful cool something that was flowing over my hand. That living word awakened my soul; gave it light, hope, joy, set it free! (1903:21–24)

Language is the means by which all humans enter the world of culture. Language is defined as *a system of symbols with standard meanings that allows members of a society to communicate with one another*. All cultures have a spoken language, although some lack a system of writing. The Yąnomamö, for example, communicate entirely through speech.

Language—in a sense, our cultural heritage in coded form—is the most important means of **cultural transmission,** *the process by which culture is passed from one generation to the next*. Just as our bodies contain

The Meanings of Gestures in Different Cultures

On his first trip to Naples, a well-meaning American tourist thanks his waiter for a meal well-served by making the "A-Okay" gesture with his thumb and forefinger. The waiter pales and heads for the manager. They seriously discuss calling the police and having the hapless tourist arrested for obscene and offensive public behavior.

What happened? Most travelers wouldn't think of leaving home without a phrase book of some kind, enough of a guide to help them say and understand "Ja," "Nein," "Grazie," and "Ou se trouvent les toilettes?" And yet, while most people are aware that gestures are the most common form of cross-cultural communication, they don't realize that the language of gestures can be just as different . . . and just as likely to cause misunderstanding as the spoken word.

Consider our puzzled tourist. The

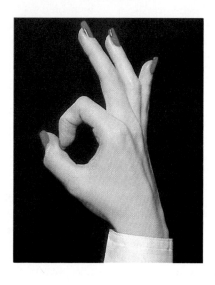

Praise or insult? The meaning of countless human gestures is strikingly different

thumb-and-forefinger-in-a-circle gesture, a friendly one in America, has an insulting meaning in France and Belgium: "You're worth zero." In parts of southern Italy it means "asshole," while in Greece and Turkey it is an insulting sexual invitation.

There are, in fact, dozens of gestures that take on different meanings as you move from one country or region to another. Is "thumbs up" always a positive gesture? Absolutely not. In northern Greece and Sardinia it has the insulting meaning "Up yours." Does nodding the head up and down always mean "yes?" No! That gesture may indicate "no" in parts of Greece and Turkey.

SOURCE: Paul Ekman, Wallace V. Friesen, and John Bear, "The International Language of Gestures," *Psychology Today*, May 1984, p. 64. Copyright May 1984 by the American Psychological Association. Reprinted by permission.

---

the genes of our ancestors, so our words and ideas are rooted in the lives of those who came before us. Language, then, offers us enormous power by providing access to the accumulated knowledge of centuries.

For most of human history, culture has been transmitted through speech alone, often called the *oral tradition*. Not until five thousand years ago was writing devised, and even then only a few people learned to read and write. Such was also the case in American history, as only a small elite was literate two centuries ago. Today, although few Americans are officially recognized as illiterate, perhaps 25 million adults in the United States cannot read and write. Indeed, a tragic fact is that many economically disadvantaged Americans rely on the oral tradition in a society that increasingly demands the symbolic skills of written language.

As the life of Helen Keller reveals, language skills are the key to human imagination. By connecting symbols in virtually infinite combinations, we can conceive

of life other than as it is. In this way, language distinguishes human beings as creatures who dream and hope, able to conceive of a future better than the present and, unique among all creatures, also aware of our own mortality.

Is Language Uniquely Human?

Are speech and writing unique to human beings? Creatures great and small make sounds and other physical signals to one another, which can be viewed as a form of language. These are largely instinctual, however, so that humans stand out as having the mental capacity to create a complex symbolic system of communication. Still, research has shown that some animals have at least some ability to use symbols in the process of communicating with one another and with humans.

Allen and Beatrice Gardner taught a chimp named Washoe to use 160 different words of the American Sign

Language. Washoe was able not only to attach words to objects but also to put words together into new and meaningful combinations. For example, when a researcher known to Washoe as Susan stepped on Washoe's doll, Washoe quickly responded: "Up Susan; mine, please up; gimme baby; shoe up; please move up." Other studies have shown that chimps understand complex instructions such as "You insert banana in pail, apple in dish" (Gardner & Gardner, 1969; Premack, 1976; Harris, 1987).

Even more remarkably, E. Sue Savage-Rumbaugh reports that a four-year-old pygmy chimpanzee named Kanzi has not only spontaneously created simple sentences but also learned to respond to spoken English she has not heard before. For example, if asked with no physical gestures whatever, "Will you get a diaper for your sister?" Kanzi is able to do so—a feat until now undocumented among nonhuman primates (Eckholm, 1985).

Chimpanzees do not have the physical ability to form the consonant sounds made by humans. Nor have these specially trained animals been able to teach their language skills to others of their kind. But these recent achievements suggest that we should not chauvinistically assume only humans have any claim to culture. With a limited ability to use symbols, some other species share at least partly in a world of culture.

Does Language Shape Reality?

To most Americans whose symbolic system is the English language, crystals of frozen water that fall from the sky simply register as one idea: *snow*. Eskimos, in contrast, have 20 specific words for particular kinds of snow—falling snow, drifting snow, damp snow, dry snow, and so forth. Does this difference in the meanings we attach to the world mean that we would experience a winter day in the Arctic differently from an Eskimo companion?

Two anthropologists who specialized in linguistic studies, Edward Sapir and Benjamin Whorf, would say "Yes!" Sapir and Whorf argued that language is more than simply attaching labels to the "real world" (Sapir, 1929, 1949; Whorf, 1956). Because language stands between us and the world, they suggested, it actually shapes the "reality" we experience. Sapir and Whorf thereby challenge the common assumption that the many human languages describe a single reality. They remind us that every language has words or expressions that have no precise counterpart in another symbolic system. In addition, each language fuses symbols with particular emotions. Thus, as multilingual people can attest, a single idea may "feel" different if spoken in Spanish rather than in English or German (Falk, 1987). Formally, then, the **Sapir-Whorf hypothesis,** as this insight has come to be called, holds that *we know the world only in terms*

All animals are expressive. Only to humans, however, do facial gestures have symbolic meaning.

of our language. Making use of different symbolic systems, a Turk, a Brazilian, and a Filipino actually experience "distinct worlds, not merely the same world with different labels attached" (Sapir, 1949:162).

Of course, the Sapir-Whorf hypothesis does not assert that human beings are absolutely constrained to understand the world in only one way. Our various senses and great mental capacity provide us with great perceptive power, and our creativity allows us to generate new symbols as well as to employ in new ways those that are familiar. Technological advances such as the invention of computers also lead to new words and phrases—*bytes*, *interface*, and *random access memory*, for instance. In addition, political controversy often causes languages to change. The desire for greater equality in a predominantly white society led African-Americans to replace the word *Negro* with the term *black* or *person of color*. After more than twenty years of increasing usage, this symbolic change has helped improve white people's perceptions of African-Americans. Similarly, adult males in English-speaking societies have long been called *men*, while adult females have often been referred to condescendingly as *girls*. The recent emphasis on calling women *women* is both a cause and an effect of the changing position of women in our culture. In short, a system of language generates strong *tendencies* to understand the world in a particular way, but it does not *determine* how we do so.

Values

What accounts for the popularity among Americans of films featuring characters such as Dirty Harry and Rambo? Each is based on a ruggedly individualistic character, suspicious of "the system," who relies primarily upon his own skill and effort. Together, they suggest that Americans celebrate an ideal of sturdy individualism, especially for males. Such patterns reflect **values,** which are *standards by which members of a culture define what is desirable or undesirable, good or bad, beautiful or ugly* (Williams, 1970:27). Values are evaluations and judgments, from the standpoint of the culture, of what ought to be. These broad principles are widely evident in a people's way of life.

Our personalities develop in relation to the values of our culture, usually without our being aware that this is so. We learn from our families, schools, and religious institutions how to think and act according to cultural standards of value, what personal goals are de-

fined as worthy, and how to relate properly to our fellow human beings.

In a society as large and diverse as the United States, of course, few cultural values are shared by everyone. Over the centuries, people from all over the world have entered the United States, producing a mosaic of cultural values. This contrasts to the greater cultural homogeneity of historically isolated societies such as Japan. Even so, the American way of life is guided by a number of values that most people recognize and that tend to persist over time.

American Values

Sociologist Robin Williams (1970) suggests that the following ten values are among the most central to American culture.

1. **Equal opportunity.** Americans tend to value providing everyone with the opportunity to get ahead, although, due to varying talents and efforts, people are not expected to end up in the same situation. In other words, while not endorsing *equality of condition*, Americans do embrace *equality of opportunity*, by which everyone should have a fair chance to obtain the good things in life.

2. **Achievement and success.** American culture encourages competition. In this way, we tend to think, each person receives what is deserved on the basis of personal merit. Within American culture, to be successful in one's endeavors implies that one is a more worthy person—a "winner."

3. **Activity and work.** American heroes, from Olympic track star Jackie Joyner-Kersee to film's famed archeologist Indiana Jones, are "doers," people who get the job done. Americans prefer *action* to *reflection*, and through hard work we seek to control events rather than passively accepting our "fate." For this reason, Americans often take a dim view of cultures that appear more easygoing.

4. **Material comfort.** Activity defined as worthwhile is generally that which brings money and all it will buy. Americans may quip that "money won't buy happiness," but most eagerly pursue wealth as best they can all the same.

5. **Practicality and efficiency.** Americans value activity that solves problems and produces the greatest results in the least amount of time. "Building a better mousetrap" is praiseworthy in our culture, especially when done in the most cost-effective way.

6. **Progress.** Americans have traditionally believed that the present is better than the past, and that the future is likely to be better still. In the United States, advertising continually sparks sales with claims that the "very latest" is the "very best." Similarly, supermarkets are full of products that are advertised as "new and improved."

7. **Science.** Americans tend to be confident that science can effectively address problems and that the work of scientific experts and technologists will improve our lives. We think of ourselves as rational people, which probably explains our cultural tendency (especially among men) to devalue emotions and intuition as sources of knowledge.

8. **Democracy.** Americans see their way of life as based on the rights of the individual that cannot be overridden by government. Our political system is based on the ideal of free elections in which all adults exercise their right to vote. Similarly, the American economy is thought to meet the widely varied needs of selective, individual consumers.

9. **Freedom.** Closely related to democracy, this cultural value suggests that individual initiative is more desirable than collective conformity. Although Americans recognize that everyone has responsibilities and obligations to others, we believe that individuals should be free to pursue personal goals without unreasonable interference from anyone else.

10. **Racism and group superiority.** Although expressing a commitment to the values of equality and freedom, Americans often link personal worth to social categories based on social class, race, ethnicity, and sex. Many Americans value males above females, whites above nonwhites, and more privileged people above those who are disadvantaged. Thus, although Americans often describe themselves as a nation of equals, there is little doubt that some of us are "more equal than others."

Value Inconsistency and Value Conflict

Within any society, the values people hold are likely to vary according to age, sex, ethnicity, religion, race, and social class. Individuals are even likely to experience inconsistency and conflict within their personal values. An upper-class homosexual male, for example, may experience tension between our culture's standards of masculinity and his own sexual orientation, as well as between his class privilege and the disadvantaged status

Artist Sally Swain alters Degas' famous painting of a ballerina to make fun of our culture's tendency to ignore the everyday lives of most women.

Sally Swain, Mrs. Degas Vacuums *the* Floor. *From* *Great Housewives in Modern Art, *Penguin Books, 1988.*

he holds as a member of a sexual minority. This example also suggests that the overall culture often defines types of people in ways that conflict with how they like to think of themselves. Homosexual men and women, for instance, have become active in opposing the traditional (and often quite distorted) stereotypes generated by our culture.

Even the dominant values of a culture contain contradictions (Lynd, 1967; Bellah et al., 1985). Americans frequently find themselves torn between the "me first" attitude of an individualistic, success-at-all-costs orientation and the contradictory need to belong within some community. In addition, the value Americans place on equality of opportunity for all has long conflicted with a tendency to promote or degrade others because of their race, sex, or social background.

Such value conflicts inevitably cause strain in most of us, leading to awkward balancing acts in our views of the world. Sometimes we decide that one value is more important than another, as when we give up an enjoyable area of college study for another that promises greater financial gains. Another response is simply to ignore such contradictions. National surveys, for example, show that most Americans are aware of great differences in people's social backgrounds, even as they claim that equal opportunity in the United States is a reality (N.O.R.C., 1989). Both views obviously cannot be true, but such value conflicts are inevitable in complex societies such as ours. In some cases, at least, the only resolution to cultural complexity may lié in learning to live with contradiction.

Values in Action: The Games People Play

Cultural values affect us even when we are least aware of them. For instance, the games we play as children seem like spontaneous fun, without deep significance. But they actually provide important lessons in what a culture defines as important.

Using the sociological perspective, James Spates (1976a) finds in the familiar game King of the Mountain a clear expression of the American values of achievement and success:[1]

> In this game, the King (winner) is the one who scrambles to the top of some designated area and holds it against all challengers (losers). This is a very gratifying game from the winner's point of view, for one learns what it is like (however brief is the tenure at the top before being thrown off) to be an unequivocal success, to be unquestionably better than the entire competition. (1976a:286)

Each player thus attempts to become number one at the expense of all other players. As we all know, success is not without its costs, and King of the Mountain teaches us about these costs as well.

> The King can never relax in such a pressurized position and, psychologically, constant vigilance is very difficult to endure for long. Additionally, the sole victor is likely to feel a certain alienation from others: whom can he trust? Truly, "it is lonely at the top."

---

[1] The excerpt presented here has been slightly modified on the basis of unpublished versions of the study, with the permission of the author.

As King of the Mountain expresses our cultural emphasis on winning, other children's games teach us the plight of being a loser. Tag, Keep Away, and Monkey in the Middle are good examples of games of this kind. Spates notes that in the game of Tag, the loser is the person designated as "It." This player is singled out as lacking the ability to be a member of the group—an experience so difficult to bear that often other players will eventually allow themselves to be tagged just to end "It's" ordeal. All players thus learn the importance of competing successfully, as well as the dangers of not fitting in with the group. Such observations help explain the prominence of competitive team sports in American culture and why star athletes are often celebrated as cultural heroes.

Norms

For most of our history, Americans have viewed sex as appropriate within marriage, and then largely for the purpose of having children. By the 1960s, however, the rules of sexual behavior had changed: sexual activity had become widely redefined as a form of recreation, often involving people who hardly knew each other. By the mid-1980s, the rules had changed once again. Amidst growing fears of sexually transmitted diseases, especially the deadly acquired immune deficiency syndrome (AIDS), the "sexual revolution" was coming to an end, with more Americans limiting their sexual activity to one partner (McKusick, et al., 1985; Smilgas, 1987).

Such patterns illustrate the operation of what sociologists call norms, *rules that guide behavior.* Many norms are *proscriptive,* mandating what we must *not* do. For example, Americans are now warned to avoid casual sex. Other norms are *prescriptive,* stating what we *must* do. Following practices of "safe sex," for instance, has been broadly promoted in recent years.

Some norms apply to virtually every social situation. For example, we expect children to obey their parents consistently, regardless of setting. Other norms, however, vary from situation to situation. Applauding at the completion of a musical performance is appropriate, and even expected; applauding at the end of a classroom lecture is acceptable, but rather rare; and applauding the completion of a sermon by a priest or rabbi is generally considered inappropriate. In the same way, the norms that guide our behavior at a library, a formal dinner party, and a rock concert are all somewhat different.

Mores and Folkways

Not all cultural norms have the same degree of importance. William Graham Sumner (1959; orig. 1906), an early American sociologist, used the term **mores** (pronounced MORE-ays; the rarely used singular form is *mos*) to refer to *norms that have great moral significance.* Proscriptive mores are often simply termed *taboos*; these are illustrated by the American expectation that adults not have sexual relations with children. Mores can also be prescriptive, as in the expectation that people in public places wear sufficient clothing to conform to "standards of decency."

Because of their importance, mores usually apply to anyone, anywhere, and at any time. Indeed, most people believe that observing this type of norm is crucial to the existence of society as we know it. This also explains the strong penalties that follow a violation of many mores. For example, Americans consider the right to one's property as beyond question. Consequently, from early childhood, we learn that theft is such a serious wrong that the force of the police and the legal system can be directed against an offender.

Sumner used the term **folkways** to designate *norms that have little moral significance.* Examples include norms involving dress and polite behavior. Since they are viewed as less important than mores, folkways involve matters about which we tend to allow people considerable personal discretion. For the same reason, violations of folkways typically result in only mild penalties. For example, a male who does not wear a tie to a formal dinner party is violating one of the folkways we sometimes call "etiquette"; he might be the subject of some derisive comment, but little more. On the other hand, were he to arrive at the dinner party wearing *only* a tie, he would be violating cultural mores and inviting far more serious sanctions.

Cultural norms, then, steer our behavior by defining what is right and wrong, proper and improper. Although we sometimes object to the conformity norms demand, norms are the shared standards that make possible a sense of security and trust in our personal interactions. Norms are thus part of the symbolic road map of culture, guiding us through what are sometimes confusing social situations.

Social Control

The operation of norms promotes conformity. Outside a movie theater, for instance, you take your place at the end of the ticket line without thinking much about it. But consider the angry mutterings if you were to push directly to the front of the line. Someone might even bark, "Just what do you think you're doing!" If you were to apologize for your mistake and go to the end of the line, the expressions of outrage might turn to nods of approval. Such negative and positive responses from others, termed *sanctions*, reward us for conformity and punish us for deviance. Sanctions may be applied informally, as in this example, or in more formal ways, ranging from grades in school to arrest by the police and imprisonment by courts of law. Sanctions are an important part of a culture's system of **social control**: *various means by which members of society encourage conformity to cultural norms.*

The enforcement of norms does not always depend on the reaction of others. Recall a situation in which you were alone and did something you knew was wrong. Perhaps as a child you took something that belonged to someone else. Even if no one ever found out about it, you probably felt uncomfortable with your own behavior. In other words, once we come to believe in most of the norms of our culture, we usually respond *to ourselves* just as someone else observing our behavior would. This is a result of *internalizing* cultural norms—that is, building norms into our own personalities. The evidence that we have done so lies in our experience of *guilt*—the negative judgment we make of ourselves for having violated a norm—and *shame*—the painful acknowledgment of others' disapproval. This internalizing of norms was no doubt what writer Mark Twain had in mind when he quipped that human beings "are the only animals that blush . . . or need to."

"Ideal" and "Real" Culture

Values and norms are not descriptions of actual behavior as much as statements about how we *should* behave as members of a culture. Sociologists therefore distinguish between **ideal culture**, *social patterns described by cultural values and norms*, and **real culture**, designating *social patterns that actually occur.* This distinction is useful when we consider, for example, that while the vast majority of Americans acknowledge the importance of sexual fidelity in marriage, roughly one-third of married people are sexually unfaithful to their spouses at some point in their marriages. Such discrepancies are common to all cultural systems, as the old saying "Do as I say, and not as I do" suggests.

Moreover, like all elements of cultural systems, norms vary over time and among different segments of the population. The cultural values and norms brought to North America by English settlers centuries ago continue to shape American life, but many of our current interpretations of them would seem strange indeed to Sir Walter Raleigh or Abigail Adams. In addition, immigrants from other cultures have introduced such a variety of patterns into our society that American culture is far more diverse than any single description can convey.

Material Culture and Technology

In addition to intangible cultural elements such as values and norms, every culture includes a wide range of tangible (from Latin meaning "touchable") human creations that sociologists refer to as _artifacts._ The Yąnomamö gather material from the forest to build huts and make hammocks. They craft bows and arrows to hunt and defend themselves, fashion various tools for raising crops, and paint their bodies with colored paints. Such examples of material culture among the Yąnomamö are probably as strange to us as their nonmaterial culture—including their language, values, and norms.

Material and nonmaterial elements of culture are closely related. An examination of a society's artifacts reveals that the things people create often express their cultural values. Because warfare is a major part of their life, the Yąnomamö value militaristic skills and devote great care to making weapons. The poisoned tips of their arrows are prized possessions.

In the same way, the material elements of our own culture reflect the values we consider important. The value we place on individuality and independence, for instance, is obvious in our preference for privately owned automobiles over mass transportation. Some 140 million automobiles are registered in the United States today, which is almost one car for every licensed driver and more than one car for every two Americans. This means that, at any given moment, every American could climb into a car—and nobody would have to sit in back!

Material culture reflects not only a society's cultural values but also **technology,** which is _the application of cultural knowledge to the task of living in a physical environment._ Technology, then, links the world of nature and the world of culture. The Yąnomamö, for example, have a relatively simple technology, meaning that their way of life is largely shaped by the natural environment. Thus they are keenly aware of any change in rainfall, crops, or movement of the animals they hunt for food. In contrast, technologically complex societies (such as those of North America) have considerable ability to contend with the forces of nature, even reshaping the environment according to their own cultural values.

Because we highly value science and the sophisticated technology it has produced, Americans often judge cultures with simpler technology as less advanced. Some facts would support such a judgment. If we use average life expectancy as the measure of a society's quality of life, our technology seems to have served us well. Ameri-

Members of the Ndebele of South Africa lavishly color their surroundings. Most of the cultures of Europe and North America, in contrast, make far less use of color and seem relatively subdued in comparison. Aesthetic standards, like so many other dimensions of human life, vary significantly from one culture to another.

can males born in the late 1980s will live, on the average, over seventy-one years; American females, over seventy-eight years (U.S. Bureau of the Census, 1989). In contrast, Napoleon Chagnon estimated that the life expectancy of the Yąnomamö is only about forty years.

We must take care, however, to avoid self-serving judgments about the quality of life of people whose cultures differ from our own. Although the Yąnomamö are quite eager to gain some of the advantages of modern technology (such as steel tools and shotguns), it may surprise you to learn that they are generally well fed by world standards and are quite satisfied with their lives (Chagnon, 1983). The Yąnomamö, like other technologically simple societies, adapt to the natural world more than they manipulate the natural world to suit themselves. This is in striking contrast to our own culture, driven by a sophisticated technology that has had enormous impact on the natural world—for better or worse. Thus, while our advanced technology has produced work-reducing devices and seemingly miraculous forms of medical treatment, it has also contributed to unhealthy levels of stress, opened threatening holes in the planet's ozone layer, and created weapons capable of destroying in a flash everything that humankind has managed to achieve.

Technology, of course, is another cultural element that varies substantially even within American society. Although many of us may not be able to imagine life without stereos, televisions, and microwave ovens, some members of our society cannot afford such items, and still others will not own them on principle. The Amish are a case in point, as the box explains.

CROSS-CULTURAL COMPARISON

The Amish: Rejecting Modern Technology

Westward from the rolling farmlands of central Pennsylvania through Ohio, Indiana, and southern Ontario, live some 100,000 Old Order Amish, who came to North America in the colonial era yet have always stood apart from its dominant culture.

The Amish are descendants of sixteenth-century Germans who were driven from their homelands by religious and political persecution. Compared to the society around them, the Amish have changed little over the centuries. The Amish view of the world is captured in the phrase "The old is the best, and the new is of the devil" (Hostetler, 1980:10–11). To most North Americans, the Amish seem to be "relics of the past" who live a rigid and simple life without the technological conveniences of electricity or gasoline-powered vehicles (1980:3–4).

Amish life is highly personal. Their settlements are small enough so that people can work and worship

Using traditional horsedrawn buggies rather than high-speed automobiles allows the Amish to maintain strong local communities.

together in close, lasting relationships. This gives the Amish a secure sense of belonging, as well as a strong identity and sense of purpose. Although the conformity of Amish life can be a strain to some, most are satisfied to model themselves on those who have gone before them. They prefer to educate their children themselves rather than expose them to outside influences. They view science and technology as forces that threaten to dilute and ultimately destroy their cherished way of life.

For much of their history in North America, the Amish have been of little interest to others. In recent decades, however, their existence has become more widely known, and they now endure thousands of outsiders who come as tourists to examine these strange people who seem to live in another time. Is this simply a passing interest? Or does our heightened curiosity suggest that the Amish may have something to teach the rest of us? Perhaps in the Amish many of us see in purer form the rugged individualism and strong conviction that was once stronger in America's dominant culture. To outsiders, perhaps, the Amish represent "islands of sanity in a culture gripped by commercialism and technology run wild" (1980:4).

SOURCE: Based on John A. Hostetler, *Amish Society*, 3rd ed. (Baltimore: Johns Hopkins University Press, 1980).

CULTURAL DIVERSITY: MANY WAYS OF LIFE IN ONE WORLD

Between 1820 (when the government began keeping track of immigration) and 1990, over 55 million people came to the United States. Earlier in this century, most came from Europe; by the 1980s, most were from Asia and Latin America (Fallows, 1983; U.S. Bureau of the Census, 1989). This large-scale immigration has made the United States a land of cultural diversity.

Our cultural variety corresponds to geographical region, religion, ethnicity, and individual lifestyle. Although sociologists sometimes speak of the "cloth of culture," a more accurate description of our culture might be "patchwork quilt." Thus to understand our way of life, we must move beyond dominant cultural patterns to a consideration of cultural diversity.

Mexican artist Diego Rivera saw the factory as a setting that transformed people from various cultural backgrounds into members of a unified working class.

Diego Rivera, Detroit Industry, 1932–33. Detail, North Wall, Fresco. The Detroit Institute of Arts. Gift of Edsel B. Ford.

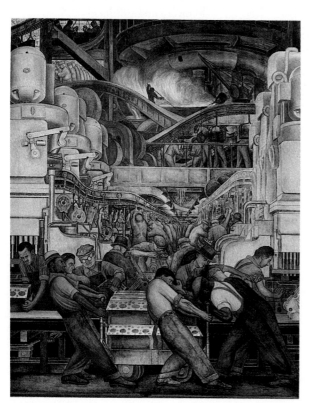

Subcultures

Sociologists use the term **subculture** to refer to *a cultural pattern that differs from the dominant culture in some distinctive way.* Teenagers, Polish-Americans, homeless people, and "southerners" are all examples of subcultures within American society. Occupations also foster subcultural differences, including specialized ways of speaking, as anyone who has ever spent time with race-car drivers, jazz musicians, or even sociologists can attest. Residents of rural areas may mock the ways of "city slickers," who in turn deride their "country cousins." Sexual orientation generates yet another subculture in our society, especially in cities such as San Francisco, Los Angeles, and New York, where large numbers of gay men and women live.

Most societies are composed of many subcultures based on ethnicity. Consider Yugoslavia, a nation in southeastern Europe that is a rather extreme case. This *one* small country (roughly the size of the state of Wyoming, with a population of about 25 million) makes use of *two* alphabets, has *three* major religions, speaks *four* major languages, contains *five* major nationalities, is divided into *six* separate republics, and absorbs cultural influences from *seven* other nations with which it shares borders. How does American culture compare to that of Yugoslavia?

We learn as children that the United States is a "melting pot" in which people of many nationalities blend into a single "American" culture. But ethnicity and race have generated greater cultural diversity—and sometimes greater controversy—than this official history suggests. More recently, cultural distinctiveness has become something to celebrate, so that many people who have come to North America want to maintain their traditional ways of life.

In 1981, Congress first considered legislation that would make English the official language of the United States. Perhaps this is surprising, since the English language has been central to American culture for centuries. Yet, by the early 1980s, over 20 million people—about one in ten Americans—spoke a language other than English in their homes. And their number will steadily increase to an estimated 40 million by the beginning of the next century. Spanish is by far the most common American language other than English. European languages, such as Italian, German, and French, also are widely used, reflecting the historical pattern of European immigration to North America. In recent decades, immigration from other world regions—notably Asia—has greatly increased the number of native speakers of Fili-

CRITICAL THINKING

An Official American Language? The Diversity Debate

To some, the idea of designating English as the official language of the United States may seem a bit silly—after all, doesn't virtually everybody speak English? The answer, in a word, is *no*. In fact, about 20 million Americans now speak a language other than English at home, and this number is growing. Furthermore, an increasing number of Americans are quite content to use *only* a language other than English.

Behind these facts is rising immigration, which we discuss in Chapter 12, "Race and Ethnicity." Not since the early decades of this century have American cities confronted such cultural diversity. According to some, this raises serious problems. Consider the experience of Emmy Schafer. In 1978, she sought assistance at a local government office in southern Florida but was unable to find a single employee who could understand English. She was angry enough to start the social movement that seeks official recognition for English.

Those in favor of this idea point out, first, that our nation is a remarkable mixture of cultural patterns. It is therefore essential, they claim, that Americans have something as basic as language in common. Government policy, therefore, should support what *unites* all people rather than what *divides* us. Second, they believe that declaring English to be our official language would ensure that all young people—whatever their cultural background—are able to learn English in school. This is important if all Americans are to have a fair chance at higher education and a good job. By the late 1980s, some 6 million school children in the United States were native speakers of a language other than English. Unless they know the language of the majority, it is argued, these children risk assuming second-class citizenship.

Opponents suggest, first, that the "official English" movement is little more than a backlash against rising immigration. More specifically, they call it an expression of *xenophobia*, a word derived from the Greek for "fear of strangers or what is strange." Those who would force all Americans to speak English, opponents claim, are simply trying to stamp out cultural diversity by imposing one cultural system on everyone. Second, they point to legal support for diversity. The Bilingual Education Act, passed by Congress in 1968, mandates that children who do not speak English at home can request to be educated in their own language as they simultaneously learn to speak English. While conceding the difficulty of securing teachers able to converse in some 125 different languages—including Spanish, Haitian Creole, and even Hmong, Khmer, and Ulithian—proponents of bilingualism maintain that only in this way can all Americans come to value their own cultural heritage.

At present, one-third of the states have recognized English as their official language. There is also support for—and opposition to—passing a constitutional amendment making English the official language of the entire country. Probably many Americans echo the sentiments of Arizona senator John McCain, who commented: "Our nation and the English language have done quite well with Chinese spoken in California, German in Pennsylvania, Italian in New York, Swedish in Minnesota, and Spanish in New York. I fail to see the cause for alarm now." But, in a nation of intense cultural diversity, controversy of this kind is likely to continue.

SOURCE: Based on Edward B. Fiske, "One Language or Two? The Controversy over Bilingual Education in America's Schools," *The New York Times*, November 10, 1985, Sect. 12, pp. 1, 45; also, Margaret Carlson, "Only English Spoken Here," *Time*, December 5, 1988:30.

---

pino, Japanese, Korean, and Vietnamese. In areas with large concentrations of non–English-speakers, ethnic subcultures often prompt parents to insist that their children be provided with a bilingual education in public schools. The box provides some dimensions of this complex and controversial issue.

Canada has long faced an especially serious problem because it is a society in which two major cultural groups—those of English ancestry and those of French ancestry—live together. Of 25 million Canadians, about 67 percent speak only English, 18 percent speak only French, and the remaining 15 percent are bilingual. The French-speaking minority experiences certain social and economic disadvantages in a society where English culture predominates. Although Canada officially recognizes both cultural groups by having two national languages, tensions between English-speaking and French-speaking Canadians continue (Esman, 1982).

Countercultures

Cultural differences within a society may also represent active opposition to at least some aspects of the dominant culture. A **counterculture** is defined as *cultural patterns that are strongly at odds with the dominant culture.* People who embrace a counterculture are likely to question the morality of the majority; not surprisingly, the majority may be swift to direct the forces of social control against them, from negative coverage in the mass media to police action.

In many societies, countercultures are linked to youth (Spates, 1976b, 1983; Spates & Perkins, 1982). Most of us are familiar with several youth-oriented countercultures that were widely publicized during the 1960s. The hippies criticized American society, calling it overly competitive, individualistic, and concerned with money. Instead, they favored a collective and cooperative lifestyle in which "being" was more important than "doing," and personal qualities such as "expanded consciousness" were prized over material possessions. Such differences led many hippies to "drop out" of the larger society, often to form large countercultural communities. The Haight-Ashbury district of San Francisco was perhaps the best-known hippie community in the world.

During the same period, other countercultures opposed the American political system and the war in Vietnam. Political organizations such as Students for a Democratic Society (SDS) organized protest marches, while more radical groups carried out sporadic acts of violence against what they viewed as an unjust and militaristic society. Similarly, the Black Panthers armed themselves in revolt against what they saw as the racism of American culture.

Countercultures may develop not only their own political principles but also their own folkways, which may include distinctive dress, forms of greeting, and musical forms. To many members of the 1960s countercultures, for instance, blue jeans and "ethnic" clothing symbolized their identification with the "common people" of our society. Rock and roll flourished as a countercultural anthem and had little of the middle-class respectability it enjoys today.

Countercultures still exist, although they are perhaps less evident than in the 1960s. In the United States, the Ku Klux Klan and other white supremacist groups promote violence and racial hatred in order to protect what they see as "real American values." In Europe, young "punks" express their contempt for established culture through styles of music and appearance—shaved heads or multicolored hairstyles, black leather and chains—intended to challenge and offend more conventional members of their societies.

Cultural Change

The Greek philosopher Aristotle stated "there is nothing permanent except change." Caught up in day-to-day concerns, we may not notice changes because we are busy living our lives, not observing them. Cultural change is continuous, however, even if it is sometimes

When we encounter members of other cultures, we cannot easily determine if they represent dominant cultural patterns or countercultures. These boys in Colombia, South America, are meeting their first American: What impressions are they likely to form of American culture?

evident only over a period of years. Consider, for example, changes in the American family over the past half-century. Government records show that the divorce rate is now more than twice as high as it was in 1940, when a family composed of a bread-winning father, a home-making mother, and their children was the norm. Between 1970 and 1990, the number of single-parent households more than doubled, so that now a majority of children in the United States will live with only one parent before they reach the age of eighteen. Moreover, as women have become a much larger proportion of the labor force, more of them are delaying marriage and children, or remaining single but perhaps having children all the same.

Table 3–1 indicates some changes in attitudes among first-year college students over a single generation: those entering college in 1968 and those entering in 1987. The figures in the table indicate that some things have not changed very much: about the same proportion of students come to college in order to "gain a general education" and to "learn more about things." But students of the late 1980s certainly appear more interested in gaining skills, especially those that will lead to a high-paying job. Moreover, the political activism of the 1960s seems to have declined significantly in favor of pursuing personal success. Note that changes have generally been greater among women than among men. This, no doubt, reflects the fact that the women's movement, concerned with social equality for the two sexes, intensified after 1968.

Generally, change in any part of a cultural system sparks other changes as well. As noted earlier, for instance, changes in women's participation in the labor force are associated with changing patterns of marriage. Such linkages illustrate the principle of **cultural integration**: that *the various parts of a cultural system are linked together.* Even so, some parts of a cultural system are likely to change more quickly than others. William Ogburn (1964) observed that technological advances tend to create new elements of material culture (such as "test-tube babies") faster than new nonmaterial elements (such as ideas about parenthood). Ogburn called this pattern **cultural lag**: *inconsistencies within a cultural system resulting from the unequal rates at which different cultural elements change.* In a culture that now has the technical ability to allow one woman to give birth to a child by using another woman's egg, which has been fertilized in a laboratory with the sperm of a total stranger, how are we to apply the traditional terms *motherhood* and *fatherhood*?

It is worth asking here how such cultural changes

Table 3–1 ATTITUDES AMONG STUDENTS ENTERING AMERICAN COLLEGES, 1968 and 1987

		1968	1987	Change
REASONS TO GO TO COLLEGE (Very Important)				
Gain a general education	male	60	61	+1
	female	67	67	0
Learn more about things	male	69	72	+3
	female	74	76	+2
Improve reading and writing skills	male	22	36	+14
	female	23	43	+20
Get a better job	male	74	83	+9
	female	70	83	+13
Prepare for graduate or professional school	male	39	44	+5
	female	29	50	+21
Make more money	male	57	75	+18
	female	42	68	+26
LIFE OBJECTIVES (Essential or Very Important)				
Develop a philosophy of life	male	79	40	−39
	female	87	39	−48
Keep up with political affairs	male	52	43	−9
	female	52	33	−19
Raise a family	male	64	56	−8
	female	72	60	−12
Help others in difficulty	male	50	50	0
	female	71	67	−4
Be successful in my own business	male	55	55	0
	female	32	46	+14
Be well off financially	male	51	80	+29
	female	27	72	+45

Note: To allow comparisons, data from early 1970s rather than 1968 are used for some items.

SOURCE: Richard G. Braungart and Margaret M. Braungart, "From Yippies to Yuppies: Twenty Years of Freshman Attitudes," *Public Opinion,* Vol. 11, No. 3 (September-October 1988):53–56.

are set in motion in the first place. Cultural change is caused in three general ways. The first is *invention,* the process of creating new cultural elements—video games, political parties, or polio vaccines, for example. The telephone (1876), the airplane (1903), and the aerosol spray can (1941) are inventions that have had a tremendous impact on our culture. The process of invention is going on constantly, as indicated by the thousands of applications received by the United States Patent Office each year.

Discovery, a second, closely related cause of cultural change, involves recognizing and understanding something already in existence—from a distant star, to the foods of a foreign culture, to the muscle power of American women. Discovery is often the result of scientific research; many medical breakthroughs happen this way. Yet discovery can also occur quite by accident, as when Marie Curie unintentionally left a "rock" on a piece of photographic paper in 1898 and thus discovered radium.

The third cause of cultural change is *diffusion*, the spread of both material and nonmaterial elements from one cultural system to another. Missionaries and anthropologists like Napoleon Chagnon have introduced many cultural elements to the Yąnomamö. Elements of American culture have spread throughout the world through diffusion: jazz, with its roots deep in the culture of black Americans; computers, first built in the mid-1940s in a Philadelphia laboratory; and even the United States Constitution, on which several other countries have modeled their own political systems. On the other hand, much of what we assume is "American" is actually borrowed from other cultures. Ralph Linton (1937) has pointed out that commonplace elements of our way of life—most of our clothing and furniture, clocks, newspapers, money, and, of course, the English language—are all derived from other cultures. Obviously, as the technology of travel and communication makes the world smaller, the rate of cultural diffusion is likely to increase.

Ethnocentrism and Cultural Relativity

A question in the popular game Trivial Pursuit asks which beverage is most popular among Americans. Milk? Soft drinks? Coffee? The answer is actually soft drinks, but all the beverages mentioned are appropriate to members of our culture.

If the Masai of eastern Africa were to join the game, however, their answer might well be "Blood!" To us, of course, the idea of drinking blood is revolting, if not downright "unnatural." On the other hand, milk, which Americans are taught is "nature's perfect food," is actually detested by billions of people in the world, including the Chinese (Harris, 1985).

In a world of many cultures, how do we come to terms with other people's ways of living when they offend our own ideas of what is proper? Recall how Napoleon Chagnon, trained as an anthropologist to have an open mind, first reacted with disgust to the Yąnomamö as "naked, sweaty, and hideous." He soon found that some of their cultural practices seemed, from his point of view, to be outrageous. For example, Yąnomamö men, who dominate Yąnomamö women, share their wives sexually with younger brothers or friends. From the Yąnomamö point of view, this common practice represents friendship and generosity. By our cultural standards, however, it can be understood only as morally perverse and grossly unfair to women.

In outdoor markets throughout the southern region of the People's Republic of China, dogs are a prized food. To an American observer, selecting a puppy for dinner may well seem cruel and inhumane. From the Chinese point of view, however, the common American practice of drinking milk provokes disgust.

Anthropologists and sociologists caution us against **ethnocentrism,** which is *the practice of judging another culture by the standards of our own culture.* The tendency to be ethnocentric is perhaps inevitable because our understanding of the world is so closely tied to our own particular way of life. Yet it can result in a biased evaluation of any unfamiliar practice not judged in its own cultural context. Ethnocentrism is a two-way street, of course. Just as we tend to define those who differ from us in negative terms, so others may judge us in the same way. The Yąnomamö, for example, initially considered Napoleon Chagnon to be little more than a "subhuman foreigner" (Chagnon, 1983:14).

An alternative to ethnocentrism is **cultural relativism,** *the practice of judging any culture by its own standards.* Cultural relativism is often a difficult attitude to achieve, since it requires not only understanding the values and norms of another culture but also suspending those of the culture we have known all our lives. Still, the effort is worth making for reasons of goodwill or self-interest. As the people of the world come into increasing contact with one another, the need to understand other cultures more fully increases. With an increasingly global economy, for instance, American business is learning that economic success depends on cultural sensitivity and sophistication. When Coors first translated their slogan "Get loose with Coors" into Spanish, would-be customers were startled to read "Get the runs with Coors." Similarly, Kentucky Fried Chicken found out that the Chinese thought that "licking one's fingers" made food seem anything but appealing. And Coca-Cola's early attempts to entice the Japanese to buy their soft drink involved a translation of "Coke adds life" that was read as "Coke brings your ancestors back from the dead," with results that are easy to imagine (Westerman, 1989:32).

Cultural sensitivity is obviously vital to successful business and generating a fair and just world order, but a culturally relative approach can also raise problems. Virtually anything one can imagine is found somewhere in a world of cultural diversity: does that mean that anything and everything has equal claim to being morally right? Consider the fact that Yąnomamö men routinely offer their wives to other men, and they often react with physical violence to a woman who allegedly commits some social impropriety. Sometimes, Chagnon reports, this goes as far as men shooting women with arrows or otherwise mutilating them. Even in the unlikely event that Yąnomamö women accept this sort of treatment, should we adopt the culturally relative view that such practices are morally right simply because the Yąnomamö themselves accept them?

The fact that there is but one human species leads us to search for some universal standards of conduct that are "fair" for people everywhere. But what are they? How can we resist the tendency to put forward our own standards of fair play as applicable to everyone else? Sociologists have no final answer to this dilemma, yet in a world in which societies confront each other amidst ever-present problems such as hunger and war, this is an issue well worth careful thought.

The tension between ethnocentrism and cultural relativism often poses difficult problems for Americans abroad. The box on page 78 looks more closely at "the traveler's dilemma."

THEORETICAL ANALYSIS OF CULTURE

Culture provides us with the means to understand ourselves and the world around us. Sociologists and anthropologists, however, have the special task of understanding culture itself. To understand something as complex as culture, we will present several widely used approaches.

Investigating culture as a broad system of symbols, values, and norms requires a *macro-level analysis.* You will recall that there are two such theoretical paradigms within sociology, the structural-functional paradigm and the social-conflict paradigm. Each provides valuable insights about culture.

Structural-Functional Analysis

As you recall from Chapter 1, structural-functional analysis sees culture as a relatively stable system of integrated parts devised to meet human needs. Any one of these parts, or *cultural traits,* is understood in terms of how it *functions* to maintain the overall cultural system. When cultural change does occur, it is most likely attributed to cultural diffusion (related, perhaps, to immigration), invention, or discovery within the culture.

The stability of cultural systems is rooted in core values, which, for American society, were specified earlier (Parsons, 1966; Williams, 1970). In this way, structural-functionalism draws on the philosophical doctrine of *idealism,* which holds that ideas (rather than, for exam-

CRITICAL THINKING

"The Traveler's Dilemma": How Should You Judge Another Culture?

Being receptive to another culture rather than ethnocentric requires resisting the temptation to judge another way of life by our own standards. But this is usually easier said than done, as an American traveler might discover in many parts of the world.

Imagine, for instance, strolling through downtown Taipei, the capital city of Taiwan, in the Republic of China. This island nation, about the size of the states of Maryland and Delaware combined, lies some 150 miles off the shore of the Chinese mainland. Although it is a rapidly developing nation, its way of life is shaped by distinctive cultural traditions and a history of great poverty.

One quickly discovers that Taipei is a city frantic with activity. Streets teem with people and motor scooters. Drivers show little concern for pedestrians, so that Americans are likely to react angrily to what seem like intentional efforts to run them down. At no time is the pace of life more frenzied than after dark, when tens of thousands of people flood into the

city's vast night market. Here, in thousands of outdoor stalls, just about everything is for sale. Vendors hawk familiar items such as clothing, fruits, and jewelry to the passing crowd; but many sights are strange indeed to the visitor. Food vendors display "snacks" such as chicken feet and, worse still, cook animals such as dogs that Americans think of as pets. Children with withered limbs lie on the ground, begging from the people who swarm around them.

If they wander into the night market's infamous "Snake Alley," Americans are likely to have their sensibilities pushed to the limit. For here—from the visitor's point of view, at least—cruelty and violence are elevated to the level of a sport. Visitors join a crowd in a stall, drawn by a man beckoning over a loudspeaker. At the back of the stall are several televisions, "warming up" the crowd by displaying dog fights in which one animal tears another to pieces, bringing cheers and whistles from some in the audience. The real show, how-

ever, is not televised but live and begins as the master of ceremonies displays dozens of huge, live snakes. "Who will drink the venom?" he taunts once in Chinese, once in Japanese, and then in English. One or two young men, who seem eager to show courage to their comrades, push

---

ple, patterns of material production) are the basis of human reality. As noted earlier, cultural values are expressed in a wide range of activities, including children's games that function to transmit core values to new members of a society. Obviously, values also serve to bind all members of a society together.

Using a structural-functional approach, let us consider once again the culture of the Amish. What is the function of such curious practices as working hundreds of acres of farmland with a horse and plow, and rejecting electricity and a host of other modern conveniences? Within the Amish cultural system, hard work—usually outside the home for men and inside for women—is an important means of maintaining the Amish value

of discipline. Long days of shared labor, along with meals and recreation at home, bind family members together. Their communal rejection of modern technology and conveniences supports the Amish desire to maintain their self-sufficient and distinctive way of life (Hostetler, 1980).

As noted in Chapter 1, elements of a culture have not only functional but *dysfunctional* consequences. The Amish trait of "shunning," by which people cease to socially interact with anyone judged to have violated Amish mores, generates conformity but also considerable community tensions. In the most extreme case, a specific cultural practice can even lead to a community's destruction. Consider the Shakers, another countercultural religious group that flourished in the nineteenth century.

forward. To capture everyone's attention, one of the snakes is raised overhead while being poked and taunted to provoke its full viciousness. Suddenly, the snake's head is punctured by a hook suspended from the ceiling and—as it continues to flash back and forth in anguish—its skin is torn from its body to be fingered eagerly by a few members of the audience. Then, using skills earned from hundreds of displays such as this one, the man in the stall squeezes venom from the body of the snake into a small glass. Another spectator pays for the prize, which is promptly consumed like so much whiskey as the crowd cheers. The process is repeated.

Looking away from this display, the American's eyes might settle on a small monkey caged at the back of the stall. The observer soon stiffens as the monkey is snatched from the cage and thrust into the center of attention. "Pay to see him die!" the man shrieks. "See *real* blood now!" More cash is passed forward. One's mind whirls in disbelief. Can he

mean it? Would he really kill the monkey? Before the observer can regain wits enough to respond, however, the monkey is struck dead. Although a few turn and walk off in shock, others continue to shout their approval, encouraging more of the same.

Incidents such as this one, in which the values of two cultures collide, reveal two kinds of dangers. On the one hand, ethnocentrism closes off insight and understanding by leading us to judge others simplistically and often unfairly. On the other hand, complete cultural relativism suggests that right and wrong are just a simple matter of convention that, in the end, seems arbitrary and meaningless.

There may be a resolution to "the traveler's dilemma," however. First, we can try to suspend judgments and to confront the unfamiliar with an *open mind*. We learn only by being receptive to others' ways of life. Second, we can try to imagine events from the standpoint of *them* rather

than *us*. Witnessing the events of the night market, for instance, one might wonder if animals have a different significance in a society in which human poverty, hunger, and suffering are commonplace. Third, after a period of careful and critical thinking, we can and should try to form a judgment of an unfamiliar cultural practice. After all, a world in which everyone observed but no one evaluated or attempted to right a wrong would be a frightening one. Even in doing so, bear in mind that, unable to "stand in the shoes" of other people, we can never experience the world as they do. Fourth, and finally, learning to take the perspective of others helps us to evaluate our own way of life more realistically as well. Would an experience in the night market of Taipei change an American's view of fox hunts or boxing in the United States?

SOURCE: Based on the author's personal experiences in Taipei.

This culture prohibited sexual relations among its members. Although they were able to survive for decades by assimilating new members from the outside world, the Shakers' failure to reproduce themselves ultimately led to their disappearance.

Since the structural-functional paradigm claims that cultures are devised to meet human needs, it also suggests that world cultures have at least some traits in common because all cultures are created by the same human species. The term **cultural universals** refers to *traits found in every culture of the world.* Comparing hundreds of different cultures, George Murdock (1945) found dozens of general traits common to all. One example of a cultural universal is the family, which functions everywhere to control sexual reproduction and to oversee the care and upbringing of children. Another cultural universal is funeral rites, which are a response to the fact that humans everywhere must deal with the reality of death. Jokes, too, exist everywhere, at least partly because they provide a relatively safe means of relieving stress. Of course, specific examples of these and other cultural universals vary from place to place. As Chapter 6 ("Social Interaction in Everyday Life") explains, particular jokes do not travel well, so what is funny to us may puzzle, or even offend, members of other cultures.

Critical evaluation. The structural-functional paradigm points out that cultures are organized systems at-

Funerals are often defined as a form of respect for the deceased. The social function of funerals, however, has much more to do with the living. For survivors, funerals reaffirm their sense of unity and continuity in the face of separation and disruption.

tempting to meet human needs. Since all cultures are created by a single species, they have much in common. At the same time, since there are many ways to meet almost any human need, cultures around the world reveal striking diversity. One limitation of the structural-functional paradigm is its tendency to stress dominant cultural patterns, while directing less attention to cultural diversity within a society. This is especially true with regard to cultural differences that arise from social inequality. In addition, this paradigm emphasizes cultural stability, perhaps underplaying the importance of cultural change.

Social-Conflict Analysis

The social-conflict paradigm suggests that culture can be analyzed as a dynamic arena of social conflict generated by inequality among categories of people. This para-

digm draws attention to the ways in which cultural traits serve the needs of some members of society at the expense of others.

The social-conflict paradigm also asks critical questions about why certain values are dominant within a society. What forces in society generate one set of values rather than another? How are these values linked to social inequality? Many who make use of this paradigm, especially sociologists influenced by the work of Karl Marx, argue that values are shaped by a society's system of economic production. "It is not the consciousness of men that determines their existence," Marx asserted, "it is their social existence that determines their consciousness" (1977:4; orig. 1859). In this sense, the social-conflict paradigm is related to the philosophical doctrine of *materialism*, which holds that the ways people deal with the material world (for instance, the American economic system of industrial capitalism) have a powerful effect on all other dimensions of their culture. Such a materialist approach contrasts sharply with the idealist leanings of structural-functionalism.

Social-conflict analysis, then, holds that America's competitive and individualistic values reflect our capitalist economy, in which factories and other productive enterprises are privately owned. Within a culture of capitalism, for instance, people are likely to believe that the rich and powerful have more talent and discipline than other people, and therefore they deserve greater wealth and privileges. This encourages people to view capitalism as somehow "natural" and to distrust any change that might lessen the great economic disparity found in American society.

Social-conflict analysis holds that eventually, however, the strains fostered by social inequality are likely to transform the cultural system. Of course, changes sought by people with few social resources are likely to provoke resistance from those with much to lose. The civil rights movement and the women's movement are two recent examples of change generated by disadvantaged segments of American society, both of which have met with opposition by defenders of the status quo.

Critical evaluation. The strength of the social-conflict paradigm lies in its suggestion that, if cultural systems address human needs, they do so unequally. Just as important, this orientation suggests that cultural elements serve to maintain the dominance of some people over others. This inequity, in turn, generates forces that promote change. A limitation of the social-conflict paradigm is that, by stressing divisiveness of culture, we may minimize ways in which cultural patterns integrate everyone. Thus it is perhaps best to use both the social-conflict paradigm and the structural-functional paradigm to gain a fuller understanding of culture.

◆ Cultural Ecology

An additional theoretical paradigm rooted in the natural sciences emphasizes that human culture is significantly shaped by the natural environment. Thus this may be described as a *naturalist analysis of culture*. Ecology is a branch of the natural sciences that explores the relationship between a living organism and its natural environment. Cultural ecology is defined as *a theoretical paradigm that explores the relationship of human culture and the physical environment*. This paradigm investigates how characteristics of the physical environment, such as climate and the availability of food, water, and other natural resources, may shape cultural patterns.

Consider the case of India, a nation with widespread hunger and malnutrition. The norms of India's predominantly Hindu culture prohibit the killing of cows, which are considered sacred animals. To North Americans who enjoy so much beef, this is puzzling. What accounts for the prohibition against killing cows?

Marvin Harris (1975) claims that, as part of India's ecological system, the cow has an importance that greatly exceeds its value as a source of food. Harris points out that cows consume grasses of little value to humans, thereby producing two valuable resources: oxen (the neutered offspring of cows) and manure. Unable to afford the high costs of farm machinery, Indian farmers depend on oxen to power their plows. For Indians, then, killing cows would be about as clever as American farmers destroying factories that build tractors. But there is more. Each year, cows also produce millions of tons of manure, which is processed into building material and burned as fuel (India has little oil, coal, or wood). To kill cows, then, would deprive millions of Indians of homes and a source of heat. In short, the cultural protection of the cow can be understood in terms of the animal's great ecological importance.

Critical evaluation. Cultural ecology adds to our understanding of the interplay between culture and the natural environment. This approach can reveal how cultural patterns arise as human beings confront a particular physical environment. A limitation of this paradigm is that the physical environment rarely shapes cultural patterns in any simple or direct way. More correctly, the cultural and physical worlds interact, each shaping the other. Finally, especially within technologically complex societies that extensively manipulate the natural world, few cultural traits may be explained in this way.

Visitors to the cities of India are often puzzled by cows, which wander the streets. Americans, accustomed to eating beef, may wonder why cows are not used as a source of food. To Indians, however, cows are defined as sacred. Marvin Harris suggests that the veneration of cows is a way of protecting a resource vital to the nation's survival. Oxen, for example, are essential to Indian agriculture. Here farmers use oxen to churn a rice paddy, a practice that greatly improves productivity.

Sociobiology

Since its origin in the nineteenth century, sociology has had a rather uneasy relationship with biology. In part, this is due to rivalry between two disciplines that study human life. A more important source of friction, however, is that in the past some biological interpretations of human behavior—for example, the belief that some categories of people were naturally "better" than others—were expressions of racism and ethnocentrism rather than legitimate science. Early sociologists often provided evidence to refute such thinking.

By the middle of this century, sociologists had demonstrated that culture rather than biology was the major force shaping human lives. Within the last decade, however, new ideas linking human behavior to the principles of biological evolution have revived old debates. This research has created **sociobiology**: *a theoretical paradigm that seeks to explain cultural patterns as the product, at least in part, of biological causes.* Not surprisingly, some sociologists are skeptical about this new paradigm, although others suspect that it may provide helpful insights into human culture.

Sociobiology and Human Evolution

The scientific understanding of the development of life on earth is based largely on the theory of evolution. First put forward by Charles Darwin in 1859 in his book *The Origin of Species*, this theory states that living organisms change over long periods of time as a result of the process of *natural selection*, which is a matter of four simple principles. First, all living organisms live and reproduce within a natural environment. Second, within each species there is a certain degree of random variability in genes, the basic units of life that carry characteristics of one generation into the next. This random genetic variation can be thought of as the way in which a species "tries out" new life patterns in a particular environment. Third, this variation leads some organisms to survive better than others; these survivors then pass on their advantageous genetic variation to offspring. Fourth and finally, over thousands of generations the characteristics that grow dominant within a species are those associated with greater success in survival and reproduction. Genetic traits that do not aid survival tend to disappear.

In brief, Darwin asserted that any natural environment favors some gene-based characteristics over others based on how well they contribute to reproductive success. As naturally selected traits become more pro-

nounced over time, a species can be said to have *adapted* to its environment, and these traits taken together can be described as the "nature" of the organism.

Applying Sociobiology to Human Culture

Darwin's insights revolutionized the study of living things, although his work cannot readily be applied to human beings. The behavior of nonhumans is regulated by encoded genetic programs. The behavior of all ants and bees, for instance, obviously reveals considerable uniformity. The complex behavior of such insects is accurately described as "social" because individual creatures perform related, specialized tasks. Therefore, ants and bees do form "societies." But, unable to freely and creatively fashion their life patterns as much as we do, they are prisoners of their own biology (Berger, 1967).

What of human beings? Freed from the tyranny of biology, humans have created diverse and changing cultures. Even so, the various cultures of the world are not nearly as different as they *could be*, as evidenced by numerous cultural universals. In other words, sociobiologists ask, if human beings are free to create any culture, why do we find so many similar cultural patterns everywhere? Perhaps the answer lies in the fact that all people are members of a single biological species. Perhaps our biological characteristics influence the culture we create.

Why is sugar sweet? With this question, David Barash reminds us that human beings everywhere favor foods that taste sweet over those that taste sour. Chemically, the answer is that sugar tastes sweet because it contains sucrose. From the sociobiological point of view, a deeper process unfolds:

> What is the evolutionary explanation for sugar's sweetness? Clearly, just as beauty is in the eye of the beholder, sweetness is in the mouth of the taster. To anteaters, ants are "sweet"; anteaters may even find sugar bitter—certainly they don't like it as much as we do. The reason is clear enough: we are primates, and some of our ancestors spent a great deal of time in trees, where they ate a great deal of fruit. Ripe fruit is more nutritious than unripe, and one thing about ripe fruit is that it contains sugars. It doesn't take much imagination to reconstruct the evolutionary sequence that selected for a strong preference among our distant ancestors for the taste that characterized ripe fruit. Genes that influenced their carriers to eat ripe fruit and reject the unripe ultimately made more copies of themselves than did those that were less discriminating. (1981:39)

Sociobiologists extend this argument to some forms of human behavior. Sex, for example, is certainly "sweet" to human beings, as it is to all forms of life. A sociobiological approach to *why* sex feels good is that sex is vital to the process of reproducing our genes in the next generation. There is no surprise here. But what about the way in which males and females characteristically approach sexuality?

We are all aware of what has been traditionally described within our culture as the "double standard," that is, the general pattern by which males everywhere engage in sexual activity more freely than females do. Sex researcher Alfred Kinsey put it, "Among all people everywhere in the world, the male is more likely than the female to desire sex with a variety of partners" (cited in Barash, 1981:49). Indeed, we are well aware that, in American culture, men are often encouraged to "sow their wild oats," while women are generally expected to be far more discriminating in their sexual relationships.

Following the sociobiological argument, nature has assigned females and males very different parts to play in the reproductive process. Females bear children that result from the joining of a woman's egg with a man's sperm. But there are striking differences in the value of a single sperm to the male and a single egg to the female. For healthy males, sperm represents a "renewable resource" produced regularly by the testes throughout much of life. A male releases hundreds of millions of sperm in a single ejaculation—technically speaking, enough "to fertilize every woman in North America," according to Barash (1981:47). A newborn female's ovaries, however, contain her entire lifetime allotment of follicles or immature eggs. Women commonly release just one mature egg cell from their ovaries each month. So, while men are biologically capable of fathering thousands of offspring, women are able to bear only a relatively small number of children. From a strictly biological point of view, then, males reproduce their genes most efficiently through a strategy of sexual promiscuity. This strategy, however, does *not* serve the reproductive interests of women. Each of a woman's relatively few pregnancies demands that she carry the child for the duration of the pregnancy, give birth, and perhaps nurse the child afterward. Thus, efficient reproduction on the part of the female is to seek selectively a male whose own qualities will contribute to her child's survival and successful reproduction (Remoff, 1984). No one doubts that the double standard is a pattern linked to the historical domination of females by males (Barry, 1983). But sociobiology suggests that this cultural pattern, like many others, has an underlying bio-logic. Simply put, it has developed widely around the world because males and females everywhere benefit from different reproductive strategies.

A pattern common to the world's cultures is for males to be more forward than females in initiating sexual relationships. Sociobiology explains this "double standard" by investigating the different reproductive strategies that benefit males and females.

Critical evaluation. Because sociobiology is a new approach, its significance is not yet entirely clear. Potentially, sociobiology offers insights about the biological roots of some cultural patterns—especially cultural universals. At present, however, it remains controversial.

First, because so-called biological facts have historically been used (or more precisely, *mis*used) to justify oppression of one race or sex, sociobiology can be suspected of attempting to do the same thing. Defenders respond, however, that sociobiology has no connection to the past pseudoscience of racial superiority. On the contrary, sociobiology serves to unite rather than divide humanity by asserting that all humans of all cultures share the same evolutionary history and thus have more in common than other theories might allow.

Sexism—the assertion that males are inherently superior to females and are therefore justified in having greater social power—is also not part of sociobiological thinking. Sociobiology does rest on the assumption that, from a biological standpoint, men and women differ in ways that no culture is ever likely to eliminate completely—if, in fact, any culture intended to. If sociobiology is considered sexist, it is only in recognizing sex-linked human difference. As Barash points out, moreover, rather than asserting that males are somehow better or more worthy than females, this approach emphasizes that the two sexes are equally vital to the reproduction of the human species.

A second issue is that sociobiology has little scientific proof of its claims. Some sociobiologists, including Edward O. Wilson (1975, 1978), who is generally considered to be the founder of this field of study, believe that future research is likely to provide the evidence necessary to demonstrate the biological roots of human culture.

Nonetheless, it is highly doubtful that biological forces will ever be shown to *determine* human behavior; human behavior is *learned* within a system of culture. More likely, the value of sociobiology will be in showing, as David Barash suggests, that biological forces make some cultural patterns more common than others. This is because, given our evolutionary history, some cultural patterns are simply *easier* to learn than others. (For example, it is easy to learn to like what our bodies tell us is sweet.) Biological forces in human beings, he claims, may well turn out to be real but subject to cultural change. The development of birth control techniques, for example, has allowed people in many cultures to separate sex from reproduction and therefore to develop sexual attitudes very different from those that prevailed in the past.

Still, biology is a vital part of human existence. We are, after all, living creatures whose large brains allow us to create the survival strategy we call culture. In this sense, the forces of "nature" (our biological being) and "nurture" (what we learn) are more intertwined than in opposition. As noted earlier, *culture is our nature* (Berger, 1967; Lewontin et al., 1984).

The final value of both cultural ecology and sociobiology lies in showing us that humans create a highly variable world of culture within a physical world. We live in ecological relationship both to other forms of life and to natural resources. Furthermore, these naturalist analyses remind us that the ability to create many different cultures is a result of the transformation of our species throughout our evolutionary past—a long history that in some ways may still be imprinted on our patterns of culture. Sociological and naturalist interpretations of human culture are not irreconcilable, nor are they neces-

sarily even inconsistent. Each provides us with a partial analysis of our world of culture, and we can increase our understanding by making use of them both.

CULTURE AND HUMAN FREEDOM

We have now taken a broad look at the elements of human culture, its complexity, and some approaches to cultural analysis. The final task of this chapter is to consider the individual in the midst of culture. Is the power of culture always beneficial for human beings?

Culture as Constraint

During the long course of human evolution, culture became our strategy for survival within the natural world. But although we could hardly live without it, culture

Always powerful, culture sometimes is experienced as an alien force that overwhelms individuals. This is vividly evident in Tom Lea's portrayal of a marine caught up in the agony of World War II.

can have negative consequences. By experiencing the world through symbols and meaning, we become detached, susceptible to the experience of alienation unknown to other forms of life. Once established, cultural systems sometimes seem to weigh heavily on us, as social inertia carries us forward to relive troubling patterns from the past. Then, too, extensive social inequality is supported by American culture, providing great privilege to some, while others face a variety of problems associated with poverty. Women of all social classes have often felt powerless in the face of cultural patterns that reflect the dominance of males.

The value American culture places on competitive achievement encourages us to strive for excellence, yet this value also serves to isolate us from one another and to discourage cooperation. Material comforts do improve our lives in many ways, yet a preoccupation with objects may divert us from the security and satisfaction that come from close relationships with others or a strong religious faith. Our emphasis on personal freedom provides a great deal of privacy and autonomy but may deny us the support of a human community in which the problems of life are shared among many people (Slater, 1976; Bellah et al., 1985).

While culture is as necessary to human beings as biological instinct is to other forms of animal life, it can detract from our well-being. Yet a fundamental difference between human beings and other animals gives us reason to see the world of culture in a more positive light, as we shall now explain.

Culture as Freedom

In certain ways, human beings may appear to be prisoners of culture, just as other animals are prisoners of biology. But careful thought about the ideas presented in this chapter suggests a crucial difference. Over millions of years of human evolution, the development of culture gradually took our species out of a world shaped largely by biology into a world we shape extensively for ourselves.

Therefore, although culture may seem to oppose human interests at times, it represents the human capacity to be creative, to shape and reshape the world according to our own goals, interests, and choices. The evidence that supports this conclusion lies all around us: great cultural diversity exists within our own society, and even richer cultural variety is found around the world. Furthermore, far from static, culture is constantly changing. And although it sometimes takes the form of constraint, culture is also a continual source of human opportunity. The more we discover about the operation of our culture, the greater will be our ability to use the freedom it offers us.

SUMMARY

1. Culture refers to the patterned way of life of human beings; although some animals have simple forms of culture, only human beings rely on culture for survival.

2. Culture emerged over the long course of human evolution as the human brain gradually enlarged. Basic elements of culture first appeared some 2 million years ago. However, the complex culture that we call civilization emerged only within the last 12,000 years.

3. Culture is based on symbols, attaching significance to objects and patterns of behavior. As the most important expression of cultural symbolism, language transmits culture in the present and from generation to generation.

4. An important element of culture is values, standards that shape our orientation to the world around us.

5. All cultures also contain norms that guide human behavior. Mores are norms of high moral significance; folkways are norms of low moral significance in which greater individual discretion is allowed.

6. Values and norms provide statements of ideal culture; in practice, real culture varies considerably from these standards.

7. Material creations often reflect cultural values. Material culture is also shaped by a culture's technology.

8. Cultures contain significant internal variation. Subcultures are cultural patterns that differ from the dominant culture; countercultures are cultural patterns that are strongly at odds with the dominant culture.

9. Culture is never static; invention, discovery, and diffusion all generate cultural change. Not all parts of a cultural system change at the same rate, however, which causes cultural lag.

10. Having learned the standards of our own culture,

we often evaluate other cultures ethnocentrically. The alternative to ethnocentrism is cultural relativism, by which different cultures are understood in terms of their own standards.

11. The structural-functional paradigm emphasizes the extent to which culture is a relatively stable system of related parts. Any cultural trait is understood in terms of its function in maintaining the entire cultural system.

12. The social-conflict paradigm draws attention to cultural systems as dynamic arenas of social inequality and conflict.

13. The cultural-ecology paradigm explores the ways in which patterns of human culture are shaped by the natural environment.

14. Like cultural ecology, sociobiology is a "naturalistic" paradigm that explores ways in which patterns of human culture are influenced by subtle biological forces rooted in the human species' evolutionary past.

15. Culture can be a constraint on human needs and ambitions; yet human beings have the capacity to shape and reshape their cultural world to better realize their own needs.

KEY CONCEPTS

counterculture cultural patterns that are strongly at odds with the dominant culture

cultural ecology a theoretical paradigm that explores the relationship of human culture and the physical environment

cultural integration the close relationship among various parts of a cultural system

cultural lag inconsistencies within a cultural system resulting from the unequal rates at which different cultural elements change

cultural relativism the practice of judging any culture by its own standards

cultural transmission the process by which culture is passed from one generation to the next

cultural universals traits found in every culture

culture the beliefs, values, behavior, and material objects shared by a particular people

culture shock the personal disorientation that may accompany entry into an unfamiliar social world

ethnocentrism the practice of judging another culture by the standards of our own culture

folkways norms that have little moral significance

ideal culture social patterns consistent with cultural values and norms

language a system of symbols with standard meanings that allows members of a society to communicate with one another

material culture tangible elements of human society such as clothing and cities

mores norms that have great moral significance

nonmaterial culture intangible elements of human society such as values and norms

norms rules and expectations by which a society guides the behavior of its members

real culture actual social patterns that are typically only an approximation of ideal cultural norms

Sapir-Whorf hypothesis the assertion that people perceive the world only in terms of the symbols provided by their language

social control the process by which members of a culture encourage conformity to cultural norms

sociobiology a theoretical paradigm that seeks to explain cultural patterns as the product, at least in part, of biological causes

subculture a cultural pattern that differs from the dominant culture in some distinctive way

symbol anything that carries a particular meaning recognized by members of a culture

technology the application of cultural knowledge to the task of living in a physical environment

values culturally defined standards of desirability, goodness, and beauty that serve as broad guidelines for social life

SUGGESTED READINGS

Napoleon Chagnon's account of the Yąnomamö is extremely interesting, both as a description of a culture very different from our own and as the story of carrying out fieldwork in a most unfamiliar setting.

> Napoleon A. Chagnon. *Yąnomamö: The Fierce People.* 3rd ed. New York: Holt, Rinehart and Winston, 1983.

Cannibalism is a practice almost impossible for Westerners to comprehend. Yet, as this book explains, this consuming passion is quite acceptable within some cultures.

> Peggy Reeves Sanday. *Divine Hunger: Cannibalism as a Cultural System.* Cambridge, UK: Cambridge University Press, 1986.

Here is an analysis of one of America's most fascinating counter-cultures.

> Calvin W. Redekop. *Mennonite Society.* Baltimore: Johns Hopkins University Press, 1989.

This book reports on the culture of the American campus, revealing both dominant values and significant cultural diversity.

> Michael Moffat. *Coming of Age in New Jersey: College and American Culture.* New Brunswick, NJ: Rutgers University Press, 1989.

This paperback presents the "tough guy" (and the much rarer "tough gal") in American culture. Including popular "tough guys" of today and of the past, this paperback explores America's "ambivalent love affair with strength."

> Rupert Wilkinson. *American Tough: The Tough-Guy Tradition and American Character.* New York: Harper & Row, 1986.

One criticism of American culture concerns the extent to which males have historically shaped the lives of women. The growing awareness of the power of women to shape their own lives within a traditionally male world is the subject of this readable paperback.

> Anne Wilson Schaef. *Women's Reality: The Emerging Female System in a White Male Society.* Minneapolis: Winston, 1981.

These two books comment on current American culture. The first emphasizes the conflict between values of individualism and a sense of community. The second suggests that core American values such as freedom and democracy may not be promoted by our social institutions.

> Robert N. Bellah, Richard Madsen, William M. Sullivan, Ann Swidler, and Steven M. Tipton. *Habits of the Heart: Individualism and Commitment in American Life.* New York: Harper & Row, 1986.

> Frances Moore Lappé. *Rediscovering America's Values.* New York: Ballantine Books, 1989.

Music is a powerful force within a cultural system. This book describes the lives and music of four popular musicians who helped develop the "protest song" in opposition to many dominant cultural values.

> Wayne Hampton. *Guerrilla Minstrels: John Lennon, Joe Hill, Woody Guthrie, Bob Dylan.* Knoxville: University of Tennessee Press, 1986.

Perhaps the least examined of America's subcultures are gypsies, the focus of this research report.

> Marlene Sway. *Familiar Strangers: Gypsy Life in America.* Urbana: University of Illinois Press, 1988.

This survey of the rich variety of humankind concludes with a collection of striking photographs.

> John Reader. *Man on Earth.* Austin: University of Texas Press, 1988.

Why have firearms had such a strong presence in the cultural history of the United States? This paperback uses the sociological perspective to provide an answer.

> William R. Tonso. *Gun and Society: The Social and Existential Roots of the American Attachment to Firearms.* Lanham, MD: University Press of America, 1982.

Since language is the key to culture, the history of the English language in the United States—in all its variety—helps to explain the interaction of various cultural forces in American history.

> J. L. Dillard. *Toward a Social History of American English* (with a chapter on Appalachian English by Linda L. Blanton). New York: Mouton Publishers, 1985.

Marvin Harris has used the cultural-ecology paradigm to explain a number of apparently strange cultural practices found around the world. The following book provides fascinating reading.

> Marvin Harris. *Good to Eat: Riddles of Food and Culture.* New York: Simon & Schuster, 1986.

The first of the following books is a direct and enjoyable account of sociobiology, exploring patterns of behavior among humans as well as other animals. The second is a critical response to sociobiology.

> David Barash. *The Whisperings Within: Evolution and the Origin of Human Nature.* New York: Penguin Books, 1981.

> R. C. Lewontin, Steven Rose, and Leon J. Kamin. *Not in Our Genes: Biology, Ideology, and Human Nature.* New York: Pantheon, 1984.

4

Society

Today, after thousands of years of human culture, only one human creation on earth is visible from outer space: the Great Wall of China. This magnificent achievement, which snakes its way more than 3,000 miles across the People's Republic of China, is actually longer than the United States is wide.

The construction of the Great Wall began during the Chou dynasty, some seven centuries before the birth of Christ. Initially, some twenty-five thousand watchtowers were built, from which soldiers could observe anyone threatening the empire from the north. In the centuries that followed, all were linked together into a massive wall roughly thirty feet high and twenty-five feet thick.

Perhaps most amazing is that the Great Wall was made by people using only simple tools, working with muscles instead of heavy machinery. By order of the emperor—a leader treated as a god—hundreds of thousands of people worked under the harshest of conditions; half perished before the task was completed. As was common to societies of this time, refusal to work or even complaint could mean death.

Sociologically, the building of the Great Wall is more than a marvel of engineering. It also provokes us to think about human societies, how they operate, and how they have changed over the course of human history. Consider, for instance, that even though the American president today commands military power vastly greater than the emperors of ancient China, no president could command such absolute obedience from "subjects." Moreover, even an average person routinely makes use of technology—from electric lighting to jet air travel to global television—that god-kings of the past could hardly have imagined.

This chapter takes a broad look at human societies, as they have existed in the past, and how they are likely to change in the future. The concept society refers to *people who interact with one another within a limited territory and who share a culture*. This deceptively simple term will be explored through four major approaches,

each of which is used in later chapters. Each identifies major *types* of societies and highlights how they operate and how they differ. Each also provides an explanation of social change by which one type is transformed into another. Because each represents a distinctive vision of society that has gained great importance in sociology, a careful examination of all four will provide a rich understanding of human society.

Gerhard and Jean Lenski describe the major types of human societies that have emerged over roughly the last ten thousand years. Their work highlights the importance of *technology* in shaping social life and shows how a technological breakthrough often has revolutionary consequences for society as a whole. Karl Marx also understood human history as a long and complex process of social change. For Marx, however, *social conflict*, rooted in the way in which human beings produce material goods, was crucial to understanding human society. Max Weber acknowledged the importance of productive forces, but he sought to demonstrate the power of *human ideas* to shape society. Weber believed that the essential quality of modern society is rationality, a world view which has transformed our way of life. Finally, Emile Durkheim investigated patterns of *social solidarity*, that is, how societies are held together. By identifying different sources of solidarity, Durkheim further reveals how modern societies are distinctive.

All four visions of society offer answers to important questions: How do societies of the past and present differ? How and why do societies change? What forces divide a society? What forces hold a society together? Are human societies improving or not? Because the theorists included in this chapter provide somewhat different answers to these questions, similarities and differences will be highlighted as we proceed.

• GERHARD AND JEAN LENSKI: SOCIETY AND TECHNOLOGY

For hundreds of years, a small society called the Ona lived at the southernmost tip of South America. As they gathered vegetation and hunted game, the Ona may well have observed the Portuguese explorer Ferdinand Magellan sail in 1520 through the straits that now bear his name. Although their society endured for many centuries with little change, the encroachment of people with more complex technology gradually deprived the

Ona of their land. Many Ona fell victim to foreign diseases; others simply gave up their way of life. The death of the last full-blooded member of the Ona was recorded in 1975 (Lenski & Lenski, 1987:127–129).

As members of the industrialized world of rapid transportation and instant global communication, we might regard the Ona merely as a curious vestige of the past. But the contrast between societies like our own and those of extinct or vanishing peoples such as the Ona raise fascinating questions. Gerhard and Jean Lenski have described the great differences among societies that have existed throughout human history. They explain how a world of technologically simple people such as the Ona—the only type of human society until about ten thousand years ago—has been transformed into a world of rapidly advancing industrial technology today.

In analyzing human society, the Lenskis use an approach that is called **sociocultural evolution**, defined as *the process of social change that results from gaining new cultural information, particularly technology* (Lenski & Lenski, 1987:75). Sociocultural evolution examines the relationship of a society to its physical environment. It applies the biological concept of evolution to suggest that societies, like living species, change over time as the effects of specific innovations ripple through them. In particular, the Lenskis see technology as vitally important in shaping cultural patterns. Societies with simple technology can support only a small population engaging in a correspondingly simple way of life. Technologically complex societies—while not necessarily "better" in many respects—can become extremely large and engage in highly diverse activities.

The Lenskis also point out that the amount of technological information within a society affects the rate at which that society changes. Because of their simple technology, societies such as the Ona change only slowly. On the other hand, highly industrialized societies change so swiftly that many people witness dramatic transformations within their lifetimes. Consider some familiar elements of North American culture that would probably puzzle, or even alarm, people who lived just a few generations ago: test-tube babies, genetic engineering, the threat of nuclear holocaust, computers, electronic surveillance, transsexualism, space shuttles, and artificial hearts (Lenski & Lenski, 1982:3).

As a society's technological information expands, the processes of invention, discovery, and diffusion (described in Chapter 3, "Culture") become more rapid. This is because a single innovation (say, controlling the power of the wind) can reshape a culture as it is applied

Gerhard Lenski and Jean Lenski

Gerhard Lenski is a contemporary American sociologist known for his research on religion and social inequality. Jean Lenski is a writer and poet who has worked closely with her husband in sociological research. Together, they have studied the importance of technology in the process of sociocultural evolution.

The Lenskis' ideas about society have much in common with those of Marvin Harris, whose ecological approach to culture was described in Chapter 3 ("Culture"). Cultural ecology, you will recall, explains how specific cultural patterns help a society to survive in a particular natural environment. Similarly, sociocultural evolution explores the changing technology devised or adopted by a society to produce material resources from the natural environment.

Cultural ecology and sociocultural evolution are different, however, in one important respect. While both emphasize that the natural environment can shape cultural patterns, the Lenskis' model of sociocultural evolution shows that this is more true of *some* societies than others. With little ability to manipulate the environment, technologically simple societies are influenced the most by their natural surroundings. Technologically complex societies have a greater ability to contend with nature or even shape the natural world according to their own designs. Therefore, technologically simple societies are much alike, with minor variations resulting from different natural environments. In contrast, technologically complex societies reveal the striking cultural diversity described in Chapter 3.

---

to many existing cultural elements (to produce windmills, kites, sailing ships, and so on). Consider, as a more recent example, how many elements of modern life have been transformed by the computer or the ability to control the power of the atom.

Based on the Lenskis' work, we can distinguish four general types of societies according to their technology: hunting and gathering societies, horticultural and pastoral societies, agrarian societies, and industrial societies.[1]

● Hunting and Gathering Societies

A **hunting and gathering society** is *a society that uses simple technology to hunt animals and gather vegetation.*

---
[1] This account examines only the major types of societies described by the Lenskis.

From the emergence of our species until about ten thousand years ago, all humans were hunters and gatherers. Although such societies remained common until several centuries ago, only a few persist today, including the Pygmies of central Africa, the Bushmen of southwestern Africa, the Aborigines of Australia, the Kaska Indians of northwest Canada, and the Tasaday of the Philippines.

Food production is relatively inefficient at this early stage of sociocultural evolution, so that the primary activity must be the search for game and edible plants. In harsh environments, this work is continual; in areas where food is plentiful, however, hunters and gatherers may enjoy considerable leisure. In any case, food production usually requires a large amount of land, so hunting and gathering societies remain at some distance from one another and are limited to several dozen people. They are also typically nomadic, moving on as they deplete the vegetation in one area, or in their pursuit of migratory animals. Although they periodically return to earlier sites, they rarely form permanent settlements.

In technologically simple societies, successful hunting brings great praise to males. However, the gathering of vegetation by females is a more abundant and dependable source of nutrition.

Hunting and gathering societies are commonly organized around the family. The family obtains and distributes food, teaches necessary skills to children, and protects its members. While most activities are common to everyone and involve seeking their next meal, some specialization is linked to age and sex. The very young and the very old are expected to contribute only what they can, while healthy adults secure most of the food. The gathering of vegetation—the primary food source—is typically carried out by women, while men do most of the hunting. Therefore, males and females have somewhat different positions, but hunters and gatherers probably see men and women as generally equal in social importance (Leacock, 1978).

Hunting and gathering societies have few formal positions of leadership. Most recognize one person as a *shaman*, or spiritual leader, but the reward of this position is prestige rather than more material possessions. Furthermore, even a shaman must help procure food. Male hunters with exceptional skills are admired, as are women who are unusually productive in gathering vegetation. Overall, however, the social organization of hunting and gathering societies is relatively simple and equal.

Hunting and gathering peoples rarely turn their handcrafted weapons—the spear, the bow and arrow, and stone knife—to the task of warfare. However, their simple way of life renders them vulnerable to the forces of nature. Storms and droughts, for instance, can easily destroy their food supply. Similarly, they have few effective ways to deal with accident and disease. Such high risks probably encourage the cooperative sharing of food, a strategy that increases the society's ability to survive. Nonetheless, many members do not outlive childhood, and perhaps half die before reaching the age of twenty (Lenski & Lenski, 1987:105).

In modern times, technologically complex societies have slowly closed in on remaining hunting and gathering societies; living within limited areas, these simple societies now face depletion of game and vegetation. The Lenskis suggest that the 1990s may well see the end of hunting and gathering societies on earth. Their plight is tragic. Fortunately, study of their way of life has already produced valuable information about humanity's sociocultural history and our fundamental ties to the natural world.

Horticultural and Pastoral Societies

Between ten and twelve thousand years ago, the technology of *horticulture*—allowing the cultivation of plants—slowly began to change many hunting and gathering societies. The **horticultural society** developed: *a society that uses hand tools to raise crops.* This gradual transition first appeared in fertile regions of the Middle East and Southeast Asia. Through cultural diffusion, horticultural technology—primarily the hoe and the digging stick to punch holes in the ground for seeds—had spread as far as Western Europe and China by about six thousand years ago. In Central and South America, the cultivation of plants appears to have emerged independently about nine thousand years ago, although horticulture was less efficient there because of the rocky soil and mountainous terrain.

Not all societies were quick to abandon hunting and gathering in favor of horticulture. Hunters and gatherers who enjoyed a plentiful supply of vegetation and game probably found little reason to embrace the new technology (Fisher, 1979). The Yąnomamö, described in Chapter 3 ("Culture"), illustrate the common practice of combining horticulture with more traditional hunt-

ing and gathering (Chagnon, 1983). Then, too, in particularly arid regions, horticulture was of relatively little value. People in these regions developed the **pastoral society,** *a society whose livelihood is based on the domestication of animals.* In some cases, horticulture and pastoralism were both used to produce more food. Today, numerous examples of horticultural-pastoral societies can be found in South America, Africa, the Middle East, and Asia.

The domestication of plants and animals transformed societies in various ways. First, producing more food allowed societies to become larger, so populations climbed into the hundreds. Societies that emphasized pastoralism remained largely nomadic, leading their herds to fresh grazing lands. Those that emphasized horticulture formed settlements of several hundred people, relocating only when the soil became depleted. As such

Pastoralism is common in arid regions of the world, where little can be grown. Pastoral people flourish today in many North African societies.

settlements became linked by trade, they formed multi-centered societies with an overall population that often exceeded five thousand.

The domestication of plants and animals enabled societies to generate a *material surplus*—more resources than necessary to sustain day-to-day living. Because not everyone had to produce food, some people could do other things such as creating crafts, engaging in trade, or serving as full-time priests. In comparison to hunting and gathering societies, horticultural and pastoral societies are marked by far more specialization and social complexity.

Of Egypt's 130 pyramids, the Great Pyramids at Giza are the largest. Each of the three major pyramids stands more than forty stories high and is composed of 3 million massive stones. Tens of thousands of people labored to build the tomb of one man, the pharaoh. Clearly, social inequality in this early agrarian society, some 4,500 years ago, was striking.

Religious beliefs among hunting and gathering societies generally recognize numerous spirits inhabiting the world. Horticulture, however, is associated with the emergence of ancestor worship and a conception of God as Creator. Pastoral societies tend to carry this belief further, viewing God as directly involved in the well-being of the entire world. This view of God is widespread within American society today because both Christianity and Judaism emerged among pastoral peoples.

The technological capacity to produce a surplus of food also results in pronounced social inequality within horticultural and pastoral societies. As some families produce more food than others, they assume positions of relative privilege and power and form alliances with other privileged families, so that social advantages endure over many generations. Out of the power of such an elite, a rudimentary form of government emerges. However, there are technological limitations to the extent of this power. Without, for example, the ability to communicate or to travel quickly, a ruler can directly control only a small number of people. Furthermore, the exercise of power often breeds opposition, and there is evidence of frequent revolts and other forms of political conflict in these societies.

The domestication of plants and animals enabled societies to become much more productive than was possible relying on hunting and gathering. But advancing technology is rarely completely beneficial. The Lenskis suggest that technological progress is sometimes accompanied by ethical regression. The production of more goods has historically been accompanied by less willingness to share resources among all members of a society. Moreover, this stage in sociocultural evolution is marked by the emergence of slavery, more frequent warfare, and, in a few cases, cannibalism.

Agrarian Societies

About five thousand years ago, further technological advance led to the emergence of the **agrarian society,** which is *a society that engages in large-scale agriculture based on the use of plows drawn by animals.* Agrarian technology first appeared in the Middle East but was gradually adopted throughout the world. The Lenskis argue that the animal-drawn plow, along with other technological advances that occurred at about the same time—including the wheel, writing, numbers, and the expanding use of metals—brought such profound change to human societies that this era is widely regarded as "the dawn of civilization" (1987:166).

The animal-drawn plow produced food far more efficiently than the hand tools used in horticultural societies. Aeration of the soil as it was turned by the plow also increased soil fertility. Land could now be farmed continuously for many decades, permitting permanent settlements. Irrigation also developed in many societies about this time. The large food surpluses produced by agriculture, combined with the use of animals and wagons for transportation, allowed agrarian societies to become far larger both in population and in geographical size. Representing an extreme case, the Roman Empire at its height (about 100 C.E.) had a population of roughly 70 million and encompassed some 2 million square miles (Stavrianos, 1983; Lenski & Lenski, 1987).

The greater surplus of food produced by agriculture enabled a large proportion of the population to engage in various specialized activities. Tasks once carried out by everyone, such as clearing land, building, processing food, and engaging in trade, became the basis of distinct occupations. Money emerges about this time, gradually replacing barter as a more efficient system for trade among people engaged in specialized activities. Expanding trade also sparked the growth of cities as economic and political centers. Ancient Rome grew to roughly 1 million people, and cities in modern agrarian societies such as India and Egypt are now many times that size. As population grew and economic activity expanded, social life gradually became more individualistic and impersonal.

Agrarian societies produce dramatic social inequality. In many cases—including the United States early in its history, especially in the South—a large proportion of the population are slaves or peasants who labor for elites. Freed from the need to work, elites are able to engage in the study of philosophy, art, and literature. This is the historical link between "high culture" and privileged segments of society.

Women in horticultural societies gain prestige from producing much of the food. The agrarian revolution, however, appears to have propelled men into a position of clear social dominance (Boulding, 1976; Fisher, 1979). The box on page 96 provides a closer look at the declining social position of women at this point in the course of sociocultural evolution.

Religion often reinforces male dominance by presenting God in masculine terms. More generally, religion tends to support the power of existing elites by propagating the belief that people are morally obligated to carry out tasks according to their place in the social order. Chinese emperors were able to mobilize their people to produce the Great Wall, the Forbidden City, and other massive undertakings only because they were defined as gods, whose power was virtually absolute. Little more than a century ago, religion was used to help elites enslave other human beings based on the claim that God had wisely placed "childlike" human beings in the care of their owners.

Within agrarian societies, then, the social power of elites greatly expands, so that they may exercise virtually absolute control over large empires. In maintaining control of such large societies, however, elites require the services of a wide range of administrators. Therefore, along with the growing economy, a political system becomes established as a distinct part of society.

In relation to other types of societies described so far, the Lenskis conclude, agrarian societies are more internally diverse and socially unequal. They are also more distinct from one another than are horticultural and pastoral societies. Advancing technology provides greater control over the natural world, allowing more extensive use of the creative elements of human culture.

Industrial Societies

An **industrial society**, such as the United States or Canada, is *a society that uses sophisticated machinery powered*

Animal power is vital to agrarian life. Throughout rural India today, oxen provide the energy for irrigating crops and a host of other tasks.

Plants, Technology, and the Status of Women

In the early stages of sociocultural evolution, evidence suggests that women made a greater contribution to food production than men did. Hunters and gatherers valued meat highly, but the hunting carried out primarily by males did not provide a dependable source of food. Thus the gathering of vegetation, undertaken mostly by females, was the primary means of ensuring the society's survival.

The tools and seeds used in horticulture developed under the control of women, who already had primary responsibility for providing and preparing food. Although men did most of the work of clearing land, women planted and tended the crops. Then the harvest provided work for every-one—male and female, young and old.

When cultivation was under the control of women, men assumed most of the responsibility for trade and tending herds of animals. About five thousand years ago, an important cultural invention took place—the development of metals. This invention spread by cultural diffusion, primarily through the network of male traders. It seems all but certain that males, who were already managing animals, were responsible for hitching the metal plow to cattle, initiating the transition from horticulture to agriculture. As this happened, men for the first time moved into a dominant position in the production of food. As Elise Boulding explains, the result was a decline in the social position of women:

> The shift of the status of the woman farmer may have happened quite rapidly, once there were two male specializations relating to agriculture: plowing and the care of cattle. This situation left women with all the subsidiary tasks, including weeding and carrying water to the fields. The new fields were larger, so women had to work just as many hours as they did before, but now they worked at more secondary tasks. . . . This would contribute further to the erosion of the status of women.

SOURCE: Based on Elise Boulding, *The Underside of History* (Boulder, CO: Westview Press, 1976), pp. 161–163; also Elizabeth Fisher, *Woman's Creation* (Garden City, NY: Anchor Press/Doubleday, 1979).

---

by advanced fuels to produce material goods. The muscle power of humans and animals is no longer the basis of production, and tools and machinery become more complex and efficient owing to the incorporation of metal alloys such as steel. The steam engine (first coupled to machinery in England in 1765) efficiently mechanized many productive tasks previously done by hand. But this was just the beginning of the Industrial Revolution, which ushered in the final stage of the Lenskis' model of sociocultural evolution. As shown in Figure 4–1, the rate of technological innovation rose rapidly during the nineteenth century, producing vast social changes and, as noted in Chapter 1 ("The Sociological Perspective"), stimulating the birth of sociology itself. Within another century, railroads and steamships revolutionized transportation, and tall buildings supported by steel frames formed towering skylines in cities of Europe and North America.

By the beginning of the twentieth century, automobiles began to further transform Western societies, and electricity was becoming a part of everyday life. New forms of communication such as the telephone, radio, and television were gradually making a large world seem smaller and smaller. Other changes occurred during the Industrial Revolution. Additional advances in transportation technology have given humanity the power to fly faster than the speed of sound and even routinely to "shuttle" away from the planet entirely. This is even more remarkable when we consider that, for all of human history until the beginning of this century, no one traveled faster than about thirty-five miles an hour—the speed of a fast horse or early steam locomotive. Nuclear power, used for destruction ten years before it was used to generate electricity, has also changed forever how we think about the world. Most recently, computers have ushered in the "information revolution," dramatically increasing humanity's ability to process information.

In agrarian societies, most occupations are carried on within the home; the development of large, industrial

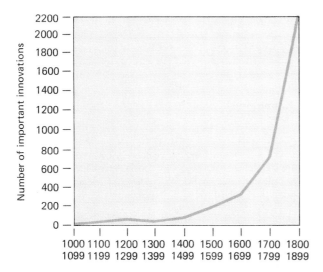

Figure 4–1 The Increasing Rate of Technological Innovation
This figure illustrates the increasing rate of technological innovation in Western Europe after the beginning of the Industrial Revolution in the mid-eighteenth century. Technological innovation occurs at an accelerating rate because each innovation combines with existing cultural elements to produce many further innovations.

(*Lenski & Lenski, 1987:67*)

machinery, however, led to the creation of factories. Individuals who had worked primarily within the family became industrial workers linked to many others only by economic necessity. Lost in the process were many traditional values, beliefs, and customs that had guided agrarian life for centuries.

Industrialism has generated societies of unparalleled size and prosperity. Although the health of people living in industrial cities was initially poor, a rising standard of living and advancing health-related technology gradually resulted in the control of diseases that had for centuries caused high death rates for both children and adults. Consequently, average life expectancy in industrial societies significantly increased, leading to population growth. Industrialization has also brought about a greater concentration of population. Within agrarian societies, population is usually dispersed over the land, with only about 10 percent of people living in cities. In industrial societies, however, a growing proportion of the population (now over 75 percent in the United States) clusters within cities.

Occupational specialization, which increased over the long course of sociocultural evolution, becomes more pronounced than ever. Indeed, in industrial societies, people often identify one another in terms of what they do for a living (or, even, what kind of car they drive) rather than in terms of family background. Similarly, cultural values have become more varied with the emergence of numerous subcultures and countercultures, as described in Chapter 3 ("Culture").

Within industrial societies, the family loses much of its traditional significance as the center of social life. It is no longer the major setting for economic production, education, and religious activity. The increasing numbers of single people, divorced people, and single-parent families also reflect the effects of technological advance, as Chapter 15 ("Family") describes in detail.

The Lenskis suggest that when a society first becomes industrialized, the benefits of advancing technology are enjoyed by only a small part of the population. The majority—especially the urban industrial workers—frequently live in poverty. Over time, however, the benefits of industrial societies are extended. Although poverty remains a very serious problem in industrial societies, economic, social, and political inequality in industrial societies today is certainly less than it was a century ago. Some social leveling, as discussed in detail in Chapter 9 ("Social Stratification"), occurs because industrial societies require an increasingly literate and skilled labor force. In contrast to the dramatic social inequality common to agrarian societies, industrial societies gradually provide more and more schooling and extend political rights to a larger proportion of people. For example, even a century ago, only in isolated areas of the United States could women vote. The Nineteenth Amendment to the Constitution in 1920 afforded voting rights equally to women and men; in Canada, women voted in national elections two years earlier. Indeed, the demand for increasing political participation often accompanies industrialization, as is evident in South Korea, Taiwan, the People's Republic of China, and, most recently, in the societies of Eastern Europe. A summary of the characteristics of industrial societies in relation to the three other types identified by the Lenskis is presented in Table 4–1 on pages 98–99. Sociocultural ecology is continuing, of course, and discussion of the character of our emerging *post-industrial* society is found in Chapter 10 ("Social Class in America") and Chapter 19 ("The Economy and Work").

The technological power of industrial societies is

Table 4–1 SOCIOCULTURAL EVOLUTION: A SUMMARY

Type of Society	Historical Period	Productive Technology	Population Size
Hunting and Gathering Societies	Only type of society until about 10,000 years ago; still common several centuries ago; the few examples remaining today are threatened by extinction	Primitive weapons	25–40 people
Horticultural and Pastoral Societies	From about 10,000 years ago, with decreasing numbers after about 3000 B.C.E.	Horticultural societies use hand tools for cultivating plants; pastoral societies are based on the domestication of animals.	Settlements of several hundred people, interconnected to form societies of several thousand people
Agrarian Societies	From about 5,000 years ago, with large but decreasing numbers today	Animal-drawn plow	Millions of people
Industrial Societies	From about 1750 to the present	Advanced sources of energy; mechanized production	Millions of people

Technology can threaten as well as serve humanity. The utter destruction of the Japanese city of Nagasaki by the armed forces of the United States at the end of World War II— using a single, "primitive" nuclear bomb—only hints at the horrors of warfare today.

Type of Society	Settlement Pattern	Social Organization	Examples
Hunting and Gathering Societies	Nomadic	Family-centered; specialization limited to age and sex; little social inequality	Pygmies of central Africa Bushmen of southwest Africa Aborigines of Australia Tasaday of the Philippines Kaska Indians of Canada
Horticultural and Pastoral Societies	Horticulturalists form relatively small permanent settlements; pastoralists are nomadic	Family-centered; religious system begins to develop moderate specialization; increased social inequality	Middle Eastern societies about 5,000 B.C.E. Various societies today in New Guinea and other Pacific islands Yąnomanö today in South America
Agrarian Societies	Cities become common, though they generally contain only a small proportion of the population	Family loses significance as distinctive religious, political, and economic systems emerge; extensive specialization; increased social inequality	Egypt during construction of the Great Pyramids Medieval Europe Numerous nonindustrial societies of the world today
Industrial Societies	Cities now contain most of the population	Distinct religious, political, economic, educational, and family systems; highly specialized; marked social inequality persists, diminishing somewhat over time	Most societies today in Europe and North America Japan

unparalleled in human history. An important historical lesson, however, is that technology by itself does not solve *social* problems. Poverty remains the plight of millions within the United States (detailed in Chapter 10, "Social Class in America") and of more than 1 billion people worldwide (Chapter 11, "Global Inequality"). Moreover, we face new problems that our ancestors could hardly have imagined. Industrial societies tend to provide more personal freedom, but, as explained in Chapter 23 ("Social Change and Modernity"), only at the cost of the traditional sense of community that characterized agrarian societies. Furthermore, humanity's ability to manipulate nature, coupled with our failure to control human greed, has wrought a staggering problem of environmental pollution. Perhaps most important, although industrial societies engage in warfare far less frequently than do societies with less developed forms of technology, war now poses unimaginable horrors. Should the current nuclear weapons of war ever be unleashed, human society would almost certainly be violently returned to a technologically primitive state if, indeed, our species survived

at all. In some respects, technological advances have brought the world's people closer together, creating a "global village." What remains, however, are daunting problems of establishing peace and justice—problems that technology alone can never solve.

KARL MARX: SOCIETY AND CONFLICT

A second, major vision of human society was provided by Karl Marx. Few observed the transformation of Europe by the Industrial Revolution as keenly as he did. There can be little doubt that Marx was awed by the productive power of industry. Not only were the countries of Europe producing more goods than ever before, but resources from around the world were being funneled through their factories at a dizzying rate. Marx spent most of his adult life in London, then the capital of a vast British

Karl Marx (1818–1883)

Few names evoke as strong a response as that of Karl Marx. Many consider him a genius and a prophet, others see only evil in his ideas. Marx is, in any event, one of the social thinkers with the greatest impact on the world's

people. Today, despite the recent transformation in the socialist societies of Eastern Europe (described in Chapter 18, "Politics and Government"), about one-fourth of humanity lives in a society that considers itself Marxist.

Controversy surrounded Marx even during his own lifetime. Born in Trier (now in West Germany), he received a doctorate in 1841 and soon began working as a newspaper editor. But his relentless social criticism led to conflict with government authorities, and he moved to Paris. Soon he was forced to leave France as well. He spent the rest of his life in London.

Along with Max Weber and Emile Durkheim, Marx is one of the major figures in the development of European sociology. However, his ideas received relatively little attention in American sociology until the 1960s.

The reason for this neglect surely lies in Marx's explicit criticism of industrial-capitalist society. Early American sociologists frequently dismissed his ideas as mere "politics" rather than serious scholarship. While most sociologists heeded Max Weber's call for a value-free sociology by attempting to minimize or conceal their own values (see Chapter 2, "Sociological Investigation"), Marx's work was explicitly value-laden. Marx did not merely *observe* society; he offered a rousing prescription for profound social *change*. As we have come to recognize the extent to which values shape all ideas, Marx's social analysis has finally received the attention it deserves as an important part of sociology in North America.

SOURCE: Based in part on George Ritzer, *Sociological Theory* (New York: Alfred A. Knopf, 1983), pp. 63–66.

Empire, and a city that symbolized the wealth and power of the new social order.

As impressive as the new industrial technology was, Marx was conscious of something more—the concentration of these new riches in the hands of a few. A walk almost anywhere in London showed only too clearly dramatic extremes of affluence and squalor. A handful of aristocrats and industrialists lived in massive mansions well staffed by servants, where they enjoyed luxury and privileges barely imaginable to most of their fellow Londoners. The majority of Londoners, however, labored long hours for low wages, living in slums or even in the streets, where many eventually succumbed to poor nutrition and disease.

Marx was both saddened and angered by the social inequities he saw around him. The technological miracles of industrialization had finally made possible human society without want. In reality, however, industrializa-

tion had done little to improve the lives of most people. To Marx, this represented a fundamental contradiction: how could a society that was so rich have a majority who were so poor? Just as important, how could this situation be changed? Many people, no doubt, think of Karl Marx as a man determined to tear societies apart, but actually he was motivated by compassion for humanity and sought to help a society already badly divided find a new and just unity.

The key-to Marx's thinking is the idea of **social conflict**, which means *struggle among segments of society over valued resources*. In fact, the social-conflict paradigm in sociology is based heavily on Marx's work. Social conflict can, of course, take many forms: individuals may quarrel, some colleges have long-standing rivalries, and nations may go to war. For Marx, however, the most significant form of social conflict arises from the way a society produces material goods.

In all societies, art commonly conveys political ideas. This is especially true of socialist countries: according to Marx's thinking, economic revolution should transform all of social life. *Friendship of the People* by Stephan Carpov was painted in 1924 to propagate the proletarian ideals of the Russian Revolution.

Society and Production

Nineteenth-century European societies familiar to Marx had industrial-capitalist economies, similar to those that exist today in various forms in North America, Western Europe, and elsewhere. Within this system, Marx designated a small part of the population as capitalists—*those who own factories and other productive enterprises.* The capitalist's goal is profit, made by selling a product for more than it costs to produce. Most people within the society are the industrial workers Marx termed the proletariat—*those who provide the labor necessary for the operation of factories and other productive enterprises.* Workers offer their labor in exchange for the wages necessary to live. In Marx's analysis, social conflict between capitalists and workers is an inevitable result of the productive process itself. To maximize profits, capitalists try to minimize wages, generally their single greatest expense. Workers, on the other hand, want wages to be as high as possible. Since profits and wages draw upon the same economic resources, social conflict results. Marx argued that this conflict would end only by fundamentally changing the capitalist system—which, he believed, would eventually occur.

Marx's analysis of society is a form of the philosophical approach called *materialism* because it asserts that the system of producing material goods can shape all of society. By this, Marx did not mean that once an economic system is established, cultural values, politics, and family patterns all fall into place in a direct chain of cause and effect. Rather, just as the Lenskis argue that technology is a crucial force that affects all dimensions of society, so Marx argued that the economic system is of special importance in shaping society:

> [T]he economic structure of society [is] the real foundation [of society]. . . . The mode of production in material life determines the general character of the social, political, and spiritual processes of life. (1959:43; orig. 1859)

Marx therefore saw the economic system as the *infrastructure* of society ("infra" comes from the Latin for "below"). Other social institutions, such as the family, the political system, and religion, are built on this foundation and become society's superstructure, thereby carrying the significance of the economic system into other areas of social life. This important idea is illustrated in Figure 4–2 on page 102. In practical terms, then, each social institution in an industrial-capitalist society reinforces the control of that society by the capitalists, who run the economy. For example, the legal system serves the interests of capitalists by protecting private property and

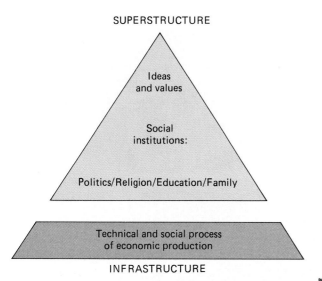

SUPERSTRUCTURE

Ideas
and values

Social
institutions:

Politics/Religion/Education/Family

Technical and social process
of economic production

INFRASTRUCTURE

Figure 4–2 Karl Marx's Model of Society

This diagram illustrates Marx's materialist approach: that the process of economic production shapes the entire society. Economic production involves both technology (industry, in the case of capitalism) and social relationships (for capitalism, the relationship between the capitalists, who control the process, and the workers, who are simply a source of labor). Upon this infrastructure, or economic foundation, are built the major social institutions, as well as core cultural values and ideas. Taken together, these additional social elements represent the society's superstructure. Marx maintained that all the other parts of the society are likely to operate in a manner consistent with the economic system.

allowing workers to be hired and fired at the discretion of those who own factories.

Most members of industrial-capitalist societies do not view their legal system, or any other part of society, as part of an ongoing social conflict. Indeed, individual rights to private property are taken for granted as "natural." To illustrate, Americans commonly think that some people live in poor-quality housing simply because they cannot afford something better. Likewise, no business is expected to provide better housing for them unless doing so would be profitable. Similarly, people who are out of work are likely to be seen as lacking the skills or the motivation to become employed. Marx argued that this kind of thinking is molded by our capitalist society, resting on "truths" defined by a social system in which human well-being is based on the operation of the marketplace. Such "truths," he insisted, are actually questionable products of a specific social context.

Poor housing and unemployment are not inevitable; nor do they reflect the fact that some people "simply don't deserve more." They are merely one set of human possibilities generated by capitalism (Cuff & Payne, 1979).

This led Marx to claim that capitalism promoted **false consciousness,** *the belief that the shortcomings of individuals themselves, rather than society, are responsible for many of the personal problems that people experience.* Marx argued, however, that industrial capitalism itself was the cause of many of the social problems he found all around him. False consciousness, he maintained, does much more than simply victimize people: it obscures the real cause of their problems and even encourages them to blame themselves for their own suffering. Marx believed, however, that false consciousness could be overcome so that people might actively improve their lives.

Conflict in History

Marx believed that ideas are powerful when linked to action. Thus he studied historical social change, noting that such change was often gradual or evolutionary, and sometimes rapid or revolutionary. Marx would have agreed with the Lenskis that social change is partly caused by technological advance. But he emphasized the greater, underlying importance of social conflict in transforming societies.

Marx believed that the earliest hunters and gatherers were characterized by primitive communism. The word *communism* means simply that the production of food and other material goods is a common effort shared more or less equal by everyone. Because the resources of nature were available to all hunters and gatherers (rather than privately owned), and because everyone carried out much the same tasks (rather than being highly specialized), there was little possibility for social conflict in such societies.

Marx noted that horticulture was a technological advance that introduced significant social inequality to human societies. Within horticultural, pastoral, and early agrarian societies—which Marx described simply as the "ancient world"—warfare produced military captives who typically became slaves. Supported by the political state, a small elite (the "masters") used the labor of these slaves to produce riches for themselves. Slaves and masters were thus locked into an irreconcilable pattern of social conflict (Zeitlin, 1981).

Agriculture brought still more wealth to elites, and social conflict persisted. In later agrarian societies—including European societies between about the twelfth

Fildes' *Awaiting Admission to the Casual Ward* shows the numbing poverty commonplace among immigrants in the rapidly growing cities soon after the Industrial Revolution. To Marx, this posed a contradiction: industrial technology for the first time promised material plenty for all, yet capitalism concentrated wealth in the hands of a few.

and eighteenth centuries—the position of laboring serfs was only slightly better than that of slaves. In Marx's view, both the church and the state supported agrarian inequality by defining the existing social order as an expression of God's will. Thus, Marx believed this system amounted to little more than "exploitation, veiled by religious and political illusions" (Marx & Engels, 1972:337; orig. 1848).

Marx continued to trace the development of social conflict as new productive forces emerged within the feudal order. Commerce steadily grew throughout the Middle Ages, carried out mostly by peasants who had settled in the cities, thereby becoming free of feudal obligations to the nobility. Such people represented a new social category, the *bourgeoisie* (a French word meaning "of the town"). Profits earned in the growing market brought the bourgeoisie considerable wealth. After the mid-eighteenth century, with the factory system brought by the Industrial Revolution at their command,

the bourgeoisie had become true capitalists with the power to rival the old feudal nobility. Although the nobility often expressed disdain for men and women "of commerce," the capitalists eventually took control of the emerging industrial-capitalist societies of Europe. Following Marx's analysis, then, technological change was only part of the Industrial Revolution. More important, the agrarian economy and its elite nobility were overthrown from below by capitalists who presided over the emerging industrial economy.

Industrialization also guided the development of the proletariat. The proletariat emerged as English capitalists converted fields once tilled by serfs into grazing land for sheep. To the capitalists, in other words, sheep were more valuable than people, since they provided the wool needed for a prospering textile industry. Serfs had little choice but to migrate to the cities to seek work in factories, thereby becoming an industrial proletariat. Marx envisioned that these workers would one day rise as a unified class to set the stage for another historical confrontation. This time, the confrontation would be between capitalists, who now controlled economic production, and the exploited workers.

Much of Marx's work identifies socially destructive aspects of industrial capitalism—especially class conflict and alienation. His analysis of each makes clearer why he believed this type of society had to be overthrown.

Capitalism and Class Conflict

"The history of all hitherto existing society is the history of class struggles." With this observation, Marx and his collaborator Friedrich Engels began their best-known statement, the "Manifesto of the Communist Party" (1972:335; orig. 1848). The idea of social class is at the heart of Marx's critique of capitalist society. Industrial capitalism, like earlier types of society, contains two major social classes based on the position people hold in the system of material production. As already noted, capitalists and proletarians are the historical descendants of dominant and oppressed classes in earlier types of societies: masters and slaves in the earliest societies, nobility and serfs in agrarian societies. In each case, one class controls the other as productive property.

Social conflict, then, is nothing new. Marx contended, however, that industrial capitalism makes oppression more obvious to all. In agrarian societies, serfs and nobles were bound together by long-rooted tradition and personal ties. Industrial capitalism dissolved such ties, so that people confronted each other concerned with only "naked self-interest" and "callous cash payment." With no personal ties to their oppressors, Marx concluded, the proletariat had little reason to tolerate their suffering.

In Marx's analysis, classes inevitably generate social conflict, as the oppressed contend with those who support the status quo. But despite the fact that industrial capitalism had brought class conflict more out in the open, Marx recognized that social change was a gradual process involving several steps. First, he claimed, workers must *become aware* of their shared oppression. Second, they must *organize and act* to address their problems. In other words, they must recognize that they suffer not from personal failings (as capitalist cultural beliefs suggest), nor because other workers compete for their jobs. Rather, their suffering is caused by capitalism itself. In short, *each* worker must gain a bit of the sociological perspective to see how social forces have placed *all* workers in the same situation. In doing so, they replace false consciousness with **class consciousness:** *the recognition by workers of their unity as a class in opposition to capitalists and, ultimately, to capitalism itself.* Because the inhumanity of early capitalism seemed so obvious to Marx, he believed that industrial workers would inevitably act in opposition to industrial capitalism. In doing so, they would cease to be merely a social class *in* themselves and become a social class acting *for* themselves.

And what of their adversaries, the capitalists? Their formidable wealth and power, protected by the institutions of society, might seem invulnerable. But Marx saw a weakness in the capitalist armor. Motivated by a desire for personal gain, capitalists fear the competition of other capitalists. Thus Marx thought that capitalists would be reluctant to band together, even though they, too, have common interests. Furthermore, he believed, the capitalist system itself would undermine the power of the capitalists. By competing with one another, capitalists keep wages low and thereby encourage workers to join together into a social class actively opposed to industrial capitalism. In the long run, Marx claimed, capitalists contribute to their own undoing.

Capitalism and Alienation

Marx also condemned capitalism for the widespread alienation it produced. He used the term **alienation** to mean *the experience of powerlessness in social life.* Dominated by capitalists and dehumanized by their jobs, workers find little satisfaction in their lives and feel individually powerless to improve their situation. A major contradiction in capitalist society, observed Marx, is that as human beings have used advanced technology to gain power over the world, the productive process itself has increasingly exerted power over human beings.

The basic problem is that workers find industrial-capitalist work unsatisfying. They feel themselves to be only a commodity, a source of labor, bought by capitalists when necessary and discarded when no longer needed. Marx cited four ways in which industrial capitalism alienates workers.

1. **Alienation from the act of working.** Ideally, work allows people to meet their needs and develop their potential. Capitalism, however, denies workers a voice in what is produced or how production takes place. Furthermore, work in industrial-capitalist societies is often tedious, involving countless repetitions of routine tasks. The fact that much human

labor in industrial societies has been replaced by machines would hardly have surprised Marx. As far as he was concerned, capitalism had turned human beings into machines long ago.

2. **Alienation from the products of work.** The products of work belong not to workers but to capitalists, who dispose of them in exchange for profits. Thus, Marx concluded, the more workers put into the products of their labor, the more they lose.

3. **Alienation from other workers.** Marx saw work as the productive affirmation of human community. Industrial capitalism, however, renders work competitive rather than cooperative. Indeed, as the box illustrates, work often provides little chance for even human companionship.

4. **Alienation from humanity.** Industrial capitalism alienates workers from their own human potential. Marx argued that a worker "does not fulfill himself in his work but denies himself, has a feeling of misery rather than well-being, does not freely develop his physical and mental energies, but is physically exhausted and mentally debased. The worker, therefore, feels himself to be at home only during his leisure time, whereas at work he feels homeless" (1964a:124–125; orig. 1844). In short, productive

SOCIOLOGY OF EVERYDAY LIFE

Alienation and Industrial Capitalism

These excerpts from the book *Working* by Studs Terkel illustrate how workers may experience social alienation in their jobs.

Twenty-seven-year-old Phil Stallings is an auto worker in a Ford Motor Company assembly plant in Chicago.

I start the automobile, the first welds. From there it goes to another line, where the floor's put on, the roof, the trunk, the hood, the doors. Then it's put on a frame. There is hundreds of lines. . . . I stand in one spot, about two- or three-feet area, all night. The only time a person stops is when the line stops. We do about thirty-two jobs per car, per unit. Forty-eight units an hour, eight hours a day. Thirty-two times forty-eight times eight. Figure it out. That's how many times I push that button.

The noise, oh it's tremendous. You open your mouth and you're liable to get a mouthful of sparks. (Shows his arms) That's a burn, these are burns. You don't compete against the noise. You go to yell and at the same time you're straining to maneuver the gun to where you have to weld.

You got some guys that are uptight, and they're not sociable. It's too rough. You pretty much stay to yourself. You get involved with yourself. You dream, you think of things you've done. I drift back continuously to when I was a kid and what me and my brothers did. The things you love most are what you drift back into.

Lots of times I worked from the time I started to the time of the break and I never realized I had even worked. When you dream, you reduce the chances of friction with the foreman or the next guy.

It don't stop. It just goes and goes and goes. I bet there's men who have lived and died out there, never seen the end of the line. And they never will—because it's endless. It's like a serpent. It's just all body, no tail. It can do things to you. . . .

Twenty-four-year-old Sharon Atkins is a college graduate working as a telephone receptionist for a large midwestern business.

I don't have much contact with people. You can't see them. You don't know if they're laughing, if they're being satirical or being kind. So your conversations become very abrupt. I notice that in talking to people. My conversation would be very short and clipped, in short sentences, the way I talk to people all day on the telephone. . . .

You try to fill up your time with trying to think about other things: what you're going to do on the weekend or about your family. You have to use your imagination. If you don't have a very good one and you bore easily, you're in trouble. Just to fill in time, I write real bad poetry or letters to myself and to other people and never mail them. The letters are fantasies, sort of rambling, how I feel, how depressed I am.

. . . I never answer the phone at home.

SOURCE: Studs Terkel, *Working* (New York: Pantheon Books, 1974), pp. 57–59; 221–222. © 1974 by Pantheon Books, A Division of Random House, Inc.

Socialist revolution did occur, as Marx expected, but not in the industrial-capitalist societies of Western Europe. Instead, socialism has transformed many agrarian societies, in which social inequality is most pronounced. In recent years, Marxist revolutionaries have struggled against government forces in El Salvador.

activity, ideally an expression of the best qualities in human beings, is perverted by industrial capitalism into a dull and dehumanizing experience.

Marx believed that alienation, in all its forms, is itself a barrier to social change. He also believed, however, that industrial workers would overcome their alienation by uniting into a true social class that was aware of the cause of its problems and prepared to change society.

Revolution

The only way out of the trap, contended Marx, was to change society. He envisioned a more humane and egalitarian type of productive system, which he termed *socialism*. Marx knew well the obstacles to a socialist revolution; even so, he was disappointed that workers in England did not act to end industrial capitalism during his lifetime. Still, believing deeply in the basic immorality of industrial capitalism, he was sure that, in time, the working majority would realize they held the key to a better future in their own hands. This transformation would certainly be revolutionary, and perhaps even violent. In the end, however, a socialist society based on meeting the needs of all would emerge.

For Marx, a socialist society promised an end to the social conflict that turns one part of society against another. The discussion of social stratification in Chapter 9 ("Social Stratification") will reveal more about changes in industrial-capitalist societies since Marx's time, and why the revolution he longed for has not yet taken place. Chapter 18 ("Politics and Government") also explains why people in the societies of Eastern Europe revolted in 1989 *against* established socialist governments. Marx, however, looked toward the future with hope (1972:362; orig. 1848): "The proletarians have nothing to lose but their chains. They have a world to win."

● MAX WEBER: THE RATIONALIZATION OF SOCIETY

With a deep understanding of law, economics, religion, and history, Max Weber produced what many regard as the greatest individual contribution to sociology. Indeed, Weber's ideas are so wide-ranging that they are difficult to summarize. For the present, we shall focus on Weber's vision of modern society, especially the ways in which our social world differs from societies of earlier times.

Weber's analysis of society reflects the philosophical approach called *idealism* because it emphasizes the importance of human ideas in shaping society. Like the Lenskis, he believed technology was responsible for important social patterns. He also shared many of Marx's ideas about social conflict (see Chapter 9, "Social Stratification"). But he departed from Marx's materialist analysis, arguing that societies differ primarily in terms of the ways in which human beings think about the world around them. For Weber, human consciousness—ideas, beliefs, and values—was a transforming power. Thus he saw modern society as the result of not just new technology and production but new ways of thinking. Weber's emphasis on nonmaterial elements of culture in contrast to Marx's focus on material culture has led his work to be described as "a debate with the ghost of Karl Marx" (Cuff & Payne, 1979:73–74).

Weber, then, was concerned with more than observing the behavior of members of a society. He investigated the *meanings* that motivate people and make their lives meaningful. This approach to sociological research is often termed **verstehen** (a German word meaning "insight" and "empathic understanding"), which is defined as *interpreting how people in a particular social setting understand themselves*. Weber believed, in other words, that *why* people act is as important as *what* they do.

Another of Weber's tools was the **ideal type**: *an abstract statement of the essential characteristics of any social phenomenon*. People can be described in terms of ideal types (for instance, as "Protestants" or "Jews"), and so can entire societies (the Lenskis describe "industrial societies" and other ideal types). Ideal types are a form of categorizing by which Weber sought to compare various patterns of human thought and behavior. His research investigated how the lives of Protestants differed from other religious categories, for example, or the differences between agrarian and industrial societies. An ideal type has much in common with the more familiar idea of stereotype, in that both are abstract distillations and exaggerations of reality. Unlike a stereotype, however, an ideal type is essentially factual rather than being unfairly positive or negative (Theodorson & Theodorson, 1969:194). Weber's use of the word *ideal* does not mean that something is "good" or "the best," since "criminals" as well as "priests" can be analyzed as ideal types.

Rationality and Industrial Capitalism

As explained earlier, the Lenskis categorize societies in terms of technology, as Marx did in terms of production

and social conflict. Max Weber took yet a third approach, highlighting differences in patterns of thought, or the way in which people view the world. In simple terms, preindustrial societies tend to be what Weber called *traditional*; industrial-capitalist societies are highly *rational*.

Tradition, to Weber, refers to *sentiments and beliefs about the world that are passed from generation to generation*. Within a traditional society, human thought and action strongly reflect the past. Therefore, people tend to believe a social pattern is right and proper precisely because it has existed for so long.

Modern society is quite different, Weber argued, because it fosters **rationality**, *deliberate, matter-of-fact calculation of the most efficient means to accomplish any particular goal*. A rational world view is largely indifferent to the past, and tradition tends to be simply a form of information without any special claims on individuals. Patterns of thought and behavior are adopted on the basis of their consequences for the present. As members of modern societies, we tend to evaluate our jobs, our schooling, and even our relationships through a "cost-benefit" analysis that weighs what we put into them in relation to what we expect them to provide for us.

In Weber's view, industrial capitalism itself is simply a grand expression of a rational orientation emerging in history. He used the term **rationalization of society** to denote *the change from tradition to rationality as the dominant mode of human thought*. Modern society, he claimed, became "disenchanted" as sentimental ties to the past gave way to greater reliance on scientific thinking and advancing technology.

Thus, Weber explained the technological transformation that we call the Industrial Revolution, as well as the highly calculating capitalist economy, as expressions of this new rationality. This implies that not every society perceives technological advance in the same way; some societies have dismissed certain technological innovations as unimportant and others have even opposed what we tend to define as "progress." Weber pointed out that, guided by a traditional—not a rational—world view, industrial technology would have little positive value. Elites in ancient Greece, for instance, had many surprisingly elaborate mechanical devices. Well served by slaves, however, they viewed such inventions as merely entertaining. The Amish of North America (described in Chapter 3, "Culture") are today guided by their traditions to reject much of modern technology.

Weber's contention, then, is that technological innovation can be encouraged or hindered by the way

Max Weber (1864–1920)

To be called merely a "sociologist" would probably have offended Max Weber. Not that he was indifferent to the study of society; indeed, he spent most of his life doing just that. But Weber's contribution to under-standing humanity is so broad and rich that no single discipline can properly claim him.

The product of a prosperous German family, Weber probably disappointed no one as he completed law school and began a legal career. But Weber found law too confining. As a college professor, his curiosity raced across the entire human condition, and he integrated many approaches into his rich scholarship.

Even so, Weber's family ties continued to influence his work. His mother's devout Calvinism may well have encouraged Weber's study of world religions and his interest in the links between Calvinism and the rise of industrial capitalism. From his father, a notable politician, Weber clearly gained an interest in the workings of bureaucracy and political life.

Weber also flirted with politics, which he found to be incompatible with his work as a scholar. Politics, he claimed, demands action and strong personal conviction, while scholarship requires patient reflection and impartiality. This led Weber to urge his fellow scholars to become involved in politics as citizens outside of the classroom, while striving for scientific neutrality in their professional work.

For many reasons, Weber's life was not very happy. He endured conflict with his parents and later suffered for years from psychological problems that sharply limited his ability to work. Even so, the exceptional number of major studies he produced has led many to regard him as the most brilliant sociologist in history.

---

people understand their world. He noted that many societies of the world held the technological keys to industry, but only in some areas of Western Europe did the Industrial Revolution actually take place (1958; orig. 1904–1905). To Weber, the key to this curious fact is that only in Western Europe did a rational world view develop.

Marx, in contrast, thought that industrial capitalism was anything but rational, claiming that this economic system failed to meet the needs of most of the people for basic food, clothing, and shelter. From Weber's point of view, however, industrial capitalism is the essence of rationality because it is based on the pursuit of profit through deliberately calculated action. Thus, without denying the existence of social conflict as emphasized by Marx, Weber believed that rationality was a more important force in shaping modern society (Gerth & Mills, 1946:49).

The Roots of Rationality

Weber began his analysis of the importance of modern rationality by noting that industrial capitalism developed where Calvinism—a Christian religious movement emerging from the Protestant Reformation—was widespread. This was a crucial observation because Weber also knew that Calvinists, as an ideal type, approached life in a highly disciplined and rational way.

Central to the religious views spread by John Calvin (1509–1564) is the doctrine of *predestination*. This means that God, with complete control over the universe, has selected some people for salvation and others for eternal damnation. With an individual's fate predestined before birth, Calvinists were taught that there was nothing people could do to alter their destiny. Nor could individuals even know their fate. The only certainty was what hung in the balance: heavenly glory or hellfire for all of eternity.

The life of Calvinists, then, was framed by visions of salvation or damnation. The anxiety of not knowing one's fate is obvious. Calvinists gradually came to a resolution of sorts: those chosen for glory in the next world should see signs of being favored in *this* world. Calvinists came to view worldly prosperity as just such a sign of divine favor. Anxious to acquire this reassuring sign of God's approval, Calvinists became absorbed in a quest for worldly success, rationally applying discipline and hard work to their lives. Their pursuit of riches was not for its own sake, since spending money self-indulgently was clearly sinful. Calvinists also had little motivation to share their wealth with the poor, since poverty was a sign of rejection by God. Their ever-present purpose was simply to carry out God's will as effectively as possible. In Weber's terms, they viewed their work as a divine *"calling."*

Calvinists established the roots of capitalism by reinvesting their profits for greater success. They deliberately and piously used wealth to generate more wealth, practicing personal thrift and readily embracing the technological advances that accompanied the Industrial Revolution.

In this way, explained Weber, Calvinism stood apart from other world religions. Catholicism, which had dominated Europe before the Protestant Reformation, encouraged a more traditional, "otherworldly" acceptance of one's lot on earth in hopes of greater rewards in the life to come. For Catholics, then, one's material wealth or poverty had little spiritual significance. And so it was, Weber explained, that industrial capitalism became well established primarily in areas of Europe in which Calvinism was strong.

Weber's study of Calvinism gives striking evidence of the power of ideas—which Marx considered to be merely a reflection of the process of material production—to shape all of society. Weber's analysis does not imply, however, that something as complex as industrial capitalism has only one cause. On the contrary, such simplicity would have offended Weber, whose work was partly an effort to broaden what he saw as Marx's narrow explanation of modern society in economic terms. Later in his career, in fact, Weber (1961; orig. 1920) stressed that the development of industrial capitalism was exceedingly complex, involving both economic and legal factors in addition to a distinctive world view (Collins, 1986).

Weber continued to believe, however, that the defining characteristic of the modern world was rationality. When the religious fervor that motivated early Calvinists weakened in later generations, he noted, success-seeking personal discipline remained. A religious ethic became simply a "work ethic," in search of profit rather than the glory of God. From this point of view, industrial capitalism can be thought of as a "disenchanted" religion, pursuing wealth for its own sake. It is revealing that the term *accounting*, which was to the early Calvinists a written record of one's daily moral deeds, is today associated simply with monetary concerns.

Rationality and Modern Society

Weber believed that, by encouraging the Industrial Revolution and the development of capitalism, rationality defined the character of modern society. Various ways in which rationality shapes modern societies are suggested below.

1. **Distinctive social institutions.** In part, rationality is evident in the emergence of distinctive **social institutions,** defined as *major structural parts of society that address one or more basic activities.* Within the earliest hunting and gathering societies, the family took responsibility for virtually everything people did. Gradually, however, other social institutions, including religious, political, and economic systems, emerged apart from the family. Within modern societies, formal education and health care have also developed. These social institutions—all of which are detailed in later chapters—are rational strategies for more efficiently addressing societal goals.

2. **Specialization.** The development of distinctive social institutions means that human activity is increasingly specialized. In traditional societies, all people typically engage in the same activities. The rational organization of modern society, however, separates human activity into numerous specialized tasks and responsibilities. Indeed, as members of modern societies, we spend our working lives in narrowly defined activity such as biology, welding, or driving a taxi. Moreover, much of our personal identity is based on our occupation.

3. **Personal Discipline.** Modern society encourages its members to be deliberate in their actions, pursuing life goals in a disciplined way. For early Calvinists, of course, discipline was rooted in religious belief. Although now somewhat disenchanted from its religious origin, discipline is still encouraged in modern society through values such as achievement, success, and efficiency. In addition, personal

discipline is encouraged by extensive rules and regulations that surround our working lives.

4. **Awareness of time.** A central quality of a modern, rational world view is awareness of time. Traditional societies mark the passing of time by observing the rhythm of the sun, the moon, and the seasons. In modern, rational societies, by contrast, people schedule many daily activities according to the *precise* time, down to the hour and minute. In societies that embrace a national world view, therefore, the wristwatch becomes an almost standard personal item. In addition, rationality turns attention from the past to the present and future as people seek to improve their lives.

5. **Technical competence.** Societies of the past evaluated their members largely on the basis of *who* they were, meaning how they were related to others within the web of kinship. Rationality within modern society, then, encourages us to judge people according to *what* they are, that is, their technical skills and personal abilities.

6. **Impersonality.** Since a rational society values technical competence above personal relationships, the world becomes impersonal. As Max Weber and

Max Weber agreed with Marx that modern society is alienating. As the painting by George Tooker suggests, however, alienation can be as much a result of rigid bureaucratic organization as social inequality.

a host of other sociologists have observed, modern societies often seem to be filled with strangers. This is because rational social organization is increasingly the interplay of specialists concerned with tasks rather than people concerned with human feelings. Weber explained that personal feelings and emotions tend to be devalued as "irrational," as they are frequently at odds with rational principles.

7. **Large-scale organizations.** Finally, rationality is evident in the increasing importance to society of large-scale organizations. As early as the horticultural era, organizations were created deliberately to organize and oversee activities such as religious celebrations, public works, and warfare. As societies became larger and more complex, such organizations also grew in size. By the time agrarian societies were established in Europe, for example, the Catholic Church had become an enormous organization with thousands of officials who maintained its political and religious influence.

Still, Weber argued, even large organizations with agrarian societies were not completely rational because their goals were primarily the preservation of tradition. Both the Catholic Church and traditional ruling monarchies, for example, were powerfully conservative forces in medieval Europe. Truly rational organizations, in which traditional concerns have been dissolved by demands for efficiency, only recently emerged in Western societies as rationality became a dominant world view. The elaborate type of social organization commonly called *bureaucracy* emerged as a result of the rationalization of society; bureaucracy, then, has much in common with industrial capitalism.

Rational Organization: Bureaucracy

Bureaucracy is central to Weber's analysis of rationality and society. Modern society involves innumerable complex tasks, and these are efficiently carried out by large-scale organizations, including businesses, government agencies, labor unions, and universities. A full discussion of bureaucracy is found in Chapter 7 ("Groups and Organizations"). What is important for the present is that Weber viewed bureaucracy as the clearest expression of a rational world view because its organizational elements—people, offices, duties, and policies—are designed to achieve specific goals as efficiently as possible. In addition, any part of the organization is likely to be modified if doing so will make the organization even more efficient. In contrast, traditional social organization, which places little emphasis on efficiency, is typically hostile to change. Weber asserted that bureaucracy had done for society as a whole what industrialization had done for the production of material goods:

> The decisive reason for the advance of bureaucratic organization has always been its purely technical superiority over any other form of organization. The fully developed bureaucratic apparatus compares with other organizations exactly as does the machine with the nonmechanical modes of production. (1978:973; orig. 1921)

Rational bureaucracy also has a natural affinity to capitalism, as Weber noted:

> Today, it is primarily the capitalist market economy which demands that the official business of public administration be discharged precisely, unambiguously, continuously, and with as much speed as possible. Normally, the very large capitalist enterprises are themselves unequalled models of strict bureaucratic organization. (1978:974; orig. 1921)

Rationality and Alienation

So far, we have emphasized the unparalleled efficiency of modern society. Worth remembering, however, is that Karl Marx reached much the same conclusion, at least as far as the productive efficiency of industrial capitalism was concerned. At the same time, however, Marx ultimately rejected this type of society based on alienation and other destructive consequences of economic inequality.

Weber, too, was highly critical of modern society, although for different reasons. For Weber, the primary problem was not the economic inequality that so troubled Marx. Rather, the price of rational efficiency appeared to be alienation and dehumanization as people were stifled by bureaucratic impersonality and regulation.

Large-scale organizations, Weber observed, tend to treat people as cases rather than as individuals. In addition, much of modern society's highly specialized work involves tedious repetition. Perhaps most important, Weber feared that the human spirit was being extinguished by rational formality. In the end, Weber envisioned modern society as a vast and growing system of rules and regulations that sought to direct rationally virtually every human activity. In this way, he worried, human beings were becoming alienated from their essential spontaneity and creativity.

The irony we found in the work of Marx appears once again: rather than serving humanity, modern society turns on its creators and enslaves them. In language reminiscent of Marx's description of the human toll of industrial capitalism, Weber portrayed the modern individual as "only a small cog in a ceaselessly moving mechanism which prescribes to him an endlessly fixed routine of march" (1978:988; orig. 1921).

Despite the obvious advantages of modern society over earlier types of societies, Weber was deeply pessimistic. More and more, modern society was coming to resemble one vast "machine," which "chained" people to their work despite their efforts to "squirm free." Weber wondered if the logical conclusion of the rationalization of society would be the reduction of people to mere robots.

EMILE DURKHEIM: SOCIETY AND FUNCTION

"To love society is to love something beyond us and something in ourselves." These are the words of Emile Durkheim, one of the founding architects of sociology, introduced in the box on page 112. In this curious phrase[2] we find another influential vision of human society.

Social Fact: Society Beyond Ourselves

The starting point for understanding the work of Emile Durkheim is the concept of **social fact,** *any part of society that is argued to have an objective existence apart from the individual and is therefore able to influence individual behavior.* Familiar examples of social facts are cultural norms and values, described in the last chapter, or the degree of social integration that Durkheim found to influence suicide rates, as noted in Chapter 1 ("The Sociological Perspective").

Durkheim's concept of social facts becomes clearer with three additional observations. First, Durkheim viewed society as *structured,* that is, as an array of social patterns in an orderly relationship to one another. Second, because humans live in the midst of society, these patterns shape our thoughts and actions. Third, these patterns can be thought of as *"facts"* because they have an objective existence or life of their own apart from any individual's subjective experience of them.

For Durkheim, then, society is more than the sum

---

[2] *Sociology and Philosophy,* 1974:55; orig. 1924.

of its parts. People, as individuals, do not represent the essence of society. Rather, society is an elaborate, collective creation, which takes on a certain "life" and momentum of its own. Society confronts its creators as something beyond themselves, demanding a measure of obedience. A first-grade classroom, a family sitting down to dinner, and a country auction are commonplace situations that have an existence apart from any particular individual who has ever participated in them. Social situations not only shape peoples' behavior, but they affect our thoughts and feelings as well; the power of society is, therefore, experienced as *morality*. For Durkheim, the nature of society lies in its separate power as something that precedes us, makes claims on us while we are here, and remains after we are gone.

Function: Society in Action

The next step in understanding Durkheim's vision of society is the concept of *function*. Along with Herbert Spencer, who was introduced in Chapter 1, Durkheim helped to formulate what we now call the "structural-functional paradigm" in sociology. The significance of social facts, Durkheim argued, is discovered, not in the experience of individuals, but in the functional contribution of social facts to the general life of society itself.

Without sociological insight, Durkheim reasoned, common sense misleads us into understanding events solely in terms of ourselves or other individuals. Crime, for instance, brings to mind the harm that offenders inflict on their victims. For Durkheim, though, the essential character of crime has little to do with particular people but involves society as a system. As Chapter 8 ("Deviance") explains in detail, only through identifying and responding to some acts as criminal can society exist as a moral system. The *social function* of crime is something most people will never recognize: generating and sustaining the moral power of society. For this reason, Durkheim rejected the view of crime as "pathological" behavior that we should seek to eliminate. On the contrary, he viewed crime as quite "normal" for the most basic of reasons: no society has ever existed without it or *could* exist without it (1964a, orig. 1895; 1964b, orig. 1893).

Emile Durkheim (1858–1917)

Why would the desire to be a sociology professor be controversial? Because there *weren't* any, at least not in France until Emile Durkheim became the first in 1887. Up to this time, human behavior had been understood almost exclusively in terms of biology and psychology. But Durkheim argued that one cannot comprehend humanity by looking simply within the individual. Instead, he urged, understanding individuals demands examining their society.

In Chapter 1 ("The Sociological Perspective"), we encountered persuasive evidence of the power of society to shape the lives of individuals. By studying suicide, among the most personal and individualistic of actions, Durkheim showed that precisely where people are embedded within society—as males or females, rich or poor, or as members of various religions—affects their suicide rates. In other words, this variation reflects not differences among *individuals*, but how *society* affects individual lives.

Durkheim is introduced here because his work, like that of the other social thinkers previously discussed, is central to the discipline of sociology and is used extensively in later chapters. Durkheim's contributions to the understanding of crime are especially significant, and they figure prominently in Chapter 8 ("Deviance"). He also spent much of his life investigating religion, and we include his ideas on this subject in Chapter 17 ("Religion"). Just as important, Durkheim is also one of the major architects of the structural-functional paradigm, which is used in almost every chapter that follows.

Durkheim's work suggests that material affluence, especially when rapidly gained, disrupts established social patterns enhancing individualism and anomie. The improving standard of living during this century has been accompanied by a rising suicide rate, especially among privileged young people.

The Individual: Society in Ourselves

We began by suggesting that while society is "beyond us," with an existence of its own, it is also "something in ourselves." Individuals, in Durkheim's view, build personalities by internalizing social facts from the surrounding society. We develop humanity only insofar as we receive moral education from society, which regulates the natural insatiability of human beings. We are in danger of being overpowered by our desires, Durkheim observed, because "the more one has, the more one wants, since satisfactions received only stimulate instead of filling needs" (1966; orig. 1897). Society, then, must necessarily make claims on each of us.

The need for societal regulation is evident in Durkheim's study of suicide (1966; orig. 1897), detailed in Chapter 1. In nineteenth-century France, as well as in the United States today, it is precisely the categories of people *least* regulated by society that suffer the *highest* rates of suicide. Today, for example, the greater autonomy afforded to males is evident in a suicide rate four times higher than that among females.

The diminishing regulation of people by society generates individualism. Such a condition was described by Durkheim as **anomie,** *a condition in which society provides little moral guidance to individuals.* People leaping from the windows of office buildings during a stock-market crash is perhaps the extreme case of anomic suicide. In this case, a radical collapse of the social environment disrupts society's support and regulation of the individual, sometimes with deadly results. Interestingly, sudden affluence does much the same, tearing individuals out of established social patterns and overwhelming them with unregulated free choice. The lives of the rock performers of recent decades who experienced sudden stardom suggest that self-destructiveness and even anomic suicide under such conditions are all too common.

Durkheim was an outspoken defender of individual rights against what he viewed as unfair social prejudices. Even so, he never doubted that the needs of the individual must be balanced by the claims and guidance of society. Nowhere has this balance become more precarious than in the modern world.

Evolving Societies: The Division of Labor

Like Karl Marx and Max Weber, Emile Durkheim experienced first-hand the rapid social changes that were breaking across Europe during the nineteenth century. Durkheim saw in this process monumental implications for the operation of society.

Looking back in time, Durkheim could see that European societies were everywhere losing their traditions. Analyzing tradition, Durkheim concluded that societies with simple technology have a strong orientation to the past, so that they are powerful moral systems

Historically, most members of human societies have engaged in the same basic activities: building shelters and obtaining food. Modern societies, claimed Durkheim, have a rapidly expanding division of labor. Increasing specialization is evident on the streets of societies beginning to industrialize: providing people with their weight is the livelihood of this man in Istanbul, Turkey; on a Bombay street in India, another earns a small fee for cleaning ears.

demanding extensive conformity. What he described as the *"collective conscience"* of such societies demands that any person who dares to differ very much from others be repressed or punished. Such intense moral consensus Durkheim termed **mechanical solidarity**, meaning *social bonds, common to preindustrial societies, based on shared moral sentiments.* In the horticultural and agrarian societies described by the Lenskis, for example, social solidarity is *based on likeness,* since everyone in these societies does much the same things and views the world mostly in the same way. Durkheim called such solidarity mechanical because people feel that they belong together more or less automatically.

For Durkheim, the decline of this kind of social solidarity marked the emergence of modern society. With modern society, he continued, came a new type of solidarity that emerged to fill some of the void left by lost tradition. Durkheim described this new social integration as **organic solidarity**, defined as *social bonds, common to industrial societies, based on specialization.* Social solidarity *based on difference* arises from people who, although no longer conforming to one another as much, find that their specialization makes them depend on one another. Therefore, the key to this entire process is the growing **division of labor,** or *specialized economic activity,* common to industrial societies. As we have already seen in Max Weber's ideas, such societies rationally promote efficiency through specialization. From Durkheim's point of view, the result is a complex web of interdependence by which each of us relies on tens of thousands of others—most entirely unknown—who help produce the products and provide the services we use every day.

Modern organic solidarity, then, has the same overall function as traditional mechanical solidarity: maintaining the unified operation of society. But there is a crucial difference: as members of modern societies, we depend more and more on anonymous people whom we feel we can trust less and less. Why, after all, should we trust those with whom we have so little in common? In part, the answer is "because we depend on them," but trust becomes hard in a world that has lost much of its moral foundation. What we might call "Durkheim's Dilemma" is that the positive benefits of modern society, including technological advance and greater personal freedom, are achieved only at the cost of undermining morality and unleashing the ever-present danger of anomie.

Durkheim certainly found much to celebrate in modern society, especially the emergence of diverse human personalities. Like Marx and Weber, though, he clearly had misgivings about the direction society was taking. Still, of the three, Durkheim was probably the most optimistic. This confidence in the future sprang from his hope that we could create for ourselves, while enjoying greater freedom, the much-needed moral support and regulation that had once been provided for us by tradition.

CRITICAL EVALUATION: FOUR VISIONS OF SOCIETY

At the beginning of this chapter, we presented several important questions about the operation of human society. To conclude, we shall see how these questions are answered within the four visions of society we have examined.

How Do Societies of the Past and Present Differ?

For the Lenskis, societies throughout human history differ primarily in terms of their productive technology. Modern society is distinctive primarily because of its industrial technology. Karl Marx also stressed historical differences in the productive system, but was more concerned with demonstrating that material production in all historical societies (except for the simple hunters and gatherers) generates social conflict. For Marx, modern society stands out only in that social conflict has become more obvious. In contrast to Marx, Max Weber distinguished societies in terms of characteristic modes of human thought. Preindustrial societies, he claimed, were traditional, while modern societies are based on a rational view of the world. Finally, for Emile Durkheim, societies differ in how they are held together. The preindustrial solidarity based on likeness gives way in industrial societies to solidarity based on difference.

How and Why Do Societies Change?

Here again, the social thinkers we have considered provide different insights. The Lenskis see social change as primarily a matter of technological innovation that, over time, can transform an entire society. Marx pointed to the struggle between classes as the "engine of history" that pushes societies toward revolutionary reorganization. Weber complemented Marx's materialism with an idealist view, showing that modes of thought are also important to social change. He demonstrated how the rational thinking characteristic of Calvinism contributed to the Industrial Revolution and reorganized much of modern

society. Finally, Durkheim viewed change in terms of an expanding division of labor, required, he claimed, by the increasing complexity of human societies.

How Are Societies United and Divided?

The Lenskis show that all societies are united by cultural patterns, although these patterns change according to a society's level of technological development. They note, too, that inequality tends to intensify with advancing technology, although diminishing somewhat with the onset of industrialization. Marx argued that material production places classes in opposition throughout history. From his point of view, social unity could only occur if production became a truly cooperative enterprise. Without denying the importance of economic divisions, Weber claimed that societies typically have a distinctive world view shared by their populations. Just as tradition has fused people together in the past, so rational, large-scale organizations now link the lives of people in modern societies. Working within the structural-functional paradigm, Durkheim focused on social solidarity. He contrasted the mechanical solidarity of preindustrial societies with modern society's organic solidarity, fostered by an increasing division of labor. Durkheim's analysis also helps us to understand why modern societies allow (and even encourage) individuals to cultivate a measure of individual distinctiveness.

Are Human Societies Improving or Not?

Based on what they see as the historical path of human societies, the social thinkers included in this chapter have different views of human progress. The Lenskis suggest that industrial societies provide important advantages, such as a higher standard of living and a longer life span. But the potential threat to our planet posed by advancing technology—through war or environmental pollution—makes the Lenskis unwilling to equate technological advance with overall quality of life. More certain is that rapid technological change means that societies of the future will experience further dramatic transformation.

Marx applauded the power of advancing technology, but he concluded that only the few would enjoy its benefits until society underwent an essential *social* reconstruction. He looked to the future for a final resolution of historical class conflict as socialism placed the productive system under the control of all the people.

Weber found little comfort in Marx's vision, fearing that socialist revolution would only intensify the power of large-scale organizations to dominate the lives of individuals. Thus, his view of the course of human society is probably the most pessimistic of all.

Durkheim, in contrast, is the most optimistic. He saw in the twilight of tradition the possibility for more freedom than individuals had ever known. Individualism has it dangers, however, as Durkheim's concern with anomie suggests. Despite his reservations, Durkheim probably comes closest to applauding the history of human societies as genuine "progress."

The significant differences among these four approaches do not mean that any one of them is, in an absolute sense, right or wrong. Society is exceedingly complex, and we shall turn again and again to the work of all of these social thinkers in later chapters.

SUMMARY

Gerhard and Jean Lenski

1. The Lenskis' model of sociocultural evolution links social change to technological advance.
2. Beginning with earliest human history, hunting and gathering societies are composed of a small number of family-centered nomads. These societies are rapidly vanishing from the world.
3. Horticultural societies, which emerged about ten thousand years ago, used hand tools for cultivation. Pastoral societies are nomadic, domesticating animals and engaging in extensive trade.
4. Agrarian societies, which appeared some five thousand years ago, use animal-drawn plows for agriculture. Often growing to vast empires, they are more specialized, richer, and more unequal.
5. Industrial societies, arising about 250 years ago in Europe, power sophisticated machinery with advanced sources of energy. Social change is typically rapid. Most people live in cities, and highly specialized activities take place apart from the family.

Karl Marx

6. Marx understood society in terms of conflict between social classes. Classes are production-based, making Marx's analysis materialist.
7. Social conflict has characterized human history since the earliest hunting and gathering societies. Conflict in "ancient" societies involved masters and slaves; in agrarian societies, nobility and serfs;

in industrial-capitalist societies, the bourgeoisie and the proletariat.
8. Industrial-capitalism alienates workers in four ways: from the act of working, from the products of work, from other workers, and from human potential.
9. Marx believed that workers could overcome resistance from elites and their own false consciousness to ultimately overthrow the industrial-capitalist system.

Max Weber

10. The idealist approach of Max Weber showed that ways of thinking have a powerful effect on society.
11. The rationality of modern society contrasts to the tradition of feudal society; Weber described this transformation as the rationalization of society.
12. Weber feared that rationality and the anonymous organizations it fosters would stifle human creativity.

Emile Durkheim

13. Durkheim claimed that society confronts the individual as an external, objective fact.
14. Various elements can be related to the operation of society as a whole through their functions.
15. Societies require solidarity; mechanical solidarity is based on traditional likeness, while organic solidarity is based on the division of labor, or productive specialization.

KEY CONCEPTS

agrarian society a society that engages in large-scale agriculture based on the use of plows drawn by animals

alienation the experience of powerlessness in social life

anomie a condition in which society provides little moral guidance to individuals

capitalists those who own factories and other productive enterprises

class consciousness the recognition by workers of their unity as a social class in opposition to capitalists and to capitalism itself

division of labor specialized economic activity

false consciousness the belief that the shortcomings of individuals themselves, rather than society, are responsible for many of the personal problems that people experience

horticultural society a society that uses hand tools to cultivate plants

hunting and gathering society a society that uses simple technology to hunt animals and gather vegetation

ideal type an abstract statement of the essential characteristics of any social phenomenon

industrial society a society that uses sophisticated machinery powered by advanced fuels to produce material goods

mechanical solidarity social bonds, common to preindustrial societies, based on shared moral sentiments

organic solidarity social bonds, common to industrial societies, based on specialization

pastoral society a society whose livelihood is based on the domestication of animals

proletariat those who provide the labor necessary for the operation of factories and other productive enterprises

rationality deliberate, matter-of-fact calculation of the most efficient means to accomplish any particular goal

rationalization of society the change from tradition to rationality as the dominant mode of human thought

social conflict struggle among segments of society over valued resources

social fact any part of society that is argued to have an objective existence apart from the individual and is therefore able to influence individual behavior

social institution a major structural part of society that addresses one or more basic activities

society people who interact with one another within a limited territory and who share a culture

sociocultural evolution the process of social change resulting from gaining new cultural elements, particularly technology

tradition sentiments and beliefs about the world that are passed from generation to generation

verstehen a German word meaning the act of interpreting how individuals in a particular social setting understand themselves

---

SUGGESTED READINGS

A comprehensive account of Gerhard and Jean Lenski's analysis of human societies is the following textbook.

> Gerhard Lenski and Jean Lenski. *Human Society: An Introduction to Macrosociology.* 5th ed. New York: McGraw-Hill, 1987.

An overview of selected world societies at varying levels of technological development, accompanied by dozens of striking photographs, is found in this recent book.

> John Reader. *Man on Earth.* Austin: University of Austin Press, 1988.

Using the theorists included in this chapter, as well as literary figures, this book examines the emergence of sociology amidst the changes of the nineteenth century.

> Bruce Mazlish. *A New Science: The Breakdown of Connections and the Birth of Sociology.* New York: Oxford University Press, 1989.

This is one of the best sources of essays by Karl Marx and Friedrich Engels.

> Robert C. Tucker, ed. *The Marx-Engels Reader.* 2nd ed. New York: W. W. Norton, 1978.

Perhaps Max Weber's best-known study is his analysis of Protestantism and capitalism.

> Max Weber. *The Protestant Ethic and the Spirit of Capitalism.* New York: Charles Scribner's Sons, 1958 (orig. 1904–05).

This collection of essays investigates various issues that show

Max Weber's skills at incorporating history, politics, and social criticism into his work.

> Wolfgang J. Mommsen. *The Political and Social Theory of Max Weber: Collected Essays.* Chicago: University of Chicago Press, 1989.

One of the best volumes on Emile Durkheim is this one.

> Steven Lukes. *Emile Durkheim, His Life and Work: A Historical and Critical Study.* New York: Harper & Row, 1972.

Much of the discussion of this chapter centers on the societies of Europe; human society, however, is a global phenomenon. This book examines the state of world societies at a time when Europe played only a minor role in world affairs.

> Janet Abu-Lughod. *Before European Hegemony: The World System A.D. 1250–1350.* New York: Oxford University Press, 1989.

Essays in this paperback develop the theme that the vitality of sociological thinking rests on its moral content.

> Mark L. Wardell and Stephen P. Turner, eds. *Sociological Theory in Transition.* Boston: Allen & Unwin, 1986.

Sociological theory has yet to respond adequately to the large number of women who entered sociology in recent decades. This book is a step in that direction.

> Ruth A. Wallace, ed. *Feminism and Sociological Theory.* Newbury Park, CA: Sage Publications, 1989.

5
Socialization

On a cold winter day in 1938, a concerned social worker paid a call to a farmhouse in rural Pennsylvania and found a five-year-old girl hidden in a second-floor storage room. The child, whose name was Anna, was wedged into an old chair with her arms tied above her head so that she could not move. She was dressed in only a few filthy garments, and her arms and legs were like matchsticks—so thin and frail that she could not use them (Davis 1940:554).

Anna's situation was both moving and tragic. She was born in 1932 to an unmarried woman of twenty-six who lived with her father. Enraged by his daughter's "illegitimate" motherhood, he initially refused to even have the child in his house. Anna therefore spent the first six months of her life in various children's homes. Finally, because her mother was unable to pay for such care, and her grandfather was unwilling to do so, Anna was returned to live with her mother and grandfather.

At this point, her ordeal intensified. The grandfather's continuing hostility and the mother's apparent indifference resulted in Anna being kept in a room that resembled an attic, where she received little attention and just enough milk to keep her alive. There she stayed, with essentially no human contact, for five years.

Upon reading of the discovery of Anna, sociologist Kingsley Davis traveled immediately to see the child, who had been taken by local authorities to a county home for children. He was appalled by her condition.

Anna was emaciated, devoid of strength, and she displayed virtually no human qualities whatever. She could not laugh, show anger, speak, or even smile. She was completely apathetic, as if the world around her did not even exist. Not surprisingly, she was initially assumed to be deaf and blind (Davis, 1940).

THE IMPORTANCE OF SOCIAL EXPERIENCE

Here is a case, at once deplorable but instructive, of a human being deprived of virtually all social contact. Although Anna was physically alive, she had none of

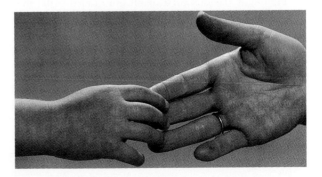

the abilities and responsiveness associated with full humanity. This incident reveals the need for social experience to endow us with the capacity for thought, emotion, and meaningful action. Without such experience we remain, like Anna, more an *object* than a *person*.

This chapter explores what Anna was deprived of: the process by which we become fully human. We call this **socialization,** *the lifelong process of social experience by which individuals develop their human potential and learn the patterns of their culture.* Unlike other species of life for which behavior is determined biologically, human beings depend on culture gained from social experience for survival. Moreover, social experience is the foundation of **personality,** which refers to *a person's fairly consistent pattern of thinking, feeling, and acting.* Personality is constructed from our social surroundings and how we learn to respond to them. As personality develops, we simultaneously become distinctive individuals and gain the ability to share in a culture. In the absence of social experience, as the case of Anna shows, personality simply does not develop.

Social experience is as vital for all of society as it is for the individual. A society has a life that extends both forward and backward in time, far beyond the life span of any individual. As explained in Chapters 3 ("Culture") and 4 ("Society"), every society teaches something of its past and present way of life to its new members. The complex and lifelong process of socialization is the fundamental way in which culture is transmitted from one generation to another (Elkin & Handel, 1984).

Human Development: Nature and Nurture

Virtually helpless at birth, the human infant needs care and nourishment from others to survive. A child also relies on others to learn patterns of culture. Although Anna's short life makes these facts very clear, for many years the importance of social experience to individual development was obscured by an unfounded belief that human behavior was directed almost entirely by biology.

Chapter 3 ("Culture") described Charles Darwin's ground-breaking work in the mid-nineteenth century. In brief, Darwin's theory of evolution held that a species gradually changes over many generations as genetic variations lead to more successful survival and reproduction. As Darwin's influence grew, his ideas were applied to the understanding of human behavior. "Naturalists" claimed that all human behavior was instinctive, or part of the "nature" of the human species. By the end of the nineteenth century, most human behavior was under-

stood in this way—and such notions are still with us. It is sometimes claimed, for example, that our economic system is a reflection of "instinctive human competitiveness," that some people are "born criminals," or that females are more emotional while males are more rational (Witkin-Lanoil, 1984). The term *human nature* is often used in this way to mean personality traits that people are supposedly born with, just as we are born with five senses. However, correctly understood, human nature involves the creation and learning of cultural traits, as we shall see.

The naturalist argument was also adapted to explain how entire societies differed from one another. Centuries of world exploration and empire building brought Western Europeans into contact with people who were quite different from themselves. Usually, they attributed the differences to biological characteristics rather than to cultural diversity. Thus Europeans and North Americans viewed the members of technologically simple societies as biologically less evolved (and, thus, less human) forms of life. This self-serving and ethnocentric view helped them, of course, justify their colonial practices. It is easy to enter another society, exploit its resources, and perhaps enslave its people if you believe they are not truly human in the same sense you are.

In the twentieth century, naturalistic explanations of human behavior were challenged. Psychologist John B. Watson (1878–1958) developed an approach called *behaviorism,* claiming that human behavior is not instinctive but learned within a social environment. Arguing that all of the world's cultures have the same biological foundation, Watson also rejected the idea that cultural variations reflect any evolutionary distinctions. In short, Watson viewed human behavior as malleable, open to the influence of any imaginable environment.

> Give me a dozen healthy infants . . . and my own specified world to bring them up in, and I will guarantee to take any one at random and train him to become any type of specialist that I might select—doctor, lawyer, artist, merchant-chief, and yes, even beggar-man and thief—regardless of his talents, penchants, tendencies, abilities, vocations, and race of his ancestors. (1930:104)

Watson was aware that he was somewhat overstating his case, but he was convinced that the widespread view that linked human behavior to biology was fundamentally wrong and that nurture—or learning—was far more influential than "nature."

Watson's assertions were supported by more and more research. Anthropologists were able to show that cultural patterns were highly variable, even among soci-

Present at birth, reflexes are behavioral patterns that enhance the likelihood of survival. The sucking reflex, which may begin before birth, clearly assists the infant in obtaining nourishment. The grasping reflex can be demonstrated by placing a finger in the infant's palm, causing the hand to close. This reflex helps the infant to maintain contact with a parent as well as to grasp objects. The Moro reflex, which occurs when an infant is startled, causes the arms to spread outward and then come together on the chest. This grasping action, which disappears after several months, probably developed among our evolutionary ancestors so that a falling baby would grasp the body hair of a parent.

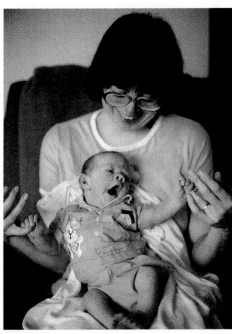

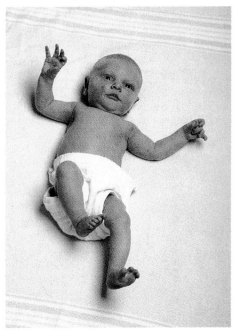

eties using similar technology. An outspoken proponent of the "nurture" view of human behavior, noted anthropologist Margaret Mead summed up the evidence: "The differences between individuals who are members of different cultures, like the differences between individuals within a culture, are almost entirely to be laid to differences in conditioning, especially during early childhood, and this conditioning is culturally determined" (1963:280; orig. 1935).

Today, social scientists are cautious about describing *any* human behavioral trait as instinctive. Even the development of sociobiology, discussed in Chapter 3

("Culture"), has not challenged the conclusion that human behavior is primarily a consequence of learning within a cultural system. This does not mean that biology has no part in human behavior. Obviously, all life depends on the functioning of the human body. We also know that children share some of the biological traits of their parents, especially physical characteristics such as height, weight, hair and eye color, and facial features. Heredity probably also has some importance in the transmission of intelligence and personality characteristics (such as how one reacts to stimulation). The potential to excel in such activities as art and music may also have a genetic component. Of course, whether or not any inherited potential is developed will depend upon the opportunities associated with social position (Plomin & Foch, 1980; Goldsmith, 1983). Overall, then, there is little doubt that nurture is far more important than nature in shaping human behavior. But bear in mind, as suggested in Chapter 3, that what we call human nature is the creation, learning, and modification of culture. Thus, nature and nurture are not so much in opposition as they are inseparable.

Social Isolation

For obvious ethical reasons, researchers cannot conduct experiments involving the social isolation of human beings. Consequently, much of what we know about this issue comes from rare cases of children like Anna subjected to this kind of abuse. Even then, researchers typi-

The research of Harry and Margaret Harlow demonstrates the importance of physical contact to emotional development. The Harlows found that the infant monkey's ability to hug even a soft artificial "mother" lessened the detrimental effects of social isolation.

cally enter the picture at the end of an ordeal and have to piece together what happened over a period of years. For this reason, research into the effects of social isolation has made use of animals.

Effects of Social Isolation in Nonhuman Primates

Classic research in social isolation with nonhuman primates was carried out by psychologists Harry and Margaret Harlow (1962). The Harlows placed rhesus monkeys—whose behavior is in some ways surprisingly similar to that of human beings—in various conditions of social isolation to observe the consequences.

They found that complete social isolation for a period of even six months (though adequate nutrition was provided) was sufficient to produce serious disturbances in the monkeys' development. When subsequently introduced to others of their kind, these monkeys were fearful and unable to defend themselves against aggression.

The Harlows also placed infant rhesus monkeys in cages with an artificial mother constructed of wire mesh and a wooden head, with the nipple of a feeding tube where the breast would be. These monkeys survived physically, but they, too, were subsequently unable to interact with other monkeys. Interestingly, however, when the artificial mother was covered with soft terry cloth, the infant monkeys clung to it and appeared to derive some emotional benefit from the closeness, resulting in less emotional disturbance. The Harlows concluded that normal emotional development depends on affectionate cradling as part of mother-infant interaction.

The Harlows also made two other discoveries. First, even deprived of mother-infant contact, monkeys surrounded by other infant monkeys did not suffer adversely. This shows that it is the lack of all social experience, rather than the specific absence of maternal contact, that produces devastating effects. Second, the Harlows found that infant monkeys socially isolated for shorter periods of time (about three months) eventually regained normal emotional patterns after rejoining other monkeys. Thus they concluded that the effects of short-term isolation can be overcome; longer-term isolation, however, appeared to cause irreversible emotional and behavioral damage to the monkeys.

Effects of Social Isolation in Children

The case of Anna, described at the beginning of this chapter, is the best-known instance of the long-term social isolation of a human infant. Her discovery led to extensive social contact, and Anna soon began to show some improvement. When Kingsley Davis (1940) visited her in the county home after ten days, he noted that she was more alert and showed some human expression, even smiling with obvious pleasure. During the next year, Anna made slow but steady progress, as she experienced the humanizing effects of socialization, showing increasing interest in other people and gradually gaining the ability to walk. After a year and a half, she was able to feed herself, walk alone for short distances, and play with toys.

Consistent with the observations of the Harlows, however, it was becoming apparent that Anna's five years of social isolation may have left her permanently damaged. At the age of eight she had the mental and social development of a typical child of a year and a half. Only as she approached the age of ten did she show the first signs of using language. Complicating the problem is the fact that Anna's mother was thought to be mentally retarded, so that Anna may have been similarly disadvantaged. The puzzle was never untangled, however, because Anna died at age ten of a blood disorder, possibly related to her long years of abuse (Davis, 1940).

A second, quite similar case reveals more about the long-range effects of social isolation. At about the same time that Anna was discovered, another girl about the same age was found under strikingly similar circumstances. After over six years of virtual isolation, this girl—known as Isabelle—revealed the same lack of human responsiveness that had characterized Anna (Davis, 1947). Unlike Anna, though, Isabelle benefited from intensive efforts by psychologists to aid her development. One week after this program began, Isabelle was attempting to speak, and a year and a half later, her vocabulary was approaching two thousand words. The psychologists concluded that Isabelle had managed to progress through what is normally about six years of development in two years of intensive effort. By the time she was fourteen, Isabelle was attending sixth-grade classes in school, apparently well on her way to at least an approximately normal life.

A final case of childhood isolation involves a thirteen-year-old girl in California who was isolated in a small room from the age of about two (Pines, 1981). Upon discovery, her condition was similar to that of the other two children we have described. She was emaciated (weighing only fifty-nine pounds) and had the mental development of a one-year-old. Genie, as she came to be known, was afforded intensive treatment under the direction of specialists and is alive today. Yet even after

years of care, her ability to use language is no better than that of a young child (Pines, 1981).

All of the evidence clearly demonstrates that social experience is crucial for the development of human personality. Human beings are resilient creatures, sometimes able to recover from even the crushing experience of prolonged isolation. But, consistent with the Harlows' research with rhesus monkeys, there may be a point at which social isolation in infancy results in developmental damage, including the ability to gain language skills, that cannot be fully repaired. Precisely what this point is, however, remains unclear from the small number of cases that have been studied (Pines, 1981).

UNDERSTANDING THE SOCIALIZATION PROCESS

Socialization is highly complex, and explanations differ in approach and emphasis. The following sections introduce several twentieth-century thinkers who have made important contributions to our understanding of this process.

Sigmund Freud: The Elements of Personality

Sigmund Freud (1856–1939) lived in Vienna at a time when most Europeans viewed human behavior as a reflection of biological forces. Freud himself was trained in the natural sciences and began his career as a physician. His importance today, however, is based on his ground-breaking analysis of human personality. From this came Freud's crowning achievement, the development of psychoanalysis. This treatment of psychological problems involves exploring the unconscious mind through intensive dialogue between analyst and patient. Some aspects of Freud's work have a direct bearing on the process of socialization.

Basic Human Needs

Freud believed that biological factors play an important part in the human personality, although he did not share the view that human behavior reflects biological instinct. When he used the term *instinct*, he was referring to very general human needs in the form of *urges* or *drives*. Freud ultimately decided that there are two basic human needs. First, he claimed, all humans have a basic need for bonding, which he described as the life instinct, or *eros*. Second, and rather paradoxically, he asserted that people also have an aggressive drive, which he called the death instinct, or *thanatos*. Freud postulated that these opposing forces would generate tension within us, although we would not necessarily be conscious of this. Together, he maintained, these general drives provide the foundation for human life.

Freud's Model of Personality

Freud incorporated both basic needs and the influence of society into an overall model of personality. The model has three parts: id, ego, and superego. Freud claimed that the *id* represents *the human being's basic needs*, which are unconscious and demand immediate satisfaction. (The word *id* is simply Latin for "it," suggesting the tentative way in which Freud conceived of the unconscious mind). Rooted in the biological organism, the id is present at birth, which means that a newborn infant is basically a bundle of needs—for attention, touching, food, and so forth. Since society does not allow unlimited

Sigmund Freud is one of the pioneers who explored the complexities of the human personality. His daughter Anna Freud, also shown here in this 1913 photograph, further developed another of her father's achievements: the theory of psychoanalysis.

personal physical satisfaction, the id's desires inevitably encounter resistance, which is why the first word a child learns is often "no." The child must therefore learn to approach the world realistically. This is accomplished through the ego, the second part of the personality, which gradually becomes differentiated from the id. The ego (Latin for "I") represents *the conscious attempt to balance the innate pleasure-seeking drives of the human organism and the demands of society*. The ego arises, then, in the awareness of existing apart from society as a distinct entity; it develops in response to the fact that we cannot have everything we want. Finally, the human personality develops the superego (Latin meaning "above" or "beyond" the ego), which is *the presence of culture within the individual*. The superego may be thought of as our understanding of *why* we cannot have everything we want. It is based on internalized values and norms and is basically the same as conscience. The superego is initially a recognition of parental demands but enlarges its scope as the child learns that parental control is itself a reflection of the moral demands of the larger cultural system.

Initially, then, a child experiences the world as physical sensations linked to need satisfaction. With the gradual development of superego, however, the child's comprehension involves not only physical pleasure and pain but also moral ideas of right and wrong. In other words, initially a child can feel good only as a physical sensation. Later a child has the capacity to feel good for behaving in culturally appropriate ways and, of course, to feel bad (the experience of guilt) for failing to do so.

If the ego successfully manages the opposing forces of the id and the superego, the personality is considered to be well adjusted. If the conflict is not successfully resolved, personality disorders can result. Freud viewed childhood as the critical period for the formation of an individual's basic personality, and he believed that conflicts experienced during this stage of life can linger as an unconscious source of personality problems later on.

Freud termed society's controlling influence on the drives of each individual *repression*. In his view, some repression is inevitable, since society cannot permit all of the individual's urges to be met without some compromise. Often this compromise takes the form of redirecting these needs into socially approved forms. This process, which Freud called *sublimation*, transforms fundamentally selfish drives into more socially acceptable objectives. For example, the sexual urges of the individual may lead to marriage, or aggressive urges may be expressed in the form of competitive sports.

Critical evaluation. Freud's work was controversial within his own lifetime and some of it remains so today. His own European society vigorously repressed human sexuality, so that few of his contemporaries were prepared to admit that humans had basic sexual needs. Recently, it has been alleged that Freud's thinking depicts humanity in male terms, thereby representing a distorted view of women (Donovan & Littenberg, 1982). But certainly Freud provided a foundation that has influenced virtually all who subsequently examined the human personality. Of special importance to sociology is his notion that we internalize social norms, and that childhood experiences have lasting importance to the socialization process.

Jean Piaget: Cognitive Development

During his long life, Jean Piaget (1896–1980) became one of the foremost psychologists of the century. Much of his thinking centered on human *cognition*—the process of thought and understanding. Early in his career, Piaget became fascinated with the behavior of his own three children, wondering not only *what* they knew, but also *how* they understood the world. He gradually concluded that children's conception of the world depends upon their age. He identified four major stages of cognitive development, which he claimed reflected biological maturation as well as increasing social experience.

The Sensorimotor Stage

The first stage of human development in Piaget's model is the **sensorimotor stage**—*the level of human development in which the world is experienced only through sensory contact*. In this stage, which corresponds roughly to the first two years of life, the infant explores the world by touching, looking, sucking, and listening. By about four months of age, this leads children to distinguish their own bodies from the larger environment. As they near the end of this stage, children recognize what Piaget called *object permanence*, so that they know existence does not depend on direct, sensory contact. Initially, for example, infants think that an adult leaving the room (out of range of their senses) has ceased to exist. With time, as children learn that adults leave the room only to return, they comprehend the world more confidently and correctly.

Children become more adept at imitating the actions or sounds of others during the sensorimotor stage, but they do not have the capacity to understand or use symbols. Thus, at this stage, children do not think; they know the world only in terms of direct physical experience.

The Preoperational Stage

The second stage described by Piaget is the **preoperational stage:** *the level of human development in which language and other symbols are first used*. This stage typically begins by the age of two and extends to about seven. Using symbols, children can now engage the world mentally—that is, without having direct sensory contact with it. In short, they begin to attach meaning to the world. In addition, with the ability to distinguish between their ideas and objective reality, they need not believe that their dreams are real, and they recognize the element of fantasy in fairy tales (Kohlberg & Gilligan, 1971; Skolnick, 1986). Unlike adults, however, they attach names and meanings only in very specific terms. A child may describe a specific toy, for example, but be unable to describe the qualities of toys in general.

Furthermore, without the ability to generalize concepts, a child has no abstract conception of size, weight, and volume. One of Piaget's best-known experiments provides an illustration. He placed two identical glasses filled with the same amount of water on a table and asked several children aged five and six if the amount in each was the same. They acknowledged that it was. The children then watched Piaget take one of the glasses and pour its contents into a much taller, narrower glass, so that the level of water was now higher. He asked again if each glass held the same amount. The typical five- and six-year-old now claimed that the taller glass held more water. But children over the age of seven, who are able to think in more abstract terms, could usually comprehend that the amount of water remained the same.

During the preoperational stage of development, children still have a very egocentric view of the world (Damon, 1983). For example, you may have noticed young children placing their hands in front of their faces and exclaiming, "You can't see me!" They assume that if they cannot see you, then you must be unable to see them. This illustrates that they perceive the world only from their own vantage point and cannot imagine that a situation may appear different to another person.

The Concrete Operational Stage

The third stage in Piaget's model is the **concrete operational stage**, *the level of human development characterized*

In his well-known experiment, Piaget demonstrated that children over the age of seven entered the concrete operational stage of development as they were able to recognize that the quantity of liquid remained the same when poured from a wide beaker into a tall beaker.

by the use of logic to understand objects or events. During this stage, which typically corresponds to the years between about seven and eleven, children make significant strides in their ability to comprehend and manipulate their environment. As they begin to think logically, they connect events in terms of cause and effect. In addition, they attach more than one symbol to a particular event or object. For instance, if you say to a girl of six, "Today is Wednesday," she might respond, "No, it's my birthday!" indicating that she is able to think of an event in terms of only one symbol. Within a few years, however, she would be able to respond by saying, "Yes, this Wednesday is my birthday!" However, during the concrete operational stage, the thinking of children remains centered on concrete objects and events. They may understand that hitting their brothers without provocation will bring punishment, but they are generally unable to conceive of situations in which hitting a brother would be fair or why parents punish. Another important development during the concrete operational stage is that children begin to transcend their previous egocentrism and imaginatively put themselves in the position of another person. They learn to perceive a situation from another's point of view. As we shall explain shortly, this ability is the foundation for engaging in complex social activities, such as games, with a number of other people.

The Formal Operational Stage

The fourth stage in Piaget's model is the **formal operational stage**, which is *the level of human development characterized by highly abstract thought and the ability to imagine alternatives to reality.* Beginning at about the age of twelve, children begin to think of themselves and the world in highly abstract terms rather than only in terms of concrete situations. If, for example, you were to ask a child of seven or eight, "What would you like to be when you grow up?" a typical answer might be a concrete response such as "A teacher," "A doctor," or "An airplane pilot." Once the final stage of cognitive development is attained, however, the child is capable of making an abstract response, such as, "I would like a job that is exciting." At this point, the child has begun to imagine and evaluate entirely hypothetical alternatives. For this reason, children entering this stage often develop an interest in imaginative literature, such as science fiction (Skolnick, 1986). This capacity for abstract thought also allows the child to comprehend metaphors. Hearing the phrase "A penny for your thoughts" might lead a younger child to think of money, but the older child will recognize a gentle invitation to intimacy.

Critical evaluation. More than Freud, who viewed human beings as torn by the opposing forces of biology and society, Piaget believed the human mind to be active and creative. In other words, Piaget believed that people have considerable ability to shape their own social world, an assertion supported by other research (Corsaro & Rizzo, 1988). His contribution to understanding socialization lies in showing that this capacity unfolds gradually as the result of both biological maturation and increasing social experience.

There is some question as to whether human beings in every culture progress through Piaget's stages in the same time frame. For instance, living within a traditional society that changes very slowly is likely to inhibit the ability to imagine one's life or an entire world apart from what actually exists. In addition, Carol Gilligan (1982) has suggested that we have yet to examine adequately how being male or female affects the process of social development. Finally, among both males and females, a substantial proportion, estimated as 30 percent of thirty-year-olds, have not reached the formal operational stage (Kohlberg & Gilligan, 1971:1065). This underscores once again the importance of social experience in the development of personality. Regardless of biological maturity, people who are not exposed to highly creative and imaginative thinking are unlikely to develop this capacity in themselves. This important idea is found throughout the work of George Herbert Mead, whose ideals are presented next.

George Herbert Mead: The Social Self

What exactly is social experience? How does social experience enhance our humanity? Such fundamental questions guided the work of George Herbert Mead, who is introduced in the box. Within the discipline of sociology, Mead is widely regarded as having made the greatest contribution to explaining the process of socialization.

Mead's analysis (1962; orig. 1934) has often been described as *social behaviorism*, which suggests a connection with the behaviorist ideas of psychologist John B.

Watson, described earlier. Mead echoed Watson's view of the environment as a powerful influence on human behavior, but he also saw basic errors in Watson's approach. Watson focused on behavior itself, ignoring mental processes because he thought they could never be studied scientifically. Watson thus treated the behavior of humans and of other animals in essentially the same way. Mead conceded the difficulty of studying the human mind, but he maintained that this was important because mental activity is precisely what distinguishes humans from other animals.

The Self

In Mead's analysis, the basis of humanity is the **self**—*the individual's active awareness of existing in the midst*

PROFILE

George Herbert Mead (1863–1931)

There was probably little doubt that George Herbert Mead would become a college professor. He was born to a Massachusetts family with a strong intellectual tradition, and both his parents were academics. His mother served for ten years as president of Mount Holyoke College, and his father was both a preacher and teacher at a number of colleges.

But Mead also had a hand in shaping his own life, and in some unexpected ways. Early on, he rebelled against the strong religious environment of his home and community. After completing college, he traveled about the Pacific Northwest, surveying for the railroad and reading as much as he could. Restless and unsure of his future, he gradually settled on the idea of studying philosophy, which he did at Harvard and abroad.

Eventually, Mead settled into teaching at the new University of Chicago. But he was still far from conventional. For one thing, he rarely published, an activity expected of many academics. Indeed, his fame developed only since his death when a collection of his lecture notes was published. For another, Mead combined ideas from a wide range of related disciplines in new and interesting ways, helping to develop the new field of social psychology. Finally,

never content with life as it was, Mead was an active reformer often involved in controversial causes. He firmly believed in the human capacity to change. More broadly, living in Chicago at a time of explosive growth and overwhelming social problems, Mead labored to improve the lives of the city's disadvantaged.

George Herbert Mead envisioned both an individual biography and the life of an entire society as an ongoing process. In fact, his own life reveals both the power of society to shape individuals and the power of individuals to shape society. This theme, developed within the symbolic-interaction approach in sociology, is perhaps his greatest contribution to the study of socialization.

SOURCE: Based, in part, on Lewis A. Coser, *Masters of Sociological Thought* (New York: Harcourt Brace Jovanovich, 1971), pp. 333–355; also James A. Schellenberg, *Masters of Social Psychology* (New York: Oxford University Press, 1978), pp. 38–62.

of society. Mead's genius lay in seeing the self as inseparable from society, a connection that can be explained in a series of steps. First, Mead asserted, the self emerges as a result of social experience. Thus the self is not biological, it is not the same as any part of the body, and it does not exist at birth. Mead therefore rejected the view that human personality and behavior reflect biological drives (as asserted by Freud) or biological maturation (as Piaget claimed). For Mead, the self develops only through social experience—as one individual comes into contact with others. In the absence of such experience—as demonstrated by cases of isolated children—the body may grow but no self will emerge.

Second, Mead explained social experience as the exchange of symbols—meanings shared by people engaged in social interaction. Humans use a wave of the hand, a word, or a smile symbolically. Thus, while Mead agreed with Watson that human behavior can be shaped through manipulating the environment, he maintained that this ignores what is distinctively human in our behavior. A dog, for example, can be trained to respond to a specific stimulus, but the dog attaches no meaning to this behavior. Human beings, on the other hand, perceive behavior in terms of meanings and are as sensitive to intention as to action. In short, a dog

People everywhere are fascinated by photos of themselves. Perhaps this is because, as George Herbert Mead explained, imagining ourselves as others see us is the essence of our humanity and the foundation of all social behavior.

responds to *what you do*, but a human being responds to *what you have in mind* as you do it.

Return to our friendly dog for a moment. Using reward and punishment, you can train a dog to walk out on the porch and bring back an umbrella. But the dog grasps no intention behind the command. Thus, if the dog cannot find the umbrella, it is incapable of the *human* response: to go look for a raincoat instead. Human beings would do this because we understand actions in terms of underlying intentions.

The third step in Mead's analysis is that, in order to understand the intentions of others, humans assume one another's point of view. And by imaginatively putting ourselves in the other person's place, we are able to anticipate the other person's response to us. This mental process precedes even a simple social act such as telephoning a friend. To do this, we imagine the friend's response to us—the act of answering our own call. In this way, Mead explained, social interaction involves seeing ourselves as others see us—a process that he termed *"taking the role of the other."*

The Looking-Glass Self

Charles Horton Cooley, one of Mead's colleagues, offered a useful way of understanding the process of "taking the role of the other." He suggested that others represent a mirror or looking glass in which we imagine ourselves as they see us. Cooley (1964; orig. 1902) used the phrase **looking-glass self** to capture his idea that *a person's self-conception is based on the responses of others*. The social experience of imaginatively "putting ourselves in their shoes" is a powerful influence on how we think of ourselves.

The I and the Me

The notion that *the self thinks about itself* suggests an important dualism. First, there is *self as subject*, by which we initiate any social action. In other words, Mead claimed humans are innately active and spontaneous in their environment, initiating social interaction with others. For simplicity, he dubbed this subjective element of the self the *I* (the subjective form of the personal pronoun). Second, there is *self as object*, which is how we imagine ourselves from the perspective of someone else. Mead called this objective element of the self the *me* (the objective form of the personal pronoun). In other words, the self initiates interaction (as the I) which is guided as the self becomes an object to itself (the me) by "taking the role of the other." All social experience is a continuous interplay of the I and the me: we are spontaneous even as we are guided by how others respond to us.

Mead stressed that *thinking* is also social experience, even when we are alone. Our thoughts are partly creative (representing the I), but thinking also allows us to become objects to ourselves (representing the me) as we imagine how others would respond to our ideas. In both thought and interaction, then, human beings are self-conscious.

Development of the Self

For Mead, the self develops through gaining sophistication in taking the role of the other. Like Freud and Piaget, Mead believed early childhood was crucial to this process. He did not, however, link the development of self to stages linked closely to age. Both Freud and Piaget emphasized biological dimensions of personality development, while Mead consistently minimized the importance of biological forces. Thus Mead thought that the complexity of the self emerged over time due simply to more and more social experience.

Mead claimed that infants with limited social experience respond to others only in terms of *imitation*. At this point, they mimic behavior without understanding underlying intentions. Without symbolic interaction, Mead concluded, no self exists.

As children learn to use language and other symbols, the self begins to emerge in the form of *play*. At this stage, children begin to recreate complex patterns of behavior they observe around them by role playing. At first, this involves playing roles modeled on significant people—such as parents—who are sometimes termed *significant others*. Playing "Mommy and Daddy," for instance, helps children imagine the world from their parents' point of view.

Further social experience teaches children to take the roles of several others simultaneously in a single situation. In other words, the increasingly complex self is able to initiate different actions in response to different others. This makes possible moving from simple play involving one role to more complex *games* involving many roles at one time. It also means that a person's conception of self becomes more complex, as it is now based on numerous "looking-glasses." The box on page 131 applies Mead's analysis of play and games to several familiar activities.

The last step in the development of the self occurs as children become able to see themselves as society in general does. Figure 5–1 on page 130 shows how this is an extension of the ability to engage in play and games.

"Peek-a-boo" reveals the inability of very young children to accomplish what Mead calls taking the role of the other. Children assume that, "since I cannot see you, you cannot see me." Once this ability is gained, play such as "dress up" is common. This involves assuming the role of one other person, often a parent. Complex team sports require children to imaginatively take the roles of many other people. Thus, games such as soccer can be played only by children who have had considerable social experience.

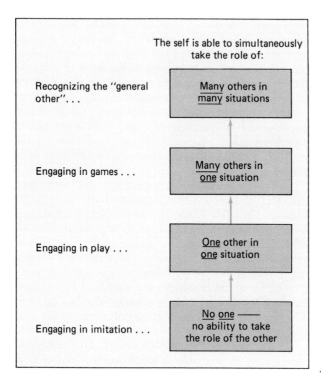

The self is able to simultaneously
take the role of:

Recognizing the "general
other"...

Many others in
many situations

Engaging in games ...

Many others in
one situation

Engaging in play ...

One other in
one situation

Engaging in imitation ...

No one ——
no ability to take
the role of the other

Figure 5–1 Building on Social Experience
George Herbert Mead described the development of self as
the process of gaining social experience. This is largely a matter
of taking the role of the other with increasing sophistication.

At this point, the individual has the capacity, at one time, to take the role of many others in many different situations. This depends on recognizing that people throughout society share cultural norms and values. As general cultural patterns are incorporated into the self, children begin to respond to themselves as they imagine *any* other person in *any* situation would. Mead used the term **generalized other** to refer to *widespread cultural norms and values used as a reference in evaluating ourselves.*

Finally, the emergence of the self is not the end of the socialization process. On the contrary, Mead considered socialization to continue as long as we have social experience. Furthermore, we may expect changing social experiences to reshape ourselves. Just as important, he stressed that social experience is *interactional:* just as society shapes us, so we act back to shape society. In other words, as active and creative beings, we play a large part in our own socialization.

Critical evaluation.   George Herbert Mead's contribution to the understanding of socialization lies in his exploration of social experience itself. He succeeded in showing how symbolic interaction is the foundation of self as well as society.

Mead's view is sometimes criticized for being radically social—meaning that it recognizes no biological element in the emergence of the self. In this, he stands apart from Freud (who identified general drives within the organism) and Piaget (whose stages of development are tied to biological maturity).

Mead's concepts of the I and the me should not be confused with Freud's concepts of the id and the superego. One difference is that Freud rooted the id in the biological organism, while Mead rejected any link between the self and biology (although he was never quite clear about the origin of the "I"). Freud's concept of the superego and Mead's concept of the me both reflect the power of society to shape the personality. But for Freud, superego and id are locked in continual combat. Mead, however, understood the I and the me as working closely together (Meltzer, 1978).

AGENTS OF SOCIALIZATION

We are affected in at least some small way by every social experience we have. In modern industrial societies, however, several agents of socialization have pronounced importance.

The Family

The family is the most important agent of socialization. As we have seen, infants are almost entirely dependent on others to meet their various needs, and this responsibility almost always falls on the family. Typically, the family is the entire social world of children, at least until the onset of schooling, and it is the agent of socialization most central to our social experiences throughout the life course (Riley, Foner, & Waring, 1988).

Family-based socialization is not all intentional. Children learn constantly from the kind of environment that is unconsciously created by adults. Whether children believe themselves to be strong or weak, smart or stupid, loved or simply tolerated—and whether they believe the world to be trustworthy or dangerous—is largely a consequence of this early environment.

The family is also central to the process of cultural

Play and Games: Taking the Roles of Others

"Playing the role" of mother, father, doctor, soldier, and so on, is the first way in which a child steps into the role of another. Often two or more children play together, perhaps as doctor and patient. Whatever else they may learn, they begin the vital human process of experiencing the world as the "other" does.

Games are a single situation in which the self takes the role of many others. An avid fan, Mead often turned to baseball to illustrate his ideas. Place yourself, then, in the role of shortstop in a baseball game. With one out and a runner on first base, the batter hits a ground ball to you, setting up the classic double-play situation. In order to respond, you have to imagine yourself through the eyes of various others. The fielder at first base normally does not expect you to throw the ball there, but the fielder at second base does, and as quickly as possible. The choice of where to throw obviously depends on viewing this process through the eyes of a *third* person, the runner moving toward second base. If this player will beat the throw, the ball goes to first in-

stead. But even that choice is contingent on a *fourth* person, the batter who is closing in on first base.

Children of four or five years of age usually have had sufficient social experience to play "catch" with one other person. But they lack the more complex social interaction characteristic of a game such as baseball, so enjoyed by older children.

SOURCE: For suggestions here and throughout the discussion of G.H. Mead, I am grateful to Howard Sacks of Kenyon College.

transmission, by which a way of life is passed from one generation to the next. In short, although parents never completely determine the development of their children, many attitudes, interests, goals, beliefs, and prejudices are acquired within the family. Also, from infancy boys and girls receive both conscious and unconscious guidance from family members in how to be "masculine" and "feminine" (Tavris & Wade, 1984; Witkin-Lanoil, 1984). In sum, much of what we consider to be innate in ourselves is actually the product of socialization within the family.

Although parenting styles obviously vary, research suggests that attention encourages the social development of children. Physical contact, verbal stimulation, and responsiveness from parents have all been shown to foster intellectual growth (Belsky, Lerner, & Spanier, 1984).

Another crucial function of the family is providing children with a social position. In other words, parents not only bring children into the physical world, they also place them within society in terms of social class, religion, race, and ethnicity. In time, all these elements of social identity also become part of our self-concept. Of course, this social placement may change in at least some respects, but it affects us throughout our lives.

Illustrating the importance of social class to socialization, Melvin Kohn (1977) conducted interviews with working-class and middle-class parents in the United States. He found that working-class parents tend to stress behavioral conformity in rearing their children. Middle-class parents, on the other hand, typically tolerate a wider range of behavior and show greater concern for the intentions and motivations that underlie their children's actions. Kohn explained such differences in terms of the education and occupations common to parents in each category. Working-class parents usually lack higher education and often have jobs in which they are closely supervised and expected to do as they are told. This leads them to expect similar obedience and conformity in their children. In contrast, with more formal education, middle-class parents usually have jobs that provide more autonomy and encourage the use of imagination. These parents are therefore likely to inspire the same qualities in their children. Such differences in patterns of socialization will obviously have long-term effects on children's ambition, partly explaining the fact that middle-class children are more likely than working-class children to go to college themselves and are generally more confident of success in college and in later careers (Wilson, 1959; Ballantine, 1983). In many ways, then, parents teach children to follow in their footsteps, adapting to the constraints or privileges of their inherited social positions.

Family members, who usually provide the earliest social experiences to children, remain important in the socialization process for much of life. A growing child's self-image, her degree of self-esteem, as well as her understanding of cultural norms and values, are strongly influenced by parents.

Schooling

Formal schooling introduces unfamiliar people and new experiences into the socialization process. In school, children learn to interact with other people who are initially strangers and who may have social backgrounds that differ from their own. As children encounter social diversity, they are also likely to become more aware of their own social identities and respond to others accordingly. For example, one study of kindergarten children showed that whites and blacks tended to form same-race play groups (Finkelstein & Haskins, 1983). Similarly, boys and girls tend to form distinct play groups, grasping more of the importance that our culture attaches to sex (Lever, 1978).

The most widely recognized task of schooling is to teach children a wide range of knowledge and skills. In the early grades, these are basic skills such as reading, writing, and arithmetic. Later, secondary schools and colleges convey highly specialized material students may need in order to function in a complex industrial society that has many specialized productive roles. But what children learn in school goes far beyond the official curriculum. What is often called the *hidden curriculum* teaches them important cultural values. As noted in Chapter 3 ("Culture"), for instance, school activities such as spelling bees and sports encourage children to be competitive and to value success. Children also receive countless subtle messages that their society's way of life is both practically and morally good. In addition, schools further socialize children into culturally approved sex roles. As Raphaela Best (1983) points out, instructional activities for boys and girls often differ, so that boys engage in more physical activities and spend more time outdoors, while girls tend to be more sedentary, often helping the teacher with various housekeeping chores. Such distinctions related to sex continue throughout the process of formal education. For example, college women may be urged to select majors in the arts or humanities, while college men may be encouraged to study the physical sciences.

Another school learning experience is being evaluated in tasks such as reading and athletic performance according to universal standards rather than on the basis of particular personal relationships, as is often the case in families. Such impersonal evaluation is used to define personal abilities, greatly affecting how children come to view themselves. At the same time, the confidence or anxiety that children develop at home can have a significant effect on how well they perform in school (Belsky, Lerner, & Spanier, 1984). Finally, the school is probably children's first experience with rigid formality. The school day is based on a strict time schedule, subjecting children to impersonal regimentation and fostering traits such as punctuality that will be expected by many large organizations later in life.

Overall, schooling plays a vital part in guiding the development of children. Schools not only help children adjust to living within a large, impersonal world but also teach them the knowledge and skills necessary for the successful performance of adult roles. In addition, schooling generally fosters support for society as it exists. As Chapter 16 ("Education") explains, schooling helps to perpetuate social inequality by linking gender and social class to the extent and type of education that children receive.

Peer Groups

By the start of schooling, children have discovered another new setting for social activity in the **peer group,** *people in regular interaction who share common interests, social position, and similar age.* A young child's peer group is generally drawn from neighborhood playmates; later, peer groups are composed of friends from school or other activities.

The peer group differs from the family and the school by allowing children an escape from the direct supervision of adults. This is, of course, much of the attraction of peer groups to their members. Within such groups, children have considerable independence, which offers valuable experience in forging social relationships of their own and developing a sense of themselves apart from their families. Peer groups also provide the opportunity for discussion of interests that may not be shared by adults (such as styles of dress and popular music) as well as topics young people may wish to avoid in the presence of parents and teachers (such as drugs and sex).

The greater autonomy of the peer group, with the ever-present possibility of activity that would not be condoned by adults, is no doubt the reason parents have long expressed concern about who their children's friends are. Especially in a society that is changing rapidly, peer groups often rival the influence of parents. This is simply because the interests and attitudes of parents and children may differ considerably—as suggested by the familiar phrase "the generation gap." The importance of the peer group is typically greatest during adolescence, when young people are beginning to break away from their families and think of themselves as responsible adults. It is during this period of life that peer groups typically pressure members toward their own brand of conformity. A sense of belonging within a peer group eases some of the anxiety provoked by breaking away from the family.

The conflict between parents and peers may be more apparent than real, however, for even during adolescence children remain strongly influenced by their parents. While the peer group may guide such short-term concerns as style of dress and musical taste, parents retain more sway over the long-term aspirations of their children. For example, one study found that parents had more influence than even best friends on young people's educational aspirations (Davies & Kandel, 1981).

Finally, a neighborhood or school is typically a social mosaic of many peer groups. As we will see in Chapter 7 ("Groups and Organizations"), members often perceive their own peer group in positive terms while viewing others negatively. Therefore, many peer groups actually are important to the socialization process as individuals seek to conform to their own groups while forming an identity in opposition to others. In some cases, too, people are strongly influenced by peer groups they would like to join. For example, upon entering a new school, a young man with a desire to excel at basketball may wish to become part of the basketball players' social crowd. He is likely to adopt what he sees as the social patterns of this group in the hope of eventual acceptance. This represents what sociologists call **anticipatory socialization,** *the process of social learning directed toward gaining a desired position.* Later in life, jobs are likely to provoke further anticipatory socialization. For instance, a young lawyer who hopes to eventually become a partner in her law firm may conform to the attitudes and behavior of other partners to encourage her acceptance into this exclusive group.

The Mass Media

The **mass media** are *impersonal communications directed to a vast audience.* Common to industrial societies, the mass media include television, radio, newspapers, and magazines. Public exposure to the mass media is extensive, so that they have an enormous effect on our attitudes and behavior. The mass media often claim to present world events in a factual manner. However, some sociologists have argued that they tend to present the interests of established elites in a favorable light, while portraying those who challenge the system in negative terms (Gans, 1980; Parenti, 1986).

First developed in 1939, television rapidly became part of the American way of life after 1950. At that time, only about 9 percent of American households had one or more television sets. By the late 1980s, this proportion had soared to 98 percent (while only 92 percent had telephones). The latest statistics show that the average household has a television turned on for seven hours a day (U.S. Bureau of the Census, 1989a). Before most children learn to read, watching television has become their regular routine, and American schoolchildren actually spend more hours in front of a television than they do in school (Anderson & Lorch, 1983; Singer, 1983). Indeed, television may very well consume more of children's time than interacting with parents does. Overall,

Spanish painter Diego Velazquez painted this portrait of Prince Baltasar Carlos at his riding school in the seventeenth century. Although barely old enough to be entering school by contemporary American standards, this little boy is depicted as having an adult-like stature. The study of historical paintings has led to the conclusion that childhood as a stage of life as we understand it emerged in Europe only after the Industrial Revolution.

television is now the most powerful mass medium (Singer & Singer, 1983).

Like other mass media, television is impersonal, so that we cannot directly respond to its content. Television clearly does more than provide us with entertainment; it also serves to program many of our attitudes and beliefs. For example, television has traditionally portrayed men and women according to cultural stereotypes, showing, for instance, males in positions of power and women only as mothers or subordinates (Cantor & Pin-

gree, 1983; Ang, 1985). As Chapter 13 ("Sex and Gender") describes in detail, advertising in the mass media further contributes to sex stereotyping (Courtney & Whipple, 1983). Similarly, television shows have long presented affluent people in favorable terms, while suggesting that less affluent people (Archie Bunker is the classic example) are ignorant and wrongheaded (Gans, 1980). In addition, although racial and ethnic minorities tend to watch more television than others, until recently they have been all but absent from programming. The successful 1950s comedy *I Love Lucy*, for example, was shunned by all the major television producers because it featured Desi Arnaz—a Hispanic—in a starring role. Even now, minorities are often portrayed in ways attractive to white middle-class Americans (as in the affluent black family on *The Cosby Show*). This situation improved during the 1980s as advertisers recognized the marketing advantages of appealing to these large segments of American society (Wilson & Gutiérrez, 1985). The box offers a critical look at how advertising in the mass media has traditionally portrayed minorities in terms of negative stereotypes.

Just as important, television also influences us through what it ignores, such as the lives of the poor and the large homosexual minority in the United States. In this way, television sends the message that these categories of people do not matter or—even more incorrectly—that they do not exist.

Television has unquestionably enriched American culture in many respects, bringing into our homes a wide range of entertaining and educational programming. Furthermore, this "window on the world" has increased our awareness of diverse cultures and provided a means of addressing current public issues. At the same time, the power of television has made this medium controversial, and especially so to the extent that it supports traditional stereotypes.

Public Opinion

Public opinion is defined as *the attitudes of people throughout a society about one or more controversial issues*. Although family and peer groups have the greatest importance in the process of socialization, our attitudes and behavior are also influenced by what we perceive to be the opinions of other members of our society. As discussed in Chapter 6 ("Social Interaction in Everyday Life"), people often conform to the attitudes of others—even complete strangers—to avoid being singled out as different. The mass media provide numerous accounts

When Advertising Offends: The Death of the Frito Bandito

Commercial advertising is obviously intended to sell products. However, some ad campaigns offend rather than attract an audience by portraying categories of people in inaccurate and unfair ways.

A century ago, the vast majority of American consumers were white Anglos, many of whom were uncomfortable with the growing racial and cultural diversity of American society. Businesses commonly exploited this discomfort, depicting racial and cultural diversity in ways that were condescending at best. In 1889, for example, a pancake mix appeared featuring a servant mammy named "Aunt Jemima." Although modified in recent years, this logo is still widely seen in the mass media, largely because the product continues to have a com- manding share of the market. Like- wise, the hot cereal "Cream of Wheat" is still symbolized by the black chef Rastus, and "Uncle Ben" is familiar to millions of Americans as a brand name for rice. To many Americans, use of such caricatures— which, after all, originally depicted the black slaves of white people—is racially insensitive at best.

However, changes in advertising have occurred in recent decades in all the mass media. The stereotypical Frito Bandito, long familiar to older television viewers, was abandoned in 1971 by Frito-Lay (a company whose first product was a corn chip ironically invented by a Hispanic in San Antonio). A host of other such images has also disappeared as American businesses confront a new reality: the growing voice and financial power of minorities. Taken together, blacks, Hispanics, and Asians now represent 20 percent of Americans, a proportion projected to reach one-third early in the next century. Even now, these Americans represent a commercial market worth almost one-half trillion dollars. Also, as immigrants, many minorities rely heavily on television to learn about their new society. This obviously makes them especially accessible to advertisers. At the same time, however, all categories of Americans are increasingly voicing a simple demand: that products not be marketed at the expense of human dignity.

SOURCE: Based on Marty Westerman, "Death of the Frito Bandito," *American Demographics*, Vol. 11, No. 3 (March 1989):28–32.

---

of the latest trends, and there is little doubt that many Americans seek to conform to such patterns. For example, the clothing industry's success in marketing new fashions several times a year illustrates people's tendency to adopt, within their budgets, what the trend makers define as desirable.

As George Herbert Mead suggested, what others think—or what we *think* they think—affects how we perceive ourselves. Because public opinion tends to reflect the dominant values and norms of a society, those who differ in some way from the majority may be devalued. Widespread American opinion suggests that if we are homosexual, we are "bad," that males who are noncompetitive "lack character," and that females who are assertive are "pushy." Thus people who fail to conform to cultural patterns may develop a sense of being social outsiders. No one, of course, ever conforms completely to the dominant values and norms. Even people who publicly conform to cultural patterns are apt to experience private anxiety about their failure to live up to ideal cultural expectations.

Within complex, industrial societies, there are numerous agents of socialization. In addition to those we have described, there are religious organizations, the workplace, the military, and social clubs. As a result, socialization inevitably involves inconsistencies as we learn different information from various kinds of social experiences. Thus socialization is not a simple process of learning, but a complex balancing act in which individuals encounter a wide range of ideas in the process of forming their own distinctive personalities.

SOCIALIZATION AND THE LIFE COURSE

Although most discussions of socialization focus on childhood, socialization actually continues throughout our lives. Our experiences are socially structured during different stages of the life course—commonly understood to include childhood, adolescence, adulthood, and, as a final stage of adulthood, old age. Socialization has distinctive characteristics within each stage.

Childhood

Charles Dickens's classic novel *Oliver Twist* is set in London early in the nineteenth century, when the Industrial Revolution was bringing sweeping changes to English society. Oliver's mother died in childbirth and, barely surviving himself, he began life as an indigent orphan, "buffeted through the world—despised by all, and pitied by none" (Dickens, 1886:36; orig. 1837–1839). What little pleasure Oliver Twist received in his early years came through charity. Long before he reached the age when we expect a young person to seek employment, he began a life of toil and drudgery in a workhouse, working long hours in exchange for filthy shelter and meager food.

Had Oliver Twist been born to an aristocratic family, his life would have been far easier. Perhaps he was fortunate to have survived at all in a society in which one-fifth of all children died in their first year of life.

Until this century, in fact, parents were less concerned with how their children would grow up than with whether they would grow up at all (Skolnick, 1986:19).

In American culture today, *childhood*—roughly the first twelve years of life—is a period of freedom from the responsibilities of the adult world. But during the Middle Ages in Europe—and, as Oliver Twist testifies, long afterward—children's lives were very much like those of adults. Historian Philippe Ariès (1965) explains that medieval Europe had little conception of childhood; as soon as children were able to survive without constant care, they were viewed as adults. This meant that children often worked long hours, just as most adults did. Although "child labor" is now scorned in American society, this pattern persists in preindustrial societies throughout Latin America, Africa, and Asia.

This may seem startling because our common sense suggests that children are very different from adults— inexperienced in the ways of the world and biologically immature. In technologically advanced societies, childhood is extended because much knowledge and many complex skills must be learned before assuming adult activities. For this reason, we attach opposing definitions

CROSS-CULTURAL COMPARISON

Sex among Children? The Social Construction of Childhood

Should children be sexual? To most Americans, sexual activity on the part of children is disturbing and unnatural. As anthropologist Ruth Benedict points out, the Zuni—a Native American society of New Mexico— also discourage childhood sexuality. This is because the Zuni view sex simply as a means of reproduction, so that they see little point in the activity before reaching the age of puberty, when reproduction is possible. Different still are the Melanesian cultures of Southeast New Guinea. Here, Benedict found sexual activity among children to be quite acceptable. Rather than reacting with alarm as Americans would, adults typically

laugh it off, believing, along with the Zuni, that no harm can result.

Obviously, the fact that children cannot reproduce while adults can is a biological reality (although the age of puberty now occurs earlier in life in response to social changes). Generally, however, much of the way the two stages of the life course are defined reflects social beliefs and learning rather than biological characteristics.

Is the way a society defines childhood important, then? Ruth Benedict suggests that, unlike many other cultures, Americans define childhood and adulthood *in opposition*. This means that socialization does not in-

volve just accumulating information as we grow. Rather, to learn to be adults in American society, we must also *unlearn* much of our childhood. Perhaps, wonders Benedict, this may hold some insight into the widespread sexual anxieties among adults in our culture:

> The adult in our culture has often failed to unlearn the wickedness or the dangerousness of sex, a lesson that was impressed upon [the child] strongly during [the] most formative years. (1938:165)

SOURCE: Ruth Benedict, "Continuities and Discontinuities in Cultural Conditioning," *Psychiatry*, Vol. 1 (May 1938): 161–167.

to children and adults, contrasting "irresponsible" with "responsible" adults (Benedict, 1938). But comparing various cultures shows that this is far from an inevitable consequence of biological maturation. Many characteristics of childhood—and even whether it exists at all—are a matter of social definition. The box provides an example.

Recently, sociologists and psychologists have found evidence that—especially in relatively affluent families—childhood is changing yet again, and becoming shorter. In other words, children are subjected to mounting pressures to dress, speak, and act like adults (Elkind, 1981; Winn, 1983). Evidence of the "hurried child" pattern includes ten-year-old boys in designer jeans and girls of the same age adorned with jewelry and makeup. The mass media now introduce into the child's world sexuality, violence, and a host of other issues that were considered to be strictly adult topics only a generation ago. Young children may routinely watch films that graphically depict violence and listen to rock music that contains sexually explicit lyrics. Pressure to grow up quickly is also exerted in the home because greater numbers of mothers work, requiring children to fend more for themselves. Furthermore, today's parents are often delighted if their children can read, spell, or discuss world events before their peers can do these things, believing that this indicates greater intelligence. Schools also encourage rapid maturation by emphasizing achievement, which reflects positively on both the child and the school. In the view of child psychologist David Elkind (1981), the "hurried child" pattern is a recent—and detrimental—change in American society's conception of childhood that results in children being confronted with issues they have little basis for understanding, let alone successfully resolving.

Adolescence

As childhood emerged as a distinct stage of life in industrial societies, adolescence became recognized as a buffer stage between childhood and adulthood corresponding roughly to the teenage years. This stage of life offers time to learn various specialized skills required for adult life.

We generally associate adolescence with emotional and social turmoil; young people experience conflict with their parents and attempt to develop their identities within adult society. Since adolescence is commonly linked to the onset of puberty, we often attribute much of the social turmoil of this stage of life to physiological changes.

Among a growing number of American families today, childhood as a stage of life is again changing. The "hurried child" pattern encourages children still in elementary school to look and act like adults.

However, thinking sociologically, the instability of adolescence also reflects inconsistencies in the socialization process. For example, adolescents are expected to be increasingly self-reliant and responsible for themselves, yet they are considered unequipped for the adult occupations that would give them financial independence from their parents. Adolescents also receive inconsistent messages about sexuality—encouragement by sex-oriented mass media to be sexually active and simultaneous messages of restraint from adults. Consider, also, that an eighteen-year-old male may have the adult responsibility of going to war thrust upon him, while simultaneously being denied the adult right to drink alcohol. In 1971, the Twenty-sixth Amendment to the United States Constitution gave eighteen-year-olds of both sexes the right to vote. By the end of the 1980s, however, the federal government pressured states to raise the drinking age to twenty-one. Without denying that biological changes mark the onset of adolescence, there are marked contradictions in the social definition of a stage of life when people are no longer children but not yet adults.

Of course, the experience of adolescence varies according to social background. Young people from working-class families often move directly into the adult world of work and parenthood upon completion of high school. However, those from wealthier families typically have the resources to attend college and perhaps graduate school, which may extend adolescence into the later twenties and even the thirties (Skolnick, 1986). Some of the poorest Americans also have an extended adolescence, although for a different reason. Especially in the inner cities, many young minorities cannot attain full adult standing because our society fails to provide them with jobs.

Further evidence that adolescence is not simply a matter of biological maturation is provided by cross-cultural research. When anthropologist Margaret Mead studied the culture of the Samoan Islands in the 1920s, she found that boys and girls were simply defined as adults when they reached their midteens. In the Samoan culture, in other words, childhood and adulthood were not defined in strong opposition, so the transition between the two stages of life was not dramatic (M. Mead, 1961; orig. 1928).

Adulthood

At the age of thirty-five, Eleanor Roosevelt, one of the most widely admired American women, wrote in her diary: "I do not think I have ever felt so strangely as in the past year . . . all my self confidence is gone and I am on the edge, though I never was better physically I feel sure" (cited in Sheehy, 1976:260). What explains Eleanor Roosevelt's self-doubt? Perhaps she was troubled by the attention her husband was paying to another, younger woman; perhaps as she looked into the future, she could not see what challenges or accomplishments might bring further satisfaction to her life. As she experienced what we might today describe as a "midlife crisis," there was much that she could not foresee. Although her husband, Franklin Delano Roosevelt, was shortly to become disabled by poliomyelitis, his rising political career would lead ultimately to thirteen consecutive years as his country's president. And Eleanor Roosevelt would become perhaps the most active and influential of all First Ladies. After her husband's death, she remained outspoken and served as a delegate to the United Nations. Her funeral in 1962 was attended by three United States presidents.

Eleanor Roosevelt's life illustrates two major characteristics of the stage of life that we call *adulthood*, which in our culture typically begins at some point during the twenties. First, adulthood is the period during which most of life's accomplishments typically occur. In other words, having been socialized into society's conception of adulthood, people embark upon careers and raise families of their own. Second, especially in later adulthood, people reflect upon what they have been able to accomplish, often coming to the sobering realization that some of the idealistic dreams of their youth will never be realized.

Early Adulthood

Personalities are largely formed by the onset of adulthood, although marked transformations in an individual's social environment—such as unemployment, divorce, or serious illness—may result in significant changes (Dannefer, 1984). Early adulthood—until about the age of forty—is generally a time of working toward many goals set earlier in life. Young adults learn to manage for themselves a host of day-to-day responsibilities that had been taken care of by parents or others. In beginning a family, we draw on the experience of having lived within the family formed by our parents, although as children we may have understood little about adult life. In addition, early adulthood typically involves learning patterns of intimate living with another person who may have just as much to learn. This is also a period of juggling conflicting priorities and demands on time: parents, spouse, children, and work (Levinson et al., 1978). Women, especially, face the realization that "doing it all" can be extremely difficult, since in our culture they are expected to assume primary responsibility for childrearing and household chores, even while they have demanding occupations outside the home. In short, women today are often caught between the traditional femin*ine* ideals they learned as children and the more contemporary femin*ist* ideals they learned as adults (Sexton, 1980; cited in Giele, 1982:121).

Middle Adulthood

Young adults usually cope with such tensions optimistically. But in middle adulthood—roughly the years between the ages of forty and sixty—they begin to feel that marked improvements in life circumstances are less likely. The distinctive quality of middle adulthood is thus greater reflection as people assess their achievements in light of earlier expectations. People become more aware of the fragility of health at this age—not typically a major concern in youth. Women who have spent the first part of their adulthood raising a family can find middle adulthood especially trying. Children have grown up and require less attention, husbands are absorbed in their careers, so that women may find spaces in their lives that are difficult to fill. Women who get divorced during middle adulthood may experience serious economic problems (Weitzman, 1985). For all these reasons, many women return to school and begin careers in middle adulthood. In fact, during the 1980s, women between thirty-five and forty-four years of age were the fastest-growing segment of the American labor force (U.S. Bureau of the Census, 1989). But neither education nor a career is easy after several decades of working primarily in the home.

The traditional conception of femininity also stresses the importance of physical attractiveness. Both older men and older women face the reality of physical decline, but our society's traditional socialization of women has made good looks so crucial that wrinkles, weight gain, and loss of hair are generally more traumatic for women than for men. Men, of course, have their own particular difficulties. Some confront their limited achievements knowing that their careers are unlikely to change dramatically over the rest of their working lives. Others, realizing that the price of career success has been neglect of family or personal health, harbor deep uncertainties about their self-worth even in the face of praise from others (Farrell & Rosenberg, 1981).

Eleanor Roosevelt's midlife crisis may well have involved some of the personal transitions we have described. But her life also illustrates the fact that the greatest productivity and personal satisfaction may occur after the middle of life. Socialization in America's youth-oriented culture has convinced many people that life ends at forty. As the average life expectancy of Americans has increased, however, such limiting notions about later life have begun to change. Major life transformations may become less likely, but the potential for learning and new beginnings continues all the same.

⅍Old Age and Dying

Old age is the later years of adulthood and the final stage of life itself, beginning in about the mid-sixties. Societies also attach different meanings to this period of life. In preindustrial societies, old age typically brings great influence and respect. As explained in Chapter 14 ("Aging and the Elderly"), this is because the elderly usually control land and other wealth, and also because in societies that change slowly, they represent a lifetime of wisdom. Thus, although the elderly face many challenging transitions in these societies, they also make important decisions for younger family members (Sheehan, 1976; Hareven, 1982).

In industrial societies, however, the fact that younger people typically work apart from the family lessens the influence of the elderly. Also, in a rapidly changing society, older people tend to be defined as marginal or even obsolete. They are thought to be unaware of new trends and fashions, and their knowledge and experience is often seen as irrelevant to the social world of younger people. As we have already noted, American society has a youth orientation in which the physical beauty, activities, and attitudes of the young are standards by which everyone is judged.

No doubt, however, this youth orientation will diminish as the proportion of older Americans steadily increases. The percentage of Americans over the age of sixty-five has almost tripled since the beginning of this century, so that today there are more Americans in old age than in their teens. Moreover, as average life expectancy increases, more Americans will live well past the age of sixty-five. Looking to the next century, the Census Bureau (1989b) predicts that the fastest-growing segment of our population will be those over eighty-five. It is projected that there will be almost six times as many people over that age a century from now as there are today.

At present, socialization in old age differs in an important way from socialization earlier in life. For the young, advancing age typically means entering new roles and taking on new responsibilities. Old age, however, involves the opposite process: leaving roles that have long provided social identity and meaningful activity. Retirement is one clear example. Although retirement sometimes fits the common image of being a period of restful activity after years of work, it often means the loss of familiar routines, and sometimes outright boredom. Like any life transition, retirement demands that a person learn new and different ways of living while simultaneously *un*learning patterns and routines of earlier stages in life. A nearly equal transition is required of the nonworking wife or husband who must change routines to accommodate a spouse now spending more time in the home.

The sociological perspective suggests that stages in the life course are shaped by society as well as by biology. In industrial societies, elderly people are deemed worthy of "retirement," which often means finishing their lives with little meaningful activity. In the People's Republic of China and other preindustrial societies, however, people of all ages represent a vital resource. Thus, productive work continues well into what Americans term "old age."

Throughout human history, death from disease and accident commonly occurred during all stages of life, usually due to a low standard of living and primitive medical technology. In industrial societies, in contrast, although death can still occur at any time (especially among the poor), it is usually linked to old age. Therefore, even though more and more Americans reaching the age of sixty-five can look forward to decades of life, patterns of socialization in old age cannot be separated from the ultimate recognition of impending death.

After observing many dying people, Elisabeth Kübler-Ross (1969) described death as an orderly transition involving five distinct stages. Because American culture tends to ignore the reality of death, people's first reaction to the prospect of their own death is usually *denial*.

This involves avoiding anything that might suggest the inevitability of death. The second stage is *anger*; the person has begun to accept the fact of impending death but views it as a gross injustice. In the third stage, anger gives way to *negotiation*, the attitude that death may not be inevitable and that a bargain might be struck with God to allow life to continue. The fourth stage is *resignation*, often accompanied by psychological depression. Finally, adjustment to death is completed in the fifth stage, *acceptance*. At this point, rather than being paralyzed by fear and anxiety, the person sets out to use constructively whatever time remains.

As the proportion of Americans in old age increases, we can expect attitudes toward death to change. Today, for example, death is more widely discussed than it was earlier in this century, and many people view death as preferable to months or even years of suffering and social isolation in hospitals and rest homes. In addition, married couples are more likely to anticipate their own deaths with discussion and planning. This may ease somewhat the disorientation that usually accompanies the death of a spouse—a greater problem for women, who usually outlive their husbands.

This brief examination of the life course leads to two general conclusions. First and most important, although linked to the biological process of aging, the essential characteristics of each stage of life are a construction of society. For this reason, any stage of life may be experienced differently within various cultures. Second, each period of the life course presents characteristic problems and transitions that involve learning something new and, in many cases, unlearning what has become familiar.

Two additional points are worth noting. The fact that social experience is organized according to age within every society in no way negates the effects of other social forces, such as those based on social background, race, ethnicity, and sex. Thus, the general patterns described are all subject to further modification as they apply to various categories of people. Finally, the social experiences accumulated over the life course also depend on when, in the history of a society, life begins. The lives of people within a particular **cohort,** meaning *a category of people born at about the same period,* are likely to be shaped by the same major events (Riley, Foner, & Waring, 1988). Americans born early in this century, for instance, are a cohort influenced by two world wars and economic depression unknown to many of their children. In this sense, too, general patterns pertaining to the life course will vary.

RESOCIALIZATION: TOTAL INSTITUTIONS

So far, this chapter has focused on socialization as it applies to the vast majority of people living within familiar settings. For almost 1 million Americans, however, a special type of socialization takes place because they are confined—often against their will—within settings such as prisons and mental hospitals. These are examples of a **total institution,** defined as *a setting in which individuals are isolated from the rest of society and manipulated by an administrative staff.*

According to Erving Goffman (1961), total institutions have three distinctive characteristics. First, they control all aspects of the daily lives of their residents (often called "inmates"), including eating, sleeping, working, and recreation. Second, they subject residents to standardized activities, food, and sleeping quarters. Third, they apply formal rules and rigid scheduling to all activities from eating to showering. Furthermore, inmates are continuously supervised by the administrative staff, which wields complete power much as adults in our society monitor the activities of young children.

The reason for this rigid control of the social environment is a policy of **resocialization:** *deliberate socialization intended to radically alter the individual's personality.* The power of a total institution to reshape personality lies in the fact that inmates have no other source of social experience. Their complete isolation is achieved through physical barriers such as walls and fences (usually with barbed wire and guard towers), barred windows, and locked doors. Cut off from the outside world in this way, the inmates' entire social world can be manipulated by the administrative staff to produce change—or at least compliance—in the inmate.

Resocialization is a two-part process. First, the staff attempts to destroy the new inmate's established conception of self. This involves a series of experiences that Goffman describes as "abasements, degradations, humiliations, and profanations of self" (1961:14). For example, inmates are required to surrender personal possessions, including clothing and grooming articles, that are normally used to maintain a person's distinctive "presentation of self." In their place, inmates receive standard-issue items that make everyone more alike. In addition, inmates are typically given standard haircuts, so that, once again, what was personalized becomes uniform. The staff also uniformly processes new inmates by searching, weighing, fingerprinting, and photographing them, and by issuing them a serial number. Individuals also surrender the right to privacy, often evident in demands that they undress publicly as part of the admission procedure and in routine surveillance and searches of their living quarters. These "mortifications of self" undermine the sense of identity and autonomy that the inmate brings to the total institution from the outside world.

The second part of the resocialization process involves efforts to systematically build a different self. The staff manipulates inmates through a system of rewards and punishments. Being allowed to keep a book or having extra cigarettes may seem trivial from the vantage point of outsiders, but in the rigidly controlled environment of the total institution, such privileges can be powerful motivations toward conformity. On the other hand, noncompliance means that privileges can quickly be withdrawn or, in more serious cases, physical pain and social isolation can result. Furthermore, the duration of confinement in a prison or mental hospital is often related to the degree of cooperation with the staff. Goffman emphasizes that demands for conformity in a total institution may involve inward motivation as well as outward behavior. A person who displays no outward violation of the rules, in other words, may still be subjected to punishment for having "an attitude problem."

Resocialization in a total institution can considerably change an inmate. The rebuilding of a person's self is extremely difficult, however, and no two people are likely to respond to the environment of any total institution in precisely the same way (Irwin, 1980). Therefore, while some inmates may experience "rehabilitation" or "recovery" (meaning change that is officially approved), others may gradually sink into an embittered state because of the perceived injustice of their incarceration. Furthermore, over a considerable period of time, the rigidly controlled environment of a total institution may render people completely *institutionalized*, incapable of the independence required for living in the outside world.

SOCIALIZATION AND HUMAN FREEDOM

This chapter has explained that socialization is the means by which society shapes how we think, feel, and act. If society has this power over us, are we free in any meaningful sense? This chapter ends with a closer look at this important question.

Children and adults throughout North America enjoy watching the Muppets, stars of television and film. Observing the expressive antics of Kermit the Frog, Miss Piggy, and the rest of the troupe, one almost believes that these puppets are real rather than passive objects animated by movements that originate backstage. The sociological perspective reveals that human beings are like puppets in that we respond to the backstage guidance of society. Indeed, more so, in that society affects not just our outward behavior but our innermost feelings.

But our analysis of socialization also reveals that the puppet analogy ultimately breaks down. Viewing human beings as the puppets of society leads into the trap that Dennis Wrong (1961) has called an "oversocialized" conception of the human being. In part, Wrong reminds us that we are biological as well as social creatures—a point that was emphasized by Sigmund Freud, who identified highly general drives within the human species. To the extent that any biological force has an impact on our being, we can never be entirely shaped by society.

The fact that human beings may be subject to *both* biological and social influences, however, hardly supports the notion of human freedom. Here is where the ideas of George Herbert Mead are of crucial importance. Mead recognized the power of society to act on human beings, but he argued that human spontaneity and creativity (conceptualized in the I) cause human beings to continually *act back* on society. On this basis, the process of socialization affirms the capacity for choice. Within society, we are continually engaged in reflection, evaluation, and action. Therefore, although the process of socialization may initially suggest that we are like puppets, Peter Berger points out that "unlike the puppets, we have the possibility of stopping in our movements, looking up and perceiving the machinery by which we have been moved" (1963:176). In doing so, we can act to change society—if we wish, to pull back on the strings. This reaffirms our individual autonomy. As Berger adds, the more we are able to utilize the sociological perspective to recognize how the machinery of our society works, the freer we are.

SUMMARY

1. Socialization is the process by which social experience confers on the individual the qualities we associate with being fully human. For society as a whole, socialization is the means of teaching culture to each new generation.

2. A century ago, patterns of human behavior were widely linked to an instinctive human nature. Today, human behavior is understood to be mostly a result of nurture rather than nature. Human nature is therefore the highly variable creation of culture.

3. The observed and damaging effects of social isola-

tion reveal the importance of social experience to human development.

4. Sigmund Freud described the human personality as composed of three conceptual parts. The id represents general human needs, which Freud claimed were innate. The superego represents cultural values and norms as internalized by the individual. The needs of the id and the cultural restraints of the superego are mediated by the ego.

5. Jean Piaget believed that human development reflects both biological maturation and increasing social experience. He asserted that socialization involves four major stages of development: sensorimotor, preoperational, concrete operational, and formal operational.

6. To George Herbert Mead, the process of socialization is based on the emergence of the self, which he viewed as partly autonomous (the I) and partly guided by society (the me).

7. Charles Horton Cooley used the term *looking-glass self* to recognize that our conception of self is influenced by perceptions of how others respond to us.

8. Commonly the first setting of socialization, the family has primary importance for initially shaping a child's attitudes and behavior.

9. The school exposes children to greater social diversity and introduces them to the experience of being evaluated on the basis of universal standards of performance. In addition to formal lessons, the hidden curriculum teaches cultural definitions of race and gender and fosters support for the existing political and economic system.

10. In peer groups, the child is subject to less adult supervision than in the family and in school. Peer groups take on increasing significance in adolescence.

11. The mass media, especially television, have considerable importance in the socialization process. The average American child now spends more time watching television than attending school.

12. Public opinion is also important in the socialization process because attitudes and values that are widespread influence individual thoughts and actions.

13. As is true of all stages of the life cycle, the characteristics of childhood are socially constructed. During the Middle Ages, European societies did not recognize childhood as a stage of life. In industrial societies such as the United States, childhood is defined in opposing terms to adulthood.

14. Americans define adolescence as the transition between childhood and adulthood. While adolescence is often a difficult period for Americans, this is not the case in all societies.

15. During early adulthood, socialization involves settling into careers and raising families. Later adulthood is often marked by considerable reflection about earlier goals in light of actual achievements.

16. Old age involves many transitions, including retirement and establishing new patterns of social life. While the elderly typically have high prestige in preindustrial societies, industrial societies are more youth-oriented.

17. Death usually occurs in old age; adjustment to the death of a spouse (an experience more common to women) and acceptance of the inevitability of one's own death are part of socialization in old age.

18. Total institutions such as prisons and mental hospitals have the goal of resocialization—radically changing the inmate's personality.

19. Socialization demonstrates the power of society to shape our thoughts, feelings, and actions. Yet, as George Herbert Mead pointed out, the relationship between self and society is a two-way process: each shapes the other within ongoing social interaction.

KEY CONCEPTS

anticipatory socialization the process of social learning directed toward gaining a desired position

cohort a category of people born at about the same period, or entering some setting such as a college at the same time

concrete operational stage Piaget's term for the level of human development characterized by the use of logic to understand objects or events

ego Freud's designation of the conscious attempt to balance the pleasure-seeking drives of the human organism and the demands of society

formal operational stage Piaget's term for the level of human development characterized by highly abstract thought and the ability to imagine alternatives to reality

generalized other George Herbert Mead's term for widespread cultural norms and values used as a reference in evaluating ourselves

id Freud's designation of the human being's basic needs

looking-glass self Cooley's term meaning a conception of self derived from the responses of others

mass media impersonal communications directed toward a vast audience

peer group people in regular interaction who share common interests, social position, and similar age

personality a person's fairly consistent pattern of thinking, feeling, and acting

preoperational stage Piaget's term for the level of human development in which language and other symbols are first used

public opinion the attitudes of people throughout a society about one or more controversial issues

resocialization deliberate socialization intended to radically alter the individual's personality

self the individual's active awareness of existing in the midst of society

sensorimotor stage Piaget's term for the level of human development in which the world is experienced only through the senses in terms of physical contact

socialization the lifelong process of social experience by which individuals develop their human potential and learn patterns of their culture

superego Freud's designation of the presence of culture within the individual in the form of internalized values and norms

total institution a setting in which individuals are isolated from the rest of society and manipulated by an administrative staff

SUGGESTED READINGS

Many of the issues discussed in this chapter are explored in the following books.

Frederick Elkin and Gerald Handel. *The Child and Society: The Process of Socialization.* 5th ed. New York: Random House, 1988.

Matilda White Riley, Beth B. Hess, and Bettina J. Huber. *Social Change and the Life Course.* Vol. 1. Newbury Park, CA: Sage Publications, 1988.

This new analysis of Freud examines the implications of his work for a broad range of social issues.

Paul Roazen. *Encountering Freud: The Politics and Histories of Psychoanalysis.* New Brunswick, NJ: Transaction Books, 1989.

George Herbert Mead's analysis of the development of self is presented in this paperback, compiled after Mead's death by many of his students.

George Herbert Mead. *Mind, Self, and Society from the Standpoint of a Social Behaviorist.* Charles W. Morris, ed. Chicago: University of Chicago, 1962; orig, 1934.

The first of the two books listed below is a classic study of the history of the family, including changing conceptions of childhood and related patterns of socialization. The second book describes the recent development of the "hurried child" pattern in the United States.

Philippe Ariès. *Centuries of Childhood: A Social History of Family Life.* New York: Vintage Books, 1965.

David Elkind. *The Hurried Child: Growing Up Too Fast Too Soon.* Reading, MA: Addison-Wesley, 1981.

This book is a collection of fourteen essays that share a concern for the distinctive elements of socialization among black children.

Harriette Pipes McAdoo and John Lewis McAdoo, eds. *Black Children: Social, Educational, and Parental Environments.* Beverly Hills, CA: Sage Publications, 1985.

Gay people lack many of the social supports that heterosexuals take for granted. As a result, a gay folklore has emerged that is influential in the social development of millions of Americans.

Joseph P. Goodwin. *More Man than You'll Ever Be: Gay Folklore and Acculturation in Middle America.* Bloomington, IN: Indiana University Press, 1989.

This paperback uses the social-conflict paradigm to analyze the mass media in the United States. Parenti asserts that the mass media are not the liberal influence many claim them to be; rather, they support the American capitalist economic system.

Michael Parenti. *Inventing the News: The Politics of the Mass Media.* New York: St. Martin's Press, 1986.

How have the mass media shaped the way Americans perceive minority groups? This book explores images of four categories of Americans—blacks, Latinos, Native Americans, and Asians—as they are presented by the mass media.

Clinty C. Wilson II and Félix Gutiérrez. *Minorities and Media: Diversity and the End of Mass Communication.* Beverly Hills, CA: Sage Publications, 1985.

"Dallas" is a popular television show, not only in the United States, but in Europe as well. This paperback provides a European perspective on "Dallas" and what it conveys about American society.

Ien Ang. *Watching Dallas: Soap Opera and the Melodramatic Imagination.* New York: Methuen, 1985.

While still in her early twenties, Margaret Mead completed what is probably the best-known book in anthropology. In this paperback, she argues that the problems of youth are socially created rather than rooted in biology.

Margaret Mead. *Coming of Age in Samoa.* New York: Dell, 1961; orig. 1928.

Derek Freeman challenges many of Margaret Mead's conclusions, suggesting that human development is not free from biological influence.

Derek Freeman. *Margaret Mead and Samoa: The Making and Unmaking of an Anthropological Myth.* Cambridge, MA: Harvard University Press, 1983.

The following two books examine the interplay of socialization and gender.

Ray Raphael. *The Men from the Boys: Rights of Passage in Male America.* Lincoln: University of Nebraska Press, 1988.

Janet Zollinger Giele, ed. *Women in the Middle Years: Current Knowledge and Directions for Research and Policy.* New York: John Wiley and Sons, 1982.

Personality is shaped by the particular times in which we live. How the 1960s influenced a generation of Americans is suggested by this historical look at a turbulent decade.

Joan Morrison and Robert K. Morrison. *The Sixties Experience: Sights and Sounds of the Decade of Change in the Words of Those Who Lived It.* New York: Times Books, 1987.

The following book examines the process of socialization, emphasizing characteristic differences in the social experiences of females and males.

Carol Gilligan. *In a Different Voice: Psychological Theory and Women's Development.* Cambridge, MA: Harvard University Press, 1982.

6

Social Interaction in Everyday Life

The automobile roared down the mountain road, tearing through sheets of windblown rain. Two people, a man and his young son, peered intently through the windshield, observing the edge of the road beyond which they could see only a black void. Suddenly, as the car rounded a bend, the headlights shone upon a large tree that had fallen across the roadway. The man swerved to the right and braked, but unable to stop, the car left the road, crashed through some brush, turned end upon end, and came to rest on its roof. Then a bit of good fortune: the noise of the crash had been heard at a nearby hunting lodge, and a telephone call from there soon brought police and a rescue crew. The driver, beyond help, was pronounced dead at the scene of the accident. Yet, the boy was still alive, although badly hurt and unconscious. Rushed by ambulance to the hospital in the town at the foot of the mountain, he was taken immediately into emergency surgery.

Alerted in advance, the medical team burst through the swinging doors ready to try to save the boy's life. Then, with a single look at his face, the surgeon abruptly exclaimed: "Oh, no! Get someone to take over for me— I can't operate on this boy. *He's my son!*"

How can the surgeon's reaction be explained?

This situation appears to contain a contradiction: if the boy's father died in the crash, how could the boy be the surgeon's son? The contradiction, however, exists only in the reader's *assumption* that the surgeon

must be male. Inconsistency is resolved if we conclude that the surgeon is simply the boy's *mother*.

This chapter provides the opportunity to explore **social interaction**: *the process by which people act and react in relation to others*. Through social interaction, human beings create meaning in any situation. Every situation, however, is also shaped by assumptions and expectations rooted in the larger society of which we are a part.

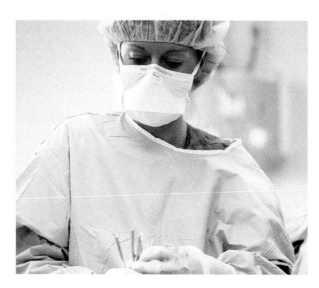

SOCIAL STRUCTURE: STATUS AND ROLE

Earlier chapters have explained that social life is an organized system in which we all participate. Chapter 3 ("Culture") examined the symbolic web that unites members of society into a culture, guiding everyday interaction with norms and values. Chapter 4 ("Society") argued that the social world is shaped by its level of technological development, its economic system, and its particular world view and moral beliefs. Chapter 5 ("Socialization") showed how individuals become human only as they become part of the system of society.

Even so, the assertion that human behavior is socially patterned often provokes some initial resistance. Living in a culture that prizes individual autonomy, few Americans readily admit to being part of any kind of system. Instead, we tend to emphasize individual responsibility for behavior and highlight the unique elements of our personalities. The fact that we behave in patterned ways, however, does not threaten our individuality. Quite the opposite: individuality is *encouraged* by the structure of society.

First, as Chapter 5 ("Socialization") explained, to live as a human being involves much more than physical existence. To become fully human is possible only through social life, which produces distinct personalities as people blend their unique qualities with the values and norms of the larger culture.

Second, in the absence of social structure, we would have no way of making sense out of any social situation. The social world can be disorienting, even frightening, when behavioral guidelines are unclear. Entering an unfamiliar setting generally inhibits us from freely expressing ourselves. Joining relative strangers at a party, for example, we feel understandable anxiety at not knowing quite what to expect. We look, therefore, to others for clues about what sort of behavior is appropriate. Only after we understand the behavioral standards that apply to the situation are we likely to feel comfortable enough to "act like ourselves."

Social structure also places some constraints on everyday life: established social patterns inevitably discourage what is unconventional. Traditional values and norms in North America, for example, still reflect the expectation that males will be "masculine" (dominant and assertive) and that females will be "feminine" (subordinate and supportive). It is because Americans do not readily link a powerful and prestigious occupation such as "surgeon" to being female that the opening to this chapter causes confusion. By pressuring each of us to fit neatly into "feminine" or "masculine" categories, social structure limits any individual's freedom to think and act according to personal preference.

Keep in mind, however, that social structure *guides* rather than *rigidly determines* human behavior. A cello and a saxophone are each designed to make only certain kinds of sounds. Similarly, "fatherhood" or any other social structure is a design that encourages a certain kind of behavior. Like musical instruments, however, any social arrangement can be "played" in a wide range of creative ways.

Status

Among the most important components of social interaction is **status**, which refers to *a recognized social position that an individual occupies within society.* Every status involves various rights, duties, or expectations that are widely recognized. Sociologists therefore use this term rather differently from its everyday meaning of "prestige." In the everyday world, a bank president has "more status" than a bank teller. Sociologically, both "bank president" and "bank teller" are statuses because they represent socially defined positions, even though one does have more power and prestige than the other.

The statuses people occupy guide the social interaction that occurs within any setting. Within the college classroom, for example, the two major statuses of professor and student have different and well-defined rights and duties. Similarly, interaction within families also reflects the statuses of mother, father, son, and daughter. Notice that statuses are defined in terms of each other, thereby forging a relationship between various individuals. A status, then, is a social definition of who and what we are in relation to specific others.

We all occupy many statuses simultaneously. The term **status set** refers to *all the statuses a particular person holds at a given time.* A girl is a *daughter* in relation to her parents, a *sister* to her siblings, a *friend* to others in her social circle, and a *goalie* to members of her hockey team. Just as status sets are complex, they are also changeable. A child becomes an adult, a student becomes a lawyer, and people marry to become husbands and wives, sometimes becoming single again as a result of death or divorce. Joining an organization or finding a job enlarges our status set; withdrawing from activities diminishes it. Individuals gain and lose many statuses over a lifetime.

Statuses also play an important part in how we define ourselves. Occupational status, for example, is a major element of the self-concept of most Americans. Long after retirement, for instance, a man may still think of himself as a professor and be similarly defined by others.

Ascribed Status and Achieved Status

Sociologists use a helpful distinction to describe how people obtain various statuses. An **ascribed status** is *a social position that is received at birth or involuntarily assumed later in the life course.* Examples of statuses that are commonly ascribed at birth are being a daughter, a Hispanic, an American, or the Prince of Wales. Becoming a teenager, a senior citizen, or a widow or widower are examples of statuses ascribed as part of the aging process. All ascribed statuses are matters about which people have little or no personal choice.

In contrast, an **achieved status** refers to *a social position that is assumed voluntarily and that reflects a significant measure of personal ability and effort.* Examples of achieved statuses are being an honors student, an Olympic athlete, a husband or wife, a computer programmer, or a thief. In each case, the individual has a definite choice in the matter.

Most statuses actually involve some combination of ascription and achievement. More specifically, people's ascribed statuses influence the statuses they are likely to achieve. Children are unlikely to be lawyers, since this status is open only to adults. Adults who complete law school are likely to have been born into relatively privileged families. Although the status of lawyer is widely viewed as achieved, it also reflects a substantial element of ascription. More generally, any person of a privileged sex, race, ethnicity, or age has far more opportunity to enter desirable achieved statuses than does someone without such privileges. In contrast, many less desirable statuses, such as criminal, welfare recipient, or drug addict are more easily "achieved" by people disadvantaged by ascription.

Master Status

Among the many statuses a person holds at any time, one often has overpowering significance to everyday life. A **master status** is *a status that has exceptional importance for social identity, often shaping a person's entire life.* A master status is usually a crucial element of one's self-concept and may be the result of any combination of ascription and achievement. In American society, a person's occupation—largely due to achievement—is of-

In rigidly hierarchical social organizations, no interaction can proceed unless people recognize each other's social standing. In traditional Indian society, each individual wears a caste mark on the forehead, which serves as a master status guiding subsequent behavior.

ten a master status. This is because occupation conveys so much information, including some idea of a person's education, income, and family background. No doubt, this is why adults typically introduce themselves by stating their occupations along with their names. Other master statuses, however, are based on ascription. For a Rockefeller or a Kennedy, family name is what stands out in the minds of others.

Serious disease can also be the basis of a master status. Many cancer patients are avoided even by lifelong friends. For persons with acquired immune deficiency syndrome (AIDS), disease is also a master status, frequently resulting in marked social isolation. Most societies of the world also limit the opportunities of women, whatever their abilities, so that sex, too, can be a master status. Additionally, the physically disabled may feel dehumanized because some perceive them as little more than the sum of their handicaps. In the box, several physically disabled people describe this problem.

Race also has traditionally been a master status in American society. A striking illustration is the life and death of Dr. Charles Drew, a medical surgeon largely responsible for the establishment of blood banks—lifesaving supplies of blood available to hospitals across the United States. In 1950, while driving to a medical conference in Alabama, Dr. Drew was seriously injured in an automobile accident. He was taken to a local hospital that was then restricted to white patients.

Although he was known to be a distinguished physician and scientist, his admission to the hospital was delayed because he was black. In the end, the hospital did treat Dr. Drew. (Ironically, it did not have the blood plasma that might have saved his life.) This incident suggests that some people are prepared to overlook substantial personal accomplishments simply because of a person's race (Low & Clift, 1981; Logan, 1982).

Role

A second major component of social interaction is **role**, which refers to *patterns of expected behavior attached to a particular status*. Ralph Linton (1937) described a role as the dynamic expression of a status. Every status involves various obligations and privileges that shape the role. The student role, for example, involves obligations to professors and other students, as well as the

SOCIOLOGY OF EVERYDAY LIFE

Physical Disability as Master Status

In the following excerpts, three people suggest that physical disability can shape a person's life, as the person is defined as "different."

Now in his later thirties, David Clark was stricken with polio when he was ten months of age. He lives and works in Corning, New York.

All the stares you get from the public used to really bother me when I was younger. But either it doesn't happen as much nowadays, or parents have taught their children better about disabilities, or else I'm older and more immune to it, I don't know. It doesn't bother me now like it used to; it used to really bother me. But I really think people are better educated now about disabilities and they don't look as much and make you feel like you're a freak, which is the way I felt when I was younger and they were looking at you like you didn't belong there, what's your problem?

Donna Finch is twenty-nine years old, holds a master's degree in social work, and lives with her husband and son in Muskogee, Oklahoma. She is also blind.

Most people don't expect handicapped people to grow up, they are always supposed to be children. . . . (Y)ou aren't supposed to date, you aren't supposed to have a job, somehow you're just supposed to disappear. I'm not saying this is true of anyone else, but in my own case I think I was more intellectually mature than most children, and more emotionally immature. I'd say that not until the last four or five years have I felt really whole.

Rose Helman is an elderly woman living near New York City. She suffers from spinal meningitis and is also blind.

You ask me if people are really different today than in the '20s and '30s. Not too much. They are still fearful of the handicapped. I don't know if fearful is the right word, but uncomfortable at least. But I can understand it somewhat; it happened to me. I once asked a man to tell me which staircase to use to get from the subway out to the street. He started giving me directions that were confusing, and I said, "Do you mind taking me?" He said, "Not at all." He grabbed me on the side with my dog on it, so I asked him to take my other arm. And he said, "I'm sorry, I have no other arm." And I said, "That's all right, I'll hold onto the jacket." It felt funny hanging onto the sleeve without the arm in it.

SOURCE: Michael D. Orlansky and William L. Heward, *Voices: Interviews with Handicapped People* (Columbus, OH: Charles E. Merrill, 1981), pp. 85, 92, 133–134, 172. Copyright 1981. Reprinted by permission of the publisher.

privilege of being able to devote much of one's time to personal enrichment through academic study. Thus, individuals *occupy* a status and *perform* a role. Cultural norms suggest how a person with a particular status ought to act, which is often called a *role expectation*. As noted in Chapter 3 ("Culture"), however, real culture only approximates ideal culture, so that actual *role performance*, therefore, will vary according to an individual's unique personality. In addition, because values and norms vary throughout a society, people may perform comparable roles quite differently.

Like status, a role is *relational*; it organizes our behavior toward some other person. The parent's role, for example, is centered on responsibilities toward a child. Correspondingly, the role of son or daughter consists largely of obligations toward a parent. Countless other examples exist of such role pairs: wives and husbands, baseball pitchers and catchers, physicians and patients, and performers and members of the audience.

Because individuals occupy many statuses simultaneously—a status set—they perform multiple roles. Yet, the total number of roles usually exceeds the number of statuses because each status can involve performing several roles in relation to various other people. Robert Merton (1968) introduced the term **role set** to identify *a number of roles attached to a single status*. Figure 6–1 illustrates the status set and corresponding role sets of one individual. Four statuses are presented, each linked to a different role set. First, this woman occupies the status of "wife," with corresponding roles toward her husband ("conjugal roles," such as confidante and sexual partner), with whom she would share a "domestic role" toward the household. Second, she also holds the status of "mother," with routine responsibilities toward her children (the "maternal role") and activities in various organizations such as the PTA (the "civic role"). Third, as a professor, she interacts with students (the "teaching role") as well as with other academics (the "colleague role"). Fourth, her work in a laboratory (the "researcher role") provides the data she uses in her publications (the "author role"). Figure 6–1 is, naturally, only a partial listing of this person's status set and role sets, since anyone generally occupies dozens of statuses at one time, each linked to a role set.

Conflict and Strain

As this example suggests, performing all the roles within an array of role sets is often demanding. Indeed, sometimes various roles seem almost incompatible. All of the roles in the example—wife, mother, teacher, researcher—draw on a person's limited time and energy. As working mothers can testify, carrying out the role of parent as well as the role of breadwinner can be difficult. Sociologists use the concept of **role conflict** to refer to *incompatibility among the roles corresponding to two or more statuses*. We experience role conflict when we find ourselves pulled in various directions while trying to respond to the many statuses we hold at the same time. A surgeon might well choose not to operate on her own son because the personal involvement of motherhood could impair her professional objectivity as a physician.

But even a single status can leave a person with this feeling. The reason is that the many roles linked to one status may make competing demands on us. The concept of **role strain** refers to *incompatibility among the roles corresponding to a single status*. A plant supervisor may wish to be a good friend and confidant to other workers. At the same time, however, a supervisor's responsibility for everyone's performance may require maintaining some measure of personal distance. In short, performing the roles attached to even one status may

Figure 6–1 Status Set and Role Set

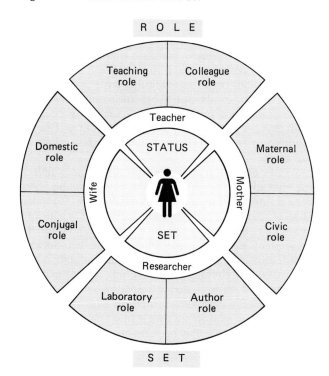

The common experience of women "trying to do it all" is one of conflict between the roles of parent and worker. Because the responsibilities of raising children still fall mostly to mothers, women executives approaching middle age are less than half as likely as their male counterparts to become a parent.

involve a "balancing act" as we attempt to satisfy various duties and obligations.

An individual may handle problems associated with multiple roles in various ways. One simple way to reduce role conflict is to define some roles as more important than others. A new mother, for instance, might devote most of her efforts to parenting and put her career on hold, at least for the present. Resolving role conflict in

this way, however, depends on being able to afford not to work—an option unavailable to many mothers.

Setting priorities is also a common way of reducing the strain among roles linked to a single status. This approach involves emphasizing one particular role, while withdrawing from another with which it conflicts. A father, for example, may decide that maintaining a close and trusting relationship with his child is more important than enforcing cultural norms as a disciplinarian.

Another way to deal with role conflict is to do what Robert Merton (1968) described as "insulating" roles from one another. No role is discarded, but people "compartmentalize" their lives so that roles linked to one status are performed in one place for part of the day, while those corresponding to another status dominate activity elsewhere or at some other time. For example, people usually try to leave their jobs behind them when they go home to assume the responsibilities of spouse or parent.

Role conflict and role strain are everyday experiences in industrial societies because people routinely assume so many statuses and perform an even greater number of roles. As we shall see presently, how we behave in one particular setting is often quite different from how we appear in another.

Role Exit

An interesting area of recent research is *role exit*, the process by which people disengage from social roles that have been central to their lives. Helen Rose Fuchs Ebaugh (1988) began to study this issue as she herself left the life of Catholic nun to become a university sociologist. Studying a range of "exes," including ex-nuns, ex-doctors, ex-husbands, and ex-alcoholics, Ebaugh found many common elements to the process of "becoming an ex."

She explains that people typically begin by reflecting critically on their existing lives, raising doubts about their ability or willingness to carry out that role. Consideration of alternative roles may ultimately lead to a turning point that initiates pursuit of a new life. Within the subsequent "ex-role," people often change their outward appearance and behavior (an ex-nun, for example, begins to wear stylish clothing and make-up). They must also learn to deal with changing responses on the part of those who may have known them in their earlier role, as well as those who do not realize how new and unfamiliar their present role may be. Creating new relationships is especially challenging for an "ex," since many new social skills must be learned. Ebaugh reports, for example, that nuns who begin dating after decades in the church are often startled to learn that sexual norms are now vastly different from those they knew as teenagers.

In modern society, fewer and fewer people expect to live within one job or one marriage. The study of role exit, therefore, seems likely to gain in importance.

THE SOCIAL CONSTRUCTION OF REALITY

Over fifty years ago, the Italian playwright Luigi Pirandello skillfully applied the sociological perspective to social interaction. In *The Pleasure of Honesty*, Angelo Baldovino—a brilliant man with a rather checkered past—enters the fashionable home of the Renni family and introduces himself in a most peculiar way:

> Inevitably we construct ourselves. Let me explain. I enter this house and immediately I become what I have to become, what I can become: I construct myself. That is, I present myself to you in a form suitable to the relationship I wish to achieve with you. And, of course, you do the same with me. . . . (1962:157–158)

This curious statement suggests that, while social interaction is guided by status and role, each human being has considerable ability to shape patterns of interaction with others. Of course, we often perceive the "reality" of society as fixed. As Emile Durkheim explained (see Chapter 4, "Society"), the social world has an objective existence: it has existed long before we were born, affects us throughout our lives, and is likely to continue long after we die. Yet, society is also the behavior of countless creative people. If society affects individuals, then individuals also affect society (Berger & Luckmann, 1967).

The phrase **social construction of reality** refers to *the process by which individuals creatively shape reality through social interaction*. This idea is familiar as an important foundation of the symbolic-interaction paradigm in sociology, as described in earlier chapters. In this context, Angelo Baldovino's remark suggests that, especially in an unfamiliar situation, quite a bit of "reality" is not yet clear in anyone's mind. Pirandello's character will simply use his ability to "present himself" in terms that he decides suit his purposes. As others do the same, reality is socially constructed. What is unusual about Baldovino is his sociological perspective: people

are not generally aware of creating reality in this way, and even when they are, they are seldom so "up front" about their deliberate efforts to foster an impression.

Social interaction, then, is a process of negotiation that generates a changing reality. Usually, interaction results in at least some agreement about how to define a situation. It is unlikely, however, that all participants will have precisely the same perception of the reality being constructed. Perceptions vary because social interaction brings together people with different purposes and interests, each of whom can be expected to seek a somewhat different shaping of reality.

Effectively shaping reality is the essence of what is commonly called "street smarts." In his biography *Down These Mean Streets*, Piri Thomas recalls moving to a new apartment in Spanish Harlem, which soon brought him into contact with the local street gang. Returning home one evening, young Piri found himself cut off by Waneko, the gang's leader, who was surrounded by a dozen others.

> "Whatta ya say, Mr. Johnny Gringo," drawled Waneko.
>
> *Think man*, I told myself, *think your way out of a stomping. Make it good.* "I hear you 104th street coolies are supposed to have heart," I said. "I don't know this for sure. You know there's a lot of streets where a whole 'click' is made out of punks who can't fight one guy unless they all jump him for the stomp." I hoped this would push Waneko into giving me a fair one. His expression didn't change.
>
> "Maybe we don't look at it that way."
>
> *Crazy, man. I cheer inwardly, the* cabron *is falling into my setup.* . . . "I wasn't talking to you," I said. "Where I come from, the pres is president 'cause he got heart when it comes to dealing."
>
> Waneko was starting to look uneasy. He had bit on my worm and felt like a sucker fish. His boys were now light on me. They were no longer so much interested in stomping me as in seeing the outcome between Waneko and me. "Yeah," was his reply. . . .
>
> I knew I'd won. Sure, I'd have to fight; but one guy, not ten or fifteen. If I lost I might still get stomped, and if I won I might get stomped. I took care of this with my next sentence. "I don't know you or your boys," I said, "but they look cool to me. They don't feature as punks."
>
> I had left him out purposely when I said "they." Now his boys were in a separate class. I had cut him off. He would have to fight me on his own, to prove his heart to himself, to his boys, and most important, to his turf. He got away from the stoop and asked, "Fair one, Gringo?" (1967:56–57)

This situation illustrates the character of all human interaction: drama—sometimes subtle, sometimes savage—in which participants creatively negotiate an outcome. We all know that there are limits to what even the most skillful personality can achieve. Should a police officer have come upon the fight that ensued between Piri and Waneko, both young men might well have ended up in jail. Obviously, not everyone enters a negotiation with equal standing; the police officer would probably have the last word simply because of a status that holds greater power than theirs (Molotch & Boden, 1985).

Piri Thomas won acceptance that evening. Having been defined as worthy, he was now one of the group, and from that moment his social identity was changed. W. I. Thomas (1966:301; orig. 1931) succinctly expressed this insight in what has come to be known as the **Thomas theorem**: *situations that are defined as real are real in their consequences*. Applied to social interaction, his insight means that although reality is initially "soft" as it is fashioned, it can become "hard" in its effects. In other words, now that he has been accepted by gang members, Piri Thomas will be treated with respect in subsequent interaction.

The Importance of Culture

Human beings construct everyday experiences in ways that are at least fairly predictable. Instead of fashioning reality "out of thin air," human creativity draws on what is available in the surrounding culture. This means, for example, that the construction of social experience in Spanish Harlem differs from that typical of the affluent East Side of Manhattan. More broadly, "reality" common to those living within ancient Greece was significantly different from that common in Iran today. The social experiences of today's Iranians may seem equally foreign to many Americans.

Because socially constructed realities are guided by culture, each society typically regards them as "given" or "natural." This is the essential point of the Thomas theorem, which claims that the emerging social world is "real" to those who fashion it. One of the benefits of the sociological perspective is the constant reminder that humans have made—and can remake—the surrounding social world, perhaps more differently than we may initially imagine.

Within a different cultural context, any object or human action is also subject to differing interpretations. The meanings attached to the two sexes, stages of the life cycle, or even the days of the week vary according to cultural context. In a recent study, for example, Wendy Griswold (1987) asked people from different cultures—the West Indies, Great Britain, and the United States—to interpret several novels. She found that reality is not "black and white" but constructed according to the basic "blueprint" of culture. What people see in a book—or anything else—is guided by their social environment.

Cultures frame reality differently. This man lay on the street in Bombay, India, for several hours and finally died. In the United States, such an event would probably have provoked someone to call the rescue squad. In a poor society where death on the streets is a daily occurrence, however, many Indians responded with simple decency by placing incense on him and continuing on their way.

Ethnomethodology

It is hardly surprising that human beings take for granted most of the reality they create. After all, what would social life be like if we questioned every situation we experienced? Some sociologists, however, attempt to learn about everyday life precisely by challenging patterns of conventional behavior.

Ethnomethodology is a specialized approach within the symbolic-interaction paradigm. The term itself has two parts: the Greek "ethno" refers to understandings of cultural surroundings that people share, and "methodology" designates a system of methods or principles. Combining them leads to defining **ethnomethodology** as *the study of the everyday, common-sense understandings that people have of the world around them.*

The term *ethnomethodology* was coined in the 1950s by Harold Garfinkel, a sociologist who was dissatisfied with the views of society that were widespread in the discipline at that time. Rather than seeing society as a broad "system" with a life of its own (as did Emile Durkheim, described in Chapter 4, "Society"), Garfinkel explored how we constantly engage in building understandings of familiar, everyday experiences (Heritage, 1984). For example, people readily expect certain behavior when sitting down to dinner in a restaurant, when beginning to take a final examination, or when driving onto a freeway. As important as such conventional understandings may be, Garfinkel (1967) maintained that few of us ever think much about them.

In the rebellious social climate of the 1960s, Garfinkel developed a distinctive technique for exposing what the typically unacknowledged patterns of everyday life are: *break the rules*. There is no better way to tease out the conventional realities, he reasoned, than to deliberately ignore them.

In a series of experiments, Garfinkel (1967) had his students map patterns of everyday life by deliberately refusing to "play the game." Some entered stores and insisted on bargaining for standard-priced items, others recruited people into simple games (like tic-tac-toe) only to intentionally flout the rules, still others initiated conversations and slowly moved closer and closer until they were almost nose to nose with their quarry. At the very least, intentional rule violation was met with bewilderment; often "victims" were provoked to anger. One of Garfinkel's students reported, for example, the following exchange (1967:44):

> Acquaintance: "How are you?"
> Student: "How am I in regard to what? My health,

my finances, my school work, my peace of mind, my . . ."
> Acquaintance (now red in the face and suddenly out of control): "Look! I was just trying to be polite. Frankly, I don't give a damn how you are."

In each case, Garfinkel maintains, a deliberate lack of social cooperation may allow the researcher to see more clearly the unspoken rules of everyday life. The importance of these rules is indicated by the fact that people find their violation unpleasant, even threatening.

The provocative character of ethnomethodology, coupled with its focus on commonplace experiences, has led some sociologists to view it as less-than-serious research. Even so, ethnomethodology has succeeded in heightening awareness of many unnoticed patterns of everyday life.

DRAMATURGICAL ANALYSIS: "THE PRESENTATION OF SELF"

Erving Goffman (1922–1982) shared with Garfinkel an interest in the patterned character of everyday life. Goffman agreed that people socially construct reality, and he attempted to show that in doing so, we have much in common with actors performing on a stage. Thus, calling to mind a director scrutinizing the action in a theater, Goffman termed his approach **dramaturgical analysis**, defined as *the analysis of social interaction in terms of theatrical performance.*

Dramaturgical analysis provides a fesh look at two now-familiar concepts. A status is very much like a part in a play, and a role is a script that supplies dialogue and action to each of the characters. Any setting of a role performance can be compared to the stage of a theater, and what unfolds is observed by an audience. The heart of Goffman's analysis is the process he called the **presentation of self**, which means *the ways in which individuals, in various settings, attempt to create specific impressions in the minds of others.* This process, also known as *impression management,* contains a number of common elements (Goffman, 1959, 1967).

Performances

As individuals present themselves to others, they convey information—consciously and unconsciously—about how they wish to be understood. Goffman called these efforts, taken together, a *performance*. Dress (costume), the objects people carry with them (props), and tone of voice and gestures are all part of a performance. Another important element of any performance is its physical location. Since many cultural norms vary according to setting, performance responds to the social context in which it occurs. People who are joking loudly on the sidewalk, for example, are likely to assume a more reverent manner when they enter a church. Equally important, individuals often design settings, such as their home or office, to invoke desired reactions in others. Like a stage, a setting can be used to enhance an individual's performance by providing numerous specific pieces of information.

Consider, for example, how a physician's office influences patterns of social interaction. This setting is carefully crafted by the physician and the medical staff to convey appropriate information to their audience of patients. Physicians enjoy considerable prestige and power in American society. Their high status is usually conveyed to the patient immediately on entering the doctor's office by the fact that the physician is nowhere to be seen. Instead, within what Goffman describes as the "front region" of the setting, the patient encounters a receptionist. This person functions as a gatekeeper, deciding if and when the patient can meet the physician. A simple survey of the doctor's waiting room, with patients—often impatiently—waiting to gain entry to the inner sanctum, leaves little doubt that the medical team is in control of events.

The physician's private office constitutes the "back region" of the setting. Here are found a wide range of props, such as medical books and framed degrees, that serve as further reminders that the physician, and not the patient, has the specialized knowledge necessary to guide their social interaction. Notice, too, that the physician usually remains seated behind a large desk—a symbol of power—while the patient is provided with only a chair.

The physician's appearance and manner convey still more information. The usual costume of white lab coat may have the practical function of keeping clothes from becoming soiled, but its primary purpose is to let others know at a glance the physician's status. A stethoscope around the neck or a black medical bag in hand has the same purpose. The doctor's highly technical terminology—frequently mystifying, if occasionally necessary—also reinforces the hierarchy in the situation. The use of the title "Doctor" by patients who, in turn, are frequently addressed by only their first names is another way of underscoring the physician's dominant position.

The overall message of a doctor's performance is clear: "I can help you, but you must agree that I am in charge." Not all medical situations are so easily defined. In some special cases, medical performances generate ambiguity in the minds of patients, which can cause misunderstanding and unnecessary discomfort. The box presents a dramaturgical analysis of a sensitive medical situation familiar to women.

Professionals often carry out their personal performances in carefully crafted settings. The prominent display of numerous degrees behind this physician's desk informs her patients that she expects to take charge of the interaction.

The Gynecological Examination: A Dramaturgical Analysis

Erving Goffman explains how individual performances convey specific information to an audience. Sociologist Joan Emerson points out that performances can sometimes be understood in more than one way. She claims that in some situations ambiguity can be especially disruptive, so people must think and act carefully to ensure that the information a performance conveys is understood correctly.

An experience familiar to many women, a gynecological examination by a male physician, is one such precarious situation. Emerson systematically observed seventy-five such examinations, concluding that this situation is subject to dangerous misinterpretation. The basis of the problem is that a male physician must touch the genitals of a female patient. Ambiguity arises because in other settings, such behavior between males and females is defined as either a consensual sexual relationship or a sexual assault. Neither of these situational definitions is acceptable in the case of a medical examination. The medical staff, therefore, must carefully structure their personal performances to remove sexual connotations as completely as possible so the patient will define the situation as a clearly medical procedure in which her dignity is fully respected.

Emerson notes several ways in which the medical staff attempts to make the exam less threatening to the patient. First, the procedure is restricted to a specific setting used for no other purpose—a room whose decor and equipment evoke only a medical definition of the situation. All personnel wear medical uniforms, never clothing that could be worn in other, nonmedical situations. The medical staff also tries to make the patient feel that such examinations are simply routine although, from the patient's point of view, they are actually highly unusual.

Rapport between physician and patient is important, but this should be established before the examination begins. Once it starts, the performance of a male physician must be extremely matter-of-fact, suggesting to the patient that examining the genitals is no different from examining any other part of the body. A female nurse is usually present during the examination. Her manifest role is to assist the physician, but she also has the important role of dispelling any impression that the situation involves a man and woman "alone in a room" (Emerson, 1970:81). The nurse usually initiates the procedure with a soothing phrase such as "The doctor wants to take a peek at you now." After the examination has begun, though, all members of the medical staff are careful to use only technical and impersonal language. Moreover, the medical staff addresses the patient solely in terms reflecting her status as patient. Instead of mentioning "*your* vagina," for example, the physician refers, more technically, to "*the* vagina." Similarly, phrases such as "let your knees fall apart" are used in place of such sexually loaded language as "spread your legs" (Emerson, 1970:81–82). Finally, physical contact between the physician and the patient is limited to what is medically necessary.

How to control situational definitions is rarely discussed in medical schools. This omission is unfortunate because, as Emerson's analysis shows, understanding social interaction in the examination room is just as crucial as mastering the medical skills involved. Fortunately, the importance of sociological insights is gradually being recognized by medical professionals. At the Southwestern Medical School in Dallas, Texas, for example, Professor David Hemsell urges all his medical students to gain a better understanding of this process from the patient's point of view by actually climbing onto an examination table and placing their feet in the metal stirrups with their legs apart. Hemsell claims, "The only way to understand women's feelings is to be there." He adds, "You can see the impact of being in that position hit them in the face like a two-by-four." Imagine the even greater impact if male medical students were required to do this without wearing their trousers.

SOURCES: Joan P. Emerson, "Behavior in Private Places: Sustaining Definitions of Reality in Gynecological Examinations," in H. P. Drietzel, ed., *Recent Sociology*, Vol. 2 (New York: Collier, 1970), pp. 74–97; Professor Hemsell's work is described in *Mother Jones*, (December 1984), p. 9.

Nonverbal Communication

Novelist William Sansom describes a fictional Mr. Preedy—an English vacationer on a beach in Spain:

> He took care to avoid catching anyone's eye. First, he had to make it clear to those potential companions of his holiday that they were of no concern to him whatsoever. He stared through them, round them, over them—eyes lost in space. The beach might have been empty. If by chance a ball was thrown his way, he looked surprised; then let a smile of amusement light his face (Kindly Preedy), looked around dazed to see that there were people on the beach, tossed it back with a smile to himself and not a smile *at* the people. . . .

> . . . (He) then gathered together his beach-wrap and bag into a neat sand-resistant pile (Methodical and Sensible Preedy), rose slowly to stretch his huge frame (Big-Cat Preedy), and tossed aside his sandals (Carefree Preedy, after all). (1956; cited in Goffman, 1959:4–5)

Through his performance, Mr. Preedy offers a great deal of information about himself to anyone caring to observe him. Notice that it is conveyed without his uttering a single word. This illustrates the process of **nonverbal communication**, which is *communication using body movements, gestures, and facial expressions rather than spoken words.*

Nonverbal communication is largely based on the use of the body to convey information to others, as sug-

---

SOCIOLOGY OF EVERYDAY LIFE

Telling Lies: Clues to Deceit

On September 15, 1938, Germany's chancellor Adolf Hitler and Britain's prime minister Neville Chamberlain met for the first time, as the world looked on with the hope of avoiding war. Although his plans for war were already well under way, Hitler assured Chamberlain that peace could be preserved. Chamberlain believed what he heard, writing soon afterward, "In spite of the hardness and ruthlessness I thought I saw in his face, I got the impression that here was a man who could be relied upon when he had given his word" (Ekman, 1985:15–16). In retrospect, we can see that Chamberlain should have paid less attention to the message Hitler *gave* and more to the contradictory non-verbal signals he *gave off*.

Telling lies is difficult because few people can skillfully manipulate their facial gestures. The grief in Figure A is probably genuine, since few people can intentionally lift the upper eyelids and inner corners of the eyebrows in this way. Likewise, the apprehension in Figure B also appears genuine, since raising the eyebrows and pulling them together in this way is also extremely difficult. In contrast, the asymmetrical smile in Figure C is probably a phony expression of pleasure since, for most people, genuine pleasure is expressed by a "balanced" smile.

Detecting lies is a difficult task, because no bodily gesture directly indicates deceit as, for example, a smile indicates pleasure. Even so, because any performance involves so many pieces of information, few people can confidently lie without allowing some element of contradictory information to raise the observer's suspicions. The key, therefore, to identifying deceit is to examine a complete performance with an eye for any discrepancies in the information conveyed.

More specifically, Ekman suggests directing attention to four types of information provided by a performer. The first is *language*, the major chan-

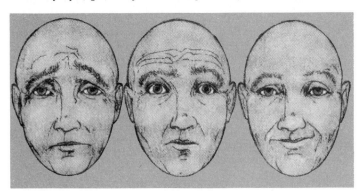

| Figure A | Figure B | Figure C |

gested by the more common phrase *body language*. Facial expressions are crucial to nonverbal communication. Smiling, for example, is a symbol of pleasure, although we distinguish between the casual, lighthearted smile of Kindly Preedy on the beach, a smile of embarrassment, and the full, unrestrained smile of self-satisfaction we often associate with the "cat who ate the canary." Other facial expressions convey an almost limitless range of human emotions, including anger, confusion, disgust, pain, sadness, and indifference.

Eye contact is another significant element of nonverbal communication. Generally, eye contact is an invitation to further social interaction. Someone across the room "catches our eye," for example, and a conversation begins. Avoiding the eyes of another, in contrast, discour-

ages communication. Our hands also speak for us. Common hand gestures within our culture can convey, among other things, an insult, a request for a ride, an invitation for someone to join us, or a demand that others stop in their tracks. Gestures also supplement spoken words. Pointing in a menacing way at someone, for example, gives greater emphasis to a word of warning, as shrugging the shoulders adds an air of indifference to the phrase "I don't know," and rapidly waving the arms lends urgency to the single word "Hurry!"

Like all symbols, nonverbal communication is largely culture-specific. Few gestures have uniform meaning among all humanity, and many significant gestures in North American culture mean nothing—or something very different—to members of other cultures,

nel of communication in social interaction. Words are relatively easy for a liar to manipulate, since they can be mentally rehearsed prior to presentation. One clue to deceit, however, is a simple slip of the tongue—something the performer did not mean to say in quite that way. For example, a young man who is deceiving his parents by claiming that his roommate is a male friend rather than a female lover might inadvertently use the word *she* rather than *he* in a conversation. The more complicated the deception, the more likely a performer will introduce contradiction into what is said.

A second type of information is *voice*—meaning all the qualities of speech other than words. Tone and patterns of speech often contain clues to deception because they are hard to control. When attempting to hide a powerful emotion, for example, a person's voice is likely to tremble or break. Similarly, the rate of speech may become unusually fast (suggest-

ing anger) or slow (suggesting sadness). In other cases, inappropriate pauses between words—or nonwords, such as *ah* and *ummm*—may suggest discomfort.

A third kind of information is a "leak" from the *body* that a performer is unable to conceal. Subtle body movements, for example, suggest nervousness, as can sudden swallowing or rapid breathing. These are especially good clues to deception because they are extremely difficult to control. Sometimes, *not* using the body in a usual manner to enhance words—as when a person tries to fake excitement—may also suggest deception.

The fourth type of information is uncontrollable *facial expression*. A sad person feigning happiness, for example, is likely to "flash" momentary frowns through a smile as concealed emotion leaks through the performance. Raising and drawing together the eyebrows is a sign of fear or worry that is virtually impossible for most

people to accomplish voluntarily. Appearing while a person claims to be at ease, this expression usually indicates deception.

These brief examples suggest that lies are detectable, although the ability to notice relevant clues usually requires training. As parents know about their children, clues to deception are easier to spot in people whose patterns of speech and behavior are familiar. Such clues to deception are also more prevalent when a person is trying to contain strong emotions. Some cases of deception, then, can be unmasked more readily than others. Many people with unusual ability to carefully manage their verbal and nonverbal performances—including both those with theatrical training and those who have spent many years deceiving others—can be quite successful in their deceptions. There are, in short, both good and bad liars.

SOURCE: Adapted from Paul Ekman, *Telling Lies: Clues to Deceit in the Marketplace, Politics, and Marriage* (New York: W. W. Norton, 1985).

as described in the box on p. 64 in Chapter 3 ("Culture"). The "thumbs up" gesture indicates approval in the United States, while in Greece the same gesture is a sexual insult. Similarly, what Americans call the "A-Okay" gesture with thumb and forefinger means "You're a zero" to the French, and symbolizes a crude word for "rectum" to many Italians (Ekman, 1984).

The examples of nonverbal communication presented in Chapter 3 so far were elements of a deliberate performance. Sometimes, however, the information we communicate verbally is contradicted by nonverbal cues that we cannot easily control. Listening to her teenage son's explanation for returning home at a late hour, for example, a mother begins to doubt his words because he is unable to hold eye contact. The guest on a television talk show claims that his recent divorce is "the best thing that ever happened to me," but the nervous swing of his leg suggests otherwise. In this manner, nonverbal communication may provide clues to verbal deception, in much the same way that a lie detector measures the subtle physical changes in breathing, pulse rate, perspiration, and blood pressure that signal the stress of telling lies. Does this mean that careful observers can detect dishonesty in another's performance? Paul Ekman believes they can, as the box on pp. 158–59 explains.

Gender and Personal Performances

An analysis of personal performances must take account of *gender*, or how society links human traits to being male and female. Because females are socialized to be less assertive than males, they tend to be especially sensitive to nonverbal communication. More generally, society leads us to make assumptions about performances simply on the basis of a person's sex. Based on the work of Nancy Henley, Mykol Hamilton, and Barrie Thorne (1989), we can extend the conventional discussion of personal performances to highlight the importance of gender.

Demeanor

Goffman (1967) has suggested that *demeanor*—general conduct or deportment—varies according to an individual's power. Simply put, people in positions of power have far greater personal discretion in how they act; in contrast, those subject to supervision usually must act more self-consciously and formally. Office behavior such as swearing, removing shoes, or putting feet up on the desk may well be considered appropriate for the boss, but not for subordinates (Henley, Hamilton, & Thorne,

1989). Similarly, people in positions of dominance can interrupt the performances of others with impunity, while those subject to their power are expected to display deference by becoming silent (Smith-Lovin & Brody, 1989).

This is especially important for women, who generally occupy positions of little power. As Chapter 13 ("Sex and Gender") explains, about half of all working women in the United States have clerical or service jobs that subject them to the direct control of supervisors, usually male. Within our society, then, women must craft their personal performances more formally than men while continually displaying expected deference. Whatever else they may wish to convey to others, women are expected to continually broadcast their subordination to men.

Use of Space

An important, albeit less commonly considered, element of personal performances is the amount of space they occupy. Here again, power is a key variable, since using more space conveys a nonverbal message of being an important person. According to Henley, Hamilton, and Thorne (1989), men tend to use significantly more space than women do. Femininity itself has traditionally been evaluated by how little space women occupy (the standard of "daintiness"), while masculinity has been enhanced by controlling as much territory as possible.

The concept of **personal space** refers to *the area around a person over which some claim to privacy is made*. In American society, personal space is somewhat greater than in more densely populated societies such as Japan, and typically involves a distance between individuals of at least several feet. But this distance varies significantly by sex. In interaction, men are more likely to intrude upon the personal space of women than the other way around. A woman's intrusion into a man's personal space is likely to be defined and responded to by the male as a sexual overture. Here again, women have less power to define a reality than men do.

Staring, Smiling, and Touching

Eye contact is an important means of encouraging interaction. Women do more to maintain interactions than men do, by sustaining more eye contact. An exception is *staring*. Women often find themselves the objects of men's stares, which reflects both the dominance of males in American society and their tendency to define women as sexual objects.

Although frequently conveying happiness, *smiling* can convey a wide range of meaning. In a male-domi-

In private interactions involving the two sexes, women tend to maintain more eye contact than men do. In public places, however, eye contact in the form of staring is common behavior among males. This reflects male dominance and the tendency of men to view women as sexual objects.

nated world, women often smile to indicate appeasement, or acceptance of submission. For this reason, Henley, Hamilton, and Thorne maintain, smiling is more common among women than men, in extreme cases even reaching the level of nervous habit.

Finally, *touching* is a significant social pattern. Mutual touching generally conveys intimacy and caring. In most situations, touching is primarily something men do to women. A male physician touches the shoulder of his female nurse as they examine a report, a young man who has just begun dating touches the back of his woman friend as he guides her across the street, or a male skiing instructor excessively and unnecessarily touches his female students. In these examples—as well as many others—the touching evokes little response, so common is it in everyday life. But each situation is also a subtle ritual by which males express their position in an assumed hierarchy that subordinates women (Henley, Hamilton, & Thorne, 1989:108–110).

Idealization

Whatever the actual motive for our actions, Goffman suggests that performances typically attempt to *idealize* our intentions. That is, people usually want to convince others that they are abiding by ideal cultural standards. Idealization is easily illustrated by returning to the world of physicians and patients.

Within the hospital, physicians engage in a routine commonly described as "making rounds." Entering the room of a patient, the physician often stops at the foot of the bed and silently examines the patient's chart. Afterwards, physician and patient briefly converse. In culturally ideal terms, this routine involves a physician making a personal visit to inquire about a patient's condition.

In reality, something less ideal is usually occurring. A physician who sees perhaps thirty-five patients a day may remember little about most of them. Immediately reading the chart provides an opportunity to rediscover who the person is and recall the patient's medical problems. Openly revealing the actual impersonality of much medical care would undermine the culturally ideal perception of the physician as deeply concerned about patients' welfare. The process of idealization also helps to explain the common pattern by which patients assume that "what the doctor orders" must be in their own best interest. No doubt this is often the case. But, as Chapter 20 ("Health and Medicine") suggests, physicians often prescribe drugs, admit patients to hospitals, and perform surgery with a keen awareness of what's in it for themselves (Kaplan et al., 1985).

Idealization is woven into the fabric of everyday life in countless ways. Physicians and other professionals typically attempt to idealize their motives for entering their chosen careers. They assert that their work is an effort to "make a contribution to science," to "answer a calling from God," or to "serve the community." Rarely do such people concede the less honorable, although common, motives of seeking the high income, power, and prestige provided by these occupations. More generally, most of us smile and make polite remarks to people we do not like. Because they are expected, such ideal cultural patterns are generally unnoticed. Even when we suspect that others are putting on an act, we are unlikely to openly challenge their performance, for reasons that the next section explains.

Embarrassment and Tact

The fashionably dressed socialite enters the room with her slip showing; the eminent professor consistently mispronounces a simple word; the visiting dignitary rises from the table to speak, unaware that his napkin still hangs from his neck. As carefully as individuals may craft their performances, slip-ups of this kind frequently occur. They may result in *embarrassment*, which in a dramaturgical analysis means recognizing that a poor performance has failed to convince an audience. As Goffman suggests, embarrassment is the experience of "losing face."

Embarrassment is an ever-present danger in social interaction. First, idealized performances typically contain some element of deception. Second, since performances are extremely complex, any inconsistent piece of information can render an entire performance inauthentic to an audience.

Curiously, an audience usually chooses to overlook flaws in a person's performance to avoid introducing embarrassment into a social situation. Pointing out that a woman's slip is showing is usually appropriate only if doing so is likely to spare her even greater embarrassment. In Hans Christian Andersen's classic fable "The Emperor's New Clothes," the child who blurts out that the emperor is naked tells the truth, but is scolded for being rude.

People not only ignore flaws in a performance, they often help the performer recover from them. Goffman suggests that this is the meaning of *tact*, which, dramaturgically speaking, is helping another person "save face." After hearing a friend make an embarrassingly inaccurate remark, for example, people may be tactful in a variety of ways. No response at all may signal that they wish to pretend the statement was never made. Mild laughter may indicate they wish to dismiss what they have heard as a joke. Or a listener may simply respond, "C'mon, I know you don't mean that," suggesting that one part of a performance will not destroy the actor's overall social image.

Why is tact so common? The answer is that embarrassment causes discomfort not simply for one person but for *everyone*. Just as members of a theater audience feel uneasy when an actor forgets a line, people who observe a poor performance are reminded of how fragile their own performances often are. Through their performances human beings construct social reality, which is like a dam holding back a sea of chaotic alternatives. Should one person's performance spring a leak, others

Gestures vary widely from one culture to another. Yet a chuckle, grin, or smirk in response to someone's personal performance is a universal sign of not taking the person seriously. Therefore, people the world over tactfully cover their faces in such situations.

can be expected to tactfully assist in making repairs. Everyone, after all, is engaged in jointly building reality, and no one wants it to be suddenly swept away.

Goffman's research shows that although individuals interact with a considerable degree of individuality and spontaneity, everyone's social interactions are constructed out of similar patterned elements. Almost four hundred years ago, Shakespeare wrote:

> All the world's a stage,
> And all the men and women are merely players.
> They have their exits and their entrances,
> And one man in his time plays many parts.
> (As You Like It, V)

Human behavior is certainly not as rigidly scripted as a stage performance. In a lifetime, though, each individual does play many parts in ways that combine social structure with expressions of a unique personality. As Goffman (1959:72) concludes, even if human behavior does not simply consist of stage and script, Shakespeare's observation still contains a good bit of truth.

INTERACTION IN EVERYDAY LIFE: TWO ILLUSTRATIONS

We have now presented a general approach to understanding social interaction. The final sections of this chapter will illustrate these ideas with two important, yet quite different, elements of everyday life.

Language: The Gender Issue

As explained in Chapter 3 ("Culture"), language is the major form of communication by which members of a society weave the symbolic web we call culture. Any use of language is likely to convey meaning on more than one level.

Everyday communication has a *manifest* content, referring to what is explicitly stated. Communication also has a *latent* content, which conveys much more information. One latent message involves the relative social definition of males and females. Language functions to define the two sexes differently in at least three ways (Henley, Hamilton, & Thorne, 1989).[1]

[1] The following sections draw primarily upon Henley, Hamilton, & Thorne, 1989. Additional material is drawn from Thorne, Kramarae, and Henley, 1983, and MacKay, 1983, and others as noted.

The Control Function of Language

A young man drives into the gas station, eager to display his new motorcycle, and proudly asks, "Isn't she a beauty?" On the surface, the question has little to do with males and females. Yet, it is curious that a common linguistic pattern is to use the female "she," rather than male "he," to refer to "admired" objects.

This pattern is significant as a means of establishing and enhancing the control of males over their surroundings. In other words, a male owner attaches a female pronoun to a motorcycle, car, yacht, or other object because it seems consistent with *possession*. Conversely, use of a male pronoun for such cases (by either a male or female owner) is rare.

Perhaps the most obvious control function of language involves the naming of people. A traditional pattern in American society, and one commonly found elsewhere, is that women take the family name of men upon marriage. While few today would view this as an explicit statement of male ownership of a female, many find it suggestive of male dominance. An increasing proportion of women have for this reason retained their own name (more precisely, the name obtained from their father) or combined in a more equitable fashion two family names.

The Value Function of Language

Language attaches value to what is defined as masculine or feminine, in a generally consistent and unequal manner. This pattern is deeply rooted in the English language, in ways that probably few men or women realize. For instance, the word "virtue," meaning moral excellence, is derived from the Latin word *vir*, meaning "man."

In numerous, more familiar ways, language also confers different values upon the two sexes. Traditional masculine terms such as "king" or "lord" have retained their high value, while some initially comparable terms, such as "queen," "madam," or "dame" have assumed more negative meanings in contemporary society. Language is thus both a mirror of social attitudes and also a means by which they are perpetuated.

Similarly, use of the prefixes "ette" and "ess" to denote femininity are generally perceived as devaluing. For example, a *major* has higher standing than a *majorette*, as does a *host* in relation to a *hostess*. And, certainly, male groups with names such as the Los Angeles Rams carry more stature than female groups with names such as the Radio City Music Hall Rockettes.

The Attention Function of Language

Language also organizes our reality, directing attention to what is masculine, while tending to ignore what is feminine. The most obvious example is the use of personal pronouns. Within the English language, the plural pronoun "they" is neutral as it refers to both sexes. But the corresponding singular pronouns "he" and "she" are sex linked.

A more subtle example of how language constructs reality in masculine terms is found in the traditional grammatical practice of using "he" (also, the possessive "his" and objective "him") to refer to *all people*. Thus, we assume that the masculine pronoun in the bit of wisdom "He who hesitates is lost" refers to females as well as to males. But are masculine pronouns truly inclusive, or do they serve to ignore what involves females? Considerable research suggests that people respond to allegedly inclusive or generic male pronouns as if only males were involved (Martyna, 1978, 1980; MacKay, 1983). To many female readers, especially those who express sympathy for the women's movement, encountering male pronouns carries the message that females are of peripheral importance (MacKay, 1983).

For a century, suggestions have been made for the creation of a gender-neutral, singular personal pronoun. In 1884, one language critic offered a new word "thon" (from "that" + "one") to solve the pronoun problem, as in "the confident person is thon who is well-prepared"(Converse, 1884; cited in Kramarae, Thorne, & Henley, 1983:175). The awkwardness of new constructions indicates how established traditional patterns have become in our everyday lives. More recently, the plural pronoun "they" has been increasingly employed as a singular pronoun. This usage remains controversial, for it violates grammatical rules. Yet, in an age of growing concern over gender-linked bias, such an evolution of the English language seems likely.

Humor: Playing with Reality

For virtually everyone, humor is a part of everyday life. Comedians are among our favorite entertainers, most newspapers contain cartoon pages, and even professors and the clergy include humor in their performances. But like much of everyday life, humor is largely taken for granted. While everyone laughs at a joke, few people think about *why* something is funny or why humor is a universal element of social life. We will now apply many of the ideas developed in this chapter to the topic of humor.[2]

The Foundation of Humor

The essence of humor lies in the contrast between two incongruous realities. Generally, one socially constructed reality can be termed *conventional* because it is consistent with the values and norms that people expect in a situation. The other reality can be called *unconventional* because it represents a significant violation of cultural patterns. Humor, therefore, arises from ambiguity and "double meanings" involving two differing definitions of a situation. Consider the following simple pieces of humor:

> Steve Martin muses: "I like a woman with a head on her shoulders. *I hate necks!*"

> A bumper sticker reads: "Insanity is hereditary—you get it from your kids!"

In each of these examples, the first sentence represents a conventional reality. A man seeks a woman who is sensible and intelligent. Mental illness can be inherited. There is nothing startling here. In contrast, the second sentence in each example provides an unconventional meaning that collides with what we take for granted. In the Steve Martin joke, the assertion "I hate necks!" suddenly transforms the entire statement into an unexpectedly grotesque image. Similarly, the line ". . . you get it from your kids!" is an absurd reversal of the hereditary process. The foundation of all humor is such contrasting realities.

The same simple pattern is evident in the humor of other well-known comedians:

> Groucho Marx, trying to sound manly: "This morning, I shot a lion in my pajamas." He then turns to the camera and adds, "What the lion was doing in my pajamas I'll *never* know . . ."

> On the television show "M*A*S*H," Hawkeye Pierce observes Colonel Henry Blake gallivanting around with a young woman half his age and dryly responds, "There's an age problem there; she's twenty-two and his wife's forty-eight."

---

[2] The ideas contained in this discussion are those of the author (1987), except as otherwise noted. The general approach draws on work presented earlier in this chapter, especially on the ideas of Erving Goffman.

Perhaps the most common format for comedy is "funny person-straight person," in which one comic disrupts social conventions to the consternation of the other. Laurel and Hardy are among the best comedians to have generated humor in this way. As the defender of conventional reality, Oliver Hardy haplessly scolded his sidekick Stan Laurel: "A fine mess *you've* gotten us into!"

Like the other two examples, each of these jokes contains two major elements, a conventional assertion followed by an unconventional one. The greater the opposition, or incongruity, between the two definitions of reality, the greater the potential for humor. When telling jokes, people can strengthen this opposition in various ways. One technique, often used by Groucho Marx, George Burns, and other comedians of the screen, is to present the first, or conventional remark, in conversation with another actor, then to turn toward the audience while delivering the second, or unconventional, line. This "shift of channel" serves to underscore the incongruity of the two parts. This also explains why comedians must pay careful attention to their performances—the precise words they use, as well as the timing of each part of the delivery. A joke, then, is "well told" by creating the sharpest possible contrast between the realities, and easily ruined by a careless performance. Since the key to humor lies in the opposition of realities, it is not surprising that the climax of a joke is termed the *punch line*.

The Dynamics of Humor: "Getting It"

Someone who does not understand both the conventional and unconventional realities embedded in a joke offers the typical complaint: "I don't get it." The significance of "getting" the humor, then, is a matter of understanding the two realities involved well enough to perceive their incongruity.

Something more is usually involved in getting a joke. All of the information necessary to get it may not be explicitly stated. The audience, therefore, must pay attention to the stated elements of the joke and then inferentially complete the joke in their own minds. An illustration is the following exchange, from the well-known television show "Cheers":

Sam: "Diane, you're drunk."
Diane: "Yes, Sam, and you're stupid, but I'll be sober in the morning."

In this case, "getting" the joke is a fairly simple process of following well enough to mentally complete Diane's line with the words ". . . *and you'll still be stupid.*"

A more complex joke is the following, written on the wall of a college restroom:

Dyslexics of the World, Untie!

This joke demands much more of the audience. One must know, first, that dyslexia is a condition in which people routinely reverse letters; second, one must identify the line as an adaptation of Karl Marx's call to the world's workers to unite; third and finally, one must recognize "untie" as an anagram of "unite," as one might imagine a disgruntled dyslexic person would write it.

Why would an audience be required to make this sort of effort in order to understand a joke? The answer is that this practice pays dividends in audience response. Simply put, as listeners, our reaction to a joke is heightened by the pleasure of having completed the puzzle necessary to "get it." This pleasure partly derives from satisfaction at our mental abilities. Additionally, "getting" the joke confers a favored status as an "insider" within the larger audience. Conversely, the frustration that accompanies not getting a joke is easy to understand: the fear of mental inadequacy coupled to a sense of being socially excluded from pleasure shared by others. Not surprisingly, "outsiders" in such a situation may fake "getting" the joke, or may quietly ask others to explain it to end their sense of being left out.

But, as the old saying goes, if a joke has to be explained, it is unlikely to be very funny. Besides taking the edge off the language and timing on which the *punch* depends, an explanation completely relieves the audience of any mental involvement, substantially reducing their pleasure.

The Topics of Humor

As a means of playing with reality, humor is set off from whatever is conventional within any culture. Since people throughout the world live within many diverse cultures, they differ in what they find to be funny. Musicians frequently travel to perform for receptive audiences around the world, suggesting that music may be the "common language" of humanity. Comedians rarely do, demonstrating that humor does not travel well.

What is humorous to the Chinese, then, may be lost on most Americans. To some degree, too, different categories of people in one society will find humor in different situations. In the United States, New Englanders, southerners, and westerners have their own brands of humor, as do blacks and whites, fifteen and forty year olds, bankers and construction workers.

In all these cases, however, humor deals with topics that lend themselves to double meanings—in short, it is closely tied to what is *controversial*. For example, the first jokes many of us learned as children were probably concerned with what American culture defines as a childhood taboo: sex. The mere mention of "unmentionable acts" or even certain parts of the body can bring paralyzing laughter to young faces.

Humor's inherent controversy is also the reason

that a thin line separates what is funny from what is considered "sick." The word *humors*, in fact, was used during the Middle Ages to refer to a balance of bodily fluids ("humor" is derived from the Latin *humidus*, meaning "moist") that determined a person's health or sickness. In most cultures, sometimes taking conventional definitions of reality lightly (in other words, having a "sense of humor") is valued. Evidence also suggests that maintaining a sense of humor contributes to a person's physical health (Robinson, 1983). At the other extreme, paying no attention to conventional reality is to risk being defined as deviant or even mentally ill.

Even in less serious instances, a person may be admonished for telling a "sick" joke, which treats lightly a situation that is expected to be handled with reverence. There are some topics, in other words, that any culture expects to be understood in only one way; consequently, they are defined as "off limits" for humor. Common examples are people's religious beliefs or tragic accidents.

The Functions of Humor

As a means of expressing opposition to cultural convention, humor can be valuable to any social system. Following structural-functional analysis, the universality of humor reflects its function as a social "safety valve," allowing the release of potentially disruptive sentiments. Jokes express sentiments that might be dangerous if taken seriously, as consideration of racial and ethnic jokes readily suggests. Called to account for a remark that could be defined as offensive, a person may diffuse the situation by simply stating, "I didn't mean anything by what I said, it was just a joke!" Likewise, a person who would be justified in taking offense at another's behavior may use humor as a form of tact, smiling, as if to say, "I could be angry at this, but I choose not to take seriously what you have done."

Like theater and art, humor also allows a society to explore alternatives to the status quo, with limited seriousness. Sometimes political jokes may, in other words, be the first step in acting to change government.

Humor and Conflict

Humor is also an expression of conflict among various categories of people. Men and women, blacks and whites, and rich and poor tend to endorse somewhat different definitions of reality. Consequently, members of any such category can employ humor to question the interests of those they oppose. Men who tell jokes about feminists, for example, are almost certainly expressing some measure of hostility to the interests of women (Benokraitis & Feagin, 1986; Powell & Paton, 1988). Similarly, jokes at the expense of homosexuals reveal the tensions surrounding sexual orientation in American society.

In these final observations, we can begin to understand the larger significance of humor in everyday life. Michael Flaherty (1984, 1990) points out that socially constructing reality is constant and demanding work. Furthermore, the reality that emerges is often less favorable than what we are able to imagine. As long as we maintain a sense of humor, we are never prisoners of the present. Indeed, we are able to fight back at the world and in doing so, perhaps, change it (and ourselves) just a little.

These very different issues—the significance of gender in our language and humor—are but two of the countless dimensions of everyday life. They are each products of people in social interaction who construct a world of meaning and then continuously react to what they have made. They also suggest the value of the sociological perspective for understanding and participating in this process.

Because humor involves challenging social realities, "outsiders"—particularly ethnic and racial minorities—have always been disproportionately represented among America's comedians. The Marx Brothers, sons of Jewish immigrants, delighted in revealing the pretensions of the Protestant upper class. A half-century later, black comedian Eddie Murphy employed a similar pattern, as suggested in this movie role as he is arrested for trespassing on a millionaire's estate in Beverly Hills.

SUMMARY

1. While social interaction is creative and spontaneous, social life is patterned in ways described as social structure. By guiding behavior within culturally approved bounds, social structure helps to make situations more understandable and predictable.
2. A major component of social structure is status. A master status stands out among an entire status set.
3. Ascribed statuses are essentially involuntary, while achieved statuses are largely earned. In practice, however, many statuses are both ascribed and achieved.
4. Role is the dynamic expression of a status. Like statuses, roles are relational, guiding people as they interact.
5. The roles that correspond to two or more statuses may be incompatible, giving rise to role conflict. Likewise, incompatibility among various roles linked to a single status (the role set) can generate role strain.
6. The phrase "social construction of reality" conveys the important idea that people build the social world as they interact.
7. The Thomas theorem points out that although reality is a human creation, it is real in its consequences for those involved.
8. People creatively generate social reality within the context of their culture and available social resources.
9. Ethnomethodology reveals how everyday social situations are defined by violating patterns of expected behavior.
10. Dramaturgical analysis explores how people construct personal performances. This approach understands everyday life in terms of theatrical performances.
11. People make use of language, nonverbal behavior, and deliberately fashioned physical settings in their performances. Within American society, males and females do so in distinctive ways. Often these performances attempt to idealize personal intentions.
12. All social behavior carries the ever-present danger of embarrassment. Tact is a common response to a "loss of face" by others.
13. Language is a major element in forming social reality. In various ways, language defines males and females in different terms, generally to the advantage of males.
14. Humor is based on the contrast between conventional and unconventional social realities. Because humor is framed by the specific culture, people throughout the world find humor in very different situations.

KEY CONCEPTS

achieved status a social position that is assumed voluntarily and that reflects a significant measure of personal ability and effort

ascribed status a social position that is received at birth or involuntarily assumed later in the life course

dramaturgical analysis the analysis of social interaction in terms of theatrical performance

ethnomethodology the study of the everyday, common-sense understandings that people have of the world around them

master status a status that has exceptional importance for social identity, often shaping a person's entire life

nonverbal communication communication using body movements, gestures, and facial expressions rather than spoken words

personal space the area around a person over which some claim to privacy is made

presentation of self the ways in which individuals, in various settings, attempt to create specific impressions in the minds of others

role patterns of expected behavior attached to a particular status

role conflict incompatibility among the roles corresponding to two or more statuses

role set a number of roles attached to a single status

role strain incompatibility among roles corresponding to a single status

social construction of reality the process by which individuals creatively shape reality through social interaction

social interaction the process by which people act and react in relation to others

status a recognized social position that an individual occupies within society

status set all the statuses a particular person holds at a given time

Thomas theorem the assertion that situations that are defined as real are real in their consequences

---

SUGGESTED READINGS

This paperback provides many examples of rich insights about everyday life that the sociological perspective offers.

David A. Karp and William C. Yoels. *Sociology and Everyday Life*. Itasca, IL: Peacock, 1986.

These two readable classics in sociology are readily available in paperback.

Erving Goffman. *The Presentation of Self in Everyday Life*. Garden City, NY: Doubleday Anchor Books, 1959.

Peter L. Berger and Thomas Luckmann. *The Social Construction of Reality: A Treatise in the Sociology of Knowledge*. Garden City, NY: Doubleday Anchor Books, 1967.

At the end of his career, Erving Goffman applied dramaturgical analysis to spoken communication.

Erving Goffman. *Forms of Talk*. Philadelphia: University of Pennsylvania Press, 1981.

A fascinating study of role conflict involves this account of the lives of Roman Catholic priests who are also homosexuals.

James G. Wolf. *Gay Priests*. San Francisco: Harper & Row, 1989.

The everyday lives of women, especially black women in America, have been largely ignored. This paperback is an oral history of one black woman's life as told to her sociologist granddaughter.

Mamie Garvin Fields with Karen Fields. *Lemon Swamp and Other Places*. New York: Free Press, 1985.

This is a recent book by a noted analyst of deceit, discussed in this chapter.

Paul Ekman. *Why Kids Lie: How to Encourage Truthfulness*. New York: Charles Scribner's Sons, 1989.

This book details the process of *leaving* roles, described in this chapter.

Helen Rose Fuchs Ebaugh. *Becoming an EX: The Process of Role Exit*. Chicago: University of Chicago Press, 1988.

Despite its centrality to our lives, human emotion is often overlooked in sociological analysis. A notable exception is the following paperback.

William H. Frey II with Muriel Langstreth. *Crying: The Mystery of Tears*. Minneapolis: Winston Press and Harper & Row, 1985.

Physical attractiveness is a topic of growing interest in social science. This book is a good introduction to this area of study.

Elaine Hatfield and Susan Sprecher. *Mirror, Mirror . . . The Importance of Looks in Everyday Life*. Albany, NY: SUNY Press, 1986.

The importance of gender in how we use language to shape everyday reality is explored in this book of essays, which also contains a comprehensive and annotated bibliography.

Barrie Thorne, Cheris Kramarae, and Nancy Henley. *Language, Gender and Society*. Cambridge, MA: Newbury House, 1983.

In the decades since World War II, shopping malls have become the new American "Main Street." This paperback examines this familiar setting.

Jerry Jacobs. *The Mall: An Attempted Escape from Everyday Life*. Prospect Heights, IL: Waveland Press, 1984.

Many units of time (including the day, month, and year) have a natural foundation, but not the week. This study examines how and why humans sometimes arbitrarily structure their lives.

Eviatar Zerubavel. *The Seven Day Circle*. Chicago: University of Chicago Press, 1989.

Art is an important dimension of everyday life that is examined sociologically in this paperback.

Arnold Hauser. *The Sociology of Art*. Chicago: University of Chicago Press, 1982.

Relatively little attention has been paid to the sociological analysis of humor. The following books introduce various approaches.

Marvin R. Koller. *Humor and Society: Explorations in the Sociology of Humor*. Houston: Cap and Gown Press, 1988.

Paul E. McGhee and Jeffrey H. Goldstein, eds. *Handbook of Humor Research*. Volumes I and II. New York: Springer-Verlag, 1983.

Chris Powell and George E. C. Paton, eds. *Humour in Society: Resistance and Control*. New York: St. Martin's Press, 1988.

7

Groups and Organizations

On March 8, 1965, a young marine named Philip Caputo landed in Danang, Vietnam. Sixteen months later, his tour of duty completed, he returned to the United States. He had made it. He was home. But he would never be the same. A decade later, telling the story of his time in Vietnam, Caputo (1977:xiv–xv) wrote:

> . . . an honorable discharge released me from the Marines and the chance of dying an early death in Asia. I felt as happy as a condemned man whose sentence has been commuted, but within a year I began growing nostalgic for the war.

> Other veterans I knew confessed to the same emotion. In spite of everything, we felt a strange attachment to Vietnam and, even stranger, a longing to return. The war was still being fought, but this desire to go back did not spring from any patriotic ideas about duty, honor, and sacrifice, the myths with which old men send young men off to get killed or maimed. It arose, rather, from a recognition of how deeply we had been changed, how different we were from everyone who had not shared with us the miseries of the monsoon, the exhausting patrols, the fear of a combat assault on a hot landing zone. We had very little in common with them. Though we were civilians again, the civilian world seemed alien. We did not belong to it as much as we did to that other world, where we had fought and our friends had died. . . .

> . . . [I also want] to describe the intimacy of life in infantry

battalions, where the communion between men is as profound as any between lovers. Actually, it is more so. It does not demand for its sustenance the reciprocity, the pledges of affection, the endless reassurances required by the love of men and women. It is, unlike marriage, a bond that cannot be broken by a word, by boredom or divorce, or by anything other than death. Sometimes even that is not strong enough. Two friends of mine died trying

to save the corpses of their men from the battlefield. Such devotion, simple and selfless, the sentiment of belonging to each other, was the one decent thing we found in a conflict otherwise notable for its monstrosities.

These words reveal the power of social experience—even in the midst of violence—to fuse human beings together into an entity greater than themselves. Notice how Caputo writes of *we* contrasted to *them*; how he stresses the sense of *belonging* shared with his fellow soldiers, and a collective intimacy, bonding, and devotion.

Social interaction, the focus of Chapter 6, implies participation in something larger than ourselves. This is often the *social group*, illustrated by the countless clusters of soldiers who forge a common identity on the battlefield. Much of modern social life also revolves around *formal organizations*. These include the Marine Corps, corporations, universities, and volunteer associations such as the American Red Cross. In this chapter, we explore both social groups and formal organizations.

SOCIAL GROUPS

Virtually no one lives without some sense of belonging and identification with other people. More simply, almost everyone participates in social groups. A **social group** is defined as *two or more people who identify with one another and have a distinctive pattern of interaction*. Human beings continually join together in couples, families, circles of friends, platoons, churches, businesses, clubs, and numerous large organizations. Although groups take many forms, they encompass people who share common experiences, loyalties, and interests. In short, while maintaining their individuality, members of social groups also think of themselves as a special "we."

Groups, Aggregates, and Categories

Not every collection of people is a social group. The term *aggregate* refers to people who are in the same place at the same time but who interact little, if at all, and have no sense of belonging together. People riding together on a subway, for example, form an aggregate, not a social group.

People also have various statuses in common, such as "mothers," "soldiers," "homeowners," or "Roman Catholics." A common status defines a *category* rather than a social group. People in some categories are aware that they share a particular status with others, yet most of them are strangers who never socially interact.

People in some aggregates and categories *could* become a social group if the right circumstances arose, giving them a common identity and creating a pattern of interaction over a period of time. If, for example, a subway train stalls beneath the streets of New York City, passengers in each car, prompted by their common plight, may build some group awareness. Similarly, combat soldiers assigned to the same unit quickly develop a distinctive set of social patterns.

Primary and Secondary Groups

Commonly, people greet one another with a smile and the simple phrase "Hi! How are you?" Usually, the response is a simple and well-scripted, "Just fine, thanks. How about you?" This answer, of course, is often far from truthful; in most cases, providing a detailed account of how you *really* are doing would prompt the other person to make a hasty and awkward exit.

Types of social groups can be distinguished according to the degree of personal concern for others in social interaction. According to Charles Horton Cooley, introduced in the box, a **primary group** is *typically a small social group in which relationships are both personal and enduring*. Bound together by strong and lasting loyalties that Cooley termed *primary relationships*, people in primary groups usually share many activities, spend a great deal of time together, and come to know one another well. Consequently, they are likely to display genuine concern for one another's welfare. The family is generally the most important primary group within any society.

Cooley called social groups of this kind *primary* because they are among the first groups we experience in life. And because the family and peer groups generate intense social activity, they are also of primary importance to the socialization process, shaping personal attitudes and behavior. We look to members of our primary groups for clues to our social identity as well, which is why members of any primary group almost always think of themselves as "we."

The strength of primary relationships gives individuals considerable comfort and security, often evident in personal performances, described in Chapter 6 ("Social Interaction in Everyday Life"). Within the familiar social circles of family or friends, people tend to feel they

Charles Horton Cooley (1864–1929)

Have you ever felt that the world was becoming so fast paced and impersonal that people were losing touch with one another? Charles Horton

Cooley shared this concern, drawn from his experience growing up in a small town as America was going through a period of great change.

Cooley lived in Ann Arbor, Michigan, most of his life, serving on the faculty of the University of Michigan from 1892 until his death. His major contribution to sociology focused on the character of the primary group. Cooley took note of a disturbing trend: as urban industrialization progressed, together with rising individualism and interpersonal competition, people's concern for the traditional family and local neighborhood waned. This transformation made him uneasy because he was convinced that small, cooperative social groups were cru-

cially important to human life. Without them, he wondered, how could we maintain a sense of belonging and develop attitudes of fairness and compassion?

Cooley believed that calling attention to the importance of primary groups would encourage the preservation of some of the traditional values of a more socially cohesive way of life, despite rapid change.

SOURCES: Some ideas drawn from Lewis A. Coser, *Masters of Sociological Thought: Ideas in Historical and Social Context*, 2nd ed. (New York: Harcourt Brace Jovanovich, 1977), Chap. 8; and Philip Rieff, "Introduction," in Charles Horton Cooley, *Social Organization* (New York: Schocken Books, 1962), pp. v–xx.

---

can be themselves without constantly worrying about the impressions they are making.

Members of primary groups generally provide one another with many forms of personal, financial, and emotional support. But people generally think of the primary group as an end in itself rather than as a means to other ends. For example, we readily call on family members or close friends to help us move into a new apartment, without expecting to pay for their services. And we would do the same for them. If we consistently help a friend who never returns the favor, however, we are likely to feel "used" and to question the depth of the friendship.

Members of primary groups are considered unique and not interchangeable with others. We usually do not care who cashes our check or approves a loan for us at the bank. Yet in primary groups—especially the family—emotion and loyalty bind us, for better or worse, to particular people. Although brothers and sisters may experience periodic conflict, they always remain siblings.

In contrast to the primary group, the **secondary group** is *a large and impersonal social group usually*

based on a specific interest or activity. Secondary groups, which are formed by *secondary relationships*, are generally larger than primary groups. For example, people who work together in an office, enroll in the same college course, live in the same city neighborhood, or belong to a particular political organization all form secondary groups.

In most respects, secondary groups have precisely the opposite characteristics of primary groups. Members of secondary groups usually have little personal knowledge of one another and weak emotional ties. Such groups vary in duration, but they are frequently of short term, beginning and ending without particular significance. Students in a college course, for instance, who may not see one another after the semester ends, exemplify the secondary group. Because secondary groups focus on a specific activity or interest, members have little chance to develop a deep concern for one another's overall welfare. In some cases, such as co-workers who share an office for many years, secondary relationships may develop more primacy with the passing of time. Generally, however, although people in a secondary

Americans tend to define business ties as secondary relationships in which little personal knowledge is necessary or even desirable. In many traditional societies, however, people routinely conduct business with others they know well. This pattern is still evident in Turkey, where a ritual of exchanging greetings and news and sharing refreshments precedes business dealings.

group sometimes think of themselves as "we," the boundary that distinguishes members from nonmembers is usually far less clear than it is in primary groups.

While secondary relationships are less intense than primary ties, they are valued as a means of achieving specific ends. If primary relationships have a *personal orientation*, then, secondary relationships have a *goal orientation*. This does not mean that secondary ties are necessarily formal and unemotional. On the contrary, social interactions with fellow students, co-workers, and business contacts can be as enjoyable as they are casual. Simply bear in mind that personal pleasure does not generate secondary groups.

Members of primary groups are important because of *who they are*; members of secondary groups have significance because of *what they can do for us*. In secondary groups, in other words, we remain aware of what we offer others and what we receive in return. This is most evident in business relationships. Likewise, secondary ties among neighbors typically are based on the expectation that a neighborly favor will be reciprocated.

The goal orientation of secondary groups shifts the focus of social interaction from personal matters to concerns outside the individual. In order to make the most of the secondary relationship, members of secondary groups tend to craft personal performances carefully, and usually expect others to do the same. In these roles, we remain characteristically impersonal and polite. The secondary relationship, therefore, is one in which the question "How are you?" may be asked with no real concern for a truthful answer.

The characteristics of primary and secondary groups are summarized in Table 7–1. Because these two types of social groups are presented in ideal terms, neither concept is likely to describe precisely most actual social groups in our lives. Some family relationships, for example, are more primary than others, and not all business relationships are equally secondary. These concepts actually form a continuum on which any group can be placed.

Finally, the balance between primary and secondary groups tends to shift as traditional societies undergo industrialization. In general, primary relationships dominate family and local village life in preindustrial societies. Strangers stand out in the social landscape. By contrast, secondary ties take precedence in modern, industrial societies, where people assume highly specialized social roles. In today's world, we all routinely engage in impersonal, secondary relationships with strangers—people about whom we know very little and may never meet again (Wirth, 1938).

Group Leadership

Leadership plays an important part in *group dynamics*, which refers to the ways in which groups operate. Social groups vary in the extent to which they designate one

Table 7–1 PRIMARY GROUPS AND SECONDARY GROUPS: A SUMMARY

	Primary Group	Secondary Group
Quality of relationships	Personal orientation	Goal orientation
Duration of relationships	Usually long-term	Variable; often short term
Breadth of relationships	Broad; usually involving many activities	Narrow; usually involving few activities
Subjective perception of relationships	As an end in itself	As a means to an end
Typical examples	Families; close friendships	Co-workers; political organizations

or more members as leaders, with responsibility to direct the activities of all members. Some friendship groups grant someone the clear status of leader; others do not. Within families, parents traditionally share leadership responsibilities, although husband and wife may disagree about who is really in charge. In many secondary groups, such as corporations, leadership is likely to involve a formal chain of command with clearly defined roles.

Leaders are commonly thought to possess extraordinary personal abilities, but research over several decades has failed to produce convincing evidence of so-called "natural leaders." Group members, in fact, often discourage an individual who tries to assume a dominant position in the group. Instead of reflecting individual traits, leadership has more to do with the needs of the group itself (Ridgeway, 1983; Ridgeway & Diekema, 1989), as we shall see.

Although Americans commonly think of a leader as a single person, research indicates that two different leadership roles emerge in groups. These are likely to be held by different individuals (Bales, 1953; Bales & Slater, 1955). **Instrumental leadership** refers to *group leadership that emphasizes the completion of tasks.* Group members look to instrumental leaders to "get things done." **Expressive leadership,** in contrast, *emphasizes collective well-being.* Expressive leaders are less concerned with the performance goals of a group than with

providing emotional support to group members and minimizing tension and conflict among them.

Because they concentrate on performance, instrumental leaders usually form a secondary relationship with other group members. Instrumental leaders give orders and discipline those who hold back the group's efforts. Expressive leaders cultivate more personal or primary relationships. They offer sympathy when a member is going through a difficult time, work to keep the group united, and lighten serious moments with humor. Expressive leaders generally receive more personal *affection* from members, while successful instrumental leaders enjoy a more distant *respect.*

This differentiation of leadership is sometimes linked to gender. Consider, for example, the traditional American family (Parsons & Bales, 1955). For generations, cultural norms have bestowed instrumental leadership on males, as fathers and husbands. In this traditional pattern, men assume primary responsibility for providing family income, making major family decisions, and disciplining children. On the other hand, expressive leadership has traditionally been assigned to women. Within the family, mothers and wives historically have been expected to lend emotional support and to maintain peaceful relationships among all family members. In this context, it is not surprising that children may have greater respect for their fathers, but closer personal relationships with their mothers (Macionis, 1978). As gender roles within the family have been changing in recent decades (see Chapter 15, "Family"), the assignment of instrumental and expressive leadership roles in the family has become much less rigid. Similarly, in other group settings, women and men are both assuming leadership roles.

Decision-making styles also distinguish leaders from one another. *Authoritarian leaders* focus on instrumental concerns, make decisions on their own, and demand strict compliance from subordinates. This leadership style rarely wins great personal affection from group members. However, the authoritarian leader may be highly effective in crisis situations requiring immediate decisions and in maintaining strong group discipline. *Democratic leaders* take a more expressive approach to leadership, seeking to include all group members in the decision-making process. While less successful during crises, when there is little time for discussion, democratic leaders draw on the ideas of other group members to forge reflective and imaginative responses to the tasks at hand. *Laissez-faire leaders* (from the French phrase meaning roughly "to leave alone") tend to downplay their position and power, allowing the group to function more or less on its own. Laissez-faire leaders generally are the least effective in promoting group goals. Clearly, the leadership style of the person who guides a social group determines, in large part, the characteristics and needs of the group itself (White & Lippitt, 1953; Ridgeway, 1983).

Group Conformity

How do groups influence the behavior of their members? In friendship groups, some amount of *group conformity* gives members a more secure feeling of belonging. In other groups, such as families, the pressure to conform may be considerable.

Even interaction with unfamiliar people can promote conformity. A classic experiment conducted some forty years ago by Solomon Asch (1952) showed that many people would "not believe their own eyes" if what they saw was challenged by others in their group.

Asch's Research

Asch recruited candidates for a group of six to eight people, allegedly to study visual perception. In reality, he was exploring patterns of group conformity. In each trial of his study, Asch arranged with all but one member of the group to create a situation in which the remaining subject would be pressured to accept conclusions that were quite unreasonable.

In the experiment, group members sat around a table, where they were asked to examine sets of cards similar to those in Figure 7–1. One at a time, subjects were asked to match a "standard" line, shown on the left card, to one of three lines on the right card. Anyone with normal vision could easily see that the line marked "A" on the second card would be the correct choice. Initially, everyone gave correct answers. Then, as the experiment progressed, Asch's secret accomplices began agreeing on an obviously wrong answer. As this occurred, the naive subject began to look bewildered and uncomfortable, as the photos reveal. Asch had created a dilemma: Should a person stand out by being right, or should a person conform to the obvious error of others? Asch reached the surprising conclusion that more than one-third of all subjects resolved this dilemma by answering incorrectly. Many later admitted they had no doubt about the right answer, but preferred to avoid the discomfort of being different from others—even people they did not know. Many of us, apparently, are prepared to

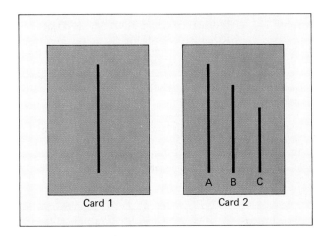

Figure 7–1 The Cards Used in Asch's Experiment in Group Conformity

(*Asch*, 1952:452–453)

compromise our own judgment in the interests of group conformity.

Milgram's Research

In the early 1960s, Stanley Milgram—who had been a student of Solomon Asch—conducted a remarkable and controversial set of experiments at Yale University. Aware that millions of innocent people had been "slaughtered on command" during World War II, Milgram was intrigued with the idea that ordinary people would inflict suffering on others simply because an authority figure or others in a group encouraged them to do so.

In Milgram's initial study (1963, 1965; Miller, 1986), a "researcher" greeted pairs of subjects, explaining that they were engaging in a study of memory. One subject took the role of "teacher" and the other the role of "learner." Actually, the person assigned to be the learner was part of the study; only the subject assigned to the position of teacher was unaware of what was really going on.

The learner was then placed in a contraption resembling an electric chair with electrodes attached to one arm. The researcher instructed the teacher to read pairs of words. Subsequently, the first word of each pair was repeated and the learner was asked to recall the correct second word. As mistakes occurred, the researcher instructed the teacher to administer a shock to the learner using a realistic-looking "shock generator," marked to indicate shocks ranging from 15 volts (labeled "mild shock") to 300 volts (marked "intense shock") to an extreme of 450 volts (marked "Danger: Severe Shock" and "XXX"). Beginning at the lowest level, the teachers were instructed to increase the shock by 15 volts every time a mistake was made. The experimenter explained to the teacher that the shocks were "extremely painful" but caused "no permanent tissue damage."

The results were striking evidence of the ability of leaders to obtain compliance. Of the forty subjects assigned in the role of teacher during the initial research, all obeyed the experimenter and administered "severe shocks" to the learners. No one even questioned the procedure before 300 volts had been applied, and twenty-six of the subjects—almost two-thirds—went all the way to 450 volts.

In later research, the proportion of subjects who applied the maximum shock varied according to specific experimental conditions. But overall, many of Milgram's subjects administered shocks to accomplices who verbally objected, many shocked accomplices who protested that they had heart conditions, and many even increased

All societies teach people to respect authority figures, but this is obviously not innate, as the often disrespectful attitudes of children show.

the voltage as accomplices screamed and then feigned unconsciousness and fell silent. Not surprisingly, many subjects found this extremely stressful, which has made the experiment controversial ever since. In some cases, Milgram reported, the person administering the shocks was "reduced to a twitching, stuttering wreck." But many followed orders all the same.

Amazed and disturbed by these results, Milgram concluded that people are likely to obey those in positions of authority, even when common sense suggests they should disobey. Milgram (1964) then extended the research with an eye toward the earlier work of Solomon Asch, his former teacher.

Milgram wondered if Asch had found a high degree of group conformity because the task of matching lines was a trivial activity. What if groups pressured people to administer electrical shocks? To investigate, he varied the experiment so that a group of three "teachers" worked together. As usual, two of the teachers were Milgram's accomplices. Milgram asked each of the three teachers to suggest a shock level when an error was made, explaining that the shock actually given would be the *lowest* of the three suggestions. This gave the naive subject the power to set the shock level without regard for what the other two subjects said. Milgram's accomplices recommended increasing the shock level with each error. This resulting group pressure caused the third member to suggest higher shock levels. Under these conditions, subjects applied voltages three to four times higher than in experiments with a subject acting alone.

Milgram's research suggests that people are surprisingly likely to follow the directions of "legitimate authority figures." They are also easily influenced by groups even when other members are just "ordinary people."

Janis's Research

High government officials, too, often succumb to pressure for group conformity, according to Irving L. Janis's (1972, 1989) examination of historical documents. Janis contends that a number of American foreign policy errors, including the failure to foresee the Japanese attack on Pearl Harbor in World War II, the disastrous U.S. attempt to invade Cuba in 1961, and our tragic involvement in the Vietnam War, may have been the result of group conformity among our highest-ranking political leaders.

Brainstorming in groups is popularly thought to contribute to better decision making. However, Janis showed that group decision making sometimes backfires.

First, rather than examining a problem from many points of view, groups often seek consensus, thereby *narrowing* the range of options. Second, groups may develop a distinctive language, adopting terms that favor a particular interpretation of events. Third, having settled on a position, members of the group may come to see anyone with another view as the "opposition." This results, Janis concluded, in **"groupthink,"** *a reduced capacity for critical thinking caused by group conformity.*

In Janis's view, "groupthink" accounted for the decision by the Kennedy administration to invade Cuba—a plan that failed, provoking international criticism of the United States. Arthur Schlesinger, Jr., former adviser to President John Kennedy, confessed guilt "for having kept so quiet during those crucial discussions in the Cabinet Room," but added that the group discouraged anyone from challenging even what appeared to be "nonsense" (Janis, 1972:30, 40).

More recently, "groupthink" was probably at work in the Iran-contra affair, in which some officials of the Reagan administration formulated a secret plan to sell weapons to Iran. They were seeking to win the release of American hostages held in Lebanon by groups loyal to Iran and to direct proceeds from the weapons sales to the contras, soldiers opposed to the Sandinista government in Nicaragua. Congressional hearings in 1987 revealed that some of the officials involved—best exemplified by Lieutenant Colonel Oliver North—became so singlemindedly committed to the plan that they disregarded the law. Further, people who were involved in the decision made extensive use of language that supported only one interpretation of events. For example, they never called the plan a strategy of "trading arms for hostages" but rather one of "opening relations with moderates in Iran." Likewise, instead of calling the Nicaraguan rebels "contras" or "guerrilla insurgents," they adopted a more positive label—"freedom fighters." The architects of the Iran-contra affair also minimized resistance to the plan by "the opposition" by refusing to share information with any key administration official who did not endorse the plan.

Reference Groups

Frequently, we make evaluations and decisions by measuring our views against the views of others. We often use social groups for this purpose. The term **reference group** signifies *a social group that serves as a point of reference for people making evaluations and decisions.*

A young man who imagines his family's response to a woman he is dating is using his family as a reference group. Similarly, a banker who assesses her colleagues' reactions to a new loan policy is using her co-workers as a standard of reference. As these examples suggest, reference groups can be both primary and secondary. And because we are often strongly motivated to conform to a group, the attitudes of group members can greatly affect personal evaluations.

Even groups of which we are *not* members can be used as points of reference. For example, people going on job interviews usually anticipate how those in the organization dress and act, and they adjust their personal performances accordingly. People are especially likely to use social groups they wish to join as reference groups, in the process known as *anticipatory socialization*

Reference groups are not only important for making specific evaluations; such groups also serve as role models, guiding the personality development of a society's young people.

(see Chapter 5, "Socialization"). By conforming, they hope to more readily win acceptance to the group.

Stouffer's Research

A classic study of reference group dynamics was conducted during World War II, when the government hired a team of sociologists to investigate the attitudes and morale of soldiers (Stouffer et al., 1949). As part of this study, a survey asked soldiers to evaluate the chances of promotion for a competent soldier in their branch of the service. Common sense suggests that soldiers in a part of the service with a relatively high promotion rate would be optimistic. Yet survey results revealed just the opposite: Soldiers in branches of the service with relatively low promotion rates were actually more optimistic about their own chances for advancement.

The key to this paradox lies in identifying the groups against which the soldiers measured their progress. Those in branches with lower promotion rates compared their advancement with people like themselves; therefore, although they had not been promoted, neither had many others, so they did not feel deprived. As a result, they expressed relatively positive attitudes about their chances for promotion. Soldiers in a service branch with a higher promotion rate, however, could easily think of people who had been promoted sooner or more often than they had. Using these people as a reference group, even soldiers who had been promoted were likely to feel they had come up short. Not surprisingly, then, soldiers in branches with higher promotion rates voiced more negative attitudes in their evaluations.

Stouffer's research demonstrates that we do not make judgments about ourselves in isolation, nor do we compare ourselves with the entire population. Instead, we use specific social groups as standards in developing individual attitudes. Regardless of our situation in *absolute* terms, then, we perceive well-being subjectively *relative* to some specific reference group (Merton, 1968; Mirowsky, 1987).

Ingroups and Outgroups

By the time children reach the early grades of school, they have discovered that life revolves around various social groups. They eagerly join some groups, but avoid—or are excluded from—others. Play groups, for example, may be segregated by sex, focusing on activities culturally defined as feminine or masculine (Lever, 1978; Best, 1983).

What makes belonging to one group more attractive than belonging to another? Perceived group differences—political outlook, social status, even manner of dress—often lead us to identify positively with one social group while opposing others. Across the United States, for example, students wear high-school jackets and place school decals on car windows to indicate their school affiliation and its meaning to them as an important social group. Students attending another school may become the targets of derision simply because they belong to a rival group.

This illustrates an important process of group dynamics: the opposition of ingroups and outgroups. An **ingroup** is *an esteemed social group commanding a member's loyalty*. An ingroup exists in relation to an **outgroup**,

The popularity of "celebrity" clothing among young people is partly explained by the desire to display ingroup solidarity.

which is *a scorned social group toward which one feels competition or opposition*. Many social groups follow this pattern. A sports team amounts to an ingroup for its members and an outgroup for members of opposing teams. A town's Democrats generally think of themselves as an ingroup in relation to the local Republicans. Although not precisely a group, all Americans share a sense of being an ingroup in relation to citizens of other nations. All ingroups and outgroups work on the principle that "we" have valued characteristics that "they" lack.

The ingroup/outgroup dynamic establishes the boundaries that define many social groups. By joining together with some people, while simultaneously avoiding contact with others, people gain a clearer sense of their place in a world of diversity. However, this process often promotes self-serving distortions of reality. Research has shown that the members of ingroups hold unrealistically positive views of themselves and unfairly negative views of various outgroups (Tajfel, 1982). Ethnocentrism, for example, may grow out of the tendency to overvalue one's own "group," while undervaluing other cultures as outgroups.

When an ingroup has greater social power than an outgroup it opposes, serious personal and social problems may result. For example, whites have historically viewed nonwhites in negative terms and subjected them to certain social, political, and economic disadvantages. Internalizing these negative attitudes, blacks, Hispanics, Asians, and Native Americans often struggle to overcome negative self-images based on stereotypes held by the larger society. The operation of individual ingroups and outgroups, therefore, may mirror patterns of social inequality in the larger society. As groups work to sharpen their specific boundaries, then, they frequently foster both loyalty (to the ingroup) and social tension and conflict (with the outgroup).

The Importance of Group Size

If you are the first person to come to a party, you can observe a fascinating process in group dynamics. Six or fewer people in one setting generally share a single conversation. But as more people arrive, the group soon divides into two or more smaller clusters. Here it is apparent that size plays a crucial role in group dynamics. The number of members in a group determines in large part how members socially interact.

To understand why, consider the mathematical connection between the number of people in a social group and the number of relationships among them, as shown in Figure 7–2. Two people create one relationship; adding a third person results in three relationships; a fourth person yields six. Adding people one at a time—a process mathematicians describe as an *arithmetic* increase—causes the number of relationships to increase very rapidly—in what is called a *geometric progression*. By the time six people join one conversation, fifteen different relationships connect them—an unwieldy number—so the group usually divides by this point.

German sociologist Georg Simmel (1858–1918) focused his research on social dynamics in the smallest social groups. Simmel (1950; orig. 1902) used the term **dyad** to designate *a social group with two members*. In American society, love affairs, marriages, and the closest friendships are dyadic. Simmel identified some special qualities of the dyad. First, dyads are typically less stable than groups with many members. In a dyad, both members must actively participate in the relationship because if either withdraws from the dyad, the group dissipates. Because the stability of marriages is important to society, the potentially fragile bond between spouses is reinforced

Figure 7–2 Group Size and Relationships

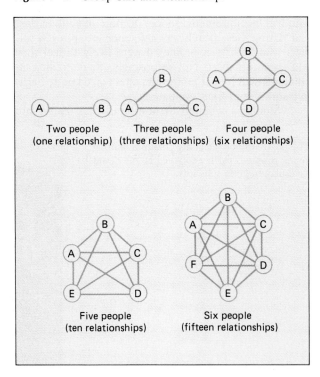

Two people
(one relationship)

Three people
(three relationships)

Four people
(six relationships)

Five people
(ten relationships)

Six people
(fifteen relationships)

A distinctive characteristic of a triad is that the social bond between two of the members can intensify, excluding the third.

with legal and often religious ties. Society thus bolsters this dyadic group in case personal interest wanes. In contrast, a large group is inherently more stable. A volunteer fire company contains many people, so even if a few dropped out the group would not collapse.

Second, social interaction in a dyad is typically more intense than in other groups. In such a one-to-one relationship, neither member shares the other's attention with anyone else. For this reason, dyads also have the potential to be the most meaningful social bonds we ever experience. Because marriage in our culture is dyadic, powerful emotional ties generally unite husbands and wives. But in Chapter 15 ("Family"), we will discover that marriage in other societies can involve more than two people. In that case, the attention of spouses is divided among several relationships, so that the strength of any one tie may diminish in relation to another.

Simmel also explored the **triad**—*a social group with three members*. A triad is composed of three relationships, each uniting two of the three members. Any two members, therefore, can form a coalition against the third and press their views as a majority. Two of the three may also intensify their relationship, transforming the triad into a dyad with a "third wheel." This often occurs, for example, among three roommates at college. For the triad to continue, all three members must take part in many routine activities. Romantic interest may easily transform a triad into a dyad. Two members now have a powerful bond that neither shares with the third person, thus, the old saying "Two's company, three's a crowd."

A triad does, however, benefit from a source of stability not found in a dyad. If the relationship between any two of the group's members becomes strained, the third can act as a mediator to restore the group's vitality. Similarly, members of a dyad (such as a married couple) often seek out a third person (a trusted friend or counselor) to resolve tensions between them.

Social groups with more than three members tend to be more stable than smaller ones because even if several members lose interest, it does not directly threaten the group's existence. Larger social groups usually develop a more formal social structure—a variety of statuses and roles, certain rules and regulations—that stabilizes their operation. Yet, larger social groups inevitably lack intense personal interaction, for these are possible only in the smallest groups.

Is there an ideal size for a social group? That depends on the group's purpose. A dyad offers unsurpassed emotional intensity, while a group of several dozen people is likely to be more stable and capable of accomplishing larger and more complex tasks. In general, research suggests that groups of about five people generate the highest degree of satisfaction among group members. Groups smaller than five require much more effort from each person, but larger ones are typically too impersonal (Slater, 1958; Ridgeway, 1983).

Networks

The term **network** refers to *a web of social ties that links people, often with little common identity and social* *interaction*. Like a social group, a network joins people in relationships. Unlike a social group, network members usually feel little sense of membership in the network and have only occasional contact. The boundaries of networks are also less clearcut than those of groups. If a group takes the form of a "circle of friends," a network is better described as a "social web" expanding outward, with most members connected indirectly through others.

Sometimes, the social ties within networks are close, as among people who attended college together and have since maintained friendships by mail and telephone. More commonly, networks involve secondary relationships. A social network may include people we *know of*—or who *know of us*—but with whom we interact infrequently, if at all. As one woman with a widespread reputation as a community organizer explains, "I get calls at home. Someone says, 'Are you Roseann Navarro? Somebody told me to call you. I have this problem . . .'" (Kaminer, 1984:94). For this reason, social networks are most commonly "clusters of weak ties" (Granovetter, 1973).

Networks are a source of power. Exclusive social clubs have traditionally reinforced the advantages of some categories of people.

Network relationships can work to personal advantage. For example, many people rely on their networks to find a job. Even the scientific genius Albert Einstein needed a hand in landing his first job. After a year of interviewing, he succeeded in obtaining employment only when the father of one of his classmates put him in touch with an office manager who hired him (Clark, 1971; cited in Fischer, 1977:19). Apparently, *who you know* is often just as important as *what you know*.

In a survey, Nan Lin (1981) determined that almost 60 percent of 399 men in an urban area of the United States had used networks to find a job—more than any other single resource. Lin also found that networks do not provide equal advantages to everyone. Men whose fathers held important occupational positions gained the greatest advantages from networks. This finding underscores the commonly held belief that networks tend to link people of similar social characteristics and social rank, thereby perpetuating social privilege.

Recent research by Peter Marsden (1987) indicates that the most extensive social networks are maintained by people who are young, well educated, and living in urban areas. The networks of men and women tend to be the same size, although women include more relatives in their networks. Women's networks, therefore, may not carry the clout that the "old-boy" networks do. Additionally, female workers often work in settings where men outnumber them and have more power than they do. In response, many women have begun to pay more attention to building networks in the world of work. Female networks provide the support and camaraderie, as well as the business contacts, that women might otherwise lack (Speizer, 1983; Coppock, 1987).

FORMAL ORGANIZATIONS

Even a century ago, most social life occurred in small social groups—the family, friendship and working groups, and the local neighborhood. Today, our lives revolve far more around **formal organizations,** *large, secondary groups that are formally organized to facilitate achieving their goals.* Formal organizations such as corporations or branches of government differ from small family or friendship groups in more than simply their numbers. Their greater size makes social relationships more impersonal; they also foster a planned or *formal* atmosphere. Formal organizations are designed to accomplish specific tasks, rather than to meet personal needs.

With a population of 250 million, American society faces countless complicated tasks ranging from educating expectant parents to delivering the mail. Most of these are carried out by large, formal organizations. The United States government, the largest formal organization in America, employs more than 5 million people in various agencies and the armed forces. Each government agency includes many smaller organizations with specific goals. Such large groups develop lives and cultures of their own, so that as members come and go, the statuses they fill and the roles they perform remain unchanged over the years.

Types of Formal Organizations

In distinguishing among formal organizations, consider *how members relate to the organization.* Amitai Etzioni (1975) uses this criterion to identify three types of formal organizations: normative, coercive, and utilitarian.

Normative Organizations

People join *normative organizations* to pursue some goal they consider morally worthwhile, deriving personal satisfaction, perhaps social prestige, but no monetary reward for their efforts. For this reason, normative organizations are also commonly called *voluntary associations.* These include community service groups (such as the PTA, the Lions Club, the League of Women Voters, Red Cross, and United Way), political parties, religious organizations, and numerous other organizations concerned with specific social issues. The United States has often been described as a society of "joiners," and Americans participate, usually part time, in tens of thousands of normative organizations. Because women have historically been excluded from much of the paid labor force, they have traditionally played a greater part than men in civic and charitable organizations.

Coercive Organizations

Etzioni claims that people are forced to join *coercive organizations* as a form of punishment (prisons) or treatment (mental hospitals). Because people usually resist such confinement, most coercive organizations have distinctive physical features, such as locked doors, barred windows, and security personnel (Goffman, 1961). Coercive organizations are designed, at the very least, to segregate people as "inmates" or "patients" for a period of time. At the extreme, they operate to radically alter people's attitudes and behavior. Recall from Chapter 5 ("Socialization") the power of coercive organizations—including total institutions—to transform a human being's overall sense of self.

Utilitarian Organizations

According to Etzioni, *utilitarian organizations* bestow material benefits on their members. Large business enterprises, for example, generate profits for their owners and income in the form of salaries and wages for their employees. Joining utilitarian organizations is usually a matter of individual choice, although, obviously, most people must join one utilitarian organization or another to make a living. While utilitarian organizations certainly offer greater individual freedom than coercive organizations, they provide less freedom than normative organizations. Membership in utilitarian organizations is generally full time and may last for many years, sometimes for a person's entire working life.

From differing vantage points, formal organizations may fall into *all* of these categories. A mental hospital, for example, serves as a coercive organization to a patient, a utilitarian organization to a psychiatrist, and a normative organization to a part-time hospital volunteer.

Bureaucracy: Origins

The origins of formal organization date back thousands of years. To a great degree, early attempts at administering religious and political affairs were intended to extend the control of elites over millions of people living in vast areas. Formal organization also allowed rulers to undertake monumental tasks never before possible, such as building the Great Wall of China, described in Chapter 4 ("Society").

Through the years, such organizations resisted change—not because the elites lacked ambition but rather because of the traditional character of preindustrial societies. Long-established cultural patterns placed greater importance on "God's will" than on organizational efficiency. Only in the last few centuries did this change in Western societies. In response to the Industrial Revolution and what Max Weber called a "rational world view," the form of organizational structure called *bureaucracy* emerged in Europe and North America.

Bureaucracy is *an organizational model rationally designed to perform complex tasks efficiently.* Through bureaucratic organization, officials deliberately enact and modify policy to make the organization as efficient as possible. To appreciate the power and scope of bureaucratic organization, consider the telephone system in the United States. Each of over 150 million telephones can be used to reach any other telephone (and millions more throughout the entire world) at any time within seconds. This major technological feat reaches far beyond the imagination of the ancient world. Of course, we cannot overlook the importance of technological developments (such as electricity) in the workings of the telephone system. But equally important is the organizational capacity to keep track of every telephone call—noting which phone was used to call which other phone, when, and for how long—and presenting all this information to millions of telephone users in monthly bills. A task of this kind clearly requires a complex form of organizational structure.

Max Weber considered "the files" to be the heart of a formal organization, since its continued operation depends on access to a vast amount of recorded information. Today, files are still vital to bureaucracies; advancing technology has merely transformed paper documents into computer records.

Characteristics of Bureaucracy

Which organizational characteristics promote the efficient completion of tasks? Max Weber (1978; orig. 1921) identified six key elements of the ideal bureaucratic organization.

1. **Specialization.** Through most of human history, people engaged in roughly the same activities: securing food and shelter. Bureaucracy, in contrast, assigns people highly specialized tasks that correspond to organizational offices.
2. **Hierarchy of offices.** The offices in a bureaucratic organization form a hierarchy, according to their responsibilities. Each person is thus supervised by "higher-ups" in the organization while, in turn, supervising others in lower positions. Most bureaucrats are keenly aware of their own power and responsibilities relative to others.
3. **Rules and regulations.** Weber emphasized that tradition plays little part in bureaucracy. Instead, operations are guided by rationally enacted rules and regulations. These rules serve to control the organization's own functioning and, as much as possible, its larger environment. Ideally, a bureaucracy seeks to operate in a completely predictable fashion.
4. **Technical competence.** Bureaucratic officials are expected to have specific technical competence. Bureaucracies typically evaluate new staff members

according to set criteria and subsequently monitor their performance. This practice of impersonal evaluation based on performance contrasts sharply with the custom, followed through most of human history, of favoring relatives—whatever their talents—over strangers.
5. **Impersonality.** In bureaucratic organizations, rules take precedence over personal feelings. Ideally, this ensures uniform treatment for each client, supervisor, or subordinate. From this detached approach also stems the notion of the "faceless bureaucrat."
6. **Formal, written communications.** Certainly, some truth lies in the adage that the heart of bureaucracy is not people but paperwork. While casual, verbal communication characterizes most human exchanges, bureaucracy demands formal, written letters, memos, and reports. Over time, this correspondence accumulates into vast *files*. Such documents guide an organization in roughly the same way that personality guides the individual.

Bureaucracy versus Small Groups

Small groups, especially primary groups like the family, have intrinsic value for their members. By contrast, the value of bureaucracy as an organizational model for large,

Table 7–2 SMALL GROUPS AND FORMAL
ORGANIZATIONS: A COMPARISON

	Small Groups	Formal Organizations
Activities	Members typically engage in many of the same activities	Members typically engage in various highly specialized activities
Hierarchy	Often informal or nonexistent	Clearly defined, corresponding to offices
Norms	Informal application of general norms	Clearly defined rules and regulations
Criteria for Membership	Variable, often based on personal affection or kinship	Technical competence to carry out assigned tasks
Relationships	Variable; typically primary	Typically secondary, with selective primary ties
Communications	Typically casual and face to face	Typically formal and in writing
Focus	Person oriented	Task oriented

secondary groups lies in its goal-oriented approach: Bureaucracy seeks efficient performance. As a form of organization, bureaucracy is a means to an end.

Bureaucratic organization works to promote efficiency by carefully recruiting personnel and limiting the variable and unpredictable effects of personal tastes and opinions. In smaller, informal groups, members have wide-ranging personal discretion, guided by general social norms. Small-group members also respond to each other personally and are more or less equal in rank. Weber believed, however, that personal considerations compromised an organization's efficiency; he concluded that a rigid and impersonal organizational system effectively overcomes this drawback. Table 7–2 summarizes the differences between small social groups and large formal organizations.

The Informal Side of Bureaucracy

Weber's ideal bureaucracy has a highly formal structure; in principle, at least, every activity is deliberately regulated. In actual organizations, however, not all human behavior precisely fits organizational rules. Sometimes informality helps to meet a legitimate need overlooked by formal regulations. In other situations, such as cutting corners in one's job, informal behavior clearly violates official rules (Scott, 1981). In any case, bureaucratic blueprints are not always observed in actual operations; large organizations, therefore, are also *natural systems*.

Consider, for example, how personality and personal characteristics affect the quality of leadership. According to an organization chart, power resides in offices, not with the people who occupy them. In practice, however, the qualities and quirks of individuals—their charisma or skill in interpersonal relations, for example—have a tremendous impact on organizational outcomes, as studies of American corporations reveal (Halberstam, 1986). Although many have held the post of president of the Soviet Union, Mikhail Gorbachev's personal leadership skills—his ability to manage (or manipulate) others—clearly have resulted in significant restructuring of Soviet society.

Authoritarian, democratic, and laissez-faire types of leadership—examined earlier in this chapter—also reflect individual personality as much as any organizational plan. Then, too, decision making within an organization does not always conform to the defined hierarchy and the official regulations. As the 1989 scandal at the United States Housing and Urban Development (HUD) agency indicates, officials and their friends may personally benefit from abuse of organizational power. In the "real world" of organizational life, officials who attempt to operate strictly by the book may even find themselves denied promotions and power, which are often based on informal alliances. In some organizations, too, people in leadership positions rely on subordinates to handle much of their own work. Many secretaries, for example, have more authority and responsibility than their official job titles and salaries suggest.

Through memos and other formal, written communications, a formal organization disseminates information through the hierarchy. In most formal organizations, however, individuals cultivate informal networks of contacts—"grapevines"—that spread information much faster than memos, if not always as accurately. Grapevines are particularly important to subordinates

An organization's formal hierarchy is often modified according to personal preferences and abilities. In the popular television show M*A*S*H, Radar O'Reilly was only an army corporal, but he was largely responsible for keeping the outfit running smoothly.

because executives often attempt to conceal important information from them.

Sometimes employees of formal organizations modify or ignore rigid bureaucratic structures to assert their individuality or to advance their own interests. A classic study of the Western Electric factory in Chicago revealed that few workers actually reported fellow workers who violated rules, as they were required to (Roethlisberger & Dickson, 1939). On the contrary, those who *did* were socially isolated, labeled by other workers as "squealers" who could not be trusted. Although the company formally set productivity standards, workers also informally created their own definition of a fair day's work, criticizing those who exceeded it as "rate-busters" and others who fell short as "chiselers."

Such informal social structures suggest that many people reject the dehumanizing aspects of bureaucratic organization. But these informal structures also show that human beings have the creative capacity to humanize even the most rigidly defined social situations.

Limitations of Bureaucracy

Weber considered the ideal bureaucracy a model of efficiency. Still, real-life formal organizations certainly have their limitations, even when it comes to efficient operation. Anyone who has ever tried to replace a lost driver's license, return defective merchandise to a discount chain store, or change an address on a magazine subscription knows that large organizations can be maddeningly unresponsive to individual needs.

Some of these problems occur because organizations are *not* truly bureaucratic. No organizational system, after all, will ever completely eradicate human failings. Weber himself recognized that even the pure form of bureaucracy has limitations. Perhaps the most serious limitation of bureaucracy is its potential to *dehumanize* those it purports to serve. To operate efficiently, each client must be treated impersonally as a standard "case." In other words, in striving for efficiency, the organization loses the ability to treat special cases with individual attention.

Weber also feared that bureaucratic impersonality would *alienate* those who worked within large organizations. A human being in a formal organization, he claimed, was often reduced to "a small cog in a ceaselessly moving mechanism" (1978:988; orig. 1921). Although formal organizations are intended to serve humanity, Weber worried that humanity would eventually serve formal organizations.

Our ambivalence toward bureaucracy, then, comes as no surprise. On the one hand, formal organizations advance many dominant American values, as noted in Chapter 3 ("Culture"), including efficiency, practicality, and achievement. On the other hand, bureaucracies may threaten cherished ideals of democracy and individual freedom. Bureaucratic organizations affect our lives in countless ways, yet we have little sense of participation in their operation. In addition, the growth of formal organizations has paralleled a decline in individual privacy (Long, 1967; Smith, 1979). The box provides details.

CRITICAL THINKING

Bureaucracy: A Threat to Personal Privacy?

A century ago, personal privacy in the United States consisted of building a fence around one's house and hanging a "Beware of Dog" sign on the gate. Today, however, fences and dogs do little to protect personal privacy. More people, in fact, have access to more information about each one of us than ever before.

Why? Mostly because of the growth of formal organizations. Few would argue that our way of life could continue without formal organizations. Automobile drivers must be licensed, for example, but doing so requires gathering information about everyone who legally operates a vehicle. Similarly, the income tax system, the Social Security system, and programs that provide benefits to veterans, loans to students, and support for poor or unemployed people require government agencies to collect extensive information.

The explosive growth of credit in the American economy has also fueled the drive for information. In the past, local merchants routinely extended credit to their customers with no more paperwork than an I.O.U. Today, almost 1 billion credit cards are in circulation, providing credit to people who are usually total strangers. This has spawned a new business:

The efficiency of modern organizations is largely due to the capacity to process information at a speed unimaginable even fifty years ago. While serving humanity, however, computers store and share a growing amount of information about people's private lives, undermining personal privacy.

maintaining files about people's place of residence, marital status, employment, income, debts, and history of paying their bills on time.

Further eroding our privacy, computers now disseminate this informa

tion more widely and more rapidly than ever before. Because our addresses can easily be added to mailing lists, most Americans are now deluged by so-called junk mail. Of greater concern, that information circulates among all sorts of organizations, generally without the knowledge or consent of the people in question.

In response, many states have adopted laws recognizing the right of citizens to examine records kept about themselves in workplaces, banks, and credit bureaus. The U.S. Privacy Act of 1974 also places limitations on government agencies seeking to exchange information about individuals. Additionally, citizens now have the right to examine the information about themselves contained in most government files, and they may offer corrections that become part of the record. While such laws limit organizational violations of personal privacy to some extent, it is unlikely that they will stem the erosion of privacy significantly. The price of relying on formal organizations, then, may be the sacrifice of much personal privacy.

SOURCE: Based on Robert Ellis Smith, *Personal Privacy: How to Protect What's Left of It* (Garden City, NY: Anchor/Doubleday, 1979).

Bureaucratic Waste and Incompetence

"Work expands to fill the time available for its completion." Enough truth underlies C. Northcote Parkinson's (1957) tongue-in-cheek assertion that it is known today as Parkinson's Law.

To illustrate, assume that a bureaucrat processes fifty applications in an average day. If one day this worker had only twenty-five applications to examine, how long

would the task take? The logical answer is half a day, but Parkinson's Law suggests that if a full day is available to complete the work, a full day is how long it will take. Because they have little personal involvement in their work, in other words, few members of formal organizations seek extra work to fill their spare time. Therefore, bureaucrats always appear busy, prompting organizations to take on more employees. The added time and expense

George Tooker's painting *Government Bureau* is a powerful statement about the human costs of bureaucracy whereby human beings are reduced to "cases" and "officials" devoid of personal distinctiveness. Note the sameness of all the people seeking assistance, how no complete faces are shown, and the bland uniformity of the setting.

George Tooker, *Government Bureau*, 1956. Egg tempera on gesso panel. 19⅝ x 29⅝ inches. The Metropolitan Museum of Art, George A. Hearn Fund, 1956. (56.78).

required to hire, train, supervise, and evaluate a larger staff makes everyone busier still, setting in motion a vicious cycle that results in bureaucratic bloat. Ironically, the larger organization accomplishes no more real work than it did before.

Laurence J. Peter (Peter & Hull, 1969) devised the Peter Principle, which states that *bureaucrats are promoted to their level of incompetence.* The logic here is simple: employees successful at any level of the organizational hierarchy are likely to be promoted to higher positions. Eventually, however, when they reach a position where they are in over their heads and perform poorly, they no longer are candidates for promotion. They are thereby doomed to a future of inefficiency. Adding to the problem, by this time they have almost certainly acquired enough power to protect their interests, avoiding demotion or dismissal by hiding behind rules and regulations and taking credit for work actually performed by their more competent subordinates.

Bureaucratic Ritualism

For many Americans, the term *bureaucracy* conjures up images of *red tape* (derived from the red tape used by eighteenth-century English officials to wrap official parcels and records; Shipley, 1985). Red tape refers to a tedious concern with organizational procedures. In Robert Merton's view (1968), red tape amounts to a

type of group conformity. He coined the term **bureaucratic ritualism** to signify a *preoccupation with rules and regulations as ends in themselves rather than as the means to organizational goals.* Bureaucratic ritualism occurs when people become so intent on conforming to rules that they thwart the goals of the organization. Besides reducing individual and organizational performance, ritualism stifles the creativity and imagination of an organization's members, robbing the organization of the talents, dynamic ideas, and innovative approaches necessary to operate more efficiently as circumstances change (Whyte, 1957; Merton, 1968). In bureaucratic ritualism, we see one form of the alienation that Max Weber feared would arise from bureaucratic rigidity.

Bureaucratic Inertia

Weber noted that "once fully established, bureaucracy is among the social structures which are hardest to destroy" (1978:987; orig. 1921). Through **bureaucratic inertia,** *the tendency of bureaucratic organizations to persist over time,* formal organizations tend to take on a life of their own and to perpetuate themselves. A formal organization that meets its organizational goals will occasionally simply disband—as the anti-British Sons of Liberty did after the American Revolution. More commonly, an organization redefines its goals so it can continue to provide a livelihood for its members. The National Association for Infantile Paralysis, the sponsor of the well-known March of Dimes, was created to help find a cure for polio. After the development of the Salk vaccine to prevent polio, in the early 1950s, the organization did not dissolve but simply redirected its efforts toward other medical problems (Sills, 1969). It still exists today.

Even formal organizations with little real purpose may remain in operation. "Sunset laws," widely enacted in the United States, require government agencies that cannot justify their existence to be terminated. In Illinois, for example, officials who reviewed the qualifications of people who shoe horses were finally relieved of their duties well into the automobile age. Despite such examples, bureaucratic inertia usually leads formal organizations to devise justifications for themselves long after they have outlived their usefulness.

Oligarchy

Early in this century, Robert Michels (1876–1936) pointed out that bureaucracy encourages **oligarchy,** *the rule of the many by the few* (1949; orig. 1911). The earliest human societies did not possess the organizational means for even the most power-hungry ruler to control everyone. As societies became more complex and devel-oped formal organizations, including bureaucratic governments, domination by a small elite became common. According to what Michels called "the iron law of oligarchy," the pyramid-like structure of bureaucracy means that organizations are ruled by a few powerful leaders.

In Weber's terms, bureaucracy's strict hierarchy of responsibility encourages efficiency. It also, according to Michels, discourages democracy in government. While organizational officials are expected to subordinate personal interests to organizational goals, people who occupy powerful positions can—and often do—use their access to information, opportunity to influence others, and numerous other advantages to promote their personal interests. Such abuse of power goes on largely hidden from the public, undermining society's control over its elected leaders.

Sociologists have documented the prevalence of oligarchy in formal organizations (Lipset, Trow, & Coleman, 1977). Political competition and governmental checks and balances in the American system of government prevent the flagrant practice of oligarchy found in less democratic societies. In 1974, for example, Richard Nixon was forced to resign as president of the United States. Two years later, Jimmy Carter, considered an outsider by the national political establishment, gained enough grass-roots support among the American people

The tumultuous events in Eastern Europe during 1989 demonstrate the vulnerability of oligarchies to popular opposition. Here, Czechs fill Wenceslau Square in Prague, demanding an end to four decades of Communist rule.

Rosabeth Moss Kanter

How did a woman who began her career studying communes and other utopian settlements end up in the board rooms of many of America's most successful corporations? Perhaps the answer lies in changing social trends that distinguish the 1990s from the 1960s. Rosabeth Moss Kanter, a professor of business administration at Harvard University, has shown that what sociologists learn in one setting may be usefully applied in another. Kanter has earned numerous honorary doctoral degrees and been featured in national publications. Her achievements rank her among the most influential American women.

Kanter's career is divided between academic duties and Goodmeasure, Inc., a consulting firm she founded with her husband, that advises many large corporations. She is the author of several widely read books that apply sociological insights to the task of making corporations more profitable. What lessons does Kanter offer corporate executives that warrant fees as high as $15,000 for a single appearance? She challenges conventional organizational wisdom by demonstrating that *people*—not technology or machinery—are a corporation's most important resource. In the long run, she maintains, an organizational environment that develops human potential will advance corporate success. Reflecting on her career, Kanter explains:

> I remember when participation was what was being talked about on college campuses by Vietnam war protestors or people looking for student power. Now it's a respectable concept in corporate America, and now very large companies are figuring out how to divide themselves into small units. Many ideas and values of the '60s have been translated into the workplace. Take, for example, the right of workers to free expression, the desirability of participation and teamwork, the idea that authority should not be obeyed unquestioningly, the idea that smaller can be better because it can create ownership and family feeling. All of these are mainstream ideas.

SOURCES: Quotation from Megan Baldridge Murray, "Innovation Without Geniuses," *Yale Alumni Magazine and Journal*, Vol. XLVII, No. 6 (April 1984): 40–43; other sources include Susan McHenry, "Rosabeth Moss Kanter," *Ms.*, Vol. 13 (January 1985):62–63, 107–108.

to carry him to the White House. When the political leadership becomes unresponsive to the needs of the majority, opposition movements often arise. Sometimes these anti-government drives succeed—as in the overthrow of the Marcos regime in the Philippines and the Somoza oligarchy in Nicaragua, as well as the popular uprisings that toppled Communist regimes in Eastern Europe. Sometimes they do not; witness the much slower pace of change in South Africa despite popular opposition to the apartheid system.

Gender and Race in Organizations

Rosabeth Moss Kanter, introduced in the box, notes that ascribed statuses such as gender and race often determine who holds power in a bureaucratic hierarchy. To the extent that an organization has a dominant social composition, the gender- or race-based ingroup enjoys greater social acceptance, respect, credibility, and access to informal social networks. In American society, the most powerful positions in both private business and public government are generally held by well-to-do white males. By contrast, females, nonwhites, and those from economically disadvantaged backgrounds tend to feel like part of socially isolated outgroups. Often uncomfortably visible, they are taken less seriously and have lower chances of promotion than others. These people generally believe that they must work twice as hard as those in dominant categories to maintain their present position, let alone advance to a higher position (Kanter, 1977; Kanter & Stein, 1979:137).

Opportunity and Power: Effects on Employees

Kanter finds that providing power and opportunity to some members of formal organizations and not others has important consequences for everyone's on-the-job performance. Although the popular wisdom holds that employees who get ahead are smart and "hustle" while those who do not are less able and less motivated, Kanter's (1977) research indicates that the *organizational environment* greatly influences employee performance.

In addition to the social composition of a corporation, the opportunity to advance is a key dimension of the organizational environment. According to Kanter, organizations that offer everyone a chance for promotion typically turn employees into "fast-trackers," raising their aspirations, self-esteem, and commitment to the organization. By contrast, "dead-end" jobs produce only "zombies" with little aspiration, poor self-concept, and little loyalty to the organization.

Following this logic, Kanter maintains that having power and opportunity for themselves encourages people to be flexible leaders who build the morale of others, including subordinates. In contrast, those holding positions of little power often jealously guard what privileges they do have, rigidly supervising subordinates. Table 7–3 summarizes Kanter's findings.

The key message of Kanter's work is that organizations must change—or "humanize"—their structure to bring out the best in their employees. The consequences for the "bottom line" are obvious.

"Humanizing" Bureaucracy

"Humanizing" bureaucracy means *fostering an organizational environment that develops human resources*. Research by Kanter (1977, 1980, 1983, 1989) and others (cf. Peters & Waterman, Jr., 1982) shows that "humanizing" bureaucracy produces both happier employees and healthier profits. We have touched on the characteristics of a more humane organizational environment in the preceding discussion. They fall into the following broad categories:

1. **Social inclusiveness.** The social composition of the organization should, ideally, make no one feel "out of place" because of gender, race, or ethnicity. As long as any categories of people are represented in various segments of organizations in merely token numbers, however, this goal remains elusive. The long-term performance of all employees will improve to the extent that no one is subject to social exclusion.

Table 7–3 KANTER'S RESEARCH: A SUMMARY

	Advantaged Employees	Disadvantaged Employees
Social Composition	Being represented in high proportions helps employees to more easily fit in and to enjoy greater credibility; they experience less stress, and are usually candidates for promotion	Being represented in low proportions puts employees visibly "on display" and results in their not being taken seriously; they tend to fear making mistakes and losing ground rather than optimistically looking toward advancement
Power	In powerful positions, employees contribute to high morale and support subordinates; such employees tend to be more democratic leaders	In positions of low power, employees tend to foster low morale and restrict opportunities for subordinates to advance; they tend to be more authoritarian leaders
Opportunity	High opportunity encourages optimism and high aspirations, loyalty to organization, use of higher-ups as reference groups, and constructive responses to problems	Low opportunity encourages pessimism and low aspirations, weak attachment to the job, use of peers as reference groups, and ineffective griping in response to problems

SOURCE: Based on Rosabeth Moss Kanter, *Men and Women of the Corporation* (New York: Basic Books, 1977), pp. 246–249.

2. **A sharing of responsibilities.** "Humanizing" bureaucracy means reducing rigid, oligarchical structures by spreading power and responsibility more widely. Managers cannot benefit from the ideas of employees who have no channels for expressing their opinions. Knowing that superiors are open to suggestions encourages all employees to think creatively, increasing organizational effectiveness.

3. **Expanding opportunities for advancement.** Expanding opportunity reduces the number of employees stuck in routine, dead-end jobs with little motivation to perform well. Employees at all levels, therefore, should be encouraged to share ideas and to try new approaches, and no position should be ruled out as the start of an upward career path.

Critical evaluation. Kanter's work provides a fresh look at the concept of bureaucracy and its application to business organizations. Perhaps rigid formality made sense in the past, when uneducated organizational employees were hired simply as a source of physical labor. But today, workers can contribute a wealth of ideas to bolster organizational efficiency if the organizational environment encourages and rewards innovation.

Although Kanter's suggested changes may encounter resistance, such efforts are likely to produce significant returns. Comparing forty-seven companies with rigid bureaucratic structures to competitors of similar size but with more flexible approaches, Kanter (1983) found that the more flexible organizations were more profitable. She argues, therefore, that bureaucratic structure limits an organization's success to the extent that it treats employees as a group to be controlled rather than as a resource to be developed. Thus, while the basic bureaucratic model may still promote efficiency, organizational effectiveness is enhanced by flexible management styles, coupled with efforts to spread power and opportunity throughout the organization (Kanter, 1985).

Formal Organizations in Japan

The limitations of bureaucracy in America also become clear in comparisons with organizational patterns in other societies. Japanese organizations have sparked considerable interest among Americans in recent decades because of the remarkable economic success of this small society. Since the end of World War II, Japan's economic growth has surged five times faster than America's. Although geographically no larger than the state of Montana, Japan's gross national product in 1990 was more than one-third the size of our entire country's.

Formal organizations in Japan reflect that culture's strong traditions of collective identity and social solidarity. While Americans prize rugged individualism, Japanese society unites individuals into a society that is socially unequal, yet well integrated. This cohesiveness results in relatively low levels of social problems—such as alcoholism, violence, and drug abuse—compared to more rootless and competitive societies like the United States. Japanese cities also lack the abject poverty and crime found in much of urban America: Even late at night, a person can walk safely through downtown Tokyo (Ouchi, 1981).

This social solidarity makes formal organizations in Japan remarkably personal. With only slight exaggeration, we may describe formal organizations in Japan as extremely large primary groups. In the United States, by comparison, although a few companies have tried to model themselves on Japanese organizational principles, even "humanized" bureaucracy is usually based on secondary relationships.

William Ouchi (1981) highlights five distinctions between formal organizations in Japan and their counterparts in industrial societies of the West. In each case, the Japanese organization reflects that society's more collective orientation.

1. **Hiring and advancement.** In American organizations, promotions and higher salaries are prizes won through individual competition. In Japanese organizations, however, new graduates from schools are hired together as a group and receive comparable salaries and responsibilities. As one employee moves ahead, so do they all. Only after many years is anyone likely to be singled out for special advancement. This corporate approach generates a common identity among employees of the same age. In fact, Japanese employees are sometimes distressed at the thought of advancing at another's expense.

2. **Lifetime security.** American employees today rarely remain with one company for their entire careers. Instead, Americans commonly move from one company to another to fulfill personal ambitions. American companies are also quick to lay off employees in the event of economic setbacks. By contrast, Japanese companies typically hire employees for life, so companies and their employees have strong, mutual loyalties. Then, too, Japanese

Japan is a fascinating blend of the old and the new. Traditional loyalties and patterns of deference—of the young toward the old and women toward men—are now displayed in corporate life. The corporation's responsibilities toward employees are also modeled on traditional family life.

workers who spend several years learning one organization's system may be unattractive to other firms. Japanese companies, moreover, avoid layoffs by providing workers with other jobs in the organization, along with any necessary retraining.

3. **Holistic involvement.** In the United States, a clear line usually separates a person's working and private lives. Japanese organizations, on the other hand, take an active part in many aspects of their employee's lives. Companies often provide dormitory housing or mortgages for the purchase of homes, sponsor recreational activities, and schedule a wide range of social events in which every worker participates. Employee interaction outside the workplace strengthens collective identity, while offering the

respectful Japanese worker an opportunity to voice suggestions and criticisms more readily.

4. **Nonspecialized training.** Bureaucratic organization in the United States is based on specialized activity; a person's entire career often has a single focus. But a Japanese organization trains employees in all phases of its operation, expecting that employees will remain with the organization for life. This nonspecialized training shows workers how each job relates to the organization's overall operation. As a result, Japanese workers generally have more technical knowledge than their American counterparts (Sengoku, 1985). Broad training also enables the company to move employees from job to job more easily as circumstances dictate.

5. **Collective decision making.** Most major decisions in American organizations are made by a handful of executives. This cultural pattern is evident in the well-known sign on the desk of President Harry Truman: "The buck stops here." Although leaders of Japanese organizations also take responsibility for their company's performance, they involve workers in any decision that affects them. Greater economic equality between management and workers also fosters a closer working relationship, and the salary differential between executives and the rank and file is about half that found in the United States. Additionally, Japanese companies typically encompass many semi-autonomous working groups, called "quality circles." Instead of responding simply to the directives of superiors, all employees in Japan share managerial responsibilities.

Because of these organizational characteristics, formal organizations in Japan generate a strong sense of loyalty to the organization among employees. The cultural emphasis on *individual* achievement in American society finds its parallel in Japanese *groupism*. Japanese organizations promote a strong collective identity through broad personal involvement with the organization. By tying their personal interests to those of the organization, workers realize ambitions through the organization.

FORMAL ORGANIZATIONS AND SOCIETY

In recent years, the emphasis in the study of formal organizations has shifted from the organizations themselves to the *organizational environment* in which they operate. Formal organizations in Japan differ markedly from those in the United States, with much of this difference attributable to the social environments in which organizations operate. Just as important, formal organizations everywhere change along with their environments.

CRITICAL THINKING

Worker Participation: Will It Work in America?

What the company wants is for us to work like the Japanese. Everybody go out and do jumping jacks in the morning and kiss each other when they go home at night. You work as a team, rat on each other, and lose control of your destiny. That's not going to work in this country.

John Brodie
President, United Paperworkers
    Local 448
Chester, Pennsylvania

Who can quarrel with the economic success of the Japanese? Increasing economic competition from Asia and Europe has forced American companies to consider novel techniques for involving their workers in day-to-day decision making. Yet some voices in the American workplace—workers, union leaders, and managers—have been no happier about importing Japanese organizational techniques than about importing Japanese cars.

There is little doubt that such policies can be applied to the American workplace. Japanese companies, including Honda, Nissan, and Toyota, have built manufacturing plants in the United States and used American workers to achieve the same degree of efficiency and quality that they do in Japan. However, American corporate culture, with its hierarchical organizational environment, its heritage of individualism, and its history of labor-management conflict makes proposals for greater worker participation highly controversial.

Many American workers dislike the concept of worker participation because they see it as increasing their personal workload. While still responsible for actually building cars, for instance, workers are now asked to worry about quality control, unit costs, and overall company efficiency—tasks traditionally shouldered by management. At the extreme, Japanese-style policies require workers to learn about the operation of the entire company. Moreover, many American employees do not

As Ouchi (1981:62–64) explains, Max Weber's analysis of bureaucracy was developed in nineteenth-century Europe, where most businesses were still small family undertakings. Primary social relationships predominated, but many people agreed with Weber that such ties (critically viewed as nepotism and personal favoritism) ran counter to organizational efficiency. Weber's model of bureaucracy, now well entrenched in European and North American societies, therefore focused on impersonal, secondary relationships emphasizing technical specialization, impartiality, and behavior strictly guided by rules and regulations.

In Japan, formal organizations also developed within the context of a socially cohesive society. But formal organizations in Japan did not undermine primary relationships as they did in the West; rather, as Japan has modernized, traditional loyalties to family and locality have been largely *transferred to the corporation*. In this way, the Japanese remain at once traditional and modern, using personal social ties as an organizational asset that promotes efficiency. In recent years, many Japanese workers have become more individualistic; some are leaving the big industrial corporations, lured by higher salaries to newer financial organizations. Yet the Japanese case shows organizations need not be impersonal.

The startling Japanese economic advancement has prompted Americans to take a closer look at their way of doing things. In fact, Japanese productivity has sparked efforts to "humanize" bureaucracy in the United States. However, calls for greater worker participation in decision making do not always earn high marks from American workers. The box suggests why.

There is another reason to study the Japanese approach carefully. American society is less socially cohesive now than the more family-based society Weber knew. A rigidly bureaucratic form of organization encourages further atomization of society. Perhaps by following the lead of the Japanese, our own formal organizations can promote—rather than diminish—a sense of collective identity and responsibility. While bolstering organizational productivity, that is, this approach may also foster a greater integration of society.

want to move from job to job, acquiring new skills that they may or may not master successfully. Many union leaders also are suspicious of new plans formulated by management, even those purporting to share power. American labor unions themselves introduced the idea of worker participation more than fifty years ago. Today, though, many union leaders are wary that an alliance of workers and managers under the banner of "worker participation" may undermine union strength, which has been declining steadily in recent decades (see Chapter 19, "The Economy and Work"). Some managers, too, have been slow to adopt worker partici-pation programs: sharing power—meaning that lower-level employees procure supplies, direct production, and even schedule their own vacations—does not come easily in light of past practices placing executives in positions of undisputed dominance. Finally, in an age of corporate takeovers and short-term profits, those who control corporations may not wish to invest the time and money in restructuring the organization.

Are worker-participation programs changing the American workplace? A recent government survey found that, despite reservations and some outright resistance, about 70 percent of large American businesses had ini-tiated at least some programs to enhance worker participation. The advantages go right to the bottom line: productivity and profits are usually higher when workers have a say in decision making. And most employees in worker-participation programs—even those who may not want to sign up for morning jumping jacks—seem significantly happier about their jobs. Workers who have long used only their bodies are now enjoying the opportunity to use their brains as well.

SOURCE: Based on John Hoerr, "The Payoff from Teamwork," *Business Week*, No. 3114 (July 10, 1989):56–62.

SUMMARY

1. Social groups, which are important building blocks of societies, foster common identity and distinctive patterns of interaction.

2. Primary groups tend to be small and person oriented; secondary groups are typically large and goal oriented.

3. Instrumental leadership is concerned with a group's goals; expressive leadership focuses on the collective well-being of the members.

4. Group conformity is a process well documented by researchers. Insofar as members seek consensus, groups do not generate a wider range of ideas than do individuals working alone.

5. Reference groups—both ingroups and outgroups—are used by individuals making decisions and evaluations.

6. Georg Simmel argued that dyads have a distinctive intensity, but lack stability because of the effort necessary to maintain them. A triad can easily dissolve into a dyad by excluding one member.

7. Social networks are grouplike structures whose members usually have little common identity and uncertain interaction.

8. Formal organizations are large, secondary groups that seek to perform complex tasks efficiently. Depending on their members' reasons for joining, formal organizations can be classified as normative, coercive, or utilitarian.

9. The organizational model of bureaucracy has been widely adopted in the United States. Ideally, bureaucratic organization promotes the efficient performance of complex tasks.

10. Bureaucracy is based on specialization, hierarchy, rules and regulations, technical competence, impersonal interaction, and formal, written communications.

11. In practice, bureaucratic weaknesses include the inability to deal efficiently with special cases, depersonalizing the workplace, and fostering ritualism among some employees. Max Weber recognized, furthermore, that bureaucracy tends to resist change.

12. Formal organizations are often oligarchies. Rosabeth Moss Kanter's research has shown that the concentration of power and opportunity in American corporations tends to diminish organizational effectiveness.

13. "Humanizing" bureaucracy means recognizing that people are an organization's greatest resource. To develop human resources, the organizational environment must reduce the significance of ascribed statuses such as gender and race, spread decision-making power more widely, and broaden opportunity.

14. Formal organization in Japan differs from the Western, bureaucratic model because of the collective spirit of Japanese culture. Formal organizations in Japan are based on more personal ties than are their counterparts in the United States.

KEY CONCEPTS

bureaucracy an organizational model rationally designed to perform complex tasks efficiently

bureaucratic inertia the tendency of bureaucratic organizations to persist over time

bureaucratic ritualism a preoccupation with organizational rules and regulations as ends in themselves rather than as the means to organizational goals

dyad a social group with two members

expressive leadership group leadership that emphasizes collective well-being

formal organization a large, secondary group that is formally organized to facilitate achieving its goals

"groupthink" a reduced capacity for critical thinking caused by group conformity

"humanizing" bureaucracy fostering an organizational environment that develops human resources

ingroup an esteemed social group commanding a member's loyalty

instrumental leadership group leadership that emphasizes the completion of tasks

network a web of social ties that links people, often with little common identity and social interaction

oligarchy the rule of the many by the few

outgroup a scorned social group toward which one feels competition or opposition

primary group typically a small social group in which relationships are both personal and enduring

reference group a social group that serves as a point of reference for people making evaluations and decisions

secondary group typically a large and impersonal social group based on some special interest or activity

social group two or more people who identify with one another and have a distinctive pattern of interaction

triad a social group with three members

SUGGESTED READINGS

These two books provide a detailed account of many of the issues considered in this chapter.

> Rhoda Lois Blumberg. *Organizations in Contemporary Society.* Englewood Cliffs, NJ: Prentice Hall, 1987.

> Cecilia L. Ridgeway. *The Dynamics of Small Groups.* New York: St. Martin's Press, 1983.

Controversy has followed the obedience experiments of Stanley Milgram for more than thirty years. This book reviews Milgram's work and other studies of this kind, and tackles the broad ethical questions such research raises.

> Arthur G. Miller. *The Obedience Experiments: A Case Study of Controversy in Social Science.* New York: Praeger, 1986.

This recent book by the originator of the term *groupthink* examines organizational leadership.

> Irving L. Janis. *Crucial Decisions: Leadership in Policymaking and Crisis Management.* New York: The Free Press, 1989.

Throughout the world, women have played a large part in informal associations. These two books explore the interplay between women's associations and more established centers of power in developing societies.

> Patricia Caplan. *Class and Gender in India: Women and Their Organizations in a South Indian City.* New York: Tavistock, 1985.

> Kathryn S. March and Rachelle L. Taqqu. *Women's Informal Associations in Developing Countries: Catalysts for Change?* Boulder, CO: Westview Press, 1986.

Here is a rare analysis of the unpaid work of American women outside the home.

> Arlene Kaplan Daniels. *Invisible Careers: Women Civic Leaders from the Volunteer World.* Chicago: University of Chicago Press, 1988.

These two books exemplify the growing trend of applying sociological analysis to problems of business management. The first, by one of the best-known sociologists in the field of formal organizations, examines the future of corporate organization. The second, by a noted futurist, argues that simply "doing more of the same" in a changing society will surely lead to declining business.

> Rosabeth Moss Kanter. *When Giants Learn to Dance: Mastering the Challenges of Strategy, Management, and Careers in the 1990s.* New York: Simon and Schuster, 1989.

> Alvin Toffler. *The Adaptive Corporation.* New York: McGraw-Hill, 1985.

This collection of essays spotlights the power of large organizations. Both corporations and government agencies, often linked by social networks, exercise enormous power in local, national, and global contexts.

> Robert Perrucci and Harry R. Potter, eds. *Networks of Power: Organizational Actors at the National, Corporate, and Community Levels.* Hawthorne, NY: Aldine de Gruyter, 1989.

This book contains thirteen essays that explore how power is distributed and used in various kinds of organizations.

> G. William Domhoff and Thomas R. Dye, eds. *Power Elites and Organizations.* Newbury Park, CA: Sage Publications, 1987.

This fascinating book contrasts formal organizations in the United States with those in Japan.

> William Ouchi. *Theory Z: How American Business Can Meet the Japanese Challenge.* Reading, MA: Addison-Wesley, 1981.

Delving into the interplay of emotion and formal organization, this study of businesses highlights such success stories as Mary Kay cosmetics and Amway products.

> Nicole Woolsey Biggart. *Charismatic Capitalism: Direct Selling Organizations in America.* Chicago: The University of Chicago Press, 1989.

8

Deviance

In 1984 Gregory L. Johnson, a twenty-seven-year-old member of the Revolutionary Communist Youth Brigade, traveled to Houston, Texas, to engage in political protest outside the hall where the Republican National Convention was being held. The demonstrators tore down a nearby American flag, soaked it in lighter fluid, set it on fire, and, as it went up in flames, chanted, "America—the red, white, and blue; we spit on you!" For his part in the episode, Johnson was convicted of violating a Texas law against defiling the flag. Initially fined $2,000 and sentenced to one year in prison, his conviction was appealed. In 1989, in a five-to-four decision, the Supreme Court ruled that the First Amendment to the Constitution, which guarantees the right to free speech, protects the burning of the flag as a form of political protest.

This decision caused a furor far beyond Johnson's act. Many Americans were outraged that Old Glory—a symbol of our nation—could be treated with such outright contempt under the protection of the law. The Senate voted a resolution expressing its "profound disappointment" with the decision, and President George Bush suggested that the Constitution be amended to negate the High Court's decision. Public opinion surveys ran three to one against the Court's stand.

The Johnson case thrust deep into the heart of the timeless tension between deviance and conformity.

On the one hand was the passionate desire to support American principles by denouncing such an attack on them. On the other hand was the idea that we honor the flag precisely by tolerating those who dishonor it. This latter view was expressed by Justice William J. Brennan, writing for the majority of the Court: "If there is a bedrock principle underlying the First Amendment, it is that the Government may not prohibit the expression of an idea simply because society finds the idea itself offensive or disagreeable" (Isaacson, 1989; Jacoby, 1989).

This chapter examines the ways in which societies confront the "offensive or disagreeable." How and why

does deviance arise? What happens when competing views of what is right and wrong collide? Are all people who violate norms defined as deviant? Why are legal standards sometimes at odds with public opinion? We shall begin with several basic concepts.

WHAT IS DEVIANCE?

Deviance is *the recognized violation of cultural norms.* Norms shape a wide range of human activities, and so the concept of deviance is correspondingly broad. One familiar type of deviance is **crime,** *the violation of norms formally enacted into criminal law.* Even criminal deviance is variable, ranging from minor traffic violations to serious offenses such as rape and murder. A special category of crime is **juvenile delinquency,** *the violation of legal standards that apply to the young.*

Deviance includes many other types of nonconformity, some viewed as mild (left-handedness, boastfulness, and Mohawk hairstyles), others as more serious (violent political protest and mental illness). To some

Deviance exists in relation to any and all normative patterns. Because many societies have traditional conceptions of femininity involving softness and submissiveness, women who develop their physical strength—and especially women body-builders—may be viewed as deviant.

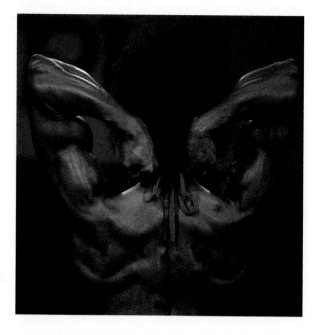

who are in the majority, being a member of a racial or ethnic minority may seem deviant. In addition, the poor—who may find it difficult to conform to many conventional middle-class patterns—are also widely defined as deviant. Even physical traits may be considered deviant. Men with many highly visible tattoos may be seen as deviant, as are women with any tattoo at all. Being unusually tall or short, or grossly fat or exceedingly thin, may be the basis of deviance. Physical disabilities are yet another reason for being defined as nonconforming.

Most of the examples of nonconformity that come readily to mind involve negative definitions. However, the opposite may also be the case. Since we all have shortcomings, we might define especially righteous people as deviant, although we accord them a measure of respect (Huls, 1987). Deviance, then, involves *difference,* both negative and positive, which causes us to react to others as "outsiders" (Becker, 1966).

The Social Foundation of Deviance

We tend to view deviance simply as a result of free choice or personal failings. As earlier chapters have emphasized, however, all social behavior—deviance as well as conformity—is shaped by society. This is evident in three ways.

1. **Deviance exists only in relation to cultural norms.** No thought or action is inherently deviant. It becomes deviant only in relation to particular norms. In the traditional village communities of Sicily, for example, norms support the use of physical violence to avenge an insult to family honor (Wolfgang & Ferracuti, 1982). In this case, *not* to avenge an insult is defined as deviant. Within most American society, in contrast, norms do not support the use of such violence. What is honorable in one place, therefore, may result in arrest and prosecution in another.

    Since cultural norms change, so does what is deviant. A century ago, American cultural norms linked women's lives to the home: women seeking business careers were likely to be considered deviant. Today women pursuing careers outside the home receive widespread support.

2. **People become deviant as others define them that way.** Each of us violates cultural norms, perhaps even to the extent of breaking the law. For example, most of us have at some time walked around talking

On May 4, 1970, National Guard troops opened fire on students who had gathered for an antiwar demonstration at Kent State University in Ohio. Four students were killed and nine were wounded. Widespread opinion held that the shooting was justified, if regrettable, as a firm response to the many campus protests taking place at that time. None of the troops or their superiors was criminally prosecuted for taking part in the event.

to ourselves or "borrowed" supplies, such as pens or paper, from the workplace. Such actions, in themselves, are insufficient to define us as mentally ill or criminal. Whether a person is defined as deviant depends on how others perceive, define, and respond to the situation.

3. **Both norms and the way people define situations involve social power.** Following the ideas of Karl Marx (introduced in Chapter 4, "Society"), we have seen that norms, and especially laws, tend to protect the interests of powerful people. For example, the owners of an unprofitable factory have a legal right to close their business, although doing so puts thousands of people out of work. If workers commit an act of vandalism that closes the same factory for a single day, they are likely to be defined as criminal. Also some people may be defined as deviant for exactly the same behavior that others engage in with impunity. A homeless person who stands on a street corner and denounces the city government risks arrest for disturbing the peace; a mayoral candidate during an election campaign can do the same while receiving extensive police protection. In short, norms and their application are linked to social inequality.

Social Control

Deviant people may be subject to **social control,** *attempts by society to regulate the behavior of individuals.* Like deviance itself, social control takes many forms. Socialization, discussed in Chapter 5, is a complex process

of social control in which family, peer groups, and the mass media influence people's attitudes and behavior. A more structured type of social control is the **criminal justice system,** *a formal reaction to alleged violations of the law through the use of police, courts, and punishment.* Social control involves a positive response to conformity as well as a negative response to deviance. Praise from parents, high grades in school, and positive recognition from people in the community encourage conformity to conventional patterns of thought and behavior.

In sum, both deviance and social control are inseparable from the operation of society.

BIOLOGICAL EXPLANATIONS OF DEVIANCE

Chapter 5 ("Socialization") noted that human behavior was understood—or, more correctly, misunderstood—during the nineteenth century as an expression of biological instincts. Not surprisingly, then, early interest in criminality emphasized biological causes.

Early Research

In 1876 Caesare Lombroso (1835–1909), an Italian physician who worked in prisons, suggested that criminals were physically distinctive—with low foreheads, prominent jaws and cheekbones, protruding ears, hairiness, and unusually long arms that made them resemble human beings' apelike ancestors. In biological terms, Lombroso viewed criminals as evolutionary throwbacks to lower forms of life. Toward the end of his career he acknowledged the importance of social forces in criminality, but his early assertion that some people were literally born criminals was extremely popular at a time when few powerful people were inclined to face up to flaws in social arrangements (Jones, 1986).

Lombroso's research was seriously defective. He identified physical features among prisoners without realizing that the same traits also existed in the population as a whole. Several decades later, the British psychiatrist Charles Buckman Goring (1870–1919) more carefully compared thousands of convicts and noncriminals. He found great physical variation within both groups, but no overall physical differences between criminals and noncriminals of the kind suggested by Lombroso (1972; orig. 1913).

Delinquency and Body Structure

Although Lombroso's work had been discredited, others continued to search for biological explanations of criminality. William Sheldon (1949) suggested that body structure was significant. He described three general types of body structure: *ectomorphs*, who were tall, thin, and fragile; *endomorphs*, who were short and fat; and *mesomorphs*, who were muscular and athletic. After analyzing the body structure and criminal history of hundreds of young men, Sheldon reported a correlation between criminality and the mesomorphic body type. Criminality, according to Sheldon, was linked to muscular, athletic body structure.

This conclusion was supported by subsequent research conducted by Sheldon and Eleanor Glueck (1950). The Gluecks, however, cautioned that mesomorphic body structure was not necessarily a *cause* of criminality. Mesomorphic males, they suggested, were somewhat more likely to be raised with little affection and understanding from family members and consequently showed less sensitivity toward others and tended to react aggressively to frustration. It is also likely that young men with muscular builds have the physical capacity to become the "bullies on the block" (Gibbons, 1981). Moreover, expecting muscular and athletic boys to be more physically aggressive than others, people may treat them accordingly, thereby provoking the very behavior that is expected.

Recent Research

Since the 1960s, increasing knowledge of genetics has rekindled interest in biological causes of criminality. Some research has explored the connection between criminal behavior and a specific pattern of chromosomes, the structures that carry the genes (see Vold & Bernard, 1986:92–99). In human development, sex is determined by chromosomes, females having two X chromosomes and males having one X and one Y. In perhaps one case in a thousand, a genetic mutation causes a male to have an extra Y chromosome, producing an XYY pattern. Males with this XYY pattern appear somewhat more often in prisons and mental institutions. Initially, this fact was taken to mean that they were prone to violent criminal behavior, but subsequent research has refuted this conclusion, indicating only that such men are significantly taller and perhaps less intelligent than average. As was noted earlier, unusually large men are more likely to be seen by others as threatening; low intelligence is often a barrier to social acceptance and a good job (Hook, 1973; Suzuki & Knudtson, 1989).

Instead of linking criminality to specific genetic flaws, recent research suggests that overall genetic composition, in combination with social influences, explains some variation in criminality (Rowe, 1983; Rowe & Osgood, 1984; Jencks, 1987). In a review of research on this topic, James Q. Wilson and Richard Herrnstein (1985) lend further support to the conclusion that biological factors have a small but real effect on whether individuals engage in crime. If this is so, the new field of sociobiology (see Chapter 3, "Culture") may offer clues to criminal patterns, such as why males engage in more violence than females do. This approach also promises to shed light on victims of violence, perhaps explaining why disabled or foster children are more likely to be victimized by family violence than healthy or natural children (Daly & Wilson, 1988). Clearly, in these instances, whatever biological forces may be at work are enhanced or inhibited by the social environment.

Critical evaluation. Biological theories attempt to explain crime in terms of individual physical traits. For this reason, biological research has produced a limited understanding of the causes of crime.

First, early biological research tended to focus on rare and abnormal cases, which comprised only a small proportion of all crimes. Second, more recent sociobiological research suggests that common biological traits may be linked to criminality but, since so little is understood about genetics and human behavior, causal connections are not yet justified. Third, in any case, an individualistic biological approach cannot address the issue of how some kinds of behaviors come to be defined as deviant in the first place.

In sum, there is much to be learned about human biology as it may affect behavior. At present, however, virtually all research places far greater emphasis on social influences on human behavior (Gibbons & Krohn, 1986; Liska, 1987).

PSYCHOLOGICAL EXPLANATION OF DEVIANCE

Like biological theories, psychological explanations of deviance tend to be individualistic, focusing on abnormalities in the individual personality. Though some abnormalities are hereditary, psychologists view most as a result of socialization. Since personality is shaped by social experience throughout life, deviance is usually understood to be the result of "unsuccessful" socialization.

Containment Theory

Walter Reckless and Simon Dinitz (1967) explained juvenile delinquency as the outcome of young boys' personality traits. They claimed that the desire to engage in delinquent activity can be contained if boys have developed strong moral values and a positive self-image. Reckless and Dinitz called their idea *containment theory*.

They asked teachers to identify, from among boys about age twelve, those who were deemed likely to engage in delinquent acts and those who were not. Interviews with both the boys and their mothers provided information on each boy's self-concept—how he viewed himself and how he related to the world around him. The "good boys" seemed to have a strong conscience (or *superego*, in Sigmund Freud's terminology), generally coped well with frustration, and identified positively with cultural norms and values. The "bad boys" had a weaker conscience, tolerated less frustration, and identified less strongly with conventional culture. Over a four-year period, the researchers found that the "good boys" had

indeed experienced fewer contacts with the police than had the "bad boys." Since all the boys studied were from areas where delinquency was widespread, the researchers concluded that boys who managed to stay out of trouble had a strong conscience and a positive self-concept that served as "an internal buffer which protects people against (violation) of the social and legal norms" (Reckless, 1970:401).

Critical evaluation. Psychological research has demonstrated that personality patterns have some relationship to delinquency and other types of deviance. Nevertheless, a number of weaknesses are common to this research.

First, the vast majority of serious crimes are committed by people who are not psychologically abnormal, so this approach cannot explain most deviance. Second, because it looks at individuals, this approach ignores how "normal" and "abnormal" personality traits vary from society to society, just as what is defined as deviant varies with cultural norms. Third, little explanation is offered for the fact that, among people with similar attitudes and behavior, some are defined as deviant while others are not.

Both biological and psychological approaches view deviance as an individual attribute without exploring how conceptions of right and wrong initially arise or without investigating the deviant person's place within the larger society. The importance of a sociological analysis of deviance lies precisely in this type of investigation.

SOCIOLOGICAL EXPLANATION: STRUCTURAL-FUNCTIONAL ANALYSIS

All sociological approaches explain deviance in terms of the operation of society rather than in terms of traits of individuals. The structural–functional paradigm examines how any social pattern is involved in the operation of society as a whole.

Emile Durkheim: The Functions of Deviance

At first glance, deviance may seem simply destructive; crime, for example, causes some $15 billion in losses to Americans each year, as well as death and personal

The arts allow members of society to explore alternatives to existing ideas and social arrangements. For this reason, artists have historically been celebrated but with a mildly deviant identity. Some provocative art has recently sparked controversy as to whether society should fund, or even permit, *any* type of artistic expression. This artistic work provoked national attention because it required observers to walk on an American flag.

injury to hundreds of thousands of people. Structural–functional theorists nevertheless argue that without some amount of deviance, society could not exist at all.

A pioneering study of the functions of deviance was carried out by Emile Durkheim (1964a, orig. 1895; 1964b, orig. 1893). He asserted that there is nothing abnormal about deviance, since it is an integral part of all societies. Durkheim pointed out four major functions of deviance.

1. **Deviance affirms cultural values and norms.** Any society requires moral definition: some attitudes and behavior must be defined as more desirable than others. However, no conception of what is morally right exists without a corresponding conception of what is morally wrong. For example, patriotism is strengthened as a society condemns those who dishonor its flag. Deviance is therefore indispensable to the process of generating and sustaining cultural values. Even the Puritans of seven-teenth-century Massachusetts Bay, a small and deeply religious society, inevitably defined some of their own as deviant. Durkheim could well have had the Puritans in mind when he asked us to

    > imagine a society of saints, a perfect cloister of exemplary individuals. Crimes, properly so called, will there be unknown; but faults which appear (insignificant) to the layman will create there the same scandal that the ordinary offense does in ordinary consciousness. . . . For the same reason, the perfect and upright man judges his smallest failings with a severity that the majority reserve for acts more truly in the nature of an offense. (1964a: 68–69)

2. **Responding to deviance clarifies moral boundaries.** Defining people as deviant also instructs everyone as to the precise position of society's moral boundaries. For example, a college marks the line between academic honesty and dishonesty by conferring deviant status on some students through disciplinary procedures. Drawing on Durkheim's ideas, Kai Erikson explains:

    > When a community calls [a person] to account for [deviance] it is making a statement about the nature and placement of its boundaries. It is declaring how much variability and diversity can be tolerated within the group before it begins to lose its distinctive shape, its unique identity. (1966:11)

3. **Responding to deviance promotes social unity.** People typically react to serious deviance with collective outrage. In doing so, Durkheim explained, they reaffirm the moral ties that bind them. For example, Americans have often reacted with a surge of patriotism to what we view as terrorist actions against the United States.

4. **Deviance encourages social change.** By "patrolling" a society's moral boundaries, deviants suggest alternatives to the status quo. In this way, no society remains static. Today's deviance, Durkheim noted, may well become tomorrow's norm (1964a:71). For example, in the 1950s, most Americans viewed rock and roll music as a corrupter of youth and an outrage against established tastes. Today, rock and roll has become a conventional part of society, perhaps more "all-American" than apple pie, and certainly more profitable, as the box explains.

An Illustration: The Puritans of Massachusetts Bay

Kai Erikson's (1966) historical research about the early Puritans of Massachusetts Bay provides support for Durk-

Rock and Roll: From Deviance to Big Business

Rock and roll exploded onto the American scene in the early 1950s, full of energy and controversy. Rock's roots were in the rhythm and blues of black America, music that few record companies or radio stations promoted at the time. Then, too, rock and roll was central to the emerging youth subculture, signifying rebellion against parental authority. By the 1960s, protest and drug-based psychedelic music questioned virtually all authority. Early rock and roll also contended with its image as the music of the poor and the working class. Among privileged people with more refined tastes, it was discredited. Also, and probably most important, rock and roll has long been synonymous with sex—the phrase itself originally meant sexual intercourse. For all these reasons, rock and roll redefined American morality.

While singers like Perry Como and Doris Day represented conventional musical tastes of the 1950s, Elvis Presley—the first superstar of rock and roll—was dismissed by one influential critic of the times as an "unspeakably . . . vulgar young entertainer" (cited in Gillett, 1983:17). Church groups, especially in the South, launched

Elvis Presley

campaigns to suppress rock and roll. In addition to the sexually suggestive gyrations of rock and roll singers, some lyrics provoked charges of obscenity. Mild by today's standards, early rock and roll lyrics were viewed as threatening in a decade when sex was rarely mentioned.

American culture gradually came to embrace rock and roll for the simple reason that there was enormous money to be made from it. In the early 1960s, the Beatles not only sold millions of records but generated a fortune through side-line products, concert tours, and successful films. Coca-Cola was the first company to use rock music in advertising, now a common practice.

Lionel Ritchie

Rock music is now bigger business than anyone could have imagined a generation ago. From 5 percent of record sales in the mid-1950s, rock is now a multibillion-dollar industry, accounting for more than 80 percent of all record sales. In the 1990s, rock will certainly become increasingly evident on television. Promoter Dick Clark looked to the bottom line when he claimed, "I don't make culture, I sell it" (cited in Chapple & Garofalo, 1977:305).

SOURCE: Based on Charlie Gillett, *The Sound of the City: The Rise of Rock and Roll* (New York: Pantheon, 1983); also Steve Chapple and Reebee Garofalo, *Rock 'n' Roll Is Here to Pay: The History and Politics of the Music Industry* (Chicago: Nelson-Hall, 1977).

heim's analysis of deviance. This highly religious "society of saints," Erikson discovered, used deviance to clarify various moral boundaries. The kind of deviance the Puritans encountered depended on the moral questions they needed to resolve. The rigors of life in Massachusetts Bay meant that they could no longer afford the lively individualism that had sustained them as religious dissenters in England. As Erikson explains, they were able to shift their moral foundations through defining as deviant several once celebrated members. Responding to the

deviance they had created, the early Puritans fostered their unity as they reaffirmed common moral values.

Erikson's research also revealed that the proportion of people in Massachusetts Bay viewed as deviant remained stable over time, even while the reasons for deviance changed. Erikson saw this stability as evidence that deviants served as moral markers, outlining the changing boundaries of conventional attitudes and behavior. The Puritan society thus ensured that the social functions of deviance were consistently carried out.

Robert Merton: Strain Theory

The analysis of the work of Emile Durkheim in Chapter 4 ("Society") noted that modern societies are prone to *anomie*, or normlessness. Such a condition leaves individuals socially unregulated and prone to deviance.

Robert Merton (1938, 1968) has applied Durkheim's concept of anomie by linking deviance to certain societal imbalances. Merton's theory begins with the observation that financial success is a widespread American *goal* and that society endorses certain *means* to that end. Ideally, then, success is achieved, on the one hand, through obtaining an appropriate education and working hard at a job. "Success" gained through theft or other dishonest activities, on the other hand, is a violation of cultural norms. Therefore, if people are socialized to want success and to play by the rules, *conformity* should result.

But American society does not provide sufficient opportunity to allow everyone who desires success to achieve it. Moreover, because of the American emphasis on wealth, even relatively successful people may be motivated by the promise of gain to violate cultural norms and perhaps the law. Corporate executives, for example, may engage in dishonest business practices or embezzle company funds; certainly, too, many wealthy Americans misrepresent their income to the Internal Revenue Service. Merton called this type of activity *innovation*—attempting to achieve culturally approved goals using unconventional means. Table 8–1 portrays innovation as accepting the goal of success while rejecting conventional means to that goal.

Such innovation results from the "strain" experienced when the value placed on wealth overpowers the norms that regulate how wealth is to be acquired. The poor obviously experience this strain to the extent that their aspirations for success are frustrated by a lack of educational and job opportunities. Not surprisingly, some resort to making their own rules, engaging in what is conventionally defined as theft, selling illegal drugs, or other kinds of street hustling and racketeering. The box illustrates the process of innovation through the life of notorious gangster Al Capone.

A second response to the inability to achieve wealth through normative means is *ritualism* (see Table 8–1). In this response, people resolve the strain of not having realized cultural goals by abandoning them while still seeking respectability by compulsively conforming to cultural norms. Ritualism, Merton suggests, is common among people of modest social standing who have little

Table 8–1 MERTON'S STRAIN THEORY OF DEVIANCE

Individual Responses to Dominant Cultural Patterns	Cultural Goals	Cultural Means
Nondeviant Response		
Conformity	Accept	Accept
Deviant Responses		
Innovation	Accept	Reject
Ritualism	Reject	Accept
Retreatism	Reject	Reject
Rebellion	Reject current goals but promote new ones	Reject current means but promote new ones

SOURCE: Based on Robert K. Merton, *Social Theory and Social Structure* (New York: Free Press, 1968), pp. 230–246.

opportunity to gain more in life but fear risking what they have through innovation. This response is illustrated by "bureaucratic ritualists," described in Chapter 7 ("Groups and Organizations") as lower-level officials who compulsively conform to rules to the point of losing sight of their overall purpose. Such people are deviant in giving up their goal of financial success, although they may be viewed as "good citizens" because of their rigid adherence to the rules.

A third response to the inability to succeed is *retreatism*—the rejection of both the goals and the norms of one's culture. Retreatists are society's dropouts. This category includes some alcoholics and drug addicts, as well as some of the street people common to American cities. The deviance of retreatists is their unconventional way of life and, perhaps more seriously, their assumed lack of desire to change.

The fourth response to the failure to achieve wealth is *rebellion*. Like retreatists, rebels reject both the cultural definition of success and the normative means of achieving it. Rebels, however, go further by advocating radical alternatives to the existing social order, proposing new, disapproved values and norms. Some seek to do this through political revolution, while others promote an unconventional religious group. Either way, as rebels withdraw from established society in favor of a counterculture, they are likely to be widely viewed as deviant.

Although Merton's theory is an influential statement of the relationship between deviance and the opera-

Al Capone: The Gangster as Innovator

All I ever did was to sell beer and whiskey to our best people. All I ever did was to supply a demand that was pretty popular.

In these words, Al Capone described his life as probably the most notorious of America's gangsters. Capone's opportunity to found a criminal empire was created by Prohibition, which outlawed alcoholic beverages in the United States between 1920 and 1933. For someone willing to take the risk, there was a lot of money to be made in bootlegging.

Capone rose to power and wealth at a time when American cities were filled with tens of millions of immigrants from Europe—mostly poor but eager to share in the American Dream of success. Defined by many as socially inferior, immigrants commonly encountered the barriers of prejudice and discrimination. The vast majority of immigrants nonetheless patiently remained conformists in Merton's terminology. Others, however, saw in organized crime a means to achieve the American Dream. So it was that Al Capone—a man of genius and ambition, born in Naples, Italy, and brought up in an Italian slum of New York City—came to dominate one of the largest criminal empires of our history, centered in Chicago.

Capone's life illustrates Merton's concept of the deviant innovator—an individual who accepts the culturally approved goal of success but rejects conventional norms, thereby signaling a lack of legitimate opportunity. In the words of one analyst of the American underworld:

The typical criminal of the Capone era was a boy who had . . . seen what was rated as success in the society he had been thrust into—the Cadillac, the big bank-roll, the elegant apartment. How could he acquire that kind of recognizable status? He was almost always a boy of outstanding initiative, imagination, and ability; he was the kind of boy who, under different conditions, would have been a captain of industry or a key political figure of his time. But he hadn't the opportunity of going to Yale and becoming a banker or broker; there was no passage for him to a law degree from Harvard. There was, however, a relatively easy way of acquiring these goods that he was incessantly told were available to him as an American citizen, and without which he had begun to feel he could not properly count himself as an American citizen. He could become a gangster. (Allsop, 1961:236)

Even if they managed to gain wealth and power, gangsters found that they were denied the prestige accorded to those who had succeeded in legitimate business. Thus many gangsters attempted to distance themselves from their poor, ethnic origins by, for example, changing their names.

Capone took his first job from an immigrant who called himself Mr. Frankie Yale. The reputed head of the national Mafia, Yale operated from an establishment on Coney Island that he named the Harvard Inn. For part of his life Capone himself demanded that he be called Anthony Brown, and according to one of his associates, he hired only men who displayed few of the ethnic traits he sought to leave behind.

The Big Fellow hires nothing but gentlemen. They have to be well dressed at all times and have to have cultured accents. They always have to say "Yes, Sir" and "No, Sir" to him. (Allsop, 1961:249)

In this way, Capone attempted to live in the manner of upper-class Americans. During the Depression he charitably provided food to many of Chicago's destitute people. Later he enrolled his son Anthony at Yale University, and subsequently he celebrated the young man's wedding to a well-to-do woman from Nashville.

Capone was one of the most notorious American criminals of the twentieth century, yet his hopes for himself and his family were modeled on the American Dream. His deviance—not unlike that of thousands of young people dealing drugs in today's cities—is of a particularly American kind: based on a strong desire for success and indicating limited opportunity in American society.

SOURCE: Kenneth Allsop, *The Bootleggers* (London: Hutchinson and Company, 1961). Other information from E. Digby Baltzell, *The Protestant Establishment* (New York: Vintage Books, 1964), pp. 214–218.

tion of society, it is subject to criticism. First, there is no clear evidence suggesting how much crime or other deviance can be attributed to the "strain" generated by the operation of society. Second, some kinds of deviance, such as crimes of passion or mental illness, are not easily explained in this way. Third, Merton provides only a few clues as to why an individual would choose one response to strain over another. Fourth, strain theory assumes that, initially at least, everyone seeks success in conventional terms of wealth. As was noted in Chapter 3 ("Culture"), American society exhibits considerable variability in cultural values and generates many different conceptions of personal success.

Deviant Subcultures

An extension of Merton's theory is a study of delinquent youth by Richard Cloward and Lloyd Ohlin (1966). They point out that criminal deviance results when there is limited legitimate opportunity to achieve success plus *available illegitimate opportunity*. In short, patterns of deviance and conformity largely reflect the *relative opportunity structure* confronted by various categories of young people.

The life of Al Capone illustrates this idea. Capone pursued a criminal career partly because, as a poor immigrant, he was denied legitimate paths to success, such as a college education. Yet his world did provide illegitimate opportunity for success as a bootlegger. Where relative opportunity favors what Merton might call "organized innovation," Cloward and Ohlin expect *criminal subcultures* to develop. Such subcultures offer the knowledge, skills, and other resources needed to succeed in unconventional ways.

Cloward and Ohlin also recognize that such organized innovation may be unlikely, especially in poor and highly transient neighborhoods. Here, delinquency may arise in the form of *conflict subcultures* in which gangs employ violence as an expression of frustration and claim to prestige. Finally, among those who have failed to achieve success even using criminal means, *retreatist subcultures* may arise. Consistent with Merton's analysis, such subcultures are supported by dropouts who may extensively use alcohol or other drugs.

Albert Cohen (1971) has suggested that delinquency is pronounced among lower-class youths because they are denied opportunity to achieve success in a conventional way. They are aware of conventional definitions of success and so find little basis for self-respect

in their impoverished condition. In response, they may develop a delinquent subculture based on values and norms that offer more favorable self-definitions. These subcultures, Cohen says, "define as meritorious the characteristics [these youths] *do* possess, the kinds of conduct of which they *are* capable" (1971:66). For example, because the dominant culture values the calculated pursuit of wealth, a delinquent subculture may extol stealing "for the hell of it" and gain prestige in the process. In short, members of a delinquent subculture may enjoy publicly flouting conventional norms while carefully conforming to their own norms.

Walter Miller (1970) agrees that delinquent subcultures are most likely to develop in the lower classes. The values and norms of delinquent gangs, he maintains, are not a reaction to a middle-class way of life but arise from the daily experiences of living with little legitimate opportunity. He describes six focal concerns of delinquent subcultures. First is *trouble*, arising from frequent conflict with teachers and police. Second, especially among males, is *toughness*, with value placed on physical size, strength, and athletic skills. Third is *smartness*, the ability to succeed on the streets, to outthink or con others, and to avoid being similarly taken advantage of. Fourth is *excitement*, the search for thrills, risk, or danger to gain needed release from a daily routine that is too predictable and unsatisfying. Fifth is a concern with *fate*, derived from the lack of control these youths feel over their own lives. Sixth is *autonomy*, or the desire for freedom, often expressed as resentment toward authority figures.

Hirschi's Control Theory

A final argument derived from Durkheim's analysis of anomie is Travis Hirschi's (1969) *control theory*. Like others who share this approach, Hirschi suggests that deviance arises from particular social arrangements, specifically the inability of society to control adequately the activities of its members. He assumes that individuals find deviance tempting; for Hirschi, what requires explanation is not deviance, but *conformity*. Hirschi suggests that conformity is a function of four types of social controls.

1. **Attachment.** Strong social attachments to others enhance conformity; weak relationships within the family, peer group, and school leave people freer to engage in deviance.

2. **Commitment.** The higher one's commitment to legitimate opportunity, the greater the advantages of conformity. A young person who seems bound for college and likely to end up with a good job, in other words, has a high stake in conformity. In contrast, someone with little confidence in future success has a low investment in conformity and is a likely candidate to engage in deviance.

3. **Involvement.** Extensive involvement in legitimate activities such as a job, going to school and completing homework, or hobbies inhibits deviance. People with little legitimate involvement—who simply "hang out" waiting for something to happen—have time and energy for deviant activity.

4. **Belief.** Strong beliefs in conventional morality and respect for authority figures also control tendencies toward deviance; people with weak beliefs are more vulnerable to whatever temptation deviance presents.

Hirschi's analysis is widely viewed as one of the most useful for explaining many kinds of deviant behavior, and it has gained support from subsequent research (Wiatrowski, Griswold, & Roberts, 1981). Here, again, a person's location in society is considered crucial in generating a stake in conformity or allowing everyday temptations to turn into actual deviance.

Critical evaluation. Structural–functional theories investigate how deviance is linked to the norms and social structures of society. The pioneering work of Emile Durkheim shows how recognizing and reacting to some form of deviance enables a society to morally define itself. Durkheim's analysis of anomie has also led others to investigate how social organization can enhance or inhibit deviant behavior.

Merton's strain theory links deviance to a lack of fit between society's goals and means. The general approach of Cloward and Ohlin, Cohen, Miller, and Hirschi—that deviance reflects the opportunity structure of society—is widely supported (cf. Allan & Steffensmeier, 1989). Some of this research suggests that disadvantaged youths may try to expand the opportunities they do have through forming deviant subcultures.

One limitation of these theories is that they assume a single cultural standard against which attitudes and behavior are defined as either legitimate or illegitimate. American society, however, upholds various, sometimes competing ideas of what is deviant. A second problem lies in our defining deviance in terms that focus attention on poor people. If crime is defined to include stock fraud as well as street theft, criminals are more likely to be people who are well integrated into American society. A third problem is that structural–functional theories imply that everyone who violates conventional cultural standards will be defined as deviant. Being defined as deviant, however, is actually a highly complex process, as is explained in the next section.

SOCIOLOGICAL EXPLANATION: SYMBOLIC-INTERACTION ANALYSIS

The symbolic-interaction paradigm directs our attention to how people in various situations generate social reality through their interaction. In the early 1950s, sociologists began to apply this theoretical orientation to the study of deviance. Their work led to the recognition that social norms vary considerably, and therefore definitions of deviance and conformity are applied with surprising flexibility.

Labeling Theory

The central contribution of symbolic-interaction analysis is **labeling theory,** *the assertion that deviance and conformity result from the response of others.* Labeling theory stresses the relativity of deviance, meaning that behavior understood in one situation may be defined differently in another. Howard S. Becker therefore claims that deviance is nothing more than "behavior that people so label" (1966:9). Consider these situations: A woman takes an article of clothing from a roommate; a married man at a convention in a distant city sleeps with a female prostitute; a member of Congress drives home intoxicated after a party. The reality of these situations depends on the response of others. The first could be defined as borrowing or as theft. The consequences of the second situation depend largely on whether the news of his behavior follows the man back home. In the third situation, the official might be defined as either an active socialite or a dangerous drunk. Reality, then, is socially created according to a variable process of detection, definition, and response.

People also may be labeled for involvement in situations completely beyond their control. For example,

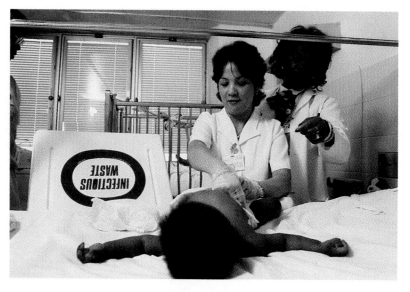

The disproportionate number of male homosexuals—people who have suffered from deviant labeling for their sexual orientation—among persons with acquired immune difficiency syndrome (AIDS) resulted in slow mobilization to fight this serious health problem. Public awareness that thousands of children are among the persons with AIDS has helped to change the way American society views this deadly disease.

victims of violent rape are sometimes subjected to deviant labeling because of the misguided assumption that they must have encouraged the offender. Similarly, people with serious diseases may be labeled as deviant by those who cannot cope with their illness. Persons with Acquired Immune Deficiency Syndrome (AIDS), for instance, are often shunned by employers, friends, and even family members.

Primary and Secondary Deviance

Edwin Lemert (1951, 1972) explains that being labeled as deviant can change a person's subsequent behavior. Lemert calls activity that is initially defined as deviant *primary deviance*. A person who accepts this label may then engage in *secondary deviance*, behavior caused by the person's incorporating the deviant label into self-concept and social identity. Initial labeling, then, can encourage the person to fulfill, for better or worse, the expectations of others. The box shows how the primary deviance of being overweight in childhood led one woman to engage in secondary deviance.

Stigma

The development of secondary deviance marks the start of what Erving Goffman (1963) called a *deviant career*. Typically, this occurs as a consequence of acquiring a **stigma,** *a powerful negative social label that radically changes a person's social identity and self-concept.*

Stigma, then, is a label that operates as a master status (Chapter 6, "Social Interaction in Everyday Life"), overpowering other dimensions of social identity so that a person is "reduced in our minds from a whole and usual person to a tainted, discounted one" (1963:3). As such, stigma often results in social isolation for the person involved. Although the stigma is generated by others, the stigmatized person (along with everyone else) may come to accept it as justified by personal failings.

Children learn to devalue stigmatized categories of people as part of the socialization process. Those stigmatized may include not only lawbreakers but people of certain races and social classes as well as those who are physically disabled or unconventional in a host of other respects.

Subsequently, individuals may learn that a particular stigma applies to them personally. Confronted with bigotry, for example, a black child learns the emotionally wrenching lesson that, in the eyes of some Americans, being different can mean being hated. Sometimes the condemnation of an entire community is conveyed through what Harold Garfinkel (1956) calls a *degradation ceremony*. A criminal prosecution, for example, has many of the same characteristics as a high-school graduation: people stand before others to be formally labeled—negatively in one situation, positively in the other.

The long-term effects of being stigmatized can be considerable. As the box explains, even after Joan had lost weight, she still viewed herself as unattractive. Yet Joan also expresses the determination to resist the judg-

SOCIOLOGY OF EVERYDAY LIFE

Being Overweight—A Study in Deviant Labeling

A female sociologist whom we shall call Joan begins the story of her life by noting that she was born to two overweight parents. Probably through no fault of her own, she became heavy as a child. Yet she was unaware of being overweight—or of what it might mean to others—until she began school.

> In the first grade, it was painfully pointed out to me—for the first time in my life—that I was different from other children. Other children's taunts of "fatty" and "pig" first brought shock, pain, tears, and later, guilt. I remember being afraid of the other children to the point of not wanting to walk home alone, and my mother frequently walked the one block from my home to the school to get me.

> The teasing, however, did not cause me to stop eating, for I still did not realize the connection between eating and being overweight. Instead, I started to develop . . . coping and protective devices which became quite elaborate later.

Ironically, Joan's "coping devices" deepened her deviant identity. She learned, for example, that she could avoid the embarrassment of engaging in sports (no one wanted her as a teammate) by pretending to be sick. Gradually, her "sick role" expanded:

> I also learned that being "sick" I could avoid facing other people. . . . While in the third grade, I was in the school nurse's office almost every day with a wide range of ailments.

Another coping mechanism was lying. When her mother asked how much she weighed, Joan answered according to what she thought her mother would believe rather than revealing her actual weight. She knew her parents disliked lying, but she preferred to think of herself as a liar than as fat. Yet, once again, her self-protection backfired:

> Like all good things, my deception came to an end when it was discovered during a visit to the doctor for a physical. Right up to the point of stepping on the scale . . . I had my mother convinced I weighed almost fifteen pounds less. The anxiety caused by the lying was terrible, but it was nothing compared with the way I felt when they found out. I cried hysterically. . . . The doctor suggested that my parents send me to a psychiatrist if I couldn't diet, which they did not do. This recommendation shocked me, and I entered high school with a much different picture of myself. At last I knew I was deviant; I accepted the fact, and I began to act accordingly.

In high school Joan continued in her deviant role, shunned and dateless. She remained unable to lose weight, having come to accept her current self-image. Her weight was no longer the problem; she saw herself simply as an outcast, someone without much for others to like. Entering college, Joan felt herself worthy of friendship only with those also labeled as deviant—her roommate was a woman who was partly blind and who was known to have had extensive psychiatric treatment; another friend was physically disabled. These were unhappy years.

> I think my college depression can best be summarized by the way I felt when both my roommate and my paraplegic friend had dates on Friday night and I didn't. The only outlet I found that night for the anger I felt was the candy vending machine in the basement of the dormitory. How ironic that I should perpetuate the very thing that was helping to keep me home by eating candy.

There is no happy ending to Joan's story. She has now lost a great deal of weight and gained considerable understanding of her past. Yet she finds that her deviance has become so incorporated into her self-concept that her life simply hasn't changed:

> I now weigh 129 pounds and plan to lose at least another 10 pounds. The loss in weight, however, has not been accompanied by any increase in dates or change of mental attitude, and I fear that it is really my internal makeup that is deviant. I still feel fat, and no matter how many times my friends or parents tell me how nice I look, I don't believe them. . . . I do not know how to get dates, let alone what type of behavior is expected on a date.

> If I sound bitter, it's because I am tired of having to do all the changing. I don't like the fact that I have allowed my life to be regulated by the opinions and expectations of other people. . . . If nothing else, I hope I have shown to what extent being obese, and others' reactions to obesity, as well as the various rationalizations one entertains under these circumstances, can influence and even create a lifestyle.

SOURCE: Adapted from Anonymous, "Losing: An Attempt at Stigma Neutralization," in Jerry Jacobs, ed., *Deviance: Field Studies and Self-Disclosures* (Palo Alto, CA: National Press Books, 1974), pp. 69–72.

ments of others. Many people with physical disabilities, gay people, and members of racial minorities have countered stigma by recognizing and emphasizing their positive personal qualities.

Retrospective Labeling

Once a stigma is acquired, a person may be subject to **retrospective labeling,** *the interpretation of someone's past consistent with present deviance* (Scheff, 1984). For example, after discovering that a woman who has worked with the Girl Scouts for years has sexually molested a child, others rethink her past, perhaps musing, "She always did want to be around young children." Obviously, retrospective labeling involves a highly selective view of a person's past, guided more by the present stigma than by an attempt to be fair. News reports covering the shooting of Beatle John Lennon by Mark David Chapman in 1980 selectively highlighted Chapman's running away from home on several occasions, his inability to hold a job, use of drugs, and compulsion to emulate Lennon. Ignoring many other facts, one reporter concluded, "The signs of [Chapman's] disintegration had been all too clear—and altogether missed" (Matthews, 1980:35).

Labeling and Mental Illness

Labeling theory is particularly useful in studying situations prone to ambiguity. Mental illness is a good example because a person's mental condition may be difficult to define. Psychiatrists have often assumed that mental disorders have a concrete reality similar to diseases of the body. It is true that factors such as heredity, diet, stress, and chemical imbalances in the body are at least partial causes of some mental disturbances. However, much of what we label "mental illness" is based on social definition (Thoits, 1985). This fact suggests that defining and treating the "mentally ill" is sometimes little more than an attempt to enforce conformity to conventional standards.

If a woman believes that Jesus rides the bus to work with her every day, is she seriously deluded or merely expressing her religious faith in a highly graphic way? If a man refuses to bathe or observe common etiquette, much to the dismay of his family, is he insane or simply choosing to ignore cultural norms? Is a homeless woman loudly denouncing the city government while shivering on a street corner mentally ill or expressing justifiable anger?

Because he chooses to express his religious convictions in an unconventional manner, should this man's actions be labeled as mental illness?

Maintaining that the label of insanity is widely applied to what is actually only "difference," psychiatrist Thomas Szasz has suggested that the notion of mental illness be abandoned (1961, 1970; Vatz & Weinberg, 1983). Illness, Szasz argues, can afflict only the body. Mental illness, therefore, is a myth. Being "different" in thought or action may irritate others, but it does not imply that someone is sick. Why, then, is this label so widely applied? Szasz claims that such labeling provides a powerful justification for encouraging—or forcing—someone to change. Thus, for example, political dissidents in the Soviet Union have reportedly been sent to mental hospitals for "rehabilitation"; so have homeless people in New York who refuse an offer of a bed in a city shelter.

Szasz's views are controversial; many of his colleagues reject the idea that all mental illness is a fiction. He has also been widely praised, however, for pointing to the danger of abusing medical practice in the interest of conformity.

Erving Goffman (1961) has also criticized the label of mental illness. He pointed out that commitment to a mental institution may reflect the needs and desires of others as much as those of the patient. Forcible commitment, he claimed, is often triggered by contingencies that have no direct bearing on the patient's mental condition:

> . . . a psychotic man is tolerated by his wife until she finds herself a boyfriend, or by his adult children until they move from a house to an apartment; an alcoholic is sent to a mental hospital because the jail is full, and a drug addict because he declines to avail himself of psychiatric treatment on the outside; a rebellious adolescent daughter can no longer be managed at home because she now threatens to have an open affair with an unsuitable companion. . . . One could say that mental patients distinctively suffer not from mental illness, but from contingencies. (1961:135)

The label of mental illness is a severe stigma that greatly transforms one's life. Most of us have experienced periods of extreme stress or other mental disability. Such episodes, although upsetting, are usually of passing importance. If, however, they form the basis of a social stigma, they may lead to a deviant career as a self-fulfilling prophecy (Scheff, 1984).

The Medicalization of Deviance

Labeling theory, particularly the ideas of Szasz and Goffman, provides the background for understanding an important shift in the way deviance is understood. Over the last fifty years, the growing influence of medicine—particularly psychiatry—within American society has resulted in the **medicalization of deviance,** *the transformation of moral and legal issues into medical matters.* In essence, this is a matter of changing labels. In moral terms, people and their behavior are seen as some combination of "bad" and "good." However, the scientific objectivity of medicine allows no such moral judgment; therefore, the medicalization of deviance involves adopting clinical terms such as "sick" and "well."

Changing views on alcoholism illustrate this process. Until the middle of this century an alcoholic was viewed widely as morally deficient, a "drunk" too weak to act responsibly. Gradually, alcoholism was redefined as a medical problem. Now it is generally viewed as a disease, affecting people who are "sick" rather than "bad." Similarly, obesity, drug addiction, child abuse, and other behaviors that used to be a matter of morality are today widely defined as illnesses for which the people need help rather than punishment.

Some cases are more complex, with moral and medical views alternating over time. For instance, homosexuality was for centuries a moral issue in American society, a straightforward example of being "bad" against a heterosexual standard of "good." By the 1950s, however, homosexuality had become largely a medical matter; in 1952, the American Psychiatric Association (APA) officially declared it a "sociopathic personality disturbance." This declaration by medical professionals was a powerful influence on public opinion; by 1970, about two-thirds of American adults had endorsed the view that homosexuality was a "sickness that could be cured." Since then, however, yet another view has emerged: that while gay people may be *different*, they are not *deviant*. Those endorsing this view point to the lack of success in "curing" homosexuality and to the growing evidence that sexual orientation is a matter of little choice. In 1974, therefore, the APA redefined homosexuality as simply a "form of sexual behavior" (Conrad

How behavior is labeled has important consequences for how people respond. If defined as an "irresponsible drunk," this man is subject to moral condemnation and also arrest. If the same behavior is viewed as resulting from illness, he may receive public sympathy and medical care for alcoholism.

& Schneider, 1980: 193–209). This shift to a more neutral view is reflected in the attempts of many gay and straight people to define unwarranted hostility toward homosexuals as "homophobia." They thereby shifted the negative label from those targeted to those on the side of convention, thus suggesting that deviance may lie in "conventional" people and not those they victimize.

The adoption of a moral or a medical approach to deviance has a number of profound consequences. First is the issue of *who responds* to deviance. For an offense against common morality, members of the community (or officials such as police) typically respond. If medical definitions are applied, however, the situation comes under the control of specialists, including counselors, psychiatrists, and physicians. Second is the issue of *how people respond* to the deviant. A moral approach defines the deviant as an "offender" subject to punishment; medically, however, "patients" are in need of treatment. Therefore, while punishment fits the crime, treatment fits the patient and may involve virtually anything that can prevent future deviance (von Hirsh, 1986). Third, and most important, is *the personal competence of the person labeled as deviant.* Morally, people are responsible for their own behavior: they may do wrong, but they understand what they are doing. Medically, "sick" people are not considered responsible for what they do. Defined as personally incompetent and unaware of what is in their own best interest, they become vulnerable to more intense, often involuntary, treatment. For this reason alone, attempts to define deviance in medical terms should be made with extreme caution.

Differential Association Theory

Edwin Sutherland (1940) suggested that all human behavior, including deviance, is learned through association with others, especially in primary groups. Because of the complexity of socialization, people are exposed to situations encouraging criminality as well as those supporting conformity. A person's likelihood of engaging in criminal activity depends upon the frequency of association with those who encourage norm violation compared with those who encourage conformity. This is Sutherland's theory of *differential association.*

Sutherland's theory is illustrated by a study of drug and alcohol use among young adults in the United States (Akers et al., 1979). Responses to a questionnaire sent to junior and senior high-school students indicated that the extent of alcohol and drug use was related to the degree that the peer group encouraged such activity.

The researchers found that young people learn delinquent patterns as they imitate others, receive praise and other rewards for delinquency, and (as Sutherland emphasized) learn to define deviance rather than conformity in positive terms.

A learning approach to deviance may also explain the persistence of juvenile delinquency in specific neighborhoods (Shaw & McKay, 1972; orig. 1942). Once they are established in delinquent subcultures, skills and attitudes favorable to deviance may be transmitted over time to generations of new members. Adolescents also develop deviant behavior independently, perhaps as a rebellion against parental control. Additionally, many deviant acts, such as cheating on an examination or shoplifting, may be spontaneous rather than evidence of commitment to a deviant career. As others have noted, many young people casually drift into and out of deviant episodes, many of which are not serious. While young people may learn patterns of deviance, therefore, they are not necessarily committed to deviant activity (Matza, 1964; Elliot & Ageton, 1980).

Critical evaluation. Interest in labeling theory derives from the fact that it focuses, not on some action itself, but on the reaction of others in creating deviance. This powerful idea suggests why some people are defined as deviant while others who think or behave in the same way are not. The concepts of stigma, secondary deviance, and deviant career demonstrate how the label of deviance can be incorporated into a lasting self-concept.

Yet labeling theory has several limitations. First, its highly relative view of deviance overlooks how some kinds of behavior, such as murder, are almost universally considered serious crimes (Wellford, 1980). Labeling theory is thus most usefully applied to less serious deviance, such as certain kinds of sexual behavior and mental illness. Second, the consequences of deviant labeling are unclear. On the one hand, labeling may promote subsequent deviance. On the other hand, however, evidence suggests that labeling in the form of arrest often discourages people from engaging in further violations (Smith & Gartin, 1989). In short, questions remain as to when and how deviant labeling initiates a deviant career. Third, the theory assumes that people always resist the label of deviance. While most probably do, some may actively seek to be defined as deviant (Vold & Bernard, 1986). For example, dressing unconventionally can be a deliberate means of establishing a distinctive identity, just as civil disobedience can effectively call attention to social injustice. Fourth, we still have much to learn about how people respond to those who are labeled. One recent study found that the stigma of being a former mental patient did not always result in social rejection: this reaction occurred only when the person was considered likely to behave dangerously (Link et al., 1987).

Sutherland's differential association theory has had considerable influence in sociology, but it provides little insight into why society's norms and laws define certain kinds of activities as deviant in the first place. This important question is addressed by social-conflict analysis, described in the next section.

SOCIOLOGICAL EXPLANATION: SOCIAL-CONFLICT ANALYSIS

The social-conflict paradigm links deviance to social inequality. This approach suggests that *who* and *what* is labeled as deviant is based primarily on relative power.

Why, Alexander Liazos (1972) asks, do we tend to think of deviants as "nuts, sluts, and 'preverts'?" The answer, he suggests, is that such terms bring to mind powerless people. Deviance is thereby linked to bag ladies (not tax evaders) and unemployed men on street corners (not those who profit from wars). Similarly, the peer groups of poor youths are likely to be defined as "street gangs," while those of affluent young people are simply called "cliques."

Social-conflict theory explains this pattern in three

ways. First, the norms—including laws—of any society generally reflect the interests of the rich and powerful. People who threaten the wealthy, either by taking their property or by advocating a more equal society, may be readily defined as "thieves" or "political radicals." As was noted in Chapter 4 ("Society"), Karl Marx argued that all social institutions tend to be supportive of the capitalist economic system and to protect the interests of the rich, capitalist class. Richard Quinney makes the point succinctly: "Capitalist justice is by the capitalist class, for the capitalist class, and against the working class" (1977:3).

Second, even if their behavior is called into question, the powerful have the resources to resist deviant labels. Corporate executives who might order or condone the dumping of hazardous wastes are rarely held personally accountable for these acts. Such acts are widely viewed as dangerous, but not necessarily criminal.

Third, the political character of norms and laws is obscured by the widespread belief that such standards are natural and good. For this reason, while the *unequal application* of the law may be seen as unjust, little thought is usually given to the fact that *laws themselves* may be inherently unfair (Quinney, 1977).

Deviance and Capitalism

Steven Spitzer (1980) claims that deviant labels are applied primarily to people who impede the operation of

Hispanic artist Frank Romero painted *The Closing of Whittier Boulevard* based on a recollection of his youth in East Los Angeles. To many young Hispanics, portrayed here by their distinctive "low-rider" cars, police represent a hostile Anglo culture, likely to use heavy-handed tactics to discourage them from venturing out of their neighborhoods.

Frank Romero. The Closing of Whittier Boulevard 1984. Oil on canvas. 72 x 120". Collection of Peter Schindler.

capitalism. As Spitzer explains, such "problem populations" include various kinds of people (1980:180).

First, capitalism is based on private control of property. People who threaten the property of others—especially the poor who steal from the rich—are therefore prime candidates for labeling as deviant. Conversely, the rich who exploit the poor are unlikely to be defined as deviant. Landlords, for example, may charge poor tenants unreasonably high rents and even legally evict those who cannot pay.

Second, capitalism depends on the productive labor of the majority of people, and therefore those who cannot or will not work risk deviant labeling. Americans commonly think of people who are out of work—even if through no fault of their own—as deviant.

Third, capitalism depends on respect for figures of authority, and so those who resist authority are likely to be labeled as deviant. Examples are children who talk back to parents and teachers or who skip school, adults who do not cooperate with employers or police, and anyone who opposes "the system."

Fourth, capitalism rests on the widespread acceptance of the status quo; those who undermine or challenge the capitalist system are subject to deviant labeling. In this category are antiwar activists, environmentalists, labor organizers, and anyone who endorses another kind of economic system.

In contrast, whatever enhances the operation of capitalism is labeled positively. Athletes, for example, are praised because they express the values of individual achievement and competition vital to capitalism. Additionally, Spitzer notes, the use of drugs for escape (marijuana, psychedelics, heroin, and crack) is likely to be defined as deviant, while drugs that encourage adjustment to the status quo (such as alcohol and caffeine) tend to be positively defined.

The strength of deviant labels depends upon the degree of threat to the capitalist system. Adolescents defying authority figures receive only a mildly deviant label: they are "immature" or "going through a phase." More serious norm violations by young people, such as theft, may be stigmatized as "delinquency." Similarly, college professors who are critical of American society are generally tolerated as long as they restrict their views to the classroom. Should they begin giving speeches at a local factory, reaction would be more negative.

Spitzer identifies two general types of "problem populations." The first is what the system tends to define as *social junk*, that is, people who are a "costly yet relatively harmless burden" to capitalist society (1980:184).

The popular "pro-democracy movement" in the People's Republic of China was brutally crushed on June 11, 1989 as 10,000 troops converged on Tiananmen Square at the center of Beijing. Thousands of Chinese people, who were demanding a greater voice in their government, were killed and wounded. The event demonstrated that "law and order," if not always moral rightness, is typically defined by the party with the greater power.

These people do not support the system by working, and they may depend on others or the government. Such nonproductive, but nonthreatening, members of society include Robert Merton's retreatists (for example, those addicted to alcohol or other drugs) and the elderly, physically disabled, mentally retarded, or mentally ill. Defined as moderately deviant, these people are typically subject to control by social welfare agencies.

The second type of problem population is the *social dynamite*, that is, people perceived as directly threatening to the capitalist system. Included are those who might actively challenge capitalism—for example, the inner-city "underclass," alienated youths, radicals, and revolutionaries. In Merton's terms, these are society's innovators and rebels. To the extent that they become threatening, such people are subject to control by the criminal justice system and, in times of crisis, by military forces such as the national guard.

Following Marx's ideas, Spitzer claims that both "social junk" and "social dynamite" are produced by capitalism. The unemployment and poverty that generate much of these populations is the inevitable outcome of the capitalist system. Having created these categories of people, capitalism must also control them—through the social welfare system and the criminal justice system. Both systems, in the process of doing so, apply deviant labels that place responsibility for social problems on the people themselves. Those who receive welfare because they have no other source of income are defined as unworthy; poor people who vent their rage at being deprived of a secure life are labeled rioters; anyone who actively challenges the government is called a radical or a communist; and those who attempt to gain illegally what they cannot otherwise acquire are called common thieves.

Deviance and the Rich: White-Collar Crime

Until 1989, few people other than Wall Street stockbrokers had ever heard of Michael Milken. Yet Milken had accomplished a stunning feat, becoming the highest-paid American in half a century. With salary and bonuses in 1987 totaling $550 million—*about $1.5 million a day*—Milken ranks behind only Al Capone, whose earnings in 1927 reportedly reached $600 million in current dollars (Swartz, 1989). Now Milken has something else in common with Capone: the government is after his fortune, accusing him of one hundred violations of securities and exchange laws.

During the last few years, federal officials have charged dozens in the financial world with illegal dealings. Such activities exemplify **white-collar crime**, defined by Edwin Sutherland in 1940 as *crimes committed by persons of high social position in the course of their occupations* (Sutherland & Cressey, 1978:44). As the Milken case suggests, white-collar crime rarely involves uniformed police converging on a scene with drawn guns, nor is it likely to involve violence. Thus it does not refer to crimes such as murder, assault, or rape that happen to be carried out by people of high social position. Instead, it refers to crimes committed by power-

ful people making illegal use of their occupational positions to enrich themselves or others, often causing significant public harm in the process (Hagan & Parker, 1985; Vold & Bernard, 1986). In short, white-collar offenses that occur in government offices and corporate board rooms are commonly termed *crime in the suites* rather than *crime in the streets*.

The public harm caused by white-collar crime—including false advertising, marketing of unsafe products, embezzlement, and bribery of public officials—is far greater than most people realize and greater than the public harm caused by more visible "street crime" (Reiman, 1990). The government estimates of the economic costs of business-related crimes range up to several hundred billion dollars a year—an amount many times that caused by common theft (Reid, 1982; Reiman, 1984; U.S. Department of Justice, 1987). Although workplace safety is primarily the responsibility of employers, some 100,000 Americans die each year from occupational hazards—five times more people than all the murders carried out by street criminals (Simon & Eitzen, 1982:27; U.S. Federal Bureau of Investigation, 1987).

Sutherland (1940) claimed this white-collar crime is commonplace: he found that all the largest American businesses at that time had broken the law, causing considerable social harm. Yet only about one case in ten was officially treated as the criminal action of a specific person. Rather, he noted, violations by corporations or government agencies are far more likely to be treated in a civil court than in a criminal court. *Civil law* refers to general regulations involving economic losses between private parties, while *criminal law* refers to specific laws that define every individual's moral responsibility to society. In civil settlements, damage or injury is paid for but no one is defined as a criminal. Further, since corporations have the legal standing of persons, white-collar offenses commonly involve the organization as a whole rather than any individuals. Today, as at the time of Sutherland's research, elite deviance rarely results in criminal labeling of powerful people (Simon & Eitzen, 1986).

Ivan Boesky, another notorious Wall Street figure involved in "insider-trading" criminality, was recently fined some $100 million and sentenced to three years in jail. But this outcome is rare: in 1987 fewer than three in ten people convicted of embezzlement in the U.S. District Court system spent a single day in prison; most were placed on probation (U.S. Bureau of Justice Statistics, 1989).

Sutherland also noted that the public displays less

concern about white-collar crime than about street crime, partly because it has little knowledge of the existence of white-collar crimes. Additionally, corporate crime may be said to victimize everyone and no one: there is no gun in anyone's ribs, and the economic costs are usually spread throughout the population.

As the "backbone of capitalism," corporations have immense power, influencing both the mass media and the political process. High corporate officials are frequently graduates of prestigious universities and professional schools, are members of exclusive social clubs, and are well connected to other powerful people in all walks of life. Many government officials, drawn from the ranks of corporate executives, regulate the very corporate enterprises in which they have spent most of their working lives. It is not surprising, then, that serious episodes of white-collar crime only occasionally come to the attention of the public.

Critical evaluation. Social-conflict theory claims that inequality of wealth and power is evident in both the creation and the application of laws and other norms. It also suggests that the criminal justice system and social welfare agencies have the political purpose of controlling categories of people perceived as threatening to the capitalist system.

Like all approaches to deviance, however, social-conflict theory is subject to criticism. First, this approach tends to assume that laws and other cultural norms are created directly by the rich and powerful. But, as Chapter 9 ("Social Stratification") explains, exactly which people fall within the capitalist elite is unclear. Besides, *many* segments of American society influence the political process. For example, laws protect workers, consumers, and the environment with apparent indifference to the interests of capitalists. A second criticism is that although social-conflict theory points out the social injury caused by the powerful, most Americans are more concerned about street crime. Third, this approach implies that criminality should exist only to the extent a society is unequal. This view is challenged by Durkheim's contention that all societies generate deviance, as well as by the presence of extensive criminality in societies far more economically equal than our own.

Various sociological explanations of crime and other types of deviance have now been presented. Table 8–2 summarizes the contributions of the structural-functional, symbolic-interaction, and social-conflict approaches.

Table 8–2 SOCIOLOGICAL EXPLANATIONS OF DEVIANCE: A SUMMARY

Theoretical Paradigm	Major Contribution
Structural–functional analysis	While what is deviant may vary, deviance itself is found in all societies; deviance and the social response it provokes serve to maintain the moral foundation of society; deviance can also direct social change.
Symbolic-interaction analysis	Nothing is inherently deviant but may become defined as such through the response of others; the reactions of others are highly variable; the label of deviance can lead to the emergence of secondary deviance and deviant careers.
Social-conflict analysis	Laws and other norms reflect the interests of powerful members of society; those who threaten the status quo are likely to be defined as deviant; social injury caused by powerful people is less likely to be defined as criminal than social injury caused by people who have little social power.

Deviance and Gender

As was noted in earlier chapters, sociological analysis has traditionally paid little attention to the importance of gender. Explanations of deviance are no exception: they tend to focus on male behavior.

Robert Merton's "strain theory," for example, defines cultural goals in terms of financial success. Traditionally, however, this materialist preoccupation has been true of men more than of women, who have been socialized to define success in relational terms of marriage and raising a family (Leonard, 1982). Indeed, the "strain" caused by American ideals of equality and the reality of gender-based inequality has only recently been raised.

Labeling theory provides a promising framework in which gender can be shown to influence how deviance is defined. Since the behavior of males and females is regulated by somewhat different standards, the process of labeling is accordingly sex-based. Further, as Edwin Schur (1983) observes, in a society in which males have power over females, men can often escape direct responsibility for their actions. Frequently males engage in sexual harassment, rape, or other assaults against women and receive only mildly deviant labels, or no response at all, or even societal encouragement. In contrast, women who are victimized may have to convince an unsympathetic audience that they are not to blame for what happened. Research confirms that people's response to some types of perceived deviance varies according to the sex of both the audience and the actors (King & Clayson, 1988).

Ironically, because of its concern with social inequality, social-conflict analysis has also neglected the importance of gender in theory building. If oppression fostered by capitalism is a primary cause of crime, why do women (who are objectively worse off than men are) account for so much *less* crime than men do? In the next section we shall examine *both* male and female patterns of crime.

CRIME AND THE CRIMINAL JUSTICE SYSTEM

Like all types of deviance, crime is highly variable. In centuries past, for a commoner simply to look upon the Chinese emperor when he appeared in public was a serious crime. Today a citizen of the People's Republic of China who expressed support for the historic royalty would likely be charged with a crime. The American legal system has also undergone considerable change, having first supported slavery and then condemned racial discrimination.

What all crime has in common is that perceived violations evoke a response by a formal criminal justice system. A system of this kind, empowered by the government, is found in every industrial society in the world. Crime, then, is the violation of criminal law enacted by local, state, or national government.

The "anatomy of a crime" contains two distinct elements. First is the act itself (or, in some cases, the failure to do what the law requires). Second, serious crimes involve criminal intent (in legal terminology, *mens rea*, or "guilty mind"). Under the law, intent is a variable concept, ranging from deliberate activity to negligence in which a person acts (or fails to act) in a manner that may reasonably be expected to produce harm. The degree of intent involved in the killing of one person by another, for example, is reflected in distinctions made among first-degree murder, second-degree murder, and negligent manslaughter (Reid, 1982).

Types of Crime

In the United States, information on criminal offenses is gathered by the Federal Bureau of Investigation and regularly reported in a publication called *Crime in the United States*. Two major types of offenses are used to generate the "crime index."

Crimes against the person (violent crimes) are *crimes against people that involve violence or the threat of violence*. Such "index" crimes include murder and nonnegligent manslaughter (legally defined as "the willful killing of one human being by another"), aggravated assault ("an unlawful attack by one person upon another for the purpose of inflicting severe or aggravated bodily injury"), forcible rape ("the carnal knowledge of a female forcibly and against her will"), and robbery ("taking or attempting to take anything of value from the care, custody, or control of a person or persons by force or threat of force or violence and/or putting the victim in fear").

Crimes against property (property crimes) are *crimes that involve theft of property belonging to others*. This type of "index" crime includes burglary ("the unlawful entry of a structure to commit a [serious crime] or a theft"), larceny-theft ("the unlawful taking, carrying, leading, or riding away of property from the possession of another"), auto theft ("the theft or attempted theft of a motor vehicle"), and arson ("any willful or malicious burning or attempt to burn the personal property of another").

A third category of offenses is **victimless crimes**—*violations of law in which there are no readily apparent victims*. Examples of "crimes without complaint" are the use of illegal drugs, prostitution, and gambling. Opinion as to the rightness or wrongness of such activities varies considerably, and so the laws regulating victimless crimes similarly vary. In the United States, gambling is legal only in Nevada and part of New Jersey; prostitution is legal only in part of Nevada; homosexual (and some heterosexual) behavior is still legally restricted in about half of the states. Furthermore, where such laws do exist, they are enforced unevenly.

Victimless crimes also vary in their costs to society. Although a majority of Americans continue to oppose legalizing marijuana, few are certain that this drug causes serious harm. In contrast, by 1990 the cocaine crisis had become acute in the United States, contributing to a rise in violent crime, family destruction, and personal injury.

Criminal Statistics

Statistics gathered by the Federal Bureau of Investigation show that crime rates increased dramatically during the 1970s, declined during the early 1980s, and rose again after 1984. Figure 8–1 displays this trend and shows the relative frequency of various crimes.

Figure 8–1 Crime Rates in the United States, 1960–1988 (*U.S. Federal Bureau of Investigation, 1989*).

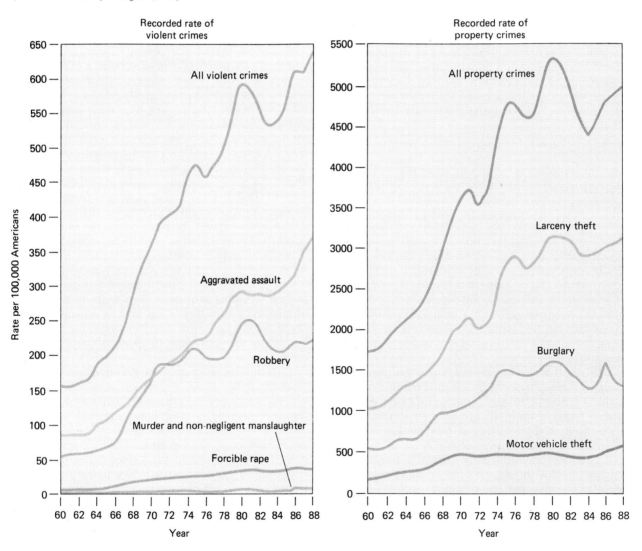

Official crime statistics are far from accurate, however. The biggest problem is that they include only what becomes known to the police. Police become aware of almost all homicides, but assaults—especially among acquaintances—are far less likely to be reported. Police records include even a smaller proportion of property crimes that occur, omitting especially those involving items of little value. Often people may not realize that they have been victimized, or they may assume they have little chance of recovering their property even if they notify the police.

Rape is an unusually difficult crime to quantify. Because of the traditional stigma attached to innocent victims, many women avoided reporting rape to the police. Improving public support for rape victims is recently reflected in a significant rise in the reporting of this crime (U.S. Federal Bureau of Investigation, 1989). Nevertheless, it is likely that only about half of all rapes are reported.

One way to evaluate official crime statistics is through a *victimization survey*, in which a representative sample of Americans is asked about being victimized. Such surveys suggest that actual criminality is almost three times what official reports indicate.

A Profile of the "Street" Criminal

Government statistics afford a general description of persons arrested as "index crime" offenders.

Age

The likelihood of engaging in crime rises sharply during adolescence and declines thereafter (Hirschi & Gottfredson, 1983; Krisberg & Schwartz, 1983). Although people between the ages of fifteen and twenty-four represent only 16 percent of all Americans, they accounted for almost half the arrests for index crimes in 1988: 41.1 percent for violent crimes and 47.6 percent for property crimes.

Sex

Official statistics suggest that crime is an overwhelmingly male activity. Although males and females each constitute roughly half of the population, males were about four times more likely than females to be arrested for index crimes in 1988: 76.0 percent of property crime

arrests were of males; 24.0 percent, females. For violent crimes, the disparity was even greater: 88.6 percent males and only 11.4 percent females. Although some research suggests that the criminal disparity between the sexes is far less in the lower social classes, this general pattern is striking (Hagan, Gillis, & Simpson, 1985).

Certain offenses are defined in such a way as to disproportionately criminalize males or females. Rape is defined so that 99 percent of those arrested are men. In contrast, two-thirds of arrests for prostitution and commercialized vice are of women.

Evidence suggests that the disparity between male and female arrest rates is somewhat greater than the actual difference in their criminality (Cernkovich & Giordano, 1980). This may indicate a reluctance of law enforcement officials to define women as criminal. Whatever the cause, the female arrest rate has been moving closer to that of men, perhaps because of increasing sexual equality in American society. Between 1979 and 1988, the increase in female arrests was greater (37.4 percent) than that for males (18.9 percent) (U.S. Federal Bureau of Investigation, 1989). Similarly, in families in which males and females are more equal, patterns of delinquency among daughters more resemble those of sons (Hagan, Simpson, & Gillis, 1987). Finally, the greatest differences in crime rates of the two sexes appear in societies that most limit the social opportunities of women (Blum & Fisher, 1980).

Social Class

Many Americans associate criminality with poverty. Sociological research suggests, however, that rich and poor alike commit crimes; people with different social standing simply commit different *kinds* of offenses.

There is little doubt that more Americans with low social standing are arrested for the index crimes (Wolfgang, Figlio, & Sellin, 1972; Elliott & Ageton, 1980; Braithwaite, 1981; Thornberry & Farnsworth, 1982; Wolfgang, Thornberry, & Figlio, 1987). Similar patterns appear in other societies as well (Clinard & Abbott, 1973). This difference may reflect the historical tendency for poor people to be arrested and convicted of crimes more often than those whose wealth and power make them "respectable" (Tittle & Villemez, 1977; Tittle, Villemez, & Smith, 1978; Elias, 1986). As this bias in the criminal justice system has steadily lessened, the argument continues, criminality among various segments of the population has become more equal.

Differing crime rates between women and men reflect the relative inequality of the two sexes. Over time, this disparity has grown smaller in American society. In strongly patriarchal societies such as Saudi Arabia, women still have little personal autonomy, and the crime rate among women is correspondingly low.

Overall, the evidence suggests that street crime does tend to involve people of lower social position—as *victims* as well as offenders. Only a small proportion of less advantaged people are ever convicted of crimes, however; most crimes are committed by relatively few hard-core offenders (Wolfgang, Figlio, & Sellin, 1972; Elliott & Ageton, 1980; Wolfgang, Thornberry, & Figlio, 1987). Additionally, as John Braithwaite notes, the connection between social standing and criminality "depends entirely on what form of crime one is talking about" (1981:47). If the definition of crime is expanded beyond street crime to include white-collar crime, the "common criminal" is of much higher social position.

Race

The relationship between race and criminality is also quite complex. Official statistics indicate that 68.6 percent of arrests for index crimes in 1988 involved whites. At the same time, blacks were arrested more often than whites in proportion to their numbers, representing about 12 percent of Americans and 35.7 percent of index crime arrests. Blacks comprised 32.6 percent of arrests for property crimes (versus 65.3 percent for whites) and 46.8 percent of arrests for violent crimes (51.7 percent for whites) (U.S. Federal Bureau of Investigation, 1989).

Just as Americans have long linked criminality to the poor, they have done so to blacks (and particularly to young black males). This is so even though most criminality involves whites. However, the proportion of index arrests of blacks has risen during the 1980s (from 21.4 percent in 1979 to 35.7 percent in 1988).

Yet no simple conclusions about crime and race are warranted, for three reasons. First, arrest records are not statements of proven guilt. Insofar as cultural prejudices lead police to arrest blacks more readily than whites, and lead white citizens more readily to report blacks to the police as potential offenders, blacks are overly criminalized. The same prejudices work in the courtroom. Even small biases by law enforcement officials and the public will, in the long run, substantially distort the official record of black crime (Liska & Tausig, 1979; Unnever, Frazier, & Henretta, 1980; Smith & Visher, 1981).

Second, race in the United States is closely related to social standing, which, as we have already shown, affects the likelihood of engaging in street crimes. Research by Judith and Peter Blau (1982) helps to sort out the links among race, poverty, and criminality. After a study of 125 large American cities, the Blaus concluded that high rates of criminality—especially violent crime—were caused primarily by income disparity. Thus, criminality is caused not so much by deviant subcultures as by poverty in the midst of affluence. In a rich society, those who suffer the hardships of poverty may perceive society and its laws as unjust. This perception, the Blaus maintain, is what provokes criminality. Because many blacks were economically hurt during the 1980s, because *almost half* of black children grow up in poverty (in contrast to about one in six white children), and because unemployment among black adults is two to three times higher than among whites, we should expect proportionately higher crime rates for blacks (Sampson, 1987).

Leona Helmsley, "queen" of a vast hotel empire, was convicted and sentenced to prison for tax fraud in 1989. She once commented that laws were only for poor people, an assertion contradicted by her own fate. Yet research shows that well-to-do people are less likely than average Americans to be convicted of a crime when they engage in wrongdoing.

Other research suggests that rigid systems of social inequality generate crime in much the same way in other societies (Messner, 1989).

Third, as was noted earlier, white-collar crimes are excluded from "index crime" statistics. Clearly, this omission contributes to the view of the typical criminal as not simply poor but black. If crime is also defined to include insider stock trading, dumping industrial wastes, embezzlement, bribery, and cheating on income tax returns, the proportion of white criminals would certainly rise.

Crime in Global Perspective

By global standards, American society has a lot of crime. Marshall Clinard (1978) observes that in Switzerland murders are relatively rare even in the largest cities. In contrast, New York City led all American cities with 1,896 murders in 1988; it is a rare day in New York when no murder occurs. Another forty-nine cities had more than fifty murders each (U.S. Federal Bureau of Investigation, 1989).

Although crime rates rose in Europe more than in the United States during the early 1980s, American society remains far more criminal. A recent comparison showed the American homicide rate to be five times that of Europe; the rape rate, seven times higher; and property crime rates, twice as high. Truly global comparisons are difficult because nations define crimes differently and because data are often not accurately reported. Figure 8–2 on the next page gives comparative data for rape and robbery. Although the patterns differ for each crime, the general conclusion is that the United States contends with more crime than virtually any other country in the world (Kalish, 1988).

Elliott Currie (1985) suggests that America's high crime rate reflects our culture's emphasis on individual economic success, frequently at the expense of family and community cohesion. Currie also notes that, unlike European nations, the United States has neither a government-guaranteed minimum family income level nor publicly funded child-care programs. Such public policy decisions, he claims, weaken the fabric of our society and thus also our defense against crime. Furthermore, Currie asserts that the high level of unemployment and underemployment tolerated by Americans (and increasingly by Europeans) helps create a large category of perpetually poor people whose opportunities to make money are often limited to crime. The key to reducing crime lies *in society*, Currie believes, not in the more politically expedient demands for more police and prisons.

Finally, American individualism has traditionally supported private ownership of guns, which encourages deadly crime. Recent controversy over proliferation of "assault rifles" has renewed attention to this critical issue, as the box on page 225 explains.

Available evidence indicates that crime rates in the nonindustrial societies of the world are also generally lower than in the United States. Some of these societies have high rates of violence (Colombia's recent drug war stands out), but property crimes are generally rare by American standards. This lower crime rate reflects the fact that nonindustrial societies are often quite traditional, with strong families and cohesive residential areas that informally control crime (Clinard & Abbott, 1973).

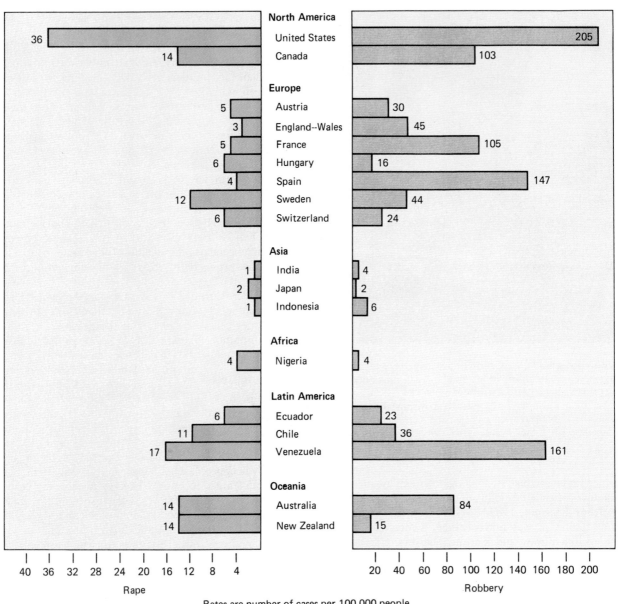

North America
United States
Canada

Europe
Austria
England--Wales
France
Hungary
Spain
Sweden
Switzerland

Asia
India
Japan
Indonesia

Africa
Nigeria

Latin America
Ecuador
Chile
Venezuela

Oceania
Australia
New Zealand

Rape

Robbery

Rates are number of cases per 100,000 people

Figure 8–2 Global Comparisons: Rates for Rape and Robbery

(Interpol data, as reported by Kalish, 1988.)

"The Other Arms Race": Are Americans Really Safer?

On the afternoon of January 31, 1989, thirty-one-year-old Patrick Purdy waited nervously in a Stockton, California, schoolyard. Just after the final bell rang, as children swarmed from the building, Purdy opened fire with a high-powered semiautomatic rifle, killing five and wounding thirty. The shocking attack will never be completely understood, since Purdy ended the slaughter by taking his own life, but this event highlighted the latest chapter in the long controversy surrounding private ownership of firearms in the United States.

Over 20,000 Americans are murdered each year, about 60 percent of them by guns. Currently, almost half of American households report owning at least one gun (N.O.R.C., 1989). In recent years, high-power military-type weaponry such as the imitation AK-47 assault rifle Patrick Purdy used are being added to the American arsenal. Capable of rapidly firing bullets through concrete walls, such devices are readily available in stores in most states. They are especially popular among drug-dealing gangs common to many cities, but increasing numbers are being purchased by "average Americans" convinced that their personal safety depends on owning a potent firearm. In the aftermath of highly publicized cases such as this, more and more Americans support the private owner-

ship of guns. A vicious circle is now operating, with more violence creating more demand for firearms, which in turn generates further violence.

The heightened controversy over privately owned firearms has sparked a number of suggested reforms. One proposal would mandate a waiting period of perhaps two weeks before a firearm can be purchased, during which a buyer's possible criminal background can be checked. Such a regulation also discourages impulsive purchases. Another proposal would consolidate the current patchwork of state and local laws into uniform federal laws; in this way, no one could bypass a law merely by crossing a state border.

To date, most legislation on such proposals has been stalled by powerful opponents of gun control. Several months after the Purdy shooting, California was only narrowly able to enact a ban on the manufacture and

sale of assault rifles. The federal government did not follow suit, instead restricting itself to blocking imports of such weapons.

Controlling guns will never, in itself, resolve the American crime problem; the number of Californians killed each year by knives, for example, exceeds the number of Canadians killed by weapons of *all* kinds (Currie, 1985). Nevertheless, greater regulation of guns can reduce the extent and intensity of American violence. There is a good chance that widespread gun control will begin with paramilitary firearms that have no legitimate sports use and which have become increasingly linked to the drug trade.

The future of gun control may well depend on the position taken by police officers, who face the sobering reality of being "outgunned" by criminals. As Daryl Gates, Los Angeles Chief of Police, recently pointed out, "There is no need for citizens to have highly sophisticated military assault rifles designed for the sole purpose of killing people on the battlefield."

SOURCE: Based on George J. Church, "The Other Arms Race," *Time*, Vol. 133, No. 6 (February 6, 1989):20–24, 25–26; Jacob V. Lamar, "Gunning for Assault Rifles," *Time*, Vol. 133, No. 13 (March 27, 1989):29; William R. Tonso, *Gun and Society: The Social and Existential Roots of the American Attachment to Firearms* (Lanham, MD: University Press of America, 1982).

Elements of the Criminal Justice System

The criminal justice system encompasses the formal reaction to crime. Important elements of this system are the police, the courts, and the punishment of convicted offenders.

The Police

The police are generally the point of contact between the public and the criminal justice system. In principle, the police maintain public order by uniformly enforcing the law. In reality, the roughly 650,000 full-time police in the United States (in 1990) cannot effectively monitor the activities of some 250 million Americans. As a result, the police exercise considerable discretion about which situations warrant their attention and how to handle them.

In a study of police behavior in five cities, Douglas Smith and Christy Visher (1981; Smith, 1987) identified six factors that affect police when confronted with apparent crime. Because they must often act quickly, police rely on external cues to guide their actions. First, they are guided by the legal seriousness of the offense. The more serious they perceive the situation to be, the more likely they are to make an arrest. Second, police assess the desire of the victim. In general, if victims demand that an arrest be made, police are more likely to do so. Third, police are more likely to arrest suspects who appear uncooperative. Fourth, they are more likely to arrest suspects with whom they have had prior contact, presumably because this suggests guilt. Fifth, the presence of bystanders increases the likelihood of arrest. According to Smith and Visher, the presence of observers encourages police to act more assertively, because they want to appear in control of the situation and also because an arrest moves the negotiation from the street to the police department. Sixth, all else being equal, police are more likely to arrest black suspects than white. Smith and Visher concluded that being black tends to suggest to police that the suspect either is more dangerous or is more likely to be guilty. Clearly, this perception contributes to the disproportionately high level of arrests of blacks.

Finally, the concentration of police relative to population is greatest in cities with high concentrations of blacks and with high income disparities between the rich and the poor (Jacobs, 1979). This finding is consistent with Judith and Peter Blau's (1982) conclusion that income disparity promotes criminal violence. Apparently, then, police are concentrated where social forces encourage social disruption.

The Courts

After arrest, a suspect's guilt or innocence is determined by a court. In principle, our court system is based on an adversarial process involving attorneys—who represent the defendant on the one side and the state on the other—in the presence of a judge who assumes responsibility for proper legal procedures being followed. In practice, however, about 90 percent of criminal cases are resolved prior to court appearance through **plea bargaining,** *a legal negotiation in which the prosecution reduces a defendant's charge in exchange for a guilty plea.* For example, a defendant charged with burglary may agree to plead guilty to the lesser charge of possession of burglary tools; another charged with selling cocaine may agree to plead guilty to mere possession.

The major reason for widespread plea bargaining is that it allows courts to avoid the time and expense of trying cases. A trial is usually unnecessary if there is little disagreement as to the facts of the case. By selectively trying only a small proportion of the cases, the courts can also channel their resources into those deemed most important (Reid, 1982).

As a result, defendants (who may be innocent) are pressured to plead guilty. Insisting on one's right to a trial carries the risk of receiving a more severe sentence if found guilty. Plea bargaining therefore undercuts the right of all defendants as it circumvents the adversarial process. According to Abraham Blumberg (1970), defendants who have little understanding of the criminal justice system, as well as those unable to afford a good lawyer, are likely to suffer from this system of "bargain-counter justice."

Punishment

In 1831 a nine-year-old English boy was hanged for the crime of setting fire to a house (Kittrie, 1971:103). American history reveals 281 youths executed for crimes committed as juveniles, most recently a young man in Texas for a murder committed when he was seventeen. Twenty-seven other juveniles are currently on death row, waiting for the Supreme Court to decide whether their age should prevent their execution (Rosenbaum, 1989).

Such cases are controversial because young people are widely regarded as having diminished capacity for crime. In addition, these cases raise the general question

Van Gogh's painting *Prisoner's Round* conveys the stark isolation and numbing depersonalization that characterized dungeon-like prisons of the late nineteenth century. A century later, our prisons remain custodial institutions in which little rehabilitation occurs.

Vincent Van Gogh, 1853–1890. Prisoner's Round. *Dutch. Pushkin State Museum, Moscow.*

of why societies punish in the first place. Four justifications are commonly offered.

Retribution. Oliver Wendell Holmes, a celebrated justice of the Supreme Court, once stated, "The first requirement of a sound body of law is that it should correspond with the actual feelings and demands of the community." Knowing that people respond to crime with a passion for revenge, Holmes concluded that "the law has no choice but to satisfy [that] craving" (cited in Carlson, 1976).

Probably the most important justification for punishing is **retribution,** *subjecting an offender to suffering comparable to that caused by the offense.* As an act of social vengeance, retribution is based on a view of society as a system of moral balance. As criminality upsets this balance, so must punishment restore the moral order, as suggested in the ancient dictum "An eye for an eye."

Retribution is the oldest justification for punishment. During the Middle Ages, crime was widely viewed as sin—an offense against God as well as society—and therefore it warranted harsh punishment. Although retribution is sometimes criticized today because it involves no effort to reform the offender, it remains a strong justification for punishment.

Deterrence. A second justification for punishment is **deterrence,** *the attempt to discourage criminality through punishment.* Deterrence is based on the Enlightenment notion that humans are calculating and rational creatures. From this point of view, people engage in deviance for personal gain, but if they think that the pains of punishment outweigh the pleasures of deviance, such behavior is unlikely.

The idea of deterrence was initially used to reform excessive punishments linked to retribution. Why put someone to death for an act of theft, for example, if the crime can be discouraged by a lesser penalty? As the usefulness of deterrence became widely accepted, execution and physical mutilation of criminals were replaced by milder forms of punishment such as imprisonment.

Punishment may deter in two ways. *Specific deterrence* demonstrates to the offender individually that crime does not pay. *General deterrence* is achieved as punishment of one person becomes an example to others.

Rehabilitation. The third justification for punishment is **rehabilitation,** *reforming the offender to preclude subsequent offenses.* This goal accompanied the development of the social sciences in the nineteenth century as the effects of social forces on individuals became recognized. Crime and other deviance were seen as the consequences of an unfavorable social environment, such as poverty or lack of parental supervision. It was thought that just as offenders learned to be deviant, so could they learn to obey the rules. Many prisons, therefore, were termed *reformatories* or *houses of correction* and afforded the offenders a controlled environment (recall the description of total institutions in Chapter 5, "Socialization").

Rehabilitation resembles deterrence by motivating the offender toward conformity, but it emphasizes constructive improvement while deterrence and retribution simply make the offender suffer. In addition, while retribution demands that the punishment fit the crime, reha-

Table 8–3   FOUR JUSTIFICATIONS
OF PUNISHMENT: A SUMMARY

Retribution	The oldest justification of punishment that remains important today. Punishment is atonement for a moral wrong by an individual; in principle, punishment should be comparable in severity to the deviance itself.
Deterrence	An early modern approach, deviance is viewed as social disruption, which society acts to control. People are viewed as rational and self-interested, so that deterrence requires that the pains of punishment outweigh the pleasures of deviance.
Rehabilitation	A modern approach linked to development of social sciences, deviance is viewed as the product of social problems (such as poverty) or of personal problems (such as mental illness). Social conditions are improved and offenders subjected to intervention appropriate to their condition.
Social Protection	A modern approach easier to effect than rehabilitation. If society is unable or unwilling to improve offenders or reform social conditions, protection from further deviance is afforded by incarceration or execution.

bilitation links punishment to the personal problems of the offender. Identical offenses might then result in similar acts of retribution but different programs of rehabilitation.

Social protection.   A final justification for punishment is **social protection,** or *rendering an offender incapable of further offenses either temporarily during a period of incarceration or permanently by execution.* Like deterrence, social protection is a rational approach to punishment and seeks to protect society from crime.

Table 8–3 summarizes these four justifications of punishment.

Critical evaluation.   Although these four justifications of punishment are widely recognized, demonstrating the actual consequences of punishment is difficult.

The value of retribution is related to Durkheim's ideas about the functions of punishment, presented earlier in this chapter. Recall that Durkheim believed that responding to deviance increases people's awareness of shared morality. When society punishes a person for what it considers a moral offense, moreover, everyone is united by a sense of retribution. For this reason punishment was traditionally carried out in public. Public executions occurred in England until 1868; the last public execution in the United States took place in Kentucky in 1936. Today the mass media ensure that the public is aware of executions carried out within prisons (Kittrie, 1971). Nonetheless, it is difficult to demonstrate scientifically that punishment upholds social morality. Often it advances one conception of social morality at the expense of another, as when people who object to military service are imprisoned.

To some degree, punishment serves as a specific deterrent. Yet American society also has a high rate of **criminal recidivism,** *subsequent offenses by people previously convicted of crimes.* One recent study of people released from prison found that within three years 63 percent had been rearrested and 41 percent had been returned to prison (U.S. Bureau of Justice Statistics, 1989). Such a high rate of recidivism raises questions about the extent to which punishment actually deters crime. Another problem is that only about one-third of all crimes are known to police, and of these, only about one in five results in an arrest. The old adage that "crime doesn't pay" rings rather hollow, since only a small portion of offenses ever result in punishment. General deterrence is even more difficult to investigate scientifically, since we have no way of knowing how people might act if they were unaware of punishments applied to others. This debate is particularly intense in the case of capital punishment, which is now permitted in thirty-seven states. Research suggests that the death penalty has limited value as a general deterrent, not only in the United States but elsewhere (Sellin, 1980; van den Haag & Conrad, 1983; Lester, 1987; Archer & Gartner, 1987; Bailey & Peterson, 1989).

Efforts at rehabilitation have also been controversial. Prisons may accomplish social protection simply by keeping offenders off the streets but they offer very little in the way of socially constructive learning. Penologists now concede that prisons do not rehabilitate inmates (Carlson, 1976). This acknowledgment is hardly surprising, since according to Sutherland's theory of differential association, placing a person among criminals for a long period of time should simply strengthen criminal attitudes and skills. The prison environment is also destructive because of its widespread physical and sexual violence.

People who are imprisoned also acquire the stigma of being ex-convicts, an obstacle to successful integration into the larger society. One study of young offenders in Philadelphia found that boys who were punished severely, and were therefore more likely to acquire a criminal stigma, later committed both more crimes and more serious ones (Wolfgang, Figlio, & Sellin, 1972).

Ultimately, we should never assume that the criminal justice system—the police, courts, and punishment—can effectively stop crime. The reason, echoed throughout this chapter, is that deviance is a product of social forces more than of individuals. Until we focus attention on the causes of crime in American society, little is likely to change.

SUMMARY

1. Deviance refers to violations of all kinds of norms—from mild breaches of etiquette to dangerous acts of violence. Crime is one important type of deviance, involving violations of the criminal law.

2. Deviance is socially generated because (a) it exists in relation to cultural norms, (b) it involves a process of social definition, and (c) both of these are influenced by the distribution of social power.

3. Biological explanations of crime, from Lombroso's research in the nineteenth century to sophisticated research in human genetics, has provided relatively little understanding of crime.

4. Psychological explanations of deviance focus on abnormalities in the individual personality, which arise from either biological causes or the social environment. Psychological theories help to explain some kinds of deviance.

5. Sociology links deviance to the operation of society rather than the deficiencies of individuals. Using the structural–functional paradigm, Durkheim identified several functions of deviance for society as a whole.

6. The symbolic-interaction paradigm is the basis of labeling theory, in which deviance is created through the reaction of others. Labeling theory has focused especially on secondary deviance, including the formation of deviant careers as a result of acquiring the stigma of deviance.

7. Social-conflict theory directs attention to the relationship between deviance and patterns of social inequality. Following the approach of Karl Marx, laws and other norms reflect the interests of the most powerful people in society. Social-conflict theory also directs attention to white-collar crimes that cause extensive social harm, although the offenders are rarely defined as criminals.

8. Official statistics indicate that arrest rates peak in adolescence, then drop steadily with advancing age. Males are arrested about four times as often as females are for serious street crimes. Three-fourths of property crime arrests are of males, as are almost nine of ten arrests for personal crimes.

9. People of lower social position tend to commit more street crime than Americans with greater social privilege. When white-collar crimes are included in the overall category of criminal offenses, however, this disparity is lessened.

10. More whites than blacks are arrested for street crimes, although blacks are arrested proportionately more often. Eliminating racial bias from the criminal justice system would lessen this disparity, as would the inclusion of white-collar crimes.

11. The police exercise considerable discretion in their work, often relying on external cues when deciding whether to make an arrest. Research suggests that factors such as a serious offense, the presence of bystanders, and the accused being male and black make arrest more likely.

12. The ideal adversarial procedure of American courts is typically replaced in practice by the system of plea bargaining. This system may be efficient, but less powerful people tend to suffer in the process.

13. Punishment has been justified in terms of retribution, deterrence, rehabilitation, and social protection. Because its consequences are difficult to evaluate scientifically, punishment—like deviance itself—is a matter of considerable controversy among sociologists and the public as a whole.

KEY CONCEPTS

crime the violation of norms formally enacted into criminal law

crimes against property (property crimes) crimes that involve theft of property belonging to others

crimes against the person (violent crimes) crimes against people that involve violence or the threat of violence

criminal justice system the formal reaction to alleged violations of the law through the use of police, courts, and punishment

criminal recidivism subsequent offenses by people previously convicted of crimes

deterrence the attempt to discourage criminality through punishment

deviance the recognized violation of cultural norms

juvenile delinquency the violation of legal standards that apply to the young

labeling theory the assertion that deviance and conformity result from the response of others

medicalization of deviance the transformation of moral and legal issues into medical matters

plea bargaining a legal negotiation in which the prosecution reduces a defendant's charge in exchange for a guilty plea

rehabilitation reforming the offender to preclude subsequent offenses

retribution subjecting an offender to suffering comparable to that caused by the offense

retrospective labeling the interpretation of someone's past consistent with present deviance

social control attempts by society to regulate the behavior of individuals

social protection rendering an offender incapable of further offenses either temporarily during a period of incarceration or permanently by execution

stigma a powerful negative social label that radically changes a person's social identity and self-concept

victimless crimes violations of law in which there are no readily apparent victims

white-collar crime crimes committed by people of high social position in the course of their occupations

SUGGESTED READINGS

These three books offer a closer look at many of the issues discussed in this chapter.

> Neil Alan Weiner and Marvin A. Wolfgang, eds. *Pathways to Criminal Violence.* Newbury Park, CA: Sage, 1989.

> Neil Alan Weiner and Marvin A. Wolfgang, eds. *Violent Crime, Violent Criminals.* Newbury Park, CA: Sage, 1989.

> Allen E. Liska. *Perspectives in Deviance.* 2nd ed. Englewood Cliffs, NJ: Prentice Hall, 1987.

These two books are valuable as efforts to include women in the study of deviance. The first explains how women have virtually been ignored up to the present; the second focuses on labeling theory and women.

> Eileen B. Leonard. *Women, Crime and Society: A Critique of Theoretical Criminology.* New York: Longman, 1982.

> Edwin M. Schur. *Labeling Women Deviant: Gender, Stigma, and Social Control.* Philadelphia: Temple University Press, 1983.

This paperback examines the history and contemporary controversies surrounding punishment in the United States.

> Charles W. Thomas. *Corrections in America: Problems of the Past and the Present.* Newbury Park, CA: Sage, 1987.

This text explores mental illness, including a discussion of the distribution of mental illness within the American population and the social role of the mental patient.

> Bernard J. Gallagher III. *The Sociology of Mental Illness.* 2nd ed. Englewood Cliffs, NJ: Prentice Hall, 1987.

A critical review of the case linking the XYY chromosome to crime is found in Chapter 6 of this study of the ethical consequences of human biology.

> David Suzuki and Peter Knudtson. *Genetics: The Clash Between the New Genetics and Human Values.* Cambridge, MA: Harvard University Press, 1989.

Poor children, the children of criminal parents, and children subject to political repression are imprisoned around the world, often in brutal environments. This book draws together reports and analyses from various societies concerning this human problem.

> Katarina Tomasevski. *Children in Adult Prisons: An International Perspective.* New York: St. Martin's Press, 1986.

This book offers a sociobiological analysis of patterns of violence.

> Martin Daly and Margo Wilson. *Homicide.* New York: Aldine de Gruyter, 1988.

Presenting evidence that the vast majority of "freaks" were fraudulent, this study asks why Americans created the grotesque in the first place, and why the practice is now rare.

Robert Bogden. *Freak Show: Presenting Human Oddities for Amusement and Profit*. Chicago: University of Chicago Press, 1988.

The extent and character of police misconduct are examined in this comparative study of New York, London, and Amsterdam.

Maurice Punch. *Conduct Unbecoming: The Social Construction of Police Deviance and Control*. New York: Tavistock, 1985.

Organized crime around the world is the focus of this collection of thirteen essays.

Robert J. Kelly, ed. *Organized Crime: A Global Perspective*. Totowa, NJ: Rowman & Littlefield, 1986.

Only recently have Americans begun to recognize the deadly combination formed by two elements central to our culture.

James B. Jacobs. *Drunk Driving: An American Dilemma*. Chicago: University of Chicago Press, 1989.

The author of this book weaves interviews into a broad portrait of dissent in the United States.

John Langston Gwaltney. *The Dissenters: Voices from Contemporary America*. New York: Random House, 1986.

A long-time "fence," one who buys and sells stolen goods, provides a lively look at the world of illegal business.

Darrell J. Steffensmeier. *The Fence: In the Shadow of Two Worlds*. Totowa, NJ: Rowman & Littlefield, 1986.

The deaf have long been defined as deviant by hearing people. Unusual insights into the relation between deafness and deviance can be drawn from this study of deaf people on Martha's Vineyard, Massachusetts. For some two hundred years this island had a high rate of deafness, so that deafness became part of "normal" life.

Nora Ellen Groce. *Everyone Here Spoke Sign Language: Hereditary Deafness on Martha's Vineyard*. Cambridge, MA: Harvard University Press, 1985.

This government publication examines the victims of crime in the United States and in selected societies around the world.

Richard Block, ed. *Victimization and Fear of Crime: World Perspectives*. Washington, DC: U.S. Department of Justice, Bureau of Justice Statistics, 1984.

Prediction is always risky, but here is an interesting vision of twenty-first–century deviance.

Georgette Bennett. *Crimewarps: The Future of Crime in America*. Garden City, NY: Doubleday, 1987.

9

Social Stratification

On April 10, 1912, the ocean liner *Titanic* left the docks of Southampton, England, on its maiden voyage across the North Atlantic to New York. A proud symbol of the new industrial age, the ship towered eleven stories above the water and boasted the most sophisticated technology of its time. Twenty-three hundred passengers were on board, some of them enjoying more luxury than most travelers today could imagine. The lower decks, however, were crowded with poor immigrants, journeying to what they hoped would be a better life in the United States.

On April 14 the crew received reports of icebergs in the area but paid little notice. Then, near midnight, as the ship steamed swiftly and silently westward, a lookout was stunned to see a massive shape rising out of the dark ocean directly ahead. Moments later, the ship collided with a huge iceberg, almost as tall as the *Titanic* itself, which ripped open the seams in the hull along the starboard side. Sea water exploded into the ship's lower levels, and within twenty-five minutes people were cramming into the lifeboats. By 2 A.M. the bow of the *Titanic* was submerged and the stern was rising high above the water. There, silently observed by those in the lifeboats, hundreds of helpless passengers solemnly passed their final moments before the ship disappeared into the frigid water (Lord, 1976).

The tragic loss of more than 1,600 lives shocked the world. Looking back at this terrible event from a sociological perspective, however, we see that some categories of passengers had much better odds of survival than others. Of those holding first-class tickets, more than 60 percent survived, primarily because they were on the upper decks, where warnings were sounded first and lifeboats were accessible. Only 36 percent of the second-class passengers survived, and of the third-class passengers on the lower decks, only 24 percent escaped

drowning. On board the *Titanic*, class turned out to mean more than the degree of luxury of accommodations: it was truly a matter of life or death.

This story dramatically illustrates the consequences of social inequality and the enormous difference it can make in the way people live—sometimes whether they live at all. This chapter introduces a number of concepts and sociological ideas concerning social stratification. Chapter 10 continues the analysis, examining social inequality in American society, and Chapter 11 explores how American society fits into a system of global inequality.

WHAT IS SOCIAL STRATIFICATION?

In every society, some people have more valued resources—money, housing, education, health, and power—than others. Such patterns are commonly called *social inequality*. Some social inequality reflects differences in people themselves—their varying abilities and efforts, for example. However, it also relates to the *society* in which they live. Sociologists use the term **social stratification** to refer to *a system by which categories of people in a society are ranked in a hierarchy*. Four key principles help explain social stratification.

1. **Social stratification is a characteristic of society, not simply a function of individual differences.** Social stratification is a society-wide system that unequally distributes social resources among categories of people. In the most technologically primitive societies—the hunting and gathering societies described in Chapter 4 ("Society")—little was produced so only rudimentary social stratification could exist. In more technologically advanced societies, however, social resources are unequally distributed to various social categories, regardless of people's individual innate abilities.

   Did a higher percentage of the first-class passengers on the *Titanic* survive because they were better swimmers than second- and third-class passengers? Hardly. They fared better because of their privileged position on the ship. Similarly, American children born into wealthy families are more likely than those born into poverty to enjoy health and to live well into old age. Neither rich nor poor children are responsible for creating social

stratification, yet this system shapes the lives of them all.

2. **Social stratification is universal but variable.** No society is completely devoid of social stratification. While social stratification in technologically primitive societies is minimal and limited to age and sex, historically, as societies develop more sophisticated technologies, they also forge more complex and often more rigid systems for distributing goods the society produces. Yet social stratification, though universal, is also highly variable. One important global pattern is that social stratification in agrarian societies is more rigid than that common in industrial societies. Less pronounced differences in systems of social inequality also distinguish today's industrial societies from one another.

3. **Social stratification persists over generations.** Social stratification is closely linked to the family; that is, children assume the social positions of their parents. As described in Chapter 6 ("Social Interaction in Everyday Life"), a person's social position, at least initially, is ascribed; therefore, systems of social stratification tend to retain considerable sta-

The social position of Americans tends to remain fairly stable over generations. This is most true at the extremes, that is, among the very rich and the very poor. The most privileged Americans—those born to great wealth—employ rituals such as debutante balls to encourage their sons and daughters to marry one another, thus extending their privileges into another generation.

bility. To some degree, however, social position can also be achieved, the result of individual effort or, occasionally, sheer chance. The concept of **social mobility** refers to *changes in people's positions within a system of social stratification.*

Social mobility may be *upward* or *downward*. Americans celebrate the achievements of a Bill Cosby, just as many of the British express pride in the accomplishments of Prime Minister Margaret Thatcher. Both rose to prominence from modest beginnings. People may also move downward socially because of business setbacks, unemployment, or illness. Nevertheless, as explained in Chapter 10 ("Social Class in America"), social position usually remains much the same over a lifetime. The pattern of *horizontal* social mobility—as people change their occupation, for example, without changing their overall social standing—appears quite frequently in class systems.

4. **Social stratification is supported by patterns of belief.** No system of social stratification is likely to persist over many generations unless it is widely viewed as fair. And just as systems of social stratification differ, so do their underpinnings of legitimacy. Not everyone, though, embraces a system of inequality to an equal degree. Typically, people with the greatest social privileges express the strongest support for their society's system of social stratification, while those with fewer social resources are more likely to challenge the system.

SYSTEMS OF CASTE AND CLASS

In comparing systems of social stratification, sociologists distinguish two general systems: those that are relatively "closed"—with little social mobility—and those that are relatively "open"—offering considerable social mobility (Tumin, 1985).

The Caste System

A **caste system** is *a system of social stratification based on ascription.* In other words, pure caste systems are closed, with no social mobility at all. Since social position at birth determines their destinies for life, people living in caste systems are very conscious of which social category they belong to.

Two quite different stratification systems have significant elements of caste: the traditional Hindu social system in rural India and racial apartheid in South Africa. In the Indian caste system, people are born into one of several thousand caste groups, which confer social position in the local community. Similarly, race largely determines social placement in South Africa. About one South African in seven is of European ancestry (approximately the same proportion as that of Americans of African descent), yet South Africa's white minority holds the dominant share of wealth and power. Representing three-fourths of South Africans, blacks have far fewer rights and privileges. Another 3 million South Africans, known as "coloreds," are of mixed race, and about 1 million are Asians. The box on page 236 explores South Africa's racially based system of social stratification.

For those living in a caste system, ascription determines the fundamental aspects of their lives. First, birth generally dictates a person's lifetime occupation. In traditional Indian society, for example, the families in each caste group perform one type of work. Although some occupations (such as farming) are open to all, castes are socially identified with the work their members do (priests, barbers, leather workers, and so on). More generally, whites in South Africa hold almost all sought-after occupational positions, while the black majority is consigned to manual labor and other less desirable work.

Second, because the family transmits social standing from one generation to the next, a rigid system of social stratification mandates that marriage unite people of the same social standing. Sociologists call this pattern *endogamous* marriage ("endo" stems from the Greek, meaning "within"). Thus partners marry within social categories rather than between them. In India parents traditionally select their children's marriage partners, often when the children are quite young. Only occasionally does a child of one caste (usually a female) marry a person of a higher position (Srinivas, 1971) in a rare instance of individual social mobility. In South Africa, laws forbidding sexual relationships and marriage between the races were eased in 1985, but interracial marriage occurs infrequently because blacks and whites are required to live in separate areas.

Third, powerful cultural beliefs underlie caste systems: people consider it a moral duty to accept their fate and carry out their life's work, whatever it is. Such beliefs foster the habits of diligence and discipline agrarian societies demand. Cultural norms also specify appropriate social relationships. Traditional Indian Hinduism defines higher caste groups as relatively "pure," while

South Africa: Race as Caste

At the southern tip of the African continent lies South Africa, a territory about the size of Alaska, with a population of some 35 million. Dutch traders settled in South Africa in the mid-seventeenth century; early in the nineteenth century, their descendants were pushed inland by British colonization. Then, at the beginning of the twentieth century, the British gained control of what became the Union of South Africa. In 1961 the Republic of South Africa won political independence.

To ensure their political control, the white European minority developed the policy of apartheid, or separation of the races. An informal practice for many years, apartheid became law in 1948 and was used to deny the black majority South African citizenship, ownership of land, and a formal voice in the government. As a racial caste, blacks hold low-paying jobs; on average, they earn only one-fourth what whites do. In the past twenty years, some 3 million blacks have been forcibly relocated to homelands—dirt-poor districts set aside to confine and control them. In short, in a land with extensive natural resources, including diamonds and precious minerals, the majority of people live in abject poverty. The prosperous white minority has traditionally defended its privileges by viewing blacks as social inferiors. Increasingly, however, whites have relied on a powerful system of military repression to maintain their power. Without formal rights, blacks suspected of opposing white rule have been subject to arbitrary arrest and indefinite detention.

Despite its severity, this repression

Recent reforms in South Africa have yet to fundamentally alter the caste barriers that divide the races in this industrial society. Whites dominate the economy and live in desirable urban areas, while blacks are constrained to live in shantytowns as poor as any in the world.

has not kept blacks—and a growing number of sympathetic whites—from challenging apartheid. Violent confrontations have become more frequent in recent years, especially among younger blacks impatient for political and economic opportunity. By the end of the 1980s, some 200 American corporations had also severed direct economic ties with South Africa. This economic pressure has prompted reforms. In 1984, South Africans of mixed race and Asians were granted a limited voice in government. Additionally, a number of "petty apartheid" regulations, separating blacks and whites in public places, have been rescinded. Blacks have also won the right to form labor unions, resulting in economic gains for some workers. In 1990, the release from prison of Nelson Mandela and

the legalization of the anti-apartheid African National Congress has raised the hope of more basic change. In defending the slow pace of reform, South African officials urge Americans to remember that America, too, has had a racial caste system in the past, and that the races are still far from equal in American society.

Yet pressure for more fundamental change is building both within and outside South Africa. Most whites fear—with good reason—that granting full legal rights to the black majority will undermine their privileged position. The black majority, however, appears unlikely to settle for anything less.

SOURCES: George M. Fredrickson, *White Supremacy: A Comparative Study in American and South African History* (New York: Oxford University Press, 1981); also recent news reports.

lower caste groups are considered symbolically "polluted." The belief that a member of a higher caste is polluted by contact with a member of a lower caste maintains social distance between the two, virtually eliminating intermarriage. In the same way, many white South Africans justify apartheid by claiming they are morally superior to the black majority and, consequently, justified in dominating them.

Since the Industrial Revolution, beliefs that rank entire categories of people in this way have gradually diminished. As later chapters explain, such views represent various "isms"—racism, sexism, ageism—whose underpinnings are increasingly denounced as unjust. Even in India, the caste system has been outlawed, although it still remains deeply embedded in rural social life. And in South Africa, where apartheid is still legally in force, the white majority is clearly on the defensive in the face of strong condemnation by almost every other society in the world.

The Class System

A caste system bolsters stable, agrarian societies; industrial social life, in contrast, depends on more individual initiative, extensive education, and specialized skills. Social inequality in industrialized societies thus takes the form of **class systems,** *systems of social stratification based on individual achievement.*

In class systems, social categories—or classes—are not as rigidly defined as they are in caste systems. This "openness" promotes the development of individual talents, leading to relatively high rates of social mobility that blur class distinctions. The breakdown of clear social categories also stems from several other factors. First, especially at the outset, industrial economies encourage migration from traditional rural villages to cities. And by producing more wealth and providing more opportunity for education, cities themselves promote social mobility (Lipset & Bendix, 1967; Cutright, 1968; Treiman, 1970). Second, industrial societies usually develop democratic political systems in which political rights are extended to more and more people (Glass, 1954; Blau & Duncan, 1967). In other words, while each category in a caste system has a different standing before the law, class systems tend to embrace the principle (though imperfectly applied) of equal standing before the law. Third, industrialization generally attracts immigrants to a society. A century ago, for example, drawn by opportunity, millions of people came to the United States and took low-paying jobs at the bottom of the social hierarchy,

The success of entertainers such as Bruce Springsteen—whose talent transformed a boy from a modest family into a superstar—encourages Americans to believe that personal merit is the key to social position.

pushing others upward to positions of higher income and greater social prestige. In time, many of these immigrants themselves were similarly promoted. Comparative research shows that societies with higher rates of immigration are likely to have greater social mobility (Tyree, Semyonov, & Hodge, 1979).

Class systems, then, rest on the belief that individual talents and abilities, rather than birth, should determine social position. Occupations are not dictated by ascription, as in caste systems. Greater individuality translates into social mobility in marriage, too, since parents have a less influential role in their child's selection of a mate.

Status consistency, *the consistent ranking across various dimensions of social standing,* also distinguishes caste systems from class systems. Because caste systems link social ranking to birth, they have high status consistency; that is, all members of a particular caste group enjoy the same perceived cultural purity, wealth, prestige, and power. Class systems, in contrast, have less status consistency. In America, some people have prestigious occupations (such as priests or professors) that yield little wealth and only moderate social power. Such inconsistencies make the boundaries between classes less clear than those separating castes.

Caste and Class Together: England

As the examples cited earlier suggest, many societies' social stratification combines elements of caste and class systems. This mixture is especially evident in societies in which a long-established agrarian economy has become industrialized. English society illustrates how traditional caste distinctions can linger in an industrial class system.

The Estate System

Unlike the United States, England (which, together with Wales, Scotland, and Northern Ireland, comprises today's United Kingdom of Great Britain and Northern Ireland) existed for many centuries as an agrarian society. In the Middle Ages, social stratification in England took the form of a caste-like system of three *estates.* A hereditary nobility, or *first estate,* which accounted for only 5 percent of the population, controlled the system, maintaining wealth and power through the ownership of land, the basis of agrarian production (Laslett, 1984). Typically, nobles had no occupation at all; indeed, to be "engaged in trade" or any other type of work for income was deemed "beneath" them. Well tended by servants, nobles cultivated refined tastes in art, music, and literature during their extensive leisure time.

The law of *primogeniture* (from Latin meaning "first born") mandated that only the eldest son inherit the property of parents. This system protected large landholdings from division among children, so that many vast estates survived for centuries. However, this forced the younger sons of nobles to find other ways to support themselves. A few entered the clergy—the *second estate*—gaining spiritual power supplemented by the church's

extensive landholdings. Others became military officers or lawyers, or took up other occupations that have come down to us today as "honorable" callings for "gentlemen." In an age when few women could expect to earn a living on their own, a daughter of the nobility typically depended for her security on marrying well.

Below the nobility and the clergy, the vast majority of English men and women formed the *third estate,* or commoners. Owning little or no land, most commoners, also known as serfs, were poor. They toiled for a lifetime on land owned by others, receiving little in return. Indeed, the phrase "one's *lot* in life" literally describes most commoners' lives at that time. Unlike the nobility and the clergy, commoners had little access to schooling, so most remained illiterate.

As the Industrial Revolution gradually transformed England's economy, some commoners, especially those who had managed to resettle in cities, gained wealth and power rivaling—and sometimes surpassing—that of the nobility. This economic transformation, along with the extension of education and legal rights to more people, soon blurred traditional social rankings. In a pointed illustration of how far the pendulum has swung, a descendant of nobility, now making a living as a writer, was asked in a recent interview if Britain's caste-like estates had finally broken down. Playfully she retorted, "Of course they have, or *I* wouldn't be here talking to someone like *you!*" (New Haven Journal-Courier, Nov. 27, 1986).

Great Britain Today

While British social stratification has become more open to individual achievement, today's class system retains traces of a long, feudal past. Members of Great Britain's small upper class now enjoy wealth largely achieved through their own efforts. At the same time, some descendants of traditional nobility still maintain inherited wealth and high status consistency, quite conscious of their privileged standing. They savor the highest prestige, attend expensive, elite universities, and wield considerable power to shape British society.

Note, too, that a monarch stands as Britain's head of state, and Parliament's House of Lords is composed of "peers" of noble birth. Actual control of government, however, resides in the House of Commons, composed of commoners who are more likely to have achieved their position through individual effort than through ascription.

Below the upper class, perhaps one-fourth of the British population falls into the "middle class." Some are moderately wealthy, with high incomes from professions and business. These richer "commoners," along with members of the upper class, make up the roughly 10 percent of Britons with investments in the form of stocks and bonds (Sherrid, 1986). Most members of today's British middle class, however, do not earn enough money to accumulate substantial wealth.

Below the middle class, across a boundary that cannot be precisely defined, lie the half of all Britons known as the "working class." As in the United States, members of the working class earn modest incomes, generally from manual labor, and they have limited opportunities to move upward. Although the British economy expanded during the 1980s, traditional industries such as coal mining and steel production declined, subjecting many working-class families to unemployment. Some slipped into poverty, joining the remaining one-fourth of Britons who are socially and economically deprived. Lower-class people—or, more simply, "the poor"—are heavily concentrated in northern and western regions plagued by economic decay.

Today's Great Britain displays typical class-system traits: unequally distributed wealth, power, and prestige, but opportunities for significant movement up and down in the overall system. In one legacy of the estate system, however, movement between social classes occurs less frequently than in America (Kerckhoff, Campbell, & Winfield-Laird, 1985). Compared with Americans, Britons are relatively more resigned to remaining in the social positions to which they were born (Snowman, 1977). The greater rigidity of British stratification is exemplified in the importance of accent as a mark of social position. Distinctive patterns of speech develop within any society as categories of people are socially segregated from one another over long periods. In Great Britain, families of long-standing affluence and those living in poverty speak with such different linguistic patterns that it hardly sounds as if they are speaking the same language.

Another Example: Japan

Social stratification in Japan also mixes the traditional and the contemporary. As in Great Britain, a modern emphasis on individual achievement has reshaped an ancient hierarchy of rank by birth.

Feudal Japan

During centuries of agrarian feudalism, Japan's was one of the most rigidly stratified societies the world has ever

seen. By the fifth century C.E., an imperial family claiming divine right to rule formally presided over the country. In fact, however, the imperial family maintained often uneasy alliances with a network of regional nobility. Military power propelled early nobles to prominence. At a time of widespread military conflict, these *shoguns*—powerful warlords—often fought among themselves, as did their counterparts in medieval England.

Below the nobility the *samurai*, or warrior caste, formed the second rank of Japanese society. These people developed elaborate martial skills, often in highly ritualized form. They stood above the common people because they defended the nobility. The *samurai*, like all Japanese, dressed and behaved according to their rank, as demanded by traditional codes of honor.

As in medieval England, the majority of Japanese were commoners, whose lifetime of labor produced only subsistence. In feudal Japan, commoners had no formal political voice, just as the European serfs were denied political power. Unlike their European counterparts, however, Japanese commoners were not the lowest in rank. The *burakumin*, or "outcasts," stood socially beneath them, considered unworthy of contact with even "common" Japanese. Much like the lowest caste groups in India, "outcasts" lived apart from the other castes, engaged in only the most unpleasant occupations, and, like everyone else, had no opportunity to change their standing.

Japan Today

Industrialization, the growth of cities, and the opening of Japanese society to outside influences in the mid-nineteenth century rapidly undermined the traditional caste structure. In 1871 the social ranking of "outcast" was legally abolished, although it is informally recognized in Japan even today. After Japan's defeat in World War II, the nobility also ceased to have legal standing, and few Japanese believe that the emperor rules by divine right. Overall, social stratification in Japan bears limited resemblance to the rigid system in force centuries ago.

Many Japanese, however, continue to revere tradition, so social inequality is still based on family background. Reforms granting all Japanese equal standing before the law, then, have not ended the centuries-old practice of ascribing particular character traits to members of various social categories.

Japan stands as a fascinating mix of the old and the new. The most prestigious universities—now gateways to success in the industrial world—admit only stu-

The extent of social inequality in Japan is not as great as in the United States. To many American visitors, in fact, Japan appears to be a true "middle-class society." Yet, differences of wealth are pronounced, and the increasing number of homeless people in Japanese cities reveals that poverty is becoming a national problem.

dents who earn outstanding scores on rigorous entrance examinations, as described in Chapter 16 ("Education"). Still, many of the highest achievers and business leaders in Japan are products of privilege: those of *samurai* or noble background. At the other extreme, "outcasts" continue to live in segregated areas throughout the nation with little opportunity to better themselves (Hiroshi, 1974; Norbeck, 1983). Further, despite legal equality of the sexes, women in Japan continue to be subordinate to men in many important respects. Women are far less likely than men to receive a university education and rarely assume powerful positions in Japan's rapidly expanding corporate world. In these respects, individual achievement in this modern class system is circumscribed by advantages rooted in the past.

Beyond Class? The Soviet Union

We have seen how traditional caste systems have been transformed into class systems by industrialization. Some industrial societies with socialist economies, such as the Union of Soviet Socialist Republics (U.S.S.R.), however, claim to be classless. The Soviet Union was created through a revolution in 1917 that ended the feudal estate system ruled by a hereditary nobility. The Russian Revolution transferred control of most farms, factories, and other productive property from private ownership to control by the state. As noted in Chapter 4 ("Society"), Karl Marx asserted that private ownership of productive property forms the basis of social classes; the Soviet Union has traditionally based its claim as a classless society on the elimination of such private ownership.

Nominally classless or not, the Soviet Union has been undeniably socially stratified (Lane, 1984). Occupations have generally fallen into four major categories, listed in descending order of income, prestige, and power: (1) high government officials; (2) the Soviet intelligentsia, including lower government officials and professional workers—engineers, scientists, college professors, and physicians; (3) manual laborers in state-controlled industries; and (4) the rural peasantry. According to Soviet doctrine, because factories, farms, colleges, and hospitals are owned and operated in the interest of everyone, socialist societies have less social inequality than capitalist societies.

Sweeping transformations of the socialist societies of Eastern Europe and the Soviet Union itself during 1989 and 1990 seriously undermined the claim of classlessness and the underpinnings of the Soviet system itself. It is now widely acknowledged that a powerful ruling class of party officials—served by military leaders and scientists—has for decades dominated socialist societies. In the Soviet Union, where the Communist party had retained a monopoly on power since 1917, roughly 18 million party members (about 6 percent of the population) had enjoyed privileges unavailable to others, such as vacation homes, chauffeured automobiles, and access to many consumer goods (Zaslavsky, 1982; Theen, 1984). The children of this elite have also had special educational advantages and occupational opportunities. The box on page 242 delves into the historic role the Communist Party has played in the Soviet system of social stratification.

Although Soviet society cannot accurately be described as classless, the extremes of wealth and poverty in Great Britain and the United States have not been found in the Soviet Union. Since elite standing in the Soviet Union is based on *power* rather than *wealth*, very few people enjoy a life free from work. Even Mikhail Gorbachev, the Soviet leader who has encouraged drastic restructuring ("perestroika") in the socialist world, earns little more than an average American and far less than American president George Bush. Though not wealthy, Gorbachev is unquestionably one of the most powerful people on earth.

Long before political change swept through Eastern Europe, Yugoslavia attempted to limit the concentration of power and privilege among a socialist government elite. The Yugoslav self-management system diffuses decision-making powers among factories and communities. Like the Soviet Union, however, Yugoslavia has historically conferred considerable power and prestige on members of the Communist party.

And what about social mobility in so-called classless societies? Evidence suggests that during this century there has been more upward social mobility in the Soviet Union than in Great Britain, Japan, or even the United States. This is so partially because Soviet society lacks the concentrated wealth passed from generation to generation in other societies. Even more important, the Soviet Union's rapid industrialization and bureaucratization during this century have pushed a large proportion of the working class and rural peasantry upward to occupations in industry and government. Recently, though, Soviet society has shown signs of decreasing social mobility. The country's earlier rate of upward mobility was

By American standards leaders in the Soviet Union are not wealthy; their elite position is based on the enormous power that falls to those who control the governmental bureaucracy.

The Soviet Union: Privilege in a "Classless" Society

Based on his travels in the Soviet Union before the current wave of change, journalist David K. Shipler argues that the Communist party has historically played a pivotal role in the Soviet system of social stratification. Understanding historical privileges enjoyed by party members helps to explain the "pro-democracy" movement recently evident in Soviet society.

Party membership, available to about 6 percent of the population, has . . . been a conduit for the rise of talent from modest backgrounds into positions of leadership, though usually in combination with higher education. Rarely, nowadays, does one find a Politburo or Central Committee member without a higher degree. . . .

Party membership alone guarantees nothing, but a nonmember is usually blocked from holding certain positions in what is called the *nomenklatura*, referring to jobs under the party's jurisdiction and control. The party makes, or at least approves, assignments in such posts as school principal and factory manager. Full-time, paid party work, as opposed to membership that is incidental to a person's main job in a school or a factory, is usually a key to perquisites such as closed shops where imported food, clothing, and electronic equipment are sold; a top spot on the long list of people waiting to buy cars; access to slightly roomier,

better-built apartments; and the chance to work or travel abroad. Leading party officials, those in the Council of Ministers, and some members of the Academy of Sciences are paid partly in "gold rubles" or "certificate rubles," coupons representing rubles exchanged for hard currency and usable in special stores selling imported goods or Soviet merchandise at reduced prices.

Party membership, acquired only upon the recommendation of Komsomol [Young Communist League] and other party officials and following a trial period, is often denied to those with some blemish on their record. The exclusivity adds luster. But nothing is categorical about the relationship between the party and the career; among successful scientists, for example, are both *partiiny* (members) and *bespartiiny* (nonmembers). Some who anticipate stepping into a garden of privilege find the fruits less succulent than imagined. This is especially so among those who remain simple card carriers, without becoming party professionals.

Sergei Polikanov, a party member, nuclear physicist, Lenin Prize winner, full member of the highly selective and elite Academy of Sciences, and head of a nuclear research laboratory at Dubna, a scientists' village north of Moscow, could not get his daughter, Katya, into an institute of psychology because she simply scored too low on the entrance examination. I'm not

sure how hard he tried to use whatever pull he had—he is a rather modest man, not given to throwing his weight around—but the fact was that Katya . . . had to go to work for a year before trying the exams again. . . .

When I asked Sergei Polikanov what privileges he got from being a party member, he couldn't think of any. In fact, his privileges—his pleasant spacious apartment in the lovely Volga River town; his large automobile; his monthly stipend above his generous salary from the academy; his tickets to the Bolshoi; his freedom to mix with Western scientists who came regularly to his institute; his access to Western scientific publications and to sophisticated equipment for his research; his occasional working trips to Western Europe—all were results of his job, his position, and his scientific skill, not of his party membership. However, without the party card he probably could not have risen to such a job. Being in the party said to his superiors, "I'm safe, you're safe, don't worry about me."

When he gave up this coveted position in an elite by becoming an open dissident, he baffled many Russian friends. One thing the citizens of this classless society understand is class.

SOURCE: David K. Shipler, *Russia: Broken Idols, Solemn Dreams* (New York: Times Books/Random House, 1984), pp. 199–200. Copyright © 1983 by David Shipler. Reprinted by permission of Times Books, a Division of Random House, Inc.

probably more a consequence of industrial development than of Soviet socialism (Dobson, 1977; Lane, 1984; Shipler, 1984).

This exemplifies what sociologists call **structural social mobility**—*social mobility by large numbers of peo-* *ple that is due primarily to changes in society and the economy rather than to the efforts of individuals.* In Soviet society, industrialization created a vast number of new jobs that drew people to cities from rural farming villages. Similarly, the growth of bureaucracy propelled countless

Soviet citizens from the fields into the offices. As Chapter 10 ("Social Class in America") explains, similar patterns have emerged during this century in the United States.

Institutions, Ideology, and Social Stratification

We might wonder how a stratified society can persist without distributing its resources more fairly. The caste systems of Great Britain and Japan lasted for centuries, placing most wealth and power in the hands of several hundred families. Even more striking, for two thousand years the Indian people apparently accepted the idea that their lives should be privileged or poor because of the accident of birth.

The ancient Greek philosopher Plato (427–347 B.C.E.) claimed that agreement as to who should have what was the foundation of justice. This means that most people in a society can be expected to view their system of social stratification as basically "fair" or just. In effect, patterns of social inequality become ingrained in a society, inhibiting any challenges to the system.

By contrast, Karl Marx believed that social institutions that create and justify concentrated wealth and power make for clear injustice. Marriage, for instance, unites well-to-do families, funneling wealth from generation to generation. Society then justifies such inherited wealth through the concept of private ownership of property, an idea backed, as necessary, by the power of the state. With both resources and ideas under the institutional control of a society's elite, Marx concluded, most efforts to establish a more equitable social order have little chance for success.

Ideology—*ideas that reflect and support the interests of some portion of a society*—links culture to social stratification. A statement is considered ideological, in other words, if it has consequences that favor some people over others. Ideology rarely consists of self-serving ideas deliberately generated by a privileged people in a conspiratorial fashion. Typically, it takes the form of established cultural patterns that support and justify specific social arrangements, thereby entitling certain categories of people to privileges denied to others. As a result of ideology, most people learn to accept the social hierarchy; those who do challenge it commonly question their own position in the hierarchy rather than the system itself.

As a society's economy and technology change, so do the ideas used to justify social stratification. Early agrarian societies depended heavily on slaves to carry out manual work. Thus the ideological assertion that humans differed greatly in their intellectual capacities carried great weight. During the "Golden Age" of ancient Greece, for example, Aristotle (384–322 B.C.E.) expressed a common view when he stated that some people deserved nothing more than slavery, under the control of their natural "betters." In the Middle Ages, as agrarian societies matured, people came to believe that their occupation should rightfully be determined by birth and was a matter of moral necessity. Both the European peasant during the Middle Ages and the farmer in a traditional Indian village were thus likely to see their respective caste systems as the products of a "natural" order. With the rise of industrial capitalism, a new elite promoted cultural values celebrating individualism and achievement. In a class system, wealth becomes nearly synonymous with intelligence and hard work, while poverty is viewed as the result of personal inadequacy. The box on page 244 probes the transition from the medieval view of divinely sanctioned stratification to the modern assertion that social inequality reflects personal effort and ability.

The history of human societies reveals that social

Those who gathered at Plato's fabled academy were no cross-section of Greek society. They were wealthy males—the only people thought to be capable of intellectual pursuits. Like many Americans today, they accepted these privileges as a matter of personal merit.

Ideology: Medieval and Modern Patterns

Inequality is not necessarily injustice, at least if inequality is consistent with a culture's definition of fairness. Justifications for social stratification, of course, vary across history and from society to society.

In medieval Europe, tradition and theology separated nobles and serfs in the estate system. The rigidly stratified social order was maintained because people were convinced that it stemmed from a divine plan. Believing they had been placed on earth to carry out God's will, most people accepted a life of harsh labor in support of the agrarian system and its noble elites. The elites took comfort in the same view; their privileges also derived from moral imperative. Ideologically, this world view conferred great advantages on a small minority and deprived everyone else. Still, the estate system endured for centuries, linked to the will of God, as expressed in these lines from an old Anglican hymn:

> The rich man in his castle,
> The poor man at his gate,
> He made them high and lowly
> And ordered their estate.
> All things bright and beautiful . . .

During the Industrial Revolution, newly rich industrialists, armed with a new ideology, gradually displaced the feudal nobility. Capitalism opposed the idea that tradition should dictate social hierarchy; according to the new thinking, elite status should accrue to those demonstrating exceptional individual merit. Wealth and privileges were now showered on the talented and hard working. The poor, who in feudal societies had been the objects of charitable assistance, were scorned as lacking ambition and ability. This transformation is evident in a commentary on his times by the early-nineteenth-century German writer Johann Wolfgang von Goethe:

> Really to own
> What you inherit,
> You first must earn it
> With your merit.

Although the precise justifications differ, throughout history ideology has supported a concentration of wealth, power, and prestige among the few.

---

stratification receives powerful institutional support. However, challenges to the status quo continue to arise. As traditions weaken, institutional arrangements are challenged. People also begin to call into question cultural "truths" when the political consequences of these "truths" are unmasked. For example, American women have long been deprived of opportunity by traditional notions of "a woman's place." Even today, women are subjected to a caste-like system in which they are expected to perform traditional tasks out of altruism and duty, while men are financially rewarded for their efforts. (Consider the differences in power, prestige, and financial rewards, for instance, between a family cook, usually female, and a chef, typically male.) Yet, while sexual equality is still not a reality in American society, there is little doubt that the sexes are steadily becoming more equal. The continuing struggle for racial equality in South Africa also exemplifies widespread rejection of apartheid which has shaped economic, political, and educational life. Apartheid has never been widely accepted by blacks, and it is losing support as a "natural" system among whites who reject ideological racism (Friedrich, 1987).

THEORETICAL ANALYSIS OF SOCIAL STRATIFICATION

Social institutions play a major part in maintaining social stratification. But why do such patterns exist? Sociologists offer two major answers.

Structural-Functional Analysis

The structural-functional approach recognizes that all societies maintain some form of social stratification, and therefore, social stratification must have important functional consequences.

The Davis–Moore Thesis

In 1945 Kingsley Davis and Wilbert Moore proposed a theory of social stratification that remains influential—and controversial—to this day. The *Davis–Moore thesis* asserts that some degree of social stratification actually serves society. To begin with, the analysis claims that societies encompass occupational positions of varying importance. Some jobs are easily performed by virtually anyone, while the most vital positions usually require scarce talents that are developed into valued skills through long and expensive education and training. Such positions also usually subject individuals to substantial pressure and day-to-day responsibility.

Motivation to discover and develop talents derives from the rewards—income, prestige, power, and leisure time—that societies bestow on those who fill these critical positions. To illustrate, if a society values a Supreme Court justice more than a government clerk, it will accord greater benefits to the Supreme Court justice. Similarly, if more skills and training are required to be a physician than to be a hospital orderly, a society will grant greater rewards to the physician. Unequal rewards, then, create a system of social stratification. According to the Davis–Moore thesis, a society can be egalitarian only to the extent that its members are prepared to have *any* person perform *any* job. Equality also demands that someone who carries out a job well is rewarded as much as one who performs badly. This would clearly reduce productive efficiency.

Far from attempting to justify social stratification, Davis and Moore were simply seeking to explain why stratification exists. They did not, therefore, suggest precisely what reward should be attached to any occupational position. Their claim was merely that those positions deemed more valuable by a society must yield sufficient reward to attract talent from less important positions.

Davis and Moore maintain that societies become more productive as they approach **meritocracy,** *a system linking rewards to personal merit.* Every society defines "merit" (from Latin, meaning "worthy of praise") differently. In agrarian societies, where the vast majority of people have low-skill positions in agriculture, the "merit" that is rewarded is more the drive to endure rather than to excel. Caste systems praise those who remain "in their place," conferring honor on those who are true to their duties whatever their rank.

Davis and Moore suggest that industrial societies, with their greater specialization and wider use of talents, can ill afford to take such a casual approach to human abilities. In class systems, then, social stratification rewards "merit"—displays of individual talents and abilities that benefit productive enterprises. No class system, however, distributes rewards solely based on individual talent and achievement, and for good reason. Individualism, after all, tends to undermine the social fabric. Family ties, for example, that confer favor on less capable people

who happen to be one's relatives maintain social stability. In short, needs for social cohesion dictate some caste elements even as societies become more like class systems.

Critical evaluation. Although the Davis–Moore thesis has made a lasting contribution to sociological analysis, Melvin Tumin (1953) argues that it is flawed in several respects. First, Tumin contends, identifying the functional importance of any occupation is difficult, especially because importance is frequently confused with social power. For example, the popular belief that physicians are very valuable to society is shaped by the bargaining power of doctors. By controlling the number of people entering the medical profession (through medical school admission policies), physicians ensure that they remain greatly in demand. How much of this demand reflects their actual importance, then, and how much results from policies of the American Medical Association?

Rewards also may have little to do with functional importance. Thomas "Tip" O'Neill retired in 1988 as Speaker of the House of Representatives. He now appears on television commercials plugging such products as

Gender plays a major role in social stratification in the United States and elsewhere. The merit-based American class system has traditionally provided opportunities to men, while women were limited by a caste-like sense of "their proper place." Only in recent decades have American women begun to assume positions of power and responsibility.

motel chains, credit cards, and beer. For a single day's work he receives $100,000, about as much money as he used to earn in a year. Yet would anyone argue that a day's work as a TV pitchman was as valuable to society as a year's work as a Congressional leader? The box looks critically at this issue.

Second, Tumin suggests that Davis and Moore distort how social stratification promotes the development of some individuals' talents and abilities. While American society partly rewards individual achievement, caste-like elements counterbalance that drive. Even if people gain wealth and power through individual merit, privilege tends to be passed from one generation to the next by categories of people, talented or not. Additionally, since opportunity often depends on the ascribed traits of race and sex, social stratification ensures that a great deal of talent and ability will *never* be tapped. For this reason, bright and ambitious children born into poor families have fewer opportunities to develop their talents than rich children do. Half the American population has historically lacked the chance to develop their abilities fully because our system of social stratification subordinates women to men. Tumin thus argues that social stratification, in American society at least, develops some people's talents to the fullest at the expense of the majority.

Third, the Davis–Moore thesis suggests that social stratification benefits society as a whole, ignoring the fact that social inequality frequently promotes conflict and even outright revolution. This conclusion leads us to the social-conflict paradigm, which offers a strikingly different explanation of the persistence of social stratification.

CRITICAL THINKING

Highly Paid Work: Boon or Boondoggle?

For an hour of work, a Los Angeles priest earns about $4, a bus driver in San Francisco makes about $15, and a Detroit auto worker earns roughly $20. John McEnroe garners about $400 an hour playing tournament tennis; actor Burt Reynolds receives about $5,000 for every hour he spends making movies; singer and actress Dolly Parton is paid about $25,000 for every hour she performs in Las Vegas nightclubs. Bill Cosby commands about $100,000 an hour to take the stage.

According to the Davis–Moore thesis, rewards reflect an occupation's value to society. But, while society pays $100,000 for each, is an hour's performance by Cosby worth as much as a year's work by a U.S. Supreme Court justice? In short, do earnings reflect the social importance of work?

In practice, monetary rewards in an industrial-capitalist society are shaped by market forces. An impartial evaluator of worth, the marketplace determines how much a person can successfully demand. Movie stars, top athletes, skilled professionals, and many business executives receive salaries fifty to one hundred times higher than the earnings of the average American. Is their work worth so much?

Some believe the market is far from impartial. First, critics maintain, the American economy is dominated by a small proportion of people who manipulate the system for their own benefit. American corporate executives, for example, pay themselves salaries and bonuses much higher than those of Japanese executives, even though many of Japan's corporations outperform their American counterparts. Second, undertakings that are extremely well paid do not necessarily address the broad interests of society. Michael Milken, described in Chapter 8 ("Deviance"), earned $550 million in 1987 selling "junk bonds," which benefited a small number of investors other than himself, while weakening the nation's overall economy, according to Wall Street analysts. In contrast, Rachel Stuart spent 1987 counseling about thirty-five pregnant, mostly poor, women in rural Louisiana. Her work helped them to deliver healthy babies. Although the cost of neonatal care for a single premature baby may be $200,000, Stuart is paid $4,000 a year for her work (Werman, 1989).

Even if we accept the basic argument of the Davis–Moore thesis, one troubling issue remains: How can we measure occupational importance? To some people, market forces represent the most accurate and responsive index of worth in a complex world. To others, they amount to a closed game, dominated by those with the money to play.

According to the Davis–Moore thesis, the importance of any social role is measured by the rewards it generates. Entertainers, who were generally viewed as disreputable during the Middle Ages, now enjoy income and prestige that exceeds that of even the leaders of American government. What does this suggest about American society?

Social-Conflict Analysis

Instead of identifying positive functions of social stratification for society as a whole, social-conflict analysis simply views social inequality as the domination of some categories of people by others. Although this analysis draws heavily on the ideas of Karl Marx, additional contributions were made by Max Weber.

Marx's View of Social Class

As explained in Chapter 4 ("Society"), Marx claimed that two major social classes arise from two basic relationships to the means of production: owning productive property and laboring for others. In feudal Europe, the nobility and clergy owned the productive land on which peasants labored. Similarly, in class systems, the capitalists (or the bourgeoisie) control industrial factories, where workers (or the proletariat) supply labor. So great are the disparities in wealth and power between the two classes, Marx maintained, that class conflict is inevitable. In time, he believed, the working majority would organize to overthrow capitalism once and for all.

Marx's analysis drew heavily on his observations of early capitalism in the nineteenth century, when society was clearly divided into capitalists and industrial workers. During this period, wealthy American capitalists like Andrew Carnegie, J. P. Morgan, and John Jacob Astor (one of the few very rich passengers to perish on the *Titanic*) lived in fabulous mansions filled with priceless art and staffed by dozens of servants. Their incomes were staggering, even by today's standards. Carnegie, for example, made more than $20 million in 1900, at a time when the average worker earned perhaps $500 a year in wages (Baltzell, 1964).

Critical evaluation. Marx's analysis of social classes has had an enormous influence on sociological thinking in recent decades. Still, it overlooks the crucial element of the Davis–Moore thesis: that unequal rewards motivate people to perform various social roles. Yet Marx separated reward from performance, advancing the social ideal "to each according to need, from each according to ability" (1972:388). This approach offers some insight into the generally low productivity that has characterized socialist economies around the world, sparking, to some degree, the upheavals in Eastern Europe and the Soviet Union. Still, even these societies have recognized the need for a measure of unequal rewards.

But the developments Marx considered inevitable failed to materialize. Here lies perhaps the most important critique of his ideas. In the next section, we shall consider why the socialist revolution Marx predicted and promoted has not occurred, at least in advanced capitalist societies.

Why No Marxist Revolution?

Obviously, capitalism is still thriving, in spite of Marx's prediction to the contrary. Yet, as we shall see, Western capitalism has evolved in some of the ways Marx anticipated.

Americans have not overthrown capitalism for several reasons (Dahrendorf, 1959). First, the American capitalist class has grown fragmented in the century since Marx's death. In the nineteenth century companies were typically owned by *families*; today they are owned by numerous *stockholders*. A large managerial class, whose members may or may not own a significant share of the companies they manage, has also emerged.

This cartoon, entitled "Capital and Labour," appeared in the English press in 1843, the time at which the ideas of Karl Marx were gaining attention. It links the plight of England's coal miners to the privileges of the owners of coal-fired factories.

Second, Marx's industrial proletariat also has been transformed by the so-called white-collar revolution. As Chapter 19 ("The Economy and Work") explains in detail, a century ago the vast majority of Americans held **blue-collar jobs,** *occupations involving mostly manual labor,* in factories or on farms. Today, most of the labor force holds **white-collar jobs,** *occupations that involve mostly mental activity and nonmanual skills.* White-collar jobs include positions in sales, management, and other service work, frequently in large, bureaucratic organizations. While some contend that these new white-collar workers have much in common with the industrial working class described by Marx, evidence suggests that most do not think of themselves in those terms. For much of this century, then, the white-collar revolution has bolstered structural social mobility, prompting many Americans to perceive their social positions as higher than those held by their parents and grandparents. As a result, to many Americans society seems less sharply divided between the rich and poor than it did to people during Marx's era; in fact, they perceive their society as largely middle class (Edwards, 1979; Gagliani, 1981; Wright & Martin, 1987).

Third, the plight of workers is not as desperate today as it was a century ago. Despite setbacks for many workers during the 1980s, the standard of living has improved since the time of Marx. Moreover, workers have won the right to organize into labor unions that can make demands of management backed by threats of work slowdowns and strikes. Although union membership has declined in recent decades, research suggests that well-established unions have substantially enhanced the economic standing of many workers (Rubin, 1986). Further, labor and management now regularly engage in contract negotiations. If not always peaceful, worker-management relations are now institutionalized.

Fourth, legal protection has been widely extended during the last century. Laws now protect workers' rights, and workers have greater access to the courts to demand enforcement of these laws. Government programs such as unemployment insurance, disability protection, and social security also provide workers with substantially greater financial security than the capitalists of the last century were willing to grant them.

These developments, taken together, suggest that despite persistent and marked stratification, some of capitalism's rough edges have been smoothed out. Consequently, social conflict today is less intense than it was a century ago.

Even so, many sociologists continue to find value in Marx's analysis, often in modified form (Miliband 1969; Edwards, 1979; Giddens, 1982; Domhoff, 1983; Stephens, 1986). First, they argue, Marx made a valid point about ownership of wealth: about half of all privately controlled corporate stock is still owned by just 1 percent of Americans. "Capitalists," then, continue to maintain their dominant social and economic position just as Marx described. Second, social-conflict theorists contend, the white-collar revolution has produced many jobs that offer little more income and security than factory jobs did a century ago. In fact, much white-collar work is as monotonous and routine as factory work, especially the low-level clerical jobs commonly held by women. Third, they suggest, while labor organizations have certainly advanced the interests of workers over the last half century, regular negotiation between workers and management does not signal the end of social conflict. Many of the concessions workers have won came about precisely through the class conflict Marx described. Moreover, workers still struggle to gain concessions from capitalists and, in the 1980s and 1990s, to hold on to the advances they have already made. Even today, for instance, half of working Americans lack a pension program. Fourth, these sociologists maintain, workers may

Table 9–1 TWO EXPLANATIONS OF SOCIAL STRATIFICATION: A SUMMARY

Structural-Functional Paradigm	Social-Conflict Paradigm
1. Social stratification keeps society operating. The linkage of greater rewards to more important social positions benefits society as a whole.	Social stratification is the result of social conflict. Differences in social resources serve the interests of some and harm the interests of others.
2. Social stratification encourages a matching of talents and abilities to appropriate positions.	Social stratification ensures that much talent and ability within the society will not be utilized at all.
3. Social stratification is both useful and inevitable.	Social stratification is useful to only some people; it is not inevitable.
4. The values and beliefs that legitimate social inequality are widely shared throughout society.	Values and beliefs tend to be ideological; they reflect the interests of the more powerful members of society.
5. Because systems of social stratification are useful to society and are supported by cultural values and beliefs, they are usually stable over time.	Because systems of social stratification reflect the interests of only part of the society, they are unlikely to remain stable over time.

SOURCE: Adapted in part from Authur L. Stinchcombe, "Some Empirical Consequences of the Davis–Moore Theory of Stratification," *American Sociological Review*, Vol. 28, No. 5 (October 1963): 808.

have gained some legal protections, but the law has not changed the overall distribution of wealth in America, nor can "average" Americans use the legal system to the same advantage as the rich do.

Therefore, social-conflict theorists conclude, the fact that no socialist revolution has taken place in the United States hardly invalidates Marx's observations about capitalism. American cultural values, emphasizing individualism and competition, may have curbed revolutionary aspirations in this country, but, as we shall see in Chapter 10 ("Social Class in America"), pronounced social inequality persists in American society, as does social conflict—albeit less overtly and violently than in the nineteenth century.

Table 9–1 summarizes the two contrasting approaches to social stratification.

Max Weber: Class, Status, and Power

As noted in Chapter 4 ("Society"), Max Weber, in critically responding to the work of Karl Marx, recognized that social stratification sparks social conflict, but his analysis took a different tack from Marx's in several important respects.

Weber considered Marx's model of two social classes simplistic. Instead, he suggested viewing social stratification in terms of three distinct dimensions. First is economic inequality, which Weber called *class* position. Weber used "class" not to designate crude categories, but as a continuum on which anyone could be ranked from high to low. Second is *status*, a ranking

of social prestige. Third, Weber noted the importance of *power*, which he also placed on a continuum from high to low.

Marx believed that social prestige and power generally derived from economic position; thus he saw no reason to treat them as distinct dimensions of social inequality. Weber disagreed, asserting that status consistency in class systems might be quite low, as we have already explained. For example, officials in growing bureaucracies might wield considerable power yet have little wealth or social prestige. Overall, then, Weber argued that social stratification in class systems could no longer be viewed as a matter of clearly defined categories. Instead, stratification takes the form of rankings on a multidimensional hierarchy. Sociologists today use the term **socioeconomic status** to refer to *a composite social ranking based on various dimensions of social inequality*.

A population that varies widely on each of these three dimensions of social inequality creates a virtually infinite array of social groupings, all of which pursue their own interests. Thus, unlike Marx, who saw a clear conflict between two classes, Weber considered social conflict as a highly variable and complex process.

Weber also suggested that each of his three dimensions of social inequality rises to prominence at different points in the development of human societies. Agrarian societies, he maintained, emphasize social prestige or *status*, typically in the form of honor or symbolic purity. Members of these societies gain such status by conforming to cultural norms corresponding to each rank. Industrialization generates striking economic differences in the population, placing greater importance on the economic dimension of *class*. Mature industrial societies (especially socialist societies) witness a surging growth of the state and accord tremendous *power* to high-ranking government officials. Over time, then, power becomes an increasingly critical dimension of social stratification (Kerbo, 1983).

Finally, recall from Chapter 4 ("Society") that Weber disagreed with Marx about the future of industrial-capitalist societies. Marx, with his focus on economics, believed that social stratification could be largely eliminated by abolishing private ownership of productive property. Weber doubted that overthrowing capitalism would significantly diminish social stratification in modern societies, because of the rising power of formal organizations. In fact, Weber asserted that a socialist revolution might actually promote social inequality as it expanded government and further concentrated power in a political elite. Recent popular uprisings against entrenched bureaucracies lend support to Weber's analysis; they also reveal that these political elites are more vulnerable than Weber imagined.

Critical evaluation. Weber's multidimensional analysis of social stratification as a means of understanding the complexity of today's class systems has won adherents among American sociologists. Other sociologists (particularly those influenced by Marx's ideas) argue that while social class boundaries have become less pronounced, striking patterns of social inequality persist in American society as they do in other industrial societies.

As we shall see in Chapter 10 ("Social Class in America"), the most privileged Americans possess enormous wealth, social prestige, and power. In contrast, millions of Americans live in poverty, barely able to meet their day-to-day needs. The upward social mobility that historically blurred class lines in America diminished after the 1970s; since then the social position of many "average" Americans has actually declined. During periods of greater economic polarization, sociologists tend to favor a model based on "classes" rather than one rooted in "multidimensional hierarchy."

The Lenskis: History and Stratification

Gerhard and Jean Lenski's model of sociocultural evolution, detailed in Chapter 4 ("Society"), describes the historical transformation of social stratification. Their analysis combines insights from both the structural-func-

tional and social-conflict approaches (Lenski, 1966; Lenski & Lenski, 1987).

Simple technology limits the production of hunting and gathering societies to only what is necessary for day-to-day living. Some individuals may be more successful as hunters or gatherers than others, but the group's survival depends on sharing by everyone. With little or no surplus, therefore, no categories of people emerge as better off than others. As a result, social stratification in hunting and gathering societies, based only on age and sex, is less pronounced than among societies with more complex technology.

Technological advances that generate societal surplus also promote social inequality. In horticultural and pastoral societies, a small elite comes to control most of the growing material surplus, and social inequality increases. Agrarian technology based on large-scale farming generates vastly greater surpluses, enabling entire categories of people to lead strikingly different lives from other members of the society. The most favored strata—typically hereditary nobility—frequently wield godlike power over the society as a whole.

In industrial societies, however, social inequality tends to diminish. Because industrial productivity relies on highly specialized skills, requiring an educated and highly trained labor force, individuals who cultivate those skills have a more equal chance to compete for desirable positions. Further, technological advances make production increasingly efficient, transforming much blue-collar labor (offering low prestige and power) into white-collar work (carrying greater prestige). This transformation helps to explain why Marxist revolutions have occurred in agrarian societies—such the Soviet Union (1917), Cuba (1959), and Nicaragua (1979)—and not in industrial societies, as Marx predicted more than a century ago.

Additionally, the domination of women by men, which generally is strongest in agrarian societies, gradually diminishes as societies become more industrialized. This drive for gender equality derives from the need for individual talent in industrial societies and the growing belief in basic human equality that undermine such categorical subordination.

Reducing the intensity of social stratification is actually functional for industrial societies. Thus, in advanced industrial societies like the United States, social inequality is somewhat less pronounced than in societies in the early stages of industrialization (the era that shaped Marx's writings), and much less pronounced than in earlier agrarian societies. This historical pattern, recognized by Nobel-Prize–winning economist Simon Kuz-

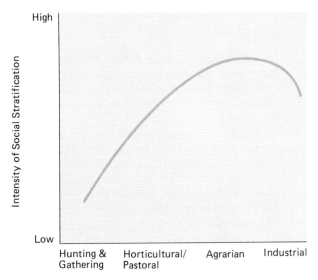

High

Low

Intensity of Social Stratification

Hunting & Gathering   Horticultural/ Pastoral   Agrarian   Industrial

Figure 9–1   Social Stratification and Technological Development: The Kuznets Curve

The Kuznets Curve suggests that greater technological sophistication is generally accompanied by greater intensity of social stratification. The trend reverses itself, however, as industrial societies gradually become more egalitarian. Rigid caste-like distinctions are relaxed in favor of greater opportunity and equality before the law. Political rights are more widely extended, and there is even some leveling of economic differences. The Kuznets Curve may also be applied to the relative social standing of the two sexes.

nets (1955, 1966), is illustrated by the "Kuznets Curve" (Figure 9–1).[1]

The trend suggested by Kuznets may or may not mean that industrial societies will gradually become even less stratified. While people widely endorse the principle of equal opportunity for all, nowhere is this ideal fully realized. The notion of equality, like all concepts related to social stratification, will no doubt remain controversial, as the final part of this chapter explains.

Social Stratification: Facts and Values

The year was 2081 and everybody was finally equal. They weren't only equal before God and the law. They were

equal every which way. Nobody was smarter than anybody else. Nobody was better looking than anybody else. Nobody was stronger or quicker than anybody else. All this equality was due to the 211th, 212th, and 213th Amendments to the Constitution and the unceasing vigilance of agents of the Handicapper General. . . .

With these words, novelist Kurt Vonnegut, Jr. (1961) begins the story of "Harrison Bergeron," an imaginary account of a future America in which social inequality no longer exists. The reader senses that Vonnegut is not celebrating this achievement. Far from it: what he describes is a social nightmare in which every personal advantage has been neutralized by agents of the government. The most physically attractive people are required to wear masks that render them average in appearance, just as the legs of the best dancers are precisely fitted with weights to compensate for whatever natural gift sets them apart from others.

Theoretical explanations of social stratification encompass more than mere facts; like Vonnegut's writing, they also advocate a position. The Davis–Moore thesis argues that social stratification is necessary in a complex society because some occupational roles have greater importance than others. Social inequality, in other words, necessarily reflects both the variation in human abilities and the various tasks of society. From this point of view, we may conclude that a degree of social stratification is critical for a "good society." Also consider how, in a world of human diversity, absolute social equality could be achieved: Vonnegut fears that it might occur through the relentless efforts of officials like the agents of his fictitious "Handicapper General."

The social-conflict analysis advocated by Karl Marx also mixes facts and values. Marx recognized that throughout history the basic institutions of society generated social stratification, which he condemned because the greed of the few was subordinating the need of the many. Guided by egalitarian values, he opposed all social arrangements that prevented everyone from sharing equally in important social resources. Marx maintained that equality enhanced humanity and could be realized if the corrupting effects of capitalism were eradicated.

The study of social stratification, then, involves a complex, ongoing debate from which no single truth is likely to emerge. Even among people who agree on basic facts, differing values may lead to opposing interpretations. This complexity remains as we turn to social stratification in the United States, in Chapter 10.

---

[1] The ideas of Simon Kuznets are explored by Peter Berger (1986:43–46), whose interpretations are reflected in the following discussion.

SUMMARY

1. Social stratification involves ranking categories of people in a hierarchy. Social stratification is: (1) a trait of society that affects the entire population; (2) universal yet variable in form; (3) persistent over many generations; and (4) supported by cultural beliefs.

2. Caste systems, common in agrarian societies, are based on ascription and permit little or no social mobility. Caste shapes a person's entire life, including occupation and marriage, and is supported by strong moral beliefs.

3. Class systems, common in industrial societies, are based on individual achievement and permit considerable social mobility. One result is less status consistency; thus, classes are less well defined than castes.

4. Socialist societies claim to be classless because they are based on public ownership of productive property. Such societies, however, are unquestionably stratified.

5. The persistence of social stratification reflects the operation of various social institutions as well as the power of ideology to define inequality as just.

6. The Davis–Moore thesis states that some degree of social stratification is universal because it helps society function. Within class systems, unequal rewards encourage the most able people to assume the most important occupational positions.

7. Criticism of the Davis–Moore thesis notes that (1) it is difficult to determine objectively the functional importance of any occupational position; (2) stratification prevents many people from developing their abilities; and (3) social stratification often generates social conflict.

8. Karl Marx had enormous influence on the social-conflict analysis of social stratification. Marx recognized two major social classes in industrial societies: the bourgeoisie, which owns the means of production and seeks profits, and the proletariat, which labors in exchange for wages.

9. The socialist revolution that Marx predicted has not occurred in industrial societies such as the United States. While some sociologists suggest that Marx's analysis was flawed, others point out that American society is still marked by pronounced social inequality and substantial class conflict.

10. Max Weber described social stratification in terms of three dimensions of social inequality: economic class, social status or prestige, and power. Taken together, these three dimensions form a complex hierarchy of socioeconomic standing.

11. Gerhard and Jean Lenski observe that, historically, technological advances have been associated with more pronounced social stratification. A limited reversal of this trend occurs in advanced industrial societies, as represented by the "Kuznets Curve."

12. Social stratification, a complex and controversial area of research, combines facts and values.

KEY CONCEPTS

blue-collar jobs occupations that involve mostly manual labor

caste system a system of social stratification based on ascription

class system a system of social stratification based on individual achievement

ideology ideas that reflect and support the interests of some portion of a society

meritocracy a system linking rewards to personal merit

social mobility changes in the position of people within a system of social stratification

social stratification a system by which categories of people in a society are ranked in a hierarchy

socioeconomic status a composite social ranking based on various dimensions of social inequality

status consistency consistent ranking across various dimensions of social standing

structural social mobility social mobility of large numbers of people that is due primarily to changes in society and the economy rather than to the efforts of individuals

white-collar jobs occupations that involve mostly mental activity and nonmanual skills

SUGGESTED READINGS

The following paperbacks examine in detail many issues raised in this chapter:

Melvin M. Tumin. *Social Stratification: The Forms and Functions of Social Inequality*. Englewood Cliffs, NJ: Prentice Hall, 1985.

Anthony Giddens and David Held, eds. *Classes, Power and Conflict: Classical and Contemporary Debates*. Berkeley: University of California Press, 1982.

These books spotlight the racial caste system in South Africa. The first describes various political movements seeking to end apartheid; the second explores ideological support for this system.

Robert Fatton, Jr. *Black Consciousness in South Africa: The Dialectics of Ideological Resistance to White Supremacy*. Albany, NY: SUNY Press, 1986.

Leonard Thompson. *The Political Mythology of Apartheid*. New Haven, CT: Yale University Press, 1985.

These books highlight gender as a dimension of social inequality. The first explains how male domination has shaped human history, and celebrates women of the past. The second examines the work of various social thinkers who focus on social inequality with respect to gender.

Rosalind Miles. *The Woman's History of the World*. Topfield, MA: Salem House, 1989.

Nancy C. M. Hartsock. *Money, Sex, and Power: Toward a Feminist Historical Materialism*. Boston: Northeastern University Press, 1985.

This paperback provides an evenhanded presentation of the ideas of Karl Marx.

Robert Freedman. *The Mind of Karl Marx: Economic, Political, and Social Perspectives*. Chatham, NJ: Chatham House, 1986.

With a focus on Great Britain, this book suggests reasons for the persistence of capitalism, in spite of Marx's predictions.

Bob Carter. *Capitalism, Class Conflict and the New Middle Class*. London: Routledge & Kegan Paul, 1985.

This report on British stratification is rich in descriptive and theoretical insights.

Gordon Marshall, Howard Newby, David Rose, and Carolyn Vogler. *Social Class in Modern Britain*. Philadelphia: Temple University Press, 1988.

This historical analysis of Swedish society explains how the rise of capitalism transformed the entire cultural system.

Jonas Frykman and Orvar Lofgren. *Culture Builders: A Historical Anthology of Middle-Class Life*. New Brunswick, NJ: Rutgers University Press, 1987.

Another analysis of Swedish society examines how values penetrate research dealing with social stratification.

Allan Carlson. *The Swedish Experiment in Family Politics: The Myrdals and the Interwar Population Crisis*. New Brunswick, NJ: Rutgers University Press, 1989.

This book explores the meanings of social equality in three very different societies.

Sidney Verba with Steven Kelman, Gary R. Orren, Ichiro Miyake, Joji Watanuki, Ikuo Kabashima, and G. Donald Ferree, Jr. *Elites and the Idea of Equality: A Comparison of Japan, Sweden, and the United States*. Cambridge, MA: Harvard University Press, 1987.

Changes in social stratification are typically gradual. This book examines an unusual period, the war years of the 1940s, when women assumed many traditionally male responsibilities.

Susan M. Hartmann. *The Home Front and Beyond: American Women in the 1940s*. Boston: Twayne Publishers, 1982.

10

Social Class in America

As John Coleman[1] stepped from Penn Station into the streets of New York City, frigid, mid-January air whipped him in the face. It was enough to make him momentarily question the wisdom of what he was about to do. But determined to begin his adventure, he raised his coat collar and pulled down his cap to keep out the wind.

Coleman had just joined the legions of homeless people found in cities across the United States. Yet there was an important difference between his situation and theirs: he had *chosen* to live on the streets. Why would a man who had a home, who had spent a decade as a college president, who had money in the bank, decide to become "homeless"? Coleman's answer was simple: he wanted to find out for himself what it is like to be "down and out" in the richest city in the world.

The early hours of the morning taught Coleman his first lesson: *becoming poor changes you in the eyes of others*. He immediately noticed a difference in the faces of those passing by. He was used to being acknowledged, to being *somebody*. Now, to a few, he was a puzzle; to most, he was not even there. When he requested attention, people usually wished he would simply go away. Entering a coffee shop, for example, he became flushed with self-consciousness as the man at the counter

scrutinized him. Cautiously, he sat down. The counterman told him he could eat, but only if he paid in advance.

The second day Coleman learned his next lesson: *becoming poor also changes you in your own eyes*. He was already walking more slowly, no longer dashing ahead to beat a traffic light, or rushing to be first through a revolving door. Habit directed his eyes to his wrist, where he normally wore a watch, but his skin was bare. It hardly mattered: Coleman was becoming much more aware of temperature than of time.

For ten days, John Coleman lived on the streets of New York. He slept on sidewalk vents when there

---

[1] This opening is a selective adaptation of Coleman's (1989) description of his urban adventure.

was heat, encountered the indifference of employment agencies, and ducked the hostility of social service workers. By the end of those ten days, he had identified a downward spiral of poverty. Coleman explains how the spiral works by describing one of his final experiences:

> Early this afternoon, I went again to [a] restaurant where I had eaten five times before. I didn't recognize the man at the cash register.
>
> "Get out," he said.
>
> "But I have money."
>
> "You heard me. Get out." His voice was stronger.
>
> "That man knows me," I said, looking toward the owner in the back of the restaurant.
>
> The owner nodded, and the man at the register said, "Okay, but sit in the back."
>
> If this life on the streets had been real, I'd have gone out the door at the first "Get out." And the assessment of me as not worthy would have been self-fulfilling: I'd have lost so much respect for myself that I wouldn't have been worthy of being served the next time. The downward spiral would have begun. (1989:87–88)

John Coleman's experiences tell us about more than homelessness; they help us see that social inequality involves not only money and power but personal worth—or personal deficiency. In short, the story of social class in America extends beyond what we have to *who we are*.

AMERICAN SOCIAL INEQUALITY

Without denying that some people have more money and power than others, Americans have long considered their society to be egalitarian, at least in comparison to most. Unlike most European societies or Japan, the United States has never had a feudal aristocracy. Except for our racial history, American society has known no caste system that rigidly separates categories of people.

Even so, American society is stratified in many crucial respects. The rich enjoy not only more money, but also more schooling, better health, as well as a greater share of almost all goods and services related to well-being. Such privilege stands out even more when compared to the stark poverty that makes simply getting by a daily struggle for millions of poor Americans. This

chapter will explain that the popular portrayal of the United States as a "middle-class society" is more vague ideal than clear reality.

Perhaps we should not be surprised that Americans tend to underestimate the extent of social inequality in the United States. First, as just noted, American society lacks the feudal legacy of nobility and commoners that marks societies elsewhere. Instead, the United States was founded on the more modern principle of equality under the law for everyone—although this goal has been elusive. Second, the American emphasis on individual autonomy and individual achievement frequently obscures the degree to which birth confers on some Americans advantages and opportunities that others could never imagine. Third, recognizing the full range of social inequality in America is difficult because our primary groups—including family, neighbors, and friends—tend to share the same social positions. In the course of daily life, different categories of people interact with one another, but the full extent of social differences rarely shows through in these brief and impersonal contacts. Fourth and finally, as Chapter 11 ("Global Inequality") explains, the standard of living in the United States is extremely high compared to the rest of the world. We tend, therefore, to see every American as at least fairly well off.

When Americans do acknowledge social inequality, they sometimes speak of a "ladder of social class" as if inequality referred to a single factor such as money. Social inequality, however, has various, distinct dimensions. *Socioeconomic status* (SES), examined in Chapter 9 ("Social Stratification"), amounts to a composite measure of social position that encompasses economic resources, power, occupational prestige, and formal education.

Income, Wealth, and Power

Economic resources are distributed unequally in American society. One important dimension of economic inequality involves **income,** *occupational wages or salaries and earnings from investments.*

The government reports that the median American family income in 1988 was $32,190 (U.S. Bureau of the Census, 1988, 1989). Figure 10–1 shows the distribution of income among all American families. Note that the 20 percent of families with the highest earnings take in 44.0 percent of all income, while the bottom 20 percent receive only about 4.6 percent. Additionally, with about 17 percent of all income, the top 5 percent

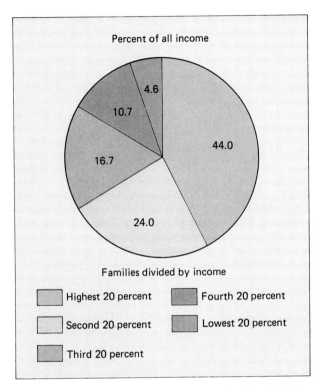

Percent of all income

4.6
10.7
16.7
44.0
24.0

Families divided by income

- Highest 20 percent
- Second 20 percent
- Third 20 percent
- Fourth 20 percent
- Lowest 20 percent

Figure 10–1 Distribution of Income in the United States, 1988

(U.S. Bureau of the Census, 1989)

of American families receive as much income as the lowest 40 percent. This means the bulk of the nation's income is earned by a small number of families, while the rest of the population makes do with much less. Although generally stable since World War II, this income disparity increased during the 1980s as a result of the Reagan administration's budgetary priorities (Levy, 1987; Reich, 1989). Between 1979 and 1988, the income of the top fifth of American families rose 12 percent in constant 1988 dollars (a real gain of $9,109 for the average wealthy family). The income share of the middle fifth remained about the same during this period, while the income share of the lowest fifth actually fell 6 percent (an average family loss of $576). By the end of the 1980s, therefore, the income gap between rich and poor was greater than at any time since the end of World War II (Jaeger & Greenstein, 1989).

Income is but one component of the broader economic factor of **wealth,** *the total amount of money and*

valuable goods that any person or family controls. Wealth—in the form of stocks, bonds, real estate, and other privately owned property—is distributed even less equally than income is. Figure 10–2 shows the approximate distribution of wealth in the United States, which was most recently calculated for 1983. The richest 20 percent of American families own more than three-fourths of the country's entire wealth. In this privileged category, the richest 5 percent of American families—America's "super-rich"—control over half the nation's wealth. Richer still—with wealth into the millions and tens of millions—one-half of one percent of American families possess about one-third of our nation's wealth. And at the very top of the wealth pyramid, the *three* richest Americans have a combined wealth totaling over $12 billion, which equals everything owned by half a million "average" Americans (Joint Economic Committee, 1986; Forbes, 1989).

Figure 10–2 Distribution of Wealth in the United States, 1983

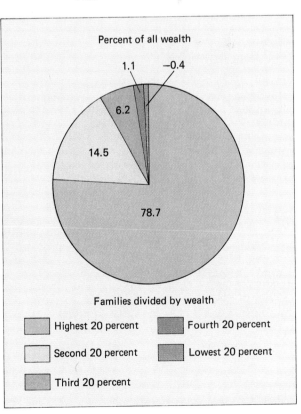

Percent of all wealth

1.1   −0.4
6.2
14.5
78.7

Families divided by wealth

- Highest 20 percent
- Second 20 percent
- Third 20 percent
- Fourth 20 percent
- Lowest 20 percent

The wealth of more typical Americans—in the second and third fifths of Figure 10–2—lies in the range of the median annual income for families, about $35,000. Lesser wealth is also different in *kind*: the richest Americans hold their wealth in the form of stocks and other income-producing investments. Other Americans' wealth resides primarily in nonincome-producing property such as a home. When financial liabilities are balanced against assets for the least wealthy 40 percent of American families, wealth simply does not exist. As the negative figure in Figure 10–2 shows, the bottom 20 percent are actually in debt.

In American society, wealth stands as an important source of power; therefore, the small proportion of families who control most of the wealth also have the ability to set the agenda for all of American society. Thomas Jefferson, the third American president and a large landholder himself, cautioned that democracy depends on

"subdividing property" among the people (1953). As we shall note in Chapter 18 ("Politics and Government"), many sociologists argue that American society has failed in this regard, as high concentrations of wealth undermine political democracy. Instead, they maintain, the political system represents and serves the interests of the small proportion of "super-rich" families.

Occupational Prestige

Occupation not only generates income (and perhaps wealth), but it also serves as an important source of social prestige. Americans commonly evaluate others according to the kind of work they do, envying and respecting some, avoiding and looking down on others.

For more than sixty years, sociologists have measured the relative social prestige of various occupations

Table 10–1   THE RELATIVE SOCIAL PRESTIGE OF ONE HUNDRED OCCUPATIONS IN THE UNITED STATES

White-collar Occupations	Prestige Score	Blue-collar Occupations	White-collar Occupations	Prestige Score	Blue-collar Occupations
Physician	82		Postmaster	58	
College/university professor	78		Union official	58	
Lawyer	76		Accountant	57	
Dentist	74		Economist	57	
Physicist/astronomer	74		Draftsman	56	
Bank officer	72		Painter/sculptor	56	
Architect	71		Actor	55	
Aeronautical/astronautical engineer	71		Librarian	55	
			Statistician	55	
Psychologist	71		Industrial engineer	54	
Airplane pilot	70		Forester and conservationist	54	
Clergy	69		Surveyor	53	
Chemist	69		Dietician	52	
Electrical engineer	69		Funeral director	52	
Geologist	67		Social worker	52	
Sociologist	66		Athlete	51	
Secondary school teacher	63		Computer specialist	51	
Mechanical engineer	62		Editor/reporter	51	
Registered nurse	62			51	Locomotive engineer
Dental hygienist	61		Radio/TV announcer	51	
Pharmacist	61		Bank teller	50	
Radiologic technician	61		Sales manager	50	
Chiropractor	60			49	Electrician
Elementary school teacher	60			48	Aircraft mechanic
Veterinarian	60			48	Machinist
				48	Police officer

SOURCE: Adapted from *General Social Surveys, 1972–1989: Cumulative Codebook* (Chicago: National Opinion Research Center, 1989), pp. 685–698.

(Counts, 1925; Hodge, Treiman, & Rossi, 1966; N.O.R.C., 1989). Table 10–1 presents the results of a recent survey involving a random sample of American adults. Note that the high-income occupations—physician, lawyer, banker, engineer—also confer high prestige. But prestigious work is not merely well paid; it also commands respect because of the ability, education, and training generally required. By contrast, less prestigious work—as a salesperson or janitor, for example—not only pays less, but usually requires less ability and education. This pattern helps explain why occupational prestige rankings follow similar patterns in all industrial societies.[2]

Overall, white-collar occupations that involve mostly mental activity free from extensive supervision

[2] Dr. Li-Chen Ma of Lamar University provided cross-cultural comparisons.

by superiors confer greater prestige than blue-collar occupations that require supervised, manual labor. However, there are exceptions to this pattern: A blue-collar locomotive engineer, for example, enjoys greater social prestige than a white-collar bank teller.

Although women are now represented in every occupation, their numbers are greatest in *pink-collar jobs* (Bernard, 1981). Primarily service occupations—such as secretary, waitress, and beautician—pink-collar jobs tend to fall near the bottom of the prestige hierarchy. Chapter 13 ("Sex and Gender") examines the link between gender and work more closely.

Formal Education

Although schooling is widely regarded as everyone's right, some Americans gain much more formal education than

White-collar Occupations	Prestige Score	Blue-collar Occupations	White-collar Occupations	Prestige Score	Blue-collar Occupations
Bookkeeper	48		Auctioneer	32	
Insurance agent	47			32	Bus driver
Musician/composer	46			32	Truck driver
	46	Secretary	Cashier	31	
	44	Fireman	File clerk	30	
Adult education teacher	43			30	Upholsterer
Air traffic controller	43			29	Drill-press operator
	42	Mail carrier		29	Furniture finisher
	41	Apprentice electrician	Retail salesperson	29	
	41	Farmer		23	Midwife
Buyer/shipper, farm products	41			22	Gas station attendant
	41	Tailor		22	Security guard
Photographer	41			22	Taxi driver
	40	Carpenter		21	Elevator operator
	40	Telephone operator		20	Bartender
	40	Welder		20	Waiter/waitress
Restaurant manager	39			18	Clothing presser
Building superintendent	38			18	Farm laborer
	37	Auto body repairperson		18	Household servant
	36			17	Car washer
	36	Brick/stone mason		17	Freight handler
	35	TV repairperson	Airline stewardess	17	Garbage collector
	34	Baker		16	Janitor
	33	Hairdresser		14	Bellhop
	33	Bulldozer operator		09	Shoe shiner

Table 10–2 EDUCATIONAL INEQUALITY IN THE UNITED STATES, 1988 (PERSONS AGED 25 AND OVER)

Not a High-School Graduate		23.8%
0–7 years	6.8	
8 years	5.2	
9–11 years	11.7	
High-School Graduate		76.2
High school only	38.9	
Some college (1–3 years)	17.0	
College graduate or more	20.3	

SOURCE: U.S. Census Bureau, 1989.

others. Table 10–2 indicates how much formal education Americans aged twenty-five and over had acquired in 1988. According to the table, 23.8 percent of adults had not completed a high-school education. Of the 76.2 percent of American adults who had completed high school, only 20.3 percent were college graduates.

Formal education promotes more than personal development: it also affects a person's occupation and income. Most (but not all) of the white-collar occupations shown in Table 10–1 that yield high income and greater social prestige require a college degree or other advanced education. Similarly, most of the blue-collar occupations that offer less income and lower social prestige are held by people with less schooling.

ASCRIPTION AND SOCIAL STRATIFICATION

The class system of social stratification in the United States rewards individual talent and effort to some degree. But, as we discovered in Chapter 9 ("Social Stratification"), class systems also rely on ascription; that is, who we are at birth influences greatly what we become later in life.

Ancestry

Nothing affects most Americans' social standing as much as the accident of birth. Ancestry—or social background—determines our point of entry into the system of social stratification. Some Americans, including du-Ponts, Rockefellers, Roosevelts, and Kennedys, are known around the world by virtue of their family name.

On a more modest scale, practically every community in North America has several families whose wealth and power have become well established over several generations.

The family into which we are born has a strong bearing on our future education, occupation, and income. Studies of the richest Americans—those with hundreds of millions of dollars in wealth—suggest that about half derived their fortunes primarily from inheritance (Thurow, 1987; Queenan, 1989). By the same token, the "inheritance" of poverty and the lack of opportunity that goes with it just as surely shapes the future for those in need. While some social mobility is certainly within reach of many Americans, it is equally true that patterns of social stratification typically persist over generations.

Race and Ethnicity

Race is strongly related to social position in American society. Whites have a higher overall occupational standing than blacks, and greater educational achievement. As a result, the median income of black families in 1988—$19,330—was only 60 percent of that earned by white families—$33,920 (U.S. Bureau of the Census, 1989). Over time, this income differential widens the gap between the wealth of blacks and whites, with average black wealth (about $4,000 in the mid-1980s) only about 10 percent of that found among whites (O'Hare, 1989). Even among affluent families, race makes a difference. The box takes a closer look.

Ethnic background also relates to social stratification (Hirschman & Wong, 1984). Traditionally, people of English ancestry have been the wealthiest and most powerful of all Americans. A detailed examination of how these factors affect social standing is presented in Chapter 12 ("Race and Ethnicity").

Gender

How society defines males and females influences individuals' social position as well. Obviously, members of both sexes are born into families at every social level. Women born into families of high social standing, therefore, draw on many more social resources than men born into disadvantaged families. Yet, women overall claim less income, wealth, and occupational prestige, and place slightly lower in educational achievement than men do (Bernard, 1981; Lengermann & Wallace, 1985). Furthermore, as we shall see later in this chapter, house-

Two Colors of Affluence: Do Blacks and Whites Differ?

The income of the typical black American family is only about 60 percent of the income of the average white family. For this reason, there is a strong link between black families and poverty. But there is another side to black America—an affluent side—that expanded dramatically during the 1980s.

Black families that are affluent—with an annual income of at least $50,000—are rapidly increasing. In 1987, some 764,000 black families were affluent, a 360 percent increase over the 212,000 families with the same income level two decades before (in constant 1987 dollars). Today, one in ten black families is affluent: over 2 million adults and their children. This is the same as the proportion of Hispanic families that are affluent, but well below the 25 percent of white families who have this much income.

But black and white affluence are not quite the same. First, rich blacks are not *as rich* as rich whites. About

one-third of the affluent whites are families that earn over $75,000 a year, which is true of only one-fourth of affluent black families. Second, blacks more than whites achieve affluence through multiple incomes—from two employed spouses, or employed parents and children. Third, affluent blacks are more likely to work

for their income than whites are. Three-fourths of affluent white families have investment income, compared to only one-half of affluent black families.

Beyond differences in income, affluent blacks still contend with social barriers based on color. Blacks with the money to purchase a home, for example, still often find they are unwelcome in many desirable neighborhoods. For this reason, affluent black families are more likely to live in central-city areas (56 percent) than in the suburbs (40 percent). Affluent whites are much more likely to live in suburbs (61 percent).

Affluent Americans come in all colors. Yet, the social significance of race affects the lives of affluent people, as it does the lives of all Americans.

SOURCE: Based on William O'Hare, "In the Black," *American Demographics*, Vol. 11, no. 11 (November 1989):25–29.

holds headed by women are ten times more likely to be poor than those headed by men. Chapter 13 ("Sex and Gender") fully examines the link between gender and social stratification.

Religion

Religion, too, has a bearing on the social standing of Americans. Among Protestant denominations, Episcopalians and Presbyterians claim higher overall social standing than Lutherans and Baptists. In recent decades, Jews, on average, have gained higher social standing, while Roman Catholics have experienced a relatively lower overall social position (Roof, 1979; Gallup, 1981). Even John Fitzgerald Kennedy—a member of one of America's

wealthiest and most powerful families—became this nation's first Catholic president in 1960 only by overcoming opposition directed against him because he belonged to a religious minority. Perhaps it is not surprising, then, that many upwardly mobile Americans convert to a higher-ranking religion (Baltzell, 1979). Chapter 17 ("Religion") presents a closer look at the importance of religion in the American system of social stratification.

SOCIAL CLASSES IN THE UNITED STATES

As Chapter 9 ("Social Stratification") explained, social rankings in a rigid caste system are usually obvious to all. Defining the social categories in a more fluid class system, however, poses a number of challenges.

Consider the joke about the fellow who orders a pizza, asking that it be cut into six slices because he isn't hungry enough to eat eight. Because the American class system lacks clear boundaries, dividing the system into distinct classes becomes problematic. Using Karl Marx's analysis, we might identify only two major social classes; however, other sociologists have suggested that there are as many as six (Warner & Lunt, 1941) or seven (Coleman & Rainwater, 1978). Another approach stems from Max Weber's identification of various dimensions of social inequality. We might reject the idea of clear classes in American society in favor of a complex status hierarchy.

The difficulty in defining classes arises from the relatively low level of status consistency in the United States. Especially toward the middle of the class system, a person's social position on one dimension of social inequality may contradict that same individual's position on another (Gilbert & Kahl, 1987). A government official, for example, may wield great power yet earn a relatively modest income and have accumulated no wealth. Similarly, a member of the clergy may enjoy substantial prestige while possessing only moderate power and little wealth. Finally, a lucky professional gambler may accumulate considerable wealth yet have little power, prestige, or education. Additionally, because of the social mobility typical of class systems—again, most pronounced near the middle—social position may change within anyone's lifetime, further complicating the task of defining social classes. Nonetheless, patterns of social stratification in the United States do emerge, with four general social classes comprising American society: the upper class, the middle class, the working class, and the lower class.

The Upper Class

No more than 3 or 4 percent of all Americans fall into the upper class. The yearly income of upper-class families is at least $100,000 and can exceed ten times that much. Such high income is often derived from inherited stocks and bonds, real estate, and other investments. In 1989, *Forbes* magazine profiled the richest four hundred people in America, estimating their combined wealth at $268 billion. The personal worth of individuals in this economic elite (including sixty-six billionaires) was a *minimum* of $275 million. The upper class thus encompasses

Members of the upper class are set apart in death as they are in life. In many cities exclusive sections of cemeteries contain the rich and famous of an earlier time. Philadelphia's Laurel Hill Cemetery, shown here, has been designated a national landmark.

what Karl Marx called "capitalists" who own most of the nation's productive property. Besides controlling a vast amount of wealth, many members of the upper class hold occupational positions—as top executives in large corporations and as high government officials—that further enhance their power to shape events in the nation and, increasingly, the entire world. The upper class also gains the most education, usually in the most expensive and highly regarded schools and colleges. Historically, the upper class has largely been composed of white Anglo-Saxon Protestants (WASPs), although this is less true today (Baltzell, 1964, 1976, 1988).

Among even the most privileged Americans, a useful social distinction can be made between the "upper-upper class" and the "lower-upper class." The *upper-upper class*, often described as "society" or "bluebloods," includes no more than 1 percent of the American population (Warner & Lunt, 1941; Coleman & Neugarten, 1971; Rossides, 1990). Membership is almost always the result of ascription by birth, as suggested by the old quip that the easiest way to become an "upper-upper" is to be born one. These families possess enormous wealth, primarily inherited rather than earned. For this reason, members of the upper-upper class are said to have *old money*, since their wealth has grown old (and even more extensive) over many generations. Noting the favor accorded to this segment of American society, C. Wright Mills commented that "prestige is the shadow of money and power" (1956:83).

Set apart from the rest of society by their wealth, members of the upper-upper class live in a world of selective social affiliations. They seek out exclusive neighborhoods, such as Beacon Hill in Boston, the Rittenhouse Square area or the Main Line in Philadelphia, the Gold Coast of Chicago, and Nob Hill in San Francisco. Schools and colleges extend this privileged environment. Children of the upper-upper class typically attend private secondary schools with others of similar background, completing their formal education at high-prestige colleges and universities. In the historical pattern of European aristocrats, such children study liberal arts rather than vocationally directed subjects. Women of the upper-upper class often engage in volunteer work for charitable organizations. For example, women from the Philadelphia Main Line were responsible for establishing the highly respected Philadelphia Museum of Art. While helping the larger community, these activities also help forge networks that enhance this elite's social power (Ostrander, 1980, 1984).

The remaining 2 or 3 percent of the upper class falls into the lower-upper class. From the point of view of most Americans, such people are every bit as privileged as the upper-upper class. But the two actually differ in several key respects.

First, for the lower-upper class earnings rather than inheritance provide the primary source of wealth. Few members of the lower-upper class inherit a vast fortune from their parents, although the majority inherit some wealth. They have certainly inherited the social advantages that helped them to become high achievers in business or the professions.

Second, wealth that is earned typically brings less social prestige, especially from "society"—the bluebloods mentioned earlier. While *new rich* Americans generally live in very expensive houses or condominiums, they may still be excluded from the highest-prestige clubs and associations of "old-money" families.

For many, the American dream of success means joining the lower-upper class through individual achievement. The aspiring young actress leaves her small town and achieves Hollywood stardom; the athlete gains a million-dollar, big-league contract after years of workouts; the clever engineer whose design for a new computer grows into a billion-dollar corporation—these lucky and talented achievers become part of the American lower-upper class. Their success stories fascinate most Americans, who have little interest in the upper-upper class. Instead, they prefer to aspire to the "lifestyles of the rich and famous," as portrayed on television shows like *Dallas*. These shows portray people who seem like the rest of us—except that they have made a lot of money.

In sum, there are two general types of "rich people" in American society. The box on page 264 further explores the differences between the two.

The Middle Class

The middle class includes 40 to 45 percent of all Americans. Because it is so large and embodies the aspirations of many more people, the middle class exerts tremendous influence on patterns of American culture. Television and other mass media usually show middle-class Americans, and most commercial advertising is directed at this category. Because of its size, the middle class encompasses far more ethnic and racial diversity than the upper class. While many upper-class people (especially "upper-uppers") are likely to know each other personally, such exclusiveness and familiarity do not characterize the middle class.

Those in the top third of this category are often distinguished as the *upper*-middle class because their income is above average: generally from $40,000 to $100,000 a year. Family income may be even greater if both husband and wife work. This allows upper-middle-class families to gradually accumulate considerable property—an elegant house in a fairly expensive area, automobiles, and some investments. Virtually all upper-middle-class people have college educations, and a sizable proportion also hold postgraduate degrees. Many work in the white-collar fields of medicine, engineering, and law, or as business executives. Less wealthy than members of the upper class, this category of Americans lacks the power to influence national or international events, but often plays an important role in local civic and political affairs.

The rest of the middle class typically works in less prestigious white-collar occupations (such as bank tellers, lower-level managers, and sales clerks), or in highly skilled blue-collar jobs (including electrical work and carpentry). These people sometimes have incomes as high as those in the upper-middle class, especially if more than one family member works. Commonly, however, family income is between $25,000 and $40,000 a year. This roughly equals the median income for Amer-

Caste and Class in America: The Social Register and Who's Who

The best indicator of membership in the upper-upper class is inclusion in the *Social Register*. The criterion for inclusion in this listing of elites, first published in 1887, has as much to do with the source of family wealth as with the extent of the family fortune. In general, only "old-money" Americans appear here. This segment of the upper class, then, works like a caste: by ascription only. Because such elite standing is inherited, families rather than individuals are listed in the *Social Register*. The listing for David Rockefeller, for example, indicates (1) the family address and home telephone number; (2) Mrs. Rockefeller's maiden name; (3) the names of the Rockefeller children (noting boarding schools and colleges attended); and (4) the exclusive social clubs to which the family belongs. No mention is made of occupation, place of business, or any other mark of individual achievement.

Another kind of elite is recognized in the national edition of *Who's Who in America*. Instead of established families, this listing features individuals of high achievement. Because many people in *Who's Who in America* have succeeded in highly paid and high-prestige occupations, this book amounts to a rough approximation of the lower-upper class. Some *Social Register* families include individuals, such as David Rockefeller, who are also listed in *Who's Who*. In *Who's Who*, however, the focus shifts markedly. David Rockefeller's entry in *Who's Who* includes a brief biography (date of birth, education, and honorary degrees), a list of accomplishments (such as various military decorations, government service, books authored), and—most important—his chairmanship of the board of Chase Manhattan Bank. The address provided is his place of business.

In sum, the caste-like *Social Register* lists families on the basis of *who they are*. The more classlike *Who's Who* lists individuals on the basis of *what they have done*. But, as the dual listings of David Rockefeller suggest, personal achievement and social privilege are frequently closely related.

---

icans (about $32,000 in 1988) and provides a secure, if modest, standard of living. People in this range of the middle class generally accumulate only a small amount of wealth over the course of their working lives. The goal of owning a house is achieved by most, but the house is unlikely to be located in a prestigious neighborhood. Most of these people have a high-school education, but they cannot count on sending their children to college. And limited income means that young people in this class who do go to college generally attend state-supported schools.

The Working Class

Including about one-third of all Americans, working-class people have lower incomes than those in the middle class and virtually no accumulated wealth. In Marxist terms, the working class forms the core of the industrial proletariat. The blue-collar occupations of the working class generally yield a family income of between $12,000 and $25,000 a year, somewhat below the national average. Working-class Americans thus find themselves vulnerable to financial problems brought on by unemployment or illness.

Besides generating less income than the occupations of the middle class, working-class jobs typically provide less personal satisfaction. The work is far less interesting and challenging, and workers are usually subject to continual supervision by superiors (Edwards, 1979). Additionally, most working-class jobs offer few benefits, such as medical insurance and pension programs. Only about half of working-class families own their homes, and their housing, which is usually less substantial than that of middle-class families, is likely to be in lower-cost neighborhoods. Most working-class people also earn no more than a high-school education.

As these facts suggest, working-class people generally lack the power to shape events. Families typically live in modest neighborhoods because they cannot afford better housing. Their children may want to attend college but lack the money to do so. Although they find little satisfaction in their jobs, they have few alternatives. Still, working-class families tend to express a great deal of pride in what they do have, especially in comparison to those who are not working at all.

Television programming has generally portrayed Americans in a narrow range of the class structure from middle class to lower-upper class. In the last decade, however, an increasing number of shows have featured working-class people. Roseanne Barr, herself from a working-class family, is the star of one of the most popular of recent new shows.

The Lower Class

The remaining 20 percent of the population belong to the lower class. Low income makes their lives unstable and insecure. Some 32 million Americans (roughly 13 percent of the population) are officially classified as poor. Of course, millions more—the so-called "working poor"—are only marginally better off. Most lower-class people in the United States are white; however, blacks, Hispanics, and other minorities are disproportionately represented at the low end of the socioeconomic scale. The American poor typically work in low-prestige jobs that provide minimal income and little intrinsic satisfaction. Educationally disadvantaged as well, only some manage to complete high school; a college degree is usually out of reach. Further limiting their chances to escape from poverty, many lower-class Americans are functionally illiterate.

The lower class also experiences considerable social segregation, especially when the poor belong to racial or ethnic minorities. Such segregation appears most starkly in urban areas where large numbers of poor people live in deteriorating neighborhoods, shunned by the other social classes. And because very few lower-class families ever amass the resources to purchase a home, they typically live in undesirable low-cost rental housing.

The socialization of upper-class children differs markedly from that of lower-class children. Upper-class children grow up in an environment that fosters and promotes their talents, abilities, and confidence to the fullest. By contrast, lower-class children learn early on the harsh reality that most people place little value on their accomplishments and consider them only marginal members of society. Observing their parents and other lower-class adults, they may conclude that their own future holds little hope for breaking the cycle of poverty. Lower-class life, then, often generates self-defeating resignation to the hard social reality of being cut off from the resources of an affluent society (Jacob, 1986).

Not surprisingly, some simply give up. Most poor people, however, work desperately, often at two or three jobs, to make ends meet. In a study conducted in a northern city, Carol Stack (1975) discovered that, far from lacking initiative and responsibility, many poor people devise ingenious means of survival. They do so, she concluded, because they simply have no choice.

THE DIFFERENCE CLASS MAKES

Social stratification affects nearly every dimension of social life. We will now look briefly at some of the ways social standing shapes our lives, beginning with the crucial issue of health.

Class and Health

The health of Americans has much to do with their individual social standing. Children born into poor families are about 50 percent more likely to die during their first year of life than children born into more privileged families (Gortmaker, 1979). Later in life, Americans with high incomes are twice as likely to describe their health as excellent as people living in poverty. Conversely, only 4 percent of high-income people describe their health as merely fair or poor, a self-assessment made by 22 percent of poor Americans (U.S. National Center for Health Statistics, 1988). The same pattern appears in Great Britain and in virtually every other industrial society (Doyal, 1981).

Social class is linked to life expectancy as well. Black children, who are about three times more likely to be poor than white children, can expect to live about seventy years, while whites can expect to live over seventy-five years (U.S. Bureau of the Census, 1989).

The striking disparity in life expectancy between rich and poor is easily explained: nutritious foods, a safe environment, and necessary medical attention cost money. Medical costs, which have risen sharply in recent years, now average over $1,500 annually per person. Such costs are obviously out of reach for a family of four with an annual income of, say, $15,000.

People in the lower social classes also tend to live and work in more dangerous environments than privileged Americans. Because poorer people work in places such as factories and mines, rather than office buildings, and they generally live in neighborhoods plagued by drugs and crime, rather than exclusive suburbs, their lives are considerably less safe.

Privilege in America also confers benefits in terms of mental health (Link, Dohrenwend, & Skodol, 1986; Mirowsky & Ross, 1989). As one study concluded, "Lower class people are exposed to more of the stressful events and situations that can lead to emotional distress than their middle and upper class counterparts" (Kessler & Cleary, 1980:476). Moreover, people with greater social resources can respond more effectively to emotional disorders, seeking out help to defuse emotional crises. Consequently, they tend to recover more quickly, avoiding the stigma of mental illness.

Class and Values

Cultural values vary somewhat from class to class. Americans in the upper-upper class, for example, have an unusually strong sense of family history since their social position is based on wealth and social prestige passed down from generation to generation (Baltzell, 1979). Many other Americans, by contrast, do not know the full names of even their four grandparents. Because their social standing is guaranteed as a birthright, the "old rich" also tend to be understated in their manners and tastes, as if to say, "I know who I am and I don't have to prove anything to anyone else."

Below the upper class, patterns of consumption take on greater importance as class boundaries start to blur. Houses, clothes, and cars are often viewed as *status symbols* that "make a statement" about their owners. Perhaps this is why designer clothing is avoided by members of "society" yet sought after by those directly below them in class.

Because of their greater personal and financial security, middle-class people display more tolerance than their working-class counterparts toward controversial be-

People who are upwardly mobile are keenly aware of patterns of consumption. A growing income has often changed their lives, and money is what sets them apart from others. Thus they use material things (and even pets) to make a statement about "what they have become."

havior such as premarital sexual activity and homosexuality (Humphries, 1984). As Chapter 5 ("Socialization") explained, working-class people grow up in an atmosphere of greater supervision and discipline, and their jobs usually offer less autonomy than those of middle-class people. Therefore, working-class people are generally more likely to conform to conventional beliefs and practices (Kohn, 1977).

Even the meaning of time varies according to social class. Supported by generations of wealth, upper-class families maintain a strong pride in the past. Middle-class people, especially those who are upwardly mobile, optimistically look to the future for a better life. By contrast, the drive for daily survival focuses the attention of lower-class people on the present. This pessimistic present-time orientation often reflects the limited opportunities open to the lower class for improving their social position (Liebow, 1967; Lamar, Jr., 1985; Jacob, 1986).

Class and Politics

There is no simple relationship between social class and political attitudes. Generally, however, Americans of higher social position support the Republican Party, while those of lower social standing tend to favor the Democrats (Wolfinger, Shaprio, & Greenstein, 1980). Looking more closely, we see that the desire to protect their wealth generally prompts people of higher social standing to take a more conservative approach to economic issues than lower-income people. Thus, for example, the higher social classes, whose members usually own or manage businesses, favor a free-market economy unregulated by government. On social issues, such as support for the Equal Rights Amendment, abortion, and other feminist concerns, however, those in a high social position tend to support the liberal agenda. People of lower social standing take the opposite positions: they favor liberal policies on economic issues and conservative approaches on social issues (Nunn, Crockett, & Williams, 1978; Erikson, Luttberg, & Tedin, 1980; Syzmanski, 1983; Humphries, 1984).

Those in a higher social position also derive political power from participation in the political process. Americans with higher incomes, more education, and white-collar jobs are most likely to vote and belong to the largest number of voluntary associations (Hyman & Wright, 1971; Wolfinger & Rosenstone, 1980).

Class, Family, and Gender

In America, marriage generally unites people of comparable social standing. Family size varies by class; in general, lower-class families have more children than middle-class families. This is because lower-class people marry at an earlier age and make less use of birth control. Upper-class families, too, have more children, partly because they can afford the added child-rearing expenses.

Working-class people encourage their children to conform to conventional norms and obey authority figures. In contrast, people of higher social standing typically motivate children to express their individuality and to use their imagination more freely. This difference reflects parents' expectations about their children's future: less privileged children are likely to take jobs demanding close adherence to specified rules, while more advantaged children will probably enter fields that demand more creativity (Kohn, 1977). In comparing the child-rearing patterns of lower-class and upper-class families, however, one key fact emerges: families with more social resources are better able to develop their children's talents and abilities. In this way, social position tends to be transmitted from generation to generation.

Divorce is more common among families of lower social standing; such factors as low income and high risk of unemployment subject these families to greater stress (Kitson & Raschke, 1981; Fergusson, Horwood, & Shannon, 1984). In marriage, working-class people maintain a more rigid division of responsibilities between husband and wife, while middle-class marriages are somewhat more egalitarian (Bott, 1971). Finally, the number of households with children headed by women has been increasing rapidly during the last decade. This pattern appears most frequently among the poor—especially poor blacks—although Americans of all classes are grappling with the economic problems of single parenthood in increasing numbers.

SOCIAL MOBILITY IN AMERICA

Ours is a dynamic society marked by a significant measure of social mobility. As we noted in the last chapter, social mobility allows individuals to move upward or downward. Earning a college degree, securing a higher-paying job, or succeeding in a business endeavor contribute to *upward social mobility*, while dropping out of school, losing a job, or having a business enterprise fail may signal *downward social mobility*.

Changes in society as a whole also affect social mobility. During the first half of this century, for example, industrialization expanded the economy, raising the standard of living for millions of Americans. Even without being very good swimmers, so to speak, people were able to "ride a rising tide of prosperity." As explained later in this chapter, *structural social mobility* in a downward direction has more recently forced many Americans to endure severe economic setbacks.

Whether an individual's social mobility stems from personal achievement or societal changes, it is experienced as a transition—for better or worse—in social position. In studying such patterns, sociologists distinguish between one-generation and multi-generational transitions. **Intragenerational social mobility** refers to *a change in social position occurring during a person's lifetime.* Of even greater concern to sociologists is **intergenerational social mobility,** *the upward or downward social mobility of children in relation to their parents.* Social mobility across generations takes on special significance because it reflects changes in society that affect virtually everyone.

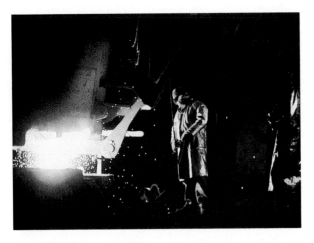

From World War II until about 1970, American industries dominated world and domestic markets. Since then, however, the "deindustrialization of America" has brought hard times to thousands of American families. Social mobility is sometimes a matter of individual effort and luck, but more often is due to major economic changes.

Social Mobility: Myth and Reality

In few societies do people dwell on social mobility as much as in the United States: historically, moving ahead has been central to the American Dream. And ideologically, the belief that people have the opportunity to realize their individual potential also undergirds American social stratification (Kleugel & Smith, 1986).

But precisely how much social mobility occurs in American society? Using the broad categories of blue-collar and white-collar jobs, studies of intergenerational mobility (which, unfortunately, have focused almost exclusively on men) show that almost 40 percent of the sons of blue-collar workers attain white-collar jobs and almost 30 percent of sons born into white-collar families accept blue-collar jobs. When comparing more specific occupational categories, about 80 percent of sons show some social mobility in relation to their fathers (Blau & Duncan, 1967; Featherman & Hauser, 1978).

These data suggest, first, that social mobility is relatively high for American males, as we would expect in a class system. Second, until recently, the trend in social mobility has more commonly been upward than downward. Structural social mobility accounted for most of this upward movement, as better-paying white-collar jobs steadily replaced the blue-collar and farming work more common several generations ago. Third, although significant changes appear over many generations, social mobility within a single generation has usually been

incremental rather than dramatic. This means that Americans rarely move "from rags to riches," or the other way around. Social mobility typically involves subtle changes *within* the social classes described already rather than dramatic changes *between* classes.

No patterns apply equally to *all* Americans, however. Black Americans have traditionally experienced less upward social mobility than whites, especially in recent years (Featherman & Hauser, 1978; Pomer, 1986). Although the United States staged an overall economic recovery during the 1980s, blacks actually lost ground in terms of income through most of the decade (Jacob, 1986). Hispanic families, too, were downwardly mobile throughout the 1980s, due to declining wage levels and the low overall age of this category of American. Women and men also differ in terms of social mobility. As we shall see in Chapter 13 ("Sex and Gender"), the majority of working women hold clerical positions (such as secretaries) and low-paying service jobs (such as waitresses). Because these jobs offer little opportunity for advancement, women appear to face more barriers to upward social mobility than men. Divorce also commonly results in downward social mobility for women—but not men—as Chapter 15 ("Family") explains.

Compared to other industrial societies, the United States has not had exceptional social mobility. Table 10–3 compares intergenerational social mobility in six industrial societies during the economically favorable decades about the middle of this century (Lipset & Ben-

Table 10–3 INTERGENERATIONAL MOBILITY IN SIX INDUSTRIAL SOCIETIES

Country	Upward Social Mobility	Downward Social Mobility
Switzerland	45%	13%
France	39	20
Japan	36	22
United States	33	26
Sweden	31	24
West Germany	29	32

In this table, intergenerational social mobility is based on the occupation of fathers and their sons. Upward social mobility indicates a father with a blue-collar occupation and a son with a white-collar occupation. Downward social mobility indicates a father with a white-collar occupation and a son with a blue-collar occupation.

SOURCE: Seymour Martin Lipset and Reinhard Bendix, *Social Mobility in Industrial Society* (Berkeley: University of California Press, 1967), p. 25.

dix, 1967). Switzerland had the most upward mobility and the least downward mobility, while West Germany experienced the least upward mobility and the most downward mobility. The United States fell near the center in this comparison. More recent research suggests that social mobility in the United States remains comparable to that of other Western, industrial societies (McRoberts & Selbee, 1981; Kaelble, 1986).

The "Middle-Class Slide"

The expectation of upward social mobility is deeply rooted in American history and the American national consciousness. For two centuries, the United States has made expansion the nation's watchword, with westward migration followed by an industrial revolution. The resulting economic growth fueled America's reputation as a land where opportunity was limited only by a person's imagination and willingness to work. The Great Depression of the 1930s wounded American optimism, but prosperity returned in the 1940s and continued through the 1960s, bolstering Americans' optimism once again. During this period, the standard of living for the typical American rose steadily.

Since the 1960s, however, our traditional confidence in upward social mobility has diminished, with some sociologists claiming that American society has entered an "age of decline" (Blumberg, 1981). A large proportion of Americans are now concentrating on simply holding on to what they have, and many are losing the economic security associated with middle-class living.

The recent shift in attitude stems from changes in the larger economy: the pace of economic gains, long taken for granted, has slowed considerably. Figure 10–3 on page 270 shows median family income for Americans between 1950 and 1988 in constant 1988 dollars. Between 1950 and 1973, median family income for Americans grew by almost 65 percent; however, it has remained roughly stable since then (U.S. Bureau of the Census, 1989).

Historically, support for the American class system was based on the steady growth of the middle class. The rapid surge in white-collar positions during this century, drawing millions of Americans from blue-collar and farming work, suggested that the United States was becoming predominantly a middle-class society (Kerckhoff, Campbell, & Winfield-Laird, 1985).

But upward structural social mobility diminished during the 1970s and 1980s (Pampel, Land, & Felson, 1977; Levy, 1987). Instead, because new jobs commonly pay less than in the past, American social mobility is now more likely to be in the *downward* direction. We saw in Figure 10–3 how this change affected income in the United States. We can spot the underlying cause of this income decline in Figure 10–4 on page 271. Between 1963 and 1973, almost half of new jobs fell into the high-income range (paying over $30,000 annually in 1988 dollars). Through the remainder of the 1970s, more than 60 percent of new jobs paid in the middle-income range (between about $15,000 and $30,000). During the first half of the 1980s, far fewer high-income jobs were created, and the proportion of middle-income jobs also fell considerably. Simultaneously, the proportion of low-income jobs (paying less than $15,000 annually) jumped sharply, to more than 40 percent. Simply stated, this means that many people—especially "average" Americans in the middle class and working class—have suffered an economic decline. This economic change is responsible for what has been called the *"middle-class slide."*

The Deindustrialization of America

Underlying the "middle-class slide" is a global economic transformation: much of the industrial production that offered Americans high-paying jobs a generation ago has been transferred overseas, while a growing proportion of new jobs in the United States require little skill and provide minimal income (Blumberg, 1981; Rosen, 1987;

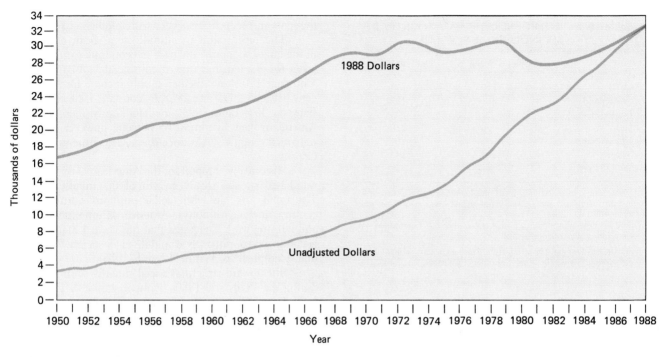

Figure 10–3 Median Family Income, 1950–1988

(U.S. Bureau of the Census)

Thurow, 1987). Major industrial goods such as cars, and popular items such as electronic equipment, are now routinely imported from Japan, Korea, and other countries; at home, McDonald's now has more employees than USX (formerly United States Steel). The increasingly global economy, further examined in Chapter 11 ("Global Inequality"), has sparked upward mobility for a small proportion of Americans—notably those who manage and invest in expanding global corporations. By contrast, this transformation has hurt a larger proportion of moderate-income Americans—mainly those whose factory jobs have been "exported" overseas (Reich, 1989).

Many Americans are painfully aware of how this change has affected their lives. Compared to a generation ago, far fewer people now expect to improve their social position, and a growing number worry that they may not be able to maintain the standard of living they knew as children in their parents' home. This is so despite the fact that about half of today's families have two or more members in the labor force, double the proportion

in 1950. Many Americans today, therefore, are working harder to hold on to the social standing they have.

How did U.S. society fare overall in the 1980s? The reviews were mixed. In the course of the decade, some families were propelled into the ranks of the rich, while nearly twice as many stalled economically or suffered setbacks. As the rich became richer and the poor became poorer, the shine dimmed on the American Dream. Not surprisingly, the problem of poverty received growing attention during the 1980s, as the next section explains.

AMERICAN POVERTY

By concentrating resources in the hands of some, social stratification deprives others of the elements necessary for a secure life. Although poverty always signifies deprivation, the concept is commonly used in two different ways. **Relative poverty** refers to *being deprived of social*

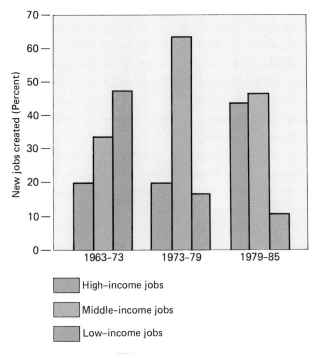

Figure 10–4 New American Jobs and Downward Mobility
(Thurow, 1987)

resources *relative to those with more.* Since all societies are stratified, relative poverty is found everywhere and, by definition, can never be eliminated. Anyone can be relatively poor (or relatively rich) depending on the standard of comparison. Much more serious is **absolute poverty,** defined as *a deprivation of social resources that is life-threatening.* Living in a state of absolute poverty does not involve merely having fewer resources than others; rather, it is nothing less than the desperate matter of staying alive. Defined this way, poverty is a pressing human problem, but one that can be solved.

As we shall note in Chapter 11 ("Global Inequality"), the global dimensions of absolute poverty place the lives of roughly 1 billion people—one in five of the earth's entire population—at risk. Even here, however, the wrenching reality of hunger pervades the American landscape, coupled with inadequate housing and poor health.

The Extent of American Poverty

Figure 10–5 shows the official American poverty rate since 1959. The poverty rate dropped overall in recent decades, although it rose during much of the 1980s. In 1988, 31.9 million people—13.1 percent of all Americans—were officially labeled as poor. For a family of four living in an urban area, the government defined being "poor" as having a total income below $12,092. Although this standard is somewhat arbitrary, it approximates three times the estimated minimum expense for food. Another 11 million Americans, who fall within 25 percent of this poverty line, are known as the *marginally poor.* One recent study noted that the proportion of very poor Americans whose income is less than half the official poverty level has increased from about 30 percent in 1975 to almost 40 percent today (Littman, 1989).

Poverty in America means hunger. Estimates suggest that for at least 20 million Americans hunger is a daily experience (Schwartz-Nobel, 1981; Physician Task Force on Hunger, 1987). According to the Children's Defense Fund (1985), some ten thousand children die each year for various reasons stemming from poverty, making this the leading cause of death among the youngest Americans. The resources to eradicate this problem appear to be within reach because, this organization estimates, one-half of just the *increase* in defense spending for one year in the mid-1980s would have been enough to rescue every child in America from poverty.

Figure 10–5 The American Poverty Rate, 1959–1988
(U.S. Bureau of the Census)

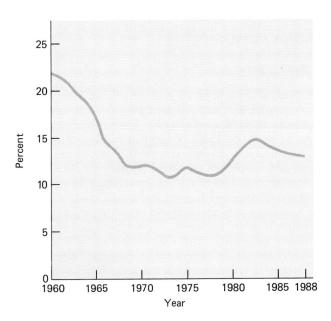

Reductions in domestic spending during much of the past decade hit poor people the hardest. Although programs intended to help the poor account for only about 10 percent of the federal budget, they absorbed nearly one-third of these federal budget cuts (Interfaith Action for Economic Justice, 1984). The richest society in the world, then, confronts the reality of widespread poverty, which many argue forms a barrier to becoming a "kinder and gentler nation."

Who Are the American Poor?

Although no single description covers all poor people, poverty is pronounced among certain categories of Americans: children, nonwhites, women, and people who live in rural areas. Where these categories overlap, the problem is especially serious.

Age

Children are more likely to be poor than Americans of any other age category. In 1988, 19.7 percent of those under the age of eighteen were officially classified as poor. From another perspective, 40 percent of the American poor are under the age of eighteen.

Children are now the poorest of the American poor. A generation ago, however, the elderly were. The poverty rate for Americans over the age of sixty-five was 12.0 percent in 1988, slightly below the overall poverty rate of about 13 percent. Nevertheless, the growing number of older Americans means that about 11 percent of the poor are elderly people.

Race and Ethnicity

About 65 percent of all poor people are white; about 30 percent are black. But in relation to their overall numbers, blacks are about three times as likely as whites to be poor. In 1988, 32 percent of black Americans lived in poverty, compared to about 28 percent of Hispanics and 10 percent of whites. During the 1980s, this "poverty gap" between the races increased (U.S. Bureau of the Census, 1989).

Since both children and nonwhites are disproportionately poor, nonwhite children are especially likely to live in poverty. About 20 percent of all Americans under the age of eighteen were poor in 1988, but 38 percent of Hispanic children felt the sting of poverty, as did 44 percent of all black children.

People usually associate poverty with nonwhites in inner cities. But most poor people are white, and many struggle to survive in rural areas, unnoticed by the vast majority of Americans.

Sex

Poverty does not affect males and females equally. Of all poor Americans over the age of eighteen, 62 percent are women and 38 percent are men. Poverty strikes hardest among women who are the heads of households. On their shoulders falls the financial burden of raising children, which makes working for income difficult. For those able to work, low-paying jobs are the norm. Some 53 percent of all poor families are headed by women with no husband present. In marked contrast, only 4.9 percent of poor families are households headed by single men. The widening of this gap in recent decades is called the **feminization of poverty**, *the trend by which females represent an increasing proportion of the poor.* The box takes a closer look at this process.

What Is the Feminization of Poverty?

In 1978, Diana Pearce first described the correlation between women and poverty as the *feminization of poverty*. This term has been widely used by sociologists ever since. What, exactly, does the term mean?

To answer this question we must carefully examine the changing profile of poor people. The government defines being poor as living in a family with an income below the official poverty level. Being female can be linked to being poor, however, in two ways. First, we can look at all poor families and determine the proportion headed by women. Second, we can begin with all families headed by women, and determine what proportion are poor. Obtaining recent data from government reports for each approach, two different pictures emerge.

The "feminization of poverty" thesis holds true only if understood in the following way: *the proportion of poor families headed by women (with no husband present) has generally risen since 1960.* The purple line in the accompanying figure represents this process. In 1960, about 25 percent of all poor families were headed by women; most of the remaining poor families had both wives and husbands present. By the end of the 1980s, however, the proportion of poor families headed by women had increased 50 percent.

If we turn the question around and investigate the proportion of families headed by women that are poor, the opposite pattern emerges. *The proportion of all female-headed families in*

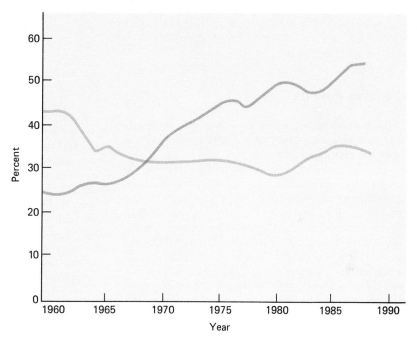

Percent of families below poverty level, headed by a female with no husband present.

Percent of female-headed families, with no husband present, below the poverty level.

(U.S. Bureau of the Census)

poverty has generally declined since 1960. The green line in the figure represents this trend. In 1960, more than 40 percent of families headed by women were poor; the figure fell to almost 30 percent during the 1970s, rising to about 35 percent in the 1980s.

Both findings result from the rapid growth in the number of families headed by women, roughly doubling since 1960. At all social levels, many more women are heads of families today; but the number of families headed by more *affluent* women is increasing faster than the number of families headed by *poor* women. The "feminization of poverty," then, is correctly used to refer to the rising proportion of poor families that are headed by women.

Area of Residence

Poverty is more common in rural areas than in cities. In 1987, 16.9 percent of Americans living outside large urban areas were poor, in contrast to 12.5 percent of people living within them (U.S. Bureau of the Census, 1989). Urban living tends to raise living standards because wealth, job opportunities, and social services are concentrated in cities. Yet, inner-city areas provide the largest pockets of poverty. Almost one in five residents of American inner cities is poor.

Explaining Poverty

America's standing as a rich society by world standards makes the presence of tens of millions of poor people a serious social and moral concern. But it also sparks considerable controversy, as suggested by Figure 10–6. A recent survey asked a representative sample of adults whether the government should act to improve the living standards of poor Americans, or whether poor people should be expected to help themselves. Almost one-third of respondents thought the government should do more, while close to one-fourth thought that people should take responsibility for themselves. More than 40 percent, however, agreed with both "solutions." We now probe the arguments underlying these two approaches to the

Figure 10–6 Asking Americans: Who Is Responsible for Poverty?

(*General Social Surveys, 1972–1989: Cumulative Codebook*. Chicago: National Opinion Research Center, 1989:328)

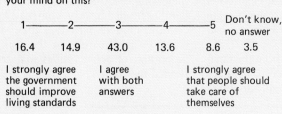

Question: "Some people think that the government in Washington should do everything possible to improve the living standards of all poor Americans [they are at point 1 below]. Other people think it is not the government's responsibility, and that each person should take care of himself [they are at point 5 below]. Where would you place yourself on this scale, or haven't you made up your mind on this?"

1	2	3	4	5	Don't know, no answer
16.4	14.9	43.0	13.6	8.6	3.5

I strongly agree the government should improve living standards / I agree with both answers / I strongly agree that people should take care of themselves

problem of poverty, which form opposing sides of a lively political debate.

The poor are primarily responsible for their own poverty. Throughout American history, popular belief has held that people are largely responsible for their own social standing. This approach assumes that American society has considerable opportunity for anyone able and willing to take advantage of it. The poor, then, are viewed as people with fewer skills, less education, lower motivation, or, perhaps, a debilitating drug addiction—in sum, people who are undeserving of more out of life. This view is expressed, in various degrees, by the selection of responses 3, 4, or 5 in Figure 10–6.

Edward Banfield (1974), an outspoken proponent of personal responsibility for poverty, recognizes that children make up a large proportion of the poor and should not be considered responsible for themselves in the same way as able-bodied adults. He claims, however, that many poor people gather in areas, especially inner cities, where a distinctive lower-class subculture inhibits personal achievement. An important element of this subculture is a present-time orientation, which dictates living for the moment rather than the future. Since hard work, saving, and other behavior likely to promote upward social mobility depend on looking toward the future, people who live largely for the moment merely perpetuate their own poverty. In Banfield's view, many of the poor are irresponsible, reaping what they deserve.

A decade earlier, anthropologist Oscar Lewis (1961) developed this approach to poverty in studies of Latin America. The *culture of poverty* Lewis described is characterized by resignation to being poor as a matter of fate. Growing up in such an environment, children eventually come to believe that there is little point in looking to the future for a better life. They become resigned to the idea that no matter what they do they will never escape a self-perpetuating cycle of poverty.

Society is primarily responsible for poverty. Americans do not believe that hard work and individual drive alone determine a person's social position. As Figure 10–6 shows, almost 75 percent of Americans express some support for action by the government to reduce poverty (responses 1, 2, and 3). William Ryan (1976) argues that society—not the poor—is primarily responsible for poverty. In his view, wealth and poverty result from the unequal distribution of resources in a society. Therefore, Ryan claims that Banfield's analysis amounts to little more than "blaming the victims" for their own suffering. Ryan maintains that for many Americans economic opportunity is sharply limited: this, and not the

A common view of the poor during the early Industrial Revolution was that they were morally deficient people who, like other offenders, deserved to be punished. Debtor's prisons were the result, as depicted in this period engraving by an unknown artist. The poor are no longer physically imprisoned, but the idea that they are morally flawed and responsible for their own poverty remains strong.

personal qualities of the poor themselves, should be the focus of attention in explaining and addressing poverty. In global terms, societies whose wealth is distributed very unequally (such as the United States and Canada) face a significant poverty problem; societies that distribute wealth more equally (like the Soviet Union, Sweden, and Japan) lack these extremes.

Ryan suggests that the characteristics associated with a "culture of poverty" are not the *causes* of poverty but rather its *consequences*. If poor people appear to lack ambition and become resigned to their plight, the fault lies with the real lack of opportunity in American society, according to Ryan.

Critical evaluation. The explanations of poverty advanced by Banfield and Ryan differ radically. Both approaches have won adherents in the American public and among government policymakers. Banfield's approach, placing responsibility for poverty primarily on the poor themselves, gives society few options to eradicate pervasive poverty. Ryan's view, however, claims that poverty could be reduced by redistributing income and opportunity in a more equal manner. This could be accomplished through programs ranging from a comprehensive child-care package to help poor mothers gain necessary skills or maintain jobs, to a guaranteed minimum income level for every American family. From

this point of view, providing real opportunity makes for the best way to stem the hopelessness, despair, and violence that perpetuate poverty.

Little hard evidence supports either of these approaches directly. But data reflecting patterns of work among the poor are suggestive. Banfield's position is supported by government data showing that more than half (52.6 percent) of the heads of poor families did not work at all during 1987. Moreover, only 18.9 percent of the heads of families in poverty worked at least fifty weeks during 1987 (U.S. Bureau of the Census, 1989). So, from this point of view, the major cause of poverty is *not holding a job*.

But the *reasons* that people do not work seem more consistent with Ryan's position. Most women who are poor do not go to work because they need to care for children. In the United States, few employers provide child-care programs for workers, and few low-paid workers can afford to obtain child care on their own. Most poor men claim there are no jobs to be found, illness or disability has sidelined them, or they have retired, in the case of the elderly. Of course, not all poor people are jobless. In fact, 46.9 percent of the poor (15 million people) comprise the *working poor*, who remain in poverty even though they are working. Of all the working poor, 18.9 percent (6 million people) worked at least fifty weeks in 1987, 10.7 percent (3.5 million people) worked 27 to 49 weeks, and 17.3 percent (5.5 million people) worked fewer than 26 weeks. Such "working poverty" places a double burden on the poor: low wages that barely make ends meet and the inability to seek training or education to better themselves because they must struggle simply to survive on a day-to-day basis. (Levitan & Shapiro, 1987). For most of the 1980s, the minimum wage remained at $3.35; it will rise to $4.25 by 1992. Even at this higher level, two adults working full time could barely support a family above the official poverty line.

Obviously, individual ability and initiative play a part in shaping everyone's social position. On balance, though, evidence points toward society—not individual character traits—as the primary source of poverty. Surely, some poor people lack ambition. Overall, however, the poor are *categories* of people—women heads of families, minorities, people isolated from the larger society in inner-city areas—without the same opportunities as others.

Homelessness

At the beginning of the 1980s, economic recession and rising poverty rates focused attention on the problem of homelessness. This problem is hardly new to America; indeed, homelessness has been much more pervasive in the past. Nor is homelessness uniquely American; as Chapter 11 ("Global Inequality") explains, the problem is far worse in many other countries. Yet, in light of the enormous wealth of the United States and its commitment to providing opportunity for everyone,

homelessness may be fairly described as a national scandal demanding an effective response (Schutt, 1989).

There is no precise count of homeless Americans. Estimates range between about 500,000 and several million (Kozol, 1989). The lower figure approximates the number of people who are homeless *on any given night*. A more meaningful estimate suggests that about one and one-half million Americans are homeless *for some time during the course of a year* (Wright, 1989).

Consider these familiar stereotypes of homeless people: men sleeping in doorways and women carrying everything they own in a shopping bag down a busy city street. In recent years, these stereotypes have been undermined by the reality of the "new homeless"—those thrown out of work because of plant closings, people forced out of apartments by rising rents or condominium conversions, and others unable to meet mortgage or rent payments because they must work for lower wages. In fact, no stereotype of the homeless paints a complete picture because such people are now a highly varied category of Americans.

But virtually all homeless people have one status in common: *poverty*. For that reason, the approaches already used in explaining poverty also apply to homelessness. One side of the debate places responsibility on *personal* traits of the homeless themselves. For instance, perhaps one-third of homeless people are mentally ill; still others are addicted to alcohol or other drugs. Others, for whatever reason, seem unable to cope in a complex and highly competitive society (Bassuk, 1984; Whitman, 1989). On the other side of the debate, advocates assert that homelessness results from *societal* factors, including a lack of low-income housing in the United States and

The increase in homelessness during the 1980s renewed the debate about American poverty. Some homeless people have personal problems that render them less capable of coping with a demanding and sometimes bewildering world. But homelessness is more a social problem reflecting changes in the American economy and cutbacks in social service programs.

the economic transition toward low-paying jobs described earlier (Kozol, 1989). Thus, one-third of all homeless people are now entire families, and children are the fastest growing category of the homeless. A minister living in a Pennsylvania town that has lost hundreds of industrial jobs due to plant closings described the underlying economic problem this way:

> Yes, there are new jobs. There's a new McDonald's and a Burger King. You can take home $450 in a month from jobs like that. That might barely pay the rent. What do you do if someone gets sick? What do you do for food and clothes? These may be good jobs for a teenager. Can you ask a thirty-year-old man who's worked for GM since he was eighteen to keep his wife and kids alive on jobs like that? There are jobs cleaning rooms in the hotel . . . Can you expect a single mother with three kids to hold her life together with that kind of work? (Kozol, 1989:6)

No one disputes that a large proportion of homeless people are personally impaired to some degree, although how much cause and how much effect is often difficult to untangle. But structural changes in the American economy, coupled with government policies reducing support for lower-income people, contribute substantially to homelessness.

In responding to homelessness, we must consider both its individual and its societal roots. Providing housing (other than shelters) for low-income people would go far toward remedying the problem. Additionally, people must have an opportunity to earn the income necessary to afford housing. The problem of homelessness, however, goes beyond housing; it is also a *human* problem. People who endure months or years of insecure living come to need various types of social services. Recall how John Coleman, the college president whose experience as a homeless man was described at the beginning of this chapter, identified the personal damage caused by even short-term homelessness. Solving the problem of homelessness also means coming to terms with the socially damaging consequences of poverty.

Class and Welfare in America: Politics and Values

This chapter has presented a great many facts about social class in American society. In the end, however, our understanding of what it means to be wealthy and privileged or poor and perhaps homeless also turns on politics and values. Not surprisingly, support for the notion that social standing reflects personal merit is strongest among well-off Americans. The idea that society should distribute wealth and other resources more equally finds greatest favor among those with relatively few advantages (Rytina, Form, & Pease, 1970; N.O.R.C., 1989).

The perceptions of *all* Americans are shaped by cultural values that hold people responsible for their own life circumstances. When a random sample of American adults was asked, "How important is hard work for getting ahead in life?" almost 90 percent responded that it was "essential" or "very important" (N.O.R.C., 1989:491). Such cultural values encourage us to see successful people as personally meritorious and the poor as personally deficient. Richard Sennett and Jonathan Cobb (1973) called this view, as applied to the poor, the *hidden injury of class*. In other words, poverty significantly lowers the self-image of disadvantaged people, while others display their affluence as a personal "badge of ability." Values supporting individual responsibility also contribute to the historically negative view of social welfare programs and those who receive such support in American society (Waxman, 1983). While advocates for the poor defend welfare programs as necessary for millions of Americans lacking opportunities and advantages, American cultural values promote the view that social welfare programs undermine initiative. Accepting assistance of this kind thus becomes personally demeaning. This anti-welfare bias discourages half the Americans eligible for various forms of needed assistance from applying for it (U.S. Bureau of the Census, 1989a).

Curiously, this same value system paints a more positive picture of government benefits provided to allegedly "deserving" wealthy Americans. Even as the Reagan administration cut government benefits to the poor in the early 1980s, for example, dozens of major corporations, including Boeing, General Electric, DuPont, Texaco, and Mobil, paid virtually no taxes on billions of dollars in earnings (Children's Defense Fund, 1985). A more recent case of government "welfare for the rich" is the Bush Administration proposal to cut the capital-gains tax, which no one denies would primarily enrich the wealthiest Americans. In the case of the capital-gains tax cut, supporters argue that such a government subsidy would spur economic growth. Clearly, government policy can aggravate or minimize social inequality, just as government policy itself is shaped by cultural and ideological definitions of rich and poor.

The drama of social stratification extends far beyond America's borders. The most striking social disparities are found not in the United States but in other parts of the world. Chapter 11 continues our investigation of social stratification, focusing on global inequality.

SUMMARY

1. Social inequality in American society involves income disparity and even greater differences of wealth.

2. Greater occupational prestige and income are generally accorded to white-collar occupations than to blue-collar occupations. The pink-collar occupations, typically held by women, offer little social prestige or income.

3. Formal education is also distributed unequally. About three-fourths of American adults complete high school, but less than one-fifth are college graduates.

4. Social standing in the United States is related to many factors, including ancestry, race and ethnicity, gender, and religion.

5. The upper class, which is small (about 4 percent), includes the richest and most powerful Americans. Included in the upper-upper class are the old rich, whose wealth is transmitted over several generations, and the lower-upper class, or new rich, whose wealth is primarily earned income.

6. The middle class includes 40 to 45 percent of Americans. The upper-middle class may be distinguished on the basis of higher income, higher-prestige occupations, and more schooling.

7. The working class includes about one-third of Americans. With below-average income, working-class families have less financial security than those in the middle class. Few working-class Americans have more than a high-school education, and they commonly work in blue-collar or lower white-collar jobs.

8. About one-fifth of Americans are in the lower class.

Most live near or below the official poverty line. Blacks, Hispanics, and women are disproportionately represented in the lower class.

9. Social class affects nearly all dimensions of life, beginning with health and life expectancy, and encompassing a wide range of attitudes and patterns of family life.

10. Social mobility is common in the United States, usually involving only small changes from one generation to the next. Patterns of social mobility in the United States differ little from those in other industrial societies.

11. Since the early 1970s, changes in the American economy have reduced the standard of living for many moderate-income Americans. This is the result of a decline in manufacturing industries in the United States, paralleling growth in low-paying service-sector jobs.

12. Some 32 million Americans are officially classified as poor. About 40 percent of the poor are children under the age of eighteen. Most poor Americans are white, but blacks and Hispanics are disproportionately represented among the poor. A growing proportion of poor families are headed by women.

13. Edward Banfield and Oscar Lewis advanced the "culture of poverty" thesis, suggesting that much poverty is perpetuated by the personal characteristics of the poor themselves. Opposing this view, William Ryan argues that poverty is caused by the unequal distribution of wealth in society. Although Banfield's view is consistent with the American cultural pattern of personalizing social position, Ryan's view is supported by more evidence.

KEY CONCEPTS

absolute poverty a state of deprivation of social resources that is life-threatening

feminization of poverty a trend by which females represent an increasing proportion of the poor

income occupational wages or salaries and earnings from investments

intergenerational social mobility a change in the social position of children in relation to that of their parents

intragenerational social mobility a change in social position occurring during a person's lifetime

relative poverty being deprived of social resources in relation to those who have more

wealth the total amount of money and valuable goods that any person or family controls

SUGGESTED READINGS

The first text below provides a detailed account of many issues raised in this chapter. Also listed is a publication that offers data on income distribution in American society.

Daniel W. Rossides. *Social Stratification: The American Class System in Comparative Perspective*. Englewood Cliffs, NJ: Prentice Hall, 1990.

Frank Levy. *Dollars and Dreams: The Changing American Income Distribution*. New York: Russell Sage Foundation, 1987.

This book describes how the decline of traditional industries in the United States has threatened the well-being of many Americans.

David Bensman and Roberta Lynch. *Rusted Dreams: Hard Times in a Steel Community*. New York: McGraw-Hill, 1987.

The first two of these books trace the history of the upper class. The third explains how the lives of privileged women differ from those of privileged men.

Edward Pessen. *Riches, Class, and Power: The United States Before the Civil War*. New Brunswick, NJ: Transaction Books, 1989.

E. Digby Baltzell. *Philadelphia Gentlemen: The Making of a National Upper Class*. Philadelphia: University of Pennsylvania Press, 1979.

Susan A. Ostrander. *Women of the Upper Class*. Philadelphia: Temple University Press, 1984.

This insider's view of the old rich is as rare as it is informative.

Nelson W. Aldrich, Jr. *Old Money: The Mythology of America's Upper Class*. New York: Alfred A. Knopf, 1988.

The working class—often ignored in research in favor of both the rich and the poor—is the focus of these books.

Reeve Vanneman and Lynn Weber Cannon. *The American Perception of Class*. Philadelphia: Temple University Press, 1987.

David Halle. *America's Working Man: Work, Home, and Politics Among Blue-Collar Property Owners*. Chicago: University of Chicago Press, 1984.

The highly variable formation of working-class political movements is examined in this collection of essays.

Ira Katznelson and Aristide Zolberg, eds. *Working-Class Formation: Nineteenth-Century Patterns in Western Europe and the United States*. Princeton, NJ: Princeton University Press, 1986.

In this book, the author takes a probing—and often amusing—look at social differences in America.

Paul Fussell. *Class: A Guide Through the American Status System*. New York: Summit Books, 1983.

This book examines the "feminization of poverty"—the link between being female and being poor.

Hilda Scott. *Working Your Way to the Bottom: The Feminization of Poverty*. Boston: Routledge & Kegan Paul/Pandora Press, 1984.

This is an analysis of the effects of poverty on personal motivation and achievement.

Jay MacLeod. *Ain't No Makin' It: Leveled Aspirations in a Low-Income Neighborhood*. Boulder, Co.: Westview Press, 1987.

Here are some of the best of recent books investigating the growing problem of homelessness in the United States.

Peter H. Rossi. *Down and Out in America: The Origins of Homelessness*. Chicago: University of Chicago Press, 1989.

Jonathan Kozol. *Rachael and Her Children: Homeless Families in America*. New York: Crown Publishers, 1988.

Kathleen Hirsch. *Songs From the Alley*. New York: Ticknor & Fields, 1989.

F. Steven Redburn and Terry F. Buss. *Responding to America's Homeless*. New York: Praeger, 1987.

Sophie Watson. *Housing and Homelessness: A Feminist Perspective*. New York: Routledge & Kegan Paul, 1986.

Here are studies that assess various social-policy approaches to fighting poverty in American society.

Leslie W. Dunbar. *The Common Interest: How Our Social-Welfare Policies Don't Work, and What We Can Do About Them*. New York: Pantheon, 1988.

Sheldon H. Danziger and Daniel H. Weinberg. *Fighting Poverty: What Works and What Doesn't*. Cambridge, MA: Harvard University Press, 1986.

11

Global Inequality

Half an hour out of Cairo, Egypt's capital city, the bus jerked to a stop at the beginning of a dirt road. It was still dark, although the Mo'edhdhins would soon climb the minarets of Cairo's many mosques to call the Islamic faithful to prayers at dawn. The driver turned to the busload of American students and their instructor, genuinely bewildered. "Why," he said, mixing English with some Arabic, "do you want to be here? And in the middle of the night?"

Why, indeed? No sooner had we left the bus than smoke and stench, the likes of which we had never before encountered, overcame us. Eyes squinting, handkerchiefs pressed against noses and mouths, we moved slowly uphill along the path to mountains of trash and garbage that extended for miles. We had reached the Cairo Dump, where the fifteen million people of one of the world's largest cities deposit their trash and garbage.[1] We walked stiffly and with great care, since the only light came from small fires smoldering all around us. Suddenly, from the shadows, shapes appeared. After a moment, we spotted dogs peering curiously through the curtain of haze. As startled as we were, they quickly turned and vanished into the thick air. Ahead of us, large fires became visible, with people clustered all around.

Human beings actually inhabit this inhuman place, creating a surreal scene, like the aftermath of the next war. As we approached, the fires cast an eerie light on their faces. We stopped some distance from them, separated by a vast chasm of culture and circumstances. But smiles eased the tension, and soon we were sharing the warmth of their flames. At that moment, the melodious call to prayer sounded across the city.

---

[1] This portrayal of the Cairo Dump is based on the author's experiences in Cairo. It also draws on the discussion found in Spates & Macionis, 1987, and conversations with James L. Spates, who has also visited the Cairo Dump.

The people of the Cairo Dump, called the Zeba-leen, belong to a religious minority—Coptic Christians—in a predominantly Muslim society. Barred by religious discrimination from many jobs, the Zebaleen use don-key-carts and small trucks to pick up refuse throughout the city and bring it here. The night-long routine reaches a climax at dawn when the hundreds of Zebaleen gather at the dump, swarming over the new piles in search of anything of value. That morning, we watched men, women, and children accumulate bits of paper and rib-bon, examine scraps of discarded food, and slowly fill their baskets with what would get them through another day. Every now and then, someone held up an especially "valuable" object that might bring the equivalent of a few dollars in the city. Watching in silence, we could no longer take our comfortable Western lives for granted. Our sturdy shoes and warm clothing meant much more than they ever had before, and we became intensely aware that our watches and cameras represented more money than most of the Zebaleen might earn in a year.

Although unfamiliar to most Americans, the Zebaleen of the Cairo Dump are hardly unique. Their counterparts live in almost every nation of the world. Such destitute people are especially numerous in the Third World, where poverty is not only more common than in North America, but also far more acute.

THE IMPORTANCE OF GLOBAL PERSPECTIVE

Why should we study unfamiliar parts of the world, especially in a course primarily concerned with North America? Chapter 1 ("The Sociological Perspective") explained that to understand ourselves we must recognize our place in American society. We are not isolated indi-viduals: our perceptions, our sense of ourselves, our entire lives are shaped by the many ways we relate to countless other Americans.

Taken one step further, the same logic applies to American society's relationship to the world. To under-stand our own society we must explore how our part of the world fits into the larger global order. Extending the sociological perspective in this way is especially im-portant today, as political changes sweep through Latin America, Eastern Europe, the Soviet Union, and South Africa, and rapid economic development reshapes many countries in Eastern Asia. All these global realignments affect the United States and the lives of every American.

This chapter focuses on how our world has grown increasingly interdependent. St. Augustine, an early leader of the Christian Church, once described the world as a book, noting that those who concentrate only on their own society read just a single page. With much of the contemporary world seized by political and eco-nomic change, looking beyond our own borders takes on greater importance than ever before.

THE THREE WORLDS

To gain a broader understanding of social inequality, then, we must look beyond the United States. As Chapter 10 ("Social Class in America") explained, American soci-ety is marked by clear social stratification. Yet, because the United States is among the richest nations in the world, the average American is very well off by world standards. Even most Americans living below our govern-ment's poverty line enjoy a much higher standard of living than the majority of people in the poorest nations on earth. We begin our study of global inequality by dividing the world's societies into three broad categories or "worlds."

First, however, a word of caution. There are roughly 185 nations on earth (the precise number changes frequently in response to political events). To place them all in only three overarching categories ignores striking differences in their ways of life. The societies in each category have rich and varied histories, speak dozens of languages, and encompass diverse peoples whose cul-tural distinctiveness serves as a source of pride. However, the three broad categories used in this chapter have long served to cluster societies together based on (1) their level of technological development and (2) their political and economic system.

The First World

The term **First World** refers to *industrial societies that have predominantly capitalist economies.* They are not called "first" because they are "better" or "more impor-tant" than other nations, but rather because the Industrial Revolution came first to these nations, beginning two centuries ago. Chapter 4 ("Society") explained that a society's productive capacity is increased one hundred-fold by industrialization. Thus, for example, in America today the economic activity surrounding the care of household pets (not to mention the computer or automo-

Japan represents the First World, in which industrial technology and economic expansion have produced material prosperity; the market is among the most powerful cultural forces as shown in this view of downtown Tokyo. The Soviet Union is the leading nation of the Second world; industrial development has been slower than in the First World, as socialist economies have performed sluggishly. Residents of Moscow, for example, have grown accustomed to waiting in long lines for their daily needs. Still, such nations have provided basic goods and services for their people in a remarkably equal fashion. Egypt represents the Third World; as this view of Cairo suggests, these nations have limited industrial development and rapidly increasing populations.

bile industries) exceeds the economic enterprise in all of Europe during the Middle Ages. Modern Americans, therefore, have a substantially higher standard of living than did Europeans several centuries ago.

Figure 11–1 identifies nations of the First World. Shown in blue, this region includes the nations of Western Europe such as the United Kingdom (made up of England, Scotland, Wales, and Northern Ireland). It was in southeastern England that industrialization began about 1775. Also part of the First World are the United States and Canada in North America, where the Industrial Revolution was under way around 1850. On the African continent, the advanced economic development of South Africa places this country (at least its *white minority*) in the First World. Also ranking in the First World is Japan, the most economically powerful nation in Asia. And, in the world region known as Oceania, the First World spans Australia and New Zealand.

Collectively, the First World covers roughly 25 percent of the land area of the earth, including parts of five continents mostly in the northern hemisphere. As of 1990, the population of the First World stood at about 700 million, just over 15 percent of the earth's people. By global standards, the First World is not densely populated.

Despite historic and cultural differences among First-World nations, they now share an industrial capacity that generates, on average, a high standard of living for their people. Of the entire world's income, most is enjoyed by the minority of humanity living in the First World.

The economies of First-World nations are predominantly capitalist. In capitalist economies, a market system (or "private enterprise") rather than government controls production. Because their economies are all market-driven, First-World nations have formed political and

Figure 11–1 The Three Worlds

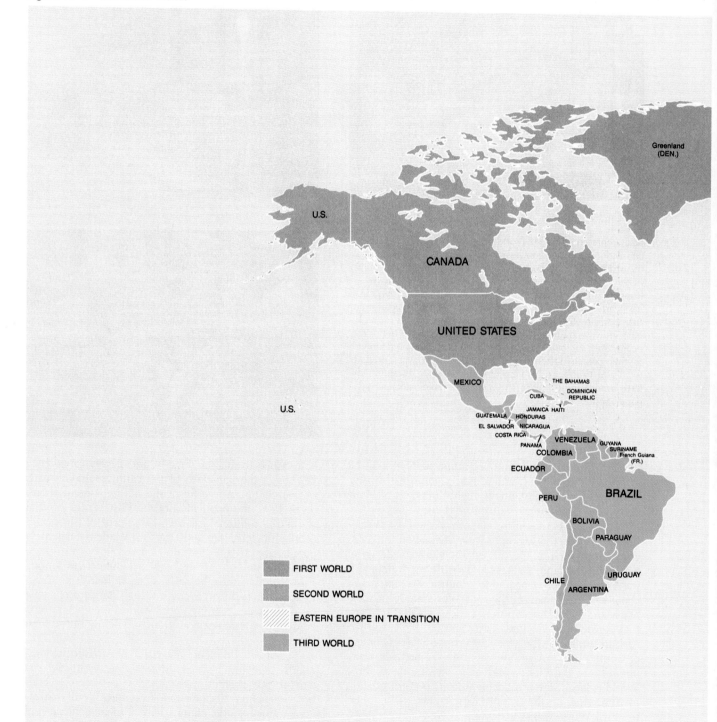

FIRST WORLD

SECOND WORLD

EASTERN EUROPE IN TRANSITION

THIRD WORLD

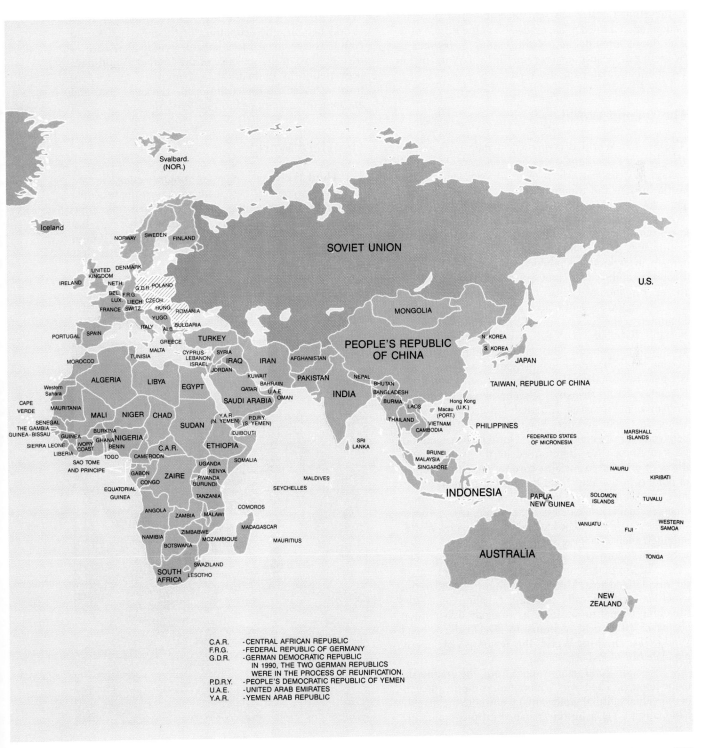

Svalbard.
(NOR.)

Iceland

NORWAY SWEDEN FINLAND

SOVIET UNION

U.S.

UNITED   DENMARK
KINGDOM
IRELAND   NETH.
BEL. F.R.G.
G.D.R. POLAND
LUX. LIECH. CZECH.
FRANCE SWITZ. HUNG.
YUGO. ROMANIA

MONGOLIA

N. KOREA
S. KOREA

PORTUGAL SPAIN
ITALY ALB. BULGARIA
GREECE
MALTA   TURKEY
CYPRUS SYRIA
LEBANON IRAQ   IRAN
ISRAEL
JORDAN

PEOPLE'S REPUBLIC
OF CHINA

JAPAN

MOROCCO
TUNISIA

KUWAIT
BAHRAIN
QATAR U.A.E. OMAN

AFGHANISTAN

TAIWAN, REPUBLIC OF CHINA

ALGERIA LIBYA EGYPT

PAKISTAN

NEPAL
BHUTAN
BANGLADESH
BURMA   LAOS

Hong Kong
Macau (U.K.)
(PORT.)

Western
Sahara

SAUDI ARABIA

INDIA

CAPE
VERDE   MAURITANIA

MALI NIGER CHAD

Y.A.R.
(N. YEMEN) P.D.R.Y.
(S. YEMEN)

THAILAND VIETNAM
CAMBODIA

PHILIPPINES

FEDERATED STATES
OF MICRONESIA

MARSHALL
ISLANDS

SENEGAL
THE GAMBIA
GUINEA-BISSAU GUINEA
BURKINA
GHANA NIGERIA
BENIN

SUDAN

DJIBOUTI

SRI
LANKA

SsIERRA LEONE
LIBERIA
IVORY
COAST
TOGO CAMEROON
C.A.R.

ETHIOPIA

BRUNEI
MALAYSIA
SINGAPORE

SAO TOME
AND PRINCIPE

SOMALIA

NAURU

KIRIBATI

GABON ZAIRE
CONGO

UGANDA
KENYA
RWANDA
BURUNDI

MALDIVES

EQUATORIAL
GUINEA

TANZANIA

SEYCHELLES

INDONESIA

PAPUA
NEW GUINEA

SOLOMON
ISLANDS

TUVALU

ANGOLA
ZAMBIA MALAWI

COMOROS

MADAGASCAR

VANUATU
FIJI

WESTERN
SAMOA

NAMIBIA
ZIMBABWE
MOZAMBIQUE
BOTSWANA

MAURITIUS

AUSTRALIA

TONGA

SWAZILAND
SOUTH
AFRICA LESOTHO

NEW
ZEALAND

C.A.R.   -CENTRAL AFRICAN REPUBLIC
F.R.G.   -FEDERAL REPUBLIC OF GERMANY
G.D.R.   -GERMAN DEMOCRATIC REPUBLIC
         IN 1990, THE TWO GERMAN REPUBLICS
         WERE IN THE PROCESS OF REUNIFICATION.
P.D.R.Y. -PEOPLE'S DEMOCRATIC REPUBLIC OF YEMEN
U.A.E.   -UNITED ARAB EMIRATES
Y.A.R.   -YEMEN ARAB REPUBLIC

economic alliances with one another. Since World War I, the United States has remained the most powerful nation (often termed a "superpower") in the First World. The dominant influence of the United States and its Western European allies has given the First-World region the shorthand name of "the West."

The Second World

The **Second World** is composed of *industrial societies that have predominantly socialist economies.* Industrialization took hold in much of this broad region of the world only in the twentieth century; this accounts, in part, for the lesser economic strength of the Second World in relation to the First World. Second-World nations have less powerful industrial capacities, and proportionately more of their people live in rural areas and remain in agricultural production. (Chapter 19, "The Economy and Work," provides a comparative look at the performance of capitalist and socialist economies.)

In Figure 11–1, the Second World appears in red. Dominating the Second World is the Union of Soviet Socialist Republics (U.S.S.R.), whose military might gives it "superpower" status. Since World War II, the Second World has also encompassed the nations of Eastern Europe including Poland, the German Democratic Republic (East Germany), Czechoslovakia, Hungary, Romania, and Bulgaria. Although not tied to the Soviet Union in recent decades, Yugoslavia and Albania also belong to the Second World. During 1989, most of Eastern Europe was transformed by the popular overthrow of established socialist governments, the opening of borders to the West, and the call for more Western-style market systems. The future of such momentous change remains unclear. For the purposes of our discussion, these nations will be included in the Second World, although their changing status is reflected by a striped pattern in Figure 11–1.

The Second World spans roughly 15 percent of the world's land area. Most of it lies in the Soviet Union, which is geographically the largest nation on earth, stretching from Europe to Asia. Roughly 500 million people or 10 percent of humanity live in the Second World. Like the First World, this region is not densely populated by global standards.

Second-World nations differ from one another in many respects. The Soviet Union itself comprises dozens of individual cultural groups, many of whom are fiercely nationalistic. Yet a historic reliance on predominantly

socialist economies has joined the nations of the Second World together. Instead of the market systems of First-World nations, the economies of these Second-World countries are directed to a large degree by their governments. Most of the societies of the Second World have been politically unified—at least until recent developments—under the leadership of the Soviet Union, and are sometimes described as the "Eastern Bloc."

The Third World

The **Third World** encompasses *primarily agrarian societies that are poor.* In these societies, a majority of people live in rural areas, engage in farming, and follow the traditions of their ancestors. Industrial technology has had only a limited impact here, mostly in the cities of the Third World. Economically, these societies are less

When natural disasters strike rich nations, property loss is great but loss of life is low; in poor societies, the converse is true. In 1985, a flood and mudslide wiped out the poor village of Armero in Colombia, killing more than 10,000 people.

productive than the rest of the world. This pattern holds true even though some Third-World countries—notably the oil-rich nations of the Middle East—have an extremely high average standard of living that reflects the great wealth of *some* of their people.

Figure 11–1 indicates that the Third World, shown in green, encompasses *most* of the globe. On the southern border of the United States lies the Third-World nation of Mexico, below which is all of Central America. The nations of South America also belong to the Third World. Moving across the Atlantic Ocean, the continent of Africa (except for South Africa) falls into the Third World as well. This category also includes the Middle East except Israel and all of Asia except Japan.

The Third World represents about 60 percent of the earth's land area including most of the nations near and below the equator. More significantly, about 75 percent of the world's 5.2 billion people live in a country of the Third World. Because of its large and rapidly increasing population, its low economic productivity, and unfavorable economic relations with rich societies, the Third World faces stunning poverty on a massive scale. Hunger, unsafe housing, high rates of disease, widespread illiteracy, and limited life choices all plague the Third World.

Despite the poverty they share, Third-World societies do not have an economic system in common. Some poor countries, such as the People's Republic of China (with 1.1 billion people, the world's most populous nation), have predominantly socialist economic systems. Other nations, like India and Egypt, blend elements of socialist and capitalist economies. Still others, including Brazil and much of Latin America, are primarily capitalist in nature. We shall explore some of the consequences of the type of economic system a country adopts later in this chapter, as well as in later chapters dealing with politics and economics. For now, our point is simply that all Third-World societies share a common plight: devastating poverty.

This identification of the "three worlds" is the foundation for understanding the problem of global inequality. For people living in an affluent nation such as the United States, the scope of the problem may be difficult to grasp. Televised scenes of famine in Ethiopia, familiar during the mid-1980s, gave many Americans a shocking look at the absolute poverty that makes daily living a life-and-death struggle in much of the world today. We now explore how poverty shapes the everyday lives of hundreds of millions of people throughout the Third World.

THIRD-WORLD POVERTY

Poverty always means struggle. Throughout the Third World, however, poverty typically involves a far greater magnitude of hardship than poverty in American society (see Chapter 10, "Social Class in America"). This does not mean that poverty in the United States is a minor issue. Especially in a rich society, the lack of food, housing, and health care for tens of millions of people—a

Poverty in the Third World falls hardest upon children, a truth that is strikingly portrayed by David Alfaro Siqueiros in his painting, *Echo of a Scream*.

David Alfaro Siqueiros, *Echo of a Scream*. 1937. Duco on wood, 48 x 36″. Collection, The Museum of Modern Art, New York. Gift of M. M. Warburg.

disproportionate percentage of them children—amounts to a national tragedy. Yet as we expand our analysis of social stratification to the entire world, two important differences become clear: poverty in the Third World is *more severe* and *more extensive* than in the United States.

The Severity of Poverty

Poverty in the Third World is more severe than it is in rich societies such as the United States. The data in Table 11–1 suggest why. The first column of figures shows the gross national product (GNP) of the nations listed (the total value of all the goods and services produced in a given year by everyone in that country). Industrial societies typically have a high gross national product simply because industrial technology makes them extremely productive. A large, First-World nation like the United States had a 1990 GNP of over $4 trillion; the GNP of the Soviet Union, a large Second-World country, stood at about $2 trillion. The rest of the table shows that Third-World countries around the globe have far lower GNPs. With little access to industrial technology, in short, these nations are less productive.

What does this lack of productivity mean for individuals? Consider the second column of figures in Table 11–1. Here we see "per-person income," calculated by dividing the country's total income by the total population. The figures for First-World nations are quite high—above $15,000 for the United States, for example. Income levels in Second-World societies are significantly lower than those in the First World. But a more dramatic difference appears when we examine the figures for Third-World countries. Here, per-person income levels are generally less than $2,000 (in many cases, below $1,000) a year. At approximately $150, the per-capita income in India amounts to only about 1 percent of that found in the United States. The typical American earns in several days what the typical person in India works all year to make.[2]

We can also visualize the scope of global inequality in Figure 11–2. This figure shows the relative share of world income earned in each of the three "worlds."

---

[2] The per-person income figures for the poorest of the world's societies are understated to some degree because a significant amount of income in the form of traded products (acquired through barter) is not included in formal accountings. But even if the figures were doubled to overcome this bias, per-capita income of Third-World countries would remain well below that of rich nations.

Table 11–1   INCOME AND WEALTH IN WORLD PERSPECTIVE

Country	Gross National Product ($ billion)	Per-Person Income ($)
First World		
United States	4,200	15,400
Canada	367	13,100
United Kingdom	453	8,300
West Germany	898	11,000
Japan	1,900	10,400
Second World		
Soviet Union	2,000	7,300
Poland	240	6,100
Hungary	80	7,300
East Germany	93	9,800
Czechoslovakia	136	8,300
Third World		
Latin America		
Mexico	126	2,100
Argentina	65	2,300
El Salvador	4	700
Bolivia	4	550
Colombia	31	1,100
Nicaragua	3	850
Africa/Middle East		
Cameroon	8	800
Egypt	30	700
Nigeria	53	800
Burkina Faso	1	150
Zaire	5	150
Saudi Arabia	98	11,500
Lebanon	3	1,150
Iran	75	1,700
Asia		
P.R. of China	270	250
Taiwan	73	3,000
South Korea	90	2,200
Thailand	40	800
India	194	150
Pakistan	32	350
Bangladesh	15	100

Note: This table shows gross national product (GNP) and yearly per-person income in U.S. dollars for various nations. Available data are not always precisely comparable, but provide a generally accurate pattern. Most data are for the mid-1980s.

SOURCE: U.S. Arms Control and Disarmament Agency, *World Military Expenditures and Arms Transfers 1986* (Washington, DC: U.S. Government Printing Office, 1987); also *World Almanac and Book of Facts 1989* (New York: Pharos Books, 1988).

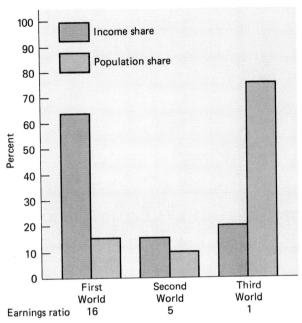

Figure 11–2 The Relative Share of Global Income by World Region

Clearly, the people of the First World are most advantaged: while representing only 15 percent of the world's population, they enjoy about two-thirds of the world's income. The people of the Second World are less well off, but they, too, claim a disproportionately large share of global income. In the Third World, three-fourths of humanity receive only about 20 percent of all income. For every dollar earned by a Third-World worker, five dollars go to a worker in the Second World. Even more advantaged is the typical member of a First-World society, who makes about sixteen dollars.

Beyond these general patterns of global inequality, every society also has significant *internal* social stratification. This means that social differences between affluent Americans and disadvantaged Third-World people, such as the Zebaleen described in the chapter opening, are especially striking. As we shall see shortly, women of both rich and poor societies also have significantly lower income levels than men.

Relative versus Absolute Poverty

A distinction made in the last chapter has an important application to global inequality. In rich societies, most discussions of poverty focus on *relative poverty*, the lack of resources some have in comparison to others who have more. By definition, relative poverty exists in every society, even in the First World. But just as important—especially in a global context—is the concept of *absolute poverty*, or a lack of resources that is life threatening. Most commonly, absolute poverty means lacking the minimum level of nutrition necessary for health.

In a rich society like the United States, poverty is often viewed in relative terms. Some degree of absolute poverty does exist, however; inadequate nutrition and even starvation are unfortunate realities in America. Yet such immediately life-threatening poverty strikes only a small proportion of the population. By contrast, societies of the Third World face a severe problem of absolute poverty, involving one-fifth of the Third World's population—some 800 million people.

The Extent of Poverty

Poverty in the Third World is more extensive than it is in the United States. As explained in Chapter 10 ("Social Class in America"), about 15 percent of the American population is officially classified as poor. In the societies of the Third World, however, *most* people live no better than the American poor, and at any given time, about 20 percent of the people face absolute poverty. In some parts of the world (such as East Asia), the extent of absolute poverty is not so great; in other regions (rural areas in Central America and Africa, for example), half the population may lack the minimum level of nutrition needed to sustain life. In the world as a whole, 100 million people have no form of shelter and approximately 1 billion people do not eat enough to allow them to work regularly. Of these, 800 million are at risk for their lives (Sivard, 1987; Helmuth, 1989).

Simply stated, these statistics mean that people are dying, every minute of every day, from lack of basic nutrition. In the ten minutes it takes to read through this section of the chapter, about three hundred people in the world will die of starvation. This amounts to more than 40,000 people a day, or 15 million people each year. Even more than in the United States, the burden of poverty in the Third World falls on children. In the entire Third World, about one child in four dies before reaching the age of five.

Two further comparisons may make these statistics more meaningful. First, at the end of World War II, the United States virtually obliterated the Japanese city of Hiroshima with an atomic bomb. The global loss of life from starvation *every three days* equals the Hiroshima

American society enjoys a large share of the world's wealth; even so, the poorest of Americans have a standard of living that is little better than that of the poor found throughout the Third World. The plight of some children growing up in New York's Harlem (right) is remarkably similar to that of children in much of Nicaragua.

death toll. Second, the number of people who have died in all the wars, revolutions, and murders during the last 150 years roughly equals the number of people who died from hunger in the last *five* years (Burch, 1983). World hunger must be considered as one of the most serious problems facing humanity today.

Third-World Women: Work and Poverty

As in the United States, the burden of poverty in the Third World falls more heavily on women than on men. Even more than in rich societies, in the Third World women are disproportionately the poorest of the poor.

In every society, women have primary responsibility for childrearing and maintaining the household. Because their families need money to survive, women are also increasingly involved in work to generate added family income. In rural areas throughout the Third World, women commonly work almost twelve hours a day, while the workday for men is typically about eight hours (House of Representatives, 1988:43).

At present, neither officials nor sociologists have devised any accurate way to measure work outside the paid labor force. Much of women's work—cleaning and repairing the home, gathering firewood, traveling to and from the market, tending to the needs of children, and preparing meals for the family—remains "invisible" to

those who monitor the labor force. And what is "invisible" is also likely to be unpaid. In comparison to rich societies, more of women's work in the Third World is not paid, making the economic position of women correspondingly weaker.

Third-World women who are paid for their work are also at a greater disadvantage than their counterparts in rich societies. As Chapter 13 ("Sex and Gender") details, in the United States and the rest of the industrialized world, women typically receive less income for paid work than men. In the largely agrarian societies of the Third World, where traditional subordination of women to men is more pronounced, the differential in salary between the two sexes is even greater. In addition, Third-World women have much less access to education than men, a pattern that is disappearing in many industrial societies (United Nations, 1988). Lacking education, women have far fewer choices about their lives.

Finally, the United Nations estimates that roughly 90 percent of land in the Third World is formally owned by males (in rich societies, the proportion is somewhat lower). In reality, as wives and mothers, women exert considerable control over property that formally belongs to males. Nevertheless, strong traditions of family and the support of law give men ultimate control of the land, which is the most valuable resource in agrarian societies.

In sum, poverty in Third-World nations is both

Life for both men and women throughout the Third World is typically a matter of continual labor simply to meet basic needs. Because social inequality between the sexes is pronounced in agrarian societies, the relative disadvantages faced by women are greater than in industrial societies.

severe and extensive. In Third-World societies, however, the burden of poverty is not shared equally; women are generally among the most disadvantaged.

Correlates of Third-World Poverty

What accounts for the massive and acute poverty in the Third World? Much of the rest of this chapter seeks to weave various facts related to poverty into explanations.

1. **Technology.** The Third World is largely agrarian, lacking the productive capacity of industrial technology. Specifically, energy is supplied by the muscles of humans and other animals rather than by steam, nuclear reactors, or other industrial energy sources capable of powering large machinery. The focus in agrarian societies on farming, rather than more specialized activities, also limits the development of human skills and abilities.

2. **Population growth.** As Chapter 21 ("Population and Urbanization") explains in detail, Third-World societies have the highest birth rates in the world. Despite high death rates from poverty, the populations of many poor societies of Africa, for example, are doubling every twenty-five years. In such societies, more than half the people are teenagers or younger, just entering their childbearing years.

Population growth in the future, therefore, is inevitable. Even a strong, industrial economy cannot absorb overwhelming surges in population. So as new jobs are created and the society's productive capacity expands, a rapidly growing population will thwart economic progress. Economic growth, then, produces no real increase in standard of living for most of the population.

3. **Cultural patterns.** Societies that have yet to experience widespread industrialization usually place great value on tradition. From generation to generation, families and neighborhood groups pass down folkways and mores virtually unchanged. Adhering to their traditions, such people tend to resist innovations—even those that promise a richer, more comfortable material life.

   Traditionalism in poor societies often means accepting one's life, although it may be poor, in order to maintain family vitality and cultural heritage. The box focuses on India, where poor people respond to their poverty differently than poor people in the United States. Westerners generally find this difference both striking and puzzling.

4. **Social stratification.** Exacerbating global poverty, Third-World societies typically distribute their limited resources very unequally within the population. Chapter 9 ("Social Stratification") explained

India: A Different Kind of Poverty

Most Americans know that India is one of the poorest societies of the world: Table 11–1 showed per-person income in India to be only $150 a year. One in three of the world's hungry lives in this vast society.

Few Americans observe (and fewer still experience) the reality of poverty in this Asian nation. There are rich people in India, just as everywhere else, but most of this nation's 750 million people live in conditions far worse than Americans who are labeled "poor." An American's first experience of Indian life is sobering and sometimes shocking; in time, the outsider also sees that, in India, people *experience* poverty differently as well.

Arriving in Madras, one of India's largest cities, a visitor immediately sees that life is not the same as in the United States. The air reeks of human sewage, which makes most of the region's water unsafe to drink. The sights and sounds, too, are strange and intense—motorbikes, trucks, carts pulled by oxen, and waves of people choke the streets. Lining the roads, vendors sitting on burlap cloth hawk fruits, vegetables, and prepared foods. And, seemingly oblivious to the urban chaos sur-

Third World societies may be poor, but their traditions strengthen families. Thus poverty is endured amidst the support of kinship, which contrasts to the often isolating poverty of the United States.

---

that social inequality is generally more pronounced in agrarian societies, where land is a vital resource, than in industrial societies. In the farming regions of Bangladesh in Central Asia, for example, just 10 percent of all landowners own more than half the land, while almost half of all farming families have almost no land of their own (Hartmann & Boyce, 1982). According to another estimate, the richest 10 percent of landowners in Central America control more than three-fourths of the land in those poor societies (Barry, 1987). Such concentration of land and wealth has prompted widespread demands for land reform in many agrarian societies, such as the Philippines.

5. **Global power relationships.** A final cause of global poverty lies in the relationships among the nations of the world. The wealth of First-World nations has grown because of the resources of Third-World nations. Historically, this is due to **colonialism,** *the process by which some nations enrich themselves through political and economic control of other na-*

tions. The nations of Western Europe colonized and maintained control over much of Latin America for more than 300 years; much of Africa endured a century of colonization; parts of Asia were also colonized for long periods. This global exploitation propelled some nations to *develop* economically while others remained *underdeveloped*.

During the nineteenth and twentieth centuries, most colonies gained their political independence; only a small number of formal colonies remain today. As we shall see, however, colonialism has assumed a new guise in **neocolonialism** ("neo" comes from Greek, meaning "new"), *a new form of economic exploitation that does not involve formal political control.* Charges of neocolonialism center on the operation of **multinational corporations** (or *transnational corporations*), *large corporations whose operations span many different nations.* As Chapter 19 ("The Economy and Work") explains, multinational corporations historically developed through rapid corporate growth and rounding them, people work, talk, defecate, and sleep in the streets where they live. The cities of India contain literally millions of homeless people.

Madras is also dotted by more than a thousand shanty settlements, where about half a million people live in shelters more primitive than most Americans could imagine. Huts are constructed of branches, leaves, and discarded material; they offer little privacy and no refrigeration, running water, or bathrooms.

The American visitor approaches a shanty community with a measure of unease, since the poorest sections of inner cities in the United States abound with frustration and, often-times, outright violence. But here,

too, India offers a sharp contrast. No one sleeps in doorways menacing passersby, no angry young men hang out at the corner, no drugs pervade the area, and there is surprisingly little danger. Instead, the outsider finds strong families—children, parents, and sometimes elderly people—who extend a smile and a welcome. In traditional societies like India, and especially among those who come to the city from rural villages, ways of life change little in generations. Moreover, the lives of traditional Indians are shaped by *dharma*—the Hindu concept of duty and destiny—that encourages people to accept their fate, whatever it may be. Mother Teresa, who has won praise for her work among the poorest of India's

people, goes to the heart of the cultural differences: "Americans have angry poverty; in India, there is worse poverty, but it is a happy poverty."

No one who lives on the edge of survival can be called truly "happy." The deadly horror of poverty in India, however, is eased by the strength of families and traditional communities, as well as a world view that encourages each person to accept whatever society offers. As a result, the American visitor comes away from the first encounter with Indian poverty in confusion: "How can people be so poor, and yet apparently content, vibrant, and so *alive?*"

SOURCE: Based on the author's research in Madras, India, November, 1988.

mergers. These corporations now wield such tremendous economic power that corporate decision makers can—and often do—influence the political systems in countries where they do business.

GLOBAL INEQUALITY: THEORETICAL ANALYSIS

There are two major explanations for the unequal distribution of the world's wealth and power—modernization theory and dependency theory. Each suggests not only why so many of the world's people are poor, but why we as North Americans enjoy such comparative advantages.

The two explanations do overlap to some extent. Both acknowledge that enormous inequality exists on our planet, and that some changes are required to guarantee the future security of humanity, rich and poor alike.

Yet, by emphasizing different factors, they reach differing conclusions about where responsibility lies for global poverty.

Modernization Theory

Modernization theory maintains that *global inequality reflects differing levels of technological development among societies.* Modernization theory evolved in the 1950s, when the United States began to fear that much of the Third World was becoming hostile to American interests. At that time, socialist nations of the Second World were arguing that Third-World countries could not make economic progress under the influence of the capitalist First World. The American response was a broad defense of the First World that has shaped official foreign policy toward poor nations ever since.[3]

_____

[3] The following discussion of modernization theory draws primarily on Rostow (1978), Bauer (1981), and Berger (1986).

In 1844, when an unknown artist produced this painting, hard and dangerous work was a fact of childhood in England. Initially, the Industrial Revolution did little to improve the lives of children, who had historically labored as adults did. Gradually, however, as machinery reduced the need for labor, the proper role of children was transformed so that they left mines and factories for schools.

Historical Perspective

According to modernization theory, as recently as several centuries ago, the *entire world* was poor. Because poverty was the norm throughout human history, then, *affluence*—not poverty—demands an explanation.

Affluence came within reach of a small part of humanity in the late Middle Ages as economic activity expanded in Western Europe. Initially, this economic growth came in the form of trade within cities. By the beginning of the sixteenth century, exploration of other parts of the world identified a vast new commercial potential. Then, the Industrial Revolution in the eighteenth and nineteenth centuries transformed Western Europe and, soon after, North America. Industrial technology and the innovations of countless entrepreneurs created new wealth on a grand scale. At the outset of the Industrial Revolution, the allocation of this new wealth was highly unequal. Yet industrial technology was so productive that gradually the standard of living of even the poorest people began to rise. The specter of absolute poverty, which had cast a menacing shadow over humanity for its entire history, was finally being routed.

Since then, the standard of living in the region where the Industrial Revolution first began has continued to improve. Today, the benefits of industrialization are enjoyed primarily in the First World and, to a lesser extent, in the Second World. Without this industrial technology, the Third World maintains the same low productivity it has had throughout history.

The Importance of Culture

Why didn't people the world over share in the Industrial Revolution so that they, too, could enjoy material plenty? Drawing on Max Weber's analysis of world religions, especially the connection between Protestantism and capitalism (explored in Chapter 4, "Society"), modernization theory holds that new technology is likely to be exploited only in a *cultural environment* that emphasizes the benefits of innovation and greater productivity.

Modernization theory suggests, therefore, that the greatest barrier to economic development is *traditionalism*. In small societies based on strong family systems, ancient ways of life provide powerful guides to understanding the present and shaping the future. Predictably, this creates a form of "cultural inertia" that keeps societies from adopting technological advances that would improve their material standard of living. For example, Western innovations and technological advances have encountered fierce resistance in Iran because they threaten traditional Islamic family relationships, customs, and religious beliefs.

In contrast, Max Weber argued, toward the end of the Middle Ages a distinctive cultural environment that favored change developed in Western Europe. This progress-oriented culture strongly characterized societies where the Protestant Reformation had transformed traditional Catholicism. Material affluence, which the Catholic Church had regarded with suspicion, became a personal virtue, and individualism steadily eroded the traditional emphasis on kinship and community. Taken together, these changing cultural patterns nurtured the Industrial Revolution, which allowed one segment of humanity to prosper.

Rostow's Stages of Modernization

Modernization theory does not condemn the poor regions of the globe to a future as poor as their past. Due to technological advances, all societies are gradually converging on one general form: the industrial model. According to W. W. Rostow (1978), the process of modernization follows four general stages.

1. **Traditional stage.** In this stage, poor societies rely on strong traditions, and their cultures resist technological innovation. People in traditional societies cannot easily conceive of how life could be different. Such societies place great significance on family and community, granting little exercise of individual freedom of the sort that initiates change. Life may be spiritually rich, therefore, but lacking in material abundance.

   A century ago, much of the world was in this initial stage of economic development. Today, according to modernization theory, the extreme poverty of societies like Bangladesh in Central Asia and Burkina Faso in Central Africa stems from their still being at the traditional, or first, stage of development.

2. **Take-off stage.** As traditions begin to weaken, the economy slowly grows. A limited market economy takes shape; people produce not only for their own consumption but in order to engage in profitable trade with others. Paralleling these developments is a greater achievement orientation, which often comes at the expense of family ties and longstanding norms and values.

   Great Britain reached this stage by about 1800, as the United States did soon afterward.

Many of the nations of the Third World have made economic gains in recent decades, and are now at this stage. Thailand in Eastern Asia is a prime example.

Rostow argues that economic "take-off" in Third-World societies depends on progressive influences—including foreign aid, introduction of advanced technology and investment capital, and schooling abroad—that only rich nations can provide.

3. **Drive to technological maturity.** At this stage, a society has become committed to the idea of an improved standard of living. An active, diversified economy thrives because the population is eager to enjoy the benefits of industrial technology. At the same time, however, people begin to recognize that industrialization is eroding traditional life in families and local communities. Great Britain reached this point by about 1840, the United States by about 1860. Today, Mexico, India, and the People's Republic of China are among the nations driving to technological maturity.

   At this stage of economic development, change comes quickly. On the one hand, absolute poverty is greatly reduced. On the other hand, cities swell to great size, occupational specialization makes relationships less personal, and heightened individualism often sparks movements pressing for greater political rights. Societies at this level of development also recognize the need to educate all their people, and to provide advanced training for some. As adherence to tradition declines with industrialization, women tend to assume a social position more equal to that of men. Initially, however, the process of development subjects women to new and unanticipated stresses, as the box on page 296 explains.

4. **High mass consumption.** Economic development through industrial technology is designed to create a higher standard of living. This becomes possible, Rostow argues, as mass production of goods allows for mass consumption. The United States reached this stage of development by the beginning of the twentieth century. Other First-World societies were not far behind. For example, Japan became a military power early in this century. After recovering from the destruction of World War II, the Japanese enjoyed high mass consumption, and Japan now rivals the United States as an economic power. The Soviet Union was approaching this stage by

Modernization and Women: What Are the Drawbacks?

As we noted previously, gender inequality is most pronounced in the poorest societies. For this reason, we would assume that economic development advances the interests of women. Modernization weakens traditional patterns of male domination and gives women more opportunities to work outside the home. Women also benefit from more formal education and from information about and access to birth control.

Yet economic development also has drawbacks for women, even as their standard of living rises. Based on research in a poor, rural district of Bangladesh, Sultana Alam (1985) identified several serious problems women face as a result of modernization.

First, economic opportunity in the cities often draws men from rural areas to urban centers in search of work, leaving women and children to fend for themselves. Men may also sell their land and abandon women, who are left with nothing but their children.

Second, the eroding strength of the family and neighborhood leaves women who are deserted in this way with few sources of economic assistance. The same holds true for women who become single through divorce or the death of a spouse. In the past, Alam suggests, a Bangladeshi woman's family or neighbors would readily take her in if she found herself alone. Today, as Bangladesh struggles to advance economically,

this is less common, producing a growing number of female-headed poor households. A greater spirit of individualism makes each person more likely to "look out only for 'number one.'" Instead of greater autonomy for women, Alam argues, this attitude reflects a loss of women's social standing.

Third, economic development often diminishes women's kinship value—as wives, sisters, and mothers—while focusing on their significance as objects of sexual attention. The traditions of Bangladesh, like those of other poor societies, define women primarily through their family roles. Today, especially under the influence of the Western mass media, the emphasis on sexuality has placed women at a decided disadvantage. More and more men (who are usually much older than their wives) are deserting aging spouses for younger, more physically attractive women.

Modernization, then, does not affect men and women in the same ways. As modern cultural patterns begin to take hold and poverty is gradually eliminated from traditional societies, men reap more benefits than women. In the long run, the evidence suggests that modernization does make the sexes more equal. In the short run, however, the economic position of many women declines, and women are also forced to contend with new problems that were virtually unknown in traditional societies.

One consequence of modernization in Third World societies might be termed "the sexualization of women." Rather then being defined in terms of traditional kinship roles, women are increasingly valued for their sexual attractiveness. Perhaps significantly, many of the growing number of prostitutes in large Third World cities have discarded traditional dress for Western styles of clothing.

SOURCE: Based on Sultana Alam, "Women and Poverty in Bangladesh," *Women's Studies International Forum*, Vol. 8, No. 4 (1985), pp. 361–371; also Barbara Mink, "How Modernization Affects Women," *Cornell Alumni News*, Vol. III, No. 3 (April 1989):10–11.

about 1950, but its sluggish economy since then still limits the availability of many goods and services. Fast approaching this level of economic development are some of the most prosperous East Asian societies of the Third World: South Korea, Taiwan, Hong Kong, and Singapore.

The Role of Rich Nations

Rich nations of the First World play an important role in global economic development, according to modernization theory. This line of thinking holds that First-World societies are not the *cause* of the abject poverty that afflicts much of humanity. Rather, modernization theory claims that rich societies form part of the *solution* to global inequality in the following respects:

1. **Assisting in population control.** A major barrier to overcoming poverty in Third-World societies is burgeoning population. As we have already noted, population growth is greatest in the poorest societies of the world and can easily overtake economic advances. First-World nations can help curb global population by exporting various types of birth control technology and promoting their use. Once economic development is under way, birth rates should decline as they have in industrialized societies.

2. **Increasing food production.** Traditional food production is relatively inefficient. Modernization theory suggests that "high-tech" farming methods, exported from rich societies to poor nations, can significantly raise agricultural yields. Such techniques—collectively referred to as the "*Green Revolution*"—involve the use of new hybrid seeds, modern irrigation methods, chemical fertilizers, and pesticides for insect control.

3. **Introducing industrial technology.** Rich nations can accelerate the economic growth of poor societies by introducing industrial technology to boost productivity. The transfer of industrial technology is one application of the concept of cultural diffusion, described in Chapter 3 ("Culture"). Over the long term, this process transforms the labor force of poor countries from lower-skill, agricultural workers to higher-skill industrial workers, paving the way for a higher standard of living.

4. **Instituting programs of foreign aid.** One vital way rich nations can address the problem of global poverty is through foreign aid. Financial assistance, in the form of investment capital, allows poor societies to reach the "take-off" stage. When developing countries use foreign aid to purchase high technology—in the form of fertilizers and irrigation projects—they raise agricultural productivity. Similarly, building power-generating plants and factories greatly improves industrial productivity.

Critical evaluation. Modernization theory has influential adherents among social scientists (Parsons, 1966; W. Moore, 1977, 1979; Bauer, 1981; Berger, 1986). By identifying how industrialization affects other dimensions of social life, it has made key contributions to our understanding of what industrialization means to a society. This approach has also shaped the foreign policy of the United States and other First-World nations. Modernization theorists cite a number of poor societies that have made impressive strides with the assistance of rich countries. For instance, the Asian nations of South Korea, Taiwan, the former British colony of Singapore, and the current British colony of Hong Kong each receive extensive First-World assistance, and each has shown significant economic development. Similarly, concerted efforts to modernize by nations like Turkey have greatly improved national living standards.

From the outset, however, modernization theory has come under fire from nations of the Second World as a thinly veiled defense of capitalism. By the 1960s, a growing number of critics in First-World societies also detected major flaws in this approach. Perhaps the most serious failing, according to critics, is that modernization theory has fallen short of its own standards of success. Instead of making the industrial model widely accessible so Third-World countries could reach the "take-off" stage, only limited modernization has occurred. As a result, global inequality remains as striking as ever.

Second, critics maintain, modernization theory tends to ignore historical facts that thwart development in the Third World today. Modernization theory holds that the opportunities for growth available to rich nations several centuries ago are still available to the Third World. (Indeed, according to this theory, opportunities today are even *greater*, since rich nations can offer assistance to the Third World.) However, as the rest of this chapter explains, many critics claim that political and economic barriers to modernization have emerged in the two centuries since Europe's Industrial Revolution; these almost ensure the perpetuation of global poverty. In essence, critics argue, the First World industrialized from a position of global *strength*; the Third World cannot be expected to modernize from a position of global *weakness*.

Third, by minimizing the connections between rich and poor societies, modernization theory offers little insight into how global development continues to affect *rich* societies. For example, many traditional American industries, such as steel and auto production, have declined in large measure because of the growth of these industries abroad, notably in Japan and South Korea. As a result, low-paid service work is replacing high-paid factory work, as explained in the last chapter.

Fourth, critics contend that by holding up the First World as the standard by which the rest of humanity should be judged, modernization theory betrays an ethnocentric bias. As Chapter 23 ("Social Change and Modernity") explains, "progress" is reducing the cultural diversity of our world, promoting a materialistic, Western way of life around the globe.

Fifth, and finally, modernization theory draws criticism for suggesting that the causes of global poverty lie almost entirely in the poor societies themselves. Instead of "blaming the victims" for their own plight, critics argue that an analysis of global inequality must focus as much attention on the behavior of *rich* nations as that of poor nations (Wiarda, 1987).

From all these concerns has emerged a second major approach to understanding global inequality: dependency theory.

Dependency Theory

Dependency theory maintains that *global poverty historically stems from the exploitation of poor societies by rich societies.* Dependency theory offers a dramatically different analysis of global inequality than modernization theory, placing primary responsibility for global poverty on rich nations. Dependency theory holds that rich societies have impoverished the Third World by making poor nations *dependent* on richer ones. This destructive process continues today, but its roots extend back several centuries.

Historical Perspective

Before the Industrial Revolution, there was little of the affluence present in some of the world today. Dependency theory argues, however, that most of the people living in what we now call the Third World were actually better off economically in the past than they are today. In the words of André Gunder Frank, a noted proponent of this approach, the development of rich societies resulted in the *underdevelopment* of poor societies:

> Underdevelopment is not just the lack of development. Before there was development there was no underdevelopment. . . . Development and underdevelopment are . . . related through the common historical process that they have shared during the past several centuries. . . . (1975:1)

Dependency theory hinges on the crucial insight that the economic positions of the rich and poor nations of the globe are linked: they cannot be correctly understood in isolation from each other. Modernization theory, its critics argue, errs by suggesting that poor societies are lagging behind rich ones on a single "path of progress." According to dependency theory, the increasing prosperity of the First World has come largely *at the expense of* the Third World. In short, some nations have become rich because others have become poor. This complex process, which began centuries ago with the onset of global commerce, continues in much of the world today.

The Importance of Colonialism

Some five hundred years ago, many early European explorers set out uncertain that anything at all lay beyond the seas; some feared that ships sailing toward the horizon would fall off the earth. Instead, explorations of the "New World" of North America to the west, the massive continent of Africa to the south, and Asia to the east yielded vast new wealth.

The economic fortunes of the First World began to rise in the late fifteenth century as much of the Third World fell under the domination of European governments. Spain and Portugal colonized nearly all of Latin America. With colonies around the world by the beginning of the twentieth century, Great Britain boasted that "The sun never sets on the British Empire." The United States, itself originally a British colony, later gained control of several other countries, including the Virgin Islands, Haiti, Puerto Rico, and part of Cuba in the western hemisphere, and Guam and the Philippines in Asia.

Colonialism no longer holds sway in the world. Most Latin American nations achieved political independence during the first half of the nineteenth century, and most African and Asian colonies gained their freedom during this century. However, according to dependency theory, *political* liberation has not meant *economic* autonomy. Far from it: poor societies of the Third World maintain economic relationships with rich nations that

According to dependency theory, the poverty of much of the world was created through centuries of unfavorable economic relations. During the so-called "Age of Exploration" beginning in the late 15th century, European societies dispatched expeditions that systematically plundered other societies, often killing many people in the process. As the conquerors reduced these societies to European colonies, an enduring global pattern was established: the First World began to prosper, while the Third World fell into a state of economic decline and dependency.

mirror the colonial pattern. This neocolonialism is fueled by a capitalist world economy.

Wallerstein's Capitalist World Economy

Immanuel Wallerstein (1974, 1979, 1983, 1984) developed a model of the *"capitalist world economy"* to explain the origins of contemporary global inequality.[4] Wallerstein's term *world economy* suggests that interacting national economies form a global economic system. According to his model, the global economic system has expanded over the last five hundred years beyond the control of the traditional political units we call nations. The dominant character of this global system is capitalism.

In this model, the nations of the First World stand at the *core* of the world economy. Colonialism originally established this core by funneling raw materials to Western Europe from the rest of the world; these raw materials fueled the Industrial Revolution. Today, most multinational corporations that operate profitably around the globe are headquartered in the core nations of North America and Western Europe. By contrast, the Third World encompasses countries at the *periphery* of the world economy. These poor countries were drawn into the world economy by colonial exploitation, and they continue to support the industrial base of the First World today. The three-fourths of the world's population who live in poor societies provide an enormous market for products of First World societies; their labor also comes at a low cost, impossible to match in the First World.

According to this approach, the world economy benefits the First World (in terms of profits) and harms the Third World (by perpetuating poverty). The world economy thus fosters a state of dependency in which poor nations remain under the control of rich ones. This dependency is caused primarily by the following three factors:

1. **Narrow, export-oriented economies.** Unlike those of core nations, the economies of Third-World countries are not diversified. Historically, colonial powers have forced local farmers to stop growing a variety of traditional crops for local consumption in favor of producing a small number of products

---

[4] While based largely on Wallerstein's ideas, this section also draws on the work of Frank (1980, 1981), Delacroix & Ragin (1981), and Bergesen (1983).

for export. In some cases, traditional farmers have lost their land entirely, becoming low-paid laborers in foreign-owned industries. Such colonial economies export only a few products—mostly raw materials. Coffee and fruits from Latin American countries, oil from Nigeria, hardwoods from the Philippines, and palm oil from Malaysia are some of the key products central to the economies of poor nations. Multinational corporations maintain this pattern today as they purchase raw materials cheaply in poor societies and process them profitably in core societies. This prevents Third-World societies from developing their own industrial capacity.

2. **Lack of industrial capacity.** Without an industrial base of their own, poor societies face a double bind: they rely on rich nations to buy their inexpensive raw materials and they also depend on rich nations to supply whatever expensive manufactured goods they can afford. In a classic example of this type of double dependency, British colonialists allowed the people of India to raise cotton, but prohibited them from manufacturing their own cloth. Instead, Indian cotton was shipped to the textile mills of Birmingham and Manchester in England, where it was woven into cloth. The manufactured garments were then shipped back for profitable sale in India. Outraged at this exploitation, the leader of the Indian independence movement, Mahatma Gandhi, urged his people to wear only cloth manufactured in their own country.

Underdevelopment theorists also blast the "Green Revolution," widely praised by modernization theory, for fostering dependency. To promote agricultural productivity, poor countries must purchase expensive fertilizers, pesticides, and mechanical equipment from core nations. In some cases, rich societies benefit more from these arrangements than poor societies do.

3. **Foreign debt.** Such unequal trade patterns have sent Third-World debt—to industrialized core societies—soaring. Collectively, the Third World owes First-World nations roughly $1 trillion; hundreds of billions of dollars are owed to the United States alone. This staggering debt—which is growing in most cases—represents a financial burden that few poor societies can bear. Excessive debt can destabilize a country's economy, and many poor nations are already reeling from high unemployment and rampant inflation. Besides further impoverishing peripheral societies, massive foreign debt makes poor countries all the more dependent on rich nations. This vicious circle, dependency theorists argue, makes rich nations richer and poor nations poorer.

Seeing no way out of the "debt trap," some Third-World countries have simply stopped making payments. Cuba, for example, refused to make further payments on its $7 billion foreign debt in 1986. Because this threatens the economic growth of rich nations, countries such as the United States strongly oppose such actions.

Struggling under massive foreign debt, the economy of Argentina has been devastated by inflation. As a result, tens of thousands of Argentinos took to the streets in 1990 to demand change. Their demands were simple, as suggested by the banner that reads "Argentinos Are Hungry."

The Role of Rich Nations

The analyses of global inequality advanced by modernization theorists and dependency theorists differ widely. Nowhere is this difference more apparent than in the role they assign to rich nations.

Modernization theory holds that rich societies *create* new wealth through technological innovation. According to this view, the economic success of the First World does not *cause* world poverty. Rather, as Third-World nations modernize, poverty will disappear. In contrast, dependency theory argues that rich societies have unjustly *seized* the wealth of the world for their own purposes. That is, the *over*development of some of the globe is directly tied to the *under*development of the rest of it.

Dependency theorists take issue with modernization theory arguments that rich nations help poor societies through programs of population control, agricultural and industrial technology, and foreign aid. Instead, dependency theory holds, rich nations enter poor societies solely in pursuit of profits. Selling technology generates profits, and foreign aid, which often goes to small, ruling elites rather than the poor, establishes a favorable "business climate" for multinational corporations (Lappé, Collins, & Kinley, 1981).

Additionally, the capitalist culture of the United States encourages people to think of poverty as natural or inevitable, dependency theory maintains. Following this line of reasoning, poverty results from "natural" processes including having (too many) children and disasters such as droughts. Denying that hunger fits into any "natural" scheme, dependency theory asserts that global hunger results from deliberate decisions by powerful people who control agricultural production and distribution. The box argues that world hunger is *not* caused by a lack of food.

CRITICAL THINKING

World Hunger: Is Scarcity the Problem?

The typical American thinks that people in the world go hungry because there isn't enough food to feed everyone. This belief seems reasonable, but is it true? The answer, according to world hunger activists Frances Moore Lappé and Joseph Collins, may surprise you.

Lappé and Collins claim that the world produces enough grain so every man, woman, and child could consume 3,600 calories a day. Such consumption, they add, would soon result in a world of grossly overweight people! Plenty of food is produced virtually everywhere. Even most of the poorest societies grow enough food for their people. The cause of world hunger, therefore, is not "too little food" or "too many people"; rather, many people cannot *afford* to buy food. Poverty, not production, is the problem.

For instance, while several hundred million people in India suffer from malnutrition, their country actually *exports* substantial amounts of beef, wheat, and rice. Similarly, millions of children go hungry in Africa, yet this vast and rich continent also exports more food than it imports. The problem in India and in Africa is not that more resources need to be *produced*, but that they need to be more equitably *distributed*. Even in South Africa, the one nation on the African continent rich enough to be counted in the First World, about 50,000 children die from hunger each year. Most are black children whose families endure severe poverty despite the bounty enjoyed by most whites.

According to Lappé and Collins, the contradiction of poverty amid plenty stems from a policy of producing food for profits, not people. That is, crops (such as coffee in much of Latin America) are selected and grown for export, earning profits for large corporations and small elites in the country. Export industries, however, have no call for corn or beans; these are consumed by local people. Governments of many poor societies promote the practice of growing for export rather than local consumption because food profits are needed to repay massive foreign debt. Capitalist corporations, Lappé and Collins conclude, serve the greedy instead of the needy. Thus much of the persistent poverty and periodic famine in the world is entirely avoidable.

SOURCE: Based on Frances Moore Lappé and Joseph Collins, *World Hunger: Twelve Myths* (New York: Grove Press/Food First Books, 1986).

Hong Kong, an economic marketplace that operates as freely as anywhere in the world, is a monument to the power of capitalism to generate wealth. Land values in Hong Kong are among the highest in the world, and many of the British colony's people are extremely wealthy. At the same time, however, there is a striking contrast between the rich and the poor. In Aberdeen, shown here, thousands of Chinese people live in a floating neighborhood where the chances of getting ahead are quite small.

Critical evaluation. Dependency theory has made a strong impact in sociology. By showing that no society develops (or fails to develop) in isolation, dependency theory has spotlighted global patterns of wealth and power that shape the destiny of all nations. Advocates of dependency theory cite cases, including many Latin American countries, where development simply cannot proceed under present international conditions. To address global poverty, they claim change within poor societies will not work; instead, the world economy must be reformed so it operates in the interests of the majority of people.

Critics of the dependency approach identify some important weaknesses in the theory. First, the theory assumes that the wealth of the First World is based solely on appropriating resources from poor societies. Farmers, small-business owners, and industrialists can and do create new wealth through their imagination and drive. Wealth is not a zero-sum resource; the *entire* world's wealth has grown during this century, largely due to technological advances and other innovations.

Second, if dependency theory were correct in condemning the First World for creating global poverty, those nations with the strongest ties to rich societies would be among the poorest in the world. However, the most impoverished nations of the world (such as Ethiopia and other countries in Central Africa) have had little contact with rich societies. Similarly, critics suggest, a long history of trade with rich countries has dramatically improved the economies of Singapore, South Korea, Japan, and Hong Kong (which became a British colony in 1841 and will remain so until 1997). Then, too, many of the nations most active as colonizers in the past (Portugal and Spain, for example) are far from "superpowers" today.

Third, critics contend that dependency theory simplistically assumes that a single factor—world capitalism—has produced global inequality. In the process of directing attention to forces *outside* of poor societies, in short, dependency theory ignores factors *within* these countries that may contribute to their economic plight. Sociologists have long recognized that culture determines much human behavior. World cultural patterns vary greatly, with some societies embracing change readily and others staunchly resisting economic development. As we noted earlier, for example, Iran's fundamentalist Islamic society deliberately avoids bolstering its economic ties with other countries. Capitalist societies could hardly be blamed for Iran's slow economic development. Nor can rich societies be saddled with responsibility for the behavior of every foreign leader. Governments of poor societies must assume some responsibility for widespread poverty insofar as leaders engage in far-reaching corruption (consider the past regimes of Marcos in the Philippines, Duvalier in Haiti, and Noriega in Panama). Some governments also use food supplies as a weapon in internal political struggles (this occurred in Ethiopia and the Sudan in Africa). Other regimes (including many nations of Latin America and Africa) fail to support programs to improve the status of women or control population growth.

Fourth, dependency theory tends to overlook economic dependency fostered by the Soviet Union, the leading power of the Second World. While the Soviet Union never colonized the Third World, it seized control of most of Eastern Europe during World War II and subsequently dominated these nations politically and economically. The popular uprisings against Soviet-installed governments, beginning in 1989, reveals the widespread belief that this domination constituted a form of exploitation that prevented economic development. Eastern European nations were forced to buy Soviet-manufactured goods and Soviet-produced energy, and they were prevented from trading more profitably on the world market.

In the Third World, Cuba and Angola are among the nations that have become economically dependent on the Soviet Union.

Fifth, dependency theory does not lend itself to clear policy making. This approach suggests that poor societies should end all contact with the First World, and perhaps nationalize foreign-owned industries. On a broader scale, however, dependency theory implies that global poverty could be eliminated by a vaguely described world overthrow of international capitalism. What form emerging economies would take, and whether they would be capable of meeting the economic needs of a growing world population (in light of the economic weaknesses of current socialist societies) are questions that remain unclear.

THE FUTURE OF GLOBAL INEQUALITY

Faced with two different explanations for global inequality, we might wonder which is "right." As with many controversies in sociology, each side makes some valid points, which form a complex set of truths. Table 11–2 summarizes important arguments made by advocates of each approach.

We must also consider empirical evidence. In some regions of the world, such as the "Pacific Rim" of Eastern Asia, the market forces endorsed by modernization theory are raising living standards rapidly. At the same time, other societies of the Third World, especially in Latin America, are experiencing unprecedented economic turmoil that frustrates hopes for market-based development.

The Third-World societies that have surged ahead economically have two factors in common. First, they are relatively small.[5] Combined, the Asian societies of South Korea, Taiwan, Hong Kong, Singapore, and Japan equal only about one-fifth of the land area and population of India. The economic problems smaller countries face can be managed more easily; consequently, small societies administer programs of development more effectively. Second, these "best case" societies have cultural traits in common, especially traditions of emphasizing individual achievement and economic success. In other areas of the world, where powerful group forces inhibit

_____

[5] This argument was advanced by Professor Alan Frishman of Hobart College.

Table 11–2 MODERNIZATION THEORY AND DEPENDENCY THEORY: A SUMMARY

	Modernization Theory	Dependency Theory
Historical Pattern	The entire world was poor just two centuries ago; the Industrial Revolution brought affluence to the First World; as industrialization gradually transforms the Third World, all societies are likely to become more equal and alike.	Global parity was disrupted by colonialism, which developed the First World and simultaneously underdeveloped the Third World; barring change in the world capitalist system, rich nations will grow richer and poor nations will become poorer.
Primary Causes of Global Poverty	Characteristics of Third-World societies cause poverty, including lack of industrial technology, traditional cultural patterns that discourage innovation, and rapid population growth.	Global economic relations—historical colonialism and the operation of multinational corporations—have enriched the First World while placing the Third World in a state of economic dependency.
Role of Rich Nations	First-World countries can and do assist Third-World nations through programs of population control, technology transfers that increase food production and stimulate industrial development, and by providing investment capital in the form of foreign aid.	First-World countries have concentrated global resources, advantaging themselves while producing massive foreign debt in the Third World; rich nations represent a barrier to economic development in the Third World.

individual achievement, even smaller nations have a limited record of development.

The picture now emerging tends to call into question arguments put forward by both approaches. Both of the major "paths of development" advanced by modernization and dependency theories are currently undergoing significant transformation. On the one hand, few societies seeking economic growth now claim that a capitalist economy should be completely free of government control. This view challenges modernization theory, which has favored a free-market approach over government-directed development. Also, as recent upheavals in the Soviet Union and Eastern Europe demonstrate, a global reevaluation of socialism is currently under way. These events, following decades of poor economic performance, make many Third-World societies reluctant to consider this path to development. Because dependency theory has historically supported socialist economic systems, changes in world socialism will surely generate new thinking here as well.

In the immediate future, no plan for development is likely to effectively reduce the pressing problems of world hunger and rapid population growth. Looking to the next century, however, there are reasons for hope. The approaches described in this chapter identify the two keys to combating global inequality. One, revealed by modernization theory, is that world hunger is at least partly a *problem of technology*, because a higher standard of living for a rapidly increasing world population will require greater agricultural and industrial productivity. The second, derived from dependency theory, is that global inequality is also a *political issue*. Even with higher productivity, crucial questions concerning how resources are distributed—both within societies and around the globe—remain.

As debate over global inequality continues, people are coming to recognize that the security of *everyone*—in rich and poor nations alike—depends on reducing the destabilizing extremes of contemporary global poverty. Perhaps the lessening of tensions between the United States and the Soviet Union at the end of the 1980s will open the way for energy and resources (the so-called "peace dividend") to be redirected to the needs of the vast majority of humanity trapped in a desperate struggle for life itself.

SUMMARY

1. We need to adopt a global perspective in order to appreciate the full extent of social stratification around the world and to understand how global changes affect American society and individual Americans.

2. The "three worlds" are broad categories of nations used to describe patterns of economic development. The First World encompasses industrialized, capitalist societies including the United States; the Second World is composed of largely industrialized, socialist societies including the Soviet Union; the Third World represents the remaining poor societies that have yet to industrialize.

3. Third-World poverty does not simply consist of relative poverty; it also involves absolute, life-threatening poverty that is widespread. The typical citizen of a Third-World nation struggles to survive on an income far below that of the typical American.

4. Poverty places about 20 percent of the Third-World population—at least 800 million people—at risk.

Some 15 million people, many of them children, die of starvation every year.

5. Women are more likely than men to be poor nearly everywhere in the world. In poor societies, women's relative and absolute disadvantages are greater than in the United States.

6. Third-World poverty is a complex problem rooted in the lack of industrial technology, rapid population growth, traditional cultural patterns, social stratification, and global power relationships.

7. Modernization theory maintains that acquiring advanced productive technology is crucial to economic development. Traditional cultural patterns are viewed as retarding modernization.

8. Modernization theorist W. W. Rostow identifies four stages of development: traditional, take-off, drive to technological maturity, and high mass consumption.

9. Arguing that rich societies create their own wealth, modernization theory cites four ways assistance can

be offered to poor societies: through population control, food-producing technologies, industrial development, and investment and other foreign aid.

10. Modernization theory comes under criticism for failing to produce widespread economic development in the world, and for assuming ethnocentrically that poor societies can follow the path to development taken by rich nations centuries ago.

11. Dependency theory sees global wealth and poverty as directly linked to the historical operation of the capitalist world economy.

12. The dependency of Third-World countries is rooted in colonialism. In this century, multinational corporations continue to exploit politically independent societies of the Third World through neocolonialism.

13. Immanuel Wallerstein views the First World as the advantaged "core" of the capitalist world economy; poor societies of the Third World form the global "periphery."

14. Three key factors—export-oriented economies, a lack of industrial capacity, and foreign debt—perpetuate Third-World dependency on rich nations.

15. Dependency theory is criticized for overlooking how some nations have created new wealth. Further, contrary to the theory's tenets, the poorest societies are not those with the strongest ties to the First World.

16. Both modernization and dependency approaches offer useful insights into the development of global inequality. Some evidence supports each view. Less controversial is the urgent need to address the various problems caused by worldwide poverty.

KEY CONCEPTS

colonialism the process by which some nations enrich themselves through political and economic control of other nations

dependency theory an approach maintaining that global inequality stems from and is perpetuated by the exploitation of poor societies by rich ones

First World a category of industrial societies with predominantly capitalist economies

modernization theory an approach maintaining that global inequality reflects differing levels of technological development among world societies

multinational corporation (transnational corporation) a large corporation that operates in many different nations

neocolonialism a new form of colonialism involving the operation of multinational corporations

Second World a category of industrial societies with predominantly socialist economies

Third World a category of primarily agrarian societies in which most people are poor

SUGGESTED READINGS

This classic statement concerning global inequality sets a radical agenda.
　　Frantz Fanon. *The Wretched of the Earth*. New York: Grove Press, 1963.

The following United Nations publication, which contains recent data on the state of the global economy, explores contrasts between the rich and poor societies of the world.
　　World Economic Survey 1990: Current Trends and Policies in the World Economy. New York: United Nations, 1990.

This useful, short paperback provides an introduction to the growing economic disparity between rich and poor societies.
　　Peter Donaldson. *Worlds Apart: The Development Gap and What It Means*. 2nd ed. New York: Penguin, 1986.

These books provide a good introduction to the issue of world hunger.
　　Arthur Simon. *Bread for the World*. Rev. Ed. New York: Paulist Press, 1984; Grand Rapids: Wm. B. Erdmans Publishing Co., 1984.
　　Frances Moore Lappé and Joseph Collins. *World Hunger: Twelve Myths*. New York: Grove Press/Food First Books, 1986.

This book offers an excellent presentation of modernization theory.
　　W. W. Rostow. *The World Economy: History and Prospect*. Austin and London: University of Texas Press, 1978.

12

Race and Ethnicity

Almost forty years ago, in the city of Topeka, Kansas, a minister walked hand in hand with his seven-year-old daughter to a public elementary school four blocks from their home. Linda Brown wanted to enroll in the second grade, but the school officials refused to admit her. Instead, she was required to attend another school two miles away. Because of their decision, the little girl had to walk six blocks every day to a bus stop, where she sometimes waited half an hour for the bus. In bad weather, she would be soaking wet by the time the bus came; one day she became so cold at the bus stop that she walked back home. Why, she asked her parents, couldn't she attend the school that was only four blocks away?

With the answer—one difficult for loving parents to give their child—came Linda Brown's realization that her skin color made her a second-class citizen in American society. Her parents were moved to begin speaking to other blacks in the city about the injustice of separate schools for black and white children. Ultimately, a suit was filed on behalf of Linda Brown and several other children, and in 1954 their case came before the Supreme Court of the United States. In *Brown* vs. *the Board of Education of Topeka*, the Supreme Court unanimously rejected the idea that schools for the two races were "separate but equal." Instead, they concluded, racially

segregated schools inevitably provide blacks with an inferior education. A generation later, Linda Brown looked back on this decision, calling it a "turning point for black America" (U.S. Commission on Civil Rights, 1974:17).

Throughout the world, skin color and cultural background are important sources of group unity; they

The range of biological variation in human beings is far greater than any system of racial classification allows. This is made obvious by trying to place all of the people pictured here into simple racial categories.

also provoke struggles that are frequently more intense than those linked to social class. In South Africa, blacks continue to press a white minority government for equal political rights. In the United Kingdom, an uneasy tension exists between whites and darker-skinned immigrants from former European colonies such as India. To the west, in Ireland, strife between Protestants and Catholics also continues. In Canada, too, conflict between people of French and English backgrounds is never far below the surface. And nowhere has ethnic conflict been more evident than in the Soviet Union. Since 1989, the Soviet government has faced continuous demands for independence from members of various ethnicities and religions in many of its fifteen republics.

In American society, as throughout the world, race and ethnicity are fundamental units of social organization, providing personal identity and group pride, but often causing struggle and even sparking violence. This chapter examines the meaning and consequences of race and ethnicity.

THE SOCIAL SIGNIFICANCE OF RACE AND ETHNICITY

Americans, like people around the world, frequently use the terms "race" and "ethnicity" imprecisely and sometimes even interchangeably. For this reason, they need to be carefully defined.

Race

A **race** is *a category composed of men and women who share biologically transmitted traits that are defined as socially significant.* Races are commonly distinguished by physical traits such as skin color, hair texture, shape of facial features, and body type. Members of a single biological species, human beings display biological variations—described as "racial characteristics"—due to living for thousands of generations in different geographical regions of the world (Molnar, 1983). People residing in hot climates, for example, tend to have darker skin for protection from the sun, while people in moderate climates, who do not need such protection, have lighter skin.

Over the course of human history, human beings intermarried as they migrated from place to place, so that genetic characteristics once common to a single region spread through much of the world. In regions that have historically been a "crossroads" of human migration like the Middle East, people display striking racial variation. More isolated people, such as the Japanese, are biologically more similar. No society, however, lacks genetic mixture and, with increasing contact among the different parts of the globe, racial mixing can be expected to increase.

Attempting to make sense of what can be bewildering human variety, nineteenth-century biologists developed a three-part scheme of racial classifications. People with relatively light skin and fine hair were called *Caucasian*. The term *Negroid* was applied to those with darker skin and coarser, curlier hair. Early biologists labeled people with yellow or brown skin and distinctive folds on the eyelids as *Mongoloid*. As we know now, however, there are no biologically pure races. In fact, the traveler moving from region to region notices gradual and subtle racial variations the world over. The people commonly called "Caucasians" or "whites" actually display skin color that ranges from very light to very dark, and the same variation occurs among the so-called "Negroids" and "Mongoloids." Some "whites" (such as the Caucasians of southern India) actually have darker skin and hair than some "blacks" (such as the blond Negroid aborigines of Australia).

Although Americans distinguish people who are "white" and "black," research confirms that many Americans are genetically mixed. Over many generations, the genetic traits typical of Negroid Africans and Caucasian Europeans have combined; the Mongoloid traits of Native Americans have also spread widely through the American population. Many "black" people, therefore, have a large proportion of Caucasian genes, and many "white" people have at least some Negroid genes. In short, race is not a black-and-white issue.

Nevertheless, biological facts may have little to do with cultural definitions of race. American society, like the rest of the world, uses biological traits to rank people in systems of social inequality. Historically, this ranking has been defended by beliefs that racial traits are linked to innate intelligence and other mental abilities, but there is no scientific foundation for such beliefs. Nevertheless, because of the social significance of race, societies simplify racial variation to make social rankings clear and enforceable. Earlier in this century, for example, many states in the South labeled as "colored" anyone who had at least one thirty-second black ancestry. That is, having at least one great-great grandparent (or any closer ancestor) was grounds for being legally "black." Because race has become less of a caste distinction in American society, state laws now allow parents to indicate the race of a child.

Ethnicity

Ethnicity is *a cultural heritage shared by a category of people.* Members of an *ethnic category* may have a common ancestral origin, language, and religion which, together, confer a distinctive social identity. The ancestors of Polish, Hispanic, and Chinese Americans, for example, lived in particular nations of the world. As Chapter 3 ("Culture") explained, millions of Americans speak Spanish, Italian, German, French, or other languages in their homes. The United States and Canada are predominantly Protestant societies, but most Americans and Canadians of Spanish, Italian, and Polish ancestry are Roman Catholic, while many others of Greek, Ukrainian, and Russian ancestry are members of the Eastern Orthodox Church. More than 6 million Americans (with ancestral ties to various nations) are Jews who share a common religious heritage.

Race and ethnicity, then, are quite different: the first is biological, and the second, cultural. But the two often go hand in hand. Japanese Americans, for example, have distinctive physical traits and—for those who maintain a traditional way of life—cultural traits as well. Sometimes people erroneously view ethnic attributes as racial. For example, Jews are sometimes described as a race although they are distinctive only in their religious heritage as well as their history of persecution by other people (Goldsby, 1977). Finally, people can change their ethnicity by adopting a different way of life. Polish immigrants who discard their cultural background over time may cease to have a particular ethnicity. The physical traits of race, in contrast, persist over generations.

Table 12–1 RACIAL AND ETHNIC CATEGORIES IN THE UNITED STATES, 1980

Racial or Ethnic Classification	Approximate Number of Americans
Black	26,495,000
Hispanic	14,609,000
Mexican American	8,740,000
Puerto Rican	2,014,000
Cuban American	803,000
Other	3,051,000
Native American	1,420,000
Chinese	806,000
Filipino	775,000
Japanese	701,000
Korean	355,000
Vietnamese	262,000
Whites of European Ancestry	
English	49,598,000
German	49,224,000
Irish	40,166,000
French	12,892,000
Italian	12,184,000
Scottish	10,049,000
Polish	8,228,000
Dutch	6,304,000
Swedish	4,345,000
Norwegian	3,454,000
Russian	2,781,000
Czech	1,892,000
Hungarian	1,777,000
Welsh	1,665,000
Danish	1,518,000
Portuguese	1,024,000

SOURCE: U.S. Bureau of the Census.

Minorities

Races and ethnicities that stand out from those dominating any society are *minorities*. A racial or ethnic **minority**[1] is *a category of people, defined by physical or cultural traits, who are socially disadvantaged*. Minorities are of many kinds, including people with physical disabilities, political radicals, and (as Chapter 13, "Sex and Gender," suggests) women. Race and ethnicity, however,

---

[1] The commonly used term "minority group" is incorrect because minorities are categories rather than groups, as explained in Chapter 7.

are the most common types of minorities. Table 12–1 presents the 1980 count of the various racial and ethnic minorities in the United States.

Minorities have two major characteristics. First, they have a *distinctive identity*. Members of a minority often refer to themselves as "we" and "us," while designating others as "they" and "them." Because race is highly visible (and virtually impossible for a person to change), members of racial minorities, such as blacks in the United States or Chinese in South Africa, are often keenly aware of their race. The significance of ethnicity (which can be changed) is more variable. Throughout American history, some people (such as many Reform Jews) have downplayed their ethnicity, while others (including many Orthodox Jews) have maintained distinctive cultural traditions and often lived within ethnic neighborhoods.

Race and ethnicity persist over generations to the extent that people marry others like themselves. The vast majority of marriages in the United States are between couples of one racial category. The pattern of *endogamy*, or marrying within one's own social category, is less pronounced among ethnic minorities, although some cultural—and especially religious—traditions oppose marrying "outsiders." If love and marriage were to completely disregard race and ethnicity, racial and ethnic minorities would cease to exist within several generations.

A second characteristic of minorities is *subordination*. Chapter 10 ("Social Class in America") explained that race and ethnicity are part of the American system of social stratification. Minorities typically have lower incomes and less occupational prestige and education. But not all members of a minority are equally disadvantaged. Some Hispanic-Americans are extremely wealthy, some Chinese Americans are celebrated business leaders, and blacks are among America's leading scholars. But even these people may be defined as socially inferior and be subjected to abuse and humiliation on the basis of their social category. Thus race or ethnicity can serve as a master status (as described in Chapter 6, "Social Interaction in Everyday Life") that overpowers other personal traits.

Minorities usually represent a small proportion of a society's population, but there are exceptions. For example, Chapter 9 ("Social Stratification") described how the black numerical majority in South Africa is grossly deprived of economic and political power by the white numerical minority. In the United States, women represent slightly more than half of the population but are still denied opportunities and privileges enjoyed by men.

Social conflict involving minorities and the majority is common around the world, as one particular category of people—blacks in the United States, Christians in Egypt, Sikhs in India, Azerbaijanis in the Soviet Union—struggles for rights that are formally guaranteed by law. Malaysia represents an unusual and interesting case: a society in which ethnic *inequality* is mandated by law. The box provides details.

Prejudice

Prejudice is *a rigid and irrational generalization about an entire category of people.* The word *prejudice* is closely related to the word *prejudgment.* Prejudice is therefore irrational insofar as people hold strong, inflexible attitudes even though they have little or no direct evidence about the target of those attitudes. Prejudice can be di-

CROSS-CULTURAL COMPARISON

Unequal Under the Law: Race and Ethnicity in Malaysia

The 16 million people of Malaysia live in a nation roughly the size of New Mexico. This small society, on the southeast tip of Asia, also includes the northern part of the island of Borneo. As a Third-World nation, Malaysia is still poor in American terms, but its standard of living is rising.

Race and ethnicity are fundamental to Malaysian society. The earliest inhabitants of the region, called Malays, now make up just over half of the population. People of Chinese ancestry account for another one-third, while an additional 10 percent are Indians whose ancestors came to work on agricultural plantations. Malaysia is truly a nation of rich and diverse cultural traditions.

Although the languages of this nation are various combinations of Malay, Chinese, English, and Indian tongues, most Malaysians can communicate with one another. When they do, they often disagree about their respective social standing. The Chinese are the wealthiest Malaysians. Concentrated in large cities, they control the largest, most prosperous businesses and live in expensive neighborhoods. Indians, too, are urban, but the majority own small busi-

nesses or work for wages. The typical Indian Malaysian earns only about two-thirds what the Chinese Malaysian does. The Malays, despite being the region's first inhabitants, are the poorest. Most live in rural areas, working as farm laborers and earning about half what the Chinese Malaysians do.

Such disparities have long fueled conflict, which erupted into violence in 1969 leading to years of martial law. Then, in an effort to socially advance the Malay majority, the government adopted policies granting them special privileges. The rapidly expanding government bureaucracy now gives hiring preference to Malays. State-supported universities are required to admit applicants according to their proportion in the population as a whole, and so half the places in the universities are reserved for Malays. Similarly, most government licenses to operate small businesses such as taxi services are given to Malays. The government also supports a visible role for traditional Malay culture in the public life of Malaysia.

Malaysia defends such unequal and categorical treatment of its people as necessary to help the Malays catch

up to the wealthy Chinese. But many Malays still feel disadvantaged and, joined by many Indians, express resentment toward the Chinese. For their part, the Chinese community has become embittered by what it sees as an official policy of favoritism for the Malays. For instance, many Chinese claim that the quota system forces them to send their children abroad for a college education. In this tense situation, many Indians feel caught between the economic power of the Chinese and the new political clout of the Malays.

Most world societies are composed of distinctive races and ethnicities, which usually have different social standing. Malaysia is one of the few societies in which different treatment for racial and ethnic categories is enshrined in the constitution. Unlike the apartheid system under attack in South Africa, however, this policy is intended not to maintain social differences, but to increase social equality. Whether it will do so—and at what cost—remains to be seen.

SOURCE: Based on information provided by Professor Steven Chee, University of Malaysia, and travel by the author in Malaysia.

rected toward persons of a particular social class, sex, sexual orientation, age, political affiliation, race, or ethnicity. Prejudices can be positive or negative, and most people hold some of each type. Positive prejudices tend to exaggerate the virtues of people like ourselves, while negative prejudices condemn people who are different from us. Prejudice is also a matter of degree, ranging from mild aversion to outright hostility. Because attitudes are shaped by culture, at least some prejudice is found in everyone.

Stereotypes

A common form of prejudice is the **stereotype** (*stereo* is derived from Greek meaning "hard" or "solid"), *a set of prejudices that characterize a category of people.* Because stereotypes often involve emotions of love (toward members of ingroups) and hate or fear (toward members of outgroups), they are hard to change even in the face of contrary evidence. For example, some people have a stereotypical understanding of the poor as lazy and irresponsible freeloaders who could support themselves if they wanted to but choose instead to rely on welfare (Waxman, 1983; N.O.R.C., 1989). As was explained in Chapter 10 ("Social Class in America"), this stereotype distorts reality: more than half of poor Americans are children and adults who do work hard but nevertheless earn little money.

Almost every racial and ethnic minority has been depicted in stereotypical form; such views can become part of a society's culture. In the United States, white people often stereotype nonwhites in much the same way that wealthy people stereotype the poor, as lacking motivation to improve their own lives (N.O.R.C., 1989:287). Such attitudes assume poverty is mostly a matter of personal deficiency, and, more to the point, they ignore the fact that most poor people in America are white and that most blacks work as hard as anyone else and are *not* poor. In this case the bit of truth in the stereotype is that blacks are more likely than whites to be poor. But by building a rigid attitude out of a few selected facts, stereotypes grossly distort reality.

Racism

One of the most powerful and destructive forms of prejudice, **racism** is *the belief that one racial category is innately superior or inferior to another.* Racism has been common in world history. The ancient Greeks, various peoples of India, and many Asian societies viewed those

unlike themselves as inferior. Racism has historically been widespread in American society; today racism has certainly declined with a more egalitarian culture, yet it persists among Americans, if not always professed as openly and directly.

The alleged innate inferiority of certain people is frequently used to justify subjecting them to *social* inferiority. By the end of the nineteenth century, Great Britain, France, Spain, and the United States had forged colonial empires throughout the Third World. Exploiting colonies often involved the ruthless oppression of their people. What better way to justify oppression than to believe that those subjugated are inferior beings? Similarly, in the past many white Americans believed in the innate inferiority of Native Americans, whose land they seized, and in the innate inferiority of black Americans, who were forced into slavery.

In the twentieth century, racism was central to the Nazi regime in Germany. Nazi racial doctrine proclaimed an "Aryan race" of blond-haired, blue-eyed Caucasians as a pure racial type—a biological fiction. This mythical Aryan race was held to be innately superior to all others and destined to rule the world. Such racism was used to justify killing "inferior beings," including some 6 million European Jews and millions of Poles, gypsies, homosexuals, and physically and mentally disabled people.

More recently, racial conflict has intensified in European societies as whites confront millions of immigrants from former colonies (Glenn & Kennedy-Keel, 1986). As one British lawyer notes, "We haven't come to terms with the fact that black people are really here. . . . White society wants to believe it's all a bad dream—that they will wake up one morning and all the blacks will be gone. Well, it's not going to happen" (cited in Nielsen, 1984:40). Similarly, in the United States the 1980s were marked by an increase in racial tensions in cities and on college campuses across the country.

Scapegoat Theory of Prejudice

If prejudice is not a rational assessment of facts, what are its origins? One explanation, commonly termed *scapegoat theory*, links prejudice to frustration and suggests that prejudice is likely to be pronounced among people who are themselves disadvantaged (Dollard, 1939). A white woman working in a textile factory for low wages, for example, may be fearful of expressing hostility at the people who operate the factory because they are, after all, powerful and capable of retaliation. A safer (if misdirected) course of action is to identify people even less powerful than she is, and blame them for her plight. Thus the woman might direct antagonism toward her black co-workers: "It's because there are so many blacks in this factory that we are treated like this!" Prejudice of this kind is not likely to improve the woman's situation in the factory, but it may allow her to feel that she is superior at least to someone.

A **scapegoat** is thus *a person or category of people unfairly blamed for the troubles of others.* Because they typically have little social power, minorities are easily used as scapegoats. Just as the Nazis used Jews as scapegoats allegedly responsible for Germany's ills, blacks and Hispanic Americans have been similarly victimized in the United States, as have Indians and Pakistanis in Great Britain.

Authoritarian Personality Theory

At the end of World War II, T. W. Adorno (1950) and others suggested that extreme prejudice may develop as a personality trait. Adorno's research led to the significant conclusion that people who displayed strong prejudice toward any minority were usually prejudiced against all minorities. Such people—described as having *authoritarian personalities*—rigidly conformed to conventional cultural values, believed most moral issues to be clear matters of right and wrong, and were strongly ethnocentric. Such people also viewed society as naturally competitive and hierarchical, with "better" people (such as themselves) inevitably dominating those who are weaker. In contrast, Adorno found that people who were tolerant toward any minority were likely to be accepting of all. They were also more flexible in their moral judgments and believed that, ideally, society should be relatively egalitarian. They felt uncomfortable in any situation in which some people are able to exercise power over others.

The researchers claimed that authoritarian personalities characterize people with little education and those raised by harsh and demanding parents. Faced with cold and insistent parents, they theorized, children may become angry and anxious, and ultimately hostile and aggressive toward scapegoats—others they define as their social inferiors.

Cultural Theory of Prejudice

A third approach suggests that while extreme prejudice may be characteristic of particular people, some prejudice takes the form of widespread cultural values. As was noted in Chapter 3 ("Culture"), the social superiority of some categories of people is a core American value (Williams, 1970).

Emory Bogardus (1968) studied this issue for more than forty years using the concept of *social distance*, or how closely people are willing to interact with members of various racial and ethnic categories. His research showed that Americans generally offered similar evaluations of various racial and ethnic categories, a result suggesting that such attitudes had become normative within our culture. Persons of English, Canadian, and Scottish background were viewed most positively: most Americans indicated a willingness to have close social relationships, including marriage, with such people. Attitudes were less positive toward people whose background is French, German, Swedish, or Dutch. Finally, Bogardus's subjects expressed reluctance even to form friendships with members of other categories, including blacks, Chinese, and Koreans.

The fact that such evaluations were widely shared suggests that prejudice is not found only in abnormal people, as Adorno's research implies, but is widespread among people well adjusted to a "culture of prejudice." These results also reflect the historical domination of American society by people of English ancestry, the original European settlers of the United States, toward whom attitudes are more positive.

Conflict Theory of Prejudice

A fourth approach maintains that prejudice results from social conflict among categories of people. According to this theory, prejudice is used as ideology, justifying the oppression of minorities. To the extent that illegal immigrants in the Southwest are devalued, for example, they deserve little more than hard work at low wages.

In Marxist terms, prejudice toward minorities also serves the interests of elites by dividing workers. There is ample evidence in American history of racial and ethnic minorities being used as scapegoats by white workers whose problems have actually been caused by elites (Geschwender, 1978; Olzak, 1989). This reduces the likelihood that all categories of people will join together to advance their interests as *workers*.

Discrimination

Closely related to prejudice is the concept of **discrimination**, *treating various categories of people unequally.* While prejudice refers to attitudes and beliefs, discrimination is a matter of behavior. Like prejudice, discrimination can be either positive (providing special advantages) or negative (subjecting categories of people to disadvantages). Discrimination is also a matter of degree, ranging from the subtle to the overt.

Often, prejudice and discrimination occur simultaneously. A personnel manager prejudiced against members of a particular minority may refuse to hire them. Robert Merton (1976) describes such a person as an *active bigot* (see Figure 12–1). But not all prejudice is expressed as discrimination. Fearing legal action, the prejudiced personnel manager may not discriminate, thereby becoming the *timid bigot* in Figure 12–1. What Merton calls *fair-weather liberals* may discriminate without being prejudiced, as in the case of our manager

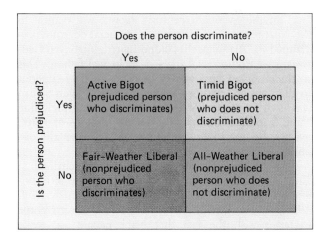

Figure 12–1 Patterns of Prejudice and Discrimination
(Merton, 1976)

discriminating when a superior demands it. Finally, Merton's *all-weather liberal* is free of both prejudice and discrimination.

Institutional Discrimination

Like prejudice, discrimination involves more than the behavior of some people. **Institutional discrimination** refers to *patterns of discrimination that are woven into the fabric of a society.* As the story of Linda Brown at the beginning of this chapter indicates, the law and traditional ideas of people's "place" have stood between minorities and quality education, good jobs, adequate housing, and even the right to own land and to vote.

Historically, many minorities faced *legal discrimination*, unequal standing under the law. Black Americans, for example, suffered from legal discrimination only two generations ago, even fighting in segregated military units during World War II to defend American freedoms. Blacks and whites are still divided by the legal discrimination of South Africa's apartheid system.

Industrial societies tend to view categorical discrimination as unjust; they embrace the ideal of legal equality for all. This view eliminates only one form of institutional discrimination, however. Sociologists have learned that all social institutions can operate to maintain discrimination, so that legal equality may have little effect on people's behavior and attitudes (Marshall et al., 1978). The 1954 Supreme Court ruling that outlawed segregated schools, for example, did not end this problem. The social separation of blacks and whites had become so deeply rooted in American society—evident in patterns of friendship, neighborhoods, workplace responsibilities, and even membership in religious organizations—that the pursuit of racial equality has been painfully slow. In the 1990s, as in the 1950s, many American students still attend racially imbalanced schools.

Prejudice and Discrimination: The Vicious Circle

Prejudice and discrimination persist in American society because they are mutually reinforcing. W. I. Thomas offered a simple explanation of this fact, noted in Chapter 6 ("Social Interaction in Everyday Life") as the Thomas theorem: *if situations are defined as real, they are real in their consequences* (1966:301; orig. 1931).

Thomas recognized that reality is a matter not of facts, but of how people define situations. Thus a category of people may become what they are defined to be. Stereotypes become very real to those who believe them, sometimes even to those victimized by them. How some minorities deal with this problem is described in the box.

By labeling a minority negatively and then acting accordingly, people make their definition of the situation real in its consequences. Thus, defining nonwhites as inferior may lead whites to withhold equal access to jobs, income, education, and political rights. While this process does not produce *innate* inferiority, it does produce *social* inferiority, constraining many nonwhites to poverty, low-prestige occupations, and poor housing in racially segregated neighborhoods.

Prejudice and discrimination thereby form a *vicious circle*—a situation that perpetuates itself over time, even from generation to generation. White people today see that many blacks, Mexican Americans, and Native Amer-

---

SOCIOLOGY OF EVERYDAY LIFE

Ethnic Therapy: Connecting Self to Society

Psychologist Judith Weinstein Klein claims that we can understand personal experiences and problems only be realizing how our society's definitions of race and ethnicity shape our everyday lives. This idea is the foundation of *ethnotherapy*, begun in the 1970s to address problems encountered by many Americans. Therapy groups, in which a small number of people talk together under the guidance of a trained professional, reveal that members of different racial or ethnic minorities often grapple with similar personal problems. According to Klein, "All ethnic minorities have to deal with self-hate and feelings of inadequacy as members of American culture."

Among blacks, racism may cause repressed anger as well as uncertainty about personal capabilities. Some successful blacks even struggle with a sense of guilt at leaving other blacks behind.

Another therapist, Joseph Giordano, leads ethnotherapy sessions for Italian Americans. Women of Italian descent often suffer due to conflict between their growing career aspirations and traditional expectations of being subordinate to their husbands. One indication of this sexual tug-of-war, Giordano finds, is that Italian-American men continue to favor women like themselves, while the women now look for partners who are not Italian Americans.

Jewish Americans explore how religious pride is tainted by self-hate: a product of being socialized within a predominantly non-Jewish society.

Some express confusion and anger as they recall attempts to become less Jewish. One woman explained that cosmetic surgery on less than perfect noses (widely called *nose jobs*) was as common as braces on teeth. Men and women also admit to confronting each other angrily with American cultural stereotypes. Accused of being self-centered, Jewish women counter that Jewish men are neurotic, dependent, and unsexual.

Ethnotherapy contains a significant element of the sociological perspective: To understand our own lives, we must understand how society shapes our attitudes and actions.

SOURCE: Adapted from John Leo, "Therapy for Ethnics," *Time*, March 15, 1982, p. 42.

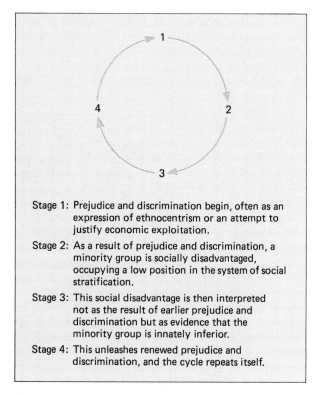

Stage 1: Prejudice and discrimination begin, often as an expression of ethnocentrism or an attempt to justify economic exploitation.

Stage 2: As a result of prejudice and discrimination, a minority group is socially disadvantaged, occupying a low position in the system of social stratification.

Stage 3: This social disadvantage is then interpreted not as the result of earlier prejudice and discrimination but as evidence that the minority group is innately inferior.

Stage 4: This unleashes renewed prejudice and discrimination, and the cycle repeats itself.

Figure 12–2 Prejudice and Discrimination—The Vicious Circle

Prejudice and discrimination can form a vicious circle, perpetuating themselves, as explained above.

icans are socially disadvantaged. If they interpret this situation as evidence that such categories of people have been innately inferior all along, they are doing what William Ryan (1976) calls "blaming the victim," which then justifies a new round of prejudice and discrimination. The results of definitions made in the past become causes of new definitions that affect the future—a cycle that can endlessly repeat itself, as is graphically illustrated in Figure 12–2.

MAJORITY AND MINORITY: PATTERNS OF INTERACTION

Patterns of interaction between minorities and more privileged members of society can be described in terms of four models.

Pluralism

Pluralism is *a state in which racial and ethnic minorities are distinct but have social parity*. Pride leads many people to maintain their distinctive social identity, but in this model no one is forced to be different by prejudice and discrimination. Agrarian caste systems, described in Chapter 9 ("Social Stratification"), ascribed rigid and unequal social standing to various categories of people. Within industrial class systems, however, pluralism emerges as a social ideal by which people are judged for what they do (personal performance), not who they are (racial or ethnic category).

Many Americans are pleased that almost all of the world's races and ethnicities are now found in American society. Large cities contain countless "ethnic villages" where people display the cultural traditions of their immigrant ancestors (Greeley, 1971; Gans, 1982). In New York these include Spanish Harlem, Little Italy, and Chinatown; in Philadelphia, Polish Kensington and Italian "South Philly"; in Chicago, Vietnamese "Little Saigon"; and in Los Angeles, Hispanic East Los Angeles. As one resident of a Hispanic neighborhood in Chicago explained, "There are people who come here and live and die and never learn English" (Kiefer, 1984:130).

Nevertheless, American society is not entirely pluralistic. First, while many Americans appreciate their cultural heritage, only a small proportion maintain a racial and ethnic identity that sets them clearly apart from others as do, say, the Amish. Relatively few Americans, furthermore, express a desire to live with only their "own kind" (N.O.R.C., 1989).

Second, American tolerance for the social diversity that does occur is limited. Chapter 3 ("Culture") described the social movement to make English the official language of the United States, which is hardly encouragement to pluralism. Almost two-thirds of Americans support religious observances in schools such as reading the Bible and reciting the Lord's Prayer—even though these reflect only some religious traditions in the United States (N.O.R.C., 1987:154).

Third, some measure of racial and ethnic identity is forced on people by others. For example, many communities in the Appalachian Mountains of the eastern United States remain culturally distinctive because their members are snubbed as "hillbillies" and subjected to discrimination that perpetuates their poverty (Sacks, 1986). Black and Hispanic Americans also continue to be socially isolated by prejudice and discrimination on the part of the white majority.

This piece of "neon art," entitled *Nation of Nations*, suggests the ethnic complexity of the United States. Various combinations of cultures provide a kaleidoscope of new cultural patterns that add to the vitality of American society.

A truer example of pluralism is found in Switzerland, a European nation of more than 6 million people with strong German, French, and Italian cultural traditions. This nation's relative success in maintaining pluralism (albeit involving only one racial and regional category) is evident in its official recognition of the languages of the three ethnicities. Just as important, no category is subjected to economic disadvantage (Simpson & Yinger, 1972).

Assimilation

Assimilation is *the process by which minorities gradually adopt patterns of the dominant culture.* Assimilation involves changing modes of dress, values, religion, language, or friends. Americans have traditionally viewed the United States as a "melting pot" in which various nationalities were fused into an entirely new way of life.

This turn-of-the-century description of the United States by one European immigrant remains influential today:

> America is God's Crucible, the great melting-pot where all races of Europe are melting and reforming. Here you stand, good folks, think I, when I see them at Ellis Island [historical entry point for many immigrants in New York], here you stand with your fifty groups, with your fifty languages and histories, and your fifty blood-hatreds and rivalries. But you won't be long like that, brothers, for these are the fires of God . . . Germans and Frenchmen, Irishmen and Englishmen, Jews and Russians, into the Crucible with you all! God is making an American! (Zangwill, 1921:33; orig. 1909)

This melting pot characterization of American society is misleading, however. Rather than everyone melting into a new cultural pattern, minorities have typically adopted the traits of the dominant culture established by the earliest settlers. They did so to improve their

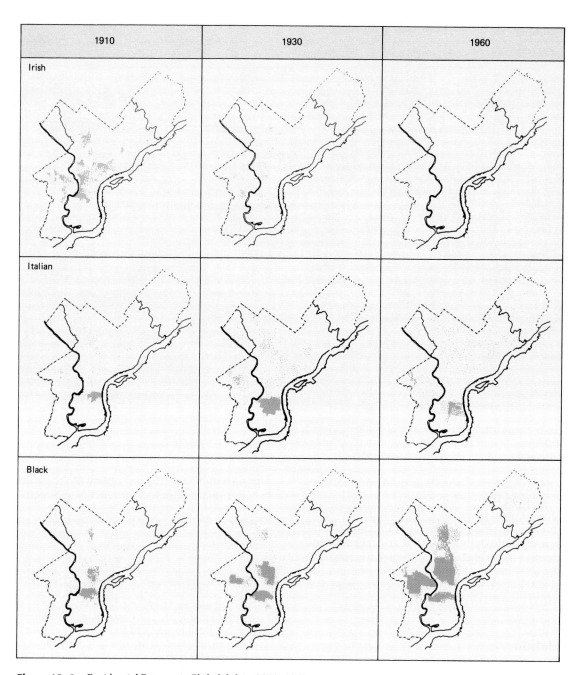

	1910	1930	1960
Irish			
Italian			
Black			

Figure 12–3 Residential Patterns in Philadelphia, 1910–1960
(*Wurman & Gallery, 1972*)

social position and to escape the prejudice and discrimination directed against foreigners (Newman, 1973). The box in Chapter 1, on page 5, shows that many well-known entertainers adopted Anglicized names early in their careers. This is not to deny the rich contributions to American culture made by various minorities; cases of cultural contact, however, generally involve more change on the part of the less powerful minority.

Over this century, some assimilation has certainly occurred in the United States. Herbert Gans (1982) argues that whereas first-generation immigrants typically retain their traditional culture, ethnicity is far less pronounced among second and subsequent generations. Figure 12–3 shows that Irish and Italian neighborhoods in Philadelphia faded during the first half of this century as members of these ethnic minorities gradually dispersed. Race may be a different matter, however, as this residential diffusion has not been true of blacks. Because some distinctive districts persist—and others are now forming—we know that race and ethnicity are still building blocks of American society (Glazer & Moynihan, 1970; Alba, 1985).

As a cultural process, assimilation involves changes in ethnicity but not in race. For example, many descendants of Japanese immigrants have discarded a traditionally Japanese way of life but still have their racial identity. However, distinguishing racial traits may also diminish over generations. **Miscegenation** is *the biological process of interbreeding among racial categories.* Although resistance to such biological mixing remains strong, miscegenation (often outside of marriage) has occurred throughout American history.

Segregation

Segregation is *the physical and social separation of categories of people.* Racial and ethnic minorities sometimes voluntarily segregate themselves, as do the Amish, described in Chapter 3 ("Culture"). Usually, however, minorities are segregated involuntarily as others choose to exclude them. Various degrees of segregation are found in residential neighborhoods and schools, as well as occupations, hospitals, and even cemeteries. While pluralism is distinctiveness without disadvantage, segregation is enforced separation to the detriment of a minority.

South Africa's system of apartheid (described in Chapter 9, "Social Stratification") illustrates racial segregation that has been both rigid and pervasive. Alien to the cultures of Africa, apartheid was created by the European minority it has served, and it has historically been enforced through the use of brutal power (Fredrickson, 1981). Apartheid is currently being eroded in South Africa by widespread opposition among blacks and a growing number of whites. Presently, however, South Africa remains essentially two different societies that touch only when blacks provide services for whites.

Racial segregation also has a long history in the United States. Under slavery, whites and blacks lived in physical proximity but were separated by enormous social distance (Hirschman, 1983). After the abolition of slavery in 1865, Jim Crow laws perpetuated a racial caste system, as in South Africa today, effectively segregating blacks and whites in their daily lives. Throughout the country, blacks were forbidden to use white hotels, railroad cars, buses, public restrooms, and drinking fountains (Woodward, 1974). Until the Supreme Court outlawed segregated schools in 1954, the law supported separate and unequal education for the two races. Other minorities, including Native Americans, Hispanics, and Asians, received similar treatment from the white majority in various parts of the United States.

Such overt and *de jure* (Latin meaning "by law") discrimination has ended in the United States. However, *de facto* ("in fact") segregation continues. A generation ago, Karl and Alma Taeuber (1965) measured the residential segregation of blacks and whites in over two hundred American cities, using a numerical index ranging from zero (a mixing of races in all neighborhoods) to 100 (total racial segregation). They calculated an *average* score of 86.2. In the decades since, segregation has decreased little, despite the documented desire of most blacks to live in racially integrated neighborhoods (Van Valey, Roof, & Wilcox, 1977; Calmore, 1986; N.O.R.C., 1989:187). Segregation persists even among minorities—especially blacks—who have achieved economic standing equal to that of whites (Hwang et al., 1985).

Recent research by Douglas Massey and Nancy Denton (1989a) suggests that segregation entails more than simply neighborhood composition. Beyond neighborhood housing, Massey and Denton discovered that racial segregation involves black neighborhoods clustered together into a larger ghetto in the inner city with little social contact between blacks and others. They concluded that *hypersegregation* was common among blacks, although far less pronounced among Hispanics. Of 60 major cities, ten (containing almost one-third of the blacks in the United States) were found to be hypersegregated with virtually all-black regions of the inner city socially cut off from the rest of the urban area.

Although blacks have become less suburbanized than Hispanics and Asian Americans, there are now millions of blacks in American suburbs (Massey & Denton, 1988). Generally, though, the white population of Americans suburbs has increased while inner cities have become progressively more black. The suburb of Dearborn, Michigan, for instance, was reported to have only eighty-three blacks among a population of over 90,000 (DeMott, 1986). At the same time, whites have a strong economic presence in black inner-city areas because they own businesses there, a pattern described by Robert Blauner (1972) as *internal colonialism*. Even blacks who manage to move to American suburbs contend with racial segregation, as well as many of the same problems of unemployment and poverty that plague inner cities (Clark, 1979; Logan & Schneider, 1984; Stahura, 1983, 1986).

Segregation is naturally opposed by minorities. The family of Linda Brown, described earlier, successfully used the court system to challenge school segregation. Sometimes the action of even a single individual can have lasting consequences. On December 1, 1955, Rosa Parks was riding a bus in Montgomery, Alabama, sitting in a section designated by law for blacks. When a crowd of white passengers boarded the bus, the driver asked four blacks to give up their seats to whites. Three did so, but Rosa Parks was tired and did not believe she should have to stand so that a white man could sit. When she refused to move, the driver left the bus and returned with police, who arrested Parks for violating the racial segregation laws. She was later convicted in court and fined $14—but her action sparked the black community of Montgomery to boycott city buses, ultimately bringing this practice of segregation to an end (King, 1969).

Genocide

Genocide is *the systematic killing of one category of people by another*. This extreme form of racism and ethnocentrism violates nearly every recognized moral standard, but it has nonetheless been common in human history.

Genocide has figured prominently in centuries of contact between Europeans and the indigenous population of the Americas. From the sixteenth century on, the Spanish, Portuguese, English, French, and Dutch forcibly established vast colonial empires. The native populations of North and South America were systematically killed so that Europeans could gain control of their

Many of us were taught that Europeans brought Christianity and civilization to the New World. The painting *Battle of the Aztecs and the Spaniards* by Mexican artist Diego Rivera is more truthful. In many cases, Europeans engaged in systematic genocide against the indigenous peoples of the Americas.

wealth. The Spanish explorer Hernando Cortez (1485–1547) razed the Aztec capital—site of today's Mexico City—slaughtering thousands of Aztecs. Similarly, the God-fearing colonists of early New England exterminated Native Americans, who were regarded as heathen savages. Diseases introduced by Europeans in addition to outright killing resulted in the death of most of this

Political regimes sometimes engage in the inhuman madness of mass murder. These shoes are silent testimony to the methodical death wrought by the Nazis during World War II against Jews, Gypsies, homosexuals, and a host of other people deemed "undesirable." More recently, the Pol Pot government turned Cambodia into "killing fields," murdering some two million people.

hemisphere's indigenous population (Hardoy, 1975; Cottrell, 1979; Butterworth & Chance, 1981; Matthiessen, 1984).

Genocide has also occurred in the twentieth century. Jews experienced unimaginable horror during World War II as the Nazi regime took control of much of Europe. Adolf Hitler used Jews as a scapegoat, blaming

them for the ills of society, leading to a reign of terror known as the Holocaust, in which more than 6 million perished. Between 1975 and 1980 the Communist regime of Pol Pot in Cambodia exterminated anyone thought to represent capitalist cultural influences. Condemned to death were people who knew any Western language and even those who wore eyeglasses, viewed as a symbol of capitalist culture. In the "killing fields" of Cambodia, 2 million people (one-fourth of the population) perished (Shawcross, 1979).

These four major types of contact between the majority and minorities exist simultaneously within a society. For example, Americans are proud to point to patterns of pluralism and assimilation but are often less willing to recognize the degree to which our society has been built on segregation and annihilation.

The remainder of this chapter employs these four types of contact to examine the history and present social standing of major racial and ethnic categories in American society.

RACE AND ETHNICITY IN THE UNITED STATES

> Give me your tired, your poor,
> Your huddled masses yearning to breathe free,
> The wretched refuse of your teeming shore,
> Send these, the homeless, tempest-tossed to me:
> I lift my lamp beside the golden door.

These words by Emma Lazarus, inscribed on the Statue of Liberty, express American ideals of human dignity, personal freedom, and opportunity. But America's golden door has opened more widely for some than for others. Social inequality has been entrenched in American society since its beginning, evident in the history of America's various racial and ethnic minorities.

White Anglo-Saxon Protestants

White Anglo-Saxon Protestants (WASPs) have historically dominated American society. Most WASPs are of English ancestry, but Scots and Welsh are also included. Those Protestants who are members of the Episcopal Church—derived from the Anglican Church in England—have the highest social standing of WASPs (Roof,

1979). WASPs predominated among early settlers; not until the nineteenth century did substantial immigration of non-WASPs begin. In 1980 there were almost 50 million Americans of English ancestry (see Table 12–1). Adding people of Scottish and Welsh ancestry, one in four Americans is at least partly WASP.

Historically, WASP immigrants were highly skilled and strongly motivated toward achievement, displaying what came to be called the Protestant work ethic. Also, as the majority, WASPs were not subject to the prejudice and discrimination experienced by other categories of people. The historical dominance of WASPs has been so great that, as was noted earlier, becoming assimilated into American society has largely meant becoming more like the WASPs (Gordon, 1964).

In the nineteenth century, some WASPs responded to growing social diversity with prejudice and discrimination toward new arrivals they saw as undesirable foreigners. Nativist political movements also sought legal limits to the rapidly growing immigration. Many wealthier WASPs pursued a personal solution to the "problem": isolating themselves from those they deemed their social inferiors. Louis Brandeis, a brilliant Jewish lawyer whose appointment to the U.S. Supreme Court represented a triumph over prejudice, recalled that wealthy WASPs in Boston advised their children that

> Boston holds nothing for you except heavy taxes and political misrule. When you marry, pick out a suburb to build a house in, join [a country club], and make your life center about your club, your home and your children. (Mumford, 1961:495)

Thus the 1880s—the decade in which the Statue of Liberty first welcomed immigrants to America—also saw the founding of the first American country club (with all WASP members). Soon afterward, WASPs established various genealogical societies—such as the Daughters of the American Revolution (1890) and the Society of Mayflower Descendants (1894)—and began publishing the *Social Register* (1887; see the box on page 264). These organizations served to socially distance wealthy WASPs from newly arrived immigrants (Baltzell, 1964).

By about 1930, the growing wealth of other categories of Americans as well as more egalitarian values forced WASPs to share their privileges (Baltzell, 1964, 1976, 1988). This changing trend was symbolized in 1960 by the election of John Fitzgerald Kennedy as the first non-WASP (Irish-Catholic) president of the United States. Even so, WASPs continue to have great influence in American society. Typically, WASPs are highly edu-

cated, work in high-prestige occupations, and enjoy above-average incomes (Neidert & Farley, 1985). Also the majority of people in the upper-upper class are WASPs (Greeley, 1974; Baltzell, 1979; Roof, 1981). The WASP cultural legacy also continues: English remains the dominant language of the United States, and Protestantism is the majority religion. Our legal system, too, reflects its English origins. Perhaps the historical dominance of WASPs is most evident in the widespread use of the terms "race" and "ethnicity" to describe everyone but them.

Native Americans

The term *Native Americans* refers to the hundreds of distinct societies that comprised the original inhabitants of the Americas, including Aleuts, Cherokee, Hopi, Sioux, Mohawk, Aztec, and Inca. Thousands of years ago, migrating peoples crossed a land bridge from Asia to North America where the Bering Strait (off the coast of Alaska) is today, and over the centuries they spread throughout the Western hemisphere. When the first Europeans arrived late in the fifteenth century, Native Americans had already inhabited the continent for 30,000 years and numbered in the millions (Dobyns, 1966).

From the start, contact with Europeans was disastrous for Native Americans. What Europeans ethnocentrically described as "taming the wilderness" was actually the destruction of many ancient civilizations. Exposure to European diseases took a terrible toll among Native Americans, and tens of thousands more were exterminated as Europeans sought wealth and land. By the beginning of the twentieth century, the "vanishing Americans" numbered a mere 250,000 (Tyler, 1973).

Use of the term *Indians* to refer to Native Americans is traced to Christopher Columbus (1446–1506), who is said to have mistaken the Antilles in the Caribbean for India. Columbus confronted indigenous Americans as a peaceful and generous people living in harmony with nature (Matthiessen, 1984). Such values clashed with those of Europeans, whose way of life was more hierarchical, competitive, and aggressive. Even as Europeans slaughtered Native-American men, women, and children and seized their land, the invaders demeaned their victims as thieves and murderers, and even as subhuman (Josephy, 1982). Among the early colonial leaders of New England, Roger Williams described Native Americans as "wolves with men's brains," William Bradford termed them "wild men," and Cotton Mather denounced

Trail of Tears was painted by Robert Lindneux (1942) to commemorate the suffering caused by the policy of forced migration—often at gunpoint—of native Americans living east of the Mississippi after 1830. Uprooted from traditional homelands, the Shawnee, Cherokee, and other peoples were marched for hundreds of miles westward to supposedly "reserved" territories on the plains. Often they arrived only to confront still more hostile whites who had already settled on what the government had promised were to be Indian lands.

Robert Lindneux, The Trail of Tears, 1942. Woolaroc Museum, Bartlesville, OK.

them as sinful "hounds of hell" (Matthiessen, 1984:3–4). Such negative stereotyping represents attempts to justify the often barbarous treatment of these people (Unruh, 1979).

After the Revolutionary War, the new United States government adopted a pluralist approach to Native American societies and sought to gain more land through treaties. Payment for their land was far from fair, however, and when Native Americans resisted surrender of their homelands, superior military power was used to evict them. Thousands of Cherokees, for example, died on a forced march—the Trail of Tears—from their homes in the southeastern United States to segregated reservations in the Midwest. By the early 1800s, few Native Americans remained east of the Mississippi River.

After 1871, the United States condescendingly made Native Americans wards of the government and tried to resolve "the Indian problem" through forced assimilation. The result was that Native Americans not only continued to lose their land, but now were losing their culture as well. Reservation life fostered dependency, replacing ancestral languages with English and eroding traditional religion in favor of Christianity. Many children were taken from their parents and placed in boarding schools, operated by the Bureau of Indian Affairs, to be resocialized into "Americans." Local control of reservations was given to the few Native Americans who supported government policies, and reservation land—traditionally held collectively—was distributed as

the private property of individual families (Tyler, 1973). In the process, whites grabbed still more land for themselves.

What Native American territories remain today are sought by outsiders wishing to develop coal, oil, natural gas, and uranium reserves (Josephy, 1982). Native Americans differ among themselves as to whether they should accept lucrative offers from big corporations for their land. Progressives favor the sale of mining leases, while traditionalists condemn mining or any other commercial activity on what they view as sacred land.

Not unil 1924 were Native Americans granted citizenship. Since then, the government has encouraged their moving from reservations. A number of them have adopted mainstream cultural patterns and married non-Native Americans. Many large cities now have sizable Native American populations. As is shown in Table 12–2, however, median family income for Native Americans in 1980 was far below the American average, and college degrees among Native Americans (7.7 percent) were less than half as common as among Americans as a whole (17.1 percent).

From in-depth interviews with Native Americans in a western city, Joan Albon (1971) concluded that many were disadvantaged by little education, few marketable skills, less than perfect English, and dark skin that provokes prejudice and discrimination. Additionally, she noted, Native Americans often lacked the individualism and competitiveness that foster success in America, a

Table 12–2 THE SOCIAL STANDING OF NATIVE AMERICANS, 1980*

	Native Americans	Entire United States
Median Family Income	$16,672	$19,917
Proportion in Poverty	27.5%	12.4%
Median Education (age 25 and over)	12.2 years	12.5 years
Completion of Four or More Years of College (age 25 and over)	7.7%	17.1%

* The data used in this chapter are the most recent available at the time of publication. Comparisons of all racial and ethnic categories are possible only through using data from the 1980 census, but more recent statistics are also included wherever possible.

SOURCE: U.S. Bureau of the Census.

result of both traditional values and long dependence on government assistance.

Like other racial and ethnic minorities in the United States, Native Americans have recently reasserted pride in their cultural heritage and sought greater rights and opportunity for themselves. They have sued the national government for return of lands forcibly taken in the past, and organizations such as the Pan-Indian American Indian Movement seek democratic control of reservation lands by Native Americans themselves. In some instances, they have also confronted federal officials violently. Few Native Americans support this means of addressing grievances, but the vast majority share a profound sense of the injustice endured at the hands of whites (Josephy, 1982; Matthiessen, 1983).

Black Americans

Although blacks accompanied Spanish explorers to the New World in the fifteenth century, the beginning of black history in the United States is usually set at 1619, when a Dutch trading ship brought twenty Africans to Jamestown, Virginia (Holt, 1980). It is unclear whether these people arrived as slaves or as indentured servants— that is, people who were obligated to work for a fixed period of time in return for passage across the Atlantic Ocean. Nevertheless, being black in America soon became virtually synonymous with being a slave. In 1661 the first law recognizing slavery was passed in Virginia (Sowell, 1981).

Slavery became the foundation of the plantation system within an agrarian plantation economy. Whites prospered as plantation owners, and also as slave traders— a legal occupation until 1808. Some 10 million Africans were forcibly brought to the Western hemisphere, and about 400,000 of them entered the United States (Sowell, 1981). During a voyage of several weeks across the Atlantic Ocean, hundreds of slaves were chained on board small sailing ships as human cargo with barely enough room to move. Filth and disease killed many; others were driven to suicide. Overall, perhaps half the Africans died en route (Tannenbaum, 1946; Franklin, 1967).

Surviving the journey was a mixed blessing, bringing a life of servitude as the economic property of white owners. Most slaves engaged in farming, although some worked in cities at a variety of trades (Franklin, 1967). Work usually lasted from morning until evening, and for up to twenty hours a day during the harvest.

The law afforded slave owners whatever discipline was needed to ensure that slaves labored continuously. Corporal punishment was widely used. Even the killing of a slave by a white owner was rarely a legal concern. Also slave families were divided at the whim of white owners as human beings were bought and sold at public auctions like any other pieces of property. This system further controlled slaves by eliminating all opportunities to gain an education and by ensuring that they remained totally dependent on their owners for their basic needs (Sowell, 1981).

There were, however, free blacks in both the North and the South. Such free people of color, as they were called, were small-scale farmers, skilled workers, and small-business owners (Murray, 1978). But the lives of most black Americans were a glaring contradiction of the principles of equality and freedom on which the United States was founded. The Declaration of Independence states:

> We hold these Truths to be self-evident, that all Men are created equal, that they are endowed by their Creator with certain unalienable Rights, that among these are Life, Liberty, and the Pursuit of Happiness. . . .

Most white Americans did not apply these ideals to blacks. In the Dred Scott case in 1857, the U.S. Supreme Court addressed the question, "Are blacks citizens?" and answered, "We think they are not, and that they are not included, and were not intended to be included, under the word 'citizens' in the Constitution, and can therefore claim none of the rights and privileges which that instrument provides for and secures for citizens of the United

States" (Blaustein & Zangrando, 1968:160). Thus arose what Swedish sociologist Gunnar Myrdal (1944) later called the *American dilemma*: the denial of basic rights and freedoms to an entire category of Americans. To resolve this dilemma, many whites simply defined blacks as innately inferior.

In 1865 the Thirteenth Amendment to the Constitution outlawed slavery. Three years later the Fourteenth Amendment reversed the Dred Scott ruling, giving citizenship to all people born in the United States. The Fifteenth Amendment, ratified in 1870, stated that neither race nor previous condition of servitude should deprive anyone of the right to vote. Even so, subsequent Jim Crow laws kept American society divided into two racial castes (Woodward, 1974). Especially in the South, violence was directed at blacks (and some whites) who advocated racial equality. Thousands of blacks were lynched or burned, often on the basis of the flimsiest allegations by whites.

The twentieth century has brought dramatic changes to black America. Overwhelmingly concentrated in the South a century ago, tens of thousands of blacks left farming for industrial jobs in northern cities in the decades after World War I. These migrants did find greater economic opportunity in the North, but they also encountered prejudice and discrimination, greater than that experienced by white immigrants arriving from Europe at the same time (Lieberson, 1980). In the 1950s and 1960s, blacks and sympathetic whites launched an attack on racism in America that became a national civil rights movement. A number of important legal battles were won during this period, including the rejection of racially segregated schools. Civil rights acts passed in the 1960s lessened overt racial discrimination in employment and public accommodations. Also the "black power movement" brought a renewed sense of purpose and pride to black Americans, making many less willing to be defined in terms of the white culture.

Nonetheless, blacks continue to occupy a clearly subordinate position in the American system of social stratification, as is shown in Table 12–3. The median income of black families in 1988 ($19,330) was substantially below that for America as a whole ($32,191). Black families are also three times as likely as white families to be poor. In 1980, median family income for blacks was about 63 percent that of whites. By 1984, the proportion had fallen to 56 percent, recovering slightly to 60 percent by 1988. In general, black Americans made significant economic gains from the 1940s through 1960s; the 1970s brought economic stagnation, and much of

Some five thousand lynchings were officially recorded in the United States between 1880 and 1930. Lynch mobs were formed by whites as a terrorist means of maintaining dominance over blacks and other minorities.

Beginning in the mid-1950s, a renewed Civil Rights movement struggled for racial equality in the United States. Resistance by whites was often fierce, as suggested by the common tactic of turning fire hoses on protesters.

Table 12–3   THE SOCIAL STANDING OF BLACK AMERICANS, 1980 AND 1988

	Black Americans	Entire United States
Median Family Income	$12,598 ($19,330 in 1988)	$19,917 ($32,191 in 1988)
Proportion in Poverty	29.9% (31.6% in 1988)	12.4% (13.1% in 1988)
Median Education (age 25 and over)	12.0 yrs (12.5 yrs in 1988)	12.5 yrs (12.8 yrs in 1988)
Completion of Four or More Years of College (age 25 and over)	8.4% (11.3% in 1988)	17.1% (22.7% in 1988)

SOURCE: U.S. Bureau of the Census.

the 1980s saw a decline in economic position (Jacob, 1986; Littman, 1989; Jaynes & Williams, 1989; Welniak & Littman, 1989).

This economic disparity results from the historical overrepresentation of blacks in low-paying occupations. Recent changes in the American economy, described in Chapter 10 ("Social Class in America"), have also hurt blacks who had gained financial security from better-paying work in factories. The 1980s saw the loss of millions of factory jobs—a vital source of employment often close to inner-city black neighborhoods. The drastic cuts in domestic spending by the Reagan administration also made retraining for these workers harder to obtain. Thus black unemployment has remained twice as high as white unemployment. Among urban black teenagers the figure exceeds 40 percent; *all* black adults struggle with this level of unemployment in rural areas (Farley, 1980; Wilson, 1984; Jacob, 1986; Lichter, 1989).

With regard to education, the median schooling for blacks over the age of 25 in 1960 was 8.2 years, well below the median of 10.9 years for whites. By 1988 the gap was much smaller: the median figure for blacks was 12.5 years, compared with 12.8 for whites. Despite the gain, as Table 12–3 shows, blacks are still only about half as likely as whites to complete four years of college. In recent years the number of blacks enrolling in college has actually fallen. In the mid-1980s, only about one-fourth of black high-school graduates entered college, compared with about one-third a decade earlier. A similar pattern of decline holds for graduate study as well (American Council on Education, 1987; *Black Issues*

in Higher Education, 1987). This educational setback is undoubtedly related to the economic reversals already described.

No less distressing is evidence that education may not solve the economic problems of black America. A generation ago, Peter Blau and Otis Duncan (1967) claimed that education offers less upward social mobility to blacks than it does to whites. Their research showed that better-educated blacks actually had a lower social standing in relation to whites with comparable education than blacks with less education had in relation to their white counterparts. This finding suggests that the barriers of prejudice and discrimination become greater as blacks gain more education, a conclusion supported by other research (Tienda & Lii, 1987). As we explained in Chapter 10, one in ten black families is now affluent, with income exceeding $50,000 a year; about one in four black families is now securely within the American middle class. The number of black physicians and lawyers has increased dramatically during the last generation. But these gains stand out against the persistent poverty of millions of blacks—especially women and children—who represent an economically desperate underclass (Wilson, 1984; O'Hare, 1989).

Black Americans have greatly increased their political power: a greater number are now registered voters and hold elective office. Black migration to cities, along with white movement to the suburbs, has resulted in black majorities in many large cities, and by 1990 half

The election of Douglas Wilder in 1989 was a symbolic victory for all black Americans. Not only was this descendant of slaves elected to the highest political office in Virginia—a state of the old Confederacy—but his achievement marked the first time in American history that a black person was elected as governor of any state.

of America's ten largest cities had elected black mayors. In 1989 Virginia elected the first black governor in American history. At the national level, however, blacks represent 11 percent of voting-age Americans and only about 1 percent of elected officials. In 1984 Jesse Jackson became the first black American to win a state presidential primary election, but after the 1988 elections only 24 blacks (of 435) sat in the House of Representatives and no black person (of 100) was in the Senate. Another issue is that, because of serious economic problems, blacks generally favor more extensive changes in American society than whites are willing to support. Thus Dianne Pinderhughes (1986) maintains that neither major political party in the United States really represents black interests.

In sum, for more than 350 years blacks have struggled for social equality in America. American society can certainly be proud of important steps in pursuit of racial equality. A century ago slavery was outlawed, and many forms of overt discrimination have been legally banned during this century. Further, research suggests that anti-black prejudice has declined in recent decades as a majority of Americans are coming to see racial justice as a matter of basic fairness (Firebaugh & Davis, 1988). For example, during the 1970s about 60 percent of Americans claimed that white home owners had the right to sell their homes only to whites if they so wished. By 1989 that proportion had fallen to under 40 percent (N.O.R.C., 1989:180).

Still, such figures also indicate that racial bigotry remains strong in America. Researchers have also concluded that the psychological well-being and overall quality of life for blacks remain below that of whites, even at equal levels of income (Thomas & Hughes, 1986). Thus race remains a powerful force in American society.

One response has been the government policy of affirmative action, or preferential treatment for categories of people historically subject to prejudice and discrimination. The box on page 328 provides details.

Asian Americans

Although they share some racial characteristics, Asian Americans represent enormous cultural diversity. The official count at the beginning of the 1980s placed their number at about 3 million—approaching 2 percent of the population. These represented several dozen cultural categories. As was shown in Table 12–1, the largest category of Asian Americans was of Chinese ancestry (about 800,000 people in 1980) followed by Filipino (775,000) and Japanese (about 700,000). Most Asian Americans live in the West. Migration from China and Japan to the United States began over a century ago; these long-established minorities are described in separate sections below.

More recent immigrants from Asia include Filipinos, Koreans, and Vietnamese. About 200,000 Vietnam-

The success of many Asians is testimony to their cultural emphasis on achievement. But such success is common only in a few fields. Immigrant minorities tend to excel in mathematics, science, or music because these pursuits do not depend on extensive knowledge of a new language or culture. Instead, they utilize systems of thought (especially numbers) that are familiar to people of all societies. Asian immigrants have won several Nobel prizes in physics, for instance, but none for literature.

Affirmative Action: Problem or Solution?

The phrase "Equal Justice Under Law" over the entrance to the Supreme Court building in Washington, D.C., has certainly not applied to many American minorities. One reaction to this historical pattern is affirmative action, which entails special efforts to enhance the opportunities of minorities. Affirmative action means, for example, that employers actively encourage applications from all racial and ethnic categories and that they carefully monitor hiring and promotion policies to ensure that they not discriminate, even unintentionally, against minorities. The goal is the representation of all categories of people in various occupations and educational programs in proportion to their population size.

The most controversial element of affirmative action is the establishment of quotas that ensure the inclusion of minorities. Under a quota system, a fixed number of minority members are guaranteed favorable treatment regardless of how they stack up against other applicants. Quota systems have been successfully challenged in the courts, but the *principle* of affirmative action has also been upheld; in other words, race and ethnicity can be considered in hiring and promotions.

Advocates see affirmative action as a fair and necessary corrective for historical discrimination. Everybody alive today, they argue, is advantaged or disadvantaged because of privileges accorded or denied to their parents and grandparents. Past discrimination affects minorities, just as past privilege affects others. "Special treatment," then, is nothing new and is necessary for those denied opportunity through no fault of their own. Only in this way, advocates claim, can we break the vicious circle of prejudice and discrimination.

Opponents of affirmative action agree that minorities have historically suffered from discrimination, but they see affirmative action as *reverse discrimination*. Why should whites today be penalized for past discrimination for which they were in no way responsible? Opponents also claim that minorities have largely overcome historical barriers to opportunity and that those who have made the greatest efforts have had the most success—which is as it should be. Giving minorities special treatment inevitably compromises standards, which is harmful to everyone.

Americans are divided on this issue as it is applied to blacks, but they generally oppose such policies:

> Some people think that blacks have been discriminated against for so long that the government has a special obligation to help improve their living standards. Others believe that the government should not be giving special treatment to blacks. (N.O.R.C., 1989:331)

The results of a 1989 survey are presented below. The numbers 1 through 5 show the range of opinion in relation to the three statements.

I strongly agree that the government is obligated to help blacks.		I agree with both answers.		I strongly agree that the government shouldn't give special treatment.
1	2	3	4	5
8.7%	9.4%	26.9%	18.4%	33.0%

No Response = 3.7%   Total = 1,035 respondents

SOURCE: Survey data from N.O.R.C., *General Social Surveys* (Chicago: National Opinion Research Center, 1989), p. 331.

ese have immigrated to the United States, a legacy of American military involvement in Southeast Asia. By 1990, estimates placed Filipinos as the largest category of Asian Americans, with 1.4 million people, outnumbering Chinese Americans (1990 estimate, 1.2 million), and Japanese Americans (800,000). Thus Asian Americans, now accounting for 40 percent of all immigrants, are the fastest-growing American minority. These newer immigrants have changed the face of western cities; during the 1970s, for example, the Asian-American population of Los Angeles more than tripled to about 750,000 people (Anderson, 1983). Lower numbers of Asian immigrants have settled in the East and across the Midwest.

Asian immigrants—especially young people—have attracted both attention and respect in recent years as high achievers. For instance, *Time* magazine recently devoted a cover story to "Asian-American Whiz Kids" (Brand, 1987). The article noted that many of the best American colleges and universities now have large numbers of Asian-American students. These 2 percent of all Americans represented 20 percent of the class of 1991 at the Massachusetts Institute of Technology. In California, although they represent only 7 percent of the population, one of every four students at the University of California at Berkeley is Asian American.

Although Asian Americans have made significant economic and social gains in recent years, the American attitude toward Asians has not always been one of pride. As will be explained presently, the "model minority" image also obscures the poverty of some Asian Americans.

Chinese Americans

Chinese immigration to America began about 140 years ago, when the California Gold Rush of 1849 sparked an economic boom in the West. People swarmed into the region in search of easy riches, and new towns and businesses developed virtually overnight. This boom created a pressing need for cheap labor, leading to the importation of about 100,000 Chinese immigrants in the decades that followed. Most were young, hard-working males willing to take lower-status jobs shunned by whites (Ling, 1971).

But the economy turned bad in the 1870s, and desperate whites began competing with the Chinese for jobs. Suddenly the industriousness of the Chinese and their willingness to work for low wages became threatening. The result was mounting prejudice and discrimination (Boswell, 1986).

Soon, laws barred the Chinese from many occupations. They also lost legal protections, including the right to testify against whites in court, just when they needed them most (Sowell, 1981). As fear of the "Yellow Peril" grew, whites directed vicious and racist campaigns against the Chinese. In 1877 thousands of whites rampaged through San Francisco's Chinatown, attacking people and property; in other towns, the entire Chinese population was driven out (Lyman, 1971). American society seemed to line up against the Chinese; thus the

saying about not having a "Chinaman's chance" became part of our folklore (Sung, 1967:56).

Backing the white majority, the U.S. government in 1882 passed the first of several laws ending Chinese immigration. This action brought further hardship because, of the 100,000 Chinese already in the United States, males outnumbered females by almost twenty to one (Hsu, 1971; Lai, 1980). This law prevented the wives and children of Chinese male immigrants from joining them in the United States. Because of this sex imbalance, the Chinese population fell to about 60,000 by 1920. Chinese women already in the United States benefited from the situation, however: being in such demand, they soon became far less submissive to men (Sowell, 1981).

In response to white oppression, some Chinese moved eastward; many more sought the relative safety of urban Chinatowns (Wong, 1971). There Chinese traditions flourished, and kinship networks called *clans* gave financial assistance to individuals and served as political organizations representing the interests of all. With the help of the clans, Chinese obtained loans to start businesses and find jobs. At the same time, however, living in a Chinatown discouraged the learning of the English language and other forms of cultural assimilation.

With the onset of World War II, hostility toward the Chinese diminished as labor was again in short supply (Lai, 1980). In 1943 President Roosevelt ended the ban on Chinese immigration and extended the rights of citizenship to Chinese Americans born abroad. Many responded by moving out of Chinatowns and seeking cultural assimilation. In Honolulu, for example, 70 percent of the Chinese people lived in Chinatown in 1900; by 1980, only 20 percent did (Lai, 1980).

By 1950, many Chinese Americans were enjoying considerable upward social mobility. Today, Americans of Chinese ancestry are no longer restricted to self-employment in laundries and restaurants; many now work in the highest-prestige occupations. Their achievement has been outstanding in science and technology fields, in which many Chinese Americans—including several Nobel Prize winners—have excelled (Sowell, 1981). As is shown in Table 12–4, the median household income of Chinese Americans in 1980 ($22,259) was above the national average ($19,917), and Chinese Americans have twice the proportion of college graduates as Americans taken as a whole.

Nevertheless, many Chinese Americans still contend with serious problems. Overt prejudice and discrimination have lessened, but racial hostility persists. Poverty

Table 12–4 THE SOCIAL STANDING OF CHINESE AND JAPANESE AMERICANS, 1980

	Chinese Americans	Japanese Americans	Entire United States
Median Family Income	$22,259	$27,354	$19,917
Proportion in Poverty	13.5%	6.5%	12.4%
Median Education (age 25 and over)	13.4 yrs.	12.9 yrs.	12.5 yrs.
Completion of Four or More Years of College (age 25 and over)	36.6%	26.4%	17.1%

SOURCE: U.S. Bureau of the Census.

among Chinese Americans is above the national average, especially among those who remain within the protective circle of Chinatowns. At the beginning of the 1980s, the poverty level of New York's Chinatown was twice as high as that of the city as a whole, with half of all Chinese males working in restaurants and three-fourths of Chinese females stuck in low-paying jobs in the garment industry (Sowell, 1981). This situation has sparked a debate over whether racial and ethnic enclaves exploit or economically assist their residents (Portes & Jensen, 1989; Zhou & Logan, 1989).

Japanese Americans

Japanese immigration to the United States began slowly in the 1860s; by 1890, only 3,000 had arrived, most of them settling in the West. Japanese immigrants were welcomed to the Hawaiian Islands (a state since 1959) as a source of cheap labor on sugar plantations. Although by 1870 hostility toward Chinese immigrants was strong, the fact that the early Japanese immigrants were few in number apparently helped them escape much anti-Asian prejudice. In later decades, however, as Japanese immigration rose along with demands for better pay, whites sought to curb their immigration (Daniels, 1971). In 1908 the United States signed an agreement with Japan limiting male immigration, which was seen as the major economic threat, while allowing Japanese women to immigrate to ease the sex-ratio imbalance. By the early 1920s, new laws virtually ended Japanese immigration. At this point, Japanese immigrants faced much the same prejudice and discrimination as did the Chinese. In some areas, laws mandated segregation and prohibited interra-

cial marriage. Foreign-born Japanese were not eligible for U.S. citizenship until 1952.

But Japanese immigrants differed from the Chinese in two significant ways. First, knowledge of the United States was much more extensive in Japan than in China. Although maintaining their ethnic identity, Japanese immigrants were therefore poised for assimilation on their arrival in the United States (Sowell, 1981). Second, Japanese immigrants did not cluster in urban areas. In response to prejudice and discrimination, some did form defensive enclaves—called Little Tokyos or Little Osakas by immigrants and simply Japtowns by hostile whites (Daniels, 1971). Many, however, began farming in rural areas.

Japanese purchase of farmland brought a swift reaction from economically threatened whites. In 1913 California began passing laws preventing any noncitizen from owning farmland. This institutional discrimination was intended to prevent Asian immigrants from entering the lucrative agricultural market. Even more basically, such laws were simply racist, as the attorney-general of California conceded in 1914 with remarkable candor:

> The fundamental basis of all legislation has been, and is, race undesirability. It seeks to limit [Japanese] presence by curtailing the privileges which they may enjoy here, for they will not come here in large numbers and abide with us if they may not acquire land. (Kitano, 1980:563).

In response, foreign-born Japanese (called the *Issei*) placed farmland in the names of their American-born children (*Nisei*), who were automatically U.S. citizens under the Constitution. Another strategy was to lease farmland, which many Japanese did with great success.

The Japanese faced an even greater struggle after December 7, 1941, when the nation of Japan destroyed much of the U.S. naval fleet at Hawaii's Pearl Harbor. The rage felt toward Japan was directed toward the Japanese living in America. Some feared the Japanese here would commit espionage and sabotage on behalf of Japan. Within a year, President Roosevelt signed Executive Order 9066, an unprecedented act intended to protect the national security of the United States. Areas of the West Coast were designated as military zones from which anyone considered likely to be disloyal would be relocated inland to remote military reservations. Thus over 110,000 people of Japanese ancestry, representing 90 percent of their total population in the United States, were interned in security camps.

This policy has since been condemned. First, the act was applied not to individuals, but to an entire cate-

The internment of Japanese Americans during World War II was justified as necessary to ensure national security, but it was also an expression of the racial hostility toward people of Asian ancestry that had long existed in the western United States.

gory of people, not one of whom was ever convicted of any disloyal act. Second, roughly two-thirds of those imprisoned were Nisei American, citizens by birth; but racism was apparently stronger than the concern for the rights of Americans, and the cry "The Japs must go" was raised by liberals and conservatives alike (Kitano, 1985:244). Third, although the United States was also at war with Germany and Italy, no such action was taken against whites of German and Italian ancestry.

Relocation meant selling homes, furnishings, and businesses on short notice for whatever price could be obtained. As a result, almost the entire Japanese-American population was economically devastated. Within the military prison camps—surrounded by barbed wire and armed soldiers—life was a great hardship. Until the end of 1944, families were crowded into single rooms, often in buildings that had previously been used for livestock (Fujimoto, 1971; Bloom, 1980). The internment ended in 1944, when it was declared unconstitutional by the Supreme Court. In 1988 Congress awarded $20,000 as compensation to each victim of this policy, token recognition of the economic loss and personal suffering endured by Japanese Americans.

After World War II, Japanese Americans made a dramatic recovery. Having lost their traditional businesses, they entered a wide range of new occupations. Because their culture places a high value on education and hard work, Japanese Americans have enjoyed remarkable success. As is shown in Table 12–4, the 1980 median income of a Japanese-American household was $27,354—more than 30 percent above the national average. The rate of poverty among Japanese Americans was also half the national average.

Upward social mobility has been accompanied by considerable cultural assimilation. The third and fourth generations of Japanese Americans (the *Sansei* and *Yonsei*) rarely live within residential enclaves, as many Chinese Americans still do, and many have married non-Japanese Americans, linking cultural assimilation to biological miscegenation. Of course, many Japanese have lost their traditions, including the ability to speak Japanese. But a high proportion of Japanese Americans participate in ethnic associations as a way of maintaining some ethnic identity (Fugita & O'Brien, 1985). Still, many appear to be caught between two worlds, belonging to neither. As one Japanese-American man claims, "I never considered myself 100 percent American because of obvious physical differences. Nor did I think of myself as Japanese" (Okimoto, 1971:14).

Hispanic Americans

In 1990, there were more than 25 million Hispanic Americans, representing 10 percent of the population of the United States. Although some are of purely Spanish descent, most are some combination of Spanish, African, and Native American ancestry. Hispanic Americans also represent a variety of cultures. About half are Mexican Americans, commonly called *Chicanos*. Puerto Ricans are next in population size (3 million), followed by Cuban Americans (1 million). Many other societies of Latin America are represented in smaller numbers. Because of a high birth rate, the Hispanic-American population is currently increasing by almost a million a year. On this basis, Hispanic Americans may outnumber blacks in the United States early in the next century (Moore & Pachon, 1985).

The social standing of Hispanics improved in some respects during the 1980s. Between 1984 and 1988, for instance, the number of Hispanic men in managerial and professional occupations jumped 42 percent; among Hispanic women, the increase was even greater: 61 percent (Schwartz, 1989). Nevertheless, family income for

Hispanics remained steady during the 1980s. Furthermore, as the following sections reveal, some categories of Hispanics have fared better than others.

Mexican Americans

Some Mexican Americans, or Chicanos, are descendants of people who were living in a part of Mexico that was annexed to the United States as a result of the Mexican-American War (1846–1848). Most Mexican Americans, however, immigrated to the United States in recent decades. During the 1970s and 1980s, immigration from Mexico was greater than from any other country in the world. By the end of the 1980s, almost 15 million Mexican Americans were officially recorded as living in the United States, most in the West and Southwest. The actual figure could be far higher because large numbers of Mexican Americans have entered the United States illegally (Weintraub & Ross, 1982). The rapid increase in the Mexican-American population has reshaped cities such as San Antonio and Los Angeles. In the last two decades, for example, the Mexican-American population of Los Angeles has roughly tripled to at least 3 million.

Attitudes toward Mexican Americans have changed over time with the need for the inexpensive labor many of them provide, especially as farm workers. As was true of Japanese and Chinese immigrants in the West a century ago, many Mexican Americans still hold low-paying jobs. Table 12–5 shows that in 1980 the median family income for Chicanos was $14,765, about the same as

for all categories of Hispanics ($14,712), but well below the national average ($19,917). Chicano income rose during the 1980s but slipped even further behind other Americans. The 1988 median family income for Mexican Americans was $19,968, which was about 65 percent of the comparable national figure, down from 74 percent at the beginning of the decade. In 1988, one-fourth of Chicano families were classified as poor, more than twice the national average, although below the figure for blacks. Finally, despite improvement since 1980, Mexican Americans have significantly less education than Americans taken as a whole.

Puerto Ricans

Puerto Rico has been a possession of the United States since the end of the Spanish-American War in 1898. In 1917, Puerto Ricans became citizens of the United States, and they move freely to and from the mainland (Fitzpatrick, 1980). Most who migrate seek greater economic opportunity, and the majority settle in New York City.

In 1910 about 500 Puerto Ricans lived in New York City; by 1940, this number had increased to about 70,000. After World War II, however, regular airline service between New York City and San Juan, the capital of Puerto Rico, sparked greater migration. Almost 40,000 Puerto Ricans came to New York during 1946 alone, and by 1950, New York's Puerto Rican population reached 187,000 (Glazer & Moynihan, 1970).

Table 12–5 THE SOCIAL STANDING OF HISPANIC AMERICANS, 1980 AND 1988

	All Hispanics		Mexican Americans		Puerto Ricans		Cuban Americans		Entire United States	
	1980	1988	1980	1988	1980	1988	1980	1988	1980	1988
Median Family Income	$14,712	$20,306	$14,765	$19,968	$10,734	$15,185	$18,245	$27,294	$19,917	$30,853
Proportion in Poverty	23.5%	25.8%	23.3%	25.5%	36.3%	37.9%	13.2%	13.8%	12.4%	10.8%
Median Education (years) (age 25 or over)	10.8	12.0	9.6	10.8	10.5	12.0	12.2	12.4	12.5	12.7
Completion of Four or More Years of College (age 25 or over)	7.6%	10.0%	4.9%	7.1%	5.6%	9.6%	16.2%	17.2%	17.1%	20.3%

SOURCE: U.S. Bureau of the Census.

Hispanic Americans represent a majority of the residents of Miami, Florida. In the Little Havana district of the city, Cuban immigrants have blended their traditional way of life with the surrounding cultures.

Life in New York may have been better than on the island, but it was less than most Puerto Ricans had hoped for. By the mid-1960s, half of the Puerto Ricans in New York were living in poverty (Moore & Pachon, 1985). Today, half of the more than 2 million Puerto Ricans in the continental United States live in New York's Spanish Harlem, and many continue to be severely disadvantaged. Adjusting to cultural patterns on the mainland—including, for many, learning English—is a major challenge; Puerto Ricans with darker skin encounter especially strong prejudice and discrimination. As a result, there are about as many Puerto Ricans now emigrating each year from the mainland to Puerto Rico as arriving here from the island.

The ease with which Puerto Ricans can return to Puerto Rico has probably limited cultural assimilation. For example, about three-fourths of Puerto Rican families on the mainland continue to speak Spanish in the home, compared with about one-half of Mexican-American families (Sowell, 1981; Stevens & Swicegood, 1987). Speaking Spanish helps maintain a strong ethnic identity but may also limit economic opportunity. Puerto Ricans also have a higher incidence of female-headed households than do other Hispanics, a statistic that is linked to American poverty (Reimers, 1984). Table 12–5 shows that in 1988 the median household income for Puerto Ricans was $15,185—about half the national average. Throughout the 1980s, therefore, poverty has been higher among Puerto Ricans (37.9 percent in 1988) than among all Hispanics (25.8 percent in 1988). In short, Puerto Ricans continue to be the most socially disadvantaged Hispanic minority.

Cuban Americans

Large numbers of Cubans immigrated to the United States after the 1959 Marxist revolution led by Fidel Castro. By 1972, aided by special legislation, 400,000 Cubans had entered the United States (Perez, 1980). Most settled in Miami, although the Cuban community in New York now numbers over 50,000. Those who fled Castro's Cuba were generally not the "huddled masses" described on the Statue of Liberty, but highly educated business and professional people. They wasted little time building much the same success in the United States that they had enjoyed in Cuba (Fallows, 1983). Table 12–5 shows that the median household income for Cuban Americans in 1988 was $27,294—well above the average for all categories of Hispanics, and almost equal to the national average. Similarly, the proportion of Cuban Americans living in poverty is well below that for all Hispanics, although slightly higher than for all Americans. Notice, too, that Cuban Americans have more education than other categories of Hispanics.

Cuban Americans have managed high achievement despite retaining much of their traditional culture. Of the categories of Hispanics we have considered, they are the most likely to speak Spanish in their homes; eight out of ten families do (Sowell, 1981). Cultural distinctiveness and living in highly visible communities provokes hostility on the part of some whites. Miami, for example, has a vibrant Cuban-American population centered in the Little Havana district. While some whites applaud the economic and social strengths of the Cuban community, others angrily assert that the city has been taken over by outsiders. As one bumper sticker said bluntly, "Will the last American to leave Miami remember to bring the flag?"

In 1988 the number of Cuban Americans was estimated to be over a million (U.S. Bureau of the Census, 1989). Substantial population growth during the 1980s followed Fidel Castro's decision in 1980 to allow immigration to the United States through Mariel Harbor. The result was a flotilla of boats—the Mariel boat lift—transporting 125,000 refugees. Several thousand of these "boat people" had been released from Cuban prisons and mental hospitals, and they became the focus of mass-media accounts, fueling prejudice toward Cuban Americans (Clark, Lasaga, & Regue, 1981; Portes, 1984).

About 90,000 of this second wave of Cuban immigrants settled in the Miami area while others—especially those with darker skin—entered cities in the Northeast (Perez, 1980). These recent immigrants are typically poorer and less educated than those who arrived a generation earlier, a difference that has caused friction between them and the more established Cuban community in Miami (Fallows, 1983). But they too are quickly becoming established. Soon after their arrival, most applied for resident status so that their relatives abroad could also be admitted to the United States.

White Ethnic Americans

Despite a century of describing the United States as a melting pot, there is little doubt that ethnicity retains considerable importance among white Americans (Rubin, 1976). In the 1960s, the term *white ethnics* was coined in recognition of the fact that many whites proudly maintain their ethnic heritage. White ethnics are people of European ancestry, although generally not the WASPs described earlier. As Table 12–1 indicated, the largest "white ethnic" categories in 1980 were people of German ancestry (49 million), Irish ancestry (40 million), and French ancestry (13 million). Overall, more than half of all Americans fall into some white ethnic category.

The huge wave of immigration from Europe in the nineteenth century greatly increased the social diversity of the United States. Initially, the Germans and Irish predominated. Italians and Jews from many European societies followed. Despite cultural differences, these Europeans shared the hope that America would offer more political freedom and economic opportunity than they had known in their homelands. The belief that the streets of America were paved with gold was, of course, a far cry from the reality experienced by the

vast majority of immigrants. Jobs were not always easy to find, and most demanded hard labor for low wages.

Economic problems were made worse by prejudice and discrimination, which swelled with the increasing tide of immigration. Nativist organizations opposed the entry of more non-WASP Europeans to America and stirred up prejudice and discrimination against those already here. Ads seeking workers in the mid-nineteenth century often carried a warning to new arrivals: "None need apply but Americans" (Handlin, 1941:67).

Some of the prejudice and discrimination really involved class, since immigrants were typically poor and often had little command of English. But hostility toward "inferior" ethnicity was directed toward even the most distinguished achievers. Fiorello La Guardia, an outstanding mayor of New York between 1933 and 1945 and the son of immigrants, half Italian and half Jewish, was once denounced by President Herbert Hoover in words that reveal unambiguous ethnic hatred:

> You should go back where you belong and advise Mussolini how to make good honest citizens in Italy. The Italians are preponderantly our murderers and bootleggers. . . . Like a lot of other foreign spawn, you do not appreciate the country that supports and tolerates you. (Mann, 1959, cited in Baltzell, 1964:30)

That such a comment would be made by the president of the United States suggests the extent to which ethnic prejudice was rooted in American society.

Nativist opposition to the "dilution of WASP America" was greatest between 1880 and 1930, decades of intensive immigration as shown in Figure 12–4. Additional sources of ethnic tension during this period were the Bolshevik Revolution in Russia and other political conflicts in Europe after World War I, which sparked a "Red Scare" in America.

Nativists were finally victorious. Between 1921 and 1968, immigration quotas were applied to each foreign country. The greatest restrictions were placed on immigration by southern and eastern Europeans—peoples likely to have darker skin and to differ culturally from the dominant WASPs (Fallows, 1983).

In response to widespread prejudice and discrimination, many white ethnics followed the pattern of forming ethnic enclaves in which opportunity and mutual assistance were available. Often an ethnic minority was able to gain a foothold in a specialized trade. Italian Americans, for example, entered the construction industry; Irish Americans often worked in various building trades and civil service occupations; Jews were heavily represented in the garment industry; many Greeks (like

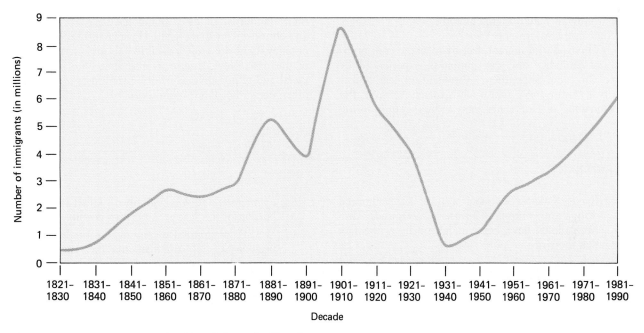

Figure 12–4 Immigration to the United States by Decade

(U.S. Immigration and Naturalization Service)

the Chinese) worked in the retail food business (Newman, 1973).

Most white ethnics who prospered were easily assimilated into the larger society. This has been far less true of working-class people, many of whom still live in traditional neighborhoods. Some of them, keenly aware of their plight, resent the national attention focused on the problems of other minorities, especially blacks. As one white ethnic Bostonian complained, "I'm working my ass off. My kids don't have a place to swim, my parks are full of glass, and I'm supposed to bleed for a bunch of people on relief" (Schrag, 1969:16).

Despite continuing problems, white ethnics have achieved considerable success of this century. Many descendants of immigrants who labored in sweatshops and lived in overcrowded tenements now have respectable positions—both socially and economically. No doubt this progress is the primary reason that ethnic heritage is now a source of pride to many white Americans.

AMERICAN MINORITIES: A HUNDRED-YEAR PERSPECTIVE

The United States has been, and is likely to remain, a land of immigrants. Its striking cultural diversity is the result of immigration, which peaked shortly after the beginning of this century and subsided with World War I (1914–1918) and with the restrictive legislation enacted between 1882 and the 1920s (Easterlin, 1980).

For most of those who came to America, the first half of this century brought gradual economic gains and at least some cultural assimilation. American society gradually granted basic freedoms where they had earlier been denied; for example, citizenship was extended to Native Americans (1924) and to foreign-born Chinese Americans (1943) and Japanese Americans (1952). In the 1950s, black Americans organized the civil rights movement in response to centuries of oppression.

As Figure 12–4 shows, immigration has risen steadily since the 1930s. The annual arrival of about 400,000 immigrants during the 1980s was about the same as during the "Great Immigration" a century before, although the newcomers were now entering a country with five times as many people. But today the names, faces, and cultural patterns of these immigrants are different. Now Latin America and Asia, rather than Europe, provide most immigrants to the United States. During the 1980s, Mexicans, Filipinos, and Koreans arrived in the largest numbers. Rather than entering the large cities on the "European" side of the United States, these new immigrants are bringing profound cultural changes to cities in the South and West.

These new immigrants face many of the same problems of prejudice and discrimination experienced by those who came before them. Also like European immigrants a century ago, many now struggle to enter the "golden door" of American society without entirely losing their traditional culture. Some have also built racial and ethnic enclaves: the Little Havana and Little Saigon of today stand alongside the Little Italy and Germantown of the past. New Americans also share the hope that racial and ethnic diversity will be viewed as a matter of difference rather than inferiority.

SUMMARY

1. Race is a matter of biological traits. The traditional distinctions among Caucasians, Negroids, and Mongoloids have been undermined by the fact that there are no pure races.

2. Ethnicity is based on shared cultural heritage and is further distinguished from race by being rather easily changed.

3. Both race and ethnicity are the bases of minority status by which a distinctive social identity is linked to social subordination.

4. A prejudice is an inflexible attitude that consists of an unfair generalization or stereotype about a category of people. Racism is a powerful type of prejudice, asserting that one race is innately superior or inferior to another.

5. Discrimination involves action—treating various categories of people differently. Although prejudice and discrimination are expressed by individuals, both are part of the fabric of American society, as they are elsewhere.

6. Pluralism recognizes social differences based on race and ethnicity but treats categories of people equally. Although American society is in some ways pluralistic, minorities do not have equal social standing.

7. Assimilation is a process by which minorities gradually adopt the patterns of the dominant culture. Instead of forming part of a true melting pot, immigrants to the United States have typically become more Anglicized.

8. Segregation is the physical and social separation of categories of people. Although some minorities seek to separate themselves, segregation is typically involuntary.

9. Genocide is the extermination of a category of people. In the history of the Americas, European colonists and settlers systemically killed a large proportion of the Native American people.

10. WASPs predominated among the original European settlers of America, and they continue to enjoy a high social position today.

11. Native Americans—the original inhabitants of the Americas—were subjected at the hands of Europeans to genocide, segregation, and forced assimilation. As a result, today the social standing of most Native Americans is well below the national average.

12. Black Americans endured over two centuries of slavery in America. After emancipation in 1865, blacks were rigidly segregated in American society by law. De facto segregation continues to this day. The typical social standing of blacks remains below the American average.

13. Chinese and Japanese Americans have been socially disadvantaged because of their racial and ethnic differences. Today, however, both categories have above-average income and education.

14. Hispanic Americans represent many ethnicities sharing a Spanish heritage. Mexican Americans are the largest Hispanic minority, heavily concentrated in the Southwest. Puerto Ricans, most of whom live in New York, are poorer. Cubans, heavily concentrated in Miami, are the most affluent category of Hispanics; their income approaches the national average.

15. White ethnic Americans include non-WASPs of European ancestry. While making gains during the last century, many white ethnics are still struggling for economic security.

16. Immigration has increased in recent years. No longer primarily from Europe, new immigrants are now mostly from Latin America and Asia.

KEY CONCEPTS

assimilation the process by which minorities gradually adopt patterns of the dominant culture

discrimination treating various categories of people unequally

ethnicity a cultural heritage shared by a category of people

genocide the systematic killing of one category of people by another

institutional discrimination patterns of discrimination that are woven into the fabric of a society

minority a category of people, defined by physical or cultural traits, who are socially disadvantaged

miscegenation the biological process of interbreeding among racial categories

pluralism a state in which racial and ethnic minorities are distinct but have social parity

prejudice a rigid and irrational generalization about a category of people

race a category composed of men and women who share biologically transmitted traits that are defined as socially significant

racism the belief that one racial category is innately superior or inferior to another

scapegoat a person or category of people unfairly blamed for the troubles of others

segregation the physical and social separation of categories of people

stereotype a set of prejudices that characterize a category of people

SUGGESTED READINGS

This paperback text provides a closer examination of issues raised in this chapter.

Harry H. L. Kitano. *Race Relations*. 4th ed. Englewood Cliffs, NJ: Prentice Hall, 1990.

The importance of race within the American system of social stratification is discussed in this recent book.

Fred R. Harris and Roger W. Wilkins. *Quiet Riots: Race and Poverty in the United States*. New York: Pantheon, 1988.

This book provides a detailed analysis of prejudice and discrimination within American society.

Joe R. Feagin and Clairece Booher Feagin. *Discrimination American Style: Institutional Racism and Sexism*. 2nd ed. Malabar, FL: Kreiger, 1986.

This collection of eleven essays examines how and why housing segregation persists in urban America.

Gary A. Tobin, ed. *Divided Neighborhoods: Changing Patterns of Racial Segregation*. Newbury Park, CA: Sage, 1987.

If cultural patterns can build community, they can also turn people against one another. Nowhere has this occurrence been truer than in the Middle East. This book examines ethnicity as central to Middle Eastern social structure.

Milton J. Esman and Itamar Rabinovich, eds. *Ethnicity, Pluralism, and the State in the Middle East*. Ithaca, NY and London: Cornell University Press, 1988.

The significance of race as it shaped the World War II conflict between the United States and Japan is examined in this book.

John W. Dower. *War Without Mercy: Race and Power in the Pacific War*. New York: Pantheon Books, 1986.

These two recent volumes review the social standing of black Americans.

Jaynes, Gerald David, and Robin M. Williams, eds. *A Common Destiny: Blacks and American Society*. Washington, DC: National Academy Press, 1989.

Janet Dewart, ed. *The State of Black America, 1989*. New York: National Urban League, 1989.

How do factors such as social class and race shape early educational experiences? This study compares a Head Start center in a black working-class neighborhood with a preschool in a white middle-class neighborhood.

Sally Lubeck. *Sandbox Society: Early Education in Black and White America—A Comparative Ethnography*. Philadelphia: Falmer Press/Taylor & Francis, 1985.

This book provides a general history of Hispanic cultures in the United States.

Lewis H. Gann and Peter J. Duignan. *The Hispanics in the United States: A History*. Boulder, CO: Westview, 1986.

13

Sex and Gender

In 1840 an American couple traveled to London to attend the World Anti-Slavery Convention. Henry Brewster Stanton, an eloquent speaker, was welcomed as a delegate—but his wife, Elizabeth Cady Stanton, was not. As a woman, she was barred at the door by people opposed to social inequality!

In London, Elizabeth Cady Stanton encountered Lucretia Mott, who had also been excluded from the meeting. The two women shared their dismay at how even abolitionists could discriminate against women of all races. Stanton and Mott discussed organizing a meeting of their own, and eight years later in Seneca Falls, New York, the first women's rights gathering was held. Delegates to this convention described how women and blacks suffered from similar prejudice and discrimination. Like black slaves, they concluded, most women could not own property, keep their earnings, enter into business, testify in court against their husbands, or legally vote.

In 1865 the Thirteenth Amendment to the Constitution outlawed slavery in the United States. Congress soon extended citizenship to all blacks (the Fourteenth Amendment), but the right to vote was granted only to black *men* (the Fifteenth Amendment). Women of all races were still denied suffrage. Elizabeth Cady Stanton

and other feminists consequently launched the National Woman Suffrage Association. In 1920 their long-sought goal was finally achieved with the adoption of the Nineteenth Amendment to the Constitution, granting women the right to vote (McGlen & O'Connor, 1983; Friedrich, 1984).

SEX AND GENDER

Now, more than seventy years later, women have made important gains but are still socially disadvantaged as men continue to hold a position of relative privilege. This inequality is often thought to reflect innate differences between the sexes, but it is actually a creation of society itself, as this chapter will explain. To begin, we shall explore the key concepts of sex and gender.

Sex: A Biological Distinction

Sex refers to *the division of humanity into biological categories of male and female.* Sex is determined at the moment a child is conceived through sexual intercourse.

Sex is a biological distinction that develops prior to birth. Gender is the meaning that a society attaches to being female or male—that is, feelings, thoughts, and behavior that are defined as feminine or masculine. Gender differences are not evident among infants, although over a lifetime the social worlds of males and females are distinguished in countless ways.

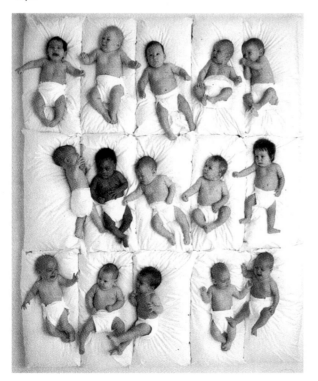

The female ovum and the male sperm, which join to form a fertilized embryo, each contain twenty-three pairs of chromosomes—biological codes that guide physical development. One of these pairs of chromosomes determines the child's sex: the mother contributes an X chromosome; the father contributes either an X or a Y. If the father contributes an X chromosome, a female embryo (XX) develops, whereas a Y results in a male embryo (XY).

Within six weeks, sex differentiation in a human embryo begins. If the embryo is male, testicular tissue produces testosterone, a chemical hormone that stimulates the development of the male genitals. Without testosterone, the embryo develops female genitals. About 105 males are born for every 100 females, but a higher death rate among males renders females a slight majority by the time people reach their mid-thirties (U.S. National Center for Health Statistics, 1988; 1988a).

At birth, males and females are distinguished by **primary sex characteristics**—*the genitals, used to reproduce the human species.* At puberty in the early teens, when people become capable of reproduction, further biological differentiation occurs in the development of **secondary sex characteristics**—*physical traits, other than the genitals, that distinguish males and females.* To accommodate pregnancy, giving birth, and nurturing infants, adolescent females develop breasts, wider hips, and soft fatty tissue, thereby providing a reserve supply of nutrition for pregnancy and breast-feeding (Brownmiller, 1984). Males, usually slightly taller and heavier than females from birth, typically develop more muscles in the upper body, more extensive body hair, and voices deeper in tone. These are only general differences, however. Many males are smaller and lighter than many females; some males have less body hair than some females; and some males speak in a higher tone than some females do.

In rare cases, hormone imbalance before birth results in a **hermaphrodite** (a word derived from Hermaphroditus, the offspring of the mythological Greek gods Hermes and Aphrodite, who embodied both sexes), *humans with some combination of male and female internal and external genitalia.* Because our culture tends to be intolerant of sexual ambiguity, we often regard hermaphrodites with confusion and even disgust. In contrast, the Pokot of Eastern Africa are indifferent to what they define as a simple biological error, and the Navaho look upon hermaphrodites with awe, seeing them as the embodiment of the full potential of both the male and the female (Geertz, 1975).

There are cases of people who choose to change their sex. Hermaphrodites may have their genitals surgically altered to gain the appearance (and occasionally the function) of a sexually normal male or female. Surgery may also be considered by **transsexuals,** *people who feel they are one sex when biologically they are the other.* Some 20,000 transsexuals in the United States have medically altered their genitals to escape the sense of being "trapped in the wrong body" (Restak, 1979, cited in Offir, 1982:146).

Sexual Orientation

Sexual orientation refers to *the manner in which people experience sexual arousal and achieve sexual pleasure.* In most life forms, sexuality is biologically programmed. In human beings, however, sexual orientation is a more complex matter of culture. The norm within all industrial societies is *heterosexuality* (*hetero* is a Greek word meaning "the other of two"), by which a person is sexually attracted to the opposite sex. However, *homosexuality* (*homo* is the Greek word for "the same"), by which a person is sexually attracted to the same sex, is not uncommon.

The meaning people attach to any sexual orientation varies according to cultural setting. All cultures endorse heterosexuality, although many tolerate—and some even encourage—homosexuality. Among the ancient Greeks, for instance, elite male intellectuals celebrated homosexuality as the highest form of relationship while devaluing relations with women, whom they considered to be incapable of philosophical discussion. Heterosexuality was thus seen as little more than a reproductive necessity. Additionally, men who did not engage in homosexuality were probably defined as deviant. But because homosexual relations do not permit reproduction, no society has been known to favor homosexuality over heterosexuality (Kluckhohn, 1948; Ford & Beach, 1951; Greenberg, 1988).

By the 1960s, homosexuals became more outspoken in opposition to heterosexual norms, and they adopted the term *gay* to describe themselves. This new terminology allowed gays to express satisfaction with their sexual orientation and to reduce the significance of sexuality to their personal identities. Although stereotypes of homosexuals abound, the personalities of gay people vary as much as those of "straights."

Tolerance of gay people has increased during this century. In 1974 the American Psychiatric Association removed homosexuality from its listing of mental disorders. Gays are still subject to both prejudice and discrimination, however, both of which increased during the 1980s, when the deadly disease AIDS became publicly identified with homosexual men. Today, although three-fourths of American adults continue to define homosexuality as morally wrong, the same proportion think American society should allow gays and straights equal workplace opportunities (N.O.R.C., 1989:258; Salholz, 1990).

Until American society becomes truly accepting of homosexuality, some gay people will understandably choose to remain "in the closet," avoiding public disclosure of their sexual orientation. Heterosexuals can begin to understand what this secrecy means by imagining never speaking about their romances to parents, roommates, or anyone else (Offir, 1982:216). Many organizations of gay people are struggling to overcome the inaccurate stereotypes of gay men and gay women (commonly called *lesbians*). In the late 1960s the term *homophobia* (with Greek roots meaning "fear of sameness") was coined to indicate irrational fear of gay people (Weinberg, 1973). Instead of asking "What's wrong with gay people," in other words, this label turns attention to society itself: "What's wrong with people who can't accept this sexual orientation?"

The pioneering research of Alfred Kinsey (1948, 1953) suggested that about 4 percent of males and 2 percent of females have an exclusively same-sex orientation. Nevertheless, perhaps 25 percent of Americans have had at least one sexual experience with someone of the same sex. Sexual orientations, then, are not mutually exclusive—many people, called *bisexuals*, are some combination of homosexual and heterosexual.

How any person gains a specific sexual orientation is not entirely understood. There is growing evidence that sexual orientation is rooted in biological factors present at birth and is further established by hormone balance as we grow (Gladue, Green & Hellman, 1984; Weinrich, 1987; Isay, 1989). Still other research points to the importance of the social environment in encouraging sexual attitudes and behaviors (Troiden, 1988). According to these researchers, humans are born with the capacity and desire to be sexual, but *how* sexuality is expressed is learned as an individual's personality develops in society. Most likely, the truth involves both approaches. To make matters more complex, sexual orientation is probably not established in precisely the same way for everyone. One influential study concluded that a complete explanation of homosexuality—or, for that matter, heterosexuality—simply does not exist at present (Bell, Weinberg, & Keifer-Hammersmith, 1981).

Gender: A Cultural Distinction

Gender is *human traits that are linked by culture to each sex*. Gender includes all culturally learned differences between males and females, including how people think about themselves, how they interact with others, and what positions they occupy in society as a whole.

Gender, therefore, is concerned not only with difference—how a society constructs masculine and feminine people—but also with the disparity of power that distinguishes two categories of humanity. This inequity, which has historically favored males, is no simple matter of biological differences between the two sexes. Males and females do, of course, differ biologically. Beyond the primary and secondary sex characteristics already noted, males have more muscle in the arms and shoulders so that the average male can lift more weight than the average female can. Furthermore, males have greater strength over short periods of time. Yet, because of the energy that females derive from greater body fat, they can outperform males in many tests of long-term endurance. Females also outperform males in life itself. According to the Bureau of the Census (1989), the average life expectancy of males born in 1987 is 71.5 years, while females born in that year can expect to live 78.3 years.

Research suggests that there is no difference in the overall intelligence of males and females. Adolescent males do seem to have greater mathematical ability, but adolescent females outperform males in verbal skills (Maccoby & Jacklin, 1974; Baker et al., 1980; Lengermann & Wallace, 1985).

Biologically, then males and females reveal limited differences, with neither sex being naturally superior. Nevertheless, the cultural notion of male superiority may seem so natural that we simply assume it is the inevitable consequence of sex itself. But society much more than biology is at work here, as several kinds of research show.

An unusual case study. In 1963 a physician was performing a routine penis circumcision on seven-month-old identical twins. While using electrocautery (surgery employing a heated needle), the physician accidentally burned off the penis of one boy. Understandably, the parents were horrified. After months of medical consultation, they decided to use further surgery to change the boy's sex and to raise him as a female.

The child was dressed as a girl, her hair was allowed to grow, and she was treated according to cultural definitions of femininity. Meanwhile, the brother—born an exact biological copy—was raised as a boy.

Because of their different socialization, each child learned a distinctive **gender identity,** *the ways males and females, guided by culture, learn to think of themselves.* In this example, one child learned to think of himself in terms that our culture defines as masculine, while the other child—despite beginning life as a male—soon began to think of herself as feminine. As the twins' mother observed:

> One thing that really amazes me is that (my daughter) is so feminine. I've never seen a little girl so neat and tidy. . . . She is very proud of herself, when she puts on a new dress, or I set her hair. She just loves to have her hair set; she could sit under the dryer all day long to have her hair set. She just loves it. . . . (My daughter) likes for me to wipe her face. She doesn't like to be dirty, and yet my son is quite different. I can't wash his face for anything. . . . She seems to be daintier. (Money & Ehrhardt, 1972:124)

The girl did display some traits associated with males, the researchers noted, including a desire to gain dominance among her peers. Later researchers following the case suggest that, by the time she was reaching adolescence, she was having difficulty with her gender identity (Diamond, 1982). Such a case is obviously complex, but it demonstrates how gender can be socially constructed.

The Israeli kibbutzim. Further evidence of society's power to create gender differences is found in studies of collective settlements in Israel called *kibbutzim.* The kibbutz (the singular form) embraces the value of social equality: everyone shares in necessary work, holds property collectively, and has a voice in decision making.

The members of kibbutzim typically oppose conceptions of gender that allow one sex to dominate the other. Therefore, both men and women do all types of work, including child care, building repair, cooking, and cleaning. Boys and girls are raised in the same way and, from the first weeks of life, live in dormitories under the care of specially trained personnel. To members of kibbutzim, then, sex is defined as irrelevant to much of everyday life.

Some observers suggest that patterns of social equality between these males and females are not as strong as they once were. Sociobiologists (see Chapter 3, "Cul-

The stereotypical view of females as "the weaker sex" is challenged by the everyday lives of women throughout the world. Especially in poor societies that depend on human labor, women perform work that would be physically challenging to most American men.

ture") wonder if subtle but persistent biological dispositions may undermine gender equality (Tiger & Shepher, 1975). Even so, the kibbutzim certainly demonstrate that cultures have considerable latitude in defining what is masculine and feminine. They also exemplify how a society can encourage sexual equality just as it can allow one sex to dominate the other.

Cross-cultural research. Another way to assess whether gender reflects culture or is inborn is to take a broad view of how the two sexes live in many cultures. To the extent that gender reflects the biological facts of sex, the human traits defined as masculine and feminine should be everywhere the same; if gender is cultural, these conceptions should vary.

The best-known research of this kind is a study of gender in three societies of New Guinea by anthropologist Margaret Mead (1963; orig. 1935). In the mountains of New Guinea, Mead observed the Arapesh, whose men and women were remarkably similar in attitudes and behavior. Both, according to Mead, were cooperative and sensitive to others. Arapesh males and females were what American culture would define as "feminine."

Moving south, Mead then observed the Mundugumor, whose culture of head-hunting and cannibalism was in striking contrast to the gentle ways of the Arapesh. Here Mead also found males and females to be alike, although quite different from the Arapesh. Both Mundugumor males and females were typically selfish and aggressive, traits that made them "masculine" according to American culture.

Finally, Mead traveled west to observe the Tchambuli and found a culture that, like our own, defined males and females differently. Yet the Tchambuli *reversed* many of our conceptions of gender: females were dominant and rational, while males were submissive, emotional, and nurturing toward children.

Mead's argument is that cultures can exaggerate or minimize social distinctions based on sex. Additionally, where differences are pronounced, what one culture defines as masculine may be considered feminine by another. Mead's research therefore strongly supports the conclusion that gender is a variable creation of society.

A broader study of gender in over two hundred preindustrial societies was carried out by George Murdock (1937). Murdock observed that all societies defined some tasks as feminine and viewed others as masculine. Hunting and warfare, he concluded, are usually the responsibilities of males, while home-centered tasks such as cooking and child care tend to be defined as females' tasks. This pattern undoubtedly has some biological basis. Males' typically greater size and short-term strength make them more suitable for hunting and warfare in preindustrial societies that rely on musclepower; because females bear children, their activities are likely to be more domestic.

Beyond these general patterns, however, Murdock found significant variation. As many societies consider agriculture—the core of preindustrial production—to be feminine as masculine. Mostly, however, it is a responsibility of both males and females. For many other tasks, from building shelters to tattooing the body, Murdock discovered considerable variation from culture to culture.

In short, only a few specific activities are overwhelmingly thought of as masculine or feminine. As societies industrialize, thereby decreasing the significance of muscle power, the distinctions between the social activities of the two sexes become even less (Lenski & Lenski, 1987). Gender, therefore, is simply too variable to be considered a simple expression of the biological categories of sex. Instead, as with many other elements of culture, what it means to be male and female is mostly a creation of society.

Patriarchy and Sexism

Although conceptions of gender are highly variable, a universal pattern is some degree of **patriarchy** (literally, "the rule of fathers"), *a form of social organization in which males dominate females*. Despite mythical tales of societies dominated by female "Amazons," the pattern of **matriarchy**, *a form of social organization in which females dominate males*, is not at present part of the human record (Gough, 1971; Harris, 1977; Kipp, 1980; Lengermann & Wallace, 1985). Even so, this universal tendency toward patriarchy involves significant variation in the relative power and privilege of males and females from society to society.

In principle, patriarchy is based on **sexism**, *the belief that one sex is innately superior to the other*. Patriarchy, then, rests on the belief that males are innately superior to females and therefore rightly dominate them. As Table 13–1 shows, sexism has much in common with racism, which was discussed in Chapter 12 ("Race and Ethnicity"). Just as racism is an ideology supporting white domination of nonwhites, so sexism is an ideology supporting (allegedly superior) males dominating (alleg-

Table 13–1 WAYS IN WHICH SEXISM AND RACISM ARE ALIKE

	Women	Blacks
Link to highly visible personal traits	Secondary sex characteristics.	Skin color.
Assertion of innate inferiority	Women are mentally inferior. Women are irresponsible, unreliable, and emotional.	Blacks are mentally inferior. Blacks are irresponsible, unreliable, and pleasure-seeking.
Assertion that those who are disadvantaged are content with their "proper place" in society	"A woman's place is in the home." All women really enjoy being treated "like a woman."	"Blacks should remain in their place." Blacks are content living just as they do.
Assertion that victims are under the protection of their oppressors	"Men put women on a pedestal."	Whites "take care of" blacks.
Coping strategies on the part of victims	Behavior flattering to men; letting men think they are better even when they are not. Hiding one's real feelings. Attempting to outwit men.	Deferential behavior toward whites; letting whites think they are better even when they are not. Hiding one's real feelings. Attempting to outwit whites.
Barriers to opportunity	Women don't need an education. Confined to "women's work." Women should stay out of politics.	Blacks don't need an education. Confined to "black occupations." Blacks should stay out of politics.
Criticism of those who do not "stay in their place"	Assertive women are "pushy." Ambitious women are trying to be like men. Women as traditional targets of violence by men.	Assertive blacks are "uppity." Ambitious blacks are trying to be like whites. Blacks as traditional targets of violence by whites.

SOURCE: Adapted from Helen Mayer Hacker, "Women as a Minority Group," *Social Forces*, Vol. 30 (October 1951): 60–69; and "Women as a Minority Group: Twenty Years Later," in Florence Denmark, ed., *Who Discriminates Against Women?* (Beverly Hills, CA: Sage, 1974), pp. 124–134.

edly inferior) females. Both racism and sexism cause people to distort their own abilities by understanding social privilege or disadvantage as personal merit or deficiency.

Sexism is a powerful force in countless daily experiences. As Chapter 6 ("Social Interaction in Everyday Life") explained, even language—by which all of humanity is often subsumed under male pronouns—is shaped by the tradition of male dominance.

In addition to the obvious costs to females, society as a whole pays a high price for maintaining sexism. Limiting the opportunities available to women ensures that the full talents and abilities of half the population will never be developed. Males derive significant benefits from sexism, including a disproportionate share of power and wealth. But men too suffer as a result of sexism. As Marilyn French (1985) argues, patriarchy demands that men relentlessly seek control—not only of women, but of themselves and the entire world. Because this is not humanly possible, the effort extracts a high price in terms of accidents, stress, heart attacks, and other diseases that result in higher death rates among males of all ages. The so-called Type A personality—characterized by impatience, drive, and competitiveness, and known to be linked to heart disease—is essentially what our culture defines as masculine (Ehrenreich, 1983). Furthermore, insofar as males seek control over others, they lose the ability to experience intimacy and trust (French, 1985). One recent study concluded that although competition is supposed to separate "the men from the boys," in practice it separates the men from the men (Raphael, 1988:184).

Overall, when human feelings, thoughts, and actions are rigidly scripted according to a culture's conceptions of gender, people are denied the opportunity to develop and freely express the full range of their humanity. Males are strongly pressured to be assertive, competitive, and in control, a task that is surely a burden to many of them. Females are constrained to be submissive, dependent, and self-effacing, regardless of their individual talents. The box on pages 346–347 illustrates how rigid conceptions of gender limit human experience.

Is Patriarchy Inevitable?

Because technologically simple societies have little control over nature, patriarchy in these societies reflects biological differences of sex. Pregnancy and childbirth limit the scope of women's lives, while men's greater height and short-term strength typically allow them to overpower females. In industrial societies, however, advanced technology reduces the significance of any natural differences between the sexes. Technological innovations cannot change the woman's responsibility for giving birth, but pregnancy is now usually a matter of choice. Industrial machinery has also made muscle power less important for accomplishing everyday tasks. Thus biological differences seem to provide little justification for patriarchy.

Categorical social inequality—whether based on race, ethnicity, or sex—also comes under attack in the more egalitarian culture of industrial societies. In Sweden and many other industrial nations, laws mandate equal opportunity for men and women in all occupations and require equal pay for equal work. Housework is also to be the responsibility of both sexes. Nonetheless, in Sweden as elsewhere, women still have primary responsibility for maintaining the household, while most economic and political power is wielded by men (Haas, 1981).

Since the socialist revolution in 1917, the Soviet Union has officially endorsed sexual equality. Soviet women are heavily represented in many occupations that are defined as masculine in the United States, including physically demanding work in construction and factories. But Soviet reforms have not included granting *political* equality to females, who remain all but excluded from the highest levels of important government. The Politburo (the key political decision-making body in the Soviet Union) had one woman (of twenty members) in 1990, and in the Communist party, men outnumbered women by three to one. As in virtually every society in the world, work defined as feminine commonly provides less income and social prestige than that performed by men. For example, most physicians in the Soviet Union are women, but this profession has a lower social ranking than it has in the United States, where the majority of physicians are men (Mamonova, 1984).

Does the persistence of patriarchy mean that it is inevitable? Some researchers claim that biologically based factors generate different behaviors and motivations in the two sexes, making the complete eradication of patriarchy difficult, if not impossible (Goldberg, 1974, 1987). The position that biologically based differences between the sexes have *some* effect on human behavior is readily acknowledged by many sociologists (Rossi, 1985), but the overwhelming opinion among sociologists is that gender is primarily a social construction. As such, it is subject to change. The fact that no society has yet eliminated patriarchy, then, does not mean that patri-

"X: A Fabulous Child's Story"

Once upon a time, a baby named X was born. This baby was named X so that nobody could tell whether it was a boy or a girl.

In a children's story by Lois Gould, "X" was given to Mr. and Ms. Jones, a couple carefully screened from thousands of applicants, as an experiment. The Joneses were to follow one rule only: X was not to be socialized as masculine or feminine but was to learn everything a child could. Assisted by a heavy *Official Instruction Manual*, the Joneses promised to follow this rule as closely as possible. They agreed to take equal turns feeding and caring for X, to spend as much time bouncing as they did cuddling the baby, and to praise X for being strong just as often as for being sweet. But trouble began almost immediately, when the Joneses' friends and relatives asked whether X was a boy or a girl.

When the Joneses smiled and said "It's an X!" nobody knew what to say. They couldn't say, "Look at her cute little dimples." And they couldn't say, "Look at his husky little biceps!" And they couldn't even say just plain "kitchy-coo." In fact, they all thought

that the Joneses were playing some kind of rude joke.

The Joneses were being quite serious, but other people became irritated and embarrassed by their behavior:

"People will think there's something wrong with it!" some of them whispered.

"There *is* something wrong with it!" others whispered back.

And what did baby X think about all the fuss? It simply finished its bottle with a loud and satisfied burp.

Finding toys for X was another problem. The first trip to the toy store brought this immediate question from the store clerk: "Well, now, is it a boy or a girl?" In the storekeeper's mind, footballs and fire engine sets were for boys, and dolls and housekeeping sets were for girls. But the Joneses knew that they had to be sure baby X had all kinds of toys to play with, including:

a boy doll that made pee-pee and cried "Pa-Pa." And a girl doll that talked in three languages and said "I am the Pres-i-dent of Gen-er-al Motors." They also bought a storybook about

a brave princess who rescued a handsome prince from his ivory tower, and another one about a sister and brother who grew up to be a baseball star and a ballet star, and you had to guess which was which.

But the biggest problem came when X was old enough to begin school, where the children were treated according to their sex. Boys and girls lined up separately, played games separately, and, naturally, used different bathrooms. The other children had never met an X before and just had to know what its sex really was. But the Joneses had raised X very carefully so that there was no easy answer:

You couldn't tell what X was by studying its clothes; overalls don't button right-to-left, like girl's clothes, or left-to-right, like boy's clothes. And you couldn't tell whether X had a girl's short haircut or a boy's long haircut. And it was very hard to tell by the games X liked to play. Either X played ball very well for a girl, or else X played house very well for a boy.

The other children found X a very strange playmate: one day it would ask boys to weave some baskets in the arts and crafts room, and the next

---

archy as it has existed in the past is an inevitable part of the human future.

To understand the persistence of patriarchy, we now turn to an examination of how gender is deeply rooted in society, from the way children learn to think of themselves, to how sexual inequality affects men and women as adults.

GENDER AND SOCIALIZATION

Gender plays a major part in the socialization process. From birth until death, human feelings, thoughts, and actions reflect social definitions of the sexes. As children interact with others, they quickly learn that males and females are thought to be different kinds of human beings, day it would ask some girls to go shoot baskets in the gym. But X tried hard to be friendly to everyone—boys and girls alike—and to do well in school. And X did very well in school, winning spelling bees and athletic events, and coming in second in a baking contest (even X's aren't perfect). As other children noticed what a good time X was having in school, they began to wonder if maybe X wasn't having twice as much fun as they were!

From then on, some really funny things began to happen. Susie, who sat next to X in class, suddenly refused to wear pink dresses to school any more. She insisted on wearing red-and-white checked overalls—just like X's. Overalls, she told her parents, were much better for climbing monkey bars. Then Jim, the class football nut, started wheeling his little sister's doll carriage around the football field. He'd put on his entire football uniform, except for the helmet. Then he'd put the helmet in the carriage, lovingly tucked under an old set of shoulder pads. Then he'd start jogging around the field, pushing the carriage and singing "Rockabye Baby" to his football helmet. He told his family that X did the same thing, so it must be

okay. After all, X was now the team's star quarterback.

But this kind of behavior in the children horrified their parents. And when Peggy started using Joe's hockey skates while Joe enjoyed using Peggy's needlepoint kit, the situation deteriorated. X was to blame for all this! So the Parents' Association at school demanded that X be identified as either a boy or a girl and be forced to act accordingly. A psychiatrist was asked to conduct a full examination and report back to the parents. If, as most suspected, X was found to be a very confused child, it should be expelled from school altogether.

The teachers were puzzled by the commotion; after all, X was one of their very best students. But the school—as well as the Joneses—finally agreed to let X be examined.

The next day the psychiatrist arrived at the school and began a long examination of X while everyone waited anxiously outside. When the psychiatrist finally emerged from the examination room, the results were not what most people expected. "In my opinion," the psychiatrist told them, "young X here is just about

the least mixed up child I've ever examined!" The doctor explained that by the time that X's sex really mattered, everyone would know what it was.

The psychiatrist's opinion naturally elated the Joneses, and delighted the scientists who had begun the experiment in the first place. And later that day, X's friends (dressed in red-and-white checked overalls) came over to X's house to play. They found X in the backyard playing with a new tiny baby.

"How do you like our new baby?" X asked the other children proudly.

"It's got cute dimples," said Jim.

"It's got husky biceps, too," said Susie.

"What kind of baby is it?" asked Joe and Peggy.

X frowned at them. "Can't you tell?" Then X broke into a big mischievous grin. "It's a Y!"

SOURCE: Adapted from Lois Gould, "X: A Fabulous Child's Story," Ms., Vol. 1 (December 1972): 74–76, 105–106.

and by about the age of three or four they apply this distinction to themselves (Bem, 1981; Kohlberg, 1966, cited in Lengermann & Wallace, 1985:37). Table 13–2 lists conventional traits that traditionally have formed the gender identity of American males and females.

Despite societal urging, not everyone conforms to cultural norms concerning gender. Larry Bernard (1980)

evaluated only about 35 percent of male college students as entirely "masculine" and 41 percent of females as consistently "feminine." Another one-fourth of males and females scored high on *both* masculine and feminine attributes. Bernard found the remaining students (about 40 percent of males and one-third of females) scored low on both sets of attributes. Overall, these results sug-

Table 13–2	TRADITIONAL GENDER IDENTITY
Masculine Traits	Feminine Traits
Dominant	Submissive
Independent	Dependent
Intelligent and competent	Unintelligent and incapable
Rational	Emotional
Assertive	Receptive
Analytical	Intuitive
Strong	Weak
Brave	Timid
Ambitious	Content
Active	Passive
Competitive	Cooperative
Insensitive	Sensitive
Sexually aggressive	Sex object
Attractive because of achievement	Attractive because of physical appearance

gest that many, but not all, males suppress the feminine side of their humanity. Similarly, females are taught to suppress their masculine side, but not all do. The fact that fewer males than females in this research conformed to ideal gender patterns suggests that gender-scripts may be more burdensome to males than to females (French, 1985).

Just as socialization incorporates gender into personal identity, so it teaches us to *act* according to cultural conceptions of what is masculine and feminine. **Gender roles** (or sex roles) are *attitudes and activities that a culture links to each sex*. Gender roles are the active expression of gender identity. In other words, because our culture defines males as ambitious and competitive, we expect them to engage in team sports and seek out positions of leadership. Females, culturally defined as deferential and emotional, are expected to be good listeners and supportive of others.

Throughout our lives, we are subject to considerable social pressure to conform to gender roles. An assertive girl who loves competitive sports more than dresses and dolls is tolerated as a "tomboy" but later may be negatively labeled as "tough" and "mannish." A sensitive boy may be derided as a "sissy" and later demeaned as "unmanly" if this pattern persists. Gender becomes a blueprint imposed on males and females by all the agents of socialization described in Chapter 5.

Gender and the Family

The first question usually asked about a newborn child is, "Is it a boy or a girl?" The question is important because the answer involves more than sex; it carries a great deal of significance for the child's entire life.

Sociologist Jessie Bernard, introduced in the box, suggests that males and females enter different worlds within a single society: the "pink world" of girls and the "blue world" of boys (1981). As earlier chapters have shown, people of different social classes and racial and

Play may appear to be simply a matter of having fun, but it is also a serious means of teaching children how their culture defines the roles of each sex.

Jessie Bernard

Now in her eighties, Jessie Bernard continues to make contributions to the discipline of sociology. Her work has long been concerned with gender.

Bernard urges sociologists to include women as well as men in their work. In the past, even sociologists critical of the status quo have tended to disregard women. Karl Marx, for instance, paid almost no attention to women in his writings. One reason for not giving balanced attention to males and females, Bernard suggests, is that sociology, like other disciplines, has developed largely under the control of men. Many familiar sociological issues and concepts thus have a built-in male bias.

Consider the topic of social stratification. As was explained in Chapter 10 ("Social Class in America"), to be within the upper class, a male must have considerable wealth. But this definition neglects the other half of humanity, since a female's social class position is traditionally derived from *men*: initially from her father and subsequently from her husband. Further, in ranking the prestige of occupations (Table 10–1), sociologists usually ignore housework—conventionally the most common activity of women. By defining the concept of occupational prestige so that it applies primarily to males, sociologists exclude women from sociological research.

In sum, sociologists must use care to ensure that their work addresses both males and females. Otherwise sociology is the study of only half of society.

SOURCE: Based on Jessie Bernard, *The Female World* (New York: Free Press, 1981), and personal communication.

---

ethnic categories may share physical space but be separated by greater *social* distance than many people realize.

In a patriarchal society, we might expect couples to prefer male children. One American survey found that even women favored having sons over daughters: 45 percent wanted a boy and 20 percent preferred a girl, while the remainder had no preference (cited in Lengermann & Wallace, 1985:61). Historically, and in China and elsewhere even today, female embryos are commonly aborted and female infants killed because parents would rather devote their resources to male children, whose social value is greater.

Parents also treat boys and girls differently. Research on parental attitudes suggests that both fathers and mothers encourage sons to be strong, aggressive achievers while expecting daughters to be weaker, delicate, and less assertive (Witkin-Lanoil, 1984:66–71). Par-

ents typically convey these expectations through the way they handle their children. A researcher at an English university presented an infant dressed as either a boy or a girl to a number of women. Videotapes revealed that the women handled the "female" child tenderly, with frequent hugs and caresses, while treating the "male" child more aggressively, often lifting him up high in the air or bouncing him on the knee (Bonner, 1984). Other research shows that mothers have more overall physical contact with their male infants than with females (Major, 1981). The message is clear: the female world is one of passivity and emotion, while the male world involves the more important characteristics of independence and action.

Parents also teach the significance of gender by encouraging their male and female children to dress and groom appropriately. In addition, toys provided to children (trucks for boys and dolls for girls) and the requests for help around the house (boys mow the lawn, girls help with dishes) reinforce gender-based social worlds.

Gender and the Peer Group

On reaching school age, children begin to interact more intensively outside the family, especially with others their own age. Peer groups further distinguish the pink and blue worlds of girls and boys. The box explains how peer groups shaped one young boy's sense of himself as masculine.

As was noted in Chapter 3 ("Culture"), children's games provide important cultural lessons. A year of observing fifth graders at play led Janet Lever (1978) to conclude that the peer groups of boys and those of girls each provide a distinctive type of socialization. Boys, Lever observed, commonly engage in team sports—such as baseball and football—that involve many roles, complex rules, and clear objectives such as scoring a run or a touchdown. These games are nearly always competitive, producing winners and losers. Such activities reinforce the traits of masculinity, notably aggression, competition, and remaining in control.

Girls, Lever found, commonly play games such as hopscotch or jump-rope in small groups, or they simply talk, sing, or dance together. These activities tend to be spontaneous and involve few formal rules. Since such games rarely have "victory" as their ultimate goal, girls rarely oppose one another. Instead of teaching girls to be competitive, female peer groups convey interpersonal skills of communication and cooperation that are the basis for life within the family.

Carol Gilligan (1982) investigated how boys and girls also develop distinctive patterns of moral reasoning. Boys learn to reason according to rules and principles: for them, "rightness" consists largely in "playing by the rules." Girls, in contrast, understand morality more in terms of responsibility to other human beings; for them, "rightness" lies in maintaining close relationships with others. These distinctive patterns of moral reasoning appear to be encouraged by the different peer-group activities of boys and girls.

Gender and Schooling

Schooling enhances distinctive gender worlds. Traditionally, this reinforcement has been accomplished through the books children read, even before they enter school. In one study, a group of researchers examined books widely read to pre-elementary school children by parents (Weitzman et al., 1972). Males rather than females were the focus of attention in most of these books. For example, for every picture of female children, more than ten pictures of male children appeared. Three times as many book titles mentioned males as females. These researchers concluded that children "are bound to receive

SOCIOLOGY OF EVERYDAY LIFE

Masculinity as Contest

By the time I was ten, the central fact in my life was the demand that I become a man. By then, the most important relationships by which I was taught to define myself were those I had with other boys. I already knew that I must see every encounter with another boy as a contest in which I must win or at least hold my own. . . . The same lesson continued (in school), after school, even in Sunday School. My parents, relatives,

teachers, the books I read, movies I saw, all taught me that my self-worth depended on my manliness, my willingness to stand up to the other boys. This usually didn't mean a physical fight, though the willingness to stand up and "fight like a man" always remained a final test. But the relationships between us usually had the character of an armed truce. Girls weren't part of this social world at all yet, just because they weren't part of this con-

test. They didn't have to be bluffed, no credit was gained by cowing them, so they were more or less ignored. Sometimes when there were no grownups around we would let each other know that we liked each other, but most of the time we did as we were taught.

SOURCE: Michael Silverstein, in Jon Snodgrass, ed., *A Book of Readings for Men Against Sexism* (Albion, CA: Times Change Press, 1977), pp. 178–179.

the impression that girls are not very important because no one has bothered to write books about them" (1972:1129). The books also presented the lives of males and females in stereotypical ways that favored males: Males engaged in diverse and interesting activities, while females usually stayed in the house. The females depicted in these books were usually concerned with pleasing males: Girls courted the favor of their father and brothers, and women endeavored to please their husbands. Males were mostly active; females were typically passive observers:

> The little boy is constantly in motion, continuously interacting with the world around him. He is jumping up to touch the scarecrow next to the cornstalk, unwrapping his baseball bat (leaving the mess of paper, string, and box for someone else to clean up), building blocks on top of his sled, reaching up on tiptoe to touch his father's workbench, and spraying the lawn (and himself) with the garden hose. In contrast the little girl relates to each of the objects around her merely by looking at them. (Weitzman et al., 1972:1137)

More like dolls than living beings, the girls in these books were mostly attractive and compliant objects, sources of support and pleasure to males.

Within the last decade, however, the growing awareness among authors, teachers, and readers that childhood learning shapes people's lives as adults has led to changes. Today's books for children portray males and females in a more balanced way.

In addition to the formal lessons of school, what Raphaela Best (1983) calls "the second curriculum"—the informal messages and experiences of school life—encourages children to adopt the identity and roles assigned to their sex. By the time children reach high school, areas of study begin to reflect the different roles males and females are expected to assume as adults. Instruction in typing and such home-centered skills as nutrition, cooking, and sewing has long been provided to classes composed almost entirely of females. Classes in woodworking and auto mechanics, conversely, are still mostly all male.

In college, males and females continue this division, tending toward different majors. Traditionally, the natural sciences—including physics, chemistry, biology, and mathematics—have been defined as part of the male world. Women have been expected to major in the humanities (such as English), the fine arts (painting, music, dance, and drama), or the social sciences (including anthropology and sociology). Even new areas of study are likely to be sex linked. Computer science, for exam-

ple, has become a predominantly male activity (Klein, 1984); new courses in gender studies, in contrast, tend to enroll females.

Extracurricular activities also segregate males and females. Athletics and other activities for men benefit from more attention and more funding. Mass media coverage of men's athletics is also far greater than that given to female sports. Because of this male dominance, females frequently assume supportive roles as observers or cheerleaders.

In many colleges and universities, fraternities (traditionally stronger than sororities) have been criticized as bastions of male power. Allegations that fraternities encourage sexism and sometimes outright violence against women have caused members increasingly to examine themselves and their organizations, often with constructive results (A. Merton, 1985).

Gender and the Mass Media

In Chapter 5 ("Socialization"), we explained that the mass media are a powerful part of the socialization process. Films, magazines, and especially television significantly affect ways we think and act.

Since becoming widespread in the 1950s, television has presented the dominant category of Americans—white males—at center stage. Racial and ethnic minorities were all but absent from television until the early 1970s, and only within the last decade have a number of programs featured female characters in major roles.

Even with both sexes now included on television shows, consider how they are portrayed. Men generally play the brilliant detectives, fearless explorers, and skilled surgeons. Males take charge; they give the orders and are seen as competent and capable. Women, in contrast, generally rely on men, are less competent, and are more often the targets of comedy (Busby, 1975). Women have also been traditionally portrayed as sex objects valued mostly for their physical attractiveness. Such stereotypes persisted during the 1980s, although more programming now involves interesting and responsible roles for women.

Like television programming directed at adults, children's programs reinforce gender stereotypes. Here again, males have been portrayed as active, ambitious, brave, competent, in control of situations, and unlikely to show fear or other emotions. Females, in contrast, have been passive, content to be what they are, timid, incapable, and emotional (Busby, 1975; Doyle, 1983). In recent years, children's television, too, has shown fewer stereotypical portrayals of the sexes.

SHE'S VERY CHARLIE.

Charlie
REVLON

Some recent advertising reverses traditional gender roles by portraying males as the sex objects of successful females. Although the role reversal is new, the use of gender stereotypes to sell consumer products is very old indeed.

Advertising is perhaps the dimension of the mass media in which change has been slowest. This is so because advertising sells products by conforming to widely established cultural patterns. Historically, television and magazine advertising has presented women in the home far more often than in the workplace. Women are used to sell household items such as cleaning products, foods, clothing, and appliances, while men predominate in ads for cars, travel, banking services, industrial companies, and alcoholic beverages. The authoritative "voiceover" in television and radio advertising is almost always male (Busby, 1975; Courtney & Whipple, 1983).

Erving Goffman (1979) studied magazine and newspaper ads, concluding that men were typically photographed to appear taller than women, implying male superiority. Women were more frequently presented lying down (on sofas and beds) or, like children, seated on the floor. The expressions and gestures of men conveyed competence and authority, whereas women were more likely to appear in childlike poses. While men tend to look favorably at the products being advertised, the attention of women is directed toward men, conveying their supportive and submissive role.

Advertising tries to persuade us that being properly masculine and feminine is of great importance and dictates what we should consume. For example, the really masculine man drives the "right" car or vacations in the "right" place. The truly feminine woman buys the kind of clothing and cosmetics that make her look younger and more attractive and—above all—capture the attention of men.

Gender and Adult Socialization

Our gender identity and gender roles typically come to feel natural well before we become adults. For this reason, appropriately feminine and masculine attitudes, behavior, and patterns of speech are commonly reinforced in the social interaction of adults (Spender, 1980; Kramarae, 1981).

In a simple but revealing bit of research, Pamela Fishman (1977, 1978) tape recorded the conversations of three young, white, middle-class married couples at their homes for up to two weeks. Even casual conversation, she discovered, reinforces male dominance over females. For example, conversation initiated by the men was more likely to be sustained. When the men began a conversation, the women usually attempted to keep it going; yet when the women initiated a conversation, the men frequently allowed it to collapse. This pattern suggests that both males and females think what males have to say is more important. Women, but rarely men, opened conversations with remarks like "This is interesting" or "Do you know what?" Fishman interpreted this pattern—also common to the speech of children—as women's way of finding out if men really want to hear what they had to say. Starting a conversation with "This is interesting," for example, is a request to the male to pay attention to what follows. Opening with "Do you know what?" is equivalent to stating, "I have something to say; are you willing to listen?"

The women also asked many more questions than the men did. Asking a question is often a sign of deference to another person, so this pattern, too, reflected the women's subordination to their husbands. Both men and women used various "minimal responses" (such as "yeah," "umm," and "huh"), but they used them differently. For the men, such responses were expressions of minimal interest, as if to say, "I guess I'll continue to listen if you insist on speaking." For the women, however, minimal responses were a form of "support work," inserted continually to express interest in the conversation and to encourage the men to continue.

Years of gender-based socialization are the groundwork for marriages between adults who inhabit different social worlds. Not surprisingly, husbands and wives often have considerable difficulty simply communicating with each other. Studies of verbal interaction within marriage confirm that both spouses are aware of this problem (Komarovsky, 1967; Rubin, 1976, 1983).

GENDER AND SOCIAL STRATIFICATION

Gender implies more than how people think and act. The concept of **gender stratification** refers to *the unequal distribution of wealth, power, and privileges between the two sexes.* More specifically, in American society as elsewhere in the world, females have less of society's valued resources than males do.

Working Men and Women

In 1989, 66.5 percent of Americans over the age of fifteen were in the labor force, which consisted of 76.4 percent of men and 57.4 percent of women (U.S. Bureau of Labor Statistics, 1990). In 1900, only about one-fifth of women were in the labor force; as is shown in Figure 13–1, the proportion has increased steadily in recent decades. Furthermore, 74.5 percent of women working in 1989 did so full time. The traditional view that earning

Figure 13–1 Men and Women in the American Labor Force
(*U.S. Bureau of Labor Statistics*)

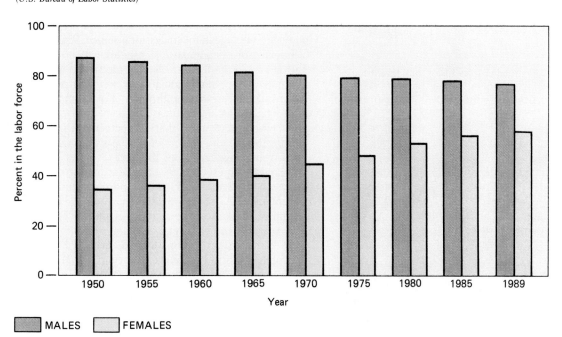

an income is a "man's job" is thus no longer valid.

Some of the factors altering the composition of the American labor force are the increasing number of service jobs in the American economy, the growth of cities, declining family size, and more flexible norms regarding appropriate roles for women. Because economic decline has reduced the income of many Americans during the last fifteen years (see Chapter 10, "Social Class in America"), an increasing proportion of families find one income insufficient to maintain a comfortable standard of living. In 1988, 63.8 percent of married couples earned two incomes.

A common—although incorrect—belief is that most women in the labor force are single or, if married, without children. In 1989, 57 percent of all married women were working. Women with children are *more* likely to be working than childless women: 72.5 percent of married women with children between six and seventeen years of age were working, as were 57.1 percent of those with children under six. For divorced women with children, the comparable figures were higher still: 83.9 percent of women with older children and 70.1 percent of those with children under six were working (U.S. Bureau of the Census, 1989). The increase in child-care support in the workplace is allowing more women and men to combine the responsibilities of being workers and parents, a trend that is especially important for divorced mothers.

Women in the American labor force historically have been concentrated in a few occupations, such as garment making, usually under the supervision of males.

Gender and Occupations

Although the proportions of men and women in the labor force are converging—and more rapidly so since 1970 (Jacobs, 1989)—the work done by females and males has historically been quite different. According to the U.S. Bureau of Labor Statistics (1990), women still have a relatively small range of jobs: almost half of working women fall within two broad occupational categories. The first is clerical work—28 percent of working women are secretaries, typists, or stenographers. These "pink-collar" jobs are considered support positions, and consequently, 80 percent of clerical workers are female. The second broad category is service work, performed by 18 percent of employed women. This includes waitresses and other food service employees as well as nurses and other health service workers. Both categories of jobs are low-paying, offer little intrinsic satisfaction, and have limited opportunity for advancement.

Table 13–3 shows the ten occupations with the highest concentration of women in 1989. Although increasing numbers of women are working, both married and single, women remain highly segregated in the labor force because American society continues to link work to gender (Roos, 1983; Kemp & Coverman, 1989; U.S. Bureau of Labor Statistics, 1990).

Men predominate in most job categories beyond the ten occupations noted in the table. The highest proportion of men are in the trades; for instance, 99.5 percent of brickmasons, stonemasons, structural metal workers, and heavy equipment mechanics are male. Males are also likely to predominate in any job that provides a lot of income, prestige, and power. For example, more than 90 percent of engineers, 80 percent of physicians and lawyers, and more than 60 percent of managers, administrators, and computer specialists are men. Only a few women appear among the top executives of America's largest corporations. Even where men and women do much the same work, titles (and consequently pay) benefit men. A "special assistant to the president," for example, is likely to be a man, while an "executive secretary" is nearly always a woman.

Gender stratification, then, is evident in the fact that males tend to hold powerful occupational positions while women are in relatively powerless occupations. This hierarchy is often apparent in the job setting itself: male physicians work with female nurses, male executives have female secretaries, and male airline pilots work with female flight attendants. Within a given occupation, the greater a job's income and social prestige, the

Table 13–3 JOBS WITH THE HIGHEST CONCENTRATIONS OF WOMEN, 1989

	Occupation	Number of Women Employed	Percent in Occupation Who Are Women
1.	Dental hygienist	79,360	99.2%
2.	Secretary	3,973,910	99.1%
3.	Dental assistant	184,943	98.7%
4.	Prekindergarten and kindergarten teachers	421,518	98.2%
5.	Receptionist	792,180	97.2%
6.	Private household child-care worker	347,618	97.1%
7.	Child-care worker	829,143	96.3%
8.	Licensed practical nurse	397,854	96.0%
9.	Teacher's aide	418,440	95.1%
10.	Typist	694,450	95.0%

SOURCE: U.S. Bureau of Labor Statistics.

more likely it is to be held by a male. In teaching, for example, women are 98 percent of the kindergarten teachers, 85 percent of teachers in the elementary grades, 53 percent of secondary school teachers, and only 39 percent of professors in colleges and universities (U.S. Bureau of Labor Statistics, 1990). At the top of the pyramid, only about 12 percent of college and university presidents are women, and these usually preside over smaller institutions, many with an all-female student body (American Council on Education, 1984).

Housework

Just as work outside the home has traditionally been required of males, so has housework—maintaining the home and caring for children—been expected of females. The importance of housework has always been a cultural contradiction: touted as essential to American life on the one hand, carrying little reward or social prestige on the other (J. Bernard, 1981).

Women's rapidly increasing participation in the labor force has caused little change in the pattern of responsibility for housework. One estimate indicates that between 1959 and 1983 the hours of housework performed by women declined only slightly and the proportion of housework shared by men remained the same (Fuchs, 1986). In a typical American household, responsibilities truly shared by the two sexes usually are limited

to disciplining the children and managing finances. Men routinely engage in a few activities such as home repairs and mowing the lawn; women do the daily tasks of shopping, cooking, and cleaning. Many women return from the workplace to perform a "second shift" of unpaid work in the home (Schooler et al, 1984; Benokraitis & Feagin, 1986; Hochschild, 1989).

Most men support women's entering the labor force as long as they do not have to modify their own gender roles to help women do so (Komarovsky, 1973). Only in rare cases, such as the Israeli kibbutzim, is housework shared to any great extent. Even in Sweden—a society with a strong belief in the social equality of the sexes—only one in five couples appears to share housework equitably (Haas, 1981).

The controversy over housework exists because few people want to do it. In a study of women in London, Anne Oakley (1974) found that 70 percent of women homemakers found housework objectionable, due to the monotony and loneliness of it. Oakley also calculated that the average homemaker worked 77 hours a week—almost twice the standard workweek.

Gender, Income, and Wealth

Because women predominate in clerical and service jobs while men hold most business and professional positions, women earn less than men do. Thus, income—a major measure of self-worth for Americans—reinforces women's disadvantaged position in the occupational hierarchy.

In 1988 the median earnings for women working full-time was $18,545, while men working full-time earned $27,342. Thus men earn in about seven days what women earn in ten days; more simply, for every dollar earned by men, women earn about 68 cents. This income disparity between males and females has declined gradually over the last two decades.

Put in different terms, one in seven women working full-time earned less than $10,000 in 1988, whereas only one in thirteen men did. Only one in four women earned more than $25,000, while one in two men did. Men were also eight times more likely than women (4.4 percent versus 0.6 percent) to earn more than $75,000 (U.S. Bureau of the Census, 1989).

The first and most important reason for this earning disparity—noted already—is the different jobs held by males and females. Considerable evidence suggests that the value of a job is affected by its composition by sex. That is, jobs typically performed by women are viewed as less worthy than jobs done by men (Parcel, Mueller, & Cuvelier, 1986). During the 1980s, this disparity was challenged by the "equal pay for equal worth" movement, advocating that women receive the same earnings as men when they perform work that has equal worth, even in different job categories. Using this standard of fairness, estimates indicate that American women are currently being underpaid some $1 billion dollars for their work.

A second cause of income disparity is family-related factors. Having children especially disadvantages female workers because it results in their having less seniority than their male counterparts (Fuchs, 1986). Pregnancy, childbirth, and raising small children keep some younger women out of the labor force altogether at a time when younger men commonly make occupational gains. Moreover, women who choose to have children may be reluctant or unable to maintain fast-paced jobs that demand evening and weekend work. Career mothers often seek less-demanding jobs that offer advantages such as a shorter commuting distance, flexible hours, and child-care services (Schwartz, 1989). The box examines a recent, controversial proposal intended to benefit corporate women.

The two factors noted so far—types of jobs held and motherhood—account for about two-thirds of the earnings disparity between women and men. A third factor, then, is assumed to be simple discrimination against women, accounting for the remaining one-third of the difference (Pear, 1987). Because it is illegal, dis-

CRITICAL THINKING

Twin Tracks for Working Women: Sensitive or Sexist?

The facts of corporate life are changing. Once the preserve of male executives and female support workers, management positions are now being occupied by women in record numbers. This is good news for corporations, because increasingly women are among the top college and business school graduates in America. The end of the baby boom of past decades, coupled with rapid growth in administrative positions within the new "information economy," means that soon there will no longer be enough men (and far fewer *good* men) to fill all the positions. In short, corporate America needs women.

Despite their increasing numbers, the corporate world remains an environment unfriendly to women. According to Felice N. Schwartz—founder and president of Catalyst, an organization that seeks to develop the careers of women—the reason is simply this: While trying to make women equal to men in the workplace, we have chosen to almost ignore *maternity*, the most crucial difference between the two sexes. Many women want to divide their time and energy between a career and young children. Currently, Schwartz claims, doing this is much more difficult for women than for men, as is evident in the fact that, by age 40, 90 percent of male executives but only 35 percent of female executives have children.

Businesses are uneasy about career women having children because, under current policies, motherhood often results in women leaving their jobs entirely. Professional women who choose to have children usually do so in their early thirties, after corporations have invested almost a decade in training them. To employers, motherhood still signals a lack of commitment to a career. Men obviously do not encounter this problem, since their wives take responsibility

crimination may be less overt today, but it remains a major cause of economic disadvantage for working women (Benokraitis & Feagin, 1986). Women in corporate America often encounter a "glass ceiling," a barrier that is not easily seen but prevents them from rising beyond middle-management positions. To some extent, this discrimination is institutionalized and self-perpetuating: The traditional dominance of males at higher corporate levels gives women little of the "old boys network" that supports many men. Then, too, men may be threatened by talented and ambitious women and uneasy about interacting with colleagues whom they find sexually attractive.

For a variety of reasons, then, differences in earnings for women and men exist even within occupational categories. As shown in Table 13–4, this ratio varies by type of work, but in no job category do women earn more than three-fourths as much as men do.

Finally, perhaps because women typically outlive men, some Americans believe that women own most of the country's wealth. Government statistics (calculated for 1982) show otherwise: 53 percent of Americans with $500,000 or more in assets were men, although widows were highly represented. Among people with more modest wealth ($100,000 or more in assets), 58 percent were men (U.S. Department of Labor, 1983; U.S. Bureau of the Census, 1985). More recently, in Forbes magazine's listing of the four hundred richest Americans in 1989, only fifty-four (13.5 percent) were women (Queenan, 1989).

for child care. After a baby is born, companies commonly pressure a woman to decide between being a mother or a businesswoman. The choice is unfair because women can, and often wish to, do *both*. Currently, however, many women leave their careers with the birth of a child, so both the corporations and the women themselves lose out.

The solution to the problem, Schwartz suggests, is for corporations to develop two tracks for women executives, a "career track" and a "career and family track." Women who wish to put their careers first should be identified early and given as much opportunity and encouragement as the best and most ambitious men.

"Career and family" women—the majority of women, in Schwartz's view—want careers, too, but are willing to give up some advancement to have a family. These women can be equally valuable to a company, especially at the middle-management positions currently staffed with less successful males. Positions of moderate responsibility, with part-time, flex-time, or job-sharing options, would allow women to combine career and childrearing. Women often bring much-needed creativity and enthusiasm to jobs traditionally held by male colleagues who have stalled in their careers. A "career and family" option also would allow mothers to return to the "career track" at a later time. Corporations would be able to recover their investment from past training and gain future benefits from loyal workers whose personal needs were being met.

Schwartz's proposal has been controversial, especially among feminists who fear that creating a "mommy track" will reinforce stereotypes that women have less attachment to careers, thereby undermining women's gains in the workplace. Because such a plan is unlikely to be applied to men, critics fear, it may simply reinforce the traditional attitude that women are unsuitable for management careers. Thus, rather than being sensitive to the needs of women, Schwartz's proposal may only encourage sexism.

Schwartz disagrees. Women, she claims, have demonstrated that they are the equal of men in any kind of work. With about 40 percent of management positions now held by women, corporations must give them more choice in the workplace. By their doing so, careers and children will no longer be in conflict.

SOURCE: Felice N. Schwartz, "Management, Women, and the New Facts of Life," *Harvard Business Review*, Vol. 89, no. 1 (January-February 1989):65–76.

Table 13–4   EARNINGS OF FULL-TIME AMERICAN WORKERS, BY SEX, 1988*

Selected Occupational Categories	Median Income (dollars)		Women's Income as a Percentage of Men's
	Men	Women	
Executives, administrators, and managers	$36,759	$23,356	63.5%
Professional specialties	$37,490	$25,789	68.8%
Technical workers	$30,369	$21,039	69.3%
Sales	$27,022	$15,474	57.3%
Precision production, craft, and repair workers	$25,746	$16,869	65.5%
Clerical and other administrative support workers	$24,399	$16,676	68.3%
Transportation workers	$23,453	$13,021	55.5%
Machine operators and tenders	$21,382	$13,289	62.2%
Service workers	$18,648	$11,032	59.2%
Farming, forestry, and fishing workers	$14,300	$9,926	69.4%
All occupations listed above	$26,656	$17,606	66.0%

* Workers aged 15 and over.

SOURCE: U.S. Bureau of the Census. *Money Income of Households, Families, and Persons in the United States: 1988.* Washington, DC: U.S. Government Printing Office, 1989, pp. 158–165.

Gender and Education

Women have traditionally been discouraged, and sometimes formally excluded, from higher education because schooling was seen as unnecessary for homemakers. In 1989, however, 54.2 percent of all college students were women, and they received 52.6 percent of all higher-education degrees awarded that year (Cohen & Croe, 1988; Kroc, 1989).

As was noted earlier, men and women often pursue different courses of study in college, although the link between gender and areas of study has been declining. For example, in 1970, only 17 percent of the bachelor's degrees in natural science, computer science, and engineering were awarded to women; by 1987 the proportion

had risen to 28 percent (U.S. Center for Education Statistics, 1989).

Postgraduate education, often a springboard to a high-prestige job, has been even more of a male preserve. In the past, women who tried to enter graduate school were frequently discouraged by professors and university officials, who expected that they would "probably just get married and drop out anyway." Such attitudes probably persist, although they are now rarer. Today, when all areas of study are counted, women earn as many master's degrees as men do. Furthermore, a growing number of women are pursuing programs that were until recently virtually all male. For example, in 1970 only a few hundred women received Masters of Business Administration (M.B.A.) degrees; in 1980 the number reached 12,000 (25 percent of such degrees); by 1987, the number exceeded 22,000 (33 percent of M.B.A.s) (Kaufman, 1982; U.S. National Center for Education Statistics, 1989).

Men also continue to receive most of the other advanced degrees that lead to high-paying occupations. In 1987, males received 64.8 percent of doctorates. Men also received 59.8 percent of law degrees (LL.B. and J.D.), 67.6 percent of medical degrees (M.D.), and 76.0 percent of dental degrees (D.D.S. and D.M.D.) (U.S. Center for Education Statistics, 1989). In a culture that still defines high-paying professions (and the drive and competitiveness needed to succeed in them) as masculine, women may be discouraged from completing professional education after having enrolled (Fiorentine, 1987). Nevertheless, the proportion of women in professional schools and the professions has steadily risen.

Gender and Politics

Throughout American history, occupational positions, income and wealth, and educational advantages have reinforced male power. This dominance is clearly evident in American politics.

A century ago women were all but excluded from politics. Virtually no women held elected office. The law barred women from voting in national elections in Canada until 1917, and in the United States until 1920. A few women were candidates for political office, however, even before they could vote. The Equal Rights Party supported Victoria Woodhull for the American presidency in 1872; perhaps it was a sign of the times that she spent election day in a New York City jail. Table 13–5 describes milestones in women's gradual movement into American politics, including the election

Table 13–5 SIGNIFICANT "FIRSTS" FOR WOMEN IN AMERICAN POLITICS

1872	First woman to run for the presidency (Victoria Woodhull) represents the Equal Rights Party.
1917	First woman elected to the House of Representatives (Jeannette Rankin of Montana).
1924	First women elected state governors (Nellie Tyloe Ross of Wyoming and Miriam Ferguson of Texas); both followed their husbands into office.
	First woman to have her name placed in nomination for the vice presidency at the convention of a major political party (Lena Jones Spring).
1931	First woman to serve in the Senate (Hattie Caraway of Arkansas); completed the term of her husband upon his death and was reelected in 1932.
1932	First woman appointed to a presidential cabinet (Frances Perkins, Secretary of Labor); as of 1990, only eight women have been so appointed.
1964	First woman to have her name placed in nomination for the presidency at the convention of a major political party (Margaret Chase Smith).
1972	First black woman to have her name placed in nomination for the presidency at the convention of a major political party (Shirley Chisholm).
1981	First woman appointed to the U.S. Supreme Court (Sandra Day O'Connor).
1984	First woman to be successfully nominated for the vice presidency (Geraldine Ferraro).
1988	First woman chief executive to be elected to consecutive third term (Madeleine Kunin, governor of Vermont).

SOURCE: Adapted from Sandra Salmans, "Women Ran for Office Before They Could Vote," *New York Times*, July 13, 1984, p. A 11.

of Jeannette Rankin to Congress in 1917, the first American woman to hold national office. Subsequently, the first two women to serve as governors and the first woman to enter the Senate did so only by succeeding their husbands.

The political power of American women has steadily increased. Several thousand have served as mayors of cities and towns across the United States, and tens of thousands have held responsible administrative posts in the federal government (Mashek & Avery, 1983; Schreiner, 1984). Less change has occurred at the highest levels of politics, although a majority of Americans now claim that they do not object to having a woman even as president. In 1990, 3 of the 50 state governors were women (6 percent); in Congress, 25 of 435 members of the House of Representatives (6 percent) and 2 of 100 senators (2 percent) were women.

Minority Women

If minorities (discussed in Chapter 12, "Race and Ethnicity") are socially disadvantaged, are minority women doubly disadvantaged? Generally, yes. First, there is the disadvantage associated with race and ethnicity. For example, in 1988, black women in the full-time labor force earned 89.6 percent as much as white women; for Hispanic women, the figure was 80.8 percent. Second, there is the disadvantage associated with sex. Thus, black women earned 81.4 percent as much as black men, while Hispanic women earned about 83.6 percent as much as Hispanic men. When these disadvantages are combined, black women earned 59.7 percent as much as white men and Hispanic women earned 53.8 percent as much (U.S. Bureau of the Census, 1989).

The low income of minority women reflects their lower position on the occupational ladder in comparison to white women. Whenever the economy sags, as it did after the early 1970s, minority women are especially likely to experience declining income and unemployment.

Chapter 10 ("Social Class in America") explained that poverty in the United States affects more females than males. In 1988, 53.0 percent of poor households were headed by women, in contrast to 4.9 percent headed by men. The feminization of poverty is especially dramatic among minority women. In 1988 about 29.3 percent of households headed by white women (with no husband present) were poor, but 52.1 percent of comparable black households and 55.1 percent of comparable Hispanic households were poor.

Are Women a Minority?

In Chapter 12 a minority was defined as a category of people whose social disadvantage is linked to physical or cultural traits. In a patriarchal society, a reasonable question is whether all women should be defined as a minority. Objectively, women must be viewed as a minority, since physical traits of sex are linked to being socially disadvantaged in various ways, as we have explained.

Even so, white women tend *not* to perceive themselves as a social minority (Hacker, 1951; Lengermann & Wallace, 1985). This is so partly because, unlike racial and ethnic minorities, which are typically in the lower social classes, white women are part of families at all social levels. Yet, within every social class, women usually have less income, wealth, education, and power than men do. The reason is that women gain much of their social standing through men—first their fathers, and later their husbands (Bernard, 1981).

Another reason that many white women do not consider themselves a minority is that they have been socialized to accept their social position as natural. A woman who accepts conventional ideas about gender believes that she should be submissive and deferential to men and that men should have power over her.

In sum, some women—especially the relatively privileged—may not think of themselves as disadvantaged. Yet as a category of Americans, women have both the distinctive identity and the social disadvantages to be validly considered a social minority.

THEORETICAL ANALYSIS OF GENDER

Both the structural-functional and social-conflict paradigms guide understandings of the significance of gender in American society.

Structural-Functional Analysis

The structural-functional paradigm views society as a complex system of many separate but integrated parts. The significance of any social structure is sought in its functional contribution to the stable operation of the overall society.

As explained in Chapter 4 ("Society"), the earliest human societies were based on hunting and gathering. Within such societies, simple technology provides humans with limited ability to challenge biological facts and forces. Superior male strength allows men to dominate women. Lacking effective birth control, women further contend with frequent pregnancies and the related responsibilities of child care (Lengermann & Wallace, 1985). As a result, social norms that encourage females to center their lives around home and children promote societal survival. Thus these cultures come to view such activities as feminine.

Additionally, the greater short-term strength of males suggests that they should have other responsibilities. Males are typically more successful in capturing

game, for instance; thus such tasks away from the home come to be defined as masculine.

As long as technology remains simple, the biological facts of sex and cultural facts of gender are likely to be closely linked. This is not a matter of biological necessity but a cultural strategy that most preindustrial societies adopt for its survival value. Over many generations, the sex-based division of labor becomes institutionalized, built into the structure of society and taken for granted.

Industrial technology opens up a vastly greater range of cultural possibilities. The muscles of humans and other animals are no longer the primary sources of energy, so the physical strength of males loses much of its earlier significance. At the same time, the ability to control reproduction provides females with greater choice in shaping their lives. Under such circumstances, societies benefit from the weakening of traditional conceptions of gender. In the process, the mental abilities of both males and females gain in importance, rivaling or surpassing physical strength and skill. Such changes are slow, however, and are resisted to the extent that gender has become institutionalized. In other words, even as conventional gender definitions become increasingly dysfunctional, many people persist in the belief that such patterns are natural.

In addition, as Talcott Parsons (1951, 1954) has explained, gender differences are a form of social fabric that contributes to integrate society—at least in its traditional form. Gender, Parsons claimed, defines a *complementary* set of roles that links males and females into family units that, in turn, support the operation of society. Females maintain the internal cohesion of the family, managing the household and taking primary responsibility for raising children; males function to connect the family to the larger world, primarily through their participation in the labor force.

Parsons further argued that, through the socialization process, societies prepare individuals to assume these differing adult responsibilities. Both males and females learn their appropriate gender identity, as well as the skills and attitudes needed to fulfill their gender roles. Because males' primary societal responsibility is achievement in the labor force, they are socialized to be rational, self-assured, and competitive—a complex of traits that Parsons described as *instrumental*. Because females take primary responsibility for childrearing, they are socialized to display what Parsons termed *expressive* qualities, such as emotion and sensitivity to others. In Parsons's scheme, then, gender identity learned early in life is the foundation of gender roles assumed later by adults.

Finally, according to Parsons, society enforces gender-linked behavior through various means of social control. This social guidance is partly internal, as people incorporate cultural definitions of gender into their own identities, so that violations of these norms generate guilt. It is also partly external: the failure to display the personal traits appropriate to one's sex can lead to shame based on criticism from others. A powerful form of social control is the belief that culturally deviant gender traits will bring rejection by members of the opposite sex. In simple terms, women are likely to view nonmasculine men as sexually unattractive, while unfeminine women risk rejection by men.

Critical evaluation. Structural-functional analysis emphasizes how masculinity and femininity are culturally defined in complementary fashion. People who accept gender norms do not necessarily find gender differences to be unjust. Consequently, gender integrates society both structurally (in terms of what people do) and morally (in terms of what people believe).

The major problem with this approach is that it assumes a singular vision of society that is unlikely to be shared by everyone. For example, many women have traditionally worked outside the home because of economic necessity. Also, as an approach supportive of the status quo, Parsons's analysis ignores the personal strains and social costs produced by rigid, traditional gender roles (Giele, 1988). Finally, as traditional norms and values that support conventional families have weakened, what Parsons termed gender "complementarity" is often seen as male "domination."

Social-Conflict Analysis

Centered on the issue of power, social-conflict analysis suggests that gender has historically benefited men and rendered women a socially disadvantaged minority (Hacker, 1951, 1974). Patriarchy subjects women to the same prejudice and discrimination experienced by racial and ethnic minorities (Collins, 1971; Lengermann & Wallace, 1985). From this point of view, gender promotes not social cohesion but rather social conflict as men protect their privileges while women challenge the status quo. Traditional gender beliefs are viewed as sexist ideology that justifies "keeping women in their place" and thereby provides substantial economic advantages to men. As racism has legitimated the oppression of nonwhites, so has sexism devalued women and their

activities. Patriarchy can persist only to the extent that men are believed to be innately superior and women are defined as less capable in the labor force or in politics. Within the home, patriarchy inhibits marital communication and contributes to family violence, mostly directed against women (F. Klein, 1982).

As was noted in earlier chapters, the social-conflict paradigm draws heavily on the ideas of Karl Marx. Marx's writings, like those of most social scientists until recently, focused almost exclusively on men, but his friend and collaborator Friedrich Engels addressed the issue of gender, linking gender stratification to the historical formation of social classes (1902; orig. 1884).

For generations, the evaluation of women in terms of physical appearance instead of job performance contributed to unequal occupational opportunities. By turning the tables, this educational poster helps people to see how grossly unfair this practice really is.

"Hire him. He's got great legs."

SEX DISCRIMINATION ISN'T FUNNY
SUPPORT THE NATIONAL ORGANIZATION FOR WOMEN
28 EAST 56 STREET N.Y.C. 10022

Engels claimed that the different activities of women and men in hunting and gathering societies were essentially of equal importance. A successful hunt may have brought males great prestige, but since most of the society's food was vegetation gathered by women, females had great importance as well (Leacock, 1978). As a surplus was generated in horticultural and agrarian societies, however, social equality and the custom of sharing goods gave way to social classes based on the idea of private property. At this point, male power over females became marked. Surplus wealth made men concerned with heirs to whom they would pass on their property. Their problem was solved with the creation of monogamous marriage and the family: men could now identify their own offspring and ensure that their property would be passed on to them, especially sons. Within families, the lives of women became centered on bearing and raising children.

Engels claimed that capitalism intensified male domination. First, capitalism created more wealth, which further empowered men. Second, expanding the capitalist economy depended on defining women as consumers and encouraging them to seek personal fulfillment through buying various products. Third, to support males working in factories, females were assigned the task of maintaining the home. Overall, capitalism exploits humanity by paying low wages for male labor, but *no* wages for female work (Eisenstein, 1979; Barry, 1983; Jagger, 1983; Vogel, 1983).

According to social-conflict analysis, those who suffer social disadvantages are likely to act to change society. Thus, efforts to transform gender roles are viewed as political acts against an oppressive system. But as William Goode (1983) points out, men are less likely than women to recognize gender as a source of social conflict. Goode suggests that women, in their subordinate role, are well aware how men shape their lives, but men, who are less influenced by women, often fail to see how much gender matters. Even those who do may think that they are not personally responsible for patriarchy. Men also tend to view anyone's success or failure simply as a result of personal merit; this is so because it is the women who commonly experience prejudice and discrimination. Men also emotionally identify with women as lovers, wives, mothers, and daughters. They define their role as protecting and providing for females so that, at worst, they are benevolent despots. For these reasons, Goode concludes, men may be hurt and confused by women's claims of being victimized.

Critical evaluation. Social-conflict analysis stresses the domination of society by males. This approach explains the growing criticism of conventional gender roles as a consequence of the inequality of the sexes.

One problem is that social-conflict analysis minimizes the extent to which males and females live together cooperatively in families. Especially those who endorse traditional notions of gender may resist redefining as "political ideology" what they view as morality. Another concern with this approach is its assertion that capitalism is the basis of gender stratification. As we shall see, even societies with socialist economic systems are strongly patriarchal.

FEMINISM

Feminism is *the support for the social equality of the sexes, leading to opposition to patriarchy and sexism.* Feminism is not new to America. As described at the beginning of this chapter, antislavery women including Elizabeth Cady Stanton and Lucretia Mott began the "first wave" of feminism in the 1840s when they drew parallels between the oppression of nonwhites and the oppression of women (Randall, 1982). The primary objective of the women's movement at that time was to gain the right to vote, but after suffrage was achieved in 1920, other disadvantages for women persisted. Thus, the "second wave" of feminism arose in the 1960s—and continues today.

Basic Feminist Ideas

Like the sociological perspective, feminism involves stepping back from conventional social patterns to gain a keener awareness of what is often taken for granted. Also like the sociological perspective, feminism links *personal* experiences to the operation of *society*. In other words, how we think of ourselves (gender identity), how we act (gender roles), and our place in society (gender stratification) represent the power of society over us.

But feminism is also decidedly political and critical, challenging conventional ideas about the two sexes, especially those that contribute to patriarchy. For example, our culture traditionally defines masculinity largely in terms of power over others. In contrast, femininity is viewed in terms of altruism—selfless responding to the needs of other people, especially males. Feminism holds that examining, and ultimately rejecting, such values can lead to equal power and dignity for both sexes.

Feminism is also committed to the "reintegration of humanity" (French, 1985:443). Feminists argue that cultural conceptions of gender divide the full range of human qualities into two distinct and limited spheres: the male world of rationality and competition, and the female world of emotions and cooperation. Feminism challenges the assertion that masculine traits are inherently more important than feminine traits. Instead, it claims that *any* human being is capable of developing *all* these traits. In short, feminism is a process of resocialization by which all people can develop and express the full range of their human potential.

Feminism is also critical of gender stratification, challenging laws and cultural norms that limit the income, education, and occupational opportunities of women. Supporters of women's rights seek to end the historical pattern by which the female half of the population has been subject to decisions made by the male half—whether in the privacy of the home or in the public world of national politics. For this reason, feminists have supported the Equal Rights Amendment (ERA) to the U.S. Constitution, which states simply:

Equality of rights under the law shall not be denied or abridged by the United States or any State on account of sex.

A final area of feminist concern is human sexuality. In a patriarchal society, sexual relationships between men and women are often an expression of male power (Millet, 1970; J. Bernard, 1973; Dworkin, 1987). One reflection of women's inequality is the widespread pattern of sexual harassment. On college campuses, for example, as many as one-third of female students report unwanted sexual advances from their male teachers (Dziech & Weiner, 1984). Another survey found that about one-fourth of college women had been victims of rape—often what is commonly called *date rape*, in which, during a date, the man forcibly imposes sex on the woman (Sweet, 1985). Surveys of men and women in the workplace also indicate that a majority of both sexes believe sexual harassment is a serious problem (Loy & Stewart, 1984).

More generally, feminism supports the right of females to control their own sexuality and reproduction. It is for this reason that feminists have advocated the right of women to obtain birth control information—something that was illegal in some states even in the

More than a century after women's movement in the United States began, a "second wave" of feminism sought to reduce gender-based inequality. Women's control of their own sexuality is widely viewed as crucial to these efforts. This accounts for the centrality of the abortion controversy to the women's movement in recent years. After declaring abortion to be a woman's choice in 1973, the Supreme Court stepped back in the 1989 Webster decision, supporting the ability of states to regulate that right.

1960s. In addition, most feminists support a woman's right to choose whether to bear children or to terminate a pregnancy. Feminism is not in favor of abortion, but it claims that the decision to bear children should be made by women themselves rather than by men—such as husbands, physicians, and legislators. Many feminists also support gay peoples' struggle to overcome prejudice and discrimination within a culture dominated by heterosexuality. Such social disadvantages are even greater for lesbians than for gay men, because lesbians violate not only the cultural norm of heterosexuality, but also the norm that men should control the sexuality of women (Deckard, 1979; Barry, 1983; Jagger, 1983).

Resistance to Feminism

Feminism has been strongly resisted by both men and women who accept the dominant cultural ideas about gender. Many men oppose feminism for the same reasons that many whites have historically opposed social equality for nonwhites: they do not want to lose privileges linked to patriarchy. Other men, including those who are neither rich nor powerful, are uneasy about a social movement that appears to attack the traditional family and established male-female relationships. Further, for some men, feminism threatens an important basis of their status and self-respect: their masculinity. Men who have been socialized to value strength and dominance can understandably feel threatened by the feminist challenge that they can also be gentle and warm (Doyle, 1983). Many other men, however, support feminist ideas. Some simply object to an entire category of human beings being treated unequally in American society. Others find in feminism encouragement for developing themselves more fully—the opportunity, in the words of army recruiters, to "be all that you can be."

Some women, as well, are uneasy about feminism. For example, women who have centered their lives around their husbands and children may perceive feminism as a threat to all they believe is valuable. From this point of view, feminism amounts to an effort to revise the law, to change the workplace, to restructure marriage and childrearing—in short, to remake all of society—according to the radical political agenda of a few rather than the traditional values that have guided American life for centuries. Additionally, some women see demands for sexual equality as threatening the conventional "feminine" spheres of life, including the home

and the family, that have traditionally provided women with power and personal identity (Marshall, 1985).

Many people's fears about feminism are based on incorrect images of what feminism is. Although change often involves conflict, feminism does not seek to set men and women against each other. Instead, in the belief that patriarchy has long fostered social conflict, feminism seeks to eliminate the element of power from human relationships.

Widespread support for at least some feminist ideas can be inferred from the endorsement of the Equal Rights Amendment by almost three-fourths of American adults (N.O.R.C., 1989:280). However, the failure of American society formally to enact the ERA, which was first proposed in Congress in 1923, shows that resistance to feminism is strong.

A final area of resistance to feminism involves *how* women's social standing can be improved. Although a large majority of Americans believe women should have equal rights, a majority also believe that women should advance individually, according to their abilities. In a national survey, 70 percent of American adults claimed that women should expect to get ahead on the basis of their own training and qualifications; only 10 percent thought women's rights groups represented the best approach (N.O.R.C., 1989:391).

Of course, these views may not be contradictory. Americans generally believe people should be rewarded for their personal merit; this is precisely what feminism is seeking.

Variations Within Feminism

A goal as general as promoting equality of the sexes can be pursued in various ways, so that more than one kind of feminism exists today. Three distinct variants of feminism can be noted, although the distinctions among them are not clear-cut, and each is continually changing as feminist thinking develops (Barry, 1983; Jagger, 1983; Stacey, 1983; Vogel, 1983).

Liberal feminism accepts the basic organization of American society but seeks to ensure that females have the same rights and opportunities as males do. Liberal feminism endorses the Equal Rights Amendment and stresses the need to eliminate the prejudice and discrimination that have historically limited women's opportunities. Liberal feminism supports reproductive freedom for all women. While accepting the family as

THE AGE OF IRON.
MAN AS HE EXPECTS TO BE

Since the emergence of feminism in the United States, some people have feared sexual equality. As this 1869 Currier and Ives drawing suggests, males may fear the loss of privileges central to their masculine identity.

a central social institution, liberal feminism advocates the availability of maternity leave and child care for women who wish to work. A striking fact is that over one hundred nations of the world guarantee maternity leaves for all working women, but the United States has no such policy (Hewlett, 1986). This, critics contend, is not unfair to women, but undermines American families.

Socialist feminism, based on the ideas of Karl Marx and Friedrich Engels, links the social disadvantages of women primarily to the capitalist economic system. Thus, socialist feminists view the reforms sought by liberal feminism as necessary but insufficient. Only a socialist revolution, these feminists claim, can provide significant equality for all men and women. (Further discussion of socialism is found in Chapter 19, "The Economy and Work.")

Radical feminism endorses liberal feminist reforms but, like socialist feminism, also views them as inadequate. Nor do radical feminists consider even socialist revolution likely to end patriarchy. This type of feminism claims patriarchy can be overcome only through the elimination of gender itself. This does not mean, of course, that males and females will not differ biologically in terms of sex, but rather that culture should not define sex in terms that divide human capacities into masculine and feminine worlds. Radical feminists, then, seek a gender-free society.

GENDER IN THE TWENTY-FIRST CENTURY

Predictions about the future are, at best, informed speculation. Just as economists disagree about the likely inflation rate a year from now, sociologists differ as to the future state of our society. Yet some general comments are possible about the future of gender in American society.

Recall, first, the position of American women more than a century ago. Husbands controlled property within most marriages, women were barred from most areas of the labor force, and no woman was able to vote. Although women remain socially disadvantaged, the movement toward greater equality has been striking.

Many factors have contributed to this change. Perhaps most important, industrialization has both broadened the range of human activity and shifted the nature of work from physically demanding tasks that favored male strength to jobs that demand human thought and imagination. Additionally, medical technology has placed reproduction under human control so that women's lives are less limited by unwanted pregnancies.

Many women and men have also made deliberate efforts to lessen the power of patriarchy. Feminism seeks to end the constraints imposed on people by a society that assigns activities and forms of self-expression simply on the basis of sex. As these efforts continue, the social changes in the twenty-first century may be even greater than those we have already witnessed.

In the midst of change, strong opposition to feminism persists. Gender is still an important foundation of personal identity and of family life, and it is deeply woven into the moral fabric of America. We should therefore, expect, that attempts to change cultural ideas about the two sexes will continue to provoke considerable anxiety, fear, and resistance.

On balance, it seems that radical change in American society's view of gender is unlikely in the near future. Yet the movement toward a society in which males and females enjoy more equal rights and opportunities seems equally certain to persist.

SUMMARY

1. Sex is a biological concept; human beings are male or female from the moment of conception. People with the rare condition of hermaphroditism combine the biological traits of both sexes. Transsexuals are people who deliberately alter their sex surgically.

2. Heterosexuality is the dominant sexual orientation in virtually every society in the world. Homosexuals make up a small proportion of the American population. Sexual orientation is not always clear-cut, however; many people are bisexual.

3. Gender involves human traits that a culture attaches to each sex. Gender varies historically and across cultures.

4. Some degree of patriarchy exists in every society. Male dominance has been defended by sexism, just as racial dominance has been defended by racism.

5. The socialization process links gender to personal identity (gender identity) and distinctive activities (gender roles). The major agents of socialization—family, peer groups, schools, and the mass media—reinforce cultural definitions of masculine and feminine.

6. Gender stratification entails numerous social disadvantages for women. Although most women are now in the paid labor force, a majority of working women are clerical workers or service workers. Unpaid housework also remains a feminine activity.

7. On the average, women earn about 68 percent as much as men do, for a number of reasons, including discrimination. This discrepancy has led to the demand for equal pay for equal worth.

8. Historically excluded from higher education, women are now a slight majority of all college students and receive half of the master's degrees.

Most doctorates and professional degrees are still received by men.

9. The number of women in politics has increased sharply in recent decades. Still, the vast majority of national officials are men.

10. Minority women have greater social disadvantages than white women. Overall, minority women earn only half as much as white men, and half of the households headed by minority women are poor.

11. Due to their distinctive identity and social disadvantages, all women can be considered social minorities.

12. Structural-functional analysis suggests that distinctive roles for males and females is a survival strategy in preindustrial societies. In industrial societies, extensive gender inequality becomes dysfunctional, although long-established cultural norms related to gender change slowly. According to Talcott Parsons, complementary gender roles increase the social integration of the family.

13. Social-conflict analysis views gender as a dimension of social inequality and conflict. Friedrich Engels linked gender stratification to the development of private property. Engels claimed that capitalism increased male dominance by devaluing females as homemakers working for no pay.

14. Feminism supports the social equality of the sexes and opposes patriarchy and sexism. Challenging the cultural division of humanity into masculine and feminine worlds, it seeks to eliminate the historical social disadvantages faced by females.

15. Because gender is a foundation of American society, feminism has met with strong resistance. Although two-thirds of Americans express support for the Equal Rights Amendment, this legislation—first proposed in Congress in 1923—has yet to become part of the U.S. Constitution.

KEY CONCEPTS

feminism the support for the social equality of the sexes, leading to opposition to patriarchy and sexism

gender human traits that are linked by culture to each sex

gender identity the ways males and females, guided by culture, learn to think of themselves

gender roles (sex roles) attitudes and activities that a culture links to each sex

gender stratification the unequal distribution of wealth, power, and privileges between the two sexes

hermaphrodite humans with some combination of male and female internal and external genitalia

matriarchy a form of social organization in which females dominate males

patriarchy a form of social organization in which males dominate females

primary sex characteristics the genitals, used to reproduce the human species

secondary sex characteristics physical traits, other than the genitals, that distinguish males and females

sex the division of humanity into biological categories of male and female

sexism the belief that one sex is innately superior to the other

sexual orientation the manner in which people experience sexual arousal and achieve sexual pleasure

transsexuals people who feel they are one sex when biologically they are the other

SUGGESTED READINGS

This classic study argues that males and females live within different, socially constructed worlds. The author also claims that sociology itself must change in order effectively to investigate gender.

> Jessie Bernard. *The Female World*. New York: Free Press, 1981.

The first of these texts presents a detailed introduction to the concept of gender. The second provides a straightforward discussion of sexuality and sexual orientation.

> Linda L. Lindsey. *Gender Roles: A Sociological Perspective*. Englewood Cliffs, NJ: Prentice Hall, 1990.

> David A. Shultz. *Human Sexuality*. 3rd ed. Englewood Cliffs, NJ: Prentice Hall, 1988.

This book explains how economic changes in American society have brought women into the workforce although the marital roles of the two sexes have changed little.

> Arlie Hochschild, with Anne Machung. *The Second Shift: Working Parents and the Revolution at Home*. New York: Viking, 1989.

Homosexuality has long been ignored by scholars, just as it has been by the general public. The first book noted below is a collection of essays focusing on homosexuality among women. The second offers a broad, historical analysis of homosexuality.

> Estelle B. Freedman, Barbara C. Gelpi, Susan L. Johnson, and Kathleen M. Weston. *The Lesbian Issue: Essays from SIGNS*. Chicago: University of Chicago Press, 1985.

> David F. Greenberg. *The Construction of Homosexuality*. Chicago: University of Chicago Press, 1988.

Efforts to increase sexual equality in Sweden are described in this study, with comparisons to American society.

> Margaret Jean Intons-Peterson. *Gender Concepts of Swedish and American Youth*. Hillsdale, NJ: Lawrence Erlbaum, 1988.

The final book written by a long-time student of Indian society examines the practice of purdah, in which women remain veiled in the presence of men.

> David G. Mandelbaum. *Women's Seclusion and Men's Honor: Sex Roles in Northern India, Bangladesh, and Pakistan*. Tucson: University of Arizona Press, 1988.

Here are three useful books on masculinity. The first combines varied essays on the topic. The second argues that American males suffer from a lack of clear and effective standards by which to judge their masculinity. The third surveys American masculinity in recent decades.

> Harry Brod, ed. *The Making of Masculinity: The New Men's Studies*. Winchester, MA: Allen & Unwin, 1987.

> Ray Raphael. *The Men from the Boys: Rites of Passage in Male America*. Lincoln and London: University of Nebraska Press, 1988.

> Barbara Ehrenreich. *The Hearts of Men: American Dreams and the Flight from Commitment*. Garden City, NY: Anchor/Doubleday, 1983.

This book examines how feminism is transforming the social sciences.

> Sue Rosenberg Zalk and Janice Gordon-Kelter. *Revolutions in Knowledge: Feminism in the Social Sciences*. Boulder, CO: Westview Press, 1989.

14

Aging and the Elderly

In 1989, the Rolling Stones toured the United States, extending the group's career into a fourth decade. Most ticket holders who thronged to their concerts paid more attention to the music than the fact that the Stones were approaching fifty years of age. But no one doubts—least of all the Stones themselves—that the rigors of touring and performing with their legendary energy are harder now than when they were younger. Perhaps some of the older fans were actually celebrating this rock group's valiant refusal to concede any power to the passing years.

At the beginning of this century, people past the age of fifty had already had a "long life," at least statistically speaking: life expectancy for Americans born in 1900 was only about forty-seven years. Those fortunate enough to live longer were hardly secure, however. Few employers provided adequate pensions for their workers, and Social Security and other federal benefits were still decades in the future.

In the 1990s, issues relating to aging and the elderly command the attention of policy makers and all Americans. On the one hand, the poverty that confronted aging Americans even a generation ago has been greatly reduced. Forty years ago, with more than one-third living in poverty, the elderly were the most likely of all age categories to be poor. Since then, the proportion of elderly Americans in poverty has fallen dramatically, so that they now have a higher standard of living than children, teens, or young adults. On the other hand, older people continue to face prejudice and discrimination in a society that generally favors youth over maturity. And, as unprecedented numbers of Americans enter old age, new and daunting problems of aging loom on the horizon.

THE GRAYING OF AMERICAN SOCIETY

A quiet but powerful revolution is reshaping American society: the number of elderly Americans—people aged sixty-five and over—is increasing more than twice as fast as the population as a whole. In 1900, half of all Americans were under twenty-three years of age and only one in twenty-five people had reached sixty-five. Now, as shown in Figure 14–1, however, the median age of Americans is steadily rising. In 1980, the median age of Americans passed thirty, and about 11 percent of the population was over sixty-five. By the mid-1980s, elderly Americans outnumbered teenagers. By the year 2050—within the lifetimes of many readers of this book—the median age of Americans will be about forty-three and almost one in four Americans will be over sixty-five (Spencer, 1989).

What is prompting this graying of America? First,

a baby boom began in the late 1940s as Americans enthusiastically settled into family life after World War II. Before this era ended in 1965, some 75 million babies had been born. By virtue of their numbers, these baby-boomers (who first gained attention by forging the youth culture of the 1960s) will continue to exert their influence on American society as they reach old age. And since the birth rate has declined dramatically since 1960, they now form a disproportionately large segment of the population. Second, the life expectancy of Americans has been steadily increasing. Males born in 1900 could expect to live, on average, only about forty-six years; females could expect to live about forty-eight years. By contrast, American males born in 1988 can expect to live 71.5 years; the life expectancy of American females has increased to 78.3 years. This striking increase reflects a rising standard of living as well as medical advances that have virtually eliminated infectious diseases such as smallpox, diphtheria, and measles, which killed many young people early in the century. More recently, medi-

Figure 14–1   The Graying of American Society

(Spencer, 1989)

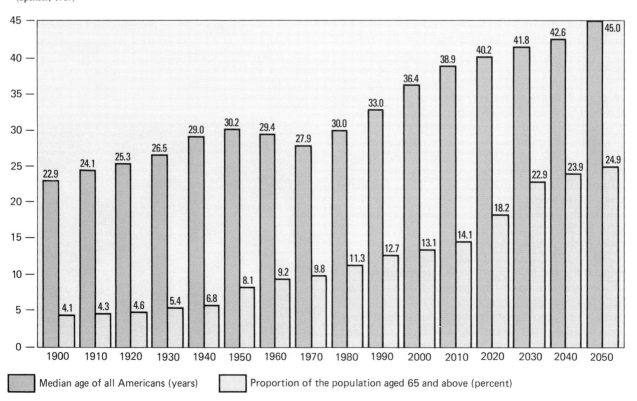

Median age of all Americans (years)   Proportion of the population aged 65 and above (percent)

Americans over the age of sixty-five, who already outnumber teenagers, will represent about one in five Americans by 2030.

cine has also made strides in combating cancer and heart disease, afflictions common among the elderly (Wall, 1980). One clear indication of this change is that the fastest-growing segment of the elderly population is people over eighty-five, who are expected to account for one in twenty Americans by the year 2050 (Spencer, 1989).

How will this transformation affect American society? We can only begin to imagine. Assuming that people over sixty-five continue to retire from the labor force, the proportion of nonemployed adults—already about ten times greater than in 1900—will soar even higher. This, in turn, will generate ever-greater demands for social resources and programs providing support for the nonworking elderly. During this century, the share of the federal budget directed to people over sixty-five has grown from 15 percent to nearly 33 percent (Callihan, 1987).

The Social Security system, the major source of retirement income, operates on a simple principle: taxes on the earnings of working people are used to support retirees. This system may falter in the future because of the growing imbalance between workers and nonworkers. In 1960, there were about five workers for every person receiving benefits. By 1980, this ratio had dropped to about three-to-one. But by the year 2030, when large numbers of "baby-boomers" will be entering old age, government projections indicate that the ratio could fall to two-to-one, casting the long-term financial strength of the system in doubt (Barberis, 1981).

The elderly also draw heavily on the health-care system, accounting for one-fourth of all medical expenditures. Older Americans make the greatest use of physicians and hospitals, and consume about one-fourth of all prescription drugs (Butler, 1975). Unless steps are taken to ensure that the medical needs of tens of millions of additional older people can be met—meaning, in many cases, providing medical care that the elderly can *afford*—our society will face a monumental crisis in the next century.

Perhaps most important, in the next century interactions with elderly people will become commonplace in everyone's daily experience. Americans are now accustomed to a considerable degree of age segregation. Young people rarely mingle in familiar settings with old people; oftentimes, in fact, the young know little about the process of growing old, which—if they are lucky—they will eventually face themselves. In the twenty-first century, when the size of the elderly population of the United States stands at twice what it is now, those who are not elderly will have extensive daily contact with those who are.

As the proportion of older Americans rises, adult children will have greater responsibility for aging parents (Gelman, 1985). Currently, about one-fourth of American adults report spending five hours or more a day caring for their aging parents (Stone, Cafferata, & Sangl, 1987). Today's younger adults may well become a "sandwich generation," spending as much time caring for their aging parents as for their own children.

GROWING OLD: BIOLOGY AND CULTURE

The graying of America has sparked the development of a relatively new field of social science. **Gerontology** (a term derived from the Greek word *geron*, meaning "an old person") is *the study of aging and the elderly*. Gerontology deals not only with the physical process of aging, but also with how individual cultures define old age.

Biological changes accompany the process of aging, of course, but so do changes in the social definitions that structure personal experience. Every society recognizes stages in the life course. Biology alone does not account for the distinctions Americans make among children, adolescents, and adults, as we can see by comparing ourselves to other cultures. In Chapter 5 ("Socialization"), Margaret Mead (1961; orig. 1928) found that the Samoan Islanders barely recognized adolescence; Philippe Ariès (1965) argued that childhood, as we know it, did not exist in medieval Europe. To fully understand old age, therefore, we must consider both the biological facts of aging and how they are perceived in a social context.

Biological Changes

Life involves ongoing bodily change. Societies label some changes as positive and others as negative. In youth-oriented American society, we tend to view biological changes that occur earlier in life as positive, and later physical changes more negatively. Growing children and maturing adolescents gain more responsibility and additional legal rights as rewards for their progress. But few are congratulated for getting old. We commiserate with those approaching old age, and make jokes about the expected onset of physical and mental decline. We assume, in other words, that after a certain point in the life cycle, people cease growing *up* and begin growing *down*.

Physical problems generally complicate old age. Yet, Americans tend to exaggerate the physical differences between the elderly and younger people (Harris, 1976). Gerontological research helps to separate the facts of aging from cultural stereotypes.

Gray hair, wrinkles, loss of height and weight, and an overall decline in strength and vitality—these all characterize the aging process that begins in middle age (Colloway & Dollevoet, 1977). After about the age of fifty, bones become more brittle; falls that would be of little consequence earlier in life can result in disabling injuries. Broken bones also take longer to heal as we get older. A substantial proportion of the elderly also suffer from chronic illnesses like arthritis, which limit physical activity, and life-threatening conditions such as heart disease and cancer. Alzheimer's disease, a devastating disability that afflicts some 3 million Americans—about 10 percent of the population over sixty-five—has received more attention in recent years. The box describes the effects of this cruel and incurable disease.

The sensory abilities—taste, sight, touch, smell, and especially hearing—tend to diminish with age. While only about 5 percent of middle-aged people have visual impairments, about 10 percent of the elderly do. Hearing problems are even more common, increasing in frequency from about 15 percent of middle-aged people to almost 30 percent of the elderly. Both types of impairments are more common among men than women (U.S. National Center for Health Statistics, 1989). Older people also experience a declining ability to taste and smell, which can adversely affect eating habits, creating health problems related to poor nutrition (Eckholm, 1985).

With advancing age, life-threatening illnesses such as heart disease and cancer occur more frequently, as do less serious disabilities like arthritis and diabetes. Even so, the vast majority of older people are not disabled by physical diseases: only about one in ten reports having trouble walking, and just one in twenty requires intensive care in a hospital or nursing home. No more than 1 percent of the elderly are bedridden. Overall, about 70 percent of people over the age of sixty-five assess their health as "good" to "excellent," while 30 percent characterize their overall condition as "fair" or "poor" (U.S. National Center for Health Statistics, 1989).

Such patterns vary greatly within the elderly population, however. As we noted in Chapter 10 ("Social Class in America"), physical health is related to social class. Those who can afford to live and work in a healthful and safe environment and who can take advantage of extensive preventive medical care fare much better than those with fewer social privileges. For instance, while over 80 percent of people aged sixty-five or over with incomes exceeding $35,000 assess their own health as "excellent" or "good," only 60 percent of people with incomes under $10,000 do. Income disparity also explains why almost three-fourths of elderly whites consider

SOCIOLOGY OF EVERYDAY LIFE

Alzheimer's Disease—A Case of Dying Twice

. . . your memory is gone, it's dead. I don't know what's missing. Your thoughts become a void, and then there's nothing.

These words were spoken by a woman experiencing the early stages of Alzheimer's disease. At fifty-three years of age, her mind is slowly dying. As the disease progresses, she will gradually lose her memory, become disoriented, and perhaps hallucinate. Ultimately, she will completely lose touch with the world around her—not knowing where she is, or whether it's day or night. She will not even recognize members of her own family. This social death, which places her beyond the reach of loved ones, precedes biological death. As her final days approach, she will lose control of her body, eventually entering a coma from which she will not recover.

Dying twice is the tragedy of Alzheimer's disease, a dementia-producing illness that causes several hundred thousand deaths each year. The incidence of Alzheimer's has soared, paralleling the increase in elderly Americans. In the past, the symptoms of Alzheimer's disease, especially the loss of memory, were often considered simply the natural result of old age. But medical research has gradu-ally revealed that this disorder—named after Alois Alzheimer, a German physician who pioneered investigation of the illness early in this century—actually stems from physical deterioration of nerve fibers in the brain. At present, only small gains have been made in understanding the disease. New research offers glimmers of hope, but there is currently no cure.

More than most illnesses, Alzheimer's disease strikes beyond the individual, drawing family members and friends into its agonizing web. Initially, those with the disease may experience only mild loss of memory (which, in itself, is certainly no sure indication of having the disease). But as the disease progresses, people with Alzheimer's become increasingly helpless, placing more and more of a burden on others. Family members must painfully watch a loved one lose the ability to work, perform simple household tasks, and interact with others.

Worse still, Alzheimer's victims may unintentionally injure themselves or other people. Families must learn to take extraordinary precautions. Confused over how to operate water faucets, sufferers may scald themselves in the shower; conse-quently, water temperatures must be adjusted to a lower range. Cars pose unimagined dangers as well: they must be disabled so the family member with Alzheimer's disease does not attempt to drive, often with tragic consequences. Danger may loom in stairways, too, requiring the installa-tion of protective gates.

Eventually, even the strongest family members find that they alone cannot provide the constant attention that people with Alzheimer's need. Institutional care, costing upwards of several thousand dollars a month, adds another crippling blow.

But perhaps the greatest pain for families is their own helplessness as they watch the gradual death of a loved one, who may be unable to respond to them. The wife of a San Diego man with Alzheimer's re-called, "One day my husband threat-ened to leave home because he wanted to go off to call his wife. He cried and begged me to let him call 'Lil.' I told him I was Lil—it was devastating."

SOURCES: Based on Matt Clark, "A Slow Death of the Mind," *Newsweek*, December 3, 1984, pp. 56–62; and Congress of the United States, *Losing a Million Minds: Confronting the Tragedy of Alzhei-mer's Disease and Other Dementias* (Washington, DC: U.S. Government Printing Office, 1987).

their health "good" or "excellent," in contrast to only about half of elderly black Americans (U.S. National Center for Health Statistics, 1989).

Psychological Changes

Despite popular assumptions, most elderly people do not suffer from mental or psychological problems. As Samuel Johnson, the famous eighteenth-century observer of British society, once noted:

> There is a wicked inclination in most people to suppose an old man decayed in his intellect. If a young or middle-aged man, when leaving a company, does not recollect where he laid his hat, it is nothing; but if the same inattention is discovered in an old man, people will shrug their shoulders and say, "His memory is going" (cited in Berger, 1983:544).

Johnson's point is that cultural assumptions about the various stages of life determine how we interpret human behavior.

Until recently, most psychologists agreed that changes in intelligence over the life cycle followed a simple rule: "What goes up must come down" (Baltes & Schaie, 1974). Mental decline, some claimed, began as early as twenty-five (Wechsler, 1972). Today, psychologists are reassessing how mental capacity changes as we age; in fact, some dimensions of intelligence may actually grow stronger in later years.

To resolve this controversy, we must clearly define the concept of *intelligence*. Certain measures of intelligence emphasize *sensorimotor coordination*, which involves, for example, the ability to arrange objects to match a drawing. These measures do show a steady decline after midlife. Similarly, tests that focus on learning new material and speed of mental performance reveal lower scores among the elderly, especially those over the age of seventy (Schaie, 1980). But tests that make use of present knowledge show little or no decline with age. Still other intelligence tests, including those measuring verbal and numerical skills, show rising ability with advancing age (Baltes & Schaie, 1974). Of course, the education and social class of the subject also affect intelligence-test results. In some cases, these factors have a greater impact on measures of intelligence than a subject's age (Botwinick, 1977; Riegel, 1977).

Psychological research has also shown that personality changes little as we grow old. People do tend to become somewhat more introverted as they age—con-

cerned with their own thoughts and feelings. But someone with a sunny disposition as a child will have an optimistic outlook on life as she approaches old age, just as a timid man will tend to remain shy throughout his life. If two people who knew each other as children met again as old people, that is, they would recognize in each other many of the same personality traits that distinguished them as youngsters (Neugarten, 1971, 1972, 1977).

Aging and Culture

Although aging involves specific biological changes, the significance of age comes from social constructs. A teen-

In Third World societies, life expectancy is significantly less than in the United States. Although not old enough to be considered "elderly" by American standards, this Indian couple displays many of the physical traits associated with advancing age. The aging process, therefore, reflects both biological and social forces.

ager may feel old in relation to a brother in elementary school, but young compared to a married sister with a career and children. To young people starting a career, forty often seems "over the hill"—until they reach that age. And a ninety-year-old may regard a newly retired person of seventy as a mere youngster.

Looking beyond our own culture, we note that the meaning of age is shaped by life expectancy in individual societies as well. Life expectancy, in turn, has a great deal to do with the society's overall standard of living and its technological ability to control disease and other threats to human life. Throughout most of human history, people's lives were relatively short by current American standards. Thomas Hobbes, the fifteenth-century British political philosopher, was referring to this when he characterized human life as "nasty, brutish, and short" in his *Leviathan*. Typically, people married and had children in their teens, those in their twenties were middle-aged, and people became old by about thirty. Few reached the age of forty until the late Middle Ages, when a rising standard of living and technological advances began to curb the infectious diseases that killed people of all ages (Mahler, 1980; Cox, 1984). As noted in Chapter 11 ("Global Inequality"), life expectancy varies significantly from one society to another. In the indus-

trialized First World, life expectancy stands at about seventy years. People in these societies are not usually regarded as old until the mid-sixties. By contrast, in the poorest societies of the Third World, people expect to live only forty years—about the same as Europeans did in the Middle Ages.

In Abkhasia, a republic of the Soviet Union, a large number of people have been reported to live to the age of a hundred and even beyond. Although such claims are probably exaggerated, Abkhasian society illustrates how social relationships—perhaps even more than technological advances—are the key to a meaningful and longlasting life. The box on pages 376–377 provides details.

Aging and Social Stratification

Like race, ethnicity, and gender, age is one basis for assigning people a social rank in every society. **Age stratification,** *the unequal distribution of wealth, power, and privileges among people of different ages,* varies from one society to another.

As explained in Chapter 4 ("Society"), hunting and gathering societies lack the technology to produce a surplus of food and are typically nomadic. Thus, they

The power and prestige of elders in preindustrial societies is based on wisdom accumulated over a lifetime. Rituals such as community storytelling provide occasions both to celebrate old people and to transmit a society's way of life to the young.

CROSS-CULTURAL COMPARISON

Growing (Very) Old in Abkhasia

Anthropologist Sula Benet was sharing wine and conversation with a man in Tamish, a small village in the Republic of Abkhasia in the southwest corner of the Soviet Union. Judging the man to be about 70, she raised her glass and offered a toast to his long life. "May you live as long as Moses," she exclaimed. The gesture of goodwill fell flat: Moses lived to 120, but Benet's companion was already 119.

An outsider—even an open-minded anthropologist—should be skeptical about the longevity claims made by the Abkhasians. In one village of twelve hundred examined by Benet, for example, almost two hundred people claimed to be at least eighty-one, and many were quite a bit older. Research has shown, however, that Abkhasia probably has about six times more people over the

age of ninety as the United States.

To her surprise, Benet discovered that some misrepresentation of age among the Abkhasians was a matter of understatement. For example, one man claimed to be 95, but his daughter (who was 81) produced a birth certificate indicating that his actual age was 108. Why the deception? In this instance, because the man was soon to be married. As another man (who, people claimed, had himself lived more than a century) explained with a wink, "A man is a man until he is 100, you know what I mean. After that, well, he is getting old."

What accounts for the Abkhasians' long life? The answer certainly is not the advanced medical technology in which Americans place so much faith; physicians are rare in Abkhasia. Nonetheless, health among all Abkhasians—including the very

Cultural patterns appear to contribute to the longevity of the Abkhasians, many of whom are reported to live well beyond what is common in the United States.

confer great value on physical strength and stamina. As people age and their strength and energy decline, so does their productivity; older members of these societies (who may actually be only thirty) are considered, therefore, an economic burden (Sheehan, 1976).

Pastoral, horticultural, and agrarian societies have the technology to produce a material surplus; consequently, individuals may accumulate considerable wealth over a lifetime. Thus, older people are generally wealthier and, therefore, more powerful. Such societies tend toward **gerontocracy,** *a form of social organization in which the elderly have the most wealth, power, and privileges.* Old people, particularly the men, are honored and sometimes feared by their families because of their wealth and power. They usually remain active members of society until they die.

Additionally, the rich folk life in preindustrial societies generates respect for the elderly, who pass down

traditional wisdom and rituals—from how to plant crops to homemaking skills to dealing with a neighboring society. These folkways play an important part in everyday life (Sheehan, 1976). Ruling "councils of elders" and the widespread practice of ancestor worship exemplify the power of old people in agrarian societies.

Industrialization—and associated advances in medical technology—gradually increase life expectancy, with the proportion of people over age sixty-five rising steadily. But industrialization also prompts a decline in the power and prestige of the elderly, as the prime source of wealth shifts from land (controlled by elder members of the society) to factories and other forms of production (owned and managed by those who are younger). Moving from rural communities to urban industrial centers also tends to divide families, forcing children to depend less on their parents and much more on their own earning power. Furthermore, cultural change accompanies advanced old—is remarkable by our standards.

Genetics may hold one possible explanation: natural selection, over many centuries of grueling warfare, may have favored those with robust physical traits. But no clear evidence supports this hypothesis. A more likely explanation is diet. Abkhasians eat little saturated fat (which is linked to heart disease) and use no sugar, but consume large amounts of fresh fruits and vegetables. They also drink no coffee or tea (but lots of buttermilk and low-alcohol wine). Few Abkhasians smoke or chew tobacco. Additionally, Abkhasians maintain an active lifestyle: regular physical work makes up much of daily life for people of all ages.

Diet and lifestyle notwithstanding, culture may actually hold the key to this remarkable longevity. A clear and consistent set of values and norms characterizes Abkhasian culture. This gives Abkhasians a strong sense of belonging; they find great significance in their lives as well. Old people are active and valued members of society—a marked contrast with our own cultural patterns. As Benet explains: "The old (in the United States), when they do not simply vegetate, out of view and out of mind, keep themselves 'busy' with bingo and shuffleboard." These words reveal the sharpest contrast between Abkhasian society and our own. The Abkhasians have no word for old people or retirement. The elderly are accorded great prestige; they are respected for their wisdom and make decisions that affect each member of their families. According to Benet:

The extraordinary attitude of the Abkhasians—to feel needed at 99 or 110—is not an artificial, self-protective one; it is a natural expression, in old age, of a consistent outlook that begins in childhood. . . .

Abkhasians expect a long and useful life and look forward to old age with good reason: in a culture which so highly values continuity in its traditions, the old are indispensable in their transmission. The elders preside at important ceremonial occasions, they mediate disputes and their knowledge of farming is sought. They feel needed because, in their own minds and everyone else's, they are. They are the opposite of burdens: they are highly valued resources.

SOURCE: Based on Sula Benet, "Why They Live to Be 100, or Even Older, in Abkhasia," *The New York Times Magazine*, December 26, 1971, pp. 3, 28–29, 31–34.

technology. The life experience of one generation may no longer apply to changing social and economic conditions. Skills and attitudes that served one generation soon become outdated, so that through the modernization process (described in Chapter 11, "Global Inequality"), *wise elders* may be redefined as the *worthless elderly*. Then, too, tradition holds less sway in industrial societies, so the elderly do not gain as much respect for perpetuating traditional values and rituals (Atchley, 1982).

In industrial societies such as the United States and Canada, economic and political leaders are usually middle-aged people with specialized training. By contrast, in the most rapidly changing areas of the economy, such as the high-tech fields, key executives are frequently just out of college. Lacking the skills currently demanded in the fast-changing marketplace, older workers may be looked on as outdated and encouraged to take an early retirement. As a result, older people predominate in traditional occupations (such as barbers, tailors, and seamstresses) and jobs that typically involve little activity (night security guards, for instance) (Kaufman & Spilerman, 1982). The tremendous productivity of industrial societies also means that the labor of everyone is not needed, so that the elderly and the very young are often assigned nonproductive roles (Cohn, 1982).

A "generation gap" common to industrial societies also reflects changes in family life. In preindustrial societies, *extended families*, in which more than two generations live together, keep the elderly involved in the lives of younger people. Industrialization, as Chapter 15 ("Family") explains, promotes *nuclear families*, usually composed of only parents and their dependent children. Older people now live with their adult children in only about 20 percent of American households, although this pattern appears to be gaining acceptance among Americans once again (N.O.R.C., 1989:224). When older

Japan is distinctive among industrial societies in that the elderly are accorded high prestige and respect by younger family members. Rapid social change and rising living costs, however, may be undermining the traditional patterns by which Japanese adults support their aging parents.

parents do live with their adult children, however, the adult children, rather than their parents, are usually the heads of the household, reversing the pattern common at the beginning of this century (Dahlin, 1980).

In a few industrial societies—especially Japan—cultural values rooted in the agrarian past still confer high (although declining) social standing on old people (Harlan, 1968; Treas, 1979; Yates, 1986). Japan's Shinto religion, for example, encourages veneration of the elderly. Most of the aged in Japan live with an adult son or daughter and continue to play a significant part in family life (Palmore, 1982). Elderly Japanese are also more likely than elderly Americans to remain in the labor force; in Japanese corporations, the oldest employees usually receive the greatest respect. Increasingly in Japan and in other industrial societies, however, growing old results in at least some loss in social standing (Cowgill & Holmes, 1972).

TRANSITION AND PROBLEMS OF AGING

Chapter 5 ("Socialization") explained that each stage of the human life cycle brings change. People unlearn self-concepts and social patterns that no longer apply to their lives and simultaneously learn to cope with new circumstances. Old age, however, presents the greatest personal challenges.

Although less serious than most people think, physical decline plays an important part in old age and causes considerable emotional stress. Pain, limits on activity, dependence on others, and reminders of our mortality (like the death of a friend or close relative) may spark frustration, fear, and self-doubt. And because American culture places great value on youth, physical vitality, and good looks, diminution of physical capabilities and signs of aging in physical appearance threaten the self-esteem of older people.

Psychologist Erik Erikson (1963, 1980) suggests that the elderly experience the tension of "integrity versus despair." No matter how much they may still be learning and achieving, older people must recognize that their lives are nearing an end. Elderly people spend much time reflecting on their past accomplishments and disappointments. Maintaining high self-esteem in the face of physical and social decline, and accepting past mistakes as well as successes can make old age a time of personal integrity, according to Erikson. Otherwise, it may turn into a time of despair—a dead end without positive meaning.

Research suggests that people who find satisfaction and meaning in earlier stages of life are also likely to achieve personal well-being in old age. In a seven-year study of people in their seventies, Bernice Neugarten

(1971) identified four different personality types and their differing adjustments to old age.

People with *disintegrated and disorganized personalities*—the smallest number of subjects in Neugarten's research—found it nearly impossible to adjust to old age. Severe psychological problems, sometimes over many years, made ongoing help from others necessary. Many people with such problems depended on support from sympathetic families or lived in hospitals or nursing homes. Despair characterized their response to old age.

People with *passive-dependent personalities* sought help with the tasks of daily life, whether or not they actually needed it. Leading lives of minimal activity—in some cases, lives bordering on withdrawal—their level of satisfaction was likewise relatively low.

People with *defended personalities* lived independently but feared advancing age. They shielded themselves from the reality of old age by fighting to stay healthy, physically fit, and youthful. While concerns about health are certainly reasonable, failing to accept the reality of aging added stress and unhappiness to their lives.

Most of Neugarten's subjects, however, had what she called *integrated personalities*, leading to successful aging. These people displayed a high level of dignity and self-confidence as they accepted the inevitability of aging; growing old did not dampen their basic optimism.

Americans tend to think that the elderly are un-happy: one national survey found that only about 1 percent of Americans under age sixty-five thought that the best years of their lives awaited them in old age (Harris, 1976). Certainly some elderly people share this dim view, but most have a more positive outlook. Neugarten's research suggests that, whatever the personal adjustments required, the aging process bears little resemblance to our familiar negative stereotypes about growing old. Rather, the experience of growing old in America varies according to individual personality, family circumstances, social class, and financial position. Research shows that people who have adapted successfully to changes earlier in life usually find satisfaction and meaning in their lives later on (Palmore, 1979a).

Social Isolation

Being alone provokes anxiety among people of every age. Although most older people continue to live productive and satisfying lives, many Americans are forced to adjust to increasing social isolation. Retirement closes off one source of social interaction, physical problems may limit the ability to leave home, and many Americans still prefer not to share a home with elderly parents. Negative stereotypes, picturing the elderly as senile and "over the hill," also discourage young people from maintaining social contact with old people.

Elderly women typically outlive their husbands. Having endured the stress of losing a spouse, widows often contend with social isolation. Ideally, however, such women discover opportunities to forge social ties as they develop new interests.

Table 14–1 LIVING ARRANGEMENTS OF THE ELDERLY, 1985

	Males	Females
Living alone	14.4%	39.6%
Living with spouse	74.0	36.9
Living with other relatives	7.4	17.8
Living with nonrelatives	2.9	2.0
Living in nursing home	1.3	3.7

SOURCE: Calculations by the author, based on data from the U.S. Bureau of the Census.

Yet most social isolation among the elderly stems from the death of significant others. Few human experiences affect people as profoundly as the death of a spouse. Widows and widowers must adjust to the loss of people with whom, in many instances, they spent most of their adult lives and shared a wealth of experiences. Some surviving spouses choose not to live at all. One study of elderly men noted a sharp increase in the incidence of death, sometimes by suicide, in the months following the death of their wives (Benjamin & Wallis, 1963).

But in most cases, women outlive their husbands. Table 14–1 shows that in 1985 three-fourths of elderly men lived with spouses, while only half of elderly women did. Put otherwise, almost 40 percent of older women lived alone, compared to about 14 percent of older men. This isolation among elderly women accounts, in part, for a research finding that, in general, the mental health of elderly women is not as strong as that of elderly men in North America (Chappell & Havens, 1980).

Living alone does not mean that the elderly lack social support from their families. Ethel Shanas (1979) found that more than half of the older people in her research lived less than ten minutes travel time from at least one adult child, and over three-fourths said they had visited with at least one of their children during the preceding week. Only 10 percent reported that they had not visited with an adult child within the past month. Women (especially daughters and daughters-in-law) are more likely than men to care for aging people (Stone, Cafferata, & Sangl, 1987). Overall, then, social activity diminishes in old age, but families lessen social isolation.

Retirement

Work determines much of our personal identity. Retirement from paid work, therefore, may entail not only loss of income and social prestige but loss of identity as well (Chown, 1977). In extreme cases, retirement can render life purposeless. Margaret Clark, for example, interviewed one retired man who talked about his life in the past tense: "I was a waiter *in my life*" (1972:134).

Some organizations strive to ease this transition. Colleges and universities, for example, confer the title of "professor emeritus" (from Latin, meaning "fully earned") on retired faculty members, giving them library, parking, and mail privileges. These honored retirees may attend faculty meetings, and sometimes a college makes office space available so they may pursue research.

For some older people, new activities and new interests minimize the personal disruption and loss of prestige brought on by retirement (Rose, 1968). Many older people find great rewards in volunteer work. The American Association of Retired Persons (AARP), with more than 15 million members over the age of fifty and more than three thousand local chapters across the United States, lists volunteer opportunities for these "experienced Americans."

A relatively modern concept, retirement became common in industrial societies only during the last century (Atchley, 1982). In contrast, most people in preindustrial societies work until they are incapacitated. Advancing technology reduces the need for labor, however, and places a premium on up-to-date skills. Retirement permits younger workers, presumably with the most current knowledge and training, to predominate in the labor force.

Sixty-five is widely viewed as the proper age for retirement in the United States. This retirement age is somewhat arbitrary: Japan, for example, links retirement to age fifty-five, although most Japanese work beyond that age (Kii, 1979; Palmore, 1982). Before the Social Security system was established in the 1930s, few Americans could afford to retire, whatever their age. As Social Security and other pension programs bolstered the financial security of older Americans, they also promoted the idea that people *should* retire, taking life easy in the later years. But should a society formally designate a specific age as the point of retirement? Given the vast differences in the interests and capacities of older people, this notion is controversial. After 1970, Congress phased out mandatory retirement policies that had been established years before, virtually ending the practice of forced retirement by 1987. Nevertheless, most American workers retire at about age sixty-five.

In the United States, the transition from work to retirement has traditionally faced men more than women. As noted in Chapter 13 ("Sex and Gender"), only in the last decade has the work force attracted a majority of women. Elderly women, who have spent their lives as homemakers, do not experience retirement per se, although the departure of the last child from home serves as a rough parallel. Even lifelong homemakers, however, must adjust to their husbands' retirement and presence at home; this has been called the "husband underfoot syndrome" (Mitchell, 1972). But in adjusting to their husbands' retirement, women may also find new joys, joining their husbands in activities they previously had little time for (Keating & Cole, 1980). As the proportion of women in the labor force continues to rise, both sexes will confront the changes brought on by retirement.

Aging and Poverty

For most Americans, retirement leads to a significant decline in income. For many, however, home mortgages and children's college expenses are paid; yet many older people also face rising expenses for medical care, household help, and home utilities. Only a small proportion of elderly Americans have significant savings or pension plans; most depend on Social Security (C.E.D., 1981). Poverty rates rise somewhat, therefore, among people over age sixty-five. Figure 14–2 graphically shows the proportion of Americans living in poverty in 1987 by age. As noted in Chapter 10 ("Social Class in America"), children are the most likely to be poor, with the incidence of poverty declining until about age fifty-five.

Official poverty rates among elderly people have fallen from about 35 percent in 1960 to 12.2 percent in 1987 (U.S. Bureau of the Census, 1970, 1989). Since 1982, in fact, poverty has been lower among elderly Americans than among the non-elderly (Stone, 1986). The decline stems from improved pension programs won by many workers and increases in Social Security benefits.

As in every other age category, elderly members of racial and ethnic minorities face the most economic disadvantages. For example, in 1987, the poverty rate among elderly Hispanics (27.4 percent) was almost three times the rate for elderly whites (10.1 percent); elderly blacks (with a poverty rate of 33.9 percent) were even more likely to be poor.

The significant difference in income between American men and women continues into old age. In 1987, the median income for men sixty-five and over working full time was $29,715, while the comparable

Figure 14–2   Poverty and the Life Course, 1987

(U.S. Bureau of the Census)

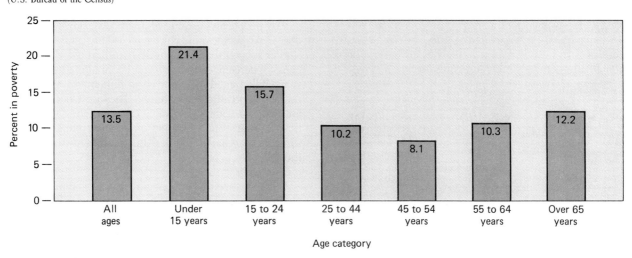

Although in the past the old grew poor, today the poor grow old. The elderly poor are typically people who have been poor throughout their lives, namely women and minorities.

figure for women was $19,178. This means that elderly women who work full time earn only about 64.5 percent as much as their male counterparts, a slightly greater disparity than that for male and female workers in general (with women across all ages earning 65.5 percent of what men earn). Table 14–2 shows the median income for *all* elderly men and women, nonworking as well as working, based on wages and salaries, Social Security, pensions, and investment income. Because nonworking people are included, income figures are lower: $11,854

for men and $6,738 for women. Comparing these figures, we note that the income of elderly women is only about 57 percent that of elderly men. The economic disadvantages of women, then, grow somewhat larger in old age. Aging is thus one dimension of the feminization of poverty discussed in Chapter 10, "Social Class in America" (Stone, 1986).

As all Americans grow old, their chances of being poor increase, especially minorities such as Hispanics, blacks, and women. Among all categories of old people, however, poverty may lurk in the shadows, effectively hidden from view. Because of personal pride and a desire to maintain the dignity of independent living—values taught to Americans from childhood—elderly people may keep financial problems a secret, even from their own families. It is often difficult for people who have supported their children for years to admit that they can no longer provide for themselves, even though it may be through no fault of their own. In addition, elderly people confined to their homes by physical disabilities or fear of street violence often suffer economic disadvantages very privately.

Abuse of the Elderly

In America, we have recognized violence and other forms of personal abuse in stages: child abuse in the 1960s, spouse abuse in the 1970s, and abuse of the elderly in the 1980s. Abuse of older people takes many forms, including passive neglect, verbal and emotional abuse, financial exploitation, and even physical assault. Most elderly people are not abused in any way; however, aging does make people more vulnerable to abuse. Government studies suggest that as many as 1 million elderly Americans (3 percent of the total) suffer maltreatment each year (Pillemer, 1988). But it is difficult to determine how widespread elderly abuse is because elderly people are understandably reluctant to talk about their victimization. Perhaps one older person in ten suffers abuse at some time (Clark, 1986). The trend is disturbing: as the proportion of elderly Americans rises, so does the incidence of abuse (Bruno, 1985:75).

Why are elderly people the targets of abuse? Much elderly abuse springs from the stress of caring—financially and emotionally—for aging parents, especially since adult children of both sexes are now typically in the labor force. Caring for one or two aging parents can mean a tremendous commitment of time and energy or the financial burden of $25,000 or more a year for

Table 14–2	EARNINGS AND TOTAL INCOME OF ELDERLY MEN AND WOMEN, 1987	
	Median Annual Income from Full-time Work (workers only)	Median Total Income for All Elderly (working and nonworking)
Males, 65 and over	$29,715	$11,854
Female, 65 and over	$19,178	$ 6,738

SOURCE: U.S. Bureau of the Census.

nursing-home care. Little wonder that even in Japan—where tradition dictates caring for aging parents at home—more and more adult children are unable to cope with the problem (Yates, 1986). Abuse appears to be most common in families with a very old parent suffering from serious health problems. The adult children are faced with long-term demands that they cannot easily meet, despite their good intentions (Douglass, 1983; Gelman, 1985).

In sum, growing old involves serious problems and transitions, but not all are brought on by physical decline. Social isolation, adjustment to retirement, limited economic resources, and abuse from family members—these are largely social problems. The next section suggests how society shapes the lives of the elderly.

THEORETICAL ANALYSIS OF AGING

Various theories—developed from the major theoretical paradigms in sociology—help to explain the process of aging in American society. We now examine several in turn.

Disengagement Theory

Disengagement theory, *an analysis linking the disengagement by elderly people from positions of social responsibility to the orderly operation of society*, represents an early attempt to explain how and why society defined the elderly differently from younger people. Applying the ideas of Talcott Parsons—an influential architect of the structural-functional paradigm—Elaine Cumming and William Henry (1961) based disengagement theory on the biological reality of human decline and eventual death. Society, they reasoned, must address the inevitable death of each of its members. Through the orderly and gradual transfer of various statuses and roles from the old to the young, social roles are performed in a more stable and dependable way. A society would experience considerable social disruption if only incompetence or death brought about a changing of the guard. Thus industrial societies arrange for status and role transfer while older people are still productive. Disengagement of the elderly also reflects the rapid change in industrial societies. Continuous replacement of older workers by younger workers keeps skills and training as up-to-date as possible.

Disengagement theory suggests that this process

benefits elderly people as well. Aging people with diminishing capacities presumably look forward to relinquishing some of the pressures of their jobs. Social norms that favor retirement at a specific age encourage older people to devote their continuing vitality to new pursuits of their own choosing (Palmore, 1979b). Society also grants the elderly greater freedom of behavior: among the elderly, unusual behavior is often construed as harmless eccentricity rather than socially dangerous deviance. Of course, the ability to disengage from paid work depends on having the necessary financial resources to forgo earned income. Most elderly Americans have had this luxury only in recent decades, and some still do not.

Critical evaluation. Disengagement theory offers one explanation for American society's tendency to define elderly people as socially marginal. According to this analysis, every society must transfer responsibilities from older to younger people.

Yet this approach tends to ignore one key fact: many elderly people do not wish to disengage. Disengagement, after all, has high costs, including loss of social prestige, social isolation, and reduced income. In addition, society loses the benefits of experience and skills gained over a lifetime. Finally, no cultural norms encouraging disengagement take into account how widely the elderly differ in terms of their abilities to continue contributing productively to society.

Activity Theory

Activity theory is *an analysis linking personal satisfaction in old age to a high level of activity*. A critical response to disengagement theory, activity theory draws heavily on the social-interaction paradigm (Friedman & Havighurst, 1954). According to this analysis, individuals build their social identity from statuses and roles. Consequently, disengagement in old age may detract from the satisfaction and meaning many elderly people find in their lives.

Cultural norms may encourage old people to disengage from society, but activity theory suggests that the elderly usually remain socially active by substituting new activities for the ones they are forced to forgo. In a society that values productive activity, the elderly are likely to find disengagement just as unsatisfying as a younger adult would. All older people obviously do not approach disengagement the same way. Activity theory suggests, therefore, that old people do not form a monolithic group, but rather have distinctive needs, interests, and physical abilities that influence their feelings about and responses to aging.

Research supports this approach (Havighurst, Neugarten, & Tobin, 1968; Neugarten, 1977; Palmore, 1979a). Old people who maintain high activity levels are the most satisfied with their lives. But this research also stresses individual differences. People seek different levels of social activity in old age; for a few older people, inactivity brings the greatest happiness.

Critical evaluation. Because it focuses attention on the elderly themselves rather than on the needs of society, activity theory provides an important counterpoint to disengagement theory. Activity theory also calls attention to the diversity among elderly people, an important consideration in formulating any social policy. Further, activity theory's assertion that the elderly generally find greater personal satisfaction in leading active lives appears to be well supported.

However, this approach ignores the risks that active elderly people pose for others as physicians, accountants, bus drivers, or in other positions of responsibility. Activity theory also fails to take into account that poor health and poverty prevent many older people from maintaining high levels of activity.

Social-Conflict Analysis

In the social-conflict approach, different age categories compete for scarce social resources. Various stages in the life course, therefore, take the form of age stratification. From this point of view, middle-aged Americans enjoy the greatest social privileges, while the elderly face relative disadvantages (Phillipson, 1982). Senior citizens, therefore, often become second-class citizens.

The social-conflict approach, derived from the ideas of Karl Marx, links the lower social standing of the elderly to the operation of industrial-capitalism. As noted in Chapter 8 ("Deviance"), Steven Spitzer (1980) argued that because a capitalist society is based on the pursuit of profit, the society devalues categories of people who are economically unproductive. Spitzer characterizes those who actively challenge the capitalist system (such as unemployed minorities or political radicals) as the most deviant and, therefore, the most likely to be subject to police controls. Those who do not threaten

the system but are also unproductive—including the elderly—are mostly ignored. In short, capitalist societies tend to define human value by what people *do* (as producers), rather than what they *are* (as human beings). Old people are devalued as nonproducers insofar as they disengage from work in a society preoccupied with material gain (Spitzer, 1980; Phillipson, 1982).

Social-conflict theorists argue that employers favor young, lower-paid workers over elderly workers who are less productive but more highly paid because of their seniority. According to this line of reasoning, employers have historically sought to replace older workers with younger, more cost-effective workers (Atchley, 1982).

Social-conflict analysis also spotlights social stratification in the elderly population. Social class, race, ethnicity, and gender divide the elderly as they do the entire population. Older people in the higher social classes have more economic security, access to better medical care, and greater options for personally satisfying activities in later life than those with fewer privileges. Likewise, elderly WASPs typically enjoy privileges denied to older people who belong to racial and ethnic minorities. And women—who become an increasing majority of the elderly population with advancing age—still suffer social and economic disadvantages stemming from sexism.

Critical evaluation. Social-conflict theory contributes to our analysis by focusing on age stratification and how capitalism devalues those who are less economically productive. This theoretical approach also emphasizes that some categories of the elderly are especially likely to be socially disadvantaged.

Yet the social standing of the elderly has greatly improved in recent decades, despite the "nonproductivity" of most old people. The theory's implication that the aged fare better in noncapitalist societies has some support (Treas, 1979). But industrialization itself is mostly responsible for the relatively low social standing of elderly people.

AGEISM

In earlier chapters, we examined how ideology seeks to justify social inequality against minorities. Sociologists use the term **ageism** to refer to *prejudice and discrimination against the elderly*. In industrial societies, cultural patterns favoring younger and middle-aged people, at the expense of older people, institutionalize ageism.

Like racism and sexism, ageism fosters negative stereotypes based on visible physical characteristics such as graying hair, wrinkled skin, and stooped posture. Ageism works in subtle ways. Defined as less capable, the elderly are expected to be deferential, allowing others to make decisions that affect their lives. Ageism uses alleged biological decline among elderly people to justify denying them full human rights and social dignity. From such tenuous assumptions, younger people may conclude that old people are incapable of handling full independence. People then feel justified in taking a condescending attitude toward the elderly, often talking down to them as if they were children (Kalish, 1979).

Familiar negative stereotypes picture the aged as helpless, confused, resistant to change, and generally unhappy (Butler, 1975). Subtle expressions of ageism include remarks intended as compliments including "My, but you certainly don't look your age!" Such comments imply that standards of youthful beauty should apply to everyone. Even supposedly positive stereotypes of the elderly sometimes deny old people the full range of their humanity. Sentimental views of sweet little old ladies and charmingly eccentric old gentlemen ignore the fact that old people are complex individuals with distinct personalities and long years of experience and accomplishment.

Like other forms of prejudice, ageism may have some foundation in reality. Some old people (like some young people) are mentally impaired, overly dependent, dirty, or senile. But ageism makes unwarranted generalizations about an entire category of people, most of whom do not conform to the stereotypes. As we noted earlier in this chapter, most elderly people do not suffer from severe physical or mental disabilities, and most have the same needs, feelings, and diversity of views as people who are younger. Elderly people in good health are also quite capable of maintaining satisfying sexual relationships, despite prejudices suggesting that anyone with gray hair and wrinkles utterly lacks sex appeal. Nevertheless, because such attitudes are widespread they have a real impact, denying millions of people full participation in American society.

As in the case of sexism, examined in Chapter 13 ("Sex and Gender"), the mass media perpetuate negative stereotypes. Media-watchers have long criticized the mass media for excluding the aged—and especially elderly women. Studies indicate that while negative stereo-

Television programming now reflects the fact that viewers—the targets of TV ads—are becoming older. Angela Lansbury's leading role on *Murder She Wrote* is only one example of shows that feature older men and women.

typing of the elderly is not as extensive as that of women, television and the print media have contributed to ageism in American society (Kubey, 1980; Buchholz & Bynum, 1982). In the last few years, television has been portraying more elderly people—some in a positive light—a change indicating that the networks recognize that older Americans make up a rapidly growing segment of the audience. Estimates hold that people aged fifty and over now buy more than 40 percent of all consumer goods, a fact well known to television advertisers (Hoyt, 1985).

Perhaps, as some research suggests, negative stereotypes about the elderly are disappearing. One reason for this trend may be that Americans are not as preoccupied with work as they were in the past, and so they are less likely to devalue elderly people as nonproductive. Older Americans have also gained political clout through organizations like the American Association of Retired Persons and the Gray Panthers. But older Americans themselves, whose ranks have been swelling, are dispelling the negative stereotypes. Remaining active, and with a positive view of their lives, the self-confidence of these older people acts as a powerful force to undermine negative social images (Tibbitts, 1979).

The Elderly: A Minority?

The evidence argues strongly that, as a category of Americans, the elderly do face social disadvantages. But sociologists differ as to whether the aged form a minority in the same way as, say, blacks, Hispanics, or women. By briefly outlining this debate, we will point up the similarities and the differences between the elderly and other categories of people that are widely known as minorities.

Three decades ago, Leonard Breen (1960) labeled the elderly as a minority. In his view, older people have a clear social identity based on the ascribed status of being old, and are typically subject to prejudice and discrimination. In addition, as we have already noted, the elderly are often socially isolated, denied equal opportunity for jobs, and are more likely than middle-aged Americans to be poor (Eitzen, 1980; Levin & Levin, 1980; Barrow & Smith, 1983).

Other sociologists, however, are not convinced that the elderly qualify as a minority. Gordon Streib (1968) points out that minority standing is usually both permanent and exclusive. That is, a person is black, Hispanic, or female for life, and this precludes being part of the dominant category of white males. Being elderly, by contrast, is an *open status* because people are elderly for only part of their lives and everyone who has the good fortune to live long enough grows old.

The elderly, then, are a diverse category of people including men and women, all races and ethnicities, and members of every social class. In other words, they are unlikely to define themselves collectively as old people. On the contrary, although aware of their age, the elderly commonly think of themselves in other social categories. Women, too, belong to various races, ethnicities, and social classes, which is one reason many women do not consider themselves a minority.

The social disadvantages faced by the elderly, Streib claims, are less substantial than those experienced by the categories of people described as minorities in earlier chapters. For example, old people have never been deprived of the right to own property, to vote, or to hold office, as blacks and women have. In fact, older men—and to a lesser extent, older women—exercise considerable political influence in American society. Some elderly people, Streib adds, do suffer from economic disadvantages, but this does not stem primarily from old age. Instead, most of the aged poor fall into categories of Americans more likely to be poor at any age. Streib concludes that "the poor grow old," *not* that "the old grow poor."

Because old age is a diverse and open category, and because the elderly are now less likely to be poor than Americans as a whole, old people do not form a minority in the same sense as other categories of Americans. Nor do they have sufficient common interests to be called a subculture, as some have suggested (Rose, 1968). Perhaps therefore, the elderly should simply be considered a *distinctive segment* of the American population.

DEATH AND DYING

To every thing there is a season,
And a time for every matter under heaven:
A time to be born and a time to die . . .

These well-known lines from the Book of Ecclesiastes in the Bible convey two basic truths about human existence: the fact of birth and the inevitability of death. Yet, just as life itself varies in striking ways across human history, so does death. We conclude this chapter with a brief look at the changing character of death—the final stage in the process of growing old.

Historical Patterns of Death

Throughout most of human history, death was a fact of everyday life. In technologically simple hunting and gathering societies, being born carried little assurance that one would stay alive for very long. Uncertainty about the survival of newborns was so great, in fact, that infants were often not named until they reached several years of age (Herty, 1960). Those who survived infancy had a very low standard of living by contemporary measures, so that illness brought on by poor nutrition, accidents, and natural catastrophes such as drought or famine combined to make life uncertain, at best.

As agricultural technology developed, societies grew in size and established permanent settlements. Yet other factors kept death within the common experience of everyone. Herds of animals in close proximity to settlements spread dangerous infectious diseases. Towns and cities devised few effective means to dispose of human waste, resulting in poor sanitation. Until about the seven-

The centrality or death to Medieval society is evident in much of the art of that period. *The Triumph of Death*, by sixteenth-century Flemish painter Pieter Brueghel, makes the point with chilling realism.

teenth century, plagues and other highly contagious diseases sometimes wiped out a city's entire population. But population growth also posed serious problems because of the low productivity of preindustrial societies. Often, this called for a drastic response. Sometimes, the least productive people were killed in the interests of the group. Most commonly, this took the form of *infanticide*—the killing of newborn infants—and *geronticide*—killing of the elderly (Newman & Matzke, 1984).

In sum, death was so much a part of the social experience of everyone that it was regarded as natural and inevitable. Religion offered the consolation that death fit into the divine plan for human existence. To illustrate, historian Philippe Ariès describes how Sir Lancelot, one of King Arthur's fearless Knights of the Round Table, prepared for his own death when he believed himself mortally wounded:

> His gestures were fixed by old customs, ritual gestures which must be carried out when one is about to die. He removed his weapons and lay quietly upon the ground. . . . He spread his arms out, his body forming a cross . . . in such a way that his head faced east toward Jerusalem. (1974:7–8)

As societies gradually gained control over many causes of death, attitudes began to change. Death was no longer an everyday experience: children rarely died at birth, and accidents and disease killed far fewer adults. Except in times of war or other catastrophes, people came to view dying as quite *extra*ordinary, except among the very old. In 1900, about one-third of all deaths in the United States occurred before the age of five, another third occurred before the age of fifty-five, so that only one-third of Americans died in what was then defined as old age. By the late 1980s, almost 85 percent of Americans died *after* the age of fifty-five (U.S. National Center for Health Statistics, 1988).

The Modern Separation of Life and Death

Less a part of everyday experience, death is now looked on as something unnatural. Religious beliefs that place both life and death in a divine scheme have been eroded by strong faith in the ability of medical technology to overcome disease and even the physical deterioration of old age. If social conditions prepared our ancestors to accept their own deaths, modern society has fostered a desire for immortality, or eternal youth. In this sense, death has become separated from life.

This denial of death, coupled with the rapid increase in the elderly population of the United States, has forced American society to confront difficult ethical questions. Should life be extended as long as technologically possible? Should American society commit an increasing share of medical resources to the task of prolonging life? In a recent book, Daniel Callahan makes the controversial assertion that society may have to devise limits on longevity, as the box explains.

Death and dying are now physically removed from the rest of life. The clearest evidence of this is that many Americans have never seen a person die. While our ancestors typically died at home, death today often occurs in unfamiliar and impersonal settings such as hospitals and nursing homes (Ariès, 1974). Even in hospitals, the process of dying is segregated from the process of healing. Dying patients are commonly kept in a special part of the hospital, and hospital morgues are located out of sight of patients and visitors (Sudnow, 1967).

While our ancestors accepted death as part of life, we now approach the prospect of dying with fear and anxiety. No doubt, this fearful attitude has propelled the rapid increase in medical research aimed at prolonging the life of the elderly. However, the fear of death may be greater among the young than among the old. For elderly people who suffer from severe and painful diseases or disabilities, death may not be feared, but welcomed as an end to suffering. In fact, in more and more cases, patients and their families are now taking the initiative, choosing not to make use of all the new medical technology available to prolong life. After long and painful deliberation, many patients and their families, together with their doctors, reach an agonizing decision: hospital staff members should use no "heroic measures" to resuscitate the patient in case a medical crisis occurs. Such "Do Not Resuscitate" (DNR) orders on a patient's chart are often cleared through special hospital ethics committees, made up of medical professionals, social service professionals, and members of the clergy.

Many elderly people accept death as a natural closure to the life span, a view that comes from a more

CRITICAL THINKING

Setting Limits: How Much Old Age Can America Afford?

For most of human history, the question "Can people live *too long*?" would have been absurd. In recent decades, however, a surge in the elderly population, widespread support for using medical technology to prolong life, and a dizzying increase in funding for medical research and treatment directed toward diseases of old age have prompted Americans to consider this question—and others never before imaginable.

The graying of America, Daniel Callahan suggests, will eventually force Americans to look critically at what proportion of our limited resources should be allocated to the needs of older people. To even raise this issue, he concedes, smacks of a lack of caring. But ignoring it poses

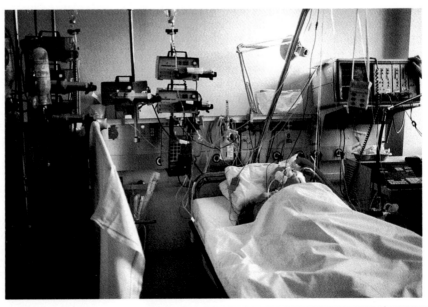

realistic approach by professionals, and also from outliving family members and friends (Kalish, 1976, cited in Atchley, 1983). Younger Americans, however, avoid even the mention of death. As a result, dying people are isolated from friends and relatives who are unable to face up to the reality of the impending death. This isolation is reinforced by the American practice of dying away from home, where hospital personnel—who may also avoid death through euphemisms such as "medical failure"—minister to the dying in place of family members and friends.

Bereavement

In Chapter 5 ("Socialization"), we described the stages by which people usually confront their own death. Elizabeth Kübler-Ross (1969) claims that people initially react with denial, followed by anger, efforts to negotiate divine intervention, gradual resignation, and final acceptance. But it is not only the dying person who must adjust to the approaching death but also those who will experience bereavement, or a sense of loss following the death.

The bereavement process parallels the stages of dying described by Kübler-Ross. Those close to a dying person, for instance, may initially deny the reality of impending death, reaching the point of acceptance only with time. This parallel has a tremendous impact because how others view death influences the attitudes of the dying person. That is, if family and friends accept the reality of approaching death, it helps the dying person do the same; conversely, a dying person may have difficulty accepting death if surrounded by loved ones who deny the reality of the situation. In some cases, too, dying people who have accepted their own death cannot share their feelings and experiences with others who deny that death is imminent.

One recent development intended to provide support to dying people is the *hospice*. While a hospital is designed to cure disease, a hospice admits only people close to death. Care centers on minimizing pain and suffering, while providing the dying person with dignity and comfort. Hospices also encourage family members to remain close to the dying person to prevent the social isolation that commonly accompanies terminal illness.

a serious threat to the well-being of the majority of Americans.

The $80 billion spent on health care for the elderly in 1981 will soar to over $200 billion by the year 2000. This dramatic boost reflects current public policies that direct a growing *proportion* of medical resources—both in research and treatment—toward disease and disability common to old age. Callahan asks, first, can we continue to increase spending on behalf of the elderly when doing so means spending less on others, especially children? At some point, American society will have to set limits. Although difficult to devise, we are fast approaching the day when such a policy will become a fiscal imperative.

Second, Callahan urges Americans to recognize that when medical technology produces *longer* life, it does not necessarily make for *better* life. Costs aside, does expensive and stressful heart surgery that may prolong the life of an 84-year-old woman for two years truly improve the quality of her life? Costs considered, would those resources yield more "quality of life" if used, say, to transplant a kidney into a 10-year-old boy?

Third, Callahan urges all of us to reconsider our conception of death. Today death is viewed as an unnatural enemy to be conquered at all costs. Yet, he suggests, to formulate any sensible health-care program in an aging society we must recognize death as a natural end to the life span. If

we cannot make peace with death for our own benefit, limited resources demand that we do so for the benefit of others.

In short, Callahan concludes, the aging of America will provoke critical thinking about death, life, and old age, leading to:

an understanding of the process of aging and death that looks to our obligations to the young and to the future, that sees old age as a source of knowledge and insight of value to other age groups, that recognizes the necessity of limits and the acceptance of decline and death, and that values the old for their age and not their continuing youthful vitality. (1987:223)

SOURCE: Daniel Callahan, *Setting Limits: Medical Goals in an Aging Society* (New York: Simon & Schuster, 1987).

Many hospice patients die in the hospice; others choose to return home before death. In either case, the hospice staff attempts to make the process of dying as comfortable as possible for the dying person and family members (Stoddard, 1978).

Bereavement is less intense among people who understand and accept the death of a loved one. And survivors who feel their relationship with the dying person reached a resolution experience a less painful grief. By not denying the inevitability of death and taking whatever opportunity is available to bring an appropriate closure to their relationship, family and friends are also better able to comfort and support one another after the death has occurred (Atchley, 1983).

Even under the most favorable circumstances, the experience of bereavement and loss may persist for some time. Besides profound grief, survivors typically experi-ence social disorientation if the dead person served as a significant point of reference in their lives. As we suggested earlier, among the elderly—especially elderly women—the loss of a spouse is perhaps the most common and difficult bereavement.

This chapter has described a number of conse-quences of the "graying of America." As the ranks of the elderly increase, they will become a more visible and vocal part of everyday life. Gerontology, the study of the elderly, will also gain in stature and medical care directed toward old people will continue to expand. As part of this transformation, we can also expect changes in the way we look at death. The growing presence of the American elderly will almost certainly shift our per-ception of death from a social taboo to a natural part of the life course. Both young and old alike may benefit.

SUMMARY

1. From 4 percent in 1900, the elderly now represent over 12 percent of Americans; by 2050, 25 percent of Americans will be over age sixty-five.

2. Gerontology is the study of aging and the elderly. It focuses on biological and psychological changes, and how aging is defined in a culture.

3. Growing old is accompanied by a rising incidence of disease and disability. The extent of disability among the elderly, however, is commonly exagger-ated by younger people.

4. Growing old does not result in overall loss of intelli-gence. Psychological research suggests that individ-ual personality changes little with advancing age.

5. The age at which people are defined as old has varied historically. Until several centuries ago, old age began as early as thirty. In poorer societies today, life expectancy is substantially lower than in North America.

6. Industrialization is generally linked to a decline in the social standing of elderly people.

7. As people age, they commonly experience social isolation brought on by retirement, physical disabil-ity, and the death of friends and sometimes a spouse. For most elderly people, family members provide considerable social support.

8. Retirement generally forces people to make various social adjustments. Although traditionally a prob-lem faced only by men, the increasing participation of women in the labor force makes retirement a concern of both sexes.

9. Since 1960, poverty among the elderly has dropped significantly. Elderly women and elderly minorities are especially likely to be poor.

10. Disengagement theory suggests that the elderly disengage from positions of social responsibility be-fore the onset of disability or death. In this way, statuses and roles are transferred from the old to the young in an orderly way.

11. Activity theory claims that people who maintain a high level of social activity experience greater personal satisfaction in old age.

12. According to social-conflict analysis, patterns of age stratification benefit middle-aged people. The emphasis on economic productivity in capitalist societies leads to a devaluing of those who are less productive, including the elderly.

13. Ageism—prejudice and discrimination against old people—serves to justify age stratification.

14. Some consider the old a minority; however, the elderly encompass people of both sexes and all races, ethnicities, and social classes.

15. Death is no longer part of everyday life, prompting widespread personal discomfort with the subject of death. Today the large majority of Americans who die are elderly. In our attempt to isolate death from life, we have segregated dying people.

KEY CONCEPTS

activity theory an analysis of aging linking personal satisfaction in old age to high levels of activity

ageism prejudice and discrimination against the elderly

age stratification the unequal distribution of wealth, power, and privileges among people of different ages

disengagement theory an analysis of aging linking the disengagement by elderly people from positions of social responsibility to the orderly operation of society

gerontocracy a form of social organization in which the elderly have the most wealth, power, and privileges

gerontology the study of aging and the elderly

SUGGESTED READINGS

These two texts provide a detailed account of issues related to aging and the elderly.

Harold Cox. *Later Life: The Realities of Aging.* 2nd ed. Englewood Cliffs, NJ: Prentice Hall, 1988.

Robert C. Atchley. *Aging: Continuity and Change.* 2nd ed. Belmont, CA: Wadsworth, 1987.

The first of these books is a Pulitzer Prize–winner, first published in 1975, criticizing America's approach to aging. The second provides a more recent assessment of the issue.

Robert N. Butler. *Why Survive? Being Old in America.* New York: Harper and Row, 1985.

Richard J. Margolis. *Risking Old Age in America.* Boulder, CO: Westview, 1989.

This comparison of communities for the elderly in the United States and England offers insights into how the transitions of aging can be eased and even made enjoyable.

Doris Francis. *Will You Still Need Me, Will You Still Feed Me, When I'm 84?* Bloomington: Indiana University Press, 1984.

This book focuses on the very old, now the fastest-growing segment of the elderly American population.

Ira Rosenwaike, with the assistance of Barbara Logue. *The Extreme Aged in America: A Portrait of an Expanding Population.* Westport, CT: Greenwood Press, 1985.

These two government studies provide an in-depth examination of two critical issues: poverty among older women, and people who care for aging Americans.

Robyn Stone. *The Feminization of Poverty and Older Women.* Washington, DC: U.S. Department of Health and Human Services, 1986.

Robyn Stone, Gail Lee Cafferata, and Judith Sangl. *Caregivers of the Frail Elderly: A National Profile.* Washington, DC: U.S. Department of Health and Human Services, 1987.

The first of these books is regarded as the "bible" for people facing the task of caring for someone with Alzheimer's disease. The second is a brief congressional report describing Alzheimer's disease and the government's response to this national problem.

Nancy L. Mace and Peter V. Rabins. *The 36-Hour Day: A Family Guide to Caring for Persons with Alzheimer's Disease, Related Dementing Illnesses, and Memory Loss in Later Life.* New York: Warner Books, 1984.

Congress of the United States. *Losing a Million Minds: Confronting the Tragedy of Alzheimer's Disease and Other Dementias.* Washington, DC: U.S. Government Printing Office, 1987.

This applied approach to health-care problems for the elderly highlights issues of public policy.

Edgar F. Borgatta and Rhonda J. V. Montgomery. *Critical Issues on Aging Policy: Linking Research and Values.* Newbury Park, CA: Sage Publications, 1987.

This historical study, centered in Boston, examines work, retirement, and social problems among older people.

Brian Gratton. *Urban Elders: Family, Work, and Welfare Among Boston's Aged, 1890–1950.* Philadelphia: Temple University Press, 1986.

This book explores the distinctive patterns of friendship among older people.

Sarah H. Matthews. *Friendships Through the Life Course: Oral Biographies in Old Age.* Newbury Park, CA: Sage, 1986.

Are the elderly a "leisure class"? This analysis of national data examines volunteer work among older Americans.

Susan Maizel Chambre. *Good Deeds in Old Age: Volunteering by the New Leisure Class.* Lexington, MA: Lexington Books/D.C. Heath, 1987.

This book presents a social-conflict approach to the problems of the elderly.

Chris Phillipson. *Capitalism and the Construction of Old Age.* London: Macmillan, 1982.

All facets of death and dying are considered here, from the common death of pets to the uncommon death of children. There is also extensive coverage of the health-care profession, including the emerging hospice movement.

Jack B. Kamerman. *Death in the Midst of Life: Social and Cultural Influences on Death, Grief, and Mourning.* Englewood Cliffs, NJ: Prentice Hall, 1988.

Faith Ringgold, *The Wedding: Lover's Quilt #1*, 1986. Oil on canvas, tie-dyed, printed, pieced fabric. 77½ x 58". Collection of Marilyn Lanfear, Texas; Photographs courtesy Bernice Steinbaum Gallery, New York City.

15

Family

Thirty years ago, one of the hottest shows on prime-time television was "Leave It to Beaver." The antics of the two Cleaver sons—"the Beaver" and his older brother Wally—delighted viewers across the country. The two boys were lovable, and only slightly mischievous by today's standards.

"Leave It to Beaver" reinforced a powerful vision of family life in America of the 1950s. Ideal families were comfortably middle class, living on quiet, tree-lined suburban streets. They had sons instead of daughters. And family life was based on the traditional complementarity between dominant, bread-winning husbands, and supportive, homemaking wives. The following exchange between Mr. and Mrs. Cleaver makes the point:

Ward Cleaver: *"What type of girl would you have Wally marry?"*

June Cleaver: *"Oh, some very sensible girl from a nice family. One with both feet on the ground, who's a good cook, and can keep a nice house and see that he's happy."*

Today, greater awareness of social diversity has changed Americans' thinking about families. Popular television shows now highlight blacks ("The Cosby Show") as well as less affluent Americans ("Roseanne"). Nor do Americans assume that the family has an ideal form. The conventional family of working husband, housewife, and children still exists, of course, but now

it represents only one in ten households. The simple fact is that no single set of characteristics accurately describes today's American family. This chapter will examine both the general traits of families and how and why families vary.

Whatever its form, the family remains a major social institution in the United States and in every other society. Recall from Chapter 4 ("Society") that social institutions are major structural parts of society that address one or more of its basic needs. Other social institutions, including the educational system, the religious system, the political system, and the economic system, are discussed in subsequent chapters of this book. We will see that all social institutions are complex and have many consequences—negative as well as positive—for the operation of a society.

THE FAMILY: BASIC CONCEPTS

Kinship refers to *social relationships based on blood, marriage, or adoption*. In small preindustrial societies, people typically rely on their kin to meet most of their everyday needs. The functional significance of kinship tends to decline in industrial societies, where people distinguish between close relatives, who interact regularly and typically live together, and distant relatives, among whom there is often little social contact.

Definitions of the family vary considerably around the world and change over time. Generally, the **family** is defined as *a relatively permanent social group of two or more people, who are related by blood, marriage, or adoption and who usually live together*. Family life tends to be cooperative: the family is a most important primary group in which members share economic resources and day-to-day responsibilities. In industrial societies, people live first within a **family of orientation**, *the family into which a person is born and receives early socialization*. Later in life, a person lives within a **family of procreation**, *a family within which people have or adopt children of their own*. In most societies of the world, families are formed by **marriage**, *a socially approved relationship, involving economic cooperation and allowing sexual activity and childbearing, that is expected to be relatively enduring*. As we shall explain, although American law recognizes marriage only as the formal union of one male and one female, marital patterns show striking variation around the world. The significance of marriage as the basis for procreation is evident in the traditional attachment of the label of *illegitimacy* to children born out of wedlock, and in the word *matrimony*, which is derived from Latin meaning "the condition of motherhood." This norm linking childbearing to marriage has

weakened considerably, however, as the proportion of children born to unmarried women has increased.

Yet even these few generalizations cannot be applied to every family in the United States today. Many Americans object to limiting the use of the term "family" to married couples and children. Thus traditional families have been increasingly complemented by various groups whose claim to being a family is that they define themselves that way. For example, an unmarried couple and their children may think of themselves as a family, even if this pattern provokes disapproval from some Americans. Many gay male and lesbian couples, perhaps living with children of one or both partners, also consider themselves to be families. Similarly, some communal groups of unrelated people who choose to live together for a period of time and share resources consider themselves a family.

Others, however, argue that because the family is central to American society, social approval should not be extended to any relationship simply because those involved wish to be defined as a family (Dedrick, 1990). What is or is not a family, then, is now a matter of political debate. Courts have a part in this controversy: they have recognized the right of partners—married or not—to make claims on each other's property. Such rulings suggest that the concept of family—legally as well as socially—is taking on a broader meaning.

THE FAMILY IN CROSS-CULTURAL PERSPECTIVE

Virtually all societies recognize families (Murdock, 1945), yet families are subject to significant cross-cultural variation.

As was noted in earlier chapters, industrial societies recognize the **nuclear family**, *a social unit composed of one or, more commonly, two parents and children*. Typically based on marriage, the nuclear family is also often called the *conjugal family*. In preindustrial societies, however, the **extended family**, *a social unit including parents, children, and other kin*, is more common. This is also called the *consanguine family*, meaning that it is based on blood ties. Extended families frequently include grandparents, aunts, uncles, and other kin.

Although many Americans live within extended families, the nuclear family has been the predominant

In modern industrial societies, members of extended families usually do not live together. However, they may assemble for family rituals such as weddings, funerals, and family reunions.

form in the United States (Laslett, 1978; Degler, 1980). Nuclear families are encouraged by industrialization because productive work is located away from the home; thus children grow up to leave families (of orientation) in order to pursue their careers and form new families (of procreation). Both geographical and social mobility tend to weaken extended families.

Yet, extended families are common among some ethnic groups, including Hispanic Americans. Additionally, about one in seven elderly people lives with a relative other than a spouse, thereby forming an extended family.

Marriage Patterns

Cultural norms, often in the form of law, regulate whom a person may marry. These norms identify categories of people that *are* or *are not* suitable as mates. One pattern that results from such norms is called **endogamy**—*marriage between people of the same social group or category*. Norms of endogamy are found in every society and endorse marriage between people of the same age, tribe, race, religion, or social class. Most religions in American society—especially Judaism and Catholicism—encourage endogamous marriage. The second

pattern, also found in every society, is **exogamy**—*marriage between people of different social groups or categories*. In traditional Indian villages, although a young person is required to marry someone from the same caste category, the mate must also be from a different village.

All societies, then, endorse some combination of endogamy and exogamy. By uniting people of similar backgrounds, endogamy encourages group solidarity and helps to maintain traditional values and norms. In contrast, exogamy may forge useful alliances with other groups and encourages cultural diffusion. American society is highly endogamous with regard to race, and only slightly less so with regard to social class, ethnicity, and age.

In every industrial society, both law and cultural norms prescribe a form of marriage called **monogamy**—*marriage that joins one female and one male*. Because divorce and remarriage are now common, however, many Americans actually engage in a pattern of *serial monogamy*, a series of monogamous marriages.

In preindustrial societies, a more common marital pattern is **polygamy** (from the Greek, meaning "many unions"), defined as *marriage that unites three or more people*. In polygamous marriage two or more nuclear families are combined to form an extended family. Polygamy takes two forms. By far the more common is **polygyny** (from the Greek, meaning "many women" or "many wives"), *marriage that joins one male with more than one female.* Islamic societies in the Middle East and Africa, for example, allow men to have up to four wives. However, in societies that endorse this marital pattern, most families are nonetheless monogamous because great wealth is required to support several wives and even more children. In the United States, polygyny is illegal although, as the box explains, followers of the Mormon religion endorsed this practice in the past.

Polyandry (from the Greek, meaning "many men" or "many husbands") is *marriage that joins one female with more than one male.* This pattern is extremely rare but does exist in a few societies, including Buddhists in Tibet. Polyandry discourages the division of land into parcels too small to support a family and divides the burdensome costs of supporting a wife among many men.

Polyandry may also emerge in societies that engage in female infanticide, which reduces the female population so that men must share women.

Although only about one-fourth of world societies consider monogamy to be the only marital pattern, most marriages are monogamous (Murdock, 1965). Monogamy predominates partly because of the financial burden of multiple spouses and partly because the numerical parity of the sexes limits the possibility for polygamy.

Residential Patterns

Societies also differ in regard to where families reside. Industrial societies typically favor **neolocality** (from the Greek, meaning "new place"), *a residential pattern in which a married couple lives apart from the parents of both spouses.* Although newlyweds may live with the

---

CROSS-CULTURAL COMPARISON

Polygyny among the Mormons

In 1856 two converts to the Mormon religion, John Vance and Lucy Stone, were married in England. Four years later they moved to Utah, the center of Mormon settlement in the United States. Lucy's friend Ellen Johnson accompanied them; a year later, she too married John Vance. In 1868 Vance took Susan Porter as his third wife. Vance slept in turn with each of his wives but never retired until he had kissed each of his wives and children good night.

Founded in 1830 in New York State by Joseph Smith, the Church of Jesus Christ of Latter-Day Saints—or more simply, the Mormons—gradually moved west, fleeing hostility sparked by their unconventional religious beliefs. Of all Mormon doctrines, none drew more criticism than the practice of polygyny, which Mormons call *plural marriage.*

Although practiced earlier, polygyny was officially sanctioned by the Mormons in 1852, after their settlement in the Utah territory. Plural marriage, the Mormons claimed, was the will of God and a necessary step toward restoring true Christianity. They pointed to biblical precedent: Abraham, David, Solomon, and Moses, for example, had more than one wife. Noting that polygyny was widely endorsed by many of the world's cultures, the Mormons also claimed it eliminated the evil of prostitution and reduced the chances that a husband would divorce a wife of many years in order to marry a younger, more attractive woman.

The expense of supporting many wives (and even more children) was high; for this reason, few Mormon males could afford to practice polygyny. For many who could, plural

marriages were successful, although often causing jealousy among a man's various wives.

The Mormon Church officially discontinued the practice of polygyny in 1890, as one of the conditions demanded by the federal government for granting statehood to Utah. Although polygyny violates church doctrine and state law, estimates suggest that between ten thousand and thirty thousand Mormons still live within plural marriages—one legal marriage and others performed by a local church.

SOURCE: Based on Kimball Young, *Isn't One Wife Enough?* (New York: Henry Holt and Company, 1954); Gary L. Bunker and Davis Bitton, *The Mormon Graphic Image, 1834–1914* (Salt Lake City: University of Utah Press, 1983); and "Polygamy Spreading Despite Laws," UPI news story, *Mount Vernon News*, April 24, 1985, p. 20.

parents of one spouse—especially if finances do not permit their setting up a new home—the American cultural norm appears to be "Honor thy mother and father—but get away from them" (Blumstein & Schwartz, 1983:26). In preindustrial societies, however, newlyweds commonly reside with one set of parents, gaining economic security and protection in the process. **Patrilocality** (Greek for "place of the father") is *a residential pattern in which a married couple lives with or near the husband's family*. This is the most common world pattern (Murdock, 1965). **Matrilocality** (meaning "place of the mother") is *a residential pattern in which a married couple lives with or near the wife's family*. This pattern is rare and occurs where families define daughters as more valuable economic assets than sons (Ember & Ember, 1971, 1985).

Patterns of Descent

Descent refers to *the system by which kinship is traced over generations*. Descent is the answer to the basic question, "To whom am I related?" Industrial societies recognize a pattern of **bilateral descent** ("two-sided descent"), *a system tracing kinship through both males and females*. In this pattern, children are linked in kinship to the families of both parents.

Preindustrial societies usually trace kinship only through one parent. Two patterns of descent thus predominate. More common is **patrilineal descent,** *a system tracing kinship through males*. In this pattern, the father's side of the family, but not the mother's, is defined as kin, and property is passed across the generations only to males. Less common is **matrilineal descent,** *a system tracing kinship through females*. Here, only the mother's side of the family is defined as kin, with property passing from mothers to daughters. Patrilineal descent is common to pastoral and agrarian societies, in which males produce the most valued resources. Matrilineal descent is common in horticultural societies, in which women are the primary breadwinners (Haviland, 1985:476).

In some societies, laws regarding citizenship are shaped by traditional practices regarding descent. For example, in the southern African nation of Botswana, the children born to a Botswanan man and a foreign woman are automatically citizens, because of the strong patrilineal history of this society; the children of a Botswanan woman and a foreign man, however, do not become citizens of Botswana (Suggs, 1989).

Patterns of Authority

The predominance of polygyny, patrilocality, and patrilineal descent in the world reflects the universal presence of some degree of patriarchy, discussed in Chapter 13 ("Sex and Gender"). Wives and mothers have considerable power in every society, but no known society is clearly matriarchal. In industrial societies such as the United States, men usually head households, just as they dominate most areas of social life. More egalitarian family patterns are gradually evolving, especially as increasing numbers of women enter the labor force, but the social status of wife is still lower than that of husband. Americans also still prefer male children, and most children are given their father's last name.

THEORETICAL ANALYSIS OF THE FAMILY

As in earlier chapters, each of several theoretical approaches will be used to provide various insights about the family.

Functions of the Family

The structural-functional paradigm suggests that the family has several important social functions. This explains why the family is sometimes described as the backbone of society.

Socialization

As was explained in Chapter 5 ("Socialization"), the family is the first agent in the socialization process, typically having more importance than peer groups, schools, churches, and the mass media. The personalities of each new generation take shape within the family, so that, ideally, children grow to be well-integrated and contributing members of the larger society (Parsons & Bales, 1955). Even then, the family continues to socialize us throughout the life cycle. Adults learn and change within marriage, and, as anyone with children knows, parents learn as much from their children as their children learn from them.

Regulation of Sexual Activity

Every culture places some restrictions on sexual behavior. Sexual intercourse is a personal matter to those involved, but as the basis of human reproduction and economic inheritance, it is also a matter of considerable social importance.

All societies enforce some type of **incest taboo,** *a cultural norm forbidding sexual relations or marriage between certain kin*. This form of exogamy is universal, but precisely which kin are subject to the incest taboo is culturally variable. The Navaho, for example, forbid marrying any relative of one's mother. Americans apply the incest taboo to both sides of the family but limit it to close relatives, including parents, grandparents, siblings, aunts, and uncles. Precisely the sexual relations that Americans view as immoral and unnatural have been condoned, or even encouraged, in still other cultures. Brother-sister marriages, for example, were common among the ancient Egyptian, Incan, and Hawaiian nobility, and male nobles of the Azande in eastern Africa are reported to have married their daughters (Murdock, 1965). Some societies forbid sexual relations between cousins, while others permit them; American Catholics reject marriage between first cousins, although American Jews do not (Murphy, 1979). Legally, as many states prohibit this practice as allow it. The incest taboo may be universal, then, but it is also quite variable among societies.

The significance of the incest taboo is primarily social rather than biological. It is true that widespread sexual activity between close relatives might have adverse mental and physical consequences for offspring. This argument by itself, however, is inadequate as an explanation of the incest taboo, which is observed by only one species of life: human beings. As Robert Murphy (1979) suggests, society more than nature punishes incest. Why? Primarily because the incest taboo serves to maintain family life. First, it minimizes sexual competition within families by restricting legitimate sexuality to spouses. Second, it forces people to marry outside of their immediate family; the resulting alliances provide political and economic advantages to some families and strengthen social ties throughout the society. Third, in every society kinship is an important system that determines people's rights and obligations toward each other. Allowing close relatives to reproduce would transform kinship into relational chaos.

"Family resemblance" means more than sharing physical features. Children's range of interests and opportunities depends on the social position of their parents. Thus each new generation in many ways "follows in the footsteps" of their predecessors, as illustrated by the careers of Kirk and Michael Douglas.

Social Placement

Although the existence of families is not biologically necessary in order for people to have children, families provide for the social placement of children. Most social statuses—including race, ethnicity, religion, and social class—are ascribed at birth through the family. This fact explains the long-standing concern that children be born of socially sanctioned marriages. Legitimate birth, especially when parents are of similar social position, clarifies inheritance rights and allows for the stable transmission of social standing from parents to children.

Material and Emotional Security

The family is expected to provide physical protection and emotional and financial support to its members. Because the family is a person's most important primary group, kin generally have intense and enduring relationships. Such personal concern seems to engender a sense of self-worth and security in each individual, evident in the fact that people living in families tend to be healthier than those living alone.

Critical evaluation. Structural-functional analysis has identified a number of the major functions of the family. From this point of view, it is easy to see that society as we know it could not exist without families.

A limitation of this approach is that it implies support for the traditional family, overlooking the great diversity of family life in American society. It also focuses little attention on the problems of family life. For example, although families provide emotional support to their members, studies of family violence show that they also have the ability to undermine the individual's self-confidence, health, and well-being.

Social Inequality and the Family

While the social-conflict paradigm too links the family to the operations of society, it does so by investigating how the family perpetuates patterns of social inequality. Still another "function" of the family, in other words, is maintaining the social dominance of certain categories of people.

As was noted in Chapter 13 ("Sex and Gender"), Friedrich Engels (1902; orig. 1884) traced the origin of the family to the desire to transmit private property from generation to generation. From this point of view, families are central to inheritance laws that concentrate wealth in the hands of a small proportion of the population. As Chapter 10 ("Social Class in America") explained, about half of the four hundred richest Americans received great wealth primarily through inheritance (Forbes, 1989). Within industrial societies, then, the operation of the family serves to restrain social mobility. Similarly, racial and ethnic inequality, described in Chapter 12 ("Race and Ethnicity"), is also perpetuated through the operation of the family. Norms of endogamy guide people at each social level to marry others in the same category, so patterns of social inequality continue across the generations.

The family, Engels explained, also reflects and perpetuates patriarchy. During his own lifetime, Engels saw marriage as a type of human struggle involving

women who had been socially (and often legally) defined as the property of men. A century ago in the United States the earnings of wives typically belonged to their husbands as heads of the household. Although this practice is no longer upheld by law, other examples of husbands' domination of their wives continue. Women continue to bear major responsibility for housework and childrearing, although most women are now in the labor force (Haas, 1981; Schooler et al., 1984; Fuchs, 1986). Although this family pattern does offer considerable benefits to men, they too are disadvantaged by having less opportunity to share in the personal satisfaction and growth derived from interaction with children.

The link between the traditional family and social inequality is related to a number of conflicts and changes that will be explored later, such as violence against women, divorce, and the growing number of women who choose to raise their children outside of marriage.

Critical evaluation. Social-conflict analysis of the family reveals another side of the family: its significant role in maintaining various kinds of social inequality. As later sections explain, inequality also shapes family life, so families vary significantly among different categories of Americans.

Almost every society that has rejected the capitalist economy condemned by Engels, however, has families all the same. Criticisms notwithstanding, therefore, the family carries out essential social functions not easily accomplished by other means.

Other Theoretical Analyses

Both structural-functional and social-conflict analyses view the family in broad terms as a central structure of society. More micro-level approaches explore individual experiences of family life.

Symbolic-interaction analysis argues that the reality of family life is constructed differently by various family members with different privileges and responsibilities. Women and men are likely to view their marriages very differently (Bernard, 1982). Similarly, parents and children are likely to perceive family life differently. For example, children usually view their parents only in terms of parental roles, with little understanding of their parents' sexual relationship. Furthermore, the experiences and perceptions of every family member change over time. Two people's expectations as they exchange their wedding vows usually evolve considerably as they confront the daily realities of married life. A change in the role of one spouse, such as a wife entering law school, may also alter the roles of other family members. Thus the symbolic-interaction approach suggests the inadequacy of describing marriage and the family in terms of any rigid characteristics.

Social-exchange analysis views courtship and marriage as a process of negotiation in which people offer each other socially valued resources and advantages (Blau, 1964). In courtship, each person assesses the likely advantages and disadvantages of taking the other as a spouse. Physical attractiveness is one critical dimension of exchange. In patriarchal societies around the world, beauty has long been a commodity offered by women on the marriage market. This social value assigned to beauty explains females' traditional concern with physical appearance and their sensitivity about revealing their age. For men, on the other hand, financial resources are more likely to be considered a valued commodity. Less attractive men may succeed in marrying attractive

In modern, industrial societies, people are typically motivated to marry by feelings of love. Luis Alberto Acuna's painting *Rural Love* testifies to the fact that romantic love is hardly a modern phenomenon. Its importance has simply increased.

women if they can offer them a high income (Melville, 1983). Dimensions of social exchange are converging for males and females as more women enter the labor force and become less dependent on men to support them and their children.

STAGES OF FAMILY LIFE

The family is dynamic; the life course of individuals, discussed in Chapter 5 ("Socialization"), generates changing patterns and problems of family life. Typically, family life begins with courtship, followed by settling into the realities of married life. Next, at least for most couples, is raising children, leading to the later years of marriage after children have left home to form families of their own.

Courtship

Because the family is a vital economic asset, preindustrial societies consider courtship too significant to be left to those who will be married (Stone, 1977; Haviland, 1985). *Arranged marriages* represent an alliance between two extended families that affects the social standing of them both. Parents often make such arrangements when their children are very young. A century ago in India, for example, children were married as early as five years of age, and half of the females were married by the age of fifteen (Mayo, 1927; Mace & Mace, 1960).

Arranged marriages are common within traditional societies in which what Emile Durkheim called "mechanical solidarity" is strong (see Chapter 4, "Society"). Because of pronounced cultural homogeneity, almost any member of the opposite sex is a suitable marriage partner, and will understand the society's way of life and the roles of spouse and parent. Thus, marriages arranged by parents are likely to join people who are culturally compatible.

With industrialization, the declining importance of extended families results in growing individuality and more personal choice in courtship. Therefore young people need to gain extensive experience in courtship before they select a marriage partner. The age at which first marriage occurs is also related to economic concerns. A century ago in the United States, as is shown in Figure 15–1, age at first marriage for men was typically twenty-six; for women, the comparable figure was twenty-two.

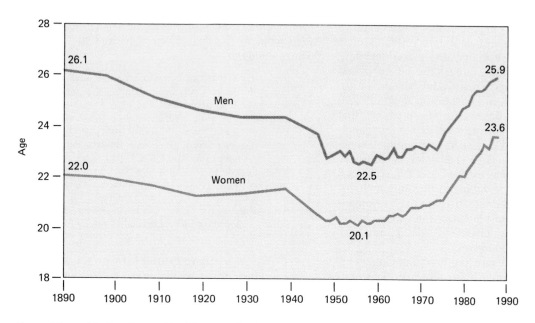

Figure 15–1 Median Age at First Marriage, by Sex: 1890–1988

(Arlene F. Saluter, *Changes in American Family Life*, Current Population Reports, Special Studies, Series P-23, No. 163. Washington, DC: United States Government Printing Office, 1990, p. 5.)

In addition to needing time to gain experience in courtship, men delayed marriage in order to accumulate some wealth that would be needed to support a family. This made them attractive to women who relied on husbands for support in a more patriarchal era. By mid-century, because American society enjoyed a higher standard of living, first marriage occurred earlier for both sexes. During the last forty years, women have entered the labor force in increasing numbers, and, particularly since 1970, income for American families has remained relatively unchanged. This economic stagnation has resulted in delaying marriage once again, in the interest of completing advanced education in order to increase economic security. Today, however, the two sexes are typically only about two years apart at first marriage, compared with a difference of four years a century ago.

Despite some variation, marriage among Americans concludes a long period of dating. This process generally begins as group dating, in which several girls and boys interact together. In time, group dating gives way to couple dating. In the United States today, courtship is frequently a period of sexual experimentation, and many couples may also live together before deciding to marry.

American culture places an enormous emphasis on *romantic love*—the experience of affection and sexual passion toward another person—as the basis for marriage. The American distaste for arranged marriages is certainly one result of this exaltation of romantic love. For us, marriage without love is difficult to imagine, and the mass media—from traditional fairy tales like "Cinderella" to contemporary paperback romance novels—present romantic love as the keystone of successful marriage. Not surprisingly, then, the vast majority of Americans view romantic love as the single most important element in courtship (Roper, 1974).

Romantic love was well established early in the Middle Ages among the nobility. It was not, however, the basis for marriage: more practical considerations of social standing guided choices of marital partners. Courtly love was actually an expression of the feudal ideal by which knights pledged themselves in service to noblewomen whom they revered from a distance but were ineligible to marry; noblewomen, in return, praised the bravery and dedication of these men. Such love was never to develop into an intimate personal relationship (Beigel, 1951). Over the centuries, however, romantic love grew in importance as the basis of marriage.

One major function of romantic love is encouraging an individual to leave the original family of orientation to form a new family of procreation. As an incentive to forming new families, romantic love is usually most intense when people first marry, and it may therefore carry a newly married couple through the difficult period of adjusting to the realities of married life (Goode, 1959). Yet, the modern American emphasis on romantic love also presents problems. Because it rests on feelings that may change, romantic love is a less stable foundation for marriage than social and economic considerations. Furthermore, as "Cinderella" and other folk tales suggest, romantic love can draw together people of different social backgrounds. Although social pressures continue to discourage such pairings, they are increasing. Thus romantic love can be a truly revolutionary force as marriages guided solely by the heart challenge racial, ethnic, religious, and social class boundaries.

Sociologists have long recognized that Cupid's arrow is aimed by society more than individualistic Americans like to believe. Even today, most married couples are about the same age and of the same race, religion, and social class. This pattern is called **homogamy** (literally, "like marrying like"), *marriage between people with the same social characteristics.*

Homogamy is common, first, because people of the same background tend to interact in the same neighborhoods, schools, and recreational settings. Second, common socialization encourages similar tastes and interests, so that we are likely to be attracted to people with the same social backgrounds as we have. Third, parents and peers often discourage marrying an "outsider." In some cases, this influence is subtle; in others, it is quite heavy-handed. Traditional Jews, for example, strongly oppose the marriage of their children to non-Jews. If sons or daughters should marry out of their category, parents may engage in the ritual of "sitting shiva," a ritual gathering to lament the loss of a loved one. Typically used after a death, it here signifies that by marrying an outsider, the child has undergone social death and may no longer be considered a member of the family.

"Falling in love," then, is usually guided by a host of social forces. Perhaps by exaggerating the importance of romantic love, we reassure ourselves that even in the midst of society we are nonetheless making a personal choice.

Settling in: Ideal and Real Marriage

Because of the social importance of marriage, socialization often instills highly idealized images of married

life. Consider the following account of a thirty-one-year-old woman, married eleven years and the mother of three children:

> When I got married, I suppose I must have loved him, but at the time, I was busy planning the wedding and I wasn't thinking about anything else. I was just thinking about this big white wedding and all the trimmings, and how I was going to be a beautiful bride, and how I would finally have my own house. I never thought about problems we might have or anything like that. I don't know even if I ever thought much about him. Oh, I wanted to make a nice home for Glen, but I wasn't thinking about how anyone did that or whether I loved him enough to live with him the rest of my life. I was too busy with my dreams and thinking about how they were finally coming true. (Rubin, 1976:69)

We do not have to read between the lines to see that for this woman family life has fallen short of earlier expectations. Such disappointment is a common result of idealizing marriage and the family. Especially for women—who, more than men, are socialized to view marriage as the key to their future happiness—the pleasures of matrimony are likely to be accompanied by disenchantment. Courtship tends to bring couples together for a limited amount of time, so they may see each other only at their best. Moreover, research suggests that romantic love involves a good deal of fantasy: people fall in love with others, not necessarily as they are, but as they want them to be (Berscheid & Hatfield, 1983). Within marriage, however, spouses confront each other regularly and realistically, for better or for worse. And only after marriage do many couples face the day-to-day challenges of maintaining a household. Sobering responsibilities include paying monthly bills, managing relationships with in-laws, and performing mundane tasks such as shopping, cooking, and cleaning. A great deal about marriage and one's spouse is therefore learned only *after* the wedding.

Newly married couples may also have to make sexual adjustments. Several generations ago, American cultural norms endorsed sexual activity only after marriage, and, no doubt, some people married simply for this reason. By the end of the 1980s, however, most nineteen-year-olds—88 percent of men and 81 percent of women—reported having had sexual intercourse (U.S. Congress, 1989). The number of sexual partners among unmarried teens is higher for men than for women.

Even for those with earlier experience, sexuality can prove disappointing in marriage. In the romantic haze of falling in love, people may anticipate marriage

Table 15–1   FREQUENCY OF SEXUAL ACTIVITY AMONG MARRIED COUPLES

Years Together	Sexual Frequency (times per month)			
	1 or less	1–4	4–12	12 or more
0–2	6%	11%	38%	45%
2–10	6	21	46	27
10 or more	16	22	45	18

SOURCE: Adapted from Philip Blumstein and Pepper Schwartz, *American Couples* (New York: William Morrow, 1983), p. 196.

as an extended sexual honeymoon, and they encounter disappointment and self-doubt when marital sex becomes less than an all-consuming passion. Although 70 percent of married people claim to be satisfied with the sexual dimension of their marriage, marital sexual activity declines over time, as Table 15–1 shows (Blumstein & Schwartz, 1983).

Research also indicates that couples with the most satisfying sexual relationships have the greatest overall satisfaction with their marriages. This does not mean that sex is the key to marital bliss, but rather that good sex and good relationships go together (Hunt, 1974; Tavris & Sadd, 1977; Blumstein & Schwartz, 1983). Sexual satisfaction is a highly relative concept, of course, based on highly variable individual needs and desires.

Infidelity—sexual activity outside marriage—is another area in which the reality of marriage may not coincide with the American cultural ideal. Traditional marriage vows "to forsake all others" appear to be strong: in a recent survey, 77 percent of American adults claimed that sex outside of marriage is "always wrong," and 13 percent thought infidelity is "almost always wrong"; about 7 percent stated that infidelity is "wrong only sometimes," while the remaining 3 percent either did not consider infidelity to be wrong at all or offered no response (N.O.R.C., 1989:258). Despite expressing support for fidelity, many married people in the United States do engage in extramarital sex. Some forty years ago Alfred Kinsey and his associates (1948, 1953) estimated that about half of married men and one-fourth of married women had engaged in extramarital sex. The percentage has subsequently remained stable for men and increased somewhat for women, especially younger wives. This rise may reflect a decline in the double standard that has long winked at male adultery while condemning females for the same activity. Additionally, as more women enter the labor force, they experience more regu-

lar contact with men (Hunt, 1974; Offir, 1982; Thompson, 1984; Saunders & Edwards, 1984). Yet during the 1980s, public disapproval of extramarital sex has increased, at least partly because of the AIDS crisis. It seems reasonable to expect some decline in infidelity not for moral reasons, but due to fear of this deadly, sexually transmitted disease.

Childrearing

The birth of a child changes marriage significantly as new demands are made on each spouse's attention, time, and energy. One thirty-year-old father described how the birth of his son had disrupted his relationship:

> Those first two years were almost perfect. . . . But when the baby was born everything began to change; it sort of all fell apart. It seemed (my wife) was busy with him all the time. And I felt like I didn't count anymore . . . and I got resentful of Danny, then I felt terrible. What kind of father am I to feel resentful at a little kid like that? But I couldn't help how I felt. (Rubin, 1983:61)

Although some may be ambivalent about the birth of children, almost all Americans think that a family should contain at least one child, as is indicated by the results of a national survey shown in Table 15–2 (N.O.R.C., 1989:211). Few Americans desire more than four children, however—a change from two centuries ago, when *eight* children was the American average (Newman & Matzke, 1984). In preindustrial societies,

Table 15–2   THE IDEAL NUMBER OF CHILDREN FOR AMERICANS, 1989

Number of Children	Proportion of Respondents
0	1.1
1	2.7
2	53.3
3	21.2
4	8.8
5	2.6
6 or more	1.4
As many as you want	5.3
No response	3.7

SOURCE: N.O.R.C., *General Social Surveys, 1972–1989* (Chicago: National Opinion Research Center, 1989), p. 253.

production is based on human labor, so children are an economic asset. In the past, having children was also regarded as a wife's duty. Birth control technology was crude and unreliable, so women frequently became pregnant whether they wanted to or not. Finally, having many babies did not necessarily mean a large family: as late as 1900, about one-third of American children died before adolescence (Wall, 1980).

With industrialization, children became less of an economic asset. Children today are rarely independent financially until at least the age of eighteen (and sometimes not until their mid-twenties), and the expense of raising them can be staggering. One estimate placed the cost of rearing one child to the age of eighteen at over $100,000, and another $50,000 to $150,000 has to be added if the child goes to college (*Family Economics Review*, 1989).

Today most American women are in the labor force and therefore want responsibility for fewer children. Birth control technology is much more effective and readily available, reducing the number of unplanned pregnancies. A great reduction in infant mortality has also lessened parents' need to have many children. Such factors explain the steadily declining American birth rate during this century to about two children per family today.

The task of raising children may be vital, but Amer-

Although women continue to take primary responsibility for parenting, many fathers are discovering the pleasures of extensive involvement in child rearing.

ican society does surprisingly little to prepare us for parenthood. Before gaining the privilege and responsibility of operating a car, for example, people must demonstrate the necessary skills, yet we have no comparable measure of fitness to be a parent. We acquire useful lessons from our family of orientation, but children often learn little of family life from a parent's point of view (Macionis, 1978; Pollak & Wise, 1979). Most new parents learn directly from their own successes and mistakes.

As was suggested in Chapter 13 ("Sex and Gender"), the recent entry of American women into the labor force has been dramatic. In 1988, 56.6 percent of women over the age of sixteen were in the workforce, and the proportion of working women with children under eighteen was higher still: 65 percent (U.S. Bureau of Labor Statistics, 1989). Unlike working men, most wives and mothers who work outside the home also bear the traditional responsibility for raising children and doing housework. Although some American men are enlarging their roles as parents, most continue to resist sharing responsibility for household tasks that our culture has historically defined as feminine (Radin, 1982).

As more women join men in the labor force, public attention has focused on what are called *latchkey kids*— children who have working parents and who are left to fend for themselves for a good part of the day. There are 7 million such children in America today; half of all nine-year-olds look after themselves after school (U.S. Women's Bureau, 1989). Defenders of the traditional American family such as Phyllis Schlafly (1984) contend that many working mothers are neglecting their responsibilities to children. Husbands and fathers are not usually subject to this criticism because their income is assumed to be necessary to support their families. However, the same now holds for most working mothers (Keniston, 1985). It is ironic that as more women have entered the labor force, more households headed by women are poor (Cahan, 1985). Chapter 10 ("Social Class in America") described this pattern as the *feminization of poverty*: over half of the poor families in the United States are households headed by single women.

Because parenting competes with other personal interests and needs, more couples are choosing to delay childbirth or to remain childless. In 1960, 12.6 percent of women between 25 and 29 who had ever been married had no children; by 1988 this proportion had risen to 29.1 percent (U.S. Bureau of the Census, 1989). Likely reasons are that many working women have low-paying jobs and cannot support children, others wish to use their income to gain more education, while still others want to become established in a career before assuming the responsibilities of parenthood (Blumstein & Schwartz, 1983).

The Family in Later Life

The increasing life expectancy of Americans means that, barring divorce, couples are likely to remain married for a long time. By about age fifty, most have completed the major task of raising children. The remaining years of marriage are commonly described as the "empty nest" because, as at the beginning of the marriage, couples have no children living in their households.

Like their birth, the departure of children causes important changes in a family. Couples must make serious adjustments, although their relationship often becomes closer and more satisfying (Kalish, 1982). Perhaps the best description of a healthy marriage at this stage of life is companionship. Years of living together may have diminished a couple's sexual passion for each other, but mutual understanding and commitment are likely to have increased.

Personal contact with children usually continues, since most older adults live within a short distance of at least one of their children (Shanas, 1979). People's incomes peak in late middle age, and the expenses of childrearing are diminished. Thus at this stage in family life, parenting may involve helping children make large purchases (a car or a house) and, of course, periodically baby-sitting for grandchildren.

Retirement, discussed in Chapter 14 ("Aging and the Elderly"), represents another change in family life. In marriages in which the wife was a homemaker and the husband worked outside the home, retirement means spouses will be spending much more time together. Although the husband's presence is often a source of pleasure to both, it may dramatically change wives' established routines. Some wives find the presence of retired husbands an intrusion, as is illustrated by one woman's blunt reaction: "I may have married him for better or worse, but not for lunch" (Kalish, 1982:96). Because retirement is becoming a common experience for both spouses, this final stage of family life provides the opportunity for them to enjoy new activities, frequently together.

The final, and most difficult, transition in married life comes with the death of a spouse. Wives typically outlive their husbands because women have a longer life expectancy than men, and also because women usu-

ally marry men who are several years older than they are. Wives can thus expect to spend a significant period of time as widows. The bereavement and loneliness accompanying the death of a spouse can be extremely challenging. This experience may be even more difficult for husbands: they usually have fewer friends than their wives do, and those who have spent their lives in traditional masculine roles must adjust to the unfamiliar responsibility of housework (Berardo, 1970).

VARIETIES OF FAMILY LIFE

Social class, race and ethnicity, and gender are powerful forces shaping the lives of Americans, as earlier chapters have explained. Together, they generate considerable variation in marriage and family life.

Social Class

As was described in Chapter 10 ("Social Class in America"), social class accounts for vast differences in standard of living. It shapes a family's financial security, range of opportunities, and patterns of interaction.

Affluence is no guarantee of personal happiness, nor does it ensure a successful family life, but economic advantages do permit a greater sense of security in an uncertain world. In a study of working-class families, Lillian Rubin reports the following observations of a working-class housewife:

> I guess I can't complain. He's a steady worker; he doesn't drink; he doesn't hit me. That's a lot more than my mother had, and she didn't sit around complaining and feeling sorry for herself, so I sure haven't got the right. (1976:33)

Being a steady worker, not drinking excessively, and refraining from violence, Rubin discovered, were the three attributes most frequently mentioned by working-class women as positive qualities in a husband. In contrast, Rubin reports, these attributes were never mentioned in evaluations of marriages by middle-class women; they were more concerned with intimacy, sharing, and communication with their husbands. Working-class women value these things, too, but recognize that they are secondary to the more basic need for economic and physical security.

Social scientists have also documented the negative

effects of unemployment on family life (Brenner, 1976). Unemployment is more common among families of lower social standing, who have fewer resources to begin with. For those who contend with economic uncertainty on a daily basis, then, unemployment serves only to heighten fears and anxieties, which can be destructive to family life. A thirty-year-old man recalls the turmoil caused by the loss of his job:

> Right after our first kid was born, I got laid off . . . and I didn't have much in the way of skills to get another job with. My unemployment [payments] ran out pretty quick, and Sue Ann couldn't work because of the baby . . . so we moved in with my folks. We lived there for about a year. What a mess. My mom and Sue Ann just didn't get along. (Rubin, 1976:73)

It may be true that money cannot buy happiness, but its absence certainly introduces strains and pressures into the lives of parents and children.

Social class also affects the relationship between spouses. Elizabeth Bott (1971) claimed that working-class couples typically have what she called a "segregated-marriage network." This means that husband and wife have distinct gender roles and carry out many daily tasks and leisure activities separately. Wives spend much of the day at home, often in the company of other women. Husbands, when not at work, usually remain away from the home, frequently with other men. Husbands, Bott concluded, are also dominant partners among the working class, making major family decisions on their own.

Middle-class spouses, in contrast, form a "joint-marriage network." They are less likely to divide tasks rigidly into "men's work" and "women's work," and they generally share leisure activities, often entertaining other couples in the home. Bott also claimed that family decision making among middle-class couples is more egalitarian.

Spouses of higher social class also are more open and expressive with each other (Komarovsky, 1967; Rubin, 1976). This is so because people of higher social standing have more education, as well as jobs that emphasize verbal skills. Additionally, each social class has a distinctive pattern of socialization. As was noted in Chapter 5 ("Socialization"), working-class parents, more than middle-class parents, teach their children to embrace conventional gender roles and to be obedient rather than to value critical self-expression (Rubin, 1976; Kohn, 1977).

Rigid adherence to gender roles causes husbands and wives to lead very different lives and to share fewer interests. Lillian Rubin (1976) explains that males who grew up with conventionally masculine ideas of self-control that stifle emotional expressiveness tend to be tight-lipped about their personal feelings. Women strictly socialized to be feminine express themselves more openly. As a result, husbands and wives may speak different languages, therefore seeking members of their own

Hispanic cultures have traditionally maintained strong kinship ties. Carmen Lomas Garza's painting, *Sandia, Watermelon*, portrays the three-generation family pattern common to Hispanic-Americans.

sex as confidants while experiencing frustration in attempting to communicate with each other.

Ethnicity and Race

As Chapter 12 ("Race and Ethnicity") indicated, ethnicity and race are powerful social forces. This factor is evident in family life.

Many Hispanic Americans maintain extended families based on strong loyalties and mutual support. Hispanic-American parents traditionally exercise considerable control over their children's courtship, seeing marriage as an alliance between two extended families rather than as a union based on romantic love. Hispanic families are also notable for relatively pronounced adherence to conventional gender roles. *Machismo*—masculine strength, daring, and sexual prowess—is strongly emphasized. Women, on the other hand, are closely supervised; those who resist such controls are likely to be stigmatized as immoral and "loose." The result is a double standard, by which men are encouraged to engage in sexual activities outside marriage while women are expected to marry as virgins and remain faithful to their husbands.

Assimilation into the larger American culture is gradually altering these traditional patterns, however. Puerto Ricans who have migrated to New York, for example, are unlikely to maintain the strong extended families found in Puerto Rico. Especially among more affluent Hispanic families, the traditional authority of males over females has diminished (Fitzpatrick, 1971; Moore & Pachon, 1985).

Black American families have been the focus of considerable attention during the last two decades. Blacks are three times as likely as whites to be poor, and household income among blacks in 1988 was only 57 percent that of white households (U.S. Bureau of the Census, 1989). Family patterns of black Americans are thus shaped by unemployment, underemployment, and poverty. One study found that 25 percent of black women born in the early 1950s have never married, compared with about 10 percent of comparable white women (Bennett, Bloom, & Craig, 1989). Economic uncertainty makes stable marriage extremely difficult. As Figure 15–2 shows, women headed 43.3 percent of black families in 1989, compared with 23.1 percent of Hispanic families and 13.0 percent of white families (U.S. Bureau of the Census, 1989). Among all categories, female-headed households have increased in recent decades. Figure

Figure 15–2 Composition of Families, 1989

(U.S. Bureau of the Census)

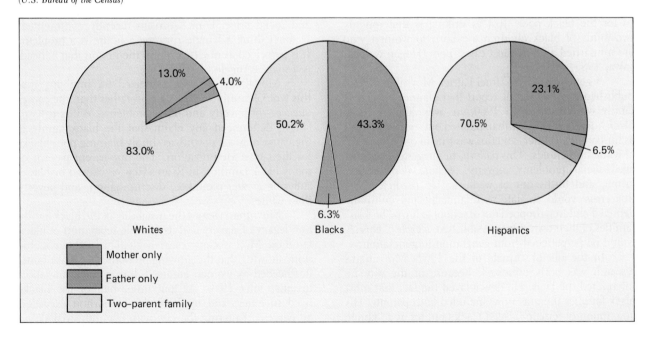

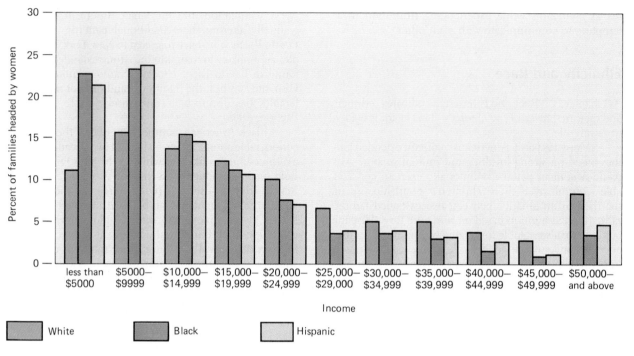

Figure 15–3 Families Headed by Women, by Income, 1989
(*U.S. Bureau of the Census*)

15–3 shows that, for whites, female-headed households are most prevalent among the poor; they are even more so for the black poor. Just as striking is that roughly two-thirds of black children are born to women who are unmarried and, in most cases, poor (Hogan & Kitagawa, 1985).

A generation ago Daniel Patrick Moynihan (1965) published a controversial report that claimed the black family was in crisis. In 1960, in over 20 percent of black households, Moynihan pointed out, no man served as husband and father, and this was true in only 5 percent of white households. This pattern, he suggested, encouraged social problems, poverty, welfare dependency, crime, and births out of wedlock. He predicted that this crisis would escalate as financially and culturally deprived children dropped out of school to form "broken" families of their own. Once established, a *cycle of poverty* would be perpetuated from generation to generation.

In the liberal climate of the 1960s Moynihan's research was hotly criticized, because of the way he interpreted the facts. He downplayed the fact that most black families then (as now) included both parents. His description of female-headed black families as a "tangle

of pathology" also struck critics as a subtle expression of prejudice against women and blacks. Black novelist and social critic Toni Morrison recently commented, "I don't think a female running a house is a problem. It is perceived as one because of the notion that a 'head' is a man" (Angelo, 1989:120).

Moynihan was also criticized for implying that this type of family was the *cause*—rather than the *consequence*—of poverty and other problems. William Ryan (1976) denounced any claim that the black family is the cause of black poverty as simply blaming poor blacks for their own victimization. The one-parent pattern of many black families, in Ryan's view, is caused by blacks suffering greater prejudice, discrimination, and poverty than whites.

Moynihan viewed the instability of the black family as a legacy of slavery and its forcible separation of black families. More recent research challenges this conclusion, showing that the growing proportion of black families headed by women emerged during black migration to cities after 1940. At that time, half of the blacks lived in cities, and by 1990 the proportion exceeded 80 percent. Entering the city with few industrial skills, and further disadvantaged by racial prejudice and discrimination, blacks were soon caught up in an economic crisis of monumental proportions. Forced to work in low-paying, unskilled jobs and constantly in danger of unemployment, many poorer blacks could not attain the financial security necessary to maintain a family (Gutman, 1976). Some scholars, therefore, conclude that the transformation of the black family is a consequence of enormous economic disadvantages and historical racism (Wilson, 1984).

The decline of traditional industries during the 1980s has hit black families hard. During a decade of prosperity for some Americans, the economic security of many blacks has declined: poor families have become poorer, and some black families' hold on middle-class standing has become tenuous (Updegrave, 1989). A black underclass now exists in urban America, increasingly cut off from opportunity and hope. Amid despair, violence has become a way of life, and the use of crack and other dangerous drugs reached epidemic proportions by the beginning of the 1990s. More than half of black children now grow up in poverty. This fact, coupled with the rise in motherhood among poor teenagers, fulfills the bitter prediction made by Moynihan of an expanding cycle of poverty among women and their children (Ladner, 1986; Furstenberg, Brooks-Gunn, & Morgan, 1987).

In light of overwhelming problems, there is remarkable strength to the family among economically disadvantaged blacks. Individuals draw upon extended family members and generate mutual-dependence networks of others, who take on kin-like roles (a substitute "aunt," for instance). Such resourcefulness has allowed people confronting tremendous barriers to care for children and meet daily needs (Stack, 1975; Cherlin & Furstenberg, 1983; Leslie & Korman, 1989).

Gender

For all social classes, ethnicities, and races, cultural definitions of masculinity and feminity affect marriage and the family. Jessie Bernard (1982) states that every marriage is actually *two* different marriages: a female marriage and a male marriage.

During the last century the extent of male domination of the family has diminished, but still few marriages are composed of two equal partners. In research by Mirra Komarovsky (1973, 1976), in the ideal marriage envisioned by most of the college seniors of both sexes, the man was dominant. Even men who claimed to believe in sexual equality, she concluded, did not want to marry a woman who might upstage them. In contrast, women are socialized to defer to men so that many women do desire a husband they view as their superior. Moreover, Americans expect men to be older as well as taller than the women they marry. Even when both spouses work, the husband's career is assumed to be more important (McRae, 1986).

In light of these patterns, a surprising fact is that American culture promotes the idea that marriage is more beneficial for women than for men (Bernard, 1982). At countless bridal showers, women congratulate one of their own on her impending marriage, yet at bachelor parties men bemoan the loss of one of their number to his new wife. Consider, too, the contrast between the positive stereotype of the carefree bachelor and the negative stereotype of spinster. In short, women are thought to pursue a husband eagerly while men may eventually—and always reluctantly—settle down.

The view that marriage is favorable to women is rooted in their historical exclusion from the labor force: a woman's financial security depended on her having a husband. But in most respects, Jessie Bernard claims, marriage has never been beneficial to women. In comparison to single women, she notes, married women have poorer mental health and more passive attitudes toward life, and they report greater personal unhappiness. It is therefore men who are the beneficiaries of marriage. Married men generally live longer than single men, have better mental health, and report greater personal happiness. After divorce, many more women than men report happier lives, and they are in fact less likely than men to remarry. Bernard (1982:24) concludes that there is no better guarantor of long life, health, and happiness for a man than a woman well socialized to perform the "duties of a wife," willing to devote her life to taking care of him and providing the regularity and security of a well-ordered home.

Bernard is not saying that marriage must be unhealthful for women. The problem, she asserts, is the "anachronistic way in which marriage is structured today": husbands dominating wives and constraining them to tedious work within the home. Under these circumstances, as the box suggests, men reap considerable advantages from marriage while women have reason to spearhead the effort to reform marital patterns in American society.

Recent research based on a random sample of American couples helps us to see the connections be-

"I Want a Wife!"

Judy Syfers, a married woman, is aware that marriage generally benefits men more than women. Let's be fair, she suggests, "I, too, want a wife!"

I am a wife. Not long ago a male friend of mine appeared on the scene fresh from a recent divorce. He is obviously looking for another wife. As I thought about him while ironing one evening, it suddenly occurred to me that I, too, would like to have a wife.

I want a wife who will work and send me to school so that I can become economically independent. And while I am going to school I want a wife to take care of the children. I want a wife to keep track of the children's doctor and dentist appointments. And to keep track of mine too. I want a wife to make sure my children eat properly and are kept clean. I want a wife who will wash the children's clothes and keep them mended.

I want a wife who will take care of my physical needs. I want a wife who will keep my house clean. A wife who will pick up after me. I want a wife who will keep my clothes clean, ironed, mended, replaced when need be, and who will see to it that my personal things are kept in their proper place so that I can find what I need the minute I need it. I want a wife who cooks the meals, a wife who is a good cook. I want a wife who will plan the menus, do the necessary grocery shopping, prepare the meals, serve them pleasantly, and then do the cleaning up while I do my studying. I want a wife who will care for me when I am sick and sympathize with my pain and loss of time from school.

When I meet people at school whom I like and want to entertain, I want a wife who will have the house clean, will prepare a special meal, serve it to me and my friends, and not interrupt when I talk about the things that interest me and my friends. And I want a wife who knows that sometimes I need a night out by myself.

I want a wife who is sensitive to my sexual needs, a wife who makes love passionately and eagerly when I feel like it, a wife who makes sure that I am satisfied. And, of course, I want a wife who will not demand sexual attention when I am not in the mood for it.

My God, who wouldn't want a wife?

SOURCE: Abridged from Judy Syfers, "I Want a Wife," *Ms.*, December 1979, p. 144.

---

tween gender, power, and happiness in marriage (Ross, Mirowsky, & Huber, 1983; Mirowsky & Ross, 1984). Four types of marriage were found to yield different levels of depression for men and women.

The first type of marriage is traditional, in which only the husband is employed and the wife does all housework and childrearing. In this marriage, both husband and wife approve of conventional gender roles. Figure 15–4 shows that this arrangement appears to favor the husband, who derives income and prestige from his work. The wife, however, has a higher level of depression, presumably because her status as homemaker carries little social prestige, even though this is her preferred role.

In the second type of marriage, both spouses work, although the wife still does all the housework and childrearing. Here the wife works out of economic necessity, although she and her husband would prefer that she stay in the home. In this situation, as Figure 15–4 shows, depression is high for the wife and higher still for the husband. The wife has two demanding jobs, one (or both) of which she does not want. The husband, believing that he should be able to support his family, suffers from being unable to. This is the only marital pattern in which husbands have poorer mental health than wives.

In the third marital arrangement, husband and wife are happy that the wife has a job, which provides psychological benefits for her; however, she is still responsible for all the housework. The husband benefits even more: the greater family income reduces the chance that his unemployment or any other unexpected setback will cause financial hardship for the family.

In the fourth kind of marriage, both husband and wife are happy to be working outside the home and they also share most family responsibilities. This pattern provides the greatest psychological benefits to husbands and wives because sharing household responsibilities reduces tensions that arise when a working wife is expected to take sole responsibility for housework and children. The fourth pattern is gradually becoming more common in American society, although it is still quite rare.

This research supports Jessie Bernard's (1982) contention that more egalitarian marriages tend to be happier

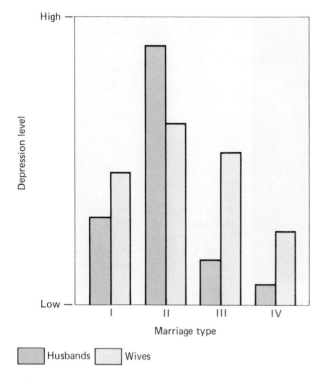

Figure 15-4 Depression in Four Types of Marriage
(*Ross, Mirowsky, & Huber, 1983*)

for husbands as well as wives. The results of this study are also consistent with Bernard's conclusion that men generally benefit from marriage more than women do. Such evidence may make us wonder why conventional and unequal marriages persist. Apparently, changing long-established cultural definitions of the two sexes is a difficult and slow process despite evidence that both men and women may benefit.

TRANSITION AND PROBLEMS IN FAMILY LIFE

Ann Landers, one of the best-known observers of the American scene, once remarked that "One marriage out of twenty is wonderful, four are good, ten are tolerable, and five are pure hell" (Landers, 1984). As has already been explained, the reality of family life often falls short of the ideal. In some cases, however, problems are serious enough to threaten family life itself.

Divorce

Figure 15–5 shows the divorce rate—the number of divorces for every one thousand people over the age of fifteen—during the last century. The rising and falling rate of divorce indicates that people's decisions are affected by changes in society itself. For example, the divorce rate fell during the Great Depression of the 1930s and rose sharply after World War II. Overall, the divorce rate has increased about tenfold since 1890. By the 1970s, half of American marriages were expected to end in divorce (for blacks, about two-thirds); recently, these rates appear to have stabilized. In global context, the American divorce rate is second to none. Marriage vows still proclaim "till death do us part," but the reality is that marriages are now as likely to be ended by divorce as by death (Cherlin, 1981; Kitson & Raschke, 1981; Weitzman, 1985).

One reason that divorce is common among Americans is that the United States has one of the highest marriage rates in the world: about nine out of ten Americans eventually marry. During the last century, however, the divorce rate has risen while the marriage rate has remained stable. This rise is due to a number of broader changes in American society (Huber & Spitze, 1980;

Figure 15–5 The Divorce Rate for the United States, 1890–1990

(*U.S. Bureau of the Census*)

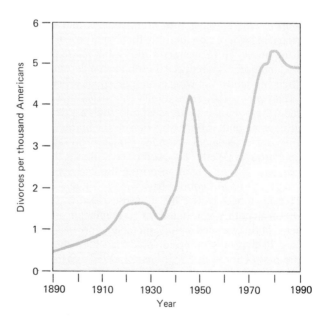

As the most important primary group, the family is typically the setting in which we form a self-concept and learn how to interact with others. Therefore, family strife can have lasting consequences, as it shapes the personality development of children.

Kitson & Raschke, 1981). First, Americans used to spend more of their time in family activities. Today parents and children work and play together less often; they are more active individually in schools, workplaces, and various recreational settings. Americans have also become more individualistic, seemingly more concerned with personal happiness than committed to the well-being of families. Second, as was noted earlier, Americans base marriage on romantic love. Because sexual passion usually subsides with time, spouses may end a marriage in favor of a relationship that renews excitement and romance. Third, women's increasing participation in the labor force has reduced their financial dependency on their husbands. Growing economic equality between the sexes may strain conventional marriages and gives women more choice about staying in such a marriage. Fourth, when both parents work outside the home, child-rearing is a considerable burden. Children do stabilize some marriages (Waite, Haggstrom, & Kanouse, 1985), but divorce is most common during the early years of marriage when many couples have young children. Fifth, divorce no longer carries the powerful negative stigma common a century ago. In today's geographically mobile society, both extended family members and neighbors are less likely to discourage divorce than they often did in the past (Thornton, 1985; Gerstel, 1987). Sixth, because the United States has a high remarriage rate, people may initiate divorce with confidence that they can find another, more suitable, partner.

Divorces are also easier to obtain now. In the past, courts required divorcing couples to demonstrate that one or both were guilty of behavior such as adultery or physical abuse. Today most states allow divorce simply because a couple believes their marriage has failed. Half of American adults now think divorce is too easy to obtain (only one-fourth think divorce procedures are too difficult) (N.O.R.C., 1989:256). Despite these changes, the emotional and financial costs of ending a marriage remain high.

Who Divorces?

Young spouses, especially teenagers, are the most likely to divorce, because usually their courtship was brief and because they have less financial stability and emotional maturity. People in lower social classes, too, are more likely to divorce because of financial strains. Divorce is more likely when a couple marries in response to an unexpected pregnancy, and when one or both have alcohol or other drug problems. Another factor related to divorce is dissimilar social backgrounds, which may introduce tensions difficult to resolve. Divorce also is more common among women who have successful careers, partly because of the strains of a two-career marriage and partly because such women are less constrained to remain in an unhappy marriage. People who divorce once also tend to divorce again, partly because problems often follow them from one marriage to another. Finally, people who move, weakening ties with family and friends, are more likely to divorce (Yoder & Nichols, 1980; Booth & White, 1980; Glenn & Shelton, 1985).

Problems of Divorce

Divorce is not necessarily a problem; it may be a transition that benefits each party. Even in the best case, however, ending a marriage brings as much change as beginning one.

Paul Bohannan (1970) suggests that divorce involves six different adjustments. First, there is the *emotional divorce*. A deteriorating marriage is often fraught with disappointment and frustration, if not outright hostility. Second is the formal, *legal divorce*, which may involve financial and further emotional burdens. Bohannan describes a third transition as *psychic divorce*. Divorced people may experience personal failure, loneliness, and a need for personal repair. Fourth, *community divorce* points to the need to reorganize friendships ("Were they really *my* friends or my spouse's?") and to adjust relations with parents and other family members who had grown accustomed to seeing someone as part of a couple.

A fifth problem, especially for women, is the *economic divorce*. Recent *no-fault* divorce laws have reduced the amount of alimony and child support paid by men to ex-wives. Divorce courts are now likely to require that homes be sold so that marital assets can be evenly divided. These legal changes, claims Lenore Weitzman (1985), have hurt women financially. In her study, in the year following divorce, women suffered a 73 percent reduction in their living standard while men experienced a 42 percent rise in theirs. For the woman, especially one who does not work, this loss usually means a marked reduction in housing quality. Ex-wives often lose other forms of financial security as well, such as insurance policies, pension programs, and credit, all of which typically remain with ex-husbands. Older women who have not been in the labor force suffer even more severe economic problems, Weitzman observes, since they generally lack job skills.

A sixth and final adjustment noted by Bohannan is *parental divorce*, in which parents must resolve the difficult issues surrounding custody of children. More than half of divorcing partners have children under eighteen, and about half of children under eighteen experience the divorce of their parents (Bumpass, 1984; Weitzman, 1985; Leslie & Korman, 1989). The practice of awarding custody to mothers is based on the conventional view of women as being better parents than men are. Recently, however, a growing number of fathers have sought to gain custody of their children. There is a trend toward joint custody, whereby children have a primary home with one parent but regularly spend time with the other, or they divide their lives more or less evenly between the two parents. Although joint custody is difficult if the divorced parents live far apart or do not get along, it does have the advantage of keeping children in regular contact with both parents (Roman & Haddad, 1978; Cherlin & Furstenberg, 1983).

Because mothers usually have custody of children but fathers typically earn more income, the well-being of children often depends on fathers making court-ordered child-support payments. Yet about half of children of divorced parents do not receive the financial support to which they are legally entitled. What has been called "an epidemic of nonsupport" has led to federal legislation mandating that parents who fail to fulfill this obligation will have the payments withheld from their earnings (Weitzman, 1985).

Conventional wisdom suggests that divorce is hardest on the children. Divorce may tear children from familiar surroundings and confront them with disturbing changes. Moreover, children may feel responsible for the divorce of their parents. There is little doubt, however, that children who experience family breakup fare better than those who remain in a family torn by tension or violence (Goetting, 1981; Zill, 1984). Recognizing this fact, Americans now express less support for the idea of staying together "for the sake of the children": 70 percent now believe that divorce is preferable to maintaining an intact family fraught with conflict (Black, 1984). Ideally, of course, children fare best in the absence of both family conflict and divorce.

Remarriage

As the divorce rate has increased, so has the rate of remarriage. Four out of five people who divorce remarry, most within five years, Men, who generally benefit more from marriage, are somewhat more likely to remarry than women are. This is especially true of older men: our culture supports their marrying younger and less economically successful women. Because women are expected to "marry up," the more education a woman has, and the better her job, the less likely she is to remarry due to difficulty in finding a suitable husband (Leslie & Korman, 1989).

Common sense suggests that what people learned from failed first marriages should make their subsequent marriages more successful. Yet remarriages are even more likely to end in divorce. One reason is that people who have already been through a divorce will be prepared to end another unsatisfactory marriage. Additionally, the first divorce may have been caused by attitudes or behavior that will undermine a subsequent marriage.

The same transitions that Paul Bohannan links to divorce are present in remarriage. According to Ann Goetting (1982), *emotional remarriage* involves reestablishing a bond based on attraction, commitment, and trust. *Legal remarriage* follows, but does not complete the remarriage process. *Psychic remarriage* suggests the need to regain personal identity as part of a couple; often individuals must relinquish the autonomy and privacy gained after an earlier divorce. *Community remarriage* involves altering relationships with friends and family based on, once again, being married. *Economic remarriage* generally increases a couple's standard of living, since two incomes now maintain only one residence. When there are children, a more complex issue is establishing and managing child-support payments, which might flow both to and from the new household. As was noted earlier, such payments are often sporadic, making economic planning difficult.

Where there are children, *parental remarriage* consists of establishing relationships with the children of the spouse, a task that often demands skill and patience. Remarriage often creates *blended families*, composed of biological parents and stepparents, so various that children in one household may have two, one, or no common parents. With one biological parent typically living elsewhere, blended families may have to make some effort to establish precisely who is part of the child's nuclear family (Furstenberg, 1984). Blended families also subject children to new relationships: an only child, for example, may suddenly find she has two older brothers. Such factors explain why remarriages involving children have more stress and conflict, contributing to the likelihood of another divorce (Kalmuss & Seltzer, 1984).

Family Violence

The ideal family is a haven from the dangers of the larger world. The disturbing reality of many real families, however, is **family violence**—*emotional, physical, or sexual abuse of one family member by another*. According to sociologist Richard J. Gelles:

The family is the most violent group in society with the exception of the police and the military. You are more likely to get killed, injured, or physically attacked in your home by someone you are related to than in any other social context. In fact, if violence were a communicable disease, the government would consider it an epidemic. (Cited in Roesch 1984:75)

Such facts are chilling, and in some cases, almost incredible. Public awareness is the first step toward solving this problem, which victimizes millions of adults and children.

Spouse Abuse

I guess the first time he hit me was when we had been married about eight years. I'd gone to my music lesson and had arranged for a babysitter to take the children to a school fair. When my husband got home from work the house was dark and no one was there. This enraged him, and in the driveway when I arrived, he greeted me with a punch in the kidneys. I doubled over. I didn't even know what I'd done. We never talked afterward. I swallowed my pain and tried to forget.

American society has reluctantly come to the conclusion that the home can be a dangerous place. This is especially true for women: at least 1 million women are the victims of family violence each year.

This incident took place in a fashionable suburb of Philadelphia in a family with plenty of money, beautiful children—and a lot of violence (Saline, 1984).

The common stereotype of a spouse abuser is a lower-class man who now and then drinks too much, loses control, and beats up his wife. In reality, spouse abuse exists among all social classes, races, and ethnic groups, though financial problems and unemployment can make the problem worse. Furthermore, as the above example suggests, in many families violence occurs without apparent explanation. Family brutality often goes unreported to police, but researchers estimate that about 9 million couples—or one in six—endure at least some violence each year. Between 1 and 2 million of these couples experience serious violence, including kicking, biting, and punching. Some research suggests that women are as likely to be violent toward men as men are toward women. But two sex-based differences have been confirmed. First, the most serious injuries affect women; second, violence against men often takes the form of women's retaliation and self-defense (Straus & Gelles, 1986). Although violence commonly involves both partners, then, the damage of spouse abuse is mostly in the form of injury to *women* (Schwartz, 1987).

Government statistics show that almost 30 percent of female murder victims and 6 percent of male murder victims are killed by spouses, ex-spouses, or unmarried partners. Some four thousand wives are killed each year in this way. Women are more likely to be injured by a family member than they are to be mugged or raped by a stranger or injured in an automobile accident.

Marital rape is a type of spouse abuse that has attracted attention in recent years. Historically, wives were considered the property of their husbands, so a man could not be legally charged with raping his wife. By 1990, however, all but ten states had outlawed rape by husbands, although in some states a marital rape charge is permissible only under specific circumstances such as after legal separation (Russell, 1982; O'Reilly, 1983; Margolick, 1984; Goetting, 1989).

Physically abused women have traditionally had few options. They may want to leave home, but many—especially those with children and without much money—have nowhere to go. Most wives are also committed to their marriages and believe (however unrealistically) that they can help abusive husbands to change. Some, unable to understand their husbands' violence, blame themselves. Others, raised in violent families, expect assault to be part of family life. The trap of family violence is seen in a study finding that one-fourth of

women who had entered a metropolitan hospital after attempting suicide had been reacting to family violence (Stark & Flitcraft, 1979).

In the past, the law regarded domestic violence as a private concern of families. Now, even without separation or divorce, a woman can obtain court protection to ensure that an abusive spouse will be punished. Medical personnel are also more aware today of the telltale signs of spouse violence and are likely to report such cases to police.

Communities across North America are establishing domestic shelters that provide counseling as well as temporary housing for women and children driven from their homes by domestic violence. The first one was established in Pasadena, California, in 1964, and almost a thousand such shelters now exist (although this number is fewer than the 3,000 animal shelters in the United States). Some men and women who abuse their partners are also joining self-help groups in an effort to understand and control their own behavior.

Child Abuse

As an adult, "Kelly" will never be able to forget the sexual abuse she suffered as a child. Her stepfather regularly separated her from other members of the family and, often in a parked car, forced her to have oral sex with him. Her mother was sick at the time, and the stepfather warned "Kelly" that telling of her sexual relationship would cause her mother to die. "I believed him," she recalls. "I thought my mother would die and I would be left with this man" (Watson, 1984).

The vicious nature of child abuse lies in adults' use of power and trust to victimize children. Child abuse is therefore both *physical* and *emotional*, undermining the core of family life. As with spouse abuse, the full extent of child abuse and neglect can only be estimated; it victimizes perhaps 2 million children each year, including several thousand who die as a result (U.S. House of Representatives, 1987). Child abuse is more common among young children—who are most vulnerable—than among teenagers (Straus & Gelles, 1986). Domestic violence against children also causes tens of thousands of them to run away from home every year.

Many abused children do not reveal their suffering to others and grow up believing that they are to blame for their own victimization. The initial abuse, coupled with years of guilt, can leave lasting emotional scars that prevent people abused as children from forming healthy relationships as adults.

About 90 percent of child abusers are men, but they conform to no simple stereotype. As one man who entered a therapy group reported, "I kept waiting for all the guys with raincoats and greasy hair to show up. But everyone looked like regular middle-class people" (Lubenow, 1984). One common trait of abusers, however, is having been abused themselves as children. Researchers have found that violent behavior within close personal relationships is *learned* (Gwartney-Gibbs, Stockard, & Bohmer, 1987). Treatment programs, then, offer legal protection to victims, although their effectiveness in assisting offenders remains unclear.

ALTERNATIVE FAMILY FORMS

In recent decades, American society has embraced greater freedom in family living. While more traditional forms are still preferred by most, marriage and the family now represent a range of legitimate lifestyles.

One-Parent Families

Figure 15–6 indicates that, in 1970, 88.9 percent of families with children under eighteen years of age had two parents in the household. By 1989, this proportion had fallen to 79.1 percent. This statistic reflects a rapid growth of *one-parent families*, which now contain almost one-fifth of all American children. Single parenthood—four times more common among women than among men—may result from divorce, but increasingly it stems from the simple desire on the part of mature women to have a child without marriage. Women's entering the labor force has provided them with the financial independence to become single parents, a choice many make either because they have not found a suitable husband or because they do not wish to marry (Kantrowitz, 1985). Not all single parents are financially secure, however. Estimates suggest that at least one-third of the women in the United States become pregnant as teenagers, and many decide to raise their children (Wallis, 1985). As was shown earlier in Figure 15–2, the proportion of one-parent families is highest among blacks. Among black Americans, 49.8 percent of families had a single parent in 1989, 43.5 percent with a mother only, and 6.3 percent with only a father. Single parenthood was less common among Hispanic families (29.6 percent)

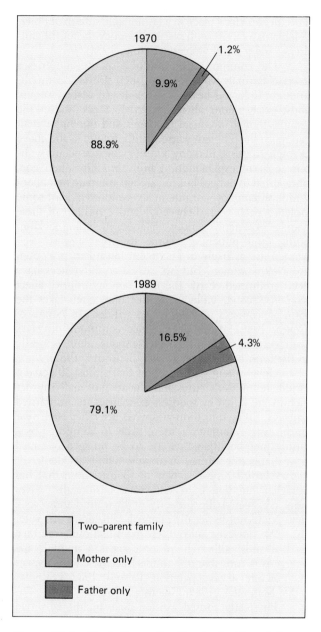

Figure 15–6 Single-Parent Families in the United States, 1970 and 1989

(*U.S. Bureau of the Census*)

and lowest among whites (17.0 percent) (U.S. Bureau of the Census, 1989).

The negative stigma attached to being born out of wedlock has certainly declined. A majority of Americans still believe, however, that a woman should not become pregnant if she does not plan to raise the child with its biological father (Kelley, 1984).

Most research supports the conclusion that growing up in a one-parent family can, but does not necessarily, have negative effects on children. Divorce is stressful for children, and many reveal emotional scars years later (Wallerstein & Blakeslee, 1989). A more common problem among families with one parent—especially if that parent is female—is poverty. This, rather than the absence of a parent, probably results in such children being more likely to become low-income adults, to divorce, and to have children outside of marriage themselves (McLanahan, 1985; Weisner & Eiduson, 1986). Some research suggests, however, that growing up in a single-parent family is linked to lower educational and occupational achievement regardless of economic circumstances (Mueller & Cooper, 1984). Such inconsistent results show the need for continuing research about this emerging family form.

Cohabitation

Cohabitation is *the sharing of a household by an unmarried couple.* A generation ago, terms such as "shacking up" and "living in sin" indicated that cohabitation was widely viewed as deviant. Yet the number of cohabiting couples in the United States has increased sharply, from about 500,000 in 1970 to over 2.5 million by the end of the 1980s. This practice is especially common on college and university campuses, where perhaps one-fourth of students cohabit at some time.

The national impact of cohabiting is unclear. One study of Lane County, Oregon, found that the proportion of married couples who had previously cohabited had increased from about one in eight in 1970 to over one-half by 1980 (Gwartney-Gibbs, 1986). Nationwide, however, most cohabitation does not lead to marriage, and cohabiting couples account for only a small percentage of all households. Although illegal in some states, cohabitation is unquestionably gaining popularity as a way to test a serious relationship while also saving the expense of maintaining a second residence.

Cohabitation does not imply as much commitment

as marriage, and for this reason cohabiting couples rarely have children. One 24-year-old woman who recently married her live-in partner of five years expressed the difference between cohabitation and marriage this way: "For me, [marriage] was deciding to make a real commitment. When we were living together I felt I could walk out at any time" (Clancy & Oberst, 1985). As this example suggests, cohabitation usually lasts only several years; at that point, perhaps 40 percent of couples marry, and the remainder split up (Blumstein & Schwartz, 1983; Macklin, 1983).

Long-term unmarried partners may have an uncertain level of commitment; court decisions, however, suggest that they do gain a claim on each other's property. In other words, as cohabitation has gained in popularity, the legal distinction between this pattern and marriage is no longer as clear.

Finally, cohabitation takes various forms. Although this relational form is most common among younger adults who are sexual partners, many elderly people choose to live together with no sexual motives. For them, cohabitation is a form of economic assistance or a source of companionship.

Gay Male and Lesbian Couples

In 1989, Denmark became the first country to legalize homosexual marriages, thereby extending to gay and lesbian couples legal advantages in inheritance, taxation, and joint property ownership. Danish law, however, does not presently allow such couples to adopt children. In the United States, recent laws in San Francisco, New York, and elsewhere confer some of the legal benefits of marriage on gay male and lesbian couples.

Despite scorn rooted in the heterosexuality of American culture and barriers to legal marriage, many gay men and lesbians form long-term, committed partnerships they themselves honor as marriages and view as the basis of families (Bell, Weinberg, & Kiefer-Hammersmith, 1981). This is especially true of lesbian couples, who are more likely than gay male couples to remain sexually exclusive (Blumstein & Schwartz, 1983).

Like heterosexual couples, gays and lesbians enter relationships with romantic ideals and then adjust to day-to-day realities; they share the strains of financial and household responsibilities; also they must deal with conventional cultural values that favor masculine attributes more than feminine traits. Some homosexual cou-

On October 1, 1989, Denmark became the first society to permit gay people to marry. Here, the first Danish couple to formalize their relationship celebrates at Copenhagen's city hall.

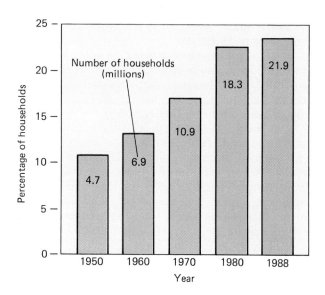

Figure 15–7 Single Adults in the United States, 1950–1988
(*U.S. Bureau of the Census*)

ples also raise children, usually from previous heterosexual relationships; artificial insemination, however, has given women the option to have children without a male partner.

Many gay men and lesbians still feel compelled to keep their relationships secret—even from other family members—to minimize prejudice and discrimination. Partners must therefore turn to each other for all the emotional, spiritual, and material support that heterosexual couples can find elsewhere. The strains placed on any relationship are obviously great in such a situation. Yet, despite these disadvantages, many partnerships between lesbians and between gay men are strong, resilient, and long-lasting.

Singlehood

Because nine out of ten Americans marry, singlehood is often seen as simply a stage prior to marriage. In recent decades, however, more Americans have deliberately chosen the freedom and independence of living alone, remaining both single and childless.

This increase is shown in Figure 15–7. In 1950 only about one household in ten contained a single person. By 1988 this proportion was approaching one

in four: a total of 22 million single adults. Most will marry at some point in their lives, but an increasing number will deliberately choose to remain single.

Perhaps the greatest change in marital status is evident among young women. In 1960 only 28 percent of women aged twenty to twenty-four were single; by 1988 the proportion had soared to 61 percent. The key to this trend is greater participation in the labor force: women who are economically secure view a husband as a matter of choice rather than a financial necessity.

By midlife, however, women confront a lack of available men. Because our culture discourages women from marrying partners much younger than they are (while encouraging men to do so), middle-aged women who do wish to marry find the odds rising against them. In 1986, there were 133 unmarried women aged forty to forty-four for every 100 unmarried men (U.S. Bureau of the Census, 1989).

NEW REPRODUCTIVE TECHNOLOGY AND THE FAMILY

Recent medical advances generally referred to as *new reproductive technology* have had a direct impact on many families. In the future, this technology promises not only widespread benefits, but difficult ethical problems surrounding the creation and manipulation of life itself.

In Vitro Fertilization

An English teenager, Louise Brown, has the distinction of being the world's first "test-tube" baby. In the fifteen years since her birth, thousands of people have been conceived in this way. Early in the next century, 2 or 3 percent of the population of industrial societies may be the result of "new birth technologies" (Vines, 1986; Ostling, 1987).

Test-tube babies are, technically speaking, the result of the process of *in vitro fertilization*: a union of the male sperm and the female ovum occurs "in glass" rather than in a woman's body. In this complex medical procedure, drugs are often used to stimulate the production of more than one egg in each ovary during a woman's reproductive cycle. Then eggs are surgically "harvested" from the ovaries and combined with sperm in a laboratory dish. The successful fusion of eggs and sperm produces embryos, which are placed in the womb of the woman who is to bear the child. The embryos may be placed immediately or may be frozen for use at a later time.

The benefits of *in vitro* fertilization are twofold. First, about one in five couples who cannot conceive children normally can be helped through this process. Second, looking to the future, many medical experts believe that new birth technologies have the potential to reduce the incidence of birth defects. In other words, by genetically screening sperm and eggs, medical specialists can reasonably predict that the baby will be born healthy (Vines, 1986).

Ethical Issues

New reproductive technology has sparked heated debate. Simply put, medical technology now provides control over life itself that would have been unthinkable only a few decades ago. The result is a classic example of "cultural lag" (see Chapter 3, "Culture"), in which society has to catch up to the moral implications of this new power.

One problem is that, as with most technological advance, benefits are expensive and available only to those who can afford them. A cost exceeding $5,000 for a single attempt at *in vitro* fertilization ensures that only a minority of Americans can even consider this procedure. A second problem is that this technology currently allows medical experts to define what constitutes a proper "family." In most cases, *in vitro* fertilization has been made available only to women who are under forty years of age and are part of a heterosexual couple. Single women, older women, and lesbian couples have so far been excluded from the opportunity.

A third ethical problem concerns *surrogate motherhood*, since this technology allows one woman to bear a child for another. Surrogate motherhood can take one of two forms. In the first type, the ovum and sperm produced by a couple are joined, and the embryo that is formed is implanted into the body of another woman, who gives birth to the child. Such a practice means a woman unable to carry a baby to term can let a second woman—her surrogate—give birth to a child that is the biological offspring of her husband and herself. In the second type, a woman and a couple agree that the woman will bear a child for the couple by having her own ovum artificially fertilized by the man's sperm.

Both types of surrogate motherhood raise difficult issues about who a baby's parents are. In some situations, lengthy and emotionally wrenching legal battles have been needed to resolve parenthood. Until society generates moral and legal standards to clarify such cases, surrogate motherhood will remain highly controversial.

An outspoken party in controversies surrounding new reproductive technologies is the Catholic Church. The Church has condemned all new reproductive technology as reducing human life to a manipulated object, as the box on page 420 explains.

THE FAMILY IN THE TWENTY-FIRST CENTURY

American family life has changed dramatically in recent decades, and new reproductive technology may cause even greater change in the future. This possibility has led some to wonder if the family may eventually disappear entirely. Controversy also continues between advocates of traditional family values and proponents of new family forms and greater personal choice (Berger & Berger, 1983).

This chapter suggests four general conclusions about the family as we look ahead to the next century. First, the traditional view that marriage lasts "till death do us part" is no longer realistic. Divorce terminates as many marriages today as death. Although the divorce

Are New Reproductive Technologies Immoral?
The Catholic Church's View

Americans tend to believe that technological advances will benefit humanity. New reproductive technologies, including *in vitro* fertilization and genetic research, have been defended because they allow more women who want children to conceive, and they promise to drastically reduce birth defects.

The Catholic Church has recently condemned all such practices. No child, a recent report concludes, should be "conceived as the product of an intervention of medical or biological techniques." Instead of serving humanity, the Church claims, such techniques treat human life as nothing more than an object of research. According to the Church, Nazi genetic experiments of the 1930s and 1940s show that new reproductive technologies may well be used to produce genetic "superhumans."

Although many scientists claim that such research can produce useful results, the Church counters that results can never justify manipulation of an embryo—a human life—in a laboratory. The Church has strong political support in this controversy; half the states in the United States currently restrict such practices, as do many European countries.

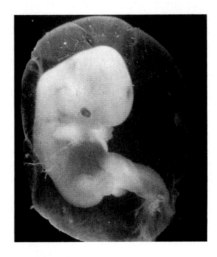

Less popular is the Church's opposition to new reproductive technologies that assist infertile couples wishing to have children. *In vitro* fertilization, the Church maintains, separates the act of procreation from the loving union of two parents. Catholics will recognize this argument as an extension of the Church's long-time prohibition of artificial contraception. Once separated from human sexuality, reproduction is in danger of becoming a business rather than a family concern.

Many people, including Catholics, are unwilling to accept sexual intercourse between husband and wife as the only moral means to conceive children. Since certain loving couples cannot conceive in this way, they argue, artificial insemination (in which a husband's sperm is used to fertilize an ovum directly in the wife's womb) or *in vitro* fertilization have obvious value. Moreover, critics complain that this prohibition strikes hardest at Catholics who accept the Church's view that Catholic families are incomplete without children.

Many Catholics will ignore the Church's recent pronouncements, just as many have overlooked prohibitions against artificial birth control in the past. But few people—whether Catholics or not—can easily dismiss the Church's concern that what is technologically possible may not always be morally desirable.

SOURCE: Based on Congregation for the Doctrine of the Faith, *Instruction on Respect for Human Life in Its Origin and on the Dignity of Procreation: Replies to Certain Questions of the Day* (Vatican City, 1987); also Richard N. Ostling, "Technology and the Womb," *Time*, Vol. 129, No. 12 (March 23, 1987):58–59; and Kenneth L. Woodward, "Rules for Making Love and Babies," *Newsweek*, Vol. 109, No. 12 (March 23, 1987):42–43.

rate stabilized in the 1980s, it is unlikely that marriage will regain the durability characteristic of the 1950s. Because increasing numbers of women are able to support themselves, a traditional marriage appeals to fewer of them. Men, too, are beginning to embrace change. The higher divorce rate of the last several decades, however, may signify a transformation of marriage rather than an end. Most divorces still lead to remarriage, suggesting

that marriage is hardly discredited in Americans' eyes. As women's and men's roles change, new forms of family life will emerge that may prove more stable and more satisfying.

The second conclusion is that family life in the twenty-first century will be highly variable. We have noted an increasing number of cohabiting couples, one-parent families, and blended families created from remarriage after divorce. Each type of family arrangement is accompanied by problems as well as satisfactions. Some alternatives, such as singlehood and childless marriage, are unlikely to be chosen by a majority of the population. Taken together, however, they represent a growing conception of family life as a matter of choice.

The third conclusion is a declining importance of American men in childrearing. Certainly many fathers today are becoming more involved in the rearing of their children, but the increasing number of women raising children outside of marriage, because of either divorce or single motherhood, means that more and more American children are growing up without social ties to their fathers. Most research suggests that the absence of fathers is not directly and significantly detrimental to children, but there is little doubt that the absence of husbands and fathers from families is a factor in the feminization of poverty in American society.

Fourth, and finally, new reproductive technology will shape families of the twenty-first century. Perhaps opposition will greatly limit such developments. More likely, however, new forms of reproduction will alter traditional meanings of parenthood. At the very least, new technology will direct a continued focus on American family life.

Despite social changes that have buffeted the American family, most Americans still report being happy as partners and as parents (Cherlin & Furstenberg, 1983). Marriage and family life may now be more socially controversial, but they are likely to remain the foundation of our society for some time to come.

SUMMARY

1. Societies are built on kinship; in industrial societies, the family is composed of close relatives. Family forms vary considerably across cultures, as they have across history.

2. Nuclear families have historically predominated in American society. As in other industrial societies, marriage in the United States is monogamous. Most preindustrial societies, however, allow polygamy, of which there are two types: polygyny and polyandry.

3. Cross-culturally, families differ in residential patterns. Industrial societies favor neolocality; patrilocality is more common throughout the world, and a few cultures have matrilocal households. Industrial societies recognize bilateral descent, while preindustrial societies tend to be either patrilineal or matrilineal.

4. Structural-functional analysis points to four major functions of the family: socialization of the young, regulation of sexual activity, social placement, and provision of emotional support.

5. Social-conflict theory draws attention to how the family perpetuates social inequality by strengthening social classes, ethnic and racial divisions, and gender distinctions.

6. Symbolic-interaction analysis highlights the dynamic nature of family life. Family life is changeable and experienced differently by various family members.

7. Families begin with the process of courtship. Unlike the United States, most societies limit the role of romantic love in the choice of a mate. Even among Americans, romantic love tends to join people with similar social backgrounds.

8. The reality of marriage often diverges from the cultural ideal. Spouses frequently discover that they have much to learn about each other as well as about married life. A majority of married men and a large minority of married women engage in sexual infidelity, although this is still a violation of cultural norms.

9. The vast majority of married couples have children, although family size has decreased over time. Industrialization has led to the transformation of children into economic liabilities, more women joining the labor force, and a reduction in infant mortality.

10. In later life, marriage changes as children leave home to form families of their own. Retirement may affect the relationship between spouses. The final stage of marriage begins with the death of one spouse, usually the husband.

11. Social class shapes family life by providing some families with more options and financial security than others.

12. Hispanics often maintain extended families and adhere to more conventional gender roles. Black

families are three times more likely to be headed by women than white families; thus, two-thirds of first children are born to black women who are unmarried. Many black families contend with poverty through extended kinship and network systems of economic support.

13. Gender affects family dynamics. Husbands continue to dominate the vast majority of families. Research suggests that marriage provides more benefits to men than to women.

14. The divorce rate today is ten times what it was a century ago; almost one-half of current marriages will end in divorce. Most people who divorce—especially men—remarry. Remarriage can create blended families that include children from previous marriages.

15. Family violence emerged as a major public issue in the 1980s. Both spouse abuse and child abuse are more widespread than is commonly recognized. Commonly, adults who abuse family members were themselves abused as children.

16. American family life has become increasingly varied. Cohabitation and one-parent families have proliferated in recent years. Gay men and lesbians cannot legally marry, but typically they form long-lasting relationships. Singlehood is also increasingly common. For many a matter of choice, singlehood—especially of older women—also reflects the lack of available men.

17. Present research suggests that divorce will continue to end close to half of all marriages, family life will continue to take many diverse forms, new reproductive technology may alter patterns of parenting, and fathers will have less importance in childrearing because of their absence from many families.

KEY CONCEPTS

bilateral descent a system tracing kinship through both males and females

cohabitation the sharing of a household by an unmarried couple

descent the system by which kinship is traced over generations

endogamy marriage between people of the same social group or category

exogamy marriage between people of different social groups or categories

extended family (consanguine family) a social unit including parents, children, and other kin

family a relatively permanent social group of two or more people, who are related by blood, marriage, or adoption and who usually live together

family of orientation the family into which a person is born and receives early socialization

family of procreation a family within which people have or adopt children of their own

family violence emotional, physical, or sexual abuse of one family member by another

homogamy marriage between people with the same social characteristics

incest taboo a cultural norm forbidding sexual relations or marriage between certain kin

kinship social relationships based on blood, marriage, or adoption

marriage a socially approved relationship, involving economic cooperation and allowing sexual activity leading to childbearing, that is expected to be relatively enduring

matrilineal descent a system tracing kinship through females

matrilocality a residential pattern in which a married couple lives with or near the wife's family

monogamy a form of marriage that joins one male and one female

neolocality a residential pattern in which a married couple lives apart from the parents of both spouses

nuclear family (conjugal family) a social unit composed of one or, more commonly, two parents and children

patrilineal descent a system tracing kinship through males

patrilocality a residential pattern in which a married couple lives with or near the husband's family

polyandry a form of marriage that joins one female with more than one male

polygamy a form of marriage that unites three or more people

polygyny a form of marriage that joins one male with more than one female

SUGGESTED READINGS

This textbook offers a detailed look at marriage and the family.

Gerald R. Leslie and Sheila K. Korman. *The Family in Social Context*. 7th ed. New York: Oxford University Press, 1989.

This book explores American families in historical context and challenges the notion that families are disappearing from American society.

Edward L. Kain. *The Myth of Family Decline: Understanding Families in a World of Rapid Social Change*. Lexington, MA: Lexington Books, 1990.

Two-career marriages are becoming increasingly common in American society. The first book argues that economic power is strongly related to domestic power. The second is a fascinating account of marriages in which women have more economic power than their husbands.

Rosanna Hertz. *More Equal Than Others: Women and Men in Dual-Career Marriages*. Berkeley: University of California Press, 1986.

Susan McRae. *Cross-Class Families: A Study of Wives' Occupational Superiority*. New York: Oxford University Press, 1986.

This collection consists of cross-cultural essays on childbearing and family life.

W. Penn Handwerker, ed. *Births and Power: The Politics of Reproduction*. Boulder, CO: Westview Press, 1989.

How does family life evolve among partners of different religious backgrounds?

Susan Weidman Schneider. *Intermarriage: The Challenge of Living with Differences between Christians and Jews*. New York: The Free Press, 1989.

The first book is one of the most influential studies of the history of the black family in America. The second is a collection of essays on the current state of black families.

Herbert G. Gutman. *The Black Family in Slavery and Freedom: 1750–1925*. New York: Pantheon Books, 1976.

Harold E. Cheatham and James B. Stewart, eds. *Black Families: Interdisciplinary Perspectives*. New Brunswick, NJ: Transaction Books, 1989.

How much does having a child change your life? The first book explores the consequences of pregnancy and childrearing for thirty working women. The second book presents the experience of parenting from a father's point of view.

Constance S. Pond. . . . *And Along Comes Baby: What Happens When the Working Woman Becomes Pregnant*. Lanham, MD: University Press of America, 1986.

Charlie Lewis. *Becoming a Father*. Philadelphia: Open University Press, 1986.

Based on interviews with one hundred families, this book explores an increasingly common family transition.

Anne C. Bernstein. *Yours, Mine, and Ours: How Families Change When Remarried Parents Have a Child Together*. New York: Charles Scribner's Sons, 1989.

One consequence of the "graying of America" is that more people have the experience of being grandparents. This is among the first pieces of research on this topic of growing importance.

Andrew J. Cherlin and Frank F. Furstenberg, Jr. *The New American Grandparent: A Place in the Family, A Life Apart*. New York: Basic Books, 1986.

The first of these two books examines recent changes in divorce law in the United States; the second reports on a decade-long study of divorced couples and their children.

Herbert Jacob. *Silent Revolution: The Transformation of Divorce Law in the United States*. Chicago: University of Chicago Press, 1988.

Judith S. Wallerstein and Sandra Blakeslee. *Second Chances: Men, Women, and Children a Decade after Divorce*. New York: Ticknor & Fields, 1989.

A source of information about child abuse is this report of a recent Congressional investigation.

U.S. House of Representatives. *Hearing before the Select Committee on Children, Youth, and Families*. May 16, 1989. Washington, DC: U.S. Government Printing Office, 1989.

16
Education

Thirteen-year-old Naoko Masuo has just returned from school to her home in a suburb of Yokohama, Japan. She does not drop off her books and head off for an afternoon of fun, as is common in the United States. Instead, she immediately settles into her homework. Within several hours, her mother reminds her that her schooling for the day is not over, and she gathers her books and departs for the *juku* or "cram school" that she attends for three hours three afternoons a week. Mother and daughter travel four stops on the subway to downtown Yokohama and climb to the second floor of an office building where Naoko joins dozens of other girls and boys for intensive training in Japanese, English, math, and science. Tuition at the *juku* costs the Masuo family several hundred dollars a month. They realize, however, that the realities of the Japanese educational system make such an investment in extra schooling a necessity.

Naoko will soon take a national examination for children her age for placement in one of the many schools that are ranked by student ability. The better the test score, the better the school. Three years later, another hurdle—the high-school examination—will, once again, determine the quality of Naoko's formal education. Then will come the chance to earn the final prize: about one-third of Japanese students who perform best on the college entrance examination are admitted to an exclusive national university.

In Japan, admission to elite universities virtually ensures that students will have high-paying, prestigious careers. Those who do not attend college will learn to settle for less. The Masuo family believes, therefore, that one cannot work too hard or begin too early in preparation for university admission (Simons, 1989).

Education has become increasingly valuable in Japan's complex and changing society, as it has in other industrial nations. **Education** refers to *the various ways*

425

in which knowledge—including factual information and skills as well as cultural norms and values—is transmitted to members of society. Within industrial societies, a vital kind of education is **schooling**—*formal instruction under the direction of specially trained teachers.* Schooling or formal education is one of the major social institutions in industrial societies.

EDUCATION IN CROSS-CULTURAL PERSPECTIVE

Like the Japanese, Americans live in a technologically advanced society and expect that children will spend much of their first eighteen years of life in school. Only a century ago, however, American schooling was a privilege restricted to a small elite. In Third World societies, even today the vast majority of people receive little or no schooling.

Chapter 4 ("Society") explained that most of human history has occurred in technologically simple hunting and gathering societies. The family was the central

Early in the twentieth century, mandatory education laws had been passed by every state. For the half of Americans who lived in rural areas, formal education meant the one-room schoolhouse, where children received a basic education from one teacher.

social institution; just as there were no governments or churches, so there was no formal system of schooling. Necessary knowledge and skills were simply taught to children by adults (Lenski & Lenski, 1987).

In more technologically complex agrarian societies—common in much of the world today—some people teach others specialized crafts and trading skills. Schooling not directly linked to the world of work is generally available only to wealthy people: the English word *school* is, in fact, derived from a Greek word for "leisure." In ancient Greece, renowned teachers such as Socrates, Plato, and Aristotle instructed aristocratic males in philosophy and science. In ancient China, the famous philosopher Confucius also taught a privileged few (Rohlen, 1983).

During the Middle Ages, the church expanded schooling by establishing the first colleges and universities (Ballantine, 1983). Until the Industrial Revolution, however, schooling remained mainly a privilege of the ruling elites in both Western Europe and North America.

The United States was among the first nations to embrace the principle of mass education. Schooling was partly a means to forge a literate citizenry able to participate in political life. Industrialization also demanded that the labor force have at least basic skills of reading, writing, and arithmetic. In the twentieth century the steady growth of bureaucracy signaled an economy based on paperwork more than on machines, so schooling became all the more important.

In 1850 only about half of Americans between the ages of five and nineteen were enrolled in school. By 1918, however, every state had **mandatory education laws**—*legal requirements that children receive a minimum of formal education* (typically to the age of sixteen or completion of the eighth grade). These laws changed the social roles of children: they left farms and factories for classrooms in schools across the country. Table 16–1 shows that by the mid-1960s, a majority of adults had completed high school. Today over 75 percent of American adults have a high-school education and 20 percent have completed four years of college.

Today, only a very small proportion of Americans are officially classified as illiterate. Illiteracy rates are similarly low in other industrial societies, including Japan, Great Britain, and the Soviet Union. In agrarian societies, however, *most* people neither read nor write. The reason, as Chapter 11 ("Global Inequality") explained, is that agrarian societies are terribly poor, with only about 5 percent of the family income enjoyed by Americans. Faced with the need simply to survive, people

Table 16–1 EDUCATIONAL ACHIEVEMENT IN THE UNITED STATES, 1910–1988*

Year	High-School Graduates	College Graduates	Median Years of Schooling
1910	13.5%	2.7%	8.1
1920	16.4	3.3	8.2
1930	19.1	3.9	8.4
1940	24.1	4.6	8.6
1950	33.4	6.0	9.3
1960	41.1	7.7	10.5
1970	55.2	11.0	12.2
1980	68.7	17.0	12.5
1988	76.2	20.3	12.7

SOURCE: National Center for Education Statistics, 1989.

* For persons twenty-five years of age and over.

in the Third World have few resources for providing educational opportunities. Except for a small number of schools that cater to privileged elites, whatever schooling does exist is of low quality, so children learn less than their peers in richer societies (Hayneman & Loxley, 1983).

Yet, striking educational successes have occurred. Before the 1960 revolution that brought the Castro regime to power, schooling in Cuba was limited to a small upper class. Despite making little progress to reduce the poverty of its people, Cuba has made a determined effort to provide some formal education to everyone and claims now to have virtually eliminated illiteracy. Such cases suggest that educational achievement is possible even in poor societies if the government defines it as a high social priority.

Industrial societies provide extensive schooling for their people, but each does so in a distinctive way, as the following brief descriptions of schooling in Japan, Great Britain, and the Soviet Union will show.

Schooling in Japan

Until the enactment of mandatory education laws in 1872, schooling in Japan was limited to the privileged few. Although Japanese society has been influenced by China, Western Europe, and the United States (which occupied Japan after World War II), Japan's educational system remains unique (Rohlen, 1983).

In the early grades, schools foster Japanese cultural

values of tradition and obligation to family (Benedict, 1974). Then, in their early teens, students encounter Japan's system of rigorous and competitive examinations. These written tests, which are believed to reward ability and hard work, resemble the Scholastic Aptitude Tests (SATs) used for college admissions in the United States. In American society, however, even students with low test scores can expect to be admitted to some college, especially if their families can afford tuition costs. In Japan, by contrast, test scores literally make or break the college aspirations of young people, rich and poor alike.

More Japanese (about 90 percent) graduate from high school than do Americans (about 76 percent). The system of competitive examinations steadily reduces the college-bound population of Japanese youths, so only about 30 percent of high-school graduates go on to college—half the figure for Americans (Simons, 1989). Understandably, then, Japanese students face entrance examinations with the utmost seriousness. Faced with this stiff competition, almost half of Japanese students attend *juku* "cram schools."

Since acceptance or rejection by a university shapes a lifetime career, Japanese mothers—far less likely than American women to be in the labor force—often devote themselves to their children's success at school (Simons, 1989). They direct special encouragement and support to sons more than to daughters (Brinton, 1988). Parents and children alike anxiously await the results of university examinations; for the Japanese public, the suspense has become something of a national pastime, as the box on page 428 explains.

Although the Japanese educational system places almost unbearable pressure on adolescents, it produces impressive results. In a number of academic areas, notably mathematics and science, Japanese students outdistance students of every other industrial society, including the United States (Hayneman & Loxley, 1983; Rohlen, 1983). Japanese cultural traditions of hard work and loyalty to family, as well as the highly competitive examination system, strongly motivate Japanese students to learn.

Schooling in Great Britain

As was noted in Chapter 9 ("Social Stratification"), the legacy of Great Britain's feudal past is evident in British society today. During the Middle Ages, schooling was a privilege of the nobility, who studied classical subjects, since they had little need for the practical skills related

University Entrance Exams: A Japanese Obsession

Pick up any of Japan's national news magazines in February and March and you will find university examinations to be lead stories, surpassing in popular interest for the moment even political scandals, economic problems, and gossip about movie stars. From the end of New Year festivities to the beginning of the new school year in April, an inordinate amount of attention is given to the trials and tribulations of the three-quarters of a million adolescents hoping to enter university. What makes this 1 percent of the population so fascinating is that their individual destinies are being shaped to a remarkable extent by just a few hours of test taking. The competition is severe and the preparations are grueling.

Ominous labels have been coined to express this concern. It is the time of the "examination hell" (*juken jigoku*). Students are enlistees in an "examination war" (*juken senso*). Twelve years of schooling culminate in this moment, which is a crucial turning point in the life cycle of most Japanese. Like other such moments, the whole nation undergoes the experience vicariously each year.

It is midnight. Families, friends, and even interested observers stand shivering in the cold on some campus waiting for the university officials to post the names of the successful candidates for admission on large, flood-lit bulletin boards. There is much nervous

chatter, and the sense of excitement is heightened by the fact that so many are braving the cold just to learn the results as soon as possible. The lists begin to go up. Flash bulbs pop, journalists scurry around, the people stand on tiptoe to search for names they know. Shouts of happy surprise are heard. Others remain intently searching, and some turn and silently disappear from the scene. . . .

SOURCE: Thomas P. Rohlen, *Japan's High Schools* (Berkeley: University of California Press, 1983), pp. 77–78.

---

to earning a living. Those in schools and colleges, then, usually shared much the same privileged background.

As the Industrial Revolution created the need for an educated labor force, schooling included an increasing proportion of the British people. The working class also successfully demanded that the British educational system be opened to their children. As a result, every British child is now required by law to attend school until age sixteen.

Yet, traditional social distinctions persist in British education. Many wealthy families send their children to what the British call *public schools*, the equivalent of American private boarding schools. Since public schools are beyond their financial reach, most British parents send their children to state-supported day schools, just as most families in the United States do. Elite public schools in Britain do more than teach academic subjects; they also socialize children from wealthy families into a distinctive way of life. Patterns of speech, mannerisms, and social graces are learned and thereby distinguish members of the upper class from other Britons.

The 1960s and 1970s saw a marked expansion in the British university system (Sampson, 1982). Today British children compete to enter universities by taking

examinations during their high-school years. In contrast to the United States, in Britain the government generally pays tuition and living expenses of those who are successful. Compared with the Japanese system, examinations are less significant in Britain, and social background plays a greater role. Thus a disproportionate number of well-to-do children attend Oxford and Cambridge, the British universities with the highest social prestige (roughly comparable to Yale, Harvard, and Princeton in the United States). Graduates of "Oxbridge" form a national elite with considerable power in business and government. For example, seventeen of the twenty-one members of Prime Minister Margaret Thatcher's first cabinet were graduates of Oxford or Cambridge, and all twenty-one had attended elite public schools (Pfaff, 1980).

Schooling in the Soviet Union

Before the socialist revolution of 1917, Russia was an agrarian society with schooling reserved primarily for nobles. In the 1930s the Soviet Union adopted mandatory education laws. In the next two decades political unrest and the costs and social disruption of World War II slowed educational programs; even so, by the end of the 1940s half of the young people in the Soviet Union were in school. In forging a national educational system, the Soviets have long contended with striking cultural diversity in the physically largest country in the world. By 1975 the Soviets finally boasted of having achieved nearly universal schooling (Ballantine, 1983; Matthews, 1983).

According to official Soviet policy, children of both sexes and every ethnic background have equal educational opportunity. Although access to higher education is roughly the same for women as for men, Soviet women are overly represented in those areas of study (such as education and medicine) with relatively low social prestige in that society, while men dominate in higher-prestige studies (such as agriculture and engineering). Similarly, although considerable strides have been made toward providing equal access to higher education for diverse ethnic groups, some (notably the Russian majority) still fare better than others (Avis, 1983).

Soviet schooling, like that in every society, reflects and reinforces important cultural values. Besides helping the country become an industrial power, Soviet education has important political purposes. Although changing as a result of *perestroika* (see Chapters 18 and 19), the Soviet educational system remains highly standardized under the direction of the central government, and therefore schools can be used to teach norms and values of socialist living (Matthews, 1983; Tomiak, 1983). Like the Japanese and the British, the Soviets employ competitive examinations to admit the most academically able students to higher education. The support of Communist party officials, however, also plays an important part in a student's educational opportunities (Ballantine, 1983).

As Chapter 9 ("Social Stratification") notes, Soviet society has less disparity of wealth than does the United States. Furthermore, the government pays most educational costs. This economic parity creates more equal educational opportunity among young people in the Soviet Union than among their American counterparts. Nevertheless, many children of families with high positions in the Communist party attend schools that offer general academic training, while children from less privileged backgrounds tend to enroll in vocational schools geared to careers in various trades. As in the United States, too, children receiving the most privileged educations tend to have the greatest opportunities later on (Avis, 1983; Matthews, 1983).

This brief comparison suggests ways in which schooling is shaped by the larger society. Societies generally adopt mandatory education laws as a consequence of industrialization. Also the operation of the educational system usually enhances cultural patterns (such as the achievement orientation and intense competition of the Japanese educational system), historical forces (such as traditional patterns of social inequality in Great Britain), and the character of the political system (such as the socialist education of the Soviet Union).

Schooling in the United States

The American educational system has also been shaped by distinctive cultural patterns. Compared with our mother country, Great Britain, the United States has a stronger tradition of widespread political participation. Such democratic ideals demand formal education so that, as Thomas Jefferson commented, the American people can "read and understand what is going on in the world" (cited in Honeywell, 1931:13). In practice, political rights were long restricted to white males and, even today, are not extended equally to women, gay people, and other minorities. However imperfectly the application of its democratic ideals, the United States has long had a larger proportion of its people attending colleges and universities than any other industrial society (Rubinson, 1986).

Schooling is a means of teaching the values and attitudes that a society deems important. Groups such as the "Young Pioneers" in the People's Republic of China meet after school to advance the political goals of socialism; the Boy Scouts and Girl Scouts represent comparable groups in the United States that teach their members our political beliefs.

Formal education in the United States is shaped by the cultural value of *equal opportunity*. National surveys show that the vast majority of Americans view schooling as crucial to personal success (Gallup, 1982). Consider that only eight of the forty men who have served as president of the United States did not graduate from college; this has been true of only four presidents since the Civil War and only one in this century (Harry Truman).

Americans also believe that our society offers extensive educational opportunity: various surveys show that 70 percent endorse the notion that people have the chance to get an education consistent with their abilities and talents, whereas only 30 percent disagree (N.O.R.C., 1989:120). The historical record is less favorable: women were effectively excluded from higher education until this century, and even today only among the higher social classes do a majority of young people attend college. More than a century ago, however, the United States initiated a policy of universal primary and secondary schooling financed by public taxes. Since then, an increasing amount of public funds have supported state colleges and universities as well. Such expenditures are made in pursuit of the ideal that all Americans should have the opportunity to achieve as much as their individual talents and efforts allow.

The cultural value of *practicality* means that American schools tend to emphasize studies that have a direct bearing on people's lives, and especially their occupations. The noted educational philosopher John Dewey (1859–1952) was probably the foremost advocate of the idea that schooling should have practical consequences. Rejecting the traditionalist emphasis on teaching a fixed body of knowledge to each generation of students, Dewey (1968; orig. 1938) endorsed *progressive education* that reflected people's changing concerns and needs.

George Herbert Mead, the architect of the symbolic-interaction paradigm in sociology and Dewey's friend, echoed these sentiments, claiming that "any education that is worthy of the name [provides] the solution to problems that we all carry with us" (1938:52). Mead further claimed that "whatever is stored up, without immediate need, for later occasion, for display, or to pass examinations is mere information [with] no enduring place in the mind" (1906:395). Reflecting this practical emphasis, today's college students select major areas of study with an eye toward future jobs. Figure 16–1 shows recent trends; note especially the rapid growth during the 1980s in the study of computer science, a consequence of America's high-tech revolution.

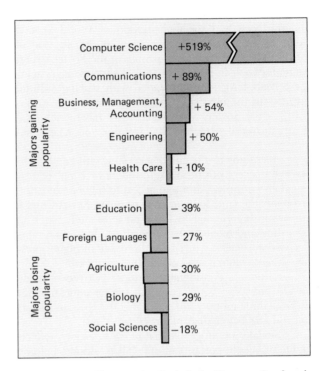

Figure 16–1   Changes in Bachelor's Degrees Conferred, 1986–1987 Compared with 1976–1977

(National Center for Education Statistics, 1979, 1989)

THE FUNCTIONS OF SCHOOLING

Structural-functional analysis directs attention to the ways in which formal education enhances the integration and stability of society. As a source of socialization, formal education helps to maintain social organization.

Socialization

Every society uses various means to transmit its way of life from one generation to the next. In technologically simple societies, the family assumes this transmission function. As societies become more technologically complex, numerous social institutions emerge to play a part in the socialization process. Within industrial societies, the family can no longer teach all that young people are required to know. Formal education, making use of specially trained personnel, is an efficient means of conveying a wide range of specialized knowledge.

Primary school begins this process, teaching children the basic language and mathematical skills that are indispensable in later life. Secondary school steadily expands this learning; for some, college continues this process. Because industrial societies change rapidly, formal education teaches students not only information (which may become obsolete), but also how to learn so that they will be able to adapt to future changes.

Schools transmit cultural values and norms as well. Civics classes, for example, explicitly instruct students in the American way of life. Important cultural lessons are also learned in subtle ways—sometimes by how the classroom itself operates. Teachers often encourage competition among students with questions such as "Who can solve this math problem?" One child's success is often at the expense of another child: the box illustrates how children learn early the cultural importance of competition.

Schools also teach cultural norms by demanding punctuality, respect for school officials, and obedience to rules. Athletic programs, too, are lessons in the values of competition and personal achievement, and also in the norms of fair play.

Formal education also has a political component. It has already been noted that Soviet formal education is a means to teach socialist principles to the young. Although American political values are different, the same process occurs in American schools. The advantages of political democracy and a free-market economy are commonly explained in the classroom, while rituals such as saluting the flag and singing "The Star-Spangled Banner" foster patriotism.

Social Integration

Schooling helps to forge a mass of people into a unified society through teaching of approved values and norms. This function is especially important in societies containing many diverse cultures, who often are indifferent or even hostile to each other. The Soviet Union contains dozens of ethnic categories, and many societies in Africa contain hundreds of culturally distinct peoples. By establishing a common language, schooling encourages broader communication and forges a national identity. Of course, some ethnic minorities resist school for exactly this reason. In the Soviet Union, for example, Lithuanians, Ukrainians, Azerbaijanis, and others have protested having to learn the Russian language, which they see as undermining their distinctive cultural traditions.

The integration function of schooling is also important in the United States, where immigration has introduced striking cultural diversity. Mandatory education laws were established in the United States a century ago with the arrival of millions of immigrants. The integrative function of formal education continues today, as people from Latin America and Asia blend their traditions with existing American culture. By the mid-1980s a majority of students in many of the largest school districts in the United States were members of racial and ethnic minority groups, and this proportion will increase in the future (Boyer, 1984).

SOCIOLOGY OF EVERYDAY LIFE

In the Classroom: A Lesson in American Culture

Boris had trouble reducing "12/16" to the lowest terms, and could only get as far as "6/8." The teacher asked him quietly if that was as far as he could reduce it. She suggested he "think." Much heaving up and down and waving of hands by the other children, all frantic to correct him left Boris pretty unhappy, probably mentally paralyzed. The teacher, quiet, patient, ignores the others and concentrates with look and voice on Boris. She says, "Is there a bigger number that you can divide into the two parts of the fraction?" After a minute or two, she becomes more urgent, but there is no response from Boris. She then turns to the class and says, "Well, who can tell Boris what the number is?" A forest of hands appears, and the teacher calls on Peggy. Peggy says that 4 may be divided into the numerator and the denominator.

SOURCE: Jules Henry, *Culture Against Man* (New York: Vintage Books, 1963), pp. 295–296.

Social Placement

Formal education channels young people into culturally approved statuses and roles that contribute to the ongoing life of society. Schooling is thus a screening and selection process that identifies and develops people's various aptitudes and abilities. Schools begin this process by evaluating students' performance primarily in terms of achievement rather than social background. Ideally, the "best and the brightest" are encouraged to pursue the most challenging and advanced studies, while students of modest abilities are guided into educational programs and occupations suited to their talents. Schooling, then, enhances meritocracy, linking social position to personal merit.

This screening and selection process has special significance to people who begin life with social disadvantages based on ascribed traits such as sex, race, ethnicity, and social class. Formal education has historically been a major avenue of upward social mobility in American society (Hurn, 1978).

Cultural Innovation

Educational systems create as well as transmit culture. Schools stimulate intellectual inquiry and critical thinking leading to the development of new ideas.

Today, for example, many college professors not only teach but engage in research that leads to discoveries and innovations. Research in the humanities, the social sciences, and the natural sciences is changing attitudes and patterns of life throughout American society. Medical research, carried on mainly in major universities, has helped to increase dramatically the life expectancy of Americans, and research by sociologists and psychologists has helped us to take advantage of this longevity.

Latent Functions of Schooling

In addition to these purposeful, manifest functions of formal education are latent functions that are not so obvious and are less widely recognized. One is child care. Schools serve the rising number of one-parent families and two-career marriages by relieving parents of some child-care duties. Among teenagers too, schooling consumes much time and considerable energy, and it thus

inhibits social disruption at a time of life when the likelihood of unlawful behavior is high. Many students attend schools well into their twenties. Schooling thus usefully engages thousands of young people for whom few jobs may be available.

Another latent function of schools is to establish lasting social relationships. High schools, colleges, and universities bring together people of marriageable age, many of whom soon meet their future spouse. Affiliation with a particular school is also the basis of lasting social networks. Such ties generate not only friendship, but also provide valuable career opportunities and resources.

Critical evaluation. Structural-functional analysis of formal education stresses the various ways in which this social institution supports the operation of an industrial society. This approach has usefully identified various manifest, as well as latent, functions of schooling.

One limitation is that functionalism tends to overlook how high-quality schooling is a privilege enjoyed by some people and barely available to others. In the next section, social-conflict analysis examines precisely this issue.

SCHOOLING AND SOCIAL INEQUALITY

Social-conflict analysis links formal education to patterns of social inequality. Schooling does enhance meritocracy to some extent by developing people's talents and abilities. Still, schools are hardly indifferent to social background, and they help to perpetuate social inequality based on sex, race, ethnicity, and social class.

Throughout the world, schooling has traditionally been considered to be more important for males than for females. Chapter 13 ("Sex and Gender") explained that the education gap between men and women has been closing in recent decades, but females and males still typically study conventionally feminine and masculine subjects. Schools also reinforce the values of dominant racial and cultural categories, to the disadvantage of minorities. Additionally, well-to-do Americans have much more educational opportunity than their poorer counterparts.

From a functionalist point of view, schooling provides children with the information and skills demanded of adults. A conflict analysis adds that schooling also instills discipline and respect for authority, thereby transforming the children of today into the docile labor force of tomorrow.

Social Control

Social-conflict analysis suggests that schooling is a means of social control that encourages acceptance of the status quo with its inherent inequities. This reproduction of the status hierarchy is not always evident to students or even teachers. The term **hidden curriculum** refers to *the content of schooling that is often unrecognized.*

    Samuel Bowles and Herbert Gintis (1976) point out that public education was expanded in the late nineteenth century to provide American capitalists with a docile, disciplined, and moderately educated work force. Mandatory education laws ensured that schools would teach immigrants with diverse cultural backgrounds the English language as well as cultural values supportive of capitalism. Compliance, punctuality, and discipline were—and still are—part of the hidden curriculum of American schools.

Testing and Social Inequality

Here is a question of the kind used to measure the intelligence and academic ability of American school-age children:

    Painter is to painting as _____ is to sonnet.

    Answers: (a) driver
                (b) author
                (c) priest
                (d) carpenter

The correct answer is (b) *author*: a painter creates a painting as an author creates a sonnet. This question purports to measure logical reasoning, but demonstrating this skill depends entirely upon knowing the meaning of each term. Unless students have been exposed to sonnets as a form of written verse, they are unlikely to answer the question correctly. An upper-middle-class student of European background is likely to have more of the experiences rewarded by such tests. The same person, however, might not score as well on an intelligence test devised by the Native American Hopi of the Southwest! Standardized tests used in the United States reflect America's dominant culture and therefore unfairly place some categories of people at a disadvantage.

Ironically, intelligence tests were developed at the beginning of this century with the intention of evaluating people's innate ability fairly, whatever their social background. But such tests have questionable validity insofar as scores also reflect a subject's cultural environment. In the United States, tests designed by white, affluent educators are likely to contain some bias in favor of white, affluent test takers (Owen, 1985; Crouse & Trusheim, 1988).

Tracking and Social Inequality

Despite the deficiencies of standardized tests, many schools in the United States and elsewhere use them as the basis for **tracking**—*categorically assigning students to different types of educational programs.* Tracking is also a common practice in Great Britain and Japan.

Defenders claim that tracking gives students an education appropriate to their individual aptitude. For a variety of reasons, including innate ability and level of motivation, some students are capable of more challenging work than others are. Also, interests differ among students, with some seeking college preparatory classes, others general education, and still others vocational and technical training. Thus a single program for all students would actually serve few of them well.

According to critics, tracking actually undermines educational meritocracy. A considerable body of research indicates that social background is a decisive factor in how students are tracked (Bowles & Gintis, 1976; Persell, 1977; Davis & Haller, 1981; Oakes, 1982). Almost all students have the capacity to succeed in any educational program, sociologist Jeannie Oakes (1985) asserts, but tracking—based on "scientific" testing—defines half of all students as below average. In practice, students from privileged social backgrounds (who in the United States are disproportionately white) are typically placed in higher tracks while those from disadvantaged backgrounds (often minorities) are likely to end up in lower tracks. Because friendship choices are influenced by the classroom, tracking also enhances segregation of privileged and disadvantaged students (Hallinan & Williams, 1989).

Those in higher tracks benefit from teachers who put more effort into classes, show more respect for students, and provide more encouragement to be active and creative in class. In contrast, students in lower tracks contend with greater memorization, classroom drill, and other unstimulating teaching techniques. Lower tracks also emphasize regimentation, emphasizing punctuality and respect for authority figures.

Not surprisingly, tracking has a major impact on students' self-concept. Young people who spend years

CRITICAL THINKING

American Schools: Is Disadvantage Labeled "Deficiency"?

Disadvantaged students labeled as "dumb" in school are likely, over time, to accept the idea that they are personally deficient. The process easily sets into motion a self-fulfilling prophecy by which students become as deficient as they are told they are. Eleven-year-old Ollie Taylor describes his situation in these words:

The only thing that matters in my life is school and there they think I'm dumb and always will be. I'm starting to think they're right. Hell, I know they put all the black kids together in one group if they can, but that doesn't make any difference either. I'm still dumb. Even if I look around and know that I'm the smartest in my group, all that means is that I'm the smartest of the dumbest, so I haven't got anywhere at all, have I? I'm right where I always was. Every word those teachers tell me, even the ones I like most, I can hear in their voice that what they're really saying is "All right you dumb kids. I'll make it as easy as I can, and if you don't get it then, you'll never get it. Ever." That's what I hear every day, man. From every one of them. Even the other kids talk that way to me too.

SOURCE: Thomas J. Cottle, "What Tracking Did to Ollie Taylor," *Social Policy,* Vol. 5, No. 2 (July–August 1974), 22–24.

in higher tracks tend to see themselves as bright and able, whereas those in lower tracks develop lower ambition and self-esteem (Bowles & Gintis, 1976; Persell, 1977; Rosenbaum, 1980; Oakes, 1982, 1985). The box describes one young boy's experience.

Inequality among Schools

Just as students are treated differently within schools, so do schools themselves vary. Private schools differ in many ways from public schools; public schools also vary from place to place.

Public and Private Schools

In 1990 almost 90 percent of America's 65 million students in primary and secondary grades were attending state-funded public schools. The remainder were in private schools.

A majority of private-school students attend Christian church schools. Most of these are *parochial* (from the Latin meaning "of the parish") schools operated by the Catholic Church, which rapidly built an educational system late in the nineteenth century as millions of Cath-

Most American children who receive a privately funded education attend parochial schools operated by the Catholic Church. These schools, which combine religious teaching with academic instruction, grew rapidly a century ago during the "Great Immigration." For many Catholic immigrants, parochial schools were a means to ensure that entering a predominantly Protestant society did not undermine their religious heritage.

olic immigrants entered the predominantly Protestant United States. More recently, fundamentalist Protestants have also established many religious schools. Christian schools are attractive to parents who want their children to receive instruction in specific religious beliefs. Some parents also favor these schools because they believe that the academic and disciplinary standards are higher than in public schools (Zigli, 1984). Recent efforts to desegregate public schools have also caused some parents to place their children in private, racially homogeneous religious schools. This has been especially true among whites in the South, as governmental policies have significantly reduced public-school segregation (James, 1989).

Additionally, a small number of American private schools enroll students mostly from the upper classes. These prestigious and expensive preparatory schools send many of their graduates to equally prestigious and expensive private universities. Prep schools not only provide a strong academic program, but also inculcate the mannerisms, attitudes, and social graces of the socially prominent. "Preppies" are likely to maintain lifelong social networks with other graduates of their school that provide numerous social advantages.

Private schools, research suggests, teach students more effectively than public schools do. Two influential reports (Coleman, Hoffer, & Kilgore, 1981; Coleman & Hoffer, 1987) indicate that students in private schools show higher rates of academic achievement than public-school students with similar social backgrounds. Private schools generate no greater interest in learning than do public schools, but classes are usually smaller. Furthermore, private schools have more academically demanding and stringent disciplinary policies that result in a safer, more orderly learning environment. Graduates of private schools are generally more likely than public-school graduates to complete college and subsequently enter high-paying occupations.

Inequality in Public Schooling

Funds allocated to public schools across the United States vary considerably. In 1987, per-student expenditures ranged from a high of $8,010 in Alaska to about $2,350 in Mississippi (U.S. Office of Educational Research and Improvement, 1989). Although much of this variation reflects cost-of-living differences, the fact is that educational opportunities are not the same, either from state to state or in different localities within a state. Generally, schools in wealthy, largely white suburbs have greater

Social inequality in the United States generates striking differences in schooling, even within a single city. Although only a few miles apart, these two schools in New York City provide students of dissimilar social backgrounds with a different quality of education.

financial resources than schools in central cities, where financially disadvantaged minority students predominate.

In 1966 a team of researchers headed by James Coleman completed an influential study of educational inequality. Four thousand public schools across the United States were investigated and survey data were gathered from more than 645,000 students. These data led the researchers to conclude that the vast majority of American students attended racially segregated schools. Although illegal since 1954, racial segregation persists, especially at the primary level, because the racial composition of schools mirrors that of their neighborhoods, which are typically racially homogeneous.

The Coleman report prompted a policy of *busing*—transporting students of one race to schools attended primarily by students of another race. This controversial policy seeks to equalize educational opportunities, although it affects only about 5 percent of American schoolchildren. Advocates see busing as a means to overcome the educational effects of urban segregation: only if more affluent white children attend schools across the entire city are adequate funds likely to be available to schools in poorer areas. Critics point to the high cost of busing and claim that it undermines the concept of neighborhood schools. Additionally, busing, to be effective, would have to involve both the cities (where blacks are concentrated) and their suburbs (which are overwhelmingly white). Within central cities, the number of white students is simply too small to make much difference in

racial composition, with or without a busing program. Officials, however, have been reluctant to consider the expansion of busing programs, which provoke strong opposition.

The Coleman report found that the races were not only separate but unequal. Predominantly white schools were better funded and had fewer students per class, more laboratories in sciences and foreign languages, more library books, and more extracurricular programs. White students also showed significantly higher academic achievement than nonwhite students did.

Coleman, however, discovered only a weak relationship between available funding and the academic quality of schools. He concluded that other factors—such as attitudes of teachers as well as the influence of students' families and peer groups—may have a greater impact on academic achievement. In other words, the academic performance of a large proportion of nonwhite children suffers from economic and cultural disadvantages. Supporting this conclusion, Christopher Jencks (1972) claimed that even if educational opportunity were equalized for all American students, academic performance would still be markedly unequal because some students have greater social advantages than others.

The conclusion is clear: Schools alone cannot overcome the broad patterns of social inequality in American society. Educational reform, therefore, would never by itself be enough to provide all young Americans with equal educational opportunities. The changes required are thus more sweeping; however, American society can no longer afford to ignore the educational needs of poor minority children, who represent a steadily increasing proportion of the American workforce (Cohen, 1989). The interests of every American are served by broader social reforms that increase educational opportunity to those historically denied this vital experience.

Unequal Access to Higher Education

Americans regard higher education as a path to occupational achievement, so that the vast majority of parents express the desire to send their children to college (Gallup, 1982). The proportion of Americans attending college has risen during this century. Government support for higher education (especially for military veterans after World War II) and the onset of the space race in the 1950s helped place increasing numbers of young people into the college classroom. Yet only 59 percent of the 1988 high-school graduates in the United States enrolled in college the following fall (U.S. Bureau of Labor Statistics, 1989), and, as was noted earlier, only about one-fifth of Americans over twenty-five are college graduates.

Parents' educational aspirations for their children clearly exceed the education children actually receive. Some high-school students, of course, do not wish to continue their education, despite parental encouragement. The intellectual demands of the college curriculum may also discourage some students with limited talents. Yet most American children wish to attend college, and doing so is certainly within the academic ability of the vast majority.

In the United States, the most crucial factor affecting access to higher education is money. Unlike primary and secondary education, which is provided by the government, higher education must be purchased. The price is high and rapidly rising. Even at state colleges and universities (partly supported by public funds), tuition is usually at least several thousand dollars a year, and in 1990 the annual tuition at the most expensive private colleges and universities reached $20,000. Additionally, although these figures may include room and board, students face extra costs for books and supplies. Government cuts in student aid programs during the 1980s made college attendance for people with modest financial means less likely.

In some respects, equal access to higher education in the United States has increased: Chapter 13 ("Sex and Gender") noted that slightly more women than men now attend college. Family income, however, continues to affect both men's and women's chances to enroll (Mare, 1981). Figure 16–2 shows, by family income, the proportion of Americans aged eighteen to twenty-four who were in college in 1986. A majority (56.3 percent) of Americans from families earning more than $50,000 a year were in college; those whose families earned under $10,000 a year comprised only 14 percent (U.S. Bureau of the Census, 1988). Most colleges offer needy students some financial aid, but many people still cannot afford to pay the remaining costs. This problem worsened during the 1980s, a decade when income declined for many Americans while college costs soared: between 1980 and 1987, expenses at public colleges and universities rose about 60 percent and those of private schools about 80 percent (Evangelauf, 1987).

One result of these rising costs is that minorities, typically with below-average incomes, have more and more difficulty attending college. Figure 16–3 shows that whites are overly represented at every stage in American education from high school to graduate school—a trend that has become more pronounced. During the 1980s the number of Hispanic students in college rose by about 50 percent; the number of black students stayed fairly steady (U.S. Bureau of the Census, 1988).

Even among those privileged enough to enroll in an institution of higher education, not everyone receives the same type and quality of schooling. People of limited financial means are likely to attend less expensive public community colleges and other government-supported schools. Certainly many students receive an excellent education in these public schools. Community colleges have the advantage of a faculty whose primary concern is teaching rather than research. Private schools, supported by high tuition and endowments, allow smaller classes as well as professors who may have national reputations. Also, a degree from a private college or university typically confers greater social prestige than one from a state-supported institution.

The most prestigious of private universities are the eight Ivy League schools—Harvard, Yale, Princeton, Pennsylvania, Dartmouth, Cornell, Columbia, and Brown. A degree from any of these is likely to impress potential employers and ensure admission to social networks of powerful people. In general, those who have attended private institutions have higher-prestige and higher-paying occupations than those who have attended state institutions (Monk-Turner, 1983; Useem & Karabel, 1986).

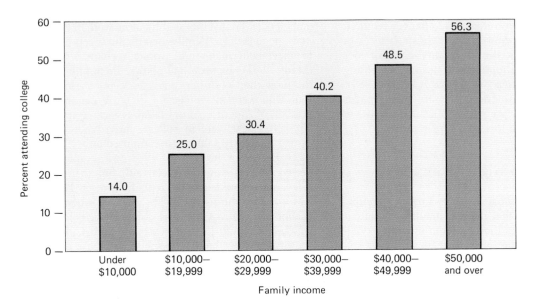

Figure 16–2 College Attendance and Family Income, 1986

* *Americans between 18 and 24 Years of Age*

(U.S. Bureau of the Census, 1988)

Before World War II, the majority of students in private colleges and universities were white, male, and wealthy. Some of these schools formally excluded females, and many also limited the number of other minorities. Today equal-opportunity policies and financial aid have opened these institutions to a broader segment of the American population. Private colleges and universities still admit socially advantaged students, but most now weigh individual talent far more than social background (Baltzell, 1976).

Whatever kind of college someone attends, higher education expands career opportunities and increases lifetime income. As Table 16–2 shows, males who do not finish high school typically earn $600,000 by age sixty-four, and each increasing level of educational achievement brings a corresponding increase in lifetime earnings. Male college graduates can expect to earn almost twice as much over a lifetime as men who do not complete high school. Among women, the financial gains of education are even greater. At each level of educational achievement, however, women earn considerably less than men. As Table 16–2 shows, the lifetime earnings of a female college graduate are typically less than those

Table 16–2 EDUCATION AND LIFETIME EARNINGS

Education	Lifetime Earnings*	
	Males	Females
College graduate (4 years)	$1,190,000	$523,000
Some college	957,000	460,000
High-school graduate	861,000	381,000
Less than 12 years	601,000	211,000

SOURCE: U.S. Bureau of the Census, 1984.

* Figures reflect earnings up to age sixty-four, in constant 1981 dollars.

of a man who did not complete high school. While education is a sound financial investment, it clearly does not overcome the earning liabilities of being female in American society.

The high earnings of college graduates are due to more than education. Americans who attend college are likely to come from relatively well-to-do families and to enjoy social and economic advantages which made college possible in the first place.

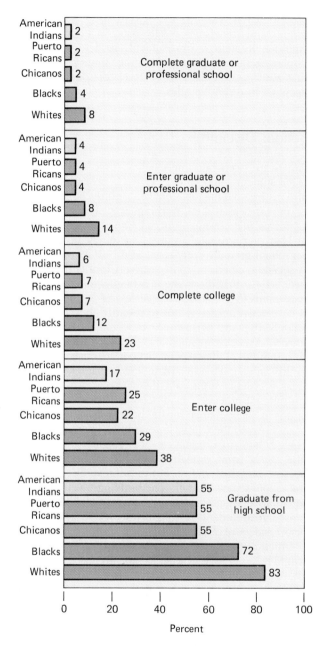

American Indians 2
Puerto Ricans 2
Chicanos 2
Blacks 4
Whites 8

Complete graduate or professional school

American Indians 4
Puerto Ricans 4
Chicanos 4
Blacks 8
Whites 14

Enter graduate or professional school

American Indians 6
Puerto Ricans 7
Chicanos 7
Blacks 12
Whites 23

Complete college

American Indians 17
Puerto Ricans 25
Chicanos 22
Blacks 29
Whites 38

Enter college

American Indians 55
Puerto Ricans 55
Chicanos 55
Blacks 72
Whites 83

Graduate from high school

0   20   40   60   80   100

Percent

Figure 16–3 Educational Achievement of Whites and Minorities

(Higher Education Research Institute, 1982)

Credentialism

Sociologist Randall Collins (1979) has called the United States a *credential society,* suggesting that Americans view diplomas and degrees as evidence of a person's ability to perform a specialized occupational role. As modern societies have become more technologically advanced, culturally diverse, and socially mobile, credentials have assumed some of the significance once attached to family background.

Credentialism, then, is *the requirement that a person hold an advanced degree as a condition of employment.* Structural-functional analysis suggests that credentialism reflects the need of a technologically complex society to fill challenging occupations with well-trained people. In contrast, social-conflict analysis contends that credentials often bear little relation to the skills and responsibilities a specific job demands. Employers in an insurance agency, for example, may require a college degree of every applicant for a managerial position, even though the company is likely to provide a comprehensive training program for all new employees. Lacking certain credentials, even someone with managerial talent and experience may find that doors are closed.

Collins (1979) argues that an important latent function of higher education is to help produce the kind of people who will support and fit into the industrial-capitalist economy, with manners and attitudes desirable for high-prestige occupations. Advanced degrees serve to advance people who are broadly and well trained, yet they may also screen out "undesirable types": people lacking the social backgrounds that would have made it possible to obtain advanced schooling. Credentials are thus a gate-keeping strategy that restricts powerful and lucrative occupations to a small segment of the population.

Finally, American society's emphasis on credentials has encouraged **overeducation,** *a situation in which workers have more formal education than the performance of their occupations requires.* Many new and specialized jobs in the American economy obviously demand advanced schooling. Research indicates, however, that educational achievement has actually outpaced the demands of the labor market (Berg, 1970; Rumberger, 1981). The expansion of low-skill service jobs during the 1980s, described in Chapter 10 ("Social Class in America"), seems inconsistent with a steady increase in higher education for Americans. Why are Americans intent on gaining more education if their jobs do not require it? Val Burris (1983) suggests that if credentials are defined as the key to getting a job, people will invest in education whether or not they really need it. One-fifth of the American labor force, Burris estimates, is overly educated. Although this excessive education may make some dissatisfied with their jobs, it also improves their chances to achieve better jobs (Shockey, 1989).

Critical evaluation. Social-conflict analysis links formal education to social inequality. Thus we see that schooling is unequal for different categories of people; schooling can also serve to transform privilege into personal ability and social disadvantage into personal deficiency.

Social-conflict analysis can be criticized for ignoring how different schooling may actually meet the needs of disparate students. This approach also minimizes the extent to which schooling does develop human talents and abilities. Moreover, significant meritocracy in the educational system has permitted upward social mobility for many talented Americans.

PROBLEMS IN AMERICAN EDUCATION

The 1980s was a decade of intense debate about American schooling. Attitudes of Americans about public schools were mixed, as is shown in Table 16–3: half of this survey's respondents gave their public schools a grade

Table 16–3 GRADING AMERICA'S PUBLIC SCHOOLS

Rating	Proportion of Respondents
A	10%
B	32
C	35
D	11
FAIL	4
Don't know	8

SOURCE: George H. Gallup, "The 16th Annual Gallup Poll of the Public's Attitudes Toward Public Schools," *Phi Delta Kappan*, Vol. 66 (September 1984), 25.

These figures reflect the responses of a national sample of American adults to the question: Students are often given the grades A, B, C, D, and FAIL to denote the quality of their work. Suppose the public schools themselves, in this community, were graded in the same way. What grade would you give the public schools here—A, B, C, D, or FAIL?

of C or below (Gallup, 1984). Certainly, violence is a serious and sometimes deadly issue in many schools. Another problem is that students tend to be passive, displaying little interest in learning. Critics also claim that academic standards at all levels of education have declined in recent decades.

School Discipline

Americans overwhelmingly believe that schools should teach students discipline (N.O.R.C., 1989:434). Many also suspect that the job is not being done. This suspicion is supported by some disturbing facts. The government estimates that several hundred thousand students and at least one thousand teachers are physically assaulted on school grounds every year. The National Education Association claims that three of every four of their members believe that discipline is a major problem in their classrooms (McGrath, 1984).

Such disorder is not necessarily the fault of the schools: they are part of a larger—and often violent—society. As was explained in Chapter 8 ("Deviance"), communities of the desperately poor are especially prone to this problem (Blau & Blau, 1982). Violence in such areas inevitably spills into the schools, disrupting the educational process. Nevertheless, schools do have the power to effect change for the better.

Early in the 1980s, for example, Thomas Jefferson High School in Los Angeles was plagued by violence, drug abuse, and vandalism. In 1982 Francis Nakano became principal and set out to improve discipline and the school's view of itself. The building was refurbished to improve its physical appearance, and Nakano and his staff held students personally responsible for any disorder. Leaders of student gangs, who were at the center of much of the disruption, were informed that violence would be suppressed by whatever means necessary. These changes brought a remarkable turnaround: Jefferson High is now getting on with the business of education (McGrath, 1984).

Examples of such constructive change exist throughout the country. The key to success appears to lie in firm disciplinary policies, supported by parents and, when necessary, law enforcement officials (Burns, 1985). Schools are unlikely to solve problems of violence that have roots deep in American society itself (Reed, 1983), but they can broaden their power to control violence by forming alliances with parents and community leaders.

Bureaucracy and Student Passivity

A problem more specific to schools themselves is pervasive *student passivity*—a lack of active participation in learning. This problem is not confined to any particular type of school: it is commonly found in both public and private schools and at all grade levels (Coleman, Hoffer, & Kilgore, 1981).

Schooling would seem a wonderful opportunity. In medieval Europe, children assumed many adult responsibilities before they were teenagers; a century ago, American children worked long hours in factories, on farms, and in coal mines for little pay. Today, however, the major responsibility faced by youths is to study their human heritage: learn the effective use of language, master the manipulation of numbers, and acquire knowledge and skills that will empower them and enhance their comprehension, enjoyment, and mastery of the surrounding world.

Yet the startling fact is that many students do not perceive the opportunities provided by schooling as a privilege, but rather as a series of hurdles that are mechanically cleared in pursuit of credentials that may open doors later in life. Students are, in short, bored. Some of the blame must be placed on students themselves, and on other factors such as television, which now takes up more of young people's time than school does. Even so, much of the pervasive passivity of American students is caused by the educational system.

In the nineteenth century, American children were typically taught in one-room schoolhouses: small and highly personal settings in their local communities. During this century, with rising costs, many local schools were dissolved; at the same time, expanding state and federal governments favored large regional schools as a more efficient means of supervising educational curricula and ensuring uniformity. Schools today, therefore, reflect the high level of bureaucratic organization found throughout American society. As Chapter 7 ("Groups and Organizations") explained, such rigid and impersonal organization can negatively affect administrators, teachers, and students.

After studying high schools across the United States, Theodore Sizer (1984) acknowledged that the bureaucratic structure of American schools is necessary to meet the massive educational demands of our vast and complex society. Yet he found that a bureaucratic educational system fosters five serious problems (1984:207–209).

First, bureaucratic *uniformity* ignores the cultural variation within countless local communities. It takes schools out of the local community and places them under the control of outside "specialists" who may have little understanding of the everyday lives of students.

Second, bureaucratic schools define success by *numerical ratings* of performance. School officials focus on attendance rates, dropout rates, and achievement test scores. In doing so, they overlook dimensions of schooling that are difficult to quantify, such as the creativity of students and the energy and enthusiasm of teachers. Such bureaucratic school systems tend to define an adequate education in terms of the number of days (or

Research suggests that pronounced bureaucracy tends to dampen student interest in learning. Not surprisingly then, students often show greater enthusiasm for learning in less formal settings.

even minutes) per year that students are inside a school building rather than the school's contribution to students' personal development.

Third, bureaucratic schools have *rigid expectations* of all students. For example, fifteen-year-olds are expected to be in the tenth grade, and eleventh-grade students are expected to score at a certain level on a standardized verbal achievement test. The high-school diploma thus rewards a student for going through the proper sequence of educational activities in the proper amount of time. Rarely are exceptionally bright and motivated students allowed to graduate early. Likewise, the system demands that students who have learned little in school graduate with their class.

Fourth, the school's bureaucratic *division of labor* requires specialized personnel. High-school students learn English from one teacher, receive guidance from another, and are coached in sports by others. No school official comes to know the "full" student as a complex human being. Students experience this division of labor as a continual shuffling among rigidly divided fifty-minute periods throughout the school day.

Fifth, the highly bureaucratic school system gives students *little responsibility* for their own learning. Similarly, teachers have little latitude in what and how they teach their classes; they dare not accelerate learning for

fear of disrupting "the system." Standardized policies dictating what is to be taught and how long the teaching should take render many teachers as passive and unimaginative as their students.

Several factors have enhanced bureaucracy in American schools. Bureaucratic schools, Sizer claims, were needed to effectively process the rapid influx of immigrant children during the last century; since then, the student population of New York City alone has grown larger than that of all of America in 1900. Cultural values are also at work: Americans tend to believe that the most effective way to accomplish any task is to formulate a system, and for better or worse, that is precisely what formal education in the United States has become.

Since bureaucracy discourages initiative and creativity, students become passive. The solution, drawing on the discussion in Chapter 7 ("Groups and Organizations"), is to "*humanize*" *bureaucracy*, or in this instance, Sizer claims, to humanize schools. He recommends eliminating rigid class schedules, reducing class size, and training teachers more broadly to enable them to become more fully involved in the lives of their students. Perhaps his most radical suggestion is that graduation from high school should depend on what a student has learned rather than simply on the length of time spent in school.

College: The Silent Classroom[1]

Consider the following observations of a bright and highly motivated freshman at a high-quality four-year college:

> I have been disappointed in my first year at college. Too many students do as little work as they can get away with, take courses that are recommended by other students as being "gut" courses, and never challenge themselves past what is absolutely necessary. It's almost like thinking that we don't watch professors but we watch television. (Forrest, 1984:10)

As this student observes, passivity is also common in colleges and universities. Sociologists have done little research on the college classroom—a curious fact considering how much time they spend there. One study carried out by David Karp and William Yoels (1976) shows that patterns of interaction in the college classroom are remarkably predictable and involve little student initiative and creative thinking.

Karp and Yoels systematically observed classes and conducted a survey of students at a coeducational university. They observed small (under forty students) and large (over forty students) classes. Although the small classes had slightly more student participation, in no case were

[1] The phrase "silent classroom" is taken from Martha E. Gimenez (1989).

more than a few students active. In small classes, only four or five students typically made more than one comment during a class period, and these few were responsible for three-fourths of the interaction in the class. In larger classes, only two or three students actively participated; they provided more than half of the discussion. Although these results suggest that smaller classes do encourage more student participation, even in smaller classes the majority of students were passive. Karp and Yoels also found that students themselves became irritated when one of their number was especially talkative.

The sex of the instructor affected classroom dynamics. In classes with equal proportions of men and women taught by men, male students were responsible for most class discussion. With women as instructors, however, the two sexes were roughly equal in terms of activity. Many women are apparently more comfortable in a class taught by a woman. Why? Perhaps because female instructors directed questions to female students as frequently as to male students, while male teachers favored their male students.

Students offered explanations of their classroom passivity; these are listed in Table 16–4. They saw passivity as mostly their own fault, in perhaps a case of the victims of a bureaucratic educational system blaming themselves. Long before reaching college, Karp and Yoels suggest, students are taught to view instructors as "experts" who provide "truth." Thus they find little value

Table 16–4 STUDENT EXPLANATIONS OF CLASSROOM PASSIVITY

	Males		Females	
	Percent	Rank	Percent	Rank
I had not done the reading assignment	80.9	1	76.3	2
The feeling that I didn't know enough about the subject matter	79.6	2	84.8	1
The large size of the class	70.4	3	68.9	4
The feeling that my ideas were not well enough formulated	69.8	4	71.1	3
The course simply isn't meaningful to me	67.3	5	65.1	5
The chance that I would appear unintelligent in the eyes of the teacher	43.2	6	41.4	7
The chance that I would appear unintelligent in the eyes of other students	42.9	7	45.4	6
The small size of the class	31.0	8	33.6	8
The possibility that my comments might negatively affect my grade	29.6	9	24.3	9
The possibility that other students might not respect my point of view	16.7	10	12.5	11
The possibility that the teacher might not respect my point of view	12.3	11	12.5	10

SOURCE: David A. Karp and William C. Yoels, "The College Classroom: Some Observations on the Meaning of Student Participation," *Sociology and Social Research*, Vol. 60, No. 4 (July 1976), 108.

in classroom discussion or debate but perceive their proper role as passively listening and taking notes. According to Karp and Yoels, these attitudes result in only 10 percent of college class time being devoted to discussion. Students also know that instructors generally come to class ready to deliver a prepared lecture. Favoring a lecture format in order to present a great deal of material in each class, instructors can ill afford to be sidetracked by student questions or comments (Boyer, 1987). Faculty lectures, then, accommodate only a few questions to the class. Early in each course a handful of students are recognized by everyone as being ready and able to provide the limited responses the instructors desire. Taken together, these facts encourage passivity on the part of the majority of college students.

Academic Standards and Educational Quality

Pervasive student passivity is not widely viewed as a serious problem, perhaps because a bureaucratic organization and its effects on individual initiative are an accepted part of American social life. More controversial and complex is a general decline in the academic performance of American students.

A comprehensive study of the academic quality of American education was prepared in 1983 by the National Commission on Excellence in Education. The report, *A Nation at Risk*, found that the quality of American education had deteriorated seriously enough to warrant strong language:

> If an unfriendly foreign power had attempted to impose on America the mediocre educational performance that exists today, we might well have viewed it as an act of war. As it stands, we have allowed this to happen to ourselves. (1983:5)

Numerous facts support this conclusion. The average scores on standardized achievement tests, including the Scholastic Aptitude Test (SAT), began to decline in the early 1960s, with a slight rebound in the 1980s. Three decades ago, average scores for American students were about 500 on the mathematical test and 480 on the verbal test; by 1989, the averages had slipped to 476 and 427. Educators have proposed various explanations for this trend, including the fact that a broader segment of American students—some of whom are less well prepared—now take the college boards (Owen, 1985). Whatever the reasons, few doubt that American education has suffered a setback.

A Nation at Risk also noted with alarm the extent of **functional illiteracy**, *the lack of basic reading and writing skills needed for everyday life.* Roughly one in eight American children completes secondary school without learning to read or write very well. For young minorities, the report estimated, the proportion is more than one in three. The box provides a closer look at this American problem.

Schools attempt to teach more than basic skills, however. Abstract and critical thinking are also important goals of formal education. Yet the report of the National Commission on Excellence in Education claimed that "nearly 40 percent of 17-year-olds cannot draw inferences from written material; only one-fifth can write a persuasive essay; and only one-third can solve mathematical problems requiring several steps" (1983:9).

A Nation at Risk recommends drastic changes in our schools. First it calls for more stringent educational requirements: schools must require every student to enroll in several years of English, mathematics, social studies, general science, and computer science courses. Second, schools at all educational levels must raise their academic standards and cease tolerating their failure to teach. Third, schools should keep students as long as necessary to teach basic skills. Fourth, teachers' salaries should be raised to attract better people into the profession, teacher training must be improved, and teachers should have support for enriching their own education through further study and research. *A Nation at Risk* concludes that educators must ensure that schools meet public expectations, and the American people must be prepared to bear the costs of good schools.

RECENT ISSUES IN AMERICAN EDUCATION

America's schools must continuously respond to changing demands, new challenges, and technological innovation. We will conclude this chapter with a brief look at several recent and significant educational issues.

Magnet Schools

During the 1970s, school districts in many American cities established **magnet schools**—*schools that attract students through special facilities and programs promoting educational excellence.* Such schools offer enriched edu-

Functional Illiteracy: Must We Rethink Education?

Imagine being unable to read the labels on cans of food, the instructions for assembling a child's toy, the dosage on a medicine bottle, or even the information on your own paycheck. These are some of the debilitating experiences of *functional illiteracy*, the inability to carry out everyday responsibilities due to inadequate reading and writing skills.

As schooling became universal among Americans, the U.S. government confidently concluded that illiteracy was virtually eliminated. Thus, the extent of functional illiteracy in recent years, even among high-school graduates, has been a shocking revelation. According to some estimates— now acknowledged by the government to be fairly accurate—some 26 million American adults read and write at no more than a fourth-grade level, and another 45 million have only eighth-grade language skills. Overall, about one-fourth of American adults are functionally illiterate, and the proportion is higher among the elderly and among many minorities.

Functional illiteracy is a complex social problem. It is caused partly by an educational system that passes children from one grade to the next whether or not they learn. Another cause is community indifference to local schools that prevents parents and teachers from working together to improve children's learning. Still another cause is the home: millions of children grow up with illiterate parents who offer little encouragement to learn language skills.

Functional illiteracy is estimated

Functional illiteracy means not only being out of touch—it often means being out of work. Finding and keeping a good job are extremely difficult for those who lack reading and writing skills.

to cost our society more than $100 billion a year. This cost includes decreased productivity (by workers who do not perform their jobs properly) and increased accidents (by people unable to understand written instructions). It also includes the human loss of those who are unable to read and write well enough to find work and often end up on public welfare or in prison.

Correcting this national problem requires one approach for the young and another for the old. The American public must demand that children not be permitted to graduate from school until they have learned basic language abilities. For adults, the answer is more complex since

many feel deep shame at their plight and avoid disclosing their need for help. Once such people are identified, however, adult education programs would have to be provided.

American society is one of the richest and most powerful nations on earth, yet more than a dozen other countries have a more literate population than we do. For those involved, functional illiteracy is a personal disaster; for all Americans, it is a national disgrace.

SOURCE: Based on Jonathan Kozol, "A Nation's Wealth," *Publisher's Weekly*, May 24, 1985, pp. 28–48; *Prisoners of Silence: Breaking the Bonds of Adult Illiteracy in the United States* (New York: Continuum, 1980); and *Illiterate America* (Garden City, NY: Doubleday, 1985).

cational opportunities by improving school buildings and providing intensive learning in subjects such as computer science, foreign languages, or science and mathematics. There are now over a thousand magnet schools throughout urban America.

One goal of magnet schools is to improve educational performance. By providing enriched learning and by demanding higher achievement, magnet schools have generally raised the academic achievement of their students. Schools that have a history of high drop-out rates now find students eagerly learning and regularly completing homework assignments.

A second purpose of magnet schools is to make inner-city schools more attractive to more affluent people—especially whites—who are likely to send their children to private schools. Magnet schools thus encourage voluntary integration, making court-ordered busing unnecessary. The performance of magnet schools in this respect has been mixed. Some cities have reported reductions in school segregation since whites and blacks alike are drawn to quality schools. But this appears to be the exception more than the rule. In 1989, for example, Kansas City concluded that there were simply not enough white students left to allow racial balance in schools. To meet court orders for racial balance, therefore, the city had to limit black enrollment in magnet schools to roughly the available number of whites (King, 1989). While magnet schools are a promising development, then, they are unlikely to solve the deeply entrenched problem of racial segregation in America's schools.

Schooling for the Disabled

Mandatory education laws not only require children to attend school, they also express the obligation of American society to provide a basic education to everyone. Nevertheless, millions of young mentally and physically disabled people receive little or no schooling. A highly bureaucratized system of mass education does not readily meet the needs of such children, and therefore many have simply been defined as uneducable.

Providing an education for disabled children raises several problems. Some children with physical disabilities have difficulty getting to and from school, and stairs and other obstacles inside school buildings are difficult to negotiate with crutches or wheelchairs. Children who are mentally retarded or who suffer from emotional problems require extensive personal attention from teachers with specialized training. As a result, many mentally

and physically disabled children have received a public education only after persistent efforts by parents and other concerned citizens.

Recently, however, there has been a trend to **mainstreaming**, *the integration of disabled students into the educational program as a whole*. Mainstreaming is an alternative to segregated "special education" classes containing only disabled students. It is especially appropriate for physically disabled students who have no difficulty keeping up academically with the rest of the class. One advantage of mainstreaming is that it allows such children to partake of the widest possible educational experiences within the limits of their abilities. A second advantage is that disabled children learn how to interact more extensively with other children and, just as important, other children learn how to interact with them. Mainstreaming may not be effective for students who have mental or emotional disabilities, however. They may have great difficulty matching the performance of other students, and they may simultaneously be deprived of special education appropriate to their needs. Under any circumstance, mainstreaming is an expensive undertaking, requiring changes in physical facilities and the hiring of teachers capable of meeting the special needs of disabled children.

Adult Education

Schooling has traditionally involved only children and adolescents. In the last several decades, this situation has changed as a growing proportion of the adult population has enrolled in school, some returning after a considerable period of time.

By the mid-1980s, 25 million American adults—more than ever before—were enrolled in school. They range in age from the twenties to well past sixty-five. Adult students are generally a fairly privileged segment of the population; most have above-average incomes.

Why do adults return to school? There are as many specific reasons as there are students, but usually the motivation is work-related. Many pursue areas of study directly linked to their current careers. Almost one-fourth of adult education students are studying business; approximately another one-fourth are enrolled in courses in health and engineering (National Center for Education Statistics, 1983). Others return to school to get a high-school diploma or college degree because they recognize its occupational advantages. Still others go back to school simply in search of intellectual stimulation.

Schooling, Computers, and the Future

The final bell has already rung at Benjamin Franklin Junior High in Ridgewood, New Jersey, yet some students are reluctant to return home. This reaction may sound unusual, and it is. The explanation for such intense student interest is Benjamin Franklin's computer science program. George Mamunes is completing a program that will graphically display every part of the human heart; Pam Miller is developing a program that simulates the operation of a nuclear reactor; Meilin Wong is debugging a business management program; Jim McGuire is developing a video game of his own. What makes this schoolroom scene unusual is explained by teacher Bob Muller: "No one told [the students] they have to be here. They're not usually doing assignments. They're experimenting. They're letting their imaginations run free" (Golden, 1982:51).

This chapter has emphasized how society as a whole shapes the educational system. Just as the Industrial Revolution had a major impact on schooling in the nineteenth century, American education is now being transformed by the computer revolution.

Computers are already used in virtually every occupation. Americans consequently express strong support for computers being part of the school curriculum (Gallup, 1983). By 1987, more than 95 percent of public schools were reported to have instructional computers (U.S. Bureau of the Census, 1989). Other industrial societies share America's enthusiasm for computers in schools: the Soviet Union began requiring computer education in its high schools in 1985 (Alexander, 1985).

The use of computers in school is not limited to the teaching of job-related skills. Computers can also improve the nature of schooling itself. In many subjects, computers have the capacity to interact with students—that is, they react directly to students' input. Computers, moreover, allow students to progress at their own pace. For disabled students unable to write with pencil and paper, computers may permit easier self-expression. The introduction of computers into schools—in some cases, as early as kindergarten—has also sparked a new passion for learning among many students. The effect of computers on learning is a topic that is commanding increasing attention in research. Initial studies suggest that computer-assisted instruction significantly increases learning speed and retention of information (Fantini, 1986).

The use of computers in the schools has dangers as well. Computers will never have the personal insight into the needs of individual students that a qualified

The number of foreign students in the United States—exceeding 350,000—has increased dramatically in recent years. Most of these students are from Third World societies, 60 percent from Asian nations. The majority will return to their countries with the goal of speeding economic development.

and motivated human teacher has. Also a computer is of little value in many areas of traditional education. As one educator noted, "There's a whole world of real problems, of human problems, which is essentially being ignored." Another teacher expressed the fear that students will be "out of touch with certain springs of human identity and creativity, which belong to the full use of language rather than mathematical and symbolical codes" (Golden, 1982:56).

The introduction of computers into American education will not solve many of the problems that plague our schools. Yet there is little doubt that computers will significantly shape the American educational system of the twenty-first century.

SUMMARY

1. Education is a major social institution for transmitting knowledge and skills, as well as cultural norms and values, to young people. In preindustrial societies, education occurs informally within the family; industrial societies develop formal systems of schooling.

2. The United States was among the first societies to develop a system of compulsory mass education, reflecting both democratic political ideals and the needs of the industrial-capitalist economy. The educational system has also been shaped by such cultural values as practicality, efficiency, and competitive individualism.

3. Structural-functional analysis suggests that schooling contributes to socialization, promotes social integration and appropriate social placement, and encourages cultural innovation. Latent functions of schooling include child care and the forging of lasting personal relationships.

4. Social-conflict analysis points out that the opportunity for formal education is unequally distributed among Americans. This approach also explains that schooling is a means of social control, instilling the discipline that produces compliant adult workers.

5. Standardized intelligence testing is criticized as being culturally biased in favor of some categories of Americans and to the disadvantage of others.

6. Allegedly based on individual talents, tracking is also strongly related to students' social background. Tracking provides greater educational resources to more privileged students, thereby perpetuating social inequality.

7. The great majority of young Americans attend state-funded public schools. Most privately funded schools are affiliated with religious organizations. A very small proportion of young people—generally of privileged social background—attend private preparatory schools.

8. School districts across America vary in the amount of resources allocated per student. Although research shows that spending money does not guarantee educational quality, schools in affluent settings are likely to offer a richer education than those in poorer areas.

9. Today one-fifth of Americans over the age of twenty-five are college graduates. Most attended state-funded institutions; private colleges and universities are usually much more expensive and enroll students from wealthier families. A college degree greatly increases lifetime earnings.

10. America has been described as a credential society. By requiring degrees for higher-paying occupations, employers are able to ensure that workers have learned norms and attitudes appropriate to the business setting. Since degrees are expensive, those able to afford higher education are also more likely ultimately to obtain the most desirable occupations.

11. Americans are critical of public schools. School violence is a highly visible problem, especially in poor neighborhoods. The bureaucratic character of American schools has also fostered widespread student passivity.

12. Declining academic standards are a major educational problem in America, reflected in lower average scores today on academic achievement tests and functional illiteracy among a significant proportion of high-school graduates.

13. Magnet schools are a recent development that have improved education in many cities. To some extent, they have lessened racial segregation in schools.

14. Mentally and physically disabled children traditionally have been schooled in special classes or not at all. In recent years, mainstreaming has afforded handicapped students greater educational opportunities.

15. Adults, usually engaged in job-related study, represent a growing proportion of students in the United States.

16. Computers are a source of effective learning, although they are not suitable for teaching every subject.

KEY CONCEPTS

credentialism the requirement that a person hold an advanced degree as a condition of employment

education the various ways in which knowledge—including factual information and skills as well as cultural norms and values—is transmitted to members of society

functional illiteracy the lack of basic reading and writing skills needed for everyday life

hidden curriculum the content of schooling that is often unrecognized

magnet schools schools that attract students through special facilities and programs promoting educational excellence

mainstreaming the integration of disabled students into the educational program as a whole

mandatory education laws legal requirements that children receive a minimum of formal education

overeducation a situation in which workers have more formal education than the performance of their occupations requires

schooling formal instruction under the direction of specially trained teachers

tracking categorically assigning students to different types of educational programs

SUGGESTED READINGS

This textbook is a good resource for the sociological analysis of education.

Jeanne H. Ballantine. *The Sociology of Education.* 2nd ed. Englewood Cliffs, NJ: Prentice Hall, 1989.

The first of the following books on schooling and gender examines how academia has been changed in recent years by feminist thinking. The second book, based on the lives of sixty-two women, asserts that women continue to have a marginal existence in the academic world.

Carol S. Pearson, Donna L. Shavik, and Judith G. Touchton. *Educating the Majority: Women Challenge Tradition in Higher Education.* New York: Macmillan, 1989.

Nadya Aisenberg and Mona Harrington. *Women of Academe: Outsiders in the Sacred Grove.* Amherst: University of Massachusetts Press, 1988.

For a scholarly book to top the best-seller list is rare indeed. This conservative critique of education captured the attention of Americans.

Allan Bloom. *The Closing of the American Mind: How Higher Education Has Failed Democracy and Impoverished the Souls of Today's Students.* New York: Simon & Schuster, 1987.

This insightful and engaging account of American schooling also made the best-seller list in 1989.

Tracy Kidder. *Among Schoolchildren.* Boston: Houghton Mifflin, 1989.

These two books offer a comparative look at schooling in two major industrial societies of the world.

J. J. Tomiak, ed. *Soviet Education in the 1980s.* London: Croom Helm, 1983.

Thomas P. Rohlen. *Japan's High Schools.* Berkeley: University of California Press, 1983.

A useful resource is this listing of over 1,000 books and articles concerning the education of women in the Third World.

David H. Kelly. *Women's Education in the Third World: An Annotated Bibliography.* New York: Garland, 1989.

In recent years the educational system of the United States has been the subject of considerable criticism and debate. The first book listed below is a recent governmental report on American education; the second is a critical appraisal of American education by a man who has spent his life in administrative positions within many levels of schools; the third, also by a long-time educator, suggests a number of educational reforms.

The National Commission on Excellence in Education. *A Nation at Risk: The Full Account.* Cambridge, MA: USA Research, 1984.

Theodore R. Sizer. *Horace's Compromise: The Dilemma of the American High School.* Boston: Houghton Mifflin, 1984.

Mario D. Fantini. *Regaining Excellence in Education.* Columbus, OH: Merrill, 1986.

A critical analysis of standardized testing, focusing on the Scholastic Aptitude Test (SAT), is the following.

David Owen. *None of the Above: Behind the Myth of Scholastic Aptitude.* Boston: Houghton Mifflin, 1985.

17

Religion

Rarely does a film—especially one about religion—cause a national furor. Even before it was released, however, the 1988 film *The Last Temptation of Christ* sparked angry controversy across the United States. On the day national screening began, thousands of enraged people staged a protest outside the gates of Paramount Studios in Hollywood. During the following weeks, smaller numbers of protestors assembled outside of theaters in cities and towns across the country. From their pulpits, many priests and ministers angrily denounced the film and urged their congregations not to see it.

Why did *The Last Temptation of Christ* offend millions of religious Americans? The reason is that the film depicts Jesus of Nazareth as torn between spiritual and earthly goals. This conflict is hardly new: the tension between spirit and flesh was part of the human record long before the life of Jesus, and can be found in the writings of Plato and other early philosophers. But hundreds of millions of Christians who believe that Jesus of Nazareth is the Christ—the Son of God—are deeply offended by the notion that he gave in—even mentally—to worldly desires such as marrying and having a family.

How and why people come to hold religious beliefs, and how organized religion is linked to other social institutions, is the focus of this chapter. We shall begin by defining several basic concepts.

RELIGION: BASIC CONCEPTS

Human beings define objects and events in various ways. For much of human history, the members of small societies attributed birth, death, and success or failure in human endeavors to supernatural forces. Before the Industrial Revolution, for example, Europeans defined many life experiences as an expression of divine will. Gradually, however, science emerged as a different world view, one that tries to explain the natural world—includ-

Every religion distinguishes the sacred from the secular. Japanese Buddhists reverently remove their shoes—which touch the profane ground—before entering this sacred temple in Kyoto.

ing human society—through systematic observation. But science has not eliminated interest in the supernatural. The more our scientific knowledge advances, in fact, the more awesome and mysterious our vast universe seems. Moreover, science can offer no insights at all about the vital issues of the *meaning and purpose* of human existence. These are largely the domain of religion.

French sociologist Emile Durkheim, whose ideas are discussed in detail in Chapter 4 ("Society"), claimed that religions the world over have a common focus on "all sorts of things that surpass the limits of our knowledge" (1965:62; orig. 1915). Human beings, Durkheim explained, define any idea, object, event, or experience in one of two ways. Most things are considered **profane** (from the Latin for "outside the temple"), meaning part of *the ordinary elements of everyday life.* Some things, Durkheim continued, are set apart as **sacred,** *that which is defined as extraordinary, inspiring a sense of awe, reverence, and even fear.* Throughout human history, distinguishing between the profane and the sacred has been the key to all religious belief. **Religion,** therefore, is *a system of beliefs and practices based upon recognizing the sacred.*

Because religion deals with ideas that transcend everyday experience, neither common sense nor science can establish religious truth. Religion is a matter of **faith,** *belief that is not based on scientific evidence.* In the New Testament of the Bible, Christians are said to "walk by faith, not by sight" (II Corinthians 5:7), and faith is

described as "the conviction of things not seen" (Hebrews 11:1).

Matters of faith vary greatly throughout the world. Nothing is placed in the category of sacred or profane by everyone on earth; anything may become one or the other depending on how a community of people defines it. Americans, for example, view most books as profane or secular, but the Torah (the first five books of the Hebrew Bible or Old Testament) is defined as sacred by Jews, as is the entire Bible by Christians and the Qur'an (Koran) by Muslims. Similarly, most cities are placed within the profane world, but Jerusalem is considered sacred by members of all three of these religions.

Durkheim (1965:62) claimed that profane things are understood in terms of their everyday usefulness; we use a computer or drive a car to get various jobs done. What is defined as sacred, however, is separated from everyday life—"set apart and forbidden"—and evokes a reverent and submissive response. For instance, Muslims demand that people remove their shoes before entering a mosque—a sacred place of worship that is not to be symbolically defiled by shoes that have touched the profane ground outside.

The sacred is usually addressed through **ritual,** *formal, ceremonial behavior.* Holy communion is the central ritual for most Christians; the wafer and wine consumed during communion are never defined as food—they are sacred symbols of the body and blood of Jesus Christ.

Religion and Sociology

The application of the sociological perspective to religion may be disturbing to some people. Yet this study of religion implies no offense or threat to anyone's religious faith. Sociologists recognize that religion is central to virtually every culture on earth, and therefore seek to understand the operation of religious beliefs and practices in human societies.

In doing this, sociology does not pass judgment on religion, nor does it make any claims about whether a particular religion is right or wrong. Sociological analysis is concerned with the social consequences of religious activity. It is true that some sociologists have interpreted these consequences as positive, others as negative, and still others in a neutral manner. But sociological analysis can never assess the *validity* of any religious doctrine, which is a matter of faith rather than empirical evidence. Perhaps this is why sociologists, like other people, have various religious orientations themselves: some are not believers, while others participate faithfully in their religions.

THEORETICAL ANALYSIS OF RELIGION

Whatever their personal religious beliefs, sociologists agree that religion is a major social institution that must be understood. Each of the major theoretical paradigms explores how religion affects social life.

The Functions of Religion

Emile Durkheim believed that confronting the power of society is a daily human experience. Society, he claimed, has an existence and power of its own beyond the lives of the people who collectively created it. Thus, Durkheim concluded, society itself is "godlike"; unlike individuals, society does not die, it has the power to shape the lives of all of us, and it evokes a sense of reverence and awe. Society demands the submission of individuals to its values and norms. Thus, according to Durkheim (1965; orig. 1915), society and the sacred are inseparable: as people develop religious beliefs, they celebrate society's awesome power.

The weakening of traditional religion, then, led Durkheim to criticize modern society. His concept of

anomie or normlessness captures the idea that modern society, with its basis in science and rational skepticism, cannot assume religion's historical functions of conferring purpose upon our lives, thereby uniting people into human communities. Thus, we moderns tend to celebrate the profane world, becoming caught up in the individualistic pursuit of money and possessions, often at the expense of our concern for spiritual values, our neighbors, or even our families.

How can people comprehend the power of their society? We do this, Durkheim continued, by transforming everyday objects into sacred symbols. The sacred symbolizes the collective immortality of individual mortal beings. Among technologically simple societies, Durkheim claimed, the power of society is typically represented by a **totem**, *an object within the natural world that is imbued with sacred qualities*. As the object of ritual activity, the totem is transformed into a sacred representation of the entire society, fusing distinct individuals into a powerful unity.

Of course, Durkheim's approach completely ignores the question of whether a divine power exists or not. Either way, he concluded, religious beliefs and practices arise to reflect the power of society. From this beginning, Durkheim went on to identify several major functions of religion for the operation of society.

Social Cohesion

Religion promotes social cohesion, uniting members of a society through shared symbolism, values, and norms. In simple societies, the visible symbol of this unity is the totem. Similar patterns are also found in complex societies. In the United States, the American eagle is a quasi-religious totem. Additionally, placing the inscription "In God We Trust" on all currency implies a collective unity based on religious belief. Similarly, local communities across the United States gain a sense of unity through totem-like symbolism attached to sports teams: from the Boston "Patriots," to the Ohio State University "Buckeyes," to the Los Angeles "Rams."

Social Control

Every society tries to promote some degree of social conformity. To do this, cultural norms, especially important *mores* that deal with reproduction and human well being, are given religious justification. In medieval Europe, monarchs often explicitly claimed to rule by divine right. Few of today's political leaders invoke religion so explicitly, but many publicly ask for God's blessing, implying to audiences that their efforts are both right and just.

Providing Meaning and Purpose

In the face of human failings, disease, and death, life can seem hopelessly chaotic. Religious beliefs offer the comforting sense that the vulnerable human condition serves some greater purpose. Strengthened by such beliefs, people are less likely to collapse with despair when confronted by life's uncertainties and calamities. Major life transitions—including birth, marriage, and death—are usually marked by religious observances that provide a context of meaning. To many people, religion also involves the vital human dimension of *love*—emotional and spiritual connection to others (Wright & D'Antonio, 1980). Religion, then, addresses ultimate issues of life, death, and attachment that transcend both common sense and science (including scientific sociology).

Critical evaluation. Durkheim's work is the basis of the structural-functional analysis of religion. This approach emphasizes that the sharing of religious beliefs—whatever they may be—produces social cohesion, stability, and a sense of meaning and purpose.

The major weakness of this approach is downplaying the dysfunctions of religion—especially the capacity of strong beliefs to generate destructive social conflict. During the early Middle Ages, for example, religious faith was a partial cause of the Crusades, in which European Christians marched against Muslims in the Middle East. Muslims, in turn, were driven by their moral duty to fight the invading Christians. Conflict among Muslims, Jews, and Christians is still a source of political instability in the Middle East today. Social divisions in Northern Ireland are also partly a matter of conflict between Protestant and Catholic religious beliefs. It is likely that humanity has historically engaged in more violence over religious beliefs than over social inequality.

The Social Construction of the Sacred

The symbolic-interaction paradigm views all of society as a human construction. "Society," asserts Peter Berger (1967:3) "is a human product and nothing but a human product, that yet continuously acts back upon its producer." Once formed through social interaction, then, society shapes the existence of its creators.

Religion, in Berger's view, is also a social construc-

tion (although perhaps inspired by divine forces). Various rituals, including religious services and saying grace before meals, teach individuals what their society defines as sacred.

The primary reason societies construct the sacred, Berger explains, is to legitimate and stabilize patterns of social life. As a human creation, society is inherently precarious and subject to disruption. Placing everyday events within a "cosmic frame of reference" confers on the fallible, transitory creations of human beings "the semblance of ultimate security and permanence" (1967:35–36).

Marriage is a good example. If it is seen only as a contract between two people, marriage can be ended as easily as it is begun. Defined as *holy* matrimony, however, confers great authority on mating patterns. Similarly, cultural norms that regulate sexual activity are made stronger if violations are defined as *sin*. But especially when humans face uncertainty and life-threatening situations—such as illness, war, and natural disaster—do sacred symbols come to the fore. Even people who are otherwise not very religious may pray when confronting the death of loved ones, and soldiers have traditionally gone to war "with God on their side." By socially creating the sacred, humanity is lifted above the ultimate reality of death, so that society—if not its individual members—becomes immortal.

Critical evaluation. The symbolic-interaction approach views religion as a social construction that places everyday life within a "sacred canopy" of meaning (Berger, 1967). But Berger cautions that the ability of the sacred to legitimate and stabilize society depends on the socially constructed character of the sacred remaining unrecognized or attributing the process to divine inspiration. The conception of holy matrimony is less compelling if we think of its creators as members of society such as ourselves. Faced with life-threatening disaster, human beings could also derive little strength from sacred beliefs they saw to be mere devices for coping with tragedy. One reason many people are uncomfortable with sociological study of religion is encountering the possibility that we have constructed the sacred in the same manner as we have created the rest of society.

Religion and Social Inequality

The social-conflict paradigm provides further analysis of religion, this time in relation to social inequality. Religion, according to Karl Marx, is a form of ideology

One way that religions support social inequality is by designating only some categories of people as eligible for leadership. Historically, this has meant the dominance of white males; but this pattern has eroded in recent years. In 1989, for example, Barbara Harris became the first black woman to be ordained as a bishop in the Episcopal Church.

that serves ruling elites by legitimating the status quo and diverting people's attention from social inequities.

In England, for example, the monarch has traditionally been crowned by the head of the Church of England, clearly illustrating the close alliance between religious and political elites. Thus, Marx claimed, opposing the status quo often means challenging the church—and, by implication, God. By learning to think of existing society as morally just, people are blinded to their power to change a system by which the privileges of the few are obtained at the expense of the many. Religion also encourages people to look hopefully to a "better world to come" while ignoring social problems of *this* world. In one of Marx's best-known statements, he offered a stinging criticism of religion as "the sigh of the oppressed creature, the sentiment of a heartless world, and the soul of soulless conditions. It is the opium of the people" (1964:27; orig. 1848).

An additional link between religion and social inequality involves gender. Virtually all the world's major religions have reflected and encouraged male dominance of social life, as the box on page 456 explains.

During Marx's lifetime, the powerful Christian nations of Western Europe used the "conversion of heathens" as one justification for colonial exploitation of societies in Africa, Asia, and the Americas. In the United States, major churches in the South pronounced the enslavement of blacks by whites to be consistent with God's will. Until well into the twentieth century, many churches supported segregation and other forms of racial inequality.

But religion has another side, one that sometimes promotes dramatic social change. A major example is found in the work of Max Weber (1958; orig. 1904–1905). As Chapter 4 ("Society") explains in detail, Weber viewed industrial-capitalist societies as the product not of social conflict but of the rational world view common to early Calvinism. In Weber's terms, the "Protestant ethic" was an engine of change: a highly disciplined approach to life that became the "spirit" of capitalism and transformed much of Western Europe.

Critical evaluation. Social-conflict analysis shows how the power of religion can legitimate social inequality. This has been true of American society as elsewhere.

Yet critics of religion's conservative face, including Karl Marx, minimize ways in which religion has promoted greater social equality. Nineteenth-century American religious groups played a key role in the abolition of slavery. During the 1950s and 1960s, both leaders and rank and file in many religious groups actively supported the civil rights movement. The black church has been especially active in the struggle for racial equality in the United States; perhaps the most outstanding leader in this movement was Martin Luther King, Jr., a minister. During the 1960s and 1970s, clergy were active opponents of the Vietnam War and, more recently, some have supported revolutionary change in Latin America and elsewhere. American churches today also offer asylum to refugees from El Salvador, Nicaragua, Guatemala, and other politically unstable countries to our south. Marx apparently did not foresee the extent to

Religion and Patriarchy: Does God Favor Males?

Passages from many of the sacred writings of major world religions provide ample evidence of religion's role in the persistence of patriarchy around the world.

The Qur'an (Koran)—the sacred text of Islam—asserts that men are to have social dominance over women:

> Men are in charge of women. . . . Hence good women are obedient. . . . As for those whose rebelliousness you fear, admonish them, banish them from your bed, and scourge them. (cited in Kaufman, 1976:163)

Christianity—the dominant religion of the Western world—has also supported patriarchy. Although Christians revere Mary, the mother of Jesus, the New Testament includes the following passages:

> A man . . . is the image and glory of God; but woman is the glory of man. For man was not made from woman, but woman from man. Neither was man created for woman, but woman for man. (I Corinthians 11: 7–9)

> As in all the churches of the saints, the women should keep silence in the churches. For they are not permitted to speak, but should be subordinate,

as even the law says. If there is anything they desire to know, let them ask their husbands at home. For it is shameful for a woman to speak in church. (I Corinthians 14:33–35)

> Wives, be subject to your husbands, as to the Lord. For the husband is the head of the wife as Christ is the head of the church. . . . As the church is subject to Christ, so let wives also be subject in everything to their husbands. (Ephesians 5:22–24)

Judaism, too, has traditionally supported patriarchy. Male Orthodox Jews include the following words in daily prayer:

> Blessed art thou, O Lord our God, King of the Universe, that I was not born a gentile. Blessed art thou, O Lord our God, King of the Universe, that I was not born a slave. Blessed art thou, O Lord our God, King of the Universe, that I was not born a woman.

The major religions have long excluded women from the clergy, although this is now being widely challenged. Islam continues to exclude women from such positions, as does the Roman Catholic Church. A growing number of Protestant denominations, however, have or-

dained women. Although Orthodox Judaism still upholds the traditional prohibition against women rabbis, Reform Judaism has long placed women in this role, and in 1985 the first woman became a rabbi in the Conservative denomination of Judaism. The proportion of women in seminary schools across the United States (now roughly one-third) has never been higher, so that further changes seem likely.

Developments such as women entering the clergy or revisions to the language in hymnals and prayers have delighted progressives while outraging traditionalists. Some religious women and men, however, believe that the recent transformations have not gone far enough. For some Christian women, for example, what is seen as patriarchal hierarchy within the church is antithetical with the largely feminine Scriptural image of Jesus Christ as "nonaggressive, noncompetitive, meek and humble of heart, a nurturer of the weak and a friend of the outcast" (Sandra Schneiders, cited in Woodward, 1989:61). Theologian Mary Daly puts the matter bluntly: "If God is male, then male is God" (cited in Woodward, 1989:58).

---

which religious social movements—such as "liberation theology"—would promote social change in the twentieth century.

Liberation Theology

Christianity shares with many world religions a history of addressing the suffering of poor and often oppressed

people. Christian efforts have traditionally sought to strengthen the faith of the believer in a better life to come. In recent decades, however, some church leaders and theologians have embraced Karl Marx's vision of social justice in *this* world. One major result has been the liberation theology movement.

Liberation theology is *a fusion of Christian principles with political activism, often Marxist in character.* This movement developed in the late 1960s within Latin

Religion has always held a special promise to the poor, reaffirming the dignity of people flogged by famine and offering hope of a better life to come. Christian churches are currently thriving in the poorest regions of southern Africa. There, Christian ideals are passionately expressed in some of the world's most inspiring religious art.

America's Roman Catholic Church. Liberation theology begins with the Church's established teaching that Christianity offers liberation from human sin. What is new—and controversial—is the assertion that the church must also help people liberate themselves from the abysmal poverty of the Third World, as described in Chapter 11 ("Global Inequality").

Although they disagree among themselves on many issues, advocates of liberation theology tend to embrace three general principles. First, human suffering in the world is tragic and beyond the imagination of most secure, comfortable people in the United States. Second, this massive suffering is inconsistent with Christian morality. Global inequality thus contradicts the Christian belief in the union of all humanity. Third, global poverty is preventable; as an expression of faith and conscience, Christians must act to reduce this suffering.

A growing number of Catholic men and women have allied themselves with the poor in a political struggle against the ruling powers in Latin American societies. The costs of opposition have been high. Many church members have been killed in the widespread violence that engulfs much of that region. Some killings are political assassinations. In 1980, Oscar Arnulfo Romero, the archbishop of San Salvador (the capital of El Salvador) and an outspoken advocate of the poor, was gunned down inside his church while celebrating Mass. In 1989, during the continuing civil unrest in El Salvador, six Jesuit priests were murdered in their home by government troops.

The radicalization of the church has, in some in-

stances, fostered more support among Latin American people (Neuhouser, 1989). Yet liberation theology has been condemned by Pope John Paul II for mixing politics with traditional church doctrine. Thus, the Vatican has forbidden church officials to participate in any political conflicts, claiming that liberation theology endangers the Catholic faith, by diverting attention from the otherworldly concerns of Christianity, and embroils the church in political controversy. Despite this opposition, the liberation theology movement continues in Latin America, fueled by the belief that Christian faith and a sense of human justice demand efforts to change the plight of the world's poor (Boff, 1984).

TYPES OF RELIGIOUS ORGANIZATION

For thousands of years, religious people have faced a world that often seems indifferent to moral concerns. The degree of tension between a religious group and society was used by Ernst Troeltsch (1931) to distinguish a church from a sect.

Church and Sect

Drawing on ideas formulated by his teacher Max Weber, Troeltsch described a **church** as *a formal religious organi-*

The formality of traditional churches is evident in the relatively subdued and passive behavior of members during worship services. In contrast, the charismatic leaders of sects encourage their followers to experience personally a divine presence, often generating strong emotion.

zation that is well integrated into the larger society. Being well established, a church typically persists for centuries. It usually includes all members of a family over many generations. Bureaucratic organization further enhances a church's stability as officials are formally ordained and work within a hierarchy of offices according to specific policies and regulations.

Although concerned with the realm of the sacred, churches accept the profane society. They advance morality in abstract terms, which enables them to overlook how specific social arrangements are inconsistent with their principles. For example, a church may claim that all human beings are brothers and sisters, but remain silent about laws that deny equal rights to people of one race or sexual orientation. Such duality minimizes conflict between the church and the political state (Troeltsch, 1931; Johnstone, 1983; O'Dea & Aviad, 1983).

A church generally takes one of two forms. An **ecclesia** is *a church that is formally allied with the state*. Ecclesias have been common in human history: the Catholic Church was for centuries allied with the Roman Empire; the Anglican Church is now the official Church of England; Confucianism was the state religion in China until early in this century; and Islam remains the official religion of Pakistan and Iran. With the state's endorsement, ecclesias are likely to claim all people in a society as members. Such membership may even be required by law, which obviously limits toleration of religious differences. Because church and state are fused, an ecclesia clearly exemplifies religious acceptance of the larger society.

A second type of church is a **denomination,** *a church that recognizes religious pluralism*. Not allied with the government, denominations usually exist within societies that formally separate church and state. The United States, for example, contains dozens of Christian denominations, including Catholics, Baptists, Methodists, and Lutherans. Each denomination holds certain religious beliefs but recognizes the right of others to disagree.

Distinct from churches are sects. A **sect** is *an informal religious organization that is not well integrated into the larger society*. Sects lack the rigid hierarchy of established churches. Sects also exalt personal experience and emotion, while churches use more formal ritual. While members of churches tend to be passive during religious services, the members of sects are often highly spontaneous and active, outwardly rejoicing in the perceived presence of God. Sects often dogmatically view established churches as having lost the true path; sect leaders, then, may seek to restore "authentic" religious beliefs and practices (Stark & Bainbridge, 1979).

Patterns of leadership also distinguish churches and sects. Churches have formal officials, such as priests, rabbis, and ministers. Leaders of sects are often anyone who displays **charisma**—*extraordinary personal qualities that can turn an audience into followers.* Charismatic leadership provokes emotional responses from members, who may view leaders as divinely inspired.

Sects also differ from churches by not accepting the established society. In some instances, sects withdraw completely in order to practice their religion without interference from outsiders. Sects see the outside world as misguided and sometimes even as evil, so that sect members are urged to remain apart from nonmembers. For example, the Amish, described in Chapter 3 ("Culture"), are a sect that has long been isolated from other Americans (Hostetler, 1980). Insofar as sects view their own beliefs as the only true religion, members are intolerant of other religious beliefs. Unlike churches, then, sects tend to reject the doctrine of religious pluralism.

To sustain their membership, many sects rely heavily on outsiders joining their ranks. They thus advocate the active recruitment, or *proselytizing,* of new members. Proselytizing leads to **conversion,** *a personal transformation resulting from new religious beliefs.* Members of Jehovah's Witnesses, for example, share their faith with others in the hope of attracting new members.

Churches and sects differ, too, in their social composition. Well-established churches tend to be composed of people of high social standing; sects often attract people of lower social position. A sect's openness to new members and promise of salvation and personal fulfillment may be especially appealing to people who perceive themselves as social outsiders.

Sects generally form as breakaway groups from established churches or other religious organizations: sects, then, are the result of religious schism (Stark & Bainbridge, 1979). Their psychic intensity and lack of formal structure render them less stable than churches; many sects, therefore, emerge only to soon disappear. The sects that do endure become more like churches, losing fervor as they become more bureaucratic, established, and respectable. Both the Puritan and the Quaker settlers of colonial America were members of breakaway English sects. Each of these sects has subsequently evolved into an established church. This transformation suggests that the terms *church* and *sect* are conceptual poles; any religious organization may be described as being churchlike or sectlike to some degree.

Cult

A **cult** is *a religious movement that is highly unconventional in terms of the surrounding society.* Whereas a sect is formed by schism from an established religious organization, a cult represents something almost entirely new. Cults typically form around a highly charismatic leader who offers a new and unorthodox message. An example is the founding of the Church of Jesus Christ of Latter-Day Saints (the Mormons) by Joseph Smith in New York State in 1830. Smith accepted many established Christian principles, but distinguished Mormonism with several unconventional religious ideas, including the practice of plural marriage as described in Chapter 15 ("Family"). In the following 150 years, however, Mormons abandoned such practices and have become an established church.

Cults can also arise from the diffusion of religious ideas from one society (where they are conventional) to another society (where they are not). Transcendental Meditation (TM) developed in the United States when Maharishi Mahesh Yogi introduced many Hindu ideas to American society in the late 1950s. During the 1970s,

Growing alienation from society, coupled with an unstable charismatic leader, led to the 1978 tragedy in Jonestown, Guyana. On the order of Jim Jones, over nine hundred members of his cult drank Kool-Aid laced with cyanide, ending one of the most bizarre cases of religious behavior.

TM had perhaps 500,000 followers, although its popularity has declined considerably since then (Bainbridge & Jackson, 1981).

Cults tend to be even more at odds with established society than sects. Many cults demand that members embrace not only religious beliefs but also an entire *lifestyle* involving a radical change in self-identity. For this reason, cults are sometimes accused of brainwashing new members into renouncing their past lives. When this happens, new converts are typically cut off from their families and friends so that the cult operates as a total institution (described in Chapter 5, "Socialization"). But this is rare: most people show only passing interest in cults and do not join; those who do only rarely experience psychological harm (Barker, 1981; Kilbourne, 1983).

Cults tend to form and disperse rather quickly, with little public notice. Some gradually become both bureaucratic and conventional. As already noted, this is the history of the Mormons, now an established church and one of the most rapidly growing religious organizations in America (Stark, 1984). As a cult becomes a church, it seeks accommodation with society, and public hostility consequently declines.

RELIGION IN HISTORY

Religion exists within every society of the world. And like every other institution, religion shows considerable variation historically and cross-culturally.

Religion in Preindustrial Societies

Religion was a part of human life even before the beginning of written history. Archaeological evidence suggests that at least forty thousand years ago our human ancestors routinely engaged in religious rituals.

Among hunting and gathering societies, religion commonly takes the form of **animism** (from the Latin meaning "the breath of life"): *the belief that natural objects are conscious forms of life that can affect humanity*. Animistic people may view forests, oceans, mountains, and the wind as spiritual forces responsible for shaping human experience. Many Native American societies that

flourished in our continent's history were animistic, which accounts for the widespread view of these peoples as deeply respectful of the environment. Characterized by little social complexity, hunting and gathering societies also carry out religious activity entirely within the family. A *shaman* or religious leader may be recognized, but shamanism is not a full-time, specialized activity.

Belief in a divine power that has created the world arose only gradually as human societies gained the technological skills of horticulture and agriculture. The belief that a supernatural power remains active in the world is the foundation of cultural morality and the sacred. A parallel development is the emergence from the family of religion as a social institution, often fused with politics: leaders such as the Egyptian pharaoh and the early Chinese emperor were regarded as both kings and priests.

Religion in Industrial Societies

In agrarian societies, religion is a distinct and powerful social institution, as evidenced by the centrality of the church in medieval Europe. The Industrial Revolution, however, brought a growing emphasis on science, diminishing the scope of religious thinking. People in distress increasingly turned to practitioners of science, such as physicians, to provide the relief they had earlier sought from religious leaders.

Yet science has not eliminated religion from industrial societies. On the contrary, religion continues because science is powerless to address issues of ultimate meaning in human life. In other words, *how* this world works is a matter of scientific investigation, but *why* we and the rest of the universe exist at all is a question about which science has nothing to say. Therefore, many traditional religions have persisted during the twentieth century, and new religions have also emerged. Whatever the benefits of science, then, religion has a unique capacity to address essential dimensions of human existence.

Because religion and science represent powerful but distinct ways of viewing the universe, the two exist in an often uneasy relationship. In recent years, this tension has emerged as controversy about the origin of humanity. This debate puts scientific "facts" about human evolution in opposition to religious "beliefs" commonly termed *creationism*. The box on pages 462–463 explores this issue more fully.

WORLD RELIGIONS

Our planet is host to thousands of different religions. Many are highly localized, with few followers. Others, termed *world religions*, have millions of adherents spread throughout the world. We shall discuss six world religions, which together represent about 3.5 billion people—roughly two-thirds of humanity. The size and geographical distribution of these religions are shown in Table 17–1.

Christianity

Christianity is the most widespread religion, involving 1.6 billion people; that is, more than one-fifth of humanity. Most Christians are Europeans and North Americans; put otherwise, about two-thirds of the people in the United States and Canada claim Christianity as their religion. Colonization by Westerners has introduced Christianity throughout the rest of the world. The tremendous influence of Christianity is suggested by the Western calendar's numbering of years beginning with the birth of Christ.

Christianity has roots in Middle-Eastern Judaism. Early Christianity was a sect, or perhaps a cult because it embraced many ideas that were entirely new. Like many cults, Christianity was fueled by the personal charisma of a leader, Jesus of Nazareth, who preached a message of personal salvation. Jesus was not a political revolutionary. He accepted the Roman Empire and admonished his followers to "Render therefore to Caesar things that are Caesar's" (Matthew 22:21). Yet Jesus' message was morally revolutionary, offering hope that a world of sin and death could be overcome through eternal life. Thus Jesus called for all people to be joined in Christian love.

Christianity is an example of **monotheism**, *religious beliefs recognizing a single divine power*. This new religion challenged the Roman Empire's traditional **polytheism**, *religious beliefs recognizing many gods*. Christianity uniquely conceives of the Supreme Being as a sacred Trinity: God the Creator; Jesus Christ, Son of God and Redeemer; and the Holy Spirit, a Christian's personal experience of God's presence.

The claim to the divinity of Jesus lies in the final events of his life on earth. Tried and sentenced to death in Jerusalem for threatening the established political leaders, Jesus endured a cruel execution by crucifixion, making the cross a sacred Christian symbol. According to Christian belief, Jesus was resurrected—that is, he rose from the dead—showing that he was the Son of God.

Peace created by the Roman Empire allowed the Apostle Paul and others to travel safely, spreading Christianity throughout the Mediterranean region. Although Christians were initially persecuted, during the fourth century Christianity became an ecclesia—the official religion of the Roman Empire. What had begun as a cult was thus transformed into an established church.

Soon afterward, Rome declined, although the east-

Table 17–1 ESTIMATED SIZE AND GEOGRAPHICAL DISTRIBUTION OF SIX WORLD RELIGIONS

Location	Religion					
	Christianity	Islam	Hinduism	Buddhism	Confucianism	Judaism
North America	232,557,080	2,698,480	885,800	186,560	100,000	8,117,900
Latin America	402,245,550	664,820	683,660	483,020	58,000	1,003,770
Europe and the Soviet Union	516,975,400	40,881,040	595,560	512,690	440,000	4,515,760
Asia	186,248,740	583,068,050	659,629,900	310,627,030	157,500,000	4,207,840
Africa	282,526,720	253,153,340	1,424,610	11,750	2,000	237,610
Oceania	21,431,200	98,480	305,920	15,120	18,000	86,460
Total	1,669,520,440	880,552,210	663,495,450	311,836,170	158,118,000	18,169,340

SOURCE: *The World Almanac and Book of Facts 1990* (New York: Newspaper Enterprise Association, 1989), p. 611.

The Creation Debate: Does Science Threaten Religion?

"In the beginning God created the heavens and the earth." So begins the book of Genesis in the Bible, the sacred text for millions of Christians and Jews. Read literally, Genesis states that life on earth began on the third day when God created vegetation; on the fifth and sixth days, God created animal life, including human beings, fashioned in God's own image.

In 1859, the English scientist Charles Darwin published *On the Origin of Species*, a biological account of the origin of human life. Darwin's theory of evolution stated that the world was not created as we find it today; instead, all life changes over time due to biological evolution (described in Chapter 3, "Culture"). From this point of view, human beings emerged not days after the earth was created, but evolved from lower forms of animal life over a billion years.

In a largely Christian society, Darwin's theory was immediately controversial. While many considered the theory a great contribution to science, others saw it as an attack against centuries-old sacred beliefs. On the surface, Darwin's scientific analysis seemed a total contradiction of biblical creation: if human beings took a billion years to evolve, they could hardly have been created when the earth was formed. This discrepancy remains at the center of the *creation debate*.

A major event in the course of this controversy occurred in the little town of Dayton, Tennessee, in 1925. At that time, a new state law forbade educators to instruct students in "any theory that denies the story of the Divine Creation of man as taught in the Bible," specifically those that claim that "man descended from a lower order of animals." One afternoon in Doc Robinson's drugstore, John Thomas Scopes, a science teacher in the local high school, conceded that he had, on occasion, violated the law by teaching evolution in the Dayton school. To test the law, Scopes agreed to stand charged with defying it.

Public interest in Scopes's eleven-day trial was heightened by the presence of two great trial lawyers of the day. William Jennings Bryan (three times a presidential candidate) was a fundamentalist Christian leading a national campaign against evolutionary science; he enthusiastically agreed to prosecute the case. Clarence Darrow, perhaps the most renowned criminal lawyer in the country, agreed to act as the defense in what came to be known as the Scopes Monkey Trial.

The trial proved to be one of Darrow's finest performances, while Bryan, aging, ill, and only days from death, did little for the creationist cause. Yet the community applauded when Scopes was found guilty and fined $100. His conviction was reversed on appeal, perhaps to prevent the case from reaching the U.S. Supreme Court. The Tennessee law for-

ern part of the empire, based in the city of Constantinople (now Istanbul, Turkey), continued until the fifteenth century. A religious division in the eleventh century resulted in twin centers of Christianity: the Roman Catholic Church based in Rome and the Orthodox Church in Constantinople.

Further divisions within Christianity occurred toward the end of the Middle Ages, when religious leaders such as Martin Luther (1483–1546) protested established church doctrine. The Reformation in Europe ushered in a period of religious pluralism from which emerged numerous Protestant denominations. More than a dozen—the Baptists and Methodists are the two largest—now command sizable followings in the United States.

Christianity is one of the oldest world religions and has most influenced Western civilization. Divisions have resulted in many variants of Christianity, but each shares the belief that a historical figure named Jesus of Nazareth was sent by God to provide salvation from sin and that he offers everlasting life to those who accept him as their personal savior (Smart, 1969; Kaufman, 1976; Stavrianos, 1983).

Islam

Islam is the second largest religion in the world, with almost 1 billion followers called Muslims (or Moslems). A majority of people in the Middle East and North Africa are Muslims. Most Muslims are actually non–

bidding the teaching of evolution remained until 1967. The following year, the U.S. Supreme Court struck down all such laws, arguing that they violated the constitutional prohibition against government-supported religion.

To sidestep the Court's ruling, creationists adopted a new line of attack: if evolution was to be discussed in schools, creationism should also be taught to balance this view. Creationism, stripped of its obvious religious qualities, became *creation science*.

Creation science lends scientific support to a literal reading of Genesis. Some state legislatures soon required that creation science be included in school curricula. Such laws, however, were rejected by the courts in 1985 as violating the constitutional separation of church and state.

The Court also declared creation science itself to be scientifically invalid. The decision was based on science having a provisional character by which any theory changes with new empirical evidence. The theory of evolution *has* continually changed as new facts have emerged from research, but creation science is religion rather than science because it is not subject to revision.

Despite the Court's ruling, many Americans continue to view the biblical account of creation as literal truth. One national poll found 44 percent endorsed the creation science belief that God created human beings in their present form within the last ten thousand years. Only 9 percent of respondents took a nonreligious evolutionary view that human life evolved from lower forms of life over millions of years, with God having no part in the process. A mixed view was held by 38 percent, who claimed that evolution is a scientific fact but believed that God directed the process. The remaining 9 percent professed no knowledge of how human beings came to exist (Severo, 1982).

Americans, therefore, remain divided over the creationism question.

But many, including church leaders, have concluded that science and religion are not in conflict at all. John S. Spong, the Episcopal bishop of Newark, New Jersey, states that scientists and biblical scholars alike must accept the "enormous amount of evidence" that humanity did evolve over a billion years. Even so, science only investigates *how* the natural world operates; only religion can address *why* we exist in terms of God's role in this process. Human creation, then, is a matter of scientific fact but also of faith.

SOURCE: Based on Harry Nelson and Robert Jermain, *Introduction to Physical Anthropology*, 3rd ed. (St. Paul, MN: West, 1985), pp. 22–24; Stephen J. Gould, "Evolution as Fact and Theory," *Discover*, May 1981, pp. 35–37; Ronald L. Numbers, "Creationism in 20th-Century America," *Science*, Vol. 218, No. 5 (November 1982): 538–544; Richard Severo, "Poll Finds Americans Split on Creation Idea," *New York Times*, August 29, 1982, p. 22. Professor J. Kenneth Smail of Kenyon College also contributed ideas to this section.

Arabs, however: the greatest concentrations are found in India, Pakistan, Indonesia, and the Soviet Union. Estimates of the Muslim population of North America range from 1.5 million to more than 4 million, and the number is rapidly growing (Roudi, 1988; Carol Stone, cited in Ostling, 1988; Weeks, 1988).

Islam is based on the life of Muhammad, born in the city of Mecca (in western Saudi Arabia) about the year 570. To Muslims, Muhammad was a prophet, not a divine being as Christians define Jesus. Muhammad's task was to record the word of Allah, the God of Islam. The Qur'an (Koran), sacred to Muslims, is Muhammad's record of the word of God. In Arabic, the word Islam means both "submission" and "peace," and the Qur'an urges submission to Allah as the path to inner peace. Muslims express this personal devotion in a daily ritual of five prayers.

Islam spread rapidly after the death of Muhammad, although divisions arose as they did within Christianity. All Muslims, however, accept the Five Pillars of Islam: (1) recognizing Allah as the one, true God, and Muhammad as God's messenger; (2) ritual prayer; (3) giving alms to the poor; (4) regular fasting; and (5) making a pilgrimage at least once to Mecca, the sacred city of Muhammad's birth (Weeks, 1988). Like many religions, Islam holds people accountable to God for their deeds on earth. Those who live obediently will be rewarded in heaven, while unbelievers will suffer infinite punishment.

Muslims are also obligated to defend their faith.

Muslims carefully study the Qur'an—often committing much of it to memory—as part of the discipline of their faith.

Sometimes this tenet has justified holy wars against unbelievers (in roughly the same way that medieval Christians joined the Crusades to recapture the Holy Land from the Muslims). Especially in Iran, Muslims have sought to rid their society of Western social influences they regard as morally compromising (Martin, 1982; Arjomand, 1988).

Like most religions, Islam is linked to the domination of women by men. Westerners often view Muslim women as among the most socially oppressed people on earth. Muslim women do lack many of the personal freedoms enjoyed by Muslim men, yet patriarchy was well established in the Middle East at the time of Muhammad's birth. Some defenders argue that Islam actually improved the social position of women by defining the obligations of husbands to wives and limiting polygyny so that a man can have no more than four wives.

Hinduism

Hinduism is probably the oldest of world religions, originating in the Indus Valley some forty-five hundred years ago. Over the centuries, Hinduism and Indian society have become intertwined so that one is not easily described apart from the other. For this reason, unlike Christianity and Islam, Hinduism has not readily diffused to other societies (Schmidt, 1980). Most of the 663 million Hindus live in India and Pakistan, with smaller numbers in other parts of the world. North American Hindus number more than 885,000.

Hinduism also differs from Christianity and Islam by not being linked to the life of a single person. Nor does Hinduism have sacred writings comparable to the Bible or the Qur'an. Therefore, Hindu beliefs and practices vary widely. Hindus generally believe, however, that a force in the universe confronts everyone with moral responsibilities termed *dharma*. Upholding the

India's Hindus believe the Ganges River to be sacred. During the *Kumbh Mela*, a major religious ritual, millions make a pilgrimage to bathe in the river's ritually purifying waters.

traditional caste system, as described in Chapter 9 ("Social Stratification"), is one responsibility that is part of dharma.

Hinduism also embraces *karma*, a belief in the spiritual progress of a person's soul. Every human action has a direct spiritual consequence; proper living causes moral improvement, while improper living results in moral decline. Karma also involves *reincarnation*, a belief that a new birth follows each death, so that one is reborn into a spiritual state corresponding to the moral quality of one's previous life. Unlike Christianity and Islam, Hinduism proclaims no ultimate justice at the hands of a supreme god, although in the cycle of rebirth, each person reaps exactly what is sown. The ultimate state of paradise—*nirvana*—is spiritual perfection in which the soul is spared further rebirth.

Hinduism is neither monotheistic nor polytheistic. An element of monotheism exists in the Hindu view of the universe as a single moral system, but Hindus perceive this moral order in all of nature. Hindu rituals are as variable as they are central to daily life. Some are private devotions, including, for example, ritual cleansing following contact with a person of lower caste. Others are massive public events, such as the Kumbh Mela, which occurs every twelve years. At this time, millions of Hindus make a pilgrimage to the Ganges River, a major sacred symbol, to bathe in the ritually purifying waters.

Because it differs from other world religions, Hinduism is unfamiliar to most Westerners. Variations of Hinduism stem from weaving religion into daily lives within countless Indian villages over thousands of years. Despite this variety, each Hindu embraces religion as a powerful force offering both explanation and guidance in life (Pitt, 1955; Sen, 1961; Embree, 1972; Kaufman, 1976; Schmidt, 1980).

Buddhism

Buddhism emerged in India about twenty-five hundred years ago. Today more than 300 million people, mostly Asians, adhere to the Buddhist religion. Resembling Hinduism in doctrine, Buddhism differs in that its inspiration is the life of one individual.

About 563 B.C.E., Siddhartha Gautama was born to a high-caste Indian family. At the age of twenty-nine, his preoccupation with spiritual matters led to a radical personal transformation. He set off for years of travel and meditation, finally reaching what Buddhists describe as *bodhi*, or enlightenment. Understanding the essence of life, Gautama became a Buddha.

Overcome by his personal charisma, followers spread Buddha's teachings—the *dhamma*—across India. During the third century B.C.E., the ruler of India became a Buddhist and sent missionaries throughout Asia, making Buddhism a world religion.

Buddhists view existence as suffering. They do not deny the experience of pleasure, but believe that joy is transitory. This belief emerged in Buddha's own travels within a society rife with poverty. Buddhism rejects wealth as a solution to suffering, seeing materialism as inhibiting spiritual development. Buddhism's answer to world problems is a personal transformation toward a spiritual existence.

Buddhism shares with Hinduism a belief in reincarnation; only full enlightenment ends the cycle of rebirth, liberating a person from the suffering of the world. Also like Hinduism, Buddhism recognizes no god of judgment, but sees spiritual consequences in all daily action.

Like Christianity and Islam, Buddhism originated in the life of a charismatic teacher. However, its conception of a highly ordered moral universe in which spiritual development occurs over many lifetimes makes Buddhism much closer to Hinduism (Schumann, 1974; Thomas, 1975).

Confucianism

From about 200 B.C.E. until the beginning of this century, Confucianism was an ecclesia—the official religion of China (McGuire, 1987). Following the 1949 revolution, the government of the People's Republic of China discouraged religion. Still, hundreds of millions of Chinese are influenced by Confucianism.

This religion was shaped by a single person, K'ung-Fu-tzu, known to Westerners as Confucius. Believed to have lived between 551 and 479 B.C.E., Confucius shared with Buddha a deep concern for the problems and suffering of the world. Buddha encouraged spiritual withdrawal from the world; Confucius, however, sought personal salvation through correct moral conduct within the world. Confucianism soon became fused with the traditional culture of China. As Hinduism has remained largely in Indian culture, Confucianism is enshrined in the Chinese way of life.

Confucianism is based on the concept of *jen*, or humaneness. In practice, this means that morality must always take precedence over self-interest. Especially within the family, individuals must be loyal and concerned for others. Personal loyalty builds strong families; strong families form a moral society. Unlike Jesus and Buddha, Confucius did not direct attention to the future and away from this world; instead, he studied the past and concluded that morality is expressed in everyday life.

Lacking a clear concept of the sacred, Confucianism is arguably less a religion and more a disciplined life based on Chinese traditions. In global perspective, then, the Chinese have long had a skeptical attitude toward the supernatural. If Confucianism is a disciplined and scholarly way of life, it shares with religion a body of beliefs and practices that strive for goodness and produce social unity (Kaufman, 1976; Schmidt, 1980).

Judaism

Judaism is a world religion with more than 18 million adherents. The largest concentration of Jews is in North America, with most others divided between Europe and the Middle East.

Like Confucianism, Judaism is historical in focus: Jews regard the past as a source of guidance in the present and for the future. Jewish history extends to the ancient cultures of Mesopotamia and Egypt, almost four thousand years before the birth of Christ. At this time, Jews were animistic; but this belief was to change after Jacob—grandson of Abraham, the earliest great ancestor—led his people to Egypt.

Under Egyptian rule, the Jews endured centuries of slavery. In the thirteenth century B.C.E., a turning point came as Moses, the adopted son of an Egyptian princess, was called by God to lead the Jews out of Egypt. This exodus (from the Latin and Greek, meaning "a marching out") is commemorated by Jews today in the ritual of Passover. As a result of the exodus, Judaism became monotheistic, recognizing a single, all-powerful God.

A distinctive element of Judaism is the *covenant*, a special relationship with God by which Jews became a "chosen people." The covenant is a body of law, centering on the Ten Commandments revealed by God to Moses. Jews regard the Bible (or, in Christian terms, the Old Testament) as both their history and the laws that all Jews must follow. Of special importance are the first five books of the Bible (Genesis, Exodus, Leviticus, Numbers, and Deuteronomy), designated as the *Torah* (a word roughly meaning "teaching" and "law").

Chanukah is an important Jewish ritual of commemoration that serves to teach young Jews their long and rich history.

In contrast to Christianity's central concern with personal salvation, therefore, Judaism emphasizes moral behavior within this world.

Like Christians, Jews are divided by interpretations of doctrine. Orthodox Jews (including more than 1 million Americans) strictly observe traditional beliefs and practices, including forms of dress, segregation of men and women at religious services, and consumption of only kosher foods. Such unconventional practices set off Orthodox Jews as sectlike. In the mid-nineteenth century, many Jews sought greater accommodation to the larger society, leading to the formation of the churchlike Reform Judaism (now including more than 1.3 million Americans). More recently, a third segment—Conservative Judaism (about 2 million Americans)—has established a middle ground between the other two categories.

All Jews, however, maintain a keen awareness of their cultural history and the historical endurance of prejudice and discrimination. A collective memory of centuries of slavery in Egypt, conquest by Rome, and persecution in Europe have shaped Jewish awareness. The denial of equal political rights and economic opportunity to European Jews was accompanied by forcible residential segregation (first in Italy) in areas of cities that came to be called *ghettos* (derived from the Italian word "borghetto," meaning small settlement outside of city walls).

Jewish emigration to America began in the mid-1600s. As large numbers arrived in the final decades of the nineteenth century during the Great Immigration, prejudice and discrimination, commonly referred to as *anti-Semitism*, increased. During this century, anti-Semitism reached its height when Jews experienced the most horrific persecution in modern times—the Holocaust, in which the Nazis systematically annihilated about 6 million people during the 1930s and 1940s. The killing was so extensive and methodical that many Americans and Europeans initially refused to recognize it for the genocide it was (Abzug, 1985).

One of the oldest world religions, Judaism has changed considerably over thousands of years. Like Christianity and Islam, Judaism recognizes a single God; like Hinduism and Confucianism, it emphasizes moral directives within this world. The history of Judaism is also a grim reminder of the extent to which religious minorities have been the target of hatred and even slaughter in human history (Bedell, Sandon, & Wellborn, 1975; Holm, 1977; Schmidt, 1980; Seltzer, 1980; B. Wilson, 1982; Eisen, 1983).

RELIGION IN THE UNITED STATES

American society has experienced remarkable changes during the past 350 years. Some wonder if the Industrial Revolution, universal education, and advancing science and technology have combined to undermine traditional religion. Yet the evidence shows that religion continues to be a central element in American society (Collins, 1982; Greeley, 1989).

Religious Affiliation

National surveys reveal that about 90 percent of Americans identify with a particular religion (Gallup, 1984; N.O.R.C., 1989). Formal affiliation with a religious organization for at least some period of life characterizes about two-thirds of the population; this proportion has

Table 17–2 RELIGIOUS IDENTIFICATION AMONG AMERICANS, 1989*

Religion	Proportion Indicating Preference
Protestant denominations	63.1%
Baptist	19.8
Methodist	9.6
Lutheran	7.3
Presbyterian	4.6
Episcopalian	2.8
All others, or no denomination	19.3
Catholic	25.1
Jewish	1.5
Other or no answer	2.5
No religious preference	7.8

SOURCE: N.O.R.C., *General Social Surveys, 1972–1989* (Chicago: National Opinion Research Center, 1989), pp. 140–141.

* Based on a national sample of persons aged 18 or over.

remained relatively stable during the past fifty years (N.O.R.C., 1989; U.S. Bureau of the Census, 1989). The rate of religious affiliation is somewhat lower in western states, where more frequent geographical movement discourages membership in religious organizations (Welch, 1983; Gallup, 1984).

The United States has no official religion; the separation of church and state is mandated by the First Amendment. American society contains more different religions than virtually any country on earth, a product of historical immigration. Despite more than 1000 distinct religions, the Christian-Judaic tradition dominates American culture to the extent that members of other religions (and those with no religion) may feel like "outsiders." In a recent survey summarized in Table 17–2, about 63 percent of Americans claimed to be Protestants, 25 percent said they were Catholics, and less than 2 percent identified themselves as Jews.

This variation—as well as the many Protestant denominations—makes American society appear to be religiously pluralistic. As Figure 17–1 suggests, however, one religious affiliation predominates within most regions of the United States. New England, urban areas of the Midwest, and the Southwest are largely Catholic. The southern states are overwhelmingly Baptist, while Lutherans stand out in the northern plains states. Members of the Church of Jesus Christ of Latter-day Saints (Mormons) are heavily concentrated in and around Utah.

Figure 17–1 Major Denominations by Counties of the United States, 1980
(Glenmary Research Center, Atlanta, Georgia)

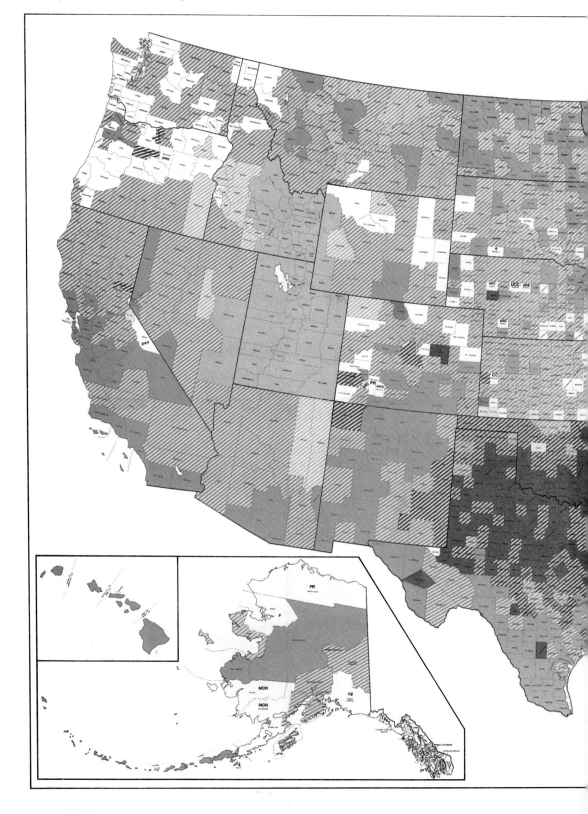

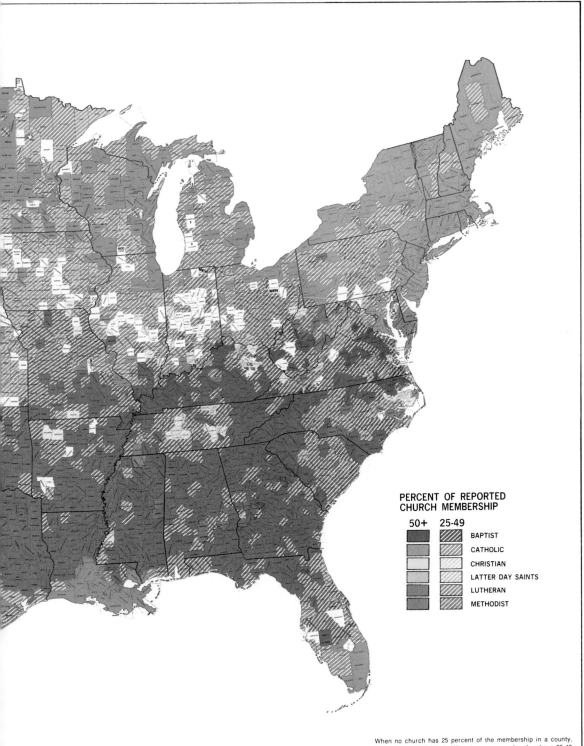

PERCENT OF REPORTED
CHURCH MEMBERSHIP

50+   25-49

BAPTIST

CATHOLIC

CHRISTIAN

LATTER DAY SAINTS

LUTHERAN

METHODIST

When no church has 25 percent of the membership in a county,
that county is left blank. When two or more churches have 25-49
percent of the membership in a county, the largest is shown.

In only a few counties (white in the figure) does no religion represent at least one-fourth of the population.

Religiosity

Religiosity is *the importance of religion in a person's life*. Americans and Canadians are a comparatively religious people; more so, for example, than Europeans or the Japanese. Quantitative measures of American religiosity vary, however, depending on how this concept is operationalized. Years ago, Charles Glock (1959, 1962) distinguished five distinct dimensions of religiosity. *Experiential* religiosity refers to a person's inward emotional tie to a religion. *Ritualistic* religiosity refers to frequency of ritual activity such as prayer and church attendance. *Ideological* religiosity concerns belief in religious doctrine. *Consequential* religiosity has to do with how evident religious beliefs are in a person's daily behavior. *Intellectual* religiosity refers to a person's knowledge of the history and beliefs of a particular religion. Anyone is likely to be more religious in some ways than in others, which compounds the difficulty of measuring a complex concept such as religiosity.

How religious, then, are Americans? Almost everyone in the United States (95 percent) claims to believe in a divine power of some kind, although only about 65 percent claim to "know that God exists and have no doubts about it" (N.O.R.C., 1989:405). As we have seen, 90 percent of Americans identify with a specific religion. And 84 percent claim to "feel closeness to God" (N.O.R.C., 1987:140). In terms of experiential religiosity, Americans do seem to be a religious people.

Americans appear to be less religious in ideological terms: only about 70 percent, for example, claim to believe in a life after death (N.O.R.C., 1989:144). Americans score even lower on dimensions of ritualistic religiosity. For example, only about half of American adults claim to pray at least once a day (N.O.R.C., 1989:150), and only about one-third attend religious services on a weekly or almost-weekly basis (N.O.R.C., 1989:142).

The degree of American religiosity, therefore, does not allow for simple answers. Because belief in God is normative within American culture, for many people such a claim may be simply a matter of conformity. Similarly, people's motives for attending religious services are not all religious. Religious organizations may provide a sense of identity and belonging, a means of serving the community, or a source of social prestige. Our general conclusion, then, is that most Americans are marginally

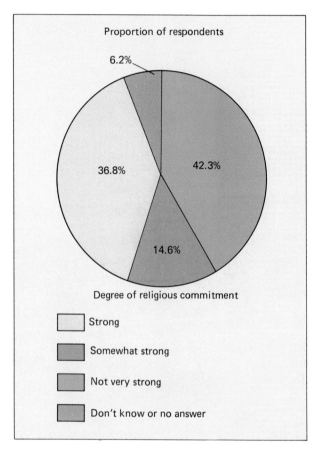

Figure 17–2 The Strength of American Religious Beliefs, 1989

(National Opinion Research Center, 1989:144)

religious, although a large minority are deeply religious. This estimation is supported by a recent survey of American adults, illustrated in Figure 17–2.

Patterns of belief also vary among different religious organizations. In a classic study, Rodney Stark and Charles Glock (1968) found that Catholics appear to be generally more religious than Protestants. And members of sects are typically more religious than members of Catholic or Protestant churches.

Correlates of Religious Affiliation

Religious affiliation is related not only to religiosity, but to other familiar social patterns as well.

Social Class

Religious affiliation is linked to social class. Wade Roof (1979) found that Jews and certain Protestant denominations (Episcopalians and Presbyterians) had the highest overall social standing in American society. In a middle position were other Protestant denominations, such as Congregationalists and Methodists. Somewhat lower social standing was typical of Catholics, Lutherans, Baptists, and various sects.

Protestant denominations with high social position are those whose members are primarily of Northern European background. The denominations contain many people whose ancestors came to the United States more than a century ago. They have encountered the least prejudice and discrimination and have had the greatest time to establish themselves socially. Roman Catholics are commonly more recent immigrants to the United States (Johnstone, 1983).

Jews have high social standing considering many are fairly recent immigrants who have confronted anti-Semitism from some members of the Christian majority. Sometimes people explain Jewish success by asserting that Jews are likely to work in banks and other financial positions. This perception is not true, however: in New York, Jews represent half of the city's college graduates, but only 2 percent of its banking officials (Schaefer, 1979). A more plausible explanation is that Jewish culture has long placed great value on achievement and education. Although a large proportion of Jews began life in the United States in poverty, an intense desire for learning often led to the extensive formal education of children, so that the social position of many Jews—although certainly not all—rose in a generation or two.

Ethnicity and Race

Throughout the world, religion is strongly linked to ethnicity. Many world religions predominate within a single geographical region, and sometimes within a single society. The Arab cultures of the Middle East are predominantly Islamic, for example, as Hinduism is virtually synonymous with Indian culture and Confucianism is with the culture of China. Elsewhere, links between religion and ethnicity are less strong. Christianity is spread throughout numerous cultures, as is Judaism.

Within American society are found *Anglo-Saxon* Protestants, *Irish* Catholics, *Russian* Jews, and *Greek* Orthodox. This fusion of nationality and religion is the result of an influx of immigrants to America from societies with a single major religion. Still, nearly every American ethnic group contains at least some religious diversity. Americans of English ancestry, for instance, include members of many Protestant denominations, as well as Roman Catholics, Jews, and followers of other religions.

The church has historically been a central element in the lives of black Americans. After arrival in the western hemisphere, most Afro-Americans became Christians—the dominant religion in the Americas—but fused Christian belief and practice with elements of African religions. This history, and the harsh discipline of slavery, generated among black Christians ritual that was—by white standards—highly emotional and spontaneous. These qualities persist in some black religious organizations in the United States today (Frazier, 1965; Roberts, 1980). Christian fellowship notwithstanding, American blacks have historically attended all-black churches or worshipped in segregated sections of predominantly white churches.

After emancipation, as blacks migrated from the rural South to the industrial cities of the North, the church addressed problems of dislocation, prejudice, and poverty. For a category of Americans often cut off from the larger society, black churches also provided opportunity for talented men and women to distinguish themselves. Black ministers, such as Ralph Abernathy, Martin Luther King, Jr., and Jesse Jackson gained national and even world recognition as distinguished leaders of black America.

Political Attitudes

On most issues, American Protestants are more conservative than Catholics. Protestants are more likely to support the (more conservative) Republican Party, while Catholics have historically been (more liberal) Democrats. Jews, too, have traditionally supported the Democratic Party (J. Wilson, 1978; Gallup, 1982). Political orientations are complex, however. Protestants, for example, are more likely to take the liberal pro-choice stand on the abortion controversy than Catholics are (Davis, 1987).

Protestant conservatism probably reflects historical privilege. Many liberal Catholics and Jews, however, are religious and ethnic minorities who have faced greater social disadvantages. Similarly, the long-standing political activism of black churches represents not only Christian ideals but a historical response to prejudice and discrimination.

RELIGION IN A CHANGING SOCIETY

Every society changes over time. Along with patterns of social inequality, family life, and formal education, religion has changed and will continue to change in the United States.

Secularization

One of the most important and controversial patterns of social change is **secularization,** *the decline in the influence of religion.* Secularization (derived from the Latin, meaning "the present age") is commonly associated with modern, technologically advanced societies (Cox, 1971; O'Dea & Aviad, 1983). Conventional wisdom holds that secularization results from the increasing importance of science to human understanding. Secularization, therefore, is a shift from a *religious* understanding of the world (based on faith) to a *scientific* understanding (based on empirical evidence).

Imagine Sir Isaac Newton (1642–1727) sitting under a tree observing apples falling to the ground. Had he followed the mode of thought that dominated Europe during the Middle Ages, Newton might have been guided by his faith to conclude that apples grow and fall according to the will of God. Newton, however, lived in an age when human beings were adopting the logic of science to understand the natural world. Thus his observations led him to formulate the law of gravity.

Today few Americans understand birth, illness, or death as the work of a divine power. All of these transitions are now more likely to occur in the presence of physicians (whose knowledge is based on science) than church leaders (whose knowledge is based on faith). In practice, then, secularization diminishes religion's sphere of influence. Theologian Harvey Cox elaborates:

> The world looks less and less to religious rules and rituals for its morality or its meanings. For some, religion provides a hobby, for others a mark of national or ethnic identification, for still others an esthetic delight. For fewer and fewer does it provide an inclusive and commanding system of personal and cosmic values and explanations. (1971:3)

If Cox is correct, should we expect that religion will someday completely disappear? Not according to many sociologists (Hammond, 1985; McGuire, 1987).

Secularization is sometimes the intentional result of repressing religion. The People's Republic of China, which controls Tibet, has used military force to undermine the influence of Buddhism in that nation. This photo, recently smuggled out of Tibet, shows a room containing desecrated Buddhist shrines and the worldly property of nine Buddhist monks killed in clashes with government troops.

Recall that the vast majority of Americans continue to profess a belief in God. Two-thirds of Americans are affiliated with a religious organization today, a proportion that is actually twice as high as in 1900 and four times as high as in 1850. Church attendance has also remained steady in recent decades (Hout & Greeley, 1987). As explained presently, American society has also recently experienced a swell of religious activity.

Secularization, therefore, is not a progressive elimination of religion. Instead, secularization is an uneven process of change in which a decline in some aspects of religion may be accompanied by an increase in others. The consequences of secularization are also unclear. Some see it as a lamentable loss of traditional American values. Others view secularization as liberation from the all-encompassing beliefs of the past, so that people now take greater responsibility for what they choose to believe. Secularization has also brought the practices of many religious organizations more in line with widespread social attitudes. The Catholic Church, for example, has abandoned Latin in religious services in favor of commonly spoken languages, and other religions have recently allowed the ordination of women.

Secularization, then, can be interpreted as either moral advance or moral decline. Whatever its significance, the fears of some that religion may disappear are almost certainly unfounded.

Civil Religion

If secularization has meant a decline in some traditional religious beliefs, it has also involved the rise of new religious forms (McGuire, 1987). Both processes can be seen in what Robert Bellah (1975) has called **civil religion,** meaning *a quasi-religious loyalty binding individuals within a basically secular society.* The term *civil* refers to the ordinary life of citizens of a political state; such patriotic ties, in other words, have many religious qualities.

A vast majority of people in the United States associate the American way of life with what is good and believe that American involvement in the world is beneficial to other nations. In contrast, most Americans believe that communism as a political system represents evil (N.O.R.C., 1983, 1989). Civil religion also includes many forms of ritual. Before the opening of sporting events, spectators rise for the playing of the national anthem. Public parades held throughout the year (including New Year's Day, Memorial Day, the Fourth of July, Labor Day, Thanksgiving Day, and Christmas) encourage the patriotic pursuit of the nation's goals. Much like the cross to Christians and the Star of David to Jews, the flag serves as a sacred symbol that Americans expect to be treated with reverence and respect.

Patriotism and religion also involve much the same personal experience. Participants in a patriotic celebration often feel the sense of reverence and awe that is shared by people at religious services. The explanation lies in Emile Durkheim's insight that all rituals allow us to experience our collective identity—the power of society.

Civil religion is not a specific religious doctrine, nor, given the political doctrine separating church and state, could it ever be. But civil religion does incorporate many elements of traditional religion into the political system of a secular society. The fact that Americans exhibit such a strong belief in the goodness of their society (based more on faith than on clear scientific evidence) is one vital religious expression in a modern, secular society.

Religious Revival in America

We have noted that religiosity, measured by belief in God and by church attendance, has changed little in recent decades. Even so, membership in established, "mainline" churches (including Episcopalian, Presbyte-

rian, and Lutheran denominations) has decreased by about 20 percent during the past twenty-five years. Yet during the same period, the memberships of other religious organizations (including the Mormons, Seventh-Day Adventists, and many Christian sects) have risen dramatically (Jacquet, 1984). Perhaps, then, secularization is a self-limiting process: as established religions decline, the timeless human need for meaning and security gives rise to new forms of religious activity (Stark & Bainbridge, 1981).

Religious Fundamentalism

Underlying the change just described is a rise in **religious fundamentalism,** *conservative religious organizations that seek to restore what are viewed as fundamental elements of religion.* In the United States, the growing significance of fundamentalism is most evident among Protestants; yet, fundamentalism is also evident among Roman Catholics and Jews.

Fundamentalism came to the attention of many Americans when conservative Christian organizations visibly supported the presidential candidacy of Ronald Reagan during the 1980s. Fundamentalism has actually been growing in importance throughout this century (Bromley & Shupe, 1984). As increasing numbers of Americans enrolled in schools, scientific thinking appeared to be replacing traditional religious beliefs. The widespread discussion of Darwin's theory of evolution was evidence to many people that science threatened traditional religion. Further, rapidly growing cities were reshaping American culture, and established traditions were thought to be endangered by the arrival of millions of immigrants from around the world.

Religious fundamentalism arose as a defense of traditional beliefs in this climate of rapid change. Opposing the perceived evils of secularization, fundamentalists seek to restore religious purity to organizations whose doctrines they believe have been eroded by tolerance for diversity and openness to change. One effective way to resist change is to insist on a literal interpretation of the Gospels (the first four books of the New Testament) as the basis of "true" religion (Johnstone, 1983). Thus, fundamentalism is appealing because it offers certainty in an uncertain world. What some—including many faithful Christians—consider dogmatic, then, others find distinctly reassuring.

Fundamentalist Christianity generally has four characteristics. First, fundamentalists literally interpret Scripture, believing that more liberal Christian clergy

Arts of the South, by American painter Thomas Hart Benton (1889–1975), suggests that religious fundamentalism is strongly integrated into the community life of rural people in the southern United States.

Thomas Hart Benton, Arts of the South. Tempera with oil glaze, 8 x 13 feet. 1953.20. From the collection of the New Britain Museum of American Art, Connecticut. Harriet Russell Stanley Fund.

offer incorrect interpretations. In the creationism debate described previously, for example, fundamentalists claim that God created the world precisely according to the account in Genesis. Second, fundamentalists tend to be less tolerant of religious diversity than are members of other religious organizations. They passionately embrace their beliefs as the only true religion, while pointing out the error in beliefs held by others. Third, fundamentalism has a sectlike emphasis on the personal experience of religion. In contrast to the reserve and self-control common to more established religious organizations, fundamentalism seeks to propagate "good old-time religion" via rituals that foster spiritual revival. To fundamentalists, being "born again" and establishing a personal relationship with Jesus is expected to be clearly evident in a person's everyday life. Fourth, fundamentalism also has a sectlike adversity toward the modern world, which is considered to be a dangerous source of "secular humanism" that undermines religious conviction.

The label "fundamentalist" applies to some religious organizations more than to others. Generally, fundamentalists are conservative Christian organizations within the larger evangelical tradition, including Pentecostals, Southern Baptists, Seventh-Day Adventists, and the Assembly of God. The precise number of Americans who can accurately be described as religious fundamentalists is a matter of informed estimate. Operationalizing the concept to include people who interpret the Bible literally, about 20 percent of American adults would

be termed Christian fundamentalists (N.O.R.C., 1989:168).

Fundamentalism has historically been strong in rural America, especially a century ago when cities in the United States were growing rapidly. The trial of John Scopes in Tennessee in 1925 again rallied fundamentalists, but soon after the movement waned. The 1950s witnessed a renewed fundamentalism with a distinctly political element: anticommunist sentiment sparked by the "cold war" between the United States and the Soviet Union (Hunter, 1985). More recent research shows that politically conservative fundamentalists are spread throughout the United States (not concentrated in the South), and include both urbanites and rural Americans (Wilcox, 1989).

During the 1980s, Christian fundamentalism once more took on a decidedly political character in the form of what is called the New Christian Right (Viguerie, 1981; Speer, 1984; Ostling, 1985). Jerry Falwell, a fundamentalist preacher who helped bring this religious movement to national attention, described its goals:

> I am seeking to rally together the people of this country who still believe in decency, the home, the family, morality, the free enterprise system, and all the great ideals that are the cornerstone of this nation. Against the growing tide of permissiveness and moral decay that is crushing our society, we must make a sacred commitment to God Almighty to turn this nation around immediately. (Falwell, 1980, cited in Speer, 1984:20)

In 1989, Falwell disbanded his "Moral Majority" and turned attention to his church in Lynchburg, Virginia. He and other fundamentalist leaders, however, continue to oppose what they see as a "liberal agenda," including the Equal Rights Amendment, abortion as a matter of choice, the civil rights of homosexuals, and the free availability of pornography. They have also sought to return prayer to American public schools, which they view as awash with a morally permissive climate of secular humanism. Finally, they have criticized the mass media for coloring presentations with liberal sentiments (Hunter, 1983).

Christian fundamentalism in the United States has expanded its educational efforts beyond the doors of the church. Thousands of Christian elementary and secondary schools exist in the United States, along with several hundred fundamentalist Bible colleges. Fundamentalist organizations also spread their message with hundreds of periodicals (Hunter, 1985). Additionally, during the 1980s, fundamentalist Christians made increasing use of the most powerful medium of communication in the United States: television.

The Electronic Church

The mass media have become vital to generating religious excitement and gaining converts to fundamentalist religion. Congregations now take the form of radio and television audiences across the nation through what is commonly called the *electronic church* dominated by prime-time preachers (Hadden & Swain, 1981). Although many members of more established churches claim "prime-time preaching" undermines religion with emotional simplicity, millions of Americans have become regular participants in this new form of religious activity.

At the beginning of the 1980s, this uniquely American religious movement claimed about fourteen hundred radio stations and sixty television stations (including many cable television channels). Aided by their electronic churches, religious leaders such as Oral Roberts, Robert Schuller, and Jim and Tammy Bakker have become better known to Americans than all but a few clergy in the past. It is likely that about 5 percent of the national television audience (about 15 million Americans) are regular viewers of religious television, while perhaps 20 percent (about 60 million) watch at least some religious programming every month (Martin, 1981; Gallup, 1982; N.O.R.C., 1989).

Using the mass media to regularly solicit contributions brought a financial windfall to many religious organizations. Broadcasting with thirty-two hundred stations in half the countries in the world, Jimmy Swaggart received $180 million in contributions in 1986.

The power of money, however, compromised some televangelists. In 1989, Jim Bakker (who began his television career in 1965, with his wife Tammy, hosting a children's puppet show) began a jail term following a conviction for defrauding contributors. The Bakkers gained national attention during the 1980s as founders of the PTL Club and developers of the twenty-three-hundred-acre Heritage, USA Christian theme park in South Carolina. As the money poured in, the couple's income soared to more than $1 million a year, sparking federal agencies to begin investigations.

In the wake of this scandal, support for television preachers has declined. Public concern—which extends

The fund-raising ability of the electronic church can be intoxicating to television preachers, as it was to Jim Bakker, founder of the PTL Ministry. In 1989, after raising tens of millions of dollars and appropriating much of it for his personal use, Bakker was convicted of mail fraud and sentenced to up to forty-five years in prison.

far beyond the PTL—is that televangelism empires remain under the control of single charismatic leaders and their families, and are accountable to no one else. No charges of improper conduct had been lodged against any other televangelists, but Americans remain wary that some televangelists are more concerned with raising cash than moral standards.

The popularity of media-ministries, the growth of cults and sects, and the adherence of millions more Americans to traditional churches strongly indicate that secularization is unlikely to eliminate religion from the modern world (Stark & Bainbridge, 1981; Bateson & Ventis, 1982; Hunter, 1985). Probably our complex and rapidly changing world creates in many people a longing for a more secure individual identity and sense of purpose. The social anonymity of modern life also generates strong feelings of isolation.

Science is simply unable to provide answers to the most central human needs and questions, and scientific technology—for example, in the form of nuclear armaments—has only increased anxiety about the future of the human species. With religion's power to provide membership and direction, no wonder that many people rely on their faith for a sense of security and hope (Cox, 1977; Barker, 1981; Johnstone, 1983).

SUMMARY

1. Religion is a major social institution based on distinguishing the sacred and the profane. Religion is a matter of faith, not scientific evidence, and involves various forms of ritual behavior.

2. Sociology analyzes religion as a social phenomenon, making no claims as to the ultimate truth or falsity of any religious belief.

3. Emile Durkheim argued that religion expresses the power of society over individuals. His structural-functional analysis suggests that religion promotes social cohesion, social control, and provides meaning and purpose to life.

4. Using the symbolic-interaction paradigm, Peter Berger explains that religious beliefs are socially constructed. They are a vital source of individual meaning and security.

5. Using the social-conflict paradigm, Karl Marx linked religion to social inequality. Religious ideals, however, have also motivated some people to seek greater equality within society.

6. Churches are formal religious organizations that are well integrated into the larger society. Two types of churches are ecclesias and denominations.

7. Sects are informal religious organizations that are not well integrated into the larger society. Sects emerge as the result of religious division and often have charismatic leadership.

8. Cults are religious organizations that embrace new and unconventional beliefs and practices.

9. Technologically simple human societies were generally animistic; more complex societies develop a distinct religious institution.

10. Followers of six major world religions—Christianity, Islam, Hinduism, Buddhism, Confucianism, and Judaism—represent two-thirds of all humanity.

11. Almost all American adults identify with a religion; about 60 percent have a formal religious affiliation, with the largest number belonging to various Protestant denominations.

12. The religiosity of the American people varies according to how this concept is operationalized. The vast majority of American adults claim to believe in God, but only about half engage in daily prayer and just about one-third attend religious services regularly.

13. Religious affiliation is related to social class, ethnicity, race, and political attitudes.

14. Secularization, an important dimension of social change, involves a diminishing importance of religion. Secularization is seen by some as a breakdown of traditional morality, and by others as a form of liberation and source of greater tolerance.

15. Although membership in many "mainline" churches has declined, other religious organizations (notably Christian sects) have gained in popularity. This casts doubt on the idea that secularization will result in the demise of religion.

16. Civil religion is a quasi-religious belief by which people profess loyalty to their society, often in the form of patriotism.

17. Fundamentalist Christianity stresses literal interpretation of the Bible, intolerance of religious diversity, and the personal experience of the power of religion. Many fundamentalist Christian organizations actively supported conservative political goals in the United States.

18. Despite the historical process of secularization, the persistence of religion suggests its unique ability to address timeless questions about human experiences and needs.

KEY CONCEPTS

animism the belief that natural objects are conscious forms of life that can affect humanity

charisma extraordinary personal qualities that can turn an audience into followers

church a formal religious organization that is well integrated into the larger society

civil religion a quasi-religious loyalty binding individuals within a basically secular society

conversion a personal transformation resulting from new religious beliefs

cult a religious movement that is highly unconventional in terms of the surrounding society

denomination a church that recognizes religious pluralism

ecclesia a church that is formally allied with the state

faith belief that is not based on scientific evidence

liberation theology a fusion of Christian principles with political activism, often Marxist in character

monotheism religious beliefs recognizing a single divine power

polytheism religious beliefs recognizing many gods

profane that which is defined as an ordinary element of everyday life

religion a system of beliefs and practices based upon recognizing the sacred

religiosity the importance of religion in a person's life

religious fundamentalism conservative religious organizations that seek to restore what are viewed as fundamental elements of religion

ritual formal, ceremonial behavior

sacred that which is defined as extraordinary, inspiring a sense of awe, reverence, and even fear

sect an informal religious organization that is not well integrated into the larger society

secularization the historical decline in the influence of religion

totem an object within the natural world imbued with sacred qualities

SUGGESTED READINGS

This text provides an overview of a sociological analysis of religion.

Meredith B. McGuire. *Religion: The Social Context*. 2nd ed. Belmont, CA: Wadsworth, 1987.

The state of American religion is explored in the first of the following books. The second consists of nine essays that survey religion globally.

Thomas Robbins and Dick Anthony. *In Gods We Trust: New Patterns of Religious Pluralism in America*. New Brunswick, NJ: Transaction, 1989.

James A. Beckford and Thomas Luckmann, eds. *The Changing Face of Religion*. Newbury Park, CA: Sage, 1989.

The study of the growth of new religious movements explains the appeal of unconventional religious organizations.

Irving Hexham and Karla Poewe. *Understanding Cults and New Religions*. Grand Rapids, MI: Wm. B. Eerdmans, 1986.

The first book explains how a fundamentalist Islamic regime rose to power in Iran. The second examines a report on five Islamic communities in the United States, providing insights into a religion about which many Americans know little.

Said Amir Arjomand. *The Turban for the Crown: The Islamic Revolution in Iran*. New York: Oxford University Press, 1988.

Yvonne Yazbeck Haddad and Adair T. Lummis. *Islamic Values in the United States: A Comparative Study*. New York: Oxford University Press, 1987.

18

Politics and Government

Not since the revolution that brought the communists to power in 1949 has the People's Republic of China experienced anything like the events of the spring of 1989. Tiananmen Square—the central landmark of the capital city of Beijing—was the scene of an unprecedented five-week demonstration in support of greater political democracy. The demonstrators, numbering in the thousands, were initially mostly students encouraged by recent economic reforms to demand a greater voice in government. Clustered together in the shadow of the Great Hall of the People, some began a hunger strike; others resolutely displayed banners and headbands that proclaimed their goals. As the days passed, their numbers steadily increased, until more than 1 million of the city's people mixed uneasily with a growing number of soldiers around the square.

Reformers among the country's leaders supported the demonstration. Hard-liners strongly opposed it, urging the use of force to crush the protest. The balance of power slowly shifted toward a policy of repression. Ominous signs appeared: troops from other regions of China (denied news of how popular the protest had become) were trucked to the outskirts of the city. Waves of soldiers periodically tried to clear sections of the square; each time, the demonstrators held their ground. Premier Li Peng then announced that the "turmoil" was to be swiftly ended. Anxiety rose as the government ordered

satellite dishes and other communication links operated by foreign news agencies shut down.

About 2 A.M. on the morning of Sunday, June 4, the political dueling ended in convulsions of violence and horror. From three sides, a fifty-truck convoy of ten thousand troops converged on the square. Soldiers leveled AK-47 assault rifles and began firing indiscriminately at the crowds. Tanks rolled over makeshift barricades, crushing the people behind them. Some demonstrators bravely fought back, but their fate had already been sealed. Within three hours, the pro-democracy

movement had ended, and Tiananmen Square was awash with the blood of thousands of people.

Events such as those in Tiananmen Square make clear a lesson often lost in the concerns of daily life: the operation of every society is shaped by those who have the power to control events. Power, of course, takes many forms, but all are not necessarily equal. As they occupied the center of their nation's capital city, the Chinese people claimed the moral power to direct their own lives. The response of their government, in words once used by Chinese leader Mao Zedong, was: "Political power grows out of the barrel of a gun."

This chapter investigates the dynamics of politics and government. As a major social institution, **politics** is *the institutionalized system by which a society distributes power and makes decisions.* **Government** refers to *formal organizations that direct political life within a society.*

POWER AND AUTHORITY

Whether power arises from "the voice of the people" or from "the barrel of a gun," all political life involves disagreement and often conflict. Early in this century, Max Weber (1978; orig. 1921) recognized this fact by defining **power** as *the ability to achieve desired ends de-*

spite possible resistance from others. History shows that sheer force—physical or psychological coercion—is surely the most basic form of power. No society can long exist, however, if power *only* derives from force, because people will break the rules at the first opportunity. Obtaining compliance through terror, then, is not only extremely difficult but limited in effectiveness. Social organization, therefore, depends on generating significant agreement about proper goals (cultural values) and the suitable means of attaining them (cultural norms). Weber was thus led to consider ways in which inequalities of power might be considered just. According to Weber, **authority** is *power widely perceived as legitimate rather than coercive.* Authority, then, is legitimated by the explicit or implicit acceptance of everyone to whom it applies.

How the use of power is perceived depends on its social context. A familiar illustration involves a teacher assigning a term paper to a class. Although students may greet the assignment by groans, they usually do the work according to the teacher's directions. Teachers and students behave as they do because making assignments is part of a teacher's role, just as completing them is part of the student role. Power used in ways consistent with cultural norms is thus transformed into authority.

A teacher who threatens a student with a poor grade in order to obtain sexual favors, however, violates cultural norms and university regulations. Such behavior

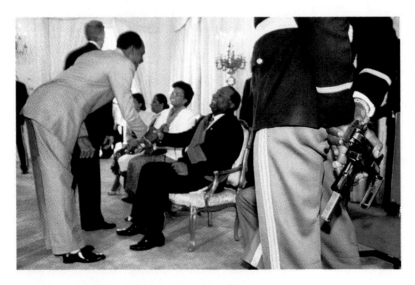

All governments desire the stability that comes from the widespread perception of legitimacy. Haiti, however, is one of the most politically volatile countries in the world. At his recent inauguration, Haitian President Manigat sought to convey a sense of confidence to well-wishers. Even so, in a climate of violence, governmental authority is often hard to distinguish from military power.

is thus coercive power rather than legitimate authority. Authority, then, demands obedience to norms not only by those who obey, but also by those who command.

Max Weber identified three general contexts in which power is commonly defined as authority. Particular everyday situations, of course, often involve some combination of the three.

Traditional Authority

Weber defined **traditional authority** as *power legitimated by respect for long-established cultural patterns*. Traditional authority is pervasive in preindustrial societies in which change is slow. Recognized by generations of people as extending back in a society's collective memory, traditional social patterns become nearly sacred. The power of Chinese emperors in antiquity was legitimated by tradition, as was the rule of nobility in medieval Europe. Traditional authority is commonly linked to families whose members, across centuries, have always ruled. The sacred character of traditional authority encourages some traditional leaders to claim a divine right to rule.

The legitimation of power by tradition declines as a society becomes industrialized. Hannah Arendt (1963) views this process as increasing cultural diversity so that no traditional beliefs are shared by everyone. Royal families still exist in several European societies, but more democratic forces have shifted power to commoners who are elected to office. As a democratic society, the United States has little heritage of traditional authority at the national level, although some upper-class American families—such as the Roosevelts, Kennedys, and Rockefellers—have a political record that has conferred on them a limited measure of traditional authority (Baltzell, 1964).

Patriarchy, the traditional domination of women by men, persists in the United States, but this form of traditional authority is increasingly challenged. The power of parents over their young children remains an example of widely supported traditional authority. In all cases of traditional authority, cultural norms require people of one status to obey those who hold a superior status. Obedience, therefore, is normally expected without discussion of the merits of the command itself. Thus when children ask *why* they should obey, a parent sometimes replies curtly, "Because I said so!"

Rational-Legal Authority

As explained in Chapter 7 ("Groups and Organizations"), Weber viewed bureaucracy as a distinctive trait of modern industrial societies. Bureaucracy expresses a rational view of the world that erodes long-established customs and practices in favor of formal rules, often in the form of law. Weber defined **rational-legal authority** (sometimes called *bureaucratic authority*) as *power legitimated by legally enacted rules and regulations*.

Rationally enacted rules underlie most authority in the United States today. The authority of classroom teachers rests primarily on holding positions in bureaucratic colleges and universities. The authority of political leaders also depends, not on family background, but on offices within vast governmental organizations. Thus a queen may always be a queen, but a president who leaves office enjoys a generous pension but loses presidential authority.

In contrast to traditional authority, bureaucratic authority stresses achievement over ascribed characteristics. An officeholder presumably exercises rational-legal authority on the basis of talent and special training, not birth. A king's brother, for example, is a prince; but brothers and sisters of American presidents rarely attract much public notice, and exercise no authority unless they, too, hold office.

Bureaucratic rules and regulations apply to every member of an organization: even the American president is subject to law. The Watergate crisis in the early 1970s occurred in the wake of unlawful actions taken by members of Richard Nixon's campaign staff, which a number of top government officials—including Nixon himself—sought to conceal. This behavior led to formal charges that Nixon had exceeded the legal limits of presidential authority, causing him to resign from office rather than face almost certain impeachment by the House of Representatives.

Charismatic Authority

Max Weber was intrigued by charisma, the exceptional personal qualities discussed in Chapter 17 ("Religion"). He defined **charismatic authority** as *power legitimated through extraordinary personal abilities that inspire devotion and obedience*. Unlike its traditional and rational-legal counterparts, charismatic authority depends little on a person's social position or office; it is an expression of individual personality.

Every society contains people regarded as especially forceful, creative, and magnetic. In modern societies, these may include famous artists, entertainers, and political leaders, as well as more obscure individuals who are admired mainly by their friends. Charisma may enhance traditional or rational-legal authority; American presidents Franklin Roosevelt and Ronald Reagan benefitted from their personal magnetism. Charisma, Weber noted, is frequently used to lead people away from traditional customs and established organizations. Leaders of religious cults, which challenge conventional beliefs and practices, often base their authority on personal charisma.

Thus people with charismatic authority may seek to—*and often can*—make their own rules, as if drawing on a higher power. This extraordinary ability is evident in religious leaders from Buddha and Jesus of Nazareth to the Ayatollah Khomeini. As different as these three were, all preached an alternative to the status quo and inspired followers to transform the existing social order. The revolutionary effects of charismatic leadership are also deeply engraved in global politics: Vladimir Lenin guided his nation's overthrow of feudal monarchy, Mahatma Gandhi inspired the struggle to free India from British colonialism, and Martin Luther King, Jr. led a decade-long civil rights movement in the United States.

Charisma may be personal, but society fosters distinctive patterns of leadership for the two sexes. Patriarchy allows men to dominate in national affairs while directing charismatic women away from politics to the arts, the family, and other social contexts traditionally defined as feminine. Yet some charismatic women such as Indira Gandhi of India, Benazir Bhutto of Pakistan, and Margaret Thatcher of the United Kingdom have gained national political prominence. Perhaps the most charismatic woman in politics during this century was Argentinean Eva Peron, described in the box.

Because charismatic authority emanates from a single individual, charismatic movements face a crisis of survival once their leader is gone. The long-term persistence of a charismatic movement, Max Weber argued, requires **routinization of charisma**, *the transformation of charismatic authority into some combination of traditional and bureaucratic authority.* Christianity, for example, began as a cult based on the personal charisma of Jesus of Nazareth. After the death of Jesus, the Roman Catholic Church gradually became established on a foundation of tradition and bureaucracy. Such a routinization

of charisma is by no means certain, however. Most charismatic movements disintegrate upon the departure of the inspirational leader. The nineteenth-century Christian sect in the Oneida region of upstate New York, founded by the charismatic clergyman John Humphrey Noyes, declined soon after its aging leader left the community.

POLITICS IN HISTORICAL PERSPECTIVE

Technologically simple hunting and gathering societies have few specialized roles and generate minimal material wealth. Such societies therefore operate like a large family. Usually a recognized leader is a male with unusual strength, hunting skill, or personal charisma. Leaders exercise only modest power over others, lacking the resources to reward supporters or punish challengers. In simple societies, then, leaders enjoy special prestige, but they have no more wealth and only slightly more power than anyone else (Lenski & Lenski, 1987).

Agrarian societies are more complex, with greater specialized activity and plentiful material surplus. Social stratification expands, with wealth and power concentrated among a small elite. Such inequality amplifies politics so that it becomes a social institution distinct from family life. Elites who maintain their social position for generations may acquire traditional authority, while Weber's rational-legal authority may further support rulers served by a bureaucratic political administration and system of law.

The power of leaders grows as political organization increases in size and scope, leading to the formation of the **political state**, *a formal government claiming the legitimate use of coercion to support its rule.* A government is not the only source of political power within a society, as proved by political revolutions that have occurred throughout human history. Yet government is distinguished from other centers of power by its claim to exercise power legitimately, based on one or more of the principles Weber described.

Initially, the power of the state is restrained by limited technology; only a few centuries ago, communication and the transportation of armies and supplies was slow and uncertain. Gaining control over a wide region, perhaps containing many distinct cultural groups, presented obvious difficulties. The earliest political empires,

Evita: Charisma, Gender, and Argentine Politics

In Argentina's strongly patriarchal culture, women are allowed little public voice in national politics. One exception to this traditional pattern was Eva Peron, whose personal charm, energy, and ambition earned her power and fame as the incomparable Evita.

Born in a poor rural village in 1919, Eva Maria Duarte had impressive personal assets: intelligence, beauty, talent as an actress, and a magnetic and forceful personality. As a young woman, she moved to Buenos Aires, Argentina's capital, and soon gained a wide following as a radio and film star. In the eyes of detractors, she used other people, including numerous men with whom she had affairs, as rungs on the social ladder she climbed to the top.

A turning point in Eva Duarte's life was meeting and entrancing Juan Peron, a powerful officer in the Argentine army. Peron was elected vice president, but in the turbulent political climate his fortunes soon swirled downward. Forced from office, he ultimately landed in jail in 1945. It

was then that Eva came into her own as his public defender. A brilliant speaker at public gatherings, she skillfully played up her poor background and forged the masses into a political movement that secured Peron's release from prison. He was shortly elected to the presidency. Within days, Eva Duarte and Juan Peron formally celebrated the advantages of their alliance by getting married.

As First Lady of Argentina, Eva Peron lacked the bureaucratic authority of her husband, but her charisma was overpowering. She won the hearts and minds of the country's poor

(whom she called *los descamisados*, or "the shirtless"), in the process, however, reaping wealth for herself.

As charismatic leaders often are, Eva Peron was highly controversial. Revered by the working class, she aroused only contempt among the middle and upper classes to whom she was an unprincipled opportunist.

After World War II, she toured Europe in an effort to build alliances between Argentina and other right-wing countries, notably Italy and Spain. By the early 1950s, in the eyes of the world Eva Peron had become synonymous with Argentina. Yet, her ambition continued to drive her, and she sought the vice presidency. Her restless quest was stopped, although not by her opponents. Stricken by uterine cancer, she rapidly declined, and in 1952 Eva Peron died at the age of forty-three. But her mystique lived on, transforming her in the eyes of her devoted followers into a saint— *Santa Evita*.

SOURCE: Partly based on Nicolas Fraser and Marysa Navarro, *Eva Peron* (New York: Norton, 1980).

---

such as Mesopotamia in the Near East about five thousand years ago, were therefore successful in establishing only small city-states (Stavrianos, 1983). This political form, also common to ancient Greece, persisted in Europe until the nineteenth century. Today, Vatican City, the center of the Roman Catholic Church inside Rome, remains as one of the few politically independent city-states. Historically, some city-states developed an unusually effective political organization and swelled into vast empires, as in the case of Rome for about five hundred years beginning in the first century B.C.E. By today's standards, such governments seem as inefficient and

cumbersome as the weapons used by their armies. The inability to effectively control its vast empire was, in the end, one reason Rome eventually collapsed.

Within the past several centuries, political organization throughout the world has evolved toward *nation-states*. Currently, the world's 185 different nation-states differ in countless ways, including their cultures and levels of technological development. In industrial societies, the state is most expansive, becoming involved in the everyday lives of the population, providing income assistance, overseeing schools, and setting safety standards in the workplace.

POLITICAL SYSTEMS

Four types of political systems manage the affairs of contemporary nation-states. In each case, government attempts to legitimate its power so that at least most people believe that the particular political system is good.

Monarchy

Monarchy is *a type of political system in which power is passed from generation to generation within a single family*. Monarchy is a very old form of government: the Bible, for example, tells of great kings such as David and Solomon. Using Weber's analysis, monarchy is legitimated primarily by tradition. In Great Britain, the royal family (as well as many members of the traditional aristocracy) trace their ancestry through centuries of nobility. The power of some monarchs was enhanced by personal charisma; most enjoyed the support of a governmental organization that served their interests. But the core of royal authority is deeply rooted tradition.

During the medieval era, *absolute monarchy*, in which hereditary rulers claimed a virtual monopoly of power based on divine right, flourished from England to China. Monarchy remained widespread into the early twentieth century. In 1910, of the seventy national leaders who assembled in London for the funeral of King Edward VII, more than fifty were royalty (Baltzell, 1964).

Since then, elected officials have gradually replaced hereditary nobility. In those European societies where royal families remain—including Great Britain, Spain, Norway, Sweden, Belgium, Denmark, and the Netherlands—they now preside over *constitutional monarchies*, in which monarchs are merely symbolic heads of state. Actual governing is now the responsibility of elected officials, led by a prime minister and guided by a constitution. In these nations, then, the nobility may reign, but elected officials rule (Roskin, 1982).

Democracy

Increasingly common in the modern world is **democracy,** *a political system in which power is exercised by the people as a whole*. In a democracy, individuals rarely participate directly in decision making, an obvious impossibility in large societies. Instead, what is more precisely termed *representative democracy* places authority in the hands of elected leaders who are accountable to the people. Legitimacy, then, is based on popular support, as deter-

mined by elections. In reality, as explained presently, many eligible voters never go to the polls. During the 1988 presidential election, for example, only 57 percent of eligible Americans voted.

Democratic political systems are most common in industrial societies that are relatively rich by world standards (Hannan & Carroll, 1981). With a highly specialized economy, industrial societies demand a literate populace. A highly educated populace generally rejects traditional rulers in favor of representative democracy, which affords them broader participation in the political system. Additionally, in every industrial society, a wide range of formal organizations seek to advance their interests within the political arena. Thus, in contrast to the high concentration of power in the absolutist monarchies common to agrarian societies, industrial societies have a more complex and diffuse political system.

The traditional legitimation of power in a monarchy gives way in democratic political systems to rational-legal patterns of authority. A rational election process places leaders within offices that provide authority limited by law. Thus democracy and rational-legal authority are linked just as monarchy and traditional authority are.

Democratic governments are far more bureaucratic than was any monarchy in the past. Bureaucracy is necessary to carry out an increasing range of governmental activities found in democracies; yet, an inherent antagonism exists between democracy and bureaucracy. The federal government of the United States, for example, employs more than 3 million people, making it one of the largest bureaucracies in the world. Another 14 million people work in some eighty thousand local governments. The great majority of these bureaucrats were never elected; doing so would be impractical given the need for specially trained people to manage government agencies. Everyday decision-making, therefore, is done primarily by career bureaucrats in an undemocratic way (Scaff, 1981; Edwards, 1985; Etzioni-Halevy, 1985).

Although having different political systems during most of this century, the East and the West have both claimed to provide freedom to their people. The East includes the Soviet Union and the nations of Eastern Europe. The West is identified with the United States, Canada, Western Europe, and other allied nations such as Japan. Dramatic changes sweeping Eastern Europe and the Soviet Union beginning in 1989 not only lessened the traditional differences between the two political camps but, as the box explains, highlighted two competing approaches to defining freedom.

The Meaning of Freedom: Changes in Eastern Europe

Underlying the changes in Eastern Europe are pivotal political and economic debates. Western societies have economies shaped by the free-market principles of capitalism. Consistent with a market system, political freedom has traditionally been defined in terms of personal *liberty*. This means *freedom to* vote or otherwise act in one's own interest with minimal interference from the government. As Chapter 19 ("The Economy and Work") explains, however, capitalism fosters considerable inequality of wealth, leading to criticism of Western societies by their Eastern counterparts. Western societies are described as neither free nor truly democratic because the rich impose their interests on others. Popular elections are unlikely to change the capitalist system, according to this view, and thus such political rituals have little practical significance. Whoever is elected presides over a society that permits some to enjoy lavish housing, extensive education, and abundant health care while necessities are denied to others.

In contrast to the Western emphasis on personal liberty, Eastern societies have traditionally pursued *freedom from* basic want, by seeking to provide every citizen with jobs, housing, education, and medical care. This version of freedom requires establishing rough economic *equality* among all people. Eastern European societies with socialist economic systems were, until recently, undemocratic; their people had no right to elect political leaders, form opposing political parties, or freely act in their own interests. But the benefits of equality were used to justify extensive government involvement in the lives of all citizens. A popular response was that government infringement on personal liberties more accurately undermined any claim to providing freedom.

Mikhail Gorbachev's restructuring of the Soviet Union provided the opportunity for the people of Eastern Europe to express widespread dissatisfaction with their political systems. Political pluralism—a system in which many political parties compete for popular support—has replaced the monopoly of power held by communist parties since World War II. These socialist economies that succeeded at maintaining economic equality only at a low standard of living are now also embracing market principles. Some Westerners have viewed this sweeping transformation as evidence of the collapse of socialism (Brzezinski, 1989). Others interpret these events as an evolution toward a political system that may meet human needs better than either the traditional Eastern or Western models.

These lines, written on the Berlin Wall shortly after its opening at the end of 1989, reveal powerful causes of change in Eastern Europe: extensive political control by socialist governments coupled with a low standard of living. Yet the market-based conception of freedom embraced by western nations may also come under fire from those who believe that political liberty depends on controlling the amount of economic inequality.

Changes in Eastern Europe suggest that political liberty and economic equality are not entirely compatible. Should these nations move toward Western-style political liberty, they may soon contend with far greater economic inequality. Should they continue to enforce economic equality, they will have to limit personal liberty. This dilemma is a topic of intense debate among leaders in Poland, Romania, Czechoslovakia and other Eastern European nations.

Authoritarianism and Totalitarianism

Authoritarianism refers to *denying the majority participation in government*. Because no society involves all its citizens in the daily activities of government, every political system is, to some degree, authoritarian. The term authoritarian, therefore, more correctly characterizes political systems that are indifferent to people's lives, in which leaders cannot be legally removed from office, and that provide the population with little institutional-

The painting by Komar and Melamid, *A Knock at the Door*, powerfully portrays the everyday reality of fear and anxiety fostered by a totalitarian government. The artists, who left the Soviet Union for the West, use their art to advocate greater openness in Soviet society.

ized means to even voice an opinion. Although they are rare, absolute monarchies are therefore highly authoritarian. Authoritarian political systems now more commonly take the form of military juntas and other dictatorships. Examples include the regime of Juan and Eva Peron in Argentina during the 1940s and 1950s, the military junta that rules Chile, and the more recent dictatorships of Ferdinand Marcos in the Philippines, the Duvalier family in Haiti, and Manuel Noriega in Panama.

More intense political control characterizes **totali-tarianism,** *denying the majority participation in a government that extensively regulates people's lives.* Totalitarian governments have emerged only within the last century with the technological means to rigidly regulate the lives of citizens. The Nazi regime in Germany, finally crushed at the end of World War II, had the technological resources to support totalitarianism. More recently, advanced electronic technology—including electronic surveillance and computers for storing vast amounts of information—has increased the potential for government manipulation of a large population.

Totalitarian governments often claim to represent the will of the people, but typically they seek to bend people to the will of the government. Such governments are *total* concentrations of power, allowing no organized political opposition. Denying the populace the right to assemble for political purposes, totalitarian regimes thrive in an environment of social atomization. Beyond widespread repression of any opposition, these governments limit the access of citizens to information: in the Soviet Union, for example, the mass media have only recently begun to act independently of the government. Further, the state weakens the public by restricting access to items such as telephone directories, accurate city maps, and copying machines. Further, totalitarian governments encourage citizens to disclose the unpatriotic activities of others. After the crackdown in the People's Republic of China, the government demanded that citizens report anyone—even their own family members—who had been involved in the pro-democracy movement.

Socialization in totalitarian societies is intensely political, seeking not just outward obedience but inward commitment to the system. In North Korea, one of the most totalitarian states in the modern world, political banners, pictures of leaders, and political messages over loudspeakers appear nearly everywhere—constant reminders that each citizen owes total support to the state. In the aftermath of the pro-democracy movement, Chinese officials subjected students at the sixty-seven Beijing universities to mandatory political "refresher" courses. The mass media further support totalitarian regimes by presenting only official versions of events (Arendt, 1958; Kornhauser, 1959; Friedrich & Brzezinski, 1965; Nisbet, 1966; Goldfarb, 1989). The bloodbath at Tiananmen Square, according to Chinese government reports, was a minor skirmish, sparked by attacks by "hooligan" and "counter-revolutionary" students on soldiers.

Totalitarian governments span the political spectrum from the far right (including Nazi Germany) to the far left (such as the People's Republic of China and

Albania). Americans tend to view socialist societies as universally totalitarian, because socialism involves greater governmental regulation of the economy. Yet socialism (an economic system) is not synonymous with totalitarianism (a political system). Extensive socialism does generally involve pervasive government involvement in everyday life. Limited socialism—as it exists in Sweden or the United Kingdom, for example—appears quite consistent with political democracy. In contrast, some societies with capitalist economies, such as Chile and South Africa, exercise sufficient control over the lives of most of their citizens to be considered totalitarian.

A century and a half ago, in his famous book *Democracy in America* (1969; orig. 1834–1840), the brilliant Frenchman Alexis de Tocqueville warned that because modern governments were growing in size and scope, they had the potential to become totalitarian. Tocqueville believed that citizens could counteract this danger by forming various voluntary associations, thereby creating centers of power apart from the government.

THE AMERICAN POLITICAL SYSTEM

The founding of the United States was one of the boldest political experiments in human history. Originally part of a colonial empire, the colonies fought a revolutionary war against Great Britain to establish an independent American political system. George Washington was elected the first president in 1789, and Congress met for the first time in New York—the nation's first capital.

Early American political leaders sought to replace the British monarchy with a democratic political system. Subsequently, the commitment of Americans to democratic principles has persisted, although our political system has grown vastly larger and more complex. The American version of democracy is also distinctive, shaped by our particular history, economy, and cultural traditions.

Culture, Economics, and Politics

American culture has traditionally prized hardy individualists—strong, self-reliant, and competitive people who seek success commensurate with their abilities and effort. Such values support the society's capitalist economy, suggesting the close relationship between economic and political institutions.

The Bill of Rights, which guarantees personal freedom to act without undue government interference, is the political foundation of this individualism. With a political tradition embracing extensive personal liberty, many Americans would express sympathy with the sentiment of nineteenth-century philosopher and poet Ralph Waldo Emerson: "The government that governs best is the government that governs least." Yet few Americans would actually want to do away with government, because almost everyone thinks that government is necessary for some purposes, including maintaining national defense, a system of schools, and public law and order. As the United States has become larger and more complex, government has expanded dramatically, regardless of which political party has been in power.

In 1789, as shown in Table 18–1, the federal budget was a mere $4.5 million; by 1988 the federal budget had passed the $1 trillion mark. Government has become so expensive that even our leaders probably cannot com-

Table 18–1 THE GROWTH OF UNITED STATES GOVERNMENT SPENDING

Year	Federal Government Expenditure (In Millions of Dollars; Unadjusted for Inflation)	Government Expenditure as Proportion of Gross National Product
1795	6	
1800	11	
1810	9	
1820	18	
1830	25	
1840	20	
1850	44	
1860	56	
1870	411	
1880	334	2.4
1890	403	2.4
1900	567	2.8
1910	676	2.0
1920	6,649	6.9
1930	4,058	3.7
1940	6,361	9.1
1950	39,485	13.9
1960	92,492	18.3
1970	193,743	20.1
1980	576,500	22.9
1988	1,117,600	23.0

SOURCE: U.S. Bureau of the Census and U.S. Bureau of Economic Analysis.

prehend its scope. The late senator Everett Dirksen once quipped that members of Congress spend a billion here and a billion there, which soon adds up to a lot of money. Government employment has also greatly expanded. During the early nineteenth century, the federal government employed only a few thousand people compared to more than 3 million today.

Growth of government has outstripped even the striking expansion of the United States in geographical size and the population. Early in the nineteenth century, one government employee served every eighteen hundred Americans; today, the corresponding ratio is one employee for every seventy-nine people (U.S. Bureau of the Census, 1989). A century ago, the presence of the federal government in most communities was limited to the local post office. Now, universal education, civil rights legislation, safety standards that protect consumers and workers, expanded support for students, veterans, and the elderly, and a larger and more complex system of national defense signify our reliance on federal, state, and local government (Devine, 1985). A majority of Americans also depend on government for at least part of their income (Caplow et al., 1982).

The results of a national survey, shown in Table 18–2, indicate that Americans are divided about the proper role of government. More than one-fourth think that government should do more to address social problems; about the same proportion claim the government is doing too much; most of the remainder express support for both views. Blacks, people with low incomes, and

young Americans tend to favor a more activist government; whites, more affluent people, and older people approve of more modest government programs (Davis, 1987).

Political Parties

Since the beginning of the nineteenth century, Americans have banded together into **political parties,** *organizations operating within the political system that seek control of the government.* In the colonial era, the merits of political parties were hotly debated. Some, including Thomas Jefferson, believed that parties representing different interests would enhance political pluralism. Others feared that parties would generate political conflict capable of tearing the new nation apart. Thus, the U.S. Constitution contains no mention of political parties (Hilsman, 1985).

Yet, political parties came and went in the early years of the republic until, on the eve of the Civil War, the two major parties we know today—the Republicans and the Democrats—were established (Burnham, 1983). The two-party system still exists, although various minor parties at times gain significant support. In the 1968 presidential election, the American Independent Party led by George Wallace gained more than 13 percent of the popular vote. In the 1988 presidential election, candidates represented a wide range of minor parties, including the Libertarian Party, the Populist Party, the Communist Party, the Workers League, and the Prohibition Party. None, however, gained more than a small share of the vote.

Functions of Political Parties

Political parties have persisted in American society because of the vital societal functions they perform.

1. **Promoting political pluralism.** Political parties create many independent centers of power. In contrast, totalitarian governments, such as the Nazi regime in Germany, ruthlessly eliminated opposing political parties. Only recently has the Communist party in the Soviet Union allowed organized political opposition.

2. **Increasing political involvement.** Parties draw people into the political process by articulating various points of view about controversial social issues. They are thus reference groups that help Americans shape their individual opinions. Political cam-

---

Table 18–2   THE ROLE OF GOVERNMENT: A NATIONAL SURVEY, 1989

QUESTION: Some people think that the government in Washington is trying to do too many things that should be left to individuals and private businesses. Others disagree and think that the government should do even more to solve our country's problems. Still others have opinions in between. What do you think?

I strongly agree that the government should do more.		I agree with both answers.	I strongly agree that government is doing too much.	
1	2	3	4	5
13.0%	14.2%	37.7%	15.4%	12.7%

Don't know, no answer: 7.1%

SOURCE: N.O.R.C., *General Social Surveys, 1972–1989* (Chicago: National Opinion Research Center, 1989), p. 310.

The numbers 1 to 5 indicate the range of opinions across the three categories.

---

paigns encourage public debate of issues, further engaging the public in the political process.

3. **Selection of political candidates.** Political parties nominate candidates to run for office. They also play a significant part in making elected officials accountable to the people.

4. **Forging political coalitions.** Parties unite supporters of various interests and issues to increase their political power. Party platforms usually incorporate many issues in general terms, thereby appealing to many while alienating few. The two major political parties in the United States are unusual because they each represent a broad coalition of people rather than a single segment of the population.

5. **Maintaining political stability.** By maintaining relatively consistent positions on a number of issues, parties promote political stability. Those who seek radical change, however, may view parties—which often favor general language over specific proposals, and which rarely mention class conflict—as helping to preserve the status quo (Wolfinger, Shapiro, & Greenstein, 1980; Irish, Prothro, & Richardson, 1981; Burnham, 1983).

The Political Spectrum in America

Many Americans claim to be either liberal or conservative. Others prefer to describe themselves as moderates or middle-of-the-roaders. Still others do not describe themselves in political terms at all.

Political labels are associated with attitudes that establish an individual's place on what is commonly called the *political spectrum*, ranging from extreme liberalism on the left to extreme conservatism on the right. Historically, the Republican Party has been more conservative while the Democratic Party has been more liberal. Within each party, however, there are conservative and liberal wings so that the difference between a liberal Republican and a conservative Democrat may be more a matter of symbols than substance.

The political views of Americans differ on two kinds of issues. *Economic issues* have to do with economic inequality and opportunity for all Americans. *Social issues* refer to moral issues and legal rights.

Economic Issues

The industrialization of American society a century ago generated enormous wealth, much of it controlled by a small elite. By the time of the Great Depression in 1929, mounting evidence suggested that, despite the productivity of American capitalism, many people had little financial security. The New Deal programs of Franklin Delano Roosevelt, the Democrat elected president in 1932, greatly expanded the role of American government. Previously limited to matters such as printing currency, financing internal improvements such as

As part of President Franklin Roosevelt's New Deal, the Work Projects Administration (WPA) created jobs for millions of Americans. Included were artists who were recruited to paint public murals. This mural, in San Francisco's Coit Tower, celebrated Americans at work at a time of catastrophic unemployment. Since the Roosevelt era, and despite greater prosperity, the expanded role of government in the American economy has continued.

roads, and maintaining the armed forces, the federal government soon became directly involved in the American economy. It regulated the stock market, provided guarantees for bank savings, and in numerous other ways increased the financial security of the American people. In 1935, the Social Security system required all workers and employers to make financial contributions to provide retirement income to the elderly.

Today, the Democratic Party tends to support more extensive government involvement in the economy than the Republican Party does. Economic liberals (likely to be Democrats) believe that such policies are the proper responsibility of government. Economic conservatives (likely to be Republicans) hold that government should interfere little with the operation of the economy in the interest of economic productivity (Burnham, 1983).

Social Issues

Social issues range from moral questions regarding abortion and the death penalty to the legal standing of women, gay people, and other minorities. Social liberals support equal rights and opportunities for every segment of American society. They usually favor individual choice regarding abortion and oppose the death penalty because, historically, it has been unfairly applied to minorities. Social conservatives support traditional social distinctions between the sexes and oppose affirmative action and other "special programs" for minority groups. Social conservatives tend to condemn abortion as a moral wrong and support the death penalty as a response to very serious crimes.

The Democratic Party is more socially liberal, and the Republican Party more socially conservative. Yet both parties favor government activity when it advances their aims. Socially liberal Democrats, for instance, support the Equal Rights amendment (ERA) to the Constitution, believing it will reduce patriarchy. Socially conservative Republicans oppose this change, arguing that existing laws protect women's rights and that the government should not aggressively undermine traditional conceptions of gender. Socially conservative Republicans *do* want government to enact legislation forbidding abortion, whereas socially liberal Democrats think this is a personal, not a governmental, decision.

Political labels are often even more complex, because many people's attitudes on economic issues may differ from their views on social issues. One estimate of American political opinions, shown in Figure 18–1, labels 10 percent of Americans as liberal on both eco-

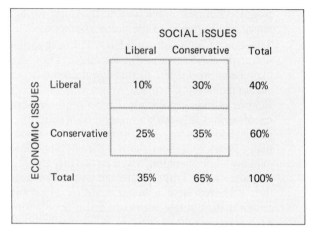

Figure 18–1 The Political Attitudes of Americans
(Barone & Ujifusa, 1982:1)

nomic and social issues, while more than one-third are conservative in both respects. Mixed attitudes are more common: 25 percent are economically conservative and socially liberal, while 30 percent are economically liberal and socially conservative.

With the most wealth to protect, well-to-do Americans tend to be conservative on economic issues. Yet their extensive education and secure social standing encourage privileged Americans to be social liberals. Americans of low social position with less education show the opposite pattern; they tend to be economically liberal and socially conservative. They seek more economic opportunity, but take pride in conforming to conventional cultural patterns. Thus, they commonly disapprove of those—such as gay people and cohabiting couples—who do not adhere to traditional American mores (Nunn, Crocket, & Williams, 1978; Erikson, Luttbeg, & Tedin, 1980; Syzmanski, 1983; Humphries, 1984).

Political attitudes vary according to race. Blacks of any social standing are likely to be socially liberal and, since the New Deal era, strongly Democratic. Because they, too, are often poor and victimized by social prejudice, ethnic minorities tend to be economically liberal and generally support the Democratic Party. Hispanic Americans and Jews provide strong support for the Democratic Party. Since about 1950, however, ethnicity—although not race—has declined as a force in American politics (Knoke & Felson, 1974).

Because most Americans are neither consistently

liberal nor conservative, party identification is understandably weak in the United States. American society, in this respect, differs from most European democracies, where people usually adhere strongly to one political party (Wolfinger, Shapiro, & Greenstein, 1980). The more well-to-do tend, nevertheless, to support the Republican Party, while the less privileged people lean toward the Democratic Party, suggesting that Americans tend to "vote their pocket-books."

Table 18–3 shows the results of a national survey of party identification among American adults (N.O.R.C., 1989). About 45 percent identified themselves—to some degree—as Democrats and about 40 percent as Republicans. Twelve percent claimed to be independents voicing no preference for either major party. Although surveys of this kind give Democrats a slight edge among the American electorate, only about one in four Americans is strongly committed to either party: 15.2 percent to the Democrats and 11.4 percent to the Republicans. In any election, then, a large proportion of Americans swings from one party to another.

One reason for this political vacillation is that the two major parties have much in common. For example, both parties support the capitalist economic system, strong national defense, and the basic principles of the U.S. Constitution. Since Roosevelt's New Deal, both parties have also favored some government involvement in the American economy.

The similarity between the two major parties and their support for the status quo means that those seeking radical change are unlikely to support either one. Some Americans, politically on the far left, advocate a socialist economy; others, on the far right, favor a market economy completely free from government regulation. Because these views are at far ends of the American political spectrum, they are not part of the political platform of either major political party.

In most other democracies, political parties represent a wider range of positions. In Great Britain, the Labour party (on the left) and the Conservative Party (on the right) are further apart politically than are the two major parties in the United States. Sweden, the Netherlands, Switzerland, Belgium, and Israel each have more than two political parties representing sizeable proportions of voters across a wide political spectrum (Roskin, 1982).

Special-Interest Groups

In 1989, President Bush proposed a tax cut on capital gains—profits from the sale of investments—that he claimed would encourage economic growth. Wealthy Americans and people in the financial industry applauded this proposal, while organizations representing less affluent people denounced it as benefiting rich Americans and likely to increase the federal debt.

The investment industry, associations of elderly people, and women's organizations are each examples of a **special-interest group**, *political alliances of people with an interest in a particular economic or social issue.* Most voluntary associations (described in Chapter 7, "Groups and Organizations") are special-interest groups seeking to shape political events. Special-interest groups flourish in societies such as the United States where political parties are relatively weak (Burnham, 1983). American society contains a vast array of special-interest groups, representing businesses and professions, religions, and recreational and leisure activities, as well as Americans of a particular race or ethnicity. Alexis de Tocqueville described the United States as a nation of joiners: in no other society, he suggested, are special-interest groups so numerous.

Many special-interest groups employ *lobbyists* who earn their living by representing the concerns of one group or another to political officials. The number of registered lobbyists in the United States—now well into the thousands—has increased rapidly in recent decades (Sheler, 1985).

Table 18–3 POLITICAL PARTY IDENTIFICATION IN THE UNITED STATES, 1989

Party Identification	Proportion of Respondents
Democrat	45.7%
Strong Democrat	15.2
Not very strong Democrat	21.8
Independent, close to Democrat	8.7
Republican	40.6
Strong Republican	11.4
Not very strong Republican	21.5
Independent, close to Republican	7.7
Independent	12.5
Other Party, No Response	1.2

SOURCE: N.O.R.C., *General Social Surveys, 1972–1989* (Chicago: National Opinion Research Center, 1989), p. 95.

During the 1980s Vietnam veterans organized into a special-interest group seeking belated recognition for their sacrifices in fighting an unpopular war.

The Agenda of Special-Interest Groups

In the United States, the most powerful special-interest groups focus on economic issues. Big business, with its tremendous wealth, exerts vast power within the American political system. Although a declining proportion (currently under 20 percent) of eligible workers are union members, labor unions still represent 20 million Americans (Goldfield, 1987). The American Federation of Labor-Congress of Industrial Organizations (AFL-CIO) is the nation's largest labor union and can draw on the talents and resources of some 14 million members. While big business directs financial support primarily to the Republican Party, the AFL-CIO channels most of its money to Democrats.

Other special-interest groups are concerned with social issues. Examples of socially oriented special-inter-

est groups are the National Organization of Women (NOW), numerous consumer-protection organizations such as those headed by Ralph Nader, environmentalist groups such as the Sierra Club, and the American Civil Liberties Union (ACLU). Special-interest groups represent virtually every social issue in American politics. The ACLU, which participated in the landmark Supreme Court decision in Brown v. Board of Education of Topeka that outlawed school segregation in 1954 (discussed in Chapter 12, "Race and Ethnicity"), is generally liberal. The National Rifle Association is a socially conservative organization with 3 million members who contribute millions of dollars annually toward the opposition of laws restricting the private ownership of firearms.

Religious organizations influence public opinion and government policy on a variety of social issues, including abortion and school prayer. Although most established churches tend to maintain a low political profile, many Christian sects are outspokenly conservative and are likely to remain active in politics during the 1990s.

Political Action Committees

Many special-interest groups do not provide votes and money directly to political parties. **Political action committees** (PACs) are *organizations formed by special-interest groups, independent of political parties, to pursue political aims by raising and spending money.* Usually, political action committees raise money, which is then channeled directly to candidates likely to support their interests.

During the early years of Roosevelt's New Deal, labor organizations formed the first political action committees. But legal reforms limiting direct contributions to candidates in the early 1970s brought PACs to the forefront of American politics. The Federal Elections Campaign Act of 1971 formally empowered special interests to form PACs, and their number has since grown rapidly. In the early 1970s, about six hundred PACs were operating; by the late 1980s, the number approached five thousand (Sabato, 1984; Jones & Miller, 1985; Federal Election Commission, 1989a).

The success of PACs is correlated to their ability to raise money (Walker, 1983). The largest spenders—and, therefore, the most powerful—focus on economic issues and support Republicans more than Democrats. Special-interest groups concerned with social issues also form PACs: the National Organization of Women (NOW) attempts to advance the social equality of women, while the National Conservative Political Action Committee (NCPAC) opposes abortion and seeks to restore traditional values to American society.

The rapid increase in the cost of campaigns has made most candidates eager to receive financial support from political action committees. Between 1972 and 1987, fifty-one U.S. senators each received more than $1 million from PACs. During the 1988 Congressional campaigns, PACs contributed $150 million—one-third of all money raised during that campaign (U.S. Federal Election Commission, 1989b).

Their power to shape American politics has made political action committees controversial. Supporters maintain that PACs represent the interests of many Americans—whose businesses, unions, or churches provide financial support—and thereby increase political participation. According to this view, PACs are a healthy reform that has the additional advantage of limiting direct contributions to candidates by organizations and wealthy individuals. These organizations therefore disperse power so that no one interest group dominates American government. Critics claim that organizations supplying cash to politicians expect to be treated favorably in return; PACs, in short, engage in buying political influence (Sabato, 1984). Thus, the political process responds not to ordinary people but to well-heeled special interests whose goals are often not in the public interest.

Politics and the Individual

The American political system is based on the participation of individuals. But how do individuals become liberals, conservatives, or independents? And to what extent do Americans use their right to participate in the political system?

Political Socialization

John F. Kennedy was the only president in this century to raise young children in the White House. From time to time, Kennedy referred to his children as "good little Democrats" although he knew well that no one is born with any particular political orientation. Like every other element of culture, we learn political attitudes through the socialization process. As discussed in Chapter 5 ("Socialization"), the family, the schools, and the mass media are instruments of socialization, each shaping political views.

The family strongly influences political attitudes, so that children come to share the opinions of their parents. The social composition of the neighborhood reinforces what is learned at home, because people of the same race and social class—and hence political orientation—tend to cluster in neighborhoods. By the time children reach elementary school, they are likely to have a conscious identification with their parents' political affiliation (Knoke & Felson, 1974; Burnham, 1983).

As described in Chapter 16 ("Education"), schools teach the culture's dominant political values. In rituals such as reciting the Pledge of Allegiance, students affirm support of their country ("I pledge allegiance to the flag of the United States of America . . .") and come to believe that its political system is good (". . . one nation, under God, with liberty and justice for all"). Schools develop discipline and respect for those in positions of authority, thereby strengthening patriotism (Bowles & Gintis, 1976). The mass media—which convey values and opinions, often under the guise of "news"—reinforce the established political system (Gans, 1980).

In spite of these influences, many Americans express indifference or even contempt for conventional political ideas. This is especially true of the poor, those unable to find employment, and people who believe that society has failed to offer them a fair shake (Zipp, 1985; Pinderhughes, 1986).

Voter Apathy

In light of the courageous desire of people around the world to gain a greater voice in government—sometimes at the cost of their lives—a disturbing fact is that many Americans seem indifferent to their own political rights. Americans are less likely to vote today than they were a century ago. *Voter apathy* was recently found to be worse in the United States than in twenty-three other industrialized democracies (Harvard/ABC News Symposium, cited in Piven & Cloward, 1988). In the 1988 presidential election, only 57 percent of eligible voters went to the polls.

Who is and is not likely to vote? Historically, sex is significant. Women gained the right to vote only in 1920, and for decades afterward they voted in lower proportions than men. In 1988, however, women (58.3 percent of those eligible voted) were slightly more likely than men (56.5 percent) to vote. The likelihood of voting also increases dramatically with age. Of eligible Americans between eighteen and twenty-four years of age in 1988, 36.2 percent voted. Among Americans over sixty-five, 68.8 percent went to the polls. Voting was also higher among whites (59.1 percent) than among blacks

During the recent Polish presidential election, the proportion of Poles voting exceeded the proportion of Americans who voted in the last presidential election in the United States. Ironically, many Americans appear to be indifferent to a political right people elsewhere in the world have risked their lives to gain.

(51.5 percent), and Hispanics (28.8 percent) were even less likely to vote. Race and ethnicity in themselves do not appear to cause this variation in voting. Rather, Americans with higher incomes, more prestigious occupations, and more schooling vote in the greatest numbers (Wolfinger & Rosenstone, 1980; U.S. Bureau of the Census, 1989).

What accounts for apparent voter apathy? Americans' failure to vote has many causes. First, at any given time, millions of people are sick or otherwise disabled; millions more are away from home having made no arrangement to submit an absentee ballot. Second, many people forget to re-register after moving from one election district to another. Third, registration and voting require the ability to read and write, which may discourage tens of millions of functionally illiterate Americans.

Conservatives claim voter apathy is *indifference* to politics, suggesting that Americans are by and large content with their lives. Thus voting levels are low despite the elimination of traditional barriers to voting such as literacy tests and poll taxes and, in 1971, the extension of the right to vote to people between the ages of eighteen and twenty-one. Radical critics counter that many Americans are so deeply dissatisfied with society that they doubt elections will significantly change anything for the better. From this perspective, voter apathy signifies *alienation* from politics. Americans may lack confidence in the political system, critics argue, but they do engage in widespread political activity such as protests, strikes, and work stoppages (Piven & Cloward, 1988).

Each of these explanations probably contains some truth. A third possibility is that many people are apathetic because our two major parties have so much in common. If the parties represented a wider spectrum of political opinion, some suggest, Americans would have more incentive to vote (Zipp & Smith, 1982; Zipp, 1985).

THEORETICAL ANALYSIS OF POWER IN SOCIETY

For more than half a century, sociologists and political scientists have debated the answers to basic questions about power in American society: How is power distributed? Who makes political decisions? In whose interest are such judgments made?

Political power is one of the most difficult topics of scientific research. Decision making is complex and often occurs informally behind closed doors. Rarely do leading decision-makers welcome the scrutiny of social scientists. Moreover, as Plato recognized more than two thousand years ago, theories about power are difficult to separate from the beliefs and interests of social thinkers themselves. From this mix of research and political debate have emerged two competing models of power in the United States.

The Pluralist Model

The first approach, linked to the structural-functional paradigm in sociology, perceives a political system as serving the needs of various constituencies within a complex society. The **pluralist model** is *an analysis of politics that views power as dispersed among many competing interest groups.*

Pluralists claim, first, that politics is an arena in which organizations with varying interests compete. Most seek specific goals, pursuing narrow agendas with little concern for most other issues. The American Association of University Professors, for example, raises and responds to issues that affect college and university faculty, leaving others to debate American health policy or gun control. Even with a limited agenda, no single organization holds sufficient power to realize all its goals. Organizations, therefore, operate as *veto groups*, keeping their competitors from achieving all of their goals. The political process, then, relies heavily on negotiating alliances and compromises that bridge differences among various interest groups so that societal conflict is minimized and resulting policies have wide support (Dahl, 1961, 1982).

Government officials play a key role in transforming various special interests into popular public policy. In doing so, the government takes account of all categories of Americans either through representative organizations or elections. The federal government also responds to countless state and local governments, which, in turn, are influenced by still more interest groups. Pluralists, then, see power as widely dispersed and deeply rooted in the complex fabric of social life.

A second pluralist assertion is that power has many sources—including wealth, political office, social prestige, and personal charisma. Only in exceptional cases are all these sources of power available to the same people. For this reason, too, power is widely diffused throughout society.

Studying the power structure of New Haven, Connecticut, Nelson Polsby (1959) found that key decisions—involving urban renewal, nominations of political candidates, and the educational system—were made by different groups. Polsby also noted that few members of the New Haven upper class—people listed in that city's *Social Register*—had major positions of economic leadership. Thus, Polsby concluded that no one segment of society is all-powerful.

Echoing Polsby's conclusions, Robert Dahl (1961) claimed that New Haven politics had once been dominated by a small number of families, but power had increasingly become dispersed. In New Haven, "no one, and certainly no group of more than a few individuals, is entirely lacking in [power]" (1961:228).

The implication of the pluralist model is that American society is democratic and fair, granting at least some power to everyone. Pluralists assert that not even the most influential Americans always get their way, and even the disadvantaged are able to band together to ensure that at least some of their political interests are addressed.

The Power-Elite Model

A second approach, closely allied with the social-conflict paradigm in sociology, is the **power-elite model,** *an analysis of politics that views power as concentrated among the rich.*

C. Wright Mills (1956) introduced the term *power elite* into America's vocabulary, arguing that the upper class (described in Chapter 10 "Social Class in America") holds most of society's wealth, prestige, and power. The power elite are America's "super-rich": families who forge alliances in corporate boardrooms and at the altar. Using these methods, a handful of families perpetuate their privileges and ensure that their priorities become national policy.

This elite is not an anti-American conspiracy, but a coalition of families who have historically overseen the three major sectors of American society—the economy, the government, and the military. According to Mills, elites circulate from one sector to another, consolidating their power. Alexander Haig, for example, has held top positions in private business, was secretary of state under Ronald Reagan as well as a 1988 presidential candidate, and is a retired army general. A large majority of national political leaders entered public life from powerful and highly paid positions in private business—and returned there later (Brownstein & Easton, 1983).

According to the power-elite model, the concentration of wealth and power in the hands of a few undermines claims of American democracy. Rejecting pluralist assertions that various centers of power serve as checks and balances on one another, the power-elite model suggests that those at the top have no real opposition.

Supporting the power-elite model, Robert and Helen Lynd (1937) studied Muncie, Indiana (which they called Middletown, to suggest that it was a typical American city). They concluded that a single family who had amassed a fortune from the manufacture of glass canning jars—the Balls—dominated many dimensions of the city's life. Thus the family name appeared on almost all the local institutions, including the bank, college, hospital, and department store. The Balls took part in dozens of other businesses and charities. In Muncie, the power elite was more or less a single family.

Floyd Hunter's (1963) study of Atlanta, Georgia, also supported the power-elite model. Atlanta, he concluded, had no single dominant family, but about forty people who held top positions in the city's economy controlled the city's politics.

Critical evaluation. The debate between proponents of these two models of power, summarized in Table 18–4, continues. The view of politics emerging from research in New Haven differs sharply from that based on the Muncie and Atlanta studies. Perhaps there is a real difference in the politics of American cities. More likely, researchers interpret facts differently. G. William Domhoff, who has advocated the power-elite model (1967, 1971, 1979), reexamined Robert Dahl's (1961) New Haven data and reached very different conclusions (Domhoff, 1983). Domhoff describes cities as "growth machines" in which wealthy landowners extensively influence the political system in pursuit of the economic growth that enhances their personal fortunes.

Research on American politics gives greater support, on balance, to the power-elite model. Even Robert Dahl (1982) — one of the stalwart supporters of the pluralist model—has recently conceded that the marked inequality of American wealth, as well as the barriers to equal opportunity faced by minorities, are basic flaws in America's quest for a truly pluralist democracy.

Does this mean that American politics entirely lacks pluralism? No, but our political system is not as democratic as many Americans would like to think it is. Although Americans have the right to vote, major candidates usually support only those positions acceptable to the most powerful segments of American society (Bachrach & Baratz, 1970). Republican and Democratic leaders may offer different approaches to helping the poor, for example, but no major-party politician has suggested radically redistributing wealth or abolishing the capitalist system.

Still, even the most powerful members of our society do not always get their way. As long as ordinary people continue to form political associations, American society will remain pluralistic. Domhoff reports that, in his own city of Santa Cruz, California, local residents and university students have joined forces to successfully oppose business interests in nearly every major decision affecting urban development (Domhoff, 1984).

Both the pluralist and the power-elite models of social power offer insights into the American political system. The size, social diversity, and political system of the United States affords each segment of the popula-

Table 18–4   THE PLURALIST AND POWER-ELITE MODELS: A COMPARISON

	Pluralist Model	Power-Elite Model
How is power distributed in the United States?	Highly dispersed.	Highly concentrated.
How many centers of power exist?	Many, each with a limited scope.	Few, with power that extends to many areas.
How do centers of power relate to one another?	They represent different political interests and thus provide checks on one another.	They represent the same political interests and face little opposition.
What is the relation between power and the system of social stratification?	Some people have more power than others, but even minority groups can organize to gain power. Wealth, social prestige, and political office are rarely combined.	Most people have little power and the upper class dominates society. Wealth, social prestige, and political office are commonly combined.
What is the importance of voting?	Voting provides the public as a whole with a political voice.	Voting cannot create significant political change.
What, then, is the most accurate description of the American political system?	A pluralist democracy.	An oligarchy—rule by the wealthy few.

tion some voice. Marked social inequality, however, ensures that some people have much more power than others.

POWER BEYOND THE RULES

Politics always concerns disagreement about goals and the means to achieve them. Yet political systems seek resolution of controversy within a system of rules. The basic rules of the American political system are written in the Constitution and its twenty-six amendments. Other rules and regulations guide every political official from the president to the county tax assessor. Sometimes, however, political activity exceeds—or even seeks to do away with—established practices.

Revolution

Political stability depends on transforming power into legitimate authority. Sometimes political systems lose legitimacy and radical change results. **Political revolution** is *the overthrow of one political system in order to establish another.*

Political revolution differs from reform. Reform involves change *within* the system's rules; revolution implies change *of the system itself.* Moreover, efforts toward reform frequently involve conflict, but rarely violence. Even when one leader overthrows another—a *coup d'etat* (in French, literally "stroke concerning the state")—violence is usually limited. In contrast, attempts at revolution often produce violence. The 1989 pro-democracy movement in the People's Republic of China led to thousands of deaths before protestors were silenced. In the successful week-long uprising against Rumanian dictator Nicolae Ceausescu in 1989, thousands of citizens perished, victims of vicious attacks by state soldiers on unarmed crowds. In other Eastern European countries, revolutionary change occurred with little or no bloodshed.

No type of political system is immune to revolution; nor does revolution invariably produce any one kind of government. The American Revolution ended colonial control by the British monarchy, resulting in a democratic government. French revolutionaries in 1789 also overthrew a monarch, summarily executing members of the feudal aristocracy, but in a few years monarchy returned in the person of Napoleon. In 1917, the Russian

Revolution replaced a system of monarchy with a socialist government fueled by the ideas of Karl Marx. And, as recent events have shown, socialist societies are vulnerable to demands for democratic reforms.

Despite such differences, revolutions reveal several general patterns (Tocqueville, 1955, orig. 1856; Davies, 1962; Brinton, 1965; Skocpol, 1979; Lewis, 1984).

1. **Rising expectations.** Although common sense suggests that revolution is more likely under conditions of extreme deprivation, history shows revolutions to be more likely when people's lives are improving. Improvement stimulates the desire for an even better life, with rising expectations often outpacing reality. Crane Brinton points out that revolutions are typically "not started by down-and-outers, by starving, miserable people"; rather, they are "born of hope and their philosophies are formally optimistic" (1965:250).

2. **Deprivation and social conflict.** Revolutionary aspiration is fueled by a sense of injustice. Seeing little chance for improving their lot within the prevailing political system, the disadvantaged may find insurgency increasingly attractive (Griffin & Griffin, 1989). Even elites may lose faith in their own claims of legitimacy, sometimes joining the forces of change.

3. **Nonresponsiveness of the old government.** Revolutions are likely when an existing political system is unable or unwilling to reform, especially when such demands are made by powerful segments of society (Tilly, 1986). The Ceausescu regime in Rumania, for example, defied popular demands for economic and political reforms, making revolution increasingly likely.

4. **Radical leadership by intellectuals.** The English philosopher Thomas Hobbes (1588–1679) observed that the center of political rebellion in seventeenth-century England was the universities. During the 1960s, students were at the forefront of much of the political unrest that marked this tumultuous decade in American history. More recently, students initiated the pro-democracy movement in the People's Republic of China. In virtually every revolution, convincing principles in support of revolution are formulated by intellectuals.

5. **Establishing a new legitimacy.** The successful overthrow of an old political system does not ensure a revolution's long-term success. Revolutionary movements may be unified primarily by hatred

of the past government. Having accomplished the objective of political overthrow, divisions within the revolutionary movement may intensify. A new political regime also faces the task of legitimating its newly-won power, even as it guards against counterrevolution led by past leaders attempting to regain political control. For this reason, victorious forces in Rumania, following a common pattern, quickly executed the deposed dictator.

We cannot categorically evaluate the effects of revolution as good or bad; the full consequences of such upheaval become evident only after many years. Revolutions have launched many nations—including the United States and the Soviet Union—to world prominence. In the wake of revolution, societies of Eastern Europe remain unsettled as the 1990s begin, with their long-term development uncertain.

Terrorism

The 1980s was a decade characterized by heightened concern over **terrorism,** *the use of violence or the threat of violence by an individual or group as a political strategy.* Like revolution, terrorism is generally understood to be political action entirely outside the rules of established political systems. Paul Johnson (1981) offers three insights about terrorism.

First, terrorism elevates violence to a legitimate political tactic. By engaging in violent intimidation, terrorists reject standards of morality and human dignity recognized by nearly every culture. They also ignore (or are excluded from) established channels of political negotiation. The seizure and holding of American hostages during the 1980s directed the world's attention on small political factions in the Middle East; this publicity is one reason powerful governments generally refuse to publicly negotiate with terrorists.

Second, although terrorism may be used by political democracies, it is especially compatible with totalitarian governments as a means of sustaining widespread fear and intimidation. The left-wing Stalinist regime in the Soviet Union and the right-wing Nazi regime in Germany each employed widespread terror.

Third, extensive civil liberties make democratic societies vulnerable to terrorism. For this reason, fear of terrorism may provoke the suspension of civil liberties. After the Japanese attack on Pearl Harbor at the outset of World War II, American fears that Japanese Americans might engage in terrorism provoked the imprisonment

Charges of "terrorism" are often traded by nations in conflict in the absence of a declared war. To many Americans, the aggressive seizure of the American embassy in 1979 and the subsequent holding of its staff as hostages, were clear acts of terrorism by Iran. A different version of truth is vividly shown by these Iranian stamps—printed in English to be circulated around the world.

of more than one hundred thousand Japanese-American citizens for the duration of the war.

During the 1980s, global terrorism increased in frequency and severity. Terrorists seized embassies and consulates of more than fifty nations; they also kidnapped (and sometimes subsequently murdered) hundreds of political officials, business leaders, teachers, and Olympic athletes, as well as several world leaders (Jenkins, 1982). Even the pope became the target of a terrorist attack in 1981.

Although many nations are victimized by terrorism, Americans are targeted in about one in four incidents worldwide. In 1983, terrorists bombed the American embassy and marine barracks in Beirut, Lebanon, killing 258 Americans. In 1985, Lebanese terrorists seized an American airliner departing from Athens, killing one American serviceman and holding the crew and passengers hostage. In 1988, the terrorist bombing of Pam Am flight 103 killed 270 people including 189 Americans. For all but nine months of the 1980s, Americans were held hostage by terrorists somewhere in the world (Jenkins, 1990).

How should a democratic nation such as the United States respond to terrorist acts? The immediate difficulty lies in identifying those responsible. Because terrorist groups are nearly always shadowy organizations with no formal connection to any established state, targeting reprisals is frequently impossible. Yet, terrorism expert Brian Jenkins warns, "Threats of retaliation that aren't carried out create unfulfilled expectations that lead to the conclusion that America is impotent. It also encourages other terrorist groups, who begin to realize that this can be a pretty cheap way to wage war on the United States" (cited in Whitaker, 1985:29). A forcible military response to terrorism, however, may broaden violence and increases the risk of confrontation with other governments.

Terrorism is not limited to groups opposing established governments. An additional form is **state terrorism,** *the use of violence without support of law against individuals or groups by a government or its agents.* State terrorism has had a long history. During the French Revolution, the government executed an estimated seventeen thousand people, many of whom had little benefit of due process as provided by law (Stohl & Lopez, 1984). Violent political repression was also used by the United States government, siding with large businesses engaged in intense conflict with labor organizations during the late nineteenth and early twentieth century. State terrorism remains widespread in the world today, notably in the case of "death squads" used by various Latin American governments to keep their populations in a state of intimidation and compliance.

The state has far greater ability to force compliance than any particular political group does. This is especially true in the case of totalitarian governments, which have almost complete control of a society. But the distinction between group and state terrorism is based on more than the number of soldiers and guns each employs. As explained earlier, the state claims to use force *legitimately,* and is therefore able to convince much of the population of the rightness of its actions. In short, groups engage in political violence as terrorists; governments, however, engage in political violence merely to "maintain law and order." This, no doubt, explains the focus of terrorism research on groups rather than on governments. But from the point of view of a government's opponents, the state can be the ultimate terrorist. Like every type of political behavior, then, terrorism concerns not only action but definitions of what is just.

WAR AND PEACE

Perhaps the most critical political issue is **war,** *armed conflict among the people of various societies, formally*

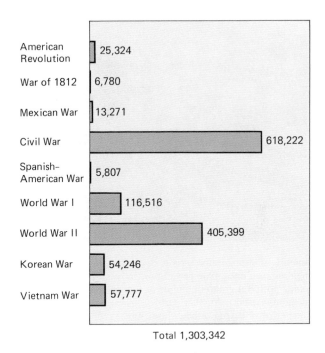

American Revolution	25,324
War of 1812	6,780
Mexican War	13,271
Civil War	618,222
Spanish-American War	5,807
World War I	116,516
World War II	405,399
Korean War	54,246
Vietnam War	57,777

Total 1,303,342

Figure 18–2 Deaths of Americans in Nine Major Wars
(Compiled from various sources by Maris A. Vinovskis, 1989:37)

initiated by their governments. War is as old as humanity; now with the technological capacity to destroy ourselves, however, war poses unprecedented danger to the entire planet. **Peace** implies *the absence of war,* although not necessarily of all conflict.

Although Americans often think of war as an extraordinary—rather than common—element of life, global peace has been rare and short-lived during this century. American history includes our involvement in nine major wars, which, as shown in Figure 18–2, resulted in the deaths of more than 1.3 million Americans and injury to many times that number (Vinovskis, 1989). Thousands of other Americans have died in "undeclared wars" and other military actions, in countries including the Dominican Republic, Lebanon, Grenada, and Panama.

Causes of War

The frequency of war in human affairs might imply something "natural" about armed confrontations. Certainly members of every culture come to embrace certain

Intensive training is necessary to transform people into efficient fighting machines. One part of this instruction involves developing powerful group discipline so that soldiers obey orders without question. Another part is learning to view others as "the enemy" devoid of basic humanity.

symbols and principles—such as patriotism and freedom—to the point that they are willing to fight to defend (or extend) them. Evidence shows that some animals are naturally aggressive (Lorenz, 1966); however, research provides no support for the conclusion that human beings inevitably go to war under any particular circumstances. As Ashley Montagu (1976) observes, governments around the world must resort to considerable coercion to enlist the support of their people for wars. Moreover, armies are deliberately constructed of small social groups in which soldiers fight to protect close companions as well as themselves. Loyalty to small groups, rather than allegiance to abstract principles, is surely the reality of war as it is experienced on the battlefield (Hruschka, 1990).

Like other forms of social behavior, warfare is the product of *society* and varies in purpose and intensity from culture to culture. The Tasaday in the Philippines, among the most peace-loving of all societies, rarely resort to violence. In contrast, the Yanomamö, described in Chapter 3 ("Culture"), readily engage in warfare with others. Napoleon Chagnon (1988) claims ferocity among Yanomamö males is encouraged by rewards such as prestige and arranged marriages to desirable women.

Under what circumstances *do* humans engage in war? According to Quincy Wright (1987), the following factors promote war.

1. **Perceived threats.** Societies commonly mobilize in response to a perceived threat to their people, territory, or culture. The likelihood of war is increased to the extent that Americans, for example, define the Soviet Union as seeking to subvert our way of life.

2. **Social problems.** Internal problems generating widespread frustration encourage a society to engage in aggressive action toward neighbors. Enemies, therefore, can be created as a form of scapegoating. The lack of economic development in the People's Republic of China, for example, has sparked that nation's hostility toward Vietnam, Tibet, and the Soviet Union.

3. **Political objectives.** War may be viewed as a desirable political strategy. Poor societies, such as Vietnam, have fought wars to end foreign domination. For powerful societies such as the United States, a periodic "show of force" (such as the invasions of Grenada and Panama) may enhance global political objectives. The escalation of conflict may also occur for the purpose of winning concessions from an opponent unwilling or unable to do the same (Patchen, 1987).

4. **Moral objectives.** Rarely do nations claim to wage war simply for tangible rewards, such as territory or wealth. They infuse military campaigns with moral urgency, so that people fight for compelling symbols, such as "freedom" or the "fatherland." An enemy defined as wicked becomes an "evil empire," as Ronald Reagan characterized the Soviet Union, or a "great satan" as Iranian officials termed the United States, that therefore deserves to be the target of hostility.

5. **The absence of alternatives.** A fifth factor that may be added to those suggested by Wright is the lack of other means to resolve international disputes. Societies establish political systems partly to reduce conflict according to the rule of law. Article 1 of the United Nation's Charter defines that organization's task as "maintaining international peace." Its ability to resolve tensions among societies that are often strongly nationalistic, however, has been limited.

Militarism and the Arms Race

The costs of militarism extend considerably beyond those of warfare. Together, the world's nations spend more than $5 billion annually on militarism. Whatever the direct consequences of such expenditures, their indirect costs must also be evaluated: militarism diverts resources needed in the struggle for survival by millions of desperately poor people throughout the world (see Chapter 11, "Global Inequality"). Assuming the desire to do so, little doubt exists that resources currently spent on militarism are sufficient to eradicate global poverty. A large proportion of the world's scientists also engage in military research; this resource, too, is thus unavailable for other activity that might benefit humanity.

In the United States, defense is the largest single category of federal government expenditures, representing about 30 percent of all spending—more than $300 billion—in 1988. Officials defend this sum—more than $1000 for every man, woman, and child in the United States—as a reasonable price to ensure American national security.

Nuclear weapons were developed by the United States, and were used in war by American forces against Japan in 1945. Directly after the war, the United States was the world's only military superpower. The Soviet Union's development of nuclear weapons in 1949 intensified the "cold war" and convinced the American military establishment that it must meet or exceed the Soviet's nuclear potential. The result has been a nuclear **arms race,** *a mutually reinforcing escalation of military might*. The irony—and the tragedy—of the arms race is that the Americans and the Soviets have, for more than forty years, pursued a policy that neither nation wanted nor could afford. The box illustrates the dynamics of the arms race.

The arms race is functional in some respects. As Sam Marullo (1987) points out, the arms race provides thousands of jobs, supports hundreds of corporations thereby stabilizing the economy, and encourages research discoveries that frequently lead to new civilian products. Yet, he concludes, the enormous resources devoted to the arms race would probably be more beneficial to Americans if invested in conventional industries.

C. Wright Mills (1956, 1958) took a more narrow view of militarism, claiming that the arms race benefits primarily the power-elite. Drawing on the ideas of Karl Marx, Mills suggested that expanding the military-industrial complex is highly profitable for the small number of capitalists who control the economy. From Mills's point of view, military expenditures are opposed to the interests of the American people but enrich the American power-elite.

Another argument against growing militarism is that it also has the potential to undermine American democracy. In his final speech as president in 1961,

CRITICAL THINKING

The Arms Race: Is Security Enhanced?

Dwight D. Eisenhower, the retired general who became our nation's thirty-fourth president, reportedly asked Soviet leader Nikita Khrushchev why they each routinely approved higher and higher military expenditures. Eisenhower began:

Perhaps first I should tell you how it is with us. It's like this. My military leaders say, "Mr. President, we need such and such a sum for such and such a program." I say, "Sorry, we don't have the funds." They say, "We have reliable information that the Soviet Union has already allocated funds for their own such program." So I give in. That's how they wring money out of me. Now tell me, how is it with you?

Khrushchev replied:

It's just the same. They say, "Comrade Khrushchev, look at this! The Americans are developing such and such a system." I tell them there's no money. So we discuss it some more, and I end up giving them the money they asked for.

Both governments have based expenditures on the assumption that military parity—at levels well beyond what is needed to destroy each other—enhances national security. Yet evidence suggests that the arms race, in which increasingly sophisticated missile systems are computer-driven and less subject to human control, may actually increase the possibility of war (Frei, 1988; Dedrick, 1990).

Source: Quotation from Clayton Fritchey, syndicated column, June 16, 1973, cited in James MacGregor Burns, J.W. Peltason, and Thomas E. Cronin, *Government by the People*. 13th ed. Englewood Cliffs, NJ: Prentice Hall, 1987:473.

Dwight Eisenhower warned of the increasing power of the **military-industrial complex,** *the close association between the federal government and defense industries.* In general agreement with the analysis of C. Wright Mills, Eisenhower claimed that a power-elite dominating both the economy and defense establishment had acquired unparalleled control over American government. The military-industrial complex, he observed, was becoming less and less responsible to the American people.

Nuclear Weapons and War

The world now contains an estimated fifty thousand nuclear weapons, representing a destructive power roughly equivalent to five tons of TNT for every human being on the planet. This state of "overkill" means that, should even a significant fraction of this arsenal be consumed in war, life as we know it will cease to exist on much of the earth. Albert Einstein, whose genius contributed to the development of nuclear weapons, reflected: "The unleashed power of the atom has changed everything save our modes of thinking, and we thus drift toward unparalleled catastrophe." In short, nuclear weap-

Figure 18–3 Area of Destruction: MX Missile Compared with Hiroshima Bomb

MX
240 sq. miles

Hiroshima bomb
4 sq. miles

ons have rendered unrestrained war unthinkable in a world not yet capable of peace.

At present, most nuclear weapons are held by the United States and the Soviet Union, although three other nations—Great Britain, France, and the People's Republic of China—have a substantial nuclear capability. The danger of catastrophic war is increasing with **nuclear proliferation,** *the acquisition of nuclear weapons technology by more and more societies.* In all likelihood, several other nations (including Israel, India, Pakistan, and South Africa) already possess some nuclear weapons. Other nations (such as Argentina, Brazil, Iraq, and Libya) are suspected to be developing nuclear weapons. By the end of this century, more than fifty nations will probably have the ability to engage in nuclear war. Because many of these nations have histories of conflict with neighboring states, nuclear proliferation is placing the entire world at greater risk (Spector, 1988).

The Pursuit of Peace

How can the world reduce the dangers of nuclear war? Several approaches are briefly described:

1. **Maintaining the status quo.** According to the logic of the present arms race, security is derived from a balance of terror between the superpowers. Thus the policy of *mutually assured destruction* (MAD) is that either superpower launching a first-strike nuclear attack against the other would itself suffer massive retaliation. Although this policy of deterrence has kept the peace for forty years, it has two major flaws. First, by encouraging the arms race, deterrence burdens the economies of the United States and the Soviet Union, and military technology become more complex, gradually raising the risk of war. Second, deterrence cannot control nuclear proliferation which, as already noted, is likely to increase in the future. For the long-term, an alternative strategy is obviously needed.

2. **High-technology defense.** One alternative that emerged during the 1980s was the *strategic defense initiative* (SDI). This proposal, initiated by the Reagan administration, is based on a complex system of satellites and ground installations that would provide a protective shield against enemy attack. In principle, enemy missiles would be detected soon after launch and destroyed by lasers and particle beams before reentering the atmosphere. If per-

fected, advocates argue, the "star wars" defense would render nuclear weapons obsolete.

This proposal has been extremely controversial. Some claim that such a program, even after years and perhaps trillions of dollars, would produce at best a leaky umbrella in the event of war. Just as serious, the Soviets have viewed SDI as an offensive system, able to assist the United States in making a first strike on them. For this reason, its development and deployment would provoke the Soviets to countermeasures, thereby provoking another costly step in the arms race (Kurtz, 1988).

3. **Diplomacy and disarmament.** This approach views the problem of achieving peace as diplomatic rather than technological (Dedrick & Yinger, 1990). Diplomacy leading to disarmament reduces rather than increases military costs and stockpiles of weapons. The idea behind disarmament is simple: a build-up of weapons in the past can lead to a mutual process of build-*down* in the future.

Disarmament also has limitations. No nation wishes to increase its vulnerability by reducing its defenses. Successful diplomacy, then, depends not on "soft" concession-making or "hard" demands, but on everyone involved sharing responsibility for a common problem (Fisher & Ury, 1988). Disarmament is most likely in a climate of mutual trust, but self-interest alone should motivate nations to examine this approach to peace.

The American and Soviet governments have a record of modest success in negotiating arms control agreements. Given the rising costs of the arms race, the pressing domestic social problems of the two superpowers, and their warming relations during the 1980s, guarded optimism about significant disarmament during the 1990s seems reasonable.

4. **Resolving underlying conflict.** Whatever success the world achieves in reducing the dangers of nuclear war will depend on resolving the issues that have fueled the arms race. Basic political differences between the superpowers are likely to remain.

The scars of combat often endure long after the guns have fallen silent. Almost a generation after American troops left Vietnam, many of the men and women who served in that conflict continue to experience the human tragedy of war.

Yet political changes such as the reduction of tensions in Europe have made nuclear war less likely than at any time since World War II.

The sources of world conflict extend beyond the superpowers, however. Regardless of improving relations between Washington and Moscow, regional conflicts continue in Latin America, Africa, the Middle East, and Asia. The world currently spends 3,000 times as much money on militarism as it does on peacekeeping efforts (Sivard, 1988). In some cases, the most powerful nations in the world can assist efforts to reach fair and reasonable settlement of regional problems. In others, powerful nations need to recognize their part in creating these problems.

The danger of war remains great: vast stockpiles of weapons, proliferating nuclear technology, and powerful military establishments at home. Forces working for peace are also great: organizations such as the United Nations, expanding international trade, and improving superpower relations. Perhaps most crucial is the growing realization that human technological progress demands non-violent solutions to the age-old problem of war.

SUMMARY

1. Politics is a major social institution involving the organization of power in society. Political systems seek legitimacy, transforming power into authority through tradition, rationally enacted rules and regulations, and personal charisma.

2. Traditional authority predominates in preindustrial

societies; industrial societies legitimate power through bureaucratic organizations and law. Charismatic authority arises in every society and may become routinized into traditional or rational-legal authority.

3. Technologically simple societies have no distinct political system. Such systems arise as societies gain the ability to generate a material surplus.

4. Monarchy based on traditional authority has been common in human history. Industrialization often transforms monarchy into a democratic political system based on rational-legal authority and extensive bureaucracy.

5. Democracy is a type of political system in which the population as a whole has considerable power.

6. Authoritarian political systems prevent popular participation in government, with indifference to the population. Totalitarian political systems also involve little popular participation, but exert extensive control over the everyday lives of the people.

7. The American government has grown dramatically during the past two centuries, reflecting population increase and wider government involvement in society.

8. The United States has two major political parties: the Republican Party is somewhat more conservative, and the Democratic Party more liberal.

9. The political spectrum—from extreme liberalism on the left to extreme conservatism on the right—involves two types of issues: economic and social. The former concerns the degree of government regulation of the economy; the latter involves the extent to which all segments of the population should enjoy rights and opportunities.

10. Special-interest groups represent segments of the population and attempt to influence the political process. Lobbyists advance the goals of such groups.

11. In recent decades, special-interest groups have formed political action committees to fund political campaigns. This development has been accompanied by a decline in the importance of political parties.

12. Many Americans do not readily describe themselves in political terms, nor are they strongly allied with one political party. Moreover, only about half of those eligible actually vote.

13. The pluralist model holds that political power is widely dispersed; the power-elite model holds that political power is concentrated in a small, wealthy segment of American society.

14. Political revolution radically transforms a political system. Political revolutions have met with varied success, and successful revolutions have established diverse political systems.

15. Terrorism employs violence in pursuit of political aims. Although attention has long focused on group terrorism, state terrorism is potentially far more powerful.

16. War is armed conflict between governments. The development of nuclear weapons and their proliferation has increased the possibility for global catastrophe. Enhancing world peace ultimately depends on resolving social problems and conflicts that underlie militarism.

KEY CONCEPTS

arms race a mutually reinforcing escalation of military might

authoritarianism denying the majority participation in a government

authority power that is widely perceived as legitimate rather than coercive

charismatic authority power legitimated through extraordinary personal abilities that inspire devotion and obedience

democracy a type of political system in which power is exercised by the people as a whole

government formal organizations that direct political life within a society

military-industrial complex the close association between the government and defense industries

monarchy a type of political system in which power is passed from generation to generation within a single family

nuclear proliferation the acquisition of nuclear weapons technology by more and more societies

peace the absence of war

pluralist model an analysis of politics that views power as dispersed among many competing interest groups

political action committee (PAC) an organization formed by a special-interest group, independent of political parties, to pursue specific aims by raising and spending money

political parties organizations operating within the political system that seek control of government

political revolution the overthrow of one political system in order to establish another

political state a formal government claiming the legitimate use of coercion to support its rule

politics the institutionalized system by which a society distributes power and makes decisions

power the ability to achieve desired ends despite possible resistance from others

power-elite model an analysis of politics that views power as concentrated among the rich

rational-legal authority (bureaucratic authority) power legitimated by legally enacted rules and regulations

routinization of charisma the transformation of charismatic authority into some combination of traditional and bureaucratic authority

special-interest group a political alliance of people with an interest in a particular economic or social issue

state terrorism the use of violence without support of law against individuals or groups by a government or its agents

terrorism the use of violence or the threat of violence by an individual or group as a political strategy

totalitarianism denying the majority participation in a government that extensively regulates people's lives

traditional authority power that is legitimated through respect for long-established cultural patterns

war armed conflict among the people of various societies, formally initiated by their governments

---

SUGGESTED READINGS

A general text dealing with politics and society is the following:
    Anthony M. Orum. *Introduction to Political Sociology: The Social Anatomy of the Body Politic.* 3rd ed. Englewood Cliffs, NJ: Prentice Hall, 1989.

This book, by a former National Security Advisor to the Carter Administration, claims the transformation of the Soviet Union and Eastern Europe is the result of a flawed political and economic system.
    Zbigniew Brzezinski. *The Grand Failure: The Rise and Fall of Communism in the Twentieth Century.* New York: Charles Scribner's Sons, 1989.

Based on study of the Polish Solidarity movement, this book explores the origins and consequences of political changes during the Gorbachev era.
    Jeffrey C. Goldfarb. *Beyond Glasnost: The Post-Totalitarian Mind.* Chicago: University of Chicago Press, 1989.

This classic analysis of politics and society is based on a journey through the United States made by a French aristocrat in the early 1830s. Many of Tocqueville's insights about the American political system remain as valuable today as they were when he wrote them.
    Alexis de Tocqueville. *Democracy in America.* Garden City, NY: Doubleday/Anchor Books, 1969; (orig. 1834–1840).

These essays examine various dimensions of black political life in the United States.

    Lucius J. Barker, ed. *Black Electoral Politics: Participation, Performance, Promise.* New Brunswick, NJ: Transaction, 1990.

An important change in American political life involves the declining power of labor unions.
    Michael Goldfield. *The Decline of Organized Labor in the United States.* Chicago and London: University of Chicago Press, 1987.

The first book below is a critical look at the pluralist model of social power; the second is the classic statement of the power-elite approach.
    Robert A. Dahl. *Dilemmas of Pluralist Democracy: Autonomy and Control.* New Haven, CT: Yale University Press, 1982.

    C. Wright Mills. *The Power Elite.* New York: Oxford University Press, 1956.

In this analysis, the arms race is viewed as a spiraling trap demanding new thinking about war and national security.
    Lester R. Kurtz. *The Nuclear Cage: A Sociology of the Arms Race.* Englewood Cliffs, NJ: Prentice Hall, 1988.

This books surveys the standing of women in the American armed services.
    Judith Hicks Stiehm. *Arms and the Enlisted Woman.* Philadelphia: Temple University Press, 1989.

19

The Economy and Work

In a joke making the rounds in the Soviet Union, Lenin (1870–1924)—architect of Soviet socialism—returns to life, but in New York. Thinking he is in Moscow, he wanders around the streets of Manhattan eagerly seeking evidence of the fate of socialism. Seeing merchandise lavishly displayed in store windows, he exclaims with joy: "Wonderful! It's exactly the way I imagined it!" (cited in Watson, 1989).

This joke provides small comfort to residents of Moscow, where, in recent years, life has been difficult. Coal for heating homes is scarce in the wake of a miners' strike; steam locomotives without coal are idle, delaying deliveries of food and other consumer goods. Many store shelves are empty, while other stores are awash with poorly made goods that no one wants to buy.

The Soviet Union's deepening crisis has led Mikhail Gorbachev to initiate a program of *perestroika*, or "restructuring" of the economy. Although Gorbachev's success is far from certain, Americans have warmly praised his plan, thinking that his reforms favor Western economic patterns. Yet, Americans have their own economic woes, having become less competitive in world markets during the 1980s.

This chapter examines the economy as a social institution, explains how the American system differs from the Soviet Union's, and suggests why the economies of nations around the world are currently undergoing extensive change.

THE ECONOMY: HISTORICAL OVERVIEW

The **economy** is *the institutionalized system for production, distribution, and consumption of goods and services.* The economy involves any material object or human activity that has value. *Goods* range from necessities (such as food, clothing, and shelter) to luxury items (such as

automobiles and swimming pools). *Services* include various activities that benefit others (such as the work of religious leaders, physicians, police officers, and telephone operators).

We value goods and services because they ensure survival or because they make life easier, more interesting, or more aesthetically pleasing. What we produce and consume is also important for our self-concepts and social identities. How goods and services are distributed, then, shapes the lives of Americans in basic ways.

The complex economies of modern industrial societies are themselves the product of centuries of technological innovation and social change. As Chapter 4 ("Society") explains, technologically simple societies of the past produced only what they immediately consumed. These small nomadic groups lived off the land—hunting game, gathering vegetation, and fashioning rudimentary clothing, tools, and shelters. Production, distribution, and consumption all took place within the family.

The Agricultural Revolution

Agriculture emerged as centuries of cultural innovation and diffusion finally brought together plows and animal power. Agrarian societies are ten to twenty times more productive than hunting and gathering societies, so that they produce a significant surplus. Because producing food no longer requires all members of a society, individuals assume specialized economic roles within permanent settlements, creating complex crafts, tools, and dwellings. Trading networks increasingly link towns, exchanging food, animals, and other goods (Jacobs, 1970). These four factors—agricultural technology, productive specialization, permanent settlements, and trade—have been the keys to a revolutionary expansion of the economy.

As noted in previous chapters, this economic expansion also increases social inequality. In contrast to relatively egalitarian hunting and gathering groups, societies in which agriculture and trade flourish are marked by a concentration of wealth in the hands of a small elite. Greater productivity, therefore, does not necessarily mean a better standard of living for everyone.

In agrarian societies, the economy becomes a social institution distinct from family life, although production usually occurs close to the home. In medieval Europe, for instance, most people farmed nearby fields. People living in cities often worked at home—a pattern called

The Grand Bazaar in Istanbul, Turkey, is an intense concentration of economic activity involving 3000 shops under one roof and virtually every product one could imagine. In operation for more than six centuries, the Grand Bazaar retains its traditional character in the form of "haggling," a ritual negotiation through which buyer and seller establish a price for an item. Haggling is rare in modern, industrial societies, where prices are typically uniform—a matter of formal policy on the part of large, commercial bureaucracies.

cottage industry. Goods produced at home were commonly sold in outdoor markets.

In England three centuries ago, for example, an urban home may have included several rooms used as a bakery, under the direction of the husband, who held the status of master baker. His wife could expect to be no more than his lifelong assistant, due to the pronounced patriarchy of the times. In addition, the household usually included several male apprentices working for wages as they developed their skills, and young men and women working as servants (Laslett, 1984).

The Industrial Revolution

Beginning in mid-eighteenth-century England, industrialization introduced five revolutionary changes to the economies of Western societies.

1. **New forms of energy.** Since the earliest hunting and gathering societies, energy had been produced by human beings and animals. At the dawn of industrialization in 1765, James Watt applied a steam engine to the production of material goods. Steam power surpassed muscle-power a hundredfold, allowing the operation of many large machines.

2. **The spread of factories.** Steam power and large equipment soon rendered cottage industry obsolete. Factories—centralized workplaces apart from the home—rapidly spread. In the factory, work was impersonal in relation to the close ties that had characterized cottage industry, and factories also physically separated the world of production from family life.

3. **Manufacturing and mass production.** Before the Industrial Revolution, most work involved producing raw materials, such as crops, wool, and wood. The industrial economy developed by manufacturing raw materials into a wide range of salable products. For example, factories converted wool into clothing and lumber into furniture. The new technology of the factories permitted mass production of more products in greater quantities than ever before.

4. **Specialization.** The Industrial Revolution also changed the character of work. A single cottage-industry worker fashioned a product from beginning to end. This required great skill, acquired only through years of apprenticeship. Factory workers, however, typically repeat a highly specialized task, which makes a small contribution to the product. While specialization in factories raised productivity, it also lowered the skill level of the average worker (Warner & Low, 1947).

5. **Wage labor.** Instead of working for themselves or under the supervision of a member of the household, workers entered factories to become wage laborers. This meant that they sold their labor to strangers to whom they often mattered less than the machines they operated. Supervision became routine and intense.

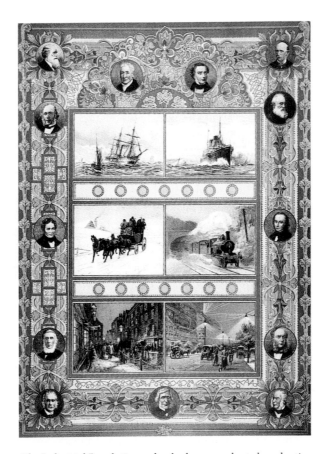

The Industrial Revolution unleashed unprecedented productive power, leading to optimistic predictions that technology would greatly improve people's everyday lives. This 1897 lithograph, *The Triumph of Steam and Electricity*, celebrates the effects of new energy sources on English society.

The Industrial Revolution gradually rippled outward from the factories to transform society as a whole. Greater productivity steadily raised the population's standard of living as countless new products and services filled an expanding economy. Especially at the outset, these benefits were very unequally shared. Some factory owners made vast fortunes, while the majority of industrial workers remained perilously close to poverty. Children were soon working as wage laborers in factories and deep in coal mines for pennies a day. Women factory workers were also among the lowest paid of all, with few opportunities and enduring special problems, as the box on page 510 explains.

Women in the Factories of Lowell, Massachusetts

The American textile industry began in 1822 in the Massachusetts town of Lowell—named for Francis Cabot Lowell, ancestor of two prominent Boston families, the Cabots and the Lowells—who brought plans for a textile factory from England.

About 75 percent of Lowell workers were women. The factory owners preferred women, first, because at about $2 to $3 a week, they received roughly half the wages men did. Second, prejudiced factory owners favored native New England women over newly-arriving male immigrants, who were also willing to work for low wages.

Women came to work in the Lowell factory from all over New England. Recruiters drove wagons through the region, encouraging parents to send their daughters to learn skills and receive moral training in the factories. The offer was attractive because many families could not provide for their children, and the few occupations open to women, such as teaching and household service, paid much less than factory work.

The Lowell factory provided dormitory-type housing and meals, de-

ducting one-third of a worker's wages for room and board. Women were subject to a curfew and, as a condition of employment, attended church regularly. Any morally questionable conduct (such as bringing men to their rooms or staying out beyond curfew) brought firm disciplinary action against offenders. These strict policies reflected more than the moral concerns of factory owners. Perhaps more important, closely supervised women were unable to organize among themselves to increase their bargaining

power. Working almost thirteen hours a day, six days a week, the Lowell employees had good reason to seek improvements in their working conditions. Yet any open criticism of the factory, or even the possession of "radical" literature, could cause a worker to lose her job and be barred from employment elsewhere.

SOURCE: Based on Benita Eisler, *The Lowell Offering: Writings by New England Mill Women 1840–1845* (Philadelphia and New York: J. B. Lippincott Company, 1977).

The Postindustrial Society

Changes continue today, more than two centuries after the beginning of industrialization. In Europe and North America, workers slowly gained power by organizing into labor unions in opposition to factory owners. During this century, governments gradually enacted legislation regulating the operation of industry, ending child labor and otherwise improving working conditions, and extending political rights to a larger segment of the population.

After mid-century, further changes signaled the emergence of a **postindustrial economy,** *an economy based on service work and high technology.* Increasingly sophisticated machinery has reduced the role of human labor in production. Simultaneously, expanding bureaucracy has increased the need for workers in clerical and managerial positions. Robert Heilbroner (1985) points out that, late in the nineteenth century, managers accounted for one in fourteen workers; by the mid-1980s, managers represented one in three employees. Service industries—such as public relations, advertising, banking, and sales—now employ most of the American labor force. As societies industrialize, then, much of the labor force shifts from generating raw materials to manufacturing. The postindustrial era is marked by a subsequent shift in which workers move from industrial production to service jobs.

The crucial technology of a postindustrial age concerns information. Computer technology has been at the center of an *information revolution* in the United States and elsewhere in the industrial world, generating a host of new, specialized occupations. Just as gaining technical skills was the key to success in the past, now Americans must enhance their literacy skills. Those unable to speak, write, or otherwise communicate effectively are increasingly at risk of being excluded from economic opportunity.

The postindustrial society also involves further change in the location of work. The earlier process of centralizing the workforce in factories was necessary because enormous machinery and energy sources were located in one place. Additionally, factory owners desired to closely supervise their employees. Today, however, computers, fax machines, and other new information technology allow workers to perform many jobs at home or even while driving in their cars. More educated and skilled workers also no longer require—and often do not tolerate—such close supervision.

Sectors of the Modern Economy

The broad historical changes just described involve a shifting balance among three parts, or sectors, of a society's economy. Which sector of the economy dominates depends on the historical level of technological development.

The **primary sector** is *the part of the economy generating raw materials directly from the natural environment*. The primary sector, which includes agriculture, animal husbandry, fishing, forestry, and mining, dominates economies of preindustrial, agrarian societies. Early in American history, for example, most work involved agriculture and other primary-sector activities. Today, in contrast, only about 3 percent of the labor force is employed in the primary sector. Globally, the economies of developing nations of the world such as India are still dominated by the primary sector.

The **secondary sector** is *the part of the economy that transforms raw materials into manufactured goods.*

This sector predominates in societies as they achieve full industrialization, such as the United States during the first half of this century. Such economic activity includes the refining of petroleum and the manufacture of metals into tools, building materials, and automobiles. In societies that are still industrializing—such as Yugoslavia and Greece—the secondary sector of the economy has grown to roughly the same size as the primary sector. In mature industrial societies, the secondary sector declines; about one-third of the American labor force today works in the secondary sector.

The **tertiary sector** is *the part of the economy generating services rather than goods*. Accounting for only a tiny share of work in preindustrial economies, the tertiary sector grows with industrialization and becomes the dominant economic sector in postindustrial societies. Almost 65 percent of the American labor force is now employed in a wide range of service occupations, including secretarial and clerical work and positions in food service, sales, law, advertising, and teaching.

The terms *primary, secondary, and tertiary* imply no ranking in importance. Each of the three types of work contributes to a society's economic well-being. The three labels simply indicate the sequence of economic development over time.

COMPARATIVE ECONOMIC SYSTEMS

The economies of world societies can be described in terms of two models: capitalism and socialism. No society has an economy that is purely capitalist or purely socialist. Instead, these models represent two ends of a spectrum on which an actual economy can be placed.

Capitalism

Capitalism is *an economic system in which natural resources and the means of producing goods and services are privately owned*. Ideally, a capitalist economy has three distinctive features.

1. **Private ownership of property.** A capitalist economy supports the right of individuals to own almost anything. Enacted into law, property rights are upheld by the power of the state. Violating property

rights is, therefore, both morally wrong and criminal.

All societies recognize some right of private property, at the very least involving small personal possessions. The more capitalist an economy is, the more private ownership extends to wealth-producing property. Factories, retail businesses, real estate, and even crucial natural resources may be privately controlled.

2. **Pursuit of personal profit.** A capitalist society encourages people to acquire the greatest amount of private property, even at the expense of others. The cultural goal of amassing wealth is embraced by individuals to different degrees and often does not guide behavior toward others in primary groups such as the family. In general, however, capitalism defines a self-centered orientation as natural and simply a matter of "doing business."

The pursuit of personal profit has also been defended on practical grounds. Scottish economist Adam Smith (1723–1790) claimed that the pursuit of profit benefits everyone. A selfish orientation on the part of individuals, Smith argued, leads an entire society to "wealth and prosperity" (1937:508; orig. 1776).

3. **Free competition and consumer sovereignty.** Adam Smith's defense of personal profit points to a third characteristic of capitalist economies—free competition and consumer sovereignty. Free competition is the principle that the economy should operate without interference from the government. The state thereby assumes a *laissez-faire* (a French expression meaning "to leave alone") approach to the marketplace. In the absence of a "guiding hand" from government, Smith argued, a freely competitive economy regulates itself by the "invisible hand" of the laws of supply and demand.

The market system is dominated by consumers, Smith maintained, who compare quality and price, buying those goods and services that provide the greatest value. Producers, competing with one another for sales, find that profits depend on offering the highest-quality goods and services at the lowest possible price. Attempting to be as efficient as possible, producers embrace technological advances in production that ultimately benefit consumers even more. Although personal gain may motivate producers and consumers, the whole society is argued to benefit as production becomes more efficient, technology advances, and consumers enjoy ever-increasing value. In Smith's time-honored phrase, from narrow self-interest comes "the greatest good for the greatest number of people." If an economy were a vast and complex ship, Smith's argument suggests, the self-interested actions of individual crew members without a captain would ensure that the ship remains on course (Albrecht, 1983:47). In contrast, government control of an economy would inevitably upset this complex market system, reducing producer motivation, diminishing the quality of goods produced, and thereby short-changing consumers.

The United States is the leading capitalist society, yet even here the guiding hand of government is a powerful economic force. Government policies affect what products are created, their quality and costs, what is imported and exported, and how the country develops or conserves natural resources. The federal government also owns and operates specific parts of the American economy. The U.S. Postal Service, the Amtrak railroad system, the Tennessee Valley Authority (a large electrical utility company), and the Nuclear Regulatory Commission (which conducts atomic research and produces nuclear materials) are branches of the federal government. The entire American military also is operated by the federal government. Federal officials may also assume partial or total control of privately owned businesses in order to prevent their collapse. This bailout approach led the government to become involved in Amtrak, Chrysler Corporation, and the American savings and loan industry. State and local governments also operate numerous large businesses, including the Port Authority of New York and New Jersey, the Los Angeles Department of Water and Power, and San Francisco's Bay Area Rapid Transit (BART) system (Herman, 1981). The government also regulates economic activity in a host of other ways: laws set minimum wage levels and safety standards for the workplace, antitrust regulations affect mergers of large corporations, price supports affect farm products, and Social Security, welfare payments, student loans, and veterans' benefits provide regular financial support to millions of Americans. Local governments also intervene in the economy by, for example, controlling rents or utility costs within a city. Finally, local, state, or federal government directly employs about 15 percent of the American labor force (U.S. Bureau of the Census, 1989).

Besides their productive performance, economic systems can also be evaluated in terms of what Peter Berger (1986) calls "mythic qualities," that is, their ability to inspire support from the people. Capitalism is weak in this regard, since self-interest is unlikely to generate collective responses. Thus, art concerned with capitalism tends to portray individuals, often in unflattering terms, as in this caricature of American capitalist Andrew Carnegie. Socialism, in contrast, has a collective orientation that inspires social movements. Socialist art, therefore, depicts "the people" as a whole, typically celebrating their productive roles. Shown here is Vassili Efanov's painting *The Meritorious People of the State*.

Socialism

Socialism is *an economic system in which natural resources, as well as the means of producing goods and services, are collectively owned.* In its ideal form, a socialist economy is antithetical to each of the three characteristics of capitalism just described.

1. **Collective ownership of property.** An economy is socialist to the extent that it limits the rights to private property, especially property used in producing goods and services. Socialist economies are argued to utilize productive property for the whole society. To ensure that what is produced goes to everyone and not just those with the most money, the means of production must be collectively owned. Housing, for example, is a social resource needed by each person. A socialist society therefore defines housing as a right of all instead of a private commodity to be traded in the marketplace for the enrichment of some people.

   Karl Marx linked the private ownership of productive property to social classes. An economy that places wealth-generating property in private hands, he claimed, invariably generates an economic elite and disadvantages the majority. Ownership of productive property also confers great political power on the bourgeoisie, who can utilize the state to further manipulate the proletariat. Because socialism regards such social class antagonism as a destructive force, socialist law prevents class formation by regulating the private ownership of property.

2. **Pursuit of collective goals.** The individualistic pursuit of personal profit is also at odds with the collective orientation of socialism. Cultural values and norms in the socialist societies define such self-serving behavior as immoral and often illegal. What capitalist societies view as entrepreneurial spirit, socialist societies define as anti-social behavior, as the box explains.

3. **Government control of the economy.** Socialism rejects the idea that a free-market economy is self-regulating. Instead of a laissez-faire approach, the government places some or all sectors of the economy under centralized control. Thus, a socialist economy is often termed a *centrally controlled economy* or a *command economy.* From a socialist point of view, individuals acting on the basis of narrow self-interest—Adam Smith's ship without

a captain—should flounder or, worse still, destroy themselves on the rocks. In the absence of the guiding hand of government, the economy will experience spasms of growth and recession. Resulting inflation and unemployment are likely to adversely affect millions of people.

Socialism rejects the notion that consumers guide capitalist production through their purchases. Consumers often lack the information necessary to evaluate the performance and potential dangers of various products. They are also manipulated by advertising, which creates artificial (and profit-producing) wants rather than meeting genuine consumer needs. Commercial advertising thus plays a small role in a socialist economy. Just as important, capitalist producers are more concerned with affluent consumers than with the poor, so that a free-market economy *creates* rather than *solves* social problems such as unemployment and poverty (Pryor, 1985). From a socialist point of view, only government—committed to serving the needs of each member of society in an equitable manner—can accomplish such goals.

The Soviet Union, the People's Republic of China, and some societies in Asia, Africa, and Latin America pattern their economies on the socialist ideal, and place almost all wealth-generating property under government control (Gregory & Stuart, 1985). Only recently has the Soviet Union, the most powerful socialist society in the world, permitted limited private ownership of productive property. Eastern European societies, under the political control of the Soviet Union since the end of World War II, were dramatically transformed during 1989. These nations—including Poland, the German Democratic Republic, Czechoslovakia, Hungary, Rumania, and Bulgaria—have rapidly introduced capitalist elements into what had for decades been centrally-controlled economies. The consequences of these recent changes are still unclear. Yugoslavia retains a socialist system that has traditionally allowed limited market forces; Albania, in contrast, continues to have a rigidly centralized economic system.

Socialism and Communism

Americans often mistakenly equate the term *socialism* with the term *communism.* As an ideal realization of the spirit of socialism, **communism** is *a hypothetical*

The Black Market of Moscow

"Good morning." The young man, smiling broadly, speaks surprisingly good English. "Would you like to change some money?" "No, thank you," responds the American visitor, curiosity outweighed by caution.

The young man turns away and, in a minute, has better luck with another tourist heading in his direction.

Few visitors to Moscow, capital of the Union of Soviet Socialist Republics (U.S.S.R.), avoid confronting the so-called "black market." On the streets, especially near hotels reserved for foreigners, thousands of young Muscovites display what Americans would call "entrepreneurial spirit" as they watch for tourists. Within a socialist society that has long denounced market forces, however, what Americans might praise as personal ambition can result in lengthy prison sentences.

In economic terms, "the *black* market" is simply "the *market*" in a society that outlaws private economic activity. In the United States, the black market or "underground economy" refers to economic transactions (themselves quite proper) involving illegal goods or in avoidance of taxes. In socialist societies, however, *any* private transaction may be outlawed.

But law cannot completely eliminate the forces of supply and demand. Some people, therefore, respond to them. Until recently, the government officially exchanged one ruble for $1.60. Because the market value of dollars was far higher, money changers on the street acquired dollars by trading at six or even eight rubles. As part of economic reforms, in 1989 the Soviets devalued rubles to about 16 cents, although the street value fell even further to about five cents, so that money changers remained busy.

Why do many Soviet citizens want dollars? They need American dollars—or other foreign currency—to buy consumer goods such as records and tapes, books in foreign languages, or fine clothing only available in special "barioska" stores catering to foreigners. For Soviets, living better means buying foreign goods, and this requires foreign currency.

Another common black market activity is "trading," a barter system used by enterprising Soviets to obtain foreign goods brought by tourists. Western jeans are a favorite item, along with cowboy boots, American college sweat shirts, and designer-label clothing of almost any kind. In exchange for "the shirt off your back," traders offer small souvenir pins (perhaps with a portrait of Lenin), fur hats, or the item of choice among many American visitors: a woolen Russian army coat.

The Soviet police tolerate some black market activity, just as police wink at a certain amount of illegal activities in the United States. For many traders, the black market is highly profitable, providing a standard of living far above that of the average Muscovite. But as financially rewarding as it may be, extensive "black marketeering" also carries substantial risk of arrest and imprisonment.

The Soviet population has wide-ranging opinions of "traders." Some express indifference to what they see as a harmless way of earning some extra money. Others, however, consider street trading to be a serious violation of law and socialist principles. Still others see it as the future of a society that is gradually introducing a market system.

SOURCE: Based on the author's travel in the Soviet Union in 1988.

economic and political system in which all members of society have economic and social equality. Karl Marx viewed socialism as a transitory stage on the path toward a communist society devoid of social conflict. In many socialist societies today, the dominant political party describes itself as communist, but nowhere has this system been achieved.

One important reason is that social stratification involves differences of power as well as wealth. Socialist societies have generally succeeded in reducing privately owned productive property only through expanding government bureaucracies, by which officials gain enormous power over the people. Karl Marx imagined communism would have no powerful government at all; in the absence of class conflict, he reasoned, the state could "wither away." A communist society, then, would have a socialist economy that would be an equal and cooperative association of all people. In Marx's vision, communist society would combine the equality of the earliest human societies with material bounty produced by modern, advanced technology. In the absence of inequality and exploitation, people would contribute to society according to ability and receive from society according to need. Rigidly specialized work would also be abandoned so that everyone could freely and fully develop their interests and abilities.

Marx would have been the first to agree that such a society is a *utopia* (from Greek words meaning "not a place"). His writings provide only a vague description of true communism. Yet Marx considered communism a worthy goal, and would certainly have regarded existing "Marxist" societies such as the Soviet Union as far from his communist ideal.

Democratic Socialism

In many Western European democracies—including Great Britain, Sweden, and Italy—socialist policies have been introduced into capitalist economies through elections rather than revolution. The result is termed **democratic socialism**: *a political and economic system in which free elections coexist with a market system modified by government policies to minimize social inequality*. Under democratic socialism, the government owns a number of the largest industries and services, such as mining, transportation, education, and health care. Privately owned industry also exists, but it is subject to extensive regulation. High taxation (aimed especially at the rich) provides funds for social welfare programs to help the less advantaged members of society.

Sweden is one such society in which roughly 13 percent of economic production is government controlled. Although Margaret Thatcher reduced government ownership of key British industries during the 1980s, about 20 percent of the British economy remains nationalized. Both Sweden and Great Britain have far larger social welfare programs than the United States. Basic health care, for example, is treated as a right of all citizens rather than as a commodity available only to those who can afford to purchase it in a free-market system.

In 1981, a socialist government was elected in France. About 12 percent of French businesses—including all but one television station—have since become state-owned. Italy has a predominantly capitalist economy, with 12 percent of Italian businesses under state control (Roskin, 1982; Gregory & Stuart, 1985; Pedersen, 1990).

Democratic-socialist societies recognize advantages in both the market economy and government regulation. They also claim that quality of life is improved through extensive social programs.

Relative Advantages of Capitalism and Socialism

The recent economic changes that are reshaping many societies of the world have heightened debate over the relative advantages of capitalism and socialism. Assessing these economic systems is difficult because nowhere can they be precisely and objectively compared. Any society's economic performance—whatever the mix of capitalism and socialism—is affected by historical and cultural patterns such as attitudes toward work. Working hours and

Table 19–1 ECONOMIC PERFORMANCE OF CAPITALIST AND SOCIALIST ECONOMIES, 1987

	Per Capita GNP (U.S. dollars)
Predominantly Capitalist Economies	
Austria	15,440
Belgium	13,940
Canada	15,550
Federal Republic of Germany (West Germany)	18,450
France	15,620
Great Britain	11,730
Greece	4,677
Hong Kong	8,260
Japan	19,410
Sweden	15,630
United States	18,570
Unweighted average	14,821
Predominantly Socialist Economies	
Czechoslovakia	9,709
German Democratic Republic (East Germany)	11,860
Hungary	8,260
Poland	6,879
Soviet Union	8,662
Yugoslavia	2,580
Unweighted average	7,992

SOURCE: U.S. Arms Control and Disarmament Agency, *World Military Expenditures and Arms Transfers 1988* (Washington, DC: U.S. Government Printing Office, 1989).

The productivity of capitalist societies is suggested by the overwhelming presence of corporate power in central cities, as in the Ginza district of Tokyo. Since social equality is a primary concern of socialist societies, "downtown" generally means government buildings rather than a central business district. In Moscow, the central location of Red Square and the Kremlin convey the unmistakable importance of government.

the size and composition of the labor force vary from one society to another. Nations also have unequal natural resources and different levels of technological development, as well as disparate patterns of trade and distinctive political alliances. Finally, the destructive effects of war burden some societies more than others (Gregory & Stuart, 1985). Despite these complicating factors, some crude comparisons are possible.

Productivity

Table 19–1 compares economic performance for a number of societies with predominantly capitalist or predominantly socialist economies. "Gross National Product" (GNP) is the total value of all goods and services produced annually by the economy; "per capita" (or per person) GNP allows comparisons among societies of different

size. Because each society uses a different currency system, the per capita GNP is presented in 1987 U.S. dollars.

Among the societies with predominantly capitalist economies, Japan had the highest per capita GNP ($19,410), closely followed by the United States ($18,570) and the Federal German Republic (West Germany) ($18,450). Greece had the lowest per capita GNP ($4,677). The considerable variation in GNP is due to complicating factors already noted. Taken together, the per capita GNP of these nine predominantly capitalist societies yields an unweighted average of $14,821 ("unweighted" means that the varying sizes of the countries is ignored). This average figure is a rough measure of the value of goods and services produced per person in predominantly capitalist societies.

Per capita GNP also varies significantly among

societies with primarily socialist economies. The German Democratic Republic (East Germany) had the highest economic output per person ($11,860), while Yugoslavia had the lowest ($2,580). Overall, these socialist economies produced considerably less than their capitalist counterparts. The unweighted average is $7,992 or 56 percent of the figure for capitalist societies. The comparison between the two Germanies is especially interesting, because this is a case of a single society divided at the end of World War II into two parts—one capitalist and one socialist. In 1987, per capita GNP in the socialist German Democratic Republic was about 64 percent that of capitalist Federal Republic of Germany.

Distribution of Income

How wealth is distributed is also important in comparing capitalist and socialist economies. Table 19–2 shows income inequality in several societies with predominantly capitalist or predominantly socialist economies. The income ratios indicate how many times more income is received by highly-paid people than is earned by poorly-paid people.[1]

Of the five primarily capitalist societies listed in Table 19–2, the United States had the greatest income inequality, with a rich person earning almost thirteen times more than a poor person. The income ratios of Canada (12.0) and Italy (11.2) are only slightly less. Both Sweden (5.5) and Great Britain (5.0) have much less income inequality, due to incorporating socialist principles into traditionally capitalist economies. The unweighted average shows a rich person earning more than nine times as much as a poor person in predominantly capitalist societies.

With an unweighted average of 4.5, primarily socialist societies have about half as much income inequality. This comparison of economic performance supports the conclusion that capitalist economies are relatively more productive but also generate greater social inequality; socialist economies produce greater social equality, but at a lower standard of living.

Economics and Politics

Chapter 18 ("Politics and Government") explained that a society's economic system shapes its political life. Capi-

---

[1] Specifically, income ratio is derived from dividing the 95th percentile income by the 5th percentile income.

Table 19–2   DISTRIBUTION OF INCOME IN CAPITALIST AND SOCIALIST ECONOMIES

	Income Ratio
Predominantly Capitalist Economies	
United States (1968)	12.7
Canada (1971)	12.0
Italy (1969)	11.2
Sweden (1971)	5.5
Great Britain (1969)	5.0
Unweighted average	9.3
Predominantly Socialist Economies	
Soviet Union (1966)	5.7
Czechoslovakia (1965)	4.3
Hungary (1964)	4.0
Bulgaria (1963–1965)	3.8
Unweighted average	4.5

SOURCE: Adapted from P. J. D. Wiles, *Economic Institutions Compared* (New York: Halsted Press, 1977), as cited in Paul R. Gregory and Robert C. Stuart, *Comparative Economic Systems*, 2nd ed. (Boston: Houghton Mifflin, 1985), p. 503.

talism depends on the freedom of producers and consumers to interact in a market setting without extensive interference from the state. Thus economic capitalism is linked to extensive civil liberties and political freedoms. From a socialist point of view, such freedom presents an obstacle to collective goals. A market-based freedom amounts to people doing what they can *afford*: consequently, some people have far more freedom than others.

In socialist societies, government tries to maximize economic and social equality. This requires considerable state intervention in the economy, limiting the personal liberty of citizens. But this is defended as necessary so that the society can more effectively meet everyone's basic needs for adequate housing, education, and health care. From the capitalist point of view, this kind of government intervention undermines any claim by socialist societies to being free and democratic.

Humanity has yet to resolve the timeless tension between the goals of personal liberty and economic equality. Some traditionally capitalist societies of Western Europe have adopted socialist policies to limit social inequality. More recently, societies in both Eastern and Western Europe, as well as the Soviet Union, have been expanding market forces in the interest of greater productivity.

Perestroika

Economic reform throughout the socialist world accelerated after 1985 when Mikhail Gorbachev assumed leadership of the Soviet Union. His approach is popularly known as *perestroika*, meaning "restructuring." The basic cause of this reform is the poor performance of the Soviet economy which, were he able to return to his homeland and witness the results of seventy-five years of socialism, would doubtlessly disappoint Vladimir Lenin. Decades of rigid centralized control of the economy and expanding bureaucracy have left the Soviet economy almost paralyzed. As noted already, the standard of living of the Soviet people remains substantially below that of nearly every Western society (Berger, 1986; Brzezinski, 1989; U.S. Bureau of the Census, 1989). Figure 19–1 shows that, between 1960 and 1988, the Soviet economy has increasingly fallen behind the economies of Japan and the United States.

More than simple reform, perestroika is actually a second socialist revolution. The Russian Revolution in 1917 sought to overthrow the aristocratic ruling class; Gorbachev's revolution is an effort to overthrow the entrenched bureaucracy that has ruled the Soviet Union ever since. Defenders of *perestroika* have criticized the rigidly centralized administration of the Soviet economy for producing mostly *plans* rather than *products*. Economic success, in other words, has been defined as meeting the goals of bureaucrats, often out of touch with the actual needs of the people. For this reason, Soviet goods have little value on world markets, while the Soviet people can find few desirable items on which to spend their earnings. Currently, for instance, food stores lack adequate supplies of meats and vegetables, while large supplies of shoddy shoes remain on the shelves; purchasing a Soviet automobile requires a wait of about seven years.

Economic restructuring has been even more rapid

Figure 19–1 Per Capita GNP 1960–1987: United States, Japan, and the Soviet Union (adjusted for inflation)

(Estimates based on Brzezinski, 1989:259 and The World Bank)

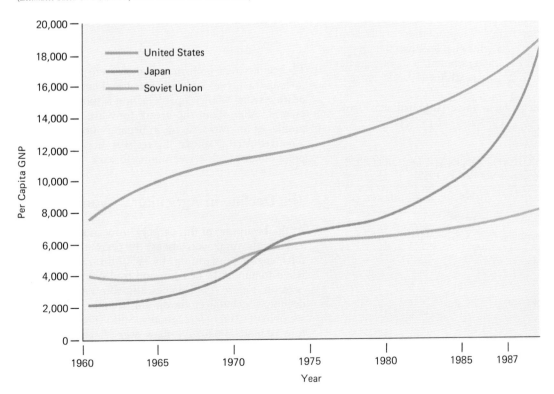

in the societies of Eastern Europe, where productivity has also been low. Restricted since the end of World War II to trading with the Soviet Union and among themselves, Eastern European societies now seek to establish economic ties to other nations and are actively courting foreign investment. Because of the stunning rate of change, the future of European *perestroika* cannot be predicted. Nevertheless, Europe is unlikely to ever return to its state at the beginning of the 1980s.

WORK IN THE POSTINDUSTRIAL ECONOMY

The economy of the United States has also changed dramatically during the last century. The Industrial Revolution transformed the American workforce a century ago; further changes are taking place today.

In 1989, 124 million Americans were in the labor force, representing two-thirds of those over the age of sixteen. As shown in Table 19–3, a larger proportion of American men (72.5 percent) than women (54.3 percent) had income-producing jobs. As noted in Chapter 13 ("Sex and Gender"), in recent decades this gap has diminished. Among males, the proportion of blacks in the labor force (71.0%) is somewhat less than the proportion of whites (77.1%); among women, a slightly greater share of blacks (58.7%) than whites (57.2%) are employed.

Age also affects labor force participation. Figure

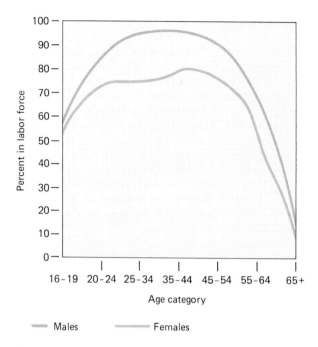

Figure 19–2 Participation in the Labor Force by Age and Sex, 1989

(U.S. Bureau of Labor Statistics, 1990)

19–2 shows that both men and women join the work force in their teens and early twenties. During the child-bearing years, women's participation is subsequently depressed. After about the age of forty-five, the working profiles of the two sexes again become similar, showing a marked decline so that, by age sixty-five, only a small proportion of each sex continues to work.

The Decline of Agricultural Work

At the beginning of this century, American society was still largely rural with almost 40 percent of the labor force engaged in farming. By 1950, this proportion had fallen to almost 10 percent, and by 1990 to less than 3 percent. Figure 19–3 graphically illustrates this rapid decline, which reflects the diminished role of the primary sector in the American economy. Still, American agriculture is more productive than ever. A century ago, a typical farmer could feed five people; today, a farmer can grow food for seventy-five. This dramatic rise in productivity is due to new types of crops, pesticides that

Table 19–3 PARTICIPATION IN THE LABOR FORCE BY SEX AND RACE, 1989

Category of the Population	In the Labor Force	
	Number (millions)	Percent
Males (aged 16 and over)	67.8	76.4
White	59.0	77.1
Black	6.7	71.0
Females (aged 16 and over)	56.0	57.4
White	47.4	57.2
Black	6.8	58.7

SOURCE: U.S. Bureau of Labor Statistics, *Employment and Earnings*, Vol. 37, No. 1 (January 1990), pp. 162–164.

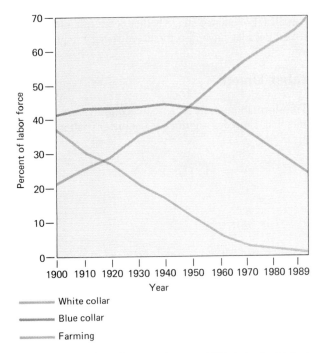

Figure 19–3   The Changing Pattern of Work in the United States, 1900–1989

(U.S. Bureau of the Census)

provide higher yields, larger and more sophisticated farm equipment, higher energy consumption, and advances in farming techniques. The average American farm has also doubled in size since 1950 to about 465 acres today. "Family farms" are declining in number and produce relatively little; more and more production is carried out by *corporate agribusinesses*. For farming communities across the United States, this change has resulted in an often painful loss of a way of life. And, despite the rising productivity of agribusiness, a growing proportion of Americans are concerned about the effect of widespread use of pesticides and chemicals on crops.

From Factory Work to Service Work

The industrialization of the American economy swelled the ranks of blue-collar occupations, especially factory work. By 1900, as shown in Figure 19–3, more than 40 percent of working Americans had blue-collar jobs—more than those employed in agriculture. By mid-cen-

tury, another transformation had occurred, as the white-collar revolution carried a majority of Americans into service occupations. By 1988, more than two-thirds of employed Americans held white-collar jobs; blue-collar work had declined to almost one-fourth of the labor force.

The growth of white-collar occupations is one reason for the widespread—if misleading—description of the United States as a middle-class society. As explained in Chapter 10 ("Social Class in America"), however, much so-called "white-collar" work is actually "service work," including sales positions, secretarial jobs, and working in fast-food restaurants. Such work yields little of the income, prestige, and other benefits of traditional white-collar occupations. Therefore, an increasing proportion of work in postindustrial America provides a modest standard of living.

Another way to describe this change is to divide work into two different *labor markets* (Edwards, 1979). The **primary labor market** includes *occupations that provide extensive benefits to workers*. This segment contains traditional white-collar occupations including professions and high management positions in business and other formal organizations. Work in the primary labor market not only provides high income and job security but is also personally challenging and satisfying. Such occupations require a broad education rather than specialized training, and offer good opportunity for advancement.

The **secondary labor market** includes *jobs providing minimal benefits to workers*. This segment of the labor force consists of low-skill, blue-collar work and low-level, white-collar jobs, usually clerical positions. The secondary labor market provides much lower income and job security. Even if they attain more education and training, workers have little opportunity for advancement. Many jobs are dead-end, non-unionized, and do not offer even the benefits of a seniority system. Workers in the secondary labor market are most likely to experience alienation and dissatisfaction (Mottaz, 1981; Kohn & Schooler, 1982). These problems are most serious for women and other minorities who suffer disadvantages in both segments of the labor force (Kemp & Coverman, 1989).

A growing proportion of the jobs being created in the emerging postindustrial economy appear in the secondary labor market and involve the same kind of unchallenging work, low wages, and poor working conditions characteristic of manufacturing jobs in factories a century ago (Edwards, 1979; Gruenberg, 1980). In the box, two workers—one with a traditional factory job and the other with a new service position—describe their occupations in terms suggestive of Karl Marx's concept of worker alienation, described in Chapter 4 ("Society").

Increasing productivity in the emerging postindustrial economy has depended on a longer work week: now averaging almost forty-nine hours (Hunnicutt, 1988, 1990). As explained in Chapter 10 ("Social Class in America"), evidence suggests that economic changes in recent decades have also increased social inequality.

Labor Unions

Transformation of the American economy in recent decades has caused a significant decline in **labor unions,**

SOCIOLOGY OF EVERYDAY LIFE

Old Factory Work and New Service Work: Much the Same

Mike Lefevre is an industrial worker in a Chicago steel mill. He is aware that jobs such as his are declining in America. He also explains that he finds little personal satisfaction in his work.

I'm a dying breed. A laborer. Strictly muscle work . . . pick it up, put it down, pick it up, put it down. We handle between forty and fifty thousand pounds of steel a day. (Laughs) I know it's hard to believe—from four hundred pounds to three- and four-pound pieces. It's dying.

. . . It's hard to take pride in a bridge you're never gonna cross, in a door you're never gonna open. You're mass-producing things and you never see the end of it. (Muses) I worked for a trucker one time. At least I could see the truck depart loaded. In a steel mill, forget it. You don't see where nothing goes.

I got chewed out by my foreman once. He said, "Mike, you're a good worker but you have a bad attitude." My attitude is that I don't get excited about my job. I do my work but I don't say whoopee-doo. The day I get excited about my job is the day I go to a head shrinker. How are you gonna get excited about pullin' steel? How are you gonna get excited when you're tired and want to sit down?

It's not just the work. Somebody built the pyramids. Somebody's going to build something. Pyramids, Empire State Building—these things just don't happen. There's hard work behind it. I would like to see a building, say, the Empire State, I would like to see on one side of it a foot wide strip from top to bottom with the name of every bricklayer, the name of every electrician, and all the names. So when a guy walked by, he could take his son and say, "See, that's me over there on the forty-fifth floor, I put the steel beam in." Picasso can point to a painting. What can I point to? Everybody should have something to point to.

Heather Lamb is also a Midwestern worker, employed in the newer service sector of the American economy. Her work as a long-distance telephone operator provides little more autonomy and personal satisfaction than Mike Lefevre finds in the steel mill.

It's a strange atmosphere. You're in a room about the size of a gymnasium, talking to people thousands of miles away. You come in contact with at least thirty-five an hour. You can't exchange any ideas with them. They don't know you, they never will. You feel like you might be missing people. You feel like they put a coin in the machine and they've got you. You're there to perform your service and go. You're kind of detached.

. . . A big thing is not to talk with a customer. If he's upset, you can't say more than, "I'm sorry you've been having trouble." If you get caught talking with a customer, that's one mark against you. You can't help but want to talk to them if they're in trouble or they're just feeling bad or something. For me it's a great temptation to say, "Gee, what's the matter?" You don't feel like you're really that much helping people.

. . . It's a hard feeling when everyone's in a hurry to talk to somebody else, but not to you. Sometimes you get a feeling of needing to talk to somebody. Somebody who wants to listen to you other than, "Why didn't you get me the right number?"

It's something to run into somebody who says, "It's a nice day out, operator. How's your day, busy?" You're so thankful for these people. You say, "Oh, yes, it's been an awful day. Thank you for asking."

SOURCE: Studs Terkel, *Working* (New York: Pantheon Books, 1974), 1–2, 65, 66, 69. Copyright © 1974 by Pantheon Books, a Division of Random House, Inc.

organizations of workers that attempt to improve wages and working conditions through various strategies, including negotiations and strikes. Membership in labor unions increased rapidly after 1935, rising to more than one-third of the non-agricultural labor force after World War II. Union membership peaked during the 1970s at almost 25 million.

Since then, it has steadily declined to about 17 percent of the non-farm labor force, or about 20 million men and women. Unions now claim a far lower proportion of workers in the United States than in other industrial societies: more than 90 percent of workers in Denmark and Sweden belong to unions, as do half in Great Britain, and about one third in Canada, Switzerland, and Japan.

Several factors have contributed to this decline. First, the highly unionized industrial sector of the American economy has suffered greatly in recent years, as already noted. Tens of thousands of unionized workers in steel, automobile, and other industries have lost their jobs. Especially during the recession in the early 1980s, some plants facing economic problems forced concessions from workers including, in many cases, the dissolution of labor unions. Second, newly created service jobs are far less likely to be unionized. Job creation during the next decade will probably continue this trend. Third, the Reagan administration, which began its eight years in office with a highly public victory over the Professional Air Traffic Controllers Organization (PATCO), fostered a national climate often hostile to union interests.

Unions are still a powerful force in the American workplace and also in national politics. Yet, the erosion of union strength is likely to continue (Goldfield, 1987).

Professions

Professional work has brought substantial benefits to some Americans in the emerging postindustrial economy of the United States. Many kinds of work are commonly termed *professional*, such as a professional exterminator or a professional tennis player. As distinct from *amateurs*, professionals pursue an activity for a living, and presumably have skills and training.

More precisely, a **profession** is *a prestigious, white-collar occupation that requires extensive formal education.* In the past, professional standing was limited to a few occupations, principally medicine, law, academia, and the ministry (W. Goode, 1960). Today, more occupations are described as professional to the extent that they have the following four characteristics (Ritzer, 1972).

1. **Theoretical knowledge.** Unlike jobs involving only technical skills, professionals claim a theoretical understanding of their field based on extensive formal training and informal interaction with their peers. Anyone can learn first-aid skills, for example, but physicians must have a theoretical understanding of human health and illness.

2. **Self-regulated training and practice.** While most workers are subject to on-the-job supervision, professionals tend to be self-employed rather than salaried employees of large organizations (Zald, 1971). Specialized training is regulated by professional associations composed of others in the profession. Formal degrees and other certificates are required of those who wish to "practice." Professionals must also conform to a formal code of ethics.

3. **Authority over clients.** Many workers are directed by the desires of their customers. In contrast, professionals claim knowledge that "lay people" do not possess; therefore, they expect clients to follow their direction and advice.

4. **Community orientation rather than self-interest.** Professionals frequently assert that they are serving the needs of clients and the community as a whole, rather than seeking personal enrichment. Most business executives readily admit to seeking financial gain for their efforts. A professional such as a minister or a college professor, however, is widely viewed as contributing to the well-being of others. It would be mildly disturbing, in fact, to think of one's priest as simply "in it for the money." Some professionals, including physicians, are even barred by professional codes from advertising. Such altruism also makes many professionals reluctant to discuss fees, although most receive high incomes all the same.

Besides the traditional professions of medicine, law, academia, and the ministry, a number of other occupations can be described as *new professions*, including architecture, psychiatry, social work, and accountancy, which share most of the characteristics just presented. Many new service occupations in America's postindustrial economy have also sought professional standing, a process termed *professionalization*.

Members of an occupational category initiate their claim to professional standing by labeling their work in a new way. The new name both suggests that they employ special, theoretical knowledge and distances them from their previously less distinguished reputation. Government administrators, for example, become "public policy analysts" and dogcatchers transform themselves into "animal control specialists." A professional association soon forms to formally attest to their individual skills. This organization begins to lobby for the right to license those who perform the work. It also develops a code of ethics, modeled on those of traditional professions, which emphasizes the occupation's contribution to the community. A professional association may also establish schools or other training facilities, and perhaps start a professional journal. All of this will help win acceptance of the occupation's professional standing (Abbott, 1988).

Not every category of workers that tries to claim professional status will succeed. In marginal cases, the term *paraprofessional* denotes work, such as that of medical technicians, with specialized skills but lacking extensive theoretical education required of professionals.

Self-Employment

Self-employment, earning a living without working for a large organization, has been an American tradition. Rural farms were family owned and operated, and in the cities, self-employed workers owned shops and other small businesses or sold their skills and labor on the open market. C. Wright Mills (1951) estimated that in the early nineteenth century about 80 percent of the American labor force was self-employed. By 1870, however, the proportion of self-employed American workers had dropped to one-third, and by 1940, to one-fifth.

Since 1970, self-employment has risen slightly, fueled by expansion in postindustrial service occupations (Steinmetz & Wright, 1989). Government statistics indicate that 8.2 percent of the labor force (9.9 percent of men and 6.2 percent of women) were self-employed in 1989. Among the shrinking number of agricultural workers, about half of all men and one-third of all women are self-employed (U.S. Bureau of Labor Statistics, 1990).

Lawyers, physicians, and other professionals have always been strongly represented among the self-employed because they possess the special education and skills that enable them to make a living without working for any organization. But most self-employed workers are not professionals. They are small business owners, plumbers, carpenters, free-lance writers, editors, artists, and long-distance truck drivers. Overall, the self-employed are more likely to have blue-collar jobs than white-collar work.

American culture has always celebrated the value of working independently: no time clocks to punch, no inflexible routines, and no supervision. For those subject to prejudice and discrimination, the strategy of self-employment tends to increase economic opportunity (Evans, 1989). The self-employed possess the potential—although rarely realized—of earning a great deal of money. Self-employed people, however, also face special problems. Many are vulnerable to fluctuations in the economy: about one-third of small businesses do not survive for five years (Form, 1982). Another common problem is that the self-employed lack pension and healthcare benefits provided to employees of large organizations.

Unemployment

Work supplies not only needed income but satisfaction, social prestige, and a sense of personal identity. Unemployment, therefore, can cause both financial hardship and social and psychological problems (Riegle, 1982).

Some unemployment is found in every society. Few young people entering the labor force find a job immediately; some workers temporarily leave the labor force while seeking a new job or because of a labor strike; others suffer from long-term illnesses; and still others who are illiterate or without skills cannot perform useful work. Unemployment, however, is also caused by the operation of the economy itself. Workers may lose their jobs due to economic recession, as a result of their occupations becoming obsolete, or because their employers close down in the face of foreign competition. During the 1980s, for example, the emergence of a postindustrial economy generated widespread unemployment among workers in many traditional blue-collar occupations (Kasarda, 1983).

In predominantly capitalist societies such as the United States, the unemployment rate rarely dips below 5 percent of the labor force. Public policymakers generally view this level of unemployment as natural, even describing it as "full employment." Typically, an "unemployment problem" is publicly acknowledged only when the unemployment rate exceeds about 8 percent (Albrecht, 1983). In contrast, predominantly socialist societies consider work to be each person's right and obligation, so the government may, if necessary, create jobs to keep the unemployment rate low. Unemployment is, nevertheless, just as great a problem in these societies.

In 1989, 6.5 million Americans over the age of sixteen were unemployed—about 5 percent of the civilian

During the Great Depression, a time of catastrophic unemployment in the United States, Isaac Soyer painted *Employment Agency* to reveal the personal collapse and despair that can afflict men and women who are out of work.

labor force. In some regions of the United States, such as parts of West Virginia and New Mexico, unemployment may be twice the national rate. Unemployment has generally declined since 1982, the year of the highest annual unemployment rate (9.7 percent) since the Great Depression ended in the early 1940s. Because American culture embraces the misleading idea that anyone who really wants to work can, we sometimes harshly judge the unemployed as unmotivated people in a land of opportunity.

Unemployment is more common in the secondary labor market than in the primary labor market. Figure 19–4 on page 526 shows the official jobless rate for various segments of the American population in 1989 (U.S. Bureau of Labor Statistics, 1990). Black unemployment was more than twice as high (11.4 percent) as white unemployment (4.5 percent), due to the historical concentration of blacks in the secondary labor market (Di-Prete, 1981). Although every category of teenager suffers from unemployment, this problem is far worse for blacks (32.4 percent) than among whites (12.7 percent). Even for college graduates, who typically work in the primary labor market, black unemployment (10.1 percent) is more than twice as high as for whites (4.8 percent). For both races, women and men had the same level of unemployment during the 1980s. Before, women experienced consistently higher unemployment than men did. The eco-

nomic recession of the early 1980s, which hit male-dominated blue-collar industrial jobs especially hard, explains this change.

Official unemployment statistics are based on monthly national surveys. These figures may understate unemployment for two reasons. First, to be termed unemployed, a person must be actively seeking work. Especially during economic recessions, many people become discouraged after failing to find a job and so stop looking. These "discouraged workers" are not counted among the unemployed. Second, many people unable to find jobs for which they are qualified take "lesser" employment: a former college professor, for example, may drive a taxi while seeking a new teaching position. Such people are considered to be employed, although they might also be described as *underemployed*. For other reasons, official statistics may overstate unemployment. Some people counted as unemployed may receive income from odd jobs or illegal activity. Overall, however, the actual level of unemployment is probably several percentage points above the official figure.

The Underground Economy

Unlike socialist economies that have traditionally condemned market forces, the capitalist American economy

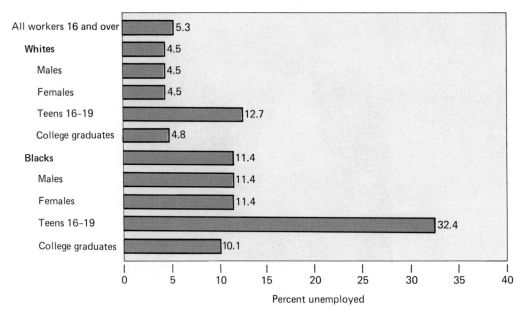

Figure 19-4 Official Unemployment Rate among Various Categories of Americans, 1989

(*U.S. Bureau of Labor Statistics, 1990*)

supports "free enterprise." Yet, even in the United States, economic transactions are subject to government regulations that require extensive records and regular reports. In violation of these regulations is the **underground economy,** *economic activity involving income or the exchange of goods and services that is not reported to the government.*

On a small scale, the underground economy operates in many familiar ways: sales representatives for different companies swap customer samples on a weekly basis; teenagers baby-sit for parents in their neighborhoods; a family makes some extra money by holding a garage sale. Any such activity that generates income that is unreported to the government becomes part of the underground economy. Another large segment of the underground economy consists of income from criminal activity, especially from the sale of illegal drugs. Income from crimes such as prostitution, bribery, theft, illegal gambling, and loan-sharking also goes unreported. Some additional transactions occur "under the table" because people wish to avoid time-consuming official paperwork.

The single largest segment of the underground economy is legally obtained income unreported on income tax forms. Self-employed persons such as carpenters, physicians, and owners of small businesses may understate their incomes; waiters, waitresses, and other service workers may not report their entire income from tips. Even relatively small omissions and misrepresentations on individual income tax returns add up to billions of dollars within the underground economy (Simon & Witte, 1982).

Exactly how big is the underground economy? Estimates suggest that perhaps 10 percent of economic activity in the United States is unreported (Gutmann, cited in Simon & Witte, 1982). In 1990, the gross national product of the United States exceeded $5 trillion, so the underground economy may have amounted to $500 billion—more than the combined GNP of all the Scandinavian countries.

CORPORATIONS

The core of today's capitalist economies is corporations. A **corporation** is *an organization with a legal existence including rights and liabilities apart from those of its members.* An organization that becomes legally incorporated is viewed as an entity unto itself able to enter into contracts and own property. Of perhaps 18 million businesses in the United States in the mid-1980s, about 3.4 million were incorporated (*Statistics of Income Bulletin*, 1989).

Legal incorporation developed about a century ago to provide two major benefits to owners of large businesses. First, incorporation helps to shield owners from legal liabilities of their businesses. It protects personal wealth from lawsuits arising from business debts or harm to consumers. Second, incorporation provides advantages under the tax laws of the United States that increase the profits of owners.

Chapter 9 ("Social Stratification") explains that many corporations are owned by millions of stockholders (and by other corporations) rather than by single families. This dispersion of corporate ownership has to some extent spread wealth by making more Americans small-scale capitalists. Ralf Dahrendorf (1959) adds that the day-to-day operation of a corporation is the task of white-collar executives who are responsible to the stockholders. In practice, however, a great deal of corporate stock is owned by a small number of the corporation's top executives and directors. These major stockholders comprise a small economic elite, which owns and operates the richest and most powerful American businesses. Thus the proliferation of corporations has not substantially changed how large businesses operate or greatly affected the distribution of American wealth (Useem, 1980).

Economic Concentration

Profit-making corporations range in size from tiny one-person businesses to veritable giants such as the major automobile manufacturers that employ hundreds of thousands of people in the United States and abroad. About half of American corporations are small, with assets worth less than $100,000. The largest corporations, however, dominate the American economy.

The first truly giant American corporation was United States Steel, formed in 1901 from the merger of several steel companies. Leading this mega-corporation, industrialist J. P. Morgan produced two-thirds of American steel in the early decades of the twentieth century. Worth billions of dollars, at that time, U.S. Steel's assets would have funded the operation of the federal government for almost two years (Baltzell, 1964; Fusfeld, 1982).

Throughout this century, the growth of corporations has resulted in a staggering concentration of national and international economic power. In 1968, for example, the one hundred largest manufacturing corporations con-trolled more productive assets than the two hundred largest firms in 1950 (Fusfeld, 1982). Of more than 3 million American corporations in 1985, 281 had total assets exceeding $1 billion, which represented two-thirds of all American corporate assets and almost 70 percent of all corporate profits (U.S. Bureau of the Census, 1987).

Table 19–5 on page 528 shows the twenty largest corporations in the United States in 1988, ranked by sales. At the top of the list, General Motors had over $120 billion in sales and $163 billion in total assets. GM's sales during that year were about as much as the combined tax revenue of half the states. GM also employed more people than did the governments of all the states on the West Coast, including Alaska and Hawaii. Such economic concentration suggests that a few giant corporations control many American markets, as shown in Table 19–6.

Conglomerates and Corporate Linkages

Economic concentration has created conglomerates, *giant corporations composed of many smaller corporations.* Conglomerates arise as corporations seek greater profits by entering new markets. In the past, corporations grew as they spawned new companies; more recently, "take-overs" of existing companies have become common. This diversification has the added benefit of protecting corporations from declining profits in their original market. Facing decreased sales of tobacco products, for example, R.J. Reynolds merged with Nabisco foods, forming RJR-Nabisco. Although its original market is still growing, Coca-Cola now produces not only soft drinks but fruit drinks, coffee, bottled water, feature films, and television programs. Beatrice Foods is a corporate "umbrella" containing more than fifty smaller corporations that manufacture well-known products such as Reddi-Whip, Wesson cooking oils, Peter Pan peanut butter, Hunt's foods, Tropicana fruit juices, La Choy foods, Orville Redenbacher pop corn, Max Factor cosmetics, Playtex clothing, and Samsonite luggage (Beatrice, 1985).

Besides conglomerates, corporate linkages also result from stock ownership by extremely wealthy families. For example, when Pittsburgh banking magnate Richard K. Mellon died in 1970, his family reportedly owned a controlling interest in six major corporations (Fusfeld, 1982). Today, linkage often takes the form of corporations owning each other's stock. Able to own property just as individuals do, corporations invest heavily in one another. Joint ventures, which promise to benefit all parties, frequently accompany stock linkages (Herman, 1981).

Table 19–5 THE TWENTY LARGEST INDUSTRIAL CORPORATIONS IN THE UNITED STATES, 1988 (RANKED BY SALES)

Corporation	Product	Sales ($ billions)	Assets ($ billions)	Number of Employees
General Motors	Motor vehicles	121.8	163.8	765,700
Ford Motor	Motor vehicles	92.4	143.2	358,900
Exxon	Oil refining	80.9	74.3	100,500
International Business Machines (IBM)	Office equipment	59.7	73.0	388,200
Sears, Roebuck	Retail stores	50.1	78.0	510,500
General Electric	Electronics	49.8	110.9	310,000
Mobil	Oil refining	48.2	38.8	68,900
Chrysler	Motor vehicles	35.5	48.6	130,200
American Telephone & Telegraph (AT&T)	Electronics	35.2	35.2	303,600
Texaco	Oil refining	33.5	26.3	46,000
E.I. du Pont de Nemours	Chemicals	32.5	30.7	140,500
Citicorp	Banks	32.0	207.7	89,500
K-mart	Retail stores	27.6	12.1	342,500
Philip Morris Co.	Tobacco products	25.9	37.0	116,500
Chevron	Oil refining	25.2	34.0	52,700
Aetna Life & Casualty	Insurance	24.3	81.4	44,500
American Express	Financial services	22.9	142.7	92,200
Amoco	Oil refining	21.2	30.0	50,100
Wal-Mart Stores	Retail stores	20.6	7.0	191,500
Procter & Gamble	Chemicals	20.4	15.8	75,300

SOURCE: "The Forbes 500 Annual Directory," *Forbes*, Vol. 143, no. 9 (May 1, 1989): Special issue.

Another type of linkage among corporations is the **interlocking directorate**, *a social network made up of people who simultaneously serve on the boards of directors of many corporations*. These connections give corporations access to insider information that can be extremely valuable. When founded in 1901, for example, U.S. Steel was linked through its board to more than one hundred other corporations. Interlocking directorates are now less extensive because antitrust laws prevent direct linkages if the corporations compete with one another. Yet beneficial linkages persist among noncompeting corporations with common interests—for example, a corporation building tractors may share directors with one that manufactures tires. Indirect linkages also occur when, for example, a member of General Motor's board of directors and a member of Ford's board of directors both sit on the board of Exxon.

Research reveals that interlocking directorates remain an important trait of corporate life (Marlios, 1975; Herman, 1981; Scott & Griff, 1985). Beth Mintz and Michael Schwartz (1981) found that General Motors is linked through board-of-director memberships to twenty-nine other major corporations. The members of these boards, in turn, serve on the boards of almost seven hundred other corporations. Indirect linkages among corporations, Mintz and Schwartz also note, commonly involve major banks and insurance companies, which seek to protect the financial well-being of American corporations as a whole.

Gwen Moore (1979) has described how social networks (discussed in Chapter 7, "Groups and Organizations") link members of the corporate elite. In other words, corporate executives participate in various other social networks that allow exchange of valuable information. Michael Useem (1979) concludes that such networks enhance the influence of corporate leaders within political, social, and charitable organizations.

Corporate linkages do not necessarily oppose the public interest, but they do concentrate power and encourage some kinds of illegal activity. Price-fixing, for example, is legal in much of the world (the Organization of Petroleum Exporting Countries—OPEC—meets reg-

Table 19–6 ECONOMIC CONCENTRATION IN MAJOR MARKETS OF THE AMERICAN ECONOMY

Market	Leading Corporations	Percent of Market	Market	Leading Corporations	Percent of Market
Motor vehicles	General Motors Ford Chrysler Volkswagen	70–75	Metal containers	American Can Continental Can	80–90
			Aircraft	Boeing McDonnell-Douglas General Dynamics	80–90
Petroleum refining	Exxon Texaco Mobil Standard Oil (Calif.) Standard Oil (Ind.)	50–60	Aircraft engines	General Electric United Technologies	90–100
			Drugs	American Home Products Merck Pfizer Lilly	70–80
Iron and steel	U.S. Corporation Bethlehem Armco LTV Corporation	50–60	Soaps and related products	Procter & Gamble Colgate Lever Brothers	60–70
Industrial chemicals	DuPont Union Carbide Dow Monsanto	60–70	Dairy products	Borden National Dairy Carnation	60–70
Aluminum	Alcoa Kaiser Reynolds	80–90	Automobile tires and tubes	Goodyear Firestone Uniroyal	70–80
Copper	Anaconda Kennecott Phelps-Dodge	60–70			

SOURCE: Daniel R. Fusfeld, *Economics: Principles of Political Economy*, 3rd ed. (Glenview, IL: Scott, Foresman, 1988), p. 407. Copyright © 1988, 1985 by Scott, Foresman, and Company. Reprinted by permission of Harper Collins Publishers.

ularly to try to set oil prices), but not in the United States. By their nature, linkages encourage price-fixing, especially when only several corporations control a market.

Corporations and Competition

The capitalist model assumes businesses operate independently within a competitive market. In the United States, the *competitive sector* of the economy is actually limited to smaller businesses and self-employed people. Large corporations at the core of the American economy fall within the *noncompetitive sector*. Corporations are not truly competitive because, first, extensive linkages mean that they do not operate independently. Second, a small number of corporations dominate many large markets.

Any business would maximize profits by achieving a **monopoly**, *domination of a market by a single producer*. Because a lack of competition allows a company to dictate prices, a century ago the federal government declared monopolies to be a danger to the public welfare and limited them by law, beginning with the Sherman Anti-Trust Act of 1890. Such legislation has eliminated true monopolies, but limited competition persists in the form of **oligopoly**, or *domination of a market by a few producers*.

Oligopoly is inherent in industrial-capitalism. Entering the automobile manufacturing market today, for example, would take a staggering investment of billions of dollars, and even then there is no certainty of competing effectively against existing automobile manufacturers that have merged to form ever-larger corporations. To big business, in short, competition means risk, which corporations seek to limit in order to secure profits.

Ideally, capitalism supports minimal government

The expansion of Western multinational corporations has changed patterns of consumption throughout the world, creating a "corporate culture" that is—for better or worse—undermining countless traditional ways of life.

intervention in the economy. But corporate power is now so great—and competition among corporations so limited—that government regulation is often the only means to protect the public interest. Yet, in general we can hardly describe government as an adversary of large corporations. The government is, in fact, the single biggest customer of large corporations (Madsen, 1980). It also frequently intervenes to support struggling corporations, as in the savings and loan bailout of the late 1980s. Corporations and government typically work together to make the entire economy more stable and more profitable.

Corporations and the Global Economy

Corporations have grown in size and power and will soon account for most of the world's economic activity. Trade has long tied together diverse cultures, but never before has so much economic activity spanned the globe. The largest corporations—the majority of which are American—have spilled across national borders and now view the entire world as one vast marketplace.

As discussed in Chapter 11 ("Global Inequality"), multinational corporations are large corporations that produce and market products in many different nations. Beatrice Foods, for example, operates factories in thirty countries that manufacture products sold in more than one hundred. Exxon is heavily multinational, earning roughly three-fourths of its profits outside the United States through the production, refining, and sale of petroleum products in one hundred countries. General Motors is multinational on a smaller scale, earning one-fourth of its profits through foreign operations in a dozen countries (Madsen, 1980).

Corporations become multinational in pursuit of their primary goal: making money. About three-fourths of the world's people live in nonindustrialized societies, where most of the planet's resources are found. Worldwide operations, then, offer access to larger markets, less costly labor, and more raw materials. Becoming international also permits corporations to lower their tax liabilities and to move money from country to country, profiting from fluctuating currency values.

The effects of capitalist expansion to the poor societies of the Third World have been controversial, as Chapter 11 ("Global Inequality") explains in detail. Modernization theorists argue that multinationals are the key to world economic development (Rostow, 1978; Madsen, 1980; Berger, 1986). In the face of staggering problems of poverty and hunger, multinationals unleash the great productivity of the capitalist economic system. For instance, by itself the Exxon corporation outproduces almost any Third-World nation. During the 1980s, Exxon's annual sales averaged several times the combined gross national product of all seven nations of Central America.

Corporate expansion, supporters argue, provides poor societies with needed employment in the secondary (manufacturing) and tertiary (service) sectors. Multinationals also import capital and new technology—especially manufacturing techniques—that accelerate economic growth. Multinationals thus offer countries in which they operate short-term advantages by paying wages and taxes, and stimulate long-term development by expanding the local economy with new products and services.

On the other side, critics claim that multinationals have intensified global inequality (Vaughan, 1978; Wallerstein, 1979; Delacroix & Ragin, 1981; Bergesen, 1983). Multinational investment, they argue, is primarily capital-intensive; in other words, a multinational's presence actually creates few jobs. Instead, tremendously powerful multinationals frequently inhibit the development of labor-intensive local industries, the real source of employment. Another argument against multinationals is that they generally produce expensive consumer goods that are exported to rich societies, rather than food and other necessities needed by local communities.

Instead of assisting economic development of Third-World societies, critics conclude, multinationals make poor societies poorer and increasingly dependent on rich societies of the capitalist First World. From this perspective, the growth of multinational corporations is an extension of historical colonialism: a neocolonialism now concerned with profit rather than political control. As one defender of multinationals asserted, "We are not without cunning. We shall not make Britain's mistake. Too wise to govern the world, we shall simply own it" (cited in Vaughan, 1978:20).

THE ECONOMY OF THE TWENTY-FIRST CENTURY

Today, the rate of economic change is accelerating as it did in 1890, as a new century approached. Many socialist economic systems have seen dramatic transformations, which will probably continue during the 1990s. While some societies, such as those of Eastern Europe, are gradually introducing market systems, other societies, such as the People's Republic of China, are pulling back toward centralized economic control. Socialism, which has involved about one-fourth of humanity, seems likely to take on highly variable forms in the coming decades.

Capitalism, too, has seen marked changes and now exists with various degrees of government regulation. Perhaps the most significant change in the capitalist system is the emergence of global corporations. In part, this means that American-based corporations have expanded into more parts of the world. It also means that foreign-based corporations are increasing their investment in the United States.

Perhaps, as some analysts suggest, we are nearing the end of "the American century." A sign of impending change was the 1989 purchase of New York's Rockefeller Center—a symbol of American capitalism—by Japan's Mitsubishi corporation. Another turning point occurred in 1990, when for the first time, foreign corporations owned more of the United States than American corporations owned abroad ("Buy America," 1989). Foreign investors now own half of commercial property in downtown Los Angeles, 40 percent in Houston, 35 percent in Minneapolis, and 25 percent in Manhattan (Selimuddin, 1989). Growing industrial production overseas, benefiting from new factories, a highly motivated workforce, and the latest technology, has also reduced American competitiveness in numerous areas. The world's largest steel corporations and automobile manufacturers are now Japanese, as is virtually the entire American market in home electronics. The overall lesson is clear: no longer can Americans afford to be uninformed about events in the rest of the world.

We can only imagine the long-term effects of all these changes. One conclusion seems clear, however: our economic future is becoming less a matter of the performance of *national* economies. Instead, the world's societies are increasingly bound together into a global economic system. The emergence of the postindustrial economy in the United States is certainly linked to increasing industrial production abroad, especially in Asia's Pacific Rim. Finally, the ever-pressing issue of global inequality remains unresolved. Whether the world economy ultimately reduces or deepens the disparity between rich and poor societies will likely steer our planet toward peace or belligerence.

SUMMARY

1. The economy is a major social institution by which goods and services are produced, distributed, and consumed.

2. In technologically simple societies, economic activity is subsumed within the family. In agrarian societies, the economy becomes distinct from the family. Industrialization sparks significant economic expansion due to new sources of energy, factories, mass production, specialization, and wage labor. In postindustrial economies, there is an increasing production of services rather than of goods.

3. The primary sector of the economy generates raw materials; the secondary sector manufactures various goods; the tertiary sector produces services. In preindustrial societies, the primary sector predominates; the secondary sector is of greatest importance in industrial societies; the tertiary sector prevails in postindustrial societies.

4. The economies of today's industrial societies may be described in terms of two models. Capitalism is based on private ownership of productive property and the pursuit of personal profit in a competitive marketplace. Socialism is based on collective ownership of productive property and the pursuit of collective well-being through government control of the economy.

5. Although the American economy is predominantly capitalist, government is widely involved in economic life. Government plays an even greater economic role in democratic socialist societies of Western Europe. The Soviet Union has slowly introduced some market forces into its historically centralized economy; many nations of Eastern Europe are doing so in dramatic and sweeping changes.

6. Capitalism is highly productive, providing a high overall standard of living. Socialist economies are less productive but generate more economic equality.

7. Agricultural work has declined in the United States during this century. The number of blue-collar jobs has also diminished; such work now involves only one-fourth of the labor force. Today, about two-thirds of American workers have white-collar service jobs.

8. A profession is a special category of white-collar work based on theoretical knowledge, occupational autonomy, and authority over clients, with an emphasis on community service.

9. Work in the primary labor market provides far more rewards than work in the secondary labor market. Service jobs in the secondary labor market have become more pronounced in recent years.

10. Today, 8 percent of Americans are self-employed. Although many professionals are in this category, most self-employed workers have blue-collar occupations.

11. Capitalist societies tend to have an unemployment rate of at least 5 percent. Socialist societies, too, struggle with high unemployment.

12. The underground economy represents about 10 percent of the economic activity in the United States, including most criminal business as well as legal income unreported on income tax forms.

13. Corporations are the core of the American economy. The largest corporations, which are conglomerates, account for most corporate assets and profits.

14. The competitive sector of the American economy contains smaller businesses. Large corporations dominate the noncompetitive sector.

15. Multinational corporations have grown in number and size during this century. The consequences for global economic development are a matter of continuing controversy.

KEY CONCEPTS

capitalism an economic system in which natural resources and the means of producing goods and services are privately owned

communism a hypothetical economic and political system in which all members of society have economic and social equality

conglomerates giant corporations composed of many smaller corporations

corporation an organization with a legal existence including rights and liabilities apart from those of its members

democratic socialism a political and economic system in which free elections coexist with a market system modified by government policies to minimize social inequality

economy the institutionalized system for production, distribution, and consumption of goods and services

interlocking directorate a social network made up of people who simultaneously serve on the boards of directors of several corporations

labor unions organizations of workers that attempt to improve wages and working conditions through various strategies, including negotiations and strikes

monopoly domination of a market by a single producer

oligopoly domination of a market by a few producers

postindustrial economy an economy based on service work and high technology

primary labor market occupations that provide extensive benefits to workers

primary sector part of the economy that generates raw materials directly from the natural environment

profession a prestigious white-collar occupation that requires extensive formal education

secondary labor market jobs that provide minimal benefits to workers

secondary sector part of the economy that transforms raw materials into manufactured goods

socialism an economic system in which natural resources, as well as the means of producing goods and services, are collectively owned

tertiary sector part of the economy that generates services rather than goods

underground economy all economic activity involving income or the exchange of goods and services that is not reported to the government

SUGGESTED READINGS

One of sociology's best contemporary thinkers examines the social consequences of capitalism.

> Peter L. Berger. *The Capitalist Revolution: Fifty Propositions about Prosperity, Equality, and Liberty.* New York: Basic Books, 1986.

This textbook focuses on work in American society, with emphasis on patterns of conflict within the workplace.

> George Ritzer and David Walczak. *Working: Conflict and Change.* 4th ed. Englewood Cliffs, NJ: Prentice Hall, 1990.

The first of these books, a sociological classic, explores the emergence of a postindustrial society. The second, published a decade later, argues that manufacturing remains crucial to the American economy and to our ability to develop high-wage service occupations.

> Daniel Bell. *The Coming of Post-Industrial Society: A Venture in Social Forecasting.* New York: Harper, 1976.

> Stephen S. Cohen and John Zysman. *Manufacturing Matters: The Myth of the Post-Industrial Economy.* New York: Basic Books, 1987.

This "issue of the eighties" is likely to remain as an issue of the nineties.

> Frances C. Hunter. *Equal Pay for Equal Worth: The Working Woman's Issue of the Eighties.* New York: Praeger, 1986.

The problems of women in the secondary labor market are detailed in this study.

> Ellen Israel Rosen. *Bitter Choices: Blue-Collar Women In and Out of Work.* Chicago: University of Chicago Press, 1987.

Labor unions have been weakened by the decline of America's industrial base.

> Michael Goldfield. *The Decline of Organized Labor in the United States.* Chicago: University of Chicago, 1987.

How have occupational groups historically claimed the right to control particular services as professional jurisdictions?

> Andrew Abbott. *The System of Professions: An Essay on the Division of Expert Labor.* Chicago: University of Chicago Press, 1988.

Although farming has received growing attention in recent decades, the role of the one million American women in farming is rarely studied. This book describes farmwork, household work, and community life among farm women today.

> Rachel Ann Rosenfeld. *Farm Women: Work, Farm, and Family in the United States.* Chapel Hill, NC: University of North Carolina Press, 1985.

This book is a comparative study of one important dimension of the economy—attitudes toward work.

> Tomotsu Sengoku. *Willing Workers: The Work Ethics in Japan, England, and the United States.* Westport, CT: Quorum Books, 1985.

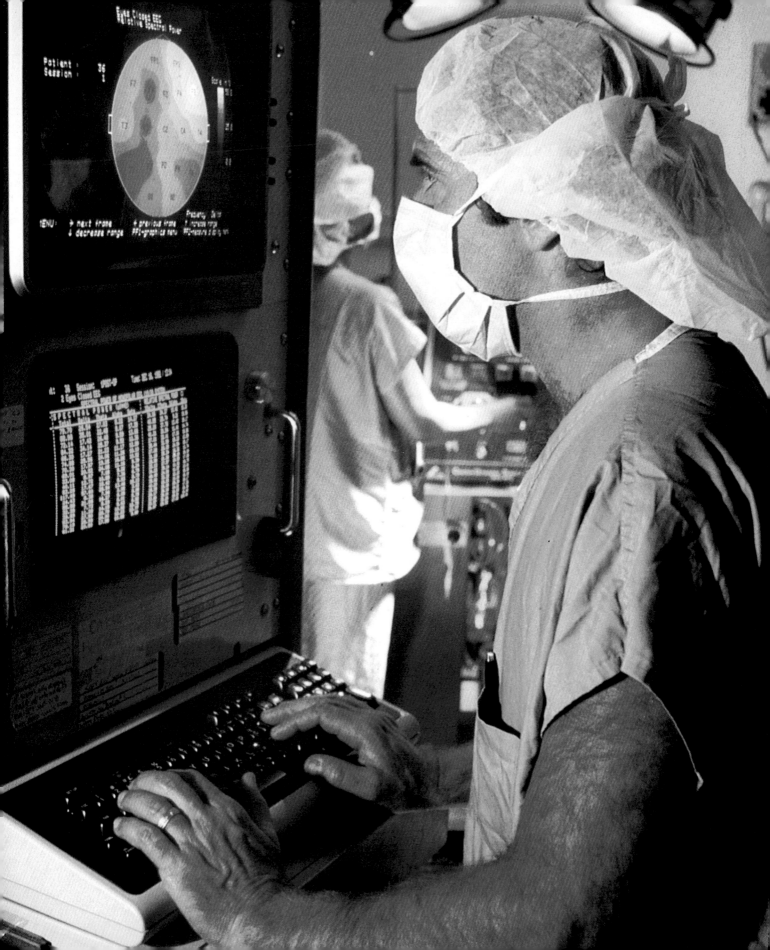

20

Health and Medicine

Melody, a nineteen-year-old sophomore at an exclusive private college in Minnesota, sits restlessly in the waiting room of the school medical clinic. She feels annoyed and fearful: her roommate had pressured her to see the doctor, and she is afraid her parents will be angry if they discover she is ill. *There isn't anything wrong*, she keeps telling herself. Her parents, both lawyers, live forty miles away in Minneapolis. They expect Melody home for the weekend, but she is trying to think up an excuse for not going.

Melody's problem is failing health due to starvation. Far from feeling that she is starving, however, she thinks of herself as *fat*. She knows that she weighs only 87 pounds, and the doctor will undoubtedly say that this is far too little for a woman five feet, five inches tall. But for over three years Melody has been concerned—her roommate would say *obsessed*—with being thin.

Melody's problem, one familiar to many college students, is *anorexia nervosa*,[1] a disorder characterized by what specialists term "severe caloric restriction," or intense, often compulsive dieting. Like many diseases, anorexia nervosa is also a sociological issue: 90 to 95

percent of its victims are *females*, most of them white and from affluent families. Many have been strongly pressured by their parents to be high achievers. Research suggests that one-third to one-half of college-aged women actively try to lose weight, although most of them would not clinically be considered overweight. About one in

[1] This profile of victims of anorexia nervosa is based on Levine, 1987. Another eating disorder, *bulimia*, is binge-eating coupled with induced vomiting to inhibit weight gain. The two diseases have similar victim profiles (cf. Striegel-Moore, Silberstein, & Rodin, 1986).

seven female teens in the United States has behaved in ways that are characteristic of an eating disorder (Levine, 1987; Robinson, 1987).

The Duchess of Windsor once observed that "A woman cannot be too rich or too thin" (Levine, 1987). Women tend to be victims of eating disorders because, in our culture, women's personal value lies in their physical appearance, and the mass media have promoted slenderness as an ideal of femininity (Parrott, 1987). Some researchers suggest that our society socializes young American women to believe that they are never "too thin to feel fat." Such an attitude encourages some women to become victims of a "mass starvation" that "compares with foot-binding, lip-stretching, and other forms of woman mutilation" found in other cultures (Wooley, Wooley, & Dyrenforth, 1979).

Patterns of health are obviously the concern of physicians and other professionals. Sociologists study them too, because, as this chapter will explain, social forces greatly shape the health of Americans just as they do people throughout the world.

WHAT IS HEALTH?

Common sense suggests that health is simply the absence of disease. The World Health Organization, however, defines the ideal of **health** as *a state of complete physical, mental, and social well-being* (1946:3). This more sociological definition underscores the major theme of this chapter: *health is as much a social as a biological issue.*

Health and Society

The health of any population is shaped by important characteristics of that society as a whole.

1. **Health relates to a society's cultural patterns.** Any society's conceptions of health are based on standards that vary from culture to culture. René Dubos (1980; orig. 1965) points out that early in this century, yaws, a contagious skin disease, was so common in tropical Africa that societies there considered it normal.

   What a society views as healthy is also closely linked to what it defines as morally good; contrarily, what is unhealthy is often perceived as morally bad. Because many Americans evaluate homosex-

uality as morally wrong, this sexual orientation is sometimes termed "sick," although it is quite natural from a medical point of view. Americans, especially men, tend to define a competitive, stressful way of life as normal, despite strong evidence that such behavior is related to perhaps two-thirds of physician visits and most heart disease—the leading cause of death in the United States (Wallis, 1983). Ideas about what constitutes good health appear therefore to be forms of social control, encouraging conformity to cultural norms.

   Because standards of health are aspects of culture, they change over time. Early in this century, prominent physicians deplored higher education for women as an unhealthy strain on the female brain, and denounced masturbation as a detriment to health (Smith-Rosenberg & Rosenberg, 1984; Money, 1985). At the same time, cigarette smoking was becoming fashionable, and cigarette manufacturers touted their products' health benefits. Today each of these issues is viewed quite differently.

2. **Health relates to a society's technology and social resources.** A society's level of health depends on the technology it applies to meeting human needs. From today's vantage point, America's history is seen as one of malnutrition, poor sanitation, occupational hazards, and infectious disease. As industrialization raised the standard of living, conceptions of health rose correspondingly.

   In contrast, what Americans would consider poor health, Third World people today take as the norm. In the most disadvantaged of these societies, half the babies born each year die in infancy, most because of hunger (George, 1977; Harrison, 1984).

3. **Health relates to social inequality.** In every society on earth, resources promoting personal well-being are unequally distributed. The physical, mental, and emotional health of wealthier Americans of all ages is far better than that of poor Americans, as we shall explain presently. Longevity, too, is a matter of social position: blacks, who are three times more likely than whites to be poor, can expect to live almost a decade less.

Historical Patterns of Health

One indication that health is a social issue is the pronounced change in well-being over the course of history.

Social changes such as the development of agriculture, the growth of cities, and the emergence of scientific medicine have had a major impact on patterns of health.

Health in Preindustrial Societies

The earliest hunting and gathering societies, described in Chapter 4 ("Society"), continually labored for an adequate supply of food. Their simple technology greatly limited their ability to sustain a healthful environment. As Gerhard and Jean Lenski (1987) suggest, because infants typically must be breastfed for several years, a food shortage or the birth of another child to a nursing mother sometimes meant the abandonment of at least one child. Children fortunate enough to survive infancy were still vulnerable to injuries or illnesses. Perhaps half of the members of hunting and gathering societies died before age twenty, and few lived past forty.

The agricultural revolution expanded the supply of food and other resources. Yet, because of increasing social inequality, elites enjoyed better health than peasants and slaves, who typically lived in crowded, unsanitary shelters. Hunger, hard work, and frequent abusive treatment took their toll on the majority. Their patterns of health were poor—in some cases, even worse than among hunting and gathering societies.

Concentrations of people and lack of sanitation in cities made them less healthful than the countryside. In medieval Europe even rich urbanites lived amid human waste and other refuse, which only became worse as the cities grew (Mumford, 1961). Efforts to restrict environmental pollution in European cities, dating from the fourteenth century, had little effect. The spread of infectious disease, including plague, periodically wiped out sizable portions of the population. Thus those who survived childhood in medieval times had a life expectancy no greater than that of their ancestors a thousand years before.

Health in Industrial Societies

The Industrial Revolution in Europe and North America initially did little to improve health. Factories in the mid-eighteenth century drew millions of people from the countryside to the cities, making sanitation problems worse. The economic elite continued to enjoy better nutrition and housing than did other segments of the population. Even the most well-paid industrial workers lived in crowded, contaminated tenements, and city streets were rife with crime. Factories continuously fouled

Medieval medical practice was heavily influenced by astrology, and diseases were often thought to arise from astral influence; this is the root of our word "influenza." Thus, as midwives attend a childbirth in this woodcut by Swiss artist Jost Amman (1580), an astrologer casts a horoscope for the newborn.

the air with smoke, a health threat unrecognized until well into the twentieth century. Accidents in the workplace became common, since the early industrialists cared little about worker safety.

Then, during the nineteenth century, patterns of health in Western Europe and North America began to improve. The change is often attributed to medical advances that occurred after mid-century, but the death rate in Western Europe and North America had begun to decline even before (Illich, 1976; McKeown, 1979; Mahler, 1980). Industrialization was the main cause of improving health; as the standard of living rose, the population enjoyed better nutrition and safer housing.

During the second half of the nineteenth century, scientific advances in medicine did improve health further, especially in the cities plagued with infectious diseases. In 1854 John Snow examined residential patterns of cholera victims in London and traced the source of this disease to contaminated drinking water (Mechanic, 1978). Within several decades, scientists understood that cholera was caused by bacteria, and they eventually developed protective vaccines. Such medical advances also raised environmental awareness and led to the curbing of age-old practices such as discharging raw sewage into rivers used for drinking water. By the early twentieth century, death rates from infectious diseases had sharply declined.

Dramatic improvement in the health of industrialized societies has continued. In 1900 influenza and pneumonia were leading killers, accounting for one-fourth of all deaths. Today these diseases cause fewer than 3 percent of deaths in the United States. As Table 20–1 indicates, other infectious diseases that were leading causes of death in 1900—including tuberculosis, stomach and intestinal disorders, diseases of early infancy, and diphtheria—no longer pose a major threat to health.

Now, however, heart disease, cancer, and cerebrovascular diseases such as stroke have become widespread

and account for almost 60 percent of deaths in the United States. The predominance of these diseases is due partly to increased use of work-saving devices that reduce healthful exercise, and partly to the consumption of more cigarettes. Also, the American diet, based heavily on meat and eggs, provides 60 percent more cholesterol than the American Heart Association recommends. Americans, consequently, are more likely to die from heart disease than are the Japanese, whose diet is based on fish (Wallis, 1984).

Because fewer Americans today die from acute infectious diseases (such as influenza and pneumonia), more die from chronic illnesses (including heart disease and cancer) associated with advancing age. In 1900, infectious diseases that attacked people at all ages limited the typical male's life expectancy to forty-eight years; females lived about fifty-one years. For Americans born in 1990, government estimates place life expectancy at seventy-six years for males and eighty-three years for females. Living longer, most Americans can expect to die of chronic illnesses common to old age, such as heart disease, cancer, and stroke.

World Health Today

Poverty sharply reduces physical and mental well-being. Because of the striking poverty in the Third World (see Chapter 11, "Global Inequality"), health in poor countries is much worse than in industrial societies. People in the Third World can expect to live less than sixty years, ten years below the average in industrial societies (Mahler, 1980). In Africa the figure is barely fifty, and in the poorest nations in the world, such as Cambodia and Ethiopia, it is only about forty.

According to the World Health Organization, 1 billion people around the world have poor health, most of them because of poverty. First of all, being poor means facing the cruel reality of hunger. Ill health is the result not only of insufficient food, but also of consuming only a single kind of food, as the box explains.

Many impoverished places lack sanitary drinking water, and this problem also contributes to the infectious diseases common in the Third World. The leading causes of death in the United States in 1900, such as influenza, pneumonia, and tuberculosis, still kill the people of nonindustrialized societies. Additionally, parasites such as hookworms, tapeworms, and roundworms cause widespread suffering in these societies (Harrison, 1984; New-

---

Table 20–1 THE CHANGING CAUSES OF DEATH IN THE UNITED STATES

The Ten Leading Causes of Death in 1900
1. Influenza and pneumonia
2. Tuberculosis
3. Stomach and intestinal diseases
4. Heart disease
5. Cerebral hemorrhage
6. Kidney disease
7. Accidents
8. Cancer
9. Diseases of early infancy
10. Diphtheria

The Ten Leading Causes of Death in 1987
1. Heart disease
2. Cancer
3. Cerebrovascular diseases
4. Accidents
5. Lung disease (noncancerous)
6. Influenza and pneumonia
7. Diabetes
8. Suicide
9. Cirrhosis and related liver disease
10. Artery disease

SOURCE: Information for 1900 is from William C. Cockerham, *Medical Sociology*, 2nd ed. (Englewood Cliffs, NJ: Prentice-Hall, 1986), p. 24; information for 1987 is from U.S. National Center for Health Statistics, *Monthly Vital Statistics Report*, Vol. 36, No. 3 (June 22, 1987): Table 6.

Hunger: The Leading Cause of Death in the Third World

Widespread famine in Africa during the 1980s brought home to Americans the image of starving children. Some of the children shown in newspapers and on television appear bloated, while others seem to have shriveled to little more than skin drawn tightly over bones. Both of these deadly conditions, Susan George explains, are the consequences of hunger.

Children with bloated bodies are suffering from protein deficiency. In West Africa this condition is known as *kwashiorkor*, which means literally "one-two." This term derives from the mothers' common practice of abruptly weaning a first child upon the birth of a second. Deprived of their mother's milk, these young children may receive virtually no protein.

The children with shriveled bodies are being deprived of both protein and calories, the result of eating little food of any kind. In both cases, the affected children usually do not die of starvation. Instead, their weakened physical state increases their vulnerability to stomach ailments such as gastroenteritis or diseases such as measles. The death rate from measles is one thousand times greater in parts of Africa than in North America.

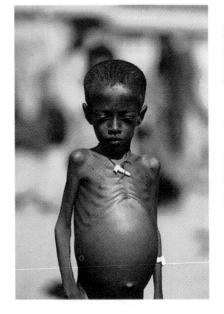

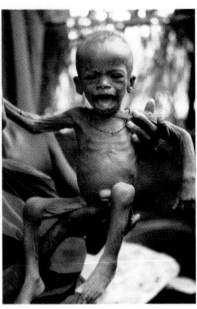

Living on a single food also causes serious medical problems linked to protein, vitamin, or mineral deficiencies. Some 3 million people in the Third World suffer from goiter, a debilitating diet-related disease of the thyroid gland. Pellagra, a disease common to people who consume only corn, is equally serious, frequently leading to madness. Those who depend only on processed rice are prone to beriberi.

A host of diseases virtually unknown to Americans is a common experience of life—and death—in the Third World.

SOURCE: Based, in part, on Susan George, *How the Other Half Dies: The Real Reasons for World Hunger* (Totowa, NJ: Rowman and Allanheld, 1977), pp. 11–12.

man & Matzke, 1984). Whereas a majority of Americans die in old age from heart disease and cancer, most people in the Third World die at any time in the life cycle from infectious and parasitic diseases. Paul Harrison (1984) estimates that in the Third World as a whole, 10 percent of children die in their first year of life; in the poorest societies, half the children do not survive into adulthood. Lacking the basic antibiotics that control many infectious diseases, children of the Third World die at the same rate as European children did in 1750 (George, 1977).

Improving Third-World health is a monumental challenge. First, poverty and poor health form a vicious circle: poverty is a breeding ground for disease, which in turn undermines economic productivity (Harrison, 1984). As was explained in Chapter 11 ("Global Inequality"), the combined effects of simple technology in the Third World and concentration of wealth in the industrialized societies make it unlikely that desperate poverty will soon be reduced. The prognosis for improving the physical, mental, and social well-being of the world's poorest people remains bleak.

An additional reason for pessimism is that as medical technology does control deadly infectious diseases, the populations of poor societies increase. Such societies lack the resources to ensure the well-being of their current populations, so this population growth only increases poverty. Health gains produced by medical advances, then, are often negated by increased disease fueled by rampant poverty. Thus, reducing death rates in this way carries with it the moral obligation to help reduce birth rates as well.

Still, the ability to address the cultural, economic, and political factors that currently undermine the health of much of the world's people is not entirely out of reach of the industrialized world.

HEALTH IN THE UNITED STATES

In comparison with people of the Third World, Americans enjoy very favorable patterns of health. Some categories of Americans, however, are far healthier than others.

Social Epidemiology: The Distribution of Health

Social epidemiology is *the study of the distribution of health and disease in a society's population.* Early social epidemiologists examined the origin and spread of epidemic diseases; John Snow's research on cholera, noted earlier, is one example. Modern social epidemiologists focus more broadly on linking patterns of health to physical and social environments (Cockerham, 1986). For example, they examine the incidence of heart disease among people in different occupations. They also relate health to age, sex, and social standing.

Age and Sex

During this century, the rising standard of living and improved medical care have enhanced the health of Americans of almost every age. One exception is young adults, who suffer more accidental deaths, frequently automobile related. Most Americans now live well past the age of sixty-five. Barring a world holocaust such as nuclear war, 73.1 percent of male Americans born in 1986 and 84.6 percent of females will live to age sixty-five (U.S. Bureau of the Census, 1989).

American females have better health than American males. Because of biological differences, males are slightly more likely than females to die before or immediately after birth. Then the socialization of children into gender roles continues to favor the survival of females. Males, encouraged to be aggressive and individualistic, are the primary victims of accidents, violence, and suicide. In order to be masculine in America, males are encouraged to compete in their occupations, repress their emotions, and engage in smoking, alcohol consumption, and other hazardous behaviors. Gender distinctions, then, explain the significant differences in the longevity of the two sexes: while providing American males with more privileges, conventionally masculine patterns of behavior also entail greater health risks.

Social Class and Race

Social epidemiology research has established a strong relationship between health and social class. Infant mortality—the death rate among newborns—is twice as high for disadvantaged than for privileged Americans. While the richest American children fare the best of all the world's children, the poorest American children are as vulnerable as those in many Third-World countries, including Libya and Lebanon.

Table 20–2 shows how Americans' perceptions of their own health are related to income. Almost 80 percent of Americans with family incomes over $35,000 evaluate their health as excellent or very good, in contrast to not quite half of those whose families earned less than $10,000. Conversely, while only about 4 percent of high-income people described their health as fair or poor, more than 20 percent of the poorest Americans made this claim.

Just as income affects health, so does poor health affect income. Americans with family income under $10,000 miss 25 days of school and work per year from illness, while those earning over $35,000 have only 10 days of medical disability (U.S. National Center for Health Statistics, 1989).

Chapter 12 ("Race and Ethnicity") stated that black Americans are three times as likely as whites to live in poverty. The consequences of this disparity appear in

Table 20–2 ASSESSMENT OF PERSONAL HEALTH BY INCOME, 1987

Family Income	Excellent	Very Good	Good	Fair	Poor
Under $10,000	25.0%	23.9%	29.2%	14.4%	7.5%
$10,000–$19,999	31.8	27.1	27.4	10.1	3.6
$20,000–$34,999	41.8	29.6	22.4	5.3	1.4
$35,000 and over	51.1	28.7	16.1	3.2	0.8

SOURCE: U.S. National Center for Health Statistics, *Current Estimates from the National Health Interview Survey United States*, 1987, Series 10, No. 166 (Washington, DC: Government Printing Office, 1988), Table 70, p. 114.

health statistics: blacks are more likely to die in infancy and to suffer from illness as adults, and blacks die about five years earlier than whites. Table 20–3 shows the average life expectancy for American children born in 1987. For whites, it exceeds seventy-five years; for nonwhites, it is about seventy-one years. Sex is an even stronger predictor of health than race, since nonwhite females born in 1987 can expect to outlive males of either race. Table 20–3 also indicates that while 75 percent of white males born in 1987 will live to sixty-five, only about 58 percent of nonwhite males will. The comparable chances for women are about 86 percent for whites and 75 percent for nonwhites.

In the United States, poverty implies life in a crowded, unsanitary environment that breeds infectious diseases. Although tuberculosis now rarely causes death in the United States, black Americans are four times as likely as whites to die from this disease. Poor people of all races also suffer from nutritional deficiencies. Perhaps 20 percent of Americans—some 45 million people—cannot afford a healthful diet and cannot purchase essential medical care. As a result, while wealthy Americans are likely to die of long-range chronic illnesses such as heart disease and cancer, poor Americans are likely to die younger from infectious diseases and illnesses resulting from poor nutrition.

Poverty also breeds stress. Often areas with a high concentration of poor people are dangerously violent. Frustration and despair have become more pronounced among America's urban underclass. The leading cause of death for black males aged fifteen to twenty-four—who are heavily represented in this disadvantaged category—is homicide. In 1988 about 4,500 black Americans were killed by other black Americans—roughly the number of black soldiers killed in the Vietnam War. Increased drug use during the 1980s, especially crack cocaine, further raised the level of inner-city violence.

Table 20-3 LIFE EXPECTANCY FOR AMERICAN CHILDREN BORN IN 1987

	Males	Females	Both Sexes
Whites	72.1	78.8	75.5
	(75%)	(86%)	(81%)
Nonwhites	67.6	75.4	71.6
	(58%)	(75%)	(66%)
All races	71.5	78.3	74.9
	(73%)	(85%)	(79%)

Figures in parentheses indicate the chances of living to age 65.

SOURCE: U.S. Bureau of the Census, 1989.

But privilege provides no immunity to illness. In fact affluence—based on stress-producing competition and offering a sedentary lifestyle and rich food—takes a toll in higher death rates from heart disease (Fuchs, 1974; Wallis, 1984). Nevertheless, wealth does provide decided health advantages: safer environment, less fear, and better medical care. Wealth also allows people to more effectively address health problems that do arise (Lin & Ensel, 1989). The facts are conclusive: affluent people live longer and suffer less from illness than do other Americans. Health, then, is a reflection of how a society operates.

Environmental Pollution

Americans have become increasingly concerned about the consequences of industrial technology on the planet's ecology.

Air pollution from automobiles and industry is a well-documented threat to health. In Los Angeles, for example, the air is considered health-threatening about half the days of the year. Modern technology, while raising Americans' standard of living, has also introduced new health hazards.

Industrial wastes are another area of public concern. For more than half a century, some industries across the country have been haphazardly disposing of poisonous chemicals. They have been pouring toxic substances into local sewage systems or into rivers and streams. Dumps that dot the American landscape now contain steel drums filled with dangerous chemicals that leach into the soil and groundwater.

National attention was drawn to the problem of toxic wastes in 1980, when the residents of Love Canal, near Niagara Falls, New York, discovered deadly dioxin seeping into their homes and yards, which had been built on an old petrochemical dump. In 1983 the entire population of Times Beach, Missouri, had to abandon their homes because oil contaminated with dioxin had been sprayed on the roads.

There are at least 30,000 hazardous waste dump sites in the United States that pose some danger to water supplies. The Environmental Protection Agency has identified 1,200 of these as requiring urgent action, but only about 27 were improved during the 1980s. Bureaucratic delays and mismanagement of public funds have slowed the cleanup; even some environmentalists argue that the problems of air pollution and global warming are more serious than that of dump sites.

Nuclear power has the potential to provide inexpensive energy without depleting the finite resources of coal and oil. In 1989, 110 nuclear reactors in the United States produced about 20 percent of the electricity consumed by Americans. One problem of nuclear power, however, is that a major malfunction could release radiation into the atmosphere for hundreds of miles, as deadly as fallout from an atomic bomb. Accidents at nuclear reactor plants have been reported since they first began operating in the early 1950s. Serious malfunctions occurred at reactors near Ottawa, Canada (1952), near Liverpool, England (1957), and at Three Mile Island near Harrisburg, Pennsylvania (1979). The most serious accident to date—a meltdown of the reactor core at Chernobyl plant near Kiev in the Soviet Union in 1986—spread radiation throughout much of the world. The immediate death toll was thirty, but long-term casualties of radiation exposure might be many thousands.

Another serious problem is that nuclear power plants produce waste materials that remain highly radio-active for hundreds of thousands of years. Currently, no means of disposing of such wastes eliminates the danger of future radioactive contamination of the environment.

Cigarette Smoking

Cigarette smoking in the United States has become prevalent only in this century. Most Americans were unaware of the potential harm posed by cigarettes, despite early evidence of its dangers. Smoking was even socially acceptable. Today smoking is recognized as the leading preventable cause of illness and death among Americans and is becoming defined as mild social deviance.

Despite continued advertising by cigarette manufacturers (banned from television and radio in 1971), per capita consumption of cigarettes has fallen since 1963. In 1988, Americans consumed 566 billion cigarettes, but the number is steadily declining. In 1970, about 37 percent of American adults smoked cigarettes. By 1987, the proportion of cigarette smokers was 29 percent; a further reduction is expected during the 1990s (U.S. Center for Disease Control, 1989).

Some smokers become physically addicted to the nicotine in cigarettes. Those who use cigarettes as a means of coping with stress develop a psychological dependence on them as well. The divorced and separated are more likely to smoke, as are the unemployed and people in the military services. Blue-collar workers are more likely to smoke than white-collar workers, and people with less education smoke more than their more educated counterparts. Black adults (40 percent) are more likely to smoke than white adults (30 percent), and males of all races (32 percent) smoke more than females (27 percent). Cigarettes are the only form of tobacco use to gain popularity among women; the number of women smokers has risen since World War II, and in 1987 lung cancer surpassed breast cancer as a cause of death among women.

Evidence of the health risks of smoking first appeared in the 1930s, about twenty years after it had gained popularity in the United States. At that time, medical researchers noted a sharp rise in smoking-related diseases such as lung cancer. The twenty-year lag represents the time generally necessary for lung cancer to develop from continual smoking. Not until the 1960s, however, did the government begin systematic study of the dangers of tobacco use. This attention was partially

Critics claim that the American tobacco industry has targeted minorities, partly accounting for higher rates of cigarette smoking among blacks. Several communities, including this neighborhood in Washington, D.C., have organized to demand removal of such billboards.

provoked by a rising incidence of lung cancer among women, who had begun smoking in large numbers during the 1940s. By the mid-1960s, government reports linked cigarettes—as well as cigars and pipes—to heart disease; cancer of the mouth, throat, and lungs; and lung diseases such as bronchitis and emphysema. Nearly 400,000 Americans die each year as a direct result of cigarette smoking—about seven times the number killed during the Vietnam War. Smokers also experience more frequent minor illnesses such as flu, and pregnant women who smoke increase the likelihood of spontaneous abortion and prenatal death. Recent research indicates that even nonsmokers exposed to cigarette smoke have a higher risk of smoking-related diseases (Shephard, 1982).

Tobacco was a $25 billion industry in the United States in 1986. The tobacco industry still maintains that because the precise link between cigarettes and disease has not been specified, the health effects of smoking remain "an open question" (Rudolph, 1985). But the American tobacco industry is not breathing as easily today as it once did. Laws mandating a smoke-free environment are rapidly proliferating. Furthermore, courts have increased the liability of cigarette manufacturers in lawsuits brought by victims of smoking-related illnesses, or their survivors.

One response of the tobacco industry has been to sell more of their products in the Third World, where regulation of tobacco sales and advertising and antismoking sentiments are less strict. In the United States, how-ever, more and more smokers are taking advantage of the fact that someone who has not smoked for ten years has about the same pattern of health as a lifelong non-smoker.

Sexually Transmitted Diseases

Sexual activity, while vital to the continuation of the species, can transmit a number of diseases. What are commonly called *venereal diseases* (from Venus, the Roman goddess of love) are as old as humanity itself: references to these illnesses are found in the Bible. American culture has traditionally viewed sex ambivalently as a source of pleasure and procreation on the one hand, and a sinful act on the other. Many Americans therefore regard venereal diseases not only as illnesses, but also as punishments for immorality.

Sexually transmitted diseases have become a major national concern since the 1960s. One reason is the increased sexual activity as a result of the "sexual revolution." In 1950, perhaps two out of three males and one in ten females had premarital sexual intercourse; by the 1980s, the figures had risen to three out of four males and two out of three females.

Sexually transmitted diseases (STDs) thus represent an exception to the general decline in infectious diseases during this century. Even more alarming, sex is now potentially deadly. Acquired immune deficiency syndrome (AIDS) has sparked a sexual counterrevolution and caused individuals to reexamine their values and behavior (Kain, 1987; Kain & Hart, 1987).

Gonorrhea and Syphilis

Gonorrhea and syphilis are very old diseases, each caused by a microscopic organism almost always transmitted by sexual contact. Untreated gonorrhea can lead to sterility, while syphilis can damage major organs and result in blindness, mental disorders, and death. In the past, American culture severely stigmatized victims of gonorrhea and syphilis, seeing these diseases as the "wages of sin" among social outcasts such as prostitutes.

More than a million cases of gonorrhea are reported annually, although the actual number is probably several times greater (Masters, Johnson, & Kolodny, 1988). Gonorrhea is more common among minorities than whites. Of the reported cases in 1988, 78 percent involved were blacks, 16 percent whites, and 5 percent Hispanics. Blacks also had the highest rate of syphilis, accounting for 76 percent of cases; whites and Hispanics each accounted for about 12 percent (Moran et al., 1989).

Gonorrhea and syphilis are now easily cured with penicillin, an antibiotic drug developed in the 1940s. Therefore neither disease currently represents a serious health problem in the United States.

Genital Herpes

Genital herpes received widespread public attention during the 1980s. An estimated one in eight American adults carries the genital herpes virus. The infection rate among blacks, however, is estimated to be about three times higher (Moran et al., 1989).

Although far less serious than gonorrhea and syphilis, herpes is currently incurable. It can be asymptomatic or it can exhibit itself by periodic, painful blisters on the genitals along with fever and headache. It is not fatal to adults. However, women with active genital herpes can transmit the disease during a vaginal delivery to children, to whom it may be deadly. Such women, therefore, often give birth by cesarean section.

AIDS

The most serious sexually transmitted disease is acquired immune deficiency syndrome, or AIDS. Although AIDS may have appeared as early as the 1960s, the disease was identified only in 1981. Currently it is incurable and fatal. Thirty-six thousand new cases were reported

in the United States during 1989, bringing the total in 1990 over 121,000; more than 70,000 of these individuals have already died.

AIDS is caused by a human immunodeficiency virus (HIV). This virus attacks white blood cells, the core of the immune system by which the body fights infections. As these cells are destroyed, a person with AIDS becomes vulnerable to a wide range of infectious diseases that eventually causes death. Technically, then, AIDS kills people by rendering them unable to fight off common infections.

According to estimates, about 1.5 million Americans in 1990 were infected with HIV. The presence of HIV does not necessarily generate AIDS, however. The majority of persons with the virus show no symptoms and are probably unaware of their infection. Symptoms of AIDS do not usually appear for at least a year. Within about five years, perhaps 25 percent of infected persons will develop AIDS; most but perhaps not all infected people will eventually develop the disease. According to estimates, about 365,000 Americans will have the active disease by 1992. AIDS thus represents a catastrophic development—potentially the most serious epidemic of modern times.

Transmission of HIV almost always occurs through blood, semen, or breast milk. This means that AIDS is not spread through casual contact with an infected person, including shaking hands or hugging. There is no known case of the virus being transmitted through coughing and sneezing, through the sharing of towels, dishes, or telephones, or through water in a bath, pool, or hot tub. The risk of transmitting AIDS through saliva (as in kissing) appears to be extremely low. Oral and especially genital sex carry risk, which can be greatly reduced by the use of condoms. There is no danger of becoming infected by donating blood, and receiving a blood transfusion is now virtually safe. Infected women can pass HIV to their newborn children, although present evidence indicates that there is less than a 50 percent chance of their doing so. In short, AIDS is a deadly disease but it is also hard to get.

There are specific behaviors that place people at high risk for AIDS. The first is anal sex, which can cause rectal bleeding and thereby allow easy transmission of HIV. This practice is therefore extremely dangerous, and, of course, the greater the number of sexual partners, the greater the risk. Anal sex is commonly practiced by gay males, in some cases with many sexual partners. For this reason, about two-thirds of persons with AIDS are homosexual and bisexual males. During the 1980s,

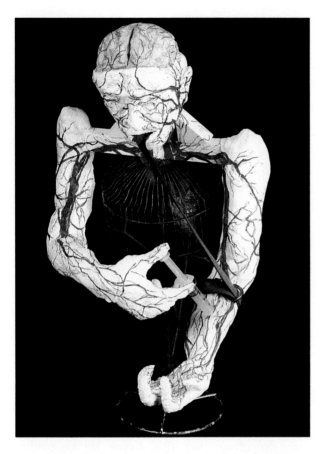

The sculpture *The Junkie*, by Paul Marcus, graphically depicts the loss of humanity that often accompanies intravenous drug use. The age of AIDS has added yet another deadly consequence to such behavior, the transmission of HIV through the sharing of needles. Many cities have proposed programs for giving clean needles to addicts, but almost all of them have been defeated by those concerned that this encourages illegal drug use.

however, promiscuity among gays (and nongays) greatly declined as a result of concern about this disease (McKusick et al., 1985).

Sharing needles used for intravenous drugs is the second high-risk behavior. At present, intravenous drug users account for 21 percent of persons with AIDS. People who have sex with such users are also at high risk. Because intravenous drug use is more common among poor Americans, AIDS is increasingly becoming a disease of the socially disadvantaged. Overall, six in ten AIDS victims are white, yet blacks (12 percent of Americans) account for 27 percent of people with AIDS, and Hispanics (7 percent of Americans) represent 15 percent of

AIDS cases (Bowles & Robinson, 1989). Among children, AIDS and minorities are even more closely linked: almost 80 percent of AIDS victims under thirteen are minorities (U.S. Department of Health and Human Services, 1989).

In 1990 only 5 percent of AIDS cases in the United States were thought to have been caused by heterosexual contact (although heterosexuals, infected in various ways, account for about 20 percent of AIDS cases). The likelihood of a runaway "breakout" of AIDS into the heterosexual population now seems less likely than it did several years ago (Fumento, 1989). Heterosexual activity can transmit AIDS, however, and the risk rises with the number of sexual partners, especially those in high-risk categories.

The "third wave" of AIDS—after gay men and intravenous drug users—is likely to occur among the urban poor. The problem is already getting out of control in cities such as Miami and New York, where the use of crack cocaine fuels casual sex and prostitution, which spreads HIV.

AIDS has become an overwhelming national financial problem. The cost of treatment already exceeds $150,000 per person and may rise further as new therapies are developed. In 1985 the national medical bill for AIDS was over $5 billion and was likely to triple within a few years. Added to the direct medical costs are tens of billions of dollars in lost earnings and productivity. Government health programs, private insurance, and personal savings will probably meet only a small fraction of this total. There is little doubt, then, that AIDS is a medical and a social problem of monumental proportions.

The government initially responded slowly to the AIDS crisis, largely because gays and intravenous drug users are widely viewed as deviant. More recently, money allocated for AIDS research has risen rapidly, and some progress is being made. For example, researchers have found that some drugs, such as AZT, slow the progress of the disease. Nevertheless, educational programs remain the most effective weapon against AIDS, since prevention is the only way to stop what currently has no cure.

Ethical Issues Surrounding Death

Health involves not only medical concerns but also ethical issues. There are a number of difficult ethical issues related to death; these arise mainly as a result of technological changes that permit human beings greater control over life itself.

When is a person dead?   Common sense suggests that life ends when breathing and heartbeat stop. Advancing medical technology, however, is rendering this view of death obsolete. A heart that has stopped beating can be revived or replaced, and respiration can be artificially sustained. Furthermore, both heartbeat and breathing may continue in the absence of any brain activity. Today, therefore, it can be difficult to distinguish between life and death. Medical and legal experts in the United States now define death as an irreversible state involving no response to stimulation, no movement or breathing, no reflexes, and no indication of brain activity (Ladd, 1979; Wall, 1980).

Do people have a right to die?   With increasing frequency, the death of a terminally ill person depends on a human decision. Who should assume this responsibility? In 1975, twenty-one-year-old Karen Ann Quinlan fell into an irreversible coma after mixing tranquilizers and alcohol. Physicians assured Quinlan's parents that she would never recover. Four months later the Quinlans sought to remove their daughter from the respirator that was helping her to breath. A New Jersey court objected, claiming that the parents had no right to make such a decision. In 1976 the state supreme court reversed the lower court, and the hospital disconnected the respirator. Even so, Quinlan lived for another nine years. In 1985, never having regained consciousness and weighing only 70 pounds, she finally stopped breathing.

Ten thousand Americans are in the same kind of permanent vegetative state as Karen Ann Quinlan was (Wallis, 1986). In 1983 a presidential commission issued guidelines outlining their rights. The commission noted, first, that physicians and hospitals must protect the patient's life rather than help to end it. Doctors must explain every medical option available to patients or, when patients are incapacitated, to family members. Nevertheless, terminally ill patients can themselves refuse heroic treatment that may extend their lives but not offer hope of recovery.

The commission also suggested that physicians honor any patient's *living will*, a statement of personal intention regarding heroic treatment of terminal illness. Laws in most states support this principle. In the absence of a living will, or if the patient is a newborn child, physicians and hospitals must provide any treatment that may be reasonably expected to sustain life. However, a parent or other close family member may, in consultation with physicians, decide to refuse further medical intervention. According to the commission, all decisions should be in the interest of the patient, not other family members.

What about mercy killing?   *Mercy killing* is the common term for **euthanasia**, *assisting in the death of a person suffering from an incurable disease.* Euthanasia (from the Greek, meaning "an easy death") poses an ethical dilemma, since it does cause the death of another person but the presumed motive is kindness. Although the patient's right to die has increasing support in the United States, assisting in the death of another person is more controversial. Withholding heroic treatment by, say, disconnecting a respirator may allow a patient to die; actively killing a patient, even as an act of mercy, is a more serious responsibility.

Those who categorically view life—even with suffering—as preferable to death totally reject euthanasia. Those who believe there are circumstances under which death is preferable may support euthanasia, but they face the practical problem of determining just when a person's life is no longer worth living. After requesting physicians to revive the heart of her dying father, one daughter recently said, "I'm glad they brought him back. He was old, but that doesn't mean he should stop living. He was still alive, and as long as he's alive, he should be saved." Another woman, however, insisted that physicians not prolong the life of her 98-year-old mother: "If my mother's heart stopped beating, I don't want them pounding on her chest and destroying her body any more than it was. For what? Revive her for another day or another two weeks?" (cited in Kleiman, 1985:11).

Both views compellingly illustrate the burden on family members who must decide whether to sustain the life of loved ones or allow them to die with dignity. In many cases, medical expenses are an additional, often unspoken, concern. Each attempt to revive a patient whose heart has stopped may cost $1,500. Two weeks of heroic lifesaving efforts may result in tens of thousands of dollars of medical expenses. Opponents of euthanasia express concern that such costs may enter into a family's decision regarding heroic treatment.

Ethical standards for dealing with dying patients are gradually emerging. Presently, wide support exists for the concept of *passive* euthanasia, illustrated by the Quinlan case, in which heroic treatment is withheld. Support appears weaker for *active* euthanasia, in which a family member or physician decisively ends a life. Who can confidently determine whether a decision to terminate someone's life is prompted by a desire to end the patient's suffering or that of the patient's family?

MEDICINE

Medicine is *an institutionalized system for combating disease and improving health.* It is part of a broader program of **health care,** which is *any activity intended to improve health.* Throughout most of human history, individuals and their families were responsible for their own health care. In traditional preindustrial societies, medicine entails knowledge about the healing properties of certain plants, often combined with astute insights into the emotional and spiritual needs of the ill (Ayensu, 1981). Traditional healers—from herbalists to acupuncturists—are sometimes dismissed by ethnocentric Americans as "witch doctors," but they do indeed improve human health, and they continue to combat some of the world's greatest health problems.

Medicine emerges as a complex social institution in technologically complex societies as people assume various formal, specialized roles as healers. As a society industrializes, both prevention and healing become the professional responsibilities of highly trained and legally licensed specialists. Although families still treat their own minor illnesses, a host of specialists—from anesthesiologists to X-ray technicians—provide health care in offices and hospitals established for those purposes.

The Rise of Scientific Medicine

Health care in the United States is now dominated by *scientific medicine,* which applies the logic of science to research and the treatment of disease and injury. In colonial America medicine was practiced by herbalists, druggists, midwives, and even ministers. About one in 600 Americans engaged in some form of healing arts—about the same proportion as today—but there was no consensus about how this work should be done (Stevens, 1971). The few who had received formal medical training in Europe still had very limited knowledge by today's standards, and often less than that of the herbalists and midwives. Unsanitary instruments, lack of anesthesia, and plain ignorance made surgery a terrible ordeal in which surgeons probably killed as many patients as they saved.

Gradually, medical specialists learned more about human anatomy, physiology, and biochemistry. Medical doctors established themselves as self-regulating, service-oriented professionals. Early in the nineteenth century, medical societies appeared across the United States.

This page from an 18th century treatise on the plague, probably created in what is today Czechoslovakia, depicts a range of medical treatments common to that era: bleeding patients, placing leeches on bodies to draw out disease, and consultations with experts. Healthful exercise was also encouraged as a means of escaping the dangers of "bad air," which gave rise to the term "malaria."

Training came under the control of medical schools: in 1800 there existed only four such schools, but by the end of the century there were more than 400. The number of hospitals also increased during the second half of the nineteenth century (Stevens, 1971). Those who wished to practice or teach medical skills were required to obtain licenses, which were available only to those who embraced specific medical standards.

The medical standards were set largely through the efforts of the American Medical Association (AMA).

The founding of this organization in 1847 signified broad acceptance of the scientific model of medicine. The AMA widely publicized the medical successes of its members in tracing the cause of life-threatening diseases to bacteria and viruses, and developing vaccines to combat disease. Still, alternative approaches to health care, such as regulating nutrition, also had many defenders.

The AMA boldly—some thought arrogantly—asserted the superiority of its approach. It won a victory in the early 1900s as state licensing boards would certify only those physicians who were competent in the scientific knowledge approved by the AMA (Starr, 1982). With control of the certification process, the AMA could close down schools teaching other approaches, and so the practice of medicine became limited mainly to those with an M.D. degree. In the process, both the prestige and income of physicians rose dramatically. They have become among the highest-paid Americans, earning an average of about $120,000 in 1987.

Some supporters of other approaches, such as osteopathic physicians, concluded that they had no choice but to accept scientific medicine. Thus osteopaths (with D.O. degrees), originally concerned only with manipulating the skeleton and muscles, today treat illness much as do medical doctors (with M.D. degrees). Other practitioners—such as chiropractors, herbal healers, and midwives—held to traditional practices and have become defined as a fringe area of the medical profession. With far less social prestige and income than physicians, such professionals now have a small, if devoted, following among Americans (Gordon, 1980).

The rise of scientific medicine also determined the kinds of people likely to become physicians. During the nineteenth century many rural medical colleges trained people of modest financial means. Alleging deficient standards and facilities, the AMA targeted these for attack. As a result, more and more of the physicians came from privileged backgrounds and practiced in cities. Furthermore, the AMA denigrated the more traditional forms of health care in which women had long played a role. Some medical schools did train women and black Americans but, with little public support or financial resources, few of these schools survived. As the number of medical schools in the United States dropped to only seventy-seven by 1950, the number of blacks and women in medicine declined as well, remaining quite low until recently (Starr, 1982; Huet-Cox, 1984).

In sum, as the AMA established physicians as scientific professionals, it simultaneously restricted the practice of medicine to a small, affluent elite favored by expensive and often discriminatory medical schools. Medicine, in effect, became dominated by white males, most of them from urban, privileged families (Stevens, 1971; Starr, 1982). The result has been a shortage of physicians in rural areas as well as a lack of physicians who are women and other minorities.

Holistic Medicine

The scientific medical establishment still has its critics. A traditional view of health that has gained support among Americans in recent decades is **holistic medicine,** *an approach to health care that emphasizes prevention of illness and takes account of the whole person within a physical and social environment.*

Holistic medicine criticizes scientific medicine's tendency to focus on diseases and injuries rather than on prevention of illness and overall well-being. Holistic practitioners claim that drugs, surgery, artificial organs, and high technology have transformed healers into narrow specialists concerned with symptoms rather than people, and with disease rather than health. Drugs and surgery are sometimes necessary, but within a broader view of health that takes account of a person's entire life and environment. In holistic medicine, a wide variety of trained personnel—physicians, physical therapists, nutritionists, counselors, clergy, and even acupuncturists and teachers of meditation—work as a team to improve the physical, mental, and social well-being of patients. In the holistic approach to health care, the following are major concerns (Gordon, 1980).

1. **Patients are people.** Holistic practitioners are concerned not only with symptoms, but with how each person's environment and lifestyle encourage or inhibit health. For example, the likelihood of illness increases under stress caused by the death of a family member, intense competition at work, or poverty (Duhl, 1980). Holistic practitioners also actively combat environmental pollution and other dangers to public health.

2. **Responsibility, not dependency.** Holistic medicine places primary responsibility for health on individuals themselves. Scientific medicine tends to view health as a complex issue only physicians can understand, thereby fostering patients' dependency on them. Holistic medicine recognizes that experts must assume immediate control in a crisis, but generally their role is to help people enhance

their own ability to engage in health-promoting behavior (Ferguson, 1980). Holistic medicine is an *active* approach to *health*, whereas scientific medicine is a *reactive* approach to *disease*.

3. **Personal treatment environment.** Conventional medicine has shifted health care from the home to impersonal offices and hospitals, which are disease-centered rather than health-oriented and which reinforce uninformed reliance on medical experts. While holistic medicine recognizes the need for hospitalization in cases of severe illness, it favors placing health care in personal, relaxed settings.

4. **Optimum health for all.** The goal of holistic medicine is the highest possible level of well-being for everyone. Beyond treating illness, the holistic approach assists people who are "well" to realize "a state of extraordinary vigor, joy, and creativity" (Gordon, 1980:17).

Perhaps most important, holistic medicine seeks to reestablish the personal social ties that united healers and patients before the era of specialists. The AMA currently recognizes more than fifty specialized areas of medical practice, and a growing proportion of M.D.s are entering these high-paying specialties rather than family practice. Thus there is a need for practitioners who are concerned with the patient in the holistic sense.

Medicine and Economics

With its reliance on high technology and scientific medicine, health care in industrial societies is extremely expensive. Different forms of government in these societies help people meet these costs in different ways.

Medicine in Socialist Societies

In societies with predominantly socialist economies, such as the Soviet Union and the People's Republic of China, the government directly controls medical care. Socialist societies agree that all citizens have the right to medical care, and this resource should be equally distributed. People do not pay physicians and hospitals directly; the government uses public funds to pay medical costs. It owns and operates medical facilities and pays salaries to practitioners, who are government employees.

The Soviet Union. In the Soviet Union, the government provides medical care paid for by taxes (Fuchs,

The transformation of Eastern Europe has revealed that some socialist societies have not placed a high value on the health of their people. Romania is perhaps the worst offender, for decades subjecting its people to industrial pollutants. In the town of Copsa Mica, death rates have been extremely high, raising doubts about the long-term health of children such as these.

1974; Knaus, 1981). People cannot choose their own physician, as in the United States, but rather report to a government health facility near their home.

Soviet physicians have lower prestige and income than their American counterparts. They receive about the same salary as do skilled industrial workers, a reflection of socialist attempts at economic equality. Also, about 70 percent of Soviet physicians are women, compared with about 18 percent in the United States, and, as in the United States, occupations dominated by women are financially less rewarded (Knaus, 1981).

The Soviet system of medical care succeeds fairly well in meeting the basic needs of a large population. However, its rigid bureaucracy results in highly standardized and impersonal medical care. This institutionalized lack of flexibility limits the Soviet system's ability to adopt the holistic approach to health.

People's Republic of China. The People's Republic of China is a poor, agrarian society that is only beginning to industrialize. The task of attending to the health of more than 1 billion people is truly monumental. Traditional healing arts, including acupuncture and the use of medicinal herbs, are still widely used in China, and the holistic concern for the interplay of mind and body has remained strong for thousands of years (Sidel & Sidel, 1982b; Kaptchuk, 1985).

China recently experimented with private medical care, but in 1989 it reestablished tight government control over every area of life. Medical facilities are government operated. China's so-called barefoot doctors, roughly comparable to American paramedics, have brought at least some modern methods of medical care to millions of peasants in remote rural villages.

Medicine in Capitalist Societies

Societies with predominantly capitalist economies limit government welfare programs, including health care. Citizens provide for themselves in accordance with their own resources and personal preferences. As Chapter 19 ("The Economy and Work") explains, capitalist societies have substantial economic inequality. Paying for good health is simply beyond the means of a large part of the population. Therefore every capitalist society provides some government assistance. Most of these nations—with the noteworthy exception of the United States—offer a comprehensive health program to the entire population.

Sweden. In 1891 Sweden instituted a compulsory, comprehensive system of government medical care. The people pay for this program through their taxes, which are among the highest in the world. Most physicians receive salaries from the government rather than fees from patients, and most hospitals are government managed. Because this medical system resembles that of socialist societies, it is often described as **socialized medicine,** *a health-care system in which most medical facilities are owned and operated by the government, and most physicians are salaried government employees.*

Great Britain. In 1948 Great Britain instituted socialized medicine as an outgrowth of a medical insurance program begun in 1911. Some physicians and hospitals do operate privately. Thus British citizens are entitled to medical care provided by the National Health Service, but those who can afford to do so may purchase more extensive care from private practitioners. This "dual system" results in basic care for all and better care for those who can afford it.

Canada. The Canadian government reimburses its people for hospitalization and physician services according to set fees. Because physicians operate privately, Canada does not offer true socialized medicine. Moreover, some physicians work entirely outside of the government-funded system, charging whatever fees they wish. The schedule of reimbursable fees is set annually by the federal government and the governments of the ten Canadian provinces in consultation with medical professional associations (Grant, 1984; Vayda & Deber, 1984).

Japan. Physicians in Japan operate privately, and a combination of private insurance and government programs pays medical costs. As Chapter 7 ("Groups and Organizations") notes, large Japanese businesses take a broad interest in the welfare of their employees, and many provide medical care as an employee benefit. For those outside such privately funded programs, government medical insurance covers 70 percent of all costs, and the elderly receive free care (Vogel, 1979).

Despite their differences, the medical-care systems of capitalist societies other than the United States have three major benefits in common. First, basic medical care is available to everyone regardless of income. Second, government programs protect citizens from the financial hardships of a major illness, which can be disastrous even for the well-to-do. Third, subsidizing care encourages even well people to use medical facilities regularly, thereby often preventing illness.

Medicine in the United States

The United States is unique among the industrialized societies in lacking a government program that ensures basic medical care to every citizen. While European governments pay for about 75 percent of their people's medical costs, the U.S. government pays about 40 percent. Although the government does pay certain medical expenses for some categories of people, for the most part American medicine is a private, profit-making industry in which more money buys better care. This **direct-fee system** is *a medical-care system in which patients pay directly for the services of physicians and hospitals.*

Because there is no comprehensive national medical-care program, and also because economic inequality is greater in the United States than in most of Western Europe, poor Americans have much less access to medical care than other Americans do. Although the United

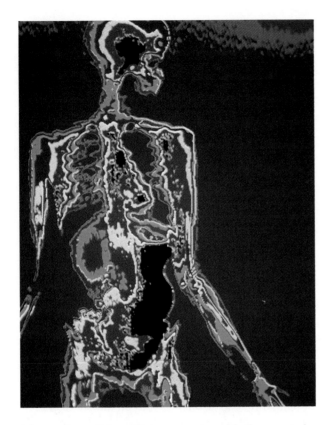

Advances in medicine utilizing computers and other new technology offer significant benefits to some Americans. But they have contributed to the soaring costs of medical care that especially harm poor people.

States is richer than any European society, in some respects our health is worse. For example, infant mortality is higher in the United States than in most of Western Europe, and the death rate for 45-year-old men is twice as high in the United States as in Sweden (Fuchs, 1974; United Nations, 1983).

Why has the United States not developed a national health-care program? First, Americans have traditionally limited government intervention in the economy and in people's personal matters; a century ago, when European societies were establishing national medical-care plans, the U.S. government had only a small role in society. Second, despite the growth of government in the last fifty years, political support for a national medical program remains limited. In Europe, organized labor and socialist political parties demanded such programs,

but Americans have traditionally mistrusted socialist ideas. Even labor unions have never made government-supported medical care a high priority, concentrating instead on winning health-care benefits from employers. A third reason for the lack of a national health-care program has been the consistent opposition of the AMA and the private insurance industry, both powerful special-interest groups (Starr, 1982).

The cost of technologically sophisticated American medicine is extremely high. As Figure 20–1 shows, expenditures for medical care increased almost forty-fold between 1950 and 1986, from just over $12 billion to more than $450 billion. Americans spent about 5 percent of the gross national product on medical care in 1950; by 1986, medical care was absorbing 11 percent of GNP. Without a program of socialized medicine or comprehen-

Figure 20–1 The Rising Cost of Medical Care in the United States

(*U.S. Bureau of the Census, 1970, 1989*)

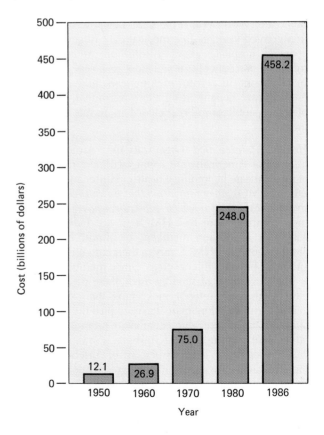

sive federal health insurance, how do Americans pay for medical care?

Private insurance programs. In 1987, 147 million Americans, or about 61 percent of the population, received some medical-care benefits from a family member's employer or labor union. Another 35 million Americans (14 percent) purchased some private coverage on their own. Most large-scale private programs such as Blue Cross and Blue Shield do not pay all medical costs, but overall, three-fourths of the American population has some private medical insurance (Health Insurance Association of America, 1989).

Public insurance programs. In 1965 Congress enacted legislation creating Medicare and Medicaid, programs that provide limited medical benefits to specific categories of Americans. Medicare pays some of the medical costs of Americans over sixty-five; in 1987 it covered almost 33 million Americans, or about 16 percent of the population. During the same year, Medicaid, a medical insurance program for the poor, provided benefits to almost 23 million Americans, or about 10 percent of the population. After World War II the U.S. Veterans Administration granted veterans free medical care in government-operated hospitals; about 10 million Americans, or roughly 4 percent of the population, receive VA benefits. In all, about 30 percent of Americans now gain some medical-care benefits from the government, but most of these people are also included in private insurance programs.

Health Maintenance Organizations. An increasing number of Americans are coping with the rising costs of medical care by joining a **health maintenance organization** (HMO), *an organization that provides comprehensive medical care for which subscribers pay a fixed fee.* In 1988 there were 653 HMOs in the United States with over 27 million members, or almost 13 percent of the population. HMOs vary in their costs and benefits, and none provides full coverage. Since membership cost is fixed regardless of services used, these organizations have a financial interest in keeping their subscribers healthy, and therefore many have adopted the principles of holistic medicine, which emphasize promoting health rather than treating illness (Ginsburg, 1983).

In all, more than 85 percent of Americans have some medical-care program. Most are privately funded, and the government provides limited care to low-income people. This combination fails in important respects, however. First, the coverage of perhaps 50 million Americans would pay only part of the costs of a serious illness, which would therefore threaten even middle-class people with financial ruin. Second, no program covers every medical need. Most private programs, as well as Medicare and Medicaid, exclude many medical services, such as dental care (Eve, 1984). Third, and perhaps most serious, some 35 million Americans (about 14 percent of the population) have no medical insurance at all (*Sourcebook of Health Insurance Data*, 1989; Altman et al., 1989). Most are poor or marginally poor people who cannot afford to become ill or to purchase the medical care they need to remain healthy.

THEORETICAL ANALYSIS OF HEALTH AND MEDICINE

Each of the major theoretical paradigms in sociology provides a means of organizing and interpreting the facts and issues presented in this chapter.

Structural-Functional Analysis

Structural-functional analysis rests on the image of society as a complex system that is stable and internally well-integrated. Talcott Parsons (1951) argued that the good health of its members is a societal imperative. Thus he viewed illness as dysfunctional, as undermining individuals' ability to contribute to the operation of society. He also recognized that every society must have an established means for dealing with those who are ill.

The Sick Role

The most important idea within structural-functional analysis of health is the **sick role**, *patterns of behavior that are socially defined as appropriate for those who are ill.* As developed by Parsons, the sick role has four characteristics.

1. **A sick person is exempted from routine responsibilities.** In everyday life, an individual performs a variety of social roles, such as student, parent, and employee. Serious illness, Parsons claims, causes a relaxation or suspension of normal social responsibilities. Presumably so this benefit is not abused, people cannot define themselves as ill;

they usually depend on the assessment of a recognized medical expert in order to assume the sick role.

2. **A person's illness is not deliberate.** Sick people are not normally responsible for their own illness; illness is something that has happened to them. Therefore, the failure of ill people to fulfill routine responsibilities does not lead to punishment.

3. **A sick person must want to be well.** Because the sick role rests on the assumption that no one wants to be ill, people suspected of feigning illness to escape responsibility or to receive special attention do not have a socially recognized sick role.

4. **A sick person must seek competent help.** An ill person, not wanting to be sick, must seek competent assistance and cooperate with health-care practitioners. A person who fails to seek medical help and to follow doctor's orders is likely to lose the sick role's exemption from routine responsibilities.

The Physician's Role

According to Parsons, the physician's role is to provide medical care as needed by the patient. Just as a person in the sick role is expected to want to become well and to seek competent help, so the physician is expected to cure illness. Sometimes doing so is impossible, but physician and patient initially envision that the patient will recover.

Parsons claimed that the physician's role requires power over the patient. This hierarchy is based on the cultural norm that those who are ill must cooperate with physicians, and it is strengthened by the physician's special knowledge. Physicians expect patients to comply with their requests and to supply personal information, even that shared with no one else. Parsons noted that patients give this information only to assist in the treatment process; physicians may not make other use of it.

The physician's role varies from society to society. In Japan, for example, physicians share less information with patients than is the case in the United States. The box on page 554 takes a closer look.

Critical evaluation. Parsons's work helps to place illness and medical care into the broader organization of society. Through the concept of the sick role, society can excuse the ill from routine responsibilities while also monitoring claims of illness. Others have noted that the sick role can also apply to some non-illness situations, such as

pregnancy (Myers & Grasmick, 1989). One objection to this concept is that it is more easily applied to the wealthy and middle classes than to the poor. Many impoverished Americans simply cannot afford effective health care, nor can they afford not to work, even when they are ill.

A limitation of Parsons's view of the physician's role is that it applies best to conventional, scientific medicine. Treatment-oriented physicians do usually assert authority over patients, but the holistic orientation tends to foster a more egalitarian partnership in which physicians encourage patients to assume considerable responsibility for their own health.

Symbolic-Interaction Analysis

According to the symbolic-interaction paradigm, life is an ongoing process of socially constructed reality. The reality of health, then, hinges on subjective perceptions.

Subjective Perceptions of Health

A personal experience of British sociologist Ann Holohan illustrates the importance of subjective perceptions of health. Visiting a physician because of what she assumed was a breast infection, Holohan was informed that she might have cancer and should enter the hospital for a biopsy. In a state of shock, she left the physician's office and reentered the outside world:

> It seemed incredible that nothing had changed—the sun was still shining, the road sweeper gathering the leaves. I sat in my car (and) immense waves of panic engulfed me. I drove blindly home and recall very little of the actual journey. . . . Yet I was no "sicker" than before my consultation. All that had changed was the possibility of a medical label for my symptom. (1977, cited in Cockerham, 1982:95)

Later Holohan learned that she did not have cancer, and her world changed again—this time for the better. As this example shows, the simple perception of illness or health is real enough to affect human behavior. Sometimes disease itself is caused by perceptions. Medical experts have long noted the existence of *psychosomatic* disorders, in which a person's state of mind affects physical well-being (Hamrick, Anspaugh, & Ezell, 1986). In other words, situations that are defined as real may become real in their consequences (Thomas, 1931).

Breaking Bad News: Comparing Japanese and American Physicians

Japanese emperor Hirohito died in 1988 reportedly without knowing that he had intestinal cancer. In Japan most physicians conceal the fact of terminal illness from patients. A Japanese specialist in bioethics explains:

> In Japan, the art of medicine is regarded as an expression of loving kindness—part of the art of Jin, the fundamental teaching of Confucian ideas. There is the belief that giving the patient hope until the last minute will give him a fighting spirit.

Physicians thus consider themselves responsible for every decision that affects their patients. Claiming to be motivated by concern for the patient, they routinely keep relevant information from the seriously ill. The Japanese are not alone in this practice: physicians throughout the Third World follow the same precepts.

American doctors did the same three decades ago. In 1961 a *Journal of the American Medical Association* report indicated that only one in eight American physicians believed in discussing terminal illness with a dying patient.

What changed this practice? The *patient rights movement,* which is most advanced in the United States, dramatically altered the traditional physician–patient relationship. American physicians have responded to public demands—often in the courts—that they readily disclose

John Collier's painting *Sentence of Death* portrays one of the most difficult ordeals faced by physicians: informing a patient of impending death. Until recently, American physicians routinely withheld such a diagnosis in the belief that it was in the patient's interest to do so. Although now less common in the United States, this practice continues in Japan and in many other countries of the world.

medical information to patients. Evidence indicates that full disclosure reduces patients' anxieties, strengthens their bond with doctors, and allows them to decide how to use whatever time is left.

European societies are following closely behind the United States in advancing patient rights. Even Japan is starting to change as physicians and laypeople are beginning to consider people's right to be told the truth, whatever that may be.

SOURCE: Based on Nina Darnton and Yuriko Hoshia, "Whose Life Is It, Anyway?" *Newsweek,* Vol. 113, No. 4 (January 13, 1989):61.

The Social Construction of Illness

Any state of health or illness is understood within a socially constructed reality, as described in Chapter 6 ("Social Interaction in Everyday Life"). In a society where most people suffer from malnutrition, an underfed child may be considered quite normal. Similarly, Americans have until recently overlooked the unhealthful effects of eating rich foods and smoking. Also our responses to serious illnesses are based as much on social definitions as on medical facts. For instance, persons with AIDS contend with fear and sometimes outright bigotry that has no basis in medical fact.

Even "expert opinions" of medical professionals are influenced by nonmedical factors. David Mechanic (1978) has observed that during periods of low worker productivity in the Soviet Union, physicians rarely excused workers from their jobs. Similarly, symptoms such as flu that may be defined as illness during peacetime may not relieve soldiers from duty in desperate times of war. And college students have been known to dismiss signs of illness on the eve of a vacation, yet readily report to the infirmary before a difficult examination. In other words, we often use medical experts to legitimate our claim to assuming the sick role so that we may be relieved of routine expectations. Defining someone as sick or well, then, is a social negotiation as much as an objective assessment.

Critical evaluation. The symbolic-interaction paradigm's strength lies in its emphasis on the relativity of the concepts of sickness and health. One problem with this approach is that it minimizes objective standards of well-being. Certain physical conditions do indeed cause concrete, negative changes in human capacities, however we define them. Even if people in poor societies perceive themselves as relatively healthy in the context of their community, they still do not live as long as people in richer societies do.

Social-Conflict Analysis

Social-conflict analysis links patterns of health and access to medical care to social inequality. This approach has developed three major criticisms of capitalist societies with regard to health.

Unequal Access to Medical Care

Health is the foundation of social life. Yet by defining medical care as a commodity for purchase, capitalist societies skew health in favor of the wealthy. As has already been noted, this problem is more serious in the United States than in capitalist societies with national medical-care programs. Health advocates, including some members of Congress, support the expansion of government-funded medical care to the entire population. Vested interests, especially the medical establishment, oppose any such program.

More radical critics claim that capitalist health problems are rooted in the class system itself. They say that the strikingly unequal distribution of wealth in America makes equal medical care impossible, even with government programs. Only a significant redistribution of economic resources would make medical care uniformly available (Bodenheimer, 1977; Navarro, 1977).

Medical Care and the Profit Motive

Many critics, then, view medical care itself positively and question only its distribution. Some social-conflict theorists, however, totally reject capitalist medical care as another big business that provides a poor product. Physicians, hospitals, and producers of drugs and medical supplies comprise multibillion-dollar corporate conglomerates (Ehrenreich, 1978). The quest for ever-increasing profits, these critics suggest, leads to questionable medical practices, including unnecessary tests and surgery and an overreliance on certain drugs (Kaplan et al., 1985). Valium, for example, is an antianxiety drug that accounts for more than 25 million doctors' prescriptions each year. Although it does reduce stress, valium also can lead to psychological addiction (Myers, 1986). Even over-the-counter drugs such as aspirin can be abused: Americans consume 20,000 tons of aspirin a year—about 225 pills per person—though overuse is known to cause a number of ailments including stomach bleeding (Gordon, 1980). Moreover, perhaps 1 million Americans enter a hospital each year with an adverse reaction to a medical drug (Illich, 1976). Some very profitable medical products have also inflicted widespread suffering. The Dalkon shield, for example, is a contraceptive intra-uterine device that the A. H. Robins Company continued to sell despite evidence that it caused pelvic inflammation that put thousands of women at risk of permanent sterility (Perry & Dawson, 1985).

Of the 26 million surgical operations performed in the United States in 1987, three-fourths were elective or not prompted by a medical emergency; they were intended to increase a patient's long-term health. Growing evidence suggests, however, that the decision to perform surgery reflects the financial interests of surgeons

Science or Sexism? The Case of Victorian Women

A century ago medical science reacted far from neutrally to the changing roles of women. American medicine, under the control of males, generally opposed greater sexual equality.

According to medical opinion, conventional gender distinctions naturally and inevitably reflected human biology. Women were weaker than men, with smaller skulls and brains and less muscular potential. Physicians also pronounced men naturally rational and intellectual while claiming that women were dominated by their emotions and hypersensitive nervous systems.

Women's proper role was said to center on childbearing and the home. One physician, writing in 1890, remarked that the physical condition of women is "as if the Almighty, in creating the female sex, had taken

Leon-Augustin Lhermitte's painting, *Claude Bernard Operates for his Students*, shows Victorian medicine to be the domain of men who commonly mixed their science with politics and patriarchal values.

and hospitals as well as the medical needs of patients (Illich, 1976). Perhaps 10 percent of this elective surgery could safely be refused or deferred, saving patients more than $1 billion each year. More important, since about one in two hundred patients dies from elective surgery (because surgery is itself dangerous), 13,000 lives a year are needlessly lost (Sidel & Sidel, 1982a).

From the social-conflict point of view, improving the performance of the American health-care system would require moving toward the model of socialized medicine, in which health, not profit, is of primary importance.

Medicine as Social Control

Social-conflict analysis also views medical care as a means of social control. Because Americans generally see sci-

ence as a path to objective truth, the scientific model of medicine dominates our understanding of health. Yet, though scientific medicine declares itself to be politically neutral, ample evidence suggests that it takes sides on significant social issues. For example, scientific medicine has resisted government health-care programs. The medical establishment also has a history of racial and sexual discrimination, having invoked "scientific" facts to protect the interests of the wealthy white males who dominate the medical profession (Leavitt, 1984). The box provides several illustrations of scientific medicine's historical sexism in the United States. Such practices decreased considerably as American females and nonwhites achieved greater social equality, but critics contend that social and political biases remain in the American medical establishment (Zola, 1978; Brown, 1979).

Even today critics view scientific medicine as a

the uterus and built up a woman around it" (cited in Smith-Rosenberg & Rosenberg, 1984:13). Furthermore, medical opinion held that childless women had a higher incidence of physical and mental illness and a shorter life span.

The Victorian medical establishment also opposed women's demands for schooling. Physicians warned that intellectual pursuits damaged a woman's health, rendering her weak and sickly and decreasing her likelihood of bearing healthy children. Describing the educated woman in 1901, one gynecologist complacently predicted, "She may become highly cultured and accomplished and shine in society, but her future husband will discover too late that he has married a large outfit of headaches, backaches, and spine aches, instead of a woman fitted to take up the duties

of life" (cited in Smith-Rosenberg & Rosenberg, 1984:16). Another physician, a member of the Harvard medical faculty, also worried about the dangers in educating women: "If she puts as much force into her brain education as a boy, the brain or the special apparatus [the reproductive system] will suffer" (cited in Bollough & Voght, 1984:30).

Victorian physicians also opposed women's efforts to control their own sexuality. Women, they argued, had no interest in sexual activity other than as a means of having children; furthermore, women had neither the desire nor the ability to achieve orgasm. Men, on the other hand, required sexual intercourse to conclude with orgasm in order to prevent the buildup of dangerous levels of nervous energy. Male orgasms unimpeded by contraceptive devices such

as condoms enhanced a woman's health by "bathing the female reproductive organs" (cited in Smith-Rosenberg & Rosenberg, 1984:19). Well into this century, in fact, the American Medical Association opposed contraception and abortion as dangerous to women's physical and mental health.

Some Victorians did challenge the conventional medical opinion. Martha Carey Thomas, president of Bryn Mawr College, denounced such ideas as "pseudo-scientific." She won much support for her conclusion that men holding such ungenerous attitudes toward women were themselves "pathological, blinded by neurotic mists of sex, unable to see that women form one-half of the kindly race of normal, healthy human creatures in the world" (cited in Bollough & Voght, 1984:34).

means of maintaining class inequality. Scientific medicine tends to explain illness in terms of bacteria, viruses, or biological processes rather than in the context of social patterns such as wealth and poverty. From the scientific perspective, in other words, poor people become ill because of little sanitation and unhealthful diet, even though poverty may be the underlying cause of these ills. In this way, critics charge, scientific medicine depoliticizes the issue of health in the United States by reducing social and political issues to simple biology.

Critical evaluation. Social-conflict analysis provides still another view of the relationship among health, medicine, and American society. There is little doubt that many Americans think of medicine in terms of artificial hearts, CAT scans, and other sophisticated technology

while overlooking the fact that many people lack the most basic medical care.

One objection to the conflict approach is that it minimizes the improvements in American health brought about by scientific medicine. Though there is plenty of room for improvement, health indicators for all Americans have unquestionably become better in recent decades.

Sociology's three major theoretical paradigms together demonstrate that health and medicine are social issues. The famous French scientist Louis Pasteur (1822–1895) spent much of his life studying how bacteria cause disease. Before his death, he is reported to have remarked that health depends much less on bacteria than on the social environment in which bacteria operate (Gordon, 1980:7). Explaining Pasteur's insight is sociology's contribution to human health.

SUMMARY

1. Health is a social and biological issue that depends on the extent and distribution of a society's resources. Culture shapes definitions of health and also shapes health care.

2. Through most of human history, health has been poor by today's standards. Health improved dramatically in Western Europe and North America in the nineteenth century, first because of a rising standard of living due to industrialization, and later because of medical advances.

3. Rising living standards and medical advances curtailed infectious diseases, major killers at the beginning of this century. Today most Americans die in old age of heart disease, cancer, or stroke.

4. Health in the Third World is generally poor, because of hunger and inadequate sanitation. Average life expectancy is about twenty years less than in the United States; in the poorest nations, half of the children do not survive to adulthood.

5. In the United States, three-fourths of children born today can expect to live to at least age sixty-five. Throughout the life course, females have relatively better health than males, and people of high social position enjoy better health than others.

6. Industrialization has raised the American standard of living and thus improved health. However, environmental pollution, especially from industrial wastes, threatens the future health of Americans.

7. Cigarette smoking increased during this century to become the greatest preventable cause of death in the United States. With the known health hazards of smoking and the decreasing social tolerance of smokers, cigarette consumption has declined.

8. Sexually transmitted diseases are a health issue of growing concern. In the 1980s the spread of genital herpes transformed patterns of sexuality. The spread of AIDS, a fatal and incurable disease, has reinforced this change.

9. Because of advancing medical technology, an increasing number of ethical issues surround death and the rights of the dying. Because of the capability to sustain life artificially, death often becomes a matter of human decision making.

10. Historically a family concern, health care is now the responsibility of trained specialists. The model of scientific medicine now dominates the American medical establishment.

11. Holistic medicine, an alternative to scientific medicine, seeks to promote health as well as treat disease. Based on personal knowledge of patients and their environment, it encourages people to assume greater responsibility for their own health.

12. Socialist societies define medical care as a right that governments offer equally to everyone.

13. Capitalist societies view medical care as a commodity to be purchased, although most capitalist governments support medical care through socialized medicine or national health insurance.

14. The United States is the only industrialized society with no comprehensive medical-care program. Within a direct-fee system, most Americans have private health insurance, government insurance, or membership in a health maintenance organization. One in five Americans cannot afford to pay for medical care.

15. A concept central to structural-functional analysis is the sick role, in which illness allows release from routine social responsibilities as long as patients seek to regain their health.

16. The symbolic-interaction paradigm states that health is largely a matter of subjective perception and social definition.

17. Social-conflict analysis focuses on the unequal distribution of health and medical care. It criticizes American medical care for overly relying on drugs and surgery and for overemphasizing the biological rather than the social causes of illness.

KEY CONCEPTS

direct-fee system a medical-care system in which patients pay directly for the services of physicians and hospitals

euthanasia (mercy killing) assisting in the death of a person suffering from an incurable illness

health a state of complete physical, mental, and social well-being

health care any activity intended to improve health

health maintenance organization (HMO) an organization that provides comprehensive medical care for which subscribers pay a fixed fee

holistic medicine an approach to health care that emphasizes prevention of illness and takes account of the whole person within a physical and social environment

medicine an institutionalized system for combating disease and improving health

sick role patterns of behavior that are socially defined as appropriate for those who are ill

social epidemiology the study of the distribution of health and disease in a society's population

socialized medicine a health-care system in which most medical facilities are owned and operated by the government, and most physicians are salaried government employees

---

SUGGESTED READINGS

These books discuss in depth many of the issues raised in this chapter.

> Meredith B. McGuire, with the assistance of Debra Kantor. *Ritual Healing in Suburban America.* New Brunswick, NJ: Rutgers University Press, 1988.

> Howard Schwartz. *Dominant Issues in Medical Sociology.* 2nd ed. New York: Random House, 1987.

> Renée C. Fox. *Essays in Medical Sociology.* 2nd ed. New Brunswick, NJ: Transaction, 1987.

This paperback is a highly readable analysis of eating disorders, emphasizing social causes.

> Michael P. Levine. *How Schools Can Help Combat Student Eating Disorders: Anorexia Nervosa and Bulimia.* Washington, DC: National Education Association, 1987.

The history of the medical establishment in the United States makes for fascinating reading. The first of these books details the emergence of the medical profession, and the second investigates the changing relations between physicians and patients.

> Paul Starr. *The Transformation of American Medicine.* New York: Basic Books, 1982.

> Edward Shorter. *Bedside Manners: The Troubled History of Doctors and Patients.* New York: Simon & Schuster, 1985.

The history of medicine is also a tale of gender conflict. The first of these books explores women's exclusion from the emerging medical establishment. The second explains how female midwives were gradually replaced by male obstetricians.

> Regina Markell Morantz-Sanchez. *Sympathy and Science: Women Physicians in American Medicine.* New York: Oxford University Press, 1985.

> Jane B. Donegan. *Women & Men Midwives: Medicine, Morality, and Misogyny in Early America.* Westport, CT: Greenwood Press, 1985.

Few issues reveal the interplay of medicine and ethics as much as abortion. The first book contrasts patterns of abortion in the United States and Great Britain. The second, based on interviews of obstetricians and gynecologists, reveals growing legal concerns among professionals.

> Colin Francome. *Abortion Practice in Britain and the United States.* Winchester, MA: Allen & Unwin, 1986.

> Jonathan B. Imber. *Abortion and the Private Practice of Medicine.* New Haven, CT: Yale University Press, 1986.

Arguing that living longer is not necessarily living better, the author asks if we should—or can afford to—provide unlimited medical care for aging people.

> Daniel Callahan. *Setting Limits: Medical Goals in an Aging Society.* New York: Simon & Schuster, 1987.

Here are three recent books concerned with the AIDS epidemic. The first is of special concern to faculty and students. The second includes a dozen essays concerned with how American society has responded to this crisis. The third criticizes the medical establishment and the press for exaggerating the scope of the AIDS epidemic.

> Jackie R. McClain and Tom E. Matteoli. *Confronting AIDS on the Campus and in the Classroom: A Guide for Higher Education.* Washington, DC: College and University Personnel Association, 1989.

> David E. Rogers and Eli Ginzberg, eds. *Public and Professional Attitudes Towards AIDS Patients: A National Dilemma.* Boulder, CO: Westview, 1989.

> Michael Fumento. *The Myth of Heterosexual AIDS.* New York: Basic Books, 1989.

This study of seventeen housewives who were institutionalized during the 1950s for emotional disturbances suggests that conventional social roles can generate illness.

> Carol A. B. Warren. *Madwives: Schizophrenic Women in the 1950s.* New Brunswick, NJ: Rutgers University Press, 1987.

This study of Eastern Europe reveals strengths and weaknesses of medical care in socialist societies.

> Alena Heitlinger. *Reproduction, Medicine and the Socialist State.* New York: St. Martin's Press, 1987.

21

Population and Urbanization

In 1519 a band of Spanish conquistadors led by Hernando Cortés reached Tenochtitlán, the capital of the Aztec empire. What they saw stunned them—a lake-encircled city, teeming with over 300,000 people, more than the population of any European city at that time. Gazing down broad streets, exploring stone temples, and entering the magnificent royal palace filled with golden treasures, Cortés and his soldiers wondered if they were dreaming.

Cortés soon woke up and set his mind to looting the city. He was unable at first to overcome the superior forces of the Aztecs and their leader Montezuma, but after spending two years raising a vast army, he finally succeeded in destroying Tenochtitlán. In its place, Cortés began construction of a new European center—*Ciudad Imperial de México*—Mexico City.

Today Mexico City is again fighting for its life. Its population has soared and is expected to reach 30 million by the end of this decade—one hundred times the number found by Cortés. This huge population is struggling within a Third-World society burdened with poverty, foreign debt, and a rapidly deteriorating environment.

Similar situations—rising populations fueling urban growth amid stunning poverty—are seen over much of the world today. This chapter examines population growth and urbanization—two powerful forces that have been changing our planet for thousands of years. Increas-

ing population will be one of the most serious problems facing the world in the coming century; more and more, this vital drama is being played out in cities of unprecedented size.

DEMOGRAPHY: THE STUDY OF POPULATION

From the emergence of the human species some 200,000 years ago until recently, the population of the earth has remained quite small and vulnerable to disease and natural disaster. Ironically, perhaps, the world population is now so large (close to 5.5 billion in 1990) and growing so rapidly that the future of humanity is again uncertain.

How this growth has come about is the focus of **demography,** *the study of human population.* Demography (from the Greek, meaning "description of people"), which is closely related to sociology, investigates the size, age, and sex composition of a population as well as people's movements from one region to another. Although much demographic research is quantitative, demography is more than a numbers game. The discipline poses crucial questions about the consequences of population growth and how it may be controlled.

Demographic analysis is based on several basic concepts, described in the following sections.

Fertility

Any study of human population must concern itself with how many people are born. **Fertility** is *the incidence of childbearing in a society's population.* Females are capable of childbearing usually from the onset of menstruation (typically in the early teens) to menopause (usually in the late forties). During this time a woman might possibly bear over twenty children, but most women's *fecundity,* or potential childbearing, is greatly reduced by poor health, financial concerns, and cultural norms.

Demographers often measure fertility using the **crude birth rate,** *the number of live births in a given year for every thousand people in a population.* A crude birth rate is calculated by dividing the number of live births in a given year by a society's total population, and multiplying the result by 1,000. In the United States in 1988 there were about 4.0 million live births within a population of 249 million (Hollman, 1990). According to this formula, then, there were 16.1 live births for every thousand people, or a crude birth rate of 16.1.

This birth rate is "crude" because included in the total population are males and also females who are not in their childbearing years. Comparing crude birth rates can be misleading if one society has a higher propor-

Four million American children were born in 1988. Fertility in the United States has been relatively low in recent decades, in part because people are waiting longer to have children.

tion of females of childbearing age than another. A crude birth rate also overlooks variation in birth rates among people of different races, ethnicities, and religions. It has the advantage, however, of being easy to calculate, and it is a good measure of a society's overall fertility. Table 21–1 shows that the crude birth rates of the United States and other industrial societies are low in world context.

Mortality

Population size is also affected by **mortality,** *the incidence of death in a society's population.* Mortality is often measured in terms of the **crude death rate,** *the number of*

Table 21–1 FERTILITY AND MORTALITY RATES AMONG WORLD SOCIETIES, 1989

	Crude Birth Rate	Crude Death Rate	Infant Mortality Rate
North America			
United States	16	9	10
Canada	14	7	7
Europe			
Belgium	12	11	8
Denmark	11	11	7
France	14	10	9
Spain	13	8	11
United Kingdom	13	12	9
U.S.S.R.	18	11	25
Latin America			
Chile	21	6	18
Cuba	17	6	14
Haiti	31	12	92
Mexico	30	6	42
Nicaragua	39	8	65
Puerto Rico	19	7	16
Africa			
Algeria	38	8	73
Cameroon	42	16	123
Egypt	35	10	93
Ethiopia	45	15	113
Nigeria	46	17	121
South Africa	35	8	53
Asia			
Afghanistan	44	21	173
Bangladesh	43	15	138
India	31	11	91
Israel	22	7	9
Japan	11	7	5
Vietnam	33	8	51

SOURCE: U.S. Bureau of the Census, *World Population Profile: 1989* (Washington, DC: Government Printing Office, 1989).

first year of life for each thousand live births in a given year. This rate is derived from dividing the number of deaths of children under one year of age by the number of live births during the same year and multiplying the result by 1,000. In 1987 there were 38,000 infant deaths and about 3.8 million live births in the United States. Dividing the first number by the second and multiplying the result by 1,000 produces an infant mortality rate of 10.0. Like other demographic variables, this rate conceals considerable variation among different segments of the American population. For example, infant mortality rates of poor Americans are twice as high as those of well-to-do Americans (Stockwell, Swanson, & Wicks, 1987).

Infant mortality offers a good general measure of overall quality of life. Table 21–1 shows that infant mortality in the United States, Canada, and other industrial societies is considerably lower than that in poor societies of the Third World.

Societies with a low infant mortality rate have a high **life expectancy,** *how long a person, on the average, can expect to live.* American males born in 1988 can expect to live 71.5 years, while females can expect to live 78.3 years. In Third-World societies with high infant mortality, however, life expectancy is about twenty years less.

Migration

Population size also changes as people move from one place to another. Demographers define **migration** as *the movement of people into and out of a specified territory.* Some migration is involuntary, such as the forcible transport of 10 million Africans to the Western Hemisphere as slaves (Sowell, 1981). Other migration is of course voluntary and is usually motivated by complex "push–pull" factors. "Push" factors sometimes begin the process; for example, rural poverty makes villagers dissatisfied with their lives. A common "pull" factor is the attraction of a big city, where opportunity is thought to be greater; as will be explained later in this chapter, such migration is a major cause of rapid urban growth in the Third World. In other cases, people frustrated by religious or political oppression may seek greater freedom elsewhere, as millions of immigrants to the United States have done. Still others simply seek a more agreeable climate, an aim that explains much of the population growth in the American Sunbelt.

People's movement into a territory—commonly termed immigration—is measured in terms of the *in-*

deaths in a given year for every thousand people in a population. The crude death rate is calculated much as the crude birth rate is: the number of deaths in a given year is divided by the total population, and the result is multiplied by 1,000. In 1988 there were 2.2 million deaths within the total U.S. population of 249 million, yielding a crude death rate of 8.8. As Table 21–1 shows, this rate is low by world standards.

Another widely used demographic measure is the **infant mortality rate,** *the number of deaths within the* *migration rate,* the number of people entering an area for every thousand people in the total population. Movement out of a territory—or emigration—is measured in terms of the *out-migration rate,* the number leaving for every thousand people in the total population. Both types of migration usually occur simultaneously; demographers describe the difference between in-migration and out-migration as the *net-migration rate.*

Population Growth

Migration, and especially fertility and mortality, affect the size of any society's population. Demographers derive the *natural growth rate* of a population by subtracting the crude death rate from the crude birth rate. The natural growth rate of the American population in 1988 was 7.3 per thousand (16.1 crude birth rate minus 8.8 crude death rate), or 0.7 percent annually. During the 1990s this growth rate is projected to be much lower than that for the world at large, as is shown in Figure 21–1.

Figure 21–1 shows that the population growth in the industrialized regions of the world—including Europe (0.2 percent), North America (0.7 percent), and Oceania (1.3 percent)—is well below the world average. In contrast, annual growth rates equal or exceed the world average in the Third World—including Asia (1.7 percent), Latin America (1.8 percent), and Africa (3.1 percent). To understand the significance of these figures, consider that an annual growth of about 2 percent (as in Latin America) will double a population in thirty-five years, and a 3 percent growth rate (as in Africa) will double a population in twenty-four years. The rapid population growth of the poorest countries is deeply troubling because they can barely support the populations they have now.

Population Composition

Demographers also study the composition of a society's population at any point in time. One simple variable is the **sex ratio,** *the number of males for every hundred females in a given population.* In 1988 the sex ratio in the United States was 95.0, or 95.0 males for every 100 females. Sex ratios are usually lower than 100 because, as was noted in Chapter 20 ("Health and Medicine"), women typically outlive men.

A more complex way to describe the composition

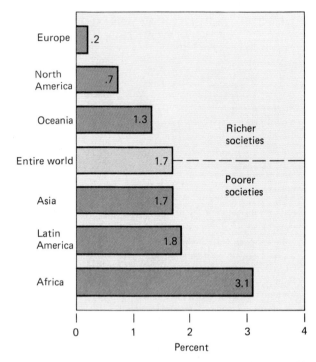

Figure 21–1   Projected Rate of Population Growth by World Region, 1990–2000

(U.S. Bureau of the Census, 1989)

of a population is the **age–sex pyramid,** *a graphic representation of the age and sex of a population.* Figure 21–2 presents the age–sex pyramid for the United States in 1989. The left side indicates the number of males of various ages, while the right side shows the corresponding number of females. The rough pyramid shape results from higher mortality as people age. After about age thirty-five, females increasingly outnumber males in the American population. The bulge in the fifteen through thirty-nine section represents the high birth rate from the mid-1940s to the late 1960s, commonly called the baby boom. The contraction just below shows that the baby boom was followed by a baby bust: a sharp decline in the birth rate. From a peak of 25.3 in 1957, the crude birth rate dropped to 15.3 in 1986.

Bulges and contractions in age–sex pyramids reveal a society's demographic history. These pyramids can also be used to predict future patterns. Figure 21–3 compares age–sex pyramids of Switzerland and Bangladesh. The relatively boxlike pyramid for Switzerland reveals a long-

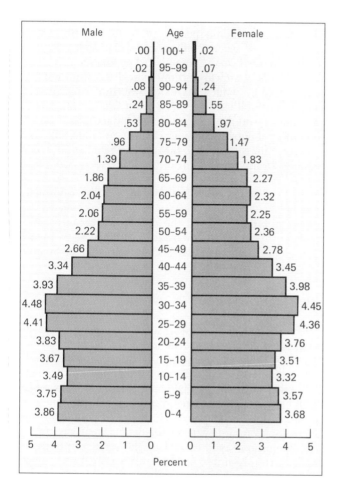

Male	Age	Female
.00	100+	.02
.02	95–99	.07
.08	90–94	.24
.24	85–89	.55
.53	80–84	.97
.96	75–79	1.47
1.39	70–74	1.83
1.86	65–69	2.27
2.04	60–64	2.32
2.06	55–59	2.25
2.22	50–54	2.36
2.66	45–49	2.78
3.34	40–44	3.45
3.93	35–39	3.98
4.48	30–34	4.45
4.41	25–29	4.36
3.83	20–24	3.76
3.67	15–19	3.51
3.49	10–14	3.32
3.75	5–9	3.57
3.86	0–4	3.68

Percent

Figure 21–2 Age–Sex Population Pyramid for the United States, 1989

(*U.S. Bureau of the Census, 1989*)

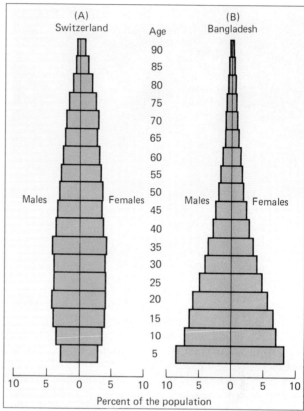

Percent of the population

Figure 21–3 The Demographic Composition of Switzerland and Bangladesh

(*Newman & Matzke, 1984*)

time low birth rate which recently dropped even further. Fewer females are entering the childbearing years, so population growth is likely to remain low, as it is in other industrial societies.

Bangladesh, a typical Third-World society, presents a dramatic contrast. The sharp point near the top of the pyramid is produced by high death rates after what we think of as middle age. The extremely wide base reveals a very high birth rate, a rate that is quite likely to rise even more, since the majority of females have yet to enter their childbearing years. When they do—unless control measures effectively limit births—the exploding population will further strain limited social resources.

HISTORY AND THEORY OF POPULATION GROWTH

Through most of human history, societies considered high birth rates desirable since human labor represented a major source of productivity. Additionally, until the development of rubber condoms 150 years ago, birth control remained uncertain at best. High death rates were the inevitable result of the inability to combat disease. High fertility and high mortality more or less balanced one another, so population growth stayed fairly low. The world's population at the dawn of civilization in about 6000 B.C.E. (perhaps 20 million) had increased tenfold by the beginning of the common era, as is shown

Among the poorest countries on earth, Bangladesh is struggling to meet the needs of approximately 115 million people in a land area smaller than the state of Wisconsin. With a high birth rate, the population problem is likely to become more serious in the future.

in Figure 21–4. In Europe the population grew slowly during the Middle Ages, as gains were periodically erased by outbreaks of deadly plague, such as the Black Death that swept across Western Europe in the mid-fourteenth century.

Then in about 1750 the earth's population turned sharply upward, reaching 1 billion a century later. As we will see, this increase was caused more by a reduction in mortality than by a rise in fertility. Forty thousand years of human reproduction were necessary to populate

Figure 21–4 The Growth of World Population
From some 20 million around 6000 B.C.E., world population reached 1 billion by 1850. Today over 5 billion people live on the earth. The world's population at the beginning of the twenty-first century is projected to be more than 6 billion.

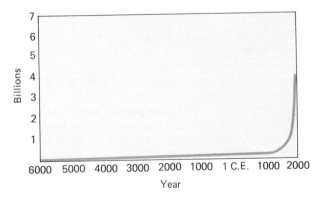

the earth with a billion people, yet by 1930—only eighty years later—a second billion had been added to the planet. In other words, not only did population increase, but the *rate* of growth also rose quickly. A third billion were added by about 1962—after just thirty-two years—and a fourth billion by 1974, a scant twelve years later. The rate of world population growth has recently slowed, but the 5 billion mark was reached in mid-1987. In no previous century did the world's population even double. In the twentieth century, it has increased *fourfold*.

Demographic projections are really informed guesswork. Currently, world population is predicted to exceed 6 billion early in the twenty-first century, and probably to reach 8 billion by 2025. Little wonder, then, that global population has become a matter of urgent concern.

Malthusian Theory

Sudden population growth some two centuries ago sparked the development of demography. Thomas Robert Malthus (1766–1834), an English clergyman and economist, developed a theory of population growth that warned of impending social chaos. Malthus (1926; orig. 1798) saw in increasing population growth the timeless passion between the sexes. He expected population to increase according to what mathematicians call a geometric progression, as illustrated by the series of numbers 2, 4, 8, 16, 32, and so on. Malthus reasoned that world population would soon soar out of control.

Food production would also increase, Malthus predicted, but only in arithmetic progression (as in the series 2, 3, 4, 5, 6, and so on) because, even with technological innovations in agriculture, farmland is limited. Malthus's analysis led to a troubling vision of the future: people reproducing beyond what the planet could feed, leading ultimately to catastrophic starvation.

Malthus saw two limits to population growth: *positive checks* such as famine, disease, and war; and *preventive checks* including artificial birth control, sexual abstinence, and delayed marriages. His religious principles precluded birth control, and his common sense told him people would not abstain from sex or marry later, unless facing imminent famine. His forecast was pessimistic indeed, earning him the title of the "dismal parson."

Critical evaluation. Fortunately, Malthus's predictions were flawed in several ways. First, by the middle of the nineteenth century the birth rate in Europe began to drop—partly because children were becoming more of an economic liability than an asset, and partly because artificial birth control was widely adopted. Second, Malthus underestimated human ingenuity: advances in irrigation, fertilizers, and pesticides greatly increased the output of farmers, and industrial technology has resulted in unforeseen increases in the production of other goods.

Malthus was also criticized for ignoring the role of social inequality as a cause of abundance or famine. His views irritated Karl Marx (1967; orig. 1867), who objected to linking human suffering to a "law of nature." To Marx, such suffering was human mischief, the results of a capitalist economy.

Still we cannot entirely dismiss Malthus's dire prediction. First, resources such as habitable land, clean water, and unpolluted air are certainly finite. In boosting economic productivity, technology has also created new and threatening problems, such as environmental pollution, described in Chapter 20 ("Health and Medicine"). Medical advances have lowered the death rate but, in so doing, have increased world population.

Second, the effects of the continuing increase in population are not evident in North America, perhaps the richest region of the world. In the poorest societies of Africa, Asia, and Latin America, however, rapid population growth is approaching the catastrophe Malthus envisioned. Throughout the Third World, perhaps one-fifth of the world's people are already in jeopardy.

Third, although the global population growth has been far below that feared by Malthus, in the long run no rate of increase is acceptable (Ehrlich, 1978). Even if humanity manages to curtail the population explosion in poor societies, all of the world must remain alert to the long-range dangers of population growth.

Demographic Transition Theory

Malthus's rather crude analysis has been superseded by **demographic transition theory,** *the thesis that population patterns are linked to a society's level of technological development.*

This relationship can be shown by a comparison of three stages of technological changes, as shown in Figure 21–5. Stage 1 is typical of preindustrial agrarian societies. Birth rates are high because children are a valuable source of labor and because there is no effective birth control. Death rates are also high: the low standard of living and the lack of advanced medical technology promote deadly infectious diseases. Because the many

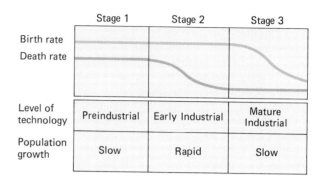

Figure 21–5 Demographic Transition Theory

deaths neutralize the many births, population growth is slight, and so population increase was modest for thousands of years before the Industrial Revolution began in eighteenth-century Europe.

Stage 2, the beginning of the demographic transition, comes with the onset of industrialization. Technology expands food supplies and helps combat disease. Birth rates remain high, but death rates fall sharply, with the predictable result of rapid population growth. It was in this era that Malthus developed his ideas, so his pessimism is understandable. Most Third-World societies today are in this high-growth stage.

In Stage 3 a fully industrial economy is established, and several factors serve to lower the birth rate. First, with a higher standard of living, children are more expensive to raise, and so large families become an economic liability rather than an asset. Smaller families are also more practical because more women are working outside the home. Furthermore, sophisticated technology makes effective birth control widely available. As birth rates begin to fall into line with low death rates, fertility and mortality are balanced and once again population growth is slow. Western industrial societies have been in this state for much of this century. Some poor societies, such as the People's Republic of China, have managed to control population through sweeping government programs, but most Third-World societies that are not yet industrialized appear to be locked into dangerously high population growth.

Critical evaluation. Demographic transition theory provides more grounds for optimism than does Malthusian theory. Instead of a runaway population increase, this analysis foresees both a lower rate of population growth and more material resources as a result of technological development.

Demographic transition theory has been incorporated into modernization theory, the approach to global development discussed in Chapter 11 ("Global Inequality"). This theory implies that the Third World will solve its population problem, since poor societies follow the path of development of European societies over past centuries. Yet, as dependency theorists argue, the current global economic system is likely to ensure that poor societies remain poor. Unless there is a significant redistribution of world resources, they claim, our planet will become increasingly divided, with the industrialized "haves" enjoying low population growth while the nonindustrialized "have-nots" struggle in vain to feed soaring populations.

World Population Today

What population patterns exist in today's world? Using demographic transition theory, we can explain important differences between industrial and nonindustrial societies.

Industrialized Societies

Soon after the Industrial Revolution began, population growth in Western Europe and North America reached a high of about 3 percent annually. Then, as industrialization proceeded, it declined, and since 1970 annual growth has remained below 1 percent in the United States. Having now reached Stage 3, these areas appear close to the population replacement level of 2.1 births per woman, a point termed **zero population growth,** *the level of reproduction that maintains population at a steady state.* Several European societies have already shown a decrease in population, prompting some analysts to suggest that there is a fourth stage, characterized by zero population growth or even population decline (van de Kaa, 1987). Because the American population is still relatively young—with a median age of 32.7 in 1989—population growth is expected to rise during the next several decades, yet the "graying of America" discussed in Chapter 14 ("Aging and the Elderly") may eventually bring us to zero population growth.

Factors contributing to declining population also include the higher costs of raising children, the increasing proportion of women in the labor force, and the growing number of people choosing to marry at a later age or to remain childless. During the last generation, contraceptive use has increased to about two-thirds of women

Il paraît que je suis un phénomène socio-culturel.

LA FRANCE A BESOIN D'ENFANTS.

The birthrate in Europe has dropped so low that some analysts foresee a decline in population. In France, the government has turned to advertising to encourage people to have children. The ad implies that children are becoming so rare that this baby can remark, "It appears that I am a sociocultural phenomenon." At the bottom right is added, "France needs children."

in the childbearing years. Similarly, voluntary sterilization has increased dramatically and is now the most common form of birth control in the United States. Even Catholics, whose religious doctrine prohibits artificial birth control, no longer differ from other Americans in their contraceptive practices (Westoff & Jones, 1977; Moore & Pachon, 1985). Abortion was legalized in 1973, and during the 1980s about 1.3 million women annually chose to abort their pregnancies (Ellerbrock et al., 1987; *Morbidity and Mortality Weekly Report*, 1989). Poor Americans still have somewhat bigger than average families and, as was noted in Chapter 10 ("Social Class in America"), the largest category of the American poor is children. Overall, however, population growth in industrial societies such as the United States does not present the pressing problem that it does in poor societies.

Nonindustrialized Societies

Today only a few societies fall within demographic transition theory's Stage 1. These isolated societies, untouched by industrial technology, have typically high birth and death rates and, consequently, low population growth. Most world societies—in Latin America, Africa, and Asia—have predominantly agrarian economies with some industrialization and are therefore in Stage 2. Advanced medical technology supplied to these areas by industrialized societies has sharply reduced death rates, but birth rates remain high. Figure 21–6 shows the result. These societies currently account for about two-thirds of the earth's people (about 80 percent of global population growth during this century has been in the Third World), and demographers predict that the percentage will increase to about three-fourths of a global population of 6 billion (Piotrow, 1980).

Birth rates are high in the Third World for many of the same reasons they were high everywhere else for thousands of years. In agrarian societies, children are important economic assets, frequently working eight- or ten-hour days to contribute to their families' income.

Figure 21–6 Population Distribution, Industrial and Nonindustrial Societies, 1750–2000

(Piotrow, 1980)

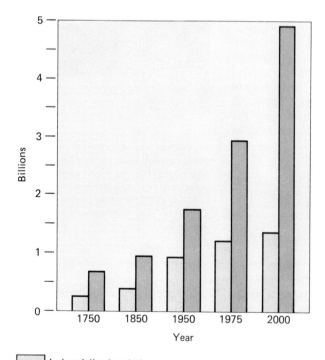

Industrialized societies

Nonindustrial societies

Parents also look to them for economic support in old age. The economic value of children, coupled with high mortality among infants and children, understandably encourages parents in these societies to have large families. Throughout the Third World, about four or five children is average for a family; in rural areas the number is frequently higher (The World Bank, 1984).

The social position of women also remains a crucial factor in today's population picture. Agrarian societies tend to be strongly patriarchal, so women's primary responsibilities are to bear and raise children. Thus in Latin America, for example, a combination of economic need, traditional patriarchy, and Roman Catholic doctrine discourages many women from using birth control devices. In much of Africa, many women in poor villages don't even know about effective forms of birth control (Salas, 1985). In some Asian countries, women have little access to effective contraception; in others, such as India and China, however, governments have launched bold programs to control birth rates. The current situation in the People's Republic of China, the world's most populous society, is examined in the box on page 570.

There is a further connection between the social position of women and population growth. Women restricted to the traditional roles of childrearing and homemaking are likely to have many children. Similarly, men with economic and educational opportunities are more likely to define their masculinity in terms other than virility. Thus formal education and rewarding work are the key not only to a society's economic development, but to population control as well. Research suggests, to cite a single example, that in Sudan (Africa) and Colombia (South America) women with seven years of schooling had half as many children as those without any education (Ross, 1985; Salas, 1985).

Efforts to control fertility have met with some success: in many Third-World societies, average family size fell by over 20 percent between 1975 and 1985. The decline will probably continue until the end of this century, although at a slower rate (Salas, 1985). Still, birth rates remain high, and since death rates are falling, population increase in the Third World is expected to continue.

Actually, *most* population growth in the Third World is due to declining death rates. After about 1920, when Europe and North America began to export to Third-World countries their advances in scientific medicine, nutrition, and sanitation, Latin America, Africa, and Asia witnessed a sharp decline in death rates. Inocula-

CROSS-CULTURAL COMPARISON

Birth Control in China

Third-World governments have responded to rapid population growth with a variety of programs aimed at reducing fertility. The People's Republic of China has one-fourth of the world's people (the population reached about 1.1 billion in 1990). Furthermore, more than half the Chinese people are under thirty, raising the specter of a baby boom without parallel in human history. Thus since 1979 the government has pursued a tough new policy limiting couples to only one child.

Local officials strongly encourage couples to delay childbirth and, once a child is born, to submit to sterilization or abort subsequent pregnancies. One-baby couples received income bonuses, and single children are promised priority in school enrollment, health care, and, later, in employment and housing. Family planning becomes each couple's social responsibility, and the birth rate dropped significantly, from 2.0 percent annually in the 1960s to about 1.8 percent in the 1980s.

The new policies spawned a number of problems, however. First, widespread sterilization during the early 1980s provoked international protest that China was forcing its people to undergo surgery. Second, the one-child policy has had the effect of encouraging abortion of female fetuses and female infanticide. In Chinese cultural tradition, sons have the responsibility of caring for elderly parents whereas daughters serve their husband's parents; with no national retirement program, few Chinese couples wish to face old age without a son. In cities where ultrasound technology allows parents to know the sex of a fetus, many women have aborted the female ones. In rural areas, couples may kill first-born girls in order to try again for a boy. A third problem is that privileges accorded to only children are now disproportionately enjoyed by sons, increasing sexual inequality in China.

By 1990, social strains had caused the government to become more lenient. Yet the price of unregulated growth appears higher: at the present rate of growth, the population will double by 2025, undermining the struggle of a vast society to raise its standard of living.

SOURCE: *World Development Report 1984* (New York: Oxford University Press, 1984); Gwenda Brophy, "China, Part I" and "China, Part II," *Population Today*, Vol. 17, no. 3 (March 1989):12 and no. 4 (April 1989):12; H. Yuan Tien, "Second Thoughts on the Second Child," *Population Today*, Vol. 17, no. 4 (April 1989):6–9.

Population policies often have unanticipated consequences. By limiting families to a single child on which parents and grandparents lavish attention, many Chinese wonder if they may be raising a generation of "little empresses" and "little emperors."

tions against infectious diseases, antibiotics, and insecticides have continued to reduce death rates with stunning effectiveness. For example, in Sri Lanka a malaria epidemic caused perhaps half of the deaths in the mid-1930s; a decade later, use of insecticide to kill malaria-carrying mosquitoes cut the malaria death toll in half (Ehrlich, 1978). Although there is reason to rejoice at such an achievement, the long-run effect was a dramatic increase in Sri Lanka's population. Similarly, India's infant mortality rate fell from 130 in 1975 to 91 in 1989, but its population now exceeds 840 million.

Infant mortality and average life expectancy in the Third World are still unfavorable by the standards of richer societies, but they have improved. More children survive to adulthood—but then they have children of their own. Newly instituted birth control programs in

Throughout the Third World, reliance on human labor to generate household income makes children an economic asset. This fact contributes to high fertility rates.

such areas attempt to limit the sharp increase in population growth caused by the successful "death control" programs several generations ago (Piotrow, 1980).

The Importance of Demography

Demographic analysis is vital for understanding how and why the earth is gaining unprecedented population. Only through such study can humankind address this pressing problem.

The technological advances that caused the populations of Europe and North America to grow during the past centuries simultaneously raised their standard of living. This is not the case in the societies presently experiencing unprecedented population growth: they lack the productive capacity to cope with their present populations, much less their future ones. Because population is growing fastest in the poorest societies, demographic forces are central to understanding global inequality, as explained in Chapter 11.

The problems of feeding a hungry world seem overwhelming. Every year the world adds almost 90 million people, who need housing, education, and employment. For years, people in rich societies have been isolated from the harsh realities of life in the Third World. The well-being of the entire planet, however, may ultimately depend on resolving many of the economic and social problems of poor, overly populated countries and bridging the widening gulf between the "have" and "have-not" societies. Describing recent population growth as "a great wave," one official of the United States government concluded:

> I see the world population movement as the effort to construct a breakwater—a structure that will stop the wave and prevent it from engulfing and sweeping away centuries of human development and civilization. (cited in Gupte, 1984:323)

URBANIZATION: THE GROWTH OF CITIES

For most of human history, people lived in small nomadic groups, moving as vegetation was depleted or following migratory game. As civilization emerged in the Middle East some eight thousand years ago, widely scattered settlements held only a small fraction of the earth's population. Today many cities contain as many people as the entire planet did then, and they will likely become even larger.

Urbanization is *the concentration of humanity into cities*. Not only does urbanization redistribute population within a society, it also transforms many patterns of social life. We will follow these changes in three urban revolutions that will be described in the remainder of this chapter.

The Evolution of Cities

Cities are a recent development in the long course of human history. After hundreds of thousands of years of evolutionary development, our ancestors grasped the idea of the city only about ten thousand years ago. Two factors set the stage for the *first urban revolution*: the emergence of permanent settlements.

The first factor was *a changing ecology*: as glaciers began to melt at the end of the last ice age, people were drawn to warm regions with fertile soil. The second was *changing technology*: at about the same time, humans discovered how to raise animals and crops. Together, these factors produced, for the first time, a surplus of food. Whereas hunting and gathering had demanded continual movement, raising food required people to remain in one place (Lenski & Lenski, 1982). Thus permanent settlements emerged. Material surplus also freed some people from food production, allowing them to build shelters, make tools and clothing, and become religious leaders. The founding of cities was truly revolutionary, resulting in a higher standard of living based on productive specialization.

The First Cities

Probably the first city was Jericho, a settlement to the north of the Dead Sea in disputed land currently occupied by Israel. About 8000 B.C.E., Jericho contained about 600 people (Kenyon, 1957; Hamblin, 1973; Spates & Macionis, 1987). By 4000 B.C.E. numerous cities were flourishing in the Fertile Crescent between the Tigris and Euphrates rivers in present-day Iraq and, soon afterward, along the Nile River in Egypt. Some, with populations of 50,000, became centers of urban empires dominating large regions. Priest-kings wielded absolute power over lesser nobility, administrators, artisans, soldiers, and farmers. Slaves, captured in frequent military campaigns, provided labor to build monumental structures such as the pyramids of Egypt (Wenke, 1980; Stavrianos, 1983; Lenski & Lenski, 1987).

Cities originated independently in at least three other areas of the world. Several large, complex cities existed in the Indus River region of present-day Pakistan in about 2500 B.C.E. Chinese cities are believed to date from 2000 B.C.E. In Central and South America, urban

Early urban settlements in Latin America often took the form of ceremonial centers. Shown here is the massive Pyramid of the Sun at Teotihuacán, near Mexico City.

centers began about 1500 B.C.E. In North America, however, significant urbanization did not begin until the arrival of European settlers in the sixteenth century (Lamberg-Karlovsky, 1973; Change, 1977; Coe & Diehl, 1980).

Preindustrial Cities in Europe

Urbanization in Europe began in about 1800 B.C.E. on the Mediterranean island of Crete and spread throughout Greece, resulting in more than one hundred city-states, of which Athens is the most famous. During its Golden Age, lasting barely a century after 500 B.C.E., Athens exemplified the positive potential of urban life. The Athenians, about 300,000 people living within roughly one square mile, devised cultural elements still central to the Western way of life, including philosophy, the arts, the principles of democracy, and a blending of physical and mental fitness symbolized by the Olympic games (Mumford, 1961; Carlton, 1977; Stavrianos, 1983). Despite such achievements, Athenian society depended on the labor of slaves, perhaps one-third of the population. Democratic principles notwithstanding, Athenian men also denied the rights of citizenship to women and foreigners (Mumford, 1961; Gouldner, 1965).

As Greek civilization faded, the city of Rome grew to almost 1 million inhabitants as it became the center of a vast empire. By the first century C.E., the militaristic Roman Empire encompassed much of northern Africa, Europe, and the Middle East. In the process, Rome widely diffused its language, arts, and technological innovations. By the fifth century C.E., the Roman Empire had fallen into disarray, a victim of its own gargantuan size, internal corruption, and militaristic appetite. Yet, between them, the Greeks and Romans had founded cities across Europe, including London, Paris, and Vienna.

The fall of the Roman Empire initiated an era of urban decline and stagnation. Cities became smaller, typically with about 25,000 people living within defensive walls. Competing warlords battled for territory, inhibiting trade between cities. Then, by the eleventh century, a semblance of peace allowed cities to become economic centers.

Medieval cities slowly removed their walls to facilitate trade but retained their narrow, winding, and usually filthy streets. As their economies expanded, London, Brussels, and Florence teemed with people from all walks of life: artisans, merchants, priests, peddlers, jugglers, nobles, and servants. Typically, different occupational groups such as bakers, keymakers, and carpenters lived in distinct sections or "quarters," and evidence of this practice remains today in some street names in old cities. In the medieval cities of Europe, cathedrals towered above all other buildings, signifying the preeminence of Christianity.

By today's standards, medieval cities were surprisingly personal (Sjoberg, 1965). Family ties were strong, and the people within each city "quarter" shared a trade and sometimes a religious and ethnic tradition. In many cases, this clustering was involuntary: religious and ethnic minorities were often legally restricted to certain districts. For example, Jews were targets of extensive prejudice and discrimination in an era dominated by the Roman Catholic Church. Laws in Venice and later in most of Europe confined Jews to areas known as *ghettos*.

Industrial-Capitalist Cities in Europe

Throughout the Middle Ages, steadily increasing commerce created an affluent urban middle class or *bourgeoisie* (French for "of the town"). By the fifteenth century, this wealth conferred such power on the bourgeoisie that it rivaled the hereditary nobility. Then European colonization of much of the rest of the world further bolstered the clout of the new trading class.

By about 1750 the Industrial Revolution was underway, triggering a *second urban revolution*, first in Europe and then in North America. Factories unleashed productive power as never before, causing cities to grow to unprecedented size, as shown in Table 21–2. During the nineteenth century the population of Paris rose from 500,000 to over 3 million, and that of London from 800,000 to 6.5 million (A. Weber, 1963, orig. 1899; Chandler & Fox, 1974). Most of this increase was due to migration from rural areas by people seeking a better standard of living.

Cities changed in other ways as well during this time. Commerce dominated the industrial-capitalist city, producing a change in urban form. Broad, straight boulevards replaced the old irregular streets to accommodate the flow of commercial traffic and, eventually, motor vehicles. Steam and electric trolleys criss-crossed the expanding European cities. Lewis Mumford (1961) explains that the city was divided into regular-sized lots as land became a commodity, bought and sold within the capitalist economy. Finally, the cathedrals that had guided the life of medieval cities were dwarfed by a central business district of factories, banks, retail stores, and offices, as ever-taller buildings proclaimed the power of the capitalist economy.

Urban social life was also new. Cities became impersonal, and increasingly crowded. People daily came into contact with vast numbers of strangers in the workplace and the neighborhood. Crime rates rose. A small

Table 21–2 POPULATION GROWTH IN SELECTED INDUSTRIAL CITIES OF EUROPE (IN THOUSANDS)

City	Year			
	1700	1800	1900	1987
Amsterdam	172	201	510	679
Berlin	100	172	2,424	3,055
Lisbon	188	237	363	807
London	550	861	6,480	6,768
Madrid	110	169	539	2,119
Paris	530	547	3,330	2,118
Rome	149	153	487	2,826
Vienna	105	231	1,662	1,489

SOURCE: Based on data from Tertius Chandler and Gerald Fox, *3000 Years of Urban History* (New York: Academic Press, 1974), pp. 17–19; and *The Statesman's Year-Book 1987–1988*, 124th ed. (New York: St. Martin's Press, 1987).

number of industrialists lived in grand style, while for most men, women, and children, factory work proved exhausting and provided bare subsistence.

Table 21–2 shows that European cities continued to grow during the twentieth century, although at a declining rate. Worker organization and political struggle brought improvements, including legal regulation of the workplace, better housing, and the right to vote. Public services such as water, sewage, and electricity further changed urban living for the better. Today poverty remains the daily plight of many workers, but a rising standard of living has partly fulfilled the historical promise of a better life in the city.

The Growth of American Cities

Although Native Americans have inhabited North America for tens of thousands of years, they established few permanent settlements. Cities began to emerge only after European colonization. The Spanish made an initial settlement at St. Augustine, Florida, in 1565, and the English founded Jamestown, Virginia, in 1607. New Amsterdam (later called New York), founded in 1624 by the Dutch, soon overshadowed these smaller settlements. Today more than three-fourths of Americans live

in urban places that cover only a tiny fraction of the country's land area. The roots of this remarkable transformation extend back to the colonial era.

Colonial Settlement: 1624–1800

Dutch New Amsterdam at the tip of Manhattan Island (1624) and English Boston (1630) were originally tiny settlements in a vast, unknown wilderness. Both resembled medieval towns of Europe, with narrow, winding streets that still exist in lower Manhattan and downtown Boston. New Amsterdam was walled on the north, the site of today's Wall Street. In 1700, Boston was the largest American settlement with a population of only 7,000.

The rational culture of capitalism soon replaced villages with thriving towns with grid-like streets. Figure 21–7 contrasts the traditional shape of New Amsterdam with the regular design of Philadelphia founded a half–century later in 1680.

Although colonial American cities grew steadily, they remained small enough to permit residents to live within a network of personal relationships. The lack of industrial technology prevented rapid movement, so pedestrians and horse-drawn wagons and carriages often clogged the cobblestone streets.

Figure 21–7   The Street Plans of Colonial New Amsterdam and Philadelphia
The plan of colonial New Amsterdam, shown on the left, reflects the preindustrial urban pattern of walls enclosing a city of narrow, irregular streets. Colonial Philadelphia, founded fifty years later, reflects the industrial urban pattern of accessible cities containing wide, regular streets to facilitate economic activity.

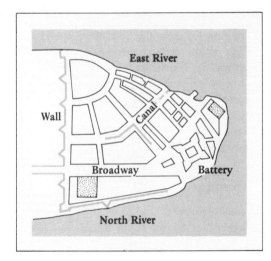
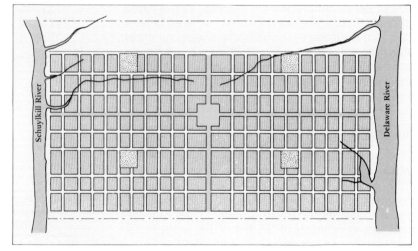

Table 21–3   THE URBAN POPULATION OF THE UNITED STATES, 1790–1986

Year	Population (millions)	Percent Urban
1790	3.9	5.1
1800	5.3	6.1
1820	9.6	7.3
1840	17.1	10.5
1860	31.4	19.7
1880	50.2	28.1
1900	76.0	39.7
1920	105.7	51.3
1940	131.7	56.5
1960	179.3	69.9
1980	226.5	73.7
1987	243.4	76.9

SOURCE: U.S. Bureau of the Census.

At this point, the United States was still an overwhelmingly rural society. In 1790 the government's first census counted roughly 4 million Americans. As Table 21–3 shows, only about 5 percent of them lived in urban places. The remainder were on farms and in small villages scattered across the Eastern seaboard.

Urban Expansion: 1800–1860

Early in the nineteenth century, dozens of new cities sprang up from coast to coast, as transportation routes opened the American West. In 1818 the National Road (now Interstate 40) linked Baltimore to the Ohio Valley. A decade later the Baltimore and Ohio Railroad transported people and products far faster. The Erie Canal (1825) connected New York to the Great Lakes and sparked the development of cities such as Buffalo, Cleveland, and Detroit. Because of the importance of water transportation during this period, most cities were established on lakes and rivers.

By 1860 about one-third of Americans were city dwellers. Some greeted this increase as progress; others mourned the passing of traditional agrarian life. Rural–urban tensions were pronounced, with negative stereotypes of "ignorant country cousins" from urbanites provoking rural people to condemn "untrustworthy city slickers" (Callow, 1969).

The Industrial Revolution in the United States began early in the nineteenth century. It centered mostly in the northern states, causing uneven urbanization: in 1850 New York City had a population ten times greater than that of Charleston. This division of American society into the industrial-urban North and the agrarian-rural South became a cause of the Civil War (Schlesinger, 1969).

The Metropolitan Era: 1860–1950

Industrialization reached its greatest intensity after the Civil War. Millions of Americans fled rural areas for the cities, with hope that factory jobs would offer greater economic opportunity. Cities also absorbed tens of millions of immigrants during this time, most from Europe. Table 21–4 shows the rapid growth of American cities in the late nineteenth century.

In 1900 New York boasted some 4 million residents, and Chicago, which had scarcely 100,000 people in 1860, was approaching 2 million. This growth marked the start of the era of the **metropolis,** *a very large city that socially and economically dominates an urban area.* Metropolises became huge commercial, manufacturing, and residential centers.

Industrial technology further changed the shape of urban America. Until 1850, few buildings exceeded three or four stories. By the 1880s, steel girders and mechanical elevators raised structures over ten stories high. In 1930, New York's Empire State Building became an urban wonder, a true "skyscraper" stretching 102 stories into the clouds. Railroads and highways enabled cities to expand outward with unprecedented efficiency (Warner, 1962). By the end of World War I, a majority of Americans lived in cities. The rural–urban controversy that had simmered throughout the nineteenth century had ended: America had become, and would remain, an urban society.

Urban Decentralization: 1950–Present

The industrial metropolis peaked about 1950. Since then, many people have moved away from the central cities in a process known as *urban decentralization* (Edmonston & Guterbock, 1984). As Table 21–4 shows, the largest central cities of the Northeast and Midwest have stopped growing and many have even lost population. New York, for example, has 600,000 fewer people than in 1950.

Urbanization in the United States nevertheless continues, in a different form. Instead of residing in densely populated central cities, Americans have spread into larger urban regions, in a migration closely tied to the growth of suburbs.

Table 21–4 POPULATION GROWTH IN SELECTED AMERICAN CITIES, 1870–1988

City	Population (in thousands)						
	1870	1890	1910	1930	1950	1970	1988
Baltimore	267	434	558	805	950	905	751
Boston	251	448	671	781	801	641	578
Chicago	299	1,100	2,185	3,376	3,621	3,369	2,978
Dallas	7	38	92	260	434	844	987
Detroit	80	206	466	1,569	1,850	1,514	1,036
Los Angeles	6	50	319	1,238	1,970	2,812	3,353
Milwaukee	71	204	374	578	637	717	599
New Orleans	191	242	339	459	570	593	531
New York*	942	2,507	4,767	6,930	7,892	7,896	7,353
Philadelphia	674	1,047	1,549	1,951	2,072	1,949	1,647
St. Louis	311	452	687	822	857	622	404
San Francisco	149	299	417	634	775	716	732

* Population figures for New York in 1870 and 1890 reflect that city as presently constituted.

SOURCE: U.S. Bureau of the Census.

Suburbs and Central Cities

Recent decades have seen rapid expansion of **suburbs,** *the urban area beyond the political boundaries of a city.* Suburbs began to grow late in the nineteenth century as railroad and trolley lines enabled people to live beyond the commotion of the city while still being able to commute to work "downtown." The first commuters were the well-to-do, imitating the pattern of the European nobility who periodically traveled between country estates and town houses (Baltzell, 1979). The growth of suburbs was also fueled by racial and ethnic intolerance: rising immigration was making the central city socially diverse, and many people fled to more homogeneous, high-prestige suburbs. In time, less-wealthy Americans also began to view a single-family house on its own piece of leafy suburban ground as part of the American Dream.

The economic boom of the late 1940s, along with increasingly affordable automobiles, placed suburbia within the grasp of many more people. After World War II Americans eagerly returned to family life, igniting the baby boom described earlier in this chapter. Since central cities contained little space for new housing construction, suburbs blossomed almost overnight. The government provided economic assistance in the form of guaranteed bank loans, further encouraging the purchase of suburban homes.

Some of the most successful postwar suburbs were designed for moderate-income Americans. Levittown, built on potato fields of New York's Long Island in the late 1940s, inaugurated a trend toward inexpensive suburban housing (Wattel, 1958). What some dismissed as prefabricated, look-alike homes were nonetheless sold

Suburban America grew rapidly after World War II. The introduction of mass-produced housing led some critics to poke fun at look-alike houses in which suburbanites allegedly lived shallow lives of superficial conformity. This didn't stop millions of Americans from buying them and enjoying a life apart from the crush and commotion of the central city.

as fast as they were built. By 1970 more Americans lived in the suburbs than in the central cities.

Not surprisingly, business also began to look to the suburbs. By 1970 the suburban mall had largely replaced the downtown stores of the metropolitan era (Rosenthal, 1974; Tobin, 1976; Geist, 1985). The interstate highway system built during the postwar period also brought industry to the suburbs. Old factory districts in the inner city not only had become expensive due to high taxes and crime, but they were also inconvenient for large trucks. Cities were soon surrounded by commercial parks containing both industry and offices.

This rapid suburban growth created financial problems for the older cities of the Northeast and Midwest. Population decline reduced tax revenues. Cities lost relatively affluent people to the suburbs and still needed to finance expensive social programs for the poor who remained (Gluck & Meister, 1979). The predictable result was the decay of the inner city after about 1950 (Sternlieb & Hughes, 1983). Some major cities, such as Cleveland and New York, reached the brink of financial bankruptcy. To many white Americans, the deteriorating inner city became synonymous with low-quality housing, crime, drugs, unemployment, the poor, and the nonwhite. This perception fueled even further "white flight," setting in motion a vicious circle of decline. Suburbs now have their own share of poor housing, congestion, and crime,

Urban renewal has transformed many decayed central-city districts into vital business centers. Baltimore's Inner Harbor, a commercial venture by developer James Rouse, is visually exciting and full of wonderful shops and restaurants. But renewal of this kind, critics claim, does little to address the basic housing needs of the American poor.

but they still appeal to many people because they have remained largely white, unlike the increasingly nonwhite central cities (Clark, 1979; Logan & Schneider, 1984; Stahura, 1986).

The government response to the plight of the central cities was **urban renewal,** *governmental programs intended to revitalize cities.* Many inner cities have been rebuilt, usually with the help of substantial federal funding. Yet these programs have been criticized for benefiting the business community far more than low-income residents in need of housing (Jacobs, 1961; Greer, 1965; Gans, 1982).

The Sunbelt: Postindustrial Cities

Not only are urban Americans spreading beyond the boundaries of central cities, they are also migrating from the traditional industrial heartland of America. In 1940 the Snowbelt (the Northeast and Midwest) contained almost 60 percent of all Americans. By 1975, however, the Sunbelt (the South and the West) passed the Snowbelt in overall population, and by 1988 it was home to 55.1 percent of the population. This regional migration, linked to the emergence of a postindustrial economy (discussed in Chapter 19, "The Economy and Work"), has further eroded the population of older Snowbelt cities.

Sunbelt cities continue their rapid growth. This demographic shift is shown in Table 21–5, which compares the ten largest cities in the United States in 1950 and in 1988. In 1950, eight of the top ten were Snowbelt industrial cities, whereas in 1988, six of ten were in the Sunbelt. The office-tower service jobs that dominate Sunbelt cities are likely to proliferate in the next decade. Thus, just as the twentieth century opened with tremendous urban growth in the North and Midwest, the twenty-first century will almost surely begin with rapid urban growth in the South and West.

Unlike industrial cities of the Snowbelt, the postindustrial cities of the Sunbelt grew *after* urban decentralization began. Since suburbs formed a ring of politically independent communities enclosing the Snowbelt cities, outward migration was at the expense of the central city. Newer Sunbelt cities, in contrast, were not surrounded by suburbs, so they have simply expanded. Chicago, for example, covers 228 square miles, whereas Houston is over 565. The physical expansion of Sunbelt cities has also enlarged their tax base and made them financially stronger than Snowbelt cities. The great

Table 21–5	THE TEN LARGEST CITIES IN THE UNITED STATES, 1950 AND 1988	

1950		
Rank	City	Population
1	New York	7,892,000
2	Chicago	3,621,000
3	Philadelphia .	2,072,000
4	Los Angeles	1,970,000
5	Detroit	1,850,000
6	Baltimore	950,000
7	Cleveland	915,000
8	St. Louis	857,000
9	Boston	801,000
10	San Francisco	775,000

1988		
Rank	City	Population
1	New York	7,352,700
2	Los Angeles	3,352,700
3	Chicago	2,977,500
4	Houston	1,698,100
5	Philadelphia	1,647,000
6	San Diego	1,070,300
7	Detroit	1,035,900
8	Dallas	987,400
9	San Antonio	941,200
10	Phoenix	923,800

SOURCE: U.S. Bureau of the Census.

The growth of urban areas is often unrecognized by Americans who live within them. Satellite photography from high above the earth, however, reveals vast urban regions formed by cities spreading outward into one another.

sprawl of the typical Sunbelt city does have drawbacks, however. Movement across town is difficult, especially for those unable to afford an automobile. Lacking a dense center, Sunbelt cities also do not generate the social intensity of New York or Chicago. For example, critics frequently contend that Los Angeles comprises a vast cluster of suburbs in search of a center.

Megalopolis: Regional Cities

The decentralization of American cities has produced large urban areas—regional cities—that contain numerous municipalities. In 1988 the Bureau of the Census (1990) recognized 283 urban regions in the United States, which they call *metropolitan statistical areas* (MSA). Each MSA contains a city with at least 50,000 people plus densely populated surrounding counties. Almost

all of the fifty fastest-growing MSAs are located in the Sunbelt.

The biggest MSAs, containing more than 1 million people, are called *consolidated metropolitan statistical areas* (CMSAs). In 1988 there were 20 CMSAs; the largest was New York and adjacent urban areas in Long Island and northern New Jersey, with a total population of about 18 million. Next in size was the CMSA in Southern California that includes Los Angeles, Riverside, and Anaheim, with a population of some 14 million (U.S. Bureau of the Census, 1989).

Many of these urban regions have grown so large that they have come into physical contact with one another. For example, the CMSA centered around New York City is part of a 400-mile supercity extending from southern New England to northern Virginia. In the early 1960s, French geographer Jean Gottmann (1961) first used the term **megalopolis** to designate *a vast urban region containing a number of cities and their surrounding suburbs.* A megalopolis is composed of hundreds of politically independent cities and suburbs; from an airplane at night, however, it appears to be one continuous city. Other such supercities are the eastern coast of Florida, much of Southern California, and the urban strip extending from Cleveland to Chicago. Future urban regions will undoubtedly emerge, especially in the Sunbelt, where urban growth is currently greatest.

European Theory: Urban Life versus Rural Life

Rapid urban growth since the Industrial Revolution has transformed American society in various ways. Several European sociologists were among the first to explore the differences between urban life and rural life.

Ferdinand Toennies

In the late nineteenth century the German sociologist Ferdinand Toennies (1855–1936) concluded that time-honored patterns of rural life were not found in the new industrial cities (1963; orig. 1887). He used the term **Gemeinschaft** (German, meaning roughly "community") to refer to *a type of social organization with strong solidarity based on tradition and personal relationships.* People who lived in rural villages, Toennies claimed, were strongly bound together by kinship, neighborhood, and friendship. *Gemeinschaft,* then, describes any social setting in which people form a more or less single primary group. This is essentially the same concept as Emile Durkheim's *mechanical solidarity,* discussed in Chapter 4 ("Society").

In contrast, **Gesellschaft** (a German word meaning roughly "association") is *a type of social organization with weak solidarity resulting from cultural pluralism and impersonal social relationships.* Within *Gesellschaft,* people are motivated by self-interest rather than the well-being of everyone. City dwellers, Toennies suggested,

Marc Chagall's painting *I and the Village* (1911) conveys the essential unity of rural life, by which people are linked by tradition and their common work on the land. In contrast, Edouard Manet's *The Bar at the Folies Bergeres* suggests the isolating character of urban life. Here a woman stands alone—despite being in the middle of a crowd—her contact with others limited to the impersonal role she performs. Note, too, that the people in the room are depicted only indirectly in a mirror.

Marc Chagall, I and the Village, *1911. Oil on canvas, 63⅝" × 59⅝". Collection, The Museum of Modern Art, New York. Mrs. Simon Guggenheim Fund.*

have little common identity and so they view each other as means of achieving their own goals. Durkheim's concept of *organic solidarity* parallels Toennies's *Gemeinschaft*. The growth of cities eroded traditional social relations in favor of the temporary and impersonal ties typical of business. Durkheim was generally more positive than Toennies about this change because it enhanced personal freedom and privacy.

Georg Simmel

Georg Simmel, the German sociologist whose analysis of small groups was discussed in Chapter 7 ("Groups and Organizations"), offered a micro-level analysis of how urban life shaped people's behavior and attitudes (1964; orig. 1905). Because the city is a crush of people, objects, and events, Simmel argued, the urbanite is easily overwhelmed with stimulation. Consequently, city people typically develop a *blasé attitude*; that is, they learn to respond selectively, tuning out much of what goes on around them in order to focus attention on what seems to be important. City dwellers are not without sensitivity and compassion for others; they simply must be discriminating in their responses because of the social intensity of the city.

American Research: Urbanism As a Way of Life

American sociologists soon joined the exploration of rapidly growing cities. The first major sociology program in the United States was founded at the University of Chicago. Chicago in the late nineteenth century was a major metropolis exploding with population and cultural diversity. These changes prompted early American sociologists to build on the ideas of Toennies and Simmel.

Perhaps the greatest urban sociologist was Robert Park, who for decades provided leadership as the discipline of sociology became established in the United States. Park is introduced in the box.

Louis Wirth

Another major figure in the Chicago School of urban sociology was Louis Wirth (1897–1952). In 1938 Wirth published an influential essay that systematically organized the ideas of Toennies, Simmel, Park, and others into a theory of urban life.

Wirth noted three factors that define urbanism: large population, dense settlement, and social diversity. These characteristics, he argued, make urban life impersonal, superficial, and transitory. Living among millions of others, a city resident has contact with many more people than a rural dweller does. Yet a city resident knows these people only in terms of what they do: driving the school bus, managing an office, working in the grocery store. Urban social relationships also form on the basis of self-interest. For example, shoppers see grocers as the source of food while grocers see the shoppers as the source of income. They may exchange greetings, but friendship is not the main reason for their interaction.

Limited interpersonal involvement and the great social diversity also make city dwellers more tolerant than rural residents are. Rural communities often vigorously enforce narrowly defined social mores, but the heterogeneous population of a city does not necessarily share moral values (Wilson, 1985).

Wirth's ideas about the city seem rather negative. The rapid urbanization of Europe and North America deeply troubled many sociologists because the personal ties and traditional morality of rural life appeared to be lost in the anonymous rush of the city. Robert Park, on the other hand, pointed out a positive side to these changes, including greater personal autonomy.

Critical evaluation. In Europe and the United States, early sociologists concerned themselves largely with the city. Decades of additional research, however, have provided mixed support for their conclusions.

Urban settings do appear to have a weaker sense of community than do rural areas, but it is easy to exaggerate the social cohesion in rural life. In reality conflict has long been a feature of the countryside as well as the city. Furthermore, while urbanites do treat many people impersonally, they also have close personal relationships. The public anonymity of cities means that some people "walk lonely in the crowd," but many others welcome such privacy (Keller, 1968; Cox, 1971; Macionis, 1978; Wellman, 1979; Lee et al., 1984).

Although urbanism does foster a certain way of life, the pioneering sociologists were wrong in implying that it neutralizes the effects of class, race, and sex. On the contrary, cities often intensify these social forces (Spates & Macionis, 1987). Herbert Gans (1968) criticized Wirth's view of urbanism as one general way of life, suggesting that rich and poor, white and black, Anglo and Hispanic, male and female lead distinctive lives in cities.

Robert Ezra Park (1864–1944)

I suspect that I have actually covered more ground, tramping about in cities in different parts of the world, than any other living man. (1950:viii)

Robert Ezra Park was a man with a consuming passion—the city. In cities, he found the full range of human expression, triumphs, and turbulence. For almost thirty years at the University of Chicago, he led a group of dedicated sociologists in direct, systematic observation of urban life.

Park was deeply influenced by European sociologists such as Ferdinand Toennies and Georg Simmel (with whom Park had studied in Germany), but he favored direct observation rather than their armchair theorizing. At Park's urging, generations of sociologists at the University of Chicago directly probed nearly every part of their city.

Park came to understand the city as a highly ordered mosaic of distinctive regions, such as ethnic communities, vice areas, and industrial districts. These "natural areas," all part of a complex social organism, developed and changed in relation to each other over time. To Park, the city was truly the human kaleidoscope.

This variety, claimed Park, is the key to the timeless attraction of people to cities:

The attraction of the metropolis is due in part to the fact that in the long run every individual finds somewhere among the varied manifestations of city life the sort of environment in which he expands and feels at ease; he finds, in short, the moral climate in which his particular nature obtains the stimulations that bring his innate dispositions to full and free expression. It is, I suspect, motives of this kind . . . which drove many, if not most, of the young men and young women from the security of their homes in the country into the big, booming confusion and excitement of city life. (1967:41, orig. 1925)

Thus what many saw as disorganized and even dangerous, Park found fascinating. His view prompted him personally to explore cities throughout the world. He firmly believed that urban places offered a better way of life—the promise of greater human freedom than could be found elsewhere.

SOURCE: Based on Robert E. Park, "The City: Suggestions for the Investigation of Human Behavior in the Human Environment," in Robert E. Park and Ernest W. Burgess, *The City* (Chicago: University of Chicago Press, 1967; orig. 1925), pp. 1–46; and Robert E. Park, *Race and Culture* (Glencoe, IL: The Free Press, 1950).

Urban Ecology

Sociologists concerned with the qualities of urban life have an interest in **urban ecology**, *study of the link between the physical and social dimensions of cities.* Chapter 3 ("Culture") discussed cultural ecology as the study of how cultural patterns are related to the physical environment. Urban ecology is an application of this approach; it shows that cities are both physical and social realities and that the two aspects may be related.

One issue is why cities are located where they are. The first cities, developed by agrarian societies, were established in fertile regions. Preindustrial societies con-

cerned with defense also built their cities on mountains or used the natural environment in other ways for self-protection. Athens is situated on an outcropping of rock; Paris and Mexico City were established on islands. After the Industrial Revolution, the unparalleled importance of economics fueled urban growth near rivers and natural harbors that facilitated trade.

A second issue studied by urban ecologists is the physical design of cities. They have developed several models explaining urban form.

The concentric zone model. In 1925 Ernest W. Burgess, a student and colleague of Robert Park, suggested that land use in Chicago and several other American cities generated a series of concentric zones. City centers, Burgess observed, are central business districts, which spill into a ring of factories. Beyond this commercial activity lie residential rings that become more expensive with greater distance from the noise and pollution of the city's center.

The sector model. Homer Hoyt (1939) investigated a greater number of cities and expanded the scope of Burgess's research. Hoyt noted that distinctive districts often form wedge-shaped sectors. For example, one fashionable area may be built next to another, or development may grow outward along a train or trolley line. Neighborhoods with specific geographic traits may also grow in the shape of sectors. For example, wealthy San Franciscans built their homes up the sides of Nob Hill, prizing its breathtaking views of San Francisco Bay.

The multiple-nuclei model. Chauncy Harris and Edward Ullman (1945) added that as cities began to decentralize, many centers of business and manufacturing emerged.

There are two major reasons that specific activities are spread across the city. First, some may be antagonistic to others. Few people wish to live close to industrial areas, for example, and owners of fashionable retail shops usually want to distance themselves from pornography and vice areas such as Boston's Combat Zone. Thus the complexity and diversity of urban life yields a mosaic of distinctive districts. Second, a city's outer fringe is often less expensive than the central area. Industry usually prefers outlying industrial parks to older, congested inner cities. Similarly, as people are drawn to lower-cost land in the suburbs, retail businesses follow them and create shopping malls miles from downtown.

Social area analysis. Social area analysis seeks to understand what people in specific neighborhoods have in common. Research in industrial cities in the United States and elsewhere has identified three significant organizing factors: family type, based on marital status and family size; social standing, based on income and prestige; and race and ethnicity (Shevky & Bell, 1955; Johnston, 1976).

These factors have been found to explain a great deal about neighborhoods. Families with children gravitate to areas offering large apartments or single-family homes and good schools. The rich generally seek high-prestige neighborhoods away from low-income people—sometimes in exclusive central-city areas. People with a common cultural heritage tend to cluster together.

The poor and some minorities, whose choices are limited, also live in distinct areas.

An integrated analysis. Each of these models provides partial understanding of the city. In an effort to integrate them all, Brian Berry and Philip Rees (1969) argue that each factor influences urban land use in a particular way. In accordance with Burgess's theory, distinctive types of families would disperse population in concentric zones, provided there were no other influences. Families with few children tend toward the city's center, while those with more children live farther away. Differences of social standing generate the sector-shaped districts described by Hoyt; that is, the rich or the poor often occupy one "side" of the city. Racial and ethnic groups cluster together at various points throughout the city, in support of Harris and Ullman's multiple-nuclei model and the findings of social area analysis.

Critical evaluation. Urban ecology, almost a century old, has succeeded in linking physical and social dimensions of urban life, but, as ecologists themselves concede, it provides an idealized picture of city life. Urban ecology has also minimized the extent to which urban development is guided by power elites rather than by the decisions of countless "average" people (Molotch, 1976; Feagin, 1983). Another problem is that urban ecologists studied American cities during a limited historical period. Preindustrial towns differ from industrial cities in critical ways, just as socialist cities vary from their capitalist counterparts. No single model is likely to account for the full range of urban diversity.

Third-World Urbanization

Twice in human history the world has experienced a revolutionary expansion of cities. The first urban revolution began about 8000 B.C.E. as the first cities emerged and spanned thousands of years as urban settlements appeared on different continents. The second urban revolution lasted for two centuries after 1750 as the Industrial Revolution sparked rapid growth of cities in Europe and North America.

A third urban revolution began about 1950, but not within the industrial societies of the world, where 75 percent of people already are city dwellers. Extraordinary urban growth is now occurring in the Third World, where only about 40 percent of the people live in cities. In 1950, about 25 percent of the Third-World population inhabited cities; by 2000, half are expected to be urbanites. In 1950, there were only seven cities in the world with a population over 5 million, and only two of these were in the Third World. By 1985, twenty-six cities had more than 5 million residents, and eighteen were in the Third World (Fornos, 1986). By the end of this century, there will probably be Third-World cities that dwarf all but a few of the cities in industrialized societies.

Table 21–6 compares the world's ten largest urban areas in 1981—cities and their densely populated surroundings—and gives estimates for the year 2000. In 1981, six of ten were in industrialized societies, three of these in the United States. By the beginning of the next century, however, only four of the top ten will be situated in industrialized societies: two in Japan, one in South Korea, and only one in the United States. Most will be in less economically developed societies of the Third World. These urban areas not only will be the world's largest, they will contain an unprecedented number of inhabitants. Relatively rich societies such as Japan may have the resources to provide for urban settlements approaching 30 million people, but this may not be true for less-developed societies such as Mexico and Brazil.

Causes of Third-World Urban Growth

To understand this third urban revolution, recall that many nonindustrial societies are now entering the high-growth stage of demographic transition. Declining death rates caused by improved technology have resulted in a population explosion in Latin America, Africa, and Asia. For urban areas, the rate of growth is *twice* as high because millions of people have been migrating from the countryside in search of a higher standard of living: jobs, health care, education, and conveniences such as running water and electricity. Additionally, the seizure of land by elites sometimes forces peasants to migrate to cities (London, 1987).

Cities do offer more opportunities than rural areas, but they provide no panacea for the massive problems generated by an escalating population and poverty. Many Third-World cities are simply unable to meet the needs of much of their population. Mexico City, described at the beginning of this chapter, receives thousands of rural people every day, although more than 10 percent of *current* residents have no running water in their homes, 15 percent lack sewage facilities, half the trash and garbage produced each day cannot be processed, and exhaust from factories and cars chokes everyone, rich and poor alike (Friedrich, 1984). As is true of other major cities throughout Latin America, Africa, and Asia, Mexico City is surrounded by wretched shantytowns—settlements of makeshift homes built from discarded materials. As was noted in Chapter 11 ("Global Inequality"), city dumps are home to thousands of poor, who pick through the waste hoping to find enough to ensure their survival for another day.

The Future of Third-World Cities

The problems now facing Third-World cities seem to defy solution, and the end of this remarkable urban growth is nowhere in sight. What hope is there of relieving the plight of people in these emerging megacities?

Table 21–6 THE WORLD'S TEN LARGEST URBAN AREAS, 1981 and 2000

1981

Urban Area	Population (in millions)
New York, U.S.	16.5
Tokyo–Yokohama, Japan	14.4
Mexico City, Mexico	14.0
Los Angeles–Long Beach, U.S.	10.6
Shanghai, China	10.0
Buenos Aires, Argentina	9.7
Paris, France	8.5
Moscow, U.S.S.R.	8.0
Beijing, China	8.0
Chicago, U.S.	7.7

2000

Urban Area	Population (in millions)
Tokyo–Yokohama, Japan	30.0
Mexico City, Mexico	27.9
São Paulo, Brazil	25.4
Seoul, South Korea	22.0
Bombay, India	15.4
New York, U.S.	14.7
Osaka-Kobe-Kyoto, Japan	14.3
Tehran, Iran	14.3
Rio de Janeiro, Brazil	14.2
Calcutta, India	14.1

SOURCE: 1981 data from various reports of the United Nations; 2000 data from U.S. Bureau of the Census, *World Population Profile: 1989* (Washington, DC: Government Printing Office, 1989), Table 15, pp. 83–84.

Many Third-World cities provide striking social contrasts: Rio de Janeiro is both a playground for the world's rich and home to millions who are desperately poor. Perhaps not surprisingly, in recent years this city has experienced a rapid rise in crime, much of it directed at affluent tourists.

Earlier chapters have suggested two different answers to this question. One view, linked with modernization theory, holds that as the Third World undergoes industrialization (as Western Europe and North America did two centuries ago), greater productivity will raise living standards and population growth will ease. A second view, associated with underdevelopment theory, argues that such progress is unlikely as long as Third-World societies remain economically dependent on rich societies.

Urbanist Jane Jacobs (1984), combining elements of each approach, thinks that expanding trade may solve these problems, but only if Third-World nations break trading ties with rich societies and build trading networks among themselves. Then their economies can move beyond providing only raw materials and inexpensive labor to wealthy corporate interests in rich societies.

Jacobs's argument remains controversial. Some warn that contact with rich societies is necessary for obtaining much-needed technology. Others assert that even breaking these ties would not resolve the growing crisis of Third-World cities: what is needed is revolutionary redistribution of the wealth that is now controlled by a small segment of the population (Gilbert & Gugler, 1983). Whatever the course of events, the drama of overpopulation in the Third World will be played out in the cities.

The Historical Importance of Cities

Historically, Americans have been ambivalent about urban life. Thomas Jefferson, as he assumed the presidency in 1800, described the city as a "pestilence to the morals, the health and the liberties of man" (cited in Glaab, 1963:52). Almost a century later Rudyard Kipling echoed those sentiments upon visiting Chicago: "Having seen it, I urgently desire never to see it again. It is inhabited by savages" (cited in Rokove, 1975:22). Other Americans have disagreed, siding with the ancient Greeks, who viewed cities as the only places where humans can find the "good life."

Why do cities provoke such spirited and divergent reactions? Probably the answer lies in their ability to encapsulate and intensify human culture. Cities have been the setting for some of the greatest human virtues (the cultural developments of classical Athens) as well as the greatest human failings (the militarism and violence of classical Rome). For over 350 years, American society has urbanized as people have sought a better way of life, but ironically, many social problems—poverty, crime, racial tensions, environmental pollution—are most serious in cities. In short, the city is an intricate weave of noble accomplishments and wretched shortcomings.

As we approach the twenty-first century, the greatest test of urban living will occur in societies of the Third World. Mexico City, Sao Paulo, and Bombay will contain almost unimaginable numbers of people. Throughout history, the city has been the most effective means of improving people's standard of living. The question is whether cities in poor societies will be able to meet the needs of their vastly larger and poorer populations in the next century. The answer is likely to affect all our lives.

SUMMARY

1. Fertility and mortality, measured as crude birth rates and crude death rates, are major components of population growth. In global terms, fertility, mortality, and population growth in North America are relatively low.

2. Migration, another key demographic concept, has special importance to the historical growth of cities.

3. Age–sex pyramids allow demographers to describe the composition of a population and to project future population patterns.

4. Historically, world population grew slowly because high birth rates were largely offset by high death rates. In about 1750, however, a demographic transition began as world population rose sharply, mostly as a result of declining death rates.

5. Malthus claimed that population would grow faster than food supplies, with the eventual result being social calamity. Contrary to Malthus's ominous predictions, demographic transition theory holds that technological advance brings gradually declining birth rates. This phenomenon has occurred in industrialized societies, where population growth is now low. In the Third World, however, declining death rates coupled with continued high birth rates are swelling population to unprecedented levels.

6. Research has shown that lowering birth rates and improving economic productivity in the Third World are closely linked to improving the social position of women.

7. World population is expected to reach 8 billion by the year 2025. If this occurs, social problems related to poverty may overwhelm Third-World societies, where population growth is now greatest.

8. Closely related to population growth is urbanization. The first urban revolution began with the appearance of cities after 8000 B.C.E.; by the start of the common era, cities had emerged in every region of the world.

9. While members of nonurban societies must continually search for food, city dwellers engage in a wide range of productive specialization.

10. Preindustrial cities are characterized by small buildings and narrow, winding streets, personal social ties, and rigid patterns of social inequality.

11. A second urban revolution began about 1750 as the Industrial Revolution caused rapid urban growth in Europe. Cities adopted wide, regular streets and social anonymity increased.

12. Urbanism came to North America with European settlers. From a string of colonial towns dotting the Atlantic coastline, by 1850 hundreds of new cities were founded from coast to coast.

13. By 1920 a majority of Americans lived in urban places, and several metropolises contained millions of inhabitants.

14. Since 1950 American cities have decentralized. The growth of the suburbs is one trait of the postindustrial city. Newer, rapidly growing Sunbelt cities are geographically larger than older, Snowbelt cities.

15. This decentralization has generated vast urban areas that the Census Bureau terms metropolitan statistical areas (MSAs), and even larger consolidated metropolitan statistical areas (CMSAs). As these urban areas expand, they may form a megalopolis—a vast urban sprawl.

16. Rapid urbanization in Europe during the nineteenth century led early sociologists to contrast rural and urban life. Ferdinand Toennies built an analysis upon the concepts of *gemeinshaft* and *gesellschaft*; Georg Simmel claimed that overstimulation produced a blasé attitude in urbanites.

17. At the University of Chicago, Robert Park saw

cities as permitting greater social freedom. Louis Wirth suggested that the size, density, and social heterogeneity of cities generated a way of life characterized by impersonality, self-interest, and tolerance.

18. Urban ecology studies the interplay of the physical and social environment of the city. The concentric zone, sector, multiple-nuclei, and social area models have advanced understanding of urban form.

19. A third urban revolution is now occurring within the Third World, where most of the world's largest urban areas will soon be found.

KEY CONCEPTS

age–sex pyramid a graphic representation of the age and sex of a population

crude birth rate the number of live births in a given year for every thousand people in a population

crude death rate the number of deaths in a given year for every thousand people in a population

demographic transition theory the thesis that population patterns are linked to a society's level of technological development

demography the study of human population

fertility the incidence of childbearing in a society's population

gemeinschaft a type of social organization with strong solidarity based on tradition and predominantly personal relationships

gesellschaft a type of social organization with weak solidarity resulting from cultural pluralism and impersonal social relationships

infant mortality rate the number of deaths within the first year of life for each thousand live births in a given year

life expectancy how long a person, on the average, can expect to live

megalopolis a vast urban region containing a number of cities and their surrounding suburbs

metropolis a very large city that socially and economically dominates an urban area

migration the movement of people into and out of a specified territory

mortality the incidence of death in a society's population

sex ratio the number of males for every hundred females in a given population

suburbs the urban area beyond the political boundaries of a city

urban ecology study of the link between the physical and social dimensions of cities

urbanization the concentration of humanity into cities

urban renewal governmental programs intended to revitalize cities

zero population growth the level of reproduction that maintains population at a steady state

---

SUGGESTED READINGS

This text provides detailed discussion of various demographic topics.

John R. Weeks. *Population: An Introduction to Concepts and Issues.* 4th ed. Belmont, CA: Wadsworth, 1989.

These two books by noted population experts describe the current state of world population and offer straightforward suggestions about how to limit population increase.

Rafael M. Salas. *Reflections on Population.* New York: Pergamon Press, 1984.

Werner Fornos. *Gaining People, Losing Ground: A Blue-*

print for Stabilizing World Population. Washington, DC: The Population Institute, 1986.

A textbook that provides a historical and contemporary analysis of cities in North America and throughout the world is this:

James L. Spates and John J. Macionis. *The Sociology of Cities.* 2nd ed. Belmont, CA: Wadsworth, 1987.

This paperback examines the nature of community in today's world and considers how sociologists study community life.

Larry Lyon. *The Community in Urban Society.* Chicago: Dorsey, 1987.

The central role of wealth and power in the growth and decline of American cities is the focus of this paperback.

Joe R. Feagin and Robert Parker. *Building American Cities: The Urban Real Estate Game*. 2nd ed. Englewood Cliffs, NJ: Prentice Hall, 1990.

This classic, although a quite long account of urban history, emphasizes how cities are shaped by historical and cultural forces.

Lewis Mumford. *The City in History*. New York: Harcourt, Brace and World, 1961.

The twenty-one essays in this book focus on Middle-Eastern cities, including Cairo, Beirut, and Jerusalem.

Abdulaziz Y. Saqqaf, ed. *The Middle East City: Ancient Traditions Confront a Modern World*. New York: Paragon House, 1987.

This collection of essays investigates the role of cities in a world becoming increasingly linked.

Richard V. Knight and Gary Gappert, eds. *Cities in a Global Society*. Newbury Park, CA: Sage, 1989.

The policies of the Reagan administration had a significant effect on America's cities during the 1980s. The following collection of essays draws on a wide range of material to examine this impact.

George E. Peterson and Carol W. Lewis, eds. *Reagan and the Cities*. Washington, DC: Urban Institute Press, 1986.

Sixteen years of walking the streets and observing how people use cities has informed this account of how to make urban places more livable.

William H. Whyte. *City: Rediscovering the Center*. New York: Doubleday, 1988.

This book examines the "female city" that has often been neglected by urban historians, with a focus on the lives of women in early New York.

Christine Stansell. *City of Women: Sex and Class in New York, 1789–1860*. New York: Knopf, 1987.

This Marxist-based analysis of cities explores the urban consequences of capitalism.

John R. Logan and Harvey L. Molotch. *Urban Fortunes: The Political Economy of Place*. Berkeley: University of California Press, 1987.

Since narrowly avoiding bankruptcy in 1975, America's leading city has continued to grapple with problems.

Herbert London. *The Broken Apple: New York City in the 1980s*. New Brunswick, NJ: Transaction Books, 1989.

This book by a well-known historian sketches the history of suburban growth in the United States.

Kenneth T. Jackson. *Crabgrass Frontier: The Suburbanization of the United States*. New York: Oxford University Press, 1985.

This case study of Detroit reveals the effects of social inequality on urban life.

Joe T. Darden, Richard Child Hill, June Thomas, and Richard Thomas. *Detroit Race and Uneven Development*. Philadelphia: Temple University Press, 1987.

This resource offers data and analysis of American housing.

Joint Center for Housing Studies. *The State of the Nation's Housing 1989*. Cambridge: Harvard University Press, 1989.

22

Collective Behavior and Social Movements

On February 1, 1990, four hungry men walked into Woolworth's in Greensboro, North Carolina. They were greeted as celebrities, and their breakfast of eggs, grits, bacon, and coffee served by a smiling waitress was news around the world.

Why? Thirty years earlier to the day, the same four—then college students—had sat at the same lunch counter and requested a meal from the same waitress. She refused to serve them because they were black and unwelcome in the segregated Greensboro Woolworth. The four young men had sat nervously, ignored by her but closely observed by a white police officer who periodically slapped his billy club into his bare hand. After one hour, they peacefully left. Their courageous action ignited the civil rights movement across the United States, helping to end legal segregation.

Social change often occurs because people engage in organized and controversial action. A major focus of this chapter is **social movements,** *organized activity that encourages or discourages social change.* Social movements are perhaps the most important type of **collective behavior,** *relatively spontaneous activity involving a large number of people that does not conform to established norms.* Other forms of collective behavior—each involving controversy and some provoking change—are fashions and fads, riots, crowds, mass hysteria, and public opinion. This chapter surveys various topics within the broad field of collective behavior. It then focuses on social movements, such as the women's movement in the United States and the democratic movements that recently swept Eastern Europe.

COLLECTIVE BEHAVIOR

Early American sociologists paid great attention to collective behavior until midcentury, when more established social patterns took center stage. In other words, because collective behavior focused on actions generally classified as unusual or deviant, this area of inquiry received less attention than social stratification and family life. In

the tumultuous 1960s, numerous social movements renewed sociological interest in the various types of collective behavior (Weller & Quarantelli, 1973; G. Marx & Wood, 1975; Aguirre & Quarantelli, 1983; Turner & Killian, 1987; McAdam, McCarthy, & Zald, 1988).

Studying Collective Behavior

Collective behavior presents several significant difficulties for the researcher. First, the concept of collective behavior is *broad*. It embraces a bewildering array of social phenomena; it is not immediately obvious, for example, what traits these fads, rumors, and mob behavior have in common. Each distinctive activity also has quite different consequences for social change. Rumors may disrupt the life of a small town, clothing fads may challenge conventional standards of appearance, and mob behavior can result in loss of life and property as people confront each other or the law.

A second difficulty is that collective behavior is *complex*. A rumor seems to come out of nowhere and circulates in countless different settings. For no apparent reason, one new form of clothing "catches on" while another does not. Similarly, why would baseball fans suddenly erupt into a near-riot at Cincinnati's Riverfront Stadium in 1988 after a quite common event: manager Pete Rose becoming involved in a heated argument with an umpire.

Third, collective behavior is often *transitory*. Sociologists have extensively studied the family because it is an established and enduring element of social life.

Fashions, rumors, and riots, in contrast, tend to arise and dissipate quickly, so they are difficult to study systematically.

Some researchers maintain that these problems apply to most of the issues sociologists study. Benigno Aguirre and E. L. Quarantelli (1983) argue that all social behavior is complex and changing. Moreover, sociologists may easily anticipate some kinds of collective behavior, such as crowds at sports events, music festivals, or protest marches, and can study them through videotapes as well as first-hand observations. Even natural disasters can be anticipated by researchers who study human response to such events. For example, statistical data indicate that forty to eighty major tornadoes occur each year; sociologists simply must be prepared to initiate research on short notice (Miller, 1985). Researchers may also use historical documents to reconstruct the details of an unanticipated natural disaster or riot.

A more serious problem, Aguirre and Quarantelli maintain, is limited theoretical analysis linking the diverse actions termed collective behavior. To clarify our focus, we can state that all collective behavior involves the action of a **collectivity,** *a large number of people who interact little if at all in the absence of well-defined and conventional norms.* In *localized collectivities,* people are in physical proximity to one another, as in crowds and riots. In *dispersed collectivities,* people influence one another often over great distances; examples are rumors, public opinion, and fashion (Turner & Killian, 1987). Sociologists distinguish these collectivities from social groups (see Chapter 7, "Groups and Organizations"), on the basis of three characteristics:

In 1989, tens of thousands of people linked hands across Estonia, Latvia, and Lithuania—Baltic republics within the Soviet Union—as a demonstration of their desire for national independence. This human chain, stretching 360 miles, provides a good example of a collectivity: people with limited social interaction, unsure of who other participants are, and unclear about precisely how they should act.

1. **Limited social interaction.** Members of groups interact directly, frequently over a considerable period. Localized collectivities such as mobs involve limited and temporary interaction, while people participating in a dispersed collectivity such as a fad may not interact at all.

2. **Unclear social boundaries.** It is generally clear who is and who is not a member of a social group. People engaged in collective behavior, in contrast, usually lack a sense of membership. Localized crowds may share an interest (such as watching a despondent person standing on a ledge high above the street) but exhibit little sense of social unity. Those involved in dispersed collectivities, such as a part of the public having the same opinion on some social issue, have even less sense of shared membership. Social movements are often an exception: people with pro-life or pro-choice views, for instance, generally form well-defined political factions.

3. **Weak and unconventional norms.** Conventional cultural norms usually regulate group behavior. A new group, such as a college debating club, probably will adopt the norms that other such groups observe. Some collectivities operate according to established social norms, such as people traveling on the same airliner, but they usually form and disband without developing much social structure. Other collectivities—such as emotional soccer fans who destroy property as they leave a stadium—rather spontaneously develop decidedly unconventional norms (Weller & Quarantelli, 1973; Turner & Killian, 1987).

Crowds

An important concept in the study of collective behavior is the **crowd,** *a temporary gathering of people who share a common focus of attention and whose members influence one another.* Historian Peter Laslett (1984) claims that in medieval Europe a crowd of 25,000 would have formed only when major armies marched into combat. Crowds of this size are routine in large, industrial societies, and are found at football stadiums and even registration halls of large universities.

Herbert Blumer (1969) has identified four types of crowds, partly on the basis of level of emotional intensity.

A *casual crowd* is a loose collection of people who interact little, if at all. People gathered on the beach or observing an automobile accident from a street corner have only a passing awareness of one another. Few social patterns are typical of casual crowds beyond the momentary sharing of an interest.

A *conventional crowd* is the result of deliberate planning of an event, such as an auction, a lecture, or a funeral. Any interaction is likely to conform to conventional norms appropriate to the situation. For example, people bid against one another at an auction according to established rules.

An *expressive crowd* forms around an event that has emotional appeal, such as a religious revival, a wrestling match, or the New Year's Eve celebration in New York's Times Square. People join expressive crowds to share in the excitement caused by the event. This focus on emotional release makes expressive crowds relatively spontaneous. The emotional energy they generate is often exhilarating.

An *acting crowd* is energetically doing something, possibly rushing into a concert hall as the doors are opened or fleeing from a building that is on fire. Acting crowds are often united by emotions even more powerful than those typical of expressive crowds, sometimes reaching feverish intensity that provokes participants to mob violence. In 1985, for example, 60,000 soccer fans assembled in a stadium near Brussels, Belgium, to watch the European Cup Finals between Italy and Great Britain. About forty-five minutes before the start of the game, British fans, many of them reportedly intoxicated, began to taunt Italians sitting beyond a fence in the adjacent section. Next the two sides threw bottles and rocks at each other, until suddenly the British surged toward the Italians, tearing down the fence in a human wave. As an estimated 400 million television viewers watched in horror, a rampaging mob trampled hundreds of helpless spectators. Within minutes, thirty-eight people were dead and another four hundred injured (Lacayo, 1985).

This example illustrates how a crowd can change from one type to another as emotions rise. Sports spectators are typically a conventional crowd, whose activity is limited to cheering and booing and who interact little with one another. In this situation, however, a conventional crowd became an expressive crowd and, provoked by a dramatic event such as name calling, was transformed into an acting crowd on a rampage.

Deliberate action by a crowd is not the product of only rising emotions. Participants in *protest crowds*— a fifth category that can be added to Blumer's list— engage in a variety of actions, such as strikes, boycotts, sit-ins, and protest marches, that have some political goal (McPhail & Wohlstein, 1983). For example, in the middle of a bitter strike in 1986, Hormel meat-packing workers from more than a dozen states marched through the streets of Austin, Minnesota, to protest what they contended were unfair practices by the company. Facing financial problems, Hormel had attempted to cut wages and benefits, and the workers decided to challenge this policy publicly.

Protest crowds vary in their emotional energy, sometimes resembling conventional crowds and other times, acting crowds. For example, many public demonstrations during the civil rights movement in the 1950s and 1960s were peaceful, yet sometimes in response to aggressive police tactics a protest was recast into a violent confrontation.

Mobs and Riots

An acting crowd that becomes violent is termed a **mob,** *a highly emotional crowd in common pursuit of some violent or destructive goal.* Despite, or perhaps because of, their intense emotion, mobs tend to dissipate quickly. The duration of mob behavior partly depends on whether its leadership raises or lowers the emotional intensity of the crowd, and on the mob's objectives.

Lynching is one of the most notorious examples of mob behavior in the United States. The term "lynch" is derived from Charles Lynch, a Virginia colonist who sought to maintain law and order in his own way before formal courts were established. The word soon became synonymous with terrorism and murder outside the legal system.

After the Civil War, freed slaves gained political rights and economic opportunities, posing a threat to many whites who had previously controlled them. Especially in the South, the effort to maintain white domination sparked formation of lynch mobs, which became a highly effective form of social control. Blacks who questioned white superiority, or were even suspected of doing so, were somtimes hanged and even burned alive by vengeful whites. These blacks and occasionally their white defenders became all-purpose scapegoats.

Lynch mobs—many of which were composed of low-status whites most threatened by black emancipation—were at a peak between 1880 and 1930: during this period about 5,000 lynchings were recorded by police. Most occurred in the Deep South, where an agrarian economy still depended on a cheap and docile black labor force, but lynchings took place in virtually every state and victimized every minority. For example, on

Jacob Lawrence, *The Migration of the Negro.* #50. "Race riots were very numerous all over the North because of the antagonism that was caused between the Negro and the white workers. Many of these riots occurred because the Negro was used as a strike breaker in many of the Northern industries." (1940–41)

(Tempera on gesso on composition board, 18 x 12". Collection, The Museum of Modern Art, New York. Gift of Mrs. David M. Levy)

the western frontier, lynch mobs frequently targeted Mexican and Asian Americans. In about 25 percent of the cases, whites lynched other whites. The lynching of women, however, was rare; only about a hundred such cases are known, and almost all involved black women (White, 1969, orig. 1929; Grant, 1975).

A violent crowd without any particular purpose is a **riot,** *a highly emotional and undirected eruption* *involving violence and destruction.* Unlike a mob action, a riot usually has no clear goal. Sometimes an apparently minor incident will trigger a riot in which long-standing anger is vented (Smelser, 1962). Rioters may then indulge in seemingly random violence against property or persons. Whereas a mob action usually ends when a specific violent goal has been achieved (or decisively prevented), a riot tends to disperse only when participants run out of steam or community leaders or police gradually bring them under control.

Throughout American history, riots have resulted from a collective expression of social injustice. Industrial workers, for example, have rioted in outrage at their working conditions. In 1886 a bitter struggle by Chicago factory workers for an eight-hour workday led to the explosive Haymarket Riot, which left eleven dead and scores injured. Rioting born of anger and despair has also been commonplace within the American penal system. In 1987 allegedly unfair treatment by the federal government sparked rioting among Cuban prisoners in Georgia and Louisiana detention centers. Throughout American history, race riots have occurred with striking regularity. Early in this century, crowds of whites attacked blacks in Chicago, Detroit, and other cities. In Los Angeles in the summer of 1965 an especially destructive riot broke out after alleged police brutality during the arrest of a black man for drunken driving. Five days of turmoil resulted in thirty-four deaths, hundreds of injuries, thousands of arrests, and millions of dollars' worth of property damage. During the summers of the late 1960s, and sporadically since, riots have rocked the black ghettos of many American cities as seemingly trivial events triggered violent anger at continuing prejudice and discrimination.

Riots can also result from positive feelings, such as the high spirits characteristic of young people who flock to resort areas during college spring break. In March 1986, for example, the exuberance of vacationing students in Palm Springs, California, erupted into a riot leading to a hundred arrests after crowds of young men began throwing rocks and bottles at passing cars and stripping the clothing off terrified women (DeMott, 1986).

Contagion Theory

Why do crowds often behave unconventionally? Social scientists have developed several different theories over the last century. One of the first, by French sociologist Gustave Le Bon (1841–1931), is *contagion theory.* Le

Bon (1960, orig. 1895) maintained that crowds can exert a hypnotic influence on their members. In the anonymity of a crowd, he claimed, people lose their individual identities and surrender personal will and responsibility to a collective mind. As a crowd assumes a life of its own, individual members slip their social restraints and become irrational automatons driven by contagious emotion. As fear or hate resonates within a crowd, emotional intensity builds, hypnotizing individuals toward a single-minded outburst of unrestrained action. The predictable result, Le Bon concluded, is destructive violence.

Critical evaluation. Le Bon's assertions that crowds are anonymous, suggestible, and emotional appear to be largely true. Yet there is little support for the idea that a crowd takes on a life of its own, separate from the thoughts and intentions of members. For example, Norris Johnson (1987), investigating the 1979 tragedy at The Who concert in Cincinnati, where eleven people died, identified several factors that contributed to the riot, such as an inadequate number of entrance doors, an open-seating policy, and too little police supervision. The crowd, he claimed, was actually composed of many small groups in which people valiantly attempted to help one another.

Convergence Theory

Convergence theory claims that the motives that drive collective action do not originate within a crowd but precede its formation. Like-minded individuals converge to form a crowd because of some common attitude or interest. In 1985 a crowd of whites in southwest Philadelphia formed for the purpose of evicting a black couple from their neighborhood. After the couple fled to safety, the crowd burned their home. In this and similar cases, convergence theory contends, the specific crowd itself did not generate the hostility and violence; rather, racial hostility had long been harbored by many local whites. This particular crowd is better understood as the convergence of people who shared an attachment to their traditionally white neighborhood, who opposed the presence of black residents, and who already had a propensity for violent action.

Critical evaluation. The value of convergence theory lies in linking crowds to broader social forces operating in a specific setting. Thus crowd behavior is not irrational, as Le Bon maintained, but the result of members' rational decision making (Berk, 1974).

Participation in a crowd, however, may encourage people to engage in behavior that normally would be restrained by social norms. Moreover, crowds intensify any sentiments simply by creating a critical mass of like-minded people.

Emergent-Norm Theory

Ralph Turner and Lewis Killian (1987) have developed an *emergent-norm theory* of crowd dynamics. While they concede that crowds may not be entirely predictable, they argue that crowds are not the irrational collectivity described by Le Bon. Similar interests may draw people to a particular crowd, but patterns of behavior emerge within the crowd itself.

Turner and Killian maintain that crowds begin as collectivities of people with mixed interests and motives. In conventional and casual crowds, members understand in advance the norms that guide behavior. The norms that steer less stable types of crowds—expressive, acting, and protest crowds—frequently emerge only within particular settings. Usually a few leaders initiate such emergent norms. For example, one member of the crowd at a rock concert holds up a lit cigarette lighter to signal praise for the performers, and others follow suit; or a few people in an angry street crowd throw bricks through store windows, and a riot ensues. In the infamous New Bedford, Massachusetts, tavern rape in 1983, a man initially assaulted a twenty-one-year-old woman who had entered the bar to buy cigarettes, then raped her on the floor. For about an hour and a half, five other men repeatedly raped the woman. Many others in the bar cheered these men on; apparently either these bystanders came to accept this brutality as normal, or they were too intimidated to voice opposition. No one in the bar responded in the conventional way by calling the police (*Time*, March 5, 1984).

Critical evaluation. Emergent-norm theory represents a symbolic-interaction approach to crowd dynamics. Turner and Killian explain that crowd behavior is not as chaotic and irrational as contagion theory suggests, nor as purposeful and rational as convergence theory implies. Crowd behavior, then, is in response to its members' motives but is often guided by norms that emerge as a situation unfolds. Thus, decision making plays a significant role in crowd behavior, although it may not be evident to casual observers. For example, frightened people clogging the exits of a burning theater may appear to be victims of irrational panic, but fleeing from a life-threatening situation can also be viewed as a rational alternative to death (1972:10). Precisely how people go

about fleeing, of course, is partly a matter of experience and common sense and partly a matter of following the direction of leaders on the scene.

Although a crowd may generate pressure toward conformity, emergent-norm theory suggests that not every participant accepts the emerging norms. Some assume leadership roles, others become their lieutenants or rank-and-file followers, and still others remain relatively inactive bystanders (Weller & Quarantelli, 1973; Zurcher & Snow, 1981).

Crowds, Politics, and Social Change

In March 1770 a crowd of Boston citizens, angry at British domination, confronted an English soldier. The soldier, in panic, called for reinforcements. The ensuing clash, which has become known as the Boston Massacre, resulted in the death of five Bostonians, as well as greatly increased support for American independence. Three years later, in angry reaction to British taxation policy, another crowd of Bostonians gathered to protest these measures. Soon afterward, some of them dressed up as Indians and dumped tea from British commercial ships into Boston harbor, an event soon dubbed the Boston Tea Party (Kelley, 1982). The British and their colonial supporters deplored these examples of "mob action," but to the colonists, the participants were patriots who were opposing injustice and thereby paving the way for a new, more democratic society.

Because crowds are linked to social change, they have often sparked controversy. Defenders of the established social order have long feared and hated them. Gustave Le Bon's negative view of crowds as "only powerful for destruction" was common among members of the aristocracy (1960:18; orig. 1895). But what some viewed as destructive, the less privileged regarded as beneficial. Those unsympathetic to the political aims of crowds generally condemn what they see as mob behavior and rioting in defiance of law and order. In contrast, those who approve of their political aims support such collective action as a public protest against a flawed system.

Crowds have long played a crucial role in both creating and opposing social change. Throngs of Romans rallying to the Sermon on the Mount by Jesus of Nazareth, bands of traditional weavers destroying new industrial machinery that was making their skills obsolete, thousands of marchers carrying banners and shouting slogans for or against abortion—these and countless other

The prodemocracy movement in the People's Republic of China in the spring of 1989 involved tens of thousands of people seeking a greater voice in their government. Were the participants patriots, as many Western news accounts suggested, or unruly hooligans, as Chinese leaders maintained? The answer is inevitably a matter of value judgments.

instances across the centuries show that crowds have been an important means through which people challenge or support their society (Rude, 1964; Canetti, 1978).

Rumor and Gossip

Collective behavior is not limited to people in physical proximity. Sociologists use the term **mass behavior** to refer to *collective behavior among people dispersed over a wide geographical area*. A common example of mass behavior is rumor.

Rumor is *unsubstantiated information spread informally, often by word of mouth*. Rumors have always been an element of social life, but the means of transmitting them have changed dramatically in the last century. Historically, rumor was spread through face-to-face communication. Although this is still frequently the case, in industrial societies telephones, computers, and the mass media have allowed rumors to be transmitted more rapidly to a greater number of people.

Rumor has three essential characteristics.

1. **Rumor thrives in a climate of ambiguity.** Rumor grows when people are deprived of definitive information about some topic of interest. For example, if people are suspicious of official authorities, ru-

mors are likely to challenge official information. Rumor, then, is an effort to define reality in a particular way in the absence of substantiated facts (Shibutani, 1966; Rosnow & Fine, 1976).

2. **Rumor is changeable.** As a rumor circulates, it is altered so that variations of the accounts add to the confusion. Which details change depends largely on the interests of those involved. For example, if a rumor is circulating concerning a confrontation between striking union members and police, people sympathetic to the union will probably place more responsibility for any violence on the police and less on the strikers.

3. **Rumor is typically difficult to stop.** The number of people who have heard the rumor increases its geometric progression as each person spreads the information to several others. Some rumors dissipate with time, others persist for years. Only clear, substantiated information that is widely disseminated is likely to stop a rumor. Even then, some may doubt such "factual" information.

Rumor can trigger the formation of crowds or other collective behavior. For this reason, authorities often establish rumor-control centers in times of crisis as a form of information management. Yet rumors may persist for years despite incontrovertible contrary evidence; the box on page 596 provides one notable example.

Closely related to rumor is **gossip**, *rumor about the personal affairs of others*. As Charles Horton Cooley (1962, orig. 1909) points out, while rumor involves issues or events of interest to a large segment of the public, gossip interests only those possessing some personal knowledge of the people being talked about. Gossip, then, is localized, while rumors may spread throughout a society.

Gossip can be an effective means of social control as its targets become aware that they are the subject of praise or scorn. People may also gossip about others to elevate their own standing as "insiders" in a social group. However, because gossiping is frequently viewed as disreputable, those who pass it on may be discredited as well.

Public Opinion

One form of highly dispersed collective behavior is public opinion, which is defined in Chapter 5 ("Socialization") as widespread attitudes toward one or more controversial

The Rumored Death of Beatle Paul McCartney

The Beatles—John Lennon, Paul McCartney, George Harrison, and Ringo Starr—were probably the most celebrated rock band in the world until their breakup in 1970. Their fame spawned a rumor that circulated over much of the world: McCartney's alleged death.

First heard in 1967, this rumor spread rapidly in 1969 after a Detroit radio station announced several curious "facts":

1. The phrase "Number 9, Number 9, Number 9" from the song "Revolution No. 9" on the Beatles' *White Album* seems to intone, "Turn me on, dead man!" when played backward.

2. At the end of the song "Strawberry Fields Forever" on the *Magical Mystery Tour* album, if background noise is filtered out, the listener hears a voice saying, "I buried Paul!"

3. In a picture inside *Magical Mystery Tour*, John, George, and Ringo are wearing red carnations, while Paul is wearing a black one.

On the basis of these clues, millions of people began to inspect Beatle albums for other hints of McCartney's demise. They found many more:

4. The cover of the *Sergeant Pep-*

per's Lonely Hearts Club Band album shows a grave with yellow flowers arranged in the shape of Paul's bass guitar.

5. On the inside of the album, McCartney wears an armpatch with the letters "OPD," which fans interpreted to mean "Officially Pronounced Dead."

6. On the back cover of the album, three Beatles are facing forward while McCartney has his back to the camera.

A report in the University of Michigan newspaper even provided the details of McCartney's "death," including a photograph of a bloodied head said to be his. The Beatle, the story claimed, had been decapitated in an automobile crash early in November 1966 and had been secretly replaced by a double.

Paul McCartney is, of course, very much alive and still jokes about the episode. Probably the Beatles intentionally provided some of the clues to encourage the interest in their fans, but this incident suggests how quickly rumors may arise, and how they persist in a climate of distrust. During the late 1960s many disaffected young people were prepared to believe that the media and other powerful interests would conceal an event such as McCartney's death. Even when McCartney himself denied the rumor in a 1969 *Life* magazine interview, a distrustful youth subculture dismissed the story as unreliable. Thousands of readers also noticed that the back of the page containing McCartney's picture had an advertisement for an automobile, and if this page was held up to the light, the car lay across McCartney's chest and blocked his head!

SOURCE: Based on Ralph L. Rosnow and Gary Alan Fine, *Rumor and Gossip: The Social Psychology of Hearsay* (New York: Elsevier, 1976), pp. 14–20.

issues. Although we frequently speak about a single public, no single issue is of concern to everyone at any given time, so societies actually contain many publics. In industrial societies publics form and dissipate around issues such as water fluoridation, air pollution, handguns, foreign relations, and thousands of other debated issues and activities. Although the members of a public may all have interest in a particular issue, typically they do not all have the same opinion about it. Public issues are thus important matters about which people disagree (Lang & Lang, 1961; Turner & Killian, 1987).

People who share a position on a public issue usually have various social traits in common. As Chapter 18 ("Politics and Government") noted, for example, conservative Republicans are likely to be affluent and white, while liberal Democrats are typically working-class and nonwhite.

Because most individuals possess a wide range of social characteristics, personal interests, and social affiliations, most belong to many publics simultaneously. At least 5 or 10 percent of the American people will offer no opinion on any public issue, because of ignorance or lack of interest. A public grows larger or smaller over time as interest in a particular issue waxes and wanes. For example, interest in the position of women in American society was strong during the years of the women's suffrage movement and declined after women won the right to vote in 1920. In recent decades, a second wave of feminism has again created a public with strong opinions for or against changes in social patterns related to the two sexes.

Some categories of people have more social influence than others because of the unequal distribution of wealth, power, and training. Many well-funded special-interest groups in the United States shape public policy even though they represent only a small minority of Americans. Physicians—just 2 percent of Americans—have enormous influence on health-care policy because of their specialized training and political organizing. In general, privileged people possess the affluence, prestige, and social contacts to promote their opinions, no matter how small their numbers may be. National surveys reveal that about two-thirds of Americans support the Equal Rights Amendment, which provides equality under the law to males and females (N.O.R.C., 1989). But ERA has not been enacted into law partly because the vast majority of public officials in the United States are male.

Political leaders, special-interest groups, and businesses attempt to influence public tastes and attitudes through **propaganda**, *information presented with the intention of shaping public opinion*. Although the term has negative connotations, propaganda is not necessarily false. What determines whether information is propaganda is the intention behind it. The goal of propaganda is to win people over to a particular viewpoint, not to encourage critical reflection on an issue. Political speeches, commercial advertising, and public relations by professional associations, labor unions, and religious organizations all disseminate propaganda.

Panic and Mass Hysteria

Panic and mass hysteria are related forms of collective behavior characterized by heightened emotions among people dispersed over a wide area. A **panic** is *a form of localized collective behavior by which people react to some stimulus with emotional, irrational, and often self-destructive behavior*. Usually, the stimulus that provokes a panic is a *threat*. For example, a fire in a crowded theater may cause members of the audience to flee in hysteria, trampling one another and blocking the exits so that few actually escape. The stimulus sparking a panic may also be something desirable. As was mentioned earlier, for example, in 1979 a crowd drawn toward the doors of Cincinnati's Riverfront Coliseum to see a concert featuring The Who surged out of control, resulting in the death of eleven people (Johnson, 1987).

Mass hysteria is *a form of dispersed collective behavior by which people respond to a real or imagined event with irrational, frantic behavior*. Mass hysteria differs from a panic in that the participants are dispersed and have little or no direct contact with each other. Mass hysteria is commonly a response to a perceived threat, although a positive event such as a rock star's appearance on campus might provoke such reaction.

The threat that sparks mass hysteria may or may not be real. The key is that a large number of people *think* they are in danger. Parents' fears that their children may become infected from a schoolmate who has AIDS may cause as much mass hysteria in a community as can the very real danger of an approaching hurricane. Moreover, actions of people in the grip of mass hysteria are likely to make the situation worse. At the extreme, mass hysteria can lead to chaotic flight and, as crowds form, panic may result. People who see others overcome by fear may become more afraid themselves, and their hysteria and panic can further intensify as they realize that their actions are ineffective.

On the night before Halloween in 1938, CBS radio

broadcast a dramatization of H. G. Wells's novel *War of the Worlds* (Cantril, Gaudet, & Herzog, 1947; Koch, 1970). From a New York studio, a small group of actors began by presenting a program of "live dance music," heard by an estimated 10 million Americans from coast to coast. The program was suddenly interrupted by a "news report" that after explosions on the surface of the planet Mars, a mysterious cylinder was found embedded in the ground near a farmhouse in New Jersey. The program then switched to an "on-the-scene reporter" who presented a chilling account of giant monsters equipped with death-ray weapons emerging from the cylinder. An "eminent astronomer," played by Orson Welles, gave scientific substantiation that Martians had begun a full-scale invasion of Earth. At a time when Americans relied on their radios for factual news and many people thought intelligent life might well exist on Mars, this episode seemed chillingly real.

At the beginning, middle, and end of the program, an announcer identified the broadcast as a fictitious dramatization. Yet apparently more than 1 million people believed the program was factual. By the time the show was over, thousands of Americans had hysterically gathered in the streets, spreading news of the "invasion" and were flooding telephone switchboards with warnings to friends and relatives. Police telephones were swamped with calls, so that most people could not be informed that the program was only drama. Among those who jumped into their cars and fled were a college senior and his roommate:

> My roommate was crying and praying. He was even more excited than I was—or more noisy about it anyway; I guess I took it out in pushing the accelerator to the floor. . . . After it was all over, I started to think about that ride, I was more jittery than when it was happening. The speed was never under 70. I thought I was racing against time. . . . I didn't have any idea exactly what I was fleeing from, and that made me all the more afraid. (Cantril, Gaudet, & Herzog, 1947:52)

Mass hysteria, then, often builds in a vicious circle. The box describes another classic example of mass hysteria, generated by totally fictitious accounts of witches in colonial Massachusetts in the late seventeenth century.

Fashions and Fads

Two other types of collective behavior among people dispersed over a large area are fashions and fads. A **fashion** is *a social pattern favored for a time by a large number of people.* In contrast to more established social norms, fashion is transitory, sometimes lasting only months. Fashion characterizes the arts (including painting, music, drama, and literature), automobiles, language, architecture, and public opinion. The most widely recognized examples of fashion are in clothing and other aspects of personal appearance.

Lyn Lofland (1973) suggests that, in preindustrial societies, clothing and other forms of personal adornment reflect traditional styles that change little over many years. Categories of people—males and females, and members of various social classes and occupations—typically wear distinctive clothes and hairstyles as visible signs of their social position.

In industrial societies, traditional style gives way to fashion, for two reasons. First, future-directed people are not concerned about threats to tradition and so eagerly embrace new social patterns. Second, the high social mobility of industrial societies causes people to judge each other according to what they buy. German sociologist Georg Simmel (1971, orig. 1904) observed that people use fashions to shape their presentations of self, seeking approval and prestige. According to Simmel, affluent people are usually the trendsetters, since they have the money to spend on trendy luxuries that advertise their position of privilege. Thus, as American sociologist Thorstein Veblen (1953, orig. 1899) explained, fashion involves *conspicuous consumption*, the practice of spending money with the intention of displaying one's wealth.

Less affluent people, aspiring to what the rich can afford, readily purchase less expensive copies of what is fashionable. As a particular fashion moves downward in society, it then loses its prestige, and wealthy consumers soon move on to something new. Fashions, then, are born at the top of the social hierarchy—on the Fifth Avenues and Rodeo Drives of the rich—rise to mass popularity in bargain stores across the country, and typically are soon forgotten.

As societies become more egalitarian in their attitudes, however, fashions may also originate among people of lower social position and then be copied by the rich who want to fit in with the masses. A classic example is the "upward mobility" of blue jeans, or dungarees (from a Hindi word for a coarse and inferior fabric). First worn by manual laborers, jeans eventually gained popularity among the affluent, especially those who identified with the socially disadvantaged. Jeans became the uniform of political activists in the civil rights and antiwar movements in the 1960s and, gradually, of college stu-

The Witches of Salem, Massachusetts

The best-known example of mass hysteria in early American history took place in 1692 in Salem, Massachusetts, a village fifteen miles north of Boston. The story began in the home of Salem minister Samuel Parris. He owned a female slave named Tituba, who had been brought to the Massachusetts Bay Colony from Barbados and was reputed to be skilled in black magic. A group of young girls met regularly to listen to Tituba spin tales that were undoubtedly beyond the bounds of conventional conversation in this devoutly pious Puritan community. Before long, two of the youngest girls began to display exceedingly strange behavior—writhing on the ground in apparent convulsions. Other young girls throughout the village soon mimicked this bizarre behavior, and horrified parents concluded that their children were bewitched.

Salem's powerful clergy demanded that the girls identify the people responsible for this "Satanic" outbreak. The girls singled out Tituba and two other older women. Brought to trial as a witch, Tituba provided a chilling, detailed account of beliefs about the "underworld" that she had learned in her youth, and she suggested that many people in Salem practiced witchcraft. The girls, pressed to identify other culprits, spewed forth

names, and the jail soon overflowed with suspects awaiting trial. The fear of being named a witch caused as much hysteria as the alleged presence of the witches themselves. As a result, few came to the defense of the accused, lest they too be labeled witches. By the end of the summer of 1692, twenty people had been convicted of witchcraft and executed. Two others died while in prison awaiting trial.

The witchcraft hysteria began to fade as Salem's citizens started to question the girls' accusations. No doubt, the young girls had been carried away by the new power they had over their patriarchal Puritan colony. Undeterred by the consequences of their actions, they had accused even strangers they had never met. Early accusations had been made against "outsiders" such as Tituba; soon, however, they pointed fingers at some of the founding fathers of the community who had the power to fight back. Only then, almost as quickly as they invaded Salem, did the "witches" depart.

SOURCE: Based on Kai T. Erikson, *Wayward Puritans: A Study in the Sociology of Deviance* (New York: John Wiley & Sons, 1966), pp. 141–150.

---

dents across the country. Author Tom Wolfe (1970) coined the phrase "radical chic" to satirize the desire of the rich to look fashionably poor. Within another decade, expensive designer jeans became the rage among Americans of every political persuasion.

A **fad** is *an unconventional social pattern that is enthusiastically embraced by a large number of people for a short time.* Fads, sometimes called *crazes,* are commonplace in industrial societies. For example, in the late 1950s, two young entrepreneurs in California produced a brightly colored plastic version of a popular Australian toy: a three-foot diameter plastic hoop that one swung around the body by gyrating the hips. Hula hoops soon became a national craze—and then disappeared almost as quickly as they emerged. Streaking—running naked in public—was a fad in the spring of 1974. Recent research suggests that, although fads have a brief existence, they are neither entirely random nor impulsive. The frequency of streaking was found to be greater where adopted by high-prestige people, and to fall where subjected to repression (Aguirre, Quarantelli, & Mendoza, 1988).

Fads and fashions have obvious similarities—both involve dispersed collectivities adopting a distinctive social pattern for a short time—but they do differ in several respects (Blumer, 1968; Turner & Killian, 1987). Fads are truly passing fancies, enthusiasms that capture the mass imagination and quickly burn out. Fashions, however, reflect fundamental human values and social patterns that *evolve* over time: values such as love, work, health, power, social status, and sexual attractiveness. A fashion, then, builds on what precedes it and influences what follows it, becoming incorporated into a society's dominant culture. Thus the fad of streaking came out of nowhere and soon vanished, whereas the fashion of blue jeans originated in the rough mining camps of Gold Rush California a century ago and will continue to influence clothing designs in the future. Because fashions show more historical continuity and ties to convention than do fads, the word *fashionable* is generally a compliment, while the word *faddish* is a mild insult.

SOCIAL MOVEMENTS

Crowds, rumors, fashions, and the other forms of collective behavior we have discussed usually do not have significant and enduring consequences for society as a whole. Social movements are far more deliberate and long-lasting forms of collective behavior.

As noted at the beginning of the chapter, a social movement involves organized activity that promotes or resists some kind of social change. Three characteristics distinguish social movements from other types of collective behavior: a higher degree of internal organization; typically longer duration, often spanning many years; and the deliberate intent to reorganize society itself.

In preindustrial societies, strong tradition unifies the population, and therefore social movements are rare. In industrial societies, however, subcultures and countercultures thrive, and so social movements easily develop

Social movements address controversial issues. Many men and women have rallied for equal rights for homosexuals, while other Americans support a countermovement that opposes greater public acceptance for gay people.

around a wide range of public issues. For example, in recent years many homosexual Americans—supported by heterosexuals sympathetic to their political aims—have organized to gain social opportunities equal to those of the heterosexual majority. The gay rights movement has already succeeded in securing legislation in several major cities forbidding various forms of discrimination based on sexual preference. Like any social movement that challenges established social patterns, this one has sparked a countermovement—in this case, an organized effort to block greater political and social acceptance of homosexuality. Almost every significant public issue similarly gives rise both to social movements favoring change and to opposing countermovements (Lo, 1982).

Types of Social Movements

Social movements have been classified in various ways (Aberle, 1966; Cameron, 1966; Blumer, 1969). One variable is *breadth*: some focus on only a part of the population, while others try to change society as a whole. A second variable is *depth*: some social movements attempt only superficial change in individuals or society, while others pursue more extensive transformations. Combining these variables produces four types of social movements, shown in Figure 22–1.

Alternative social movements pursue limited change in only certain individuals, encouraging them to discard specific attitudes and behaviors in favor of

Figure 22–1 Four Types of Social Movements
(Aberle, 1966)

	BREADTH OF CHANGE	
	Specific individuals	Entire society
Limited	1 Alternative social movement	3 Reformative social movement
Radical	2 Redemptive social movement	4 Revolutionary social movement

DEPTH OF CHANGE

alternatives. Planned Parenthood, for example, is part of an American social movement concerned with population growth. This organization encourages individuals of childbearing age to take the consequences of their sexual activity more seriously by practicing birth control.

Redemptive social movements also focus on some individuals, but attempt to change their lives radically. For example, fundamentalist Christian organizations that seek new members through conversion, as described in Chapter 17 ("Religion"), are redemptive social movements. Resulting transformation is sometimes so great that converts are described as being "born again."

Reformative social movements seek limited social change for the entire society. The holistic health-care movement, described in Chapter 20 ("Health and Medicine"), is a reformative social movement that advocates revision of American health-care practices. Reformative social movements generally work within the political system. They can be progressive (promoting a new social pattern) or reactionary (countermovements seeking to preserve the status quo or to recover past social patterns). In the ongoing debate about abortion in the United States, both the pro-life and pro-choice organizations are reformative social movements.

Revolutionary social movements seek basic transformation of an entire society. Sometimes expressing specific plans, sometimes spinning utopian dreams, they reject existing social institutions in favor of radically new alternatives. Revolutionary social movements in eighteenth-century colonial America and in Czarist Russia early in this century led to the overthrow of existing governments by new political regimes. Until recently, most Americans viewed revolution as the establishment of leftist governments, but recent events in Eastern Europe have shown that socialism, too, is subject to popular overthrow. Revolutionary social movements also emerge on the far right. The John Birch Society and the political organization headed by Lyndon LaRouche each claim that socialism is undermining the United States and therefore seek to radically alter American social institutions (Broyles, 1978).

Deprivation Theory

Because social movements are highly organized and usually endure over a long period of time, sociologists find this form of collective behavior somewhat easier to explain than fleeting incidents of mob behavior or mass hysteria. One approach to understanding social movements is *deprivation theory*, which holds that social move-

Under the domination of the Israeli government, Palestinians in the disputed territories claim they have been reduced to second-class citizens. This keen of deprivation has led to years of protest, involving violence on both sides.

ments arise as people react to feeling deprived of things they consider necessary or believe they deserve. Those who think they lack suitable income, working conditions, political rights, social dignity, or certain privileges may engage in organized collective behavior to bring about a more just state of affairs (Morrison, 1978; Rose, 1982).

The emancipation of black Americans after the Civil War seemed to signal an end to white domination. However, the economic prosperity of many Southern white farmers depended on low-cost black labor, and whites therefore felt threatened by the apparent rise in the social position of blacks. The whites' sense of loss was especially keen during economic downturns. As a result, various social movements emerged from the desire to keep black Americans "in their place" (Dollard et al., 1939). Some movements supported legal changes such as segregationist Jim Crow laws, and some favored terrorist organizations such as the Ku Klux Klan. The success of these movements enabled threatened whites to hold on to some relative advantages. Blacks, who had long experienced even greater deprivation and had even more to gain from organizing in opposition, had relatively little opportunity to do so at the time in the face of overwhelming white power. Not until well into the twentieth century did blacks successfully organize for racial justice.

The deprivation approach is also implicit in Karl Marx's expectation that industrial workers would eventu-

ally organize in opposition to capitalism. As Chapter 4 ("Society") describes, Marx claimed that capitalism deprived workers by giving them low wages and little social power, and thereby alienated them from their own creative potential. Labor unions and various political organizations of workers have arisen to address the sense of deprivation experienced by working-class Americans.

As was noted in Chapter 7 ("Groups and Organizations"), deprivation is a relative concept (Stouffer et al., 1949; Merton, 1968). Regardless of their actual money and power, people tend to evaluate themselves in relation to some category of others. **Relative deprivation** is *a perceived disadvantage based on some comparison*. Relative deprivation also arises to the extent that people imagine that they could have more than they actually do.

More than a century ago Alexis de Tocqueville (1955, orig. 1856) studied the social uprising that sparked the French Revolution. Why, he asked, did rebellion occur in France rather than in neighboring Germany, where the peasants' plight was objectively worse? Tocqueville's answer was that, as bad as the condition was, German peasants had known nothing but feudal servitude and thus had no basis for feeling deprived. French peasants, in contrast, had experienced improvements in their lives and could imagine even greater changes, and thus they felt a sense of relative deprivation. Tocqueville concluded that "steadily increasing prosperity, far from tranquilizing the population, everywhere promoted a spirit of unrest" (1955:175; orig. 1856).

Echoing Tocqueville's insight, James C. Davies (1962) suggests that as life gets better, people may take the improvements for granted and come to expect even more. Profound relative deprivation results if the standard of living stops improving or, worse, begins to drop. As Figure 22–2 illustrates, social movements aimed at changing society are most likely to occur when an extended period of improvement in the standard of living is followed by a shorter period of decline.

Critical evaluation. Deprivation theory illustrates that common sense is not always a good predictor of discontent. This approach has broad appeal, combining ideas from thinkers as diverse as Marx and Tocqueville. But knowing that most people experience some discontent all the time, we are left wondering why social movements emerge among some categories of people and not others? A second problem is that deprivation theory seems to be based on circular reasoning. That is, deprivation is assumed to cause social movements, but the only evidence of deprivation is the social movement itself (Jenkins

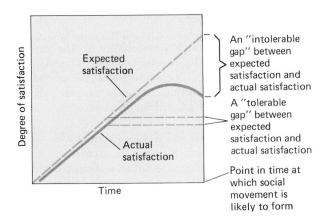

Figure 22–2 Relative Deprivation and Social Movements
In this diagram, the solid line represents a rising standard of living over time. The dotted line represents the expected standard of living, which is typically somewhat higher. Davies describes the difference between the two as "a tolerable gap between what people want and what they get." If the standard of living suddenly drops in the midst of rising expectations, however, this gap grows to an intolerable level. At this point, social movements can be expected to form.

(Davies, 1962)

& Perrow, 1977). A third criticism is that this approach tends to focus more on the setting in which a social movement develops than on the movement itself (McAdam, McCarthy, & Zald, 1988).

Mass-Society Theory

William Kornhauser's *mass-society theory* (1959) suggests that social movements attract socially isolated people who feel personally insignificant within the masses of large, complex societies. In this view, social movements are more *personal* than *political* in that they afford an individual a sense of purpose and of belonging (Melucci, 1989). Geographical areas in which social ties are weak tend to contain many people who can be readily mobilized into a social movement. Where strong social integration exists, social movements are unlikely.

Like Gustave Le Bon, discussed earlier, Kornhauser offers a conservative and critical view of social movements. He regards them as psychologically motivated groups prone to deviance, and he implies that the leaders can easily manipulate participants to subvert democratic principles. Support for extremist social movements—

both the far right and the far left—is typically greatest among people with membership in few social groups.

Critical evaluation. The strength of Kornhauser's theory is that it explains social movements in terms of both the people who join them and the characteristics of the larger society. One criticism is practical: in research, how does one measure the extent to which a setting is a "mass society"? Another criticism is political: placing the roots of social movements in psychological needs diverts attention from the injustices that people see in society. In other words, this theory views a stable, well-integrated society in positive terms and disparages movements that seek change.

Research provides inconsistent support for this approach. The Nazi movement in Germany, some claim, recruited mostly people who were *not* socially isolated (Lipset, 1963; Oberschall, 1973). Similarly, urban rioters during the 1960s typically were people with strong ties to their communities (Tilly, Tilly, & Tilly, 1975). Evidence also suggests that young people who join religious cults do not have particularly weak family ties (Wright & Piper, 1986). Additionally, Doug McAdam's (1989) study of the 1960s political activists in their later years highlights deep and continuing commitment to political goals rather than to any personal rewards. Yet research by Frances Piven and Richard Cloward (1977) shows that a dramatic breakdown of routine social patterns does contribute to social movements among poor people. Also, Bert Useem's (1985) study of the New Mexico State Penitentiary notes that after the suspension of prison programs that had promoted social ties among inmates, there was an increase in chaotic and violent protest activity.

Structural-Strain Theory

One of the most influential approaches to understanding social movements was the *structural-strain theory* developed by Neil Smelser (1962). This theory identifies six social conditions that help foster social movements. The more factors present, the greater the likelihood that a social movement will develop. His theory also offers clues as to what situations spark unorganized mobs or riots and which ones create highly organized social movements. The pro-democracy movement in Eastern Europe during the late-1980s will serve here to illustrate each of Smelser's six factors.

1. **Structural conduciveness.** Social movements are

The democratic transformation of Eastern Europe in 1989 occurred quickly, partly because of limited government repression. In Romania, however, government security forces fought troops supported by the people in a vicious house-to-house struggle that took hundreds of lives. This government resistance delayed—but ultimately could not stop—political change.

4. **Precipitating factors.** Although social movements frequently evolve over a long time, collective action is often precipitated by a specific event. The coming to power of Mikhail Gorbachev in the Soviet Union in 1985 and his program of *perestroika* offered an historic opportunity to reorganize political and economic life in Eastern Europe as Moscow relaxed its rigid control.

5. **Mobilization for action.** Once there is widespread concern about a public issue, collective action will probably be expressed in rallies, leafleting, building of alliances with sympathetic organizations, and similar activities. After the initial success of the Solidarity movement in Poland, people mobilized across Eastern Europe. Also the rate of change accelerated as reform movements gained strength: what had taken years in Poland required only months in Hungary, and only weeks elsewhere in Eastern Europe.

6. **Lack of social control.** The responses of established authorities, such as political officials and police, largely determine the outcome of any such movement. Powerful repression by the state can weaken or even destroy a social movement, as was seen by the crushing of pro-democracy forces in the People's Republic of China. In contrast, Gorbachev's policy of nonintervention in Eastern Europe increased the possibility for change there.

Critical evaluation. Smelser's approach recognizes the complexity of social movements and suggests how various factors encourage or inhibit their development. Structural-strain theory also explains how social problems may give rise to either organized social movements or more spontaneous mob action or rioting. It also is distinctly *social*, rather than psychological, in focus. Yet Smelser's theory contains much the same circularity of argument found in Kornhauser's analysis: social movements are caused by strain, but we assume strain exists only because of the emerging social movement. Finally, this theory is incomplete, ignoring the important role of resources such as the mass media in the success or failure of a social movement (Oberschall, 1973; Jenkins & Perrow, 1977; McCarthy & Zald, 1977).

Resource-Mobilization Theory

Resource-mobilization theory adds another important consideration to the discussion of social movements. They are unlikely to succeed—or even emerge—without

rooted in significant social problems within a society. The generally low standard of living in Eastern European countries since World War II, coupled with the lack of political participation by the majority of people, created widespread dissatisfaction.

2. **Structural strain.** Social movements are fueled by strains within society, especially when reality falls short of expectations. The pro-democracy movement in Eastern Europe was strengthened by the fact that the quality of life there was far lower than in Western Europe, and also by the failure of the Soviet bloc nations to realize the goal of a prosperous socialism.

3. **Growth and spread of an explanation.** Social movements require a clear statement of the problem, its causes, and likely solutions. If these are well articulated, people are likely to express their dissatisfaction in an organized way. If not, frustration may lead to unorganized rioting. Intellectuals taught the Eastern European people that their plight was linked to flaws in their society, and at the same time movement leaders suggested strategies to increase democracy.

necessary resources, including money, human labor, office and communications facilities, contacts with the mass media, and a positive public image. The fate of any social movement depends on how effectively it is organized to attract resources and mobilize people. The four young men who requested service at the Greensboro, North Carolina, Woolworth store, described in the opening to this chapter, were instrumental in mobilizing blacks and whites to expand the civil rights movement. The media attention they received attracted people and resources from across the country.

Outsiders as well as insiders have a crucial role in supplying a social movement's resources (McCarthy & Zald, 1977; Killian, 1984). Socially disadvantaged people by definition lack the money, contacts, leadership skills, and organizational know-how that a successful movement requires, and often sympathetic outsiders fill the resource gap. Well-to-do whites, including college students, performed an active part in the black civil rights movement in the 1960s, and affluent men as well as women have taken a leading role in the current women's movement. Even a few core resource people can sometimes link a developing social movement to a large, sympathetic population through extensive social networks (Snow, Zurcher, & Ekland-Olson, 1980; Snow, Rochford, Jr., Worden, & Benford, 1986).

There was little governmental response at the outset of the AIDS epidemic in the early 1980s. To a large extent, gay communities in large cities such as San Francisco and New York were forced to shoulder the responsibility of developing educational programs. As the number of AIDS victims rapidly increased, state and local governments began to allocate more resources. Rising public concern about AIDS after 1985 encouraged the federal government to provide increased funding for fighting this disease. Members of the entertainment industry have also contributed significant financial support and publicity. The ability to attract extensive resources has transformed this social movement from a small and uncertain beginning to a national coalition of political leaders, educators, and medical specialists.

Critical evaluation. The strength of resource-mobilization theory lies in its recognition that resources as well as discontent are necessary to a social movement's success. This theory also emphasizes the interplay between any social movement and other groups and organizations capable of providing or withholding valuable resources.

Critics of this approach maintain that even relatively powerless segments of a population can promote successful social movements if they are able to organize effectively and have strongly committed members. Research by Aldon Morris (1981) shows that black people and resources within the black community largely supported the black civil rights movement of the 1950s and 1960s. A second problem with this theory is that influential members of society often oppose any effort to challenge the status quo. Some powerful whites did provide valuable resources to the black civil rights movement, but white elites remained generally unsympathetic (McAdam, 1982, 1983). Thus the success or failure of a social movement is the outcome of political struggle between challengers and supporters of the status quo. A strong and united establishment, perhaps aided by a countermovement, decreases the success of a social movement seeking social change. If, on the other hand, established powers are divided, the movement's chances of success increase.

"New Social Movements" Theory

During the 1980s another theoretical approach to social movements emerged to attempt to explain how and why many recent social movements differ from those in the past. This *new social movements theory* investigates the distinctive features of social movements within the mature industrial societies of North America and Western Europe (Melucci, 1980; McAdam, McCarthy, & Zald, 1988; Kriesi, 1989).

New social movements are concerned with global ecology, women's and gay rights, the risks of nuclear war, animal rights, and other issues. One feature of these movements is their national scope. As Chapter 18 ("Politics and Government") explained, the state now is the dominant center of power, setting policies that affect entire populations. Not surprisingly, then, social movements also assume national (and sometimes even international) proportions. Second, unlike traditional social movements such as labor organizations, which are concerned primarily with economic issues, the new movements tend to focus on quality of life. The international ecology movement, for example, confronts practices that contribute to global warming and other environmental dangers. Third, whereas traditional social movements with economic interests tend to elicit strong support from working-class people, the new social movements with lesser economic focus usually draw disproportionate support from middle-class people.

Critical evaluation. Because the "new social movements" theory is a recent development, sociologists are

Environmentalists are a prominent example of what are called "new social movements." Such efforts for change typically involve people in many countries, and are concerned with "quality of life" issues that participants believe are vital to the future of humanity. Here, throngs of people in Paris celebrate Earth Day, 1990.

still assessing its utility. One clear strength of this analysis is its recognition of the increasing power of the state to shape society and affect individuals, and therefore to be the target of large-scale social movements. This approach also highlights the power of the mass media to unite people around the world in pursuit of political goals. A criticism is that the theory may exaggerate the differences between "traditional" and "new" social movements. The women's movement, for example, focuses on many of the same issues—workplace conditions and pay—that have consumed the energies of labor organizations for decades.

Each of the five major theories discussed explains part of the complex process by which social movements arise. Table 22–1 summarizes these theories.

Stages in Social Movements

The effectiveness and longevity of any social movement depend on the strength of its organizational foundation. Some social movements deliberately avoid extensive organization. The Yippie movement of the 1960s, an outgrowth of the hippie movement, embraced a "do your own thing" philosophy that was hostile to any organization at all (Hoffman, 1968). Consequently, the movement had little success and soon dissolved. In contrast, the black civil rights movement, the women's movement, and the gay rights movement are well-established organizations that continue to change American society.

While each social movement is unique, most move through four defined stages (Blumer, 1969; Mauss, 1975; Tilly, 1978).

Stage 1: Emergence. Social movements are driven by the perception that all is not well. Some, such as the civil rights and women's movements, are born of widespread dissatisfaction. Others emerge only as a small group increases public awareness of some issue, as gay activists have done with regard to the threat posed by AIDS.

Stage 2: Coalescence. After emerging, a social movement must define itself clearly and develop a strategy for becoming public. Leaders must determine policies and tactics, build morale, and recruit new members. At this stage, collective action in the form of rallies or demonstrations may promote public awareness, especially if the mass media carry the movement's message to the entire society. Additionally, the movement may form alliances with other organizations to gain necessary resources.

Stage 3: Bureaucratization. To become established, a social movement must assume bureaucratic traits, as described in Chapter 7 ("Groups and Organizations"). As it becomes "routinized," a social movement depends less on the charisma and talents of a few leaders and more on a capable staff. Some social movements do not become established in this way, however. Many activist organizations on college campuses during the

Table 22–1 THEORIES OF SOCIAL MOVEMENTS: A SUMMARY

Deprivation Theory	People join as a result of experiencing relative deprivation. Social movement is a means of seeking change that brings participants greater benefits. Social movements are especially likely when rising expectations are frustrated.
Mass-Society Theory	People who lack established social ties are easily mobilized into social movements. Periods of social breakdown are likely to spawn social movements. Social movement is a means of gaining a sense of belonging and social participation.
Structural-Strain Theory	People join because of their shared concern about the inability of society to operate as they believe it should. The growth of a social movement reflects many factors, including a belief in its legitimacy and some precipitating event that provokes action.
Resource-Mobilization Theory	People may join for all of the reasons noted above and also because of social ties to existing members. The success or failure of a social movement depends largely on the resources available to it. Also important is the extent of opposition to its goals within the larger society.
"New Social Movement" Theory	People join motivated by a concern for "quality of life," not necessarily economic issues. Mobilization is national or international in scope. New social movements are a response to the expansion of the mass media, and also the power of the state in modern industrial societies to affect people's lives for good or ill.

late 1960s developed around charismatic leaders and did not endure for long. On the other hand, the National Organization for Women (NOW), despite changing leadership, offers a steady voice on behalf of the women's movement.

Sometimes bureaucratization can hinder a social movement. Frances Piven and Richard Cloward (1977), in reviewing social movements in American history, noted that leaders can become so engrossed in building an organization that they neglect to foster sentiments of insurgency among movement members. In such instances, the radical edge of protest can be lost.

Stage 4: Decline. Social movements are inherently dynamic, so a decline is not necessarily a demise (Wright, 1987). Eventually, however, most social movements reach a point of decline. Frederick Miller (1983) suggests four reasons why this may occur.

First, after accomplishing many of its goals, a social movement may have no further reason to exist. For example, the women's suffrage movement declined after it won for American women the right to vote. Such outright successes are rare, however, since few social movements have a single specific goal. Moreover, gaining one victory often leads to new campaigns. Because issues related to gender extend far beyond voting, the women's movement has a been reborn.

Second, a social movement may fail because of political factors, such as poor leadership, loss of interest

in its goals, exhaustion of resources, repression by authorities, or bureaucratization. Some people attracted by the excitement of a new social movement may lose interest when formal organization replaces personal relationships and activities become routine. Fragmentation resulting from internal conflicts over goals and tactics is another common problem. Students for a Democratic Society (SDS), which developed out of the civil rights and antiwar movements of the 1960s, was weakened by fragmentation as some members decided to pursue more radical and often violent strategies while others reverted to supporting traditional political parties. As this example suggests, fragmentation may cause one social movement to decline while simultaneously giving birth to others.

Third, a social movement may decline if the established power structure, through offers of money, prestige, and other rewards, succeeds in diverting leaders from their goals. "Selling out" is one application of the iron law of oligarchy, noted in Chapter 7 ("Groups and Organizations"), by which organizational leaders may use their positions to enrich themselves. Jerry Rubin, a political activist of the late 1960s, used his celebrity status as a rebel to build a career in the New York financial world. Conversely, people have left lucrative, high-prestige occupations to become active in social movements. Cat Stevens, a famous rock star of the 1970s, became a Muslim, changed his name to Yusuf Islam, and promotes the spread of the Islamic religion.

Fourth, the decline of a social movement may

result from repression. Those in power may frighten away participants, discourage new recruits, and imprison or even kill leaders. Often the state reacts repressively to social movements that it considers revolutionary. The government of South Africa, for example, banned the African National Congress (ANC), a political organization seeking to overthrow the state-supported system of apartheid, and even suspicion of involvement in the ANC could lead to arrest. In 1990 the ban was lifted, and ANC leader Nelson Mandela was released after twenty-seven years of imprisonment.

Beyond the reasons noted by Miller, a fifth cause of a social movement's decline is that it may become established. Some social movements become an accepted part of the system—typically after realizing at least some of their goals—and they no longer challenge the status quo. For example, the American labor movement is now well established; its leaders control vast sums of money and resemble the business tycoons they opposed a century ago.

Figure 22–3 provides a graphic summary of the various stages of social movements.

Social Movements and Social Change

Social movements exist to encourage—or to inhibit—social change. Their degree of success naturally varies. Racial equality in the United States, although an unrealized goal, has increased, a testimony to the success of the civil rights movement and the failure of white supremacist countermovements such as the Ku Klux Klan.

We sometimes overlook the success of past social movements and take for granted the changes they wrought. Early labor movements in the United States, for example, eventually ended child labor in factories, limited working hours, made workplaces safer, and established the right to collectively bargain with employers. Legislation protecting the environment is also the product of successful social movements during this century. The American women's movement has yet to attain full equality under the law for men and women, but it has extended the legal rights and social opportunities of American women to the extent that many young people are sur-

During twenty-seven years of imprisonment, Nelson Mandela served as the symbol of a racially democratic South Africa. After his release in 1990, Mandela and the African National Congress began negotiations with the government seeking an end to apartheid.

Figure 22–3 Stages in the Lives of Social Movements

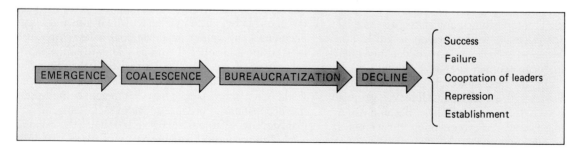

EMERGENCE ▷ COALESCENCE ▷ BUREAUCRATIZATION ▷ DECLINE ▷ Success
Failure
Cooptation of leaders
Repression
Establishment

prised to learn of social inequities that existed until recently.

Social movements and social change are closely linked. Efforts to extend workers' rights themselves sparked social changes such as the Industrial Revolution and the rise of capitalism. Conversely, social gains forged by various segments of the American population—including women, racial and ethnic minorities, and gay people—have significantly reshaped American society. Thus social change characteristic of large and complex societies is both the cause and the consequence of social movements.

SUMMARY

1. A collectivity differs from a social group in its limited social interaction, unclear social boundaries, and weak and frequently unconventional social norms.

2. Crowds, an important type of collective behavior, take five major forms: casual crowds, conventional crowds, expressive crowds, acting crowds, and protest crowds.

3. Mobs and riots are emotionally intense and often violent crowds. Mobs pursue a specific goal; rioting is undirected destructiveness.

4. Contagion theory views crowds as anonymous, suggestible, and subject to emotional contagion. Convergence theory links crowd behavior to traits of participants. Emergent-norm theory states that crowds develop their own behavioral norms.

5. Crowds have figured heavily in historical social change. Depending on the political orientation of the observer, crowds are perceived as acting either destructively or constructively.

6. Rumor, which thrives in a climate of ambiguity, is concerned with public issues; gossip, closely related to rumor, deals with personal issues of local interest.

7. Public opinion consists of various positions on issues of widespread social importance. People's opinions tend to reflect their social background, although on any public issue a small proportion of the population claims no opinion.

8. Mass hysteria is a type of collective behavior in which people anxiously respond to a significant event, real or imagined. In a spiral of panic, hysteria may lead to ineffective action, which in turn increases the hysteria.

9. Within industrial societies, fashion is a common device used to gain social prestige. A fad is more unconventional than fashion, less long-lived, and greeted with greater enthusiasm.

10. A social movement entails deliberate activity intended to promote or discourage social change. Social movements vary in the breadth and depth of their goals.

11. According to deprivation theory, social movements are a response to subjective deprivation regardless of absolute circumstances.

12. Mass-society theory suggests that people join social movements to gain a sense of belonging and social significance.

13. Structural-strain theory explains the development of social movements as a cumulative consequence of six factors. Well-formulated grievances and goals encourage the organization of social movements; undirected anger and frustration foster rioting.

14. Resource-mobilization theory ties the success or failure of a social movement to the availability of resources such as money and human labor, as well as to alliances with other organizations.

15. A social movement typically proceeds through consecutive stages. First, emergence involves defining a public issue requiring action; second, coalescence represents a movement's entry into public life; third, bureaucratization refers to a movement's increasingly formal organization; and fourth, a movement declines as a result of its success, failure, cooptation of leaders, repression, or establishment within the society.

16. The success of social movements is evident in characteristics of society that people now take for granted. Additionally, social change itself sparks social movements, so the two are strongly related.

KEY CONCEPTS

collective behavior relatively spontaneous activity involving a large number of people that does not conform to established norms

collectivity a large number of people who interact little if at all in the absence of well-defined and conventional norms

crowd a temporary gathering of people who share a common focus of attention and whose members influence one another

fad an unconventional social pattern that is enthusiastically embraced by a large number of people for a short time

fashion a social pattern favored for a time by a large number of people

gossip rumor about the personal affairs of others

mass behavior collective behavior among people dispersed over a wide geographical area

mass hysteria a form of dispersed collective behavior by which people respond to a real or imagined event with irrational, frantic behavior

mob a highly emotional crowd in common pursuit of some violent or destructive goal

panic a form of localized collective behavior by which people react to some stimulus with emotional, irrational, and often self-destructive behavior

propaganda information presented with the intention of shaping public opinion

relative deprivation a perceived disadvantage based on some comparison

riot a highly emotional and undirected eruption involving violence and destruction

rumor unsubstantiated information spread informally, often by word of mouth

social movement organized activity that encourages or discourages social change

SUGGESTED READINGS

These books provide further detail on topics covered in this chapter.

Ralph H. Turner and Lewis M. Killian. *Collective Behavior.* 3rd ed. Englewood Cliffs, NJ: Prentice-Hall, 1987.

William Gamson. *The Strategy of Social Protest.* 2nd ed. Belmont, CA: Wadsworth, 1990.

This book is one of the few academic examinations of gossip, including supermarket tabloids and various types of "idle talk."

Jack Levin and Arnold Arluke. *Gossip: The Inside Scoop.* New York: Plenum Press, 1987.

A collective behavior classic is this story of the 1938 *War of the Worlds* broadcast.

Howard Koch. *The Panic Broadcast: Portrait of an Event.* Boston: Little, Brown, 1970.

This broad investigation of black politics in the United States compares various political movements from the 1940s to the present.

Manning Marable. *Black American Politics: From the Washington Marches to Jesse Jackson.* London: Verso, 1985.

This examination of Chicano protest in the western United States focuses on how some people express their suffering and why others may or may not respond.

John C. Hammerback, Richard J. Jensen, and Jose Angel Gutierrez. *A War of Words: Chicano Protest in the 1960s and 1970s.* Westport, CT: Greenwood Press, 1985.

This recent analysis further develops the mass-society approach to social movements.

Alberto Melucci. *Nomads of the Present: Social Movements and Individual Needs in Contemporary America.* Philadelphia: Temple University Press, 1989.

These two books examine political movements of the 1960s and 1970s. The first describes the history of Students for a Democratic Society, a central force in the political events of that turbulent period. The second book traces the legacy of 1960s activism and explores the later lives of many activists.

James Miller. *"Democracy in the Streets" from Port Huron to the Siege of Chicago.* New York: Simon & Schuster, 1987.

Jack Whalen and Richard Flacks. *Beyond the Barricades: The Sixties Generation Grows Up.* Philadelphia: Temple University Press, 1989.

This study explains how the New Left movement of the late 1960s affected one Canadian city.

Richard Harris. *Democracy in Kingston: A Social Movement in Urban Politics, 1965–1970.* Kingston/Montreal: McGill–Queen's University Press, 1988.

This collection of essays explores a wide range of social movements in recent American history.

Jo Freedman, ed. *Social Movements of the Sixties and Seventies.* New York: Longman, 1983.

The first of these books contains an historical overview of the gay and lesbian movements in the United States. The second concludes that, when compared with the black civil rights movement, the gay movement has failed because of poor strategies.

Barry D. Adam. *The Rise of a Gay and Lesbian Movement.* Boston: Twayne, 1987.

Marshall Kirk and Hunter Madsen. *After the Ball.* Garden City, NY: Doubleday, 1989.

This book describes one of the most stunning examples of collective behavior in recent years: the mass suicide of some 900 members of a sect called the People's Temple in Jonestown, Guyana.

John R. Hall. *Gone from the Promised Land: Jonestown in American Cultural History.* New Brunswick, NJ: Transaction, 1987.

Here is a personal account of a teenager's experiences during the Cultural Revolution in China between 1966 and 1969, which has been dubbed a mass movement out of control.

Gao Yuan. *Born Red: A Chronicle of the Cultural Revolution.* Stanford, CA: Stanford University Press, 1987.

Unlike political leaders with big bankrolls, most people concerned with political change must mobilize extensive popular support. This book describes the role of social workers in community change.

Karen S. Haynes and James S. Mickelson. *Affecting Change: Social Workers in the Political Arena.* New York: Longman, 1986.

These two books look at social movements in world perspective, with special attention to the Third World.

Robert P. Weller and Scott E. Guggenheim, eds. *Power and Protest in the Countryside: Studies of Rural Unrest in Asia, Europe, and Latin America.* Durham, NC: Duke Press Policy Studies, 1982.

John Walton. *Reluctant Rebels: Comparative Studies of Revolution and Underdevelopment.* New York: Columbia University Press, 1984.

A noted global activist argues for a broad-based movement toward renewal of American society's core cultural values.

Frances Moore Lappé. *Rediscovering America's Values.* New York: Ballantine Books, 1989.

23

Social Change and Modernity

The firelight flickers in the gathering darkness as Chief Kanhonk sits, as he has done every evening for many years, to begin an evening of animated talk and storytelling.[1] This is the hour when the Kaiapo, a small society of Brazil's Amazon region, celebrate their culture. Because the Kaiapo are a traditional people with no written language, the elders use such occasions to instruct their grandchildren in their history and way of life. In the past, evenings like this have been filled with tales of brave Kaiapo warriors fighting off Portuguese traders in pursuit of slaves and gold.

But as the minutes pass, only a few villagers assemble for the evening ritual. "It is the Big Ghost," one grumbles. "Big Ghost" has indeed descended upon them: its presence is evident in the soft glow spilling from windows of homes. The Kaiapo are watching television. The consequences of installing a satellite dish in the village three years ago have been greater than anyone imagined. What outsiders failed to do to the Kaiapo with guns may be accomplished with prime-time programming. Those around the fire sit silently, knowing that their culture is once again under attack and may soon be destroyed (Simons, 1989).

The Kaiapo are distinctive among the 230,000 na-

tive people of Brazil. They are easily identified by their striking body paint and ornate ceremonial dress. Recently, they have become rich as profits from goldmining and cutting mahogany trees have flowed into the settlement. The Kaiapo wonder whether their new-found fortune is a blessing or a curse. To some, affluence means the opportunity to learn about the outside world through television and travel. Others, like Chief Kanhonk, express a different view. Sitting by the fire, he thinks aloud, "I have been saying that people must buy useful things

[1] This opening is a selective adaptation of the account provided by Simons (1989).

like knives and fishing hooks. Television does not fill the stomach. It only shows our children and grandchildren white people's things." Bebtopup, the oldest priest, agrees: "The night is the time the old people teach the young people. Television has stolen the night" (Simons 1989:37).

The transformation of the Kaiapo raises profound questions about what causes social change; their current plight forces us to wonder whether change—even toward a higher material standard of living—is always for the better. Moreover, the drama of the Kaiapo is being played out around the globe as more and more traditional cultures are drawn away from their past toward a more materialistic way of life modeled on the rich societies of the First World.

This chapter examines social change, a process that has both positive and negative consequences. Of particular interest to Americans is what sociologists call *modernity*, the product of social changes beginning with the Industrial Revolution. As a modern society, the United States is transforming much of the rest of the world. Modern societies can boast of solving many age-old human problems, yet its members confront new problems of their own making, problems beyond the imagination of people living centuries ago.

Increasing technological sophistication has made the world seem smaller, as familiar products are now widely sold on the other side of the globe. Are the thousands of historically distinct human cultures likely to become more alike? What are the advantages and drawbacks of such an expansion of Western corporate power?

WHAT IS SOCIAL CHANGE?

The organization of complex human societies has been the focus of this book. We have examined social structure, that is, relatively *static* social patterns involving status and roles, social stratification, and various social institutions. We have also discussed *dynamic* forces that recast human consciousness, behavior, and needs: social conflict, innovations in technology, the development of formal organizations, the growth of cities, and social movements. All of these factors are linked to **social change,** *the transformation of culture and social institutions over time.* The process of social change has four general characteristics.

1. **Social change is universal although the rate of change varies.** "Nothing is constant except death and taxes," so the saying goes. However, social patterns related to death and dying have changed in recent centuries, as Chapter 5 ("Socialization") explained. Additionally, people today die at a much later age than in the past. Taxes were unknown

for most of human history and emerged only with complex social organization.

Every society changes, but some do so faster than others. As was explained in Chapter 4 ("Society"), hunting and gathering societies changed little over thousands of years. As technology becomes more complex, a society's rate of social change increases (Lenski & Lenski, 1987) because technological advance multiplies the effect of discovery as any new invention is combined with existing cultural elements.

Moreover, various cultural elements change at different rates. William Ogburn's (1964) theory of *cultural lag* states that material culture usually changes faster than nonmaterial culture (see Chapter 3, "Culture"). For example, medical devices that prolong the life of seriously ill people have developed more rapidly than have ethical standards for deciding when and how to employ this technology.

2. **Social change is both intentional and unplanned.** Industrial societies actively encourage much social change. For example, scientists seek more efficient forms of energy, advertisers try to convince consumers that a new appliance is a "necessity," and government officials seek ways to increase equality of opportunity among various categories of people. Yet even the experts rarely comprehend all the consequences of a social change. Designers of automobiles early in this century did not foresee the many ways in which their work would reshape American society. Perhaps they imagined that people would travel in a single day distances that had required weeks or months a century before, but surely they had little understanding of how the mobility provided by automobiles would affect American families and reshape cities and suburbs.

3. **Social change is often controversial.** The results of social change may be viewed as both good and bad. Certainly, the Kaiapo have reasons for both praising and condemning the introduction of television to their society. Similarly, while Americans appreciate the mobility provided by automobiles, they have been a major cause of air pollution and contribute to almost 50,000 accidental deaths each year.

   Any transformation of society is likely to win support from some and spark opposition from others. Capitalists welcomed the Industrial Revolution, because advancing technology meant greater productivity and higher profits. Many workers, however, feared that machines would make their skills obsolete, and they strongly resisted "progress." Political changes also benefit some more than others. Most blacks celebrated the weakening of apartheid in South Africa in 1990, while these changes were unsettling to many whites. In the United States, changing social patterns between blacks and whites, between women and men, and between gays and heterosexuals also remain controversial public issues.

4. **Social change has variable consequences.** Some social changes have only passing significance whereas others endure for generations. At one extreme, fads, such as "teenage mutant Ninja turtles," arise and dissipate quickly with little long-term effect. At the other, Americans are still adjusting to powerful technological advances such as television half a century after its introduction. Today we can scarcely imagine how the computer revolution will transform the entire world during the next century. Like the automobile and television, computers will probably have both positive and negative effects, providing new kinds of jobs while eliminating old ones, and allowing easier processing of information while reducing personal privacy.

Causes of Social Change

The causes of social change lie both inside and outside a society. Advancing communication and transportation technology is linking the nations of the world ever more closely and affecting the ecosystem of the planet. As it does so, change in one place begets change elsewhere.

Cultural Processes

Culture is a dynamic system of symbols that continually gains new elements and loses others. As explained in Chapter 3 ("Culture"), cultural change results from three basic processes. First, *invention* of mechanical objects, ideas, and social patterns helps reshape society. Rocket propulsion research, beginning in the 1940s, has produced increasingly sophisticated vehicles for space flight. Today we take such technology for granted, and during the next century a significant number of Americans will likely travel in space.

A second process, *discovery*, occurs when people recognize existing elements of the world or learn to see them in a new way. For example, medical advances offer a growing understanding of how the human body operates, although we are still unable to cure many kinds of cancer or control the virus that causes AIDS. Medical discoveries also affect society in indirect ways: the capacity to enhance health has added decades to average life expectancy, contributing to the "graying of America" described in Chapter 14 ("Aging and the Elderly").

Finally, *diffusion* creates change as cultural elements spread from one society to another through trade, migration, and mass communication. Ralph Linton (1937) recognized that many cultural elements central to American life have come to us from elsewhere—for example, cloth (developed in Asia), clocks (invented in Europe), and coins (a product of Turkey). Generally, elements of material culture diffuse more readily than nonmaterial cultural traits. The Kaiapo have been quick to adopt television but are reluctant to embrace the materialism and individualism that this new device has introduced from the outside.

For its entire history, the United States has been transformed by immigration. For more than a decade, new arrivals from Latin America and Asia have been introducing cultural change, clearly evident in the sights, smells, and sounds of cities across the country (Fallows, 1983; Muller & Espenshade, 1985). Conversely, American creations from hamburgers to Harlem rap music to Harvard M.B.A. degrees have diffused to other societies.

Social Structure

Another source of social change is tension and conflict within a society. The link between social structure and social change formed the core of Karl Marx's ideas (see especially Chapter 4, "Society" and Chapter 9, "Social Stratification"). Marx claimed that conflict between the social classes is the engine of social change. In industrial-capitalist societies, he maintained, struggle between capitalists and workers drives society toward a system of socialist production. In the century since Marx's death, this model has proven simplistic, yet he was correct in foreseeing that social conflict arising from patterns of inequality (involving race and gender as well as social class) would modify every society, including the United States. As was described in Chapter 22 ("Collective Behavior and Social Movements"), social movements often emerge from the experience of deprivation. The labor, civil rights, women's, and gay rights movements developed in this manner, and each has changed American society.

Ideas

Max Weber believed that complex transformations of society have many causes, as Chapter 4 ("Society") explains. Weber acknowledged the importance of social conflict in transforming societies, but rather than tracing the roots of social change to material production, as Marx did, Weber argued that nonmaterial culture—ideas—are the key to change. He illustrated this point by showing how charisma (described in Chapters 17, "Religion," and 18, "Politics and Government") sets some people apart as extraordinary and capable of truly changing the world. Weber also embodied this thesis in describing how the world view of early Protestants fostered the rise of industrial capitalism (see Chapter 4, "Society").

By showing that industrial capitalism developed primarily in areas of Western Europe where the Protestant work ethic was strong, Weber (1958) demonstrated that the disciplined rationality of Calvinist Protestants was instrumental in this change.

Ideas are also vital to the development of social movements. Chapter 22 explained that a social movement may emerge from the decision to modify society in some manner (say, to clean up the environment) or from a sense that existing social arrangements must be reformed (Smelser, 1962). The international gay rights movement has gained strength from the belief that homosexuals have been the targets of prejudice and discrimination, and that lesbians and gay men should enjoy rights equal to those of the heterosexual majority. The persisting opposition to the gay rights movement indicates the power of ideas—as ideology—to inhibit as well as to advance social change.

The Natural Environment

Human societies are closely related to their natural environment, so change in one tends to produce change in the other.

Many traditional Native American cultures believed strongly in preserving the natural environment, while most European colonizers saw nature as an adversary to be tamed and then molded to human purposes. Confronting a wilderness, the newcomers systematically cut down forests to provide space and materials for building, established towns, extended roads in every direction, and dammed rivers as a source of water and energy. Early in the seventeenth century, Manhattan Island was covered with woods and streams; today the center of New York City is twenty-two square miles of almost unbroken concrete and buildings that soar thousands of feet into the sky. Such human construction not only reveals the American determination to master the natural environment, but also suggests how central economic activity is to American society. This industrial transformation has wrought enormous benefits but has also strained the natural environment to a degree that threatens human society.

In addition to being acted upon, the natural environment also acts upon human societies, sometimes with devastating effect. A thriving civilization in ancient India was destroyed in about 1500 B.C.E. as the waters of the Indus River gradually rose. Four centuries later, devastating earthquakes ended an early civilization on the island of Crete (Hamblin, 1973; Stavrianos, 1983). As any resi-

Americans have achieved a high standard of living partly through indifference to the long-term consequences of our way of life for the natural environment. Some resources are in danger of being depleted, clean air and water can no longer be taken for granted, and only a small fraction of waste materials is currently recycled in urban centers now awash in their own refuse.

dent of the American Gulf Coast knows, life is periodically disrupted by tropical storms, hurricanes, and tornadoes. In 1988 a major earthquake left thousands of Armenians dead; periodic drought in central Africa has killed thousands and devastated the lives of millions.

Population

Demographic factors (described in Chapter 21, "Population and Urbanization") also cause social change. Increasing population has put escalating demands on the natural environment. In many small countries, notably the Netherlands and Japan, limited space influences social patterns. For example, staircases in Amsterdam homes are steep by American standards in order to use less space; Japanese bus drivers routinely negotiate city streets that many American commuters would consider dangerously narrow. Although the United States and Canada have enjoyed a bounty of physical space, changing settlement patterns have affected American living as well. Small-town life, the norm a century ago, has been eclipsed by large-scale urban living. As the box explains, what remains of small-town America often shudders at the influx of "city slickers."

Profound change also results from the shifting composition of a population. Chapter 14 ("Aging and the Elderly") described some consequences of the aging of Americans. In 1990 almost 13 percent of Americans were over sixty-five, three times the proportion in 1900. By the year 2030, the percentage is expected to double

to about 25 percent (U.S. Bureau of the Census, 1989). Medical research and health-care services will increasingly focus on the elderly, and common stereotypes about old people will be challenged as more Americans enter this stage of life (Barberis, 1981).

Migration within and among societies is another demographic factor that promotes social change. It accelerates cultural diffusion as large numbers of people leave some areas and resettle elsewhere. Between 1870 and 1930, tens of millions of foreign immigrants swelled the industrial cities in the United States. Millions of rural Americans joined them. As a result, farm communities declined as metropolises expanded, and the United States became a predominantly urban society. Another change is taking place today, with small towns across the Sunbelt swelling with people as industries relocate there from Snowbelt states.

MODERNITY

Perhaps the key concept in the study of social change is **modernity**, *patterns of social life linked to industrialization*. In everyday usage, modernity designates the present in relation to the past. Sociologists include within this catch-all concept the social patterns that arose in the wake of the Industrial Revolution that began in Western Europe in the late eighteenth century. **Modernization**, therefore, is *the process of social change initiated by indus-*

Change in Rural America: The Invasion of the City Slickers

Historically, population increase in the United States has gone hand in hand with the development of cities. Urbanization sometimes brings dramatic changes to people living in rural villages and small towns that are drawn into the orbit of expanding cities. While some small-town residents may applaud this change, others resist it.

When city people move to the country, Noel Perrin explains, they bring with them "a series of unconscious assumptions. It might be better for rural America if they brought a few sticks of dynamite. . . ."

Take a typical example. Mr. and Mrs. Nice are Bostonians. They live a couple of miles off Route 128 in a four-bedroom house. He's a partner in an ad agency; she has considerable talent as an artist. For some years they've had a second home in northern New Hampshire. The kids love it up there in Grafton County.

For some years, too, both Nices have been feeling they'd like to simplify their lives. They look with increasing envy on their New Hampshire neighbors, who never face a morning traffic jam, or an evening one, either; who don't have a long drive to the country on Friday night and a long drive back on Sunday; who aren't cramped into a suburban lot; who live in harmony with the natural rhythm of the year; who think the rat race is probably some minor event at a county fair.

One Thursday evening Don Nice says to Sue that he's been talking to the other partners, and they've agreed there's no reason he can't do some of his work at home. If he's in the office Wednesday and Thursday every week, why, the rest of the time he can stay in touch by telephone. Sue, who has been trapped all year as a Brownie Scout leader and who has recently had the aerial snapped off her car in Boston, is delighted. She reflects happily that in their little mountain village you don't even need to lock your house, and there is no Brownie troop.

So the move occurs. In most ways Don and Sue are very happy. They raise practically all their own vegetables the first year; Sue takes up cross-country skiing. Don personally splits some of the wood they burn in their new woodstove.

But there are some problems. The first one Sue is conscious of is the school. It's just not very good. It's clear to Sue almost immediately that the town desperately needs a new school building—and also modern playground equipment, new school buses, more and better art instruction at the high school, a different principal. Don is as upset as Sue when they discover that only about 40 percent of the kids who graduate from that high school go on to any form of college. The rest do native things like becoming farmers, and mechanics, and joining the Air Force. An appalling number of the girls marry within twelve months after graduation. How are Jeanie and Don, Jr., going to get into good colleges from this school? . . . Pretty soon Sue and Don join an informal group of newcomers in town who are working to upgrade education. All they want for starters is the new building ($5.6 million) and a majority of their kind on the school board.

As for Don, though he really enjoys splitting the wood—in fact, next year he's planning to get a chainsaw and start cutting a few trees of his own—he also likes to play golf. There's no course within twenty miles. Some of the nice people he's met in the education lobby feel just as he does. They begin to discuss the possibility of a nine-hole course. The old farmer who owns the land they have in mind seems to be keeping only four or five cows on it, anyway. Besides, taxes are going up, and the old fellow is going to have to sell, sooner or later. (Which is too bad, of course. Don and Sue both admire the local farmers, and they're sincerely sorry whenever one has to quit.)

Over the next several years, Don and Sue get more and more adjusted to rural living—and they also gradually discover more things that need changing. For example, the area needs a good French restaurant. And it needs a much better airport. At present there are only two flights a day to Boston, and because of the lack of sophisticated equipment, even they are quite often canceled. If Don wants to be sure of getting down for an important meeting, he has to drive. Sue would be glad of more organized activities for the kids. There's even talk of starting a Brownie troop.

In short, if enough upper-middle-class people move to a rural town, they are naturally going to turn it into a suburb of the nearest city. For one generation it will be a nice and truly rustic suburb, with real farms dotted around it, and real natives speaking their minds at town meeting. Then as the local people are gradually taxed out of existence (or at least out of town), one more piece of rural America has died.

SOURCE: Noel Perrin, "Rural Area: Permit Required," *Country Journal*, April 1980, pp. 34–35.

trialization. Peter Berger (1977) notes four general characteristics of modernization.

1. **The decline of small, traditional communities.** Modernity involves "the progressive weakening, if not destruction, of the concrete and relatively cohesive communities in which human beings have found solidarity and meaning throughout most of history" (Berger, 1977:72). For thousands of years, in the camps of hunters and gatherers and in the rural villages of early North American settlers, humans lived in small-scale settlements with family and neighbors. Each person had a well-defined place in a traditional world, and sentiments and beliefs were widely shared and passed from generation to generation. Living in small primary groups limited the range of personal experience but conferred a strong sense of identity, belonging, and purpose. Although small, isolated communities still exist in many societies, including the United States, they are not typical of industrialized societies. Population growth and more efficient communication and transportation have expanded the scale of social life. The family is no longer the unrivaled center of everyday life; as Talcott Parsons (1966) noted, modern life is now carried out within distinct social institutions repre-

sented by schools, workplaces, hospitals, prisons, and places of worship.

2. **The expansion of personal choice.** People in traditional preindustrial societies view their lives as being shaped by forces beyond human control—gods, spirits, or simply fate. These societies jealously guard their traditions and afford members a narrow range of personal choices.

    As the power of tradition declines, a society's members come to see their lives as an unending series of options. Berger calls this process *individualization*. Americans, for instance, embrace multiple "lifestyles"; a way of life that feels comfortable to one person may be of little interest to another. Berger suggests that recognizing alternatives in everyday life is synonymous with a willingness to embrace change. Modern people, then, readily imagine that "things could be other than what they have been" (1977:77).

3. **Increasing diversity in beliefs.** In preindustrial societies, strong family ties and powerful religious beliefs enforce conformity, discouraging diversity and change. Modernization promotes a more rational, scientific world view, in which traditional beliefs weaken and morality becomes a matter of individual attitude. The growth of cities, expansion of impersonal, formal organizations, and mix of im-

In response to the rapid change in the industrial world, Paul Gauguin left France for the South Seas, where he was captivated by a simpler and seemingly timeless way of life. He romanticized this environment in his 1894 painting *Mahana no Atua* (*Day of the Gods*).

Paul Gaugin, *Day of the Gods* (*Mahana no Atua*), 1894. Oil on canvas, 68.3 x 91.5 cm. The Art Institute of Chicago, Helen Birch Bartlett Memorial Collection.

migrants from around the world foster in modern societies a diversity of beliefs and behavior as well as a tolerant openness to those who differ from ourselves.

Chapter 17 ("Religion") discussed *secularization* as the historical decline of the importance of religion. Religion does play only a limited role in many Americans' lives, but modern societies do not entirely abandon religious beliefs. Support for the more established churches has declined in the United States, but at the same time fundamentalist religious activity has flourished (Stark & Bainbridge, 1981; Johnstone, 1983).

4. **Future orientation and growing awareness of time.** People in modern societies have a distinctive appreciation of time. First, we tend to think more about the future than about the past. Preindustrial people are guided by traditions. Modern people, however, lack the traditional roots and look toward the future imagining that life will be improved by inventions and discoveries. Second, modern societies organize daily routines according to precise units of time.

Preindustrial societies measured time according to the day or the season. Europeans began thinking in terms of hours and minutes when clocks were introduced late in the Middle Ages. The precise measurement of time became steadily more important; shortly after the Industrial Revolution, people were claiming "Time is money!" Berger suggests that the wearing of wristwatches is one sign that a traditional society is industrializing.

In sum, Berger sees modernization as human emancipation from tightly knit communities in which traditional religious beliefs provide each person with a strong sense of belonging but little individual freedom. Modern societies offer far more autonomy but less personal and enduring social ties.

Finally, recall that modernization is one of the causes of sociology itself. As was noted in Chapter 1 ("The Sociological Perspective"), sociology emerged in the wake of the Industrial Revolution in Western Europe, precisely where social change was most intense. Early European and American sociologists attempted to describe and explain the rise of modern society.

PROFILE

Ferdinand Toennies (1855–1936)

What happens to traditional human virtues such as selflessness and honor in the modern world? This question is answered in the work of Ferdinand Toennies, who, along with Max Weber and Georg Simmel, helped to establish sociology as an academic discipline in Germany.

Toennies was born to a wealthy family in the German countryside, and he received an extensive education. During his lifetime the Industrial Revolution was transforming Germany and other European countries. Toennies's work divulges deep concern with the quality of life in modern societies. His influential book *Gemeinschaft and Gesellschaft* is both an account of modernization and a reaction to an increasingly impersonal world.

Toennies's thesis is that traditional societies, built on kinship and neighborhood, nourish collective sentiments, morality, and honor, whereas modernization erodes human community and fosters individualism. He did not claim that modern society was "worse" than societies of the past; in fact, he celebrated the new rational, scientific thinking. Nevertheless, he was critical of growing individualism. Knowing that there could be no return to the past, he looked to the future, hoping that new forms of social organization would combine traditional collective responsibility and modern rationality.

SOURCE: Based on Werner J. Cahnman and Rudolf Heberle, "Introduction," in *Ferdinand Toennies on Sociology: Pure, Applied, and Empirical* (Chicago: University of Chicago Press, 1971), pp. vii–xxii.

Toennies: The Loss of Community

The German sociologist Ferdinand Toennies, who is introduced in the box, produced a highly influential account of modernization, discussed at length in Chapter 21 ("Population and Urbanization"). Like Peter Berger, whose work he influenced, Toennies viewed modernization as the progressive loss of human community, or *Gemeinschaft*, by which personal ties provided a sense of group membership and loyalty. The Industrial Revolution undermined this strong social fabric by introducing a businesslike emphasis on facts and efficiency. European and North American societies gradually became rootless and impersonal and people came to associate mostly on the basis of self-interest—a state Toennies termed *Gesellschaft* (1963; orig. 1987).

Much of American society early in this century approximated Toennies's concept of *Gemeinschaft*. Families that had lived in small villages and towns for many generations had become deeply bound together. Members of these families knew each other personally and participated in a hard-working, slow-moving way of life. The social world was limited in space as well as in its way of life. Telephones (invented, in 1876) were rare; not until 1915 could an American place a coast-to-coast call across the United States. Living without television (introduced in 1939, and rare until the 1950s) encouraged families to entertain themselves, and they often gathered with friends in the evening—much like Brazil's Kaiapo—

to share stories, sorrows, or song. Without rapid transportation (Henry Ford's assembly line began in 1908, but cars became common only after World War II), many people perceived their own town as their entire world.

Past communities had inevitable tensions and conflicts, often based on race, ethnicity, and religion. According to Toennies, however, the traditional ties of *Gemeinschaft* caused the people of a community to "remain essentially united in spite of all separating factors" (1963:65).

Modern societies are closer to Toennies's concept of *Gesellschaft*, with people being "essentially separated in spite of united factors" (1963:65). In large cities, for example, most people live among strangers, ignore those they pass on the street, and do not expect others to understand the world as they do or even to treat them fairly. No wonder, as one recent news report indicated, 15 million Americans attend weekly support groups—also made up of strangers—in which they establish temporary emotional ties and find someone who is willing simply to *listen* (Leerhsen, 1990).

A major contributor to American society's rootlessness is geographic mobility. Table 23–1 shows that almost 20 percent of Americans change their residence each year because of a new job, divorce, or simply a desire for something better.

Gemeinschaft is not completely absent in modern life. Even in a world of strangers, friendships are often lasting and powerful, and many ethnic neighborhoods

George Tooker's painting *The Subway* depicts a common problem of modern life: weakening social ties and traditions that may leave us strangers to one another, anxious about who we are.

Table 23–1 MOVING ON IN MODERN AMERICA

| | Residence in 1987 | | | | |
Region	Same House as 1986	Different House than in 1986	Different House Same County	Different County Same State	Different State
Northeast	87.6%	11.9%	7.6%	2.7%	1.6%
Midwest	83.0	16.7	10.7	3.6	2.4
South	79.4	20.3	12.9	4.0	3.4
West	76.6	22.4	14.5	4.5	3.4
Total U.S.	81.4	18.1	11.6	3.7	2.8

SOURCE: U.S. Census Bureau, *Geographical Mobility: March 1986 to March 1987.* (Washington, D.C.: Government Printing Office, 1989), pp. 16–17.

share a strong sense of local community. Particularly in cosmopolitan districts of large cities, however, an indifference to those outside of an immediate circle—the attitude that disturbed Toennies in the 1880s—raises difficult ethical questions today, as the box explains.

Critical evaluation. Toennies's theory of *Gemeinschaft* and *Gesellschaft* is perhaps the most widely cited model for describing the rise of modern societies. The theory's strength lies in its synthesis of various dimensions of change—growing population, the rise of cities, greater impersonality. A limitation of Toennies's approach is that it does not specify which factors are cause and which are effect. Critics have also asserted that Toennies favored—perhaps even romanticized—traditional societies.

Durkheim: The Division of Labor

The French sociologist Emile Durkheim, whose work is discussed in Chapter 4 ("Society"), shared Toennies's interest in the profound social changes wrought by the Industrial Revolution. Durkheim based his analysis of the rise of modernity on the increasing *division of labor*, or specialized economic activity, that accompanies industrialization (1964b; orig. 1893). Whereas traditional societies involve everyone in many of the same activities, modern societies assign highly distinctive productive roles.

Durkheim claimed that *mechanical solidarity*—social bonds that result from shared moral sentiments—

is common to small preindustrial societies, where people perceive themselves as being alike and therefore belonging together. Mechanical solidarity persists as long as the division of labor is minimal, that is, as long as everyone engages in the same traditional activities. Durkheim's mechanical solidarity is essentially the same as Toennies's *Gemeinschaft*.

As the division of labor becomes more pronounced in a society, according to Durkheim, mechanical solidarity changes to *organic solidarity*—social bonds of mutual dependency based on specialization. Thus modern societies are held together not by likeness but by *difference*. Since specialization is characteristic of such societies, individuals engage in only a single activity and are dependent on others to meet their various needs. Organic solidarity is similar to Toennies's concept of *Gesellschaft*.

Despite obvious similarities, Durkheim and Toennies interpreted modernity somewhat differently. Toennies viewed the modern world of *Gesellschaft* as the loss of social solidarity—the gradual change from "natural" and "organic" traditions of the rural past to "artificial" and "mechanical" patterns of contemporary cities. Durkheim maintained that the city is as natural as the village. He made this point by reversing Toennies's use of the terms organic and mechanical; he labeled modern social life "organic" and traditional societies as "mechanical" because they were so regimented. Thus Durkheim viewed modernization not as a loss of community but as a *change* in the basis of community—from bonds of likeness (kinship and neighborhood) to economic interdependence (the division of labor). Durkheim's view of modernity is both more complex and more positive than that of Toennies.

Modern Society: What Do We Owe Others?

In an impersonal society, how much should we involve ourselves in the lives of others? Probably few want to maintain the "tyranny of the tribe" by which people in traditional communities suspiciously monitor each other. Nevertheless, inhabitants of modern societies experience a social isolation fostered by anonymity.

Especially in very large cities, Americans sometimes become too caught up in their own lives to recognize any responsibility toward others. The 1964 murder of Kitty Genovese in New York City offered a stunning example. Returning from work late at night, Genovese was stabbed to death in the parking lot near her apartment building. At least thirty-eight of her neighbors observed the prolonged attack over more than half an hour—and not one tried to help her or even called the police. Bystander apathy occurs often enough to raise troubling questions about people's proper responsibility for others in a world that often puts personal concerns ahead of community needs.

In the New Testament book of Luke (10:30–37), Jesus responded to the question "Who is my neighbor?" with the tale of the Good Samaritan.

A man on the road to Jericho was robbed and left for dead; several travelers passed by without offering him any help. Then a Samaritan stopped, attended to the man's wounds, took him to an inn, and left money to pay for further care. Although the Samaritan had no personal relationship with the victim and did not even know his name, he responded to the man's need with a compassionate human act. Perhaps it is possible for members of modern society to express their common humanity without surrendering their privacy.

Critical evaluation. Durkheim's work stands alongside that of Toennies, which it closely resembles, as a highly influential analysis of modernity. Of the two, Durkheim is clearly the more optimistic about modernity, but still, he feared that modern societies would become so internally diverse that they would collapse into *anomie,* a condition of weak and inconsistent norms and values so that society provides little moral guidance to individuals. As was noted in Chapter 4 ("Society"), modern individuals prone to anomie will tend toward egocentrism, placing their own needs above those of others.

There is evidence that anomie is a problem of modern societies. Suicide rates, which Durkheim viewed as an index of anomie, have risen during this century. Even so, shared norms and values are still strong enough to give our lives meaning, despite the rise of egocentrism. Additionally, whatever the hazards of social atomization, most people seem to value the privacy and personal autonomy it affords.

Weber: Rationalization

Max Weber held that ideas and beliefs cause social change, as discussed in Chapter 4 ("Society"). For Weber, modernity is the progressive replacement of tradition by rationality in the way people view the world.

Strong tradition acts as a constant brake to change. To members of traditional societies, "truth" is more or less synonymous with what has always been (1978:36; orig. 1921). Modern societies, in contrast, see truth as something that continually changes as a result of deliberate calculation. Where efficiency is valued, a society readily adopts whatever new social patterns will allow individuals to achieve their goals most easily. With a rational view of the world, then, we can assess a range of options according to their specific consequences rather than according to an absolute standard.

Weber agreed with Toennies and Durkheim about the steady weakening of tradition and declared that modern society had become "disenchanted." What used to be unquestioned truths have, in a rational world view, become variable and calculable. Modern society, Weber stressed, is secular because it has turned away from the gods toward rational, scientific thought.

In the process, Weber continued, modern society has become even more bureaucratic. Whereas traditional social organization relies on personal loyalties and past practices, modern bureaucracy devises policies to accomplish its tasks efficiently. As is recounted in Chapter 7

("Groups and Organizations"), formal organizations deliberately foster impersonality in order to operate more efficiently.

Critical evaluation. Compared with Toennies, and especially Durkheim, Weber was a profound critic of modern society. He recognized that science could produce technological wonders but also that it was unable to answer basic questions about the meaning and purpose of human existence. Weber feared that rationalization, especially in bureaucracies, would erode the human spirit with endless rules and regulations. Some critics of Weber believe that the alienation that he attributed to bureaucracy was actually a product of social inequality. This was the contention of Karl Marx.

Marx: Capitalism

While other analysts of modernity examined shifting patterns of moral consensus and social stability, Marx stressed social conflict. For Marx, modern society was synonymous with capitalism, and he saw the Industrial Revolution as being primarily a *capitalist revolution.* As was explained in Chapter 4 ("Society"), Marx claimed that the bourgeoisie emerged in medieval Europe as a social class intent on wresting control of society from the traditional nobility. The bourgeoisie were finally successful when the Industrial Revolution placed a powerful new productive system under their control.

One indication of modernization is that all people no longer engage in traditional activities such as farming. Instead, individuals assume increasingly specialized roles. Hoping to secure a day's work in Mexico City, these men offer their services as electricians, contractors, painters, and plumbers.

Marx agreed that modernity weakened small-scale communities (as described by Toennies), increased the division of labor (as noted by Durkheim), and fostered a rational world view (as asserted by Weber). But he saw these factors simply as conditions necessary for capitalism to flourish: capitalism draws population from rural areas and small towns into an ever-growing market system centered in the cities; specialization forms the foundation for the operation of factories; and rationality is most clearly expressed in modern society's unending quest for greater profits.

Earlier chapters have shown that Marx relentlessly criticized capitalist society, but his vision of modernity contains a crucial element of optimism. Unlike Weber, who viewed modern society as an "iron cage" of bureaucracy, Marx believed that social conflict within capitalist social systems would produce revolutionary social change and ultimately lead to the establishment of a socially equal communist society. Such a society, he claimed, would allow the wonders of industrial technology to enrich the lives of the many rather than the few—and thereby rid the world of social conflict and dehumanization. While Marx's evaluation of modern capitalist society was highly negative, he anticipated a future with greater human freedom and a renewed sense of human community.

Critical evaluation. The strength of Marx's analysis is that it identifies various dimensions of social change as products of a single dominant factor: the rise of capitalism. Marx therefore may have underestimated the significance of bureaucracy in shaping modern societies. The stifling effects of bureaucracy on humanity may well be worse in socialist societies with their expanded governmental apparatus; recent political unrest in Eastern Europe and the Soviet Union has certainly been a popular struggle against entrenched bureaucracies.

Understanding Modernity: The Theory of Mass Society

The rise of modernity is a complex process involving many kinds of transformations, described in previous chapters and summarized in Table 23–2. One broad approach combining the various dimensions of change holds that modernization has spawned *mass societies* (Dahrendorf, 1959; Kornhauser, 1959; Nisbet, 1966, 1969; Baltzell, 1968; Stein, 1972; Berger, Berger, & Kellner, 1974).

Table 23–2 TRADITIONAL AND MODERN SOCIETIES: DIMENSIONS OF DIFFERENCE

	Characteristics of Traditional Societies	Characteristics of Modern Societies
Scale of Life	Small scale; population typically small and widely dispersed in rural villages and small towns	Large scale; population typically large and concentrated in cities
Social Structure		
Status and role	Few statuses, most ascribed; few specialized roles	Many statuses, some ascribed and some achieved; many specialized roles
Relationships	Typically primary; little anonymity and privacy	Typically secondary; considerable anonymity and privacy
Communication	Face-to-face	Face-to-face communication supplemented by extensive mass media
Social control	Informal gossip	Formal police and legal system
Social stratification	Rigid patterns of social inequality; little mobility	Fluid patterns of social inequality; considerable social mobility
Gender patterns	Pronounced patriarchy; few women in the paid labor force	Declining patriarchy; increasing number of women in the paid labor force
Family	Extended family as the primary means of socialization and economic production	Nuclear family retains some socialization function but is a unit of consumption rather than production
Religion	Religion guides world view; little religious pluralism	Religion weakens with the rise of science; extensive religious pluralism
Education	Formal schooling limited to elites	Basic schooling becomes universal, with growing proportion receiving advanced education
State	Small-scale government; little state intervention into society	Large-scale government; considerable state intervention into society
Economy	Based on agriculture; some manufacturing within the home; little white-collar work	Based on industrial mass production; factories become centers of production; increasing white-collar work
Health	High birth and death rates; brief life expectancy because of low standard of living and simple medical technology	Low birth and death rates; longer life expectancy because of higher standard of living and complex medical technology
Cultural Patterns		
Values	Homogeneous; sacred character; few subcultures and countercultures	Heterogeneous; secular character; many subcultures and countercultures
Norms	High moral significance; little tolerance of diversity	Variable moral significance; high tolerance of diversity
Orientation	Present linked to past	Present linked to future
Technology	Preindustrial; human and animal energy	Industrial; advanced energy sources
Social Change	Slow; change evident over many generations	Rapid; change evident within a single generation

A **mass society** is *a society in which industrialization and expanding bureaucracy have weakened social ties.* As people become socially isolated or atomized in modern societies, they experience feelings of uncertainty and personal powerlessness. Mass-society theory draws upon the ideas of Ferdinand Toennies, Emile Durkheim, and Max Weber. This analysis argues, first, that the scale of modern life has increased so that impersonality and cultural diversity overwhelm the individual and draw meaning out of people's lives. Second, the government has expanded to the point that it manages many aspects of people's lives, so that tasks that used to be carried out by strong families and cohesive neighborhoods are now regulated by strangers—nameless officials in distant and unresponsive bureaucracies. We will discuss each of these two arguments in turn.

Expanding Scale of Social Life

Before the Industrial Revolution, Europe and North America were an intricate mosaic of countless rural villages and small towns. In these small communities, which inspired Toennies's concept of *Gemeinschaft*, people lived together for their entire lives with little personal privacy. Gossip was an informal, yet highly effective, means of enforcing rigid conformity to community standards. Limited community size, social isolation, and a strong, traditional religion combined to generate homogeneous cultural values—the mechanical solidarity described by Durkheim. For example, in England before 1690, law and local custom demanded that everyone attend church and partake in the Christian ritual of Holy Communion (Laslett, 1984). Similarly, New England's colonies offered little support for religious dissent. Because social differences were repressed, subcultures and countercultures rarely flourished and social change proceeded slowly. Also social stratification was rigidly rooted in birth, and there was little social mobility.

The rise of population, the growth of cities, and the specialization of economic activity during the Industrial Revolution expanded the scale of social life. People came to be known by their function (for example, as the "doctor" or the "bank clerk") rather than by their kinship group or home town. Beyond their business ties, the majority of people were a mass of strangers to each other. Gradually, the face-to-face communication of the village was replaced by the mass media: newspapers, radio, and television. Large organizations assumed more responsibility for daily needs that had once been fulfilled by family, friends, and neighbors; universal public edu-

cation enlarged the scope of learning; police, lawyers, and formal courts supervised a criminal justice system; and even charity became the work of impersonal bureaucracies such as the Red Cross and public welfare agencies.

As people became more mobile, had access to expanded communications, and were exposed to many different cultural values and norms, their traditional values were eroded. Less certain about what was worth believing, they became more tolerant of cultural diversity and placed greater value on individual rights and freedom of choice. Subcultures and countercultures thrived. As categorical distinctions among people came under increasing attack, women and racial and ethnic minorities gained broader participation in society, including the right to vote. These greater opportunities, within an expanding economy, stimulated social mobility for some.

The Rise of the State

In the small-scale, preindustrial societies of Europe, government amounted to little more than the local nobility. A single royal family formally presided over all of England but had little actual control over society, since communication and transportation were so inefficient.

As the centuries passed, government became centralized and grew in size and importance. As was noted in Chapter 18 ("Politics and Government"), at the time of U.S. independence the federal government was a tiny fraction of its present size and its function was largely national defense. Since then, government has entered more and more areas of social life: regulating wages and working conditions, educating the population, and providing financial assistance to the ill and the unemployed. Taxes have correspondingly increased, and the average American now works four months a year to pay for these expanded services.

As a consequence of these changes, power now resides in large bureaucracies, and people in local communities feel they have little control over their lives. For example, the federal government now requires schools to have standardized educational programs, products to carry specific labels, and businesses to keep extensive records. While such regulations may protect people and enhance uniformity of treatment, they depersonalize human decision making and limit the autonomy of neighborhoods, families, and individuals.

Critical evaluation. The theory of mass society views the transformation of small-scale societies as both a positive and a negative development. Modern societies increase individual rights, magnify toleration of social differences, and raise standards of living. But they seem prone to what Max Weber feared most—excessive bureaucracy—and to what Emile Durkheim called anomie. Their size and complexity cause individuals to feel isolated and powerless. As was noted in Chapter 18 ("Politics and Government"), only about half of the population eligible to vote do so. This voter apathy suggests that within such a political system—as in many dimensions of large-scale societies—people feel overwhelmed by the scope of social life and conclude that no one person can make a difference.

A criticism of this interpretation of modernity is that it tends to be indifferent to deliberate changes that would lessen social inequality. Mass-society analysis thus attracts considerable support from social and economic conservatives, who defend conventional morality and oppose extensive government regulation of social life.

Understanding Modernity: The Theory of Class Society

A second interpretation of modernity is derived largely from the ideas of Karl Marx. A **class society** is *a society in which capitalism has generated pronounced social stratification.* According to this theory, social inequality is the cause of widespread feelings of powerlessness. This approach recognizes that modern societies have enlarged to a mass scale but claims that the heart of modernization is an expanding capitalist economy. Capitalist societies still contain pronounced inequality and social conflict, even if the inequality is somewhat less than it was a century ago (Miliband, 1969; Habermas, 1970; Polenberg, 1980; Blumberg, 1981; Harrington, 1984).

Capitalism

According to Marx, the Industrial Revolution was not the main reason for the increasing scale of social life during the nineteenth century in Europe and North America. He attributed this growth to the insatiable appetites of capitalism. Because a capitalist economy pursues ever-increasing profits, both production and consumption expand. Marx considered the Industrial Revolution to be a significant stage in the enlarging capitalist economic system.

According to Marx, capitalism is driven by the profit motive and emphasizes "naked self-interest" and individual greed, even at the expense of others (1972:337; orig. 1848). In the process, it undermines the social ties that once cemented small-scale communities. Capitalism employs impersonality and anonymity to transform people into commodities—either a source of labor or a market for the expanding economy. In this way, capitalism gradually reduced human beings to cogs in the machinery of material production.

Science, too, plays a role in this analysis. In preindustrial Europe the nobility defended their rule with traditional conceptions of obligation and responsibility supported by religion. Although science does rival religion in modern society, it also legitimates the status quo by encouraging us to view social well-being as a technical puzzle to be solved by engineers and other experts rather than a social problem requiring greater equality (Habermas, 1970). In other words, class-society theory claims, science proposes a "technical fix" in place of meaningful change, such as combating poor health through high-technology medicine rather than through elimination of the poverty that undermines health in the first place.

Businesses also use scientific logic in claiming that efficiency demands continual growth. As was described in Chapter 19 ("The Economy and Work"), industrial-capitalist corporations have reached enormous size and control almost unimaginable wealth. Nevertheless, to increase their profits even more, they have transformed themselves into multinationals operating throughout the world. From the class-society point of view, then, the expanding scale of life is the inevitable and destructive consequence of capitalism.

The Persistence of Social Inequality

Modernity has gradually decreased rigid categorical distinctions that divided preindustrial societies. Class-society theory maintains, however, that elite groups persist, now as capitalist millionaires rather than family-based nobles. Recall from Chapter 10 ("Social Class in America") that the richest 5 percent of Americans control more than half of this nation's wealth. As Paul Blumberg (1981) notes, even the rising standard of living in the United States during this century has not altered the fact that a very small minority still controls most of the wealth while a significant minority continues to live in poverty.

What of the expanding state, which mass-society theory suggests has an expanding role in addressing social problems? The capitalist state, Marx argued, usually defends the wealth and privileges of capitalists; the greater their wealth, the more powerful their political defense. Working Americans and minorities do enjoy greater political rights and economic benefits today, but these are more the fruits of political struggle than expressions of government benevolence. Throughout the 1980s conservative political leaders, in the name of economic growth and free-market efficiency, attempted to curtail government funding for programs that benefited less-privileged Americans (Harrington, 1984; Jacob, 1986).

Critical evaluation. Class-society theory interprets the rise of modernity very differently than does mass-society theory, as is seen in the summary in Table 23-3. Instead of emphasizing the increasing scale of social life and the rise of large formal organizations, this approach stresses the expansion of capitalism. Rejecting mass-society theory's claim that many social problems have been addressed, class-society theory asserts that social inequality persists. Class-society theory also dismisses Durkheim's argument that people in modern societies suffer from the moral collapse of anomie. Instead, the malaise of modern life is argued to be alienation and powerlessness caused by persistent social inequality. Not surprisingly, then, the class-society interpretation of modernity enjoys widespread support among social and economic liberals who favor greater equality and desire more extensive regulation of the capitalist marketplace.

A criticism of this theory is that it ignores the many ways in which modern societies have grown more egalitarian. Moreover, the categorical distinctions based on race, ethnicity, religion, and sex that do persist are now widely defined as social problems. As was noted in Chapter 10 ("Social Class in America"), while the

overall amount of social inequality remains great, it has decreased since the early Industrial Revolution.

The Individual in Modern Society

Mass- and class-society theories focus primarily on *broad* patterns of social change since the Industrial Revolution. These "macro-level" approaches also offer "micro-level" insights into how modernity affects the lives of individuals.

Mass Society: Problems of Identity

Large-scale societies of the modern world have liberated individuals from the tightly knit small communities of the past. Modern Americans possess greater privacy and unprecedented freedom to express their individuality and choose their lifestyle. Mass-society theory suggests, however, that resulting social diversity, atomization, and rapid social change make it difficult for many people to establish an identity (Wheelis, 1958; Riesman, 1970; Berger, Berger, & Kellner, 1974).

Chapter 5 ("Socialization") explains that people forge distinctive personalities from the surrounding social world. The small, homogeneous, and slowly changing societies of the past provided a firm foundation that offered clear direction for an individual's personal identity and life experience. For example, the Amish communities that still flourish in the United States and Canada (see the box in Chapter 3) support a well-defined identity by teaching traditions and limiting personal choice. Members of these communities know the meaning of being Amish—that is, how the Amish think and behave—and have learned to view this type of life as "natural" and right. Not everyone born into an Amish community can tolerate these demands for conformity, but most members establish a coherent personal identity (Hostetler, 1980).

Large, culturally diverse, and rapidly changing societies, in contrast, provide only shifting sands to serve as a foundation on which individuals attempt to form personal identity. People make their own decisions about how to live, and they confront a bewildering range of options from which to choose. With such autonomy, and a lack of social standards, generally no one choice seems more compelling than any other. Not surprisingly, then, many people shuttle from one identity to another, changing their lifestyle in search of an elusive "true self." The problem is not psychological, although it is

Table 23–3 TWO INTERPRETATIONS OF MODERNITY: A SUMMARY

	Key Process of Modernization	Key Effects of Modernization
Mass-society theory	Industrialization; growth of bureaucracy	Increasing scale of life; rise of the state and other formal organizations
Class-society theory	Rise of capitalism	Expansion of capitalist economy, persistence of social inequality

Affluent Americans confront such a wide range of choices about how to live that they often speak of their "lifestyles" as something they shape for themselves. For most of humanity, however, tradition and lack of opportunity generate a more fixed existence and a more well-defined personal identity.

often treated as an individual problem. More accurately, such people are suffering from the widespread "relativism" of modern societies; they have lost the security and certainty once provided by tradition.

David Riesman (1970; orig. 1950) has described modernization in terms of changing **social character,** that is, *personality patterns common to members of a society.* Social character takes one form among people living in traditional societies and another among those in modern societies. Preindustrial societies, Riesman claims, promote **tradition-directedness,** *rigid personalities based on conformity to time-honored ways of living.* Members of such societies model their lives on what has gone before: what is "good" is equivalent to "what has always been." Thus tradition-directedness is the experience of cultural conservatism associated with Toennies's *Gemeinschaft* and Durkheim's mechanical solidarity. Tradition-directed people tend to think and act alike. Their conformity, however, unlike that of modern people, is not an effort to mimic one another, but rather a result of everyone drawing on the same cultural foundation, which is held to be the one proper way to live. For the tradition-directed Amish, for example, a rigidly prescribed life means "submission to the will of God" (Hostetler, 1980:172).

In culturally diverse and rapidly changing industrial societies, a rigid personality becomes a liability. Such societies prize personal flexibility, the capacity to adapt, and sensitivity to others. Riesman calls this type of social character **other-directedness,** *highly changeable personality patterns among people open to change and likely to imitate the behavior of others.* Because their socialization occurs within societies that are continuously in flux, other-directed people develop identities characterized by superficiality, inconsistency, and change. They try different identities, engaging, as Chapter 6 ("Social Interaction in Everyday Life") explains, in various "performances" as they move from setting to setting (Goffman, 1959). In a traditional society, such shifting behavior marks a person as untrustworthy, but in a modern society, the ability to fit in virtually anywhere is a valued personal trait (Wheelis, 1958). If conformity among tradition-directed people such as the Amish is an expression of unchanging morality, morality among other-directed people is sometimes little more than conforming to changing public opinion.

Other-directed Americans conform to peers and readily embrace fads. In societies that value the up-to-date rather than the traditional, the most significant role models are people of one's own generation, not a person's elders. Similarly, being liked by others may seem more important than being true to oneself. When social surroundings change so rapidly, however, what is the self to which one should be true? This problem is at the root of the identity crisis so familiar to Americans today. "Who Am I?" is a nagging question to many people throughout their lives. In sociological terms, this personal problem reflects the inherent instability of modern society itself.

Class Society: Problems of Powerlessness

Class-society theory maintains that persistent social inequality undermines modern society's promise of individual freedom. The unequal distribution of wealth and power, discussed in Chapters 9 ("Social Stratification") and 10 ("Social Class in America"), means that the privileges of some stand out against the powerlessness of others. Chapter 12 ("Race and Ethnicity") explains that members of racial and ethnic minorities remain disadvan-

Mass-society theory explains weak social ties as a result of rapid social change and the erosion of tradition. Class-society theory, in contrast, suggests that social inequality diminishes the likelihood of meaningful human community.

taged in modern America. Women enjoy increasing participation in modern societies, but as Chapter 13 ("Sex and Gender") establishes, they continue to experience traditional barriers of sexism. Elderly people as well encounter the prejudice and discrimination that Chapter 14 ("Aging and the Elderly") describes as ageism. Thus, whereas the theory of mass society suggests that people suffer from too much freedom, class-society theory holds that a majority of people in American society are still denied full participation in social life.

Demands for greater participation in decision making are therefore common. For example, workers seek greater power in the workplace, consumers press for more control over the marketplace, and citizens attempt to make government more responsive to their needs (Toffler, 1981).

On a global scale, as Chapter 11 ("Global Inequality") explained, the expanding scope of world capitalism has placed more of the earth's population under the influence of multinational corporations. As a result, about two-thirds of the world's income is concentrated in the richest societies, which contain only about 15 percent of its people. Class-society theorists therefore ask: Is it any wonder that throughout the Third World people are seeking greater power to shape their own lives?

Such problems led Herbert Marcuse (1964) to challenge Max Weber's contention that modern society is rational. Marcuse viewed modern society as irrational

because it fails to meet the basic needs of many people. While modern capitalist societies produce unparalleled wealth, poverty remains the daily plight of millions of their people and, in global terms, billions of people are poor. Moreover, technological advances have not empowered people, but rather reduced their control over their own lives. High technology, as the term is used in corporate energy production, favors control by elites who consider the public ill-equipped to share in decision making. Not only are most people rendered powerless, but a threat of nuclear annihilation still hangs over the entire globe. Despite the common view that technology *solves* the world's problems, Marcuse claims, it may be more accurate to say it *causes* them. In sum, class-society theory concludes, people suffer because modern societies have concentrated wealth as well as power.

Modernity and Progress

In modern societies, social change is generally applauded and is even expected. People link modernity to the idea of *progress* (from the Latin, meaning "a moving forward"), which they view as improvement. Stability, in contrast, is tied to the idea of stagnation.

This chapter began with a brief look at the plight of the Kaiapo of Brazil, for whom affluence has broadened opportunities but weakened individual identity. The erosion of their past will probably continue. As this example suggests, equating modernity with progress ignores the complexity of social change. Whether or not we see a given change as an improvement depends on our underlying values. A rising standard of living among the Kaiapo—or, historically, among Americans—has helped make lives longer and more comfortable, but also fueled materialism at the expense of spiritual life.

One of the reasons Americans tend to celebrate modern society is that it recognizes basic human rights. The idea that people have rights simply by virtue of being human, rather than having duties based on their social position, appears as a distinctly modern idea reflected in such documents as the American Declaration of Independence and the United Nations' Declaration of Human Rights (Berger, Berger, & Kellner, 1974). The contrast between the traditional notion of personal honor and the modern idea of individual dignity is highlighted in the box.

In principle, Americans support the idea that individuals should have considerable autonomy in shaping their own lives. Yet social diversity—the inevitable result of freedom of choice—seems to be a source of social conflict. For example, people may choose not to marry, but rather to remain single, live together without marrying, have children outside of marriage, or form a partnership with a member of their own sex. Thus personal

SOCIETY IN HISTORY

Traditional Honor and Modern Dignity

Honor occupies about the same place in contemporary usage as chastity. An individual asserting it hardly invites admiration, and one who claims to have lost it is an object of amusement rather than sympathy. (1974:83)

Honor is one of the vestiges of our heritage that seems distinctly out of place in modern society. The concept of *honor* is related to acting according to the traditional cultural norms of people within certain categories. Honor, then, cannot be separated from the strong morality and rigid social distinctions—between males and females, nobles and serfs, one's own people and those of other nations—characteristic of traditional societies. During the European Middle Ages, members of the nobility claimed honor when they carried out their feudal obligations to their social inferiors and displayed proper respect for their peers. Similarly, commoners were considered honorable to the extent that they fulfilled their duties to their superiors and abided by community norms.

Honor also lay at the heart of the relationship between men and women. To be honorable, men had to deal with women as females rather than as people; the medieval cultural norm was to display a fatherly, protective attitude and under no circumstances "take advantage" of them. For their part, women were honorable to the degree that they observed proper morals and manners in their affairs with men. In a traditional society, to suffer dishonor is to be stigmatized as ineligible for further social contact.

In modern societies, cultural norms are weaker and more variable, and growing egalitarianism undermines categories so that all people become basically alike. While the concept of honor survives among some ethnic groups and traditional occupations such as the military, it has far less significance for most members of modern societies.

Modernization enhances concern for people as *individuals*, which is expressed in the concept of *dignity*. Whereas there are different codes of honor that apply to various categories of people, dignity is a universal human trait, originating in the inherent value of everyone. We recognize the dignity of others when we acknowledge our common humanity despite any social differences.

In a society that prizes dignity, many women object to men treating them as females rather than as individuals. The traditional male practices of holding open a door for a woman and paying for a shared meal may be an affront to the dignity of women by underscoring social differences based on sex.

In sum, honor is the key to motivating people to conform to traditional cultural norms. However, cultural diversity and rapid social change in modern societies render the idea of honor suspect. In contrast, human beings are now viewed as having self-worth apart from any categories of society; this is the essence of dignity.

SOURCE: Based on Peter Berger, Brigitte Berger, Hansfried Kellner, *The Homeless Mind: Modernization and Consciousness* (New York: Vintage Books, 1974), pp. 83–96.

choice has weakened the traditional family. To supporters of individual choice, such changes symbolize progress, but those who value traditional family patterns as the backbone of society greet these developments with despair (Wallis, 1985).

Even technological advance has controversial aspects. Rapid transportation, efficient and extensive communications, the ability to combat disease, and other technological innovations have improved the lives of Americans in many ways. However, advanced technology has also unleashed an unprecedented threat to the natural environment and, in the form of nuclear weapons, to the future of all humanity.

Is social change the same as progress? Futurist Alvin Toffler claims it is not, suggesting that people who study social change "must resist the temptation to be seduced by straight lines" (1981:129). He means that social change does not proceed in a predictable, linear fashion. The present in some ways extends the past and in other respects is totally unexpected. Because social change is uncertain, complex, and controversial, we cannot simply assume the modern world is becoming better—or worse.

MODERNIZATION IN GLOBAL PERSPECTIVE

Social change proceeds sometimes haphazardly, sometimes deliberately. Some change that is desperately needed has not occurred at all, as in much of the Third

To some analysts, modernization is within the reach of all of the world's people; to others, the current global economy makes such improvement unlikely. Whether the majority of humanity living in the Third World is confronting a dawn of development or a dusk of dependency is a vital question likely to affect the lives of Americans as well.

World, where almost 1 billion people struggle with poverty that is life-threatening.

Two competing views of the causes of global poverty are presented in Chapter 11 ("Global Inequality"). *Modernization theory* claims that in the past the entire world was poor and that technological change, especially the Industrial Revolution, has greatly enhanced human productivity and raised the standard of living for many. From this point of view, the solution to global poverty is to encourage technological development elsewhere.

For reasons suggested earlier, however, global modernization may be difficult. Recall that David Riesman portrayed the social character of preindustrial peoples as *tradition-directed*. By embracing a way of life rooted in the past, such societies may resist change. Modernization theory therefore advocates that the world's rich societies deliberately intervene in such societies to encourage productive innovation. First-World nations should export technology to poor nations, welcome students from abroad, and provide generous foreign aid in order to stimulate movement away from tradition.

The review of modernization theory in Chapter 11 suggests that these policies have achieved only limited success. Where dramatic change has occurred, controversy has erupted. Traditional people such as Brazil's Kaiapo have gained wealth from the sale of resources to outsiders, but only at the cost of being drawn into the "global village" where concern for money replaces traditional values. In some societies, such as Iran and Ethiopia, rapid modernization has sparked a powerful backlash from segments who want to restore traditional culture.

A daunting problem within modernization theory, then, is that modernization may raise the living standards but, in the process, may turn a traditional society into a materialistic mass society, sweeping it into the global mass culture of Western pop music, fashions, and fast-food. One Brazilian anthropologist expressed uncertainty about the future of the Kaiapo: "At least they quickly understood the consequences of watching television. . . . Now [they] can make a choice" (Simons, 1989:37).

But is modernization really a choice? According to a second approach to global inequality, *dependency theory*, poor societies currently have little ability to improve, whether they want to or not. From this point of view, the major barrier to economic development is not traditionalism but rather a world economic system that has emerged over the last several centuries that benefits the rich societies of the First World at the expense of the Third World. Initially, as Chapter 11 explains, this system took the form of colonialism whereby European societies claimed ownership of much of Latin America, Africa, and Asia. Trading relationships soon enriched England, Spain, and other colonial powers, but simultaneously impoverished the colonies. Although most societies subjected to this form of domination are now politically independent, colonial ties continue in the form of multinational corporations operating throughout the world.

In effect, dependency theory asserts, rich societies achieved their modernization at least partly at the expense of poor nations, which provided valuable resources and human labor. Even today, poor societies remain locked in a disadvantageous economic relationship with the First World, dependent on rich societies to buy their raw materials and in return provide them with affordable manufactured products. Continuing ties with rich societies appear likely to perpetuate current patterns of global inequality.

Dependency theory implies that social change is not under the control of individual societies. On the contrary, the fate and fortune of individual nations worldwide is tied to their position in the global economy. Thus, change to improve the plight of people in the Third World will involve corresponding changes in First-World societies.

For this reason, we can no longer separate the study of American society from that of social patterns throughout the world. At the beginning of the twentieth century a majority of people in even the richest and most technologically complex societies lived in relatively small settlements and had a limited range of experience. Now, at the threshold of the twenty-first century, people everywhere participate in a far larger human drama. The world is smaller and the lives of all its people are increasingly linked. We now discuss the relationships among societies in the same way that people a century ago considered the expanding ties among towns and cities.

The twentieth century has witnessed unparalleled human achievement. Yet solutions to many of the timeless problems of human existence—including the problems of finding meaning in life, of poverty, and of tensions and conflict within societies—remain elusive. To this list of pressing matters, new concerns have been added, such as managing the global environment and maintaining world peace. One source of optimism as we approach the twenty-first century is that we look ahead with an unprecedented understanding of human society.

SUMMARY

1. Every society continuously changes, although with varying speed and consequences. Social change may be intentional or unplanned, but it is usually controversial.

2. One cause of social change is cultural processes, including invention and discovery within a society, and cultural diffusion from one society to another. Another cause is found in social structure—tensions and conflicts within society itself. The ways in which societies perceive the world can either encourage or inhibit social change. Finally, the natural environment and population dynamics contribute to social change.

3. Modernity is a social consequence of industrialization. Peter Berger notes that the general characteristics of modernity are the weakening of small traditional communities, the expansion of personal choice, the increasing diversity in patterns of belief, and a keener awareness of time, especially the future.

4. Ferdinand Toennies described modernization as the transition from *Gemeinschaft* to *Gesellschaft*. This process signifies the progressive loss of community amid growing individualism.

5. Emile Durkheim linked modernization to an expanding division of labor in productive activity. Mechanical solidarity, based on common activities and shared beliefs, gradually gives way to organic solidarity, in which specialization makes people interdependent.

6. Max Weber described the rise of modernity as the replacement of traditional patterns of thought by rationality. He feared that rational organization would dehumanize modern society.

7. Karl Marx's view of modernity was shaped by the triumph of capitalism over feudalism. Viewing capitalist societies as fraught with social conflict, he anticipated revolutionary change to a more egalitarian socialist society.

8. The theory of mass society emphasizes the growing scale of modern life and maintains that government and other formal organizations carry out many social tasks previously performed informally by the family and neighbors.

9. The theory of class society considers the development of capitalism to be the central element of modernization and stresses the persistence of social inequality in modern societies.

10. Mass-society theory explains that cultural diversity and rapid social change lead individuals in modern societies to develop variable personal identities and to have difficulty discovering certainty and significance in their lives.

11. Class-society theory claims the modern problem of gaining a sense of meaningful participation in society is a consequence of capitalism's concentration of wealth and power in the hands of a few.

12. Americans commonly link modernity to the idea of social progress. This simplified view overlooks the fact that social change is rarely entirely good. Social change is highly complex; from virtually any point of view, the consequences of modernity can be perceived as good and bad.

13. In a global context, modernization theory advocates intentional intervention to stimulate the transformation of poor societies. Global poverty is considered primarily a consequence of traditionalism.

14. Dependency theory argues that modernization greatly depends on a society's position in the world economic system. Poor societies are unlikely to follow the path of modernization that rich societies did because development is inhibited by their economic dependency on these rich societies.

KEY CONCEPTS

class society a society in which capitalism has generated pronounced social stratification

mass society a society in which industrialization and expanding bureaucracy have weakened social ties

modernity patterns of social life linked to industrialization

modernization the process of social change initiated by industrialization

other-directedness highly changeable personality patterns among people open to change and likely to imitate the behavior of others

social change the transformation of culture and social institutions over time

social character personality patterns common to members of a society

tradition-directedness rigid personalities based on conformity to time-honored ways of living

---

SUGGESTED READINGS

This paperback text surveys social change in a world perspective.

Daniel Chirot. *Social Change in the Modern Era*. New York: Harcourt Brace Jovanovich, 1986.

Americans tend to think of growth as necessarily good. The notion is hardly simple, however, as this book explains.

Henry Teune. *Growth*. Newbury Park, CA: Sage, 1988.

The following books are highly readable and filled with interesting insights about the modern world.

Peter Berger, Brigitte Berger, and Hansfried Kellner. *The Homeless Mind: Modernization and Consciousness*. New York: Vintage Books, 1974.

Peter L. Berger. *Facing Up to Modernity: Excursions in Society, Politics, and Religion*. New York: Basic Books, 1977.

It is easier to grasp the implications of modernity through detailed comparisons with preindustrial England.

Peter Laslett. *The World We Have Lost: England Before the Industrial Age*. 3rd ed. New York: Charles Scribner's Sons, 1984.

The nuclear arms race illustrates the modern problem of controlling human technology. This paperback examines the causes and the consequences of the growing stockpile of nuclear weapons.

Lester R. Kurtz, with Robert D. Benford and Jennifer E. Turpin. *The Nuclear Cage: A Sociology of the Arms Race*. Englewood Cliffs, NJ: Prentice Hall, 1988.

This book examines recent transformations in the U.S. medical-care system, especially the role of physicians in encouraging and opposing change.

John Colombotos and Corrine Kirchner. *Physicians and Social Change*. New York: Oxford University Press, 1986.

Many of the consequences of major events in history are unpredictable. This book examines changes in American society—attitudes toward sex, gender, and homosexuality—that were part of the legacy of World War II.

John Costello. *Virtue Under Fire: How World War II Changed Our Social and Sexual Attitudes*. Boston: Little, Brown, 1986.

This book takes a popular-culture approach to social change in the United States, exploring the transformations in roadside architecture during the twentieth century.

Chester H. Liebs. *Main Street to Miracle Mile: American Roadside Architecture*. Boston: New York Graphic Society/Little, Brown, 1985.

These two books—the first a collection of articles by many well-known thinkers—point out technological changes during this century and suggest likely future developments.

Albert H. Teich, ed. *Technology and the Future*. 5th ed. New York: St. Martin's Press, 1990.

O. B. Hardison, Jr. *Disappearing Through the Skylight: Culture and Technology in the Twentieth Century*. New York: Viking, 1989.

This book is an examination of social change in traditional societies with a focus on music: how Western music is influencing traditional musical patterns in a number of countries.

Bruno Nettl. *The Western Impact on World Music: Change, Adaptation, and Survival*. New York: Schirmer Books, 1985.

This analysis of the American economy and workforce offers projections about change over the 1990s.

William B. Johnston and Arnold E. Packer. *Workforce 2000: Work and Workers for the Twenty-first Century*. Indianapolis: Hudson Institute, 1987.

This analysis of economic development and accompanying changes contrasts rural and urban development as well as its different consequences for men and women.

Tony Barnett. *Social and Economic Development: An Introduction*. New York: Guilford Press, 1989.

Glossary

absolute poverty a state of deprivation of social resources that is life-threatening

achieved status a social position that is assumed voluntarily and that reflects a significant measure of personal ability and effort

activity theory an analysis of aging linking personal satisfaction in old age to high levels of activity

ageism prejudice and discrimination against the elderly

age-sex pyramid a graphic representation of the age and sex of a population

age stratification the unequal distribution of wealth, power, and privileges among people of different ages

agrarian society a society that engages in large-scale agriculture based on the use of plows drawn by animals

alienation the experience of powerlessness in social life

animism the belief that natural objects are conscious forms of life that can affect humanity

anomie a condition in which society provides little moral guidance to individuals

anticipatory socialization the process of social learning directed toward gaining a desired position

arms race a mutually reinforcing escalation of military might

ascribed status a social position that is received at birth or involuntarily assumed later in the life course

assimilation the process by which minorities gradually adopt patterns of the dominant culture

authoritarianism denying the majority participation in a government

authority power that is widely perceived as legitimate rather than coercive

bilateral descent a system tracing kinship through both males and females

blue-collar jobs occupations that involve mostly manual labor

bureaucracy an organizational model rationally designed to perform complex tasks efficiently

bureaucratic inertia the tendency of bureaucratic organizations to persist over time

bureaucratic ritualism a preoccupation with organizational rules and regulations as ends in themselves rather than as the means to organizational goals

capitalism an economic system in which natural resources and the means of producing goods and services are privately owned

capitalists those who own factories and other productive enterprises

caste system a system of social stratification based on ascription

cause and effect a relationship between two variables in which change in one (the independent variable) causes change in another (the dependent variable)

charisma extraordinary personal qualities that can turn an audience into followers

charismatic authority power legitimated through extraordinary personal abilities that inspire devotion and obedience

church a formal religious organization that is well integrated into the larger society

civil religion a quasi-religious loyalty binding individuals within a basically secular society

class consciousness the recognition by workers of their unity as a social class in opposition to capitalists and to capitalism itself

class society a society in which capitalism has generated pronounced social stratification

class system a system of social stratification based on individual achievement

cohabitation the sharing of a household by an unmarried couple

cohort a category of people born at about the same period, or entering some setting such as a college at the same time

collective behavior relatively spontaneous activity involving a large number of people that does not conform to established norms

collectivity a large number of people who interact little if at all in the absence of well-defined and conventional norms

colonialism the process by which some nations enrich themselves through political and economic control of other nations

communism a hypothetical economic and political system in which all members of society have economic and social equality

concept an abstract idea that represents some aspect of the world, inevitably in a somewhat ideal and simplified form

concrete operational stage Piaget's term for the level of human development characterized by the use of logic to understand objects or events

conglomerates giant corporations composed of many smaller corporations

control the ability to neutralize the effect of one variable so that the relationships among other variables can be more precisely determined

conversion a personal transformation resulting from new religious beliefs

corporation an organization with a legal existence including rights and liabilities apart from those of its members

correlation a relationship between two (or more) variables

counterculture cultural patterns that are strongly at odds with the dominant culture

credentialism the requirement that a person hold an advanced degree as a condition of employment

crime the violation of norms formally enacted into criminal law

crimes against property (property crimes) crimes that involve theft of property belonging to others

crimes against the person (violent crimes) crimes against people that involve violence or the threat of violence

criminal justice system the formal reaction to alleged violations of the law through the use of police, courts, and punishment

criminal recidivism subsequent offenses by people previously convicted of crimes

crowd a temporary gathering of people who share a common focus of attention and whose members influence one another

crude birth rate the number of live births in a given year for every thousand people in a population

crude death rate the number of deaths in a given year for every thousand people in a population

cult a religious movement that is highly unconventional in terms of the surrounding society

cultural ecology a theoretical paradigm that explores the relationship of human culture and the physical environment

cultural integration the close relationship among various parts of a cultural system

cultural lag inconsistencies within a cultural system resulting from the unequal rates at which different cultural elements change

cultural relativism the practice of judging any culture by its own standards

cultural transmission the process by which culture is passed from one generation to the next

cultural universals traits found in every culture

culture the beliefs, values, behavior, and material objects shared by a particular people

culture shock the personal disorientation that may accompany entry into an unfamiliar social world

deductive logical thought a logical process in which general theory yields specific hypotheses suitable for scientific testing

democracy a type of political system in which power is exercised by the people as a whole

democratic socialism a political and economic system in which free elections coexist with a market system modified by government policies to minimize social inequality

demographic transition theory the thesis that population patterns are linked to a society's level of technological development

demography the study of human population

denomination a church that recognizes religious pluralism

dependency theory an approach maintaining that global inequality stems from and is perpetuated by the exploitation of poor societies by rich ones

dependent variable a variable that is changed by another (independent) variable

descent the system by which kinship is traced over generations

deterrence the attempt to discourage criminality through punishment

deviance the recognized violation of cultural norms

direct-fee system a medical-care system in which patients pay directly for the services of physicians and hospitals

discrimination treating various categories of people unequally

disengagement theory an analysis of aging linking the disengagement by elderly people from positions of social responsibility to the orderly operation of society

division of labor specialized economic activity

dramaturgical analysis the analysis of social interaction in terms of theatrical performance

dyad a social group with two members

ecclesia a church that is formally allied with the state

economy the institutionalized system for production, distribution, and consumption of goods and services

education the various ways in which knowledge—including factual information and skills as well as cultural norms and values—is transmitted to members of society

ego Freud's designation of the conscious attempt to balance the pleasure-seeking drives of the human organism and the demands of society

empirical evidence evidence we are able to verify with our senses

endogamy marriage between people of the same social group or category

ethnicity a cultural heritage shared by a category of people

ethnocentrism the practice of judging another culture by the standards of our own culture

ethnomethodology the study of the everyday, common-sense understandings that people have of the world around them

euthanasia (mercy killing) assisting in the death of a person suffering from an incurable illness

exogamy marriage between people of different social groups or categories

experiment a research method that investigates cause-and-effect relationships under highly controlled conditions

expressive leadership group leadership that emphasizes collective well-being

extended family (consanguine family) a social unit including parents, children, and other kin

fad an unconventional social pattern that is enthusiastically embraced by a large number of people for a short time

faith belief that is not based on scientific evidence

false consciousness the belief that the shortcomings of individuals themselves, rather than society, are responsible for many of the personal problems that people experience

family a relatively permanent social group of two or more people, who are related by blood, marriage, or adoption and who usually live together

family of orientation the family into which a person is born and receives early socialization

family of procreation a family within which people have or adopt children of their own

family violence emotional, physical, or sexual abuse of one family member by another

fashion a social pattern favored for a time by a large number of people

feminism the support for the social equality of the sexes, leading to opposition to patriarchy and sexism

feminization of poverty a trend by which females represent an increasing proportion of the poor

fertility the incidence of childbearing in a society's population

First World a category of industrial societies with predominantly capitalist economies

folkways norms that have little moral significance

formal operational stage Piaget's term for the level of human development characterized by highly abstract thought and the ability to imagine alternatives to reality

formal organization a large, secondary group that is formally organized to facilitate achieving its goals

functional illiteracy the lack of basic reading and writing skills needed for everyday life

Gemeinschaft a type of social organization with strong solidarity based on tradition and predominantly personal relationships

gender human traits that are linked by culture to each sex

gender identity the ways males and females, guided by culture, learn to think of themselves

gender roles (sex roles) attitudes and activities that a culture links to each sex

gender stratification the unequal distribution of wealth, power, and privileges between the two sexes

generalized other George Herbert Mead's term for widespread cultural norms and values used as a reference in evaluating ourselves

genocide the systematic killing of one category of people by another

gerontocracy a form of social organization in which the elderly have the most wealth, power, and privileges

gerontology the study of aging and the elderly

Glossary   637

Gesellschaft a type of social organization with weak solidarity resulting from cultural pluralism and impersonal social relationships

gossip rumor about the personal affairs of others

government formal organizations that direct political life within a society

"groupthink" a reduced capacity for critical thinking caused by group conformity

Hawthorne effect any distortion in research caused by subjects' awareness that they are being studied

health a state of complete physical, mental, and social well-being

health care any activity intended to improve health

health maintenance organization (HMO) an organization that provides comprehensive medical care for which subscribers pay a fixed fee

hermaphrodite humans with some combination of male and female internal and external genitalia

hidden curriculum the content of schooling that is often unrecognized

holistic medicine an approach to health care that emphasizes prevention of illness and takes account of the whole person within a physical and social environment

homogamy marriage between people with the same social characteristics

horticultural society a society that uses hand tools to cultivate plants

"humanizing" bureaucracy fostering an organizational environment that develops human resources

hunting and gathering society a society that uses simple technology to hunt animals and gather vegetation

hypothesis an unverified statement of a relationship between any facts or variables

id Freud's designation of the human being's basic needs

ideal culture social patterns consistent with cultural values and norms

ideal type an abstract statement of the essential characteristics of any social phenomenon

ideology ideas that reflect and support the interests of some portion of a society

incest taboo a cultural norm forbidding sexual relations or marriage between certain kin

income occupational wages or salaries and earnings from investments

independent variable a variable that causes change in another (dependent) variable

inductive logical thought a logical process in which specific research observations are organized into general theory

industrial society a society that uses sophisticated machinery powered by advanced fuels to produce material goods

infant mortality rate the number of deaths within the first year of life for each thousand live births in a given year

ingroup an esteemed social group commanding a member's loyalty

institutional discrimination patterns of discrimination that are woven into the fabric of a society

instrumental leadership group leadership that emphasizes the completion of tasks

intergenerational social mobility a change in the social position of children in relation to that of their parents

interlocking directorate a social network made up of people who simultaneously serve on the boards of directors of several corporations

interview a series of items or questions administered personally by a researcher to respondents

intragenerational social mobility a change in social position occurring during a person's lifetime

juvenile delinquency the violation of legal standards that apply to the young

kinship social relationships based on blood, marriage, or adoption

labeling theory the assertion that deviance and conformity result from the response of others

labor unions organizations of workers that attempt to improve wages and working conditions through various strategies, including negotiations and strikes

language a system of symbols with standard meanings that allows members of a society to communicate with one another

latent functions the unrecognized and unintended consequences of any social pattern

liberation theology a fusion of Christian principles with political activism, often Marxist in character

life expectancy how long a person, on the average, can expect to live

looking-glass self Cooley's term meaning a conception of self derived from the responses of others

macro-level orientation a concern with large-scale patterns that characterize society as a whole

magnet schools schools that attract students through special facilities and programs promoting educational excellence

mainstreaming the integration of disabled students into the educational program as a whole

mandatory education laws legal requirements that children receive a minimum of formal education

manifest functions the recognized and intended consequences of any social pattern

marriage a socially approved relationship, involving economic cooperation and allowing sexual activity leading to childbearing, that is expected to be relatively enduring

mass behavior collective behavior among people dispersed over a wide geographical area

mass hysteria a form of dispersed collective behavior by which people respond to a real or imagined event with irrational, frantic behavior

mass media impersonal communications directed toward a vast audience

mass society a society in which industrialization and expanding bureaucracy have weakened social ties

master status a status that has exceptional importance for social identity, often shaping a person's entire life

material culture tangible elements of human society such as clothing and cities

matriarchy a form of social organization in which females dominate males

matrilineal descent a system tracing kinship through females

matrilocality a residential pattern in which a married couple lives with or near the wife's family

mean the arithmetic average of a series of numbers

measurement the process of determining the value of a variable in a specific case

mechanical solidarity social bonds, common to preindustrial societies, based on shared moral sentiments

median the value that occurs midway in a series of numbers or, simply, the middle case

medicalization of deviance the transformation of moral and legal issues into medical matters

medicine an institutionalized system for combating disease and improving health

megalopolis a vast urban region containing a number of cities and their surrounding suburbs

meritocracy   a system linking rewards to personal merit

metropolis   a very large city that socially and economically dominates an urban area

micro-level orientation   a concern with small-scale patterns of social interaction within specific settings

migration   the movement of people into and out of a specified territory

military-industrial complex   the close association between the government and defense industries

minority   a category of people, defined by physical or cultural traits, who are socially disadvantaged

miscegenation   the biological process of interbreeding among racial categories

mob   a highly emotional crowd in common pursuit of some violent or destructive goal

mode   the value that occurs most often in a series of numbers

modernity   patterns of social life linked to industrialization

modernization   the process of social change initiated by industrialization

modernization theory   an approach maintaining that global inequality reflects differing levels of technological development among world societies

monarchy   a type of political system in which power is passed from generation to generation within a single family

monogamy   a form of marriage that joins one male and one female

monopoly   domination of a market by a single producer

monotheism   religious beliefs recognizing a single divine power

mores   norms that have great moral significance

mortality   the incidence of death in a society's population

multinational corporation   (transnational corporation) a large corporation that operates in many different nations

neocolonialism   a new form of colonialism involving the operation of multinational corporations

neolocality   a residential pattern in which a married couple lives apart from the parents of both spouses

network   a web of social ties that links people, often with little common identity and social interaction

nonmaterial culture   intangible elements of human society such as values and norms

nonverbal communication   communication using body movements, gestures, and facial expressions rather than spoken words

norms   rules and expectations by which a society guides the behavior of its members

nuclear family (conjugal family)   a social unit composed of one or, more commonly, two parents and children

nuclear proliferation   the acquisition of nuclear weapons technology by more and more societies

objectivity   the state of complete personal neutrality in conducting research

oligarchy   the rule of the many by the few

oligopoly   domination of a market by a few producers

operationalizing a variable   specifying exactly what is to be measured in assigning a value to a variable

organic solidarity   social bonds, common to industrial societies, based on specialization

other-directedness   highly changeable personality patterns among people open to change and likely to imitate the behavior of others

outgroup   a scorned social group toward which one feels competition or opposition

overeducation   a situation in which workers have more formal education than the performance of their occupations requires

panic   a form of localized collective behavior by which people react to some stimulus with emotional, irrational, and often self-destructive behavior

participant observation   a method in which researchers systematically observe people while joining in their routine activities

pastoral society   a society whose livelihood is based on the domestication of animals

patriarchy   a form of social organization in which males dominate females

patrilineal descent   a system tracing kinship through males

patrilocality   a residential pattern in which a married couple lives with or near the husband's family

peace   the absence of war

peer group   people in regular interaction who share common interests, social position, and similar age

personality   a person's fairly consistent pattern of thinking, feeling, and acting

personal space   the area around a person over which some claim to privacy is made

plea bargaining   a legal negotiation in which the prosecution reduces a defendant's charge in exchange for a guilty plea

pluralism   a state in which racial and ethnic minorities are distinct but have social parity

pluralist model   an analysis of politics that views power as dispersed among many competing interest groups

political action committee (PAC)   an organization formed by a special-interest group, independent of political parties, to pursue specific aims by raising and spending money

political parties   organizations operating within the political system that seek control of government

political revolution   the overthrow of one political system in order to establish another

political state   a formal government claiming the legitimate use of coercion to support its rule

politics   the institutionalized system by which a society distributes power and makes decisions

polyandry   a form of marriage that joins one female with more than one male

polygamy   a form of marriage that unites three or more people

polygyny   a form of marriage that joins one male with more than one female

polytheism   religious beliefs recognizing many gods

population   the people about whom a researcher seeks knowledge

positivism   Comte's system for understanding the world based on science

postindustrial economy   an economy based on service work and high technology

power   the ability to achieve desired ends despite possible resistance from others

power-elite model   an analysis of politics that views power as concentrated among the rich

prejudice   a rigid and irrational generalization about a category of people

preoperational stage   Piaget's term for the level of human development in which language and other symbols are first used

presentation of self   the ways in which individuals, in various settings, attempt to create specific impressions in the minds of others

primary group   typically a small social group in which relationships are both personal and enduring

primary labor market   occupations that provide extensive benefits to workers

primary sector part of the economy that generates raw materials directly from the natural environment

primary sex characteristics the genitals, used to reproduce the human species

profane that which is defined as an ordinary element of everyday life

profession a prestigious white-collar occupation that requires extensive formal education

proletariat those who provide the labor necessary for the operation of factories and other productive enterprises

propaganda information presented with the intention of shaping public opinion

public opinion the attitudes of people throughout a society about one or more controversial issues

qualitative research research based heavily on subjective impressions

quantitative research research that emphasizes the analysis of numerical data

questionnaire a series of questions or items to which subjects are asked to respond

race a category composed of men and women who share biologically transmitted traits that are defined as socially significant

racism the belief that one racial category is innately superior or inferior to another

rationality deliberate, matter-of-fact calculation of the most efficient means to accomplish any particular goal

rational-legal authority (bureaucratic authority) power legitimated by legally enacted rules and regulations

rationalization of society the change from tradition to rationality as the dominant mode of human thought

real culture actual social patterns that are typically only an approximation of ideal cultural norms

reference group a social group that serves as a point of reference for people making evaluations and decisions

rehabilitation reforming the offender to preclude subsequent offenses

relative deprivation a perceived disadvantage based on some comparison

relative poverty being deprived of social resources in relation to those who have more

reliability the quality of consistency in measurement

religion a system of beliefs and practices based upon recognizing the sacred

religious fundamentalism conservative religious organizations that seek to restore what are viewed as fundamental elements of religion

religiosity the importance of religion in a person's life

replication the process by which a study is repeated by other researchers

research method a systematic strategy for carrying out research

resocialization deliberate socialization intended to radically alter the individual's personality

retribution subjecting an offender to suffering comparable to that caused by the offense

retrospective labeling the interpretation of someone's past consistent with present deviance

riot a highly emotional and undirected eruption involving violence and destruction

ritual formal, ceremonial behavior

role patterns of expected behavior attached to a particular status

role conflict incompatibility among the roles corresponding to two or more statuses

role set a number of roles attached to a single status

role strain incompatibility among roles corresponding to a single status

routinization of charisma the transformation of charismatic authority into some combination of traditional and bureaucratic authority

rumor unsubstantiated information spread informally, often by word of mouth

sacred that which is defined as extraordinary, inspiring a sense of awe, reverence, and even fear

sample part of a population, selected to be representative of the entirety, from whom data are obtained

Sapir-Whorf hypothesis the assertion that people perceive the world only in terms of the symbols provided by their language

scapegoat a person or category of people unfairly blamed for the troubles of others

schooling formal instruction under the direction of specially trained teachers

science a logical system that bases knowledge on direct, systematic observation

secondary analysis a research method involving analysis of data originally collected by others

secondary group typically a large and impersonal social group based on some special interest or activity

secondary labor market jobs that provide minimal benefits to workers

secondary sector part of the economy that transforms raw materials into manufactured goods

secondary sex characteristics physical traits, other than the genitals, that distinguish males and females

Second World a category of industrial societies with predominantly socialist economies

sect an informal religious organization that is not well integrated into the larger society

secularization the historical decline in the influence of religion

segregation the physical and social separation of categories of people

self the individual's active awareness of existing in the midst of society

sensorimotor stage Piaget's term for the level of human development in which the world is experienced only through the senses in terms of physical contact

sex the division of humanity into biological categories of male and female

sexism the belief that one sex is innately superior to the other

sex ratio the number of males for every hundred females in a given population

sexual orientation the manner in which people experience sexual arousal and achieve sexual pleasure

sick role patterns of behavior that are socially defined as appropriate for those who are ill

social change the transformation of culture and social institutions over time

social character personality patterns common to members of a society

social conflict struggle among segments of society over valued resources

social-conflict paradigm a theoretical framework based on the assumption that society is a complex system characterized by inequality and conflict that generate social change

social construction of reality the process by which individuals creatively shape reality through social interaction

social control the process by which members of a culture encourage conformity to cultural norms

social dysfunction the undesirable consequences of any social pattern for the operation of society

social epidemiology the study of the distribution of health and disease in a society's population

social fact any part of society that is argued to have an objective existence apart from the individual and is therefore able to influence individual behavior

social function the consequences of any social pattern for the operation of society

social group two or more people who identify with one another and have a distinctive pattern of interaction

social institution a major structural part of society that addresses one or more basic activities

social interaction the process by which people act and react in relation to others

socialism an economic system in which natural resources, as well as the means of producing goods and services, are collectively owned

socialization the lifelong process of social experience by which individuals develop their human potential and learn patterns of their culture

socialized medicine a health-care system in which most medical facilities are owned and operated by the government, and most physicians are salaried government employees

social marginality the state of being excluded from social activity as an "outsider"

social mobility changes in the position of people within a system of social stratification

social movement organized activity that encourages or discourages social change

social protection rendering an offender incapable of further offenses either temporarily during a period of incarceration or permanently by execution

social stratification a system by which categories of people in a society are ranked in a hierarchy

social structure a relatively stable pattern of social behavior

society people who interact with one another within a limited territory and who share a culture

sociobiology a theoretical paradigm that seeks to explain cultural patterns as the product, at least in part, of biological causes

sociocultural evolution the process of social change resulting from gaining new cultural elements, particularly technology

socioeconomic status a composite social ranking based on various dimensions of social inequality

sociology the scientific study of human social activity

special-interest group a political alliance of people with an interest in a particular economic or social issue

spurious correlation a relationship between two (or more) variables not based on direct cause and effect

state terrorism the use of violence without support of law against individuals or groups by a government or its agents

status a recognized social position that an individual occupies within society

status consistency consistent ranking across various dimensions of social standing

status set all the statuses a particular person holds at a given time

stereotype a set of prejudices that characterizes a category of people

stigma a powerful negative social label that radically changes a person's social identity and self-concept

structural-functional paradigm a theoretical framework based on the assumption that society is a complex system whose parts work together to promote stability

structural social mobility social mobility of large numbers of people that is due primarily to changes in society and the economy rather than to the efforts of individuals

subculture a cultural pattern that differs from the dominant culture in some distinctive way

suburbs the urban area beyond the political boundaries of a city

superego Freud's designation of the presence of culture within the individual in the form of internalized values and norms

survey a research method in which subjects respond to a series of items or questions in a questionnaire or interview

symbol anything that carries a particular meaning recognized by members of a culture

symbolic-interaction paradigm a theoretical framework based on the assumption that society involves interaction by which individuals actively construct reality in everyday life

technology the application of cultural knowledge to the task of living in a physical environment

terrorism the use of violence or the threat of violence by an individual or group as a political strategy

tertiary sector part of the economy that generates services rather than goods

theoretical paradigm a set of fundamental assumptions that guides thinking and research

theory an explanation of the relationship between two or more specific facts

Third World a category of primarily agrarian societies in which most people are poor

Thomas theorem the assertion that situations that are defined as real are real in their consequences

total institution a setting in which individuals are isolated from the rest of society and manipulated by an administrative staff

totalitarianism denying the majority participation in a government that extensively regulates people's lives

totem an object within the natural world imbued with sacred qualities

tracking categorically assigning students to different types of educational programs

tradition sentiments and beliefs about the world that are passed from generation to generation

traditional authority power that is legitimated through respect for long-established cultural patterns

tradition-directedness rigid personalities based on conformity to time-honored ways of living

transsexuals people who feel they are one sex when biologically they are the other

triad a social group with three members

underground economy all economic activity involving income or the exchange of goods and services that is not reported to the government

urban ecology study of the link between the physical and social dimensions of cities

urbanization the concentration of humanity into cities

urban renewal governmental programs intended to revitalize cities

validity the quality of measurement gained by actually measuring what one intends to measure

values culturally defined standards of desirability, goodness, and beauty that serve as broad guidelines for social life

variable a concept with a value that changes from case to case

Verstehen a German word meaning the act of interpreting how individuals in a particular social setting understand themselves

victimless crimes violations of law in which there are no readily apparent victims

war armed conflict among the people of various societies, formally initiated by their governments

wealth the total amount of money and valuable goods that any person or family controls

white-collar crime crimes committed by people of high social position in the course of their occupations

white-collar jobs occupations that involve mostly mental activity and nonmanual skills

zero population growth the level of reproduction that maintains population at a steady state

References

ABBOTT, ANDREW. *The System of Professions: An Essay on the Division of Expert Labor.* Chicago: University of Chicago Press, 1988.

ABERLE, DAVID F. *The Peyote Religion Among the Navaho.* Chicago: Aldine, 1966.

ABZUG, ROBERT H. *Inside the Vicious Heart: Americans and the Liberation of Nazi Concentration Camps.* New York: Oxford University Press, 1985.

ADORNO, T. W., et al. *The Authoritarian Personality.* New York: Harper and Brothers, 1950.

AGUIRRE, BENIGNO E., and E. L. QUARANTELLI. "Methodological, Ideological, and Conceptual-Theoretical Criticisms of Collective Behavior: A Critical Evaluation and Implications for Future Study." *Sociological Focus.* Vol. 16, No. 3 (August 1983):195–216.

AGUIRRE, B. E., E. L., QUARANTELLI, and JORGE L. MENDOZA. "The Collective Behavior of Fads: Characteristics, Effects, and Career of Streaking." *American Sociological Review.* Vol. 53, No. 4 (August 1988):569–584.

AKERS, RONALD L., MARVIN D. KROHN, LONN LANZA-KADUCE, and MARCIA RADOSEVICH. "Social Learning and Deviant Behavior." *American Sociological Review.* Vol. 44, No. 4 (August 1979):636–655.

ALBA, RICHARD D. *Italian Americans: Into the Twilight of Ethnicity.* Englewood Cliffs, NJ: Prentice-Hall, 1985.

ALBON, JOAN. "Retention of Cultural Values and Differential Urban Adaptation: Samoans and American Indians in a West Coast City." *Social Forces.* Vol. 49, No. 3 (March 1971):385–393.

ALBRECHT, WILLIAM P., JR. *Economics.* 3rd ed. Englewood Cliffs, NJ: Prentice-Hall, 1983.

ALEXANDER, CHARLES P. "Playing Computer Catch-Up." *Time.* Vol. 125, No. 15 (April 15, 1985):84–85.

ALLAN, EMILIE ANDERSEN, and DARRELL J. STEFFENSMEIER. "Youth, Underemployment, and Property Crime: Differential Effects of Job Availability and Job Quality on Juvenile and Young Adult Arrest Rates." *American Sociological Review.* Vol. 54, No. 1 (February 1989):107–123.

ALTMAN, DREW, et al. "Health Care for the Homeless." *Society.* Vol. 26, No. 4 (May/June 1989):4–5.

AMERICAN COUNCIL ON EDUCATION. "Senior Women Administrators in Higher Education: A Decade of Change, 1975–1983." Washington, DC: 1984.

AMERICAN COUNCIL ON EDUCATION, as reported in "Number of Black Students Still Falling, Study Finds." *The Chronicle of Higher Education.* Vol. XXXIV, No. 11 (November 11, 1987):2.

AMERICAN SOCIOLOGICAL ASSOCIATION. "Code of Ethics." Washington, DC: 1984.

ANDERSON, DANIEL R., and ELIZABETH PUGZLES LORCH. "Look at Television: Action or Reaction?" In Jennings Bryant and Daniel R. Anderson, eds., *Children's Understanding of Television: Research on Attention and Comprehension.* New York: Academic Press, 1983:1–33.

ANDERSON, HARRY. "Fuming Over College Costs." *Newsweek.* (May 18, 1987):66–68, 70, 72.

ANDERSON, KURT. "The New Ellis Island." *Time.* Vol. 121, No. 24 (June 13, 1983):18–22, 24–25.

ANG, IEN. *Watching Dallas: Soap Opera and the Melodramatic Imagination.* London: Methuen, 1985.

ANGELO, BONNIE. "The Pain of Being Black" (an interview with Toni Morrison). *Time.* Vol. 133, No. 21 (May 22, 1989):120–122.

ARCHER, DANE, and ROSEMARY GARTNER. *Violence and Crime in Cross-National Perspective.* New Haven: Yale University Press, 1987.

ARENDT, HANNAH. *The Origins of Totalitarianism.* Cleveland, OH: Meridian Books, 1958.

ARENDT, HANNAH. *Between Past and Future: Six Exercises in Political Thought.* Cleveland, OH: Meridian Books, 1963.

ARIÈS, PHILIPPE. *Centuries of Childhood: A Social History of Family Life.* New York: Vintage Books, 1965.

ARIÈS, PHILIPPE. *Western Attitudes Toward Death: From the Middle Ages to the Present.* Baltimore, MD: The Johns Hopkins University Press, 1974.

ARJOMAND, SAID AMIR. *The Turban for the Crown: The Islamic Revolution in Iran.* New York: Oxford University Press, 1988.

ASCH, SOLOMON. *Social Psychology.* Englewood Cliffs, NJ: Prentice-Hall, 1952.

ATCHLEY, ROBERT C. "Retirement as a Social Institution." *Annual Review of Sociology.* Vol. 8. Palo Alto, CA: Annual Reviews, Inc., 1982:263–287.

ATCHLEY, ROBERT C. *Aging: Continuity and Change.* Belmont, CA: Wadsworth, 1983; also 2nd ed., 1987.

AVIS, GEORGE. "Access to Higher Education in the Soviet Union." In J. J. Tomiak, ed., *Soviet Education in the 1980s.* London: Croom Helm, 1983:199–239.

AYENSU, EDWARD S. "A Worldwide Role for the Healing Powers of Plants." *Smithsonian.* Vol. 12, No. 8 (November 1981):87–97.

BABBIE, EARL. *The Practice of Social Research.* Belmont, CA: Wadsworth, 1983.

BACHRACH, PETER, and MORTON S. BARATZ. *Power and Poverty.* New York: Oxford University Press, 1970.

BAILEY, WILLIAM C., and RUTH D. PETERSON. "Murder and Capital Punishment: A Monthly Time-Series Analysis of Execution Publicity." *American Sociological Review.* Vol. 54, No. 5 (October 1989):722–743.

BAINBRIDGE, WILLIAM SIMS, and DANIEL H. JACKSON. "The Rise and Decline of Transcendental Meditation." In Bryan Wilson, ed., *The Social Impact of New Religious Movements.* New York: The Rose of Sharon Press, 1981:135–158.

BALES, ROBERT F. "The Equilibrium Problem in Small Groups." In Talcott Parsons et al., eds., *Working Papers in the Theory of Action.* New York: Free Press, 1953:111–115.

BALES, ROBERT F., and PHILIP E. SLATER. "Role Differentiation in Small Decision-Making Groups." In Talcott Parsons and Robert F. Bales, eds., *Family, Socialization and Interaction Process.* New York: Free Press, 1955:259–306.

BALLANTINE, JEANNE H. *The Sociology of Education: A Systematic Analysis.* Englewood Cliffs, NJ: Prentice-Hall, 1983.

BALTES, PAUL B., and K. WARNER SCHAIE. "The Myth of the Twilight Years." *Psychology Today.* Vol. 7, No. 10 (March 1974):35–39.

BALTZELL, E. DIGBY. *Philadelphia Gentlemen: The Making of a National Upper Class.* Philadelphia, PA: University of Pennsylvania Press, 1979; orig. 1958.

BALTZELL, E. DIGBY. *The Protestant Establishment: Aristocracy and Caste in America.* New York: Vintage, 1964.

BALTZELL, E. DIGBY. "The Protestant Establishment Revisited." *The American Scholar.* Vol. 45, No. 4 (Autumn 1976):499–518.

BALTZELL, E. DIGBY. *Puritan Boston and Quaker Philadelphia*. New York: Free Press, 1979.

BALTZELL, E. DIGBY, ed. *The Search for Community in Modern America*. New York: Harper & Row, 1968.

BALTZELL, E. DIGBY. "The WASP's Last Gasp." *Philadelphia Magazine*. Vol. 79 (September 1988):104–107, 184, 186, 188.

BANFIELD, EDWARD C. *The Unheavenly City Revisited*. Boston, MA: Little, Brown, 1974.

BARASH, DAVID. *The Whispering Within*. New York: Penguin Books, 1981.

BARBER, BEN. "Guilty Verdict in 'Mercy Killing.'" *USA Today* (May 10, 1985):3A.

BARBERIS, MARY. "America's Elderly: Policy Implications." *Population Bulletin*. Vol. 35, No. 4 (January 1981), Population Reference Bureau.

BARKER, EILEEN. "Who'd Be a Moonie? A Comparative Study of Those Who Join the Unification Church in Britain." In Bryan Wilson, ed., *The Social Impact of New Religious Movements*. New York: The Rose of Sharon Press, 1981:59–96.

BARROW, GEORGE M., and PATRICIA A. SMITH. *Aging, the Individual, and Society*. 2nd ed. St. Paul, MN: West, 1983.

BARRY, KATHLEEN. "Feminist Theory: The Meaning of Women's Liberation." In Barbara Haber, ed., *The Women's Annual 1982–1983*. Boston, MA: G. K. Hall, 1983:35–78.

BASSUK, ELLEN J. "The Homelessness Problem." *Scientific American*. Vol. 251, No. 1 (July 1984):40–45.

BATESON, C. DANIEL, and W. LARRY VENTIS. *The Religious Experience: A Social-Psychological Perspective*. New York: Oxford, 1982.

BAUER, P. T. *Equality, the Third World, and Economic Delusion*. Cambridge, MA: Harvard University Press, 1981.

BEATRICE COMPANY, INC. *Annual Report 1985*. Chicago: Beatrice, 1985.

BECKER, HOWARD S. *Outside: Studies in the Sociology of Deviance*. New York: Free Press, 1966.

BEDELL, GEORGE C., LEO SANDON, JR., and CHARLES T. WELLBORN. *Religion in America*. New York: Macmillan, 1975.

BEIGEL, HUGO G. "Romantic Love." *American Sociological Review*. Vol. 16, No. 3 (June 1951):326–334.

BELL, ALAN P., MARTIN S. WEINBERG, and SUE KIEFER-HAMMERSMITH. *Sexual Preference: Its Development in Men and Women*. Bloomington, IN: Indiana University Press, 1981.

BELL, DANIEL. *The Coming of Post-Industrial Society: A Venture in Social Forecasting*. New York: Harper Colophon, 1976.

BELLAH, ROBERT N. *The Broken Covenant*. New York: Seabury, 1975.

BELLAH, ROBERT N., RICHARD MADSEN, WILLIAM M. SULLIVAN, ANN SWIDLER, and STEVEN M. TIPTON. *Habits of the Heart: Individualism and Commitment in American Life*. New York: Harper & Row, 1985.

BELSKY, JAY, RICHARD M. LERNER, and GRAHAM B. SPANIER. *The Child in the Family*. Reading, MA: Addison-Wesley, 1984.

BEM, SANDRA LIPSITZ. "Gender Schema Theory: A Cognitive Account of Sex-Typing." *Psychological Review*. Vol. 88, No. 4 (July 1981):354–364.

BENEDICT, RUTH. "Continuities and Discontinuities in Cultural Conditioning." *Psychiatry*. Vol. 1 (May 1938):161–167.

BENEDICT, RUTH. *The Chrysanthemum and the Sword: Patterns of Japanese Culture*. New York: New American Library, 1974; orig. 1946.

BENJAMIN, BERNARD, and CHRIS WALLIS. "The Mortality of Widowers." *The Lancet*. Vol. 2 (August 1963):454–456.

BENNETT, NEIL G., DAVID E. BLOOM, and PATRICIA H. CRAIG. "The Divergence of Black and White Marriage Patterns. *American Journal of Sociology*. Vol. 95, No. 3 (November 1989):692–722.

BENOKRAITIS, NIJOLE, and JOE FEAGIN. *Modern Sexism: Blatant, Subtle and Overt Discrimination*. Englewood Cliffs, NJ: Prentice-Hall, 1986.

BERARDO, F. M. "Survivorship and Social Isolation: The Case of the Aged Widower." *The Family Coordinator*. Vol. 19 (January 1970):11–25.

BERG, IVAR. *Education and Jobs: The Great Training Robbery*. New York: Praeger, 1970.

BERGER, BRIGITTE, and PETER L. BERGER. *The War Over the Family: Capturing the Middle Ground*. Garden City, NY: Anchor/Doubleday, 1983.

BERGER, KATHLEEN STASSEN. *The Developing Person Through the Lifespan*. New York: Worth, 1983.

BERGER, PETER L. *Invitation to Sociology*. New York: Anchor Books, 1963.

BERGER, PETER L. *The Sacred Canopy: Elements of a Sociological Theory of Religion*. Garden City, NY: Doubleday & Company, Inc., 1967.

BERGER, PETER L. *Facing Up to Modernity: Excursions in Society, Politics, and Religion*. New York: Basic Books, 1977.

BERGER, PETER L. *The Capitalist Revolution: Fifty Propositions About Prosperity, Equality, and Liberty*. New York: Basic Books, 1986.

BERGER, PETER, BRIGITTE BERGER, and HANSFRIED KELLNER. *The Homeless Mind: Modernization and Consciousness*. New York: Vintage Books, 1974.

BERGER, PETER L., and HANSFRIED KELLNER. *Sociology Reinterpreted: An Essay on Method and Vocation*. Garden City, NY: Anchor Books, 1981.

BERGER, PETER L., and THOMAS LUCKMANN. *The Social Construction of Reality: A Treatise in the Sociology of Knowledge*. Garden City, NY: Anchor, 1967.

BERGESEN, ALBERT, ed. *Crises in the World-System*. Beverly Hills, CA: Sage Publications, 1983.

BERK, RICHARD A. *Collective Behavior*. Dubuque, IA: Wm. C. Brown, 1974.

BERNARD, JESSIE. *The Future of Marriage*. New Haven, CT: Yale University Press, 1982; orig. 1973.

BERNARD, JESSIE. *The Female World*. New York: Free Press, 1981.

BERNARD, LARRY CRAIG. "Multivariate Analysis of New Sex Role Formulations and Personality." *Journal of Personality and Social Psychology*. Vol. 38, No. 2 (February 1980):323–336.

BERRY, BRIAN L., and PHILIP H. REES. "The Factorial Ecology of Calcutta." *American Journal of Sociology*. Vol. 74, No. 5 (March 1969):445–491.

BERSCHEID, ELLEN, and ELAINE HATFIELD. *Interpersonal Attraction*. 2nd ed. Reading, MA: Addison-Wesley, 1983.

BESHAROV, DOUGLAS J., ALISON QUIN, and KARL ZINSMEISTER. "A Portrait in Black and White: Out-of-Wedlock Births." *Public Opinion*. Vol. 10, No. 1 (May/June 1987):43–45.

BEST, RAPHAELA. *We've All Got Scars: What Boys and Girls Learn in Elementary School*. Bloomington, IN: Indiana University Press, 1983.

BINGHAM, AMY. "Division I Dilemma: Making the Classroom a Priority for Athletes." *The Kenyon Journal*. Vol. II, No. 3 (November 1987):2.

BLACK, GORDON S., INC., Rochester, NH. National poll reported in *USA Today*. December 20, 1984:5D.

Black Issues in Higher Education. "Black Graduate Students Decline." Vol. 4, No. 8 (July 1, 1987):1–2.

BLAU, JUDITH R., and PETER M. BLAU. "The Cost of Inequality: Metropolitan Structure and Violent Crime." *American Sociological Review*. Vol. 47, No. 1 (February 1982):114–129.

BLAU, PETER M. *Exchange and Power in Social Life*. New York: Wiley, 1964.

BLAU, PETER M., and OTIS DUDLEY DUNCAN. *The American Occupational Structure*. New York: John Wiley, 1967.

BLAUNER, ROBERT. *Racial Oppression in America*. New York: Harper & Row, 1972.

BLAUSTEIN, ALBERT P., and ROBERT L. ZANGRANDO. *Civil Rights and the Black American*. New York: Washington Square Press, 1968.

BLOOM, LEONARD. "Familial Adjustments of Japanese-Americans to Relocation: First Phase." In Thomas F. Pettigrew, ed., *The Sociology of Race Relations*. New York: Free Press, 1980:163–167.

BLUM, ALAN, and GARY FISHER. "Women Who Kill." In Delos H. Kelly, ed., *Criminal Behavior: Readings in Criminology*. New York: St. Martin's Press, 1980:291–301.

BLUMBERG, ABRAHAM S. *Criminal Justice*. Chicago: Quadrangle Books, 1970.

BLUMBERG, PAUL. *Inequality in an Age of Decline*. New York: Oxford University Press, 1981.

BLUMER, HERBERT G. "Fashion." In David L. Sills, ed., *International Encyclopedia of the Social Sciences*. Vol. 5. New York: Macmillan and Free Press, 1968:341–345.

BLUMER, HERBERT G. "Collective Behavior." In Alfred McClung Lee, ed., *Principles of Sociology*. 3rd ed. New York: Barnes & Noble Books, 1969:65–121.

BLUMSTEIN, PHILIP, and PEPPER SCHWARTZ. *American Couples*. New York: William Morrow, 1983.

BODENHEIMER, THOMAS S. "Health Care in the United States: Who Pays?"

In Vicente Navarro, ed., *Health and Medical Care in the U.S.: A Critical Analysis*. Farmingdale, NY: Baywood Publishing Co. 1977:61–68.

BOFF, LEONARD and CLODOVIS. *Salvation and Liberation: In Search of a Balance Between Faith and Politics*. Maryknoll, NY: Orbis Books, 1984.

BOGARDUS, EMORY S. "Comparing Racial Distance in Ethiopia, South Africa, and the United States." *Sociology and Social Research*. Vol. 52, No. 2 (January 1968):149–156.

BOHANNAN, PAUL. *Divorce and After*. Garden City, NY: Doubleday & Company, 1970.

BOLLOUGH, VERN, and MARTHA VOGHT. "Women, Menstruation, and Nineteenth Century Medicine." In Judith Walzer Leavitt, ed., *Women and Health in America*. Madison, WI: The University of Wisconsin Press, 1984:28–37.

BONNER, JANE. Research presented in "The Two Brains." Public Broadcasting System telecast, 1984.

BOOTH, ALAN, and LYNN WHITE. "Thinking About Divorce." *Journal of Marriage and the Family*. Vol. 42, No. 3 (August 1980):605–616.

BOSWELL, TERRY E. "A Split Labor Market Analysis of Discrimination Against Chinese Immigrants, 1850–1882." *American Sociological Review*. Vol 51, No. 3 (June 1986):352–371.

BOTT, ELIZABETH. *Family and Social Network*. New York: Free Press, 1971; orig. 1957.

BOTWINICK, JACK. "Intellectual Abilities." In James E. Birren and K. Warner Schaie, eds., *Handbook of the Psychology of Aging*. New York: Van Nostrand Reinhold, 1977:580–605.

BOULDING, ELISE. *The Underside of History*. Boulder, CO: Westview Press, 1976.

BOWEN, ELENORE SMITH. *Return to Laughter*. Garden City, NY: Doubleday, 1964.

BOWEN, EZRA. "The Worst of Two Worlds." *Time*. Vol. 126, No. 17 (October 28, 1985):64.

BOWLES, JACQUELINE, and WILLIAM A. ROBINSON. "PHS Grants for Minority Group HIV Infection Education and Prevention Efforts." *Public Health Reports*. Vol. 104, No. 6 (November-December 1989):552–559.

BOWLES, SAMUEL, and HERBERT GINTIS. *Schooling in Capitalist America: Educational Reform and the Contradictions of Economic Life*. New York: Basic Books, 1976.

BOYER, ERNEST L. "The Test of Growing Student Diversity." *The New York Times Magazine*. (November 11, 1984):63.

BOYER, ERNEST L. *College: The Undergraduate Experience in America*. Prepared by The Carnegie Foundation for the Advancement of Teaching. New York: Harper & Row, 1987.

BRAITHWAITE, JOHN. " 'The Myth of Social Class and Criminality' Reconsidered." *American Sociological Review*. Vol. 46, No. 1 (February 1981):36–57.

BRAND, DAVID. "The New Whiz Kids." *Time*. Vol. 130, No. 9 (August 31, 1987):42–46, 49, 51.

BREEN, LEONARD Z. "The Aging Individual." In Clark Tibbitts, ed., *Handbook of Social Gerontology*. Chicago: University of Chicago Press, 1960:145–162.

BRENNER, HARVEY. *Estimating the Social Costs of National Economic Policy: Implications for Mental and Physical Health and Criminal Aggression*. Joint Economic Committee, 94th Congress, October 26, 1976.

BRINTON, CRANE. *The Anatomy of Revolution*. New York: Vintage Books, 1965.

BRINTON, MARY C. "The Social-Institutional Bases of Gender Stratification: Japan as an Illustrative Case." *American Journal of Sociology*. Vol. 94, No. 2 (September 1988):300–334.

BROMLEY, DAVID G., and ANSON D. SHUPE, JR. *New Christian Politics*. Macon, GA: Mercer University Press, 1984.

BROWN, E. RICHARD. *Rockefeller Medicine Men: Medicine and Capitalism in America*. Berkeley, CA: University of California Press, 1979.

BROWNMILLER, SUSAN. *Femininity*. New York: Linden Press, Simon and Schuster, 1984.

BROWNSTEIN, RONALD, and NINA EASTON. *Reagan's Ruling Class: Portraits of the President's Top One Hundred Officials*. New York: Pantheon, 1983.

BROYLES, J. ALLEN. "The John Birch Society: A Movement of Social Protest of the Radical Right." In Louis E. Genevie, ed., *Collective Behavior and Social Movements*. Itasca, IL: F. E. Peacock, 1978:338–345.

BRUNO, MARY. "Abusing the Elderly." *Newsweek* (September 23, 1985):75–76.

BRZEZINSKI, ZBIGNIEW. *The Grand Failure: The Birth and Death of Communism in the Twentieth Century*. New York: Charles Scribner's Sons, 1989.

BUCHHOLZ, MICHAEL, and JACK E. BYNUM. "Newspaper Presentation of America's Aged: A Content Analysis of Image and Role." *The Gerontologist*. Vol. 22, Number 1 (February 1982):83–88.

BUMPASS, L. "Children and Marital Disruption: A Replication and Update." *Demography*. Vol. 21, No. 1 (February 1984):71–82.

BURCH, ROBERT. Testimony to House of Representatives Hearing in "Review: The World Hunger Problem." October 25, 1983, Serial 98–38.

BURGESS, ERNEST W. "The Growth of the City." In Robert E. Park and Ernest W. Burgess, eds., *The City*. Chicago: University of Chicago Press, 1925:47–62.

BURNHAM, WALTER DEAN. *Democracy in the Making: American Government and Politics*. Englewood Cliffs, NJ: Prentice-Hall, 1983.

BURNS, JAMES A. "Discipline: Why Does It Continue To Be a Problem? Solution Is in Changing School Culture." *National Association of Secondary School Principals Bulletin*. Vol. 69, No. 479 (March 1985):1–47.

BURRIS, VAL. "The Social and Political Consequences of Overeducation." *American Sociological Review*. Vol. 48, No. 4 (August 1983):454–467.

BUSBY, LINDA J. "Sex Role Research on the Mass Media." *Journal of Communications*. Vol. 25 (Autumn 1975):107–131.

BUTLER, ROBERT N. *Why Survive? Being Old in America*. New York: Harper & Row, 1975.

BUTTERWORTH, DOUGLAS, and JOHN K. CHANCE. *Latin American Urbanization*. Cambridge (UK): Cambridge University Press, 1981.

"Buy America while Stocks Last." *The Economist*. Vol. 313, No. 7633 (December 16, 1989):63–66.

CAHAN, VICKY. "The Feminization of Poverty: More Women Are Getting Poorer." *Business Week*. No. 2878 (January 28, 1985):84–85.

CALLAHAN, DANIEL. *Setting Limits: Medical Goals in an Aging Society*. New York: Simon & Schuster, 1987.

CALLOW, A. B., JR., ed. *American Urban History*. New York: Oxford University Press, 1969.

CALMORE, JOHN O. "National Housing Policies and Black America: Trends, Issues, and Implications." In *The State of Black America 1986*. New York: National Urban League, 1986:115–149.

CAMERON, WILLIAM BRUCE. *Modern Social Movements: A Sociological Outline*. New York: Random House, 1966.

CANETTI, ELIAS. *Crowds and Power*. New York: The Seabury Press, 1978.

CANTOR, MURIAL G., and SUZANNE PINGREE. *The Soap Opera*. Beverly Hills, CA: Sage Publications, 1983.

CANTRIL, HADLEY, HAZEL GAUDET, and HERTA HERZOG. *Invasion from Mars: A Study in the Psychology of Panic*. Princeton, NJ: Princeton University Press, 1947.

CAPLOW, THEODORE, et al. *Middletown Families*. Minneapolis, MN: University of Minnesota Press, 1982.

CAPUTO, PHILIP. *A Rumor of War*. New York: Holt, Rinehart and Winston, 1977.

CAREY, MAX L. "On Occupational Employment Growth Through 1990." *Monthly Labor Review*. Vol. 104, No. 8 (August 1981):42–55.

CARLSON, NORMAN A. "Corrections in the United States Today: A Balance Has Been Struck." *The American Criminal Law Review*. Vol. 13, No. 4 (Spring 1976):615–647.

CARLTON, ERIC. *Ideology and Social Order*. London: Routledge & Kegan Paul, 1977.

C.E.D. *See* COMMITTEE FOR ECONOMIC DEVELOPMENT.

CERNKOVICH, STEPHEN A., and PEGGY C. GIORDANO. "A Comparative Analysis of Male and Female Delinquency." In Delos H. Kelly, ed., *Criminal Behavior: Readings in Criminology*. New York: St. Martin's Press, 1980:112–129.

CHAGNON, NAPOLEON A. *Yąnomamö*. 3rd ed. New York: Holt, Rinehart and Winston, 1983.

CHAGNON, NAPOLEON A. "Life Histories, Blood Revenge, and Warfare in a

Tribal Population." *Science.* Vol. 239, No. 4843 (February 26, 1988):985–992.

CHANDLER, TERTIUS, and GERALD FOX. *3000 Years of Urban History.* New York: Academic Press, 1974.

CHANG, KWANG-CHIH. *The Archaeology of Ancient China.* New Haven, CT: Yale University Press, 1977.

CHAPPELL, NEENA L., and BETTY HAVENS. "Old and Female: Testing the Double Jeopardy Hypothesis." *The Sociological Quarterly.* Vol. 21, No. 2 (Spring 1980):157–171.

CHERLIN, ANDREW. *Marriage, Divorce, Remarriage.* Cambridge, MA: Harvard University Press, 1981.

CHERLIN, ANDREW, and FRANK F. FURSTENBERG, JR."The American Family in the Year 2000." *The Futurist.* Vol. 17, No. 3 (June 1983):7–14.

CHILDREN'S DEFENSE FUND. *A Children's Defense Budget: An Analysis of the President's FY 1986 Budget and Children.* Washington, DC: 1985.

CHIROT, DANIEL. *Social Change in the Modern Era.* New York: Harcourt Brace Jovanovich, 1986.

CHOWN, SHEILA M. "Morale, Careers and Personal Potentials." In James E. Birren and K. Warner Schaie, eds., *Handbook of the Psychology of Aging.* New York: Van Nostrand Reinhold, 1977:672–691.

CLANCY, PAUL, and GAIL OBERST. "First Comes Love, Then Comes Live-In." *USA Today.* (March 28, 1985):1A, 2A.

CLARK, CURTIS B. "Geriatric Abuse: Out of the Closet." In *The Tragedy of Elder Abuse: The Problem and the Response.* Hearings before the Select Committee on Aging, House of Representatives, July 1, 1986, pp. 49–50.

CLARK, JUAN M., JOSE I. LASAGA, and ROSE S. REGUE. *The 1980 Mariel Exodus: An Assessment and Prospect: Special Report.* Washington, DC: Council for Inter-American Security, 1981.

CLARK, MARGARET. "An Anthropological View of Retirement." In Frances M. Carp, ed., *Retirement.* New York: Behavioral Publications, 1972.

CLARK, THOMAS A. *Blacks in Suburbs.* New Brunswick, NJ: Rutgers University Center for Urban Policy Research, 1979.

CLINARD, MARSHALL B. *Cities with Little Crime: The Case of Switzerland.* Cambridge (UK): Cambridge University Press, 1978.

CLINARD, MARSHALL, and DANIEL ABBOTT. *Crime in Developing Countries.* New York: Wiley, 1973.

CLOWARD, RICHARD A., and LLOYD E. OHLIN. *Delinquency and Opportunity: A Theory of Delinquent Gangs.* New York: Free Press, 1966.

COAKLEY, JAY J. *Sport in Society: Issues and Controversies.* 3rd ed. St. Louis, MO: C. V. Mosby, 1986; also 4th ed., 1990.

COCKERHAM, WILLIAM C. *Medical Sociology.* 2nd ed. Englewood Cliffs, NJ: Prentice-Hall, 1982; 3rd ed. 1986.

COE, MICHAEL D., and RICHARD A. DIEHL. *In the Land of the Olmec.* Austin, TX: University of Texas Press, 1980.

COHEN, ALBERT K. *Delinquent Boys: The Culture of the Gang.* New York: Free Press, 1971; orig. 1955.

COHEN, MICHAEL. "Restructuring the System." *Transaction.* Vol. 26, No. 4 (May/June 1989):40–48.

COHEN, MICHAEL, and E. ELAINE CROE. *Early Estimates: National Estimates of Higher Education: School Year 1988–89.* Washington, DC: U.S. Government Printing Office, 1988.

COHN, RICHARD M. "Economic Development and Status Change of the Aged." *American Journal of Sociology.* Vol. 87, No. 2 (March 1982):1150–1161.

COLEMAN, JAMES, et al. *Equality of Educational Opportunity* ("The Coleman Report"). U.S. Department of Health, Education, and Welfare. Washington, DC: U.S. Government Printing Office, 1966.

COLEMAN, JAMES S., and THOMAS HOFFER. *Public and Private High Schools: The Impact of Communities.* New York: Basic Books, 1987.

COLEMAN, JAMES, THOMAS HOFFER, and SALLY KILGORE. *Public and Private Schools: An Analysis of Public Schools and Beyond.* Washington, DC: National Center for Education Statistics, 1981.

COLEMAN, JOHN R. "Diary of a Homeless Man." *New York Magazine* (Feburary 21, 1983):26–35.

COLEMAN, RICHARD P., and BERNICE L. NEUGARTEN. *Social Status in the City.* San Francisco, CA: Jossey-Bass, 1971.

COLEMAN, RICHARD P., and LEE RAINWATER. *Social Standing in America.* New York: Basic Books, 1978.

COLLINS, RANDALL. "A Conflict Theory of Sexual Stratification." *Social Problems.* Vol. 19, No. 1 (Summer 1971):3–21.

COLLINS, RANDALL. *The Credential Society: An Historical Sociology of Education and Stratification.* New York: Academic Press, 1979.

COLLINS, RANDALL. *Sociological Insight: An Introduction to Nonobvious Sociology.* New York: Oxford University Press, 1982.

COLLINS, RANDALL. *Weberian Sociological Theory.* Cambridge (UK): Cambridge University Press, 1986.

COLLOWAY, N. O., and PAULA L. DOLLEVOET. "Selected Tabular Material on Aging." In Caleb Finch and Leonard Hayflick, eds., *Handbook of the Biology of Aging.* New York: Van Nostrand Reinhold, 1977:666–708.

COMMITTEE FOR ECONOMIC DEVELOPMENT (C.E.D.)."Reforming Retirement Policies." New York: 1981.

COMTE, AUGUSTE. *Auguste Comte and Positivism: The Essential Writings.* Gertrud Lenzer, ed. New York: Harper Torchbooks, 1975.

CONRAD, PETER, and JOSEPH W. SCHNEIDER. *Deviance and Medicalization: From Badness to Sickness.* Columbus, OH: Merrill, 1980.

COOLEY, CHARLES HORTON. *Human Nature and the Social Order.* New York: Schocken Books, 1964; orig. 1902.

COOLEY, CHARLES HORTON. *Social Organization.* New York: Schocken Books, 1962; orig. 1909.

COPPOCK, MARJORIE L. "Women's Leadership Involvement in Community Volunteer Organizations." Paper presented to Southwestern Sociological Association, Dallas, Texas, 1987.

CORSARO, WILLIAM A., and THOMAS A. RIZZO. "*Discussione* and Friendship: Socialization Processes in the Peer Culture of Italian Nursery School Children." *American Sociological Review.* Vol. 53, No. 6 (December 1988):879–894.

COSER, LEWIS A. *Masters of Sociological Thought: Ideas in Historical and Social Context.* 2nd ed. New York: Harcourt Brace Jovanovich, 1977.

COTTRELL, JOHN, and THE EDITORS OF TIME-LIFE. *The Great Cities: Mexico City.* Amsterdam: 1979.

COUNTS, G. S. "The Social Status of Occupations: A Problem in Vocational Guidance." *School Review.* Vol. 33 (January 1925):16–27.

COURTNEY, ALICE E., and THOMAS W. WHIPPLE. *Sex Stereotyping in Advertising.* Lexington, MA: D. C. Heath, 1983.

COWGILL, DONALD, and LOWELL HOMLES. *Aging and Modernization.* New York: Appleton-Century-Crofts, 1972.

COX, HAROLD. *Later Life: The Realities of Aging.* Englewood Cliffs, NJ: Prentice-Hall, 1984.

COX, HARVEY. *The Secular City.* Rev. ed. New York: Macmillan, 1971; orig. 1965.

COX, HARVEY. *Turning East: The Promise and Peril of the New Orientalism.* New York: Simon and Schuster, 1977.

CROUSE, JAMES, and DALE TRUSHEIM. *The Case Against the SAT.* Chicago: University of Chicago Press, 1988.

CUFF, E. C., and G. C. F. PAYNE, eds. *Perspectives in Sociology.* London: George Allen and Unwin, 1979.

CUMMING, ELAINE, and WILLIAM E. HENRY. *Growing Old: The Process of Disengagement.* New York: Basic Books, 1961.

CURRIE, ELLIOTT. *Confronting Crime: An American Challenge.* New York: Pantheon, 1985.

CUTRIGHT, PHILLIP. "Occupational Inheritance: A Cross-National Analysis." *American Journal of Sociology.* Vol. 73, No. 4 (January 1968):400–416.

DAHL, ROBERT A. *Who Governs?* New Haven, CT: Yale University Press, 1961.

DAHL, ROBERT A. *Dilemmas of Pluralist Democracy: Autonomy vs. Control.* New Haven, CT: Yale University Press, 1982.

DAHLIN, MICHAEL. "Perspectives on Family Life of the Elderly in 1900." *The Gerontologist.* Vol. 20, No. 1 (February 1980):99–107.

DAHRENDORF, RALF. *Class and Class Conflict in Industrial Society.* Stanford, CA: Stanford University Press, 1959.

DALY, MARTIN, and MARGO WILSON. *Homicide.* New York: Aldine De Gruyter, 1988.

DAMON, WILLIAM. *Social and Personality Development.* New York: W. W. Norton, 1983.

DANIELS, ROGER. "The Issei Generation." In Amy Tachiki et al., eds., *Roots:*

An Asian American Reader. Los Angeles: UCLA Asian American Studies Center, 1971:138–149.

DANNEFER, DALE. "Adult Development and Social Theory: A Reappraisal." *American Sociological Review.* Vol. 49, No. 1 (February 1984):100–116.

DAVIES, JAMES C. "Toward a Theory of Revolution." *American Sociological Review.* Vol. 27, No. 1 (February 1962):5–19.

DAVIES, MARK, and DENISE B. KANDEL. "Parental and Peer Influences on Adolescents' Educational Plans: Some Further Evidence." *American Journal of Sociology.* Vol. 87, No. 2 (September 1981):363–387.

DAVIS, JAMES A. *Social Differences in Contemporary America.* New York: Harcourt Brace Jovanovich, 1987.

DAVIS, KINGSLEY. "Extreme Social Isolation of a Child." *American Journal of Sociology.* Vol. 45, No. 4 (January 1940):554–565.

DAVIS, KINGSLEY. "Final Note on a Case of Extreme Isolation." *American Journal of Sociology.* Vol. 52, No. 5 (March 1947):432–437.

DAVIS, KINGSLEY, and WILBERT MOORE. "Some Principles of Stratification." *American Sociological Review.* Vol. 10, No. 2 (April 1945):242–249.

DAVIS, SHARON A., and EMIL J. HALLER. "Tracking, Ability, and SES: Further Evidence on the 'Revisionist-Meritocratic Debate.'" *American Journal of Education.* Vol. 89 (May 1981):283–304.

DEAN, DWIGHT G., and BRENT T. BRUTON. "Alienation and Emotional Maturity." *Sociological Focus.* Vol. 22, No. 4 (October 1989):221–230.

DECKARD, BARBARA SINCLAIR. *The Women's Movement: Political, Socioeconomic, and Psychological Issues.* 2nd ed. New York: Harper & Row, 1979.

DEDRICK, DENNIS K. Personal communication, 1990.

DEDRICK, DENNIS K., and RICHARD E. YINGER. "MAD, SDI, and the Nuclear Arms Race." Manuscript in development. Georgetown, KY: Georgetown College, 1990.

DEFLEUR, MELVIN. "Diffusing Information." *Social Science and Modern Society.* Vol. 25, No. 2 (January/February 1988):72–81.

DEGLER, CARL. *At Odds: Women and the Family in America From the Revolution to the Present.* New York: Oxford University Press, 1980.

DELACROIX, JACQUES, and CHARLES C. RAGIN. "Structural Blockage: A Cross-national Study of Economic Dependency, State Efficacy, and Underdevelopment." *American Journal of Sociology.* Vol. 86, No. 6 (May 1981):1311–1347.

DEMOTT, JOHN S. "Shop Here, but Don't Stop Here." *Time.* Vol. 127, No. 10 (March 10, 1986):46.

DEMOTT, JOHN S. "Wreaking Havoc on Spring Break." *Time.* Vol. 127, No. 14 (April 7, 1986):29.

DENTON, NANCY A., and DOUGLAS S. MASSEY. "Racial Identity Among Caribbean Hispanics: The Effect of Double Minority Status on Residential Segregation." *American Sociological Review.* Vol. 54, No. 5 (October 1989):790–808.

DEVINE, JOEL A. "State and State Expenditure: Determinants of Social Investment and Social Consumption Spending in the Postwar United States." *American Sociological Review.* Vol. 50, No. 2 (April 1985):150–165.

DEWEY, JOHN. *Experience and Education.* New York: Collier Books, 1968; orig. 1938.

DIAMOND, MILTON. "Sexual Identity, Monozygotic Twins Reared in Discordant Sex Roles and a BBC Follow-Up." *Archives of Sexual Behavior.* Vol. 11, No. 2 (April 1982):181–186.

DICKENS, CHARLES. *The Adventures of Oliver Twist.* Boston, MA: Estes and Lauriat, 1886; orig. 1837–1839.

DICKENS, CHARLES. *Hard Times.* New York: W. W. Norton, 1966; orig. 1854.

DIPRETE, THOMAS A. "Unemployment over the Life Cycle: Racial Differences and the Effect of Changing Economic Conditions." *American Journal of Sociology.* Vol. 87, No. 2 (September 1981):286–307.

DOBSON, RICHARD B. "Mobility and Stratification in the Soviet Union." *Annual Review of Sociology.* Vol. 3. Palo Alto, CA: Annual Reviews, Inc., 1977:297–329.

DOBYNS, HENRY F. "An Appraisal of Techniques with a New Hemispheric Estimate." *Current Anthropology.* Vol. 7, No. 4 (October 1966):395–446.

DOERNER, WILLIAM R. "In the Dead of the Night." *Time.* Vol. 127, No. 17 (April 28, 1986):28–31.

DOLLARD, JOHN, et al. *Frustration and Aggression.* New Haven, CT: Yale University Press, 1939.

DOMHOFF, G. WILLIAM. "The Growth Machine and the Power Elite: A Theo-

retical Challenge to Pluralists and Marxists Alike." Paper presented to the American Political Science Association. Washington, DC: 1984.

DOMHOFF, G. WILLIAM. *Who Rules America?* Englewood Cliffs, NJ: Prentice-Hall, 1967.

DOMHOFF, G. WILLIAM. *The Higher Circles: The Governing Class in America.* New York: Vintage, 1971.

DOMHOFF, G. WILLIAM. *The Powers That Be: Processes of Ruling Class Domination in America.* New York: Vintage, 1979.

DOMHOFF, G. WILLIAM. *Who Rules America Now? A View of the 80s.* Englewood Cliffs, NJ: Prentice-Hall, 1983.

DONALDSON, PETER. *Worlds Apart: The Development Gap and What It Means.* 2nd ed. New York: Penguin Books, 1986.

DONOVAN, VIRGINIA K., and RONNIE LITTENBERG. "Psychology of Women: Feminist Therapy." In Barbara Haber, ed., *The Women's Annual 1981: The Year in Review.* Boston: G. K. Hall, 1982:211–235.

DOUGLASS, RICHARD L. "Domestic Neglect and Abuse of the Elderly: Implications for Research and Service." *Family Relations.* Vol. 32 (July 1983):395–402.

DOYAL, LESLEY, with IMOGEN PENNELL. *The Political Economy of Health.* London: Pluto Press, 1981.

DOYLE, JAMES A. *The Male Experience.* Dubuque, IA: Wm. C. Brown, 1983.

DUBOS, RENÉ. *Man Adapting.* New Haven, CT: Yale University Press, 1980; orig. 1965.

DUHL, LEONARD J. "The Social Context of Health." In Arthur C. Hastings et al., eds., *Health for the Whole Person: The Complete Guide to Holistic Medicine.* Boulder, CO: Westview Press, 1980: 39–48.

DURKHEIM, EMILE. *The Division of Labor in Society.* New York: Free Press, 1964a; orig. 1895.

DURKHEIM, EMILE. *The Rules of Sociological Method.* New York: Free Press, 1964b; orig. 1893.

DURKHEIM, EMILE. *The Elementary Forms of Religious Life.* New York: Free Press, 1965; orig. 1915.

DURKHEIM, EMILE. *Suicide.* New York: Free Press, 1966; orig. 1897.

DURKHEIM, EMILE. *Selected Writings.* Anthony Giddens, ed. Cambridge (UK): Cambridge University Press, 1972.

DURKHEIM, EMILE. *Sociology and Philosophy.* New York: Free Press, 1974; orig. 1924.

DWORKIN, ANDREA. *Intercourse.* New York: Free Press, 1987.

DZIECH, BILLIE WRIGHT, and LINDA WEINER. *The Lecherous Professor: Sexual Harassment on Campus.* Boston, MA: Beacon Press, 1984.

EASTERLIN, RICHARD A. "Immigration: Economic and Social Characteristics." In *Harvard Encyclopedia of American Ethnic Groups.* Cambridge, MA: Harvard University Press, 1980:476–486.

EBAUGH, HELEN ROSE FUCHS. *Becoming an EX: The Process of Role Exit.* Chicago: University of Chicago Press, 1988.

ECKHOLM, ERIK. "Pygmy Chimp Readily Learns Language Skill." *The New York Times* (June 24, 1985):A1, B7.

ECKHOLM, ERIK. "Malnutrition in Elderly: Widespread Health Threat." *The New York Times* (August 13, 1985):19–20.

EDMONSTON, BARRY, and THOMAS M. GUTERBOCK. "Is Suburbanization Slowing Down? Recent Trends in Population Deconcentration in U.S. Metropolitan Areas." *Social Forces.* Vol. 62, No. 4 (June 1984):905–925.

EDWARDS, DAVID V. *The American Political Experience.* 3rd ed. Englewood Cliffs, NJ: Prentice-Hall, 1985.

EDWARDS, HARRY. *Sociology of Sport.* Homewood, IL: Dorsey Press, 1973.

EDWARDS, RICHARD. *Contested Terrain: The Transformation of the Workplace in the Twentieth Century.* New York: Basic Books, 1979.

EHRENREICH, BARBARA. *The Hearts of Men: American Dreams and the Flight from Commitment.* Garden City, NY: Anchor, 1983.

EHRENREICH, JOHN. "Introduction." In John Ehrenreich, ed., *The Cultural Crisis of Modern Medicine.* New York: Monthly Review Press, 1978:1–35.

EHRLICH, PAUL R. *The Population Bomb.* New York: Ballantine Books, 1978.

EICHLER, MARGRIT. *Nonsexist Research Methods: A Practical Guide.* Winchester, MA: Unwin Hyman, 1988.

EISEN, ARNOLD M. *The Chosen People in America: A Study of Jewish Religious Ideology.* Bloomington, IN: Indiana University Press, 1983.

EISENSTEIN, ZILLAH R., ed. *Capitalist Patriarchy and the Case for Socialist Feminism.* New York: Monthly Review Press, 1979.

EITZEN, D. STANLEY. *Social Problems.* Boston: Allyn and Bacon, 1980.

EKMAN, PAUL. *Telling Lies: Clues to Deceit in the Marketplace, Politics, and Marriage.* New York: W. W. Norton, 1985.

EKMAN, PAUL, WALLACE V. FRIESEN, and JOHN BEAR. "The International Language of Gestures." *Psychology Today* (May 1984):64–69.

ELIAS, ROBERT. *The Politics of Victimization: Victims, Victimology and Human Rights.* New York: Oxford University Press, 1986.

ELKIN, FREDERICK, and GERALD HANDEL. *The Child and Society: The Process of Socialization.* 4th ed. New York: Random House, 1984.

ELKIND, DAVID. *The Hurried Child: Growing Up Too Fast Too Soon.* Reading, MA: Addison-Wesley, 1981.

ELLIOT, DELBERT S., and SUZANNE S. AGETON. "Reconciling Race and Class Differences in Self-Reported and Official Estimates of Delinquency." *American Sociological Review.* Vol. 45, No. 1 (February 1980):95–110.

EMBER, CAROL, and MELVIN M. EMBER. *Anthropology.* 4th ed. Englewood Cliffs, NJ: Prentice-Hall, 1985.

EMBER, MELVIN, and CAROL R. EMBER. "The Conditions Favoring Matrilocal versus Patrilocal Residence." *American Anthropologist,* Vol. 73, No. 3 (June 1971):571–594.

EMBREE, AINSLIE T. *The Hindu Tradition.* New York: Vintage Books, 1972.

ENGELS, FRIEDRICH. *The Origin of the Family.* Chicago: Charles H. Kerr and Company, 1902; orig. 1884.

ERIKSON, ERIK H. *Childhood and Society.* New York: W. W. Norton, 1963; orig. 1950.

ERICKSON, ERIK H. *Identity and the Life Cycle.* New York: W. W. Norton, 1980.

ERIKSON, KAI T. *Wayward Puritans: A Study in the Sociology of Deviance.* New York: John Wiley, 1966.

ERIKSON, KAI T. *Everything in Its Path: Destruction of Community in the Buffalo Creek Flood.* New York: Simon and Schuster, 1976.

ERIKSON, ROBERT S., NORMAN R. LUTTBEG, and KENT L. TEDIN. *American Public Opinion: Its Origins, Content, and Impact.* 2nd ed. New York: Wiley, 1980.

ESMAN, MILTON J. "The Politics of Bilingualism in Canada." *Political Science Quarterly.* Vol. 97, No. 2 (Summer 1982):233–253.

ETZIONI, AMITAI. *A Comparative Analysis of Complex Organization: On Power, Involvement, and Their Correlates.* Revised and enlarged ed. New York: Free Press, 1975.

ETZIONI-HALEVY, EVA. *Bureaucracy and Democracy: A Political Dilemma.* Rev. ed. Boston: Routledge & Kegan Paul, 1985.

EVANGELAUF, JEAN. "Student Financial Aid Reaches $20.5 Billion, but Fails to Keep Pace with Rising College Costs, Study Finds." *The Chronicle of Higher Education.* Vol. XXXIV, No. 14 (December 2, 1987):A33, A36.

EVANS, M. D. R. "Immigrant Entrepreneurship: Effects of Ethnic Market Size and Isolated Labor Pool." *American Sociological Review.* Vol. 54, No. 6 (December 1989):950–962.

EVE, SUSAN BROWN. "Age Strata Differences in Utilization of Health Care Services among Adults in the United States." *Sociological Focus.* Vol. 17, No. 2 (April 1984):105–120.

FALK, GERHARD. Personal communication, 1987.

FALLOWS, JAMES. "Immigration: How It's Affecting Us." *The Atlantic Monthly.* Vol. 252 (November 1983):45–52, 55–62, 66–68, 85–90, 94, 96, 99–106.

Family Economics Review. "Updated Estimates of the Cost of Raising a Child." Vol. 2, No. 4 (1989):30–31.

FANTINI, MARIO D. *Regaining Excellence in Education.* Columbus, OH: Merrill, 1986.

FARLEY, REYNOLDS. "The Long Road: Blacks and Whites in America." *American Demographics.* Vol. 2, No. 2 (February 1980):11–17.

FARRELL, MICHAEL P., and STANLEY D. ROSENBERG. *Men at Midlife.* Boston, MA: Auburn House, 1981.

FEAGIN, JOE. *The Urban Real Estate Game.* Englewood Cliffs, NJ: Prentice-Hall, 1983.

FEATHERMAN, DAVID L., and ROBERT M. HAUSER. *Opportunity and Change.* New York: Academic Press, 1978.

FERGUSON, TOM. "Medical Self-Care: Self Responsibility for Health." In Arthur C. Hastings et al., eds., *Health for the Whole Person: The Complete Guide to Holistic Medicine.* Boulder, CO: Westview Press, 1980:87–109.

FERGUSSON, D. M., L. J. HORWOOD, and F. T. SHANNON. "A Proportional Hazards Model of Family Breakdown." *Journal of Marriage and the Family.* Vol. 46, No. 3 (August 1984):539–549.

"Final Report of the Commission on the Higher Education of Minorities." Los Angeles, CA: Higher Education Research Institute, 1982.

FINKELSTEIN, NEAL W., and RON HASKINS. "Kindergarten Children Prefer Same-Color Peers." *Child Development.* Vol. 54, No. 2 (April 1983):502–508.

FIORENTINE, ROBERT. "Men, Women, and the Premed Persistence Gap: A Normative Alternatives Approach." *American Journal of Sociology.* Vol. 92, No. 5 (March 1987):1118–1139.

FIREBAUGH, GLENN, and KENNETH E. DAVIS. "Trends in Antiblack Prejudice, 1972–1984: Region and Cohort Effects." *American Journal of Sociology.* Vol. 94, No. 2 (September 1988):251–272.

FISCHER, CLAUDE S. *The Urban Experience.* 2nd ed. New York: Harcourt Brace Jovanovich, 1984.

FISCHER, CLAUDE S., et al. *Networks and Places: Social Relations in the Urban Setting.* New York: Free Press, 1977.

FISHER, ELIZABETH. *Woman's Creation: Sexual Evolution and the Shaping of Society.* Garden City, NY: Anchor/Doubleday, 1979.

FISHER, ROGER, and WILLIAM URY. "Getting to YES." In William M. Evan and Stephen Hilgartner, eds., *The Arms Race and Nuclear War.* Englewood Cliffs, NJ: Prentice-Hall, 1988:261–268.

FISHMAN, PAMELA M. "Interactional Shitwork." *Heresies: A Feminist Publication on Art and Politics.* Vol. 2 (May 1977):99–101.

FISHMAN, PAMELA M. "The Work Women Do." *Social Problems.* Vol. 25, No. 4 (April 1978):397–406.

FITZPATRICK, JOSEPH P. *Puerto Rican Americans: The Meaning of Migration to the Mainland.* Englewood Cliffs, NJ: Prentice-Hall, 1971.

FITZPATRICK, JOSEPH P. "Puerto Ricans." In *Harvard Encyclopedia of American Ethnic Groups.* Cambridge, MA: Harvard University Press, 1980: 858–867.

FLAHERTY, MICHAEL G. "A Formal Approach to the Study of Amusement in Social Interaction." *Studies in Symbolic Interaction,* Vol. 5. New York: JAI Press, 1984:71–82.

FLAHERTY, MICHAEL G. "Two Conceptions of the Social Situation: Some Implications of Humor." *The Sociological Quarterly.* Vol. 31, No. 1 (Spring 1990), in press.

Forbes. "The Forbes Four Hundred." Vol. 144, No. 9 (October 23, 1989):152–154.

FORD, CLELLAN S., and FRANK A. BEACH. *Patterns of Sexual Behavior.* New York: Harper & Row, 1951.

FORM, WILLIAM. "Self-Employed Manual Workers: Petty Bourgeois or Working Class?" *Social Forces.* Vol. 60, No. 4 (June 1982):1050–1069.

FORNOS, WERNER. "Growth of Cities Is Major Crisis." *Popline.* Vol. 8, No. 3 (March 1986):4.

FOWLER, FLOYD J., JR., and THOMAS W. MANGIONE. *Standardized Survey Interviewing: Minimizing Interviewer-Related Error.* Newbury Park, CA: Sage, 1989.

FRANK, ANDRE GUNDER. *On Capitalist Underdevelopment.* Bombay: Oxford University Press, 1975.

FRANK, ANDRE GUNDER. *Crisis: In the World Economy.* New York: Holmes & Meier, 1980.

FRANK, ANDRE GUNDER. *Reflections on the World Economic Crisis.* New York: Monthly Review Press, 1981.

FRANKLIN, JOHN HOPE. *From Slavery to Freedom: A History of Negro Americans.* 3rd ed. New York: Vintage Books, 1967.

FRAZIER, E. FRANKLIN. *Black Bourgeoisie: The Rise of a New Middle Class.* New York: Free Press, 1965.

FREDRICKSON, GEORGE M. *White Supremacy: A Comparative Study in American and South African History.* New York: Oxford University Press, 1981.

FREI, DANIEL. "Risks of Unintentional Nuclear War." In William M. Evan and Stephen Hilgartner, eds., *The Arms Race and Nuclear War.* Englewood Cliffs, NJ: Prentice-Hall, 1988:19–24.

FRENCH, MARILYN. *Beyond Power: On Women, Men, and Morals.* New York: Summit Books, 1985.

FRIEDMAN, EUGENE A., and ROBERT J. HAVIGHURST.*The Meaning of Work and Retirement*. Chicago: University of Chicago Press, 1954.

FRIEDRICH, CARL J., and ZBIGNIEW BRZEZINSKI. *Totalitarian Dictatorship and Autocracy*. 2nd ed. Cambridge, MA: Harvard University Press, 1965.

FRIEDRICH, OTTO. "Braving Scorn and Threats." *Time*. Vol. 125, No. 30 (July 23, 1984):36–37.

FRIEDRICH, OTTO. "A Proud Capital's Distress."*Time*. Vol. 124, No. 6 (August 6, 1984):26–30, 33–35.

FRIEDRICH, OTTO. "United No More." *Time*. Vol. 129, No. 18 (May 4, 1987):28–37.

FUCHS, VICTOR R. *Who Shall Live*. New York: Basic Books, 1974.

FUCHS, VICTOR R. "Sex Differences in Economic Well-Being." *Science*. Vol. 232 (April 25, 1986):459–464.

FUGITA, STEPHEN S., and DAVID J. O'BRIEN. "Structural Assimilation, Ethnic Group Membership, and Political Participation among Japanese Americans: A Research Note." *Social Forces*. Vol. 63, No. 4 (June 1985):986–995.

FUJIMOTO, ISAO. "The Failure of Democracy in a Time of Crisis." In Amy Tachiki et al., eds., *Roots: An Asian American Reader*. Los Angeles: UCLA Asian American Studies Center, 1971:207–214.

FUMENTO, MICHAEL. *The Myth of Heterosexual AIDS*. New York: Basic Books, 1989.

FURSTENBERG, FRANK F., JR. "The New Extended Family: The Experience of Parents and Children after Remarriage." Paper presented to the Changing Family Conference XIII: The Blended Family. University of Iowa, 1984.

FURSTENBERG, FRANK F., JR., J. BROOKS-GUNN, and S. PHILIP MORGAN. *Adolescent Mothers in Later Life*. New York: Cambridge University Press, 1987.

FUSFELD, DANIEL R. *Economics: Principles of Political Economy*. Glenview, IL: Scott, Foresman, 1982.

GAGLIANI, GIORGIO. "How Many Working Classes?" *American Journal of Sociology*. Vol. 87, No. 2 (September 1981):259–285.

GALLUP, GEORGE H. "The 16th Annual Gallup Poll of the Public's Attitudes toward the Public Schools." *Phi Delta Kappan*. Vol. 66 (September 1984):23–38.

GALLUP, GEORGE, JR. *Religion in America*. Princeton, NJ: Princeton Religion Research Center, 1982.

GALLUP, GEORGE, JR. *Religion in America: The Gallup Report*. Report No. 222. Princeton, NJ: Princeton Religion Research Center, March 1984.

GALLUP OPINION INDEX. "Religion in America, 1977–78," Report 145 (January 1978); and "Religion in America," Report 184 (January 1981).

GANS, HERBERT J. *People and Plans: Essays on Urban Problems and Solutions*. New York: Basic Books, 1968.

GANS, HERBERT J. *Deciding What's News: A Study of CBS Evening News, NBC Nightly News, Newsweek and Time*. New York: Vintage, 1980.

GANS, HERBERT J. *The Urban Villagers: Group and Class in the Life of Italian-Americans*. New York: Free Press, 1982; orig. 1962.

GARDNER, R. ALLEN, and BEATRICE T. GARDNER."Teaching Sign Language to a Chimpanzee." *Science*. Vol. 165, 1969:664–672.

GARFINKEL, HAROLD. "Conditions of Successful Degradation Ceremonies." *American Journal of Sociology*. Vol. 61, No. 2 (March 1956):420–424.

GARFINKEL, HAROLD. *Studies in Ethnomethodology*. Cambridge (UK): Polity Press, 1967.

GARTON ASH, TIMOTHY. *The Polish Revolution: Solidarity*. New York: Charles Scribner's Sons, 1983.

GEERTZ, CLIFFORD. "Common Sense as a Cultural System." *The Antioch Review*. Vol. 33, No. 1 (Spring 1975):5–26.

GEIST, WILLIAM. *Toward a Safe and Sane Halloween and Other Tales of Suburbia*. New York: Times Books, 1985.

GELMAN, DAVID. "Who's Taking Care of Our Parents?" *Newsweek* (May 6, 1985):61–64, 67–68.

GEORGE, SUSAN. *How the Other Half Dies: The Real Reasons for World Hunger*. Totowa, NJ: Rowman & Allanheld, 1977.

GERSTEL, NAOMI. "Divorce and Stigma." *Social Problems*. Vol. 43, No. 2 (April 1987):172–186.

GERTH, H. H., and C. WRIGHT MILLS, eds. *From Max Weber: Essays in Sociology*. New York: Oxford University Press, 1946.

GESCHWENDER, JAMES A. *Racial Stratification in America*. Dubuque, IA: Wm. C. Brown, 1978.

GIBBONS, DON C. *Delinquent Behavior*. 3rd ed. Englewood Cliffs, NJ: Prentice-Hall, 1981.

GIBBONS, DON C., and MARVIN D. KROHN. *Delinquent Behavior*. 4th ed. Englewood Cliffs, NJ: Prentice-Hall, 1986.

GIDDENS, ANTHONY. *Sociology: A Brief but Critical Introduction*. New York: Harcourt Brace Jovanovich, 1982.

GIELE, JANET ZOLLINGER. "Women's Work and Family Roles." In Janet Zollinger Giele, ed., *Women in the Middle Years: Current Knowledge and Directions for Research and Policy*. New York: John Wiley and Sons, 1982:115–150.

GIELE, JANET Z. "Gender and Sex Roles." In Neil J. Smelser, ed., *Handbook of Sociology*. Newbury Park, CA: Sage, 1988:291–323.

GILBERT, ALAN, and JOSEF GUGLER. *Cities, Poverty, and Development*. New York: Oxford University Press, 1983.

GILBERT, DENNIS, and JOSEPH A. KAHL. *The American Class Structure: A New Synthesis*. 3rd ed. Homewood, IL: The Dorsey Press, 1987.

GILLETT, CHARLIE. *The Sound of the City: The Rise of Rock and Roll*. New York: Pantheon, 1983.

GILLIGAN, CAROL. *In a Different Voice: Psychological Theory and Women's Development*. Cambridge, MA: Harvard University Press, 1982.

GIMENEZ, MARTHA E. "Silence in the Classroom: Some Thoughts about Teaching in the 1980s." *Teaching Sociology*. Vol. 17, No. 2 (April 1989):184–191.

GINSBURG, PAUL B. "Market-Oriented Options in Medicare and Medicaid." In Jack B. Meyer, ed., *Market Reforms in Health Care: Current Issues, New Directions, Strategic Decisions*. Washington, DC: American Enterprise Institute for Public Policy Research, 1983:103–118.

GIOVANNINI, MAUREEN. "Female Anthropologist and Male Informant: Gender Conflict in a Sicilian Town." In John J. Macionis and Nijole V. Benokraitis, eds., *Seeing Ourselves: Classic, Contemporary, and Cross-Cultural Readings in Sociology*. Englewood Cliffs, NJ: Prentice Hall, 1989:30–35.

GLADUE, BRIAN A., RICHARD GREEN, and RONALD E. HELLMAN. "Neuroendocrine Response to Estrogen and Sexual Orientation." *Science*. Vol. 225, No. 4669 (September 28, 1984):1496–1499.

GLASS, DAVID V., ed. *Social Mobility in Britain*. London: Routledge & Kegan Paul, 1954.

GLAZER, NATHAN, and DANIEL P. MOYNIHAN. *Beyond the Melting Pot*. 2nd ed. Cambridge, MA: M.I.T. Press, 1970.

GLENN, CHARLES L., and FRANMARIE KENNEDY-KEEL."Commentary." *Education Week*. Vol. V, No. 21 (February 5, 1986):21.

GLENN, NORVAL D., and BETH ANN SHELTON. "Regional Differences in Divorce in the United States." *Journal of Marriage and the Family*. Vol. 47, No. 3 (August 1985):641–652.

GLOCK, CHARLES Y. "The Religious Revival in America." In Jane Zahn, ed., *Religion and the Face of America*. Berkeley, CA: University of California Press, 1959:25–42.

GLOCK, CHARLES Y. "On the Study of Religious Commitment." *Religious Education*. Vol. 62, No. 4 (1962):98–110.

GLOCK, CHARLES Y., and RODNEY STARK. *Religion and Society in Tension*. Chicago: Rand McNally, 1965.

GLUCK, PETER R. and RICHARD J. MEISTER. *Cities in Transition*. New York: New Viewpoints, 1979.

GLUECK, SHELDON, and ELEANOR GLUECK. *Unraveling Juvenile Delinquency*. New York: Commonwealth Fund, 1950.

GOETTING, ANN. "Divorce Outcome Research." *Journal of Family Issues*. Vol. 2, No. 3 (September 1981):350–378.

GOETTING, ANN. "The Six Stations of Remarriage: Developmental Tasks of Remarriage after Divorce." *Family Relations*. Vol. 31, No. 2 (April 1982):213–222.

GOETTING, ANN. Personal communication, 1989.

GOFFMAN, ERVING. *The Presentation of Self in Everyday Life*. Garden City, NY: Anchor, 1959.

GOFFMAN, ERVING. *Asylums: Essays on the Social Situation of Mental Patients and Other Inmates*. Garden City, NY: Anchor, 1961.

GOFFMAN, ERVING. *Encounters: Two Studies in the Sociology of Interaction*. Indianapolis, IN: Bobbs-Merrill, 1961.

GOFFMAN, ERVING. *Stigma: Notes on the Management of Spoiled Identity*. Englewood Cliffs, NJ: Prentice-Hall, 1963.

GOFFMAN, ERVING. *Interactional Ritual: Essays on Face to Face Behavior.* Garden City, NY: Anchor, 1967.

GOFFMAN, ERVING. *Gender Advertisements.* New York: Harper Colophon, 1979.

GOLDBERG, STEVEN. *The Inevitability of Patriarchy.* New York: William Morrow and Co., 1974.

GOLDBERG, STEVEN. Personal communication, 1987.

GOLDEN, FRÉDERIC. "Here Come the Microkids." *Time.* Vol. 119, No. 18 (May 3, 1982):50–56.

GOLDFARB, JEFFREY C. *Beyond Glasnost: The Post-Totalitarian Mind.* Chicago: University of Chicago Press, 1989.

GOLDFIELD, MICHAEL. *The Decline of Organized Labor in the United States.* Chicago and London: University of Chicago Press, 1987.

GOLDSBY, RICHARD A. *Race and Races.* 2nd ed. New York: Macmillan, 1977.

GOLDSMITH, H. H. "Genetic Influences on Personality from Infancy." *Child Development.* Vol. 54, No. 2 (April 1983):331–335.

GOODE, WILLIAM J. "The Theoretical Importance of Love." *American Sociological Review.* Vol. 24, No. 1 (February 1959):38–47.

GOODE, WILLIAM J. "Encroachment, Charlatanism, and the Emerging Profession: Psychology, Sociology and Medicine." *American Sociological Review.* Vol. 25, No. 6 (December 1960):902–914.

GOODE, WILLIAM J. "Why Men Resist." In Arlene S. Skolnick and Jerome H. Skolnick, eds., *Family in Transition.* 4th ed. Boston, MA: Little, Brown, 1983:201–218.

GORDON, JAMES S. "The Paradigm of Holistic Medicine." In Arthur C. Hastings et al., eds., *Health for the Whole Person: The Complete Guide to Holistic Medicine.* Boulder, CO: Westview Press, 1980:3–27.

GORDON, MILTON M. *Assimilation in American Life.* New York: Oxford University Press, 1964.

GORING, CHARLES BUCKMAN. *The English Convict: A Statistical Study.* Montclair, NJ: Patterson Smith, 1972; orig. 1913.

GOTTMANN, JEAN. *Megalopolis.* New York: Twentieth Century Fund, 1961.

GOUGH, KATHLEEN. "The Origin of the Family." *Journal of Marriage and the Family.* Vol. 33, No. 4 (November 1971):760–771.

GOULDNER, ALVIN. *Enter Plato.* New York: Free Press, 1965.

GOULDNER, ALVIN. "The Sociologist as Partisan: Sociology and the Welfare State." In Larry T. Reynolds and Janice M. Reynolds, eds., *The Sociology of Sociology.* New York: McKay, 1970a:218–255.

GOULDNER, ALVIN. *The Coming Crisis of Western Sociology.* New York: Avon Books, 1970b.

GRANOVETTER, MARK. "The Strength of Weak Ties." *American Journal of Sociology.* Vol. 78, No. 6 (May 1973):1360–1380.

GRANT, KAREN R. "The Inverse Care Law in the Context of Universal Free Health Insurance in Canada: Toward Meeting Health Needs Through Public Policy." *Sociological Focus.* Vol. 17, No. 2 (April 1984):137–155.

GRANT, DONALD L. *The Anti-Lynching Movement.* San Francisco, CA: R and E Research Associates, 1975.

GRANT, NIGEL. *Soviet Education.* New York: Pelican Books, 1979.

GRAY, ROBERT. *A History of London.* London: Hutchinson, 1978.

GREELEY, ANDREW M. *Why Can't They Be Like Us? America's White Ethnic Groups.* New York: E. P. Dutton, 1971.

GREELEY, ANDREW M. *Ethnicity in the United States: A Preliminary Reconnaissance.* New York: John Wiley, 1974.

GREELEY, ANDREW M. *Religious Change in America.* Cambridge: Harvard University Press, 1989.

GREENBERG, DAVID F. *The Construction of Homosexuality.* Chicago: University of Chicago Press, 1988.

GREER, SCOTT. *Urban Renewal and American Cities.* Indianapolis: Bobbs-Merril, 1965.

GREGORY, PAUL R., and ROBERT C. STUART. *Comparative Economic Systems.* 2nd ed. Boston, MA: Houghton Mifflin, 1985.

GRIFFIN, LARRY J., MICHAEL E. WALLACE, and BETH A. RUBIN. "Capitalist Resistance to the Organization of Labor Before the New Deal: Why? How? Success?" *American Sociological Review.* Vol. 51, No. 2 (April 1986):147–167.

GRIFFIN, RICHARD WAYNE, and SANDRA KERANEN GRIFFIN. "Theoretical Aspects of Insurgency Among the Powerless." Paper presented to the Southwestern Sociological Association, Little Rock, Arkansas, 1989.

GRISWOLD, WENDY. "The Fabrication of Meaning: Literary Interpretation in the United States, Great Britain, and the West Indies." *American Journal of Sociology.* Vol. 92, No. 5 (March 1987):1077–1117.

GRUENBERG, BARRY. "The Happy Worker: An Analysis of Educational and Occupational Differences in Determinants of Job Satisfaction." *American Journal of Sociology.* Vol. 86, No. 2 (September 1980):247–271.

GUPTE, PRANAY. *The Crowded Earth: People and the Politics of Population.* New York: W. W. Norton, 1984.

GUTMAN, HERBERT G. *The Black Family in Slavery and Freedom, 1750–1925.* New York: Pantheon Books, 1976.

GWARTNEY-GIBBS, PATRICIA A. "The Institutionalization of Premarital Cohabitation: Estimates from Marriage License Applications, 1970 and 1980." *Journal of Marriage and the Family.* Vol. 48, No. 2 (May 1986):423–434.

GWARTNEY-GIBBS, PATRICIA A., JEAN STOCKARD, and SUSANNE BOHMER. "Learning Courtship Aggression: The Influence of Parents, Peers, and Personal Experiences." *Family Relations.* Vol. 36, No. 3 (July 1987):276–282.

HAAS, LINDA. "Domestic Role Sharing in Sweden." *Journal of Marriage and the Family.* Vol. 43, No. 4 (November 1981):957–967.

HABERMAS, JÜRGEN. *Toward a Rational Society: Student Protest, Science, and Politics.* Jeremy J. Shapiro, trans. Boston, MA: Beacon Press, 1970.

HACKER, HELEN MAYER. "Women as a Minority Group." *Social Forces.* Vol. 30 (October 1951):60–69.

HACKER, HELEN MAYER. "Women as a Minority Group: 20 Years Later." In Florence Denmark, ed., *Who Discriminates Against Women.* Beverly Hills, CA: Sage, 1974:124–134.

HADDEN, JEFFREY K., and CHARLES E. SWAIN. *Prime Time Preachers: The Rising Power of Televangelism.* Reading, MA: Addison-Wesley, 1981.

HAGAN, JOHN, A. R. GILLIS, and JOHN SIMPSON. "The Class Structure of Gender and Delinquency: Toward a Power-Control Theory of Common Delinquent Behavior." *American Journal of Sociology.* Vol. 90. No. 6 (May 1985):1151–1178.

HAGAN, JOHN, and PATRICIA PARKER. "White-Collar Crime and Punishment: The Class Structure and Legal Sanctioning of Securities Violations." *American Sociological Review.* Vol. 50, No. 3 (June 1985):302–316.

HAGAN, JOHN, JOHN SIMPSON, and A. R. GILLIS. "Class in the Household: A Power-Control Theory of Gender and Delinquency." *American Journal of Sociology.* Vol. 92, No. 4 (January 1987):788–816.

HALBERSTAM, DAVID. *The Reckoning.* New York: Avon, 1986.

HALLINAN, MAUREEN T., and RICHARD A. WILLIAMS. "Interracial Friendship Choices in Secondary Schools." *American Sociological Review.* Vol. 54, No. 1 (February 1989):67–78.

HALLOWELL, CHRISTOPHER. "New Focus on the Old." *The New York Times Magazine* (December 15, 1985):42, 44, 48, 50, 109–111.

HAMBLIN, DORA JANE. *The First Cities.* New York: Time-Life, 1973.

HAMMOND, PHILIP E. "Introduction." In Philip E. Hammond, ed., *The Sacred in a Secular Age: Toward Revision in the Scientific Study of Religion.* Berkeley, CA: University of California Press, 1985:1–6.

HAMRICK, MICHAEL H., DAVID J. ANSPAUGH, and GENE EZELL. *Health.* Columbus, OH: Merrill, 1986.

HANDLIN, OSCAR. *Boston's Immigrants 1790–1865: A Study in Acculturation.* Cambridge, MA: Harvard University Press, 1941.

HANEY, CRAIG, CURTIS BANKS, and PHILIP ZIMBARDO. "Interpersonal Dynamics in a Simulated Prison." *International Journal of Criminology and Penology.* Vol. 1 (1973):69–97.

HANNAN, MICHAEL T., and GLENN R. CARROLL. "Dynamics of Formal Political Structure: An Event-History Analysis." *American Sociological Review.* Vol. 46, No. 1 (February 1981):19–35.

HARDOY, JORGE E. "Two Thousand Years of Latin American Urbanization." In Jorge E. Hardoy, ed., *Urbanization in Latin America: Approaches and Issues.* Garden City, NY: Anchor Books, 1975.

HAREVEN, TAMARA K. "The Life Course and Aging in Historical Perspective." In Tamara K. Hareven and Kathleen J. Adams, eds., *Aging and Life Course Transitions: An Interdisciplinary Perspective.* New York: Guilford Press, 1982:1–26.

HARLAN, WILLIAM H. "Social Status of the Aged in Three Indian Villages."

In Bernice L. Neugarten, ed., *Middle Age and Aging: A Reader in Social Psychology*. Chicago: University of Chicago Press, 1968:469–475.

HARLOW, HARRY F., and MARGARET KUENNE HARLOW. "Social Deprivation in Monkeys." *Scientific American*. Vol. 207 (November 1962):137–146.

HARRINGTON, MICHAEL. *The New American Poverty*. New York: Penguin Books, 1984.

HARRIS, CHAUNCEY D., and EDWARD L. ULLMAN. "The Nature of Cities." *The Annals*. Vol. 242 (November 1945):7–17.

HARRIS, LOUIS, and ASSOCIATES. *The Myth and Reality of Aging in America*. Washington, DC: National Council on Aging, 1976.

HARRIS, MARVIN. *Cows, Pigs, Wars and Witches: The Riddles of Culture*. New York: Vintage Books, 1975.

HARRIS, MARVIN. "Why Men Dominate Women." *New York Times Magazine* (November 13, 1977):46, 115–123.

HARRIS, MARVIN. *Good to Eat: Riddle of Food and Culture*. New York: Simon and Schuster, 1985.

HARRIS, MARVIN. *Cultural Anthropology*. 2nd ed. New York: Harper & Row, 1987.

HARRISON, PAUL. *Inside the Third World: The Anatomy of Poverty*. 2nd ed. New York: Penguin Books, 1984.

HARTMANN, BETSY, and JAMES BOYCE. *Needless Hunger: Voices from a Bangladesh Village*. San Francisco: Institute for Food and Development Policy, 1982.

HAVIGHURST, ROBERT J., BERNICE L. NEUGARTEN, and SHELDON S. TOBIN. "Disengagement and Patterns of Aging." In Bernice L. Neugarten, ed., *Middle Age and Aging: A Reader in Social Psychology*. Chicago: University of Chicago Press, 1968:161–172.

HAVILAND, WILLIAM A. *Anthropology*. 4th ed. New York: Holt, Rinehart and Winston, 1985.

HAYNEMAN, STEPHEN P., and WILLIAM A. LOXLEY. "The Effect of Primary-School Quality on Academic Achievement Across Twenty-nine High- and Low-Income Countries." *American Journal of Sociology*. Vol. 88, No. 6 (May 1983):1162–1194.

HEALTH INSURANCE ASSOCIATION OF AMERICA. *Sourcebook of Health Insurance Data 1989*. Washington, DC, 1989.

HEILBRONER, ROBERT L. *The Making of Economic Society*. 7th ed. Englewood Cliffs, NJ: Prentice-Hall, 1985.

HELMUTH, JOHN W. "World Hunger Amidst Plenty." *USA Today*. Vol. 117, No. 2526 (March 1989):48–50.

HENLEY, NANCY, MYKOL HAMILTON, and BARRIE THORNE. "Womanspeak and Manspeak: Sex Differences in Communication, Verbal and Nonverbal." In John J. Macionis and Nijole V. Benokraitis, eds., *Seeing Ourselves: Classic, Contemporary, and Cross-Cultural Readings in Sociology*. Englewood Cliffs, NJ: Prentice-Hall, 1989:105–111.

HERITAGE, JOHN. *Garfinkel and Ethnomethodology*. Cambridge (UK): Polity Press, 1984.

HERMAN, EDWARD S. *Corporate Control, Corporate Power: A Twentieth Century Fund Study*. New York: Cambridge University Press, 1981.

HERTY, ROBERT. "The Collective Representation of Death." In *Death and the Right Hand*. Aberdeen: Cohen and West, 1960:84–86.

HEWLETT, SYLVIA ANN. *A Lesser Life: The Myth of Women's Liberation in America*. New York: William Morrow, 1986.

HILSMAN, ROGER. *The Politics of Governing America*. Englewood Cliffs, NJ: Prentice-Hall, 1985.

HIROSHI, MANNARI. *The Japanese Business Leaders*. Tokyo: University of Tokyo Press, 1974.

HIRSCHI, TRAVIS. *Causes of Delinquency*. Berkeley, CA: University of California Press, 1969.

HIRSCHI, TRAVIS, and MICHAEL GOTTFREDSON. "Age and the Explanation of Crime." *American Journal of Sociology*. Vol. 89, No. 3 (November 1983):552–584.

HIRSCHMAN, CHARLES. "America's Melting Pot Reconsidered." *Annual Review of Sociology*. Vol. 9. Palo Alto, CA: Annual Reviews, Inc., 1983:397–423.

HIRSCHMAN, CHARLES, and MORRISON G. WONG. "Socioeconomic Gains of Asian Americans, Blacks, and Hispanics: 1960–1976." *American Journal of Sociology*. Vol. 90, No. 3 (November 1984):584–607.

HOCHSCHILD, ARLIE, with ANNE MACHUNG. *The Second Shift: Working Parents and the Revolution at Home*. New York: Viking, 1989.

HODGE, ROBERT W., DONALD J. TREIMAN, and PETER H. ROSSI. "A Comparative Study of Occupational Prestige." In Reinhard Bendix and Seymour Martin Lipset, eds., *Class, Status, and Power: Social Stratification in Comparative Perspective*. 2nd ed. New York: Free Press, 1966:309–321.

HOFFMAN, ABBIE. *Revolution for the Hell of It*. New York: The Dial Press, 1968.

HOGAN, DENNIS P., and EVELYN M. KITAGAWA. "The Impact of Social Status and Neighborhood on the Fertility of Black Adolescents." *American Journal of Sociology*. Vol. 90, No. 4 (January 1985):825–855.

HOLLMAN, FREDERICK W. *U.S. Population Estimates, by Age, Sex, Race, and Hispanic Origin: 1989*. Washington, DC: U.S. Government Printing Office, 1990.

HOLT, THOMAS C. "Afro-Americans." In *Harvard Encyclopedia of American Ethnic Groups*. Cambridge, MA: Harvard University Press, 1980:5–23.

HONEYWELL, ROY J. *The Educational Work of Thomas Jefferson*. Cambridge, MA: Harvard University Press, 1931.

HOOK, ERNEST B. "Behavioral Implications of the XYY Genotype." *Science*. Vol. 179 (January 12, 1973):139–150.

HOSTETLER, JOHN A. *Amish Society*. 3rd ed. Baltimore: Johns Hopkins University Press, 1980.

HOUSE OF REPRESENTATIVES. *A.I.D. and Third World Women, the Unmet Potential*. Hearing held May 11, 1988. Washington, DC: U.S. Government Printing Office, 1988.

HOUT, MICHAEL, and ANDREW M. GREELEY. "The Center Doesn't Hold: Church Attendance in the United States, 1940–1984." *American Sociological Review*. Vol. 52, No. 3 (June 1987):325–345.

HOYT, HOMER. *The Structure and Growth of Residential Neighborhoods in American Cities*. Washington, DC: Federal Housing Administration, 1939.

HOYT, MARY FINCH. "The New Prime Time." *USA Weekend* (December 13–15, 1985):4.

HRUSCHKA, PETER D. Personal communication, 1990.

HSU, FRANCIS L. K. *The Challenge of the American Dream: The Chinese in the United States*. Belmont, CA: Wadsworth, 1971.

HUBER, JOAN, and GLENNA SPITZE. "Considering Divorce: An Expansion of Becker's Theory of Marital Instability." *American Journal of Sociology*. Vol. 86, No. 1 (July 1980):75–89.

HUET-COX, ROCIO. "Medical Education: New Wine in Old Wine Skins." In Victor W. Sidel and Ruth Sidel, eds., *Reforming Medicine: Lessons of the Last Quarter Century*. New York: Pantheon Books, 1984:129–149.

HULS, GLENNA. Personal communication, 1987.

HUMPHRIES, HARRY LEROY. *The Structure and Politics of Intermediary Class Positions: An Empirical Examination of Recent Theories of Class*. Unpublished PhD. dissertation. Eugene, OR: University of Oregon, 1984.

HUNNICUTT, BENJAMIN K. *Work Without End*. Philadelphia: Temple University Press, 1988.

HUNNICUTT, BENJAMIN K. "Are We All Working Too Hard: No Time for God or Family." *The Wall Street Journal*. January 4, 1990.

HUNT, MORTON. *Sexual Behavior in the 1970s*. Chicago: Playboy Press, 1974.

HUNTER, FLOYD. *Community Power Structure*. Garden City, NY: Doubleday, 1963; orig. 1953.

HUNTER, JAMES DAVISON. *American Evangelicalism: Conservative Religion and the Quandary of Modernity*. New Brunswick, NJ: Rutgers University Press, 1983.

HUNTER, JAMES DAVISON. "Conservative Protestantism." In Phillip E. Hammond, ed., *The Sacred in a Secular Age*. Berkeley, CA: University of California Press, 1985:50–66.

HURN, CHRISTOPHER. *The Limits and Possibilities of Schooling*. Boston: Allyn and Bacon, 1978.

HWANG, SEAN-SHONG, STEVEN H. MURDOCK, BANOO PARPIA, and RITA R. HAMM. "The Effects of Race and Socioeconomic Status on Residential Segregation in Texas, 1970–80." *Social Forces*. Vol. 63, No. 3 (March 1985):732–747.

HYMAN, HERBERT H., and CHARLES R. WRIGHT. "Trends in Voluntary Association Memberships of American Adults: Replication Based on Secondary Analysis of National Sample Survey." *American Sociological Review*. Vol. 36, No. 2 (April 1971):191–206.

ILLICH, IVAN. *Medical Nemesis: The Expropriation of Health*. New York: Pantheon Books, 1976.

INTERFAITH ACTION FOR ECONOMIC JUSTICE. "End Results: The Impact of Federal Policies Since 1980 on Low Income Americans." Washington, DC: 1984.

IRISH, MARIAN D., JAMES W. PROTHRO, and RICHARD J. RICHARDSON. *The Politics of American Democracy*. 7th ed. Englewood Cliffs, NJ: Prentice-Hall, 1981.

IRWIN, JOHN. *Prison in Turmoil*. Boston, MA: Little, Brown, 1980.

ISAACSON, WALTER. "O'er the Land of the Free." *Time*. Vol. 134, No. 1 (July 3, 1989):14–15.

ISAY, RICHARD A. *Being Homosexual: Gay Men and Their Development*. New York: Farrar, Straus, Giroux, 1989.

JACOB, JOHN E. "An Overview of Black America in 1985." In James D. Williams, ed., *The State of Black America 1986*. New York: National Urban League, 1986:i–xi.

JACOBS, DAVID. "Inequality and Police Strength." *American Sociological Review*. Vol 44, No. 6 (December 1979):913–925.

JACOBS, JANE. *The Death and Life of Great American Cities*. New York: Random House, 1961.

JACOBS, JANE. *The Economy of Cities*. New York: Vintage, 1970.

JACOBS, JANE. *Cities and the Wealth of Nations*. New York: Random House, 1984.

JACOBS, JERRY A. "Long-Term Trends in Occupational Segregation by Sex." *American Journal of Sociology*. Vol. 95, No. 1 (July 1989):160–173.

JACOBY, TAMAR. "A Fight for Old Glory." *Newsweek*. (July 3, 1989):18–20.

JACQUET, CONSTANT H., JR., ed., *Yearbook of American and Canadian Churches, 1983*. Nashville, TN: Abingdon Press, 1984.

JAEGER, ART, and ROBERT GREENSTEIN. "Poverty Rate and Household Income Stagnate as Rich-Poor Gap Hits Post-War High." Washington, DC: Center on Budget and Policy Priorities, 1989.

JAGGER, ALISON. "Political Philosophies of Women's Liberation." In Laurel Richardson and Verta Taylor, eds., *Feminist Frontiers: Rethinking Sex, Gender, and Society*. Reading, MA: Addison-Wesley, 1983.

JAMES, DAVID R. "City Limits on Racial Equality: The Effects of City-Suburb Boundaries on Public-School Desegregation, 1968–1976." *American Sociological Review*. Vol. 54, No. 6 (December 1989):963–985.

JANIS, IRVING. *Victims of Groupthink*. Boston, MA: Houghton Mifflin, 1972.

JANIS, IRVING L. *Crucial Decisions: Leadership in Policymaking and Crisis Management*. New York: Free Press, 1989.

JAYNES, GERALD DAVID, and ROBIN M. WILLIAMS, eds. *A Common Destiny: Blacks and American Society*. Washington, DC: National Academy Press, 1989.

JEFFERSON, THOMAS. Letter to James Madison, October 28, 1785. In Julian P. Boyd, ed., *The Papers of Thomas Jefferson*. Princeton: Princeton University Press, 1953:681–683.

JENCKS, CHRISTOPHER. "Genes and Crime." *The New York Review* (February 12, 1987):33–41.

JENCKS, CHRISTOPHER, et al. *Inequality: A Reassessment of the Effect of Family and Schooling in America*. New York: Basic Books, 1972.

JENKINS, BRIAN M. "Statements About Terrorism." In *International Terrorism, The Annals of the American Academy of Political and Social Science*. Vol. 463 (September 1982). Beverly Hills, CA: Sage Publications:11–23

JENKINS, BRIAN M. "Terrorism Remains a Threat." Syndicated column, *The Columbus Dispatch* (January 14, 1990):D–1.

JENKINS, J. CRAIG, and CHARLES PERROW. "Insurgency of the Powerless: Farm Worker Movements (1946–1972)." *American Sociological Review*. Vol. 42, No. 2 (April 1977):249–268.

JOHNSON, NORRIS R. "Panic at 'The Who Concert Stampede': An Empirical Assessment." *Social Problems*. Vol. 34, No. 4 (October 1987):362–373.

JOHNSON, PAUL. "The Seven Deadly Sins of Terrorism." In Benjamin Netanyahu, ed., *International Terrorism*. New Brunswick, NJ: Transaction Books, 1981:12–22.

JOHNSTON, R. J. "Residential Area Characteristics." In D. T. Herbert and R. J. Johnston, eds., *Social Areas in Cities. Vol. 1: Spatial Processes and Form*. New York: Wiley, 1976:193–235.

JOHNSTONE, RONALD L. *Religion in Society: A Sociology of Religion*. 2nd ed. Englewood Cliffs, NJ: Prentice-Hall, 1983.

JOINT ECONOMIC COMMITTEE. *The Concentration of Wealth in the United States: Trends in the Distribution of Wealth Among American Families*. Washington, DC: United States Congress, 1986.

JONES, DAVID A. *History of Criminology: A Philosophical Perspective*. Westport, CT: Greenwood Press, 1986.

JONES, RUTH S., and WARREN E. MILLER. "Financing Campaigns: Macro Level Innovation and Micro Level Response." *The Western Political Quarterly*. Vol. 38, No. 2 (June 1985):187–210.

JONES, TERRY. "Foul Ball in the Front Office: Racial Practices in Baseball Management." *The Black Scholar*. Vol. 18, No. 3 (May/June 1987):16–24.

JOSEPHY, ALVIN M., JR. *Now That the Buffalo's Gone: A Study of Today's American Indians*. New York: Alfred A. Knopf, 1982.

KAELBLE, HARTMUT. *Social Mobility in the 19th and 20th Centuries: Europe and America in Comparative Perspective*. New York: St. Martin's Press, 1986.

KAIN, EDWARD L. "A Note on the Integration of AIDS Into the Sociology of Human Sexuality." *Teaching Sociology*. Vol. 15, No. 4 (July 1987):320–323.

KAIN, EDWARD L., and SHANNON HART. "AIDS and the Family: A Content Analysis of Media Coverage." Presented to National Council on Family Relations, Atlanta, 1987.

KALISH, CAROL B. "International Crime Rates." Bureau of Justice Statistics *Special Report*, May 1988. Washington, DC; U.S. Government Printing Office, 1988.

KALISH, RICHARD A. "The New Ageism and the Failure Models: A Polemic." *The Gerontologist*. Vol. 19, No. 4 (August 1979):398–402.

KALISH, RICHARD A. *Late Adulthood: Perspectives on Human Development*. 2nd ed. Monterey, CA: Brooks/Cole, 1982.

KALMUSS, DEBRA, and JUDITH A. SELTZER. "Continuity of Marital Behavior in Remarriage: The Case of Spouse Abuse." Unpublished paper. November 1984.

KAMINER, WENDY. "Volunteers: Who Knows What's in It for Them." *Ms*. (December 1984):93–94, 96, 126–128.

KANTER, ROSABETH MOSS. *Men and Women of the Corporation*. New York: Basic Books, 1977.

KANTER, ROSABETH MOSS. *The Change Masters: Innovation and Entrepreneurship in the American Corporation*. New York: Simon and Schuster, 1983.

KANTER, ROSABETH MOSS. "All That Is Entrepreneurial Is Not Gold." *The Wall Street Journal* (July 22, 1985):18.

KANTER, ROSABETH MOSS. *When Giants Learn to Dance: Mastering the Challenges of Strategy, Management, and Careers in the 1990s*. New York: Simon and Schuster, 1989.

KANTER, ROSABETH MOSS, and BARRY A. STEIN. "The Gender Pioneers: Women in an Industrial Sales Force." In R. M. Kanter and B. A. Stein, eds., *Life in Organizations*. New York: Basic Books, 1979:134–160.

KANTER, ROSABETH MOSS, and BARRY STEIN. *A Tale of "O": On Being Different in an Organization*. New York: Harper & Row, 1980.

KANTROWITZ, BARBARA. "Mothers on Their Own." *Newsweek*. (December 23, 1985):66–67.

KAPLAN, ERIC B., et al. "The Usefulness of Preoperative Laboratory Screening." *Journal of the American Medical Association*. Vol. 253, No. 24 (June 28, 1985):3576–3581.

KAPTCHUK, TED. "The Holistic Logic of Chinese Medicine." In Shepard Bliss et al., eds., *The New Holistic Health Handbook*. Lexington, MA: The Steven Greene Press/Penguin Books, 1985:41.

KARP, DAVID A., and WILLIAM C. YOELS. "The College Classroom: Some Observations on the Meaning of Student Participation." *Sociology and Social Research*. Vol. 60, No. 4 (July 1976):421–439.

KASARDA, JOHN D. "Entry-Level Jobs, Mobility and Urban Minority Employment." *Urban Affairs Quarterly*. Vol. 19, No. 1 (September 1983):21–40.

KAUFMAN, POLLY WELTS. "Women and Education." In Barbara Haber, ed., *The Women's Annual, 1981: The Year in Review*. Boston, MA: G. K. Hall and Company, 1982:24–55.

KAUFMAN, ROBERT L., and SEYMOUR SPILERMAN. "The Age Structures of Occupations and Jobs." *American Journal of Sociology*. Vol. 87, No. 4 (January 1982):827–851.

KAUFMAN, WALTER. *Religions in Four Dimensions: Existential, Aesthetic, Historical and Comparative*. New York: Reader's Digest Press, 1976.

KEATING, NORAH C., and PRISCILLA COLE. "What Do I Do with Him 24 Hours a Day? Changes in the Housewife Role After Retirement." *The Gerontologist*. Vol. 20, No. 1 (February 1980):84–89.

KELLER, HELEN. *The Story of My Life*. New York: Doubleday, Page and Company, 1903.

KELLER, SUZANNE. *The Urban Neighborhood*. New York: Random House, 1968.

KELLEY, ROBERT. *The Shaping of the American Past. Vol. 2: 1865 to the Present*. 3rd ed. Englewood Cliffs, NJ: Prentice-Hall, 1982.

KEMP, ALICE ABEL, and SHELLEY COVERMAN. "Marginal Jobs or Marginal Workers: Identifying Sex Differences in Low-Skill Occupations." *Sociological Focus*. Vol. 22, No. 1 (February 1989):19–37.

KENISTON, KENNETH. "Working Mothers." In James M. Henslin, ed., *Marriage and Family in a Changing Society*. 2nd ed. New York: Free Press, 1985:319–321.

KENYON, KATHLEEN. *Digging Up Jericho*. London: Ernest Benn, 1957.

KERBO, HAROLD R. *Social Stratification and Inequality: Class Conflict in the United States*. New York: McGraw-Hill, 1983.

KERCKHOFF, ALAN C., RICHARD T. CAMPBELL, and IDEE WINFIELD-LAIRD. "Social Mobility in Great Britain and the United States." *American Journal of Sociology*. Vol. 91, No. 2 (September 1985):281–308.

KESSLER, RONALD C., and PAUL D. CLEARY. "Social Class and Psychological Distress." *American Sociological Review*. Vol. 45, No. 3 (June 1980):463–478.

KIEFER, MICHAEL. "New Faces Old Dreams." *Chicago*. Vol. 33, No. 3 (March 1984):127–135.

KII, TOSHI. "Recent Extension of Retirement Age in Japan." *The Gerontologist*. Vol. 19, No. 5 (October 1979):481–486.

KILBOURNE, BROCK K. "The Conway and Siegelman Claims Against Religious Cults: An Assessment of Their Data." *Journal for the Scientific Study of Religion*. Vol. 22, No. 4 (December 1983):380–385.

KILLIAN, LEWIS M. "Organization, Rationality and Spontaneity in the Civil Rights Movement." *American Sociological Review*. Vol. 49, No. 6 (December 1984):770–783.

KING, KATHLEEN PIKER, and DENNIS E. CLAYSON. "The Differential Perceptions of Male and Female Deviants." *Sociological Focus*. Vol. 21, No. 2 (April 1988):153–164.

KING, MARTIN LUTHER, JR. "The Montgomery Bus Boycott." In Walt Anderson, ed., *The Age of Protest*. Pacific Palisades, CA: Goodyear, 1969:81–91.

KING, PATRICIA. "When Desegregation Backfires." *Newsweek*. Vol. 144, No. 5 (July 31, 1989):56.

KINSEY, ALFRED, et al. *Sexual Behavior in the Human Male*. Philadelphia: W. B. Saunders, 1948.

KINSEY, ALFRED, et al. *Sexual Behavior in the Human Female*. Philadelphia: W. B. Saunders, 1953.

KIPP, RITA SMITH. "Have Women Always Been Unequal?" In Beth Reed, ed., *Towards a Feminist Transformation of the Academy: Proceedings of the Fifth Annual Women's Studies Conference*. Ann Arbor, MI: Great Lakes Colleges Association, 1980:12–18.

KITANO, HARRY H. L. "Japanese." In *Harvard Encyclopedia of American Ethnic Groups*. Cambridge, MA: Harvard University Press, 1980:561–571.

KITANO, HARRY H. L. *Race Relations*. 3rd ed. Englewood Cliffs, NJ: Prentice-Hall, 1985.

KITSON, GAY C., and HELEN J. RASCHKE. "Divorce Research: What We Know; What We Need to Know." *Journal of Divorce*. Vol. 4, No. 3 (Spring 1981):1–37.

KITTRIE, NICHOLAS N. *The Right To Be Different: Deviance and Enforced Therapy*. Baltimore, MD: The Johns Hopkins University Press, 1971.

KLEIMAN, DENA. "Changing Way of Death: Some Agonizing Choices." *The New York Times*. (January 14, 1985):1, 11.

KLEIN, FREDA. "Violence Against Women." In Barbara Haber, ed., *The Women's Annual, 1981: The Year in Review*. Boston, MA: G. K. Hall and Company, 1982:270–302.

KLEIN, SUSAN SHURBERG. "Education." In Sarah M. Pritchard, ed., *The Women's Annual, Number 4, 1983–1984*. Boston, MA: G. K. Hall and Company, 1984:9–30.

KLEUGEL, JAMES R., and ELIOT R. SMITH. *Beliefs About Inequality: Americans' Views of What Is and What Ought to Be*. New York: Aldine de Gruyter, 1986.

KLUCKHOHN, CLYDE. "As An Anthropologist Views It." In Albert Deutch, ed., *Sex Habits of American Men*. New York: Prentice-Hall, 1948.

KNAUS, WILLIAM A. *Inside Russian Medicine: An American Doctor's First-Hand Report*. New York: Everest House, 1981.

KNOKE, DAVID, and RICHARD B. FELSON. "Ethnic Stratification and Political Cleavage in the United States, 1952–1968." *American Journal of Sociology*. Vol. 80, No. 3 (November 1974):630–642.

KOBLER, JOHN. *Ardent Spirits: The Rise and Fall of Prohibition*. New York: G. P. Putnam's Sons, 1973.

KOCH, HOWARD. *The Panic Broadcast: Portrait of an Event*. Boston, MA: Little, Brown, 1970.

KOENIG, FREDRICK. *Rumor in the Market Place: The Social Psychology of Commercial Hearsay*. Dover, MA: Auburn House, 1985.

KOHLBERG, LAWRENCE, and CAROL GILLIGAN. "The Adolescent as Philosopher: The Discovery of Self in a Postconventional World." *Daedalus*. Vol. 100 (Fall 1971):1051–1086.

KOHN, MELVIN L. *Class and Conformity: A Study in Values*. 2nd ed. Homewood, IL: The Dorsey Press, 1977.

KOHN, MELVIN L., and CARMI SCHOOLER. "Job Conditions and Personality: A Longitudinal Assessment of Their Reciprocal Effects." *American Journal of Sociology*. Vol. 87, No. 6 (May 1982):1257–1283.

KOMAROVSKY, MIRRA. *Blue Collar Marriage*. New York: Vintage Books, 1967.

KOMAROVSKY, MIRRA. "Cultural Contradictions and Sex Roles: The Masculine Case." *American Journal of Sociology*. Vol. 78, No. 4 (January 1973):873–884.

KOMAROVSKY, MIRRA. *Dilemmas of Masculinity: A Study of College Youth*. New York: W. W. Norton, 1976.

KORNHAUSER, WILLIAM. *The Politics of Mass Society*. New York: Free Press, 1959.

KOZOL, JONATHAN. *Prisoners of Silence: Breaking the Bonds of Adult Illiteracy in the United States*. New York: Continuum, 1980.

KOZOL, JONATHAN. *Illiterate America*. Garden City, NY: Anchor/Doubleday, 1985a.

KOZOL, JONATHAN. "A Nation's Wealth." *Publisher's Weekly*. (May 24, 1985b):28–30.

KOZOL, JONATHAN. *Rachel and Her Children: Homeless Families in America*. New York: Crown Publishers, 1988.

KRAMARAE, CHERIS. *Women and Men Speaking*. Rowley, MA: Newbury House, 1981.

KRAMARAE, CHERIS, BARRIE THORNE, and NANCY HENLEY. "Sex Similarities and Differences in Language, Speech, and Nonverbal Communication: An Annotated Bibliography." In Barrie Thorne, Cheris Kramarae, and Nancy Henley, eds., *Language, Gender and Society*. Cambridge: Newbury House, 1983:150–331.

KRIESI, HANSPETER. "New Social Movements and the New Class in the Netherlands." *American Journal of Sociology*. Vol. 94, No. 5 (March 1989):1078–1116.

KRISBERG, BARRY, and IRA SCHWARTZ. "Rethinking Juvenile Justice." *Crime and Delinquency*. Vol. 29, No. 3 (July 1983):333–364.

KROC, ELAINE. *Early Estimates, National Higher Education Statistics: Fall 1989*. Washington, DC: National Center for Education Statistics, 1989.

KUBEY, ROBERT W. "Television and Aging: Past, Present, and Future." *The Gerontologist*. Vol. 20, No. 1 (February 1980):16–35.

KÜBLER-ROSS, ELISABETH. *On Death and Dying*. New York: Macmillan, 1969.

KUHN, THOMAS. *The Structure of Scientific Revolutions*. 2d ed. Chicago: University of Chicago Press, 1970.

KURTZ, LESTER R. *The Nuclear Cage: A Sociology of the Arms Race*. Englewood Cliffs, NJ: Prentice-Hall, 1988.

KUZNETS, SIMON. "Economic Growth and Income Inequality." *The American Economic Review*. Vol. XLV, No. 1 (March 1955):1–28.

KUZNETS, SIMON. *Modern Economic Growth: Rate, Structure, and Spread*. New Haven, CT: Yale University Press, 1966.

LACAYO, RICHARD. "Blood in the Stands." *Time*. Vol. 125, No. 23 (June 10, 1985):38–39,41.

LADD, JOHN. "The Definition of Death and the Right to Die." In John Ladd, ed., *Ethical Issues Relating to Life and Death*. New York: Oxford University Press, 1979:118–145.

LADNER, JOYCE A. "Teenage Pregnancy: The Implications for Black Americans." In James D. Williams, ed., *The State of Black America 1986*. New York: National Urban League, 1986:65–84.

LAI, H. M. "Chinese." In *Harvard Encyclopedia of American Ethnic Groups*. Cambridge, MA: Harvard University Press, 1980:217–233.

LAMAR, JACOB V., JR. "Redefining the American Dilemma." *Time*. Vol. 126, No. 19 (November 11, 1985):33, 36.

LAMBERG-KARLOVSKY, C. C., and MARTHA LAMBERG-KARLOVSKY. "An Early City in Iran." In *Cities: Their Origin, Growth, and Human Impact*. San Francisco: Freeman, 1973:28–37.

LANDERS, ANN. Syndicated Column: *The Dallas Morning News* (July 8, 1984):4F.

LANE, DAVID. "Social Stratification and Class." In Erik P. Hoffman and Robbin F. Laird, eds., *The Soviet Polity in the Modern Era*. New York: Aldine, 1984:563–605.

LANG, KURT, and GLADYS ENGEL LANG. *Collective Dynamics*. New York: Thomas Y. Crowell, 1961.

LANGAN, PATRICK A., and CHRISTOPHER A. INNES. *The Risk of Violent Crime*. Special Report from the Bureau of Justice Statistics. Washington, DC: U.S. Government Printing Office, 1985.

LAPPE, FRANCES MOORE, JOSEPH COLLINS, and DAVID KINLEY. *Aid as Obstacle: Twenty Questions about Our Foreign Policy and the Hungry*. San Francisco: Institute for Food and Development Policy, 1981.

LASLETT, BARBARA. "Family Membership, Past and Present." *Social Problems*. Vol. 25, No. 5 (June 1978):476–490.

LASLETT, PETER. *The World We Have Lost: England Before the Industrial Age*. 3rd ed. New York: Charles Scribner's Sons, 1984.

LEACOCK, ELEANOR. "Women's Status in Egalitarian Societies: Implications for Social Evolution." *Current Anthropology*. Vol. 19, No. 2 (June 1978):247–275.

LEAVITT, JUDITH WALZER. "Women and Health in America: An Overview." In Judith Walzer Leavitt, ed., *Women and Health in America*. Madison, WI: University of Wisconsin Press, 1984:3–7.

LE BON, GUSTAVE. *The Crowd: A Study of the Popular Mind*. New York: The Viking Press, 1960; orig. 1895.

LEE, BARRETT A., R. S. OROPESA, BARBARA J. METCH, and AVERY M. GUEST. "Testing the Decline of Community Thesis: Neighborhood Organization in Seattle, 1929 and 1979." *American Journal of Sociology*. Vol. 89, No. 5 (March 1984):1161–1188.

LEERHSEN, CHARLES. "Unite and Conquer." *Newsweek* (February 5, 1990):50–55.

LEMERT, EDWIN M. *Social Pathology*. New York: McGraw-Hill, 1951.

LEMERT, EDWIN M. *Human Deviance, Social Problems, and Social Control*. 2nd ed. Englewood Cliffs, NJ: Prentice-Hall, 1972.

LENGERMANN, PATRICIA MADOO, and RUTH A. WALLACE. *Gender in America: Social Control and Social Change*. Englewood Cliffs, NJ: Prentice-Hall, 1985.

LENSKI, GERHARD. *Power and Privilege: A Theory of Social Stratification*. New York: McGraw-Hill, 1966.

LENSKI, GERHARD, and JEAN LENSKI. *Human Societies: An Introduction to Macrosociology*. 3rd ed. New York: McGraw-Hill, 1978; also 4th ed., 1982; also 5th ed., 1987.

LEONARD, EILEEN B. *Women, Crime, and Society: A Critique of Theoretical Criminology*. New York: Longman, 1982.

LESLIE, GERALD R., and SHEILA K. KORMAN. *The Family in Social Context*. 7th ed. New York: Oxford University Press, 1989.

LESTER, DAVID. *The Death Penalty: Issues and Answers*. Springfield, IL: Charles C. Thomas, 1987.

LEVER, JANET. "Sex Differences in the Complexity of Children's Play and Games." *American Sociological Review*. Vol. 43, No. 4 (August 1978):471–483.

LEVIN, JACK, and WILLIAM C. LEVIN. *Ageism: Prejudice and Discrimination Against the Elderly*. Belmont, CA: Wadsworth, 1980.

LEVINE, MICHAEL P. *Student Eating Disorders: Anorexia Nervosa and Bulimia*. Washington, DC: National Educational Association, 1987.

LEVINSON, DANIEL J., with CHARLOTTE N. DARROW, EDWARD B. KLEIN, MARIA H. LEVINSON, and BRAXTON McKEE. *The Seasons of a Man's Life*. New York: Alfred A. Knopf, 1978.

LEVITAN, SAR A., and ISAAC SHAPIRO. *Working but Poor: America's Contradiction*. Baltimore: Johns Hopkins University Press, 1987.

LEVY, FRANK. *Dollars and Dreams: The Changing American Income Distribution*. New York: Russell Sage Foundation, 1987.

LEWIS, FLORA. "The Roots of Revolution." *The New York Times Magazine*. (November 11, 1984):70–71, 74, 77–78, 82, 84, 86.

LEWIS, OSCAR. *The Children of Sanchez*. New York: Random House, 1961.

LEWONTIN, R. C., STEVEN ROSE, and LEON J. KAMIN. *Not In Our Genes: Biology, Ideology, and Human Nature*. New York: Pantheon, 1984.

LIAZOS, ALEXANDER. "The Poverty of the Sociology of Deviance: Nuts, Sluts and Preverts." *Social Problems*. Vol. 20, No. 1 (Summer 1972):103–120.

LICHTER, DANIEL R. "Race, Employment Hardship, and Inequality in the American Nonmetropolitan South." *American Sociological Review*. Vol. 54, No. 3 (June 1989):436–446.

LIEBERSON, STANLEY. *A Piece of the Pie: Black and White Immigrants Since 1880*. Berkeley, CA: University of California Press, 1980.

LIEBOW, ELLIOT. *Tally's Corner*. Boston, MA: Little, Brown, 1967.

LIN, NAN, and WALTER M. ENSEL. "Life Stress and Health: Stressors and Resources." *American Sociological Review*. Vol. 54, No. 3 (June 1989):382–399.

LIN, NAN, WALTER M. ENSEL, and JOHN C. VAUGHN. "Social Resources and Strength of Ties: Structural Factors in Occupational Status Attainment." *American Sociological Review*. Vol. 46, No. 4 (August 1981):393–405.

LING, PYAU. "Causes of Chinese Emigration." In Amy Tachiki et al., eds., *Roots: An Asian American Reader*. Los Angeles: UCLA Asian American Studies Center, 1971:134–138.

LINK, BRUCE G., FRANCIS T. CULLIN, JAMES FRANK, and JOHN F. WOZNIAK. "The Social Rejection of Former Mental Patients: Understanding Why Labels Matter." *American Journal of Sociology*. Vol. 92, No. 6 (May 1987):1461–1500.

LINK, BRUCE G., BRUCE P. DOHRENWEND, and ANDREW E. SKODOL. "Socio-Economic Status and Schizophrenia: Noisome Occupational Characteristics As a Risk Factor." *American Sociological Review*. Vol. 51, No. 2 (April 1986):242–258.

LINTON, RALPH. "One Hundred Percent American." *The American Mercury*. Vol. 40, No. 160 (April 1937):427–429.

LINTON, RALPH. *The Study of Man*. New York: D. Appleton-Century, 1937.

LIPSET, SEYMOUR MARTIN. *Political Man: The Social Bases of Politics*. Garden City, NY: Doubleday Anchor Books, 1963.

LIPSET, SEYMOUR MARTIN, and REINHARD BENDIX. *Social Mobility in Industrial Society*. Berkeley, CA: University of California Press, 1967.

LIPSET, SEYMOUR MARTIN, MARTIN TROW, and JAMES COLEMAN. *Union Democracy: The Inside of the International Typographical Union*. New York: Free Press, 1977; orig. 1956.

LISKA, ALLEN E. *Perspectives on Deviance*. 2nd ed. Englewood Cliffs, NJ: Prentice-Hall, 1987.

LISKA, ALLEN E., and MARK TAUSIG. "Theoretical Interpretations of Social Class and Racial Differentials in Legal Decision Making for Juveniles." *Sociological Quarterly*. Vol. 20, No. 2 (Spring 1979):197–207.

LITSKY, FRANK. "Baseball Consultant Hired to Find Minority Jobs." *International Herald Tribune* (June 15, 1987):21.

LITTMAN, MARK S. "Poverty in the 1980s: Are the Poor Getting Poorer?" *Monthly Labor Review*. Vol. 112, No. 6 (June 1989):13–18.

LO, CLARENCE Y. H. "Countermovements and Conservative Movements in the Contemporary U.S." *Annual Review of Sociology*. Vol. 8. Palo Alto, CA: Annual Reviews, Inc., 1982:107–134.

LOFLAND, LYN. *A World of Strangers*. New York: Basic Books, 1973.

LOGAN, JOHN R., and MARK SCHNEIDER. "Racial Segregation and Racial Change in American Suburbs, 1970–1980." *American Journal of Sociology*. Vol. 89, No. 4 (January 1984):874–888.

LOGAN, RAYFORD W. "Charles Richard Drew." In Rayford W. Logan and Michael R. Winston, eds., *Dictionary of American Negro Biography*. New York: W. W. Norton, 1982:190–192.

LONDON, BRUCE. "Structural Determinants of Third World Urban Change: An Ecological and Political Economic Analysis." *American Sociological Review*. Vol. 52, No. 1 (February 1987):28–43.

LONG, EDWARD V. *The Intruders: The Invasion of Privacy by Government and Industry*. New York: Frederick A. Praeger, 1967.

LORD, WALTER. *A Night to Remember*. Rev. ed. New York: Holt, Reinhart, and Winston, 1976.

LORENZ, KONRAD. *On Aggression*. New York: Harcourt, Brace and World, 1966.

LOW, W. AUGUSTUS, and VIRGIL A. CLIFT. "Charles Richard Drew." *Encyclopedia of Black America*. New York: McGraw-Hill, 1981:325–326.

LOY, PAMELA HEWITT, and LEA P. STEWART. "The Extent and Effects of Sexual Harassment of Working Women." *Sociological Focus*. Vol. 17, No. 1 (January 1984):31–43.

LUBENOW, GERALD C. "A Troubling Family Affair." *Newsweek*. (May 14, 1984):34.

LYMAN, STANFORD. "Strangers in the City: The Chinese in the Urban Frontier." In Amy Tachiki et al., eds., *Roots: An Asian American Reader*. Los Angeles: UCLA Asian American Studies Center, 1971:159–187.

LYND, ROBERT S. *Knowledge For What? The Place of Social Science in American Culture*. Princeton, NJ: Princeton University Press, 1967.

LYND, ROBERT S., and HELEN MERRELL LYND. *Middletown in Transition*. New York: Harcourt, Brace & World, 1937.

LYND, ROBERT S., and HELEN MERRELL LYND. *Middletown: A Study in Modern American Culture*. New York: Harcourt, Brace & World, 1956; orig. 1929.

MACCOBY, ELEANOR EMMONS, and CAROL NAGY JACKLIN. *The Psychology of Sex Differences*. Palo Alto, CA: Stanford University Press, 1974.

MACE, DAVID, and VERA MACE. *Marriage East and West*. Garden City, NY: Doubleday (Dolphin), 1960.

MACIONIS, JOHN J. "Intimacy: Structure and Process in Interpersonal Relationships." *Alternative Lifestyles*. Vol. 1, No. 1 (February 1978):113–130.

MACIONIS, JOHN J. "The Search for Community in Modern Society: An Interpretation." *Qualitative Sociology*. Vol. 1, No. 2 (September 1978):130–143.

MACIONIS, JOHN J. "A Sociological Analysis of Humor." Presentation to the Texas Junior College Teachers Association, Houston, 1987.

MACKAY, DONALD G. "Prescriptive Grammar and the Pronoun Problem." In Barrie Thorne, Cheris Kramarae, and Nancy Henley, eds., *Language, Gender and Society*. Cambridge: Newbury House, 1983:38–53.

MACRAE, SUSAN. *Cross-Class Families: A Study of Wives' Occupational Superiority*. New York: Oxford University Press, 1986.

MADSEN, AXEL. *Private Power: Multinational Corporations for the Survival of Our Planet*. New York: William Morrow, 1980.

MAGNET, MYRON. "The Fortune 500 Special Report: The Dollar Dampens the Profit Party." *Fortune*. Vol. 111, No. 9 (April 29, 1985):252–258, 260, 262, 265–286.

MAGNUSON, ED. "Champion of the Elderly." *Time*. Vol. 121, No. 117 (April 25, 1983):20–23, 26, 29.

MAHLER, HALFDAN. "People." *Scientific American*. Vol. 243, No. 3 (September 1980):67–77.

MAJOR, BRENDA. "Gender Patterns in Touching Behavior." In Clara Mayo and Nancy M. Henley, eds., *Gender and Nonverbal Behavior*. New York: Springer-Verlag, 1981:15–37.

MAKLIN, ELEANOR D. "Nonmarital Heterosexual Cohabitation: An Overview." In Eleanor D. Macklin and Roger H. Rubin, eds., *Contemporary Families and Alternative Lifestyles: Handbook on Research and Theory*. Beverly Hills, CA: Sage, 1983:49–74.

MALTHUS, THOMAS ROBERT. *First Essay on Population 1798*. London: Macmillan, 1926; orig. 1798.

MAMONOVA, TATYANA. *Women and Russia*. Boston, MA: Beacon Press, 1984.

MANGAN, J. A., and ROBERTA J. PARK. *From Fair Sex to Feminism: Sport and the Socialization of Women*. London: Frank Cass, 1987.

MANN, ARTHUR. "When Tammany Was Supreme." In William L. Riordan. *Plunkitt of Tammany Hall*. New York: E. P. Dutton, 1963:vii–xxii.

MARCUSE, HERBERT. *One-Dimensional Man*. Boston, MA: Beacon Press, 1964.

MARE, ROBERT D. "Change and Stability in Educational Stratification." *American Sociological Review*. Vol. 46, No. 1 (February 1981):72–87.

MARGOLICK, DAVID. "Rape in Marriage Is No Longer Within the Law." *The New York Times*. (December 13, 1984):6E.

MARLIOS, PETER. "Interlocking Directorates and the Control of Corporations: The Theory of Bank Control." *Social Science Quarterly*. Vol. 56, No. 3 (December 1975):425–439.

MARSDEN, PETER. "Core Discussion Networks of Americans." *American Sociological Review*. Vol. 52, No. 1 (February 1987):122–131.

MARSHALL, R., C. B. KNAPP, M. H. LIGGET, and R. W. GLOVER. *Employment Discrimination: The Impact of Legal and Administrative Remedies*. New York: Praeger, 1978.

MARSHALL, SUSAN E. "Ladies Against Women: Mobilization Dilemmas of Antifeminist Movements." *Social Problems*. Vol. 32, No. 4 (April 1985):348–362.

MARTIN, RICHARD C. *Islam: A Cultural Perspective*. Englewood Cliffs, NJ: Prentice-Hall, 1982.

MARTIN, WILLIAM. "The Birth of a Media Myth." *The Atlantic*. Vol. 247, No. 6 (June 1981):7, 10, 11, 16.

MARULLO, SAM. "The Functions and Dysfunctions of Preparations for Fighting Nuclear War." *Sociological Focus*. Vol. 20, No. 2 (April 1987):135–153.

MARX, GARY T., and JAMES L. WOOD. "Strands of Theory and Research in Collective Behavior." In Alex Inkeles, et al., eds., *Annual Review of Sociology*. Vol. 1. Palo Alto, CA: Annual Reviews, Inc., 1975:363–428.

MARX, KARL. Excerpt from "A Contribution to the Critique of Political Economy." In Karl Marx and Friedrich Engels. *Marx and Engels: Basic Writings on Politics and Philosophy*. Lewis S. Feuer, ed. Garden City, NY: Anchor Books, 1959:42–46.

MARX, KARL. *Karl Marx: Early Writings*. T. B. Bottomore, ed. New York: McGraw-Hill, 1964a.

MARX, KARL. *Karl Marx: Selected Writings in Sociology and Social Philosophy*. T. B. Bottomore, trans. New York: McGraw-Hill, 1964b.

MARX, KARL. *Capital*. Friedrich Engels, ed. New York: International Publishers, 1967; orig. 1867.

MARX, KARL. "Critique of the Gotha Program." Robert C. Tucker, ed. *The Marx-Engels Reader*. New York: Norton, 1972:382–398.

MARX, KARL. "Theses on Feuer." In Robert C. Tucker, ed., *The Marx-Engels Reader*. New York: W. W. Norton, 1972:107–109; orig. 1845.

MARX, KARL, and FRIEDRICH ENGELS. "Manifesto of the Communist Party." In Robert C. Tucker, ed., *The Marx-Engels Reader*. New York: W. W. Norton, 1972:331–362; orig. 1848.

MARX, KARL, and FRIEDRICH ENGELS. *The Marx-Engels Reader*. Robert C. Tucker, ed. New York: W. W. Norton, 1977.

MASHEK, JOHN W., and PATRICIA AVERY. "Women Politicians Take Off the White Gloves." *U.S. News & World Report* (August 15, 1983):41–42.

MASSEY, DOUGLAS S., and NANCY A. DENTON. "Suburbanization and Segregation in U.S. Metropolitan Areas." *American Journal of Sociology*, Vol. 94, No. 3 (November 1988):592–626.

MASSEY, DOUGLAS S., and NANCY A. DENTON. "Hypersegregation in U.S. Metropolitan Areas: Black and Hispanic Segregation Along Five Dimensions." *Demography*. Vol. 26, No. 3 (August 1989):373–391.

MASTERS, WILLIAM H., VIRGINIA E. JOHNSON, and ROBERT C. KOLODNY. *Human Sexuality*. 3rd ed. Glenview, IL: Scott, Foresman/Little, Brown, 1988.

MATHEWS, TOM. "Lennon's Alter Ego." *Newsweek* (December 22, 1980):34–35.

MATTHEWS, MERVYN. "Long Term Trends in Soviet Education." In J. J. Tomiak, ed., *Soviet Education in the 1980s*. London: Croom Helm, 1983:1–23.

MATTHIESSEN, PETER. *In the Spirit of Crazy Horse*. New York: Viking Press, 1983.

MATTHIESSEN, PETER. *Indian Country*. New York: Viking Press, 1984.

MATZA, DAVID. *Delinquency and Drift*. New York: John Wiley, 1964.

MAUSS, ARMAND L. *Social Problems of Social Movements*. Philadelphia, PA: Lippincott, 1975.

MAYO, KATHERINE. *Mother India*. New York: Harcourt, Brace and Co., 1927.

McADAM, DOUG. *Political Process and the Development of Black Insurgency, 1930–1970*. Chicago: University of Chicago Press, 1982.

McADAM, DOUG. "Tactical Innovation and the Pace of Insurgency." *American Sociological Review.* Vol. 48, No. 6 (December 1983):735–754.

McADAM, DOUG. "The Biographical Consequences of Activism." *American Sociological Review.* Vol. 54, No. 5 (October 1989):744–760.

McADAM, DOUG, JOHN D. McCARTHY, and MAYER N. ZALD. "Social Movements." In Neil J. Smelser, ed., *Handbook of Sociology.* Newbury Park, CA: Sage, 1988:695–737.

McCARTHY, JOHN D., and MAYER N. ZALD. "Resource Mobilization and Social Movements: A Partial Theory." *American Journal of Sociology.* Vol. 82, No. 6 (May 1977):1212–1241.

McGLEN, NANCY E., and KAREN O'CONNOR. *Women's Rights: The Struggle for Equality in the Nineteenth and Twentieth Centuries.* New York: Praeger Publishers, 1983.

McGRATH, ELLIE. "Preparing to Wield the Rod." *Time.* Vol. 121, No. 4 (January 23, 1984):57.

McGUIRE, MEREDITH B. *Religion: The Social Context.* 2nd ed. Belmont, CA: Wadsworth, 1987.

McKEOWN, THOMAS. *The Role of Medicine: Dream, Mirage, or Nemesis?* Princeton, NJ: Princeton University Press, 1979.

McKUSICK, LEON, et al. "Reported Changes in the Sexual Behavior of Men at Risk for AIDS, San Francisco, 1982–84—The AIDS Behavioral Research Project." *Public Health Reports.* Vol. 100, No. 6 (November–December 1985):622–629.

McLANAHAN SARA. "Family Structure and the Reproduction of Poverty." *American Journal of Sociology.* Vol. 90, No. 4 (January 1985):873–901.

McLANAHAN, SARA S., ANNEMETTE SORENSEN, and DOROTHY WATSON. "Sex Differences in Poverty." *Signs: Journal of Women in Culture and Society.* Vol. 15, No. 1 (Autumn 1989):102–122.

McPHAIL, CLARK, and RONALD T. WOHLSTEIN. "Individual and Collective Behaviors Within Gatherings, Demonstrations, and Riots." *Annual Review of Sociology.* Vol. 9. Palo Alto, CA: Annual Reviews, Inc., 1983:579–600.

McROBERTS, HUGH A., and KEVIN SELBEE. "Trends in Occupational Mobility in Canada and the United States: A Comparison." *American Sociological Review,* Vol. 46, No. 4 (August 1981):406–421.

MEAD, GEORGE HERBERT. Teaching of Science in College." *Science.* Vol. 24 (1906):390–397.

MEAD, GEORGE HERBERT. *Philosophy of the Act.* Charles W. Morris, ed. Chicago: University of Chicago Press, 1938.

MEAD, GEORGE HERBERT. *Mind, Self, and Society.* Charles W. Morris, ed. Chicago: University of Chicago Press, 1962; orig. 1934.

MEAD, MARGARET. *Coming of Age in Samoa.* New York: Dell, 1961; orig. 1928.

MEAD, MARGARET. *Sex and Temperament in Three Primitive Societies.* New York: William Morrow, 1963; orig. 1935.

MECHANIC, DAVID. *Medical Sociology.* 2nd ed. New York: Free Press, 1978.

MELTZER, BERNARD N. "Mead's Social Psychology." In Jerome G. Manis and Bernard N. Meltzer, eds., *Symbolic Interaction: A Reader in Social Psychology.* 2nd ed. Boston, MA: Allyn & Bacon, 1977:15–27; also 3rd ed., 1978.

MELUCCI, ALBERTO. "The New Social Movements: A Theoretical Approach." *Social Science Information.* Vol. 19, No. 2 (May 1980):199–226.

MELUCCI, ALBERTO. *Nomads of the Present: Social Movements and Individual Needs in Contemporary Society.* Philadelphia: Temple University Press, 1989.

MELVILLE, KEITH. *Marriage and Family Today.* 3rd ed. New York: Random House, 1983.

MERTON, ANDREW. "Return to Brotherhood." *Ms.* (September 1985):60, 62, 64–65, 121–122.

MERTON, ROBERT K. "Social Structure and Anomie." *American Sociological Review.* Vol. 3, No. 6 (October 1938):672–682.

MERTON, ROBERT K. *Social Theory and Social Structure.* New York: Free Press. 1968.

MERTON, ROBERT K. "Discrimination and the American Creed." In *Sociological Ambivalence and Other Essays.* New York: The Free Press, 1976:189–216.

MESSNER, STEVEN F. "Economic Discrimination and Societal Homicide Rates: Further Evidence of the Cost of Inequality." *American Sociological Review.* Vol. 54, No. 4 (August 1989):597–611.

MICHELS, ROBERT. *Political Parties.* Glencoe, IL: Free Press, 1949; orig. 1911.

MILGRAM, STANLEY. "Behavioral Study of Obedience." *Journal of Abnormal and Social Psychology.* Vol. 67, No. 4 (1963):371–378.

MILGRAM, STANLEY. "Group Pressure and Action Against a Person." *Journal of Abnormal and Social Psychology.* Vol. 69, No. 2 (August 1964):137–143.

MILGRAM, STANLEY. "Some Conditions of Obedience and Disobedience to Authority." *Human Relations.* Vol. 18 (February 1965):57–76.

MILIBAND, RALPH. *The State in Capitalist Society.* London: Weidenfield and Nicolson, 1969.

MILLER, ARTHUR G. *The Obedience Experiments: A Case of Controversy in Social Science.* New York: Praeger, 1986.

MILLER, DAVID L. *Introduction to Collective Behavior.* Belmont, CA: Wadsworth, 1985.

MILLER, FREDERICK D. "The End of SDS and the Emergence of Weatherman: Demise Through Success." In Jo Freeman, ed., *Social Movements of the Sixties and Seventies.* New York: Longman, 1983:279–297.

MILLER, WALTER B. "Lower Class Culture as a Generating Milieu of Gang Delinquency." In Marvin E. Wolfgang, Leonard Savitz, and Norman Johnston, eds., *The Sociology of Crime and Delinquency.* 2nd ed. New York: John Wiley, 1970:351–363; orig. 1958.

MILLET, KATE. *Sexual Politics.* Garden City, NY: Doubleday, 1970.

MILLS, C. WRIGHT. *White Collar: The American Middle Classes.* New York: Oxford University Press, 1951.

MILLS, C. WRIGHT. *The Power Elite.* New York: Oxford University Press, 1956.

MILLS, C. WRIGHT. *The Causes of World War Three.* New York: Simon and Schuster, 1958.

MILLS, C. WRIGHT. *The Sociological Imagination.* New York: Oxford University Press, 1959.

MINTZ, BETH, and MICHAEL SCHWARTZ. "Interlocking Directorates and Interest Group Formation." *American Sociological Review.* Vol. 46, No. 6 (December 1981):851–869.

MINTZ, BETH, and MICHAEL SCHWARTZ. *The Power Structure of American Business.* Chicago: University of Chicago Press, 1985.

MIROWSKY, JOHN. "The Psycho-Economics of Feeling Underpaid: Distributive Justice and the Earnings of Husbands and Wives." *American Journal of Sociology.* Vol. 92, No. 6 (May 1987):1404–1434.

MIROWSKY, JOHN, and CATHERINE ROSS. "Working Wives and Mental Health." Presentation to the American Association for the Advancement of Science. New York, 1984.

MIROWSKY, JOHN, and CATHERINE ROSS. *The Social Causes of Psychological Distress.* Hawthorne, NY: Aldine de Gruyter, 1989.

MITCHELL, WILLIAM L. "Lay Observations on Retirement." In Frances M. Carp, ed., *Retirement.* New York: Behavioral Publications, 1972:199–217.

MOLNAR, STEPHEN. *Human Variation: Races, Types, and Ethnic Groups.* 2nd ed. Englewood Cliffs, NJ: Prentice-Hall, 1983.

MOLOTCH, HARVEY. "The City as a Growth Machine." *American Journal of Sociology.* Vol. 82, No. 2 (September 1976):309–333.

MOLOTCH, HARVEY L., and DEIRDRE BODEN. "Talking Social Structure: Discourse, Domination, and the Watergate Hearings." *American Sociological Review.* Vol. 50, No. 3 (June 1985):273–288.

MONEY, JOHN. *The Destroying Angel: Sex, Fitness & Food in the Legacy of Degeneracy Theory, Graham Crackers, Kellogg's Corn Flakes & American Health History.* Buffalo, NY: Prometheus Books, 1985.

MONEY, JOHN, and ANKE A. EHRHARDT. *Man and Woman, Boy and Girl.* New York: New American Library, 1972.

MONK-TURNER, ELIZABETH. "Sex, Educational Differentiation, and Occupational Status: Analyzing Occupational Differences for Community and Four-Year Entrants." *The Sociological Quarterly.* Vol. 24, No. 3 (July 1983):393–404.

MONTAGU, ASHLEY. *The Nature of Human Aggression.* New York: Oxford University Press, 1976.

MOORE, GWEN. "The Structure of a National Elite Network." *American Sociological Review.* Vol. 44, No. 5 (October 1979):673–692.

MOORE, JOAN, and HARRY PACHON. *Hispanics in the United States*. Englewood Cliffs, NJ: Prentice-Hall, 1985.

MOORE, WILBERT E. "Modernization as Rationalization: Processes and Restraints." In Manning Nash, ed., *Essays on Economic Development and Cultural Change in Honor of Bert F. Hoselitz*. Chicago: University of Chicago Press, 1977:29–42.

MOORE, WILBERT E. *World Modernization: The Limits of Convergence*. New York: Elsevier, 1979.

MORAN, JOHN S., S. O. ARAL, W. C. JENKINS, T. A. PETERMAN, and E. R. ALEXANDER. "The Impact of Sexually Transmitted Diseases on Minority Populations." *Public Health Reports*. Vol. 104, No. 6 (November–December 1989):560–565.

Morbidity and Mortality Weekly Report. "Abortion Surveillance: Preliminary Analysis—United States, 1986 and 1987." Vol. 38, No. 38 (September 29, 1989):662.

MORRIS, ALDON. "Black Southern Sit-in Movement: An Analysis of Internal Organization." *American Sociological Review*. Vol. 46, No. 6 (December 1981):744–767.

MORRISON, DENTON E. "Some Notes Toward Theory on Relative Deprivation, Social Movements, and Social Change." In Louis E. Genevie, ed., *Collective Behavior and Social Movements*. Itasca, IL: F. E. Peacock, 1978:202–209.

MOTTAZ, CLIFFORD J. "Some Determinants of Work Alienation." *The Sociological Quarterly*. Vol. 22, No. 4 (Autumn 1981):515–529.

MOYNIHAN, DANIEL. *The Negro Family: The Case for National Action*. Office of Policy Planning and Research, United States Department of Labor. Washington, DC: U.S. Government Printing Office, 1965.

MUELLER, DANIEL P., and PHILIP W. COOPER. "Children of Single Parent Families: How Do They Fare as Young Adults?" Presentation to the American Sociological Association. San Antonio, Texas, 1984.

MULLER, THOMAS, and THOMAS J. ESPENSHADE. *The Fourth Wave: California's Newest Immigrants*. Washington, DC: The Urban Institute Press, 1985.

MUMFORD, LEWIS. *The City in History: Its Origins, Its Transformations, and Its Prospects*. New York: Harcourt, Brace & World, 1961.

MURDOCK, GEORGE P. "Comparative Data on the Division of Labor by Sex." *Social Forces*. Vol. 15, No. 4 (May 1937):551–553.

MURDOCK, GEORGE P. "The Common Denominator of Cultures." In Ralph Linton, ed., *The Science of Man in World Crisis*. New York: Columbia University Press, 1945:123–142.

MURDOCK, GEORGE PETER. *Social Structure*. New York: Free Press, 1965; orig. 1949.

MURPHY, ROBERT F. *An Overture to Social Anthropology*. Englewood Cliffs, NJ: Prentice-Hall, 1979.

MURRAY, PAULI. *Proud Shoes: The History of an American Family*. New York: Harper & Row, 1978.

MYERS, DAVID G. *Psychology*. New York: Worth, 1986.

MYERS, SHEILA, and HAROLD G. GRASMICK. "The Social Rights and Responsibilities of Pregnant Women: An Application of Parsons' Sick Role Model." Paper presented to Southwestern Sociological Association, Little Rock, Arkansas, March 1989.

MYRDAL, GUNNAR. *An American Dilemma: The Negro Problem and Modern Democracy*. New York: Harper and Brothers, 1944.

NATIONAL CENTER FOR EDUCATION STATISTICS. *Digest of Education Statistics 1983–84*. Washington, DC: U.S. Government Printing Office, 1983.

NATIONAL COMMISSION ON EXCELLENCE IN EDUCATION. *A Nation at Risk*. Washington, DC: U.S. Government Printing Office, 1983.

NAVARRO, VICENTE. "The Industrialization of Fetishism or the Fetishism of Industrialization: A Critique of Ivan Illich." In Vicente Navarro, ed., *Health and Medical Care in the U.S.: A Critical Analysis*. Farmingdale, NY: Baywood Publishing Co., 1977:38–58.

NEIDERT, LISA J., and REYNOLDS FARLEY. "Assimilation in the United States: An Analysis of Ethnic and Generation Differences in Status and Achievement." *American Sociological Review*. Vol. 50, No. 6 (December 1985):840–850.

NEUGARTEN, BERNICE L. "Grow Old with Me. The Best Is Yet to Be." *Psychology Today*. Vol. 5 (December 1971):45–48, 79, 81.

NEUGARTEN, BERNICE L. "Personality and the Aging Process." *The Gerontologist*. Vol. 12, No. 1 (Spring 1972):9–15.

NEUGARTEN, BERNICE L. "Personality and Aging." In James E. Birren and K. Warren Schaie, eds., *Handbook of the Psychology of Aging*. New York: Van Nostrand Reinhold, 1977:626–649.

NEUHOUSER, KEVIN. "The Radicalization of the Brazilian Catholic Church in Comparative Perspective." *American Sociological Review*. Vol. 54, No. 2 (April 1989):233–244.

New Haven Journal-Courier. "English Social Structure Changing." November 27, 1986.

NEWMAN, JAMES L., and GORDON E. MATZKE. *Population: Patterns, Dynamics, and Prospects*. Englewood Cliffs, NJ: Prentice-Hall, 1984.

NEWMAN, WILLIAM M. *American Pluralism: A Study of Minority Groups and Social Theory*. New York: Harper & Row, 1973.

New York Times, The. "Judge Acquits Mother of Stealing Her Son." May 19, 1987:A20.

NIELSEN, JOHN. "Rising Racism on the Continent." *Time*. Vol. 125, No. 6 (February 6, 1984):40–41, 44–45.

NISBET, ROBERT A. *The Quest for Community*. New York: Oxford University Press, 1969.

NISBET, ROBERT A. *The Sociological Tradition*. New York: Basic Books, 1966.

NISBET, ROBERT. "Sociology as an Art Form." In *Tradition and Revolt: Historical and Sociological Essays*. New York: Vintage Books, 1970.

NORBECK, EDWARD. "Class Structure." In *Kodansha Encyclopedia of Japan*. Tokyo: Kodansha, 1983:322–325.

N.O.R.C. *General Social Surveys, 1972–1983: Cumulative Codebook*. Chicago: National Opinion Research Center, 1983.

N.O.R.C. *General Social Surveys, 1972–1987: Cumulative Codebook*. Chicago: National Opinion Research Center, 1987.

N.O.R.C. *General Social Surveys, 1972–1989: Cumulative Codebook*. Chicago: National Opinion Research Center, 1989.

NUNN, CLYDE Z., HARRY J. CROCKETT, JR., and J. ALLEN WILLIAMS, JR. *Tolerance for Nonconformity*. San Francisco, CA: Jossey-Bass Publishers, 1978.

OAKES, JEANNIE. "Classroom Social Relationships: Exploring the Bowles and Gintis Hypothesis." *Sociology of Education*. Vol. 55, No. 4 (October 1982):197–212.

OAKES, JEANNIE. *Keeping Track: How High Schools Structure Inequality*. New Haven, CT: Yale University Press, 1985.

OAKLEY, ANNE. *The Sociology of Housework*. New York: Random House/Pantheon Books, 1974.

OBERSCHALL, ANTHONY. *Social Conflict and Social Movements*. Englewood Cliffs, NJ: Prentice-Hall, 1973.

O'DEA, THOMAS F., and JANET O'DEA AVIAD. *The Sociology of Religion*. 2nd ed. Englewood Cliffs, NJ: Prentice-Hall, 1983.

OFFIR, CAROLE WADE. *Human Sexuality*. New York: Harcourt Brace Jovanovich, 1982.

OGBURN, WILLIAM F. *On Culture and Social Change*. Chicago: University of Chicago Press, 1964.

O'HARE, WILLIAM. "In the Black." *American Demographics*. Vol. 11, No. 11 (November 1989):25–29.

OKIMOTO, DANIEL. "The Intolerance of Success." In Amy Tachiki et al., eds., *Roots: Asian American Reader*. Los Angeles: UCLA Asian American Studies Center, 1971:14–19.

OLZAK, SUSAN. "Labor Unrest, Immigration, and Ethnic Conflict in Urban America, 1880–1914." *American Journal of Sociology*. Vol. 94, No. 6 (May 1989):1303–1333.

O'REILLY, JANE. "Wife Beating: The Silent Crime." *Time*. Vol. 122, No. 10 (September 5, 1983):23–24, 26.

OSTLING, RICHARD N. "Jerry Falwell's Crusade." *Time*. Vol. 126, No. 9 (September 2, 1985):48–52, 55, 57.

OSTLING, RICHARD N. "Power, Glory—And Politics." *Time*. Vol. 127, No. 7 (February 17, 1986):62–69.

OSTLING, RICHARD N. "Technology and the Womb." *Time*. Vol. 129, No. 12 (March 23, 1987):58–59.

OSTLING, RICHARD N. "God and Money." *Time*. Vol. 130, No. 5 (August 3, 1987):48–49.

OSTLING, RICHARD N. "Americans Facing Toward Mecca." *Time*. Vol. 131, No. 21 (May 23, 1988):49–50.

OSTRANDER, SUSAN A. "Upper Class Women: The Feminine Side of Privilege." *Qualitative Sociology*. Vol. 3, No. 1 (Spring 1980):23–44.

OSTRANDER, SUSAN A. *Women of the Upper Class*. Philadelphia, PA: Temple University Press, 1984.

OUCHI, WILLIAM. *Theory Z: How American Business Can Meet the Japanese Challenge*. Reading, MA: Addison-Wesley, 1981.

OWEN, DAVID. *None of the Above: Behind the Myth of Scholastic Aptitude*. Boston, MA: Houghton Mifflin, 1985.

PALMORE, ERDMAN. "Predictors of Successful Aging." *The Gerontologist*. Vol. 19, No. 5 (October 1979a):427–431.

PALMORE, ERDMAN. "Advantages of Aging." *The Gerontologist*. Vol. 19, No. 2 (April 1979b):220–223.

PALMORE, ERDMAN. "What Can the USA Learn from Japan About Aging?" In Steven H. Zarit, ed., *Readings in Aging and Death: Contemporary Perspectives*. New York: Harper & Row, 1982:166–169.

PAMPEL, FRED C., KENNETH C. LAND, and MARCUS FELSON. "A Social Indicator Model of Changes in the Occupational Structure of the United States: 1947–1974." *American Sociological Review*. Vol. 42, No. 6 (December 1977):951–964.

PARCEL, TOBY L., CHARLES W. MUELLER, and STEVEN CUVELIER. "Comparable Worth and Occupational Labor Market: Explanations of Occupational Earnings Differentials." Paper presented to the American Sociological Association, New York, 1986.

PARENTI, MICHAEL. *Inventing Reality: The Politics of the Mass Media*. New York: St. Martin's Press, 1986.

PARKINSON, C. NORTHCOTE. *Parkinson's Law and Other Studies in Administration*. New York: Ballantine Books, 1957.

PARROTT, JULIE. "The Effects of Culture on Eating Disorders." Paper presented to Southwestern Social Science Association, Dallas, Texas, March 1987.

PARSONS, TALCOTT. *Essays in Sociological Theory*. New York: Free Press, 1954.

PARSONS, TALCOTT. *The Social System*. New York: Free Press, 1964; orig. 1951.

PARSONS, TALCOTT. *Societies: Evolutionary and Comparative Perspectives*. Englewood Cliffs, NJ: Prentice-Hall, 1966.

PARSONS, TALCOTT, and ROBERT F. BALES, eds. *Family, Socialization and Interaction Process*. New York: Free Press, 1955.

PATCHEN, MARTIN. "The Escalation of Inter-Nation Conflicts." *Sociological Focus*: Vol. 20, No. 2 (April 1987):95–110.

PEAR, ROBERT. "Women Reduce Lag in Earnings, But Disparities With Men Remain." *The New York Times* (September 4, 1987):1, 7.

PEARCE, DIANA. "The Feminization of Poverty: Women, Work and Welfare." *Urban and Social Change Review*. Vol. 11, No. 1 (February 1989):28–36.

PEDERSEN, DANIEL. "The Swedish Model: Lessons for the Left." *Newsweek* (March 5, 1990):30–31.

PÉREZ, LISANDRO. "Cubans." In *Harvard Encyclopedia of American Ethnic Groups*. Cambridge, MA: Harvard University Press, 1980:256–260.

PERRY, SUSAN, and JIM DAWSON. *Nightmare: Women and the Dalkon Shield*. New York: Macmillan, 1985.

PERSELL, CAROLINE HODGES. *Education and Inequality: A Theoretical and Empirical Synthesis*. New York: Free Press, 1977.

PESCOSOLIDO, BERNICE A., and SHARON GEORGIANNA. "Durkheim, Suicide, and Religion: Toward a Network Theory of Suicide." *American Sociological Review*. Vol. 54, No. 1 (February 1989):33–48.

PETER, LAURENCE J., and RAYMOND HULL. *The Peter Principle: Why Things Always Go Wrong*. New York: William Morrow, 1969.

PETERS, THOMAS J., and ROBERT H. WATERMAN, JR. *In Search of Excellence: Lessons From America's Best-Run Companies*. New York: Warner Books, 1982.

PETERSON, NORMA. "Coming to Terms With Gay Parents." *USA Today* (April 30, 1984):3D.

PFAFF, WILLIAM. "Reflections: Aristocracies." *The New Yorker* (January 14, 1980):70, 72–78.

PHILLIPSON, CHRIS. *Capitalism and the Construction of Old Age*. London: The Macmillan Press, 1982.

PHYSICIAN TASK FORCE ON HUNGER IN AMERICA. "Hunger Reaches Blue-Collar America." Report issued 1987.

PILLEMER, KARL. "Maltreatment of the Elderly at Home and in Institutions: Extent, Risk Factors, and Policy Recommendations." In U.S. Congress. House, Select Committee on Aging and Senate, Special Committee on

Aging. *Legislative Agenda for an Aging Society: 1988 and Beyond*. Washington, DC: U.S. Government Printing Office, 1988.

PINDERHUGHES, DIANNE M. "Political Choices: A Realignment in Partisanship Among Black Voters?" In James D. Williams, ed., *The State of Black America 1986*. New York: National Urban League, 1986:85–113.

PINES, MAYA. "The Civilization of Genie." *Psychology Today*. Vol. 15 (September 1981):28–34.

PIOTROW, PHYLLIS T. *World Population: The Present and Future Crisis*. Headline Series 251 (October 1980). New York: Foreign Policy Association.

PIRANDELLO, LUIGI. "The Pleasure of Honesty." In *To Clothe the Naked and Two Other Plays*. New York: Dutton, 1962:143–198.

PITT, MALCOLM. *Introducing Hinduism*. New York: Friendship Press, 1955.

PIVEN, FRANCES FOX, and RICHARD A. CLOWARD. *Poor People's Movements: Why They Succeed, How They Fail*. New York: Pantheon, 1977.

PIVEN, FRANCES FOX, and RICHARD A. CLOWARD. *Why Americans Don't Vote*. New York: Pantheon, 1988.

PLOMIN, ROBERT, and TERRYL T. FOCH. "A Twin Study of Objectively Assessed Personality in Childhood." *Journal of Personality and Social Psychology*. Vol. 39, No. 4 (October 1980):680–688.

POLENBERG, RICHARD. *One Nation Divisible: Class, Race, and Ethnicity in the United States Since 1938*. New York: Pelican Books, 1980.

POLLACK, OTTO, and ELLEN S. WISE. *Invitation to a Dialogue: Union and Separation in Family Life*. New York: SP Medical and Scientific Books, 1979.

POLSBY, NELSON W. "Three Problems in the Analysis of Community Power." *American Sociological Review*. Vol. 24, No. 6 (December 1959):796–803.

POMER, MARSHALL I. "Labor Market Structure, Intragenerational Mobility, and Discrimination: Black Male Advancement Out of Low-Paying Occupations, 1962–1973." *American Sociological Review*. Vol. 51, No. 5 (October 1986):650–659.

PORTES, ALEJANDRO. "The Rise of Ethnicity: Determinants of Ethnic Perceptions Among Cuban Exiles in Miami." *American Sociological Review*. Vol. 49, No. 3 (June 1984):383–397.

PORTES, ALEJANDRO, and LEIF JENSEN. "The Enclave and the Entrants: Patterns of Ethnic Enterprise in Miami Before and After Mariel." *American Sociological Review*. Vol. 54, No. 6 (December 1989):929–949.

PORTES, ALEJANDRO, and SASKIA SASSEN-KOOB. "Making It Underground: Comparative Material on the Informal Sector in Western Market Economies." *American Journal of Sociology*. Vol. 93, No. 1 (July 1987):30–61.

POWELL, CHRIS, and GEORGE E. C. PATON, eds. *Humour in Society: Resistance and Control*. New York: St. Martin's Press, 1988.

PREMACK, DAVID. *Intelligence in Ape and Man*. Hillsdale, NJ: Lawrence Erlbaum Associates, 1976.

PRESIDENT'S COMMISSION FOR THE STUDY OF ETHICAL PROBLEMS IN MEDICINE AND BIOMEDICAL AND BEHAVIORAL RESEARCH. *Deciding to Forego Life-Sustaining Treatment*. Washington, DC: U.S. Government Printing Office, 1983.

PRYOR, FREDERIC L. *A Guidebook to the Comparative Study of Economic Systems*. Englewood Cliffs, NJ: Prentice-Hall, 1985.

QUEENAN, JOE. "The Many Paths to Riches." *Forbes*. Vol. 144, No. 9 (October 23, 1989):149.

QUINNEY, RICHARD. *Class, State and Crime: On the Theory and Practice of Criminal Justice*. New York: David McKay, 1977.

RADIN, NORMA. "Primary Caregiving and Role-Sharing Fathers." In Michael E. Lamb, ed., *Nontraditional Families: Parenting and Child Development*. Hillsdale, NJ: Lawrence Erlbaum Associates, 1982:173–204.

RANDALL, VICKI. *Women and Politics*. London: Macmillan Press, 1982.

RAPHAEL, RAY. *The Men from the Boys: Rites of Passage in Male America*. Lincoln and London: University of Nebraska Press, 1988.

RECKLESS, WALTER C. "Containment Theory." In Marvin E. Wolfgang, Leonard Savitz, and Norman Johnstone, eds., *The Sociology of Crime and Delinquency*. 2nd ed. New York: John Wiley, 1970:401–405.

RECKLESS, WALTER C., and SIMON DINITZ. "Pioneering with Self-Concept as a Vulnerability Factor in Delinquency." *Journal of Criminal Law, Criminology, and Police Science*. Vol. 58, No. 4 (December 1967):515–523.

REED, RODNEY J. "Administrator's Advice: Causes and Remedies of School Conflict and Violence." *National Association of Secondary School Principals Bulletin*. Vol. 67, No. 462 (April 1983):75–79.

REICH, ROBERT B. "As the World Turns." *The New Republic* (May 1, 1989):23, 26–28.

REID, SUE TITUS. *Crime and Criminology.* 3rd ed. New York: Holt, Reinhart and Winston, 1982.

REIMAN, JEFFREY. *The Rich Get Richer and the Poor Get Prison: Ideology, Class, and Criminal Justice.* 3rd edition. New York: Macmillan, 1990.

REIMAN, JEFFREY H. *The Rich Get Richer and the Poor Get Prison: Ideology, Class, and Criminal Justice.* 2nd ed. New York: John Wiley & Sons, 1984.

REIMERS, CORDELIA W. "Sources of the Family Income Differentials Among Hispanics, Blacks, and White Non-Hispanics." *American Journal of Sociology.* Vol. 89, No 4 (January 1984):889–903.

REINHARZ, SHULAMIT. "Feminist Distrust: Problems of Context and Content in Sociological Work." In Davis N. Berg and Kenwyn K. Smith, eds., *Exploring Clinical Methods for Social Research.* Beverly Hills, CA: Sage, 1985: 153–172.

REMOFF, HEATHER TREXLER. *Sexual Choice: A Woman's Decision.* New York: Dutton/Lewis, 1984.

RIDGEWAY, CECILIA, and DAVID DIEKEMA. "Dominance and Collective Hierarchy Formation in Male and Female Task Groups." *American Sociological Review.* Vol. 54, No. 1 (February 1989):79–93.

RIDGEWAY, CECILIA L. *The Dynamics of Small Groups.* New York: St. Martin's Press, 1983.

RIEGEL, KLAUS F. "History of Psychological Gerontology." In James E. Birren and K. Warner Schaie, eds., *Handbook of the Psychology of Aging.* New York: Van Nostrand Reinhold, 1977:70–102.

RIEGLE, DONALD W., JR. "The Psychological and Social Effects of Unemployment." *American Psychologist.* Vol. 37, No. 10 (October 1982):1113–1115.

RIESMAN, DAVID. *The Lonely Crowd: A Study of the Changing American Character.* New Haven, CT: Yale University Press, 1970; orig. 1950.

RILEY, MATILDA WHITE, ANNE FONER, and JOAN WARING. "Sociology of Age." In Neil J. Smelser, ed., *Handbook of Sociology.* Newbury Park, CA: Sage Publications, 1988:243–290.

RITZER, GEORGE. *Man and His Work: Conflict and Change.* New York: Appleton-Century-Crofts, 1972.

ROBERTS, J. DEOTIS. *Roots of a Black Future: Family and Church.* Philadelphia, PA: The Westminster Press, 1980.

ROBINSON, DAWN. "Toward a Synthesis of Sociological and Psychological Theories of Eating Disorders." Paper presented to Southwestern Social Science Association, Dallas, Texas, March 1987.

ROBINSON, VERA M. "Humor and Health." In Paul E. McGhee and Jeffrey H. Goldstein, eds., *Handbook of Humor Research, Vol. II, Applied Studies.* New York: Springer-Verlag, 1983:109–128.

ROESCH, ROBERTA. "Violent Families." *Parents.* Vol. 59, No. 9 (September 1984):74–76, 150–152.

ROETHLISBERGER, F. J., and WILLIAM J. DICKSON. *Management and the Worker.* Cambridge, MA: Harvard University Press, 1939.

ROHLEN, THOMAS P. *Japan's High Schools.* Berkeley, CA: University of California Press, 1983.

ROKOVE, MILTON L. *Don't Make No Waves, Don't Back No Losers.* Bloomington, IN: Indiana University Press, 1975.

ROMAN, MEL, and WILLIAM HADDAD. *The Disposable Parent: The Case for Joint Custody.* New York: Holt, Rinehart and Winston, 1978.

ROOF, WADE CLARK. "Socioeconomic Differentials Among White Socioreligious Groups in the United States." *Social Forces.* Vol. 58, No 1 (September 1979):280–289.

ROOF, WADE CLARK. "Unresolved Issues in the Study of Religion and the National Elite: Response to Greeley." *Social Forces.* Vol. 59, No. 3 (March 1981):831–836.

ROOS, PATRICIA. "Marriage and Women's Occupational Attainment in Cross-Cultural Perspective." *American Sociological Review.* Vol. 48. No. 6 (December 1983):852–864.

ROPER ORGANIZATION. *The Virginia Slims American Women's Public Opinion Poll.* New York, 1974.

ROSE, ARNOLD M. "The Subculture of the Aging: A Topic for Sociological Research." In Bernice L. Neugarten, ed., *Middle Age and Aging: A Reader in Social Psychology.* Chicago: University of Chicago Press, 1968:29–34.

ROSE, JERRY D. *Outbreaks.* New York: Free Press, 1982.

ROSEN, ELLEN ISRAEL. *Bitter Choices: Blue-Collar Women in and out of Work.* Chicago: University of Chicago Press, 1987.

ROSENBAUM, JAMES E. "Track Misperceptions and Frustrated College Plans: An Analysis of the Effects of Tracks and Track Perceptions in the National Longitudinal Survey." *Sociology of Education.* Vol. 35, No. 2 (April 1980):74–88.

ROSENBAUM, RON. "A Tangled Web for the Supreme Court." *The New York Times Magazine.* March 12, 1989:60.

ROSENTHAL, JACK. "The Rapid Growth of Suburban Employment." In Lois H. Masotti and Jeffrey K. Hadden, eds., *Suburbia in Transition.* New York: New York Times Books, 1974:95–100.

ROSKIN, MICHAEL G. *Countries and Concepts: An Introduction to Comparative Politics.* Englewood Cliffs, NJ: Prentice-Hall, 1982.

ROSNOW, RALPH L., and GARY ALAN FINE. *Rumor and Gossip: The Social Psychology of Hearsay.* New York: Elsevier, 1976.

ROSS, CATHERINE E., JOHN MIROWSKY, and JOAN HUBER. "Dividing Work, Sharing Work, and In-Between: Marriage Patterns and Depression." *American Sociological Review.* Vol. 48. No. 6 (December 1983):809–823.

ROSS, SUSAN. "Education: A Step Ladder to Mobility." *Popline.* Vol. 7, No. 7 (July 1985):1–2.

ROSSI, ALICE S. "Gender and Parenthood." In Alice S. Rossi, ed. *Gender and the Life Course.* New York: Aldine, 1985:161–191.

ROSSIDES, DANIEL W. *Social Stratification: The American Class System in Comparative Perspective.* Englewood Cliffs, NJ: Prentice-Hall, 1990.

ROSTOW, WALT W. *The World Economy: History and Prospect.* Austin, TX: University of Texas Press, 1978.

ROUDI, NAZY. "The Demography of Islam." *Population Today.* Vol. 16, No. 3 (March 1988):6–9.

ROWE, DAVID C. "Biometrical Genetic Models of Self-Reported Delinquent Behavior: A Twin Study." *Behavior Genetics.* Vol. 13, No. 5 (1983):473–489.

ROWE, DAVID C., and D. WAYNE OSGOOD. "Heredity and Sociological Theories of Delinquency: A Reconsideration." *American Sociological Review.* Vol. 49, No. 4 (August 1984):526–540.

RUBIN, BETH A. "Class Struggle American Style: Unions, Strikes and Wages." *American Sociological Review.* Vol. 51, No. 5 (October 1986):618–631.

RUBIN, LILLIAN B. *Intimate Strangers: Men and Women Together.* New York: Harper & Row, 1983.

RUBIN, LILLIAN BRESLOW. *Worlds of Pain: Life in the Working-Class Family.* New York: Basic Books, 1976.

RUBINSON, RICHARD. "Class Formation, Politics, and Institutions: Schooling in the United States." *American Journal of Sociology.* Vol. 92, No. 3 (November 1986):519–548.

RUDÉ, GEORGE. *The Crowd in History: A Study of Popular Disturbances in France and England, 1730–1848.* New York: John Wiley & Sons, 1964.

RUDOLPH, BARBARA. "Tobacco Takes a New Road." *Time.* Vol. 126, No. 20 (November 18, 1985):70–71.

RUMBERGER, RUSSELL. *Overeducation in the U.S. Labor Market.* New York: Praeger, 1981.

RUSSELL, DIANA E. H. *Rape in Marriage.* New York: Macmillan, 1982.

RUSSELL, GEORGE. "People, People, People." In *Time.* Vol. 124, No. 6 (August 6, 1984):24–25.

RYAN, WILLIAM. *Blaming the Victim.* Rev. ed. New York: Vintage, 1976.

RYTINA, JOAN HUBER, WILLIAM H. FORM, and JOHN PEASE. "Income and Stratification Ideology: Beliefs About the American Opportunity Structure." *American Journal of Sociology.* Vol. 75, No. 4 (January 1970):703–716.

SABATO, LARRY J. *PAC Power: Inside the World of Political Action Committees.* New York: Norton, 1984.

SACKS, HOWARD L. Letter to the author, 1986.

SAGAN, CARL. *The Dragons of Eden.* New York: Ballantine, 1977.

SALAS, RAFAEL M. "The State of World Population 1985: Population and Women." *Popline.* Vol. 7, No. 7 (July 1985):4–5.

SALHOLZ, ELOISE. "The Future of Gay America." *Newsweek* (March 12, 1990): 20–25.

SALINE, CAROL. "Bleeding in the Suburbs." *Philadelphia.* Vol. 75, No. 3 (March 1984):81–85, 144–151.

SAMPSON, ANTHONY. *The Changing Anatomy of Britain.* New York: Random House, 1982.

SAMPSON, ROBERT J. "Urban Black Violence: The Effects of Male Joblessness and Family Disruption." *American Journal of Sociology*. Vol. 93, No. 2 (September 1987):348–382.

SAPIR, EDWARD. *Selected Writings of Edward Sapir in Language, Culture, and Personality*. David G. Mandelbaum, ed. Berkeley: University of California Press, 1949.

SAPIR, EDWARD. "The Status of Linguistics as a Science." *Language*. Vol. 5 (1929):207–214.

SAUNDERS, JANICE MILLER, and JOHN N. EDWARDS. "Extramarital Sexuality: A Predictive Model of Permissive Attitudes." *Journal of Marriage and the Family*. Vol. 46, No. 4 (November 1984):825–835.

SCAFF, LAWRENCE A. "Max Weber and Robert Michels." *American Journal of Sociology*. Vol. 86, No. 6 (May 1981):1269–1286.

SCHAEFER, RICHARD T. *Racial and Ethnic Groups*. Boston: Little, Brown, 1979.

SCHAIE, K. WARNER. "Intelligence and Problem Solving." In James E. Birren and R. Bruce Sloane, eds., *Handbook of Mental Health and Aging*. Englewood Cliffs, NJ: Prentice-Hall, 1980:262–284.

SCHEFF, THOMAS J. *Being Mentally Ill: A Sociological Theory*. 2nd ed. New York: Aldine, 1984.

SCHLAFLY, PHYLLIS. "Mothers, Stay Home; Your Kids Need You." *USA Today*. (May 30, 1984):10A.

SCHLESINGER, ARTHUR. "The City in American Civilization." In A. B. Callow, Jr., ed., *American Urban History*. New York: Oxford University Press, 1969:25–41.

SCHMIDT, ROGER. *Exploring Religion*. Belmont, CA: Wadsworth, 1980.

SCHOOLER, CARMI, JOANNE MILLER, KAREN A. MILLER, and CAROL N. RICHTAND. "Work for the Household: Its Nature and Consequences for Husbands and Wives." *American Journal of Sociology*. Vol. 90, No. 1 (July 1984):97–124.

SCHRAG, PETER. *Out of Place in America*. New York: Random House, 1969.

SCHREINER, TIM. "Your Cost to Bring Up Baby: $142,700." *USA Today*. (October 19, 1984):1D.

SCHUMANN, HANS WOLFGANG. *Buddhism: An Outline of Its Teachings and Schools*. Wheaton, IL: The Theosophical Publishing House, Quest Books, 1974.

SCHUR, EDWIN M. *Labeling Women Deviant: Gender, Stigma, and Social Control*, Philadelphia: Temple University Press, 1983.

SCHUTT, RUSSELL K. "Objectivity versus Outrage." *Society*. Vol. 26, No. 4 (May/June 1989):14–16.

SCHWARTZ, JOE. "Rising Status." *American Demographics*. Vol. 11, No. 1 (January 1989):10.

SCHWARTZ, MARTIN D. "Gender and Injury in Spousal Assault." *Sociological Focus*. Vol. 20, No. 1 (January 1987):61–75.

SCHWARTZ-NOBEL, LORETTA. *Starving in the Shadow of Plenty*. New York: McGraw-Hill, 1981.

SCOTT, JOHN, and CATHERINE GRIFF. *Directors of Industry: The British Corporate Network, 1904–1976*. New York: Blackwell, 1985.

SCOTT, W. RICHARD. *Organizations: Rational, Natural, and Open Systems*. Englewood Cliffs, NJ: Prentice-Hall, 1981.

SELIMUDDIN, ABU K. "The Selling of America." *USA Today*. Vol. 117, No. 2525 (March 1989):12–14.

SELLIN, THORSTEN. *The Penalty of Death*. Beverly Hills, CA: Sage Publications, 1980.

SELTZER, ROBERT M. *Jewish People, Jewish Thought: The Jewish Experience in History*. New York: Macmillan, 1980.

SEN, K. M. *Hinduism*. Baltimore, MD: Penguin, 1961.

SENGOKU, TAMOTSU. *Willing Workers: The Work Ethics in Japan, England, and the United States*. Westport, CT: Quorum Books, 1985.

SENNETT, RICHARD, and JONATHAN COBB. *The Hidden Injuries of Class*. New York: Vintage, 1973.

SHANAS, ETHEL. "Social Myth as Hypothesis: The Case of the Family Relations of Old People." *The Gerontologist*. Vol. 19, No. 1 (February 1979):3–9.

SHAW, CLIFFORD R., and HENRY D. McKAY. *Juvenile Delinquency in Urban Areas*. Chicago: University of Chicago Press, 1972; orig. 1942.

SHAWCROSS, WILLIAM. *Sideshow: Kissinger, Nixon and the Destruction of Cambodia*. New York: Pocket Books, 1979.

SHEEHAN, TOM. "Senior Esteem as a Factor in Socioeconomic Complexity." *The Gerontologist*. Vol. 16, No. 5 (October 1976):433–440.

SHEEHY, GAIL. *Passages: Predictable Crises of Adult Life*. New York: E. P. Dutton, 1976.

SHELDON, WILLIAM H., EMIL M. HARTL, and EUGENE McDERMOTT. *Varieties of Delinquent Youth*. New York: Harper, 1949.

SHEPHARD, ROY J. *The Risks of Passive Smoking*. London: Croom Helm, 1982.

SHERRID, PAMELA. "Hot Times in the City of London." *U.S. News & World Report* (October 27, 1986):45–46.

SHEVKY, ESHREF, and WENDELL BELL. *Social Area Analysis*. Stanford, CA: Stanford University Press, 1955.

SHIBUTANI, TAMOTSU. *Improvised News: A Sociological Study of Rumor*. Indianapolis, IN: Bobbs-Merrill, 1966.

SHIPLER, DAVID K. *Russia: Broken Idols, Solemn Dreams*. New York: Penguin Books, 1984.

SHIPLEY, JOSEPH T. *Dictionary of Word Origins*. Totowa, NJ: Roman & Allanheld, 1985.

SHOCKEY, JAMES W. "Overeducation and Earnings: A Structural Approach to Differential Attainment in the U.S. Labor Force (1970–1982)." *American Sociological Review*. Vol. 54, No. 5 (October 1989):856–864.

SIDEL, RUTH, and VICTOR W. SIDEL. *The Health Care of China*. Boston, MA: Beacon Press, 1982b.

SIDEL, VICTOR W., and RUTH SIDEL. *A Healthy State: An International Perspective on the Crisis in United States Medical Care*. Rev. ed. New York: Pantheon, 1982a.

SILLS, DAVID L. "The Succession of Goals." In Amitai Etzioni, ed., *A Sociological Reader on Complex Organizations*. 2nd ed. New York: Holt, Rinehart and Winston, 1969:175–187.

SIMMEL, GEORG. *The Sociology of Georg Simmel*. Kurt Wolff, ed., New York: Free Press, 1950:118–169.

SIMMEL, GEORG. "The Mental Life of the Metropolis." In Kurt Wolff, ed., *The Sociology of Georg Simmel*. New York: Free Press, 1964:409–424; orig. 1905.

SIMMEL, GEORG. "Fashion." In Donald N. Levine, ed., *Georg Simmel: On Individuality and Social Forms*. Chicago: University of Chicago Press, 1971; orig. 1904.

SIMON, CARL P., and ANN D. WITTE. *Beating the System: The Underground Economy*. Boston, MA: Auburn House, 1982.

SIMON, DAVID R., and D. STANLEY EITZEN. *Elite Deviance*. Boston, MA: Allyn & Bacon, 1982; also 2nd ed., 1986.

SIMONS, CAROL. "Japan's *Kyoiku* Mamas." In John J. Macionis and Nijole V. Benokraitis, eds., *Seeing Ourselves: Classic, Contemporary, and Cross-Cultural Readings in Sociology*. Englewood Cliffs, NJ: Prentice Hall, 1989:281–286.

SIMPSON, GEORGE EATON, and J. MILTON YINGER. *Racial and Cultural Minorities: An Analysis of Prejudice and Discrimination*. 4th ed. New York: Harper & Row, 1972.

SINGER, DOROTHY. "A Time to Reexamine the Role of Television in Our Lives." *American Psychologist*. Vol. 38, No. 7 (July 1983):815–816.

SINGER, JEROME L., and DOROTHY G. SINGER. "Psychologists Look at Television: Cognitive, Developmental, Personality, and Social Policy Implications." *American Psychologist*. Vol. 38, No. 1 (July 1983):826–834.

SIPES, RICHARD G. "War, Sports and Aggression: An Empirical Test of Two Rival Theories." *American Anthropologist*. Vol. 75, No. 1 (January 1973):64–86.

SIVARD, RUTH LEGER. *World Military and Social Expenditures, 1987–88*. 12th ed. Washington, DC: World Priorities, 1988.

SIZER, THEODORE R. *Horace's Compromise: The Dilemma of the American High School*. Boston, MA: Houghton Mifflin, 1984.

SJOBERG, GIDEON. *The Preindustrial City*. New York: Free Press, 1965.

SKOCPOL, THEDA. *States and Social Revolutions: A Comparative Analysis of France, Russia, and China*. Cambridge (UK): Cambridge University Press, 1979.

SKOLNICK, ARLENE. *The Psychology of Human Development*. New York: Harcourt Brace Jovanovich, 1986.

SLATER, PHILIP E. "Contrasting Correlates of Group Size." *Sociometry*. Vol. 21, No. 2 (June 1958):129–139.

SLATER, PHILIP. *The Pursuit of Loneliness*. Boston, MA: Beacon Press, 1976.

SMART, NINIAN. *The Religious Experience of Mankind*. New York: Charles Scribner's Sons, 1969.

SMELSER, NEIL J. *Theory of Collective Behavior*. New York: Free Press, 1962.

SMILGAS, MARTHA. "The Big Chill: Fear of AIDS." *Time*. Vol. 129, No. 7 (February 16, 1987):50–53.

SMITH, ADAM. *An Inquiry into the Nature and Causes of the Wealth of Nations*. New York: The Modern Library, 1937; orig. 1776.

SMITH, DOUGLAS A. "Police Response to Interpersonal Violence: Defining the Parameters of Legal Control." *Social Forces*. Vol. 65, No. 3 (March 1987):767–782.

SMITH, DOUGLAS A., and PATRICK R. GARTIN. "Specifying Specific Deterrence: The Influence of Arrest on Future Criminal Activity." *American Sociological Review*. Vol. 54, No. 1 (February 1989):94–105.

SMITH, DOUGLAS A., and CHRISTY A. VISHER. "Street-Level Justice: Situational Determinants of Police Arrest Decisions." *Social Problems*. Vol. 29, No. 2 (December 1981):167–177.

SMITH, ROBERT ELLIS. *Privacy: How to Protect What's Left of It*. Garden City, NY: Anchor Press/Doubleday, 1979.

SMITH-LOVIN, LYNN, and CHARLES BRODY. "Interruptions in Group Discussions: The Effects of Gender and Group Composition." *American Journal of Sociology*. Vol. 54, No. 3 (June 1989):424–435.

SMITH-ROSENBERG, CAROL, and CHARLES ROSENBERG. "The Female Animal: Medical and Biological Views of Woman and Her Role in Nineteenth Century America." In Judith Walzer Leavitt, ed., *Women and Health in America*. Madison, WI: University of Wisconsin Press, 1984:12–27.

SNOW, DAVID A., E. BURKE ROCHFORD, JR., STEVEN K. WORDEN, and ROBERT D. BENFORD. "Frame Alignment Processes, Micromobilization, and Movement Participation." *American Sociological Review*. Vol. 51, No. 4 (August 1986):464–481.

SNOW, DAVID A., LOUIS A. ZURCHER, JR., and SHELDON EKLAND-OLSON. "Social Networks and Social Movements: A Macrostructural Approach to Differential Recruitment." *American Sociological Review*. Vol. 45, No. 5 (October 1980):787–801.

SNOWMAN, DANIEL. *Britain and America: An Interpretation of Their Culture 1945–1975*. New York: Harper Torchbooks, 1977.

SOWELL, THOMAS. *Ethnic America*. New York: Basic Books, 1981.

SPATES, JAMES L. "Sociological Overview." In Alan Milberg, ed., *Street Games*. New York: McGraw-Hill, 1976a:286–290.

SPATES, JAMES L. "Counterculture and Dominant Culture Values: A Cross-National Analysis of the Underground Press and Dominant Culture Magazines." *American Sociological Review*. Vol. 41, No. 5 (October 1976b):868–883.

SPATES, JAMES L. "The Sociology of Values." In Ralph Turner, ed., *Annual Review of Sociology*. Vol. 9. Palo Alto, CA: Annual Reviews, 1983:27–49.

SPATES, JAMES L., and JOHN J. MACIONIS. *The Sociology of Cities*. 2nd ed. Belmont, CA: Wadsworth, 1987.

SPATES, JAMES L., and H. WESLEY PERKINS. "American and English Student Values." *Comparative Social Research*. Vol. 5. Greenwich, CT: Jai Press, 1982:245–268.

SPECTOR, LEONARD S. "Nuclear Proliferation Today." In William M. Evan and Stephen Hilgartner, eds. *The Arms Race and Nuclear War*. Englewood Cliffs, NJ: Prentice Hall, 1988:25–29.

SPEER, JAMES A. "The New Christian Right and Its Parent Company: A Study in Political Contrasts." In David G. Bromley and Anson Shupe, eds., *New Christian Politics*. Macon, GA: Mercer University Press, 1984:19–40.

SPEIZER, JEANNE J. "Education." In Barbara Haber, ed., *The Women's Annual 1982–1983*. Boston: G. K. Hall, 1983:29–54.

SPENCER, GARY. *Projections of the Population of the United States, by Age, Sex, and Race: 1988 to 2080*. Washington, DC: U.S. Government Printing Office, 1989.

SPENDER, DALE. *Man Made Language*. London: Routledge & Kegan Paul, 1980.

SPITZER, STEVEN. "Toward a Marxian Theory of Deviance." In Delos H. Kelly, ed., *Criminal Behavior: Readings in Criminology*. New York: St. Martin's Press, 1980:175–191.

SRINIVAS, M. N. *Social Change in Modern India*. Berkeley, CA: University of California Press, 1971.

STACEY, JUDITH. *Patriarchy and Socialist Revolution in China*. Berkeley: University of California Press, 1983.

STACK, CAROL B. *All Our Kin: Strategies for Survival in a Black Community*. New York: Harper & Row, 1975.

STACK, STEVEN. "Publicized Executions and Homicide, 1950–1980." *American Sociological Review*. Vol. 52, No. 4 (August 1987):532–540.

STAHURA, JOHN M. "Determinants of Change in the Distribution of Blacks Across Suburbs." *Sociological Quarterly*. Vol. 24, No. 3 (Summer 1983):421–433.

STAHURA, JOHN M. "Suburban Development, Black Suburbanization and the Black Civil Rights Movement Since World War II." *American Sociological Review*. Vol. 51, No. 1 (February 1986):131–144.

STAPLES, BRENT. "Where Are the Black Fans?" *New York Times Magazine* (May 17, 1987):26–34, 36.

STARK, EVAN, and ANN FLITCRAFT. "Domestic Violence and Female Suicide Attempts." Presentation to American Public Health Association, New York, 1979.

STARK, RODNEY. "The Rise of a New World Faith." *Review of Religious Research*. Vol. 26, No. 1 (September 1984):18–27.

STARK, RODNEY, and WILLIAM SIMS BAINBRIDGE. "Of Churches, Sects, and Cults: Preliminary Concepts for a Theory of Religious Movements." *Journal for the Scientific Study of Religion*. Vol. 18, No. 2 (June 1979):117–131.

STARK, RODNEY, and WILLIAM SIMS BAINBRIDGE. "Secularization and Cult Formation in the Jazz Age." *Journal for the Scientific Study of Religion*. Vol. 20, No. 4 (December 1981):360–373.

STARK, RODNEY, and CHARLES Y. GLOCK. *American Piety: The Nature of Religious Commitment*. Berkeley, CA: University of California Press, 1968.

STARR, PAUL. *The Social Transformation of American Medicine*. New York: Basic Books, 1982.

Statistics of Income Bulletin. Vol. 9, No. 1 (Summer 1989).

STAVRIANOS, L. S. *A Global History: The Human Heritage*. 3rd ed. Englewood Cliffs, NJ: Prentice-Hall, 1983.

STEIN, MAURICE R. *The Eclipse of Community: An Interpretation of American Studies*. Princeton, NJ: Princeton University Press, 1972

STEINMETZ, GEORGE, and ERIK OLIN WRIGHT. "The Fall and Rise of the Petty Bourgeoisie: Changing Patterns of Self-Employment in the Postwar United States." *American Journal of Sociology*. Vol. 94, No. 5 (March 1989):973–1018.

STEPHENS, JOHN D. *The Transition from Capitalism to Socialism*. Urbana IL: University of Illinois Press, 1986.

STERNLIEB, GEORGE, and JAMES W. HUGHES. "The Uncertain Future of the Central City." *Urban Affairs Quarterly*. Vol. 18, No. 4 (June 1983):455–472.

STEVENS, GILLIAN, and GRAY SWICEGOOD. "The Linguistic Context of Ethnic Endogamy." *American Sociological Review*. Vol. 52, No. 1 (February 1987):73–82.

STEVENS, ROSEMARY. *American Medicine and the Public Interest*. New Haven, CT: Yale University Press, 1971.

STOCKWELL, EDWARD G., DAVID A. SWANSON, and JERRY W. WICKS. "Trends in the Relationship Between Infant Mortality and Socioeconomic Status." *Sociological Focus*. Vol. 20, No. 4 (October 1987):319–327.

STODDARD, SANDOL. *The Hospice Movement: A Better Way to Care for the Dying*. Briarcliff Manor, NY: Stein and Day, 1978.

STOHL, MICHAEL, and GEORGE A. LOPEZ, eds. *The State as Terrorist: The Dynamics of Governmental Violence and Repression*. Westport, CT: Greenwood Press, 1984.

STONE, LAWRENCE. *The Family, Sex and Marriage in England 1500–1800*. New York: Harper & Row, 1977.

STONE, ROBYN. *The Feminization of Poverty and Older Women*. Washington, DC: U.S. Department of Health and Human Services, 1986.

STONE, ROBYN, GAIL LEE CAFFERATA, and JUDITH SANGL. *Caregivers of the Frail Elderly: A National Profile*. Washington, DC: U.S. Department of Health and Human Services, 1987.

STOUFFER, SAMUEL A., et al. *The American Soldier: Adjustment During Army Life*. Princeton, NJ: Princeton University Press, 1949.

STRAUS, MURRAY A., and RICHARD J. GELLES. "Societal Change and Change in Family Violence from 1975 to 1985 as Revealed by Two National Surveys." *Journal of Marriage and the Family*. Vol. 48, No. 4 (August 1986):465–479.

Streib, Gordon F. "Are the Aged a Minority Group?" In Bernice L. Neugarten, ed., *Middle Age and Aging: A Reader in Social Psychology*. Chicago: University of Chicago Press, 1968:35–46.

Sudnow, David N. *Passing On: The Social Organization of Dying*. Englewood Cliffs, NJ: Prentice-Hall, 1967.

Suggs, David. Personal communication, 1989.

Sumner, William Graham. *Folkways*. New York: Dover, 1959; orig. 1906.

Sung, Betty Lee. *Mountains of Gold: The Story of the Chinese in America*. New York: Macmillan, 1967.

Sutherland, Edwin H. "White Collar Criminality." *American Sociological Review*. Vol. 5, No. 1 (February 1940):1–12.

Sutherland, Edwin H., and Donald R. Cressey. *Criminology*. 3rd ed. Philadelphia: J. B. Lippincott, 1930; 8th ed. 1970; 10th ed. 1978.

Suzuki, David, and Peter Knudtson. *Genethics: The Clash Between the New Genetics and Human Values*. Cambridge, MA: Harvard University Press, 1989.

Swartz, Steve. "Why Michael Milken Stands to Qualify for Guinness Book." *The Wall Street Journal*. Vol. LXX, No. 117 (March 31, 1989):1, 4.

Sweet, Ellen. "Date Rape: The Story of an Epidemic and Those Who Deny It." *Ms./Campus Times* (October 1985):56–59, 84–85.

Syzmanski, Albert. *The Logic of Imperialism*. New York: Praeger, 1981.

Syzmanski, Albert. *Class Structure: A Critical Perspective*. New York: Praeger, 1983.

Szasz, Thomas S. *The Manufacturer of Madness: A Comparative Study of the Inquisition and the Mental Health Movement*. New York: Dell, 1961.

Szasz, Thomas S. *The Myth of Mental Illness: Foundations of a Theory of Personal Conduct*. New York: Harper & Row, 1970, orig. 1961.

Taeuber, Karl, and Alma Taeuber. *Negroes in Cities*. Chicago: Aldine, 1965.

Tajfel, Henri. "Social Psychology of Intergroup Relations." *Annual Review of Psychology*. Palo Alto, CA: Annual Reviews, 1982:1–39.

Tannenbaum, Frank. *Slave and Citizen: The Negro in the Americas*. New York: Vintage Books, 1946.

Tavris, Carol, and Susan Sadd. *The Redbood Report on Female Sexuality*. New York: Delacorte Press, 1977.

Tavris, Carol, and Carole Wade. *The Longest War: Sex Differences in Perspective*. 2nd ed. New York: Harcourt Brace Jovanovich, 1984.

Theen, Rolf H. W. "Party and Bureaucracy." In Erik P. Hoffmann and Robbin F. Laird, eds., *The Soviet Polity in the Modern Era*. New York: Aldine, 1984:131–165.

Theodorson, George A., and Achilles G. Theodorson. *A Modern Dictionary of Sociology*. New York: Barnes and Noble Books, 1969.

Thio, Alex. *Deviant Behavior*. 2nd ed. Boston: Houghton Mifflin, 1983.

Thoits, Peggy A. "Self-labeling Processes in Mental Illness: The Role of Emotional Deviance." *American Journal of Sociology*. Vol. 91, No. 2 (September 1985):221–249.

Thomas, Edward J. *The Life of Buddha as Legend and History*. London: Routledge & Kegan Paul, 1975.

Thomas, Melvin E., and Michael Hughes. "The Continuing Significance of Race: A Study of Race, Class, and Quality of Life in America, 1972–1985." *American Sociological Review*. Vol. 51, No. 6 (December 1986):830–841.

Thomas, Piri. *Down These Mean Streets*. New York: Signet, 1967.

Thomas, W. I. "The Relation of Research to the Social Process." In Morris Janowitz, ed., *W. I. Thomas on Social Organization and Social Personality*. Chicago: University of Chicago Press, 1966:289–305; orig. 1931.

Thompson, Anthony Peter. "Emotional and Sexual Components of Extramarital Relations." *Journal of Marriage and the Family*. Vol. 46, No. 1 (February 1984):35–42.

Thornberry, Terrance, and Margaret Farnsworth. "Social Correlates of Criminal Involvement: Further Evidence on the Relationship Between Social Status and Criminal Behavior." *American Sociological Review*. Vol. 47, No. 4 (August 1982):505–518.

Thorne, Barrie, Cheris Kramarae, and Nancy Henley, eds. *Language, Gender and Society*. Cambridge: Newbury House, 1983.

Thornton, Arland. "Changing Attitudes Toward Separation and Divorce: Causes and Consequences." *American Journal of Sociology*. Vol. 90, No. 4 (January 1985):856–872.

Thurow, Lester C. "A Surge in Inequality." *Scientific American*. Vol. 256, No. 5 (May 1987):30–37.

Tibbitts, Clark. "Can We Invalidate Negative Stereotypes of Aging?" *The Gerontologist*. Vol. 19, No. 1 (February 1979):10–20.

Tienda, Marta, and Ding-Tzann Lii. "Minority Concentration and Earnings Inequality: Blacks, Hispanics, and Asians Compared." *American Journal of Sociology*. Vol. 93, No. 1 (July 1987):141–165.

Tiger, Lionel, and Joseph Shepher. *Women in the Kibbutz*. New York: Harcourt Brace Jovanovich, 1975.

Tilly, Charles. *From Mobilization to Revolution*. Reading, MA: Addison-Wesley, 1978.

Tilly, Charles. "Does Modernization Breed Revolution?" In Jack A. Goldstone, ed., *Revolutions: Theoretical, Comparative, and Historical Studies*. New York: Harcourt Brace Jovanovich, 1986:47–57.

Tilly, Charles, Louise Tilly, and Richard Tilly. *The Rebellious Century, 1830–1930*. Cambridge, MA: Harvard University Press, 1975.

Time. "The Crime That Tranished a Town." Vol. 123, No. 10 (March 5, 1984):19.

Tittle, Charles R., and Wayne J. Villemez. "Social Class and Criminality." *Social Forces*. Vol. 56, No. 22 (December 1977):474–502.

Tittle, Charles R., Wayne J. Villemez, and Douglas A. Smith. "The Myth of Social Class and Criminality: An Empirical Assessment of the Empirical Evidence." *American Sociological Review*. Vol. 43, No. 5 (October 1978):643–656.

Tobin, Gary A. "Suburbanization and the Development of Motor Transportation: Transportation Technology and the Suburbanization Process." In Barry Schwartz, ed., *The Changing Face of the Suburbs*. Chicago: University of Chicago Press, 1976.

Tocqueville, Alexis de. *The Old Regime and the French Revolution*. Stuart Gilbert, trans. Garden City, NY: Doubleday Anchor Books, 1955; orig. 1856.

Tocqueville, Alexis de. *Democracy in America*. Garden City, NY: Doubleday Anchor Books, 1969; orig. 1834–1840.

Toennies, Ferdinand. *Community and Society (Gemeinschaft und Gesellschaft)*. New York: Harper & Row, 1963; orig. 1887.

Toffler, Alvin. *The Third Wave*. New York: Bantam Books, 1981.

Tomiak, Janusz. "Introduction." In J. J. Tomiak, ed., *Soviet Education in the 1980s*. London: Croom Helm, 1983:vii–x.

Treas, Judith. "Socialist Organization and Economic Development in China: Latent Consequences for the Aged." *The Gerontologist*. Vol. 19, No. 1 (February 1979):34–43.

Treiman, Donald J. "Industrialization and Social Stratification." In Edward O. Laumann, ed., *Social Stratification: Research and Theory for the 1970s*. Indianapolis: Bobbs-Merrill, 1970.

Troeltsch, Ernst. *The Social Teaching of the Christian Churches*. New York: Macmillan, 1931.

Troiden, Richard R. *Gay and Lesbian Identity: A Sociological Analysis*. Dix Hills, NY: General Hall, 1988.

Tukufu, Darryl S. "Race, Gender, and Status Differences in Voluntary Association Membership." Paper presented to Southwestern Sociological Association, Dallas, TX, 1987.

Tumin, Melvin M. "Some Principles of Stratification: A Critical Analysis." *American Sociological Review*. Vol. 18, No. 4 (August 1953):387–394.

Tumin, Melvin M. *Social Stratification: The Forms and Functions of Inequality*. 2nd ed. Englewood Cliffs, NJ: Prentice Hall, 1985.

Turner, Ralph H., and Lewis M. Killian. *Collective Behavior*. 2nd ed. Englewood Cliffs, NJ: Prentice Hall, 1972; 3rd ed., 1987.

Tygiel, Jules. *Baseball's Great Experiment: Jackie Robinson and His Legacy*. New York: Oxford University Press, 1983.

Tyler, S. Lyman. *A History of Indian Policy*. Washington, DC: United States Department of the Interior, Bureau of Indian Affairs, 1973.

Tyree, Andrea, Moshe Semyonov, and Robert W. Hodge. "Gaps and Glissandos: Inequality, Economic Development, and Social Mobility in 24 Countries." *American Sociological Review*. Vol. 44, No. 3 (June 1979):410–424.

UHLENBERG, PETER. "Older Women: The Growing Challenge to Design Constructive Roles." *The Gerontologist.* Vol. 19, No. 3 (June 1979):236–241.

UNITED NATIONS. *Demographic Yearbook 1983.* New York: United Nations, 1983.

UNITED NATIONS. *World Economic Survey 1988: Current Trends and Policies in the World Economy.* New York: United Nations Publications, 1988.

UNNEVER, JAMES D., CHARLES E. FRAZIER, and JOHN C. HENRETTA. "Race Differences in Criminal Sentencing." *The Sociological Quarterly.* Vol. 21, No. 2 (Spring 1980):197–205.

UNRUH, JOHN D., JR. *The Plains Across.* Urbana: University of Illinois Press, 1979.

U.S. BUREAU OF THE CENSUS. *Statistical Abstract of the United States 1970.* 91st ed. Washington, DC: U.S. Government Printing Office, 1970.

U.S. BUREAU OF THE CENSUS. *Household and Family Characteristics: March 1985.* P-20, No. 411. Washington, DC: U.S. Government Printing Office, 1986a.

U.S. BUREAU OF THE CENSUS. *Statistical Abstract of the United States 1986.* 106th ed. Washington, DC: U.S. Government Printing Office, 1986b.

U.S. BUREAU OF THE CENSUS. *Fertility of American Women: June 1986.* P-20, No. 421. Washington, DC: U.S. Government Printing Office, 1987a.

U.S. BUREAU OF THE CENSUS. *The Hispanic Population in the United States: March 1986 and 1987 (Advance Report).* Washington, DC: U.S. Government Printing Office, 1987b.

U.S. BUREAU OF THE CENSUS. *Marital Status and Living Arrangements: March 1986.* P-20, No. 418. Washington, DC: U.S. Government Printing Office, 1987c.

U.S. BUREAU OF THE CENSUS. *Money Income and Poverty Status of Families and Persons in the United States: 1986.* P-60, No. 157. Washington, DC: U.S. Government Printing Office, 1987d.

U.S. BUREAU OF THE CENSUS. *School Enrollment—Social and Economic Characteristics of Students, October 1986.* P-20, No. 429. Washington, DC: U.S. Government Printing Office, 1988.

U.S. BUREAU OF THE CENSUS. *Characteristics of Persons Receiving Benefits from Major Assistance Programs.* P-70, No. 14. Washington, DC: U.S. Government Printing Office, 1989a.

U.S. BUREAU OF THE CENSUS. *Fertility of American Women: June 1988.* Washington, DC: U.S. Government Printing Office, 1989b.

U.S. BUREAU OF THE CENSUS. *The Hispanic Population in the United States: March 1988.* P-20, No. 438. Washington, DC: U.S. Government Printing Office, 1989c.

U.S. BUREAU OF THE CENSUS. *Household and Family Characteristics: March 1988.* Washington, DC: U.S. Government Printing Office, 1989d.

U.S. BUREAU OF THE CENSUS. *Households, Families, Marital Status, and Living Arrangements: March 1989 (Advance Report).* Washington, DC: U.S. Government Printing Office, 1989e.

U.S. BUREAU OF THE CENSUS. *Marital Status and Living Arrangements: March 1988.* Washington, DC: U.S. Government Printing Office, 1989f.

U.S. BUREAU OF THE CENSUS. *Money Income and Poverty Status in the United States: 1988.* Washington, DC: U.S. Government Printing Office, 1989g.

U.S. BUREAU OF THE CENSUS. *Money Income of Households, Families, and Persons in the United States, 1987.* P-60, No. 162. Washington, DC: U.S. Government Printing Office, 1989h.

U.S. BUREAU OF THE CENSUS. *Patterns of Metropolitan Area and County Population Growth: 1980 to 1987.* Washington, DC: U.S. Government Printing Office, 1989i.

U.S. BUREAU OF THE CENSUS. *Per Capita Income Up, Median Family Income and Poverty Rate Unchanged in 1988, Census Bureau Reports.* (Press Release) Washington, DC: The Bureau, 1989j.

U.S. BUREAU OF THE CENSUS. *Poverty in the United States 1987.* P-60, No. 163. Washington, DC: U.S. Government Printing Office, 1989k.

U.S. BUREAU OF THE CENSUS. *Projections of the Population of the United States, by Age, Sex, and Race: 1988 to 2080.* Series P-25, No. 1018. Washington, DC: U.S. Government Printing Office, 1989l.

U.S. BUREAU OF THE CENSUS. *Public Employment in 1988.* Washington, DC: U.S. Government Printing Office, 1989m.

U.S. BUREAU OF THE CENSUS. *Statistical Abstract of the United States 1989.* 109th ed. Washington, DC: U.S. Government Printing Office, 1989n.

U.S. BUREAU OF THE CENSUS. *Voting and Registration in the Election of November 1988.* Washington, DC: U.S. Government Printing Office, 1989o.

U.S. BUREAU OF THE CENSUS. *Population Estimates for Metropolitan Statistical Areas, July 1, 1988, 1987, and 1986.* Washington, DC: U.S. Government Printing Office, 1990.

U.S. BUREAU OF JUSTICE STATISTICS. *Capital Punishment, 1985.* Washington, DC: U.S. Government Printing Office, 1986.

U.S. BUREAU OF JUSTICE STATISTICS. *Recidivism of Prisoners Released in 1983.* Washington, DC: U.S. Government Printing Office, 1989.

U.S. BUREAU OF LABOR STATISTICS. *Employment and Earnings.* Vol. 36, No. 1 (January 1989a). Washington, DC: U.S. Government Printing Office, 1989a.

U.S. BUREAU OF LABOR STATISTICS. *Employment and Earnings.* Vol. 36, No. 4 (April). Washington, DC: U.S. Government Printing Office, 1989b.

U.S. BUREAU OF LABOR STATISTICS. *Nearly Three-Fifths of the High School Graduates of 1988 Enrolled in College.* Washington, DC: U.S. Government Printing Office, 1989c.

U.S. BUREAU OF LABOR STATISTICS. *Employment and Earnings.* Vol. 37, No. 1 (January 1990).

U.S. CENTER FOR DISEASE CONTROL. *The Surgeon General's 1989 Report on Reducing the Health Consequences of Smoking: 25 Years of Progress: Executive Summary.* Washington, DC: U.S. Government Printing Office, 1989.

U.S. CENTER FOR EDUCATION STATISTICS. *Early Estimates: National Estimates of Higher Education, School Year 1988–1989.* Washington, DC: U.S. Government Printing Office, 1988.

U.S. CENTER FOR EDUCATION STATISTICS. *The Condition of Education 1989.* Washington, DC: U.S. Government Printing Office, 1989.

U.S. CENTER FOR HEALTH STATISTICS. *Vital Statistics of the United States 1986 Vol. 1—Natality.* Washington, DC: U.S. Government Printing Office, 1988.

U.S. COMMISSION ON CIVIL RIGHTS. *Twenty Years After Brown: The Shadows of the Past.* Washington, DC: U.S. Government Printing Office, 1974.

U.S. CONGRESS. HOUSE. SELECT SUBCOMMITTEE ON CHILDREN, YOUTH, AND FAMILIES. *U.S. Children and Their Families: Current Conditions and Recent Trends, 1989.* Washington, DC: U.S. Government Printing Office, 1989.

U.S. DEPARTMENT OF EDUCATION. Center for Statistics. *Digest of Educational Statistics 1985–86.* Washington, DC: U.S. Government Printing Office, 1986.

U.S. DEPARTMENT OF HEALTH AND HUMAN SERVICES. *Alcohol, Drug Abuse, and Mental Health News.* Vol. 15, No. 8 (October 1989).

U.S. DEPARTMENT OF JUSTICE. *Criminal Victimization in the United States, 1987.* Washington, DC: U.S. Government Printing Office, 1987.

U.S. DEPARTMENT OF LABOR. *Time of Change: 1983 Handbook on Women Workers.* Bulletin 298, Washington, DC: U.S. Government Printing Office, 1983.

USEEM, BERT. "Disorganization and the New Mexico Prison Riot of 1980." *American Sociological Review.* Vol. 50, No. 5 (October 1985):677–688.

USEEM, MICHAEL. "The Social Organization of the Corporate Business Elite and Participation of Corporate Directors in the Governance of American Institutions." *American Sociological Review.* Vol 44, No. 4 (August 1979):553–572.

USEEM, MICHAEL. "Corporations and the Corporate Elite." In Alex Inkeles et al., eds., *Annual Review of Sociology.* Vol. 6. Palo Alto, CA: Annual Reviews, 1980:41–77.

USEEM, MICHAEL, and JEROME KARABEL. "Pathways to Corporate Management." *American Sociological Review.* Vol. 51, No. 2 (April 1986):184–200.

U.S. FEDERAL BUREAU OF INVESTIGATION. *Crime in the United States 1988.* Washington, DC: U.S. Government Printing Office, 1989.

U.S. FEDERAL BUREAU OF PRISONS. *Statistical Report Fiscal Year 1986.* Washington, DC: U.S. Government Printing Office, 1987.

U.S. FEDERAL ELECTION COMMISSION. *FEC Final Report on 1988 Congressional Campaigns Show $459 Million Spent.* Washington, DC: The Commission, 1989a.

U.S. FEDERAL ELECTION COMMISSION. *Federal Election Commission Record.* Vol. 15, No. 8 (August 1989b).

U.S. House of Representatives, Select Committee on Children, Youth, and Families. *Abused Children in America: Victims of Neglect*. Washington, DC: U.S. Government Printing Office, 1987.

U.S. National Center for Education Statistics.*Projections of Education Statistics to 1992–93*. Washington, DC: U.S. Government Printing Office, 1985.

U.S. National Center for Education Statistics.*The Condition of Education: 1986 Edition Statistical Report*. Washington, DC: U.S. Government Printing Office, 1987.

U.S. National Center for Education Statistics.*Digest of Education Statistics: 1989*. Washington, DC: U.S. Government Printing Office, 1989.

U.S. National Center for Health Statistics.*Monthly Vital Statistics Reports*. Vol. 36, No. 3 (June 22, 1987).

U.S. National Center for Health Statistics.*Current Estimates from the National Health Interview Survey United States, 1987*. Series 10, No. 166. Washington, DC: U.S. Government Printing Office, 1988a.

U.S. National Center for Health Statistics. *Vital Statistics of the United States 1986*. Vol. II, Pt. A. Washington, DC: U.S. Government Printing Office, 1988b.

U.S. National Center for Health Statistics.*Current Estimates from the National Health Survey, 1988*. Washington, DC: U.S. Government Printing Office, 1989.

U.S. Office of Educational Research and Improvement. *The Condition of Education 1989*. Vol. 1 *Elementary and Secondary Education*. Washington, DC: U.S. Government Printing Office, 1989.

U.S. Women's Bureau. *Employers and Child Care: Benefiting Work and Family*. Washington, DC: U.S. Government Printing Office, 1989.

van de Kaa, Dirk J. "Europe's Second Demographic Transition." *Population Bulletin*. Vol. 42, No. 1 (March 1987). Washington, DC: Population Reference Bureau.

van den Haag, Ernest, and John P. Conrad. *The Death Penalty: A Debate*. New York: Plenum Press, 1983.

Van Valey, T. L., W. C. Roof, and J. E. Wilcox. "Trends in Residential Segregation." *American Journal of Sociology*. Vol. 82, No. 4 (January 1977):826–844.

Vatz, Richard E., and Lee S. Weinberg. *Thomas Szasz: Primary Values and Major Contentions*. Buffalo, NY: Prometheus Books, 1983.

Vaughan, Mary Kay. "Multinational Corporations: The World as a Company Town." In Ahamed Idris-Soven et al., eds., *The World as a Company Town: Multinational Corporations and Social Change*. The Hague: Mouton Publishers, 1978:15–35.

Vayda, Eugene, and Raisa B. Deber. "The Canadian Health Care System: An Overview." *Social Science and Medicine*. Vol. 18, No. 3 (1984):191–197.

Veblen, Thorstein. *The Theory of the Leisure Class*. New York: The New American Library, 1953; orig. 1899.

Viguerie, Richard A. *The New Right: We're Ready to Lead*. Falls Church, VA: The Viguerie Company, 1981.

Vines, Gail. "Whose Baby Is It Anyway?" *New Scientist*. No. 1515 (July 3, 1986):26–27.

Vinovskis, Maris A. "Have Social Historians Lost the Civil War? Some Preliminary Demographic Speculations." *Journal of American History*. Vol. 76, No. 1 (June 1989):34–58.

Vogel, Ezra F. *Japan as Number One: Lessons for America*. Cambridge, MA: Harvard University Press, 1979.

Vogel, Lise. *Marxism and the Oppression of Women: Toward a Unitary Theory*. New Brunswick, NJ: Rutgers University Press, 1983.

Vold, George B., and Thomas J. Bernard. *Theoretical Criminology*. 3rd ed. New York: Oxford University Press, 1986.

von Hirsh, Andrew. *Past or Future Crimes: Deservedness and Dangerousness in the Sentencing of Criminals*. New Brunswick, NJ: Rutgers University Press, 1986.

Vonnegut, Kurt, Jr. "Harrison Bergeron." In *Welcome to the Monkey House*. New York: Delacorte Press/Seymour Lawrence, 1968:7–13; orig. 1961.

Waite, Linda J., Gus W. Haggstrom, and David E. Kanouse. "The Consequences of Parenthood for the Marital Stability of Young Adults." *American Sociological Review*. Vol. 50, No. 6 (December 1985):850–857.

Walker, Jack L. "The Origins and Maintenance of Interest Groups in America." *The American Political Science Review*. Vol. 77, No. 2 (June 1983):390–406.

Wall, Thomas F. *Medical Ethics: Basic Moral Issues*. Washington, DC: University Press of America, 1980.

Wallerstein, Immanuel. *The Modern World-System: Capitalist Agriculture and the Origins of the European World-Economy in the Sixteenth Century*. New York: Academic Press, 1974.

Wallerstein, Immanuel. *The Capitalist World-Economy*. New York: Cambridge University Press, 1979.

Wallerstein, Immanuel. "Crises: The World Economy, the Movements, and the Ideologies." In Albert Bergesen, ed., *Crises in the World-System*. Beverly Hills, CA: Sage Publications, 1983:21–36.

Wallerstein, Immanuel. *The Politics of the World Economy: The States, the Movements, and the Civilizations*. Cambridge, UK: Cambridge University Press, 1984.

Wallerstein, Judith S., and Sandra Blakeslee.*Second Chances: Men, Women, and Children a Decade After Divorce*. New York: Ticknor & Fields, 1989.

Wallis, Claudia. "AIDS: A Growing Threat." *Time*. Vol. 126, No. 6 (August 12, 1985b):40–47.

Wallis, Claudia. "Children Having Children." *Time*. Vol. 126, No. 23 (December 9, 1985a):78–82, 84, 87, 89–90.

Wallis, Claudia. "Stress: Can We Cope?" *Time*. Vol. 121, No. 23 (June 6, 1983):48–54.

Wallis, Claudia. "Hold the Eggs and Butter," *Time*. Vol. 123, No. 13 (March 26, 1984):56–63.

Wallis, Claudia. "To Feed or Not to Feed?" *Time*. Vol. 127, No. 13 (March 31, 1986):60.

Warner, Sam Bass, Jr. *Streetcar Suburbs*. Cambridge, MA: Harvard University and M.I.T. Presses, 1962.

Warner, W. Lloyd, and J. O. Low. *The Social System of the Modern Factory*. Yankee City Series, Vol. 4, New Haven, CT: Yale University Press, 1947.

Warner, W. Lloyd, and Paul S. Lunt. *The Social Life of a Modern Community*. New Haven, CT: Yale University Press, 1941.

Watson, John B. *Behaviorism*. Rev. ed., New York: W. W. Norton, 1930.

Watson, Russell. "A Hidden Epidemic." *Newsweek*. (May 14, 1984):30–36.

Watson, Russell. "Riding the Tiger." *Newsweek*. Vol. CXIV, No. 23 (December 4, 1989):40–42, 44.

Wattel, H. "Levittown: A Suburban Community." In William Dobriner, ed., *The Suburban Community*. New York: G. P. Putnam's Sons, 1958:287–313.

Waxman, Chaim I. *The Stigma of Poverty: A Critique of Poverty Theories and Policies*. 2nd ed. New York: Pergamon Press, 1983.

Weber, Adna Ferrin. *The Growth of Cities*. New York: Columbia University Press, 1963; orig. 1899.

Weber, Max. *Economy and Society*. G. Roth and C. Wittich, eds. Berkeley, CA: University of California Press, 1978.

Weber, Max. *General Economic History*. Frank H. Knight, trans. New York: Collier Books, 1961; orig. 1919–1920.

Weber, Max. *Max Weber: Essays in Sociology*. H. H. Gerth and C. Wright Mills, eds. and trans., New York: Oxford University Press, 1946.

Weber, Max. *The Protestant Ethic and the Spirit of Capitalism*. New York: Charles Scribner's Sons, 1958; orig. 1904–1905.

Wechsler, D. *The Measurement and Appraisal of Adult Intelligence*. 5th ed. Baltimore, MD: Williams and Wilkins, 1972.

Weeks, John R. "The Demography of Islamic Nations." *Population Bulletin*. Vol. 43, No. 4 (December 1988).

Weinberg, George. *Society and the Healthy Homosexual*. Garden City, NY: Anchor Books, 1973.

Weinrich, James D. *Sexual Landscapes: Why We Are What We Are, Why We Love Whom We Love*. New York: Charles Scribner's Sons, 1987.

Weintraub, Sidney, and Stanley R. Ross. *"Temporary" Alien Workers in the United States: Designing Policy from Fact and Opinion*. Boulder, CO: Westview Press, 1982.

Weisner, Thomas S., and Bernice T. Eiduson. "The Children of the 60s as Parents.'" *Psychology Today*. (January 1986):60–66.

Weitzman, Lenore J. *The Divorce Revolution: The Unexpected Social and*

Economic Consequences for Women and Children in America. New York: Free Press, 1985.

WEITZMAN, LENORE J., DEBORAH EIFLER, ELIZABETH HODAKA, and CATHERINE ROSS. "Sex-Role Socialization in Picture Books for Preschool Children." *American Journal of Sociology.* Vol. 77, No. 6 (May 1972):1125–1150.

WELCH, KEVIN. "Community Development and Metropolitan Religious Commitment: A Test of Two Competing Models." *Journal for the Scientific Study of Religion.* Vol. 22, No. 2 (June 1983):167–181.

WELLER, JACK M., and E. L. QUARANTELLI. "Neglected Characteristics of Collective Behavior." *American Journal of Sociology.* Vol. 79, No. 3 (November 1973):665–685.

WELLFORD, CHARLES. "Labeling Theory and Criminology: An Assessment." In Delos H. Kelly, ed., *Criminal Behavior: Readings in Criminology.* New York: St. Martin's Press, 1980:234–247.

WELLMAN, BARRY. "The Community Question: Intimate Networks of East Yorkers." *American Journal of Sociology.* Vol. 84, No. 5 (March 1979):1201–1231.

WENKE, ROBERT J. *Patterns of Prehistory.* New York: Oxford University Press, 1980.

WERMAN, JILL. "Who Makes What?" *Working Woman* (January 1989):72–76, 80.

WESTERMAN, MARTY. "Death of the Frito Bandito." *American Demographics.* Vol. 11, No. 3 (March 1989):28–32.

WESTOFF, CHARLES F., and ELISE F. JONES. "The Secularization of U.S. Catholic Birth Control Practices." *Family Planning Perspective.* Vol. X, No. 5 (September/October 1977):203–207.

WHEELIS, ALLEN. *The Quest for Identity.* New York: W. W. Norton, 1958.

WHITAKER, MARK. "Ten Ways to Fight Terrorism." *Newsweek.* (July 1, 1985):26–29.

WHITE, RALPH, and RONALD LIPPITT. "Leader Behavior and Member Reaction in Three 'Social Climates.'" In Dorwin Cartwright and Alvin Zander, eds., *Group Dynamics.* Evanston, IL: Row, Peterson, 1953:586–611.

WHITE, WALTER. *Rope and Faggot.* New York: Arno Press and The New York Times, 1969; orig. 1929.

WHITMAN, DAVID. "Shattering Myths about the Homeless." *U.S. News & World Report* (March 20, 1989):26, 28.

WHORF, BENJAMIN LEE. "The Relation of Habitual Thought and Behavior to Language." In *Language, Thought, and Reality.* Cambridge: The Technology Press of M.I.T./New York: Wiley, 1956:134–159; orig. 1941.

WHYTE, WILLIAM FOOTE. *Street Corner Society.* 3rd ed. Chicago: University of Chicago Press, 1981; orig. 1943.

WHYTE, WILLIAM H., JR. *The Organization Man.* Garden City, NY: Anchor, 1957.

WIARDA, HOWARD J. "Ethnocentrism and Third World Development." *Society.* Vol. 24, No. 6 (September-October 1987):55–64.

WIATROWSKI, MICHAEL A., DAVID B. GRISWOLD, and MARY K. ROBERTS. "Social Control Theory and Delinquency." *American Sociological Review.* Vol. 46, No. 5 (October 1981):525–541.

WILCOX, CLYDE. "Support for the Christian Right Old and New: A Comparison of Supporters of the Anti-Communism Crusade and the Moral Majority." *Sociological Focus.* Vol. 22, No. 2 (May 1989):87–97.

WILLIAMS, ROBIN M., JR. *American Society: A Sociological Interpretation.* 3rd ed. New York: Alfred A. Knopf, 1970.

WILSON, ALAN B. "Residential Segregation of Social Classes and Aspirations of High School Boys." *American Sociological Review.* Vol. 24, No. 6 (December 1959):836–845.

WILSON, BRYAN. *Religion in Sociological Perspective.* New York: Oxford University Press, 1982.

WILSON, CLINT C., II, and FÉLIX GUTIÉRREZ. *Minorities and Media: Diversity and the End of Mass Communication.* Beverly Hills, CA: Sage Publications, 1985.

WILSON, EDWARD O. *Sociobiology: The New Synthesis.* Cambridge, MA: Belknap Press of the Harvard University Press, 1975.

WILSON, EDWARD O. *On Human Nature.* New York: Bantam Books, 1978.

WILSON, JAMES Q., and RICHARD J. HERRNSTEIN. *Crime and Human Nature.* New York: Simon and Schuster, 1985.

WILSON, JOHN. *Religion in American Society: The Effective Presence.* Englewood Cliffs, NJ: Prentice-Hall, 1978.

WILSON, LOGAN. *American Academics Then and Now.* New York: Oxford University Press, 1979.

WILSON, THOMAS C. "Urbanism and Tolerance: A Test of Some Hypotheses Drawn from Wirth and Stouffer." *American Sociological Review.* Vol. 50, No. 1 (February 1985):117–123.

WILSON, WILLIAM JULIUS. "The Black Underclass." *The Wilson Quarterly.* Vol. 8 (Spring 1984):88–99.

WINN, MARIE. *Children Without Childhood.* New York: Pantheon Books, 1983.

WIRTH, LOUIS. "Urbanism As a Way of Life." *American Journal of Sociology.* Vol. 44, No. 1 (July 1938):1–24.

WITKIN-LANOIL, GEORGIA. *The Female Stress Syndrome: How to Recognize and Live with It.* New York: Newmarket Press, 1984.

WOLFE, TOM. *Radical Chic.* New York: Bantam, 1970.

WOLFGANG, MARVIN E., and FRANCO FERRACUTI. *The Subculture of Violence: Towards an Integrated Theory in Criminology.* Beverly Hills, CA: Sage Publications, 1982.

WOLFGANG, MARVIN E., ROBERT M. FIGLIO, and THORSTEN SELLIN. *Delinquency in a Birth Cohort.* Chicago: University of Chicago Press, 1972.

WOLFGANG, MARVIN E., TERRENCE P. THORNBERRY, and ROBERT M. FIGLIO. *From Boy to Man, From Delinquency to Crime.* Chicago: University of Chicago Press, 1987.

WOLFINGER, RAYMOND E., and STEVEN J. ROSENSTONE. *Who Votes?* New Haven, CT: Yale University Press, 1980.

WOLFINGER, RAYMOND E., MARTIN SHAPIRO, and FRED I. GREENSTEIN. *Dynamics of American Politics.* 2nd ed. Englewood Cliffs, NJ: Prentice-Hall, 1980.

WONG, BUCK. "Need for Awareness: An Essay on Chinatown, San Francisco." In Amy Tachiki et al., eds., *Roots: An Asian American Reader.* Los Angeles: UCLA Asian American Studies Center, 1971:265–273.

WOODWARD, C. VANN. *The Strange Career of Jim Crow.* 3rd rev. ed. New York: Oxford University Press, 1974.

WOODWARD, KENNETH L. "Feminism and the Churches." *Newsweek.* Vol. 13, No. 7 (February 13, 1989):58–61.

WOOLEY, ORLAND W., SUSAN C. WOOLEY, and SUE R. DYRENFORTH. "Obesity and Women—II: A Neglected Feminist Topic." *Women's Studies International Quarterly.* Vol. 2 (1979):81–92.

THE WORLD BANK. *World Development Report 1984.* New York: Oxford University Press, 1984.

WORLD HEALTH ORGANIZATION. *Constitution of the World Health Organization.* New York: World Health Organization Interim Commission, 1946.

WRIGHT, ERIK OLIN, and BILL MARTIN. "The Transformation of the American Class Structure, 1960–1980." *American Journal of Sociology.* Vol. 93, No. 1 (July 1987):1–29.

WRIGHT, JAMES D. "Address Unknown: Homelessness in Contemporary America." *Society.* Vol. 26, No. 6 (September/October, 1989):45–53.

WRIGHT, QUINCY. "Causes of War in the Atomic Age." In William M. Evan and Steven Hilgartner, eds., *The Arms Race and Nuclear War.* Englewood Cliffs, NJ: Prentice-Hall, 1987:7–10.

WRIGHT, STUART A. "Social Movement Decline and Transformation: Cults in the 1980s." Paper presented to the Southwestern Social Science Association, Dallas, Texas, March 1987.

WRIGHT, STUART A., and WILLIAM V. D'ANTONIO. "The Substructure of Religion: A Further Study." *Journal for the Scientific Study of Religion.* Vol. 19, No. 3 (September 1980):292–298.

WRIGHT, STUART A., and ELIZABETH S. PIPER. "Families and Cults: Familial Factors Related to Youth Leaving or Remaining in Deviant Religious Groups." *Journal of Marriage and the Family.* Vol. 48, No. 1 (February 1986):15–25.

WRONG, DENNIS H. "The Oversocialized Conception of Man in Modern Sociology." *American Sociological Review.* Vol. 26, No. 2 (April 1961):183–193.

YATES, RONALD E. "Growing Old in Japan; They Ask Gods for a Way Out." *Philadelphia Inquirer* (August 14, 1986):3A.

YODER, JAN D., and ROBERT C. NICHOLS. "A Life Perspective: Comparison of Married and Divorced Persons." *Journal of Marriage and the Family.* Vol. 42, No. 2 (May 1980):413–419.

YOUNGMAN, HENNY. "That Don't Look Jewish to Me." *VIS a VIS*. Vol. 1, No. 2 (April 1987):136.

ZALD, MAYER N. *Occupations and Organizations in American Society*. Chicago: Markham, 1971.

ZANGWILL, ISRAEL. *The Melting Pot*. Macmillan, 1921; orig. 1909.

ZASLAVSKY, VICTOR. *The Neo-Stalinist State: Class, Ethnicity, and Consensus in Soviet Society*. Armonk, NY: M. E. Sharpe, 1982.

ZEITLIN, IRVING M. *The Social Condition of Humanity*. New York: Oxford University Press, 1981.

ZHOU, MIN, and JOHN R. LOGAN. "Returns of Human Capital in Ethnic Enclaves: New York City's Chinatown." *American Sociological Review*. Vol. 54, No. 5 (October 1989):809–820.

ZIGLI, BARBARA. "Enrollment: What's the Score?" *USA Today*. (December 20, 1984):D1.

ZILL, NICHOLAS. National Survey conducted by Child Trends, Inc., Washington, DC, 1984. Reported by Marilyn Adams. "Kids Aren't Broken by the Breakup." *USA Today* (December 20, 1984):5D.

ZIMBARDO, PHILIP G. "Pathology of Imprisonment." *Society*. Vol. 9 (April 1972):4–8.

ZIPP, JOHN F. "Perceived Representativeness and Voting: An Assessment of the Impact of 'Choices' vs. 'Echoes.'" *The American Political Science Review*. Vol. 79, No. 1 (March 1985):50–61.

ZIPP, JOHN F., and JOEL SMITH. "A Structural Analysis of Class Voting." *Social Forces*. Vol. 60, No. 3 (March 1982):738–759.

ZOLA, IRVING KENNETH. "Medicine as an Institution of Social Control." In John Ehrenreich, ed., *The Cultural Crisis of Modern Medicine*. New York: Monthly Review Press, 1978:80–100.

ZURCHER, LOUIS A., and DAVID A. SNOW. "Collective Behavior Social Movements." In Morris Rosenberg and Ralph Turner, eds., *Social Psychology: Sociological Perspectives*. New York: Basic Books, 1981:447–482.

Acknowledgments

Photographs

CHAPTER 1 Superstock, xxii; Kirk Condyles/Photoreporters, 1; Paul Liebhardt, 2; Catherine Ursillo/Photo Researchers, 4; Frank Siteman/Taurus Photos, 9; George Bellerose/Stock, Boston, 9; Paul Liebhardt, 10; Brown Brothers, 11; New York Public Library, 13; The Pierpont Morgan Library, 14; Frederic Lewis Photographs, 14; The Bettmann Archive, 15; Philip Jon Bailey/The Picture Cube, 19; Private collection, courtesy of Pucker Safrai Gallery, Boston. Photograph by David N. Israel, 22; AP/Wide World Photos, 23.

CHAPTER 2 United Nations photo, 28; AP/Wide World Photos, 29; Heard Museum, Phoenix, AZ, 31; Tony Stone/Worldwide, 34; Paul Liebhardt, 38; H. E. Edgerton, 39; David Turnley/Black Star, 42; AP/World Wide Photos, 43; Paul Liebhardt, 47; Paul Liebhardt, 49; Joel Gordon, 51; Sotheby's, 55.

CHAPTER 3 Paul Liebhardt, 58; Napoleon A. Chagnon, 59; Paul Liebhardt, 61; Dario Perla/International Stock Photo, 64; Paul Liebhardt, 65; From *Great Housewives in Modern Art*, Penguin Books, 1988, 67; M. Courtney-Clarke, 70; Tom Hollyman/Photo Researchers, 71; The Detroit Institute of Arts, Gift of Edsel B. Ford, 72; Paul Liebhardt, 74; Gerd Ludwig, 76; Paul Liebhardt, 78; Paul Liebhardt, 80; Paul Liebhardt, 81; Randy Matusow/Monkmeyer Press, 83; U.S. Department of Defense, Still Media Records Center, 84.

CHAPTER 4 Paul Liebhardt, 88; Paul Liebhardt, 89; Courtesy of the Lenskis: photo by Will Owens, 91; Four By Five, Inc., 92; Anthro-Photo, 92; James R. Holland/Stock, Boston, 93; Robert Frerck/Woodfin Camp & Associates, 94; Paul Liebhardt, 95; U.S. Air Force Photo/Photo Researchers, 98; Brown Brothers, 100; Scala/Art Resource, 101; Bridgeman Art Library/Art Resource, 103; Bob Nicklesbert/Woodfin Camp & Associates, 106; New York Public Library Picture Collection, 108; Private Collection, 110; New York Public Library, 112; Richard Steedman, 113; Paul Liebhardt, 114.

CHAPTER 5 Yale University Art Gallery, Gift of Stephen C. Clark, B.A. 1903, 118; Dede Lynn, 119; Lew Merrim/Monkmeyer Press, 121; Mimi Forsyth/Monkmeyer Press, 121; Tom Pollak/Monkmeyer Press, 121; Harry F. Harlow, University of Wisconsin Primate Laboratory, 122; Mary Evans/Sigmund Freud Copyrights, courtesy of W. E. Freud, 124; Elizabeth Crews, 126; Courtesy of the University of Chicago Archives, 127; Paul Liebhardt, 128; L. Morris-Nantz, 129; Randy Duchaine/The Stock Market, 129; Martin Rogers/Woodfin Camp & Associates, 129; Richard Hutchings/Photo Researchers, 132; By kind permission of His Grace The Duke of Westminster, DL, 134; L.L.T. Rhodes/TSW, Click/Chicago Ltd., 137; Paul Liebhardt, 140.

CHAPTER 6 Steve Liss, 147; Jan Halaska/Photo Researchers, 147; Paul Liebhardt, 149; David Woo/Stock, Boston, 152; Paul Liebhardt, 154; Mark Antman/The Image Works, 156; David Johnson, *Time* Magazine, April 22, 1985, p. 59, 158; Larry Lawfer/The Picture Cube, 161; Paul Liebhardt, 162; The Kobal Collection, 165; The Museum of Modern Art/Film Stills Archive, 167; Paramount Pictures Corporation, 167.

CHAPTER 7 Photoreporters, 170; W. Marc Bernsau/The Image Works, 171; Michael Verbois, 174; Paul Liebhardt, 177; The Picture Cube, 178; Michele Agins/NYT Pictures, 179; Paul Liebhardt, 181; Carroll Seghere/Photo Researchers, 182; Joseph Nettis/Photo Researchers, 184; Yoram Kahana/Shooting Star, 186; Courtesy Cray Research, 187; The Metropolitan Museum of Art, George A. Hearn Fund, 1956, 188; Juraj Groch/Sygma, 189; Julie Houck, 190; Ethan Hoffman, 193.

CHAPTER 8 Pana-Vue, 198; John Keating, 199; Dennis Brack/Black Star, 200; UPI/Bettmann Newsphotos, 201; AP/Wide World Photos, 204; Springer/Bettmann Film Archive, 205; Courtesy PepsiCo Inc., 205; UPI/Bettman Newsphotos, 207; Jacques M. Chenet/Woodfin Camp & Associates, 210; Bill Bachman/Photo Researchers, 212; Andrew Holbrooke/Black Star, 213; Collection of Peter Schindler, 215; David Turnley/Black Star, 216; David Austen/Stock, Boston, 222; A. Tannenbaum/Sygma, 223; Alon Reininger/Woodfin Camp & Associates, 225; Pushkin State Museum, Moscow (Superstock), 227.

CHAPTER 9 Dagmar Fabricius/Stock, Boston, 232; Ken Marschall; collection of Joseph M. Ryan, 233; Ted Spiegel/Black Star, 234; William Campbell/*Time* Magazine, 236; Neal Preston/Outline, 237; Toshifuma Kitamura/Agence France-Presse, 240; Peter Turnley/Black Star, 241; Art Resource, 243;

Alan Carey/ The Image Works, 245; Henry Gris/FPG International, 247; The Granger Collection, 248.

CHAPTER 10 Richard Howard/Black Star, 254; Paul Liebhardt, 255; Michael Grecco/Stock, Boston, 261; C. Vergara/Photo Researchers, 262; Henry Gris/FPG International, 265; Chuck Fishman/Woodfin Camp & Associates, 266; Mark Sherman/Bruce Coleman, 268; Jeffrey D. Smith/ Woodfin Camp & Associates, 268; FPG International, 272; Bettmann Archive, 275; Mark Peterson, 276.

CHAPTER 11 Paul Liebhardt, 280; James Spates, 281; Timothy Eagan/Woodfin Camp & Associates, 283; Peter Turnley/ Black Star, 283; Paul Liebhardt, 283; J. Langevin/Sygma, 286; Collection, The Museum of Modern Art, New York. Gift of Edward M. M. Warburg, 287; Viviane Moos/The Stock Market, 290; Bonnie Freer/Rapho/Photo Researchers, 290; Paul Liebhardt, 291; Paul Liebhardt, 292; ARCHIV/Photo Researchers, 294; Paul Liebhardt, 296; The Granger Collection, 299; C. Carrion/Sygma, 300; Paul Liebhardt, 302.

CHAPTER 12 Scala/Art Resource, 306; Don White/*Time* Magazine, 307; Paul Liebhardt, 308; Martin Williams Advertising, Minneapolis, 312; Patricia Upchurch, 317; Kenyon College, 320; Raymond Depardon/Magnum Photos, 321; Wally McNamee/Woodfin Camp & Associates, 321; Woolaroc Museum, Bartlesville, Oklahoma, 323; UPI/Bettmann Newsphotos, 325; Bob Adelman, 325; Joanna Pinneo/Black Star, 326; Sepp Seitz/Woodfin Camp & Associates, 327; Library of Congress, 331; Randy Taylor/Sygma, 333.

CHAPTER 13 Paul Liebhardt, 338; Library of Congress, 339; Michel Tcherevkoff/The Image Bank, 340; Paul Liebhardt, 343; Filman/FPG International, 348; Jim Weiner/Photo Researchers, 348; Courtesy of Pennsylvania State University, 349; Courtesy of Revlon, 352; Library of Congress, 354; Steve McCuny/Magnum Photos, 356; Courtesy of National Organization of Women, 361; Sylvia Johnson/Woodfin Camp & Associates, 363; Library of Congress, 365.

CHAPTER 14 Jeffrey Myers/Southern Stock Photos, 368; Michael Putland/Retna Pictures Ltd., 369; Spencer Grant/Photo Researchers, 371; Bruce Gordon/Photo Researchers, 374; N. R. Farbman/LIFE Magazine; © 1947, 1975 Time Inc., 375; Eve Arnold/Magnum Photos, 376; Bruno J. Zehnder/United Nations, 378; Jeff Lowenthal/Woodfin Camp & Associates, 379; James Balog/Black Star, 382; Stan Aggi/Picture Group, 385; Scala/Art Resource, 387; Jan Halaska/Photo Researchers, 388.

CHAPTER 15 Collection of Marilyn Lanfear; photograph courtesy of Bernice Steinbaum Gallery, New York City, 392; Photofest, 393; Farrel Grehan/Photo Researchers, 395; Barry King/Gamma-Liaison, 398; Luis Alberto Acuña, 400; Peter Papadopolous/The Stock Market, 404; Wolfgang Dietze, 406; Sybil Shockman/Monkmeyer Press, 412; Will & Deni McIntyre/Photo Researchers, 414; Sygma, 418; Petit-Format/Nestle/ Science Source/Photo Researchers, 420.

CHAPTER 16 Robert Caputo, 424; Richard Kalvar/Magnum Photos, 425; TVA, Hine/Photo Researchers, 426; Jeffrey Agronson, 429; The Bettmann Archive, 433; Milton Potts/Photo Researchers, 435; Joseph Rodriguez/Black Star, 436; Chris Pullo, 436; Richard Hutchings/Photo Researchers, 441; Copyright 1985 G. B. Trudeau, 442; Michael Grecco/Stock, Boston, 445; Erich Hartmann/Magnum Photos, 447.

CHAPTER 17 Paul Liebhardt, 450; Barbara Alper/Stock, Boston, 451; Paul Liebhardt, 452; Ira Wyman/Sygma, 455; Sepp Seitz/Woodfin Camp & Associates, 458; Anthony Suau/Black Star, 458; Gamma-Liaison, 459; R. & S. Michaud/Woodfin Camp & Associates, 464; Peter Menzel, 464; Jan Lukas/Photo Researchers, 466; Jeffrey Aaronson, 472; From the collection of the New Britain Museum of American Art, Connecticut. Harriet Russell Stanley Fund, 474; Mark Sluder/Charlotte Observer/Sygma, 475.

CHAPTER 18 B. Bossu/Sygma, 478; Eric Bouvet/Gamma-Liaison, 479; JB Pictures, 480; UPI/Bettmann Newsphotos, 483; David Becker/Photoreporters, 485; Photo by D. James Dee, 486; Ellis Herwig/Stock, Boston, 489; Bettye Lane/Photo Researchers, 492; J. Kosnik/Gamma-Liaison, 494; Richard Stack/Black Star, 500; Christopher Morris/Black Star, 503.

CHAPTER 19 Robert D. Tonsing/Picture Group, 506; Sygma, 507; Robert Frerck/Woodfin Camp & Associates, 508; The Granger Collection, 509; Museum of American Textile History, 510; The Granger Collection, 513; Scala/Art Resource, 513; Marcello Bertinetti/Photo Researchers, 517; Gilda Schiff/ Photo Researchers, 517; Collection of Whitney Museum of American Art. Purchase 37.44. Photo by Geoffrey Clements, N.Y., 525; Gamma-Liaison, 530.

CHAPTER 20 Hank Morgan/Science Source/Photo Researchers, 534; Susan Rosenberg/Photo Researchers, 535; The Granger Collection, 537; W. Campbell/Sygma, 539; Peter Magubane/Black Star, 539; Paul Fetters, 543; P.P.O.W. Gallery, New York 545; Giraudon/Art Resource, 547; Anthony Suau/Black Star, 549; Howard Sochurek/Woodfin Camp & Associates, 551; The Mansell Collection Limited, 554; Lauros-Giraudon/Art Resource, 556.

CHAPTER 21 Museum Folkwang Essen, 560; Stephanie Maze/Woodfin Camp & Associates, 561; Hella Hammid/Photo Researchers, 562; Bruce Brander/Photo Researchers, 566; N. Maceschal/The Image Bank, 568; Anderson/Gamma-Liaison, 570; United Nations Photo, 571; Monkmeyer Press, 572; Tom Hollyman/Photo Researchers, 576; George Hall/Woodfin Camp & Associates, 577; NASA, 578; Collection, The Museum of Modern Art, N.Y. Mrs. Simon Guggenheim Fund, 579; Courtauld Institute, London/Four By Five, 579; The University of Chicago Library, 581; Allan Tannenbaum/ Sygma, 584.

Acknowledgments   667

Index

673

SUBJECT INDEX

Caste system, 235–37, 252
   class system and, 238–39
   upper class, 264
Casual crowd, 591
Categories, 172
Catholic Church, 419, 457, 472, 568
Caucasians, 309
Cause and effect, 34, 35, 38, 56
C.E.D. (*see* Committee for Economic
   Development)
Central cities, 577
Change, 613–35 (*see also* Social change;
   Transition)
   cultural, 74–76
   rumor and, 595
   scientific sociology and, 38
Charisma, 459, 477
Charismatic authority, 481–82, 483, 504
Chicago, 580, 584
Chicanos, 33–, 332
Child abuse, 415–16
Child care, 432
Children, 403–5
   divorce and, 412, 413, 414
   fathers and, 421
   homosexual couples and, 418
   one-parent families and, 417
   socialization of, 119, 122–23, 136–
     37
Children's Defense Fund, 277
Chimpanzees, 64–65
China (*see* People's Republic of China)
Chinese Americans, 327, 328, 329–30,
   335
Chinese Malaysians, 311
Choice, 619, 631
Cholera, 537–38
Christianity, 456, 461–62, 482
Church, 457–58, 459, 477
   black, 455, 471
   electronic, 475–76
Cigarette smoking, 542–43
Cities, 571–85
   American, 274, 408–9, 574–75
   evolution of, 572–74
   historical importance of, 584–85
   postindustrial, 577–78
   regional, 578–79
   sociology and, 14
   suburbs and, 576–77, 586, 320
   theories of, 579–82
   Third-World, 582–84, 585
City slickers, 618
City-states, 483
Civilization, 94
Civil law, 217
Civil religion, 473, 477
Civil rights, 335, 498, 589, 592, 605,
   608
Civil War, 575
Class, 255–79 (*see also* Social class)
Class consciousness, 104, 116
Classless society, 240–42
Class society, 627–28, 629–30, 634
Class system, 237–38, 239, 252
Closed-ended format, 45
CMSA (*see* Consolidated metropolitan
   statistical area)
Coalescence, 606
Coca-Cola, 527
Coercive organizations, 183
Cognition, 125–27
Cohabitation, 417, 422
Cohesion, 453
Cohort, 141, 143
Collective behavior, 589–611
   crowds in, 591–95, 610
   defined, 610

social movements in, 589, 600–609
   (*see also* Social movement)
   studying, 590–91
   types of, 595–600
Collective conscience, 114
Collective decision making, 194
Collective goals, 514
Collectivity, 590–91, 610
College students, 4–5, 75 (*see also*
   Higher education)
   gender of, 351, 358
   passivity of, 443–44
Colonialism, 292, 298–99, 305, 320
Coming of Age in Samoa (Mead), 36
Commitment, 209
Committee for Economic Development
   (C.E.D.), 381
Common sense, 31–32
Communication, 158–60, 184, 626
Communism, 102, 429, 514–16, 532
Community, 523, 619, 621–22
Community divorce, 413
Community remarriage, 414
Companionship, 405, 417
Competence, 184, 214
Competition, 350, 512, 529–30
Complementarity, 360, 361
Computers, 447, 615
Concentric zone model, 581–82
Concept, 32, 56
Concrete operational stage, 125–26, 143
Conflict, 99–106 (*see also* Social conflict)
   role, 151–52, 168
   value, 67–68
Conflict subcultures, 208
Conflict theory of prejudice, 314
Conformity, 176–78, 206, 208
Confucianism, 465–66
Conglomerates, 527, 533
Consanguine family, 377, 394, 409, 422
Conscience, 114
Consciousness, false, 102, 117
Consensus, 30
Conservatives, 627
Consolidated metropolitan statistical
   area (CMSA), 578
Conspicuous consumption, 598
Constantinople, 462
Constitutional monarchies, 484
Constraint, 84–85
Consumer, 512, 514
Consumption, 295–97
Contagion theory, 593
Containment theory, 203
Control, 35, 56 (*see also* Social control)
Control function of language, 163
Control theory, 208
Controversy, 166
Conventional crowd, 591
Conventional reality, 164
Convergence theory, 593–94
Conversation, 352–53
Conversion, 459, 477
Coordination, 374
Corporation, 526–31
   agribusiness in, 521
   defined, 533
   multinational, 292–93
   women in, 256–57
Correlation, 34–35, 56
Cosby Show, The, 134
Cottage industry, 508
Counterculture, 74, 86
Coup d'etat, 497
Couples survey, 46
Courts, 226
Courtship, 400–402
Covenant, 466
Creationism, 460, 462–63

Creation science, 463
Credentialism, 439–40, 449
Crime, 219–29
   defined, 200, 230
   against persons, 219, 230
   against property, 219, 230
   secondary analysis of, 52
   social forces in, 6
   social function of, 112
   underground economy and, 526
   white-collar, 217–18
Crime index, 219
Crime in the United States, 219
Criminal justice system, 201, 226–29,
   230
Criminal law, 217
Criminal recidivism, 228, 230
Crisis, 9
Critical thinking (*see* Critical Thinking
   boxes and Critical Evaluation
   sections throughout text)
Crowd, 591–95, 610
Crude birth rate, 562, 586
Crude death rate, 562–63, 586
Cuba, 300, 303, 427
Cuban Americans, 333–34
Cult, 455–60, 477, 482
Cultural ecology, 81, 86, 91
Cultural integration, 75, 86
Cultural lag, 75, 86, 614
Cultural relativism, 77, 86, 629
Cultural theory of prejudice, 313–14
Cultural traits, 77
Cultural transmission, 63, 86
Cultural universals, 79, 86
Culture, 59–87
   aging and, 374–78
   components of, 62–71
   defined, 60–62, 86
   diversity in, 8, 10, 72–77
   education in, 432
   freedom and, 84–85
   gender and, 342–44, 360
   global inequality and, 291, 294, 302
   health and, 536
   politics and, 74, 487–88
   of poverty, 274, 275
   reality and, 154
   social change and, 615–16
   theoretical analysis of, 77–84
Culture shock, 60, 86

Dallas, 263
Date rape, 363
Dating, 401
Davis-Moore thesis, 244–46
Dawn of civilization, 94
Death, 140–41, 386–90
   ethics and, 545–46
   social isolation and, 380
   of spouse, 405
Death rates, 562–63, 569, 586
Debt, Third World, 300
Deceit, 158–59
Decision making, 194
Declaration of Independence, 324
Deductive logical thought, 54, 56
De facto segregation, 319
Defended personalities, 379
Degradation ceremony, 210
Dehumanization, 186
Deindustrialization, 269–70
De jure discrimination, 319
Delinquency, 200
Demeanor, 160
Democracy, 67, 484, 504

Democracy in America (Tocqueville),
   487
Democratic leaders, 175
Democratic Party, 490, 491
Democratic socialism, 516, 533
Demographic transition theory, 567–68,
   586
Demography, 562–65, 586
Denial, 140
Denmark, 417
Denomination, 458, 477
Dependency theory, 298–303
   defined, 305
   population and, 568
   social change and, 633
Dependent variable, 34
Depression, 410
Deprivation theory, 601–3
Descent, 397, 422
Descriptive research, 44
Descriptive statistics, 32
Deterrence, 227, 230
Development, 120–22
   cognitive, 125–27
   self, 129–30
Deviance, 199–231
   biology of, 201–3
   crime and, 219–29 (*see also* Crime)
   defined, 200–201, 230
   psychology of, 203
   social-conflict analysis of, 215–19
   structural-functional analysis of,
     203–9
   symbolic-interaction analysis of, 209–
     15
Dhamma, 465
Dharma, 464
Dictionary of American Biography, 52
Diet, 377
Difference, 200
Differential association theory, 214–
   15
Diffusion, 76, 615–16
Dignity, 631
Diplomacy, 503
Direct-fee medical system, 550, 558
Disability, 150, 446
Disarmament, 503
Discipline, 109–10, 440
Discovery, 75–76, 615
Discrimination, 319, 328, 337
   age, 384–86
   gender, 356–57
   institutional, 314–15, 330, 337
Disease, 149–50, 555
Disengagement theory, 383, 391
Disorganized personalities, 379
Dispersed collectivities, 590
Diversity, 8, 10, 72–77
Divine right, 481
Division of labor, 113–15, 117
   modernity and, 622–23
   schools and, 442
Divorce, 5–7, 411–13
   class and, 267
   remarriage and, 414
Domestic violence, 414–16
Double standard, 41, 83
Down These Mean Streets (Thomas),
   153
Dramaturgical analysis, 20, 155–63,
   168
Dred Scott decision, 324, 325
Drinking water, 538
Drives, 123–24
Drugs, 545, 555
Dyad, 180, 196
Dysfunctions, 18, 21, 78

About the Author

John J. Macionis (pronounced ma-SHOW-nis) is a native of Philadelphia, Pennsylvania. He received his bachelor's degree from Cornell University and his doctorate in sociology from the University of Pennsylvania. He is the author of articles and papers on topics such as community life in the United States, interpersonal relationships in families, effective teaching, and humor. An area of particular interest is urban sociology; he is coauthor of a well-received text, *The Sociology of Cities*. He has also coedited the new companion volume to this text: *Seeing Ourselves: Classic, Contemporary, and Cross-Cultural Readings in Sociology*.

John Macionis is currently associate professor of sociology at Kenyon College in Gambier, Ohio. He recently served as chair of the Anthropology-Sociology Department, as director of Kenyon's multidisciplinary program in humane studies, and as chair of Kenyon's faculty.

Professor Macionis teaches a wide range of upper-level courses, but his favorite course is Introduction to Sociology, which he teaches every semester. He enjoys extensive contact with students on his home campus, as a frequent visitor to other campuses, and as a regular participant in teaching programs abroad.

The FORGETFUL BEARS

by Larry Weinberg ✦ illustrated by Randy Cecil

A Golden Book ✦ New York
Golden Books Publishing Company, Inc., New York, New York 10106

To my wonderful grandson,
Nicholas Baer
—L.W.

For Audrey Noelle
—R.C.

One spring morning Mrs. Forgetful woke up
and went to the window. "What a beautiful day,"
she said. "Wake up, everyone! Let's go to the
country and have a picnic."

"Hooray!" shouted Sally and Tommy Forgetful.
"We'll make the lemonade."

They ran to the kitchen
and squeezed lots of lemons.

They added sugar. They added
water. Soon the lemonade was ready.

But they forgot about the picnic and drank it all themselves.

"I'll wake up Grandpa," said Mr. Forgetful. But he forgot where Grandpa's room was and walked into a closet. There on the shelf was his bowler hat. "Just what I'm looking for!" he said, and put it on. Then he closed the door behind him and forgot to come out.

Soon Mrs. Forgetful was ready to leave. "All right, everybody," she called. "Let's go!" But she forgot where the front door was. Instead she opened the door to the closet.

"Ah, there you are!" said Mr. Forgetful, who was standing inside. "Have you forgotten that we're going on a picnic?"

At last the four Forgetfuls found their way out of the house. They piled into their car and drove off.

Suddenly Mrs. Forgetful cried out, "Turn back! I forgot the food!"

Mr. Forgetful headed back for town. But he forgot what street they lived on and couldn't find the house.

Finally Mr. Forgetful suggested they look for their house on foot. They walked up one street and down another.

"There's our house," cried Tommy Forgetful.

"No! Our house is red," said Sally Forgetful.

"Hmmm. I thought it was blue," said Mr. Forgetful.

"Well, maybe we've moved," said Mrs. Forgetful. "I'm tired. Let's go back to the car."

But where was the car? Nobody could remember.

Tommy Forgetful had a bright idea. "Let's split up," he said. "Each bear will walk in a different direction. The first bear to find the car will honk the horn, and let the rest of us know where it is."

And so the four Forgetful Bears went their separate ways.

Mrs. Forgetful walked down a street where there were many stores. A supermarket sign said, "Big Sale Today." She forgot about the car and hurried inside to shop.

Sally Forgetful walked down another street where there was a park. She forgot about the car and sat down to rest.

Tommy Forgetful came to a bus stop. He forgot about the car and hopped on a bus.

Mr. Forgetful kept walking and walking. He forgot about the car and walked straight out of town.

Meanwhile Grandpa Forgetful woke up.
He rubbed his eyes and got out of bed.
"Where is everybody?" he shouted.

He went outside to look. There, across the street, was the family car. "What luck," said Grandpa. And he drove off to find the other Forgetfuls.

Soon he saw Sally Forgetful, asleep on a bench.
"Poor child, she's tired," he said to himself.
He stopped and carried Sally to the car.

A little while later Grandpa saw Mrs. Forgetful leaving the supermarket. "Poor woman, she sure is loaded down," he said. He took some of her packages and helped her into the car.

Grandpa stopped for a light and saw Tommy
Forgetful. "Poor boy, why is he riding on the bus?"

Grandpa honked the horn. "Come with us, Tommy."
So Tommy hopped off the bus and slid in next
to Sally. "Where are we going?" Tommy asked.
   "It's such a nice day," Grandpa said. "How would
you like to go for a picnic in the country?"
   "What a wonderful idea!" said Mrs. Forgetful.
"Why didn't *I* think of that?"

So they drove out into the country. Along the road they spotted Mr. Forgetful, walking very slowly. Grandpa stopped the car. "Poor man! You look tired. Hop in!" he said.

"Thank you," Mr. Forgetful said. "But I never accept rides from strangers."

"We're your FAMILY!" shouted Mrs. Forgetful. "I'm your wife, and this is your son, and this is your daughter, and this is your father!"

"Well, in that case," said Mr. Forgetful, "I guess I will get in the car. But don't tell me your names. I'm sure they will come to me."

So they drove to a lovely spot by the river. They made sandwiches from the groceries Mrs. Forgetful had bought. And they all had a wonderful time . . .

which they never forgot.